ליקוטי מוהר"ן

LIKUTEY MOHARAN

ליקוטי מוהר"ן

LIKUTEY MOHARAN

Volume 2 (Lessons 7-16)

by

Rebbe Nachman of Breslov

translated by

Moshe Mykoff

edited by

Moshe Mykoff and Ozer Bergman

annotated by

Chaim Kramer

published by
BRESLOV RESEARCH INSTITUTE
Jerusalem/New York

ISBN 0-930213-77-7
Copyright © 1993 Breslov Research Institute

all rights reserved

No part of this publication may be translated,
reproduced, stored in any retrieval system or transmitted,
in any form or any means,
electronic, mechanical, photocopying, recording or otherwise,
without prior permission in writing from the publishers.

First Edition

for further information:
Breslov Research Institute
POB 5370
Jerusalem, Israel, 91053
or:
Breslov Research Institute
POB 587
Monsey, NY 10952-0587
U.S.A.

cover design: Ben Gasner

For their generous support
in disseminating the teachings of

Rebbe Nachman of Breslov

we extend our deepest thanks and appreciation to

Steve & Beryl Reich

and to their son and daughter-in-law
Ezra & Tehilla Reich
and their granddaughter
Orah Rose Reich

Table of Contents

Likutey Moharan #7 2

Likutey Moharan #8 32

Likutey Moharan #9 82

Likutey Moharan #10 114

Likutey Moharan #11 160

Likutey Moharan #12 202

Likutey Moharan #13 246

Likutey Moharan #14 294

Likutey Moharan #15 342

Likutey Moharan #16 370

Appendix 379

ליקוטי מוהר"ן

LIKUTEY MOHARAN

LIKUTEY MOHARAN #7:1

ליקוּטֵי מוהר"ן סימן ז'

לְשׁוֹן רַבֵּנוּ, זִכְרוֹנוֹ לִבְרָכָה

וְאֵלֶּה הַמִּשְׁפָּטִים אֲשֶׁר תָּשִׂים לִפְנֵיהֶם (שְׁמוֹת כא):
אָמְרוּ חֲכָמֵינוּ, זִכְרוֹנָם לִבְרָכָה: הֻשְׁווּ אִשָּׁה לְאִישׁ (קִדּוּשִׁין לה: בָּבָא
קַמָּא טו.). וְאִיתָא בִּמְכִילְתָּא: "יָכוֹל יִהְיוּ הַתַּלְמִידִים לוֹמְדִין וְאֵינָם
מְבִינִים – תַּלְמוּד לוֹמַר: "אֲשֶׁר תָּשִׂים לִפְנֵיהֶם" – עָרְכֶם לִפְנֵיהֶם
כְּשֻׁלְחָן עָרוּךְ':

א. דַּע, כִּי עִקַּר הַגָּלוּת אֵינוֹ אֶלָּא בִּשְׁבִיל חֶסְרוֹן אֱמוּנָה, כְּמוֹ
שֶׁכָּתוּב (שִׁיר־הַשִּׁירִים ד): "תָּבוֹאִי, תָּשׁוּרִי מֵרֹאשׁ אֲמָנָה". וֶאֱמוּנָה
הוּא בְּחִינַת תְּפִלָּה, כְּמוֹ שֶׁכָּתוּב (שְׁמוֹת י"ז): "וַיְהִי יָדָיו אֱמוּנָה",
וְתַרְגּוּמוֹ: 'פְּרִישָׁן בִּצְלוֹ'.
וְזֶה בְּחִינַת נִסִּים לְמַעֲלָה מֵהַטֶּבַע, כִּי הַתְּפִלָּה לְמַעֲלָה מֵהַטֶּבַע, כִּי
הַטֶּבַע מְחַיֵּב כֵּן, וְהַתְּפִלָּה מְשַׁנָּה הַטֶּבַע, וְזֶה דְּבַר נֵס, וְלָזֶה צָרִיךְ

---

longer any men of faith (*Shabbat* 119b). Similarly, the Midrash teaches: In the merit of their faith, the Jews will be redeemed from exile (*Tanchuma, BeShalach* 10).

In Hebrew, *emunah* begins with the letter *alef* (א). An *alef* can be pronounced as the *e* in "egg," as the *a* in "what," and so on, depending on the vowel point. To highlight the connection between *emunah* (אמונה) and *amanah* (אמנה), the antiquated æ combination has been used.

3. **AMaNaH.** Amanah is the name of a towering mountain which overlooks the Land of Israel. The Talmud teaches that in future times, when returning from exile, the Jews will arrive at this mountain and begin to sing (*Yerushalmi, Sh'viit* 6:1). On this verse (*loc. cit.*) Rashi comments: Amanah: "When the Jews return from their exile, they will realize that it was only their faith in God which brought them such great reward."

4. **spread out in prayer.** When Yehoshua went into battle against Amalek, Moshe ascended to the top of a hill together with Aharon and Chur. Moshe turned to God and spread his hands out in prayer. While his hands remained raised the Jews were successful in combat. When they were lowered, Amalek succeeded. Aharon and Chur therefore held Moshe's hands *emunah* (steady) until sundown and the Jews were victorious (Exodus 17). The Talmud asks (*Rosh HaShanah* 29a): Was it Moshe's hands which won or lost the battle? No. But, when the Jews raised their eyes to Heaven in supplication the battle went in their favor. Hence the connection between *emunah* and prayer.

LIKUTEY MOHARAN # 7[1]

"V'eileh HaMishpatim (And these are the laws) that you must place before them."

(Exodus 21:1)

Our Sages taught: [The words "before them" indicate that in regard to all Torah laws,] woman is equated with man (*Kiddushin* 35a). **The *Mekhilta* (21:1) comments: It might be that the students study but fail to comprehend. [Scripture] therefore states: "that you must place before them"—spread it out before them as a fully set table.**

Know! the essential reason for exile is nothing other than a lack of *ÆMuNaH* (faith),[2] as is written (Song of Songs 4:8), "Come, gaze from the peak of AMaNaH."[3] And *emunah* is synonymous with prayer, as in (Exodus 17:12), "his hands were *emunah*," which Onkelos renders: "[his hands] were spread out in prayer."[4]

And [prayer] corresponds to miracles, the supernatural. For prayer transcends nature; the natural course dictates a certain thing, but prayer changes nature's course. This is a miracle. And for this,

---

1. **Likutey Moharan #7.** Rebbe Nachman had a vision in which his great-grandfather, the Baal Shem Tov, came to him and said, "When people spoil things in the Land of Israel, they fall into exile. This is alluded to in the verse (Genesis 49:24), 'And from there the Shepherd, the Rock of Israel.'" Rebbe Nachman explains this vision here and again in Lesson #9. Both teachings were given during the winter of 5563 (1802-03). See *Tzaddik* #129; *Until the Mashiach*, p.93.

This lesson opens with the first verse of the Torah portion *Mishpatim* (Laws). Rebbe Nachman quotes both a Talmudic passage and a *Mekhilta*, each of which explains what the words "that you must place before them" come to teach. The Talmudic passage in *Kiddushin* (also in *Bava Kama* 15a) focuses on the implication of the word "them," which is plural. The *Mekhilta*, on the other hand, explains the directive itself: "that you must place before them." Rebbe Nachman unites both these explanations and weaves them into his lesson.

This lesson is *leshon Rabbeinu z'l.* Any lesson designated as such was either a) copied verbatim from Rebbe Nachman's manuscripts which Reb Noson had in his possession, or b) dictated by Rebbe Nachman to Reb Noson. The remaining lessons (excluding the few which were written down by some of the other followers) were recorded by Reb Noson after he had heard the teaching from the Rebbe. He would prepare the written version and present it to Rebbe Nachman for approval.

2. **ÆMuNaH, faith.** Our Sages taught: Jerusalem was only destroyed when there were no

LIKUTEY MOHARAN #7:1

אֱמוּנָה, שֶׁיַּאֲמִין שֶׁיֵּשׁ מְחַדֵּשׁ וּבְיָדוֹ לְחַדֵּשׁ דָּבָר כִּרְצוֹנוֹ.

וְעִקַּר אֱמוּנָה, בְּחִינַת תְּפִלָּה, בְּחִינַת נִסִּים, אֵינוֹ אֶלָּא בְּאֶרֶץ-יִשְׂרָאֵל, כְּמוֹ שֶׁכָּתוּב (תְּהִלִּים ל"ז): "שְׁכָן אֶרֶץ וּרְעֵה אֱמוּנָה". וְשָׁם עִקַּר עֲלִיּוֹת הַתְּפִלּוֹת, כְּמוֹ שֶׁכָּתוּב (בְּרֵאשִׁית כ"ח): "וְזֶה שַׁעַר הַשָּׁמָיִם".

וּבִשְׁבִיל זֶה, כְּשֶׁפָּגַם אַבְרָהָם "בַּמָּה אֵדַע" (שָׁם ט"ו), וּבְזֶה פָּגַם בִּירֻשַּׁת אֶרֶץ, שֶׁהִיא בְּחִינַת אֱמוּנָה, בְּחִינַת תְּפִלָּה, הָיָה גָּלוּת מִצְרָיִם. וְדַוְקָא יַעֲקֹב וּבָנָיו יָרְדוּ מִצְרַיְמָה, כִּי הֵם בְּחִינַת שְׁנֵים-עָשָׂר נֻסְחָאוֹת הַתְּפִלָּה, וְהוֹרִיד אוֹתָם בַּגָּלוּת.

וּמִצְרַיִם הוּא הֵפוּךְ הַנִּסִּים, כְּמוֹ שֶׁכָּתוּב (שְׁמוֹת י"ד): "וּמִצְרַיִם נָסִים לִקְרָאתוֹ", שֶׁאֵין שָׁם מְקוֹם הַנִּסִּים, וְאֵין שָׁם מְקוֹם הַתְּפִלָּה,

9. **in Egypt.** The exile began at Yitzchak's birth, for he was Avraham's offspring. He did not own the land he lived in. The actual descent to Egypt, however, took place 190 years later (when Yaakov was 130 years old). The Children of Israel remained there for 210 years.

10. **Yaakov.** As their father, Yaakov was the root of the twelve tribes. This explains why he was included, though not numbered, with them. In Lesson #9 (*Likutey Moharan* 9:4) Rebbe Nachman explains that one must bind his prayer to the tzaddik of the generation for he knows how to elevate each prayer to its proper gate. This was Yaakov. He knew the "source" of every tribe, i.e., the appropriate place for the prayers which they offered.

11. **twelve versions of prayer.** The *Zohar* (*loc. cit.*) explains that each of the Jewish tribes has its own unique path through which its prayers enter heaven. Kabbalistically, this can be derived from God's holiest name, the Tetragrammaton: *YHVH* (יהוה). A word of four letters is permutable in 24 different ways unless any of the letters is duplicated. Thus, *YHVH* (with only 3 different letters) can be rearranged in 12 different ways, with each tribe corresponding to a different permutation. These are the twelve possible versions of prayer. See *Likutey Moharan* II, 73 for a fuller explanation and how each person can reach *his* correct path.

12. **fleeing against it.** Fleeing implies putting a distance between oneself and another. Here, however, the Egyptians *nasim* (were fleeing) against, i.e., towards, the water. As Rashi (*loc. cit.*) explains, this was because of the great confusion which came upon the Egyptian army. This in itself was a miracle. And, as mentioned earlier, Israel is the land of *nisim* (miracles). It is the place of holiness, the site of the Holy Temple, and is synonymous with faith. Egypt, on the other hand, represents everything contrary to holiness. It is the place of impurity and idolatry. It was with the intent to break these false beliefs that God performed the miracles of the Ten Plagues and the Red Sea. For Egypt is the very antithesis of the land of miracles (*Mai HaNachal*). Compare this with *Likutey Moharan* I, 9:5 and accompanying notes.

LIKUTEY MOHARAN #7:1

one needs faith. A person has to believe that there is a *M'chadesh* (an Originator) with the power to originate as He sees fit.[5]

Now, the quintessence of faith, and thus prayer and miracles, is only in the Land of Israel, as is written (Psalms 37:3), "Dwell in the Land and cultivate *emunah*."[6] The principal elevation of the prayers is there, as in (Genesis 28:17), "*This* is the gate of heaven."[7]

Because of this, when Avraham erred in saying (Genesis 15:8), "How shall I know [that I will inherit it]?"[8]—thus blemishing his inheritance of the Land, which corresponds to faith/prayer—< he brought on > the exile in Egypt.[9] And it was specifically "Yaakov[10] and his [twelve] sons who descended into Egypt" (Joshua 24:4; see Genesis 46), for they correspond to the "twelve versions of prayer" (*Zohar* III, 170a).[11]

And, [God] exiled them < to Egypt, because > the Land of Egypt is the antithesis of [the Land of Israel, the place of] *NiSiM* (miracles), as is written (Exodus 14:27), "And the Egyptians *NaSiM* (were fleeing) against it."[12] For [Egypt] is not the place of miracles. It is also not the

---

5. **He sees fit.** "The miracles which Elisha performed were achieved through prayer" (*Megillah* 27a). Rebbe Nachman points to the need for belief in God. With faith—believing that God oversees everything and can alter the course of nature as He sees fit—a person can pray to Him wholeheartedly and thereby accomplish miracles through his prayers. This was Elisha. His faith was perfect and accordingly he performed miracles through his prayers (*Mai HaNachal*).

6. **emunah.** The verse begins, "Have faith in God...then you will merit to dwell in the Land...." From this Rebbe Nachman learns that this land, the Land of Israel, can only be possessed through faith. Commenting on a similar verse (Leviticus 25:18), "You will be secure in your Land," Rashi writes: "Exile is a punishment for not having kept the Sabbatical year." This also indicates that we can only dwell securely in the Land when our faith is whole. Indeed, what greater expression of faith in God could there have been for an agrarian-based society than to leave its land fallow during the entire Sabbatical year.

7. **gate of heaven.** This verse, from Yaakov's dream of a ladder ascending to heaven, alludes to the Holy of Holies in the Temple. It is from there that all the prayers of the Jewish people ascend to God. We are taught that the Land of Israel has ten levels of holiness (*Keilim* 1:6-9), each deriving its degree of holiness from the level above it. The Talmud teaches (*Berakhot* 28b, 30a): A person should face the Holy of Holies when praying. However, if one is in the Diaspora, he should face the Land of Israel when praying. This indicates the direct relationship which the Land of Israel has with prayer.

8. **inherit it.** Prior to this, God had told Avraham that he would be blessed with children "as many as the stars of the heavens" (Genesis 15:5,6). And Avraham believed. However, when he was informed that he would inherit the Land, he questioned God. This was considered a shortcoming in his faith. God then said (Genesis 15:13), "Know for sure that your descendants will be foreigners in a land that is not theirs for 400 years."

LIKUTEY MOHARAN #7:1

כְּמוֹ שֶׁכָּתוּב (שָׁם ט): "וְהָיָה כְּצֵאתִי אֶת הָעִיר אֶפְרֹשׁ אֶת כַּפַּי".
וְכָל הַגָּלֻיּוֹת מְכֻנִּים בְּשֵׁם מִצְרַיִם, עַל שֵׁם שֶׁהֵם מְצֵרִים לְיִשְׂרָאֵל.
וּכְשֶׁפוֹגְמִין בָּאֱמוּנָה, בִּתְפִלָּה, בְּאֶרֶץ־יִשְׂרָאֵל, הוּא יוֹרֵד לְגָלוּת.

וְזֶה שֶׁאָמְרוּ חֲכָמֵינוּ, זִכְרוֹנָם לִבְרָכָה (סַנְהֶדְרִין צז.): 'אֵין מָשִׁיחַ בֶּן־
דָּוִד בָּא, אֶלָּא עַד שֶׁתִּכְלֶה פְּרוּטָה מִן הַכִּיס'; הַיְנוּ, שֶׁיִּכְלוּ
הָאֶפִּיקוֹרְסִים שֶׁאֵין לָהֶם אֱמוּנָה בְּנִסִּים, וּמְכַסִּים כָּל הַנִּסִּים בְּדֶרֶךְ
הַטֶּבַע. כִּי עִקַּר הַנִּסִּים בְּאֶרֶץ־יִשְׂרָאֵל, כִּי (תַּעֲנִית י.) 'אֶרֶץ־יִשְׂרָאֵל
שׁוֹתָה תְּחִלָּה', וּשְׁתִיָּתָהּ מֵהַתְּהוֹמוֹת, שֶׁהֵם לָשׁוֹן: "וַתֵּהֹם כָּל
הָעִיר" (רוּת א), שֶׁעַל דְּבַר נִסִּי תְּמֵהִין הָעוֹלָם.

וְזֶה (תְּהִלִּים מ"ב): "תְּהוֹם אֶל תְּהוֹם קוֹרֵא", כִּי יֵשׁ נִסִּין עִלָּאִין,
שֶׁהוּא בְּחִינַת תְּהוֹם עִלָּאָה; וְיֵשׁ נִסִּים תַּתָּאִין, שֶׁהֵם בְּחִינַת
תְּהוֹמָא תַּתָּאָה.

---

16. **drinks first.** As in the verse (Job 5:10), "Who gives rain upon the Land, and sends water upon the *chutzot* (Diaspora)" (*Taanit, loc.cit.*). The Land of Israel receives first, not only sequentially, but also in quality.

17. **t'home, depths.** This refers to the "upper waters" from which the Land of Israel receives its rain (*Taanit* 10a). Interestingly, significant sections of the tractate *Taanit* are devoted to the laws of fasting and prayer when, God forbid, there is a shortage of rain. Rainfall, as discussed by our Sages, is appreciated as a miracle from God, and is compared to both childbirth (another commonly accepted "natural" miracle) and resurrection of the dead.

18. **amazes everyone.** The straightforward meaning of the text is that everyone in the city was amazed at what had happened to Naomi. She, her husband Elimelekh and their two sons had departed the Holy Land as wealthy people. But now, Naomi was returning to her homeland an impoverished widow and a bereaved mother. Rebbe Nachman incorporates this within his lesson, explaining that everyone was amazed when Naomi returned with Ruth to the Land of Israel, the land of miracles (*Mai HaNachal*).

19. **upper...lower t'home.** The "upper miracles" can be understood as open miracles, the *amazing* things which everyone sees as clearly out of the ordinary. The "lower miracles," on the other hand, are the concealed miracles which appear as *natural* occurrences.

LIKUTEY MOHARAN #7:1

place of prayer, as in (Exodus 9:29), "When I go outside the city I will spread out my hands [in prayer]."[13]

[Our Sages taught:] All exiles are known as *MitZRayIM* (Egypt), because they *MetZeiRIM* (cause anguish and suffering) to the Jewish people (*Bereishit Rabbah* 16:4). Thus, when a person blemishes faith/ < miracles > /prayer/the Land of Israel, he descends into < the depths of > exile.

This is the meaning of what our Sages taught: The Mashiach son of David will not come until the [last] penny is gone from the pocket (*Sanhedrin* 97a)[14]—i.e., gone are the atheists who have no faith in miracles and explain away all miracles as natural phenomena.[15] And the quintessence of miracles is in the Land of Israel, for the Land of Israel drinks first (*Taanit* 10a).[16] Its drink is from the *t'home* (depths),[17] which connotes [the miraculous and amazing, as in] (Ruth 1:19), "the entire city *TeiHoMe* (was amazed)." Something that is miraculous amazes everyone.[18]

And this is (Psalms 42:8), "Deep calls to deep." There are "upper miracles," which correspond to the upper *t'home,* and there are "lower miracles," which correspond to the lower *t'home* (*Shemot Rabbah* 5:9).[19]

{I saw the Angel of Rain. It had the appearance of an *egla* (ox) and *prita sifevatei* (its lips were split open). It was standing between *t'home* (the deep) and *t'home* (*Taanit* 25b).}

---

13. **my hands in prayer.** As Rashi explains (*loc. cit.*), Egypt was filled with idolatry and hence unsuitable for prayer. Moshe therefore emphasized that he would be going "outside" to pray. Again we see the connection between faith, prayer, miracles (this verse appears in connection with the plague of miraculous hail) and the Land of Israel. This is in contrast with other lands, especially Egypt. Actually, as Rebbe Nachman explains, prayer itself was in exile in Egypt. The Jews were unable to open their mouths to talk to God (*Rabbi Nachman's Wisdom* #68).

14. **the pocket.** The Talmud (*loc. cit.*) comments on the troubles which will befall the Jews before the coming of the Mashiach. The simple meaning of "the last penny is gone from the pocket" is that inflation will render the available money valueless. Rebbe Nachman's explanation is that "there will be an end to the atheists who explain away all miracles." Also see *Likutey Moharan* I, 23.

15. **natural phenomena.** In Hebrew this is *HaTeVA* (הטבע), which has a numerical value of 86, as does God's name *ELoHIM* (אלהים, see Appendix: Gematria Chart). For the truth is that God is found in nature, albeit in a concealed manner. This is why people are sometimes awed and overwhelmed by nature, which in its essence is only a different manifestation of Godliness in our world.

LIKUTEY MOHARAN #7:1,2

וּמַלְאָךְ שֶׁכָּלוּל מִכָּל הַנִּסִּים, מִשְּׁנֵי הַתְּהוֹמוֹת, דָּמְיָא לְעֶגְלָא (תַּעֲנִית כה:), שֶׁהוּא בְּחִינַת עֲגוּלִים, בְּחִינַת אֱמוּנָה, כְּמוֹ שֶׁכָּתוּב (תְּהִלִּים פ"ט): "וֶאֱמוּנָתְךָ סְבִיבוֹתֶיךָ"; וּפְרִיטָא שְׂפָוָתֵהּ, שֶׁהוּא בְּחִינַת תְּפִלָּה, כְּמוֹ שֶׁכָּתוּב (שָׁם נ"א): "אֲדֹנָי שְׂפָתַי תִּפְתָּח", וְהוּא כְּלָלוּת הַנִּסִּים.

וְזֶה פֵּרוּשׁ: 'עַד שֶׁתִּכְלֶה פְּרוּטָה מִן הַכִּיס'; כִּי יֵשׁ בְּנֵי־אָדָם הַמְכַסִּים כְּלָלִיּוּת הַנִּסִּים, הַכְּלוּלִים בַּמַּלְאָךְ דִּפְרִיטָא שְׂפָוָתֵהּ, מְכַסִּים בְּדֶרֶךְ הַטֶּבַע. וּכְשֶׁתִּכְלֶה זֹאת וְתִתְרַבֶּה אֱמוּנָה בָּעוֹלָם, אָז יָבוֹא מָשִׁיחַ, כִּי עִקַּר הַגְּאֻלָּה תָּלוּי בָּזֶה, כְּמוֹ שֶׁכָּתוּב: "תָּבוֹאִי, תָּשׁוּרִי מֵרֹאשׁ אֲמָנָה".

ב. אֲבָל אִי אֶפְשָׁר לָבוֹא לֶאֱמוּנָה אֶלָּא עַל־יְדֵי אֱמֶת, כַּמּוּבָא בַּזֹּהַר (בָּלָק קצח:): "וְהָיָה צֶדֶק אֵזוֹר מָתְנָיו וֶאֱמוּנָה" וְכוּ' (יְשַׁעְיָהוּ י"א) — הַיְנוּ צֶדֶק, הַיְנוּ אֱמוּנָה. וְאָמְרוּ שָׁם: 'אֱמוּנָה אִתְקְרִיאַת, כַּד אִתְחַבַּר בָּהּ אֱמֶת'.

In review: The essence of faith, which corresponds to prayer and miracles, is in the Land of Israel. Its antithesis is Egypt, exile, which typify a blemish of faith and miracles. Redemption, the coming of Mashiach, is dependent upon abundant faith.

25. **except through truth.** Reb Noson explains: Essentially, faith applies in those areas where a person lacks understanding, for if one does comprehend through logic what need is there of faith? The question is, if a person does not understand, how can he know what to have faith in? For this reason, faith is dependent upon truth. If a person really seeks the truth, the real truth, he will of necessity come to believe in God, the true tzaddikim and the Torah—even if he cannot logically understand why he should (*Likutey Eitzot, Emet V'Emunah* 4). Rebbe Nachman warns, however, that one must couple his faith with intellect, for otherwise he can be a fool and believe in everything, even that which is forbidden (*Parparaot LeChokhmah*). See also *Mayim* (Breslov Research Institute, 1988).

26. **belt...band for his loins.** Both a belt and a band circle the body, much like faith, which is itself likened to a circle. Rebbe Nachman returns to this point at the end of the lesson, where the concept of *makifin* (surrounding intellect) is mentioned. The question here is, how can this encircling of the body apply to both justice and faith?

27. **justice is called faith....** The *Zohar* (*loc. cit.*) explains that *tzedek* (justice) and *emunah* (faith) are both forms of judgment. In the terminology of the Kabbalah, they both relate to the feminine principle of *Malkhut*. The difference between them is that *tzedek* refers to a

LIKUTEY MOHARAN #7:1,2

Encompassing all miracles, both *t'home,* is an angel that has "the appearance of an *EGLa* (ox)."[20] This corresponds to *EeGuLim* (circles), which is an aspect of faith, as is written (Psalms 89:9), "Your faith encircles you."[21] "And its lips were split open" alludes to prayer, as in (Psalms 51:17), "Lord, open my lips."[22] Thus, [the angel] encompasses all miracles.[23]

This is the meaning of, "until *TiKhLeH PRuTaH min haKiS* (the [last] penny is gone from the pocket)." For there are people who conceal all miracles, which are encompassed in the angel whose "lips were *PRiTaH.*" They *m'KhaSim* (conceal) [all miracles] with natural explanations. When this is *TiKhLeH* (gone), and there is abundant faith in the world, then Mashiach will come. For the redemption essentially depends upon this [abundant faith], as is written, "Come, gaze from the peak of Amanah."[24]

2. Yet it is impossible to come to faith except through truth.[25] As is brought in the *Zohar* (III, 198b): "And justice will be a belt for his hips, and faith a band for his loins" (Isaiah 11:5).[26] What then is the difference between justice and faith? The answer given there is: [justice] is called faith when it is bound with truth.[27]

20. **EGLa, ox.** The Maharsha explains that Taurus, the ox, is the constellation for Iyar, the month when the rains stop falling in the Land of Israel. This is the reason why the angel in charge of distributing rainfall appears as an ox. The Midrash (*Bereishit Rabbah* 10:7) teaches that every blade of grass has a star and an angel in charge of it. Moreover, the angel above the star constellation will have the appearance of the constellation it controls. In this case, it appears as the ox. (Compare this interpretation of the Talmudic passage with the one Rebbe Nachman offers prior to the conclusion of Lesson #9.)

21. **EeGuLim...encircles you.** Faith resembles a circle. A circle is a continuous line without protrusions. It has no edge which one can take hold of. So, too, faith applies only where one cannot understand—i.e., there is no way to take hold of it with logic (*Parparaot LeChokhmah*).

22. **open my lips.** These are the introductory words of the *Amidah* (Eighteen Benedictions) which is the central point of each of the three daily prayers.

23. **all miracles.** Prayer with one's lips, together with faith in God, generates miracles. This was the case with Moshe, who prayed for each of the miracles God performed, and Elisha, as explained above (n.5). Our Sages made a further connection between faith and the rains, saying: The rains only fall in the merit of those with faith (*Taanit* 8a).

24. **Amanah.** As mentioned earlier in notes 2 and 3, "In the merit of their faith, the Jews will be redeemed from exile," and, "When the Jews return from their exile, they will realize that it was only the power of faith which brought about the redemption." This is the faith they carried with them when they left Egypt and became a nation, and it is the faith they have always carried with them until the present day.

LIKUTEY MOHARAN #7:3   10

ג. וְאִי־אֶפְשָׁר לָבוֹא לֶאֱמֶת אֶלָּא עַל־יְדֵי הִתְקָרְבוּת לְצַדִּיקִים וְיֵלֵךְ בְּדֶרֶךְ עֲצָתָם; וְעַל־יְדֵי שֶׁמְּקַבֵּל מֵהֶם עֲצָתָם, נֶחְקָק בּוֹ אֱמֶת, כְּמוֹ שֶׁכָּתוּב (תְּהִלִּים נ״א): "הֵן אֱמֶת חָפַצְתָּ" – כְּשֶׁאַתָּה חָפֵץ אֱמֶת; "בַּטֻּחוֹת וּבְסָתֻם חָכְמָה תוֹדִיעֵנִי". כִּי הָעֵצוֹת שֶׁמְּקַבֵּל מֵהֶן הוּא בְּחִינַת נִשּׂוּאִין וְזִוּוּג,

וּכְשֶׁמְּקַבְּלִין עֵצוֹת מֵרְשָׁעִים, הוּא בְּחִינַת נִשּׂוּאִין בַּקְּלִפָּה. "הַנָּחָשׁ הִשִּׁיאַנִי" (בְּרֵאשִׁית ג) – לְשׁוֹן נִשּׂוּאִין, עֲצוֹת הַנָּחָשׁ שֶׁקִּבְּלָה הוּא בְּחִינַת נִשּׂוּאִין, וְעַל־יְדֵי נִשּׂוּאִין הֵטִיל בָּהּ זֻהֲמָא. וּבְמַעֲמַד הַר־סִינַי פָּסְקָה זֻהֲמָתָן (שַׁבָּת קמו). עַיֵּן רַשִׁ״י שָׁם), כִּי שָׁם קִבְּלוּ תַּרְיַ״ג עֲטִין דְּקֻדְשָׁה (זֹהַר יִתְרוֹ פ״ב), וְהָיְתָה לָהֶם נִשּׂוּאִין בִּקְדֻשָּׁה. וְלָמָּה נִקְרָא עֵצָה בִּבְחִינַת נִשּׂוּאִין? כִּי (בְּרָכוֹת סא.) 'הַכְּלָיוֹת יוֹעֲצוֹת', וּכְלָיוֹת הֵם כְּלֵי הַהוֹלָדָה, כְּלֵי הַזֶּרַע. נִמְצָא, כְּשֶׁמְּקַבְּלִין עֵצָה מֵאָדָם, כְּאִלּוּ מְקַבְּלִין מִמֶּנּוּ זֶרַע; וְהַכֹּל לְפִי אָדָם, אִם רָשָׁע אוֹ צַדִּיק.

---

32. wedding of holiness. The Torah tells us (Exodus 19:17) that "Moshe led the people out of the camp towards the Divine Presence and they stood transfixed at the foot of the mountain." Quoting the *Mekhilta*, Rashi comments: "This is to tell us that the Divine Presence came out to meet them just as a groom comes out to meet his bride."

33. the kidneys advise. Where is it taught that the kidneys advise? The verse states, "I will bless God who counsels me, even at night my kidneys admonish me" (Psalms 16:7; see *Rashi*). The Talmud (*loc. cit.*) lists 13 internal parts of the body (the tongue, lung, trachea, spleen, etc.), of which only the kidneys are duplicated. The Maharsha comments that this duplicity alludes to man's free will, his ability to choose right from wrong. It is also pointed out that the main function of the kidneys, the processing and purifying of the "polluted" blood in the body, occurs at night. This is alluded to in ". . . even at *night* my kidneys admonish me" (see *Chidushei HaGaonim* on *Eyn Yaakov, loc. cit.*).

The Midrash teaches: Avraham had no teacher, how then did he study Torah? The answer is that God caused his two kidneys to act as two teachers, and they taught him Torah and wisdom, as in [the verse quoted above], "I will bless...my kidneys... (*Bereishit Rabbah* 61:1).

34. reproductive organs.... Here Rebbe Nachman explains the connection between receiving advice and marital union. They share the common goal of "giving birth to," or producing, something new. See note 73.

LIKUTEY MOHARAN #7:3

3. {**"Behold, You want truth in the inner parts; in the innermost places teach me wisdom"** (Psalms 51:8).}

Yet is impossible to achieve truth except through attachment to the tzaddikim and by following their advice. The person who accepts their advice has the truth etched inside him. As is written, "Behold, You want truth"—when truth is what you desire[28]—"in the inner parts, in the innermost places, teach me wisdom." For the advice received from [the tzaddikim] is an aspect of marriage and union < of holinesss >.[29]

But when one accepts advice from the wicked, this corresponds to a marriage < and union of > the *kelipah* (husks). [As Chavah said] (Genesis 3:13), "The Serpent *advised* me"—this being a euphemism for marriage.[30] Her acceptance of the Serpent's advice is likened to a marriage. Through < this > marriage, the Serpent polluted her [and all her descendants]. However, with the revelation at Mount Sinai, this pollution ceased (*Shabbat* 146a).[31] For it was there that they received the six hundred thirteen counsels of holiness (*Zohar* II, 82b)—< a wedding of holiness >.[32]

And why is advice called marriage? This is because the kidneys advise (*Berakhot* 61a),[33] and the kidneys are reproductive organs, producers of sperm (*Zohar* III, 235a).[34] We can therefore conclude that by accepting advice from a person, it is as if we are receiving seed

---

harsh decree, when punishment is meted out with severity. However, when *emet* (truth), the masculine principle of *Tiferet* (see n.57), is coupled with *tzedek,* it then becomes faith.

In review: The essence of faith, which corresponds to prayer and miracles, is in the Land of Israel. Its antithesis is Egypt, exile, which typify a blemish of faith and miracles. Redemption, the coming of Mashiach, is dependent upon abundant faith (§1). Faith is achieved through truth. When justice is complemented by truth, it becomes faith (§2).

28. **You...you desire.** In the verse, King David is addressing God. Rebbe Nachman, however, applies this to the person's own desire for truth; thus changing the capitalized *Y* to the lower case.

29. **marriage and union of holiness.** This will be explained further on in the lesson.

30. **for marriage.** The Hebrew for "advised me," *HiShiANI,* is similar to the word for "married me," *HiSiANI* (see *Rashi, Shabbat* 146a, *s.v. k'sheba*).

31. **pollution ceased.** The Talmud (*loc. cit.*) teaches that the Serpent actually cohabited with Chavah, polluting her and therefore all of mankind, her descendants. When the Jewish people stood at Mt. Sinai and received the Torah—the 613 pure "counsels"—directly from God, they were cleansed of this pollution.

LIKUTEY MOHARAN #7:3

וּבִשְׁבִיל זֶה הַתּוֹרָה מַתִּישׁ כֹּחַ (סַנְהֶדְרִין כו:) וְנִקְרֵאת 'תּוּשִׁיָּה', כִּי הֵם תַּרְיַ"ג עֵטִין, כְּמוֹ שֶׁכָּתוּב (מִשְׁלֵי ח): "לִי עֵצָה וְתוּשִׁיָּה". וְעֵצוֹת הֵם בִּמְקוֹם נְשׂוּאִין, בְּחִינַת זִוּוּג הַמַּתִּישׁ כֹּחַ.

וַעֲצַת הַצַּדִּיק הוּא כֻּלּוֹ זֶרַע אֱמֶת. וְזֶה פֵּרוּשׁ (יִרְמְיָה ב): "וְאָנֹכִי נְטַעְתִּיךְ שׂוֹרֵק" – בְּחִינַת הַגְּאֻלָּה, כְּמוֹ שֶׁכָּתוּב (זְכַרְיָה י): "אֶשְׁרְקָה לָהֶם וַאֲקַבְּצֵם", וְעַל־יְדֵי מָה? עַל־יְדֵי: "כֻּלּוֹ זֶרַע אֱמֶת" (שָׁם בְּיִרְמְיָה סִיּוּם הַפָּסוּק "וְאָנֹכִי נְטַעְתִּיךְ" הַנַּ"ל) – עַל־יְדֵי עֲצַת הַצַּדִּיקִים תָּבוֹא לֶאֱמֶת. וְעַל־יְדֵי־זֶה נִקְרֵאת אֱמוּנָה, כַּד אִתְחַבַּר בַּהּ אֱמֶת, וְעַל־יְדֵי־זֶה תָּבוֹא הַגְּאֻלָּה כַּנַּ"ל, כִּי הוּא מְקַבֵּל טִפֵּי הַשֵּׂכֶל שֶׁל הַצַּדִּיק עַל־יְדֵי עֵצָה שֶׁמְּקַבֵּל מִמֶּנּוּ.

וְזֶה: "הֵן אֱמֶת חָפַצְתָּ בַטֻּחוֹת" – בַּכְּלָיוֹת; "חָכְמָה תוֹדִיעֵנִי" – שֶׁאֶזְכֶּה לְקַבֵּל טִפֵּי הַמֹּחַ, טִפֵּי הַשֵּׂכֶל, עַל־יְדֵי עֵצָה שֶׁאֲקַבֵּל מֵהֶם; וְאָז אֶזְכֶּה לֶאֱמֶת, כִּי הַטִּפֵּי הַשֵּׂכֶל נִקְרָא "כֻּלּוֹ זֶרַע אֱמֶת".

---

usable (the lower *sefirot* of *Netzach* and *Hod*, the kidneys). This in itself *saps the strength* of the tzaddik who strives to get people to repent.

37. **gather them in.** Concerning the word *sorek* (שורק), which has a numerical value of 606 (see Appendix: Gematria Chart), Rashi quotes a Midrash that teaches: The meaning of "I have planted you a *sorek*" is that God told the Jews, "I have given you another 606 mitzvot above the 7 Noahide laws" which are universal. These 613 mitzvot, which the *Zohar* refers to as *eitzot,* are the "counsels" and advice mentioned in the lesson.

38. **accepts from him.** The tzaddik's advice is pure, absolute truth. When a person accepts the tzaddik's advice, even without understanding the reasoning behind it (an expression of faith), he then has the truth engraved in him. This will lead him to the correct path. This person's desire for truth, as we've seen, builds up his faith, and this causes him to be directed properly. Ultimately, this will also bring on the redemption (*Parparaot LeChokhmah*). This ties into the beginning of the lesson, connecting faith to truth and accepting advice from the tzaddik.

39. **drops of the intellect...true seed.** The *Zohar Chadash* (15a) states that all seed originates in the mind. The purer the thoughts of the couple engaging in marital union, the more the child they conceive will be receptive to holiness. This is the reason it is called drops of the intellect.

In review: The essence of faith, which corresponds to prayer and miracles, is in the Land of Israel. Its antithesis is Egypt, exile, which typify a blemish of faith and miracles. Redemption, the coming of Mashiach, is dependent upon abundant faith (§1). Faith is achieved through truth. When justice is complemented by truth, it becomes faith (§2). Truth is only possible

LIKUTEY MOHARAN #7:3

from him. And [the nature of union] depends entirely upon the nature of person < giving the advice > : whether wicked or righteous.

This is the reason the Torah is *maTiSh* (saps) one's strength (*Sanhedrin* 26b).[35] It is also called *TuShiyah* (insight), for there are six hundred thirteen counsels, as in (*Proverbs* 8:14), "Mine is counsel and insight." Advice is therefore likened to marriage, an aspect of matrimonial union, which also saps one's strength.[36]

{"I have planted for you a *sorek* (a vine), an entirely true seed" (Jeremiah 2:21).}

The tzaddik's advice is "entirely true seed." This is the meaning of, "I have planted for you a *SoReK*"—this alludes to the redemption, as is written (*Zakhariah* 10:8), "*eShR'Kah* (I will whistle) to them and gather them in."[37] How will this be achieved? [They will be gathered in] through "entirely true seed"—the advice of the tzaddikim brings to truth. For through this [advice, justice] becomes faith, because it is bound up with truth. And this brings the redemption, for he receives the drops of the tzaddik's intellect through the advice which he accepts from him.[38]

This is the meaning of, "Behold, You want truth, [then] in the inner parts"—the kidneys—"...teach me wisdom." Let me merit receiving the drops of the mind, the drops of the intellect [of the tzaddikim], through the advice I will accept from them. Then I will merit the truth, for the drops of the intellect are called "entirely true seed."[39]

---

35. **saps one's strength.** Torah saps the strength because it diminishes the evil inclination's power to coerce a person to sin. Various commentators note that this is true only in the beginning, when a person first enters the realm of Torah study. Later, as one's diligence increases, his strength increases to an even greater level than what he had before beginning.

36. **also saps...strength.** "If the entire body does not feel the ejaculation, then it is not considered seed" (*Niddah* 43a). Maimonides explains that the seed is formed from the entire body and thus it is the "strength" of the entire body. Improper use of the reproductive capabilities therefore causes one's strength to be diminished (*Yad HaChazakah, Hilkhot De'ot* 4:19; *Shulchan Arukh, Orach Chaim* 240:14).

We can also infer from this comparison between advice and marital union that a person must work to create an intimate relationship with the tzaddik, similar to that of a husband and wife. Thus, in order to receive advice, one must come to love the tzaddik and desire to be close to him. Rebbe Nachman tells us (see *Tzaddik* #471) that the tzaddik's "love for his followers is very great," despite the continual effort and strength he must expend on their behalf (*ibid.*, 94). As will be made even clearer by the end of the lesson, the "entirely true seed" of advice emanates from a very high level (the upper *sefirot* of *Chokhmah* etc., the brain). It is no easy matter for the tzaddik to draw it down to a level where it becomes readily

LIKUTEY MOHARAN #7:4

14

ד. וְדַע, שֶׁעַל־יְדֵי מִצְוַת צִיצִית הָאָדָם נִצּוֹל מֵעֲצַת הַנָּחָשׁ,
מִנִּשּׂוּאִין שֶׁל רָשָׁע, מִבְּחִינַת נִאוּף, כִּי צִיצִית שְׁמִירָה לְנָאוּף;
כַּמּוּבָא בַּתִּקּוּנִים (תִּקּוּן יח): "וַיִּקַּח שֵׁם וָיֶפֶת אֶת הַשִּׂמְלָה וַיָּשִׂימוּ
עַל שְׁכֶם שְׁנֵיהֶם" (בְּרֵאשִׁית ט) – זֶה בְּחִינַת צִיצִית. "וְעֶרְוַת אֲבִיהֶם
לֹא רָאוּ" – כִּי צִיצִית מְכַסָּה עַל עֲרָיִין. אֲבָל חָם, דְּהוּא יֵצֶר הָרָע,
דִּמְחַמֵּם גּוּפֵהּ דְּבַר־נָשׁ בַּעֲבֵרָה, הוּא אָרוּר, כְּמוֹ שֶׁכָּתוּב (שָׁם):
"אָרוּר כְּנַעַן", כְּמוֹ שֶׁכָּתוּב (שָׁם ג): "אָרוּר אַתָּה מִכָּל הַבְּהֵמָה".
וְהַשִּׂמְלָה הַיְנוּ צִיצִית, הוּא שְׁמִירָה מֵעֲצַת הַנָּחָשׁ, מִזֻּהֲמַת הַנָּחָשׁ.

וְזֶה בְּחִינַת (שָׁם מ"ט): "בֵּן פֹּרָת עֲלֵי עָיִן" – בִּשְׁבִיל צִיצִית, לְשׁוֹן
(שִׁיר־הַשִּׁירִים ב): "מֵצִיץ מִן הַחֲרַכִּים", עַל־יְדֵי־זֶה זָכָה לְבֵן פֹּרָת,
שֶׁנִּשְׁמַר מִנִּשּׂוּאִין שֶׁל נָחָשׁ, מִזִּוּוּג שֶׁל הַסִּטְרָא־אָחֳרָא, וְזָכָה
לְזִוּוּגָא דִּקְדֻשָּׁה.

---

43. Kanaan. Because Kanaan initiated this action (n.40) he was the recipient of the curse. Rashi (Genesis 10:13-14) points out that Cham's offspring carried on their father's illicit ways.

44. all the animals. Rebbe Nachman quotes this verse about the curse of the Serpent, likening it to the curse put upon Cham (Kanaan). Both are said to embody the evil inclination. This effectively ties into the concept of "advice of the wicked" discussed earlier in the lesson. The Serpent and Cham (Kanaan) gave "counsel" promoting illicit sexual acts and both were immediately condemned for this. Our Sages taught: The Serpent was cursed with a gestation period of seven years (*Bekhorot* 8b). Just as its "seed" is long in coming, so too, the true nature of its advice may only be seen later on.

45. Serpent's pollution. Because the *tzitzit* protects against immorality, it automatically protects against the Serpent's pollution, which is immorality and illicit sexuality.

46. ...through the cracks. This shows how *tZItZit* corresponds to "looking." The implication is that the *tzitzit* provide, as it were, the proper "outlook"; this way of seeing things being necessary for dispensing true advice. Yosef, the tzaddik, had this outlook. It was this that protected him and through it he merited being the "fruitful bough" of Yaakov's blessing. See following notes.

47. union of holiness. Potifar was Yosef's master. When his wife tried to seduce Yosef, Yosef refused her and was subsequently incarcerated for twelve years. Later, after he became viceroy of Egypt, he took Potifar's daughter for a wife (Genesis 39:12*ff*, 41:45). Rashi explains (*ibid.*, 39:2) that Potifar's wife's astrologers informed her that she was destined to have seed from Yosef [the tzaddik], but it was not clear whether this would be through her or

LIKUTEY MOHARAN #7:4

15

4. {"Shem and Yafet took the garment and put it on both their shoulders. Walking backwards, they then covered their father's nakedness. They faced away from him and did not see their father naked" (Genesis 9:23).}

Know! through [keeping] the mitzvah of *tzitzit,* a person is protected from the Serpent's advice, from a "marriage of wickedness," from immorality. *Tzitzit* protects against immorality, as is brought in the *Tikkuney Zohar* (#18): "Shem and Yafet took the garment and put it on both their shoulders"—this is a reference to *tzitzit;* "and did not see their father naked"[40]—for *tzitzit* covers over nakedness.[41] But ChaM—the personification of the evil inclination, for he is *m'ChaMeim* (heats) a person's body to sin[42]—is cursed. As is written (Genesis 9:25), "Cursed is Kanaan"[43]; and, as in (Genesis 3:14), "Cursed are you [the Serpent] more than all the animals."[44] Thus "the garment," the *tzitzit,* is a protection against the Serpent's advice, the Serpent's pollution.[45]

This corresponds to (Genesis 49:22): "*Ben porat aley ayin* (A fruitful bough by a well)." It was because of the *tZItZit,* similar to (Song of Songs 2:9), "*meitZItZ* (he looks) through the cracks,"[46] that [Yosef] merited being a fruitful bough. For he was protected from the Serpent's marriage, from a union < of wickedness >, and merited [instead] to a union of holiness.[47]

And this is "*PoRat*"—it connotes union, similar to (Genesis 1:28),

---

through attachment to tzaddikim and carrying out their advice. Accepting their counsel is a form of holy union, whereas receiving counsel from the wicked is a form of pollution. Through the tzaddik's counsel—his "entirely true seed"—comes faith and, ultimately, redemption (§3).

40. **father naked.** After the flood, Noach planted a vineyard and then imbibed of the wine made from its grapes. He fell asleep naked and drunk. Kanaan *advised* his father Cham of this. Cham sodomized and then castrated Noach so as to prevent him from having more children. This destroyed Noach's chance to father additional offspring—i.e., the "true seed" which the tzaddik, Noach, could have produced (Genesis 9:18-27 according to *Rashi* and *Midrashim*).

41. **covers over nakedness.** The mitzvah of *tzitzit* requires placing the fringes on all four-cornered garments. This is to remind a person of all the other mitzvot of the Torah, as explained in the text (§4 below). The *tzitzit* garment covers the body and therefore protects a person from exposure to sin. Had Noach been clothed in the *tzitzit* he would have been protected from his son's immorality.

42. **m'ChaMeim...sin.** In Hebrew, the word *cham* (חם) means hot and is the root of *m'chameim* (מחמם). This is the reason Rebbe Nachman tells us that Cham is the personification of the evil inclination. He arouses the body to seek physical pleasure and brings it to sin.

LIKUTEY MOHARAN #7:4,5

וְזֶה: "פְּרָת", לְשׁוֹן זִוּוּג, לְשׁוֹן: "פְּרוּ וּרְבוּ". וְעִקַּר הַנִּאוּף תָּלוּי
בָּעֵינַיִם, כְּמוֹ שֶׁאָמְרוּ (סוֹטָה ט:): 'שִׁמְשׁוֹן הָלַךְ אַחַר עֵינָיו', וּכְמוֹ
שֶׁכָּתוּב (בְּמִדְבָּר ט"ו): "וְלֹא תָתוּרוּ אַחֲרֵי לְבַבְכֶם וְאַחֲרֵי עֵינֵיכֶם",
וּשְׁמִירַת צִיצִית, שֶׁהוּא בְּחִינַת עֵינַיִם, הוּא שְׁמִירָה מֵעֲצַת הַנָּחָשׁ,
וְיָכוֹל לְקַבֵּל הָעֵצוֹת מִצַּדִּיק, שֶׁהוּא כֻּלּוֹ זֶרַע אֱמֶת.

ה. וְזֶה פֵּרוּשׁ: אָמַר רַבָּה בַּר בַּר־חָנָה: אָמַר
לִי הַהוּא טַיָּעָא, תָּא אַחֲוֵי לָךְ טוּרָא דְסִינַי.
אַזְלִי וַחֲזָאי דְּהַדְרָן לֵהּ עַקְרַבֵּי וְקָיְמִין כִּי
חַמְרֵי חִוָּרְתָּא. וְשָׁמַעְתִּי בַּת־קוֹל שֶׁאוֹמֶרֶת:
אוֹי לִי שֶׁנִּשְׁבַּעְתִּי; וְעַכְשָׁו שֶׁנִּשְׁבַּעְתִּי, מִי מֵפֵר לִי.

רַשְׁבַּ״ם:
"שֶׁנִּשְׁבַּעְתִּי" — מִן
הַגָּלוּת, כְּדִכְתִיב קְרָאֵי
טוּבֵי בִּנְבִיאִים.

תָּא וְאַחֲוֵי לָךְ טוּרָא דְסִינַי, שֶׁהוּא בְּחִינַת עֵצוֹת, כִּי שָׁם קִבְּלוּ
תַּרְיַ״ג עֵטִין.

---

of the command to wear *tzitzit*, informing us thereby that wearing the *tzitzit* protects one from being misguided by these evil traits.

This Torah section (Numbers 15:37-41) is the third paragraph of the *Shema* and is also known as "The Exodus from Egypt"—the first redemption of the Jewish people. As Rebbe Nachman has pointed out, an essential key for redemption is truth—the "entirely true seed" and "pure counsel" of the tzaddik—this, too, being connected to the *tzitzit*.

51. ...**true seed.** It is therefore not enough for a person to remove himself from wicked advice and immorality. One must also make serious attempts, making genuine sacrifices, to achieve truth—i.e., to receive all his advice from the tzaddik. This will, in turn, bring complete faith, synonymous with an ability to pray properly, generate miracles and merit the holiness of the Land of Israel.

In review: The essence of faith, which corresponds to prayer and miracles, is in the Land of Israel. Its antithesis is Egypt, exile, which typify a blemish of faith and miracles. Redemption, the coming of Mashiach, is dependent upon abundant faith (§1). Faith is achieved through truth. When justice is complemented by truth, it becomes faith (§2). Truth is only possible through attachment to tzaddikim and carrying out their advice. Accepting their counsel is a form of holy union, whereas receiving counsel from the wicked is a form of pollution. Through the tzaddik's counsel—his "entirely true seed"—comes faith and, ultimately, redemption (§3). In particular, the mitzvah of tzitzit protects from the pollution of the wicked—i.e., immorality. It protects the eyes, so that one merits a union of holiness (§4).

52. **Mount Sinai...613 counsels.** The merchant (tzaddik) took him to Mt. Sinai for it is there that the "pure counsels" (Torah) were given. And it is from the Torah that the tzaddik draws this advice.

LIKUTEY MOHARAN #7:4,5

"P'ru u'Revu (be fruitful and multiply)." [And *"aley AYiN,"*] because immorality stems primarily from the *AYNayim* (eyes),[48] as our Sages taught: Shimshon strayed after his eyes (*Sotah* 9b).[49] It is also written (Numbers 15:39), "You will not stray after your heart or after your eyes."[50]

Thus the *tzitzit*—the eyes < of holiness > —is a protection against the Serpent's advice. A person is then able to receive advice from the tzaddik, which is "entirely true seed."[51]

5. This is the explanation:

Rabbah bar bar Chanah recounted: This merchant said to me, "Come, I will show you Mount Sinai." We went and saw that it was encircled by scorpions as tall as *chamrei chivarta* (white mules). I heard a Heavenly voice saying, "Woe to Me that I took an oath! But now that I have taken an oath, who can nullify it for Me?" (*Bava Batra* 74a).

Rashbam:

[merchant - an Ishmaelite trader:] **took an oath** - about [the Jews being] exiled, as attested to by numerous verses in the Prophets:

Come, I will show you Mount Sinai — This is an allusion to advice, for [at Mount Sinai] the Jews received the six hundred thirteen counsels.[52]

---

her daughter. Though her seductive behavior had a positive motive, it was nevertheless the "Serpent's counsel," a "marriage of wickedness," for she was another man's wife. Her daughter, on the other hand, had not been married, and was fitting for a "union of holiness."

48. **AYNayim, the eyes.** Literally, the word *ayin* means an eye. It also means a well, as in Yaakov's blessing. Here again we see a connection between *tzitzit*, the eyes and protection against immorality; though this time, by virtue of keeping one's eyes from looking out. In order to be a "fruitful bough" with "true seed"—i.e., true advice—it is necessary to rise above the immoral desires of the eyes.

49. **after his eyes.** Our Sages taught: Shimshon strayed after his eyes in taking a Philistine woman (*Sotah* 9b, 10a). Quite fittingly, the punishment for this "marriage of wickedness" came when the Philistines gouged out his eyes (Judges 14-16). Further discussion in the Talmud reveals that Shimshon's parents had *advised* him against such a union, but that he felt obligated to follow his own counsel.

50. **after your heart....** The conclusion of this verse reads, "...which lead you to immorality." The Talmud teaches (*Berakhot* 12b): "After your heart" refers to idolatry; "after your eyes" refers to immorality. This ties in very well with the themes discussed earlier in the lesson. Idolatry, as we've seen, is a lack of faith and the reason for exile. Immorality, we've been taught, serves as an obstacle to accepting the tzaddik's advice and therefore prevents us from coming to truth and complete faith. Not coincidentally, the verse forms part

LIKUTEY MOHARAN #7:5

18

חֲזַאי דְּהָדְרָן לֵהּ עַקְרַבָּא, הַיְנוּ שֶׁיֵּשׁ עֲצַת נָחָשׁ, עֲצַת רְשָׁעִים, שֶׁעַל־יְדֵיהֶם אֵין יְכוֹלִים לְקַבֵּל עֲצַת צַדִּיקִים, זֶרַע אֱמֶת.

וְקָיְמוּ כִּי חַמְרֵי חִוַּרְתָּא – זֶה בְּחִינַת צִיצִית, שֶׁהוּא שְׁמִירָה מֵעֲצַת הַנָּחָשׁ, מִנְּאוּף;

כְּמוֹ שֶׁאָמְרוּ חֲכָמֵינוּ, זִכְרוֹנָם לִבְרָכָה (מְנָחוֹת מג:): 'אֵיזֶה עָנְשׁוֹ גָּדוֹל, שֶׁל לָבָן אוֹ שֶׁל תְּכֵלֶת? וְאָמְרוּ: מָשָׁל לְאֶחָד, שֶׁצִּוָּה לְהָבִיא לוֹ חוֹתָם שֶׁל זָהָב, הַיְנוּ תְּכֵלֶת, וְחוֹתָם שֶׁל טִיט, הַיְנוּ לָבָן'. וְזֶה: "חַמְרֵי" – לְשׁוֹן חֹמֶר וָטִיט; "חִוַּרָא" – הַיְנוּ לָבָן, כִּי עַכְשָׁו זֶה עִקַּר הַצִּיצִית.

וְשָׁמַעְתִּי בַּת־קוֹל שֶׁאוֹמֶרֶת, אוֹי לִי שֶׁנִּשְׁבַּעְתִּי. פֵּרֵשׁ רַבֵּנוּ שְׁמוּאֵל: עַל הַגָּלוּת, הַיְנוּ, עַל־יְדֵי צִיצִית יְכוֹלִין לָבוֹא לַעֲצַת צַדִּיקִים, לִבְחִינַת אֱמֶת; וְעַל־יְדֵי אֱמֶת בָּאִים לֶאֱמוּנָה כַּנַּ"ל; וְעַל־יְדֵי אֱמוּנָה בָּא הַגְּאֻלָּה כַּנַּ"ל. וְזֶה שֶׁשָּׁמַע חֲרָטַת הַשֵּׁם יִתְבָּרַךְ עַל הַגָּלוּת, כִּי הַצִּיצִית שֶׁהֵם 'חַמְרֵי חִוַּרָא' גָּרַם כָּל זֶה.

---

the sky, the sky resembles a sapphire and the sapphire resembles the Heavenly Throne" (*Menachot* 43b). Now the Throne is associated with *Malkhut* (Kingship), which, as the Kabbalah teaches, corresponds to faith. The white threads are likened to truth in that whereas colored threads are produced by a dyeing process, white threads occur naturally. This truth is the advice given by the tzaddikim, the "true seed" and the white drops of the mind (see n.72 and *Likutey Moharan* I, 5).

Thus, when the Jews dwelled in the Land of Israel and the Holy Temple stood (see §1 above), t'kheilet was abundant and there was a union between sky-blue and white, faith and truth. This enabled the Jewish people to overcome the "advice of the wicked" and attach themselves to the tzaddikim (the *Sanhedrin,* the High Rabbinical Court, were the accepted leaders of the time). But when the Jews went into exile because of their lack of faith, the *chilazon* (the fish from which t'kheilet is derived) disappeared. All that was left, and all that we have today, are the white threads—truth. Consequently, without the faith which once predominated, our only hope of overcoming the "advice of the wicked" depends upon how much we accept the "white"—i.e., the advice of the tzaddikim. Indeed, as Rebbe Nachman has shown, doing so will also lead to true faith, which, in turn, will bring the redemption and the return of the *chilazon (Be'Ibey HaNachal).*

LIKUTEY MOHARAN #7:5

we saw that it was encircled by scorpions — In other words, there is the advice of the Serpent, the counsel of the wicked, which makes it impossible to receive the advice, the "true seed," of the tzaddikim.[53]

as tall as chamrei chivarta (white mules) — This alludes to the *tzitzit,* which protects against the Serpent's advice, against immorality.[54]

> {Rabbi Meir said: Not having the white threads on the *tzitzit* deserves greater punishment than not having the *t'kheilet* (sky-blue threads). Liken this to a king who issued instructions to two of his servants: one was told to bring him a seal made of clay, the other was told to bring him a seal made of gold. Each transgressed the king's order and failed to bring the seal. Whose crime was the greater? Say, then, that the servant who failed to bring the seal of clay deserves the greater punishment, for clay is more readily available (*Menachot* 43b; *Rashi, loc. cit.*).}

As our Sages taught: Which deserves greater punishment, the white or the blue? They explained: Liken it to someone who commanded that he be brought a gold seal—i.e., the blue threads— and a clay seal—i.e., the white threads. [Interpret this] as follows: *ChaMRei* refers to *ChoMeR v'tit* (clay and lime); *chivarta* is white, since nowadays this is the principal [requirement of the] *tzitzit.*[55]

I heard a Heavenly voice saying, Woe to Me that I took an oath! — The *Rashbam* explains this [as God's oath] concerning the exile. For through the *tzitzit* one can come to the advice of the tzaddikim, to truth. And with truth a person can achieve faith. And faith brings the redemption, as explained. This is why [Rabbah bar bar Chanah] heard God regretting the exile: The *tzitzit*—the *chamrei chivarta*— caused all this.

---

53. **scorpions...tzaddikim.** Satan is "the Serpent," and his "wife," Lilit, is a scorpion (*Tikkuney Zohar,* Introduction). The huge scorpions standing around Mt. Sinai are an allusion to those things which prevent a person from reaching the source of true advice and good counsel.

54. **tall...white mules...immorality.** The scorpions stood as huge as the mules. In other words, the wicked advice seems just like true advice. This is because (Ecclesiastes 7:14) "God made one to parallel the other," with man being given the free will to choose between holiness and immorality. See *Mayim* (Breslov Research Institute, 1988).

The *tzitzit* is what enables one to stand up to the "scorpions," to the wicked advice (*Mai HaNachal*).

55. **white...of the tzitzit.** The *t'kheilet* (sky-blue) and white threads represent faith and truth. The sky-blue coloring is likened to faith because "it resembles the sea and the sea resembles

LIKUTEY MOHARAN #7:6

20

ו. וְזֶה פֵּרוּשׁ: "וְאֵלֶּה" – כָּל מָקוֹם שֶׁנֶּאֱמַר 'וְאֵלֶּה' מוֹסִיף; זֶה בְּחִינַת יוֹסֵף, בְּחִינַת שְׁמִירַת הַבְּרִית, בְּחִינַת צִיצִית. הַמִּשְׁפָּטִים – זֶה בְּחִינַת 'כֻּלּוֹ זֶרַע אֱמֶת', כְּמוֹ שֶׁכָּתוּב (תְּהִלִּים י"ט): "מִשְׁפְּטֵי ה' אֱמֶת", שֶׁזּוֹכֶה לַעֲצַת צַדִּיקִים, לִבְחִינַת אֱמֶת.

אֲשֶׁר תָּשִׂים לִפְנֵיהֶם – זֶה בְּחִינוֹת 'כַּד אִתְחַבַּר בַּהּ אֱמֶת', וְזֶה בְּחִינַת 'הֵשָׁווּ אִשָּׁה לְאִישׁ', כִּי זֶה אִישׁ וְאִשָּׁה הֵם בְּחִינַת הִתְחַבְּרוּת אֱמֶת וֶאֱמוּנָה, וּבָזֶה תָּלוּי הַגְּאֻלָּה כַּנַּ"ל.

וְזֶה: 'יָכוֹל שֶׁיִּהְיוּ הַתַּלְמִידִים לוֹמְדִים וְאֵין מְבִינִים – תַּלְמוּד לוֹמַר וְכוּ', עָרְכֶם לִפְנֵיהֶם כְּשֻׁלְחָן עָרוּךְ', זֶה בְּחִינַת הַגְּאֻלָּה, שֶׁלֶּעָתִיד יִתְגַּלּוּ כָּל הַחָכְמוֹת כְּשֻׁלְחָן עָרוּךְ, כְּמוֹ שֶׁכָּתוּב (יְשַׁעְיָהוּ י"א): "וּמָלְאָה הָאָרֶץ דֵּעָה".

(עַד כָּאן לְשׁוֹן רַבֵּנוּ, זִכְרוֹנוֹ לִבְרָכָה)

---

61. **truth and faith.** Concerning the verse (Isaiah 43:6), "Bring My sons from afar and My daughters from the ends of the earth," the Talmud teaches (*Menachot* 110a): "Sons" alludes to those whose minds are clear; "daughters" to those who lack clarity of mind. Clarity of mind corresponds to truth, to a clear understanding. A lack of clarity corresponds to faith, which applies when the mind cannot understand clearly. This is the reason man and woman are likened to truth and faith, respectively.

62. **wisdoms will be revealed.** The *Zohar* (III, 23a) teaches that at the time of the Mashiach's coming, God will reveal all the great wisdoms, as in, "And the earth shall be filled with knowledge...." They will be set out for man to partake of as he pleases.

63. **filled with knowledge.** How can a student receive and accept his teacher's advice when he does not understand its reasoning? Furthermore, even if he does accept it, what value will it have if he lacks the comprehension needed to apply this advice in other, yet similar, situations? However, it should be realized that when the student accepts his master's teaching despite his failure to comprehend it, this is an act of faith. Through this faith, the student is molded into a vessel for receiving the "true seed," the tzaddik's advice, in as pure a form as is possible. This eventually enables him to attain a higher perception and comprehension—a deeper knowledge—of the tzaddik's advice, which, in turn, brings him to an even greater level of faith. And then, with this still greater level of faith he receives an even higher degree of the "true seed," and so on.

Earlier (see §4), Rebbe Nachman explained that the tzaddik's advice can be likened to the blessing to "be fruitful and multiply." By accepting this advice the student grows mentally and spiritually, to the point where he can understand the tzaddik's words in a broader

21 **LIKUTEY MOHARAN #7:6**

6. This is the explanation [of the opening verse]:
{*"V'eileh* (And these) are the laws that you must place before them."}

V'eileh — Wherever the term *v'eileh* (*and* these) is used, it comes to add.[56] This alludes to: Yosef,[57] guarding the Covenant,[58] and the *tzitzit*.[59]

are the laws — This corresponds to "entirely true seed," as in (Psalms 19:9), "God's laws are truth." One merits receiving the counsel of the tzaddikim—the aspect of truth.

that you shall place before them — That is, when [justice] is bound with truth.

And this is: **woman is equated with man.**[60] For < the aspect of > "man" and "woman" allude to the joining of truth and faith,[61] and it is on this that the redemption depends.

And this is: **It might be that the students study but fail to comprehend. [Scripture] therefore states: "that you must place before them"—spread it out before them as a fully set table** — This is a reference to the redemption. For in the future, all wisdoms will be revealed[62] as a fully set table, as in (Isaiah 11:9), "And the earth shall be filled with knowledge...."[63]

---

56. **V'eileh...add.** Wherever the term *v'eileh* [*v'* (and), *eileh* (these)] is used, it comes to add to that which is prior to it (*Bereishit Rabbah* 30:3).

57. **Yosef.** "[Rachel] named the child yOSeF, saying, 'May God grant me an additional son' " (Genesis 30:24); the word *l'hOSiF* means to add. The letter *vav* (in *v'eileh*), with its numerical value of six, also alludes to the tzaddik/Yosef, in that the Kabbalah teaches that tzaddik corresponds to *Yesod*, which is the sixth *sefirah* of the persona *Z'er Anpin* (the masculine principle; see Appendix: The Divine Persona; The Seven Supernal Shepherds).

58. **Covenant.** Yosef is called "the tzaddik" because he guarded the Covenant by keeping his sexual purity, not succumbing to the entreaties of Potifar's wife (*Zohar* II, 23a). Also see *Likutey Moharan* I, 2:2.

59. **tzitzit.** See beginning of section 4: The mitzvah of *tzitzit* has the power to protect a person from the Serpent's advice, from a "marriage of wickedness," from immorality.

60. **woman is equated with man.** Rebbe Nachman now shows how the two explanations of "before them" (see n.1) come together as part of the unified tapestry of his lesson. He begins with the first explanation: "before them" teaches us that woman is equated with man. As we've seen (n.27), *tzedek* (justice) and *emunah* (faith) are both forms of judgment—both corresponding to the feminine principle. Now that the harsher quality of justice has been tempered with the truth—the "true seed," the counsel of the tzaddik—it has become faith. Truth (*Tiferet*) and faith (*Malkhut*), man and woman, are thus equal.

LIKUTEY MOHARAN #7:7

22

(הַשְׁמָטוֹת הַשַּׁיָּכִים לְהַתּוֹרָה הַזֹּאת) :

ז. הַתְּפִלָּה הוּא בְּחִינַת אֱמוּנָה, וְהוּא בְּחִינַת הַנִּסִּים, כִּי נֵס לְמַעְלָה מִטֶּבַע, וְלָזֶה צָרִיךְ אֱמוּנָה כַּנַּ"ל, עַיֵּן שָׁם.
וּבִשְׁבִיל זֶה, הַתְּפִלָּה מְסֻגָּל לְזִכָּרוֹן, כִּי תְּפִלָּה הוּא בְּחִינַת אֱמוּנָה כַּנַּ"ל. וְשִׁכְחָה הוּא עִנְיָן, שֶׁהָיָה לְפָנֵינוּ דְּבַר-מָה וְנִשְׁכַּח וְעָבַר מֵאִתָּנוּ. (וְהִיא דֶּרֶךְ הַהַנְהָגָה עַל-פִּי מַעֲרֶכֶת הַמַּזָּלוֹת, שֶׁמִּתְנַהֵג כְּסֵדֶר יוֹם אַחַר יוֹם, וְהוּא הֵפוּךְ הָאֱמוּנָה. מַה שֶּׁאֵין כֵּן אִם מַאֲמִין שֶׁיֵּשׁ מְחַדֵּשׁ הַכֹּל בִּרְצוֹנוֹ בְּכָל יוֹם תָּמִיד, וְהוּא מְחַיֶּה וּמְקַיֵּם הַכֹּל תָּמִיד, וְהוּא לְמַעְלָה מֵהַזְּמַן, אֵין כָּאן שִׁכְחָה, וְדוּ"ק).

וּמֵעַתָּה תִּרְאֶה נִפְלָאוֹת בְּדִבְרֵי רַבּוֹתֵינוּ, זִכְרוֹנָם לִבְרָכָה (שַׁבָּת קד.) : 'מֵ"ם וְסָמֶ"ךְ שֶׁבַּלוּחוֹת בְּנֵס הָיוּ עוֹמְדִין'; כִּי מֵס הוּא בְּחִינַת הַשִּׁכְחָה, וְעַל זֶה אָמְרוּ רַבּוֹתֵינוּ, זִכְרוֹנָם לִבְרָכָה (חֲגִיגָה ט:) : 'אֵין דּוֹמֶה הַשּׁוֹנֶה פִּרְקוֹ מֵאָה פְּעָמִים לְמֵאָה פְּעָמִים וְאֶחָד'. כִּי מֵס בְּגִימַטְרִיָּא מֵאָה, וְעַד מֵאָה שׁוֹלֵט הַשַּׂר שֶׁל שִׁכְחָה. וְזֶה שֶׁהִמְתִּיקוּ

66. **held...miracle.** All the letters of the Ten Commandments were engraved on the Tablets through to the other side. As the final-*mem* (ם) and *samakh* (ס) are hollow in their center, how could they stay in place? The Talmud answers that they were held in place through a miracle (*Shabbat, loc. cit.*).

67. **one hundred and one times.** "You shall see the difference between a tzaddik and a wicked person, one who served God and one who did not serve Him" (Malakhi 3:18). Our Sages (*Chagigah* 9b) question the apparent redundancy in the verse. Their answer is that the second half of the verse is not speaking about a wicked man, but about two different levels of tzaddik, one "who served" and one who, relatively speaking, is known as "not having served." The tzaddik who served God reviewed his studies 101 times. The tzaddik who did not serve reviewed them but 100 times. Here Rebbe Nachman shows that it is only the person who can elevate himself to the level of "memory" who is considered as having served God.
The numerical difference between *zachor* (remembering, זכר = 227) and *shakhach* (forgetting, שכח = 328) is 101 (*Rabbi Elchonon Spector*).

68. **one hundred.** The *mem* has a numerical value of 40, and the *samakh* a value of 60.

69. **Angel...reigns.** *Samakh-Mem* is an acrostic for the name of the angel (whose name we are cautioned not to mention) *SaMael*. He is alternatively referred to as Samakh-Mem, Satan, or the Serpent, and is the Angel of Forgetfulness who tries to make a person forget God.

23 *LIKUTEY MOHARAN #7:7*

7. (Excerpts belonging to this lesson.)

Prayer is synonymous with faith, which in turn is synonymous with miracles. This is because a miracle is supernatural, it is something for which one needs to have faith. {See [section 1] above.} Because of this, prayer is beneficial for memory; for, as mentioned, prayer corresponds to faith. But forgetfulness entails having had something in mind, its lapsing from memory and being no longer a part of us.[64] {This can be likened to [seeing as pre-determined] the movements of the constellations, which follow a prescribed pattern day after day. And this is the very opposite of faith. Whereas, if a person believes that there is One who daily renews everything in accordance with His will, who perpetually sustains and supports everything, and who is above [the limitations of] time, then forgetfulness has no place.[65]}

See, now, the wonders in the words of our Sages: The [letters] *mem* and *samakh* which were on the Tablets were held in place through a miracle (*Shabbat* 104a).[66] *Mem-samakh* corresponds to forgetfulness. Concerning this our Sages taught: Someone who reviews his lesson one hundred times cannot be compared to someone who reviews one hundred and one times (*Chagigah* 9b).[67] For *mem-samakh* has a numerical value of one hundred,[68] [alluding to the fact that] for the first one hundred times the Angel of Forgetfulness reigns.[69] This is

[handwritten margin note: if one connects to H' there is no concept of time, therefore no forgetfulness]

---

perspective and thus apply them to different situations. This is the implication of "be fruitful and multiply" in that the true advice enables the recipient to expand the context of the original teaching to include other [diverse and timely] circumstances (*Parparaot LeChokhmah*). (To this point in the lesson is *leshon Rabbeinu z'l*, see n.1 above.)

64. **no longer a part of us.** It is very important that we accept and remember all the teachings of the Torah and the advice of the true tzaddikim. But, after centuries of exile and persecution, the "power of forgetfulness" has increased immensely, as in, "In the days to come, all is forgotten" (Ecclesiastes 2:16). The result is that even while studying, our ability to remember fails us, sometimes instantly, so that before long everything has been forgotten. Because of this it is imperative that we follow the teaching in this lesson: to wear the *tzitzit* and, while putting them on, pray that we merit to receive and remember the advice of the true tzaddikim, so that we can put it into practice. By doing so we will attain truth and faith, as well as prayer and miracles—all of which supersede the dictates of nature and time. On the level above time, [just as there is no before and after,] there is no forgetting. Then, all the true advice received and all the Torah learned will be remembered. This coincides with the Torah chapter regarding the *tzitzit* (see n.50) in which the verse states (Numbers 15:39), "You shall see the *tzitzit* and remember all the mitzvot..." (*Mai HaNachal*).

65. **forgetfulness has no place.** This is because through prayer one is attached to God, who is above time, and so nothing is ever in the past. There is no before and no after; only the present, in which there is no forgetfulness, as explained in the previous note.

LIKUTEY MOHARAN #7:7

חֲזַ"ל: מֵ"ם וְסָמֶ"ךְ, הַיְנוּ מַס שֶׁהוּא בְּחִינַת הַשִּׁכְחָה, בְּנֵס הָיוּ עוֹמְדִין, כִּי נֵס הוּא הֵפֶךְ הַשִּׁכְחָה, כִּי נִסִּים הֵם בְּחִינַת הַתְּפִלָּה, בְּחִינַת אֱמוּנָה, שֶׁהִיא הֵפֶךְ הַשִּׁכְחָה, כַּנַּ"ל.

וְדַע וְכוּ' כִּי צִיצִית שְׁמִירָה לְנִאוּף וְכוּ', עַל שְׁכֶם שְׁנֵיהֶם זֶה בְּחִינַת צִיצִית וְכוּ'. וְזֶה (בְּרֵאשִׁית ל"ז): "הֲלֹא אַחֶיךָ רֹעִים בִּשְׁכֶם", הַיְנוּ בְּחִינַת צִיצִית כַּנַּ"ל, שֶׁהִיא שְׁמִירָה לְנִאוּף, וְהוּא בְּחִינַת שְׁמִירַת הַבְּרִית, שֶׁהִיא בְּחִינַת יוֹסֵף. עַל כֵּן אָמַר יַעֲקֹב לְיוֹסֵף: "הֲלוֹא אַחֶיךָ רֹעִים בִּשְׁכֶם", שֶׁהוּא בְּחִינָה שֶׁלְּךָ; "לְכָה וְאֶשְׁלָחֲךָ אֲלֵיהֶם".

וְזֶה פֵּרוּשׁ: "וְאָנֹכִי נְטַעְתִּיךְ שׂוֹרֵק" וְכוּ', כִּי הוּא מְקַבֵּל טִפֵּי הַשֵּׂכֶל שֶׁל הַצַּדִּיק עַל־יְדֵי עֵצָה שֶׁמְּקַבֵּל מִמֶּנּוּ. וְזֶה שׂוֹרֵק הוּא בְּחִינַת שׁוּרֵק, שֶׁהוּא תְּלָת טִפִּין, כְּמוֹ שֶׁכָּתוּב בַּזֹּהַר (וּבַתִּקּוּנִים, תִּקּוּן נ"ו), וְהוּא תְּלָת מֹחִין. כִּי הוּא עִנְיָן אֶחָד, כִּי הַטִּפָּה בָּאָה מֵהַמֹּחַ וּמַגִּיעָה לְהַכְּלָיוֹת, שֶׁהֵן כְּלֵי הַהוֹלָדָה, שֶׁמְּבַשְּׁלִין הַזֶּרַע. כֵּן הַשֵּׂכֶל נוֹלָד גַּם כֵּן בַּמֹּחַ וּמַגִּיעַ עַד הַכְּלָיוֹת הַיּוֹעֲצוֹת.

---

considered a punishment. Each of the 10 brothers died during the Egyptian bondage, and so the exile of the Jewish people was shortened to 210 years (as in n.9). Prior to this episode, the Torah relates that Yosef had told his [prophetic] dreams to his brothers. However, the brothers were not willing to accept Yosef's [the tzaddik's] "advice." Now, when Yaakov sent Yosef to Shekhem, he was suggesting that they were perhaps ready to receive his counsel; "Shekhem" being Yosef's quality. Had the brothers accepted Yosef, the family's descent into Egypt, though still necessary (see *The Breslov Haggadah, passim*, Breslov Research Inst., 1989), would have been under entirely different circumstances.

72. **ShuRuK...mochin...brains.** Physically, the brain is divided into three main parts: the cerebrum, the cerebellum and the medulla. In Kabbalistic terminology, the body is aligned with the ten *sefirot* broken into two categories, the *mochin* (the three *sefirot* of Wisdom, Understanding and Knowledge) and the *guf* (the body of seven lower *sefirot*). The three dots which make up the vowel point known as the *shuruk* (ֻ) allude to the three brains and correspond to the "three drops," the seed which emanates from the brain.

73. **intellect...kidneys which advise.** By extension, the *kley holadah* (reproductive organs) can be understood as "parts of the body which *give birth* to new ideas." Rebbe Nachman therefore focuses on the correlation between the first stages in the conception of a child and

LIKUTEY MOHARAN #7:7

what our Sages brought out so artfully: "The [letters] *mem* and *samakh*"—the one hundred of forgetfulness—"were held in place through a miracle"; miracles being the very opposite of forgetfulness. For, as mentioned above, miracles are synonymous with prayer and faith, [faith] being the very opposite of forgetfulness.[70]

Know!...tzitzit protects against immorality...on both their SheKheM (shoulders)...a reference to tzitzit. [See section 4, above.] This is (Genesis 37:13), "Your brothers are shepherding in SheKheM"— an allusion to the *tzitzit,* which protects against immorality. [The *tzitzit*] corresponds to guarding the Covenant, which in turn applies to Yosef. Yaakov therefore said to Yosef, "Your brothers are shepherding in Shekhem"—which is *your* aspect. "Come, let me send you to them."[71]   *tikkun habns*

This is the meaning of: **"I have planted you a sorek, an entirely true seed"...for then, one receives the drops of the tzaddik's intellect through the advice which he accepts from him.** This *"SoReK"* alludes to the *ShuRuK,* which the *Zohar* (*Tikkuney Zohar* #56) calls "three drops." Conceptually, this is the same as the three *mochin* (brains).[72] For the drop emanates from the brain and descends to the kidneys, the organ in the reproductive system which prepares the seed. Similarly, the intellect is also formed in the mind and descends to the kidneys, which advise.[73]

---

70. **opposite of forgetfulness.** In short: Faith, prayer, miracles, the Land of Israel, the redemption and memory have all been shown to interconnect. They can be achieved through truth, by receiving the "entirely true seed," the advice of the tzaddikim. Rebbe Nachman has also shown that this advice has the power to negate the effects of idolatry, natural phenomena, exile and forgetfulness, all of which stem from the Samakh-Mem, advice of the wicked and the Serpent.

71. **Shekhem...to them.** Shekhem (also Nablus) is the name of a city in the Land of Israel. It is located in the tribal territory of Yosef's son Efraim, and Yosef is buried there. The word *shekhem* also means shoulder. The connection between these two meanings is as follows: Shem and Yafet, as a sign of their modesty, placed the garment on their shoulder so as not to see their father's nakedness. This was symbolic of guarding the Covenant, synonymous with both the tzaddik, Yosef, and Shekhem itself. This is why Yaakov told Yosef that his brothers were in Shekhem, Yosef's quality, and then said, "Come, let me send you to them."

This can be further understood in light of the commentary offered by the *Zohar* (*Zohar Chadash* p.36a): When Yosef came to his brothers, they sold him into slavery. He was taken to Egypt and was separated from his father for a period of 22 years. Ten brothers were involved in this sale and each one had to atone individually for the 22 years of Yaakov's suffering. Thus, the total exile should have been 220 years, were it not that death itself is

LIKUTEY MOHARAN #7:7

וּתְלַת מֹחִין, הוּא בְּחִינַת (יְשַׁעְיָהוּ ו): "הַשְׁמֵן לֵב וְכוּ' וְאָזְנָיו וְכוּ' וְעֵינָיו וְכוּ', פֶּן יִרְאֶה בְעֵינָיו וּבְאָזְנָיו יִשְׁמַע וּלְבָבוֹ יָבִין וָשָׁב וְכוּ'", כְּלוֹמַר, שֶׁאֵינוֹ רוֹצֶה לְדַבֵּק עַצְמוֹ לַצַּדִּיקִים פֶּן יִרְאֶה וְכוּ'. אֲבָל כְּשֶׁמְּדַבֵּק עַצְמוֹ לְצַדִּיקִים וּמְקַבֵּל מֵהֶם עֵצָה, אֲזַי הוּא בְּחִינַת כְּלָיוֹת יוֹעֲצוֹת, שֶׁהֵם כְּלֵי הַהוֹלָדָה, שֶׁמְּקַבֵּל הַטִּפָּה מֹחַ הַמִּתְחַלֶּקֶת לִתְלַת טִפִּין, תְּלַת מֹחִין כַּנַּ"ל; וְאָז יִרְאֶה בְעֵינָיו וּבְאָזְנָיו יִשְׁמַע וּלְבָבוֹ יָבִין וְכוּ', שֶׁהֵם בְּחִינַת הַשְּׁלֹשָׁה מֹחִין – וָשָׁב וְרָפָא לוֹ. וְזֶהוּ: "וְאָנֹכִי נְטַעְתִּיךְ שׂוֹרֵק כֻּלֹּה זֶרַע אֱמֶת", וְהָבֵן.

וְזֶה פֵּרוּשׁ: אָמַר רַבָּה בַּר בַּר־חָנָה וְכוּ', וְזֶה רָמַז גַּם כֵּן בְּפֶתַח דְּבָרָיו: אָמַר לִי הַהוּא טַיְעָא, וּפֵרֵשׁ רַבֵּנוּ שְׁמוּאֵל: בְּכָל מָקוֹם סוֹחֵר יִשְׁמָעֵאל; כִּי יִשְׁמָעֵאל הוּא בְּחִינַת הַתְּפִלָּה, כְּמוֹ שֶׁכָּתוּב (בְּרֵאשִׁית ט"ז): "כִּי שָׁמַע ה' אֶל עָנְיֵךְ", וְתַרְגּוּמוֹ: 'אֲרֵי קַבִּיל ה' יָת צְלוֹתִיךְ',

וְהוּא בְּחִינַת אֱמוּנָה כַּנַּ"ל. וְזֶהוּ סוֹחֵר, מִלְּשׁוֹן סָחוֹר סָחוֹר (בְּחִינַת מַקִּיפִים), שֶׁהוּא בְּחִינַת אֱמוּנָה כַּנַּ"ל, "וֶאֱמוּנָתְךָ סְבִיבוֹתֶיךָ" (תְּהִלִּים פ"ט).

---

personal level, by receiving the tzaddik's advice he will experience redemption because of the deeper knowledge in his heart, and it can therefore be said that he will "understand with his heart."

75. **makifin.** Man's intellect works on two levels, the *pnimi* (internal and inner) and the *makif* (external and surrounding). The *pnimi* relates to that knowledge which a person has already grasped and incorporated. The *makif* relates to that deeper knowledge which he is still attempting to understand, and which is, as it were, yet "surrounding" him. This connection between the *makifin* and faith which *encircles* a person indicates that the surrounding knowledge—i.e., all the great wisdoms to be revealed at the time of Mashiach's coming (see n.62)—will be achieved through truth and faith, as explained above.

76. **...encircles You.** The interpretation of Rabbah bar bar Chanah's statement would then be: "This merchant"—an iShMAelite (trader), i.e., prayer—"said to me." He said, "Come, I will show you Mt. Sinai"—prayer cannot be achieved unless one comes to receive true advice.

The *Parparaot LeChokhmah* adds the following insight, based on Ashkenazic custom:

— We recite the morning prayers [itself a form of union with God] adorned with a *tallit* bearing *tzitzit*.

— When putting on the *tallit* one is obligated to wrap it around himself, *k'atifat Ishmaelim* (as an Arab would put on his kaffiyeh).

LIKUTEY MOHARAN #7:7

And the three *mochin* correspond to (Isaiah 6:10), "Make the heart of this people gross, its ears heavy, and cover over its eyes; lest it see with its eyes, hear with its ears, understand with its heart and repent and be healed." [The prophet] says this of one who refuses to attach himself to the tzaddikim, 'lest he see...and repent.'

But when a person attaches himself to the tzaddikim and accepts their advice, this is the concept of "the kidneys advise," for they are reproductive organs. He receives the drop/brain that separates into three drops—three brains. And then, 'He *will* see with his eyes, hear with his ears, understand with his heart'—these corresponding to the three brains—'and repent and be healed.' This is: "I have planted you a *sorek*, an entirely true seed." Understand this.[74]

This is the explanation of **Rabbah bar bar Chanah recounted** etc. [The connection to prayer] is also alluded to in Rabbah bar bar Chanah's opening words, "This merchant said to me." The Rashbam explains that this is always an allusion to *socher Yishmael* (an Ishmaelite trader). For *yiShMAel* connotes prayer, as is written (Genesis 16:11), "[You shall name him Yishmael] for God has *SheMA* (heard) your affliction," which Onkelos renders: "for God has accepted your prayers."

[Prayer] is also synonymous with faith. This is [alluded to by the word] *SoCheR,* which connotes *S'ChoR s'chor* (round and round) {corresponding to the concept of *makifin.*[75]} And this corresponds to faith, as in, "Your faith encircles You."[76]

---

those in the conception of ideas. When conceiving a child, the "drop" emanates from the brain and descends to the reproductive organs which "prepare" the seed. In the process of conceiving new ideas, the drops of the intellect are formed in the mind from where they descend to the kidneys "which advise."

74. **eyes...ears...heart....Understand this.** The *Parparaot LeChokhmah* explains how these three allude to truth, faith and a deeper knowledge as discussed throughout the lesson and in note 38 and 63 above. When a person receives advice from the tzaddik, he is engraved with truth. To some degree his intellect can actually perceive this truth. In a sense, he *sees* it. Because of the connection between intellectual comprehension and the mind's eye, it can therefore be said that "he will see with his eyes." Faith, on the other hand, relates to the ears. When a person believes in something he *hears* from others, but which he himself does not comprehend, this is faith. Though he may lack the ability to intellectually comprehend what he's been told, he does hear it as something worth believing in. This is the implication of the *Shema*—"Hear O Israel!"—and it can therefore be said that he will "hear with his ears." Finally, with truth and faith a person comes to a more complete understanding, to the deeper knowledge and wisdom which will only be revealed to all in the time of the redemption. On a

LIKUTEY MOHARAN #7:7

וְזֶהוּ (רוּת ג): "וּפָרַשְׂתָּ כְנָפֶךָ עַל אֲמָתְךָ", כִּי צִיצִית דִּקְדֻשָּׁה, שֶׁהֵם כַּנְפֵי מִצְוָה, הוּא שְׁמִירַת הַבְּרִית וְהוּא בְּחִינַת זִוּוּג דִּקְדֻשָּׁה. וְזֶהוּ שֶׁשָּׁאַל חַגַּי הַנָּבִיא (חַגַּי ב): "הֵן יִשָּׂא אִישׁ בְּשַׂר־קֹדֶשׁ בִּכְנַף בִּגְדוֹ וְנָגַע בִּכְנָפוֹ אֶל הַלֶּחֶם", כִּי פְּגַם הַבְּרִית – הֶעְדֵּר הַלֶּחֶם, כְּמוֹ שֶׁכָּתוּב (מִשְׁלֵי ו): "בְּעַד אִשָּׁה זוֹנָה עַד כִּכַּר לָחֶם", וְהָבֵן: "וַתֵּשֶׁב בְּאֵיתָן קַשְׁתּוֹ וְכוּ', מִשָּׁם רוֹעֶה אֶבֶן יִשְׂרָאֵל" (בְּרֵאשִׁית מ"ט)

marriage of Ruth to Boaz—prayer to truth—the redemption (through the redeemer, the son of David) will come. See *Parparaot LeChokhmah* and *Mai HaNachal*.

The name RUTh (רות) has the same numerical value as the word *SOReK* (see above n.37), and thus is also indicative of the additional 606 mitzvot which she took upon herself when she converted and which God gave the Jews as "counsels" for bringing the redemption.

79. **contact with bread.** While the Second Temple was being rebuilt, Hagai, a prophet and member of the Great Assembly, placed certain questions before the *kohanim* (priests) to test their familiarity with the laws of purity and impurity. According to the *Chokhmat Shelomoh* (on *Pesachim* 16b) the question quoted in the text concerns the law for consecrated meat sitting in the corner of a garment which had become impure through contact with a reptile (which is impure). This meat then touched a piece of bread or some pottage etc. What affect does this indirect impurity have, when the last item comes in contact with consecrated food?

80. **Understand this.** Rebbe Nachman interprets this question as a veiled reference to "guarding the Covenant," i.e., sexual purity. Thus: "consecrated meat" alludes to the sign of the Covenant, the mitzvah of circumcision. The "corner of his garment" refers to the *tzitzit*, which guards against immorality. However, this "garment" (the protective *tzitzit*) has itself become impure through contact with the reptile (immoral behavior). When it then comes in contact with the meat (the Covenant), the meat also becomes impure. All this alludes to defiling of one's sexual purity—the blemishing of the Covenant "by means of a harlot." Now, "[this meat in] the corner came in contact with bread," making it also impure. This indicates that his bread, his livelihood, has also been blemished. He will then never have sufficient income and, as the verse quoted in the text concludes, "...a man is brought to [go searching] for a loaf of bread."

In notes 6 and 14 above, we've seen a partial indication of the relationship which truth and faith have with one's livelihood. The connection here is that by seeking the truth, a person will come to complete faith: that God provides and that all his needs will be met. This is because he has come to receive the true advice of the tzaddik—Yosef, the *tzitzit*—and as a result *his own* garment has remained pure. And indeed, because of this faith, miracles will occur (see connection in §1) to provide him with whatever he needs. This, in fact, is what happened to Yosef. Because he was the tzaddik who guarded the Covenant, Yosef—through the true advice which he gave—was made viceroy over Egypt. He was thus put in charge of the livelihood of his entire generation.

However, if a person presumes that not God, but his own efforts and the course of natural events are what provide him with his livelihood, then he has accepted the unholy advice of the Serpent. Through this polluted union, this blemishing of the Covenant, his garment and therefore his bread have been made impure. Rebbe Nachman teaches that it is

LIKUTEY MOHARAN #7:7

This is also the meaning of (Ruth 3:9), "Spread, therefore, *K'NaFekha* (your garment) over your maidservant." For the holy *tzitzit*—the *KaNFey* (garment corners of) mitzvah—corresponds to guarding the Covenant[77] and to a union of holiness.[78]

And this is the explanation of what the prophet Hagai asked (2:12), "If one carried consecrated meat in the *K'NaF* of his garment, and [this meat in] the corner came in contact with bread...."[79] For desecrating the Covenant diminishes one's bread, as is written (Proverbs 6:26), "For a harlot, a man is brought to [go searching for] a loaf of bread." Understand this.[80]

"His bow held firm...from there the Shepherd, the *evan* (Rock) of Israel" (Genesis 49:24). [Onkelos renders "*ÆVaN*" as a composite word,]

— One does not begin wearing the large *tallit* until he is married. In the Talmud, marriage is known as *kiddushin*, from the same root as the word *kedushah* (holiness). Based on our lesson, this can be understood as a reference to the "union of holiness" created when one accepts advice from the tzaddik (sections 3 and 4 of lesson).

— This also ties into the custom (according to the *Rokeach*) that for the *chupah* (wedding canopy) a *tallit* should be used, because it is symbolic of the "union of holiness" created through the *tzitzit*, the tzaddik's advice.

77. **KaNFey mitzvah...guarding the Covenant.** Aside from the *tallit*, the prayer shawl Jewish men wear while praying, it is a mitzvah to wear another four-cornered garment at all times. This smaller garment, to which fringes are attached at each of the corners, is colloquially known as "*arba kanfot*." As mentioned above (n.41), the mitzvah of placing *tzitzit* on all four-cornered garments is connected to the concept of modesty. By covering the body, we protect it from exposure to sin.

On one level, when Ruth said to Boaz, "Spread, therefore, your garment over your maidservant," she was telling him to cover her, his maidservant, with the garment of mitzvah. On another level, Ruth was warning Boaz to protect himself from sin. The Hebrew word for maidservant, *amah,* is also used as a reference to the procreative organ, the *brit*. She was telling him to exercise modesty by, as it were, covering the *amah* with the garment of mitzvah. This, in essence, is the connection to guarding the Covenant which Rebbe Nachman points out (see n.71).

78. **union of holiness.** Our Sages taught: She was called Ruth (רות) because it would one day be said of her descendant King David that he *ravah* (רוה, satiated) God with song and prayers of praise (*Berakhot* 7b). Accordingly, Ruth is synonymous with prayer. Boaz, to whom the statement quoted in the text was made, was being tested with "guarding the Covenant"—a test of morality even greater than Yosef's (see *Sanhedrin* 19b). He is also referred to as tzaddik (*Likutey Moharan* I, 11; *Tikkuney Zohar* #31). With this, we can understand that prayer (Ruth) was asking that the tzaddik (Boaz) spread the *tzitzit* (his garment), the true advice, over it. This, in order to bring about a union of holiness between prayer and truth (between Ruth and Boaz). Thus, the verse "Spread therefore your garment over you maidservant" concludes, "...for you are a redeemer." This indicates that through the

LIKUTEY MOHARAN #7:7,8

– אֲבָהָן וּבְנִין, בְּחִינַת הַתְּפִלָּה יַעֲקֹב וּבָנָיו.

סְגֻלָּה לְחוֹלֶה – לְהִסְתַּכֵּל עַל הַצִּיצִית. וְהַסּוֹד בַּפָּסוּק (שָׁם מ״ח): "הִנֵּה בִנְךָ יוֹסֵף בָּא אֵלֶיךָ". כִּי כָּל אֵלּוּ הַתֵּבוֹת מְרַמְּזִין עַל הַצִּיצִית, דְּהַיְנוּ מִנְיַן הַחוּטִין וְהַחֲלָיוֹת וְהַקְּשָׁרִים, (כַּמְבֹאָר בִּ״פְרִי-עֵץ-חַיִּים" בְּשַׁעַר הַצִּיצִית, פֶּרֶק ד', בַּהַגָּ״ה, עַיֵּן שָׁם.) ז"ל הפע"ח: ט"ל כריכות הם קנ"ו כמנין יוסף וסמ"ך גודלין יש בכל הכנפות עם הציצית כמנין הנה וכמנין בנך חוליות וקשרים. והחוטין הם ל"ב והם שזורין הרי ס"ד כמנין בא אליך ע"כ: וְזֶהוּ: "הִנֵּה בִנְךָ יוֹסֵף בָּא אֵלֶיךָ", דְּהַיְנוּ בְּחִינַת צִיצִית כַּנַּ״ל, עַל-יְדֵי-זֶה "וַיִּתְחַזֵּק יִשְׂרָאֵל".

83. **strings, loops and knots....** This explanation appears in the *Pri Etz Chaim, Shaar HaTzitzit* 4, note 4. The verse reads, "*Hiney binkha Yosef ba eilekha*" (Behold, your son Yosef is coming to you). The explanation is as follows:

— For each of the 4 fringes, one *tzitzit* string is wound around the others (in groups of 7,8,11,13) a total of 39 times, for a sum total of 156. The letters of the name YOSeF (80 = ף 60 = ס 6 = ו 10 = י) also equal 156.

— Each of the 4 fringes should be a total of 15 *gudlen* (about 15 inches) long for a total of 60. This is equivalent to the word *hiney* (5 = ה 50 = נ 5 = ה).

— There are 5 knots on each of the 4 fringes, totalling 20. The 13 loops on each of the 4 fringes total 52. Together, this gives a sum total of 72. The word *binkha* (20 = ך 50 = נ 2 = ב) also equals 72.

— The strings of the *tzitzit* are each woven from (a minimum) 2 strands so that the 8 strings total 16 strands per corner. Times the 4 fringes, this totals 64. The words *ba eilekha* (20 = ך 10 = י 30 = ל 1 = א, 1 = א 2 = ב) also equal 64.

84. **strengthened.** Yisrael, who is Yaakov, was ill at the time. He was visited by Yosef who, as we've seen, corresponds to the *tzitzit*. Yisrael looked at him and was strengthened (*Mai HaNachal*).

31   *LIKUTEY MOHARAN #7:7,8*

AVhan u'VeNin (father and sons), corresponding to prayer—Yaakov and his sons.[81]

8. It is a *segulah* (special remedy) for someone who is ill to gaze at the *tzitzit*.[82] This is the hidden meaning of the verse (Genesis 48:2), "Behold, your son Yosef is coming to you." For these words hint to the *tzitzit:* to the amount of strings, loops and knots, {as explained in the *Pri Etz Chaim*}.[83] This is: "Behold, your son Yosef is coming to you"— corresponding to the *tzitzit,* as a result of which, "Yisrael was strengthened."[84]

this lack of faith, the negation of miracles, that leads a person into exile, searching for a piece of bread.

81. **Yaakov and his sons.** This is the continuation of the blessing which Yaakov gave Yosef. See section 4 above, where Rebbe Nachman discusses the first part of the blessing. There we see that the "fruitful bough" alludes to the tzaddik's advice, and *aley ayin,* the eyes, alludes to the *tzitzit*. Here, we have the continuation of the blessing. "His bow held firm" alludes to the guarding of the Covenant, as the *Zohar* (I, 71b) teaches: "His bow," this is Yosef, because the bow refers to the sign of circumcision and Yosef guarded his sexual purity. And "the *evan*" alludes to Yaakov and his sons, the twelve versions of prayer mentioned earlier. (The spelling of *evan* as *ævan* is based upon the principle explained in note 2 above.)

In Rebbe Nachman's vision, it was this verse that the Baal Shem Tov quoted to show that when people spoil things in the Land of Israel, they fall into exile.

82. **gaze at the tzitzit.** Whoever is careful to fulfill the mitzvah of *tzitzit* will merit seeing the *Shekhinah* (Divine Presence) (*Menachot* 43b). Our Sages also taught: The *Shekhinah* rests at the head of a sick person and supports one who is not well (*Nedarim* 40a). Accordingly, Rebbe Nachman teaches that one who is not well should look carefully at the tzitzit (*Mul HaNachal*).

LIKUTEY MOHARAN #8:1 · 32

ליקוטי מוהר"ן סימן ח'

רָאִיתִי וְהִנֵּה מְנוֹרַת זָהָב כֻּלָּהּ וְגֻלָּהּ עַל רֹאשָׁהּ וְכוּ' (זְכַרְיָה ד', וְהוּא
הַפְטָרַת שַׁבָּת חֲנֻכָּה).

א. הִנֵּה יָקָר גְּנוּחֵי וְנֹהַ (שְׁקוֹרִין קְרֶעכְצְן) מֵאִישׁ יִשְׂרְאֵלִי, כִּי הוּא
שְׁלֵמוּת הַחֶסְרוֹנוֹת. כִּי עַל־יְדֵי בְּחִינַת הַנְּשִׁימָה, שֶׁהוּא הָרוּחַ חַיִּים,
נִבְרָא הָעוֹלָם, כְּמוֹ שֶׁכָּתוּב (תְּהִלִּים ל"ג): "וּבְרוּחַ פִּיו כָּל צְבָאָם".
וְחִדּוּשׁ הָעוֹלָם יִהְיֶה גַּם־כֵּן בִּבְחִינַת הָרוּחַ, כְּמוֹ שֶׁכָּתוּב (שָׁם ק"ד):
"תְּשַׁלַּח רוּחֲךָ יִבָּרֵאוּן וּתְחַדֵּשׁ פְּנֵי אֲדָמָה".
וְהוּא גַּם כֵּן חִיּוּת הָאָדָם, כִּי חִיּוּת הָאָדָם הוּא הַנְּשִׁימָה, כְּמוֹ
שֶׁכָּתוּב (בְּרֵאשִׁית ב): "וַיִּפַּח בְּאַפָּיו נִשְׁמַת חַיִּים", וּכְתִיב (שָׁם ז):

4. renewal of the world. The world was created to exist for 7,000 years, 6,000 years in the state we now know it followed by 1,000 years of void, corresponding to the Shabbat (*Sanhedrin* 97a). Following the seventh millenium, an entirely new world—a spiritual world in which the reward for one's actions will be immediate—will be created. Differing views on this subject of *chidush haolam* (renewal of the world) are found throughout Rabbinic literature.

5. by means of the ruach. "The world was created for the sake of the tzaddikim" (*Bereishit Rabbah* 2:7). This is indicative of just how precious sighing is. God foresaw that the world would have in it tzaddikim who would turn to Him with prayers and sighing, and because of this He created the world. So, too, the renewal of the world will come about through the prayers and sighing of the tzaddikim of this world (*Mai HaNachal*). In addition, since man's soul is a "a Godly portion," extending one's breath in this world causes a "lengthening of breath" in the upper worlds, thereby bringing wholeness in place of the lack (*Biur HaLikutim*).

6. renew...the earth. The verse immediately preceding this reads: "You hide Your face, they panic; *tosif rucham* (You take their breath), they die and return to the earth." The *Zohar* adds the following: "...they panic"—this is sickness; "earth"—symbolizes death; "Your breath..."—the Resurrection; "renew...the earth"—this is *chidush haolam*.

7. ...breath of life. The fundamental levels of the human soul are three: *nefesh, ruach* and *neshamah* (see Appendix: Levels of Existence). *NeShiMaH* (breath), man's life-force, has the same root as *NeShaMaH*, the highest of these levels. The *neshamah* was given to man so that he would rise above the physical and aspire to spiritual heights. His every breath should bring him closer to God. The *Zohar Chadash* (22b) comments: Man was created with a *nishmat chaim*, but through his actions lowered himself to the lowest of levels, *nefesh chayah* (Genesis

33   *LIKUTEY MOHARAN #8:1*

LIKUTEY MOHARAN #8[1]

"*Ra'iti menorat zahav* (I looked, and behold a candelabrum all of gold) and a bowl on top of it."

(Zekhariah 4:2)

See how precious is the sigh and groan {the *krekhtz*} of a Jewish person.[2] It provides wholeness [in place] of the lack.[3] For through the breath, which is the *ruach*-of-life, the world was created. As is written (Psalms 33:6), "...and by the *ruach* of His mouth, their entire hosts [were created]." The renewal of the world[4] will also come about by means of the *ruach*,[5] as in (Psalms 104:30), "You will send Your *ruach*—they will be created; You renew the face of the earth."[6]

This [*ruach*] is also the vital force of human life. This is because man's breath is his life-force. As is written (Genesis 2:7), "He breathed into his nostrils *nishmat* (the breath of) life,"[7] and (Genesis 7:22), "All in

---

1. **Likutey Moharan #8.** This lesson was taught in Breslov on the 30th of Kislev, 5563 (Dec. 25, 1802). This was Shabbat Chanukah, and the opening verse, which is from the Book of Zekhariah, appears in the *haftorah* reading recited on that day. In giving the lesson, Rebbe Nachman brought about the downfall of a notorious sinner in Nemirov. This man had been persecuting Rebbe Nachman's followers and the Rebbe addressed this issue in his discourse. "Should you be asked what you accomplished here," Rebbe Nachman advised his departing chassidim, "tell them *ruach!*" (*Tzaddik* #130).

Because this *ruach* carries at least three different but interrelated meanings, it has been left untranslated.

— "...and by the *ruach* of His mouth, their entire hosts."
— "And the *ruach* of God hovers over the waters' surface."
— "The northern *ruach* which blows upon King David's harp."

Each of these three quotes appears in our text. Each necessitates a different translation for *ruach* (breath, spirit and wind, respectively). And each directly relates to the *ruach*-of-life, the predominant concept of Rebbe Nachman's lesson.

2. **Jewish person.** When a person prays to God for his needs, sighing deeply and frequently over his wants and inadequacies [both spiritual and material], these deficiencies are removed (*Mai HaNachal*).

3. **wholeness in place of the lack.** Our text reads *shleimut hachesronot*. As used in this context, neither of these terms are easily translated. *Hachesronot* implies that which a person lacks. It is a state of incompleteness, be it due to spiritual inadequacies or material deficiencies of any kind. *Shleimut* can be rendered as complete, perfect, fulfilled; the idea being that something has been made whole. Wholeness has replaced the lack.

LIKUTEY MOHARAN #8:1,2

"כֹּל אֲשֶׁר נִשְׁמַת רוּחַ חַיִּים בְּאַפָּיו". וּכְמוֹ שֶׁאָמְרוּ חֲכָמִים: 'אִם תֶּחְסַר הַנְּשִׁימָה – תֶּחְסַר הַחַיִּים'.

נִמְצָא, כִּי עִקַּר חִיּוּת כָּל הַדְּבָרִים הוּא בִּבְחִינַת רוּחַ; וּכְשֶׁיֵּשׁ חִסָּרוֹן בְּאֵיזֶה דָּבָר, עִקַּר הַחִסָּרוֹן הוּא בִּבְחִינַת הַחִיּוּת שֶׁל אוֹתוֹ הַדָּבָר, שֶׁהוּא בְּחִינַת הָרוּחַ-חַיִּים שֶׁל אוֹתוֹ הַדָּבָר, לַאֲשֶׁר הָרוּחַ הוּא הַמְקַיֵּם הַדָּבָר.

וְהָאֲנָחָה הוּא אֲרִיכַת הַנְּשִׁימָה, וְהוּא בִּבְחִינַת "אֶרֶךְ אַפַּיִם", דְּהַיְנוּ מַאֲרִיךְ רוּחֵהּ. וְעַל כֵּן כְּשֶׁמִּתְאַנֵּחַ עַל הַחִסָּרוֹן וּמַאֲרִיךְ רוּחֵהּ, הוּא מַמְשִׁיךְ רוּחַ-הַחַיִּים לְהַחִסָּרוֹן, כִּי עִקַּר הַחִסָּרוֹן הוּא הִסְתַּלְּקוּת הָרוּחַ-חַיִּים כַּנַּ"ל, וְעַל כֵּן עַל-יְדֵי הָאֲנָחָה מַשְׁלִים הַחִסָּרוֹן.

ב. אַךְ מֵאַיִן מְקַבְּלִין הָרוּחַ-חַיִּים? דַּע, שֶׁעִקַּר הָרוּחַ-חַיִּים מְקַבְּלִין מֵהַצַּדִּיק וְהָרַב שֶׁבַּדּוֹר, כִּי עִקַּר רוּחַ-הַחַיִּים הוּא בְּהַתּוֹרָה, כְּמוֹ שֶׁכָּתוּב (שָׁם א): "וְרוּחַ אֱלֹקִים מְרַחֶפֶת עַל פְּנֵי הַמָּיִם" – הוּא הַתּוֹרָה, וְהַצַּדִּיקִים דְּבֵקִים בַּתּוֹרָה, וְעַל כֵּן עִקַּר הָרוּחַ-חַיִּים הוּא אֶצְלָם.

11. **essence of the ruach-of-life.** The essence mentioned here is the *ruach* drawn from the side of holiness, as opposed to the *ruach se'arah*, its counterpart drawn from the side of evil, as discussed in the following section.

12. **tzaddik/rav.** Rebbe Nachman uses the term *rav* (rabbi), contrasting it with the *rav* of the *kelipah*, the "rabbi" from the Other Side which he introduces in section 3. The point being made here is that because all *ruach* is drawn from the Torah, the highest levels of Torah knowledge are required in order to attain the goals mentioned in this lesson. Hence the term *rav* is used, because it is the title of one who has achieved such knowledge. (It is rare for Rebbe Nachman to use the title *rav*/rabbi in his lessons; see *Likutey Moharan* I, 111; *Parparaot LeChokhmah, loc. cit.*)

13. **waters...Torah.** There are many references both in Scripture and the Talmud which compare the Torah to water. As Rabbi Akiva taught in his well known parable (*Berakhot* 61b): "Just as fish cannot survive without water, the Jewish nation cannot survive without Torah."

14. **tzaddikim are bound to the Torah.** The tzaddik is one whose sole desire in life is to elevate himself to his transcendant root. This root is the "spirit of God"—i.e., the *nishmat chaim* (breath of life)—which "hovers over the waters' surface"—i.e., the Torah. The tzaddik spends his life attempting to ascend to these spiritual heights and consequently becomes

LIKUTEY MOHARAN #8:1,2

whose nostrils was a *nishmat* (breath of) *ruach*-of-life."[8] Regarding this the wise men said: To the extent breath is lacking, so is life (*Maaseh Tuviah, Bayit Chadash* 2; cf. *Zohar* II, 24b).[9]

We find then that the quintessential life-force of everything is its *ruach*. Whenever a lack exists, it is essentially in the life-force, which corresponds to the *ruach*-of-life of that thing. This is because it is the *ruach* which gives that thing its existence.

And sighing is the extension of the breath. It corresponds to *erekh apayim* (patience)—i.e., extended *ruach*.[10] Therefore, when a person sighs over the lack and extends his *ruach*, he draws *ruach*-of-life to that which he is lacking. For the lack is in essence a departure of the *ruach*-of-life. Therefore, through the sigh, the lack is made whole.

2. The question is, from where does one take the *ruach*-of-life? Know! the essence of the *ruach*-of-life[11] is received from the tzaddik/*rav*[12] of the generation. This is because the essence of the *ruach*-of-life can be found in the Torah, as in (Genesis 1:2), "And the *ruach* of God hovers over the waters' surface"—this is the Torah (*Tikkuney Zohar* #36).[13] And the tzaddikim are bound to the Torah,[14] which is why the essence of the *ruach*-of-life is with them.

2:7). Through this verse Rebbe Nachman teaches that by sighing and extending his breath, his life-force, with the intent to serve God, man can return to his elevated position. This brings him closer to the level of "He breathed into his nostrils the breath of life." As long as God "breathes" life into man—allowing him to keep his soul—man can draw in this breath in order to rise above the material world.

8. nishmat ruach-of-life. Through the nostrils one draws the *ruach*-of-life to his *neshamah*. The Ari taught that the breath of the nose corresponds to the element of air and the letter *Vav* of God's holy name *YHVH* (*Etz Chaim, Shaar* 4 ch.1). The connection between these concepts shall become clearer as Rebbe Nachman's lesson unfolds (see below, n.39).

9. breath is lacking.... This refers to the wicked, of whom is written, (Proverbs 13:25), "The belly of the wicked is forever lacking." Rashi comments that the wicked are never satiated.

Until this point, Rebbe Nachman has focused on the positive aspects of *ruach*. Now he quotes the epigram, "To the extent that *ruach* is lacking, so is life." This teaches that there is no middle ground. In the following section the Rebbe will show that the *ruach* comes from the tzaddik. Thus, if a person were to say to himself, "I do not want the *ruach*-of-life from the tzaddik, I can do without it," to this Rebbe Nachman answers, "You must draw *ruach* from somewhere. If not from the *rav* of *kedushah* (holiness), then you must draw it from the *rav* of the *kelipah* (husks). For, 'If *ruach* is lacking, life is lacking.'"

10. erekh apayim...extended ruach. Here Rebbe Nachman introduces a major point of the lesson: the origins of *ruach* for the righteous and the wicked. In section 4 he will explain this in the context of the Talmudic teaching that God extends His *ruach*, being "slow to anger both for the righteous and the sinner" (*Eruvin* 22a).

LIKUTEY MOHARAN #8:2   36

וּכְשֶׁהוּא מְקַשֵּׁר לְהַצַּדִּיק וְהָרַב שֶׁבַּדּוֹר, כְּשֶׁהוּא מִתְאַנַּח וּמַאֲרִיךְ רוּחֲהּ, מַמְשִׁיךְ רוּחַ־הַחַיִּים מֵהַצַּדִּיק שֶׁבַּדּוֹר, שֶׁהוּא דָּבוּק בְּהַתּוֹרָה אֲשֶׁר שָׁם הָרוּחַ.

וְזֶהוּ שֶׁנִּקְרָא הַצַּדִּיק (בְּמִדְבַּר כ"ז): "אִישׁ אֲשֶׁר רוּחַ בּוֹ" – 'שֶׁיּוֹדֵעַ לַהֲלֹךְ נֶגֶד רוּחוֹ שֶׁל כָּל אֶחָד וְאֶחָד' (כְּמוֹ שֶׁפֵּרֵשׁ רַשִׁ"י שָׁם). כִּי הַצַּדִּיק מַמְשִׁיךְ וּמַשְׁלִים הָרוּחַ־חַיִּים שֶׁל כָּל אֶחָד וְאֶחָד כַּנַּ"ל.

וְזֶה בְּחִינַת (בְּרָכוֹת ג:): 'רוּחַ צְפוֹנִית הַמְנַשֶּׁבֶת בַּכִּנּוֹר שֶׁל דָּוִד' – כִּי כִּנּוֹר שֶׁל דָּוִד הָיָה שֶׁל חָמֵשׁ נִימִין, כְּנֶגֶד חֲמִשָּׁה חֻמְשֵׁי תוֹרָה; וְרוּחַ צָפוֹן שֶׁהָיְתָה מְנַשֶּׁבֶת בּוֹ הוּא בְּחִינַת "וְרוּחַ אֱלֹקִים מְרַחֶפֶת עַל פְּנֵי הַמָּיִם" הַנַּ"ל, כִּי רוּחַ צָפוֹן הוּא בְּחִינַת הָרוּחַ הַצָּפוּן בְּלִבּוֹ שֶׁל אָדָם. שֶׁהוּא בְּחִינַת הָרוּחַ־חַיִּים.

כִּי צָפוֹן חָסֵר (בָּבָא בַּתְרָא כה:), וְהַחִסָּרוֹן הוּא בַּלֵּב, כְּמוֹ שֶׁכָּתוּב (תְּהִלִּים ל"ז): "וְיִתֶּן לְךָ מִשְׁאֲלֹת לִבֶּךָ"; "יְמַלֵּא ה' כָּל מִשְׁאֲלוֹתֶיךָ" (שָׁם כ). וְעִקַּר הָרוּחַ־חַיִּים הוּא בַּלֵּב, וּכְמוֹ שֶׁכָּתוּב בְּתִקּוּנֵי־זֹהַר

connection which is further detailed in section 6 below. (The holy Ari explains that whereas the mitzvot in general, such as sitting in a sukkah or wearing tefillin, relate to the "external" aspect of each World, prayer and Torah study relate the "inner" aspect. When applied to the different levels of the soul, the performance of general mitzvot correspond to *nefesh*, while prayer and Torah correspond to *ruach*; cf. *Etz Chaim, Heichal Nukva d'Z'er Anpin* 40:2).

18. **hidden spirit...ruach-of-life.** We now begin to see the development of the lesson's theme. "Just as people's faces are different, so, too, their thoughts are entirely different" (cf. *Sanhedrin* 38a). Each person has his own thoughts hidden in his heart. As explained, the heart is the dwelling place of the *ruach*-of-life and each individual must see to develop his heart according to *his* capabilities so as to receive as much of this life-force as is possible. This is achieved through Torah and prayer, the abode of the *ruach*. But this is not all. A person must also attach himself to the tzaddik, who is the proper conduit for the *ruach*-of-life. Only he knows how to "deal with"—provide the appropriate *ruach* for—each and every individual. Because of this, he is capable of bringing each person that much closer to his transcendant root (see n.15).

19. **Tzafon is lacking.** The sun crosses from east to west through the southern part of the sky, so that even on the very long summer days it sets in the northwest never reaching due north. Hence, the "north is lacking," as it never fully receives the sun's light. The *ruach tzafon*, as we've seen, is the aspect of one's heart. Rebbe Nachman connects this to the *ruach hatzafun*, the hidden thoughts in man's heart, pointing out that here lies the root cause of his lack.

37 *LIKUTEY MOHARAN #8:2*

When the person who is tied to the tzaddik/*rav* of the generation sighs and extends his *ruach,* he draws the *ruach*-of-life from the generation's tzaddik. For [the tzaddik] is bound to the Torah—which is where the *ruach* is.

This is why the tzaddik is called "a man in whom there is *ruach*" (Numbers 27:18)—who knows how to deal with the *ruach* of each individual (*Rashi, loc. cit.*). For the tzaddik draws and completes the *ruach*-of-life of each and every person, as above.[15]

And this corresponds to: The *ruach tzefonit* (northern wind) that blows upon King David's harp (*Berakhot* 3b).[16] King David's harp had five strings, paralleling the Five Books of the Torah (*Zohar* III, 32a).[17] The "northern *ruach*" which blew upon it alludes to "the *ruach* of God [that] hovers over the waters' surface." This *ruach tZeFoNit* corresponds to the *ruach hatZaFuN* (hidden spirit) in man's heart (cf. *Tikkuney Zohar* #69)—this being the *ruach*-of-life.[18]

Our Sages taught: *Tzafon* is lacking (*Bava Batra* 25b).[19] And the lack is in the heart, as is written (Psalms 37:4), "He will give you that which your heart lacks," and (Psalms 20:6), "God will fulfill all your requests." And the essence of the *ruach*-of-life is located in the heart. As we find

---

totally bound up and one with the Torah. Hence, drawing the *ruach*-of-life from the tzaddik is one and the same as drawing it from the Torah.

15. **every person....** Each tzaddik or rabbi must know his "flock" and direct each member according to his individual needs. The leading tzaddik must be able to reach out to all Jews and provide each one with *his* life-force. In this sense, he is the "Moshe Rabbeinu" of his generation, or his community, or his congregation. Prior to Moshe's passing, he pleaded with God to appoint as his successor a leader who would be sensitive to the very different thoughts and feelings—the "unique heart"—of each and every individual. It was on this basis that Yehoshua was chosen, for he knew "how to deal with the *ruach* of each individual." He was able to give each one the *ruach*-of-life needed for his survival. In fact, when Moshe officially appointed Yehoshua, he did so with a reminder that patience, *erekh apayim,* was of the utmost importance in dealing with the Jewish nation (*Rashi,* Numbers 27:19).

16. **King David's harp.** The Talmud teaches (*Berakhot* 3b): King David had a harp which hung above his bed. At midnight, a northern *ruach* would blow upon the strings. King David would rise from his sleep and study Torah until daybreak. In the morning, the Sages would enter before him and say, "King David, the Jewish people are in need." He would answer, "Go out, and do battle with the enemy" (see n.22).

17. **Five Books of the Torah.** This is the Pentateuch. The Book of Psalms, the prayers and supplications of King David, also consists of five books, corresponding to the Five Books of the Toruh. We've already seen that sighing is an aspect of prayer and that the Torah draws its life-force from this prayer. Here again we see the connection between Torah and prayer; a

LIKUTEY MOHARAN #8:2,3

(תִּקּוּן יג): 'כֻּלְּהוּ שַׁיְפִין מִתְנַהֲגִין בָּתַר לִבָּא כְּמַלְכָּא' כוּ', כְּמָא דְאַתְּ
אָמַר (יְחֶזְקֵאל א): "אֶל אֲשֶׁר יִהְיֶה שָׁמָּה הָרוּחַ לָלֶכֶת" כוּ'.
כִּי הָרוּחַ הוּא בַּלֵּב, וְהַחִסָּרוֹן הוּא הִסְתַּלְּקוּת הָרוּחַ שֶׁמְּקוֹמוֹ בַּלֵּב,
וְעַל כֵּן נִרְגָּשׁ הַחִסָּרוֹן בַּלֵּב. וְעַל כֵּן כְּשֶׁנִּתְמַלֵּא הַחִסָּרוֹן שֶׁהוּא
בִּבְחִינַת הָרוּחַ כַּנַּ"ל – נֶאֱמַר: "וְיִתֵּן לְךָ מִשְׁאֲלֹת לִבֶּךָ, יְמַלֵּא ה'"
וְכוּ', הַיְנוּ כַּנַּ"ל. וְעַל כֵּן יִשְׂרָאֵל, שֶׁהֵם מְקַבְּלִין הָרוּחַ-חַיִּים
מֵהַתּוֹרָה, נִקְרָאִים עַל שֵׁם צָפוֹן, כְּמוֹ שֶׁכָּתוּב (תְּהִלִּים פ"ג): "עַל
עַמְּךָ יַעֲרִימוּ סוֹד וְיִתְיָעֲצוּ עַל צְפוּנֶיךָ".

ג. אַךְ רְשָׁעִים הַדּוֹבְרִים עַל צַדִּיק עָתָק בְּגַאֲוָה וָבוּז, מֵאַיִן מְקַבְּלִין
הֵם הָרוּחַ לְהַשְׁלִים הַחִסָּרוֹן? אַךְ דַּע שֶׁיֵּשׁ רַב דִּקְלִפָּה וְהוּא בְּחִינַת

was able to provide wholeness in place of their lack. (His advising them to engage in battle with the enemy will be made clear in the ensuing text.) The *Biur HaLikutim* in a lengthy commentary to this lesson makes constant reference to King David. He shows how the goal of rectification will only be completed by the Mashiach, who is synonymous with King David himself.

In review: The essential life-force of everything, that which gives it its existence, is the *ruach/breath*. Sighing, the extension of the breath/patience, brings life into all that is lacking (§1). This *ruach*-of-life is received from the tzaddik/*rav* of the generation, for he is bound to the Torah, the source of the *ruach*. When one who is attached to the tzaddik sighs, he draws the *ruach* from the heart to fill the lack in the heart (§2).

23. **wicked...fill the lack.** Not only are they distant from the Torah, they are also against the tzaddik, who possesses the *ruach*. This gives rise to the question, "From where do they receive the *ruach*?"

24. **kelipah, husks.** This term, which appears often in the Kabbalistic and Chassidic writings, literally means husks or shells. It takes this name from the fact that the forces of evil, the Other Side, so to speak, cover over the good, the Side of Holiness, with layers of husks; thereby making holiness less accessible. The *rav* of the *kelipah* is thus representative of the force of evil, the root of unholiness—Esav.

"God made one to contrast the other" (Ecclesiastes 7:14). "If one is deserving, the Torah is for him an elixir of life; if not, it is for him a potion of death" (*Yoma* 72b). The study of Torah, especially the Codes of Law (explained in §6), is likened to a double-edged sword. Many fine points are involved in the decision-making process of the law; decisions concerning the factors for determining permitted or forbidden, pure or impure, kosher or unkosher. If one acquires the capabilities for such determination, then the Torah becomes his elixir of life. If, on the other hand, he does not acquire these capabilities, then he should avoid making legal decisions. Rather, he must attach himself to the tzaddik/*rav* of the generation who will advise him correctly. In this way, the Torah will also be an elixir of life for him.

[handwritten top:] apikorus   derogatorily
→ Rabbi Eliezer – confronted with non-Jews who kept asking why if we are tachlis of the world [to] we seem to suffer the most. Says only in the future will we be stood up!

39   LIKUTEY MOHARAN #8:2,3

[handwritten right:] humble themselves

in the *Tikkuney Zohar* (#13): All the body's organs are directed by the heart, which is like a king,[20] while the arteries are like soldiers, as is said (Ezekiel 1:20), "To wherever the *ruach* intended to go...."[21]

[handwritten left margin: Because the Jew is [to] heart of ruach Adam Chaim Kadmon so [to] the world.]

For the *ruach* is in the heart, and the lack is a departure of the *ruach*, whose place is in the heart. This is why the lack is felt [specifically] in the heart. Therefore, when the lack—which is an aspect of *ruach*—is filled, it is said, "He will give you that which your heart lacks," and, "God will fulfill all your requests." And so, the Jews, who receive the *ruach*-of-life from the Torah, are called *tzafun*, as in (Psalms 83:4), "They plot against Your people, and take counsel against *tzfunekha* (Your hidden ones)."[22]

[handwritten left margin: Jew is sensitive to all the lack in the world & therefore we suffer more]

3. But what of the wicked people "who speak arrogantly, haughtily and contemptuously of the tzaddik" (Psalms 31:19)? From where do they receive the *ruach* to fill the lack?[23] But know! there is a *RaV* of the *kelipah* (husks).[24] He corresponds to Esav, as is written in connection

---

20. **like a king.** The *Tikkuney Zohar* continues: The *ruach* in the heart is the "northern wind" which blew upon King David's harp of five strings. The *Kisey Melekh* adds: This *ruach* brings life to the entire body. Because the heart rules over the body, wherever the heart's desires take it, the body follows. Therefore, a person who desires good—he desires to fill the lack in his heart—must draw upon himself the *nishmat chaim* (breath of life). This is the great value of the *krekhtz* (sigh and groan) of a Jewish person, as mentioned at the outset.

21. **the ruach intended to go.** This verse refers to the *Merkavah*, the vision of the Chariot seen by the prophet Yechezkel (Ezekiel, chapter 1). "To wherever the *ruach*"—i.e., God's will— "intended to go, there will go the *ruach* [of the angels]." Indeed, we see that Yechezkel's vision begins by his sighting a "storm wind from the north" accompanied by clouds and fire, etc. (see §3 below). By remaining steadfast, he merited seeing the Chariot with its *ruach*-of-life. With regard to our text, this establishes the point that the heart, the place of the *ruach*, rules the body. By channeling one's heart in the appropriate direction, one merits receiving a *ruach* from the highest levels.

22. **...Your hidden ones.** Every living being, without exception, must have *ruach*-of-life in order to exist. However, this does not mean that everyone draws the *ruach* equally. The Jew, by virtue of his being close to the Torah, the wellspring of this *ruach*, has a more direct access to it. Precisely because of this, he encounters opposition from those who are distant from the wellspring and envious of his position. Thus, "They take counsel against Your hidden ones," against those who are attached to the Source of all life.

We can now appreciate the connection to King David's harp and the northern wind. Each night at midnight, the northern wind, the *ruach* which resides in every human heart, would awaken King David, crying for him to fulfill the needs and wants of his people. With the playing of the harp (the concept of song and prayer) and Torah study he would draw the *ruach* of life for the entire Jewish people. In the morning, the Sages would come requesting that he see to the people's needs. Having spent the night in Torah and prayer, King David

LIKUTEY MOHARAN #8:3

עֵשָׂו, כְּמוֹ שֶׁכָּתוּב בְּעֵשָׂו (בְּרֵאשִׁית ל"ג): "יֵשׁ לִי רָב"; וְהוּא בְּחִינַת
אַלּוּפֵי עֵשָׂו, וּכְמוֹ שֶׁתִּרְגֵּם אוּנְקְלוֹס: "רַבְרְבֵי עֵשָׂו" – בְּחִינַת הָרַב
דִּקְלִפָּה.

וּמֵהֶם מְקַבְּלִין הָרְשָׁעִים הָרוּחַ, וְהוּא בְּחִינַת רוּחַ הַטֻּמְאָה, בְּחִינַת
רוּחַ סְעָרָה, כְּמוֹ שֶׁכָּתוּב (שָׁם כ"ז): "הֵן עֵשָׂו אָחִי אִישׁ שָׂעִיר". וְעַל
כֵּן הָרוּחַ שֶׁלָּהֶם גָּדוֹל וְתַקִּיף לְפִי שָׁעָה כְּמוֹ רוּחַ-סְעָרָה שֶׁהוּא
גָּדוֹל בִּשְׁעָתוֹ.

וְעַל כֵּן: "כָּל צוֹרְרָיו יָפִיחַ בָּהֶם" (תְּהִלִּים י) – "יָפִיחַ" דַּיְקָא,
שֶׁמִּתְגַּבֵּר עֲלֵיהֶם עַל-יְדֵי בְּחִינַת רוּחַ פִּיו, שֶׁהוּא גָּדוֹל בִּשְׁעָתוֹ, אַךְ
שֶׁאֵין לוֹ קִיּוּם כְּלָל וְלַסּוֹף כָּלֶה וְנֶאֱבָד, וּמְסָגֵר גּוּפָה וְנִשְׁמָתָה;
וּכְמוֹ שֶׁכָּתוּב (דְּבָרִים ז): "וּמְשַׁלֵּם לְשֹׂנְאָיו אֶל פָּנָיו לְהַאֲבִידוֹ";
'וּמְשַׁלֵּם' – לָשׁוֹן שְׁלֵמוּת הַחֶסְרוֹן שֶׁנִּמְשָׁךְ לוֹ, דְּהַיְנוּ בְּחִינַת
אֲרִיכַת הָרוּחַ. וְזֶהוּ: 'אֶל פָּנָיו', כִּי פָּנָיו הוּא בְּחִינַת הָרוּחַ, כְּמוֹ
שֶׁכָּתוּב (יְשַׁעְיָהוּ ג): "הַכָּרַת פְּנֵיהֶם עָנְתָה בָּם" – זֶה הַחֹטֶם (יְבָמוֹת
קכ.), שֶׁהוּא בְּחִינַת הָרוּחַ, כְּמוֹ שֶׁכָּתוּב: "וַיִּפַּח בְּאַפָּיו נִשְׁמַת
חַיִּים", "כֹּל אֲשֶׁר נִשְׁמַת רוּחַ חַיִּים בְּאַפָּיו". אַךְ הוּא לְהַאֲבִידוֹ, כִּי
אַף שֶׁהוּא גָּדוֹל לְפִי שָׁעָה – לַסּוֹף נֶאֱבָד כַּנַּ"ל.

rendering *alufey* as *ravrevay*, the *rav* of the husks. The *Biur HaLikutim* points out that there are thirteen tribal chiefs of Esav listed in Genesis (36:15-19). These, he says, parallel the Thirteen Attributes of Mercy discussed in the next section of the lesson.

Here Rebbe Nachman is focusing on one of the greatest dangers facing the Jewish people: false leaders. They appear learned and wise, knowledgeable and eminently capable of dispensing advice to their innocent "flocks." In actual fact, they mislead thousands upon thousands. See *Tzaddik* #109, #212, #455, #537. Rebbe Nachman once commented, "I am frightened by false leaders because of the terrible destruction which they can cause" (*Aveneha Barzel*, p.44, n.64).

27. the nose. The Talmudic law referred to here concerns giving testimony regarding a corpse found with its nose missing. Without the nose, the identity of the deceased cannot be definitively established. In our context, the nose "bears witness" as to which *rav* a person identifies with, the tzaddik/*rav* or the *rav* of the husks. His *ruach*, his life-force, reveals his true attachment; so that arrogance, for example, is indicative of a blowing storm wind from the Other Side.

LIKUTEY MOHARAN #8:3

to Esav (Genesis 33:9), "I have *RaV* (a lot)."[25] This also corresponds to (Genesis 36:40), "...the *alufey* (tribal chiefs of) Esav," which Onkelos renders: "*RaVrevay Esav*"—who is the *RaV* of the husks.[26]

The wicked receive their *ruach* from him. And he corresponds to the impure *ruach*, a *ruach Se'ARah* (storm wind), as in (Genesis 27:11), "But my brother Esav is an *ish SA'iR* (hairy man)." This is why their *ruach* is temporarily strong and mighty, much like the storm wind which blows strongly while it lasts.

Therefore, "he blows away all his enemies" (Psalms 10:5)— specifically "blows." The wicked man overpowers them through the [blowing] *ruach* of his mouth, which is mighty while it lasts. But he has no permanence at all, and in the end is spent and disappears; his body and soul left wasted (cf. *Tikkuney Zohar* #18).

{"But He is *m'shalem* (repays) His enemies to their face [in this world] in order to destroy them [in the next]" (Deuteronomy 7:10).}

It is also written, "But He is *m'shalem* His enemies to their face in order to destroy them." The word "*m'ShaLeM*" denotes the *Sh'LeyMut* (wholeness [in place]) of the lack which is drawn to him—i.e., the aspect of extended *ruach*. This is also the meaning of "to their face." The face corresponds to *ruach*, as our Sages taught: "Their facial expression bears witness against them" (Isaiah 3:9)—this refers to the nose (*Yevamot* 120a).[27] [The nose] corresponds to *ruach*, as in, "And He breathed into his nostrils the breath of life," and, "All in whose nostrils was a breath of the *ruach*-of-life." But [His intention] is "in order to destroy them." For even though at the moment he is mighty, in the end [God's enemy] will be destroyed.

However, it is the possibility of a mistaken decision which is the origin of the *ruach* for the *rav* of the husks. When a person who is incapable of making the correct determination in any case decides on his own, he causes the *ruach* of the Torah, the root of his life-force, to transfer from the tzaddik/*rav* of *kedushah* to the *rav* of the *kelipah* (*Parparaot LeChokhmah*).

25. **I have RaV.** In responding to Yaakov's gift offering, Esav made it seem as though he had no need for it, that he already had *a lot*. From Rebbe Nachman's interpretation we learn that, in fact, Esav admitted to feeling a lack; although he desired more, he would not take it from Yaakov. Yaakov, however, answered, "I have *enough*" (Genesis 33:11), indicating that he had completeness and was not lacking.

26. **alufey...RaVrevay...husks.** The Hebrew word *aluf* also carries the connotations "thousands" and "learned." Up until the age of thirteen Esav and Yaakov both studied Torah. However, unlike his brother, Esav used his knowledge of Torah to mislead those around him (see *Rashi*, Genesis 25:27; *Likutey Moharan* I, 1). This explains Onkelos'

LIKUTEY MOHARAN #8:3,4

וְזֶהוּ בְּחִינַת (יְרוּשַׁלְמִי תַּעֲנִית פ״ב ה״א): אֶרֶךְ אַפַּיִם לָרְשָׁעִים. כִּי הָרוּחַ הַנְּשִׁימָה הוּא בִּבְחִינַת אֶרֶךְ אַפַּיִם; וְהַיְנוּ מַאֲרִיךְ אַפֵּהּ וְגַבֵּי דִילֵהּ, כִּי אַף שֶׁלְּפִי שָׁעָה הָרוּחַ גָּדוֹל וְתַקִּיף, בְּחִינַת מַאֲרִיךְ אַפֵּהּ, אַךְ לַסוֹף גַּבֵּי דִילֵהּ כַּנַּ״ל.

וְעַל כֵּן נִקְרָאִים יִשְׂרָאֵל (יְשַׁעְיָהוּ נ״ד) ״עֲנִיָּה סֹעֲרָה״, כִּי הֵם עַכְשָׁו תַּחַת מֶמְשֶׁלֶת עֵשָׂו אִישׁ שָׂעִיר, בְּחִינַת רוּחַ־סְעָרָה הַנַּ״ל. אַךְ הַדִּבּוּק בְּצַדִּיקִים מְקַבֵּל הָרוּחַ־חַיִּים, שְׁלֵמוּת הַחִסָּרוֹן, מֵהַצַּדִּיק וְהָרַב דִּקְדֻשָׁה.

ד. וְעַל כֵּן ״וְאִישׁ חָכָם יְכַפְּרֶנָּה״ (מִשְׁלֵי ט״ז), כִּי הַחִסָּרוֹן הוּא מֵחֲמַת עֲווֹנוֹת, כְּמוֹ שֶׁאָמְרוּ חֲכָמֵינוּ, זִכְרוֹנָם לִבְרָכָה (שַׁבָּת נה.): ׳אֵין מִיתָה בְּלֹא חֵטְא וְאֵין יִסוּרִים בְּלֹא עָוֹן׳, כְּמוֹ שֶׁכָּתוּב (תְּהִלִּים פ״ט): ״וּפָקַדְתִּי בְשֵׁבֶט פִּשְׁעָם וּבִנְגָעִים עֲוֹנָם״. וְעַל כֵּן הַצַּדִּיק, הַמַּמְשִׁיךְ רוּחַ הַחַיִּים וּמַשְׁלִים הַחִסָּרוֹן, מְכַפֵּר הֶעָוֹן. וְהוּא מִגְדָּל רַחֲמָנוּת וַחֲנִינוּת מֵהַבּוֹרֵא יִתְבָּרַךְ שְׁמוֹ, שֶׁצִּמְצֵם עַצְמוֹ לִהְיוֹת הָרוּחַ־חַיִּים אֵצֶל הַצַּדִּיקִים, דְּהַיְנוּ שֶׁהֵם יְקַבְּלוּ הָרוּחַ־חַיִּים מֵהַתּוֹרָה, וְהֵם מַמְשִׁיכִין רוּחַ הַחַיִּים אֶל הַחֶסְרוֹנוֹת וּבָזֶה מְכַפְּרִין הָעֲווֹנוֹת.

---

29. rav of kedushah. In review: The essential life-force of everything, that which gives it its existence, is the *ruach*/breath. Sighing, the extension of the breath/patience, brings life into all that is lacking (§1). This *ruach*-of-life is received from the tzaddik/*rav* of the generation, for he is bound to the Torah, the source of the *ruach*. When one who is attached to the tzaddik sighs, he draws the *ruach* from the heart to fill the lack in the heart (§2). Conversely, the wicked receive *ruach* from the *rav* of the Other Side. Theirs is an impure *ruach*, which is temporarily powerful but is ultimately destroyed. This results in a lack, as opposed to the wholeness received through the *rav* of holiness (§3).

30. ...atonement for the sin. The *ruach* is in the Torah. By sinning, by transgressing the Torah, one blemishes his *ruach* and consequently experiences feelings of deficiency and lack. However, because the very great tzaddik receives the *ruach* at its wellspring, he can bring it down to the person who sinned and thus undo the lack. And through this, he can bring about forgiveness for the sin, for there is no longer any lack or blemish in the *ruach* of the Torah. Compare this with *Likutey Moharan* I, 4:7 and notes.

43   *LIKUTEY MOHARAN #8:3,4*

This corresponds to: *Erekh apayim* (patience) for the wicked (*Yerushalmi, Taanit* 2:5).[28] For the *ruach,* the breath, is an aspect of *erekh apayim.* And this is: [God] is patient, but He collects His due (*Bereishit Rabbah* 67:4). Even though for the moment [the wicked man's] *ruach* is strong and mighty—an aspect of, "He is patient"—nevertheless, ultimately "He collects His due."

And this is why the Jews are called "afflicted and *SoARah* (assaulted)" (Isaiah 54:11), for they are presently under the rule of Esav *ish SA'iR*—the *ruach Se'ARah*. However, someone who is attached to the tzaddikim receives the *ruach*-of-life—the wholeness [in place] of the lack—from the tzaddik/*rav* of holiness.[29]

4. {**"The wrath of a king is as messengers of death, but a wise man shall pacify it"** (Proverbs 16:14).}

Therefore, "But a wise man shall pacify it." The lack [a person feels] results from his sins. As our Sages taught: There is no death without [there first being] transgression; nor suffering without sin, as in (Psalms 89:33), "I will punish their transgression with the rod, and their sin with plagues" (*Shabbat* 55a). Therefore, the tzaddik, who draws the *ruach*-of-life and provides wholeness [in place] of the lack, is capable of winning atonement for the sin.[30] This stems from the great mercy and compassion of the Creator, blessed be His name. For He contracts Himself into being the *ruach*-of-life for the tzaddikim—i.e., that they will receive the *ruach*-of-life from the Torah and draw the *ruach*-of-life to the lack; and with this they atone the sins.

{**"God, God, Omnipotent, merciful and compassionate,** *erekh apayim* **(patient), with** *rav chesed* **(great kindness) and truth. He is** *notzer chesed* **(keeps [in mind] the deeds of kindness)** *l'alafim* **(for thousands [of generations]), forgiving of sin and rebellion and error. Cleansing sin...**" (Exodus 34:6).}

28. **erekh apayim for the wicked.** In section 1 Rebbe Nachman introduced the concept of *erekh apayim* as the root of extended *ruach* of the righteous. Here we see that the wicked also have extended *ruach*. This appears contradictory. However, it is important to realize that this paradox is precisely the source of our "free will"; presenting us with the possibility of choosing right from wrong. If it were only the righteous who received God's *erekh apayim,* His patience, it would then be only too obvious which is the correct path to follow. That the wicked generally have a "good life" allows us to presume that perhaps their path is the appropriate or desirable one. Thus, the wicked are shown God's patience for one of two reasons: to afford them time to repent, which is what God really wants; or, to reward them in this world for the good which they performed, so that in the future, at the time of the world's *chidush* (renewal), God will exact payment from them for all their sins.

LIKUTEY MOHARAN #8:4

וְזֶהוּ בְּחִינַת שְׁלֹשׁ־עֶשְׂרֵה מִדּוֹת (שְׁמוֹת ל"ד): "ה' ה' אֵל רַחוּם
וְחַנּוּן אֶרֶךְ אַפַּיִם". 'אֶרֶךְ אַפַּיִם' – הוּא בְּחִינַת הָרוּחַ, שֶׁהוּא
מַאֲרִיךְ רוּחֵהּ, בְּחִינַת אֲנָחָה עַל הַחִסָּרוֹן;
וְהַיְנוּ "וְרַב חֶסֶד וֶאֱמֶת", כְּמוֹ שֶׁאָמַרְנוּ, שֶׁמְּקַבְּלִין הָרוּחַ־חַיִּים
מֵהַצַּדִּיק רַב דִּקְדֻשָּׁה, שֶׁהוּא "רַב חֶסֶד", הֵפֶךְ עֵשָׂו רַב דִּקְלִפָּה,
שֶׁהוּא אַדְמוֹנִי, תֹּקֶף הַדִּין. וְהַיְנוּ "וֶאֱמֶת", כִּי הַצַּדִּיק מְקַבֵּל הָרוּחַ־
חַיִּים מֵהַתּוֹרָה, שֶׁנִּקְרֵאת (מַלְאָכִי ב): "תּוֹרַת אֱמֶת הָיְתָה בְּפִיהוּ".

וְהַיְנוּ "נֹצֵר חֶסֶד לָאֲלָפִים"; 'לָאֲלָפִים' – זֶה בְּחִינַת אַלּוּפֵי עֵשָׂו,
רַבְרְבֵי עֵשָׂו שֶׁהֵם רַב דִּקְלִפָּה. וְזֶהוּ: "נֹצֵר חֶסֶד" – שֶׁהַחֶסֶד,
בְּחִינַת הָרַב דִּקְדֻשָּׁה, נוֹצֵר וּמַמְתִּיק בְּחִינַת אַלּוּפֵי עֵשָׂו, רַבְרְבֵי
עֵשָׂו.

וְעַל כֵּן "נֹשֵׂא עָוֹן וָפֶשַׁע", כִּי עַל־יְדֵי רוּחַ הַחַיִּים, שְׁלֵמוּת
הַחִסָּרוֹן, שֶׁמַּמְשִׁיכִין מֵהַצַּדִּיק עַל־יְדֵי אֲנָחָה, עַל־יְדֵי־זֶה נִתְכַּפְּרִין
הָעֲווֹנוֹת, שֶׁזֶּהוּ בְּחִינַת "וְאִישׁ חָכָם יְכַפְּרֶנָּה" כַּנַּ"ל. וְזֶהוּ "נֹשֵׂא
עָוֹן וָפֶשַׁע", כַּנַּ"ל.

---

genesis of wisdom, as explained in section 7 below. Prayer is thus the very first step in achieving a connection to the Source.

34. **merciful and compassionate.** This aligns with what appears earlier in the section that atonement "comes from the Holy One's great mercy and compassion." He allowed His *ruach* to be contracted into the Torah, from where the tzaddikim draw their *ruach*. Concerning these two Attributes, our Sages taught: God is merciful even to one who does not deserve His mercy; compassionate even to one who does not deserve His compassion (*Berakhot* 7a). The *Iyun Yaakov* explains that this includes not just the sinner, but even those who are totally evil. Even *they* can be shown this mercy.

35. **reddish...stern judgment.** The *Zohar* (III, 51a) teaches that the color white denotes *chesed* (lovingkindness)/*chasadim* (benevolences), whereas red denotes *gevurah* (strength)/*gevurot* (severities). The Torah tells us that when Rivkah gave birth, "the first one came out reddish, as hairy as a fur coat" (Genesis 25:25). This was Esav, stern judgment incarnate.

36. **wise man...forgiving....** The thirteenth Attribute, "cleansing sin," though not mentioned outright is alluded to in the next section. There, Rebbe Nachman makes clear that only a tzaddik who is completely "clean of sin" can enter into the conduit of the wicked (*Mai HaNachal; Biur HaLikutim*).

The Thirteen Attributes were revealed to Moshe after the sin of the Golden Calf. The

45   *LIKUTEY MOHARAN #8:4*

[The atonement of sin] corresponds to the Thirteen Attributes of Mercy:[31] "God, God,[32] Omnipotent,[33] merciful and compassionate,[34] *erekh apayim....*" "*Erekh apayim*" is an aspect of *ruach* < -of-life >, in that [God] extends His breath—sighing over [man's] lack.

This is the meaning of "with *rav chesed.*" As we have said, a person receives the *ruach*-of-life from the tzaddik/*rav* of holiness. He is *RaV chesed*; the antithesis of Esav, the *RaV* of the husks, who is "reddish," [from the side of] stern judgment.[35] And this is, "and truth." For the tzaddik receives the *ruach*-of-life from the Torah, which is called "the Torah of truth [that] was in his mouth" (Malakhi 2:6).

And this is the meaning of, "He keeps [in mind] the deeds of kindness *l'alafim.*" [The word] "*l'ALaFim*" alludes to the *ALuFey* (tribal chiefs of) Esav, the *RaVrevay* Esav—they are the *RaV* of the husks. And this is, "*notzer chesed.*" "*Chesed*" corresponds to the *rav* of holiness. He "keeps" [in check] and mitigates the tribal chiefs of Esav, *ravrevay* Esav.

And therefore, "[He is] forgiving of sin and rebellion." For as a result of the *ruach*-of-life, the wholeness [in place] of the lack, that we draw from the tzaddik by sighing, sins are atoned. This is the meaning of, "...but a wise man shall pacify it"; which is, "forgiving of sin and rebellion."[36]

---

31. **Thirteen Attributes of Mercy.** The Thirteen Attributes are synonymous with prayer and correspond to the thirteen exegetical rules in the *Beraita* of Rabbi Yishmael (Morning Liturgy). This is an additional connection between Torah and prayer, one of the fundamental themes of this lesson (*Mai HaNachal*). Rebbe Nachman binds together the Thirteen Attributes, presenting them as a step-by-step process for restoring the *ruach*-of-life to the sinner.

32. **God, God.** Our Sages taught: He was *YHVH* (God) before one sins, He is *YHVH* (God) even after one sins (*Rosh HaShanah* 17b). In the next section Rebbe Nachman explains that the root of all character traits is found in the four elements, corresponding to the *YHVH*, the ineffable four letter name of God. God's name is thus repeated to teach as follows: Prior to the sin being committed the *YHVH* is perfect and unblemished. Should one think that after the sin the *YHVH* has become tarnished, God forbid, we are therefore told that "He is *YHVH* even after one sins"—God's name remains without blemish. As the ultimate Source of everything (see below, n.39), the *YHVH* is above creation. This enables the tzaddikim, who draw their *ruach* from the Source, to bring this *ruach* to the person who has sinned and blemished his *ruach*. This, in turn, effects forgiveness for his sins (*Mai HaNachal*).

33. **Omnipotent.** There are different opinions as to which words signify the Thirteen Attributes. According to the Kabbalah, the first attribute is *El*, Omnipotent. The *Zohar* (III, 30b) states that *El* corresponds to the "light of the Upper Wisdom." This is prayer, the

LIKUTEY MOHARAN #8:5

ה. וְהִנֵּה, כְּשֶׁמִּתְאַנֵּחַ מַמְשִׁיךְ רוּחַ הַחַיִּים אֶל הַחִסָּרוֹן, שֶׁמִּתְאַנֵּחַ עָלָיו וּמַשְׁלִים אוֹתוֹ. אַךְ לְהִתְגָּרוֹת בָּרְשָׁעִים אִי אֶפְשָׁר, כִּי כְּשֶׁמִּתְגָּרֶה בְּהָרָשָׁע, וְהוּא מִתְאַנֵּחַ וּמַמְשִׁיךְ הָרוּחַ מֵהָרַב שֶׁלּוֹ דִקְלִפָּה, וְהָרוּחַ שֶׁלּוֹ גָּדוֹל בִּשְׁעָתוֹ, וְעַל כֵּן "כָּל צוֹרְרָיו יָפִיחַ בָּהֶם", כַּנַּ"ל, וְיוּכַל לְהַדִּיק לוֹ, חַס וְשָׁלוֹם.

וְעַל כֵּן לָאו כָּל אָדָם יָכוֹל לְהִתְגָּרוֹת בָּרְשָׁעִים, אִם לֹא מִי שֶׁהוּא צַדִּיק גָּמוּר. וְצַדִּיק גָּמוּר הוּא, כְּשֶׁהוּא בִּבְחִינַת (מִשְׁלֵי י"ב): "לֹא יְאֻנֶּה לַצַּדִּיק כָּל אָוֶן", דְּהַיְנוּ שֶׁכְּבָר גֵּרֵשׁ וּבִטֵּל כָּל הָרָע שֶׁלּוֹ, עַד שֶׁבָּטוּחַ שֶׁלֹּא יְאָרַע לוֹ שׁוּם מִכְשׁוֹל עֲבֵרָה:

וְהָעִנְיָן – כִּי יֵשׁ אַרְבָּעָה יְסוֹדוֹת: אֵשׁ, רוּחַ, מַיִם, עָפָר; וּלְמַעְלָה בְּשָׁרְשָׁם הֵם אַרְבַּע אוֹתִיּוֹת הֲוָיָ"ה. וּלְמַטָּה הֵם מְעֹרָבִים טוֹב וָרָע. וְהַצַּדִּיק גָּמוּר שֶׁהִבְדִּיל וְהִפְרִישׁ הָרַע מִן הַטּוֹב לְגַמְרֵי, עַד שֶׁלֹּא

---

37. **provoke the wicked.** We've seen that a person should draw his *ruach* from the tzaddik/*rav* in order to bring wholeness in place of the lack. But the *rav* of the husks also has a *ruach,* and that *ruach* interferes with the person's attempt to sustain himself through the tzaddik/*rav.* Faced with this obstacle, one may be tempted to try and remove it, using force. Rebbe Nachman therefore warns against such an approach. Not everyone is capable of doing battle with his enemies the way King David did (see above, n.22).

38. **a perfect tzaddik.** Our Sages taught: When Moshe requested of God that He reveal His divine Attributes of Mercy, he asked, "Why is it that one tzaddik receives good while another tzaddik must suffer?" God answered him, "The tzaddik who receives good is a perfect tzaddik" (*Berakhot* 7a). It is only the perfect tzaddik who can reveal the Thirteen Attributes, which is why only he can successfully enter the wicked man's conduit, as will be explained.

39. **good and bad.** All creation is included in these four elements. Man himself is made up of these four elements. The *ruach*-of-life also carries the aspect of four, as in (Ezekiel 37:9), "From the four *ruchot* (directions/winds) comes the *ruach*[-of-life]" (explained in §8). As Rebbe Nachman quotes from the *Tikkuney Zohar,* the four elements correspond to the four letters *YHVH,* the Source—the building blocks—of creation. As the *YHVH* permeates creation, it cloaks itself in ever increasing degrees of corporeality, thereby allowing for the development of good and the potential existence of evil. A lack of clarity in Torah law transforms this potential evil into reality. This is the case whenever the law is not properly discerned: the power of the Torah itself is used to create incorrect laws and falsehood—i.e., the *ruach se'arah.* This is why below, in this world, there is "a mixture of good and bad" (*Parparaot LeChokhmah*).

5. Now, by sighing, a person draws the *ruach*-of-life to the lack about which he sighs. This makes it whole. Nevertheless, one cannot [attempt to] provoke the wicked.[37] For when a person provokes the wicked man, and he then sighs and draws *ruach* from his *rav* of the husks—his *ruach* being momentarily mighty, so that "he blows away all his enemies"—he is capable of harming him, God forbid.

Therefore, not everyone may confront the wicked; only someone who is a perfect tzaddik.[38] A perfect tzaddik is someone who is on the level of (Proverbs 12:21), "No sin will befall the tzaddik." In other words, he has already expelled and eliminated whatever bad he may have had, to the point where he is certain that he will in no way be brought to sin.

This matter [of eliminating the bad] is as follows: There are four fundamental elements: fire, air, water, earth. Above, in their transcendent root, they correspond to the four letters [of God's holy name] *YHVH* (cf. *Tikkuney Zohar* #22). But, below [in our world], they are a mixture of good and bad.[39] The perfect tzaddik, however, has completely distinguished and separated the bad from the good, so

---

kelipot and forces of evil were so powerful at the time, they were able to draw the *ruach* into an inanimate object, i.e., a cast-metal calf. It came to life and they worshipped it (see *Rashi*, Exodus 32:5). The calf itself was forged from gold, as "Gold comes from the north" (Job 37:22). This refers to the northern *ruach* which is hidden in the heart. The "mixed multitude" (*alufey* Esav) wanted to destroy the holiness of the *ruach*-of-life. In essence, the sin of the Golden Calf was an attempt to lower this *ruach*, forcing it into the domain of the *rav* of the husks (*Likutey Halakhot, HaOseh Shaliach Ligvot Chovo* 3:26). The *Mai HaNachal* adds that this is why Moshe broke the Tablets of the Testimony. These Tablets contained the Torah, the wellspring of the *ruach*-of-life. His intention was to demonstrate clearly the severity of their sin. Even so, Moshe then ascended to heaven in order to pray and beseech God to forgive their sin. He not only succeeded in evoking a new *ruach*, he was also again given the Torah—the *ruach*-of-life—on behalf of all the Jews. All this was alluded to in the Thirteen Attributes, which were revealed to him only after his having obtained forgiveness for their sin.

In review: The essential life-force of everything, that which gives it its existence, is the *ruach*/ breath. Sighing, the extension of the breath/patience, brings life into all that is lacking (§1). This *ruach*-of-life is received from the tzaddik/*rav* of the generation, for he is bound to the Torah, the source of the *ruach*. When one who is attached to the tzaddik sighs, he draws the *ruach* from the heart to fill the lack in the heart (§2). Conversely, the wicked receive *ruach* from the *rav* of the Other Side. Theirs is an impure *ruach*, which is temporarily powerful but is ultimately destroyed. This results in a lack, as opposed to the wholeness received through the *rav* of holiness (§3). All lack stems from sin. The tzaddik who draws *ruach* to fill the lack therefore has the power to atone for sin. In this he resembles the Holy One, for atonement relates to God's 13 Attributes of Mercy (§4).

LIKUTEY MOHARAN #8:5
48

נִשְׁאַר לוֹ שׁוּם רַע מֵאֶחָד מֵאַרְבָּעָה יְסוֹדוֹת הַנַּ"ל, שֶׁהֵם כְּלָל הַמִּדּוֹת כַּיָּדוּעַ, וּכְשֶׁהוּא בִּבְחִינָה זוֹ מֻתָּר לְהִתְגָּרוֹת בָּרְשָׁעִים:

וְהָעִנְיָן – כִּי כָל רָשָׁע, הַהֶכְרֵחַ שֶׁיִּהְיֶה לוֹ צִנּוֹר שֶׁיְּקַבֵּל דֶּרֶךְ שָׁם הָרוּחַ שֶׁלּוֹ לְהַשְׁלִים הַחִסָּרוֹן, וְהַצִּנּוֹר הוּא – דֶּרֶךְ הַמִּדָּה רָעָה מֵאַרְבָּעָה יְסוֹדוֹת שֶׁהִמְשִׁיךְ וְהִגְבִּיר – הוּא הַדֶּרֶךְ וְהַצִּנּוֹר שֶׁמְּקַבֵּל דֶּרֶךְ שָׁם הָרוּחַ-חַיִּים שֶׁלּוֹ לְהַשְׁלִים חֶסְרוֹנוֹ. וּכְשֶׁהַצַּדִּיק רוֹצֶה לְהַשְׁפִּילוֹ, הוּא מֻכְרָח לֵירֵד לְהַמִּדָּה רָעָה הַהִיא שֶׁהִגְבִּיר עָלָיו הָרָשָׁע, לְהַכְנִיעָהּ וּלְקַלְקֵל הַצִּנּוֹר הַהוּא שֶׁל הָרָשָׁע, שֶׁמְּקַבֵּל מִשָּׁם הַחַיּוּת שֶׁלּוֹ.

וְעַל כֵּן מֻכְרָח שֶׁיִּהְיֶה זֶה הַצַּדִּיק צַדִּיק גָּמוּר, שֶׁאֵין בּוֹ שׁוּם רַע, לְמַעַן לֹא יִהְיֶה כֹּחַ לְהָרוּחַ-סְעָרָה, שֶׁהוּא הָרוּחַ-חַיִּים שֶׁל הָרָשָׁע, לְשַׁלֵּט וּלְהַזִּיק, חַס וְשָׁלוֹם, לְהַצַּדִּיק בְּעֵת שֶׁיּוֹרֵד לְהַמִּדָּה רָעָה שֶׁל הָרָשָׁע לְקַלְקְלָהּ, כִּי אֵין לְהָרַע שׁוּם תְּפִיסָה וַאֲחִיזָה בְּהַצַּדִּיק גָּמוּר, וְאֵין לוֹ מָקוֹם לֶאֱחֹז בּוֹ. (וְגַם מֵהַמִּדָּה רָעָה בְּעַצְמָהּ שֶׁיּוֹרֵד לְהַכְנִיעָהּ אֵין לוֹ שׁוּם תְּפִיסָה, חַס וְשָׁלוֹם, רַק מַה שֶּׁיּוֹרֵד לְתוֹכָהּ הוּא לְהַכְנִיעָהּ וּלְהַשְׁפִּילָהּ, בִּבְחִינַת (בְּרֵאשִׁית י"ג): "וַיַּעַל אַבְרָם מִמִּצְרָיִם"):

וְזֶהוּ (תְּהִלִּים קמ"ז): מַ'שְׁפִּיל רְ'שָׁעִים עֲ'דֵי אָ'רֶץ – רָאשֵׁי-תֵבוֹת: אֵשׁ, רוּחַ, מַיִם, עָפָר, שֶׁהֵם כָּל הָאַרְבָּעָה יְסוֹדוֹת, שֶׁהֵם כְּלָל כָּל הַמִּדּוֹת, שֶׁצְּרִיכִין לְבָרְרָם בְּבֵרוּר גָּמוּר, עַד שֶׁלֹּא יִהְיֶה בּוֹ שׁוּם אֲחִיזָה מִשּׁוּם רַע שֶׁבְּשׁוּם מִדָּה מֵהָאַרְבָּעָה יְסוֹדוֹת הַנַּ"ל, וַאֲזַי הוּא צַדִּיק גָּמוּר כַּנַּ"ל. וְאָז דַּיְקָא, כְּשֶׁמַּבְדִּיל הָרַע מֵאַרְבָּעָה יְסוֹדוֹת – אֵשׁ, רוּחַ, מַיִם, עָפָר – אֲזַי הוּא מַשְׁפִּיל רְשָׁעִים עֲדֵי אֶרֶץ כַּנַּ"ל.

---

42. **Avraham ascended....** "Abraham descended to Egypt" (Genesis 12:10). His going down into Egypt was in order to subdue and humble the wickedness of the land. After succeeding, he ascended from there, complete and without lack.

LIKUTEY MOHARAN #8:5

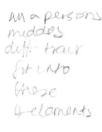
All a persons middos [different traits] fit into those 4 elements

that he is without even a residue of bad from any one of these four elements—which encompass all the traits, as is known. When he is on this level, [the tzaddik] is permitted to provoke the wicked. < And those who are attached to such a tzaddik may also provoke them. >[40]

The matter is this: Every wicked man has to have a conduit through which he receives his *ruach* in order to provide wholeness [in place] of the lack. This conduit is the particular bad trait from the four elements which he drew [upon himself] and [with which he is] empowered. Through this conduit and path he receives the *ruach*-of-life needed to fill this lack. And when the tzaddik wants to humble him, he must descend into that bad trait[41] with which the wicked man has empowered himself, to subdue and destroy the conduit < through > which the wicked man receives his < *ruach* >.

This is why the tzaddik must be a perfect tzaddik, without any bad whatsoever; so that the storm wind, which is also the wicked man's *ruach*-of-life, cannot, God forbid, overpower and harm the tzaddik when he descends into the wicked man's bad trait in order to destroy it. For the bad has no hold or grasp on the perfect tzaddik; there isn't anywhere [for the bad] to attach itself to him.

{Even the bad quality itself into which the tzaddik descends in order to bring about its destruction has no hold on him. His entry there is solely for the purpose of subduing and casting it down, as in (Genesis 13:1), "And Avraham ascended from Egypt."}[42]

{"*Mashpil* (He casts down) *resha'im* (the wicked) *adey eretz* (to the ground)" (Psalms 147:6).}

This is: "*Mashpil Resha'im Adey Eretz*," the initial letters of which are [also the initial letters of] *Esh, Ruach, Mayim, Afar* (fire, air, water, earth). These are all the four elements, which encompass all qualities and traits. A person has to totally purify these [traits] so that none of the bad found in any trait of the four elements has any hold on him. At that point, as mentioned, he is a perfect tzaddik. And only then, when he separates the bad from the four elements—fire, air, water, earth—does he "cast down the wicked to the ground."

---

40. **provoke the wicked....** Being attached to the very Source, to the *YHVH*, the tzaddik transcends the origin of the wicked man's *ruach*. This explains why the perfect tzaddik remains unaffected by the wicked man's *ruach*. His followers, provided they are truly attached to him, also enjoy this protection (see below, n.44).

41. **bad trait.** The fundamental adverse character traits are four: arrogance (fire), idleness and idle chatter (air), evil passions (water) and melancholy (earth) (*Mishnat Chassidim, Mesekhta HaHarkavah*). See *Likutey Moharan* I, 4:8.

LIKUTEY MOHARAN #8:5

מַה שֶּׁאֵין כֵּן צַדִּיק שֶׁאֵינוֹ גָּמוּר, אַף שֶׁאֵין לוֹ שׁוּם עֲבֵרָה, אַף־עַל־
פִּי־כֵן עֲדַיִן לֹא הִבְדִּיל הָרַע לְגַמְרֵי וְהָרַע עֲדַיִן בְּכֹחַ, וְעַל כֵּן אָסוּר
לוֹ לְהִתְגָּרוֹת בָּרְשָׁעִים, כִּי יֵשׁ מָקוֹם לְהָרַע לֶאֱחֹז בּוֹ, וְיוּכַל לְהַזִּיק
לוֹ, חַס וְשָׁלוֹם, הָאֲרִיכוּת־רוּחַ שֶׁל הָרָשָׁע, שֶׁהוּא גָּדוֹל בִּשְׁעָתוֹ
בִּבְחִינַת רוּחַ־סְעָרָה כַּנַּ״ל.

וְזֶהוּ שֶׁאָמְרוּ רַבּוֹתֵינוּ, זִכְרוֹנָם לִבְרָכָה (בְּרָכוֹת ז׃): וְהַכְּתִיב: ״אַל
תִּתְחַר בִּמְרֵעִים״? (תְּהִלִּים ל״ז) ׳מִי שֶׁלִּבּוֹ נוֹקְפוֹ אוֹמֵר כֵּן׳; פֵּרֵשׁ
רַשִׁ״י: ׳הַיָּרֵא מֵעֲבֵרוֹת שֶׁבְּיָדוֹ׳ – ׳שֶׁבְּיָדוֹ׳ דַּיְקָא. זֶהוּ שֶׁאָמַרְנוּ, כִּי
בֶּאֱמֶת אֵין לוֹ שׁוּם עֲבֵרָה, רַק שֶׁהוּא יָרֵא עֲדַיִן מֵעֲבֵרוֹת שֶׁבְּיָדוֹ
וְכֹחוֹ לַעֲשׂוֹת, כִּי הָרַע עֲדַיִן בְּכֹחַ, כִּי לֹא זָכָה עֲדַיִן לִבְחִינַת לֹא
יְאֻנֶּה לַצַּדִּיק כָּל אָוֶן, וְאֵינוֹ בָּטוּחַ עֲדַיִן שֶׁלֹּא יֶאֱרַע לוֹ מִכְשׁוֹל
עֲבֵרָה, חַס וְשָׁלוֹם, וְעַל כֵּן אָסוּר לוֹ לְהִתְגָּרוֹת בָּרְשָׁעִים כַּנַּ״ל.

וְזֶהוּ: ״תַּחֲרִישׁ כְּבַלַּע רָשָׁע צַדִּיק מִמֶּנּוּ״ (חֲבַקּוּק א), וְאָמְרוּ
רַבּוֹתֵינוּ, זִכְרוֹנָם לִבְרָכָה (בָּבָא מְצִיעָא עא): ׳צַדִּיק מִמֶּנּוּ בּוֹלֵעַ׳ –
׳בּוֹלֵעַ׳ דַּיְקָא, כִּי הוּא בּוֹלֵעַ אוֹתוֹ מַמָּשׁ בַּאֲרִיכַת הָרוּחַ שֶׁלּוֹ,
שֶׁהוּא גָּדוֹל בִּשְׁעָתוֹ; אֲבָל צַדִּיק גָּמוּר אֵינוֹ בּוֹלֵעַ, כִּי אֵין לִבּוֹ
נוֹקְפוֹ מֵחֲשַׁשׁ מִכְשׁוֹל עֲבֵרָה כַּנַּ״ל, כִּי כְּבָר בִּטֵּל הָרַע לְגַמְרֵי מִכָּל
הַמִּדּוֹת וְהַתַּאֲווֹת שֶׁל כָּל הָאַרְבָּעָה יְסוֹדוֹת.

וְעַל כֵּן זֶה הַצַּדִּיק גָּמוּר וְכָל הַנִּלְוִים אֵלָיו מֻתָּרִים לְהִתְגָּרוֹת
בָּרְשָׁעִים, כִּי זֶה הַצַּדִּיק יָכוֹל לֵירֵד לְתוֹךְ כָּל הַצִּנּוֹרוֹת שֶׁל כָּל
הַמִּדּוֹת רָעוֹת שֶׁלָּהֶם, שֶׁהִגְבִּירוּ עַל עַצְמָם וּלְשַׁבְּרָם וּלְבַטְּלָם, וְעַל־
יְדֵי־זֶה הוּא מַשְׁפִּיל רְשָׁעִים עֲדֵי אָרֶץ, כַּנַּ״ל:

---

warriors, all of whom were outstanding in their ability to take the initiative in battle. This
supports Rebbe Nachman's statement that even the followers of the tzaddik/rav can
"provoke" the wicked.

In review: *Ruach*/breath is the life-force of everything. Sighing brings life into all that is

LIKUTEY MOHARAN #8:5

This is not the case for the tzaddik who lacks perfection. Even if he is not guilty of any sin, he still has not totally separated out the bad. The bad still exists in potential and it is therefore forbidden for him to antagonize the wicked. For the bad has where to attach itself to him. The extended *ruach* of the wicked man, which is mighty in its moment, just as the storm wind, has the power to harm him, God forbid.

As our Sages taught: [If someone asks,] "Is it not written (Psalms 37:1), 'Do not engage in conflict with those who are wicked?' " [answer him] that this is said by someone whose heart worries (Berakhot 7b). Rashi explains: "This is someone who fears because of the sins in his hand." Specifically "in his hand," because, as we have said, in reality he is not guilty of any sin. It is just that he is still afraid of the sins which are in his hand and his power to commit.[43] Potentially, the bad still exists. He has not as yet merited the level of "no sin will befall the tzaddik"; he cannot yet be certain that he will in no way be brought to sin, God forbid. It is therefore forbidden for him to provoke the wicked.

And this is (Habakkuk 1:13), "Why do You hold Your peace, as the wicked man devours a tzaddik greater than he." Our Sages taught: He devours "a tzaddik greater than he," [but not a perfect tzaddik] (Berakhot, ibid.). Specifically "devours," because [the wicked man] literally devours him by extending his *ruach,* which is mighty in its moment. But the perfect tzaddik is not devoured. This is because *his* heart is not made anxious by a concern that he might in some way be brought to sin. For he has already totally eliminated the bad from all the traits and desires of each of the four elements.

Therefore, this perfect tzaddik—and all those joined with him— are permitted to provoke the wicked. For this tzaddik is capable of descending into the conduits of all their bad traits with which they have empowered themselves, to break and eliminate them. And, by means of this, he "casts down the wicked to the ground," as mentioned above.[44]

---

43. **power to commit.** Because the heart is *tzafun,* the place of the *ruach* is hidden. It is this hidden potential for sinning which can cause the person to be devoured by the storm wind of the wicked.

44. **all those joined with him...above.** In 2 Samuel (23:8-23) we find a list of King David's

LIKUTEY MOHARAN #8:6,7

ו. וְלָבוֹא לָזֶה – לְהַפְרִישׁ וּלְהַבְדִּיל וּלְבַטֵּל הָרָע מֵהַטּוֹב – הוּא עַל־יְדֵי תּוֹרָה וּתְפִלָּה, וְלִמּוּד הַתּוֹרָה יִהְיֶה לָלוּן לְעָמְקָהּ שֶׁל הֲלָכָה. הַיְנוּ לִלְמֹד פּוֹסְקִים. כִּי יֵשׁ בְּהַתּוֹרָה אֲחִיזַת הַטּוֹב וְהָרָע, שֶׁנֶּאֱחָזִין מִבְּחִינַת אִסּוּר וְהֶתֵּר, טָמֵא וְטָהוֹר, כָּשֵׁר וּפָסוּל, שֶׁיֵּשׁ בְּהַתּוֹרָה; וְכָל זְמַן שֶׁאֵינוּ מְבָרֵר הַהֲלָכָה הוּא מְעֹרָב טוֹב וָרָע; וְעַל כֵּן אֵינוּ יָכוֹל לְהַפְרִישׁ וּלְבַטֵּל הָרָע מֵהַטּוֹב, וְהוּא בִּבְחִינַת (מִשְׁלֵי י״א): "וְדֹרֵשׁ רָעָה תְבוֹאֶנּוּ"; עַד אֲשֶׁר הוּא מְעַיֵּן וּמְבָרֵר הַפְּסַק־הֲלָכָה וּמְבָרֵר הָאָסוּר וְהַמֻּתָּר וְכוּ', דְּהַיְנוּ עַל־יְדֵי לִמּוּד פּוֹסְקִים, אֲזַי מַפְרִישׁ הַטּוֹב מֵהָרָע. אַךְ לִזְכּוֹת לָזֶה הַשֵּׂכֶל, שֶׁיּוּכַל לָלוּן לְעָמְקָהּ שֶׁל הֲלָכָה, הוּא עַל־יְדֵי תְּפִלָּה, כִּי מִשָּׁם נִמְשָׁךְ הַשֵּׂכֶל:

ז. וְהָעִנְיָן, כְּמוֹ שֶׁכָּתוּב בְּתִקּוּנֵי־זֹהַר (תִּקּוּן י״ד, כט:): 'גַּן – דָּא אוֹרַיְתָא', כִּי הַתּוֹרָה נִקְרֵאת גַּן, וְנִשְׁמוֹת יִשְׂרָאֵל הַמְעַיְּנִים וּמְבִינִים בְּהַתּוֹרָה הֵם בְּחִינַת עֲשָׂבִין וּדְשָׁאִין דְּאִתְרַבִּיאוּ בַּגָּן. וּמֵאַיִן הֵם גְּדֵלִים? הוּא מִמַּעְיָן, דָּא חָכְמָה, כְּמוֹ שֶׁכָּתוּב (שִׁיר־הַשִּׁירִים ד): "מַעְיַן גַּנִּים."

---

46. **seeks...come to him.** One who does not clarify the Codes is in the category of "seeks bad." He is incapable of distinguishing good from bad, right from wrong. Therefore, because he may not recognize evil for what it is, he cannot engage in the attempt to destroy the wicked man's conduit, lest he himself be destroyed. Likewise, he cannot draw the *ruach* necessary to bring wholeness in place of the lack (*Mai HaNachal*).

47. **Gan...Torah.** The Torah (Pentateuch) is divided into 53 portions read weekly over the course of the year. *GaN* (גן) has the numerical value of 53 (see Appendix: Gematria Chart).

48. **grasses which grow....** Cf. *Eruvin* 54a, that people are likened to the grasses of the field. More precisely, the *Tikkuney Zohar* (#14, p.30) says that the grasses in the garden are the Torah scholars. Thus, Rebbe Nachman calls them the Jewish souls who delve into and understand the Torah. For it is the Torah which nourishes them spiritually.

49. **fountain of gardens.** This is the language of the *Tikkuney Zohar* (*ibid.*): What is it that waters the garden and makes the trees and grasses grow? It is the "fountain of gardens," which is wisdom. See note 53 that, actually, the fountain itself is wisdom. When this wisdom has watered the garden, the garden—the Torah—becomes "a fountain of gardens."

The next words in the verse (*loc. cit.*) are, "a well of flowing water." On this, the Midrash

53 · LIKUTEY MOHARAN #8:6,7

6. To achieve this, to be able to distinguish, separate and eliminate the bad from the good, one must engage in Torah and prayer. This Torah study should be delving into the depths of the law *(Megillah 4b)*—i.e., studying the Codifiers.[45] For good and bad have a hold on the Torah. They are attached through the aspects of forbidden and permitted, impure and pure, kosher and unkosher, which appear in the Torah. And as long as one does not clarify the law, he is a mixture of good and bad.

This is why he cannot separate and eliminate the bad from the good. He is in the aspect of *(Proverbs 11:27)*, "He who seeks bad, it will come to him."[46] Only once he delves into and clarifies the law in practice, and determines <the permitted, the kosher and the pure>—i.e., by studying the Codifiers—can he separate <the bad from the good> *(cf. Tikkuney Zohar #50, p.98b)*. However, being worthy of the intellect necessary for "delving into the depths of the law" only comes through prayer, because it is from there that intellect is drawn.

7. This matter [of Torah and prayer] is as follows: The *Tikkuney Zohar (#13, p.29b; #14, 30a)* states: "*Gan* (the garden) is the Torah."[47] The Torah is called a garden. The Jewish souls who *M'AYeNim* (delve into) and understand the Torah are the various types of grasses which grow in the garden.[48] What makes them grow? [They draw] from the *MaAYaN* (fountain), which is *chokhmah* (wisdom), as in *(Song of Songs 4:15)*, "A fountain of gardens...."[49]

---

lacking (§1). This *ruach*-of-life is received from the tzaddik/*rav* of the generation. When one who is attached to the tzaddik sighs, he draws the *ruach* from the heart to fill the lack in the heart (§2). Conversely, the wicked receive *ruach* from the *rav* of the Other Side. Theirs is an impure *ruach,* which is temporarily powerful but is ultimately destroyed. This results in a lack, as opposed to the wholeness received through the *rav* of holiness (§3). All lack stems from sin. The tzaddik who draws *ruach* to fill the lack therefore has the power to atone for sin. In this he resembles the Holy One, for atonement relates to God's 13 Attributes of Mercy (§4). A person must avoid provoking the wicked, whose sighs draw *ruach* from the *rav* of the husks and so cause the one who provokes them to sin. Only a perfect tzaddik, one who has expelled all evil, has the power to counter the temporary strength of the wicked. This by virtue of his having separated good from bad in the 4 elements, which encompass all the traits (§5).

45. **depths of the law...Codifiers.** Before Yehoshua went into battle against the city of Ai (Joshua 8) we are told that he spent the night "delving into the depths," studying Torah. Then, by virtue of his having drawn the *ruach* from the Torah and having separated the good from the bad, he was able to enter into battle against the wicked and defeat them. In section 2 above Rebbe Nachman mentions the "tzaddik who can stand up to the *ruach* of each and every one." This was Yehoshua.

LIKUTEY MOHARAN #8:7

54

וּמֵהֵיכָן מְקַבְּלִין הַחָכְמָה וְהַשֵּׂכֶל שֶׁהוּא בְּחִינַת הַמַּעְיָן? הוּא
מֵהַתְּפִלָּה, כְּמוֹ שֶׁכָּתוּב (יוֹאֵל ד): "וּמַעְיָן מִבֵּית ה' יֵצֵא" – הוּא
הַתְּפִלָּה, כְּמוֹ שֶׁכָּתוּב (יְשַׁעְיָהוּ נ"ו): "כִּי בֵיתִי בֵּית תְּפִלָּה".
וְהוּא בְּחִינַת מֵבִיא מִכֹּחַ אֶל הַפֹּעַל. כִּי תְּפִלָּה הוּא בְּחִינַת חִדּוּשׁ
הָעוֹלָם, כִּי תְּפִלָּה הוּא שֶׁמַּאֲמִין שֶׁיֵּשׁ מְחַדֵּשׁ אֲשֶׁר בְּיָדוֹ לַעֲשׂוֹת
כִּרְצוֹנוֹ לְשַׁנּוֹת הַטֶּבַע, וְהוּא בְּחִינוֹת בְּרִיאָה בְּכֹחַ, כְּמוֹ שֶׁכָּתוּב
(תְּהִלִּים ק"ד): "כֻּלָּם בְּחָכְמָה עָשִׂיתָ", שֶׁהוּא בְּחִינַת הַתְּפִלָּה שֶׁמִּשָּׁם
יוֹצֵא מַעְיָן הַחָכְמָה כַּנַּ"ל;

וְהַתּוֹרָה הִיא בְּחִינַת בְּרִיאָה בְּפֹעַל, כְּמוֹ שֶׁכָּתוּב (מִשְׁלֵי ח): "וָאֶהְיֶה
אֶצְלוֹ אָמוֹן" – אָמָּן, לְשׁוֹן פּוֹעֵל, כִּי בְּהַתּוֹרָה נִבְרָא הָעוֹלָם.
וּכְשֶׁמִּתְפַּלֵּל עַל אֵיזֶה דָבָר, הוּא בְּחִינַת חִדּוּשׁ הָעוֹלָם וְהוּא בְּחִינַת
בְּרִיאָה בְּכֹחַ, וְהוּא בְּחִינַת הִתְעוֹרְרוּת הַחָכְמָה שֶׁהוּא בַּתְּפִלָּה,
כַּנִּזְכָּר לְעֵיל: "וּמַעְיָן מִבֵּית ה' יֵצֵא", זֶה הַתְּפִלָּה, כִּי שָׁם נִתְעוֹרֵר
הַחָכְמָה כַּנַּ"ל, וּמִשָּׁם נִמְשָׁךְ הַמַּעְיָן הוּא הַחָכְמָה אֶל הַתּוֹרָה, וְשָׁם
יוֹצֵא אֶל הַפֹּעַל, כְּמוֹ שֶׁכָּתוּב (מִשְׁלֵי ב): "מִפִּיו דַּעַת וּתְבוּנָה", כִּי
בְּהַתּוֹרָה הוּא הִתְגַּלּוּת הַחָכְמָה, וְעַל-יְדֵי-זֶה נַעֲשֶׂה מַעְיָן גַּנִּים,
שֶׁהַמַּעְיָן מַשְׁקֶה הַגַּן, וְעַל-יְדֵי-זֶה אִתְרְבִיאוּ עֲשָׂבִין וּדְשָׁאִין כַּנַּ"ל.

---

53. **fountain of gardens is made.** The *Tikkuney Zohar* quoted earlier (n.49) indicates that the
"fountain of gardens" is wisdom. This would seem to contradict what Rebbe Nachman said
that the fountain itself is wisdom. However, later on in the *Tikkuney Zohar* (#52, p. 87b) we
find the following: Just as trees cannot grow without water, so too, the Jewish people cannot
survive without the wellsprings of Torah.... As relates to the *sefirot*, the fountain is
Chokhmah (the second Divine emanation, Wisdom). When *Keter* (the highest Divine
emanation, a reference to God Himself)—the amazing Architect—wanted to plant the Tree
in the Garden, He saw there was no source of water anywhere. What did He do? He said,
"First I will send forth a fountain and then plant, so that the Tree will grow." This is why it is
called the "fountain of gardens": at first, it is referred to as a "fountain," and later, we call it
"gardens." Thus, "fountain of gardens"—the watered garden—is made when the wisdom
which flows from prayer into the Torah is revealed there. This is the actualization of creation
mentioned earlier. With it, the garden is watered and the grasses, the Jewish souls, are
nurtured and grow.

LIKUTEY MOHARAN #8:7

From where do they receive the wisdom and intellect—this fountain? It comes from prayer, as is written (Joel 4:18), "A fountain will flow from the house of God." And this ["house of God"] is prayer, as in (Isaiah 56:7), "For My house is a house of prayer."[50]

[Prayer] is the medium for actualizing the potential. Prayer is the aspect of "renewing the world." This is because prayer < corresponds to faith, > for he believes that there is a *M'chadesh* (an Originator) capable of changing nature as He pleases. Thus [prayer] corresponds to potential creation, as in (Psalms 104:24), "You made them all with wisdom." This alludes to prayer, from where the fountain of wisdom flows.[51]

And Torah corresponds to actualized creation, as in (Proverbs 8:30), "I was as His *amone* (nurseling)." < Do not read this *AMoNe* but > *UMaN* (architect), which connotes actualized [creation], for with the Torah the world was created.[52]

Thus, when a person prays for something, it is an aspect of renewing the world and is synonymous with creation in potential. It also corresponds to an arousal of wisdom, which is in the prayer. As previously mentioned, "A fountain will flow from the house of God"—this is prayer, for that is where the wisdom is aroused. From there the fountain, the wisdom, is drawn to the Torah. And there [in the Torah] it goes < from potential > to actual, as in (Proverbs 2:6), "[For God gives wisdom]: from His mouth comes knowledge and understanding." < The Torah is > the revelation of the wisdom, and through this the "fountain of gardens" is made.[53] The fountain waters the garden and causes the grasses to grow.

(*Shir HaShirim Rabbah* 4:15) teaches: Rabbi Yochanan said, "The word *well* appears 48 times in the Torah. This corresponds to the 48 Ways through which the Torah is acquired" (cf. *Avot* 6:5).

50. **My house...prayer.** Because God's House is one of prayer and the fountain flows from it, it follows that the fountain's origin is prayer itself.

51. **prayer...wisdom flows.** Prayer corresponds to "renewing the world"—a new creation. Thus, prayer gives rise to the fountain, wisdom, with which to bring forth the "renewal"—the actual creation.

52. **with the Torah...created.** The Midrash (*Bereishit Rabbah* 1:1) attributes this verse to the Torah, who tells us that she is God's architect (אומן), encompassing, as she does, the blueprint of creation. As the *Zohar* (II, 161a) teaches: God looked at each and every word [of the Torah] and from them created the different parts of the world. The Torah thus corresponds to actualized creation.

LIKUTEY MOHARAN #8:7

וְזֶהוּ שֶׁאָמְרוּ רַבּוֹתֵינוּ, זִכְרוֹנָם לִבְרָכָה (בְּרָכוֹת לב:): 'הַמְעַיֵּן
בִּתְפִלָּתוֹ בָּא לִידֵי כְּאֵב לֵב' וְכוּ', שֶׁנֶּאֱמַר (מִשְׁלֵי י"ג): "תּוֹחֶלֶת
מְמֻשָּׁכָה מַחֲלָה לֵב". מַאי תַּקַּנְתֵּהּ? יַעֲסֹק בַּתּוֹרָה, שֶׁנֶּאֱמַר: (שָׁם)
"וְעֵץ חַיִּים תַּאֲוָה בָאָה".

זֶהוּ שֶׁאָמַרְנוּ, כִּי בְּהַתְּפִלָּה עֲדַיִן הוּא בְּכֹחַ וְאֵינוֹ יוֹצֵא אֶל הַפֹּעַל,
עַד שֶׁבָּא אֶל הַתּוֹרָה, שֶׁהִיא בְּחִינַת בְּרִיאָה בְּפֹעַל, וַאֲזַי נַעֲשֶׂה
בַּקָּשָׁתוֹ, עַל-יְדֵי שֶׁיּוֹצֵא מִכֹּחַ אֶל הַפֹּעַל.

וְהַיְנוּ דִכְתִיב: וְנָהָר יֹצֵא מֵעֵדֶן לְהַשְׁקוֹת אֶת הַגָּן, וּמִשָּׁם יִפָּרֵד
וְהָיָה לְאַרְבָּעָה רָאשִׁים.

עֵדֶן – הוּא בְּחִינַת הַתְּפִלָּה, כִּי עֵדֶן "עַיִן לֹא רָאָתָה", כְּמוֹ שֶׁאָמְרוּ
רַבּוֹתֵינוּ, זִכְרוֹנָם לִבְרָכָה (בְּרָכוֹת לד:), שֶׁזֶּהוּ בְּחִינַת תְּפִלָּה שֶׁהוּא
לְמַעְלָה מִן הַטֶּבַע, כִּי עַל-יְדֵי תְּפִלָּה מְשַׁנֶּה הַטֶּבַע כַּנַּ"ל [שֶׁזֶּהוּ
בְּחִינַת עֵדֶן "עַיִן לֹא רָאָתָה", כִּי לְמַעְלָה מֵהַטֶּבַע אֵין לָנוּ שׁוּם
תְּפִיסָא].

וְהַיְנוּ: וְנָהָר יֹצֵא מֵעֵדֶן – הַיְנוּ מֵהַתְּפִלָּה, כַּנַּ"ל: "וּמַעְיָן מִבֵּית ה'
יֵצֵא"; לְהַשְׁקוֹת אֶת הַגָּן – הוּא הַתּוֹרָה כַּנַּ"ל, "מַעְיַן גַּנִּים".

וְכַאֲשֶׁר נִמְשָׁךְ מַעְיַן הַחָכְמָה מֵהַתְּפִלָּה אֶל הַגָּן שֶׁהוּא הַתּוֹרָה, אֲזַי
אִתְרְבִּיאוּ עֲשָׂבִין וּדְשָׁאִין – נִשְׁמוֹת יִשְׂרָאֵל, כְּלוֹמַר שֶׁגְּדֵלִים בְּהַגָּן
וּמְבִינִים וּמַשְׂכִּילִים בְּהַתּוֹרָה, וַאֲזַי זוֹכֶה לָלוּן בְּעָמְקָהּ שֶׁל הֲלָכָה
לְבָרֵר הַדִּין, הָאָסוּר וְהַמֻּתָּר, הַטָּהוֹר וְכוּ', וּבָזֶה מַפְרִישׁ הַטּוֹב
מֵהָרַע כַּנַּ"ל.

looks deeply into his prayers does so because he feels a lack and therefore yearns to remove
this deficiency. However, the very fact that he awaits an answer indicates a lack of faith in his
having created a "new" order of things through his prayer. This is his heartache—feeling the
lack in his heart, because the heart is where the *ruach*, drawn from the Torah, resides. He has
not succeeded in drawing the *ruach*, the Torah, through his prayers. What is his cure? Torah
study!—a renewal of the *ruach* in order to remove the deficiency. Doing so brings wholeness
in place of the lack. He can then pray and his prayers will renew the creation—providing him
with that which he wants (see *Mai HaNachal*).

LIKUTEY MOHARAN #8:7

{"Extended longing makes the heart ache, but with the Tree of Life desire is fulfilled" (Proverbs 13:12).}

This is the meaning of what our Sages taught: Someone who is *M'AYaiN* (looks deeply) into his prayers comes to heartache. As is written, "Extended longing makes the heart ache..." (*Berakhot* 32b).[54] What is his cure? Let him engage in Torah study, as is written, "...but with the Tree of Life desire is fulfilled."[55]

As we have said, [as long as that which a person wants] is in prayer, it is still in potential. It only becomes concretized when it comes to the Torah, which is the aspect of actualized creation. Then, that which he asks for is done—having gone from potential to actual.[56]

This is as is written, "A river flows from Eden to water the garden. And from there it separates, becoming four tributaries" (Genesis 2:10).

"Eden" corresponds to prayer. As our Sages taught (*Berakhot* 34b): Eden—"No eye has seen it" (Isaiah 64:3). And ["no eye has seen it"] applies to prayer, which transcends nature. For nature can be changed through prayer. {Eden is "no eye has seen it" because we cannot fathom that which transcends nature.}

And this is: "A river flows from Eden"—i.e., from prayer, as mentioned above, "A fountain will flow from the house of God." "...to water the garden"—this is the Torah, as mentioned, the "fountain of gardens."

And when the fountain of wisdom from prayer is drawn to the garden—the Torah—then it causes the grasses—the Jewish souls—to grow. In other words, [the Jewish souls] grow in the garden, they gain understanding and intelligence of the Torah. Then they merit "delving into the depths of the law," in order to determine < the correct > law: < the permitted, kosher and pure from the impure, unkosher and forbidden >. By doing so, they separate the good from the bad.

---

54. **M'AYaiN...heart ache.** This refers to a person who prays and looks deeply, i.e., longs for his prayers to be immediately answered. See note 56.

55. **Torah...Tree of Life....** This verse appears as part of a chapter in Proverbs which begins, "My son, forget not My Torah...." "Desire fulfilled" is creation actualized, as opposed to the potential of "longed for" prayers. A later verse in the same chapter states clearly of the Torah that "she is a Tree of Life to those who take hold of her."

56. **potential to actual.** This Talmudic passage can be understood as follows: The person who

LIKUTEY MOHARAN #8:7,8

וְזֶהוּ: וּמִשָּׁם יִפָּרֵד, כִּי עַל־יְדֵי־זֶה נִפְרָד הָרָע מֵהָאַרְבָּעָה יְסוֹדוֹת
וְלֹא נִשְׁאָר רַק הַטּוֹב, וַאֲזַי: וְהָיָה לְאַרְבָּעָה רָאשִׁים – הֵם אַרְבַּע
אוֹתִיּוֹת הֲוָיָ"ה, שֶׁהֵם שֹׁרֶשׁ הַטּוֹב שֶׁל הָאַרְבָּעָה יְסוֹדוֹת כַּנַּ"ל:

ח. וְזֶהוּ בְּחִינוֹת אַרְבַּע צִיצִית, כִּי אַרְבַּע צִיצִית הֵם בְּחִינַת הָרוּחַ־
חַיִּים, וּכְמוֹ שֶׁכָּתוּב (יְחֶזְקֵאל ל"ז): "כֹּה אָמַר ה' מֵאַרְבַּע רוּחוֹת בֹּאִי
הָרוּחַ", שֶׁעַל־יְדֵי־זֶה מַכְנִיעִין הָרוּחַ־סְעָרָה, שֶׁהוּא הָרוּחַ שֶׁל
הַמִּתְנַגְּדִים הַחוֹלְקִים עַל הַצַּדִּיקִים אֲמִתִּיִּים,
[וְאֵלּוּ] שֶׁמַּמְשִׁיכִין אֲרִיכַת הָרוּחַ שֶׁלָּהֶם מֵהָרַב דִּקְלִפָּה, שֶׁהוּא
בְּחִינַת עֵשָׂו אִישׁ שָׂעִיר כַּנַּ"ל. וְעַל־כֵּן צִיצִית הוּא לְשׁוֹן שֵׂעָר, כְּמוֹ
שֶׁכָּתוּב (שָׁם ח): "וַיִּקָּחֵנִי בְּצִיצִית רֹאשִׁי". כִּי עַל־יָדָם נִכְנָע עֵשָׂו
אִישׁ שָׂעִיר, בְּחִינַת רוּחַ־סְעָרָה כַּנַּ"ל.

וְזֶה בְּחִינַת טַלִּית לָבָן שֶׁנִּתְעַטֵּף הַקָּדוֹשׁ־בָּרוּךְ־הוּא וְסֵדֶר שְׁלֹשׁ־
עֶשְׂרֵה מִדּוֹת (כְּמוֹ שֶׁאָמְרוּ רַבּוֹתֵינוּ, זִכְרוֹנָם לִבְרָכָה, רֹאשׁ הַשָּׁנָה י"ז:), כִּי
הַשְּׁלֹשׁ־עֶשְׂרֵה מִדּוֹת הֵן בְּחִינוֹת הָרוּחַ־חַיִּים דִּקְדֻשָּׁה כַּנַּ"ל. וְזֶהוּ
בְּחִינַת טַלִּית, שֶׁהוּא אַרְבַּע כְּנָפוֹת, בְּחִינוֹת הָרוּחַ מֵאַרְבַּע רוּחוֹת
כַּנַּ"ל. וְהַיְנוּ טַלִּית לָבָן – הֵפֶךְ בְּחִינוֹת רוּחַ דִּקְלִפָּה, בְּחִינַת עֵשָׂו,
שֶׁהוּא "אַדְמוֹנִי כֻּלּוֹ כְּאַדֶּרֶת שֵׂעָר" (בְּרֵאשִׁית כ"ה), וּפֵרֵשׁ רַשִׁ"י:
'כְּטַלִּית' – כְּטַלִּית דַּיְקָא, בְּחִינַת טַלִּית דִּקְלִפָּה, שֶׁהוּא בְּחִינַת

---

to separate the good from the bad and thereby draw the ruach-of-life upon himself.

Rebbe Nachman next shows how the "four tributaries" and the four letters of God's name are connected to the four cornered garment with its four *tzitzit*.

In review: *Ruach*/breath is the life-force of everything. Sighing brings life into all that is lacking (§1). This *ruach*-of-life is received from the tzaddik/rav of the generation. When one who is attached to the tzaddik sighs, he draws the *ruach* from the heart to fill the lack in the heart (§2). Conversely, the wicked receive *ruach* from the *rav* of the Other Side. Theirs is an impure *ruach,* which results in a lack (§3). All lack stems from sin. The tzaddik who draws *ruach* to fill the lack therefore has the power to atone for sin (§4). A person must avoid provoking the wicked, whose sighs draw *ruach* from the *rav* of the husks and so cause the one who provokes them to sin. Only a perfect tzaddik, one who has expelled all evil, has the power to counter the temporary strength of the wicked. This, by virtue of his having

59　　　　*LIKUTEY MOHARAN #8:7,8*

This is the meaning of, "...from there it separates." By [clarifying the law] the bad is separated out of the four elements. Only the good remains. Then, "...becoming four tributaries." These are the four letters *YHVH,* which are the root of the good found in the four elements, as above.[57]

8. This corresponds to the four *tzitzit* (corner fringes). The four *tzitzit* correspond to the *ruach*-of-life, as in (Ezekiel 37:9), "Thus says God: From the four directions comes the *ruach.*" It is through [the *tzitzit*] that the *ruach se'arah*—i.e., the *ruach* of the opponents who militate against the true tzaddikim—is subdued.

[These opponents] draw their extended *ruach* from the *rav* of the husks, who corresponds to "Esav is an *ish sa'ir* (hairy man)." This is why the *tzitzit* are synonymous with *Sei'AR* (hair), as in (Ezekiel 8:3), "And He took me by the *tzitzit* (locks) of my head." For through [the *tzitzit*], Esav *ish SA'iR*—i.e., the *ruach Se'ARah*—is subdued.

And this is the concept of the white *tallit* (prayer shawl) that God donned when He set [before Moshe] the Thirteen Attributes (see *Rosh HaShanah* 17b). For the Thirteen Attributes corresponds to the holy *ruach*-of-life; and the *tallit* with its four corners alludes to the *ruach* from the four corners [of the earth]. This is "the white *tallit,*" which is the antithesis of the *ruach* of the husks—corresponding to Esav, who is "reddish, as hairy as a fur coat" (Genesis 25:25). Rashi explains: "[The hair covered him] like a *tallit.*" Specifically "like a *tallit*"—the *tallit* of

---

57. **four elements, as above.** Reb Noson in his *Likutey Halakhot* (*HaOseh Shaliach Ligvot Chovo* 3:29) interprets the Biblical depiction of the creation of man in light of this lesson. "...no plants grew...did not rain...man was not as yet created...breathed life into him...Gan in Eden...Tree of Life...Tree of Knowledge...A river flows...to work and guard it...do not eat from the Tree of Knowledge...." (Genesis 2:2-17). God created man and breathed into him the *ruach*-of-life. Man was charged to keep it pure. Therefore, he was placed in the Garden of Eden—that is, man was charged to pray and bring wisdom into the Torah. Then he would draw the *ruach* of the Torah into himself. This was to be accomplished by engaging in "working and guarding" the Garden—i.e., arriving at the proper decisions when studying the Codes of Law. These Codes allude to the Tree of Knowledge, and their study implies separating the good from the bad and destroying the conduits of the wicked. And this is why no rain fell to water the Garden until man was created. It was necessary for there to be a creature who, through his prayers, could arouse wisdom, the fountain, with which to water the Garden properly. This was man. And, as Reb Noson points out, it is still man's mission in life to "be created." That is, man is charged with "renewing himself," just as he is charged with the "renewal of the world." How is this to be accomplished? It can only be achieved by man always praying that he be given a clear understanding of the Torah in order

LIKUTEY MOHARAN #8:8 — 60

טַלִּית אָדֹם, שֶׁמִּשָּׁם נִמְשָׁךְ הָרוּחַ שֶׁל הָרְשָׁעִים כַּנַּ״ל.
וְעַל־יְדֵי טַלִּית דִּקְדֻשָּׁה, שֶׁהוּא בְּחִינַת טַלִּית לָבָן, מַכְנִיעִין אוֹתוֹ,
כִּי מִשָּׁם נִמְשָׁךְ הָרוּחַ־חַיִּים דִּקְדֻשָּׁה, שֶׁהוּא בְּחִינַת שְׁלֹש־עֶשְׂרֵה
מִדּוֹת שֶׁל רַחֲמִים כַּנַּ״ל. וְעַל כֵּן נִתְעַטֵּף הַקָּדוֹשׁ־בָּרוּךְ־הוּא בְּטַלִּית
לָבָן דַּיְקָא וְסִדֵּר לִפְנֵי מֹשֶׁה שְׁלֹש־עֶשְׂרֵה מִדּוֹת שֶׁל רַחֲמִים, הַיְנוּ
כַּנַּ״ל, כִּי עַל־יְדֵי טַלִּית דִּקְדֻשָּׁה, שֶׁהוּא בִּבְחִינוֹת מַקִּיף, שֶׁהוּא
בְּחִינַת הָרוּחַ־חַיִּים, בְּחִינוֹת (קֹהֶלֶת א): ״סוֹבֵב סֹבֵב הוֹלֵךְ הָרוּחַ״,
נִכְנָע טַלִּית דִּקְלִפָּה, בְּחִינַת הָרוּחַ דִּקְלִפָּה:

וְזֶהוּ (אִיּוֹב ל״ח): ״לֶאֱחֹז בְּכַנְפוֹת הָאָרֶץ וְיִנָּעֲרוּ רְשָׁעִים מִמֶּנָּה״ —
כִּי עַל־יְדֵי הָאַרְבַּע כְּנָפוֹת, שֶׁהֵם בְּחִינַת הָרוּחַ־חַיִּים דִּקְדֻשָּׁה, שֶׁהֵם
בְּחִינַת הָאַרְבַּע רָאשִׁים הַנַּ״ל, עַל־יָדָם וְיִנָּעֲרוּ רְשָׁעִים, בְּחִינַת
מַשְׁפִּיל רְשָׁעִים עֲדֵי אָרֶץ, רָאשֵׁי־תֵבוֹת: אֵ׳שׁ, ר׳וּחַ, מַ׳יִם,
עָ׳פָר, כַּנַּ״ל.

וְזֶה פֵּרוּשׁ: אָמַר רַבָּה בַּר בַּר־חָנָא:
אָמַר לִי הַהוּא טַיָּעָא, תָּא וְאַחֲוֵי לָךְ
מֵתֵי מִדְבָּר. אַזְלִי וַחֲזֵיתִינְהוּ, וְדָמוּ
כְּמָאן דְּמִבַּסְּמוּ. וְגָנוּ אַפַּרְקִיד, וַהֲוָה

רַשְׁבַּ״ם:

טַיָּעָא – סוֹחֵר יִשְׁמָעֵאל: אַזְלִי
וַחֲזֵיתִינְהוּ וְדָמוּ כְּמָאן דְּמִבַּסְּמוּ
– שֶׁהָיוּ שׁוֹכְבִין בְּפָנִים צְהֻבּוֹת
כְּשִׁתּוּיֵי יַיִן: אַפַּרְקִיד – פְּנֵיהֶם

---

partake of *Gan* (Torah) *Eden* (prayer), as Rebbe Nachman taught above (see §7). The *Yerushalmi* therefore states that God Himself will remove Esav, for he is not worthy. His red *tallit* is that of the wicked, from the side of stern judgment, and he is the *rav* of the *kelipah*.

59. **makif, surrounding.** When donning the *tallit* before praying, one is *makif* (envelopes) himself in it. Rebbe Nachman also uses the term *makif* to indicate a level or thought which "surrounds" (is above) the person and which he has not yet achieved or understood. This *makif* is prayer, which, by virtue of its transcendant root, is even higher than wisdom. It thus reaches all the way to the level of the *YHVH*, the very Source of all life.

60. **subdued.** Our Sages taught that the mitzvah of *tzitzit* is equivalent to all the 613 commandments of the Torah. This can be understood by relating to the *tzitzit* as the *ruach-of-life*. In this light, the *tzitzit*, too, have the power to bring wholeness in place of the lack, subdue the *ruach* of the husks, and separate the good from the bad in the four elements. It is therefore advisable when donning the *tallit* to sigh deeply over all one's deficiencies, for this will certainly bring wholeness in place of the lack (*Mai HaNachal*).

61   *LIKUTEY MOHARAN #8:8*

the husks, which is a red garment.[58] For from there, the *ruach* of the wicked is drawn.

But through the *tallit* of holiness, the white *tallit,* [the wicked man] is subdued. This is because the holy *ruach*-of-life—i.e., the Thirteen Attributes of Mercy—is drawn from there. Therefore, God specifically donned a white *tallit* when He set before Moshe the Thirteen Attributes of Mercy. For through the *tallit* of holiness— corresponding to both the *makif* (surrounding)[59] and the *ruach*-of-life, as in (Ecclesiastes 1:6), "The *ruach* goes round and round"—the *tallit* of the husks, the *ruach* of the husks, is subdued.[60]

This is (Job 38:13), "To take hold of the corners of the earth, that the wicked be shaken off it." The four corners correspond to the holy *ruach*-of-life and to the "four tributaries." Through them, "the wicked are shaken," corresponding to "*Mashpil Resha'im Adey Eretz* (He casts down the wicked to the ground)"—the first letters of *Esh, Ruach, Mayim, Afar,* as above.

This is the explanation:

Rabbah bar bar Chanah recounted: This merchant said to me, "Come, I will show you the dead [of the Generation] of the Desert." I went and saw them. They resembled drunkards, lying flat out. One of them had his knee raised up, and the merchant went under his knee while riding a *gamal* (a camel).	*Rashbam:* merchant - an Ishmaelite trader: I went and saw them. They resembled drunkards - they were laying there, their faces flushed, like those who drink too much wine: lying flat out - facing upwards: and the merchant went under his knee - that is, I saw that

separated good from bad in the 4 elements, which encompass all the traits (§5). To separate good from bad one must engage in Torah study—i.e., clarification of the law in practice— and prayer—i.e., the drawing of wisdom and intellect (§6). Through prayer/potential creation and Torah/actualized creation, Jewish souls gain the intelligence to separate the good from the bad (§7).

58. **white tallit...red garment.** As explained in note 35 above, white denotes *chasadim* (benevolences), whereas red is *gevurot* (severities). The tzaddik/*rav* of *chesed* strives to draw the *ruach*-of-life no matter what sins the person may have transgressed. The *rav* of the husks, on the other hand, draws the *ruach se'arah.* This storm wind appears mighty in its moment, and it would seem to be a "powerful" life-style to live. However, as Rebbe Nachman stated earlier (§3), nothing will remain of those who follow this path.

The Talmud *Yerushalmi* (*Nedarim* 3:8) teaches: In the future, Esav will wrap himself in a *tallit* and attempt to join the tzaddikim in Gan Eden. But God will drag him out. Esav will assume that his *tallit* can make him worthy—a *rav* no less! He will presume that he, too, can

זְקִיפָא בְּרָכָּה דְּחַד מְנַיְהוּ, וְעַיֵּל טַיְעָא תּוּתָה בְּרָכָּה, כִּי רָכִיב גַּמְלָא וּזְקִיפָא רָמְחָה וְלָא נְגַע בָּה. פַּסְקֵי חֲדָא קַרְנָא דִּתְכֶלְתָּא דְּחַד מְנַיְהוּ וְלָא הֲוֵי מִסְתַּגֵּי לָן. אָמַר לִי: דִּלְמָא שָׁקַלְתְּ מִידֵי מְנַיְהוּ? דִּגְמִירֵי, דְּמָאן דְּשָׁקִיל מִידֵי מְנַיְהוּ לָא מִסְתַּגֵּי לֵהּ. אַזְלֵי אַהֲדַרְתֵּהּ, וְהֲדַר מִסְתַּגֵּי לָן.

לְמַעְלָה: וְעַיֵּל טַיְעָא תּוּתָה בְּרָכָּה – כְּלוֹמַר, רָאִיתִי שֶׁטַּיְעָא הָיָה הוֹלֵךְ תַּחַת בִּרְכֵּי הַמֵּת, רָכוּב עַל הַגָּמָל וְרָמְחוּ בְּיָדוֹ, וְלָא נָגַע בֵּהּ בַּבִּרְכֵּהּ: שָׁקְלָא חֲדָא קַרְנָא – כְּנַף הַטַּלִּית לְהַרְאוֹתוֹ לַחֲכָמִים, לִלְמֹד מִמֶּנּוּ דִּין צִיצִית, אִי כְּבֵית־שַׁמַּאי אִי כְּבֵית־הֶלֵּל, כְּדִלְקַמָּן: וְלָא הֲוֵי קָא מִסְתַּגֵּי לָן – בְּהֵמוֹת שֶׁהָיִינוּ רוֹכְבִין לֹא הָיוּ יְכוֹלִין לַהֲלֹךְ.

תָּא וְאַחְוֵי לָךְ מֵתֵי מִדְבָּר – הַיְנוּ שֶׁהֶרְאָה לוֹ הָרְשָׁעִים שֶׁאֵינָם דְּבֵקִים בַּצַּדִּיקִים, וְהֵם נִקְרָאִין מֵתֵי מִדְבָּר, כִּי מִדְבָּר לֹא הָיְתָה רוּחַ צְפוֹנִית מְנַשֶּׁבֶת בּוֹ (יְבָמוֹת עב.) – הַיְנוּ בְּחִינַת רוּחַ הַחַיִּים דִּקְדֻשָּׁה, שֶׁהִיא בְּחִינַת רוּחַ צְפוֹנִית שֶׁהָיְתָה מְנַשֶּׁבֶת בַּכִּנּוֹר שֶׁל דָּוִד כַּנַּ"ל. וְהָרְשָׁעִים הַלָּלוּ, שֶׁאֵינָם דְּבֵקִים בַּצַּדִּיקִים, וְאֵין לָהֶם הָרוּחַ דִּקְדֻשָּׁה, וְהֵם בְּחַיֵּיהֶם קְרוּאִים מֵתִים; וְהֶרְאָה לוֹ מֵהֵיכָן מַגִּיעַ לָהֶם שְׁלֵמוּת הַחֶסָּרוֹן. וְזֶהוּ שֶׁהֶרְאָה לוֹ:

דַּהֲווֹ דָּמוּ כִּמְבַסְּמֵי – פֵּרֵשׁ רַבֵּנוּ שְׁמוּאֵל, כִּשְׁתוּיֵי יַיִן, בְּחִינַת עֵשָׂו אַדְמוֹנִי, שֶׁהוּא הָרַב דִּקְלִפָּה, אֲשֶׁר מִשָּׁם מְקַבְּלִין הָרְשָׁעִים הָרוּחַ־חַיִּים שֶׁלָּהֶם לְהַשְׁלִים הַחֶסָּרוֹן. וְזֶהוּ:

וְגָנוּ אַפַּרְקִיד – פֵּרֵשׁ רַבֵּנוּ שְׁמוּאֵל, פְּנֵיהֶם לְמַעְלָה – פְּנֵיהֶם זֶה

---

63. **northern wind did not blow....** "Because the north wind did not blow in the desert, the Jews were unable to circumcise their children" (*Yevamot, loc. cit.; Kiddushin* 37b). This is yet another reference to the need for being attached to the tzaddik. He is the true "guardian of the Covenant" and can draw the *ruach*-of-life to his followers. See *Likutey Moharan* I, 7; and below, note 71.

64. **drunkards...rav of the husks.** A person who is drunk, even if he is able to function properly and engage in conversation, is still not in complete control of his intellect. So too, the *rav* of the husks. Though he may appear in control and quite learned, he is not in possession of true Torah knowledge. That which he does know, that which has enabled him to gain prominence and be called *rav,* is superficial at best.

LIKUTEY MOHARAN #8:8

He held up his *romach* (spear), but still could not touch it. I cut off a corner from the *tzitzit* of one of them. [After this,] we were not able to leave. The merchant asked me, "Did you perhaps take something from them? We have a tradition: Anyone who takes something from them cannot depart." So I went and put back [the *tzitzit* corner]. Then we were able to leave (*Bava Batra* 73b).

the merchant went under the knee of the dead person. He was riding on a camel and had a spear in his hand, and he could still not touch his knee: **I cut off a corner** - the corner of the *tallit,* in order to show it to the Rabbis so that they would learn from it whether the laws of *tzitzit* follow the School of Shamai or the School of Hillel:[61] **we were not able to leave** - the animals we were riding could not walk:

Come, I will show you the dead of the desert — In other words, he showed him the wicked people who are not attached to the tzaddikim.[62] They are referred to as "the dead of the desert," for the "*ruach tzefonit* (northern wind) did not blow in the desert" (*Yevamot* 72a)[63]—i.e., the aspect of the holy *ruach*-of-life, corresponding to the *ruach tzefonit* which blew upon King David's harp. But these wicked people, who do not attach themselves to the tzaddikim, and do not have the *ruach* of holiness, are "even when alive, considered dead" (*Berakhot* 18b). The [merchant] showed him from where [the wicked] draw wholeness [in place] of their lack. This is what he showed him:

They resembled drunkards — Rashbam explains that they were like those who drink too much wine. This corresponds to Esav the "reddish [one]," who is the *rav* of the husks.[64] From there the wicked get their *ruach*-of-life in order to fill that which they lack. Thus:

lying flat out — Rashbam explains that their faces were directed upwards. **Their faces** corresponds to *ruach,* as in, "Their facial

---

61. **Shamai...Hillel.** This debate in the Talmud (*Menachot* 41b) concerns how many strings are necessary for the *tzitzit,* how far the fringes are to be placed from the corner of the garment, etc. See below, note 99.

62. **not attached to the tzaddikim.** This refers to those who were redeemed from Egypt. They died in the desert. Rabbah bar bar Chanah visited there some 1500 years later and found their corpses intact. This Generation of the Desert had as their *rav* and leader none other than Moshe Rabbeinu himself. Even so they did not show complete faith, neither in Moshe nor in God's promise that they would be taken into the Land of Israel. They said (Numbers 14:4), "Let us make a new leader...." Rashi explains: "a new leader" alludes to idolatry. By separating themselves from the rightful leader, Moshe Rabbeinu, they automatically attached themselves to *rav* of the husks, from whom they then drew their *ruach.*

LIKUTEY MOHARAN #8:8

בְּחִינַת הָרוּחַ כַּנַּ"ל: הַכָּרַת פְּנֵיהֶם וְכוּ'; וְהַיְנוּ לְמַעְלָה, כִּי הָרוּחַ
שֶׁלָּהֶם גָּדוֹל לְפִי שָׁעָה עַד אֲשֶׁר עוֹלָה הַצְלָחָתָם לְמַעְלָה כַּנַּ"ל,
בְּחִינַת כָּל צוֹרְרָיו יָפִיחַ בָּהֶם כַּנַּ"ל.

וַהֲוָה זְקִיפָא בְּרְכֵּהּ דְּחַד מִנַּיְהוּ – זֶה מוֹרֶה עַל גֹּדֶל הַהַצְלָחָה שֶׁל
הָרְשָׁעִים, כִּי הֶעְדֵּר הַהַצְלָחָה נִקְרָא "בִּרְכַּיִם כּוֹשְׁלוֹת" (יְשַׁעְיָהוּ
נ"ה): 'וְגָבַהּ בְּרְכֵּהּ' הַיְנוּ רוּם הַהַצְלָחָה.

וְעַיֵּל טַיְעָא תּוּתֵהּ בִּרְכֵּהּ – הַיְנוּ הַצַּדִּיק שֶׁנִּקְרָא טַיְעָא, כְּמוֹ שֶׁפֵּרֵשׁ
רַבֵּנוּ שְׁמוּאֵל בְּכָל מָקוֹם: 'סוֹחֵר יִשְׁמָעֵאל', וְסוֹחֵר הוּא בְּחִינַת
הָרוּחַ, כְּמוֹ שֶׁכָּתוּב (קֹהֶלֶת א): "סוֹבֵב סֹבֵב הוֹלֵךְ הָרוּחַ", וְהַיְנוּ
הַצַּדִּיק שֶׁמְּקַבֵּל הָרוּחַ מֵהַקְּדֻשָּׁה. וְזֶהוּ: 'סוֹחֵר יִשְׁמָעֵאל' – עַל
שֵׁם (בְּרֵאשִׁית ט"ז): "כִּי שָׁמַע ה' אֶל עָנְיֵךְ", כִּי הַצַּדִּיק שׁוֹמֵעַ כָּל
הָאֲנָחוֹת שֶׁל הַדְּבֵקִים בּוֹ, כִּי מִמֶּנּוּ תּוֹצָאוֹת חַיִּים לְכָל אֶחָד, כִּי
הוּא אִישׁ אֲשֶׁר רוּחַ בּוֹ כַּנַּ"ל.

כִּי רָכִיב גַּמְלָא – בְּחִינַת (מִשְׁלֵי י"א): "גּוֹמֵל נַפְשׁוֹ אִישׁ חָסֶד" –
זֶה בְּחִינַת רַב חֶסֶד כַּנַּ"ל.

וּזְקִיף רָמְחָא – רוֹמַח הוּא בְּחִינַת רוּחַ מֵ"ם, בְּחִינַת "וְרוּחַ אֱלֹקִים

person himself" (*Rabbi Nachman's Wisdom* #188). Once, when Rebbe Nachman's grandson was ill, the Rebbe said, "I can feel his each and every groan in my heart" (*ibid.*, #189).

69. **above.** See section 4: A person receives the *ruach*-of-life from the tzaddik/*rav* of the generation. He is *rav chesed.* Thus, this merchant/tzaddik was riding on a *gamal*, alluding to his being the man of *chesed* (lovingkindness) who is *gomel* (does good) for his soul.

70. **RuaCh Mem.** The letter *mem* has a numerical value of 40. When Pinchas was possessed by a *ruach* (spirit) of zealousness (Numbers 25), he took the *mem*—corresponding to the four *ruchot* (see next note)—to give him the special strength needed to subdue evil. "This *Mem* (מ) he added to the *RuaCh* (רוח), creating a *RoMaCh* (spear, רומח)" with which he killed Zimri (*Zohar* III, 237a). Thus, Pinchas prepared himself for battle by readying a weapon: the weapon of prayer and Torah (cf. *Likutey Moharan* I, 2:1,2).

Our Sages taught that Pinchas undertook this, saying, "I have received this teaching (the Torah) from Moshe..." (*Sanhedrin* 82a). Pinchas had acquired his spirit of zealousness from Moshe, the tzaddik who is the "guardian of the Covenant" (see n.63). It was this spirit which prompted him to challenge Zimri who had violated the Covenant by living with a Midianite woman.

LIKUTEY MOHARAN #8:8

expression bears witness against them."[65] This is the meaning of **upwards**: for the moment, their *ruach* is mighty, so that their fortune is ascendant, as in, "he blows away all his enemies."

One of them had his knee raised up — This alludes to the great good fortune of the wicked. A lack of good fortune is known as "weak knees" (Isaiah 35:3); whereas **his knee raised up** indicates heightened good fortune.[66]

And the merchant went under his knee — Namely, the tzaddik, who is called a merchant. As Rashbam explains, ["merchant"] is always a reference to an Ishmaelite *socher* (trader). The word *socher* corresponds to the *ruach,* as in (Ecclesiastes 1:6), "Round and round goes the wind."[67] This refers to the tzaddik, who receives the *ruach* <-of-life of holiness>. And this is "an *iShMAelite* trader," similar to (Genesis 16:11), "[You shall call his name Yishmael,] for *SheMA Hashem* (God has heard) your plaint." For the tzaddik hears all the sighs of those attached to him. From him life goes out to each one, because he is "a man in whom there is *ruach*."[68]

while riding a GaMaL (camel) — As in (Proverbs 11:17), "*GoMeL nafsho* (he does good to his soul), *ish chesed* (the man of kindness)"—this is the aspect of *rav chesed,* as mentioned above.[69]

He stretched out his romach (spear) — *RoMaCh* corresponds to *RuaCh Mem*[70]—"the *ruach* of God [that] hovers over the waters'

---

65. **against them.** See above, section 3: "But He is *m'shalem* His enemies to their face"— providing them with *ruach*—but this is short lived, for God's intention is "in order to destroy them." Thus, even though at the moment the wicked man's *ruach* is strong and mighty, a veritable storm wind because "God extends His face," nevertheless, in the end God "collects His due."

66. **knee raised up....** The word *BeReKh* (knee, ברך) comes from the same root as *B'RaKhah* (blessing, ברכה). This can be understood in the sense that man's ability to stand on his own feet is likened to a strong, unfaltering knee. And our Sages taught: One who is [blessed] with possessions is thus able to stand on his feet (*Sanhedrin* 110a).

67. **goes the wind.** Onkelos translates "round and round" as *s'chor, s'chor.* Thus, Rebbe Nachman connects the *ruach,* which goes *S'ChoR,* to the *SoCheR* (merchant)—i.e., the tzaddik. He is from the side of holiness and opposes the "raised up" fortune of the wicked.

68. **man...ruach.** Rebbe Nachman once said, "I prayed to God that I might become more sensitive, so as to feel the pain and suffering of another Jew. Now, I feel it even more than the

LIKUTEY MOHARAN #8:8

מְרַחֶפֶת עַל־פְּנֵי הַמַּיִם", הַיְנוּ הַתּוֹרָה שֶׁנִּתְּנָה לְמ' יוֹם, שֶׁשָּׁם הָרוּחַ־חַיִּים כַּנַּ"ל; כְּלוֹמַר, שֶׁהַצַּדִּיק הָיָה לוֹ בְּחִינַת הָרוּחַ שֶׁמְּקַבֵּל מֵהַתּוֹרָה כַּנַּ"ל, וְעִם כָּל זֶה נָחִית תְּחוֹת בִּרְכֵּהּ, תַּחַת הַצַּלָחַת הָרָשָׁע, בְּחִינַת "כְּבַלַּע רָשָׁע צַדִּיק מִמֶּנּוּ".

וְקָא פַסְקֵי קַרְנָא דִתְכֶלְתָּא דְּחַד מִנַּיְהוּ – הַיְנוּ שֶׁפָּסַק וְשִׁבֵּר הַמִּדָּה רָעָה מֵאָחָד מֵאַרְבַּע יְסוֹדוֹת שֶׁהִגְבִּיר וְהִמְשִׁיךְ הָרָשָׁע עַל עַצְמוֹ, שֶׁהוּא הַצַּנּוֹר שֶׁלּוֹ כַּנַּ"ל. וְזֶהוּ: 'וְקָא פַסְקֵי קַרְנָא דִתְכֶלְתָּא' וְכוּ', הַיְנוּ שֶׁפָּסַק אַחַת מִן הַצִּיצִית שֶׁלָּהֶם, שֶׁזֶּה בְּחִינַת מַה שֶׁפָּסַק וְשִׁבֵּר הַמִּדָּה רָעָה שֶׁלָּהֶם שֶׁהוּא הַצַּנּוֹר שֶׁלָּהֶם, כִּי כָל הַמִּדּוֹת רָעוֹת נִמְשָׁכִין מֵאַרְבָּעָה יְסוֹדוֹת, שֶׁשָּׁרְשָׁם אַרְבַּע צִיצִית כַּנַּ"ל.

וְלָא מִסְתַּגֵּי לָן – כְּלוֹמַר, שֶׁאַף־עַל־כֵּן לֹא עָלְתָה לוֹ לְהַשְׁפִּיל אֶת הָרָשָׁע וְלָצֵאת מִתַּחַת בִּרְכָּיו, אַף־עַל־פִּי שֶׁפָּסַק וְשִׁבֵּר הַמִּדָּה רָעָה שֶׁל הָרָשָׁע שֶׁנִּמְשֶׁכֶת מֵאַרְבָּעָה יְסוֹדוֹת שֶׁשָּׁרְשָׁם אַרְבַּע צִיצִית כַּנַּ"ל, שֶׁזֶּהוּ בְּחִינַת 'וְקָא פַסְקֵי קַרְנָא דִתְכֶלְתָּא דְּחַד מִנַּיְהוּ' כַּנַּ"ל, אַף־עַל־פִּי־כֵן לֹא הָיָה יָכוֹל לְהַשְׁפִּילוֹ וְלָצֵאת מִתַּחַת בִּרְכָּיו, בְּחִינַת 'וְלָא מִסְתַּגֵּי לָן', שֶׁפֵּרוּשׁוֹ שֶׁלֹּא הָיוּ יְכוֹלִין לָצֵאת מִשָּׁם, הַיְנוּ כַּנַּ"ל.

אָמַר לִי: דִּלְמָא שַׁקְלִית מִידֵי מִנַּיְהוּ? – הַיְנוּ, שֶׁמָּא יֵשׁ לְךָ אֶחָד מֵאַרְבַּע יְסוֹדוֹת שֶׁלֹּא תִקַּנְתָּ בִּשְׁלֵמוּת לְהַפְרִיד מִמֶּנּוּ הָרַע לְגַמְרֵי, וְעַל כֵּן לָא מִסְתַּגֵּי לָן; כַּמְבֹאָר לְעֵיל, שֶׁכָּל זְמַן שֶׁנִּשְׁאָר בּוֹ אֵיזֶה אֲחִיזָה בְּעָלְמָא מֵהָרַע שֶׁל אֵיזֶה מִדָּה, אֵינוֹ יָכוֹל לְהַכְנִיעַ אֶת הָרָשָׁע. וְזֶהוּ: 'דִּלְמָא שַׁקְלִית מִידֵי מִנַּיְהוּ' – שֶׁמָּא לָקַחְתָּ קְצָת מֵהֶם, הַיְנוּ, שֶׁמָּא יֵשׁ בְּךָ עֲדַיִן אֵיזֶה אֲחִיזָה מֵאֵיזֶה מִדָּה רָעָה שֶׁל הָרְשָׁעִים, שֶׁלָּקַחְתָּ לְעַצְמְךָ אֵיזֶה מִדָּה וְתַאֲוָה שֶׁלָּהֶם, וְעַל כֵּן 'לָא מִסְתַּגֵּי לָן' – וְעַל כֵּן אֵין אָנוּ יְכוֹלִין לָצֵאת מֵהֶם כַּנַּ"ל.

---

73. **explained above.** See section 5: Otherwise the wicked man's storm wind would be able to overpower and harm the less than perfect tzaddik when he descends into the bad trait in order to destroy it.

67   *LIKUTEY MOHARAN #8:8*

surface." This is the Torah, which was given in a period of *Mem* (forty) days[71] and is the source of the *ruach*-of-life. In other words, this tzaddik had the *ruach* which is received from the Torah. Even so, he came under the knee—under the good fortune—of the wicked man, as in, "The wicked man devours a tzaddik greater than he."

I cut off a corner from the tzitzit of one of them — In other words, he separated and broke the bad trait in one of the four elements which the wicked man had empowered and drawn upon himself. This was his conduit of evil. **I cut off a corner from the tzitzit**: he separated one of their *tzitzit*. This is the aspect of separating and breaking their bad trait, their conduit. For all the bad traits stem from the four elements, the root of which, as we have said, is the four *tzitzit*.[72]

we were not able to leave — That is, even though [he separated the *tzitzit*] he was not able to subdue the wicked man and emerge from under his knee. Even though he had separated and broken the wicked man's bad trait, which is drawn from the four elements, whose root is in the *tzitzit*—thus he **cut off a corner from the tzitzit of one of them**— still, he was unable to subdue him and move out from under his knee. This corresponds to, **we were not able to leave**: we could not depart from there, as above.

The merchant asked me, Did you perhaps take something from them? — In other words, perhaps you still have < a bad trait from one of> these four elements which you have yet to completely rectify by entirely separating out the bad. This is why **we were not able to leave**. As explained above,[73] as long as the bad of some trait has even the slightest hold on him, he cannot subdue the wicked man. Thus: **Did you perhaps take something from them?** Do you perhaps still have in you a slight attachment to some bad trait of the wicked? Have you taken to yourself some bad trait or desire of theirs? Therefore, **we were not able to leave**. This was why we are unable to depart from them, as above.

---

71. **Mem, forty days.** In section 9 below, Rebbe Nachman tells us that *ruach* corresponds to the *yud* with its numerical value of 10. Four *ruchot* (four directions or winds) are equivalent to the letter *mem* (מ) with its value of 40. The *mem* alludes to the Torah which was given to Moshe when he ascended to heaven for 40 days and 40 nights (Exodus 24:18).

72. **four tzitzit.** See above, this section: The four tributaries and four letters of God's name correspond to the four *tzitzit*,... as in, "From the four directions (corners) comes the *ruach*." Through the *tzitzit* that...it is possible to "shake the wicked"...corresponding to the first letters of the four elements.

LIKUTEY MOHARAN #8:8

דִּגְמִירֵי, דְּמָאן דְּשָׁקִיל מִידֵי מִנַּיְהוּ לָא מִסְתַּגֵּי לֵהּ. – הַיְנוּ כַּנַּ"ל, שֶׁיֵּשׁ לָנוּ קַבָּלָה, שֶׁכָּל מִי שֶׁלּוֹקֵחַ לְעַצְמוֹ אֵיזֶה דָּבָר תַּאֲוָה וּמִדָּה רָעָה שֶׁל הָרְשָׁעִים, הַיְנוּ שֶׁיֵּשׁ בּוֹ עֲדַיִן אֵיזֶה אֲחִיזָה מֵהַמִּדּוֹת רָעוֹת שֶׁלָּהֶן, אֵינוֹ יָכוֹל לָצֵאת מֵהֶם וּלְהַכְנִיעָם כַּנַּ"ל.

אַזְלִי אַהֲדַרְתֵּהּ – הַיְנוּ שֶׁהֶחֱזַרְתִּי מַה שֶׁהָיָה אֶצְלִי אֵיזֶה מְעַט אֲחִיזַת הָרַע מֵהַמִּדּוֹת רָעוֹת שֶׁלָּהֶם, הֶחֱזַרְתִּי וְהִפְרַשְׁתִּי מִמֶּנִּי. וְהַדַר מִסְתַּגֵּי לָן – שֶׁאָז עָלְתָה בְּיָדֵינוּ לָצֵאת מִתַּחַת בִּרְכָּיו לְהַכְנִיעוֹ וּלְהַשְׁפִּילוֹ; כַּמְבֹאָר לְעֵיל, שֶׁצַּדִּיק גָּמוּר שֶׁמַּפְרִישׁ מֵעַצְמוֹ כָּל אֲחִיזַת הָרַע שֶׁלָּהֶם לְגַמְרֵי, הוּא יָכוֹל לָצֵאת מֵהֶם וּלְהַכְנִיעָם וּלְהַשְׁפִּילָם, בִּבְחִינַת "מַשְׁפִּיל רְשָׁעִים עֲדֵי אָרֶץ" כַּנַּ"ל:

וְזֶהוּ: רָאִיתִי וְהִנֵּה מְנוֹרַת זָהָב – הִיא הַתּוֹרָה, הַנֶּחֱמָדִים מִזָּהָב. וְגֻלָּהּ עַל רֹאשָׁהּ – פֵּרֵשׁ רַשִׁ"י: 'מַעְיָן', הוּא הַמַּעְיָן הַיּוֹצֵא מִבֵּית ה', הוּא הַתְּפִלָּה.

וְשִׁבְעָה נֵרֹתֶיהָ – הֵם הַנְּשָׁמוֹת דְּאִתְרְבִיאוּ בַּגָּן, הַנֶּחֱלָקִים לְשֶׁבַע כִּתּוֹת.

שִׁבְעָה וְשִׁבְעָה מוּצָקוֹת – הֵם מ"ט אוֹרוֹת, שֶׁהוּא אוֹר הַגָּנוּז לֶעָתִיד (כְּמוֹ שֶׁפֵּרֵשׁ רַשִׁ"י שָׁם), בְּחִינַת עֵדֶן עַיִן לֹא רָאֲתָה, שֶׁהוּא בְּחִינַת הַתְּפִלָה כַּנַּ"ל.

וּשְׁנַיִם זֵיתִים עָלֶיהָ – פֵּרֵשׁ רַשִׁ"י: 'שְׁנֵי אִילָנוֹת', הַיְנוּ אִילָנָא דְּחַיֵּי וְאִילָנָא דְּמוֹתָא, הַיְנוּ טוֹב וָרָע כַּנַּ"ל. וְזֶהוּ:

---

soul is God's lamp." The *Midrash Shocher Tov* (#11) teaches that there are seven groups of tzaddikim in the World to Come, each with its own level, and an equal number of levels for the groups of the wicked in Gehennom.

76. forty-nine lights.... "... and the light of the sun will be sevenfold" (Isaiah 30:26). In the time of Redemption, the sun's light will shine seven times brighter than at present. This refers to the Light of Creation, which was created on the first day and subsequently hidden away. It is reserved exclusively for the tzaddikim (*Chagigah* 12a), and is kept in the Torah (*Maharsha, loc. cit.*). Eden is prayer, the origin of everything. The tzaddik/*rav* has the power to draw Eden into the Gan, the Torah.

77. good and bad. This is an allusion to the Tree of Knowledge which, with its potential for both good and bad, is the root of man's free will.

LIKUTEY MOHARAN #8:8

We have a tradition: Anyone who takes something from them cannot depart — That is, we have a tradition that whoever takes for himself any desire or bad trait from the wicked—in other words, their bad traits still have some hold on him—can neither leave nor subdue them.

So I went and put back the tzitzit corner — That is, I returned whatever little bit of their bad traits which I had. I returned and separated it from me.

Then we were able to leave — Then we were successful in emerging from under his knee to subdue and humble him. As explained, the perfect tzaddik entirely removes from himself any attachment to their evil. He is able to depart from them; he can subdue and humble [the wicked], as in, "He casts down the wicked to the ground."

This is the explanation [of the opening verse]:

"I looked, and behold a candelabrum all of gold, and a bowl on its top. {With seven lamps and seven pipes to the seven lamps that are on its top. And there are two olives near it, one to the right of the bowl and one to the left. And I said to the angel who spoke with me, saying, 'What are these?...' Then the angel who spoke with me answered, 'This is the word of God to Zerubavel: Not by might, nor by power, but by My *ruach*, says the God of Hosts. Who are you, O great mountain? Before Zerubavel become a plain!'}"

I looked, and behold a candelabrum all of gold — This is the Torah which is "more desired than gold" (Psalms 19:11).[74]

and a bowl on its top — Rashi explains: "This is a *MaAYaN* (fountain)." It is the fountain that flows from "the house of God," which is prayer.

With seven lamps — These are the souls which grow in the garden. They divide into seven categories.[75]

and seven pipes to the seven lamps — These are the forty-nine lights: the Light [of Creation] hidden away for the Future (cf. *Rashi, loc. cit.*).[76] This corresponds to "Eden—No eye has seen it," the aspect of prayer, as explained.

And there are two olives near it — Rashi explains: "These were two trees." This alludes to the Tree of Life and the tree of death; i.e., good and bad.[77] Thus:

---

74. **more desired than gold.** When a person's desire for the Torah is greater than his desire for wealth, the Torah itself elevates him above all base desires and breaks the conduit from which such desires are drawn.

75. **souls...seven categories.** The soul is likened to a lamp, as in (Proverbs 20:27), "A man's

LIKUTEY MOHARAN #8:8,9 70

אֶחָד מִיָּמִין וְאֶחָד מִשְּׂמֹאל – כַּנַּ"ל. "וּמִשָּׁם יִפָּרֵד", שֶׁנִּפְרָד הָרַע
מֵהַטּוֹב, זֶה לְיָמִין וְזֶה לִשְׂמֹאל.

וְאֹמֶר אֶל הַמַּלְאָךְ מָה אֵלֶּה. וַיַּעַן וְכוּ' לֹא בְחַיִל וְלֹא בְכֹחַ כִּי אִם
בְּרוּחִי – הַיְנוּ בְּחִינַת הָרוּחַ־חַיִּים הַנַּ"ל, בְּחִינַת "כֹּה אָמַר ה'
מֵאַרְבַּע רוּחוֹת בֹּאִי הָרוּחַ" וְכוּ' כַּנַּ"ל;
כִּי עַל־יְדֵי תּוֹרָה וּתְפִלָּה, שֶׁעַל־יְדֵי־זֶה מְבָרְרִין הַטּוֹב מִן הָרָע
כַּנַּ"ל, שֶׁזֶּה בְּחִינַת כָּל מַרְאֵה הַמְּנוֹרָה כַּנַּ"ל, עַל־יְדֵי־זֶה זוֹכֶה לְרוּחַ
הַחַיִּים וְנִשְׁלָם כָּל הַחֶסְרוֹנוֹת כַּנַּ"ל.

(וְזֶהוּ: "לֹא בְחַיִל וְלֹא בְכֹחַ כִּי אִם בְּרוּחִי אָמַר ה' צְבָאוֹת. מִי
אַתָּה הַר הַגָּדוֹל לִפְנֵי זְרֻבָּבֶל לְמִישֹׁר" וְכוּ' – כִּי זְרֻבָּבֶל הָיָה אָז
הַצַּדִּיק־הַדּוֹר, וְעָמְדוּ כְּנֶגְדּוֹ כַּמָּה רְשָׁעִים לְבַטְּלוֹ מֵעֲבוֹדָתוֹ,
כַּמְבֹאָר בִּפְסוּקִים רַבִּים. וְעַל זֶה נֶאֱמַר שָׁם: "לֹא בְחַיִל וְלֹא בְכֹחַ
כִּי אִם בְּרוּחִי" וְכוּ', שֶׁעַל־יְדֵי בְּחִינַת הַמְשָׁכַת הָרוּחַ־חַיִּים הַנַּ"ל
שֶׁמַּמְשִׁיךְ הַצַּדִּיק הַגָּמוּר וְכוּ' כַּנַּ"ל, עַל־יְדֵי־זֶה יַכְנִיעַ וְיַפִּיל כָּל
הַשּׂוֹנְאִים, בְּחִינַת "מִי אַתָּה הַר הַגָּדוֹל לִפְנֵי זְרֻבָּבֶל לְמִישֹׁר", שֶׁכָּל
הַמּוֹנְעִים הָעוֹמְדִים לְפָנָיו כְּהַר, כֻּלָּם יִתְבַּטְּלוּ עַל־יְדֵי בְּחִינַת
הָרוּחַ־חַיִּים הַנַּ"ל, כַּנַּ"ל).

ט. וְהִנֵּה מְבֹאָר לְמַעְלָה, כִּי הָרוּחַ־חַיִּים הוּא בְּהַתּוֹרָה, בְּחִינַת
"וְרוּחַ אֱלֹקִים מְרַחֶפֶת עַל־פְּנֵי הַמָּיִם" כַּנַּ"ל. וְעַל כֵּן בְּמִצְרַיִם,

---

80. **all be eliminated....** Zerubavel led the return to the Holy Land following the Babylonian
exile (Hagai 1; Nechemiah *passim*). His repeated attempts to rebuild the Holy Temple were
constantly thwarted by the wicked people of his time. They were paying "mighty fortunes" to
the authorities in order to disrupt the reconstruction. Thus, the angel prophesized: "Not by
might...but by My *ruach*." That is, Zerubavel will succeed in completing the Temple, the
House of Prayer [the Holy of Holies is the fountain (see *Biur HaLikutim*)], and thereby bring
wholeness in place of the lack. It can also be understood that the angel was advising
Zerubavel that his success depended not on mighty wealth and power, but on prayer alone.
Only prayer would enable him to overcome his opponents and subdue their mighty fortunes.

In review: *Ruach*/breath is the life-force of everything. Sighing brings life into all that is

71   *LIKUTEY MOHARAN #8:8,9*

one [tree] to the right and one to the left — As above. And, "from there it separates"—the bad was separated from the good—this to the right and that to the left.[78]

And I said to the angel who spoke with me, saying, What are these? Then the angel who spoke with me answered, This is the word of God to Zerubavel: Not by might, nor by power, but by My ruach — Namely, the *ruach*-of-life, as in, "Thus says God: From the four directions comes the *ruach*."[79]

This is because through Torah and prayer, by means of which the good is selected from the bad—this being the vision of the candelabrum—one merits the *ruach*-of-life and provides wholeness [in place] of the lack.

{This is: **Not by might, nor by power, but by My ruach, says the God of Hosts. Who are you, O great mountain? Before Zerubavel become a plain!** — Zerubavel was then the tzaddik of the generation. He encountered opposition from a number of wicked people who wanted to prevent him from serving God. This is explained in a number of verses. In this regard it is written: **Not by might, nor by power, but by My ruach.** As we have seen, through the *ruach*-of-life which the perfect tzaddik draws, all enemies are subdued and humbled. Thus, **Who are you, O great mountain? Before Zerubavel become a plain!** All those opponents who stood before him like a mountain, they will all be eliminated by the *ruach*-of-life.}[80]

9. {**"I am God your Lord who brought you up out of the land of Egypt; open your mouth wide *v'amalayhu* (and I will fill it)"** (Psalms 81:11).}

It has been explained that the *ruach*-of-life is in the Torah, corresponding to, "And the *ruach* of God hovers over the waters'

---

78. **right...left.** "The heart of the righteous is to the right and the heart of the wicked to the left" (Ecclesiastes 10:2). The Midrash (*Bamidbar Rabbah* 22:9) teaches: The "right" is the good inclination, the "left" is the evil inclination. Further, the Midrash comments: The "right" refers to the tzaddikim who put their heart [*their ruach*] into the Torah, whereas the "left" refers to the wicked who put their heart [*their ruach*] into making fortunes.

79. **My ruach....** Everyone (the righteous and the wicked) draws from the *ruach*-of-life. However, at its root the *ruach* is still in potential, and has not yet been clearly defined between right and left. The angel therefore answered, "Not by might..."—not by the might of wealth or power on the left; "but by My *ruach*"—through the Torah and prayer, which is the *ruach* on the right.

LIKUTEY MOHARAN #8:9

72

שֶׁהָיָה קֹדֶם קַבָּלַת הַתּוֹרָה, וְלֹא הָיָה לָהֶם מֵהֵיכָן לְקַבֵּל הָרוּחַ־
חַיִּים, נֶאֱמַר בָּהֶם (שְׁמוֹת ו): "מִקֹּצֶר רוּחַ", כִּי לֹא הָיָה לָהֶם מֵאַיִן
לְקַבֵּל הָרוּחַ־חַיִּים שֶׁהוּא בְּחִינַת אֶרֶךְ אַפַּיִם, מַאֲרִיךְ רוּחֵהּ כַּנַּ"ל,
וְעַל כֵּן נֶאֱמַר בָּהֶם 'מִקֹּצֶר רוּחַ', שֶׁהוּא הֶפֶךְ אֶרֶךְ אַפַּיִם, שֶׁהוּא
בְּחִינַת הָרוּחַ־חַיִּים שֶׁמַּמְשִׁיכִין עַל־יְדֵי אֲנָחָה לְהַשְׁלִים הַחִסָּרוֹן
כַּנַּ"ל, כִּי הָרוּחַ הוּא שְׁלֵמוּת הַחִסָּרוֹן כַּנַּ"ל, בְּחִינַת "וְיִתֶּן לְךָ
מִשְׁאֲלֹת לִבֶּךָ".

וְזֶהוּ בְּחִינַת: "הַרְחֶב פִּיךָ וַאֲמַלְאֵהוּ" – שֶׁנִּתְמַלֵּא הַחִסָּרוֹן. וְזֶהוּ
בְּחִינַת מְלֹאפוּם – מְלֹא פוּם.

וְהָעִנְיָן, כִּי מְלֹאפוּם הוּא יוּד וָאו, וְהוּא בְּחִינַת יו"ד מִינֵי דְּפִיקִין,
כְּנֶגֶד יו"ד הַדִּבְּרוֹת. וְהַדֹּפֶק הוּא עַל־יְדֵי הָרוּחַ, כַּיָּדוּעַ. וְעַל כֵּן הֵם
עֲשָׂרָה מִינֵי דְּפִיקִין, כְּנֶגֶד עֲשֶׂרֶת הַדִּבְּרוֹת, כִּי הָרוּחַ שֶׁהוּא הַדֹּפֶק
הוּא בְּהַתּוֹרָה כַּנַּ"ל, וְהַנָּאו הוּא בְּחִינַת הַמְשָׁכַת הָרוּחַ.

These correspond to the Thirteen Attributes of Mercy (*Etz Chaim, Heikhal HaNikudim, Shaar D'rushei Nikudot* 1). Thus, the dot of the *m'lapum* denotes the last Attribute, *v'nakeh* (cleansing sin). This alludes to the perfect tzaddik. He is "clean" of all sin and can enter into the conduits of the wicked.

83. **yud vav.** The *m'lapum* is a dot in the center of the letter *vav* (ו). The dot is likened to the letter *yud* which has a numerical value of 10.

84. **in the Torah.** The Hebrew word for pulse, *DoFeK*, is similar to the word *DaFaK* (to knock or pulsate). This is the meaning of the verse (Song of Songs 5:2), "The voice of my beloved knocks." Sometimes, the heart yearns and pulsates for holiness, the Torah, and other times it turns away from Torah and that which is holy. This entirely depends on the person's desires. Rebbe Nachman therefore tells us that it is very important to long for and sigh over the holiness which one lacks. This in itself has the power to bring holiness and wholeness in place of the lack. And conversely, by sighing over and desiring evil, a person draws that evil into himself (see *Likutey Moharan* I, 60). Rebbe Nachman also taught that there are two life-supporting conduits, one from the side of holiness and the other from the side of the husks. Just as it is necessary to constantly draw air in order to breathe, so it is necessary to constantly draw from one of these conduits in order to go on living. He explains that the gain which comes from being attached to the conduit of holiness and drawing life from it source in the holy Torah far outweighs any temporary material benefits won by being attached to the conduit of evil (see *Likutey Moharan* I, 109 for a fuller explanation).

85. **vav...drawing the ruach.** The letter *vav* is shaped like an elongated *yud*. Because the *yud* represents the *ruach*, the *vav* therefore indicates a drawing and extending of the *ruach*. It is also the drawing and flowing of the river from Eden (prayer) to the Garden (Torah) (see above, §7).

LIKUTEY MOHARAN #8:9

surface." Therefore, [when the Jews were] in Egypt, which was before they were given the Torah, they did not have from where to receive the *ruach*-of-life. Of them the verse states (Exodus 6:9), "[But they did not hearken to Moshe] for their *ruach* was short." This was because they did not have from where to draw the *ruach*-of-life, which is the aspect of *erekh apayim* (patience), extended *ruach*. It was therefore said of them that "their *ruach* was short." This is the antithesis of patience, which is the *ruach*-of-life drawn through sighing in order to provide wholeness [in place] of the lack, as above. For *ruach* is wholeness [in place] of the lack, corresponding to, "He will give you what your heart lacks."[81]

And this is: "Open your mouth wide *v'amalayhu*"—the lack is filled. This alludes to the [Hebrew vowel point] *M'LaPUM*[82]: *M'Lo PUM* (a full mouth).

The matter is as follows: The *m'lapum* is *yud vav*.[83] [The *yud*] corresponds to the *yud* types of pulse, paralleling the *yud* Commandments (*Zohar* III, 257a). It is common knowledge that the pulse comes from the *ruach*. This is why the types of pulse are ten, paralleling the Ten Commandments; for the *ruach*, which corresponds to the pulse, is in the Torah.[84] And the *vav* is the aspect of drawing the *ruach*.[85]

---

lacking (§1). This *ruach*-of-life is received from the tzaddik/*rav* of the generation. When one who is attached to the tzaddik sighs, he draws the *ruach* from the heart to fill the lack in the heart (§2). Conversely, the wicked receive *ruach* from the *rav* of the Other Side. Theirs is an impure *ruach*, which results in a lack (§3). All lack stems from sin. The tzaddik who draws *ruach* to fill the lack therefore has the power to atone for sin (§4). A person must avoid provoking the wicked, whose sighs cause the one who provokes them to sin. Only a perfect tzaddik has the power to counter the wicked, by virtue of his having separated good from bad in the 4 elements, which encompass all the traits (§5). To separate good from bad one must engage in Torah study—i.e., clarification of the law in practice—and prayer—i.e., the drawing of wisdom (§6). Through prayer/potential creation and Torah/actualized creation, Jewish souls gain the intelligence to separate the good from the bad (§7). The 4 tzitzit, the 4 corners of the world, correspond to the *ruach*-of-life, which defeats the opponents of the tzaddik and the *ruach* of the Other Side (§8).

81. **erekh apayim, extended ruach....** The role which *erekh apayim* (patience) plays in drawing the *ruach* in order to bring wholeness in place of the lack has been discussed earlier in the lesson. See above, sections 1 and 4.

82. **M'LaPUM.** This is the ninth of the Hebrew vowels and corresponds to the *sefirah* of *Yesod* (Foundation), also known as tzaddik. Rebbe Nachman goes on to incorporate this within the lesson's context.

In Hebrew, the vowels are represented as dots and dashes. There are thirteen dots in the vowel system: *tzerei* (2) *segol* (3), *sh'va* (2), *cholem* (1), *chirik* (1), *shuruk* (3), *m'lapum* (1).

LIKUTEY MOHARAN #8:9

74

וְהָיִינוּ מְלָאפוֹם – מְלֹא פוֹם כִּי עַל־יְדֵי הַמְשָׁכַת הָרוּחַ נִשְׁלָם הַחִסָּרוֹן, שֶׁזֶּהוּ בְּחִינַת "הַרְחָב פִּיךָ וַאֲמַלְאֵהוּ" – שֶׁנִּתְמַלֵּא הַחִסָּרוֹן כַּנַּ"ל, שֶׁזֶּהוּ בְּחִינַת מְלָאפוֹם – מְלֹא פוֹם כַּנַּ"ל.

וְזֶהוּ שֶׁדִּקְדֵּק: (תְּהִלִּים פ"א): "אָנֹכִי ה' אֱלֹקֶיךָ הַמַּעַלְךָ מֵאֶרֶץ מִצְרָיִם", וְקִבְּלוּ הַתּוֹרָה אֲשֶׁר שָׁם הָרוּחַ, וַאֲזַי דַּיְקָא "הַרְחָב פִּיךָ וַאֲמַלְאֵהוּ", בְּחִינַת מְלָאפוֹם כַּנַּ"ל, בְּחִינַת שְׁלֵמוּת הַחִסָּרוֹן. כִּי דַּיְקָא אַחַר יְצִיאַת מִצְרַיִם, בְּחִינַת "הַמַּעַלְךָ מֵאֶרֶץ מִצְרָיִם", שֶׁאָז נִתְבַּטֵּל בְּחִינַת מִקֹּצֶר רוּחַ הַנַּ"ל, כִּי קִבְּלוּ הַתּוֹרָה שֶׁשָּׁם הָרוּחַ־חַיִּים כַּנַּ"ל, עַל כֵּן אָז דַּיְקָא: "הַרְחָב פִּיךָ וַאֲמַלְאֵהוּ", בְּחִינַת שְׁלֵמוּת הַחִסָּרוֹן, בְּחִינַת מְלֹא פוֹם, בְּחִינַת "יְמַלֵּא ה' כָּל מִשְׁאֲלוֹתֶיךָ" כַּנַּ"ל. וְעַל כֵּן נִזְכָּר יְצִיאַת מִצְרַיִם בְּפָרָשַׁת צִיצִית, כִּי צִיצִית בְּחִינַת הָרוּחַ־חַיִּים, בְּחִינַת מֵאַרְבַּע רוּחוֹת וְכוּ' כַּנַּ"ל.

גַּם דִּבֵּר אָז מֵעִנְיַן שְׁתֵּים־עֶשְׂרֵה שָׁעוֹת הַיּוֹם וּשְׁתֵּים־עֶשְׂרֵה שָׁעוֹת הַלַּיְלָה, שֶׁיֵּשׁ בָּהֶם שְׁנֵים־עָשָׂר צֵרוּפֵי הֲוָיָ"ה, בְּכָל שָׁעָה יֵשׁ צֵרוּף

those who heeded Moshe's words (not all the Jews were redeemed) did indeed draw their *ruach* from the Torah. All this is implied in the verse quoted here: "I am God your Lord" — these are also the opening words of the Ten Commandments, alluding to God's promise that He would give them the Torah; "who brought you up out of the land of Egypt" — the Exodus; "open your mouth wide and I will fill it" — filling the lack with wholeness.

88. **fill...which you ask for.** Egypt was the land of "mighty fortunes" where even the livestock were bedecked in gold and precious stones (*Mekhilta, BeShalach*). Pharaoh said, "Who is God that I should listen to him" (Exodus 5:2). He presumed himself to be a god and relied on the great wealth of Egypt for protection. His *ruach*, his spirit, was mighty but only for the moment. When the Jews left Egypt, they not only broke his mighty power, they also took with them great booty. God had Moshe tell the Jews, "let each man ask...let every woman ask...." With this, they "drained Egypt of all its mighty fortune" (Exodus 3:22, 11:2).

89. **Chapter of Tzitzit.** This reading (Numbers 15:37-41) is the third paragraph of the *Shema* and is also known as "The Exodus from Egypt."

90. **twelve...YHVH.** A word of four letters is permutable in 24 different ways unless one of the letters is duplicated, in which case it can form only 12 different combinations. The Tetragrammaton, God's ineffable name *YHVH*, thus has 12 different permutations and 24 in total. These correspond to the 24 hours of the day (12) and night (12).

LIKUTEY MOHARAN #8:9

This is the *m'lapum—m'lo pum*. By drawing the *ruach* there is wholeness [in place] of the lack. As is written, "Open your mouth wide and I will fill it"—that which was lacking is filled, corresponding to *m'lapum*: a full mouth.[86]

And this is why [the verse] specifies, "I am God your Lord who brought you up out of the land of Egypt"—they received the Torah, in which there is the *ruach*; and then concludes, "...open your mouth *v'aMaLAyhu*." This is the abovementioned *M'LApum*, the aspect of wholeness [in place] of the lack.[87]

It was specifically *after* leaving Egypt—corresponding to "who brought you up from the land of Egypt"—that *ruach* was no longer "short," for they had received the Torah in which there is the *ruach*-of-life. Then, and only then, [was there] "open your mouth and I will fill it," the aspect of wholeness [in place] of the lack—i.e., a full mouth, as in, "God will *fill* all that which you ask for."[88]

This is why the redemption from Egypt is mentioned in the Chapter of *Tzitzit*.[89] For *tzitzit* corresponds to the *ruach*-of-life, as in, "From the four directions comes the *ruach*."

At the time he [gave this lesson, Rebbe Nachman] also spoke of the twelve hours of the day and the twelve hours of the night. They align with the twelve permutations of *YHVH*,[90] with each hour

---

Based on the verse "A river flows from Eden to water the Garden," the Kabbalah prescribes a very specific way for a scribe to write the holy name of God. This entails a "drawing" of the very first letter—the *yud*, representing *chokhmah* and *ruach*—into the next letter, the *heh*. After having written the *yud* (י), the scribe is to begin the *heh* (ה) by making another *yud* and then drawing it out and elongating it into the full roof of the *heh*. This is the repeated when, after writing the third letter, a *vav* (ו), a second *vav* is elongated and drawn into the final *heh* of the *YHVH*.

86. **full mouth.** This ties into the very beginning of the lesson (§1) where we find, "And by the *ruach* of His mouth, their entire hosts were created." The *ruach* is drawn, as it were, from God's mouth. It is His *ruach* which fills that which is lacking, as in, "Open your mouth wide and *I* will fill it."

87. **the Torah...in place of the lack.** As Rebbe Nachman goes on to say, the actualization and realization of providing wholeness in place of the lack could only be achieved after the Jews had departed from Egypt and received the Torah. Even so, potentially this was already in place much earlier. When Moshe returned to Egypt in order to redeem them, he had already acquired God's promise that the Jews were to receive the Torah (Exodus 3:12). Thus, Moshe knew that even while in Egypt, the Jews would already be able to draw their *ruach* from the Torah—albeit on a seminal level. It was this "potential" *ruach* from the Torah that enabled them to overcome Pharaoh's mighty *ruach* which had been keeping them in bondage. For

LIKUTEY MOHARAN #8:9-11

אַחֵר, וְכָל שָׁעָה נֶחֱלֶקֶת לְתתר"ף חֲלָקִים, וְכָל חֵלֶק וָחֵלֶק מִתתר"ף חֲלָקִים יֵשׁ בּוֹ גַּם כֵּן צֵרוּף הַשֵּׁם, וְכָל זֶה הוּא בְּחִינַת רוּחַ הַחַיִּים שֶׁבַּדֹּפֶק. וְלֹא זָכִיתִי לִשְׁמֹעַ בֵּאוּר עִנְיָן זֶה הֵיטֵב. גַּם שָׁכַחְתִּי קְצָת מִזֶּה, וְהַמַּשְׂכִּילִים יָבִינוּ.

י. "רֶכֶב אֱלֹקִים רִבֹּתַיִם אַלְפֵי שִׁנְאָן" (תְּהִלִּים ס"ח), 'אַלְפֵי' – בְּחִינַת אַלּוּפֵי עֵשָׂו, וְעַל־יְדֵי 'רֶכֶב אֱלֹקִים רִבֹּתַיִם' – בְּחִינַת קַבָּלַת הַתּוֹרָה, שֶׁמִּשָּׁם מְקַבְּלִין הָרוּחַ־חַיִּים הָרַבָּנִים דִּקְדֻשָּׁה – עַל־יְדֵי־זֶה 'אַלְפֵי שִׁנְאָן', כְּמוֹ שֶׁדָּרְשׁוּ חֲכָמֵינוּ, זִכְרוֹנָם לִבְרָכָה (עֲבוֹדָה זָרָה ג:): 'אַל תִּקְרֵי שִׁנְאָן אֶלָּא שֶׁאֵינָן', הַיְנוּ שֶׁעַל־יְדֵי קַבָּלַת הַתּוֹרָה, שֶׁשָּׁם הָרוּחַ דְּהָרַב דִּקְדֻשָּׁה, עַל־יְדֵי־זֶה נִתְבַּטְּלִין וְנִכְנָעִין אַלּוּפֵי עֵשָׂו, רַבְרְבֵי עֵשָׂו, שֶׁהֵם בְּחִינַת הָרַב דִּקְלִפָּה, בִּבְחִינַת 'אַלְפֵי שֶׁאֵינָן', שֶׁאַלּוּפֵי עֵשָׂו, רַבְרְבֵי עֵשָׂו, נִתְבַּטְּלִין וְאֵינָן:

יא. "מִכְּנַף הָאָרֶץ זְמִרֹת שָׁמַעְנוּ צְבִי לַצַּדִּיק וָאֹמַר רָזִי־לִי רָזִי־לִי אוֹי לִי, בֹּגְדִים בָּגָדוּ וּבֶגֶד בּוֹגְדִים בָּגָדוּ" (יְשַׁעְיָהוּ כ"ד). "מִכְּנַף

emanates from the *YHVH*/the Source of all life (*Parparaot LeChokhmah*). Thus, the previous passage from the *Reishit Chokhmah* concludes that man takes 1,080 breaths per hour and each of these breaths draws from its own specific permutation of God's holy name.

94. **understand.** Now we can understand that it is the *YHVH* which provides wholeness in place of the lack. Rebbe Nachman has told us that this is only accomplished when the conduits of the wicked have been completely destroyed. We've seen that in order to destroy the wicked, it is necessary to have totally separated out all evil from the good in the four elements/traits whose Source is the *YHVH*. The twelve permutations of God's name, corresponding to the twelve hours of day or night, are the *ruach*-of-life of the pulse, the life-force, which the tzaddik then draws down. With this *ruach* he enters the conduits of the wicked and destroys them. Then, and only then, can the tzaddik draw the full *ruach*-of-life directly from the *YHVH* and bring wholeness in place of the lack (*Mai HaNachal*).

95. **...giving of the Torah.** The verse quoted here is from Psalm 68, which depicts the giving of the Torah at Sinai. Also see Rashi's commentary to this psalm.

96. **defeated and are not.** "When one rises, the other falls" (*Rashi, Genesis 25:23*). A person who attempts to immerse himself in Torah, in holiness, gains the *ruach* necessary for subduing the *ravrevay* Esav. However, if he does not seek holiness, he is automatically overcome by the *rav* of the husks.

Reshut Chochma – day is a permutation itself.
Every minute relate to one of permutations of H's name

LIKUTEY MOHARAN #8:9-11

having a different permutation. Furthermore, each hour is divided into 1,080 parts,[91] with each part of the 1,080 parts also having a permutation of the Name.[92] All this corresponds to the *ruach*-of-life which is in the pulse.[93] However, I [Reb Noson] was not fortunate enough to hear the explanation of this clearly. I've also forgotten some details. Those with wisdom [in these matters] will understand.[94]

10. "God's chariots are twice ten thousand, *alfey shinan* (thousands upon thousands)" (Psalms 68:18).

ALFeY alludes to *ALuFeY* Esav. As a result of "God's chariots are twice ten thousand"—corresponding to the giving of the Torah,[95] from which the rabbis of holiness receive the *ruach*-of-life—"*alfey shinan*." As our Sages taught: Do not read *ShiNAN,* but *She'AiNaN* (are not) (*Avodah Zarah* 3b). That is, through the giving of the Torah, which contains the holy *ruach* of the rabbis of holiness, the tribal chiefs of Esav/*ravrevay* Esav—the aspect of the *rav* of the husks—are subdued and defeated. This is the implication of *alfey shinan:* the *alufey* Esav/*ravrevay* Esav are defeated and *ainan* (are not).[96]

11. "From the *k'naf* (corner) of the earth we heard songs, *tzvi latzaddik* (glory to the righteous). But I said, 'A secret to me, a secret to me, woe to me! Traitors have betrayed; and *beged bogdim bagadu*

Yidden will suffer for than goyim

91. **1,080 parts.** Our Sages taught that an hour consists of 1,080 parts. This figure when divided by 60 minutes yields 18 parts per minute. When each of these is further divided by 60 seconds, each part equals .3 of a second. The hour has been broken into 1,080 parts because 1,080 has as its factors: 2, 3, 4, 5, 6, 8, 9, 10. These divisions are necessary for calculating the revolutions of the sun, moon, zodiac signs etc., providing exact determinations for the seasonal changes and holidays (*Yad HaChazakah, Hilkhot Kiddush HaChodesh* 6:2; see *ibid.* #4, chapters 6-19 for examples).

92. **a permutation....** The *Kavanot,* the Kabbalistic meditations, are based upon the various permutations of the names of God. One method of permutation combines a given name with a vowel point, particularly as applied to the ten *sefirot* (Divine emanations). So, for example, the holy name *YHVH* as applied to the *sefirah* of *Yesod* takes on the vowel point of *m'lapum* (יִי הִי וִי הִי).

Now, when the specific permutation of the *YHVH* for the hour is combined with each of the vowel points and with each letter of the *aleph-bet*, its sum total is 1,080. This is as follows: The 4 letters of the Tetragrammaton, *YHVH*, when punctuated with the vowel points of the 10 *sefirot* total 40. And when these are then combined with each of the 27 letters in the Hebrew alphabet (22 regular and 5 final letters), this totals 1,080—the 1,080 parts of the hour (*Reishit Chokhmah, Shaar HaYirah* 10).

93. **in the pulse.** This is because all life/*ruach*, and therefore every breath which a person takes,

LIKUTEY MOHARAN #8:11

הָאָרֶץ" – זֶה בְּחִינַת כַּנְפֵי הַצִּיצִית, שֶׁשָּׁם הָרוּחַ־חַיִּים, שֶׁהוּא בְּחִינַת כִּנּוֹר שֶׁל דָּוִד שֶׁהָיָה מְנַגֵּן עַל־יְדֵי הָרוּחַ צְפוֹנִית וְכוּ' כַּנַּ"ל. כִּי הַנְּגִינָה וְהַזְּמִירוֹת נִמְשָׁכִין מֵהָרוּחַ־חַיִּים שֶׁבְּכַנְפֵי רֵאָה כַּיָּדוּעַ. וְזֶהוּ: "זְמִרַת שָׁמַעְנוּ", בְּחִינַת הַנִּגּוּן שֶׁל כִּנּוֹר שֶׁל דָּוִד, שֶׁהוּא בְּחִינַת הָרוּחַ־חַיִּים, שֶׁהוּא בְּחִינָה בְּחִינַת כַּנְפֵי הַצִּיצִית, בְּחִינַת מִכְּנַף הָאָרֶץ כַּנַּ"ל. וְעַל־יְדֵי־זֶה מַכְנִיעִין הָרְשָׁעִים, בִּבְחִינַת "לֶאֱחֹז בְּכַנְפוֹת הָאָרֶץ וְיִנָּעֲרוּ רְשָׁעִים מִמֶּנָּה".

וְזֶהוּ: "צְבִי לַצַּדִּיק", פֵּרֵשׁ רַשִׁ"י: 'עָתִיד לִהְיוֹת מַצָּב וּתְקוּמָה לַצַּדִּיקִים' – הַיְנוּ כַּנַּ"ל, כִּי עַל־יְדֵי הָרוּחַ־חַיִּים הַנַּ"ל מִתְגַּבְּרִין הַצַּדִּיקִים עַל הָרְשָׁעִים כַּנַּ"ל.

וְזֶהוּ: "וַאֹמַר רָזִי־לִי" וְכוּ' אוֹי לִי – פֵּרֵשׁ רַשִׁ"י, 'שֶׁנִּגְלוּ לִי שְׁנֵי רָזִים: רַז פֻּרְעָנִיּוֹת וְרַז יְשׁוּעָה, וַהֲרֵי תִּרְחַק הַיְשׁוּעָה עַד' וְכוּ' – הַיְנוּ כַּנַּ"ל, כִּי הָרוּחַ שֶׁל הָרָשָׁע גָּדוֹל בִּשְׁעָתוֹ, בִּבְחִינַת רוּחַ־סְעָרָה, שֶׁמִּשָּׁם כָּל הַצָּרוֹת וַאֲרִיכַת הַגָּלוּת שֶׁל יִשְׂרָאֵל.

וְזֶהוּ: "בֹּגְדִים בָּגָדוּ וּבֶגֶד בּוֹגְדִים בָּגָדוּ" – כִּי יְנִיקַת הַבּוֹגְדִים וְהָרְשָׁעִים הוּא מִבְּחִינַת פְּגַם הַבְּגָדִים, דְּהַיְנוּ פְּגַם הַצִּיצִית, שֶׁהֵם בְּכַנְפֵי הַבֶּגֶד, דְּהַיְנוּ מִפְּגַם הָאַרְבָּעָה יְסוֹדוֹת, שֶׁאֲחִיזָתָן וְשָׁרְשָׁם הָעֶלְיוֹן הוּא בְּחִינַת אַרְבַּע צִיצִית כַּנַּ"ל.

one overcome all these?' he said.... However, a spark will come from Yosef [the tzaddik] that will destroy all of them." For the tzaddik has "clean clothes," that is, he is completely clean of all evil traits, and is therefore able to draw the *ruach* necessary for eliminating the lack. We see this clearly of Yosef, the tzaddik. He became viceroy over Egypt and, by providing grain during the famine, drew life to the world (*ibid.*, 42:6).

Yaakov took comfort knowing that, together with Yosef, he would be able overcome Esav. The numerical values of Yaakov, 182, and Yosef, 156, together total 338 (see Appendix: Gematria Chart). The same result is achieved by multiplying the holy name *YHVH* (26) by the 13 Attributes. In other words, together, Yaakov and Yosef represent the Thirteen Attributes of Mercy drawn from the Source of everything. This being so, they have the power to subdue Esav, the *rav* of the husks (*Biur HaLikutim*). See above, note 26.

99. **four tzitzit.** This relates back to Rabbah bar bar Chanah. In cutting off the corner of the garment he hoped to clarify certain laws regarding the *tzitzit*, such as how many strings were

79   *LIKUTEY MOHARAN #8:11*

(those who betrayed the traitors have betrayed). [Fear, and the pit, and the trap are upon you, O inhabitant of the earth]' " (Isaiah 24:16,17).

"From the *K'NaF* (corner) of the earth" corresponds to *KaNFey* (corners of) *tzitzit*, in which there is the *ruach*-of-life—the aspect of King David's harp, which was played by the northern *ruach*, as explained. This is because melody and song are drawn from the *ruach*-of-life in the *KaNFey reiah* (lungs). And this is the meaning of "we heard songs," which corresponds to the song of King David's harp, the *ruach*-of-life. This also corresponds to the corners of the *tzitzit*, as in, "From the corner of the earth." And through this the wicked are subdued, as in, "To take hold of the corners of the earth, that the wicked be shaken off of it."   ruach chayim of Kedusha

And this is "*tZVi latzaddik*." Rashi explains: "There will be a *matZaV* (firm positioning) and a standing up for the tzaddikim." As we've seen, through the *ruach*-of-life the tzaddikim overcome the wicked.[97]

"But I said, 'A secret to me, a secret to me, woe to me!' " Rashi explains: "Two secrets were revealed to me, the secret of suffering and the secret of salvation. However, the salvation remains distant, until...." For the *ruach* of the wicked is mighty while it lasts, just like the *ruach se'arah* from which come all the suffering and the lengthy exile of the Jews.

And so, "Traitors have betrayed; and *BeGeD bogdim bagadu*." The traitors and wicked people draw from a blemish in the *BeGaDim* (garments)—i.e., a blemish of the *tzitzit*,[98] which are on the corners of the garment—which is a blemish in the four elements, whose attachment and transcendent root correspond to the four *tzitzit*.[99]

---

97. **we've seen....** Above, section 5: Therefore, the perfect tzaddik—and all those joined with him—are permitted to provoke the wicked. For he is capable of descending into the conduits of their bad traits with which they have strengthened themselves. He can break and eliminate them, and thereby "cast down the wicked to the ground."

98. **BeGaDim...tzitzit.** The words of the prophet refer to the plundering of Jerusalem during and after its destruction. The *bogdim* were the traitors, the wicked men, who plundered the spoils. The phrase "*beged bogdim*" thus alludes to the wicked people whose power comes from their blemishing the garment (*beged*)/the *tzitzit* through sin (cf. *Likutey Moharan* I, 29 and n.121).

The *Mai HaNachal* comments: Yosef, the tzaddik, is the personification of the *sefirah* of *Yesod* (see Appendix: The Seven Supernal Shepherds). When grabbed by Potifar's wife, he abandoned his *beged* (garment) and fled (Genesis 39:12). In subduing these evil traits, he was later rewarded by being dressed in *bigdei sheish* (garments of fine linen) (*ibid.*, 41:42). Rashi comments (*ibid.*, 37:1): "When Yaakov saw all the *alufey* Esav he was frightened. 'How can

LIKUTEY MOHARAN #8:11

אֲבָל סוֹף כָּל סוֹף: "פַּחַד וָפַחַת וָפָח עָלֶיךָ יוֹשֵׁב הָאָרֶץ" וְכוּ' – כִּי
כָל הָרְשָׁעִים יִכָּרְעוּ וְיִפּלוּ, כִּי לַסּוֹף כָּלֶה וְנֶאֱבָד וְכוּ' כַּנַּ"ל, כִּי
הַצַּדִּיקִים גְּמוּרִים מַכְנִיעִין אוֹתָם וּמַשְׁפִּילִים רְשָׁעִים עֲדֵי אֶרֶץ עַל־
יְדֵי הָרוּחַ־חַיִּים שֶׁלָּהֶם, שֶׁהוּא בְּחִינַת צִיצִית, בְּחִינַת "מִכְּנַף הָאָרֶץ
זְמִרֹת שָׁמַעְנוּ" כַּנַּ"ל.

כִּנּוֹר שֶׁל חָמֵשׁ נִימִין – בְּחִינַת הַתּוֹרָה; וְכֵן כָּתוּב בַּזֹּהַר (צו לב.):
'וְתוֹפְשֵׂי הַתּוֹרָה – אִלֵּין דְּתָפְשִׁין בְּכִנּוֹרָא'.

חָמֵשׁ אֲנִי אִית לָרֵאָה (חֻלִּין מ"ז.) – כִּי רוּחַ הַחַיִּים הוּא בְּהָרֵאָה,
וּמִשָּׁם הַמְשָׁכַת הָרוּחַ שֶׁל הָאֲנָחָה, כַּיָּדוּעַ בְּחוּשׁ, וְעַל־כֵּן אִית לָהּ
חָמֵשׁ אֲנִי לָרֵאָה, כְּנֶגֶד חֲמִשָּׁה־חֻמְשֵׁי־תּוֹרָה. ה' נִימִין דְּכִנּוֹר דְּדָוִד,
שֶׁשָּׁם הָרוּחַ־חַיִּים כַּנַּ"ל: (עַיֵּן בַּתִּקּוּנִים, תִּקּוּן י: כַּנְפֵי מִצְוָה, אִנּוּן ה'
קִשְׁרִין לְקַבֵּל שְׁמַע וְכוּ', דְּאִנּוּן לְקַבֵּל ה' נִימִין דְּכִנּוֹר דְּדָוִד וְכוּ', עַיֵּן שָׁם. גַּם
עַיֵּן בְּהַשְׁמָטוֹת הַזֹּהַר:)

on each fringe of the *tzitzit*. In this way, the *tzitzit* allude to the *Shema Yisrael*, the Jewish
creed which expresses our belief in God's unity and that everything emanates from His holy
name *YHVH*.

The *Zohar* (III, 301a) teaches: The 32 strings of the *tzitzit* are compared to 32 Paths of
Wisdom. This ties in with our lesson in that *maayan* (fountain) is *chokhmah* (wisdom).

Chokhmah has 32 paths (*Sefer Yetzirah* 1:1). Thus, the *tzitzit* are directly related to
wisdom.

A further connection to Rebbe Nachman's lesson can be seen from the following: The 5
knots and 13 bows on each fringe together total 18, and because the *tzitzit* have a fringe on
each of its 4 corners, its sum total is 72. This alludes to the concept of *chesed* (חסד), which also
totals 72. The five words of the *Shema* are said to allude to the five *partzufim* (five archetype
personas; see Appendix: The Divine Persona), which are united in the final word, *echad*.
Thus, the Jews, by fulfilling the mitzvah of *tzitzit*, bring about this unification Above. This, in
turn, draws down an influx of *chesed* to the world (*Or Yisrael, Tikkuney Zohar, ibid.*). In
terms of this lesson, the thirteen of *echad* corresponds to the Thirteen Attributes of Mercy/the
ruach-of-life. Of these Thirteen Attributes, it is the attribute of *rav chesed* which is the source
of the *ruach* (see text, §4), and therefore has the power to subdue the wicked and bring about
the recognition that *YHVH* is One.

81   *LIKUTEY MOHARAN #8:11*

But in the end, "Fear, and the pit, and the trap are upon you, O inhabitant of the earth." All the wicked will be subdued and humbled, for they will eventually be destroyed and disappear. The perfect tzaddikim subdue them and "cast down the wicked to the ground" through their *ruach*-of-life/the *tzitzit*, corresponding to, "From the corner of the earth we heard songs."

King David's harp had five strings.[100] They are representative of the Five Books of the Torah. The *Zohar* (III, 32a) likewise teaches: Those who grasp the Torah are like players of the harp.

"There are five lobes to the lungs" (*Chullin* 47a). This is because the *ruach*-of-life resides in the lungs, and it is from there that the *ruach* of the sigh is drawn, as is known empirically. Thus, the lungs have five lobes, paralleling the Five Books of the Torah, the five strings of King David's harp in which there is the *ruach*-of-life. (See *Tikkuney Zohar* #10: "The corners of mitzvah have five knots, corresponding to the words *Shema Yisrael YHVH Eloheinu YHVH*, which correspond to the five strings of King David's harp....")[101]

necessary for the *tzitzit*, how far the fringes were to be placed from the corner of the garment, etc. (above, n.61). Now, even though he had taken hold of the corner/the trait in an attempt to subdue it, due to the dispute between the tzaddikim/the Schools of Shamai and Hillel, he was unable to differentiate between "good" and "bad" and come to the proper Torah decision. Consequently, he was also unable to draw the proper *ruach*-of-life for himself. The Talmud teaches that, though they were the greatest scholars and the teachers of their time, the students of Shamai and Hillel did not master their studies to the extent that the preceding generations had (*Sotah* 47b). Based on what we've seen in this lesson, we can conclude that on their own they did not have the power to enter the conduits to destroy the wicked.

100. **five strings.** This relates to section 2, where Rebbe Nachman initially mentioned King David's harp.

101. **corners of mitzvah have five knots....** The *Tikkuney Zohar* (*loc. cit.*, p.25b) teaches: Each fringe of the *tzitzit* consists of eight strings which are tied together by five knots. These five knots correspond to the five strings of the harp—songs/prayer—and to the Five Books of the Torah. They also align with the five words "*Shema Yisrael YHVH Eloheinu YHVH* (Hear O Israel, God is our Lord, God....)" (Deuteronomy 6:4). This verse concludes with the word *echad* ("is One," אחד), which has a numerical value of 13, corresponding to the 13 bows

ליקוטי מוהר"ן סימן ט'

(לְשׁוֹן רַבֵּנוּ, זִכְרוֹנוֹ לִבְרָכָה)

תְּהֹמֹת יְכַסְיֻמוּ, יָרְדוּ בִמְצוֹלֹת כְּמוֹ אָבֶן (שְׁמוֹת ט"ו).

א. כִּי עִקַּר הַחִיּוּת מְקַבְּלִין מֵהַתְּפִלָּה, כְּמוֹ שֶׁכָּתוּב (תְּהִלִּים מ"ב): "תְּפִלָּה לְאֵל חַיָּי". וּבִשְׁבִיל זֶה צָרִיךְ לְהִתְפַּלֵּל בְּכָל כֹּחוֹ, כִּי כְּשֶׁמִּתְפַּלֵּל בְּכָל כֹּחוֹ וּמַכְנִיס כֹּחוֹ בְּאוֹתִיּוֹת הַתְּפִלָּה, אֲזַי נִתְחַדֵּשׁ כֹּחוֹ שָׁם, בִּבְחִינַת (אֵיכָה ג): "חֲדָשִׁים לַבְּקָרִים (רַבָּה אֱמוּנָתֶךָ")‏ וְכוּ'. כִּי אֱמוּנָה הִיא תְּפִלָּה, כְּמוֹ שֶׁכָּתוּב (שְׁמוֹת י"ז): "וַיְהִי יָדָיו אֱמוּנָה", תַּרְגּוּמוֹ: 'פְּרִישָׁן בִּצְלוֹ':

ב. וְדַע, שֶׁיֵּשׁ שְׁנֵים־עָשָׂר שְׁבָטִים, כְּנֶגֶד שְׁנֵים־עָשָׂר מַזָּלוֹת (תִּקּוּן יח, וּבְתִקּוּן כא), וְכָל שֵׁבֶט וָשֵׁבֶט יֵשׁ לוֹ נֻסְחָא יֵשׁ לוֹ נֻסְחָא מְיֻחֶדֶת וְיֵשׁ לוֹ שַׁעַר

---

soul to God. In this sense, sleep corresponds to death, as our Sages taught: Sleep is one-sixtieth of death. In the morning, when he awakens, man's renewed soul is returned to him (see *Berakhot* 57b). The Midrash teaches that with this act God exhibits His faithfulness to us. It is a model of the way He will return our souls to us at the time of the Resurrection (*Eikhah Rabbah* 3:8). Rebbe Nachman tells us that our souls are given this life-force anew and fresh each day. Why? because of faith, which is prayer. Thus the verse "Prayer to the God of my life" can also be understood according to its more homiletic translation: "Prayer to God is my life!" The Midrash quoted above concludes: That You give us renewed [hope] in exile, we know that You will redeem us. The connection will become obvious as this lesson unfolds.

5. hands were emunah. When Yehoshua went into battle against Amalek, Moshe ascended to the top of a hill together with Aharon and Chur. Moshe turned to God and spread his hands out in prayer. While his hands remained raised the Jews were successful in combat. When they were lowered, Amalek succeeded. Aharon and Chur therefore held Moshe's hands *emunah* (steady) until sundown and the Jews were victorious (Exodus 17). The Talmud asks (*Rosh HaShanah* 29a): Was it Moshe's hands which won or lost the battle? No. But, when the Jews raised their eyes to Heaven in supplication the battle went in their favor. Hence the connection between *emunah* and prayer.

6. spread out in prayer. Therefore, through prayer—faith—with all one's energy, a person's strength is renewed (*Mai HaNachal*). Thus far, we have been introduced to three interrelated concepts: life-force, faith and prayer.

83   *LIKUTEY MOHARAN #9:1,2*

LIKUTEY MOHARAN #9[1]

"*T'homot Y'chasyumu* (The deeps covered them); they sank into the depths like a stone."

(Exodus 15:5)

The essence of life-force comes from prayer, as is written (Psalms 42:9), "Prayer to the God of my life."[2] This is why a person should pray with all his energy.[3] When a person prays with all his strength and concentrates his energy into the letters making up the prayers, his energy is renewed there. This corresponds to (Lamentations 3:23), "They are renewed each morning; great is Your *emunah* (faith)."[4] And faith is prayer, as in (Exodus 17:2), "And his hands were *emunah*,"[5] which Onkelos renders: "[his hands] were spread out in prayer."[6]

2. And know! there are twelve tribes [in Israel], corresponding to the twelve constellations (*Tikkuney Zohar* #18, #21). Each tribe has its own individual version [of the prayers], and its very own gate through

---

1. **Likutey Moharan #9.** Rebbe Nachman gave this lesson on Shabbat Shirah, 13 Shevat 5563 (Feb. 5, 1803) (see *Tzaddik* #129; *Until The Mashiach,* p.93). This teaching and Lesson #7 above share the similar themes of prayer, faith and truth, and exile. However, in the earlier teaching Rebbe Nachman focuses on the faith and truth which emanate from the tzaddik's advice and here he focuses on seeking the truth in prayer. (When studying this lesson it is advisable to refer to the footnotes of Lesson #7, particularly those in the last section.)

This entire lesson is *leshon Rabbeinu z'l.* See note 1 to Lesson #7 where this terminology has been explained.

2. **the God of my life.** Reb Naftali had a dream in which a soul came to him asking that he repeat one of Rebbe Nachman's lessons. He recalled the last discourse he had heard and began by reciting the opening words, "The essence...God of my life." Upon hearing these words, the soul grew excited and ascended towards heaven. When Reb Naftali related his dream to Rebbe Nachman, the Rebbe exclaimed: "It's no wonder! Do you think the way my lesson is heard in this world is the way it's heard in the worlds Above?! There, they understand it altogether differently."

3. **all his energy.** This may be understood in various ways:
    - total concentration on the words being said
    - pronouncing the words audibly, with all one's strength
    - trying one's best despite difficult circumstances
    Actually, where applicable, praying with all one's energy may well imply all three at once.

4. **renewed each morning...Your faith.** Each night, when a person goes to sleep, he returns his

LIKUTEY MOHARAN #9:2

84

מְיֻחָד לְכָנֵס דֶּרֶךְ שָׁם תְּפִלָּתוֹ, וְכָל שֵׁבֶט מְעוֹרֵר בִּתְפִלָּתוֹ כֹּחַ מַזָּלוֹ
שֶׁבִּשְׁנֵים־עָשָׂר מַזָּלוֹת; וְהַמַּזָּל מֵאִיר לְמַטָּה וּמְגַדֵּל הַצֶּמַח וּשְׁאָר
דְּבָרָיו הַצְּרִיכִים אֵלָיו.

Ctand

וְזֶה פֵּרוּשׁ (בְּמִדְבַּר כ״ד): "דָּרַךְ כּוֹכָב מִיַּעֲקֹב וְקָם שֵׁבֶט מִיִּשְׂרָאֵל".
'וְקָם' – זֶה בְּחִינַת עֲמִידָה, בְּחִינַת תְּפִלָּה. כְּשֶׁשֵּׁבֶט מִיִּשְׂרָאֵל עוֹמֵד
לְהִתְפַּלֵּל, עַל־יְדֵי־זֶה מְעוֹרֵר כּוֹכָב, וְהַכּוֹכָב הוּא דוֹרֵךְ וּמַכֶּה
הַדְּבָרִים שֶׁיִּגְדְּלוּ, כְּמוֹ שֶׁאָמְרוּ חֲכָמֵינוּ, זִכְרוֹנָם לִבְרָכָה (בְּרֵאשִׁית־
רַבָּה, פָּרָשָׁה י): 'אֵין לְךָ עֵשֶׂב מִלְּמַטָּה שֶׁאֵין לוֹ כּוֹכָב וּמַלְאָךְ
מִלְמַעְלָה, שֶׁמַּכֶּה אוֹתוֹ וְאוֹמֵר לוֹ: גְּדַל!'.

וְזֶה שֶׁאָמְרוּ חֲכָמֵינוּ, זִכְרוֹנָם לִבְרָכָה (פְּסָחִים קיח.): 'קָשִׁין מְזוֹנוֹתָיו
כִּקְרִיעַת יַם־סוּף וְקָשֶׁה זִוּוּגוֹ [כִּקְרִיעַת יַם־סוּף]' וְכוּ' (סוֹטָה ב).
כִּי הַיַּם־סוּף נִקְרַע לִשְׁנֵים־עָשָׂר קְרָעִים, כְּנֶגֶד שְׁנֵים־עָשָׂר שְׁבָטִים
(פִּרְקֵי דְּרַבִּי אֱלִיעֶזֶר, מב; עַיֵן תִּקּוּן כ״א נט.), וּבְנֵי־יִשְׂרָאֵל בִּתְפִלָּתָם
גּוֹרְמִים זִוּוּגָא דְּקֻדְשָׁא־בְּרִיךְ־הוּא וּשְׁכִינְתֵּהּ, כְּמוֹ שֶׁכָּתוּב (תְּהִלִּים

---

11. **splitting the Red Sea.** After pointing out how prayer can control the forces of nature, Rebbe Nachman now shows its influence over the "forces" governing one's livelihood and matters relating to marriage. Man actually has little control over these major areas of his life, for he can neither govern economic factors nor control whom he is destined to meet. Yet, prayer can succeed here as well (*Mai HaNachal*). The Talmudic teachings: "Providing a person with a living is as difficult...." and "Providing a person with a marriage partner is as difficult...," indicate that both these personal matters are in the realm of the miraculous and thus beyond our ability to govern. This is why our Sages likened them to the miracle which God performed when He split the Red Sea. Even so, through prayer it is possible to prevail upon God to act on our behalf—to perform miracles for us personally. However, to achieve this, our prayers must be pure (as will be explained in §2-4).

12. **twelve lanes...twelve tribes.** When the Egyptians chased after them, "the Jewish people [the twelve tribes] cried out to God" (Exodus 14:10). Their prayer altered nature, and each tribe was given its own path through which to cross the Red Sea. Thus, the splitting of the sea was a direct result of prayer (*Mai HaNachal*). The Midrash teaches that at Creation, God made a stipulation with the Red Sea that it should split for the Jews when they came to cross it on their way to the Holy Land. Still, the Red Sea refused to split until God Himself directly intervened (*Shemot Rabbah* 21:6). God did this after the twelve tribes prayed to him with all their energy.

LIKUTEY MOHARAN #9:2

which its prayers enter.[7] And, through its prayers, each tribe arouses the power of its constellation from among the twelve constellations.[8] This constellation then radiates downwards, causing the vegetation, as well as the other things dependent on it, to grow.

This is the meaning of (Numbers 24:17), "A star steps forth out of Yaakov, and a tribe stands up out of Israel." "Stands up," < because *Amidah* is nothing other than prayer > (*Berakhot* 6b).[9] When a tribe of Israel stands up to pray, it thereby arouses a star and the star steps forth and strikes things to make them grow. As our Sages taught: There is not a blade of grass below that does not have a star and an angel Above, which strike it and tell it, "Grow!" (*Bereishit Rabbah* 10:7).[10]

Our Sages taught: Providing < a person > with his livelihood is as difficult as splitting the Red Sea (*Pesachim* 118a); and < also > : Providing a person with his marriage partner is as difficult as splitting the Red Sea (*Sotah* 2a).[11]

The Red Sea was divided into twelve lanes, paralleling the twelve tribes (*Pirkey d'Rebbi Eliezer* 42).[12] Through their prayers, the Children of Israel bring about a < supernal > union, < a unification > between the Holy One and His *Shekhinah* (Divine Presence),[13] as is written

---

7. own gate...enter. The *Zohar* (III, 170a) explains that each of the twelve tribes has its own unique path via which its prayers enter heaven. This is derived from the Tetragrammaton, God's holy name *YHVH*. There are twelve different permutations of this name (see *Likutey Moharan* 7, n.11), with each tribe having its own unique gate corresponding to one of the possible combinations.

The *Zohar* (II, 251a) also tells us that this is the reason for the custom of having 12 windows in the synagogue. Just as in the "synagogue" of Above there are 12 gates through which the prayers enter, so, too, in our synagogues there should be 12 openings through which the prayers ascend.

8. arouses the power.... The forces of nature come together to foster the formation and growth of all physical creation as we know it. Because prayer can transcend nature and override the influences of the Zodiac (see §5), it has the power to control the course of nature.

9. Amidah...prayer. This refers to the *Shemoneh Esrei* (Eighteen Benedictions), which is recited while standing. Throughout the Talmud, the *Amidah* is known simply as *Tefillah*, Prayer.

10. Grow. Each physical creation, even a blade of grass, is ruled over by a star, which is in turn ruled over by some angel. They are all, however, dependent upon prayer, from which they draw their energy and life-force. This is because prayer alone reaches to God, Who creates and governs everything. Thus, when a person's prayers are accepted, he has the power to control the dictates of nature (such as the splitting of the Red Sea, see nn.11,12) (*Mai HaNachal*).

LIKUTEY MOHARAN #9:2

86

ס"ח): "סַלּוּ לָרֹכֵב עֲרָבוֹת" – 'רוֹכֵב', דָּא קֻדְשָׁא־בְּרִיךְ־הוּא,
'עֲרָבוֹת', דָּא שְׁכִינְתֵּהּ, שֶׁנִּתְעָרֵב בָּהּ כָּל הַגְּוָנִין; וּלְפִי הַזִּוּוּג שֶׁגּוֹרֵם
בִּתְפִלָּתוֹ, כֵּן זוֹכֶה לְזִוּוּגוֹ; וְהַתְּפִלָּה הֵם שְׁתֵּים־עֶשְׂרֵה נֻסְחָאוֹת,
לְפִיכָךְ הַזִּוּוּג כִּקְרִיעַת יַם־סוּף שֶׁהֵם שְׁנֵים־עָשָׂר.

וְגַם יִשְׂרָאֵל מְפַרְנְסִים לַאֲבִיהֶם שֶׁבַּשָּׁמַיִם בִּתְפִלָּתָם, כְּמוֹ שֶׁכָּתוּב
(שָׁם ק"ה): "וַיַּעֲמִידֶהָ לְיַעֲקֹב לְחֹק", 'וְחֹק לְשָׁנָא דִּמְזוֹנָא הוּא'
(בֵּיצָה ט"ז.), 'וְאֵין עֲמִידָה אֶלָּא תְּפִלָּה' (בְּרָכוֹת ו:).

וְזֶה פֵּרוּשׁ (תְּהִלִּים צ"ט): "שָׁמְרוּ עֵדֹתָיו וְחֹק נָתַן לָמוֹ" – 'עֵדוּת'
זֶה תְּפִלָּה, כְּמוֹ שֶׁכָּתוּב (שָׁם קכ"ב): "שִׁבְטֵי יָהּ עֵדוּת לְהֹדוֹת לְשֵׁם
ה'". גַּם אָמְרוּ חֲכָמֵינוּ, זִכְרוֹנָם לִבְרָכָה (שְׁבוּעוֹת ל.): 'אֵין עֵדוּת
אֶלָּא בַּעֲמִידָה'; וַעֲמִידָה זֶה תְּפִלָּה, שֶׁאָנוּ מְעִידִין עַל אַחְדוּתוֹ.
וּכְפִי שֶׁמְּפַרְנֵס לְאָבִיו שֶׁבַּשָּׁמַיִם בִּתְפִלָּתוֹ, כֵּן נוֹתְנִין לוֹ פַּרְנָסָתוֹ.
וְזֶה: 'קָשִׁין מְזוֹנוֹתָיו כִּקְרִיעַת יַם־סוּף', הַיְנוּ מְזוֹנוֹת נִתְחַלֵּק
לִשְׁנֵים־עָשָׂר שְׁבִילִים, לְפִי שְׁתֵּים־עֶשְׂרֵה שִׁבְטֵי יָהּ.

and other relationships, even the connection a person has to inanimate objects and his environment, all come into the category of *zivvugim*. This puts a broader perspective on the idea that "commensurate with the divine union one brings about through his prayer, so he, in turn, is granted his own *zivvug*." The *Mai HaNachal* writes: 'Rebbe Nachman is teaching that the way a person offers his prayers, directly determines the type of *zivvug* (unification) he brings about in heaven. And this, in turn, is what makes him worthy of finding his own *zivvug*.' Nor is this to be understood only as it relates to the finding of one's mate. The role which prayer plays in the building and preserving of a lasting relationship is of no less importance.

16. **nothing other than prayer.** The verse would then read: "By standing to pray, Yaakov provided sustenance." God, as it were, asks that we serve Him (for our benefit). With this service, so to speak, we provide *Him* with sustenance. See next note.

17. **testify to His unity.** "They guarded His testimonies" indicates that they kept God's commandments (*EiDoTav*). God's purpose in creating the world was in order to reveal Himself. By keeping His commandments, which Rebbe Nachman here connects to prayer, the Jews bear witness (*EiDuT*) to His unity and thereby help to fulfill this purpose. And in this sense, they "sustain God."

18. **sustenance.** Just as when a person prays he brings about a unification Above and thereby earns his own *zivvug*, so too, by "sustaining God" through his prayers he is likewise rewarded with his own sustenance and livelihood (*Mai HaNachal*).

LIKUTEY MOHARAN #9:2

(Psalms 68:5), "Praise [i.e., pray to] the One who rides upon the *aravot* (highest heavens)." The "One who rides" is the Holy One; "*ARaVot*" refers to the *Shekhinah*, in whom all the supernal colors are *nitAReV* (blended).[14] Commensurate with the divine union a person brings about through his prayer, so he, in turn, is granted his marriage partner <and livelihood>.[15] And, because there are twelve different versions of <the prayers>, finding one's marriage partner is therefore compared to the splitting of the Red Sea, which was <also> [divided] into twelve.

In addition, with their prayers, the Jewish people provide sustenance for their Father in heaven. As is written (Psalms 105:10), "*vayaAMiDehah* (He made it stand) for Yaakov as a *chok* (statute)." The word *chok* denotes livelihood (*Beitzah* 16a), and *AMiDah* is nothing other than prayer.[16]

This is the meaning of (Psalms 99:7), "They guarded His testimonies and He gave them a *chok*." The word "testimony" refers to prayer, as in (Psalms 122:4), "...the tribes of God, a testimony for Israel, to give praise [i.e., to pray] to the name of God." In addition, our Sages taught: Testimony can only be given when standing (*Shavuot* 30a), and standing is prayer: we testify to His unity.[17]

And to the extent a person sustains his Father in heaven with his prayer, so he, in turn, is given his sustenance.[18] Thus [the Sages taught]: ... <a person's> livelihood is as difficult as splitting the Red Sea. In other words, sustenance is divided up into twelve pathways, in accordance with the twelve [prayer versions of the] tribes of God.

{Abba Binyamin said, "All my days I was very concerned about two things: about my prayer, that it should be close to my *mitah* (my bed); and about my *mitah*, that it should be positioned between north and south" (*Berakhot* 5b).}

---

13. **supernal union....** Throughout the teachings of the *Zohar* and the writings of the holy Ari we find that everything good which a Jew does in this world causes a unification in the worlds Above. See *Rabbi Nachman's Stories*, Second Introduction (pp.11*ff*) for a detailed explanation of this. Also see *ibid.*, Story #1 (pp.31-54).

14. **ARaVot...blended.** The *Zohar* (II, 165a) teaches that *aravot* (ערבות) is the hidden firmament. It spans north and south (see n.22) and is a synthesis of fire and water—i.e., a blending (התערבות) of all the color variations. Because the Jewish soul is a "Godly portion," these various supernal colors correspond to the twelve tribes.

15. **marriage partner and livelihood.** The word *zivvug* means pairing or coupling, and applies to both physical and spiritual unions. Although the word refers particularly to marriage partners, it carries a much broader connotation as well. Friendships, business partnerships

LIKUTEY MOHARAN #9:2
88

וְצָרִיךְ לָזֶה זְכוּת גָּדוֹל, שֶׁיִּזְכֶּה אָדָם לְהַעֲלוֹת תְּפִלָּתוֹ דֶּרֶךְ שַׁעַר הַשַּׁיָּךְ לְשִׁבְטוֹ. וְזֶה שֶׁאָמַר אַבָּא בִּנְיָמִין (בְּרָכוֹת ה:): 'כָּל יָמַי הָיִיתִי מִצְטַעֵר עַל שְׁנֵי דְבָרִים: עַל תְּפִלָּתִי שֶׁתְּהֵא סָמוּךְ לְמִטָּתִי' – הַיְנוּ כַּנַּ"ל, שֶׁיִּתְפַּלֵּל דֶּרֶךְ שַׁעַר הַמִּטָּה שֶׁלּוֹ, כִּי יֵשׁ שְׁנֵים-עָשָׂר מִטּוֹת, וְכָל אֶחָד יֵשׁ לוֹ שַׁעַר מְיֻחָד, וְהִתְפַּלֵּל עַל שֶׁלֹּא תִּתְרַחֵק תְּפִלָּתוֹ מִמַּטָּה שֶׁלּוֹ.

וְזֶה לְשׁוֹן מַטֶּה, כִּי מַטֶּה לְשׁוֹן זִוּוּג, כְּמַאֲמָר הַסָּמוּךְ: עַל מִטָּתִי שֶׁתְּהֵא נְתוּנָה וְכוּ', וּמִטָּה הוּא בְּחִינַת זִוּוּג.

גַּם מַטֶּה הִיא בְּחִינַת פַּרְנָסָה, כְּמוֹ שֶׁכָּתוּב (וַיִּקְרָא כ"ו): "בְּשִׁבְרִי לָכֶם מַטֵּה לֶחֶם", כִּי שְׁנֵים-עָשָׂר מַטּוֹת גּוֹרְמִין זִוּוּג וּמְפַרְנְסִין כַּנַּ"ל: 'קָשֶׁה זִוּוּגָן וְקָשִׁין מְזוֹנוֹתָיו' וְכוּ'.

גַּם הִתְפַּלֵּל עַל שִׁבְטוֹ, שֶׁיִּזְכּוּ לִשְׁנֵי שֻׁלְחָנוֹת. וְזֶהוּ: 'וְעַל מִטָּתִי שֶׁתְּהֵא נְתוּנָה בֵּין צָפוֹן לְדָרוֹם', וְאָמְרוּ חֲכָמֵינוּ, זִכְרוֹנָם לִבְרָכָה (בָּבָא בַּתְרָא כה:): 'הָרוֹצֶה לְהַחְכִּים וְכוּ', הָרוֹצֶה לְהַעֲשִׁיר' וְכוּ'.

וְיַעֲקֹב, שֶׁהוּא כָּלוּל כָּל הַשְּׁנֵים-עָשָׂר שְׁבָטִים, וְהָיָה יוֹדֵעַ כָּל מַטֶּה וּמַטֶּה בְּשָׁרְשׁוֹ – בִּשְׁבִיל זֶה כְּתִיב בֵּהּ (בְּרֵאשִׁית מ"ט): "וַיֶּאֱסֹף

---

provide him with his livelihood and his *zivvug*. This indicates that when a person's prayers enter through the proper gate, they "provide" for Above, as it were. The prayers then have the power to direct those forces of nature already in place to work for his benefit. If, however, the prayers do not ascend through the proper gate, then they do not "provide" for Above and consequently he will not be properly provided for down below.

22. **south...north.** The Showbread symbolizes prosperity. Its position in the Holy Temple is on the Table, to the north of the entrance of the Holy of Holies. The Menorah symbolizes wisdom and its position is to the south of the entrance of the Holy of Holies. Our Sages therefore taught that a person wanting riches and prosperity should favor north when praying; the person wanting wisdom should favor south. Abba Binyamin hoped that his tribe's prayer would enter its appropriate gate (corresponding to the entrance to the Holy of Holies, the place towards which all prayers are directed), inclusive of both north and south. This is the meaning of the abovementioned teaching from the *Zohar* (see also n.14) that the *Shekhinah* is *aravot*, the hidden firmament spanning north and south. The *Yikara D'Shabbata* on this lesson adds that the Showbread consists of twelve loaves and thus corresponds to the twelve tribes of Israel.

It takes considerable merit for a person to be able to send his prayer up through his tribe's appropriate gate.[19] This is what Abba Binyamin said: "All my days I was concerned about two things: about my prayer that it should be close to my *MiTaH* (bed)...."[20] In other words, he wanted to pray through the gate of his *MaTeH* (tribe). For there are twelve tribes and each one has its very own gate. He prayed that his prayer should not be separated from his tribe.

Hence the word *mateh,* because "*mateh*" alludes to marital union. This is indicated in the ensuing [part of his] statement: "...about my *mitah* (bed), that it should be positioned between north and south"— *mitah* corresponding to marital union.

Furthermore, *mateh* corresponds to sustenance, as is written (Leviticus 26:26), "When I break your *MaTeh* (staff) of bread." For the twelve *MaTot* (tribes) bring about a < supernal > union [of the Holy One and the *Shekhinah*] and provide sustenance < for their Father in heaven >, as in the abovementioned: "...his marriage partner is as difficult...his livelihood is as difficult...."[21]

[Abba Binyamin] also prayed that < he > merit the "two tables" [of wisdom and prosperity]. This is the meaning of, "that my bed should be positioned between north and south." For our Sages taught: Someone who wants to become wise should face south, and someone who wants to become wealthy should face north (*Bava Batra* 25b).[22]

And Yaakov—in whom all twelve tribes were collectively embodied—knew each and every tribe at its root. This is why it is written of him (Genesis 49:33), "And Yaakov gathered up his feet onto

19. **tribe's appropriate gate.** See *Likutey Moharan* II, 73, where Rebbe Nachman teaches that by reciting the Psalms a person can come to his correct path.

20. **close to my mitah.** Rashi gives the literal explanation that Abba Binyamin was careful to pray as soon as he got out of bed in the morning, before engaging in any of his daily activities. This ties directly into our text. Rebbe Nachman has shown that each of a person's needs benefits from prayer. Success in all areas, whether personal, economic etc., is governed by prayer. This is the implication of what Abba Binyamin said. Before engaging in even the most simple activity, he would pray to God that his undertaking prove successful (see n.23). Rebbe Nachman himself said that when he rose in the morning he would pray and give over to God all the activities of his day (*Rabbi Nachman's Wisdom* #2).

21. **...marriage partner...livelihood....** Rebbe Nachman builds on the connection between the words *mitah* and *mateh*. Therefore, Abba Binyamin's request that his prayer be close to his bed carries a double meaning. He was concerned that his prayer should ascend through the gate of his tribe, and that he bring about the appropriate unifications needed in order to

LIKUTEY MOHARAN #9:2,3

יַעֲקֹב רַגְלָיו אֶל הַמִּטָּה". 'רַגְלָיו' – זֶה בְּחִינַת תְּפִלָּה, כְּמוֹ שֶׁכָּתוּב
(תְּהִלִּים פ"ה): "צֶדֶק לְפָנָיו יְהַלֵּךְ", הַיְנוּ, שֶׁהָיָה מְאַסֵּף כָּל הַתְּפִלּוֹת,
כָּל אַחַת לְשָׁרְשָׁהּ.

גַּם הָיָה כֹּחַ בְּיָדוֹ לִתֵּן חֵלֶק מֵחֶלְקֵי עוֹלָם לְיוֹסֵף, כְּמוֹ שֶׁכָּתוּב
(בְּרֵאשִׁית מ"ח): "וַאֲנִי נָתַתִּי לְךָ שְׁכֶם אַחַד עַל אַחֶיךָ" וְכוּ', כִּי עַל-
יְדֵי תְּפִלָּתוֹ הָיָה מַשְׁפִּיעַ חִיּוּת לְכָל שְׁלֹשָׁה חֶלְקֵי עוֹלָם, שֶׁהֵם
עוֹלָם הַשָּׁפָל וְעוֹלָם הַכּוֹכָבִים וְעוֹלָם הַמַּלְאָכִים. וְזֶה: שְׁכֶ"ם –
שָׁפָל, כּוֹכָב, מַלְאָךְ, כִּי כָּל זֶה זָכָה עַל-יְדֵי תְּפִלָּתוֹ, כְּמוֹ שֶׁכָּתוּב
(שָׁם): "אֲשֶׁר לָקַחְתִּי מִיַּד וְכוּ' בְּתַפְלָתִי וּבְקַשְׁתִּי":

ג. אֲבָל כְּשֶׁאָדָם עוֹמֵד לְהִתְפַּלֵּל, אֲזַי בָּאִים מַחֲשָׁבוֹת זָרוֹת וּקְלִפּוֹת
וּמְסַבְּבִין אוֹתוֹ, וְנִשְׁאָר בַּחֹשֶׁךְ וְאֵין יָכוֹל לְהִתְפַּלֵּל, כְּמוֹ שֶׁכָּתוּב
(אֵיכָה ג): "סַכֹּתָ בֶעָנָן לָךְ מֵעֲבוֹר תְּפִלָּה",

enemies was prayer, and this power he bequeathed to Yosef (cf. *Likutey Moharan* I, 2:1).

In review: A person should pray with total energy and concentration. By doing so, his energy is renewed in the letters of prayer, which are the source of all life-force (§1). Each of the 12 tribes of the Jewish people has a different version of prayer and a corresponding gate through which its prayer passes. These 12 paths also correspond to the 12 constellations, by means of which livelihood is channeled to each particular tribe. Thus through prayer an influx of life-force is provided for all parts of the universe (§2).

29. **to pray.** Now that prayer is the life-force which brings man whatever he desires, the question "Why can't everyone just pray and wait for their needs to be answered?" must be addressed. This is what Rebbe Nachman focuses on in section 3.

30. **external thoughts and kelipot....** Prayer encounters two distinct "opposing forces": external thoughts and *kelipot*. External thoughts imply anything which is foreign to whatever the person is praying for and concentrating on at that moment. Thus, whether he is suddenly beset by memories of past occurrences or anxieties over the future, or whether while praying for one holy thing he thinks about some other equally holy desire, in either case his prayer has been clouded by a foreign and external thought. The *kelipot* which disturb and interfere with a person's prayer can come from within a person's mind, such as evil and immoral thoughts, or they can oppose his prayer from without as is the case when wicked people purposely interfere with someone while he prays (*Rabbi Eliyahu Chaim Rosen*).

31. **dark...unable to pray.** This inability to pray often brings a person to a point where he does not even want to pray. This "darkness" is falsehood and, like a cloud, gives the impression that it cannot be penetrated. It is the opposite of the truth, which is "light," as Rebbe Nachman will soon explain.

32. **cloud...no prayer could pass through.** This alludes to the "opposing force" of external

LIKUTEY MOHARAN #9:2,3

the *mitah.*" "His feet" corresponds to prayer, as is written (Psalms 85:14), "Righteousness will *go* before him."[23] In other words, [Yaakov's gathering up his feet alludes to] his gathering all the prayers < to their roots > .[24]

[Yaakov] also had the power to give a portion of < the three portions of > the world to Yosef, as is written (Genesis 48:22), "And I have given you one shekhem (one portion) over and above your brothers."[25] For through his prayer, he sent an influx of life-force[26] into all three parts of the universe[27]—the lowest world, the world of the stars and the world of the angels. This is [indicated in the word] *SheKheM: Shafel* (lowly), *Kokhav* (star) and *Malakh* (angel). All this [Yaakov] achieved through his prayer, as the verse continues, "...[the portion] which I took from the hand of the Emorite with my sword and my bow"—< which Onkelos renders: > "with my prayer and supplication."[28]

3. But when a person stands up to pray,[29] he is beset by external thoughts and *kelipot* (husks) surround him < on all sides > .[30] He is left in the dark, unable to pray,[31] as is written (Lamentations 3:44), "You covered Yourself with a cloud so that no prayer could pass through."[32]

---

23. ...**before him.** On this verse, "Righteousness will go before him and walk in the way of his steps," the Talmud teaches (*Berakhot* 14a): "Righteousness will go before him"—before going to do anything one should first pray (righteousness); and only then—"walk in the way of his steps"—to take care of his needs. See note 20.

24. **to their roots.** Yaakov was the father, the root, of the twelve tribes. This explains why he was included among them even though he was not one of them. Later on in the lesson (§4), Rebbe Nachman explains that one must bind his prayers to the tzaddik of the generation for he knows how to elevate each prayer to its proper gate. This was Yaakov. He knew the "source" of every tribe—i.e., the right place for the prayers which they offered.

25. **Yosef...over and above....** Once the tribe of Levi was selected for the priesthood and service in the Temple, it meant that there were only eleven tribes left in the general populace. The tribe of Yosef was then divided into two, Efraim and Menashe, thereby restoring the number to twelve. Thus Yosef received "one *extra* portion." This provided his tribe with one *extra* prayer-gate and greater control, through their prayer, over those "forces" affecting life (see n.11). The Levites, because of their holy service, correspond to the tzaddik of the generation, for the Temple is the place to where all prayers are directed.

26. **life-force.** As we've seen in section 1: The essence of life-force comes from prayer.

27. **parts of the universe.** See note 10 that the grass (the lowest world) is governed by a star (the world of stars) which is, in turn, governed by an angel (the world of angels).

28. **prayer and supplication.** The Hebrew term *b'KaShTy* (with my bow) can also be read *baKaShaTy* (my supplication). This teaches that the weapon Yaakov used for conquering his

LIKUTEY MOHARAN #9:3

וּכְתִיב (תְּהִלִּים י״ב): "סָבִיב רְשָׁעִים יִתְהַלָּכוּן", שֶׁהָרְשָׁעִים, הַיְנוּ הַקְּלִפּוֹת, מְסַבְּבִין אוֹתוֹ. 'כְּרֻם זֻלֻּת' – הַיְנוּ בִּשְׁעַת הַתְּפִלָּה, 'שֶׁהִיא עוֹמֶדֶת בְּרוּמוֹ שֶׁל עוֹלָם' (בְּרָכוֹת ו:).

וְדַע, שֶׁיֵּשׁ פְּתָחִים הַרְבֵּה בַּחֹשֶׁךְ הַזֶּה לָצֵאת מִשָּׁם, כְּמוֹ שֶׁאָמְרוּ חֲכָמֵינוּ, זִכְרוֹנָם לִבְרָכָה (יוֹמָא לח:): 'הַבָּא לְטַמֵּא, פּוֹתְחִין לוֹ – יֵשׁ לוֹ פְּתָחִים הַרְבֵּה.' נִמְצָא, שֶׁיֵּשׁ פְּתָחִים הַרְבֵּה בַּחֹשֶׁךְ גַּם לָצֵאת מִשָּׁם. אֲבָל הָאָדָם הוּא עִוֵּר וְאֵין יוֹדֵעַ לִמְצֹא הַפֶּתַח.

וְדַע, שֶׁעַל־יְדֵי אֱמֶת זוֹכֶה לִמְצֹא הַפֶּתַח, כִּי עִקַּר אוֹר הַמֵּאִיר הוּא הַקָּדוֹשׁ־בָּרוּךְ־הוּא, כְּמוֹ שֶׁכָּתוּב (תְּהִלִּים כ״ז): "ה' אוֹרִי וְיִשְׁעִי"; וְעַל־יְדֵי שֶׁקֶר הוּא מְסַלֵּק אֶת הַקָּדוֹשׁ־בָּרוּךְ־הוּא, כְּמוֹ שֶׁכָּתוּב (שְׁמוֹת כ): "לֹא תִשָּׂא אֶת שֵׁם ה' לַשָּׁוְא", כִּי עַל־יְדֵי שָׁוְא מְסַלֵּק אֶת הַקָּדוֹשׁ־בָּרוּךְ־הוּא, כִּי "דֹּבֵר שְׁקָרִים לֹא יִכּוֹן לְנֶגֶד עֵינָיו." אֲבָל עַל־יְדֵי אֱמֶת, הַקָּדוֹשׁ־בָּרוּךְ־הוּא שׁוֹכֵן עִמּוֹ, כְּמוֹ שֶׁכָּתוּב (תְּהִלִּים קמ״ה): "קָרוֹב ה' לְכָל קוֹרְאָיו לְכֹל" וְכוּ'; וּכְשֶׁהַקָּדוֹשׁ־בָּרוּךְ־הוּא עִמּוֹ, הוּא מֵאִיר לוֹ אֵיךְ לֵיצֵא מֵהַחֹשֶׁךְ הַמּוֹנֵעַ אוֹתוֹ בִּתְפִלָּתוֹ, כְּמוֹ שֶׁכָּתוּב: "ה' אוֹרִי".

---

35. **openings for him.** God's mercy is very great. When a person finds himself distant from holiness and inundated by the "flood-waters" of empty values, if he but asks for God's help he will receive it. And not only this. Even if a person comes to defile himself, when it would seem that this should cause God to turn away from him, he is still afforded many openings through which he can get out of the darkness (*Shabbat* 104a, *Tosafot s.v. iss d'garsy*).

36. **blind and does not. . . find the opening.** This refers also to a person's doubts and questions which cloud his ability to perceive the proper path—the opening.

37. **my light and my help.** If a person sees the light, the openings, then he is already on the road to finding help and salvation.

38. **in My sight.** Commenting on this verse, the Talmud teaches that people who lie and speak falsely will never merit seeing the Divine Presence (*Sotah* 42a). Though our Sages are referring to not being in God's sight in the World to Come, Rebbe Nachman explains that this principle is equally valid in this world. When a person speaks falsely, his sight is impaired and he is no longer able to discern the truth, God's "light." For a fuller explanation of this concept, see *Mayim* (Breslov Research Inst., 1987).

93   *LIKUTEY MOHARAN #9:3*

{**"The wicked go round on every side; that which is exalted is degraded by the sons of man"** (Psalms 12:9).}

It is written, "The wicked go round on every side...." "The wicked," i.e., the *kelipot,* surround the person.[33] "That which is exalted is degraded"—i.e., while [standing] in prayer, for [prayer] stands at the very summit of the universe (*Berakhot* 6b).[34]

But know! the darkness itself contains many openings from which to exit. As our Sages taught: When someone comes to defile himself, they open up for him (*Yoma* 38b)—there are many openings for him.[35] We see that even in the darkness there are many openings through which to leave. The problem is that the person [caught up in the darkness] is blind and does not know how to find the opening.[36]

And know! a person merits finding the opening through truth. For the main light that illuminates [the openings] is God, as is written (Psalms 27:1), "God is my light and my help."[37] But through falsehood, a person dismisses God, as in (Exodus 20:7), "You shall not swear falsely by the name of God." Through falsehood one removes [himself from] God, for (Psalms 101:7), "He that speaks falsely will not stand in My sight."[38]

Through truth, on the other hand, God dwells with him, as in (Psalms 145:18), "God is near to all who call Him, to all who call Him in truth." And when God is with a person, He enlightens him on how to get out of the darkness that disturbs him when he prays, as in, "God is my light."

{**"God said to Noach: 'Make for yourself a *teivah* (an ark). . . . Make a light for the ark, and to an *amah* (a cubit) *techalenah* (finish it) *milemaalah* (up above); and put the opening of the ark *b'tzidah* (in its side), and make it with a lower, second and third stories'** " (Genesis 6:14-17).}

thoughts which becloud a person's mind and make him forget what he was praying for.

---

33. surround the person. This alludes to the *kelipot,* the "opposing force" which surrounds a person, disturbing and interfering with his prayers.

34. summit of the universe. The verse teaches that the wicked have great strength, while that which ought to be exalted is despised. Rashi (*loc. cit.*) explains that this refers to prayer, which, as we've seen, can reach to the highest levels and control all the "forces" affecting a person's life (see nn.11,25). And yet, prayer is "degraded by the sons of man." People reach a point of not even wanting to pray. Actually, a person can go for hours and days with a desire to pray, but when the time comes he finds that he cannot even open his mouth. If so, why the desire? The answer is that a person can sense, even know, the greatness of prayer. Then why not pray? He cannot pray because of the darkness, the "opposing forces," which confound all his attempts.

LIKUTEY MOHARAN #9:3

וְזֶה פֵּרוּשׁ: (בְּרֵאשִׁית ו) "צֹהַר תַּעֲשֶׂה לַתֵּבָה", פֵּרֵשׁ רַשִׁ״י: יֵשׁ
אוֹמְרִים חַלּוֹן, וְיֵשׁ אוֹמְרִים אֶבֶן טוֹב׳; וְהַחִלּוּק שֶׁבֵּין חַלּוֹן לְאֶבֶן
טוֹב – כִּי הַחַלּוֹן אֵין לוֹ אוֹר בְּעַצְמוֹ, אֶלָּא דֶּרֶךְ שָׁם נִכְנָס הָאוֹר,
אֲבָל כְּשֶׁאֵין אוֹר, אֵין מֵאִיר; אֲבָל אֶבֶן טוֹב, אֲפִלּוּ כְּשֶׁאֵין אוֹר
מִבַּחוּץ הוּא מֵאִיר בְּעַצְמוֹ. כֵּן יֵשׁ בְּנֵי-אָדָם שֶׁדִּבּוּרָם הוּא חַלּוֹן,
וְאֵין כֹּחַ לְהָאִיר לָהֶם בְּעַצְמָם; וְזֶה: יֵשׁ אוֹמְרִים, וַאֲמִירָתָם נַעֲשֶׂה
חַלּוֹן; וְיֵשׁ שֶׁאֲמִירָתָם נַעֲשֶׂה אֶבֶן טוֹב וּמֵאִיר.

וְדַע, שֶׁהַכֹּל לְפִי גֹדֶל הָאֱמֶת, כִּי עִקַּר הָאוֹר הוּא הַקָּדוֹשׁ-בָּרוּךְ-
הוּא, וְהַקָּדוֹשׁ-בָּרוּךְ-הוּא הוּא עֶצֶם הָאֱמֶת, וְעִקַּר הִשְׁתּוֹקְקוּת שֶׁל
הַשֵּׁם יִתְבָּרֵךְ אֵינוֹ אֶלָּא אֶל הָאֱמֶת.

וְזֶה: "וְאֵל אַמָּה תְּכַלֶּנָּה מִלְמַעְלָה", לְשׁוֹן (שְׁמוּאֵל-ב י״ג): "וַתְּכַל
נֶפֶשׁ דָּוִד". אַמָּה – הִיא ה׳ מוֹצָאוֹת, הַכְּלוּלִים מֵאֵשׁ וּמַיִם, הַיְנוּ
שֶׁתִּרְאֶה שֶׁיֵּצְאוּ הַדִּבּוּרִים מִפִּיךְ בֶּאֱמֶת, וְאָז יִשְׁתּוֹקֵק הַקָּדוֹשׁ-
בָּרוּךְ-הוּא מִלְמַעְלָה לִשְׁכֹּן אֶצְלְךָ; וּכְשֶׁיִּשְׁכֹּן אֶצְלְךָ, הוּא יָאִיר לְךָ.

This understanding of how God's instructions to Noach relate to each individual even today now becomes the focus of Rebbe Nachman's lesson. Here he clarifies the concept of the ark, while the meaning of the rains will be explained towards the end of the teaching.

40. **window...precious jewel....** Most people have their stronger and weaker moments. One whose life is a succession of ups and downs is likened to a window. He can pray properly and enthusiastically, but only for a while. Afterwards his resolve slackens and he needs an awakening, a boost, from others. If he is open to this arousal, he is like a window into which the "light" shines. There are, however, those rare individuals who have reached a level where they no longer have to endure this ongoing struggle to maintain their strong moments and enthusiasm. Their "light" shines constantly, not only for themselves, but even to others as well. Such an individual is compared to a precious stone which radiates on its own. It is most likely that he knows his tribe/ source, and his prayers rise up to God/the Source of truth. This is why Rebbe Nachman goes on to say (§4) that we must bind our prayers to the tzaddik. For even if our prayers are not offered with complete truth, those of the tzaddik are, and he can thus elevate even our prayers to their source. For a fuller explanation of this concept see *Tsohar* (Breslov Research, 1986), which covers this teaching and Lesson #112 together with further insights from *Likutey Halakhot*.

41. **articulators.** The *Sefer Yetzirah* (2:3) teaches that the letters of the Hebrew alphabet are divided into five groups according to the five different parts of the mouth used in their pronunciation. They are: the throat (אחהע), the palate (גיכק), the tongue (דטלנת), the teeth (זסשרץ), and the lips (בומפ).

42. **fire and water.** The holy letters of the Hebrew alphabet carry numerous meanings and

95   *LIKUTEY MOHARAN #9:3*

This is the explanation of, "Make a light for the ark."[39] Rashi explains: "some say a window, and some say a precious jewel." The difference between a window and a precious jewel is that a window has no light of its own. It is simply [a medium] for the light to enter through. But when there is no light, the window does not give light. With a precious jewel, however, even when there is no outside light the jewel shines of itself. So, too, there are people whose words are [like] a window, incapable of giving them light on their own. This is [what Rashi means by] "some say." Their "saying" becomes a window. And there are some whose "saying" becomes a precious jewel and [their words] radiate.[40]

And know! everything depends on the degree of truth [a person has]. For the main light is God, and God is the essence of truth. God's primary yearning is for nothing but the truth.

"...to an *amah* (cubit) *techalenah* (finish it) *milemaalah* (up above)." [The word *TeChaLenah*] has the same connotation as "And David's soul *TeChaL* (longed)" (cf. 2 Samuel 13:39). [And the letters of the word] *AMaH* allude to the *Heh* (five) articulators,[41] which consist of *Aish* (fire) and *Mayim* (water).[42]

---

39. **Make a light for the ark.** Aside from "ark," *teivah* also means "word." Building on this Rebbe Nachman teaches that we must make the words of our prayers shine like a light. (The dimensions of Noach's ark were 300 x 50 x 30 cubits. This parallels the Hebrew word for speech/tongue, *LaShoN*, 50 = ן 300 = ש 30 = ל. Thus, the construction of the ark itself alludes directly to prayer; *Rabbi Yaakov Meir Shechter*.)

The *Parparaot LeChokhmah* comments: These instructions were given to Noach. He was to build an ark to protect him from the flood-waters. Rashi (Genesis 7:12) explains that the flood-waters began as normal rainfall, a blessing. Had the people repented, they would have survived. But they did not heed this warning and the rains became violent, turning from gentle rain into a destructive force unparalleled in the annals of mankind. Only Noach and those with him in the ark survived. Rebbe Nachman tells us that the ark alludes to the words of our prayers; the flood-waters are the "opposing forces," the external thoughts and *kelipot* which overwhelm a person.

Actually, some of these thoughts and disturbances are integral to a person's serving God. He needs them, but must first clarify them and place them in their proper perspective in order to realize their helpful potential. Other thoughts are totally unnecessary and even bad for a person. These he must completely overcome. In this sense, the "opposing forces" correspond to the rainfall and the flood-waters. If a person prays properly, the rains are a blessing; if not, he is overwhelmed by them. When this happens, when his mind is completely inundated and "flooded" with these forces, the only solution is to enter into the words of the prayer—the ark—with all his energy and powers of concentration. He should recite the words with great truth. The greater this truth, the more he will enter into and be protected by this ark. The truth will then enable him to see past the "opposing forces" and pray properly.

LIKUTEY MOHARAN #9:3

וְזֶה: אַמָּה תְכַלֶּנָּה מִלְמַעְלָה – רָאשֵׁי־תֵבוֹת אֱמֶת,
כִּי עַל־יְדֵי אֱמֶת הַקָּדוֹשׁ־בָּרוּךְ־הוּא חוֹמֵד מִלְמַעְלָה לִשְׁכֹּן עִם
הָאָדָם, כְּמוֹ שֶׁכָּתוּב: "קָרוֹב ה' לְכָל קוֹרְאָיו" וְכוּ'.
וְאָז: "וּפָתַח הַתֵּבָה בְּצִדָּהּ תָּשִׂים", הַיְנוּ הַתֵּבָה הַיּוֹצֵאת בֶּאֱמֶת,
הִיא תָּשִׂים לְךָ פֶּתַח בַּחֹשֶׁךְ שֶׁאַתָּה נָצוֹד בּוֹ. וְזֶה: "בְּצִדָּהּ" – הַיְנוּ
הַקְּלִפָּה הַצָּד צַיִד, כְּמוֹ שֶׁכָּתוּב (בְּרֵאשִׁית כ"ה): "כִּי צַיִד בְּפִיו",
כִּי מִתְּחִלָּה לֹא הָיָה יָכוֹל לְדַבֵּר מֵחֲמַת הַחֹשֶׁךְ הַסּוֹבֵב אוֹתוֹ, וְעַל־
יְדֵי שֶׁיּוֹצֵא מִתּוֹךְ הַחֹשֶׁךְ וּמִתְפַּלֵּל הֵיטֵב, עַל־יְדֵי־זֶה הוּא מְתַקֵּן
"תַּחְתִּים שְׁנִים וּשְׁלִשִׁים", הַיְנוּ עוֹלָם הַשָּׁפָל וְעוֹלָם הַגַּלְגַּלִּים
וְעוֹלָם הַשֵּׂכֶל. (אַךְ אִי אֶפְשָׁר לְהִתְפַּלֵּל, רַק כְּשֶׁלּוֹמֵד תּוֹרָה, כִּי 'לֹא

begins saying the prayers with great fervor. His prayers, at that moment, are recited with a level of truth. This person, whoever he may be and whatever spiritual level he may have reached, is then providing life and sustenance to all levels of creation.

Rebbe Nachman particularly stressed the importance of clapping while praying (see *Likutey Moharan* I, 44; *Tzaddik* #204). Yet, there are those who find their own concentration disturbed when a neighbor claps. However, it is said in the name of Rabbi Eliyahu Chaim Rosen, that when a person hears someone else clapping this should actually remind him to concentrate on his prayers.

46. **world of the intellect.** Earlier (end of §2) this was referred to as the world of the angels. The simple explanation is that the angels, because they are souls without bodies, correspond to pure intellect. On a deeper level, in the Talmud we find two separate references (*Shabbat* 53b and *Bava Kama* 2b) to man having *mazal*. In *Shabbat* Rashi explains that *mazal* indicates a guardian angel; in *Bava Kama* he interprets *mazal* as man's intellect. When a person begins following the path of truth, he can be likened to a child first learning to walk. He must have a "guardian angel," i.e., support from Above. However, after walking on this path for some time, one gains the strength which truth brings and can thus follow his own intellect.

47. **Torah.** This paragraph did not appear in Rebbe Nachman's original manuscript, but was recorded by one of Rebbe Nachman's followers and was afterwards appended to the text (*Parparaot LeChokhmah*). Though Rebbe Nachman has as yet not mentioned Torah in the lesson, he will refer to it later on, in his commentary to Rabbah bar bar Chanah's story. Reb Noson explains that Torah is truth—the total embodiment of Truth. He points out that before reciting the *Amidah* prayer we first read the *Shema*—which appears in the Torah. (This refers to the morning and evening prayers. The afternoon *Amidah* is also preceded by a section from the Torah, viz. *Ashrei*, Psalm 145.) This is because we must attach ourselves to truth before we pray, so that our words will then shine like a "light." We can therefore understand that by mentioning the need for truth, Rebbe Nachman has, in fact, already introduced the concept of Torah (*Likutey Halakhot, Hilkhot Dayanim* 3:9).

48. **ignoramus cannot be pious...abomination.** A person who does not study Torah cannot be attached to truth, for Torah is truth. The result is that his prayers can neither be offered

97   *LIKUTEY MOHARAN #9:3*

In other words: See to it that the words leave your mouth in truth, and then, from Above, God will long to dwell with you. And when He dwells with you, He will shine for you. Thus, the initial letters of *"Amah Techalenah Milemaalah"* spell *ÆMeT* (truth).[43] For it is through truth that, from Above, God desires to dwell with man, as in, "God is near to all who call Him, to all who call him in truth."

And then, ". . .and put the opening of the *teivah* (ark) *b'tZiDah* (in its side)." That is, ["the *teivah*" corresponds to] the *teivah* (word) that emerges in truth. This [true word] will put an opening for you in the darkness in which you are trapped.[44] And this is *"b'tZiDah"*—i.e., the *kelipah* which is *tZaD tZayiD* (traps prey), as is written [of Esav], "he was a trapper with his mouth" (Genesis 25:28).

At first, [the person praying] could not even speak because of the darkness surrounding him. But, by emerging from the darkness and praying properly,[45] he rectifies the "lower, second and third storys"— i.e., the lowest world, the world of the stars and the world of the intellect.[46]

{However, it is impossible to pray without studying Torah.[47] For an ignoramus cannot be pious (*Avot* 2:6).[48] And, as is written (Proverbs

allusions on many different levels. Aside from their shapes, sounds and numerical values, their names and position in the word also have meaning. In any given word, it is generally its first letter which is primary and most important. Here Rebbe Nachman tells us that the *alef* (א) and *mem* (מ) of the word *AMah* (אמה) stand for *Aish* (אש) and *Mayim* (מים). Fire and water represent those qualities of the body, heat and moisture, which produce speech. They are also indicative of the way a person should try to pray: with *warm* emotions and with his words *flowing* freely.

43. *ÆMeT*, **truth.** In Hebrew, *emet* begins with the letter *alef* (א). Depending upon its vowel point, an *alef* can be pronounced as the *e* in "egg," as the *a* in "what," etc. To highlight the connection between *emet* (אמת) and *amah* (אמה), the antiquated æ construction has been used.

44. . . . **trapped.** Based on Rebbe Nachman's interpretation, the verse reads: **Make a light for the ark** — Put truth into your words of prayer; **and finish it to a cubit up above** — and this truth, in the warm and flowing expression of your speech, will make your words be desired Above; **and put the opening of the ark in its side** — then your prayers will make an opening for you in the darkness in which you find yourself trapped. And, as Rebbe Nachman explains next, **and make it with a lower, second and third storys** — so that now your prayers will bring sustenance to all three levels of creation.

45. **praying properly.** The *Mai HaNachal* adds: From here it is possible to understand the different "tempos" of one's own prayer. At times a person finds that he has very little desire to pray. This is due to the "opposing forces" which surround him. He tries to pray properly, only to forget himself in other thoughts or distractions. Then he remembers, and attempts to recite his words with concentration and involvement. This can go back and forth any number of times. Eventually, because of his desire and effort, energy and enthusiasm pick up and he

LIKUTEY MOHARAN #9:3,4

עַם־הָאָרֶץ חָסִיד' (אָבוֹת ב); וּכְתִיב (מִשְׁלֵי כ"ח): "מֵסִיר אָזְנוֹ מִשְּׁמֹעַ תּוֹרָה גַּם תְּפִלָּתוֹ תּוֹעֵבָה" – כְּתַב יַד הַחֲבֵרִים).

ד. וְצָרִיךְ כָּל אָדָם לְקַשֵּׁר אֶת תְּפִלָּתוֹ לְצַדִּיק הַדּוֹר. וְהַצַּדִּיק יוֹדֵעַ לְכַוֵּן הַשְּׁעָרִים וּלְהַעֲלוֹת כָּל תְּפִלָּה וּתְפִלָּה לַשַּׁעַר הַשַּׁיָּךְ. כִּי כָּל צַדִּיק וְצַדִּיק הוּא בְּחִינַת מֹשֶׁה־מָשִׁיחַ, כְּמוֹ שֶׁאָמְרוּ: 'מֹשֶׁה, שַׁפִּיר קָאָמַרְתָּ', וּכְתִיב (בְּרֵאשִׁית מ"ט): "עַד כִּי יָבֹא שִׁילֹה" – 'דָּא מֹשֶׁה'. וּמָשִׁיחַ הוּא כָּלוּל כָּל הַתְּפִלּוֹת, וּבִשְׁבִיל זֶה יִהְיֶה מָשִׁיחַ 'מוֹרַח וְדָאִין' (כְּמוֹ שֶׁאָמְרוּ רַבּוֹתֵינוּ, זִכְרוֹנָם לִבְרָכָה סַנְהֶדְרִין צג:), כִּי הַתְּפִלּוֹת הֵם בְּחִינַת חֹטֶם, כְּמוֹ שֶׁכָּתוּב (יְשַׁעְיָהוּ מ"ח): "וּתְהִלָּתִי אֶחֱטָם לָךְ."

---

51. **Moshe, you said it well.** This is how the leading Sages of the Talmud would compliment one another. They would refer to each other as Moshe, the implication being "You are to your generation what Moshe was to his" (*Rashi, loc. cit.*).

52. **Shiloh...Moshe....** Quoting Onkelos, Rashi comments that Shiloh refers to Mashiach. ShILoH (שילה) and MoShE (משה) both have a numerical value of 345 (see Appendix: Gematria Chart). After beginning the lesson by discussing the significance of an individual's prayer, Rebbe Nachman now turns to another dimension: prayer in its totality—the prayers of the entire Jewish people. All Jews must pray. And yet, as individuals, their prayers can only accomplish just so much. However, by attaching the prayer to the tzaddik, the one who encompasses all the paths of prayer, one's own words can ascend through the correct gate and reach its proper place together with all the prayers of the Jewish people. This is symbolized in the Torah's account of the erection of the holy Tabernacle. Everyone brought their own donation and contributed their share of the work, but it was only Moshe, the tzaddik of the generation, who was capable of assembling the Tabernacle properly (see *Likutey Moharan* I, 2:6). This will also be true of the Mashiach, hence Moshe is referred to as Mashiach.

53. **Mashiach...all the prayers.** The name *MaShIaCh* resembles the word *MaSIaCh*, which means speech and prayer. Indeed, "the basic weapon of the Mashiach is prayer" (see *Likutey Moharan* I, 2, where this and its connection to the power of smell/the nose are explained in greater detail).

54. **power of smell.** "[The Mashiach] shall breathe of the fear of God; he will not judge by sight nor by what he hears" (Isaiah 11:3). The Talmud (*loc. cit.*) explains that Mashiach will be given the power to judge just by his sense of smell.

55. **nose...anger from you.** *Echtom* literally means "I will plug My nose" so as to prevent the smoke of anger from escaping (see *Rashi, loc. cit.*). Just as a person's lifeline is his nose— without breathing he cannot live—so too, one's spiritual lifeline is prayer. Mashiach's strength will be prayer, symbolized by the nose. Thus, our long awaited redemption, which Rebbe Nachman refers to at the end of the lesson, is contingent upon our prayers and their being bound to the tzaddikim.

LIKUTEY MOHARAN #9:3,4

28:9), "When a person turns his ear from hearing Torah, his prayer is also an abomination."}

4. And every person must bind his prayers to the <tzaddikim> of the generation.[49] <For the> tzaddik knows how to match the gates [to the prayers] and raise each and every prayer to its appropriate gate.[50] For each and every tzaddik is an aspect of Moshe-Mashiach. As <the Sages would say>, "Moshe, you said it well" (*Shabbat* 101b).[51] And it is written (Genesis 49:10), "Until Shiloh [i.e., Mashiach] comes"— this is Moshe (*Zohar* I, 25b). <They have the same numerical value.>[52]

And Mashiach <is comprised of> all the prayers.[53] This is why [the Sages said that] the Mashiach will judge through the power of smell (*Sanhedrin* 93b).[54] For <prayer> corresponds to the *ChoTeM* (nose), as in (Isaiah 48:9), "For My praise [i.e., prayer], *eChToM* (I will restrain My anger) for you."[55]

---

properly nor provide sustenance. However, this does not apply to one who is unlearned but who, nevertheless, tries to understand Torah as best he can. Such a person is attempting to seek the truth, and he will find it at his own level.

In review: A person should pray with total energy and concentration. By doing so, his energy is renewed in the letters of prayer, which are the source of all life-force (§1). Each of the 12 tribes of the Jewish people has a different version of prayer and a corresponding gate through which its prayer passes. These 12 paths also correspond to the 12 constellations, by means of which livelihood is channeled to each particular tribe. Thus through prayer an influx of life-force is provided for all parts of the universe (§2). But the *kelipot* (husks) envelop a person in darkness and prevent him from praying. The only way out is through truth/Torah. God then shines His light to show him the way out of the darkness and falsehood (This is the inner meaning of God's instructions to Noach concerning the construction of the ark.) (§3).

49. **tzaddikim of the generation.** In any area requiring special knowledge, the wise thing to do is to go to an expert. When a person has to appear in court to seek justice, he looks for a lawyer who is familiar with law and court procedure to help him win his case. So, too, in coming before God in prayer. We need to bind our prayer to the tzaddik, so that he will present our case Above. We do this in a general sense by studying the tzaddik's teachings on prayer and following his guidance when we pray. At Rebbe Nachman's behest, before each prayer the Breslover Chassidim make a special request to bind their prayer to the tzaddikim: "I bind myself in my prayer to all the tzaddikim of this generation" (cf. *Rabbi Nachman's Wisdom* #296).

50. **appropriate gate.** See above, note 24, that Yaakov was the root of the twelve tribes. In this sense, he is synonymous with the tzaddik/prayer-source of the generation. Reb Noson thus explains (*Likutey Halakhot, ibid.*) that the prayers of the Jewish people as a whole are likened to a "window," in comparison to the tzaddik's prayers which are considered to be a "precious jewel." The true tzaddik has the power to radiate the truth into everyone and thereby raise every prayer to its appropriate gate.

LIKUTEY MOHARAN #9:4 — 100

וְזֶה פֵּרוּשׁ: אָמַר רַבָּה בַּר בַּר־
חָנָא: זִמְנָא חֲדָא הֲוֵי קָאָזְלִינַן
בְּמַדְבְּרָא, וְאִתְלַוֵּי בַּהֲדָן הַהוּא
טַיָּעָא, דַּהֲוָה שָׁקִיל עַפְרָא וּמוֹרַח
לֵהּ. וְאָמַר: הָא אָרְחָא לְדוּכְתָּא פְּלָן וְהָא אָרְחָא לְדוּכְתָּא פְּלָן.
אָמְרִינַן לֵהּ: כַּמָּה מְרַחֲקִינַן מִמַּיָּא? וְאָמַר לָן: הָבוּ לִי עַפְרָא.
יָהֲבִינַן לֵהּ. אָמַר לָן: תְּמַנְיָא פַּרְסֵי. תָּנֵינַן וְיָהֲבִינַן לֵהּ, אָמַר לָן:
דִּמְרַחֲקִינַן תְּלָתָא פַּרְסֵי. אֲפֵכִית לֵהּ וְלָא יָכֵלִית לֵהּ.

זִמְנָא חֲדָא אִתְלַוִּין בַּהֲדָן הַהוּא טַיָּעָא, סוֹחֵר יִשְׁמָעֵאל – זֶה
בְּחִינַת צַדִּיק הַדּוֹר, שֶׁהוּא כָּלוּל כָּל הַתְּפִלּוֹת כְּמָשִׁיחַ. וּתְפִלּוֹת זֶה
בְּחִינַת סוֹחֵר יִשְׁמָעֵאל, כְּמוֹ שֶׁכָּתוּב (בְּרֵאשִׁית ט"ז): "כִּי שָׁמַע ה'
אֶל עָנְיֵךְ", וְתַרְגּוּמוֹ: 'קַבִּיל ה' צְלוֹתַיִךְ'. וְזֶה סוֹחֵר, כִּי סָבִיב –
תַּרְגּוּמוֹ סְחוֹר. וְזֶה בְּחִינַת אֱמוּנָה, כְּמוֹ שֶׁכָּתוּב (תְּהִלִּים פ"ט):
"וֶאֱמוּנָתְךָ סְבִיבוֹתֶיךָ".

וְאִתְלַוִּין בַּהֲדָן הַהוּא טַיָּעָא, – שֶׁקְּשַׁרְנוּ אֶת עַצְמֵנוּ עִם צַדִּיק
הַדּוֹר, שֶׁהוּא בְּחִינַת מָשִׁיחַ, כְּלָלִיּוּת הַתְּפִלָּה.

וְשָׁקִיל עַפְרָא וּמוֹרַח וְאָמַר: הָא לְדוּכְתָּא פְּלָן וְהָא לְדוּכְתָּא פְּלָן.
עַפְרָא – זֶה בְּחִינַת תְּפִלָּה, כְּמוֹ שֶׁכָּתוּב (יְשַׁעְיָהוּ מ"א): "יִתֵּן כֶּעָפָר
חַרְבּוֹ", וְחֶרֶב זֶה בְּחִינַת תְּפִלָּה, כְּמוֹ שֶׁכָּתוּב: "בְּחַרְבִּי וּבְקַשְׁתִּי".
וּמוֹרַח – כִּי יֵשׁ לוֹ כֹּחַ הַזֶּה לְהָרִיחַ, עַל־יְדֵי שֶׁהוּא כָּלוּל כָּל
הַתְּפִלּוֹת, וּכְתִיב: "וּתְהִלָּתִי אֶחֱטָם לָךְ".

וְאָמַר: הָא לְדוּכְתָּא פְּלָן – שֶׁהָיָה יוֹדֵעַ שַׁעֲרֵי תְּפִלּוֹת, וְהָיָה יוֹדֵעַ
כָּל תְּפִלָּה הַשַּׁיָּךְ לְשִׁבְטוֹ.

(margin, top right)

רַשְׁבַּ"ם:
טַיָּעָא – סוֹחֵר יִשְׁמָעֵאל: וְהִפְכִּינַן
– הַאי עַפְרָא בְּהַאי עַפְרָא, לִנְסוֹתוֹ
אִם יִהְיֶה בָּקִי כָּל כָּךְ.

---

strong he realizes that God is everywhere and with him at all times, then he is no longer
affected by the "opposing forces" which surround him on every side.

57. **sword...as earth....** The Midrash explains this verse in connection to Avraham, when

LIKUTEY MOHARAN #9:4

This is the explanation:

Rabbah bar bar Chanah recounted: Once, we were travelling in the wilderness accompanied by a merchant. He would pick up earth, smell it and say, "This is the way to such-and-such

Rashbam:

merchant - an Ishmaelite *socher* (trader): **switched them around** - the samples of earth one with the other, to see if he really was an expert:

a place, and that is the way to some other place." We asked him, "How far are we from water?" He said to us, "Bring me some earth." We brought it and he said, "Eight miles." [Later] *taneinon* **(we again) brought him some. He said that we were three miles away. I switched them around, but still could not get the better of him** (*Bava Batra* 73b).

Once, we were travelling...accompanied by a merchant — This "Ishmaelite *socher*" (trader) corresponds to the tzaddik of the generation. He encompasses all the prayers, like Mashiach. And prayer corresponds to an *iShMAelite* trader, as is written (Genesis 16:11), "[You shall call his name Ishmael,] for God *SheMA* (has heard) your affliction." Onkelos renders this: "God has accepted your prayers." And this is the reason [he is called a] *SoCheR: SaChoR* is Aramaic for "surround," which corresponds to faith <to prayer>, as in (Psalms 89:9), "Your faith surrounds You."[56]

We were accompanied by a merchant — We bound ourselves to the tzaddik of the generation, for he is the aspect of Mashiach, the embodiment of prayer.

He would pick up earth, smell it and say, This is the way to such-and-such a place, and that is the way to some other place — "Earth" corresponds to prayer, as is written (Isaiah 41:2), "His sword will make them as earth." The sword is prayer, as in, "...my sword and my bow."[57] He would smell [the earth], for [the tzaddik] has this power of smell because he encompasses all the prayers. And it is written, "For My praise [i.e., prayer] *eChToM* for you," [and *ChoTeM* is the nose].

and say, This is the way to such-and-such a place — He knew the gates of the prayers, and he knew to which tribe each prayer related.

---

56. **surrounds You.** Faith resembles a circle. A circle is a continuous line without protrusions. It has no edge which one can take hold of. So, too, faith applies only where one cannot understand—there is no way to take hold of it with logic (*Parparaot LeChokhmah*). This "merchant" or trader is the tzaddik whose prayer is complete because his faith is perfect (cf. *Likutey Moharan* I, 7:end and n.76). When a person is encircled by faith, when his faith is so

LIKUTEY MOHARAN #9:4

וְאָמְרִינַן לֵהּ: כַּמָּה מְרַחֲקִינַן מִמַּיָּא? וְאָמַר לָן: הָבוּ לִי עַפְרָא.

יְהַבִינַן לֵהּ. אָמַר לָן: תְּמַנְיָא פַּרְסֵי. תָּנֵינַן וְיָהַבִינַן לֵהּ, אָמַר לָן:

תְּלָתָא פַּרְסֵי. אֲפֵכִית וְלֹא יָכְלִית לֵהּ. – הַיְנוּ,

אָמְרִינַן לֵהּ: כַּמָּה אֲנַן מְרַחֲקִינַן מִמַּיָּא – מִבְּחִינַת (אֵיכָה ב): "שִׁפְכִי

לְבֵּךְ כַּמַּיִם נֹכַח פְּנֵי ה'".

אָמַר לָן, תְּמַנְיָא בְּחִינוּת – הַיְנוּ לִמּוּד הַתּוֹרָה, שֶׁהוּא חֲמִשָּׁה חֻמְשֵׁי

תּוֹרָה, וְשָׁלשׁ תְּפִלּוֹת.

תָּנֵינַן וְיָהַבִינַן לֵהּ – תָּנֵינַן, לְשׁוֹן לִמּוּד, וְאַחַר הַלִּמּוּד, יָהַבִינַן לֵהּ

לְהָרִיחַ, כַּמָּה מְרַחֲקִינַן מִזּאת הַבְּחִינָה שֶׁל מַיִם.

וְאָמַר לָן, תְּלָתָא פַּרְסֵי – הַיְנוּ שְׁלשָׁה בְּחִינוּת תְּפִלּוֹת. וְהֶרְאָה לָנוּ

סִימָן עַל זֶה, שֶׁעֲדַיִן לֹא הִגַּעְנוּ לְמַדְרֵגָה זֹאת שֶׁנִּתְפַּלֵּל כָּל כָּךְ

בְּכַוָּנָה עַד שֶׁנִּשְׁפֹּךְ לִבֵּנוּ לְפָנָיו כַּמַּיִם. וְהָא רְאָיָה:

אֲפֵכִית – כְּמוֹ שֶׁכָּתוּב (תְּהִלִּים פ"ט): "אַף תָּשִׁיב צוּר חַרְבּוֹ וְלֹא

הֲקֵמוֹתוֹ בַּמִּלְחָמָה", כִּי כָּל הַתְּפִלּוֹת הֵם בְּחִינַת חֶרֶב אֵצֶל מָשִׁיחַ;

וְאִם הָיוּ הַתְּפִלּוֹת בַּבְּחִינָה הַנַּ"ל, בְּוַדַּאי לֹא הָיָה מֵשִׁיב צוּר חַרְבּוֹ,

---

60. **three daily prayers.** These are: *Shacharit* (morning), *Minchah* (afternoon), and *Maariv* (night). Thus, the eight miles allude to these three prayers together with the Five Books of the Torah.

61. **Taneinon denotes study.** In Aramaic, the word *tanna* means to "review" or "repeat." It thus connotes study.

62. **three prayers.** Simply, this refers to the three daily prayers. They can also be understood as follows: 1) *Shacharit* can be compared to a time when everything *shines* brightly, like the morning, when a person can clearly focus his prayers on all his needs and wants. This is the level of the "precious jewel." 2) *Minchah* can be compared to an *in-between* time, the afternoon, when a person finds himself surrounded with problems and distractions, yet to some degree can still focus his prayers on his needs and wants. This is the level of the "window." 3) *Maariv* can be compared to a time when everything is *dark,* like the night, when a person feels himself and his prayers inundated by "forces" and difficulties which he finds insurmountable. In all three cases, one must bring himself to pray with all his energy and with whatever degree of concentration he can muster. This will bring life into each of these levels. Thus, Rabbah bar bar Chanah asked the merchant, "How far are we from prayer?" And he was told, "Three miles"—three levels!

103   *LIKUTEY MOHARAN #9:4*

We asked him, How far are we from water? — Namely, [how far are we] from (Lamentations 2:19), "Pour out your heart like water before God."[58]

he said, Eight [aspects] — This alludes to Torah study [and prayer]: the Five Books of the Torah[59] and the three daily prayers.[60]

Taneinon (we again) brought him some — "*Taneinon*" denotes study.[61] Thus, after studying Torah we again brought him earth to smell [so that he would tell us] how far we were from this aspect of "water," [i.e., from the level where the prayer pours forth like water].

He said, Three miles — Namely, the three < prayers > .[62] Then he proved to us that we had not yet reached the level where we prayed with such concentration that we poured out our hearts before Him like water. The proof was:

I switched them around — As is written (Psalms 89:44), "But, You have turned back the edge of his sword, and You have not let him stand in battle." For all the prayers are a sword for Mashiach, and if the prayers had been as described above, [i.e., offered with true devotion,] God would certainly not have "turned back the edge of his sword."

---

he chased after the four kings in order to save his nephew Lot (Genesis 14). When he picked up earth and threw it at his enemies, the earth turned into swords and arrows (*Bereishit Rabbah* 43:3). Because Avraham's prayer was pure, he was able utilize this earth, which alludes to prayer, to save Lot. It will be from Lot's descendants (through Moab, Ruth and King David) that Mashiach, the source of prayer, will descend (*Mai HaNachal*). The understanding of sword and bow as prayer has been explained above (end of §2 and n.28).

58. **pour out your heart....** This refers to heartfelt prayer with total concentration. A person's needs are many, so that even while standing in prayer one tends to forget any number of the things he may have very much wanted to ask for. However, when a person attains truth, he finds that he can open himself up to God's light—God who is *Ein Sof* (the Infinite One)—so that his words flow freely and he merits praying from his heart for all his spiritual and physical needs, without exception.

59. **Five Books of the Torah.** We've already seen that in order to pray properly, a person must attach himself to the absolute truth, the Torah. This requires his engaging in study for the sake of truth and in a truthful manner. Further, one must also bind himself to the truth at other times, even when not involved in Torah study or prayer. This includes daily relationships with people, in business, etc. He must take great care to let nothing false pass through his lips, even accidentally or unwittingly. By being bound to truth throughout his day, a person draws upon himself God's infinite light. This, in turn, arouses God's compassion so that all his prayers and requests are answered from Above.

LIKUTEY MOHARAN #9:4,5 104

וְזֶה סִימָן שֶׁעֲדַיִן לֹא הִגַּעְנוּ לְמַדְרֵגַת "שִׁפְכִי כַמַּיִם לִבֵּךְ נֹכַח פְּנֵי ה'".

ה. וּתְפִלָּה הוּא בְּחִינַת נִסִּים, שֶׁהוּא אֵין דֶּרֶךְ הַטֶּבַע; כִּי לִפְעָמִים הַטֶּבַע מְחַיֵּב אֵיזוֹ דָבָר, וְהַתְּפִלָּה מְהַפֶּכֶת אֶת הַטֶּבַע. וְעִקַּר הַנִּסִּים, הַיְנוּ עִקַּר הַתְּפִלָּה, אֵינוֹ אֶלָּא בְּאֶרֶץ־יִשְׂרָאֵל, כְּמוֹ שֶׁכָּתוּב (תְּהִלִּים ל"ז): "שְׁכָן אֶרֶץ וּרְעֵה אֱמוּנָה", וֶאֱמוּנָה זֶה תְּפִלָּה, כְּמוֹ שֶׁכָּתוּב (שְׁמוֹת י"ז): "וַיְהִי יָדָיו אֱמוּנָה" כְּתַרְגּוּמוֹ.

וּבִשְׁבִיל זֶה הִיא גָּבוֹהַּ מִכָּל הָאֲרָצוֹת (זְבָחִים נד:), עַל שֵׁם שֶׁעִקַּר הַנִּסִּים שָׁם הֵם, וּכְתִיב (יְשַׁעְיָהוּ ס"ב): "הָרִימוּ נֵס". וּבִשְׁבִיל זֶה נִקְרֵאת אֶרֶץ כְּנַעַן; כְּנַעַן – לְשׁוֹן סוֹחֵר, בְּחִינַת אֱמוּנָה, כְּמוֹ שֶׁכָּתוּב: "וֶאֱמוּנָתְךָ סְבִיבוֹתֶיךָ".

וְזֶה שֶׁאָמְרוּ חֲכָמֵינוּ, זִכְרוֹנָם לִבְרָכָה (תַּעֲנִית י.): אֶרֶץ־יִשְׂרָאֵל שׁוֹתָה תְּחִלָּה. וְהַגְּשָׁמִים בָּאִים מִתְּהוֹמוֹת, כְּמוֹ שֶׁכָּתוּב (תְּהִלִּים מ"ב): "תְּהוֹם אֶל תְּהוֹם קוֹרֵא"; וּתְהוֹם לְשׁוֹן נֵס, כְּמוֹ שֶׁכָּתוּב (רוּת

between faith, prayer, miracles, and the Land of Israel (which Rebbe Nachman addresses next) has been more fully explained in Lesson #7, section 1 and notes.

66. **higher than all other lands.** "As God lives, who *brought up* the Children of Israel from...all the lands...back to their Land" (Jeremiah 16:15). From here we understand that the Land of Israel is higher than all other lands (*Zevachim, loc. cit., Rashi, s.v. v'eretz Yisrael*).

67. **Lift up a sign.** The Hebrew word *neis* can be translated as sign, banner or miracle, and indicates raising up. Because the Land of Israel is the land of miracles, it is elevated. This also implies that one must raise up the miracles—that is, bring them into the open and not have them covered up and explained away as natural occurrences.

68. **surrounds you.** Kanaan, besides being the earlier name of the Land of Israel, also translates as *socher* (a trader) (cf. Hosea 12:8, *Rashi, s.v. Kanaan b'yado*). Above we've seen that "trader" corresponds to both prayer and faith, the inherent qualities of the Land of Israel (see n.56).

69. **drinks first.** As it is written (Job 5:10), "Who gives rain upon the Land [of Israel], and sends water upon the *chutzot* (outside lands)" (*Taanit, loc.cit.*).

70. **t'home, deep.** This refers to the "upper waters" from which the Land of Israel receives its rain (*Taanit* 10a). (See also *Likutey Moharan* I, 7, n.17.)

105 LIKUTEY MOHARAN #9:4,5

This was the sign that we had not yet reached the level of "Pour out your heart like water before God."[63]

5. Now, prayer corresponds to miracles, for it [too] <is supernatural>.[64] Sometimes, the natural order necessitates one thing, whereas prayer overrides nature's course. And the quintessence of miracles—i.e., the quintessence of prayer—is only in the Land of Israel, as in (Psalms 37:3), "Dwell in the Land and cultivate faith." And faith is prayer, as is written, "And his hands were *emunah* (faith)," which Onkelos renders: ["his hands were spread out in prayer."][65]

This is the reason why [the Land of Israel] is higher than all other lands (*Zevachim* 54b)[66]—because the quintessence of *NiSim* (miracles) occurs there. And it is written (Isaiah 62:10), "Lift up [high] a *NeiS* (sign)."[67] This also explains why [the Land of Israel] is called the Land of Kanaan. *Kanaan* connotes a *socher* (trader), which corresponds to faith, as in, "Your faith surrounds You."[68]

Thus, our Sages taught: The Land of Israel drinks first (*Taanit* 10a).[69] [This refers to] the rains, which come from the *t'home* (deep),[70] as is written (Psalms 42:8), "Deep calls to deep." *T'HoMe* connotes the miraculous [and amazing], as in (Ruth 1:19), "and the entire city

---

63. **had not yet reached....** Because we are in exile, our prayers are "turned back"—not yet capable of reaching their proper place (*Mai HaNachal*).

In review: A person should pray with total energy and concentration. By doing so, his energy is renewed in the letters of prayer, which are the source of all life-force (§1). Each of the 12 tribes of the Jewish people has a different version of prayer and a corresponding gate through which its prayer passes. These 12 paths also correspond to the 12 constellations, by means of which livelihood is channeled to each particular tribe. Thus through prayer an influx of life-force is provided for all parts of the universe (§2). But the *kelipot* (husks) envelop a person in darkness and prevent him from praying. The only way out is through truth/Torah. God then shines His light to show him the way out of the darkness and falsehood (This is the inner meaning of God's instructions to Noach concerning the construction of the ark.) (§3). Every person must bind his prayers to the tzaddik of the generation. The tzaddik—who is Moshe-Mashiach—elevates the prayer to its appropriate gate (§4).

64. **supernatural.** With prayer, a person has control over the world of the angels and that which is below it—i.e., nature. This has already been explained at length, see notes 9 and 10.

65. **emunah...in prayer.** The verse from Psalms begins, "Trust in God...." It is this trust and faith in God which will cause you to "dwell in the Land [of Israel]." And faith, as Rebbe Nachman tells us, corresponds to prayer (see n.5 above). The interrelationship that exists

LIKUTEY MOHARAN #9:5

א): "וַתֵּהֹם כָּל הָעִיר", כִּי עַל נֵס, הַיְנוּ עַל דָּבָר חִדּוּשׁ, מַתְמִיהִין. וְזֶה שֶׁאָמְרוּ חֲכָמֵינוּ, זִכְרוֹנָם לִבְרָכָה (תַּעֲנִית כה:): 'קוֹל הַתּוֹר נִשְׁמַע בְּאַרְצֵנוּ' לְעִנְיַן גְּשָׁמִים, כִּי עִקַּר הַגְּשָׁמִים נִשְׁמָע בְּאֶרֶץ־יִשְׂרָאֵל, כִּי שָׁם הַתְּהוֹמוֹת, הַיְנוּ הַנִּסִּים, הַיְנוּ אֱמוּנָה, תְּפִלָּה.

וְזֶה לְעֻמַּת זֶה עָשָׂה אֱלֹקִים – וּמִצְרַיִם הוּא הֵפֶךְ אֶרֶץ־יִשְׂרָאֵל, זֶה לְעֻמַּת זֶה, כְּמוֹ שֶׁכָּתוּב (שְׁמוֹת י"ד): "וּמִצְרַיִם נָסִים לִקְרָאתוֹ", שֶׁמִּצְרַיִם לְעֻמַּת אֶרֶץ־יִשְׂרָאֵל, לְעֻמַּת הַנִּסִּים. וּבִשְׁבִיל זֶה אֵין מָקוֹם תְּפִלָּה בְּמִצְרַיִם, כְּמוֹ שֶׁכָּתוּב (שָׁם ט): "וְהָיָה כְּצֵאתִי אֶת הָעִיר אֶפְרֹשׂ כַּפָּי".

בִּשְׁבִיל זֶה, כְּשֶׁפָּגַם אַבְרָהָם בְּאֶרֶץ־יִשְׂרָאֵל, בְּשָׁעָה שֶׁהִבְטִיחַ לוֹ הַקָּדוֹשׁ־בָּרוּךְ־הוּא עַל יְרֵשַׁת אָרֶץ אָמַר (בְּרֵאשִׁית ט"ו): "בַּמָּה אֵדַע" – עַל־יְדֵי־זֶה יָרְדוּ אֲבוֹתֵינוּ לְמִצְרַיִם, כִּי פָּגַם בֶּאֱמוּנָה, הַיְנוּ אֶרֶץ־יִשְׂרָאֵל, בְּחִינַת נִסִּים, וְיָרַד יַעֲקֹב וּבָנָיו לְמִצְרַיִם, שֶׁשָּׁם הֵפֶךְ הַנִּסִּים, שֶׁזֶּה לְעֻמַּת זֶה.

no black magic like the black magic of Egypt" (*Avot d'Rabbi Natan*, ch. 28).

75. **my hands in prayer.** Moshe said, "When I go outside the city . . . ." As long as he remained inside the Egyptian metropolis, Moshe could not pray. Rashi explains that Egypt was filled with idolatry and hence unsuitable for prayer. Again we see the connection between faith, prayer, miracles and the Land of Israel. This is in contrast with other lands, especially Egypt. Actually, as Rebbe Nachman explains, prayer itself was in exile in Egypt. The Jews were unable to open their mouths to talk to God (*Rabbi Nachman's Wisdom #68*).

76. **down to Egypt.** Prior to this, God had told Avraham that he would be blessed with children "as many as the stars of the heavens" (Genesis 15:5,6). And Avraham believed. However, when he was informed that he would inherit the Land, he questioned God. This was considered a shortcoming in his faith. God then said (Genesis 15:13), "Know for sure that for 400 years your descendants will be foreigners in a land that is not theirs."

77. **antithesis of the Land of Israel.** The reason why rain does not normally fall in the Land of Egypt (*Rashi*, Deuteronomy 11:10) is because it is the antithesis of Land of Israel, the place of miracles (*Parparaot LeChokhmah*). In addition, Scripture warns, "Lest you forget God and worship idols; rain will not fall . . . you will be lost from the Land" (Deuteronomy 11:16-17). When a person strays from God, it is considered a form of idolatry. The result is that the heavens withhold their rain—miracles/the Land of Israel etc.—and the punishment is exile.

TeiHoMe (was amazed)." This is because over a miracle, something new and original, people are amazed.[71]

This is also why the Sages said that "the voice of the dove is heard in our land" (Song of Songs 2:12) refers to the rains (cf. *Taanit* 25b). For in the Land of Israel—the place of the deeps/miracles/faith/prayer—the quintessence of rains "is heard."[72]

And, "God made one to contrast the other" (Ecclesiastes 7:14). The Land of Egypt is thus the antithesis of the Land of Israel, "one to contrast the other," as in (Exodus 14:27), "And the Egyptians *NaSim* (were fleeing) against it."[73] Egypt is the converse of the Land of Israel, the converse of *NiSim* (miracles).[74] This is why prayer has no place in Egypt, as in, "When I go outside the city I will spread out my hands [in prayer]" (Exodus 9:29).[75]

This is why when Avraham blemished the Land of Israel—when God promised him the inheritance of the land and Avraham asked (Genesis 15:8), "How shall I know?"—it became necessary for our ancestors to go down to Egypt.[76] It was [Avraham's] blemishing of faith, of the Land of Israel, the aspect of miracles, which resulted in Yaakov and his sons descending to Egypt, < the antithesis of the Land of Israel > .[77]

[margin: know up / opposite / or / enural / ↓]

[bottom: Eretz Yisrael is enural —above the natural considerations of parnassah etc]

---

71. **people are amazed.** Everyone was amazed when Naomi returned with Ruth to the Land of Israel, the land of miracles (*Mai HaNachal*; cf. *Likutey Moharan* I, 7, n.18).

72. **Land...rains is heard.** For the rains first come to the Land of Israel, the place of the "deep waters"/miracles/faith/prayer. Just as the voice of the dove is heard in the Land, so too, the quintessence of rains is heard there. With this, Rebbe Nachman has shown that rainfall is itself a miracle, to be prayed for and not to be seen as part of nature's course.

73. **fleeing against it.** Fleeing implies putting a distance between oneself and another. Here, however, the Egyptians *nasim* (were fleeing) against, i.e., towards, the water. As Rashi (*loc. cit.*) explains, this was because of the great confusion which came upon the Egyptian army. This in itself was a miracle. And, as mentioned earlier, Israel is the land of *nisim* (miracles). It is the place of holiness, the site of the Holy Temple, and is synonymous with faith. Egypt, on the other hand, represents everything contrary to holiness. It is the place of impurity and idolatry. It was with the intent to break these false beliefs that God performed the miracles of the Ten Plagues and the Red Sea. For Egypt is the very antithesis of the land of miracles (*Mai HaNachal*).

74. **converse of miracles.** Whereas the Land of Israel is the source of faith and miracles, Egypt symbolizes everything which denies miracles and faith in God (cf. *Sanhedrin* 67b). It is the place where the forces of nature, particularly in the guise of magic, reign supreme. "There is

LIKUTEY MOHARAN #9:5

וְיָרְדוּ דַּוְקָא יַעֲקֹב וּבָנָיו, כִּי הוּא פָּגַם בְּאֶרֶץ־יִשְׂרָאֵל, בְּחִינַת תְּפִלָּה, וְיָרְדוּ יַעֲקֹב וּבָנָיו, שֶׁהֵם בְּחִינַת תְּפִלָּה, שֶׁהֵם בְּחִינַת שְׁנֵים־עָשָׂר שַׁעֲרֵי תְפִלָּה.

וְעַל־יְדֵי שֶׁעִקַּר הַתְּפִלָּה הֵם יַעֲקֹב וּבָנָיו כַּנַּ"ל, עַל־יְדֵי־זֶה לֹא זָכָה לְאֶרֶץ־יִשְׂרָאֵל, לִבְחִינַת תְּפִלָּה, אֶלָּא יַעֲקֹב וּבָנָיו, כְּמוֹ שֶׁכָּתוּב (בְּרֵאשִׁית כ"א): "כִּי בְיִצְחָק יִקָּרֵא לְךָ זָרַע", וְלֹא כָל יִצְחָק (נְדָרִים לא.).

וְזֶה שֶׁאָמְרוּ חֲכָמֵינוּ, זִכְרוֹנָם לִבְרָכָה (תַּעֲנִית ח.): 'אֵין הַגְּשָׁמִים יוֹרְדִין אֶלָּא בִּשְׁבִיל אֲמָנָה', הַיְנוּ בְּחִינַת אֶרֶץ־יִשְׂרָאֵל, שֶׁהוּא בְּחִינַת תְּפִלָּה, בְּחִינַת אֱמוּנָה; וְהִיא שׁוֹתָה תְחִלָּה, שֶׁשָּׁם הַתְּהוֹמוֹת בְּחִינַת נִסִּים, כְּמוֹ שֶׁכָּתוּב: "וַתֵּהֹם כָּל הָעִיר".

וְזֶה שֶׁאָמְרוּ חֲכָמֵינוּ, זִכְרוֹנָם לִבְרָכָה (שָׁם ח:): 'בְּשָׁעָה שֶׁהַגְּשָׁמִים יוֹרְדִין, אֲפִלּוּ פְּרוּטָה שֶׁבַּכִּיס מִתְבָּרֶכֶת'; 'פְּרוּטָה' – זֶה בְּחִינַת קוֹל הַתּוֹר. וְאָמְרוּ חֲכָמֵינוּ, זִכְרוֹנָם לִבְרָכָה: 'הַאי רוֹדְיָא דָּמְיָא לְתוֹר, וּפְרִיטָא שִׂפְוָתֵהּ', וְהוּא עוֹמֵד בֵּין תְּהוֹמָא לִתְהוֹמָא, שֶׁהוּא כָּלוּל מִשְּׁנֵי הַתְּהוֹמוֹת, שֶׁהוּא כְּלָלִיּוּת הַנִּסִּים.

וְזֶה: 'פְּרוּטָה שֶׁבַּכִּיס', שֶׁפְּעָמִים נִתְכַּסֶּה כֹּחַ הַנִּסִּים; וְעַל־יְדֵי הַגְּשָׁמִים נִתְבָּרֵךְ הַפְּרוּטָה, הַיְנוּ הַנִּסִּים, 'דִּפְרִיטָא שִׂפְוָתֵהּ'.

explanation for the spelling of *emunah* as *æmunah* appears in *Likutey Moharan* I,7 note 2; cf. n.43 above.)

81. **an ox.** The Maharsha explains that Taurus, the ox, is the constellation for Iyar, the month when the rains stop falling in the Land of Israel. This is the reason why the angel in charge of distributing rainfall appears as an ox. We've already seen (above, §2) that even a blade of grass has its own star and angel in charge of it. Moreover, the angel above the constellation will have the appearance of the constellation it controls. In this case, it is the ox.

Although the exact language of the Talmud reads that the Angel of Rain resembled an *egla*, all the commentaries equate this with the *tor*, the Aramaic term for ox. Comparing this with *Likutey Moharan* 7:1 (where this entire passage has also been quoted), we see that when Rebbe Nachman wanted to make a connection to *eegulim* (circles) he chose *egla* and when he wanted to relate to the Hebrew word for a dove, *tor*, he favored the Aramaic for ox, *tor*.

82. **lips were open.** Corresponding to faith/miracles/the Land of Israel and particularly prayer, as in, "Lord, open my lips"—the introductory words of the *Amidah* prayer. With the lips open, with the *prutah* blessed, miracles are uncovered for all to see.

LIKUTEY MOHARAN #9:5

And, it was specifically Yaakov and his sons who went down. [Avraham] blemished the Land of Israel/prayer, and Yaakov and his [twelve] sons—who correspond to prayer and its twelve gates—descended.

Moreover, because the quintessence of prayer is [embodied in] Yaakov and his sons,[78] no one merited the Land of Israel and prayer other than Yaakov and his sons. As it is written (Genesis 21:12), [Avraham was told that] "in Yitzchak shall your seed be called"—[in Yitzchak,] but not all of Yitzchak (Nedarim 31b).[79]

{The rains only fall on account of *baaley amanah* (men of faith) (Taanit 8a).}

This is the explanation of what our Sages taught: The rains only fall on account of *amanah*. ["*AMaNaH*"] corresponds to the Land of Israel, which corresponds to prayer and *ÆMuNaH* (faith).[80] And [the Land of Israel] "drinks first" because that is where the *T'HoMot/* miracles are, as in, "and the entire city *TeiHoMe*."

{I saw the Angel of Rain. It had the appearance of a *tor* (ox), and *prita sifevatei* (its lips were split open). It was standing between *t'home* (deep) and *t'home*" (Taanit 25b).}

This is the meaning of what our Sages taught: When the rains are falling, even a *prutah* (small coin) in the purse is blessed (Taanit 8b). The "*PRuTaH*" corresponds to "the voice of the *tor* (dove)" [which proclaims miracles], as the Sages also taught: [I saw] the Angel of Rain. It had the appearance of a *tor* (ox),[81] and its lips were *PRiTaH* (split open). It was standing between [the upper] deep and [the lower] deep—i.e., it comprised the two deeps, the embodiment of all miracles.

And this is: "a *prutah* in the *KiS* [is blessed]." Sometimes, the power of miracles is *nitKaSeh* (covered up). But with the [advent of the] rains, the *prutah,* the miracle, "is blessed"—for "its lips were open."[82]

---

78. **Yaakov and his sons.** As explained above in section 2 and note 7.

79. **not all of Yitzchak.** This excludes Esav. Though he was also Yitzchak's son, Esav was an idolator, the opposite of faith and prayer, and was therefore excluded from the Land of Israel.

80. **AMaNah...Land of Israel....ÆMuNaH.** As explained, rain is dependent upon *emunah*, the aspect of the Land of Israel from where all rains "begin." Egypt, on the other hand, is devoid of faith and is not the place of miracles, and so the rains do not fall there. The Midrash (*Yalkut, Ekev*) teaches: "The land of Egypt does not yield its produce without labor. But the Land of Israel, even if its people remain asleep in bed, receives rain from the Holy One and so produces." The implication is clear: the Land of Israel is blessed with Divine Providence (miracles), while the Land of Egypt follows the dictates of nature. (An

LIKUTEY MOHARAN #9:5,6 — 110

וְאֵלּוּ בְּנֵי־אָדָם הַמַּכְחִישִׁים כָּל הַנִּסִּים וְאוֹמְרִים שֶׁהַכֹּל דֶּרֶךְ הַטֶּבַע, וְאִם רוֹאִים אֵיזֶהוּ נֵס, הֵם מְכַסִּים אֶת הַנֵּס עִם דֶּרֶךְ הַטֶּבַע, שֶׁאוֹמְרִים שֶׁזֶּה דֶּרֶךְ הַטִּבְעִים – נִמְצָא שֶׁפּוֹגְמִים בַּתְּפִלָּה, כִּי הַתְּפִלָּה הִיא נִסִּים, שֶׁמְּשַׁנָּה אֶת הַטֶּבַע; וּפוֹגְמִים בָּאֱמוּנָה, שֶׁאֵין מַאֲמִינִים בְּהַשְׁגָּחַת הַבּוֹרֵא יִתְבָּרַךְ; וּפוֹגְמִים בְּאֶרֶץ־יִשְׂרָאֵל, שֶׁהוּא מְקוֹם הַנִּסִּים, כְּמוֹ שֶׁכָּתוּב: "וְקוֹל הַתּוֹר נִשְׁמַע בְּאַרְצֵנוּ", וּכְמוֹ שֶׁאָמְרוּ: 'אֶרֶץ־יִשְׂרָאֵל שׁוֹתָה תְּחִלָּה', כִּי שָׁם הַתְּהוֹמוֹת מְקוֹם הַנִּסִּים, כְּמוֹ שֶׁכָּתוּב: "וַתֵּהֹם כָּל הָעִיר".

וְעַל־יְדֵי־זֶה צָרִיךְ לִפֹּל בְּגָלוּת מִצְרַיִם, כִּי זֶה לְעֻמַּת זֶה עָשָׂה כַּנַּ״ל, וְכָל הַגָּלֻיּוֹת מְכֻנִּים בְּשֵׁם מִצְרַיִם, עַל שֵׁם שֶׁהֵם מְצֵרִים לְיִשְׂרָאֵל.

ו. וְזֶה פֵּרוּשׁ: תְּהֹמֹת יְכַסְיֻמוּ – מִי שֶׁמְּכַסֶּה אֶת הַנִּסִּים, וּמַרְאֶה לְכָל דָּבָר שֶׁהוּא דֶּרֶךְ הַטֶּבַע.

יָרְדוּ בִמְצוֹלֹת כְּמוֹ אָבֶן – (בְּרֵאשִׁית מ״ט) "מִשָּׁם רֹעֶה אֶבֶן יִשְׂרָאֵל" תַּרְגּוּמוֹ: 'אָב וּבְנָן'.

מְצוֹלֹת – זֶה בְּחִינַת מִצְרַיִם, שֶׁנֶּאֱמַר (שְׁמוֹת י״ב): "וַיְנַצְּלוּ אֶת מִצְרָיִם".

place in heaven, the exile, with all its anguish and suffering, continues. However, all is not lost. With this teaching Rebbe Nachman has shown us that by putting energy and enthusiasm into our prayers and by binding our words to the tzaddik, it is possible and within our grasp to bring the redemption (*Mai HaNachal*).

In review: A person should pray with total energy and concentration. His energy is then renewed in the letters of prayer, the source of all life-force (§1). Each of the 12 tribes has a different version of prayer and a corresponding gate through which its prayer passes. These 12 paths also correspond to the 12 constellations, by means of which livelihood is channeled to each particular tribe. Thus through prayer an influx of life-force is provided for all parts of the universe (§2). But the *kelipot* (husks) envelop a person in darkness and prevent him from praying. The only way out is through truth/Torah. God then shines His light to show him the way out of the darkness and falsehood (§3). Every person must bind his prayers to the tzaddik of the generation. The tzaddik—who is Moshe-Mashiach—elevates the prayer to its appropriate gate (§4). Prayer corresponds to miracles, an overriding of nature, the essence of which is in the Land of Israel. The antithesis of this is Egypt, exile, a place bereft of miracles and prayer (§5).

111 · LIKUTEY MOHARAN #9:5,6

There are people who deny all miracles and say that everything comes about naturally. Even if they witness a miracle, they cover it up with natural explanations, attributing it to the natural course of things. By doing so, they blemish prayer, because prayer corresponds to miracles, which alter nature. They also blemish faith, because they do not believe in Divine Providence. And they blemish the Land of Israel, the place of miracles, as in, "the voice of the dove is heard in our Land"—and [the Sages] taught: The Land of Israel drinks first. For the *T'HoMot* are there, [it being] the place of miracles, as in, "and the entire city *TeiHoMe*."

And as a result of this [blemish to the Land of Israel], < one falls into the depths of > the exile of "Egypt," because "God made one to contrast the other." < As the Midrash states: > All exiles are known as *MitZRayIM* (Egypt), because they *MetZeiRIM* (cause anguish and suffering) to the Jewish people *(Bereishit Rabbah 16:4).*[83]

6. This is the explanation [of the opening verse]:
{*"T'homot Y'chasyumu* (The deeps covered them); they sank into the *metzolot* (depths) like an *evan* (a stone)."*[84]}

The deeps covered them — This refers to people who cover up the miracles and try to show that everything follows a natural order.

they sank into the metzolot like an evan — "...from there the Shepherd, the *evan* (Rock) of Israel" (Genesis 49:24). Onkelos renders ["*ÆVaN*" as a compound word]: *AVhan u'VeNin* (father and sons).[85]

metZoLot — This alludes to Egypt, as is written (Exodus 12:36), "And they *natZLu* (despoiled) Egypt."

---

83. **All exiles....** This lesson began with an explanation of the power which prayer has to control the course of nature. Rebbe Nachman developed this theme, showing in particular how and why proper prayer can influence the "forces" governing one's livelihood and matters relating to marriage. Indeed, through prayer it is possible to successfully petition God to act on our behalf—to perform miracles for us personally—in all aspects of our lives. However, to achieve this our prayers must be pure, as Rebbe Nachman explained in sections 2-4. Here, he concludes the lesson by focusing on what happens when prayer is not as it should be. We see that because prayer, faith, miracles and the Land of Israel are closely interrelated, not praying properly is really an indication of a lack of faith, a denial of miracles, and a blemish in the Land of Israel. The result of all this is exile; both personal and for the Jewish people as a whole. As long as our prayers fail to ascend to their appropriate

LIKUTEY MOHARAN #9:6

112

כְּמוֹ 'אָב וּבָנָן' – הַיְנוּ יַעֲקֹב וּבָנָיו, שֶׁהֵם בְּחִינַת תְּפִלָּה, בְּחִינַת נִסִּים, בְּחִינַת אֶרֶץ־יִשְׂרָאֵל. לְפִי יְרִידָתָם וּלְפִי הַפְּגַם שֶׁפָּגַם בַּתְּפִלָּה וּבָאֱמוּנָה וּבְאֶרֶץ־יִשְׂרָאֵל, כֵּן צָרִיךְ לֵירֵד לְעֹמֶק הַגָּלוּת שֶׁל מִצְרַיִם, כְּמוֹ שֶׁיָּרְדוּ יַעֲקֹב וּבָנָיו לְמִצְרַיִם, כְּשֶׁאָמַר אַבְרָהָם בַּמָּה אֵדַע עַל יְרֻשַּׁת אָרֶץ.

(עַד כָּאן לְשׁוֹנוֹ, זִכְרוֹנוֹ לִבְרָכָה)

miracles; **covered them** — by saying that everything follows the course of nature; **they sank into the depths** — such people fall into exile; **like an evan** — just like Yaakov and his sons went down into Egypt. This is because exile is the punishment for a lack of faith and prayer. However, when a person has faith he prays. He searches for the truth, for the light of God. This radiant light will guide him and he will then be deserving of redemption. For such is the power of prayer, in it everything is renewed. In the words of the Midrash quoted above (n.4): That You give us renewed hope in exile, we know that You will redeem us.

LIKUTEY MOHARAN #9:6

like an evan — This is *avhan u'venin*. It alludes to Yaakov and his sons, who correspond to prayer/miracles/the Land of Israel. < In exact proportion > to the blemish cast on prayer/faith/the Land of Israel, they must accordingly go into the depths of the exile of "Egypt"—just as Yaakov and his sons descended into Egypt because Avraham asked, "How will I know?" with regard to inheriting the Land.[86]

emunah = Eretz Yisroel

84. ...**like a stone.** This verse is part of the *Az Yashir* ("Song of the Sea"). It was recited by the Jewish people after God had miraculously saved them from the Egyptians at the Red Sea, a miracle which came about through prayer (*Mai HaNachal*).

85. **evan...father and sons.** The word *evan* has been spelled *ævan* based upon the principle explained in note 43 above.

86. ...**inheriting the Land.** Thus, the opening verse of the lesson now reads: **The deeps** — the

ליקוטי מוהר"ן סימן י'

וְאֵלֶּה הַמִּשְׁפָּטִים אֲשֶׁר תָּשִׂים לִפְנֵיהֶם וְכוּ'. (שְׁמוֹת כ"א):

א. כְּשֶׁיֵּשׁ , חַס וְשָׁלוֹם, דִּינִים עַל יִשְׂרָאֵל – עַל־יְדֵי רְקוּדִים וְהַמְחָאַת כַּף אֶל כַּף נַעֲשֶׂה הַמְתָּקַת הַדִּינִים:

ב. כִּי עִקַּר גְּדֻלָּתוֹ שֶׁל הַקָּדוֹשׁ־בָּרוּךְ־הוּא הוּא, שֶׁגַּם הָעַכּוּ"ם יֵדְעוּ שֶׁיֵּשׁ אֱלֹקִים שַׁלִּיט וּמוֹשֵׁל, כַּמּוּבָא בַּזֹּהַר: 'כַּד אֲתָא יִתְרוֹ וַאֲמַר: "כִּי עַתָּה יָדַעְתִּי כִּי גָדוֹל ה'" וְכוּ', כְּדֵין אִתְיַקַּר וְאִתְעַלָּא שְׁמָא עִלָּאָה':

the world is filled with sorrow and suffering. (In essence, this in itself is the greatest suffering: that because He is hidden, we can neither know nor experience Him at all.)

This, then, is the meaning of the word *dinim*. They occur when, because of man's actions (as explained throughout the lesson), Divine anger is aroused. This leads to His relating to the world not with Divine mercy, but with Divine judgment. Nor should it be presumed, though it generally is, that only the catastrophic and tragic are examples of Divine judgment. Our Sages taught that even when one intends to take three coins from his pocket and removes only two, this is also a form of punishment from Above (*Erkhin* 16b). Accordingly, as far as the origin and source are concerned, it is a mistake to differentiate between suffering of holocaust proportions and one's minor daily annoyances. It would be wrong to view a plague as coming from God, but a governmental decree or edict as coming from the hands of man. Thus, at its inception, all decrees stem from Divine judgment. Understanding this, Rebbe Nachman explains how it is possible to pacify Divine anger and thus mitigate the *dinim*. As evidenced by his own actions (see previous note), Rebbe Nachman realized that the only way to undo even those decrees which to us seem to be of human origin, is to deal with them at their spiritual root and cause.

3. **governs the world.** In order for God to give of His good, which is His purpose in creating the world, man has to come to know Him. This recognition of the Almighty as the Sovereign over the entire creation is incumbent upon all. When the Jews accepted the Torah at Mt. Sinai, it bore testimony to their realization that God rules and governs. However, recognition by the Jewish people alone is not sufficient. The non-Jew must also come to recognize God's sovereignty and greatness.

4. **more exalted above and below.** Yitro (Jethro) was a high priest and engaged in every known form of contemporary idol worship. After hearing of the wondrous miracles which had been performed on behalf of the Jews, he gave praise to God, saying, "Now [even] *I* know...." When someone who is close to God recognizes Him, it is natural and to be expected. But when a Yitro—who is very distant from holiness—comes to praise God, it produces a manifestation of God's glory which is revealed to even the lowest levels.

LIKUTEY MOHARAN #10[1]

"*V'eileh* (And these) are the laws that you must place before them."

(Exodus 21:1)

When, God forbid, there are Divine judgments/decrees[2] affecting the Jewish people, through dancing and hand-clapping these Divine judgments/decrees can be mitigated.

2. For the essence of God's greatness is that the idolators, as well, should know there is an Almighty who rules and governs [the world].[3] As it is brought in the *Zohar* (II, 69a): When Yitro came, he said, "Now I know that God is great." With this His Name grew greater and more exalted < above and below >.[4]

1. Likutey Moharan #10. This lesson was taught shortly before Purim 5563 (1803), while Rebbe Nachman was making his annual visit to Terhovitza, a town in Ukraine. Rebbe Nachman had a number of followers who lived there, the most prominent of whom was the community leader, Reb Yekusiel, the Terhovitza Magid. At the time, an *ukase* (Russian for decree) to draft a set of regulations called "Enactments Concerning the Jews" was issued by Czar Alexander I. These *punkten* ("points"), as the Enactments were known in Yiddish, presaged the legislation concerning forced conscription and compulsory secular education, which eventually materialized. The Rebbe expressed his great concern over the severity of these decrees and warned of the devastating effect they would have on Russian Jewry.

Throughout that winter, Rebbe Nachman gave a number of lessons concerning these decrees, each one offering some different advice on how to postpone or even cancel their effect. After giving this lesson, he remarked, "This is what I said! We are hearing news of decrees against the Jews. But the days of Purim are near and Jews will dance and clap, and thereby mitigate the decree!" The Rebbe then repeated himself, emphasizing the words, "This is what I said." His intention was to emphasize to his chassidim the need for sincerely following all his lessons, abiding by the simple meaning of his words. Actually, he himself set the example by making it a point to dance more than usual that year. Afterwards, Rebbe Nachman said, "I have delayed the decrees for twenty-odd years." In fact, these decrees were only put into law in 1827, twenty-five years after the Rebbe's remark and sixteen years after he passed away. See *Rabbi Nachman's Wisdom* #131; *Tzaddik* #127, #132, #398.

2. Divine judgments/decrees. To understand the word *dinim*, which has been translated as Divine judgment/decrees, it is first necessary to realize that absolutely everything is of Divine origin. From great to small, there is no aspect of existence which stands outside God's domain. Nothing happens, unless He first allows it. And this applies equally to the good and the bad in the world. However, whereas the good is the direct work of His hand, the bad is actually the result of God's *haster panim* (hiding His face), as it were. In His turning away, the forces of evil are given free reign (see *Zohar* I, 68b). When this is the case, God forbid, then

LIKUTEY MOHARAN #10:3

116

ג. וּלְעַכּוּ"ם אִי אֶפְשָׁר לָהֶם לֵידַע גְּדֻלָּתוֹ שֶׁל הַקָּדוֹשׁ-בָּרוּךְ-הוּא, כִּי אִם עַל-יְדֵי בְּחִינַת יַעֲקֹב, כְּמוֹ שֶׁכָּתוּב (יְשַׁעְיָהוּ ב): "בֵּית יַעֲקֹב לְכוּ וְנֵלְכָה בְּאוֹר ה'", כִּי הוּא גִּלָּה אֱלֹקוּתוֹ שֶׁל הַקָּדוֹשׁ-בָּרוּךְ-הוּא יוֹתֵר מִשְּׁאָר הָאָבוֹת.

כִּי אַבְרָהָם קְרָאוֹ הַר, וְיִצְחָק קְרָאוֹ שָׂדֶה. (פְּסָחִים פח.) וְשָׂדֶה הוּא יוֹתֵר מָשָׁג וְנִצְרָךְ לָהָעוֹלָם מֵהַר; וְיַעֲקֹב קְרָאוֹ בַּיִת, שֶׁהוּא מָקוֹם יִשּׁוּב לִבְנֵי-אָדָם יוֹתֵר מִשָּׂדֶה, הַיְנוּ שֶׁיַּעֲקֹב קָרָא אֶת מְקוֹם הַבֵּית-הַמִּקְדָּשׁ, שֶׁהוּא מְקוֹם הַתְּפִלָּה – בַּיִת, שֶׁהוּא מָקוֹם יִשּׁוּב לִבְנֵי-אָדָם,

כִּי הֶעֱלָה אֶת הַתְּפִלָּה מֵהַר וְשָׂדֶה לִבְחִינַת בַּיִת, שֶׁיֵּשׁ בּוֹ תְּפִיסָה לִבְנֵי-אָדָם יוֹתֵר מֵהַר וְשָׂדֶה; כִּי בִּבְחִינַת בַּיִת יֵשׁ גַּם לְעַכּוּ"ם הַשָּׂגָה, כְּמוֹ שֶׁכָּתוּב (יְשַׁעְיָהוּ נ"ו): "כִּי בֵיתִי בֵּית תְּפִלָּה יִקָּרֵא לְכָל

---

succeeded in places where his father had not—hence the term "field," which is closer and "more useful" than a mountain—nevertheless, he was unable to bring his teachings to a level appreciated by all people.

10. **house.** "Yaakov called the name of that place the house of God (*Beit El*)" (Genesis 28:19). This was when Yaakov awoke from his dream and realized that had gone to sleep on Mt. Moriah.

11. **than a field.** Yaakov was able to reveal God's presence to the world to such a degree that now everyone is capable of experiencing and serving God. This can be compared to a house, a place for which everyone has use. It also indicates the necessity of praying to God for even one's most basic needs—health, children, livelihood—as opposed to its being reserved for only the more "abstract" goals of spiritual achievement and human perfection.

12. **place of prayer.** Each of the Patriarchs knew the site of the Holy Temple and prayed in that place (*Sanhedrin* 95b). Cf. Rashi (28:17), who says that Yaakov's calling it the "gate of heaven" indicates that this was the place from which prayers ascend to heaven, for, as the Midrash explains, the Holy Temple below is aligned with the Holy Temple Above.

13. **have an understanding.** While it is true that there are some individuals who even from distant places and under difficult circumstances—the mountains and the fields—would come to recognize and serve God on their own, nevertheless, the vast majority of people are in need of support—the "security and comforts" of a house—for they are not willing to fully devote and abandon themselves to serving God. When, however, they become aware of the advantages that devotion to God brings to their daily lives—this being the aspect of house— then they, too, come to recognize His greatness.

LIKUTEY MOHARAN #10:3

3. But it is impossible for the idolators to know of the Holy One's greatness except through the aspect of Yaakov[5], as is written (Isaiah 2:5), "O House of Yaakov, come let us go in God's light."[6] This is because [Yaakov] revealed the Holy One's greatness even more than the other patriarchs.

[Our Sages taught:] Avraham called it a mountain[7] and Yitzchak called it a field (*Pesachim* 88a).[8] People have a better understanding of and more need of a field than of a mountain.[9] Yaakov, on the other hand, referred to it as a house (*ibid.*),[10] which is even more suitable for human habitation than a field.[11] For the place of the Holy Temple, the place of prayer,[12] Yaakov called a house—a place which people inhabit.

[Yaakov] elevated prayer from mountain and field to the aspect of house, which is more comprehensible to people than either mountain or field. For in the concept of house, idolators, too, have an understanding,[13] as in (Isaiah 56:7), "for My house shall be called a

---

In review: Decrees/judgments against the Jewish people are mitigated by means of dancing and clapping (§1). The essence of God's greatness is that idolators come to recognize Him (§2).

5. **Yaakov.** Conceptually, Yaakov is almost always said to correspond to Torah (*Zohar* I, 146b). Torah is the means by which one can come to understand God's will in order to then serve Him. The gentiles, however, do not have the Torah. How can they recognize God? Rebbe Nachman, as we shall see, introduces another dimension to which Yaakov corresponds—i.e., prayer. And, whereas Torah was given to the Jews, prayer is available to all.

6. **House of Yaakov....** The prophet Yeshayahu (Isaiah 2:3,5) said, "Many nations will say, 'Let us go to the mountain of God and to the house of the God of Yaakov...O House of Yaakov, come let us go in God's light.'" This refers to the time of the Mashiach, when all the nations will recognize God through the concept of Yaakov.

7. **mountain.** We find that at the *akeidah*, when Avraham brought Yitzchak as a sacrifice on Mt. Moriah, the verse states, "Avraham called the name of that place...the mountain where God will appear" (Genesis 22:14).

8. **field.** "Yitzchak went out to the field to pray" (Genesis 24:63). This was also Mt. Moriah.

9. **than a mountain.** Avraham was the first one to argue for the belief in one God, monotheism, and among the first to serve Him. Even so, during his time, very few people accepted his teachings. This is the implication of "mountain," that despite Avraham's efforts his insights remained distant, high above and "useless" for the vast majority of people. Yitzchak, too, sought to reveal God's presence in the world. And though to some degree he

LIKUTEY MOHARAN #10:3,4

הָעַמִּים"; וּכְשֶׁהוּא בִּבְחִינַת בַּיִת, כְּדֵין אִתְיַקַּר שְׁמָא עִלָּאָה כַּנַּ"ל:

וְזֶה פֵּרוּשׁ: (תְּהִלִּים מ"ח): "גָּדוֹל ה' וּמְהֻלָּל מְאֹד", כְּלוֹמַר – אֵימָתַי גָּדוֹל ה'? כְּשֶׁהוּא מְהֻלָּל מְאֹד מִסִּטְרָא דְמוֹתָא, שֶׁהוּא בְּחִינַת עַכּוּ"ם (כְּמוֹ שֶׁאָמְרוּ רַבּוֹתֵינוּ, זִכְרוֹנָם לִבְרָכָה (בְּרֵאשִׁית רַבָּה ט) עַל פָּסוּק (בְּרֵאשִׁית א): "וְהִנֵּה טוֹב מְאֹד", 'זֶה מַלְאַךְ הַמָּוֶת'), כְּשֶׁהוּא מְהֻלָּל מֵהֶם, אֲזַי הוּא גָּדוֹל, כִּי הוּא עִקַּר גְּדֻלָּתוֹ. וְאֵימָתַי הוּא מְהֻלָּל מֵהֶם? "בְּעִיר אֱלֹקֵינוּ הַר קָדְשׁוֹ", דְּהַיְנוּ כְּשֶׁבְּחִינַת הַר נַעֲשֶׂה עִיר אֱלֹקֵינוּ, שֶׁהוּא יִשּׁוּב בְּנֵי־אָדָם, בְּחִינַת בַּיִת, שֶׁהוּא מְשֻׁגָּ יוֹתֵר מֵהַר וְשָׂדֶה; דְּהַיְנוּ כְּשֶׁמַּעֲלִין אֶת בְּחִינַת הַתְּפִלָּה מִבְּחִינַת הַר לִבְחִינַת עִיר וּבַיִת, שֶׁאָז יֵשׁ גַּם לָעַכּוּ"ם הַשָּׂגָה כַּנַּ"ל, אָז דַּיְקָא גָּדוֹל ה', כִּי זֶה עִקַּר גְּדֻלָּתוֹ יִתְבָּרַךְ, כְּשֶׁגַּם הָרְחוֹקִים יוֹדְעִים מִמֶּנּוּ יִתְבָּרַךְ כַּנַּ"ל.

ד. וְעִנְיָן זֶה – לְהַעֲלוֹת הַתְּפִלָּה מִבְּחִינַת הַר וְשָׂדֶה לִבְחִינַת בַּיִת, בְּחִינַת עִיר אֱלֹקֵינוּ, כְּדֵי שֶׁיִּתְגַּלֶּה מַלְכוּתוֹ גַּם לָעַכּוּ"ם, שֶׁיִּהְיֶה לָהֶם גַּם כֵּן הַשָּׂגָה בֶּאֱלֹקוּתוֹ יִתְבָּרַךְ שְׁמוֹ – אִי אֶפְשָׁר לְהַעֲשׂוֹת כִּי אִם עַל־יְדֵי צַדִּיקֵי הַדּוֹר, כְּמוֹ שֶׁאָמְרוּ חֲכָמֵינוּ, זִכְרוֹנָם לִבְרָכָה (בָּבָא בַּתְרָא קטז): 'מִי שֶׁיֵּשׁ לוֹ חוֹלֶה בְּתוֹךְ בֵּיתוֹ, יֵלֵךְ אֵצֶל חָכָם וִיבַקֵּשׁ עָלָיו רַחֲמִים';

17. **greatness…know of Him.** This will be when even the lowest levels recognize Him. It is not enough that all Jews who are distant from God return to Him. Non-Jews, even idolators, must also come to recognize His greatness and sovereignty. And this will only happen when the son of David, the true tzaddik, arrives. For he, the Mashiach, is capable of perfect prayer and will therefore be the one to elevate the levels of mountain and field to that of house.

In review: Decrees/judgments against the Jewish people are mitigated by means of dancing and clapping (§1). The essence of God's greatness is that idolators come to recognize Him (§2). Those far from God can only know Him through prayer in the aspect of "house," the immanent and comprehensible (§3).

18. **arouse mercy for him.** In this Talmudic passage (*loc. cit.*), the following verse is applied: "The wrath of a king is as messengers of death, but a wise man shall pacify it. In the light of the King's countenance is life" (Proverbs 16:14-15). The different commentaries explain that the "king" is the King of all kings, God; the "messengers" refers to His emissary, the Angel

LIKUTEY MOHARAN #10:3,4

house of prayer for all the nations."[14] And when it is on the level of house, then—"with this His exalted name grew still greater."[15]

{"God is great, and highly praised in the city of our God, in the mountain of His holiness" (Psalms 48:2).}

This is the meaning of "God is great, and *m'ode* (highly) praised." That is, when is it that God is great?—when He is *highly* praised by the side of death, the idolators.[16] {As our Sages taught: In the verse (Genesis 1:31), "…and behold, it was *m'ode* good," the word *m'ode* alludes to the Angel of Death (*Bereishit Rabbah* 9:5).} When *they* praise Him, then He is great; this being the quintessence of His greatness.

And when is it that they praise Him? "…in the city of our God, in the mountain of His holiness." [The idolators will praise God] when mountain becomes "the city of our God," a place of habitation/house, which is more understood than a mountain or a field. In other words, when prayer is elevated from the level of mountain to that of city and house—so that the idolators will also gain understanding—precisely then, "God is great…." For this is the essence of the Holy One's greatness: when those who are distant also know of Him.[17]

4. And this matter of elevating prayer from the levels of mountain and field to that of house and "city of our God," so that His sovereignty will also be revealed to the idolators in order for them to have an understanding of His Godliness, can only be achieved through the <true> tzaddikim of the generation. As our Sages taught: When a person has someone sick at home, let him turn to a wise man who will arouse mercy for him (*Bava Batra* 116a).[18]

---

14. **all the nations.** When King Solomon completed the building of the Holy Temple, he beseeched God to immediately accept prayers offered there by the gentiles. His intention was to instill the need for prayer amongst the nations (1 Kings 8:41-43; see *Rashi, loc. cit.*).

15. **name…greater.** Thus we see that the revelation of God's greatness comes through prayer. When an individual prays and merits seeing his prayers answered, his recognition of God increases immeasureably. This is even more explicit in the case of a community. When, as a result of their prayers, God even alters the dictates of nature, this makes His Kingship and rule all the more exalted and recognized by mankind. Yet, the ultimate revelation of His greatness comes when prayer reaches the level of house, at which time the gentiles and those Jews who are distant join in exalting His name (*Parparaot LeChokhmah*).

16. **side of death….** The Jews, because they are attached to the Torah, are considered alive, as in (Proverbs 3:18), "Torah is a tree of life for those attached to it." But those distant from God and His Torah are likened to the Other Side, the side of death, as in (*Zohar* III, 42a): One who worships idolatry departs from the side of life.

LIKUTEY MOHARAN #10:4　　120

כִּי עִקַּר הַתְּפִלָּה אֵינָם יוֹדְעִים כִּי אִם צַדִּיקֵי הַדּוֹר. כִּי יֵשׁ בַּעֲלֵי גַּאֲוָה,
שֶׁאֵינָם רוֹצִים שֶׁיֵּלְכוּ לְצַדִּיקִים, וְאוֹמְרִים שֶׁהֵן בְּעַצְמָם יְכוֹלִים
לְהִתְפַּלֵּל, וּמוֹנְעִים גַּם אֲחֵרִים כְּשֶׁיֵּשׁ לָהֶם צַעַר אוֹ חוֹלֶה לֵילֵךְ
לְצַדִּיקִים – עֲלֵיהֶם נֶאֱמַר (בְּרֵאשִׁית כ): "הָשֵׁב אֵשֶׁת הָאִישׁ" וְכוּ',
כִּי זֶה הַבַּעַל־גַּאֲוָה מְכֻנֶּה בִּלְשׁוֹן אֲבִימֶלֶךְ: אֲבִי לְשׁוֹן רָצוֹן, כִּי
הוּא רוֹצֶה לִמְלֹךְ, וְהַיְנוּ אֲבִימֶלֶךְ. כִּי בֶּאֱמֶת צַדִּיק מוֹשֵׁל בִּתְפִלָּתוֹ,
כְּמוֹ שֶׁכָּתוּב (שְׁמוּאֵל־ב כג): "צַדִּיק מוֹשֵׁל" וְכוּ'; וְהוּא מִתְגָּאֶה
בְּעַצְמוֹ שֶׁיָּכוֹל לְהִתְפַּלֵּל וְיֵשׁ לוֹ הַמֶּמְשָׁלָה, וְעַל כֵּן מְכֻנֶּה בְּשֵׁם
אֲבִימֶלֶךְ, כִּי הוּא רוֹצֶה לִמְלֹךְ וְאוֹמֵר: אֲנָא אֶמְלֹךְ.

וְזֶה פֵּרוּשׁ: "הָשֵׁב אֵשֶׁת הָאִישׁ". אֵשֶׁת – רָאשֵׁי־תֵּבוֹת "אֲדֹנָי
שְׂפָתַי תִּפְתָּח" - זֶה: בְּחִינַת תְּפִלָּה; דְּהַיְנוּ הָשֵׁב אֵשֶׁת – בְּחִינַת
הַתְּפִלָּה, לְהַצַּדִּיק, כִּי נָבִיא הוּא;

these individuals from admitting that there are others greater than themselves who *can* pray.

20. **return the man's wife.** ... Avraham went to live in Gerar. While there, the Philistine king, Avimelekh, took Sarah, Avraham's wife, into his home. For having done this, God punished Avimelekh and his nation, "sealing up every womb" until he returned "the man's wife" to Avraham, who then prayed on his behalf (Genesis 20). The name *SaRah* has the same root as the word *SaR* (ruler), corresponding to *Malkhut* (Kingship) which is also prayer. When a person prays, it is because he believes in the Kingship of God. Avraham is the tzaddik, Avimelekh is the haughty individual, as Rebbe Nachman goes on to explain (*Parparaot LeChokhmah*).

21. **avi...desire.** *AVi* connotes desiring, as in (Deuteronomy 23:6), "But God did not *AVa* (desire) to listen to Bilaam." Rebbe Nachman quotes this verse at the very end of the lesson.

22. **tzaddik rules.** ... "God issues decrees against man, however, the tzaddik [through his prayers] can overrule Heaven and thereby nullify these decrees" (*Moed Katan* 16b). *MeLeKh* (king and ruler) corresponds to *MaLKhut,* implying that he can rule with his prayer (*Parparaot LeChokhmah*).

23. **I will m'lokh.** Because he was a *melekh,* Avimelekh had some degree of authority and therefore claimed the *Malkhut* was rightfully his. Similarly, the degree of authority which the undeserving leader has makes him haughty. He boasts of his ability to pray on behalf of someone else when, in fact, he is incapable of praying even for himself.

24. **the aspect of prayer.** The central point in each of the three daily prayers is the *Amidah* (Eighteen Benedictions). In the Talmud, it is known simply as *Tefillah,* Prayer. By way of introduction, the first benediction is preceded with a verse from Psalms (51:17): "*Adonay sefatai tiftach* (Lord, open my lips) and my mouth will speak of Your praise." Thus, these words are also an aspect of prayer.

121 *LIKUTEY MOHARAN #10:4*

{**"Now *hashev* (return) *aishet ha'ish* (the man's wife), for he is a *navi* (a prophet). He will pray for you, and you will live"** (Genesis 20:7).}

For the essence of prayer is only known to the tzaddikim of the generation. But there are haughty individuals[19] who do not want to go to the tzaddikim. They say that they themselves can pray. They also prevent other people—when they experience suffering and sickness—from turning the tzaddikim. Of such individuals it is said, "return the man's wife, for he is a prophet. He will pray for you, and you will live."[20]

This haughty individual is called "Avimelekh." *Avi* connotes "desire,"[21]; he desires to *m'lokh* (rule). Hence, *Avi-melekh* (I desire to rule). For the truth is that the tzaddik rules through his prayer, as is written (2 Samuel 23:3), "The tzaddik rules...."[22] But [this haughty individual] boasts that he can pray and that rulership is his. This is the reason why he is called "Avimelekh," for he desires to rule and says, "I will *m'lokh.*"[23]

And this is the explanation of *hashev aishet ha'ish.* The letters of *AiSheT* (wife) are an acrostic for *Adonay Sefatai Tiftach,* which is the aspect of prayer.[24] In other words, "return the wife"—the aspect of prayer—to the tzaddik, "for he is a prophet."

---

of Death; and the "wise man" who pacifies Divine anger is the tzaddik. Thus, when the side of death—a distancing from God—exists, there is Divine anger, and Divine decrees are issued from heaven. The tzaddik knows how to evoke forgiveness, just as one who knows how to appease and pacify the king. He does this through prayer. For the tzaddik knows the proper way to pray and can elevate the prayers to the proper place. There, they serve to mitigate Divine judgment and thus nullify the decrees. The verse therefore continues, "In the light...life," because the decree which comes from the side of death is eliminated and replaced with life (cf. *Maharsha s.v. yeilekh*; also *Likutey Moharan* I, 4:7).

19. haughty individuals. Jewish history is replete with cases of the Children of Israel turning to their leaders (Moshe, the Judges, Shmuel, the Prophets, the Sages of the Talmud etc.) to pray on their behalf. The *Nimukei Yosef* (*Bava Batra* 116a) mentions the custom prevalent in France in his time (10th century c.e.): "A person facing difficulties would turn to the Dean of the Yeshivah to pray for him." The *Biur HaLikutim* reminds us that one is forbidden to use anyone or anything as an intermediary between God and himself. But to ask for someone's help in prayer, especially a tzaddik who knows the proper way to pray, is not only permitted but recommended.

Here Rebbe Nachman is referring to leaders of communities who pride themselves in how they "tend to the needs of their flocks." However, these personalities are not true leaders and when they are called upon to deal with some real crisis, God forbid, they find themselves incapable of nullifying the decrees against their constituents. They have no idea of the correct way to pray. What is worse, these leaders also prevent "their flocks" from turning to those who really can help. Rebbe Nachman tells us that this is due to their own haughtiness, which prevents

LIKUTEY MOHARAN #10:4

כִּי 'הַקָּדוֹשׁ־בָּרוּךְ־הוּא מִתְאַוֶּה לִתְפִלָּתָן שֶׁל צַדִּיקִים' (חֻלִּין ס:)
וּמְשַׁגֵּר תְּפִלָּה סְדוּרָה בְּפִיו, כְּדֵי שֶׁיֶּהֱנֶה מִתְּפִלָּתוֹ. וְזֶה: כִּי נָבִיא
הוּא, לְשׁוֹן נִיב שְׂפָתַיִם, כְּמוֹ שֶׁאָמְרוּ חֲכָמֵינוּ, זִכְרוֹנָם לִבְרָכָה
(בְּרָכוֹת לד:): "בּוֹרֵא נִיב שְׂפָתַיִם" – אִם שְׂגוּרָה תְּפִלָּתוֹ בְּפִיו וְכוּ'.
וְזֶה:

הָשֵׁב רָאשֵׁי־תֵבוֹת: הַר שָׂדֶה, בַּיִת; זֶה רֶמֶז שֶׁתְּפִלַּת הַצַּדִּיק הִיא
בִּשְׁלֵמוּת, שֶׁמַּעֲלֶה אוֹתָהּ מִבְּחִינַת הַר וְשָׂדֶה לִבְחִינַת בַּיִת כַּנַּ"ל.

אֲבָל אֵלּוּ הַבַּעֲלֵי־גַּאֲוָה מְעַכְּבִים תַּאֲוָתוֹ שֶׁל הַשֵּׁם יִתְבָּרֵךְ וְאֵינָם
מְבַקְשִׁים מִצַּדִּיקִים שֶׁיִּתְפַּלְּלוּ עֲלֵיהֶם, כִּי חוֹשְׁבִים שֶׁהִתְעַנּוּ וְסִגְּפוּ
אֶת עַצְמָם, וּבָזֶה הֵם צַדִּיקִים; אֲבָל הָאֱמֶת אֵינוֹ כֵן, כִּי כָל
הַתַּעֲנִיתִים שֶׁהִתְעַנּוּ, אֵין זֶה אֶלָּא כְּמוֹ שַׂק שֶׁיֵּשׁ בּוֹ חוֹרִים הַרְבֵּה,
וּכְשֶׁמְּרִיקִים אֶת הַשַּׂק, אַף־עַל־פִּי־כֵן נִשְׁאֲרוּ בּוֹ הַחוֹרִים.
וְהַגּוּף נִקְרָא שַׂק, כְּמַאֲמַר הַתַּנָּא: שִׁינָנָא, שְׁרֵי שַׂקָּךְ (שַׁבָּת קנב.).

---

30. **into tzaddikim.** As explained in note 18, this refers to those individuals who mistakenly see themselves as leaders and representatives of the Jewish community. Rebbe Nachman raises this point often, in many different lessons, as does the Talmud: If one sees a generation which has been beset by numerous decrees and troubles, go and investigate the judges of Israel...they are wicked but [appear] to trust in God...therefore the Temple will be destroyed...they are haughty and self-proclaimed... (*Shabbat* 139a). The entire passage is devoted to a severe condemnation of these "leaders" who are false, and who in turn support others equally unworthy of such prominence. Indeed, this ties in very well to our text. Those who the Talmud criticizes are one and the same as the haughty leaders who keep people away from the truth—from the true tzaddikim—and who claim leadership for themselves. That "the Temple will be destroyed" also appears in the lesson, as Rebbe Nachman alludes to this in his reference to "a house of prayer for all."

31. **not so.** For even when a person has fasted and lived a life of asceticism entirely for the sake of God, there can still be many desires and *wants* from which he has yet to be purified, though this may not be obvious to others. A person may also fool himself into thinking that he has successfully overcome all worldly attachments, when it is only his own haughtiness which has led him to believe so.

32. **holes remain.** It is possible to empty a sack containing undesirable objects by shaking out its contents, though the holes which were in the sack before it was emptied will remain. The same is true of the human body. Even if one has succeeded in "shaking out" all his evil traits, complete rectification of the body itself has not yet been achieved (*Parparaot LeChokhmah*).

33. **open your sack.** The *Tanna* was telling his comrade to "...open your *sakh* (body) and eat

LIKUTEY MOHARAN #10:4

For God desires the prayers of the tzaddikim (*Yevamot* 64a).[25] He sends a well arranged prayer into [the tzaddik's] mouth, so that He might derive pleasure from his prayer. This is, "...for he is a *NaVi*," which denotes *NiV sefataim* (an expression of the lips). As our Sages taught: "I will create an expression of the lips" (Isaiah 57:19)—if his prayer was fluent in his mouth, [he knew he was accepted] (*Berakhot* 34b).

And this is *HaSheV*, the letters of which form an acrostic for *Har* (mountain), *Sadeh* (field) and *Bayit* (house).[26] This alludes to the perfect nature of the tzaddik's prayer, which he elevates from the levels of mountain and field to the level of house, as explained above.[27]

But these haughty individuals prevent God from having this pleasure.[28] They do not ask the tzaddikim to pray on their behalf.[29] They think that because they fasted and mortified themselves, this has made them into tzaddikim.[30] It is not so.[31] All the fasts they fasted are only like a sack with many holes. Even when the sack is emptied, the holes remain.[32]

And the body is called a sack, as in the words of the *Tanna:* "Sharp scholar, open your sack" (*Shabbat* 152a).[33] Were they to look

---

25. **prayers of the tzaddikim.** Our Sages said of the Patriarchs that they were actually destined to not bear children. God desired their prayers and knew that their barrenness would bring them to persistently pray to be blessed with offspring. The Talmud then states: Why does God desire the prayers of the tzaddikim? because they transform judgment into mercy! In other words, they know how to mitigate Divine judgments/decrees. Thus, Avimelekh was punished in such a way as to highlight his inability to pray on behalf of the women of his nation. His haughtiness and power proved to be of little worth. The Patriarchs, on the other hand, did have the power of prayer, so that even though they were physically incapable of bearing children, they were, nevertheless, able to benefit from the miraculous nature of prayer (cf. *Likutey Moharan* 7:1) and were eventually blessed with offspring.

26. **Bayit, house.** The Hebrew letter *bet* (ב) without a *dagesh* (the point inside) is pronounced *vet*. Hence the letters of the word *HaSheV* (השב) are the first letters of *Har* (הר), *Sadeh* (שדה), *Bayit* (בית).

27. **level of house....** The verse concludes, "he will pray for you, and you will live." When Avimelekh (the haughty individual) returned Sarah (prayer) to Avraham (the tzaddik), it was an admission of his impotence and thus a sign of his repentance. By breaking his haughtiness (idolatry, see below) he merited having the tzaddik pray on his behalf. This brought him life, for he was then attached to the side of life—the very opposite of the side of death, as explained in note 15 (*Mai HaNachal*). The *Biur HaLikutim* adds that this is why we recite the verse "Lord, open my lips..." prior to the *Amidah* prayer. We too must return prayer to its proper place.

28. **pleasure.** As we've seen previously, God desires and draws pleasure from the prayers of the tzaddikim.

29. **pray on their behalf.** They will not even request for themselves. "On themselves they have no pity, how much more so [do they not have pity] on others" (*Yerushalmi, Peah* end).

LIKUTEY MOHARAN #10:4

124

וְאִם הִתְבּוֹנְנוּ בְּעַצְמָן הָיוּ רוֹאִים, אַחַר כָּל הַתַּעֲנִיתִים עֲדַיִן נִשְׁאֲרוּ
אֶצְלָם כָּל תַּאֲוָתָם קְשׁוּרִים בְּשַׁקָּם, הַיְנוּ בְּגוּפָם; וְלֹא תַּאֲוָתָם
בִּלְבַד נִשְׁאַר קָשׁוּר בְּגוּפָם, כִּי אִם גַּם תַּאֲוַת אֲבִיהֶם שֶׁיֵּשׁ אֶצְלָם
מִשְּׁעַת הַהוֹלָדָה, מֵחֲמַת שֶׁלֹּא נִתְקַדֵּשׁ אָבִיו בִּשְׁעַת זִוּוּג, גַּם זֶה
קָשׁוּר בְּגוּפָם עֲדַיִן. וּבְוַדַּאי אִלּוּ הָיוּ רוֹאִים אֶת כָּל זֶה, חֲרָדָה
גְדוֹלָה הָיָה נוֹפֵל עֲלֵיהֶם, כִּי הָיוּ רוֹאִים אֵיךְ הֵם עוֹמְדִים בְּמַדְרֵגָה
פְּחוּתָה וּשְׁפָלָה.

וְזֶה פֵּרוּשׁ: (בְּרֵאשִׁית מב): וַיְהִי הֵם מְרִיקִים שַׂקֵּיהֶם וְהִנֵּה אִישׁ
צְרוֹר כַּסְפּוֹ בְּשַׂקּוֹ – אַחַר כָּל הַתַּעֲנִיתִים, שֶׁהוּא הֲרָקַת הַשַּׂק,
בְּחִינַת הַגּוּף, עֲדַיִן – וְהִנֵּה אִישׁ צְרוֹר כַּסְפּוֹ – שֶׁקָּשׁוּר וְצָרוּר
כַּסְפּוֹ וְתַאֲוָתוֹ בְּשַׂקּוֹ וְגוּפוֹ; וַיִּרְאוּ אֶת צְרֹרוֹת כַּסְפֵּיהֶם הֵמָּה
וַאֲבִיהֶם – הַיְנוּ, לֹא דַּי צְרוֹרוֹת כַּסְפֵּיהֶם, שֶׁהוּא תַּאֲוֹות עַצְמָן, כִּי
אִם גַּם הֵמָּה וַאֲבִיהֶם, הַיְנוּ הַתַּאֲוֹות שֶׁל אֲבִיהֶם, גַּם הֵמָּה לֹא נָפְלוּ
מֵהֶם. וְזֶהוּ: וַיִּירָאוּ – כִּי חֲרָדָה נָפְלָה עֲלֵיהֶם, וַאֲזַי לֹא הָיוּ רוֹצִים
לְהִשְׂתָּרֵר וְלִמְלֹךְ:

וְזֶה פֵּרוּשׁ: וַיֹּאמֶר לָהֶם יַעֲקֹב אֲבִיהֶם אֹתִי שִׁכַּלְתֶּם, יוֹסֵף אֵינֶנּוּ

---

35. father did not sanctify.... A couple's thoughts during cohabitation affect the child they conceive and play an important role in their offspring's future development (*Zohar Chadash* 15a).

36. low level. For they return to their desires with additional passion, as in note 33.

37. desires and passions. Yosef's brothers sold him into slavery for twenty pieces of silver (Genesis 37:28). The connection between money and passion is indicated in the resemblance between *kesef* (כסף) and *kisufin* (כסופין). Hence Rebbe Nachman's teaching that avarice encompasses all passions.

38. no longer wanted to take power.... The brothers were tzaddikim, albeit not on the level of Yaakov or Yosef. When they discovered the bundles of money still in their sacks, they recognized this as a sign of their own shortcomings (that they had not cleansed their bodies of desire) and so they became frightened. Most people, however, are not capable of recognizing or admitting their deficiencies. They therefore are not even aware of the need to be afraid of having gone beyond their personal limitations and taken undue power—prominence—for themselves.

LIKUTEY MOHARAN #10:4

carefully at themselves they would see that even after all the fasting, they still have all their passions tied up in their sack—i.e., their bodies.[34] And, not only are their own passions still bound to their bodies, but also their father's passion. This has been with them from birth, because their fathers did not sanctify themselves during cohabitation.[35] This, too, is still bound to their bodies. Were they aware of all this, they would undoubtedly be overcome by fright. For they would realize that they are standing on an inferior and very low level.[36]

{"And it happened as they began emptying their sacks, that behold, each one's bundle of money was [found] in his sack. And when they and their father saw the bundles of money, they became afraid. *Avihem* (Their father) Yaakov said to them, '*Otee shekaltem* (You're making me lose my children). Yosef is gone. Shimon is gone. And now you want to take Binyamin! All these things are happening to me!'" (Genesis 42:35-36).}

This is the explanation of, "And it happened as they began emptying their sacks, that behold, each one's bundle of money was [found] in his sack." Even after all the fasts—which is "emptying the sack," the body—"each one's bundle of *KeSeF* (money) was found"—his < *KiSuFin* (desires) > and passions[37] were bound and tied "in his sack" and his body. "And when they and their father saw the bundles of money"—in other words, [they realized that] not only their own bundles of money, their own passions, but also "they and their father," their father's passion had also not fallen from them. Thus, "they became afraid"—they were overcome by fright, and so no longer wanted to take power and rule.[38]

[so that your body will have strength]." And, just as a sack has an opening, the body has a mouth. Its connection here is twofold, in that the mouth is also used in prayer.

34. **their sack...bodies.** Fasting and leading a life of asceticism does not necessarily guarantee freedom from one's physical desires. Indeed, Rebbe Nachman taught: A person who abstains from worldly pleasures and then retracts from his asceticism, falls into even greater physical desire than beforehand (*Aleph-Bet Book, Prishut* 1). This is understood from the Midrash: "Adam *again* knew his wife" (Genesis 4:25). That is, after abstaining from Chavah for 130 years he had even greater desires than previously (*Bereishit Rabbah* 23:5). It is clear from this that it takes more than just fasting and abstinence to break the attachment to physical desires.

It is noteworthy that Rebbe Nachman himself, after having fasted a great deal in his youth, later remarked, "Had I then known the power of prayer, I never would have destroyed my body with fasting." In this lesson, he extolls the virtues and power of prayer, while conversely showing that fasting and separation from the physical is not always the means to achieve greatness.

LIKUTEY MOHARAN #10:4

126

וְכוּ' – זֶה רֶמֶז עַל תּוֹכַחַת הַשֵּׂכֶל, כִּי הַשֵּׂכֶל מוֹכִיחַ אֶת הַבַּעֲלֵי־גַאֲוָה הָרוֹצִים לְהִתְגַּדֵּל. כִּי יַעֲקֹב הוּא בְּחִינַת הַשֵּׂכֶל, כְּמוֹ שֶׁתִּרְגֵּם אוּנְקְלוֹס (בְּרֵאשִׁית כז): "וַיַּעְקְבֵנִי" – 'וְחַכְּמַנִי'.

וְזֶה: אֲבִיהֶם, כִּי אָב בְּחָכְמָה: וְהַיְנוּ שֶׁהַשֵּׂכֶל מוֹכִיחָם וְאוֹמֵר לָהֶם: אַתֶּי שֶׁכַּלְתֶּם, כִּי 'כָּל הַמִּתְגָּאֶה – חָכְמָתוֹ מִסְתַּלֶּקֶת מִמֶּנּוּ'.

יוֹסֵף אֵינֶנּוּ – זֶה בְּחִינַת תִּקּוּן הַמְעַט, הַיְנוּ עֲדַיִן לֹא תִּקַּנְתֶּם הַמְעַט שֶׁהוּא לְחֶרְפָּה וּלְקָלוֹן, וְיֵשׁ לָכֶם לְהִתְבַּיֵּשׁ מֵחֲמָתוֹ, כִּי תִּקּוּן הַמְעַט הוּא בְּחִינַת יוֹסֵף, עַל שֵׁם (בְּרֵאשִׁית ל): "אָסַף אֱלֹקִים אֶת חֶרְפָּתִי".

וְשִׁמְעוֹן אֵינֶנּוּ – הַיְנוּ, עַל־יְדֵי שֶׁאֵין לְךָ בְּחִינַת יוֹסֵף, אֵין לְךָ בְּחִינוֹת שִׁמְעוֹן; וְשִׁמְעוֹן הוּא בְּחִינַת (שָׁם כ"ט): "כִּי שָׁמַע ה' כִּי שְׂנוּאָה אָנֹכִי", כִּי אַתָּה אֵינְךָ שָׂנוּא, כִּי מֵחֲמַת שֶׁלֹּא תִּקַּנְתָּ אֶת עַצְמְךָ, בְּוַדַּאי אֵינְךָ יָכוֹל לְהוֹכִיחַ אֲחֵרִים, כִּי יֹאמְרוּ לְךָ קְשֹׁט עַצְמְךָ תְּחִלָּה וְכוּ'; וְעַל כֵּן אֵינְךָ שָׂנוּא, כִּי הַמּוֹכִיחַ הוּא שָׂנוּא, כְּמוֹ שֶׁאָמְרוּ חֲכָמֵינוּ, זִכְרוֹנָם לִבְרָכָה (כְּתֻבּוֹת קה:): 'הַאי צוֹרְבָא מֵרַבָּנָן דִּמְרַחֲמֵי לֵהּ בְּנֵי מָתָא, לָאו מִשּׁוּם דְּמַעֲלֵי טְפֵי, אֶלָּא מִשּׁוּם דְּלָא מוֹכַח לְהוּ בְּמִלֵּי דִּשְׁמַיָּא'; נִמְצָא שֶׁהַמּוֹכִיחַ הוּא שָׂנוּא.

spiritual, the only way to bring oneself closer to Him is by developing one's own spirituality. This can only be achieved through humility and self-negation. However, when a person is haughty, God does not stay with him. Hence, his wisdom—the knowledge/Torah—leaves him.

41. **yOSeF...humiliation.** Therefore, when the aspect of Yosef is missing, there can be no rectification. Even with fasting, so long as a person does not have a binding attachment with the tzaddik—the quality of Yosef—he cannot hope to achieve a true *tikkun* (restoration).

42. **First adorn yourself.** When a person still has far to go in perfecting himself, it is a sure sign that he lacks true wisdom. How then can he presume the mantle of leadership and attempt to advise and rectify—"adorn"—others? "First adorn yourself," they will tell him, "and then worry about adorning others!"

43. **fails to rebuke....** Were he truly a fitting leader, he would have advice and teachings filled with the "fear of heaven" with which to instruct and guide his followers. His silence in these matters is the clearest indication that he lacks the qualities required, this being attested to by his unquestioned popularity. On the other hand, when a leader does address his

LIKUTEY MOHARAN #10:4

127

This is the explanation of: "*Avihem* (Their father) Yaakov said to them, '*Otee shekaltem* (You're making me lose my children). Yosef is gone....'" This is an allusion to the intellect's rebuke, because the intellect reproves the haughty individuals who seek prominence. For *YaAKoV* corresponds to intellect, as Onkelos renders *YaAKVeiny* ("he went behind my back"): "he outsmarted me" (Genesis 27:36).

And this is "*AVihem*," because *AV* (father) indicates wisdom (*Megillah* 13a).[39] In other words, the *SeKheL* (intellect) rebukes them, saying, "*otee SheKaLtem*." For whenever someone is haughty, his wisdom leaves him (cf. *Pesachim* 66b).[40]

"Yosef is gone." This corresponds to making amends. In other words, you have still not rectified that which is awry, and this is a humiliation and a disgrace. You should be ashamed because of this. Because making amends corresponds to *yOSeF*, as in (Genesis 30:23), "God *OSaF* (has gathered up) my humiliation."[41]

"Shimon is gone." That is, because you do not have the quality of Yosef, you therefore do not have the quality of Shimon. *ShiMAon* corresponds to, "for God *ShaMA* (has heard) that I am despised" (Genesis 29:33). But you are not despised because you have not rectified yourself. As such, you certainly cannot rebuke others, for they will say to you: "First adorn yourself..." (*Bava Metzia* 107b).[42] This is why you are not despised. For the person who gives reproof is despised, as our Sages taught: When the people of a city are fond of a rabbinical scholar, it is not due to his excellence, but because he fails to rebuke them in spiritual matters (*Ketuvot* 105b).[43] This shows that one who gives reproof is despised.

---

39. **AV indicates wisdom.** Aside from "father," *av* carries the meaning "to desire." How can one tell that Yaakov—intellect/wisdom—is complete? This can be recognized when the source of the desire is wisdom and not emotion (passion).

40. **...his wisdom leaves him.** The Talmud teaches that both Moshe and Hillel spoke of their own knowledge vis-a-vis their colleagues' with some degree of haughtiness and conceit. As a result, they each lost some of their own wisdom (*Pesachim* 66b). Rebbe Nachman taught that when a person has rid himself of all earthly interests he can then grasp the entire Torah. This is because the Torah is spiritual and beyond the restrictions of time and space. To the degree that he has succeeded in eliminating his attachments to the corporeal, the person himself becomes increasingly spiritual and free of physical restrictions. But if one uses Torah for physical purposes and earthly desires, then, just as corporeality conforms to time and space, so too, the Torah comes under these restrictions and becomes impossible to be mastered entirely (*Likutey Moharan* I, 110). In a similar vein, because God Himself is, as it were, totally

LIKUTEY MOHARAN #10:4,5

וְאֶת בִּנְיָמִין תִּקָּחוּ – זֶה מוֹרֶה עַל גַּדְלוּת, כִּי פֵּרֵשׁ רַשִׁ"י (ד):
בִּנְיָמִין, עַל שֵׁם אֶרֶץ־יִשְׂרָאֵל, בֶּן יָמִין, וְאֶרֶץ־יִשְׂרָאֵל הוּא גָּבוֹהַּ
מִכָּל הָאֲרָצוֹת.

וְהַיְנוּ, לֹא דַי שֶׁאֵין לָכֶם כָּל הַבְּחִינוֹת הַלָּלוּ, עִם כָּל זֶה – וְאֶת
בִּנְיָמִין תִּקָּחוּ, שֶׁאַתֶּם לוֹקְחִים לְעַצְמְכֶם גַּדְלוּת. וְהַיְנוּ דְּסַיֵּם הַשֵּׂכֶל
הַמּוֹכִיחַ אוֹתָם: עָלַי הָיוּ כֻלָּנָה – כִּי הַכֹּל נוֹפֵל עָלַי, כִּי כָּל
הַמִּתְגָּאֶה – חָכְמָתוֹ מִסְתַּלֶּקֶת מִמֶּנּוּ:

ה. וְהָעֵצָה הַיְעוּצָה לְבַטֵּל (נ"א: לְבַּעֵל) הַגַּאֲוָה, שֶׁהִיא הָעֲבוֹדָה
זָרָה, כְּמוֹ שֶׁכָּתוּב (מִשְׁלֵי ט"ז): "תּוֹעֲבַת ה' כָּל גְּבַהּ לֵב" (כְּמוֹ
שֶׁדָּרְשׁוּ רַבּוֹתֵינוּ, זִכְרוֹנָם לִבְרָכָה סוֹטָה ד:), הָעִקָּר הוּא עַל־יְדֵי הִתְקָרְבוּת

"wisdom" and follow their "advice" in serving God, it is not only justified but vital that he stand up to them with holy arrogance. This will become clearer in section 8, where Rebbe Nachman incorporates into the lesson the Purim story and the confrontation between Mordekhai and Haman.

48. **happening to me....** Failing to correct shortcomings and perfect oneself is definitely to the detriment of one's intellect. The converse is also true; rectifying one's faults, a person expands his wisdom and improves his intellect. Thus, even when a person finds himself personally lacking and therefore incapable of properly directing others, he should nevertheless make every effort to speak to others and assist them in serving God. The attempt alone is beneficial, as it will help him correct his shortcomings and perfect his intellect. This is not so in the case of the false leader. He does not speak to others about serving God and self-improvement, but rather seeks to direct others for his own benefit. This only serves to increase his own haughtiness and therefore blemishes whatever wisdom this incompetent leader does possess, eventually causing his wisdom to disappear entirely (*Parparaot LeChokhmah*).

In review: Decrees/judgments against the Jewish people are mitigated by means of dancing and clapping (§1). The essence of God's greatness is that idolators come to recognize Him (§2). Those far from God can only know Him through prayer in the aspect of "house," the immanent and comprehensible (§3). Elevating prayer to the aspect of "house" can only be accomplished through the tzaddikim, whose prayers God desires. But the haughty, who renounce having the tzaddik pray for them, deny God this pleasure. Their wisdom leaves them and they are rebuked by the intellect (§4).

49. **haughtiness...idolatry....** In Deuteronomy (7:25) we see that the term abomination is applied to idolatry. This helps us understand Rebbe Nachman's equation, for in essence the verse quoted here is saying that God considers haughtiness and idolatry conceptually the same. Furthermore, the Talmud teaches that haughtiness is to be likened to idolatry (*Sotah* 4b). This can be understood quite easily. When a person recognizes God's greatness and His sovereignty, he can then appreciate how insignificant he himself is within the total creation. But, when a person considers himself significant and important, when he seeks prominence

129 LIKUTEY MOHARAN #10:4,5

"And now you want to take Binyamin!" This indicates prominence, as Rashi explains (Genesis 35:18): "*BiNYaMIN*—he was called this because of the Land of Israel: *BeN YaMIN*."[44] And the Land of Israel is higher than all other lands (Zevachim 54b).[45]

In other words, not enough that you lack all these qualities,[46] but on top of this "you want to take Binyamin"—you want to take prominence for yourselves.[47] And this is how the intellect concluded its reproof of them: "All these things are happening to me!" Everything is happening to me, because "whenever someone is haughty, his wisdom leaves him."[48]

5. Now, the main solution for eliminating haughtiness—itself considered idolatry, as in (Proverbs 16:5), "God considers an abomination anyone whose heart is haughty"[49]—is to draw close to the

---

followers with the "fear of heaven," he is despised; though it is *his* leadership that is to be respected and valued. This was Yosef. At first, his brothers differed with him because he rebuked them and attempted to give them advice. They did not feel he was worthy of such a position. However, because they were great tzaddikim in their own right, they recognized their personal deficiencies, accepted Yaakov's admonishment (as indicated in the text of this lesson), and set about improving themselves. This is what later enabled them to recognize Yosef's greatness and accept his leadership.

44. **Land of Israel, BeN YaMIN.** Rashi explains that of Yaakov's twelve sons only his youngest was born in the Land of Israel. The others were born to the north of his homeland, in Aram Naharayim (present day Iraq). Yaakov thus gave him the name Ben Yamin, son of the south.

45. **higher than all other lands.** "As God lives, who raised up the Children of Israel from...all the lands...back into their Land" (Jeremiah 16:15). From here we understand that the Land of Israel is higher than all other lands (*Zevachim, loc. cit., Rashi, s.v. v'eretz Yisrael*).

46. **all these qualities.** This refers to lost wisdom (Yaakov), lack of rectification (Yosef) and no leadership and admonishment (Shimon).

47. **Binyamin...prominence for yourselves.** This is the leader who thinks that his followers respect and admire him for his achievements and good qualities, when actually they do so only because, in his failure to rectify himself, he does not move them to perfect their service of God. This arrogance and haughtiness misleads him and is, in point of fact, the source of his shame. For, as long as he has not yet rectified himself, [his prominence] is nothing but shame and humiliation (*Parparaot LeChokhmah*).

The *Parparaot LeChokhmah* asks: How is it that Binyamin, who was undoubtedly a tzaddik, should imply or be compared to haughtiness and arrogance, an indication of evil? He answers that there is another type of arrogance, which comes from the side of holiness. This *azut d'kedushah* (holy arrogance) is a must in serving God. Though a person has to know his place and readily defer to the wisdom of those greater than he, he must never defer to those whose arrogance is from the side of evil. When they try to get him to accept their

LIKUTEY MOHARAN #10:5

130

לַצַּדִּיקִים, כַּמּוּבָא בַּתִּקּוּנִים (תִּקּוּן כא מ״ח:): 'בִּתְרוּעָה דְּאִיהוּ רוּחָא, אִתְעֲבִיר אֵל אַחֵר';

וְצַדִּיק הוּא בְּחִינַת רוּחָא, כְּמוֹ שֶׁכָּתוּב (בְּמִדְבַּר כ״ז): "אִישׁ אֲשֶׁר רוּחַ בּוֹ", וְעַל-יָדוֹ נִכְנָע רוּחַ גָּבוֹהַּ, אֵל אַחֵר, וְנַעֲשֶׂה מֵאַחֵר, אֶחָד, כִּי הוּא קוֹצָא דְאוֹת ד' (תִּקּוּן כא נ״ה:), שֶׁמִּמֶּנּוּ אַרְבַּע רוּחוֹת, כְּמוֹ שֶׁכָּתוּב (יְחֶזְקֵאל ל״ז): "כֹּה אָמַר ה' מֵאַרְבַּע רוּחוֹת בֹּאִי הָרוּחַ". וְזֶה לְשׁוֹן תְּרוּעָה, לְשׁוֹן (תְּהִלִּים ב): "תְּרֹעֵם בְּשֵׁבֶט בַּרְזֶל" (תִּקּוּן י״ח וְתִקּוּן כ״א), כִּי הוּא מְשַׁבֵּר רוּחַ גָּבוֹהַּ, אֵל אַחֵר, כְּפִירוֹת:

to its upper right-hand corner. This back-point, though just a small addition, can make all the difference between "one" (אחד, God's unity) and "other" (אחר, idolatry). It is a very fine line which separates the two, and not everyone is capable of clearly making the distinction. It is likewise very difficult to discern between the true tzaddik and the false leader, the *one* who promotes God's unity and the *other* who diminishes it. Because he possesses the *ruach*—the *yud* of *chokhmah* (see *Likutey Moharan* I, 8 n.84; see Appendix: Levels of Existence), through which the spirit of idolatry is countered—the tzaddik himself is referred to as the back-point of the *dalet*. With his *ruach*, the tzaddik transforms the *reish*—the *ruach*—of idolatry into the *dalet* of unity.

54. four ruchot.... The tzaddik is "a man in whom there is *ruach*," the one who turns the *reish* of *acher* (אחר) into the *dalet* of *echad* (אחד). Thus, because he reveals God's spirit to the *dalet* (=4) corners of the earth, it is said that the four *ruchot* come from him.

55. TeRuAh. From here we see the great value of drawing closer to and following the advice of the true tzaddik; never despairing, no matter how far one is from God. Thus, by binding himself to his son-in-law Moshe, even Yitro, the greatest idolator of his time (above, n.3), had his haughtiness broken and was able to repent completely (*Mai HaNachal*).

56. ...atheism. See Maimonides (*Yad HaChazakah, Hilkhot Teshuvah* 3:7) that belief in other gods, i.e., idolatry, and atheism, not believing in God at all, are essentially one and the same.

Thus far in the lesson, Rebbe Nachman has connected the following concepts: that the most complete revelation of God's greatness comes when even non-Jews recognize Him (§2); that this depends upon prayer being elevated to the aspect of Yaakov/house so that everyone can appreciate and participate in prayer (§3); that this is brought about by the efforts of the true tzaddikim of the generation (§4); that their efforts are thwarted by false leaders whose haughtiness, a sign of idolatry, prevents others from serving God (§4); that nonetheless this haughty and idolatrous spirit can be overcome by searching for the true tzaddik and binding oneself to him (§5). Rebbe Nachman now returns to the opening statement (§1), "Through dancing and hand-clapping these Divine judgments/decrees can be mitigated," showing its connection to the above.

131　　　　*LIKUTEY MOHARAN #10:5*

tzaddikim.[50] As is brought in the *Tikkuney Zohar* (#21 p.49a): With a *teruah* (shofar blast), which is *ruach,* [belief in an] "other god" disappears.[51]

And the tzaddik corresponds to *ruach,* as in (Numbers 27:18), "a man in whom there is < the Lord's > *ruach* (spirit)."[52] Through him, the haughty spirit—the "other god"—is humbled; the *acheR* (other) is transformed into *echaD* (one). This is because [the tzaddik] is the back-point of the letter *dalet* (*Tikkuney Zohar, p.55b*).[53] From him are the four *ruchot,* as in (Ezekiel 37:9), "Thus says God: Come from the four winds, O spirit."[54] And this is the connotation of *TeRuAh.*[55] It is similar to (Psalms 2:9), "You shall *TRoAim* (break them) with a rod of iron" (*Tikkuney Zohar #18, p.36a*), because it breaks the haughty spirit/ "other god"/atheism.[56]

[handwritten margin notes: short notes — v f; broken heart; lev nishbar]

and acclaim, then directly proportional to this, his perception of God's greatness is diminished. This is the essence of idolatry: the worshipping of the self—haughtiness—and the lessening of the Holy One's sovereignty.

50. **close to the tzaddikim.** By drawing close to a tzaddik and following his advice, a person indicates his recognition and acceptance that there is someone greater, wiser and more accomplished than himself. This automatically reduces his haughtiness. Rebbe Nachman will now explain this process, showing how closeness to the tzaddikim actually breaks one's arrogance and haughtiness.

51. **teruah...ruach...other god disappears.** The *teruah* is a series of tremolo, or broken breaths on the shofar. Within the lesson's context, the word *ruach* can alternatively be translated as breath, wind or spirit (see *Likutey Moharan* I, 8, n.1). As the *Parparaot LeChokhmah* adds: "The effect of crying and a broken *ruach* (spirit), which the *teruah*—the broken breath—convey, stands counter to and destroys the haughty spirit." Thus, the *teruah* is sounded in order to defeat other gods—i.e., idolatry. The *Tikkuney Zohar* (*loc. cit.*) goes on to explain that herein lies the Torah's power to purify. This will be further touched upon in section 7, where Rebbe Nachman points out the connection between Torah study and this lesson.

52. **there is ruach.** The tzaddik has this spirit—this *teruah*—which counters the spirit of idolatry. These words (*loc. cit.*) were said by Moshe, the tzaddik and leader of his generation, shortly before his passing. He was appealing to God to appoint a successor who would lead the Jewish people as he had. For this, the new leader would also have to be a man of spirit. God selected Yehoshua. Aside from being Moshe's most devoted disciple, Yehoshua was devoid of haughtiness. The *Parparaot LeChokhmah* adds that of Moshe it is written, "And the man Moshe was very humble" (Numbers 12:3), indicating that the true leader must be truly humble—without any haughtiness.

53. **back-point of the letter dalet.** The letters *dalet* (ד) and *reish* (ר) are similar in form. The difference between them is that the back of the *reish* is rounded-off, whereas the right tip of the head of the *dalet* extends past the leg of the letter; as though the *reish* had a *yud* attached

LIKUTEY MOHARAN #10:6

ו. וְזֶה בְּחִינַת רִקוּדִין וְהַמְחָאַת כַּף. כִּי רִקוּדִין וְהַמְחָאַת כַּף נִמְשָׁכִין מִבְּחִינַת הָרוּחַ שֶׁבַּלֵּב, כַּנִּרְאֶה בְּחוּשׁ, כִּי עַל־יְדֵי שִׂמְחַת הַלֵּב הוּא מְרַקֵּד וּמַכֶּה כַּף אֶל כַּף; וְכַמּוּבָא בַּתִּקּוּנִים (תִּקּוּן כא נ"א): 'וְהַאי רוּחָא נָשֵׁב בְּשִׁית פִּרְקִין דִּדְרוֹעָא וּבְשִׁית פִּרְקִין דְּשׁוֹקִין', וְהִיא בְּחִינַת הַמְחָאַת כַּף וּבְחִינַת רִקוּדִין. וְזֶהוּ בְּחִינַת: "לִבּוֹ נָשָׂא אֶת רַגְלָיו" (בְּרֵאשִׁית־רַבָּה, וַיֵּצֵא, פָּרָשָׁה ע), הַיְנוּ עַל־יְדֵי הָרוּחַ שֶׁבַּלֵּב בָּאִים הָרִקוּדִין;

הַיְנוּ עַל־יְדֵי הַצַּדִּיק שֶׁהוּא בְּחִינַת רוּחַ כַּנַּ"ל, נִתְבַּטֵּל הַגַּאֲוָה כַּנַּ"ל, כְּמוֹ שֶׁכָּתוּב (תְּהִלִּים ל"ו): "אַל תְּבוֹאֵנִי רֶגֶל גַּאֲוָה", וְנִתְבַּטֵּל הָעֲבוֹדַת אֱלִילִים, כְּמוֹ שֶׁכָּתוּב: "וְרַחֲצוּ רַגְלֵיכֶם" (בְּרֵאשִׁית י"ח) — זֶה עֲבוֹדַת אֱלִילִים'.

וּכְשֶׁנִּתְעַלֶּה הָרַגְלִין עַל־יְדֵי הָרִקוּדִין, בְּחִינַת נָשָׂא לִבּוֹ אֶת רַגְלָיו, וְנִתְבַּטֵּל הַגַּאֲוָה, הַיְנוּ הָעֲבוֹדָה זָרָה, עַל־יְדֵי־זֶה נִמְתָּקִין הַדִּינִים; כִּי 'כָּל זְמַן שֶׁיֵּשׁ עֲבוֹדָה זָרָה בָּעוֹלָם, חֲרוֹן־אַף בָּעוֹלָם' (סִפְרִי, רְאֵה), וּכְשֶׁנִּתְעַבֵּר הָעֲבוֹדָה זָרָה, נִתְעַבֵּר הַחֲרוֹן־אַף וְנִמְשָׁכִין חֲסָדִים, וְאָז הָרַגְלִין הֵם בִּבְחִינַת רַגְלֵי חֲסִידָיו (שְׁמוּאֵל־א ב), הַיְנוּ

LeChokhmah explains this in greater detail. The feet are the lowest part of the body and hence understood to be closest to the *kelipot*, the forces of evil and impurity. When we say that the heart elevates the feet, it means exactly that: it elevates the feet from the *kelipot*. These evil forces are actually the cause of the Divine anger—the Divine judgments/decrees—which can only be mitigated and eliminated when haughtiness and arrogance are done away with.

63. **wash your feet...idolatry.** Rashi explains that Avraham presumed that his visitors worshipped idolatry and therefore asked them to "wash their feet" so as not to bring their mistaken beliefs into his home (Genesis 18:4). In this sense, cleansing the feet indicates the elimination of idolatry. In fact, the word *rachatzu*, which in Hebrew means wash, in Aramaic translates as trust. The person who had previously put his trust in idolatry now washes himself—more specifically, his feet (see previous note)—and puts his trust in God.

64. **anger in the world.** This Midrashic passage relates to a city in which the majority of its inhabitants have worshipped idolatry. In such a case, the entire city, including inanimate objects, must be destroyed (Deuteronomy 13:13-19). Failing to eliminate even one of these objects is in essence leaving a reminder of idolatry in the world. In terms of our lesson, this indicates that even the slightest degree of haughtiness is forbidden. Accordingly, failing to eliminate even the smallest amount leaves a reminder of Divine anger, and prevents the Divine judgments/decrees from being mitigated.

65. **feet of ChaSiDav...ChaSaDim.** The Kabbalah speaks of the five *chasadim*

6. And this is the aspect of dancing and hand-clapping, because dancing and clapping are drawn from the spirit in the heart. As is readily observable, when a person's heart is happy he dances and claps his hands.[57] And, as is brought in the *Tikkuney Zohar* (#21, p.51b): "This *ruach*[58] blows in the six sections of the arms and the six sections of the legs"[59]—the aspect of clapping and dancing.[60] This corresponds to "his heart carried his feet" (*Bereishit Rabbah* 70:8).[61] In other words, the spirit in the heart produces dancing.

Thus, through the tzaddik/the *ruach,* haughtiness is eliminated, as explained. As is written (Psalms 36:12), "Let not the foot of pride come against me."[62] Idolatry is also eliminated. As is written (Genesis 18:4), "...and wash your feet"—this alludes to idolatry (*Bava Metzia* 86b).[63]

And when the feet are lifted up in dance, corresponding to "his heart carried his feet," haughtiness—i.e., idolatry—is eliminated. Through this, Divine judgments/decrees are mitigated. For "As long as there is idol worship in the world, there is *charon af* (Divine anger) in the world" (*Sifri* 13:18).[64] But when idolatry disappears, Divine anger disappears and *chasadim* (benevolences) are drawn [to the world]. Then the feet are "the feet of *ChaSiDav* (His pious ones)" (1 Samuel 20:9)—i.e., the aspect of *ChaSaDim*.[65] This corresponds to (Isaiah 55:3),

---

57. **as is readily observable....** Even in the rare instances when Rebbe Nachman offers an empirical proof for some point in his lesson, as he does here, he also provides additional support from Scripture and Rabbinical literature.

58. **this ruach....** This alludes to the tzaddik, as explained above in section 5 (*Mai HaNachal*).

59. **six sections...arms...legs.** The six sections of the arms are the two upper arms, two forearms and the hands. The six sections of the legs are the two thighs, two calves, and the feet.

60. **...dancing.** The sections of the arms, in particular the hands, come together in clapping; the sections of the legs, in particular the feet, move together in dance. The blowing spirit which brings the different sections together is happiness and joy (*Mai HaNachal*).

61. **his heart carried his feet.** The Midrash teaches that God gave Yaakov a guarantee he would one day safely return to the Holy Land (Genesis 28). Yaakov carried the joy of this tiding in his heart. He felt it when he came to the house of Lavan, and it gave him the confidence and security he needed for overcoming his idolatrous uncle (see Genesis 24:31, *Rashi*; Genesis 31:19). While working for Lavan, marrying and raising a family, Yaakov revealed—by example—the concept of bringing one's prayers to the level of house. This was a complete revelation of God's greatness, because Yaakov, the tzaddik, is the *ruach* which counters idolatry and causes His holy name to be exalted still further (*Mai HaNachal*).

62. **foot of pride....** Haughtiness is likened to a foot. Just as a man physically relies on his feet to support his body, so too, he emotionally depends upon his haughty spirit to hold him up. Such haughtiness can be negated and countered by means of the "dancing feet"— provided the *ruach* which moves them is drawn from the heart, the tzaddik. The *Parparaot*

LIKUTEY MOHARAN #10:6

בְּבְחִינַת חֲסָדִים, הַיְנוּ בְּחִינַת "חַסְדֵּי דָוִד הַנֶּאֱמָנִים" (יְשַׁעְיָהוּ נ"ה) –
'הַנֶּאֱמָנִים' דַּיְקָא, כִּי נִתְבַּטְּלוּ הַמִּינוּת וְהַכְּפִירוֹת.

וְגַם זֶה בְּחִינַת הַמְחָאַת כַּף, כִּי עַל־יְדֵי הָרוּחַ נִתְגַּלֶּה הֶאָרַת הַיָּדַיִם,
כְּמוֹ שֶׁכָּתוּב (שִׁיר־הַשִּׁירִים ה): "קוֹל דּוֹדִי דוֹפֵק"; 'דּוֹפֵק' – זֶה
בְּחִינַת רוּחַ, כַּמּוּבָא בַּתִּקּוּנִים (תִּקּוּן כה ס"ח.), וְסָמִיךְ לֵהּ: "דּוֹדִי
שָׁלַח יָדוֹ מִן הַחוֹר" – זֶה בְּחִינַת הִתְגַּלּוּת הֶאָרַת הַיָּדַיִם, הַיְנוּ
בְּחִינַת הַמְחָאַת כַּף, וְאָז נִתְבַּטֵּל הָעֲבוֹדָה זָרָה, הַיְנוּ הַכְּפִירוֹת, וְזֶה
בְּחִינַת (שְׁמוֹת י"ז): "וַיְהִי יָדָיו אֱמוּנָה".

נִמְצָא, שֶׁעַל־יְדֵי הַצַּדִּיק, הַיְנוּ בְּחִינַת רוּחַ שֶׁבַּלֵּב, נִתְגַּלֶּה הֶאָרַת
הַיָּדַיִם וְהָרַגְלַיִם, הַיְנוּ בְּחִינַת רִקּוּדִין וְהַמְחָאַת כַּף, וְנִתְבַּטֵּל הַגַּאֲוָה
וְהַכְּפִירוֹת, וְנִתְרַבֶּה הָאֱמוּנָה, וְאָז נִתְקַיֵּם (תְּהִלִּים כ"ו): "רַגְלִי
עָמְדָה בְמִישׁוֹר", שֶׁהוּא בְּחִינַת אֱמוּנָה. כִּי הַמִּינוּת הִיא בְּחִינַת
נָטָיוּ רַגְלָי, כְּמַאֲמַר אָסָף (שָׁם ע"ג): "כִּמְעַט נָטָיוּ רַגְלָי", שֶׁנֶּאֱמַר
שָׁם עַל שֶׁהִשִּׂיאוּ לִבּוֹ לְמִינוּת, כַּמְבֹאָר שָׁם; "וְרַגְלָי עָמְדָה

(Beauty, encompassing the six lower *sefirot*). It then comes to *Malkhut,* which at that point resembles four [the four *ruchot* or winds mentioned earlier]. From this we see that the *ruach*—in this case the tzaddik or the power of the hands—is the source of the *tikkun* of *Malkhut*/ prayer, as mentioned earlier. And when prayer is complete, the Divine judgments/decrees are mitigated or nullified entirely.

70. **Dofeik...ruach.** The word *DoFeiK* (דופק, knocks or pulsates) has the same root as *DoFeK* (דפק, the pulse). We again see that it is *ruach*—the breath, wind and spirit—which causes the heart to beat and pulsate and is the source of the pulse in the hands.

71. **heresy is eliminated.** Thus, the *ruach*—by bringing about both the emanation of the power in the hands which clapping expresses and the joy in the heart which dancing expresses—is the force capable of negating all idolatry. The *Mai HaNachal* adds that the verse quoted here, "...put his hand in by the hole," is metaphorically speaking about the elimination of idol worship, as Rashi (v.3) explains.

72. **hands were faith.** ...Revealing faith is the opposite of heresy and idolatry. We see here that the *ruach* which manifests itself in the hands and feet is indicative of the spirit of faith in God.

73. **in context....** See Rashi (73:2). In other words, whereas faith is a straight, strong and supportive "foot," heresy is bent and weak and gives false support to those who depend and "stand" on it.

LIKUTEY MOHARAN #10:6

135

"...the kindnesses of David are faithful."[66] Specifically "faithful," because heresy and atheism are eliminated.[67]

And [*ruach*] also corresponds to hand-clapping.[68] For through the *ruach,* the emanation of the hands is revealed, as in (Song of Songs 5:1), "The sound of my beloved *dofeik* (pulsates)."[69] *Dofeik,* as the *Tikkuney Zohar* (#25, p.70a) brings, is an aspect of *ruach.*[70] The verse adjacent to this, "My beloved put his hand in through the hole" (Song of Songs 5:4), alludes to the revelation of the hands' emanation—i.e., hand-clapping. And then idol worship—i.e., heresy—is eliminated.[71] As it is written (Exodus 17:2), "And his hands were faith."[72]

We find, therefore, that through the tzaddik—i.e., the *ruach* in the heart—the emanation of the hands and feet—i.e., clapping and dancing—is revealed. Haughtiness and atheism are thus eliminated, and faith is increased. And then, "My foot stands in an even place" (Psalms 26:11) is fulfilled. ["My foot stands"] is a reference to faith, whereas heresy is called "a bent foot." As Asaf said (Psalms 73:2), "My feet were almost bent," which in context refers there to his having turned his heart to heresy.[73] But, "My foot stands in an even place"

(benevolences). "These spiritual energies are forces of kindness and benevolence, and have their root in *daat* (holy knowledge). The benevolences permeate the different parts of the body [paralleling the five *sefirot* (Divine emanations) from *Chesed* to *Hod,* with *Netzach* and *Hod* being the feet]" (*Shaar Ruach HaKodesh,* The Sixth *Kavanah*).

66. **are faithful.** The ultimate revelation of the *chasadim* is in *Malkhut* (Kingship), which is the final *sefirah,* corresponding to the manifestation of this physical world (see Appendix: Levels of Existence). David, King of Israel and author of the Psalms, represents the epitome of sovereignty and prayer. By destroying idolatry, haughtiness, and binding oneself to the true tzaddik, a person can merit prayer and thus partake in the revelation of God's *Malkhut,* His sovereignty.

67. **are eliminated.** For faith is also *Malkhut.* By achieving *Malkhut* one negates atheism and idolatry.

68. **hand-clapping.** Until now, Rebbe Nachman has been explaining the connection which dancing has with mitigating decrees. He now does the same for hand-clapping.

The *Parparaot LeChokhmah* explains that the hands, because they are in a higher position on the body, are less susceptible than the feet to being blemished by the forces of the *kelipot* (above, n.62). Still, when the *kelipot* are abundant and succeed in attaching themselves to the feet, the hands are also in danger and must be hidden. However, with the power of the *ruach* the emanation of the hands is manifested, and this has the ability to negate the *kelipot* and mitigate the decrees.

69. **sound of my beloved pulsates.** The *Tikkuney Zohar* (*loc. cit.*) states: "The sound of my beloved pulsates"—it knocks on the gate of the heart six times to indicate that it is *Tiferet*

LIKUTEY MOHARAN #10:6-8

בְּמִישׁוֹר" מוֹרֶה עַל אֱמוּנָה, וְאָז נִתְקַיֵּם "וַיְהִי יָדָיו אֱמוּנָה":

ז. וְהַתּוֹרָה הִיא גַּם כֵּן בְּחִינַת יָדַיִן וְרַגְלַיִן, כִּי יֵשׁ בְּהַתּוֹרָה נִגְלֶה
וְנִסְתָּר: נִגְלֶה הוּא בְּחִינַת יָדַיִם, כְּמוֹ שֶׁכָּתוּב: "דּוֹדִי שָׁלַח יָדוֹ מִן
הַחוֹר" – 'מִן הַחוֹר', הַיְנוּ חָרוּת עַל הַלּוּחוֹת (שְׁמוֹת ל"ב), שֶׁהוּא
בִּנְגְלֶה; וְנִסְתָּר הֵם בְּחִינוֹת רַגְלַיִן, כְּמַאֲמַר חֲכָמֵינוּ, זִכְרוֹנָם לִבְרָכָה
(סֻכָּה מט:): "חַמּוּקֵי יְרֵכַיִךְ" – 'מַה יָרֵךְ בַּסֵּתֶר' וְכוּ'.
וּכְלָלִיּוּת הַתּוֹרָה נִקְרֵאת לֵב, שֶׁמַּתְחֶלֶת בְּ"בֵית" וּמְסַיֶּמֶת בְּ"לָמֶד",
שֶׁשָּׁם מִשְׁכַּן הָרוּחַ דְּנָשִׁיב בְּשִׁית פִּרְקִין דִּדְרוֹעִין וְשִׁית פִּרְקִין
דְּרַגְלַיִן, הַיְנוּ בְּנִגְלֶה וּבְנִסְתָּר:

ח. וְזֶה בְּחִינַת מָרְדְּכַי וְאֶסְתֵּר, וְהָמָן, בְּחִינוֹת פּוּרִים, בְּחִינַת גּוֹרָל
שֶׁהִפִּיל הָמָן, בְּחִינַת עֹמֶר שְׂעוֹרִים.
כִּי הָמָן בְּחִינַת הָעֲבוֹדַת אֱלִילִים, כְּמַאֲמַר חֲכָמֵינוּ, זִכְרוֹנָם לִבְרָכָה,

revealed to all of Israel, correspond to the revealed Torah. In addition, the hands are generally a revealed part of the body, as opposed to the feet which are generally concealed.

77. **thigh is hidden...Torah.** The *Iyun Yaakov* on this passage in *Sukkah* (*loc. cit.*) teaches that "...hidden, so too, the words of Torah" refers to the esoteric teachings of Torah, the Kabbalah.

78. **Bet...Lamed.** The first word of the Torah (Pentateuch), *Bereishit*, begins with the letter *Bet*. The last word of the Torah, *yisraeL*, concludes with a *Lamed*. Together, these two letters form the word *LeV*, (לב, heart; see n.26 that *bet* and *vet* are the same). Thus, the heart, the seat of *ruach*, corresponds to the Torah in its entirety. In the terminology of the Kabbalah, the primary revelation of the Torah comes from *Binah* (Understanding), which also corresponds to the heart (*Parparaot LeChokhmah*).

79. **revealed...hidden.** From this we can see that Torah, like *ruach* (and tzaddik, as in §5), blows into and arouses the hands and feet to mitigate Divine judgment and nullify decrees.

It is worth noting that the Talmud (*Eruvin* 54a) lists various types of illnesses and hardships which people encounter, and then states that the remedy for all of them is Torah study. From Rebbe Nachman's explanation we can understand how this in fact stems from the power which study of Torah has to mitigate judgment and nullify decrees (see above, n.2).

In review: Decrees/judgments against the Jewish people are mitigated by means of dancing and clapping (§1). The essence of God's greatness is that idolators come to recognize Him (§2). Those far from God can only know Him through prayer in the aspect of "house," the immanent and comprehensible (§3). Elevating prayer to the aspect of "house" can only be accomplished through the tzaddikim. But the haughty renounce having the tzaddik pray for them. Their wisdom leaves them and they are rebuked by the intellect (§4). A haughty spirit,

each part of body represents diff. mitzvos, reflects middos.
either enhances or diminishes emuna

137   LIKUTEY MOHARAN #10:6-8

indicates faith. And then, "His hands were faith" is fulfilled.[74]

7. The Torah, too, corresponds to hands and feet.[75] For the Torah consists of both revealed and hidden [teachings]. The revealed corresponds to the hands, as in, "My beloved put his hand in through the *chor* (hole)." "In by the *ChoR*" alludes to "*ChoRut* (engraved) on the tablets" (Exodus 32:16)—this being the revealed.[76] The hidden corresponds to the feet, as our Sages said: "The rounded thighs" (Song of Songs 7:2)—just as the thigh is hidden, so too, the words of Torah (*Sukkah* 49b).[77]

Supposed to be ← Covered up

And the Torah in its entirety is called *lev* (heart), because it begins with a *Bet* and concludes with a *Lamed*.[78] [The heart] is the dwelling place of the spirit "which blows in the six sections of the arms and the six sections of the legs"—i.e., in the revealed and the hidden.[79]

8. And [all] this corresponds to Mordekhai and Esther, Haman, the aspects of Purim, the lots which Haman cast and the measure of barley offering.

---

74. faith is fulfilled. This verse appears in connection with the first battle which the Jewish nation faced after being redeemed from Egypt; an encounter with the idolatrous nation of Amalek (cf. *Rashi*, Deuteronomy 25:18). During the battle, Moshe stood with his hands extended in prayer. This enabled the Jews to defeat their enemy. Thus, Moshe, the tzaddik, had revealed the power of prayer through his hands. And, right after hearing about this battle against Amalek (Exodus 18:1)—the revelation of God's greatness—Yitro the priest abandoned his idolatry and came to join the Jewish people. This teaches that the tzaddik/ *ruach* can eliminate haughtiness/idolatry and bring about a revelation of faith in the world. This is why each person must see to bind himself to the tzaddik. The *Parparaot LeChokhmah* points out that Amalek (עמלק) has the same numerical value as *el acher* ("other god" or heresy, אל אחר), 240 (see Appendix: Gematria Chart).

In review: Decrees/judgments against the Jewish people are mitigated by means of dancing and clapping (§1). The essence of God's greatness is that idolators come to recognize Him (§2). Those far from God can only know Him through prayer in the aspect of "house," the immanent and comprehensible (§3). Elevating prayer to the aspect of "house" can only be accomplished through the tzaddikim, whose prayers God desires. But the haughty, who renounce having the tzaddik pray for them, deny God this pleasure. Their wisdom leaves them and they are rebuked by the intellect (§4). A haughty spirit, which is idolatry, is eliminated by being attached to the tzaddik, who is *ruach* (§5). Through the heart's *ruach*/the tzaddik, the feet dance and the hands clap, and this joy eliminates haughtiness/idolatry—i.e., mitigates Divine judgments/decrees (§6).

75. hands and feet. See above, note 51, that *ruach* corresponds to Torah.

76. hole...revealed. This verse appears in connection with the giving of the stone tablets at Sinai. The Tablets containing the Ten Commandments, which were given to Moshe and thus

LIKUTEY MOHARAN #10:8

שֶׁעָשָׂה עַצְמוֹ עֲבוֹדַת אֱלִילִים (מְגִילָה י:), וּבִשְׁבִיל זֶה הִפִּיל פּוּר הוּא הַגּוֹרָל בַּחֹדֶשׁ שֶׁמֵּת בּוֹ מֹשֶׁה (שָׁם י"ג:), כִּי מֹשֶׁה הוּא מְבַטֵּל הָעֲבוֹדָה זָרָה, וּבִשְׁבִיל זֶה נִקְבַּר מוּל בֵּית פְּעוֹר, כְּדֵי לְבַטֵּל הָעֲבוֹדָה זָרָה שֶׁבַּפְּעוֹר, כְּמוֹ שֶׁדָּרְשׁוּ רַבּוֹתֵינוּ, זִכְרוֹנָם לִבְרָכָה (סוֹטָה יד.). כִּי מֹשֶׁה גִּימַטְרִיָּא חֲרוֹן־אַף כִּי הוּא מְבַטֵּל חֲרוֹן־אַף שֶׁל הָעֲבוֹדָה זָרָה, כִּי הוּא קִבֵּל הַתּוֹרָה, שֶׁהוּא בְּחִינַת יָדַיִן וְרַגְלַיִן כַּנַּ"ל, שֶׁעַל יְדֵיהֶם נִתְבַּטֵּל הָעֲבוֹדַת אֱלִילִים כַּנַּ"ל.

וְעַל כֵּן הִפִּיל פּוּר בַּיֶּרַח שֶׁמֵּת בּוֹ מֹשֶׁה, כִּי חָשַׁב כִּי כְּבָר מֵת מֹשֶׁה הַמְבַטֵּל כֹּחַ הָעֲבוֹדַת אֱלִילִים, וְאֵין עוֹד מִי שֶׁיּוּכַל לְבַטֵּל כֹּחַ הָעֲבוֹדַת אֱלִילִים:

---

commemorating some Jewish merit—other than Adar. He was also pleased when the lottery fell on Adar, because he thought it symbolized the death of the tzaddik who has the power to counter the *ruach* of haughtiness, idolatry—i.e., Haman's quality. Indeed, our Sages taught: Haman, a one time barber, had sold himself to Mordekhai as a slave in exchange for some bread (*Megillah, ibid.*). It was his abundant arrogance and haughtiness (see previous note) which brought him to seek revenge, not only against Mordekhai, but against all the Jews.

82. **Pe'or.** This is the idol which the Jews were seduced into serving (Numbers 25). Moshe was subsequently buried opposite the site where the idol Pe'or was located. When the memory of their transgression rises to accuse the Jewish people and bring decrees upon them, Moshe rises up to counter and destroy it (*Sotah* 14a, *Tosafot, s.v. mipnei*). This indicates that Moshe is the true tzaddik, with the power to eliminate idolatry.

83. **Moshe...charon af.** The *gematria* of the name MoShE (משה) is 345, as is numerical value of the term *ChaRON AF* (חרון אף) (see Appendix: Gematria Chart).

84. **counter the power of this idol worship.** The Talmud teaches: Why were the Jews deserving of annihilation [at Haman's hands]? This was a punishment for their having worshipped idols in the time of Nebuchadnezzar (*Megillah* 12a). The explanation is this. Earlier in the lesson, Rebbe Nachman discusses the level of house and quotes the verse, "For My house shall be called a house of prayer for all the nations." God's house refers to the Holy Temple and it was Nebuchadnezzar who destroyed it. During his reign he instituted the worship of idolatry throughout his kingdom, with the intention of destroying the faith which the Jews had in God. By bowing to Nebuchadnezzar's idol, the Jewish people gave strength and support to the side of evil. This is what enabled Haman/Amalek (see n.74) to rise to power. Furthermore (*Megillah* 11b), Achashveirosh's giving Haman permission to annihilate the Jews stemmed from his belief that the time for the prophesied redemption had passed unfulfilled. The 70 years of exile which the prophet Yirmiyahu prophesied had, according to Achashveirosh's reckoning, come and gone without the predicted rebuilding of the Holy Temple. This led him to believe in the feasibility of Haman's wicked plan.

139   *LIKUTEY MOHARAN #10:8*

Haman corresponds to idol worship, as our Sages taught: [Haman] made himself into an object of worship (*Megillah* 10b).[80] This is the reason "the *pur*-lottery he cast" (*Esther* 3:7) [fell] in the month which Moshe died (*Megillah* 13b).[81] For Moshe is the one who counters idolatry. This is why he was buried "opposite Bet Pe'or" (*Deuteronomy* 34:6), as our Sages expounded: This was in order to eliminate the idolatry that was Pe'or (*Sotah* 14a).[82] For the letters of the name Moshe have the same numerical value as those of *charon af* (Divine anger).[83] He is the one who counters the Divine anger resulting from idolatry, because it was [Moshe] who received the Torah—the hands and feet through which idol worship is eliminated.

This is why [Haman rejoiced when] the lot fell in the month of Moshe's passing. He presumed that [the power of] Moshe, the one who eliminates the power of idolatry, had already passed from the world and that there was no one else who could counter the power of this idol worship.[84]

which is idolatry, is eliminated by being attached to the tzaddik, who is *ruach* (§5). Through the heart's *ruach*/the tzaddik, the feet dance and the hands clap, and this joy eliminates haughtiness/idolatry—i.e., mitigates Divine judgments/decrees (§6). Torah, which is the spirit in the heart, also corresponds to the hands and the feet, the revealed and the hidden, respectively (§7). Rebbe Nachman next shows how all these concepts correspond to story of Purim.

80. **Haman...worship.** The Midrash (*Esther Rabbah* 2:5) teaches:

Haman hung an idol around his neck so that people would bow down to him. This is the reason Mordekhai refused to bow before Haman, as everyone else was doing (Esther 3:2). The *Parparaot LeChokhmah* points out that Mordekhai descended from the tribe of Binyamin whose quality is holy arrogance (above, n.47). This arrogance was necessary if Mordekhai was to overcome the haughtiness of Haman, himself a descendant of Amalek—the arrogance of evil and idolatry incarnate.

Mordekhai, through his holy arrogance, was able to make amends for the mistake of King Shaul, who was also from the tribe of Binyamin. King Shaul had been commanded to utterly destroy the Amalekites and all they possessed (1 Samuel 15:2), but after having been victorious in battle, he was cowed by his soldiers into saving the flocks of the enemy. He also spared Agag, the Amalekite king. The prophet Shmuel admonished him, "Though you may be small in your own eyes, you were, however, made leader...why have you not obeyed the voice of God?" (1 Sam. 15:17,19). King Shaul should have used the authority of his position and his "inherited" quality of holy arrogance to entirely destroy Amalek as God had commanded. Instead of being killed immediately, Agag was imprisoned. This gave him the opportunity to father a child from whom Haman descended. It took Shaul's descendant, the tzaddik Mordekhai, to rectify this.

81. **month which Moshe died.** Moshe passed away on the 7th of Adar. In reviewing the Jewish calendar before casting lots, Haman saw that every month had at least one day

LIKUTEY MOHARAN #10:8

140

אֲבָל מָרְדְּכַי וְאֶסְתֵּר הָיָה לָהֶם כֹּחַ לְבַטֵּל הָעֲבוֹדַת אֱלִילִים שֶׁל הָמָן, וּבִשְׁבִיל זֶה בִּימֵיהֶם קִבְּלוּ יִשְׂרָאֵל הַתּוֹרָה מֵחָדָשׁ, כְּמַאֲמַר חֲכָמֵינוּ, זִכְרוֹנָם לִבְרָכָה (שַׁבָּת פח.): "קִיְּמוּ וְקִבְּלוּ" – 'קִיְּמוּ מַה שֶּׁקִּבְּלוּ כְּבָר'.

וְזֶה: קִיְּמוּ וְקִבְּלוּ. קִיְּמוּ – זֶה בְּחִינַת רַגְלַיִן, וְקִבְּלוּ – זֶה בְּחִינַת יָדַיִן, וְהוּא בְּחִינַת הַתּוֹרָה בְּעַצְמָהּ כַּנַּ"ל.

וְזֶה בְּחִינַת מָרְדְּכַי וְאֶסְתֵּר. 'מָרְדְּכַי' – מָר דְּרוֹר' (חֻלִּין קלט:) – דְּרוֹר, לְשׁוֹן חֵרוּת, זֶה בְּחִינַת יָדַיִם, כְּמוֹ שֶׁכָּתוּב: "דּוֹדִי שָׁלַח יָדוֹ מִן הַחוֹר" כַּנַּ"ל; וְאֶסְתֵּר הוּא בְּחִינַת שׁוֹקַיִן, מַה יָּרֵךְ בַּסֵּתֶר כַּנַּ"ל. וְזֶה לְשׁוֹן פּוּרִים, הַיְנוּ בִּטּוּל הָעֲבוֹדַת אֱלִילִים, כְּמוֹ שֶׁכָּתוּב (יְשַׁעְיָהוּ ס"ג): "פּוּרָה דָרַכְתִּי לְבַדִּי וּמֵעַמִּים אֵין אִישׁ אִתִּי". וְעַל-יְדֵי הֶאָרַת מָרְדְּכַי וְאֶסְתֵּר, הַיְנוּ בְּחִינַת הַיָּדַיִן וְרַגְלַיִן, נִתְבַּטְּלוּ הַכְּפִירוֹת וְנִתְרַבָּה אֱמוּנָה בָּעוֹלָם עַל-יְדֵיהֶם, כְּמוֹ שֶׁכָּתוּב (אֶסְתֵּר ב): "וַיְהִי אֹמֵן אֶת הֲדַסָּה", וּבָהּ כְּתִיב (שָׁם): "כַּאֲשֶׁר הָיְתָה

(above, §6 and §7) which, because they are generally above any contact with the *kelipot,* are an indication of freedom (*Parparaot LeChokhmah*).

90. **Esther....** The name *eSTheR* carries the connotation *haSTeR* which means hidden (*Chullin* 139a). The implication is that just as the thighs and feet are hidden and concealed, so too, was Esther; keeping her Jewish identity hidden as Mordekhai had instructed her to do. Thus, the combinations of Mordekhai and Esther, revealed and hidden Torah, the hands and the feet, all correspond to *ruach*: the spirit which counters atheism and idolatry.

91. **PuRim...PuRah...with Me.** This verse is an allegorical description of the way God will destroy and tread upon the Edomites, the way one treads upon the grapes in a winepress.

God mitigates and nullifies decrees on behalf of the Jews. Furthermore, He turns the decrees themselves back on those responsible for issuing them, the idolators. Thus, [the Egyptians were drowned for having decreed that all the newborn boys of the Jews be thrown into the Nile, and] Haman, who hoped to use the power of the *PuR* (lottery) against the Jews, had the lottery turn against him and into the festival of *PuRim* for God's chosen ones (*Parparaot LeChokhmah*). The *Mai HaNachal* adds that from this we can better understand Rebbe Nachman's remark that the days of Purim are near...(see above, n.1), for the Purim season has the power negate Divine judgment, idolatry and evil decrees.

92. **faith is thus increased....** The Midrash (*Shir HaShirim Rabbah* 7:8) states: In the days of Mordekhai and Esther, idolatry was destroyed.

LIKUTEY MOHARAN #10:8

But Mordekhai and Esther had the power to counter Haman's idolatry. This is why, in their day, the Jews received the Torah anew. As our Sages taught: "[The Jews] fulfilled and took upon themselves" (Esther 9:27)—they fulfilled that which they had previously taken upon themselves (*Shabbat* 88a).

This is the meaning of "they fulfilled and took upon themselves." "They fulfilled" corresponds to the feet,[85] and "took upon themselves" corresponds to the hands.[86] This is the very aspect of the Torah.[87]

This also corresponds to Mordekhai and Esther. *MoRDekhai* is "*MoR D'ror*"[88] (Exodus 30:23; cf. *Chullin* 139b). The word *d'ror* denotes *CheRut* (freedom),[89] which is an allusion to the hands, as in, "My beloved put his hand in by the *ChoR*." And Esther corresponds to the thighs, as in, "Just as the thigh is hidden," as mentioned above.[90]

And this is the connotation of [the festival's name,] *PURim*. It alludes to the elimination of idol worship, as is written (Isaiah 63:3), "The *PURah* (winepress) I have trodden alone; and of the nations, there was none with Me."[91]

Through the emanation of Mordekhai and Esther, the aspects of the hands and the feet, atheism is eliminated. Faith is thus increased in the world because of them.[92] As it is written (Esther 2:7), "And [Mordekhai] *ŒMeiN* (raised) Hadassah"—[i.e., Esther]—of whom it

---

85. **fulfilled...feet.** The Hebrew *Kiy'Mu* (they fulfilled) is akin to the word *l'haKiM* (to make stand), something which is done with, and thus alludes to, the feet.

86. **took upon...hands.** The Hebrew *KiBLu* (they took) is from the same root as the word *l'KaBeL* (to receive), something which is done with, and thus alludes to, the hands.

87. **aspect of the Torah.** The Torah is the hands and the feet, as above, in section 7. Our Sages taught that after the miracle of Purim, the Jews accepted the Torah with an entirely new and more total commitment, even greater than the one which they had exhibited at Mt. Sinai. It is worth noting that just as at Mt. Sinai, so too on Purim, the Torah was received only after a battle with Amalek.

88. **MoR D'ror.** The full text in *Chullin* (*loc. cit.*) reads: "Where is Mordekhai alluded to in the Five Books of Torah? It is written (Exodus 30:23), 'You must take the finest fragrances...*mor d'ror* (myrrh, free of impurities),' and Onkelos translates this into Aramaic as *MeiRa DaKhIa*." This is *MoRDeKhaI*. In addition, the word *MoR* (מר) has the same numerical value as *AMaLeK* (עמלק), 240 (see Appendix: Gematria Chart), symbolizing Mordekhai's ability to counter the power of Amalek.

89. **d'ror denotes freedom.** Both *d'ror* and *cherut* mean freedom. This implies the hands

בָּאֱמָנָה אִתּוֹ", כִּי שְׁנֵיהֶם הֵם בְּחִינַת אֱמוּנָה.

וְזֶה נַעֲשָׂה עַל־יְדֵי הָרוּחַ כַּנַּ"ל. וְזֶה בְּחִינַת (מְגִלָּה ז.): 'אֶסְתֵּר בְּרוּחַ־הַקֹּדֶשׁ נֶאֶמְרָה', הַיְנוּ בְּחִינַת "לִבּוּ נָשָׂא אֶת רַגְלָיו", כִּי עִקַּר הָעַכּוּ"ם תָּלוּי בָּהּ, שֶׁהִיא בְּחִינַת רַגְלַיִן, כְּמוֹ שֶׁכָּתוּב (מִשְׁלֵי ה): "רַגְלֶיהָ יוֹרְדוֹת מָוֶת", וְעַל כֵּן עִקַּר תִּקּוּן הָעֲבוֹדַת אֱלִילִים עַל־ יָדָהּ.

וְעַל כֵּן דַּיְקָא 'אֶסְתֵּר – בְּרוּחַ־הַקֹּדֶשׁ נֶאֶמְרָה'; אַף שֶׁבֶּאֱמֶת תִּקּוּן הָעֲבוֹדַת אֱלִילִים הוּא גַּם־כֵּן עַל־יְדֵי מָרְדְּכַי כַּנַּ"ל, רַק מֵחֲמַת שֶׁעִקַּר הָעֲבוֹדַת אֱלִילִים תְּלוּיָה בָּהּ, וְעַל כֵּן עַל־יָדָהּ עִקַּר הַתִּקּוּן. וְעַל כֵּן נִקְרֵאת הַמְּגִלָּה עַל שֵׁם אֶסְתֵּר, וְהַיְנוּ דְּדַיְקָא 'אֶסְתֵּר – בְּרוּחַ־הַקֹּדֶשׁ נֶאֶמְרָה', כִּי הָרוּחַ הוּא בַּלֵּב, וְעַל־יָדוֹ נִתְגַּלֶּה הָאָרַת הַיָּדַיִם וְהָרַגְלַיִם, רַק הָעִקַּר תְּלוּיָה בָּרַגְלַיִם, בְּחִינַת אֶסְתֵּר.

וְזֶה בְּחִינוֹת עֹמֶר שְׂעוֹרִים. עֹמֶר – זֶה בְּחִינַת מָרְדְּכַי – עַיִן מֹר, מָר דְּרוֹר – דְּרוֹר לְשׁוֹן חֵרוּת, הַיְנוּ בְּחִינַת חָרוּת עַל הַלֻּחֹת [כְּמוֹ

In the language of the Kabbalah, the forces of evil subsist on and are dependent upon *Malkhut*, the lowest of the *sefirot*. When the side of evil takes *Malkhut* into its domain— symbolizing the Divine Presence's exile amongst the idolators—it is said that "Her feet go down to death."

97. **through her.** The Talmud teaches: [Because she kept her true identity hidden,] it seemed to each person that Esther came from his nation (*Megillah* 13a). This can be understood from our lesson. Rebbe Nachman tells us that Esther was capable of descending into each of the different idolatries of the nations and destroy it. This came from her ability to make it seem as though she was associated with and had a share in it. Thus, the elimination of idolatry came through her.

98. **Mordekhai.** Many people converted to Judaism as a result of Mordekhai and his role in the miracle of Purim (Esther 8:17, see *Rashi; ibid.,* 9:3-4). Mordekhai, like Esther, rectified the sin of idolatry by bringing about a revelation of faith.

99. **rectification is through her.** Esther/the feet are closer to the *kelipot* than Mordekhai/the hands. This makes them not only more susceptible, but also more capable of bringing about a *tikkun* for the gentiles.

100. **omer of barley.** This sacrificial offering was brought on the second day of Pesach, the 16th of Nissan, as described in Leviticus 23:10-15.

LIKUTEY MOHARAN #10:8

is written (Esther 2:20), "just as when she was *ŒMNah* (raised) by him."
For both [Mordekhai and Esther] correspond to *EMuNah* (faith).[93]

And, as mentioned above, [elimination of atheism and an increase
of faith] is achieved by means of the *ruach*.[94] This corresponds to: The
Book of Esther was dictated with *ruach*-of-holiness (Megillah 7a), an
aspect of, "his heart carried his feet."[95] For, in the main, the idolators
are dependent upon [Esther], she being synonymous with the feet, as
in (Proverbs 5:5), "Her feet go down to death."[96] Therefore, the primary
rectification of idol worship comes through her.[97]

And so, specifically "The Book of Esther was dictated with *ruach*-
of-holiness." Even though it is true that idolatry is also rectified
through Mordekhai,[98] nevertheless, since the idolators are mainly
dependent upon < the feet >, the main rectification is through her.[99]
The book was therefore named after Esther (Megillah, ibid.). This is the
reason that specifically "The Book of Esther was dictated with the
spirit-of-holiness." For the spirit is in the heart, and through it the
emanation of the hands and feet is revealed. It is just that the primary
dependence is upon the feet/Esther.

This ties into the concept of the *omer* (sacrificial measure) of
barley.[100] The *AoMeR* corresponds to *MoRDekhai*: its letters *Ayin
MoR* [suggest] *MoR D'ror*. The word *d'ror* denotes *CheRut* (freedom),

---

93. **ŒMeiN...ŒMNah...EMuNah, faith.** The one who raised and brought up Hadassah—
i.e., Esther—was Mordekhai (*Megillah* 13a). The words *æmen* (אומן) and *æmnah* (אמנה) are
similar to the word *emunah* (אמונה), indicating not only the faith which they themselves had
but also their ability to "raise up" everything into faith (*Tikkuney Zohar* #21, p.57).

94. **ruach.** As above, in section 6, the *ruach* counters atheism and idolatry through the "hands
and feet."

95. **heart carried his feet.** As mentioned previously, it is the *ruach* in the heart/the tzaddik
which raises up the feet/Esther and causes them to dance, thus mitigating decrees. This *ruach*
in the heart corresponds to Divine *ruach* (spirit or inspiration) which is akin to prophecy. It
was therefore said of the Book of Esther that it was Divinely inspired and thus incorporated
into the Sacred Writings (Hagiographa).

96. **idolators...feet go down to death.** The feet, because they are the lowest part of the body,
are said to be closest to the forces of evil and impurity (n.62). This is why Rebbe Nachman
teaches that the idolators are dependent upon Esther (who corresponds to the feet), as she is
closest to them. The *Parparaot LeChokhmah* adds that this explains why our Sages connected
Esther with Sarah, for just as Esther was taken to the palace of Achashveirosh (Esther 2:16),
Sarah had been taken to the house of Avimelekh (Genesis 20:2).

LIKUTEY MOHARAN #10:8　144

שֶׁאָמְרוּ רַבּוֹתֵינוּ, זִכְרוֹנָם לִבְרָכָה (ערובין נד.): אַל תִּקְרֵי חָרוּת אֶלָּא חֵרוּת], שֶׁהוּא בְּחִינַת הַתּוֹרָה בְּנִגְלֶה, שֶׁהוּא בְּחִינַת "עַיִן בְּעַיִן" (בְּמִדְבָּר י"ד).

שְׂעוֹרִים – זֶה בְּחִינַת אֶסְתֵּר בְּרוּחַ־הַקֹּדֶשׁ, כְּמוֹ שֶׁכָּתוּב (דְּבָרִים ל"ב): "כִּשְׂעִירִים עֲלֵי־דֶשֶׁא", שֶׁהוּא לְשׁוֹן רוּחַ.

וּבִשְׁבִיל זֶה, כְּשֶׁבָּא הָמָן לְמָרְדְּכַי, מְצָאוֹ עוֹסֵק בְּעֹמֶר שְׂעוֹרִים, אָמַר לָהֶם: עֹמֶר שְׂעוֹרִים דִּידְכוּ אָתֵי וְנִצַּח אוֹתוֹ וְאֶת בָּנָיו, כַּמְבֹאָר בַּמִּדְרָשׁ (אֶסְתֵּר רַבָּה פָּרְשָׁה י; מְגִילָה טז.); כִּי עַל־יְדֵי עֹמֶר שְׂעוֹרִים, שֶׁהוּא בְּחִינַת יָדַיִן וְרַגְלַיִן, שֶׁהֵם בְּחִינַת הַמְחָאַת כַּף וְרִקּוּדִין, נִתְבַּטֵּל הָעֲבוֹדָה זָרָה, שֶׁהוּא בְּחִינַת הָמָן, בְּחִינַת גֵּאוּת כַּנַּ"ל.

וּבִשְׁבִיל זֶה צִוָּה הָמָן לַעֲשׂוֹת עֵץ גָּבֹהַּ חֲמִשִּׁים אַמָּה, כִּי רָצָה לְבַטֵּל כֹּחַ שֶׁל חֲמִשִּׁים יוֹם שֶׁל סְפִירַת הָעֹמֶר, שֶׁהוּא הַכֹּחַ שֶׁל מָרְדְּכַי וְאֶסְתֵּר:

---

omer sacrifice, and he found him studying the laws relating to the sacrifice with his students. Realizing that events were beginning to turn against him and his plot to destroy Mordekhai and the Jews, he said, "The measure of your barley offering came and defeated..." (cf. *Megillah* 16a).

104. **barley...dancing...haughtiness is eliminated.** In review: The barley measurement corresponds to Mordekhai and Esther, who, in turn, are synonymous with the hands and feet, the power of clapping and dancing. These all connect to the concept of *ruach,* through which a haughty spirit, and thus idolatry and Haman, are countered and eliminated.

105. **Mordekhai and Esther....** The 50 day Omer-Counting culminates with the holiday of Shavuot, commemorating the giving of the Torah at Mt. Sinai. Here again Rebbe Nachman adds to the structure of connections, showing, in yet another way, that Mordekhai and Esther are connected to the Torah (see n.87) and to the *ruach* for countering idolatry. Haman's intention had been to uproot the Torah and overcome the 50 day Omer-Counting. In the end, Haman's plot to hang Mordekhai was turned against him (see n.91). On the 16th of Nissan—the very day of the *omer* offering and the beginning of the Omer-Counting— Haman himself was hanged on this tree of 50 cubits; overcome by the power which Mordekhai and Esther drew from the Omer-Counting.

The *Mai HaNachal* adds that by fulfilling the commandment of Omer-Counting, or by being very joyous on Purim, a person merits receiving the Torah—the hidden and the revealed.

LIKUTEY MOHARAN #10:8

which is "*ChoRut* (engraved) on the tablets." {As our Sages taught: Do not read that the tablets were *chorut*, but rather that they provided the Jews with *cherut* (Eruvin 54a).} And [*chorut*] corresponds to revealed Torah, an aspect of "*Ayin b'Ayin* (eye to eye)" (Numbers 14:14).[101]

And *Se'ORim* (barley) corresponds to "The Book of Esther was dictated with *ruach*-of-holiness." As it is written (Deuteronomy 32:2), "Like *Se'IRim* (*wind*blown rains) upon the grass," which denotes *ruach*.[102]

This is why the Midrash teaches that when Haman came to Mordekhai, he found him teaching the laws of the barley offering. [Haman] said to them, "The measure of your barley offering will one day come to defeat" him and his sons (Esther Rabbah 10:4).[103] Through the measured barley offering, which corresponds to the hands and feet— i.e., clapping and dancing—idolatry/Haman/haughtiness is eliminated.[104]

And this is the reason why Haman ordered the preparation of "a tree of fifty cubits" [on which to hang Mordekhai] (Esther 5:14). He hoped to undermine the influence of the fifty days of Omer-Counting from which Mordekhai and Esther drew their power.[105]

---

101. **AoMeR...Ayin MoR...Ayin b'Ayin, eye to eye.** With this, Rebbe Nachman reviews a series of previous connections and proofs, and at the same time provides additional links to the lesson's structure. The letters of the word *AoMeR* (עמר) are *A[yin] MoR* (ע. מר). This alludes to *MoRDekhai*, as in "*MoR D'ror*" (see n.88). As mentioned earlier, *d'ror* is *cherut* (n.89). Rebbe Nachman here interchanges this with *chorut* (engraving), which applies to the Torah engraved on the Tablets of Testimony. Specifically, this refers to the revealed Torah about which it can be said that it is seen "*Ayin b'Ayin*" (eye to eye).

The Torah is said to have *ayin panim* (ע = 70 "faces") of interpretation. Furthermore, the *Tikkuney Zohar* (#18, p.36a) which states that *teruah* corresponds to *ruach*, which Rebbe Nachman quoted previously (§5), also teaches that *TeRuAH* (תרועה) is *ToRaH Ayin* (ע. תורה). This likewise highlights the connection *ayin* has to Torah and *ruach*.

102. **Se'IRim...ruach.** Onkelos translates *se'irim* as *ruchey mitra* (windblown rains). Thus, the likeness between *se'irim* and *se'orim* indicates that *ruach* (spirit)-of-holiness is connected to the barley offering, which in itself is related to the story of Purim, as Rebbe Nachman will next explain.

103. **defeated him and his sons.** Achashveirosh sent Haman to honor Mordekhai, ordering him to mount Mordekhai on the king's horse and parade him through the city of Shushan (Esther 6:11). When Haman came to Mordekhai it was the 16th of Nissan, the day of the

LIKUTEY MOHARAN #10:9

146

ט וְזֶה פֵּרוּשׁ:

אָמַר רַבָּה בַּר בַּר־חָנָה: אָמַר לִי הַהוּא טַיָּעָא: תָּא וְאַחֲוֵי לָךְ בְּלוּעֵי דְקֹרַח. אַזְלִי וַחֲזַאי תְּרֵי בִּזְעֵי דַהֲוֵי נָפִיק מִנַּיְהוּ קֻטְרָא. שְׁקַל גְּבָבָא דְעַמְרָא וּמַשְׁיֵהּ בְּמַיָּא וְאַנְּחֵהּ בְּרֵישֵׁהּ דְּרָמְחָה וְעַיְּלֵהּ הָתָם, וְכִי אַפִּיק, הֲוֵי אִחֲרַךְ אִחֲרוּכֵי. אָמַר לִי: אַצִּית! מָה שָׁמָעִית? וְשָׁמְעֵת דַּהֲוֵי אָמְרִין: מֹשֶׁה וְתוֹרָתוֹ אֱמֶת וְהֵן בַּדָּאִין. אָמַר לִי: כָּל שְׁלֹשִׁים יוֹמָא מְהַדְּרָא לְהוּ גֵּיהִנֹּם לְהָכָא כְּבָשָׂר בְּקַלַּחַת, וְאָמְרִי הָכִי: מֹשֶׁה וְתוֹרָתוֹ אֱמֶת וְהֵן בַּדָּאִין.

בְּלוּעֵי דְקֹרַח – כִּדְאִיתָא בַּמִּדְרָשׁ (בְּמִדְבַּר רַבָּה פָּרָשָׁה יח; יְרוּשַׁלְמִי סַנְהֶדְרִין פֶּרֶק חֵלֶק): 'קֹרַח מִין הָיָה', הַיְנוּ בְּחִינַת הָעֲבוֹדַת אֱלִילִים, מִינוּת.

apikorsos/heretic

וַחֲזַאי תְּרֵי בִּזְעֵי דַהֲוֵי נָפִיק מִנַּיְהוּ קֻטְרָא. – הַיְנוּ בְּחִינַת הַחֲרוֹן־אַף שֶׁגּוֹרְמִים בְּמִינוּת, כְּמַאֲמַר חֲכָמֵינוּ, זִכְרוֹנָם לִבְרָכָה: 'כָּל זְמַן שֶׁעֲבוֹדַת אֱלִילִים בָּעוֹלָם, חֲרוֹן־אַף בָּעוֹלָם'; 'וּתְרֵי בִּזְעֵי', זֶה בְּחִינוֹת תְּרֵי נִקְבֵי הָאַף, שֶׁיּוֹצֵא מֵהֶם הֶעָשָׁן, כְּמוֹ שֶׁכָּתוּב (תְּהִלִּים י"ח): "עָלָה עָשָׁן בְּאַפּוֹ".

וְשָׁקֵיל גְּבָבָא דְעַמְרָא – זֶה בְּחִינַת עֹמֶר כַּנַּ"ל,

וּמַשְׁיֵהּ בְּמַיָּא – זֶה בְּחִינַת שְׂעוֹרִים, בְּחִינַת אֶסְתֵּר בְּרוּחַ־הַקֹּדֶשׁ,

---

רַשְׁבַּ"ם:

בִּזְעֵי – בְּקָעִים, דִּכְתִיב: "וַתִּבָּקַע הָאֲדָמָה" וְגוֹ'. קֻטְרָא – עָשָׁן. שְׁקַל גְּבָבָא דְעַמְרָא – לָקַח גַּזַּת צֶמֶר וּשְׂרָאָהּ בְּמַיִם. וְאִחֲרַךְ אִחֲרוּכֵי – הֲנֵי גְבָבֵי, וְאַף־עַל־פִּי שֶׁשָּׂרוּ אוֹתָהּ בְּמַיִם. אַצִּית – הַסְכֵּת וּשְׁמַע. וְשָׁמְעֵת דְּקָאָמְרֵי – שֶׁהֲרֵי יָרְדוּ חַיִּים שְׁאוֹלָה. כָּל תְּלָתִין יוֹמִין – כָּל רֹאשׁ־חֹדֶשׁ. בְּקַלַּחַת – שֶׁמְּהַפְּכִין אוֹתוֹ כְּדֵי שֶׁיִּתְבַּשֵּׁל:

---

expression of the heretical beliefs which he came to because of his haughtiness.

107. **Smoke went up....** The smoke of Divine anger, brought on by "Korach"/heresy and idolatry, emanates, as it were, from the nose. Being the antithesis of Divine patience (*erekh apayim*) and *ruach* which is the source of the life-force (see *Likutey Moharan* I, 8:1,4,9), Divine anger is the source of Divine judgement/decrees.

LIKUTEY MOHARAN #10:9

9. This is the explanation:

Rabbah bar bar Chanah recounted: This merchant said to me, "Come, I will show you those swallowed up with Korach." I went and saw two cracks from which fumes were coming out. [The merchant] took a ball of *omra* (wool) and washed it in water. Then he put it on the head of his *romach* (spear) and inserted it there. When he removed it, it was *ichrakh* (scorched) entirely. He said to me, "Listen! What do you hear?" I heard them saying, "Moshe and his Torah are true, and we are false." [The merchant] said to me, "Once every thirty days Hell brings them back to here, like meat in a pot. And this is what they say, that Moshe and his Torah are true and they are false" *(Bava Batra 74a).*

Rashbam:

cracks - splits, as in, "And the earth split open": **fumes** - smoke: **took a ball of omra** - he took a clump of wool and soaked it in water: **scorched entirely** - the ball of wool, even though it had been soaked in water: **Listen!** - pay attention and hear: **I heard them saying** - for they had descended to Hell alive: **Once every thirty days** - every New Moon: **in a pot** - which is stirred so that it cooks:

those swallowed up with Korach — As we find in the Midrash: Korach was a heretic *(Bamidbar Rabbah 18).*[106] And heresy is similar to idol worship.

I saw two cracks from which fumes were coming out — This alludes to the Divine anger brought on by heresy. As our Sages taught: As long as there is idol worship in the world, there is Divine anger in the world. The **two cracks** correspond to the two *nostrils* from which smoke emanates, as in (Psalms 18:9), "Smoke went up out of his nostrils."[107]

took a ball of OMRa (wool) — This is synonymous with the *OMeR,* as mentioned above. [It refers to Mordekhai/revealed Torah/hands, which is joined with hidden Torah, as in:]

washed it in water — This is the *se'orim* (barley), which corresponds to "The Book of Esther was dictated with *ruach*-of-holiness"/the feet.

---

106. **Korach was a heretic.** Like Moshe and Aharon, Korach was a Levite. This led him to believe that he would be chosen for a position of prominence similar to his cousins. When this did not happen, his haughtiness prevented him from accepting God's will and he led a rebellion against Moshe's authority. He separated himself from the tzaddik and claimed that he, too, was God's chosen (Numbers 16). The Talmud (*Yerushalmi, Sanhedrin,* chap. *Chelek*) teaches that Korach then made light of the Torah's mitzvot. Apparently, this was an

LIKUTEY MOHARAN #10:9

148

שֶׁהוּא בְּחִינַת רַגְלַיִן כַּנַּ"ל. כִּי הָרַגְלַיִן הֵם אֲפִיקֵי מַיִם, כִּי הֵם בְּחִינַת עַרְבֵי נַחַל, כְּמַאֲמַר חֲכָמֵינוּ, זִכְרוֹנָם לִבְרָכָה (סֻכָּה נג.): 'רַגְלוֹהִי דְּבַר-נָשׁ אִנּוּן עָרְבִין לֵהּ'; 'עָרְבִין' – זֶה בְּחִינַת עַרְבֵי נַחַל, אֲפִיקֵי מַיִם, הַיְנוּ בְּחִינַת מָרְדֳּכַי וְאֶסְתֵּר, בְּחִינַת יָדַיִם וְרַגְלַיִם, בְּחִינַת הַמִּחְאַת כַּף וְרִקּוּדִין כַּנַּ"ל.

וְאַנְחֵהּ בְּרֵישֵׁהּ דְּרָמְחָא – רֹמַח, דָּא רוּחַ מֵ"ם, שֶׁהוּא מֵאַרְבַּע רוּחוֹת בָּאֵי הָרוּחַ, כִּי הַמֵּ"ם הִיא אַרְבַּע רוּחוֹת, שֶׁהִיא בְּחִינַת רוּחַ הַצַּדִּיק דְּנָשַׁב בְּיָדַיִן וְרַגְלַיִן כַּנַּ"ל; וְרֹאשׁ הָרֹמַח הוּא הַצַּדִּיק, כִּי מִמֶּנּוּ תּוֹצְאוֹת הָרוּחַ, כְּמוֹ שֶׁכָּתוּב: "אִישׁ אֲשֶׁר רוּחַ בּוֹ" כַּנַּ"ל.

וְאַפְקִינְהוּ, וְאִחְדָּךְ אַחֲרוּכֵי – אִחְדָּךְ, לְשׁוֹן חַיִּים וַאֲרִיכוּת יָמִים, כְּמַאֲמַר חֲכָמֵינוּ, זִכְרוֹנָם לִבְרָכָה (עֵרוּבִין נד:): 'לֹא יַחֲרֹךְ רְמִיָּה צֵידוֹ' – 'לֹא יִחְיֶה וְלֹא יַאֲרִיךְ', וְהַיְנוּ: 'וְאִיחְדָּךְ אִיחֲרוּכֵי', לְשׁוֹן חַיִּים וַאֲרִיכַת יָמִים; כִּי עַל-יְדֵי בִּטּוּל הַגַּאֲוָה, הַיְנוּ הָעֲבוֹדָה זָרָה, עַל-יְדֵי-זֶה הַחָכְמָה עַל תִּקּוּנָהּ כַּנַּ"ל, וְעַל-יְדֵי חָכְמָה יִחְיֶה וְיַאֲרִיךְ יָמִים, כְּמוֹ שֶׁכָּתוּב (קֹהֶלֶת ז): "הַחָכְמָה תְּחַיֶּה" וְכוּ'.

---

111. ... **mem refers to the four winds.** The word *romach* (רומח) is a composite of *ruach* (רוח) and *mem* (מ). The *mem* is a four-sided letter and thus corresponds to the four directions of the earth from which the winds—*ruchot*—come. Now the source of this *ruach,* as Rebbe Nachman reminds us here (see §5), is the tzaddik. The *Parparaot LeChokhmah* explains that we can now understand the connection between the joy which the heart feels from performing a mitzvah and expresses through the physical acts of clapping and dancing, and the nullifying of decrees. Very simply, creating joy while performing God's will arouses the corresponding spiritual forces in heaven, and this can actually overturn the stern judgments that lead to decrees.

In addition, the words *yada'im v'ragla'im* (hands and feet, ידים ורגלים) have the same numerical value as the word *simchah* (joy and happiness, שמחה), 353 (*Rabbi Moshe Kramer*).

112. **neither live nor....** This passage from the Talmud (*loc. cit.*) appears as part of a discussion about a person who is hypocritical in his observance and Torah study. Such a person, our Sages taught, will not be successful, nor will he live and have length of days. Rebbe Nachman applies this to the false leaders who do not bring life to their followers. Eventually, the "houses of prayer" which they have established will fall and come apart. In contrast, those who bind themselves to the true tzaddik *do* achieve life. They draw *ruach* and "water," Mordekhai and Esther, and can thereby eliminate and overcome the decrees and hardships which they encounter in life.

113. **wisdom gives life....** As we have seen (above §4 end), when a person grows haughty, he

149   *LIKUTEY MOHARAN #10:9*

This is because the feet are the "water brooks" (Psalms 42.2), in that they correspond to willows of the stream.[108] As our Sages taught: A person's feet are *arvin* (guarantors) for him (*Sukkah* 53a). *ARVin* corresponds to *ARVey* (willows) of the stream, the "water brooks."[109] [Thus the wool in water] alludes to Mordekhai and Esther/the hands and the feet/clapping and dancing.[110]

Then he put it on the head of his romach (spear) — *RoMaCh* is *RuaCh Mem* (cf. *Zohar* III, 237a), as in, "Come from the four *RuChot* (winds), O spirit." This is because the *mem* refers to the four winds,[111] which corresponds to the *ruach* of the tzaddik that "blows in the arms and the legs." And **the head of the romach** is the tzaddik from whom the *ruach* comes, as in, "A man in whom there is < the Lord's > *ruach*."

When he removed it, it was ichrakh (scorched) entirely — The word *iChRaKh* has the connotation of life and length of days. As our Sages taught: "The slothful man will not *YaChaRoKh* (roast) his catch" (Proverbs 12:27)—he will neither *YiChyeh* (live) nor *YaaRiKh* (have length of days) (*Eruvin* 54b).[112] This is the meaning of **scorched entirely**: it alludes to life and length of days. By eliminating haughtiness—i.e., idolatry—[one's] wisdom is as it should be. And with wisdom, a person lives long, as is written (Ecclesiastes 7:12), "Wisdom gives life to those who possess it."[113]

---

108. **water brooks...willows of the stream.** The *Zohar* (III, 68a) teaches that all the streams flow together into two springs which are called *afikey mayim* (water brooks). The same passage in the *Zohar* comments that these two brooks allude to the *sefirot* of *Netzach* and *Hod* (see above, n.65). According to the Kabbalah, these two Divine emanations are represented in the human form as the feet. In addition, the Four Species of the Sukkot holiday—the palm branch, citron, myrtle branch and willows—also correspond to different parts of the human form. The *arvey nachal* (willows of the stream), which are the "lowest" of the four, are said to represent the feet. In this sense, they are also *Netzach* and *Hod,* and are thus known as *afikey mayim.* ("Water brooks" is a term from Psalms 42 which begins *Maskil livnei Korach.*)

109. **feet...guarantors...willows...brooks.** Rebbe Nachman points to another connection between the feet and *arvey nachal.* The Sages teach that a person's feet are his *arvin* (guarantors). The interpretation given here is that when they are strong, a person's feet keep him firm and guarantee that he will not descend into the realm of evil and impurity.

110. **clapping and dancing.** The wool, which is Mordekhai, is washed in the water, Esther. It implies the combining of the revealed and the hidden Torah. This combination also indicates a joining of the hands and the feet, or clapping and dancing, and results in the mitigating of Divine judgment/decrees.

LIKUTEY MOHARAN #10:9

אָמַר לִי: אַצִּית לְהוּ וְשִׁמְעַת דְּאָמְרִין: מֹשֶׁה וְתוֹרָתוֹ אֱמֶת – שֶׁהֵן מוֹדִין עַל הָאֱמֶת; כִּי כְּשֶׁמִּתְקָרֵב אֶת עַצְמוֹ לְצַדִּיקִים כְּדֵי לְקַבֵּל מֵהֶם הָרוּחַ כַּנַּ"ל, וְעַל-יְדֵי-זֶה נִשְׁבָּר הַגַּאֲוָה וְהָעֲבוֹדָה זָרָה, וְאָז מַכִּירִין אֲפִלּוּ אֵלּוּ שֶׁהֵם מִסִּטְרָא דְּמוֹתָא אֶת גְּדֻלַּת הַבּוֹרֵא יִתְבָּרַךְ שְׁמוֹ כַּנַּ"ל.

וְאָמַר לִי: כָּל שְׁלֹשִׁים יוֹמִין מְהַדְּרָא לְהוּ גֵּיהִנֹּם לְהָכָא וְאָמְרֵי הָכִי: מֹשֶׁה וְתוֹרָתוֹ אֱמֶת – פֵּרֵשׁ רַבֵּנוּ שְׁמוּאֵל: בְּכָל רֹאשׁ-חֹדֶשׁ. כִּי כָּל דָּבָר יֵשׁ לוֹ שֹׁרֶשׁ, וְשֹׁרֶשׁ הַתְּשׁוּבָה הוּא רֹאשׁ-חֹדֶשׁ, כִּי בְּרֹאשׁ-חֹדֶשׁ אָמַר הַקָּדוֹשׁ-בָּרוּךְ-הוּא: הָבִיאוּ עָלַי כַּפָּרָה, כְּמוֹ שֶׁדָּרְשׁוּ רַבּוֹתֵינוּ, זִכְרוֹנָם לִבְרָכָה, וְזֶה בְּחִינַת תְּשׁוּבָה, וְהַתְּשׁוּבָה הַזֹּאת נִשְׁתַּלְשְׁלָה בְּכָל הַנִּבְרָאִים בְּרֹאשׁ-חֹדֶשׁ, וּבִשְׁבִיל זֶה גַּם קֹרַח וַעֲדָתוֹ מְכָרְחִים לְאֵיזֶה חֲרָטָה בְּרֹאשׁ-חֹדֶשׁ; אֲבָל הַתְּשׁוּבָה אֵינָהּ מוֹעִיל לָהֶם, כִּי

search for the truth—for the tzaddik. His attempts, when sincere and tireless, will lead him to the right path. And, the "truth" of a person's quest itself becomes apparent when his searching brings him to repent. Seeing that those who had been swallowed up with Korach were repenting once every thirty days for rebelling against Moshe, the Rashbam therefore concluded that this must have been on the New Moon—the root of all repentance.

117. **repentance.** At Creation, the moon complained to God that He had created two celestial bodies which gave off the same amount of light. The moon likened this to two kings having to wear the same crown. This can be understood as an exhibition of haughtiness, much as when Korach, in reality seeking to gain prominence for himself, took issue with God's plan. In response, God ordered that the moon make itself smaller. This symbolized a humbling of the moon's haughtiness. Later, God sought to appease the moon. But the moon would not be pacified. Finally, God said that a sacrifice should be brought on the New Moon to atone, as it were, for His having diminished the moon. The lesson of this Talmudic teaching is that the very first one to repent was God Himself, and that this repentance is in conjunction with the New Moon, when the moon is "reborn." Thus the root of all repentance is the New Moon (*Parparaot LeChokhmah*).

118. **into all of creation.** God's designation of the New Moon as a time for repenting automatically makes it a propitious time for returning to Him. But that is not all. Because all of creation emanates from God, a desire to repent is felt by all the different parts of creation on the New Moon. Accordingly, all creatures experience a "thought" of repentance at the beginning of each month, much as they do on Rosh HaShanah, the onset of the new year.

151   *LIKUTEY MOHARAN #10:9*

He said to me, Listen! What do you hear? I heard them saying, Moshe and his Torah are true — They admitted to the truth.[114] This happens when a person draws closer to the < tzaddik > in order to receive *ruach* from < him >. As a result, [the spirit of] haughtiness and idolatry are shattered. Then even those [distant from God]—who are from < the Other Side > —recognize the greatness of the Holy One.[115]

[The merchant] said to me, Once every thirty days Hell brings them back to here.... And this is what they say, that Moshe and his Torah are true — Rashbam explains that this happened every New Moon. This is because everything has its root <Above>, and the root of repentance is the New Moon.[116] As our Sages expounded: On the New Moon, the Holy One says, "Bring an atonement offering on My behalf [for My having caused the moon to be diminished]" (*Chullin* 60a). This is an aspect of repentance.[117] And on the New Moon, this repentance is projected down [from God] into all of creation.[118] Thus, even Korach and his followers must feel some remorse on the New Moon. But repentance does not help them, because essentially

loses his wisdom. Without wisdom a person is incapable of achieving "length of days," even if he lives to be 120. This is because extended days are dependent upon Torah study (cf. *Likutey Moharan* I, 56:3) and increased holiness (*ibid.,* 60:2), both of which relate to wisdom.

114. **admitted to the truth.** The merchant now tells Rabbah bar bar Chanah to listen to their confession. This merchant is a *socher Ishmael,* the tzaddik who encompasses all the prayers (see *Likutey Moharan* I, 9:4). As soon as someone draws closer to him, even if the person is so far from God and truth that he is associated with the side of death, even so, he will repent and admit to the truth. See note 116.

115. **the greatness of the Holy One.** Aside from referring to those swallowed up with Korach, this also relates back to Yitro. He, too, had been on the side of death because of his attachment to idolatry and impurity. However, he *did* bind himself to the tzaddik, Moshe, and therefore came to recognize God's greatness during his lifetime.

116. **New Moon.** Rebbe Nachman quotes the Rashbam that this takes place every New Moon. Yet, there seems to be nothing in the Talmudic text which would necessitate such an interpretation. To answer this, Rebbe Nachman shows how it is connected to what he said earlier (§5): To eliminate haughtiness it is necessary to be bound to the tzaddik. But this is not always as easy as it sounds. What does the person do when he feels himself distant, either physically or spiritually, from the tzaddik? And what if he simply does not know who the tzaddik is; "blinded" by the handicaps of his own desires, the barriers created by derisiveness and quarreling, or any of the other obstacles which keep a person from perceiving the truth?

The resolution of such difficulties lies in the effort and yearning a person puts into his

LIKUTEY MOHARAN #10:9,10

עִקַּר הַתְּשׁוּבָה הִיא רַק בָּעוֹלָם הַזֶּה, כִּי מִי שֶׁטָּרַח בְּעֶרֶב־שַׁבָּת וְכוּ'.
וְנִמְצָא בְּוַדַּאי לֹא נִפְטָרִין בְּזֶה הַהוֹדָאָה שֶׁהֵן מִתְחָרְטִין וּמוֹדִין
מִדִּין גֵּיהִנּוֹם, וְעַל כֵּן מְהַדְּרָא לְהוּ גֵּיהִנּוֹם לְהָכָא, כִּי אֵין נִפְטָרִין
בָּזֶה. וְאַף־עַל־פִּי־כֵן אֵין גֵּיהִנּוֹם בְּרֹאשׁ־חֹדֶשׁ כְּמוֹ בִּשְׁאָר יָמִים
(זֹהַר תְּרוּמָה קנ:), וְהַגֵּיהִנּוֹם שֶׁל רֹאשׁ־חֹדֶשׁ אֵינוֹ אֶלָּא הַחֲרָטָה,
שֶׁמִּתְחָרְטִים וּמוֹדִים וּמִתְבַּיְשִׁין, זֶה בְּעַצְמוֹ גֵּיהִנּוֹם שֶׁלָּהֶם. וְזֶהוּ
דְּדָיֵּק: מְהַדְּרָא לְהוּ גֵּיהִנּוֹם לְהָכָא, דְּהַיְנוּ מַה שֶּׁמְּהַדְּרָא לְהוּ
לְהָכָא, שֶׁחוֹזְרִים וּמוֹדִים, הוּא הַגֵּיהִנּוֹם שֶׁלָּהֶם.

י. וְזֶה פֵּרוּשׁ: וְאֵלֶּה הַמִּשְׁפָּטִים אֲשֶׁר תָּשִׂים לִפְנֵיהֶם. כִּי אִיתָא
בִּמְכִילְתָּא: 'אֲשֶׁר תָּשִׂים לִפְנֵיהֶם – הָשְׁווּ אִשָּׁה לְאִישׁ לְכָל דִּינִים
שֶׁבַּתּוֹרָה'; פֵּרוּשׁ, לְכָל דִּינִים שֶׁבַּתּוֹרָה שֶׁצָּרִיךְ לְהַמְתִּיקָם, צָרִיךְ
לְהַשְׁווֹת, הַיְנוּ לְיַחֵד, קֻדְשָׁא־בְּרִיךְ־הוּא וּשְׁכִינְתֵּהּ, שֶׁהוּא בְּחִינַת
אִשָּׁה וְאִישׁ, בְּחִינַת מָרְדְּכַי וְאֶסְתֵּר.

repenting here in this world.

The same is true of the haughty individuals. To effect their *tikkun* (rectification), they must come to the tzaddik. He possesses the *ruach,* and through him their haughty *ruach* (spirit) is humbled. Indeed, the wicked man's accepting and submitting himself to the tzaddik's authority is itself the breaking of his haughtiness, his repenting, and his suffering of Hell, all in one.

This also applies to anyone who feels remorse and shame for having transgressed, in whatever way, against God. These feelings can be likened to experiencing Hell in this world. This in itself counters the haughtiness and pride which served as the catalyst for sin in the first place. His repenting causes the *Malkhut,* God's Divine Presence, to be revealed all the more. And this, in essence, is the objective of all repentance.

122. **dinim...which need to be mitigated.** The Hebrew word *dinim* has two meanings: laws, civil and ritual; judgments, Divine or human. This *Mekhilta* teaches us that men and women have an equal obligation to fulfill the Torah's laws. Rebbe Nachman reads the *Mekhilta* as a prescription for mitigating and countering *dinim,* those judgments of Divine nature which are manifested in decrees of human origin (see n.2 above).

123. **equate...unite....** Equating woman with man alludes to a unification of the Holy One, the masculine principle, and His Divine Presence, the feminine principle. If, God forbid, there is a separation of the Holy One from His *Shekhinah,* then it is certain that the *kelipot,* the forces of evil and impurity, are governing and initiating decrees in the world. When such is the case, a person should see to bring about a Divine unification either by means of some holy act or through prayer. In Kabbalistic terminology this is known as returning the *Malkhut* to *Tiferet,* or *tefillah* (prayer) uniting with Torah, in order to mitigate the Divine anger which leads to Divine judgment/decrees.

124. **...Mordekhai and Esther.** Our Sages taught that Mordekhai took Esther for a wife

LIKUTEY MOHARAN #10:9,10

repentance is only in this world. For he who toiled on the eve of Shabbat will eat on Shabbat (*Avodah Zarah* 3a).[119]

It follows, certainly, that this confession, the remorse and admission [of Korach and his followers], does not absolve them from the punishment of Hell. This is why **Hell brings them back to here.** For they are not exempt with this.[120] Even so, there is no [suffering in] Hell on the New Moon as on other days (*Zohar* II, 150b). Hell on the New Moon is only remorse: feeling sorry, confessing and feeling shame. This itself was their Hell. The language is precise: **Hell brings them back to here.** In other words, this that they are brought back to here, that they return and admit—this is their Hell.[121]

10. This is the explanation [of the opening verse]:
"*V'eileh* (And these) are the laws that you must place before them."
The *Mekhilta* (21:1; *Bava Kama* 15a) comments: **that you must place before them** — Woman is equated with man in regard to all < punishments and > *dinim* (laws) of the Torah. The explanation is as follows: For all the *dinim* (Divine judgments/decrees) in the Torah which need to be mitigated,[122] one must equate < woman with man > —i.e., unite the Holy One and His Divine Presence.[123] This is the aspect of Mordekhai and Esther.[124] Thus:

---

119. **eat on Shabbat.** Rashi (*loc. cit.*) explains that the eve of Shabbat alludes to this world. Vis-a-vis the World to Come, which is likened to Shabbat, this world is seen as the six days of the week. Those who labor and prepare themselves during the week will have what to eat on Shabbat; those who strive for God and repent in this world will enjoy the fruits in the World to Come. But those connected to Korach did not repent before being swallowed up by the earth.

120. **not exempt with this.** Even though they now regret their actions and admit that Moshe— the tzaddik—is righteous, it is to no avail. The earth has already swallowed them up. They could only make amends if they were still alive. This is the meaning of "Hell brings them back to here." In other words, God shows His mercy for the followers of Korach and they are returned "to here," to this world. This is what is meant by "the children of Korach did not die..." (*Sanhedrin* 110a). And yet, to absolve them completely of their transgression would also not be right. We are forbidden to even entertain the notion that God is lax in exacting judgment. The solution is that once every thirty days, on the New Moon, they return to confess their sin and repent.

This teaches us that a person seeking to better himself should try to take advantage of the particularly propitious times, such as on the New Moon and the New Year, and make the most of them. In the case of *Rosh Chodesh*, one should see to reflect on his deeds of the month gone by and look for ways to improve himself during the month now beginning. It is therefore customary to recite the *Yom Kippur Katan* (Minor Day of Atonement) prayer on the eve of the New Moon.

121. **their Hell.** By feeling obliged to confess their mistake and admit that "Moshe and his Torah are true and they are false," Korach's followers were actually experiencing Hell and

LIKUTEY MOHARAN #10:10

וְזֶה פֵּרוּשׁ: וְאֵלֶּה – 'כָּל מָקוֹם שֶׁנֶּאֱמַר וְאֵלֶּה, מוֹסִיף עַל
הָרִאשׁוֹנִים' (בְּרֵאשִׁית רַבָּה, נֹחַ פָּרָשָׁה ל), בְּחִינַת תּוֹסֶפֶת וְרִבּוּי, בְּחִינַת
גַּאֲוָה, עֲבוֹדָה זָרָה, כְּמוֹ שֶׁכָּתוּב (דְּבָרִים ז): "לֹא מֵרֻבְּכֶם חָשַׁק ה'",
שֶׁפֵּרוּשׁוֹ גַּאֲוָה. וְזֶה בְּחִינַת: 'מוֹסִיף עַל הָרִאשׁוֹנִים', שֶׁהוּא בְּחִינַת
הָמָן-עֲמָלֵק, כְּמוֹ שֶׁכָּתוּב (בְּמִדְבַּר כ"ד): "רֵאשִׁית גּוֹיִם עֲמָלֵק",
וְתִקּוּנוֹ:

הַמִּשְׁפָּטִים, בְּחִינַת רוּחַ, כְּמוֹ שֶׁכָּתוּב (יְשַׁעְיָהוּ כח): "וּלְרוּחַ מִשְׁפָּט
וְכוּ' מְשִׁיבֵי מִלְחָמָה", כִּי עַל-יְדֵי הָרוּחַ נִתְתַּקֵּן הַגַּאֲוָה וְהָעֲבוֹדַת
אֱלִילִים כַּנַּ"ל. וְעַל-יְדֵי-זֶה:

אֲשֶׁר תָּשִׂים לִפְנֵיהֶם, הַיְנוּ 'הַשְׁווּ אִשָּׁה לְאִישׁ לְכָל דִּינִים
שֶׁבַּתּוֹרָה', הַיְנוּ בְּחִינַת הַמְתָּקַת הַדִּינִים, כִּי 'כָּל זְמַן שֶׁיֵּשׁ עֲבוֹדַת
אֱלִילִים בָּעוֹלָם, חֲרוֹן-אַף וְדִינִים בָּעוֹלָם'; וְעַל-יְדֵי הָרוּחַ הַנַּ"ל
נִתְיַחֵד קֻדְשָׁא-בְּרִיךְ-הוּא וּשְׁכִינְתֵּהּ וְנִמְתָּקִין הַדִּינִים, וְנִסְתַּלֵּק
חֲרוֹן-אַף מִן הָעוֹלָם.

127. **ruach of judgment.** The laws of the Torah (both revealed and hidden Torah) are the *"ruach* of judgment" in the hands and the feet (above, §7). Through the *ruach*, haughtiness and idolatry—the root causes of Divine judgment/decrees—are checked.

128. **battle.** This principally refers to those who do battle in Torah (*Rashi, loc.cit.*). That is, they engage in the give and take of Torah study for its own sake. In order to do this, a person must overcome his own haughtiness and self-worship. The humility which he acquires enables him to take hold of the *ruach* in the Torah so as to subdue haughtiness and idolatry, and thereby reveal God's greatness in the world (*Mai HaNachal*).

It is worth noting that each of the tzaddikim mentioned in this lesson encountered major battles during his lifetime. Avraham battled the Four Kings, including Nimrod who had declared himself a deity (Genesis 14); Yaakov battled the angel of Esav, Amalek's guardian angel (Genesis 32); Moshe went to war against Amalek, the archenemy of the Jews; Mordekhai and Esther had to battle Haman and his sons, and overcome the evil decrees which they had instigated against the Jewish people. Each of these tzaddikim had the power of this *ruach*. And with it, he was able to subdue the enemy both physically and spiritually.

129. **...Divine anger then departs from the world.** In relation to "Moshe," i.e. every true tzaddik, those attached to him are the aspect of the feet, as in (Exodus 11:8), "And all the people that are at your feet." He teaches them the Torah's laws and fills them with the *ruach*-of-holiness. By doing so, haughtiness and idolatry are eliminated, a unification of the Holy One and His Divine Presence takes place, and *dinim* are mitigated (*Parparaot LeChokhmah*).

We now have a deeper understanding of the opening verse: **V'eileh** — when there is an

LIKUTEY MOHARAN #10:10

V'eileh — Wherever the term *v'eileh* ("*and* these") is used, it comes to add to what went first (*Bereishit Rabbah* 30:3). [Thus, *v'eileh*] indicates an increase and a multiplicity, which correspond to haughtiness and idolatry. As it is written (Deuteronomy 7:7), "It was not because you had great numbers that God embraced you"—["great numbers"] being explained as haughtiness. This is the meaning of "it comes to add to what went first."[125] This is the aspect of Haman/Amalek,[126] of whom it is written (Numbers 24:20), "First among nations is Amalek." And [Haman/Amalek] is rectified by means of:

the laws — This corresponds to *ruach,* as is written (Isaiah 28:6), "And for a *ruach* (spirit) of judgment[127]...to them that turn back the battle."[128] It is with the *ruach* [of the Torah] that haughtiness and idolatry are rectified. And through this:

that you must place before them — This is, "Woman is equated with man in regard to all *dinim* of the Torah"—i.e., mitigating all the Divine judgments/decrees. For "As long as there is idolatry in the world, there is Divine anger—i.e., Divine judgments/decrees—in the world." But, by means of the abovementioned *ruach* there is a union between the Holy One and His Divine Presence, and the Divine judgments/decrees are mitigated. Divine anger then departs from the world.[129]

(*Megillah* 13a; see also *Zohar* III, 48). Thus, Rebbe Nachman tells us that in order to counter decrees it is necessary to bring about a Divine unification—to unite the revealed/the hands/ Mordekhai with the hidden/the feet/Esther: man and woman.

125. **haughtiness...first.** Rashi (*loc. cit.*) explains that Moshe Rabbeinu was telling the Jews that God loved them because they did not become haughty when He showed them favor.

This "adding to what went first" applies to both types of haughtiness or arrogance: i.e., holy arrogance and arrogance from the Other Side (above, n.47). This latter arrogance is such that because his haughtiness has not been rectified, the person grows more and more arrogant by "adding to what went first." This is the very opposite of how the tzaddik reacts. His holy arrogance is also "adding to what went first." But in his case, he adds holiness to all his previous degrees of holiness. Despite this, with each additional perception he grows increasingly humble (*Parparaot LeChokhmah*).

126. **Haman/Amalek.** Amalek was the first nation to wage war against the Jews after God had redeemed them from Egypt. In this sense, the Amalekites—and their descendant Haman—also correspond to "adding to what went first," and were the quality of haughtiness incarnate. The Midrash (*Bamidbar Rabbah* 13:51) teaches that the verse (Proverbs 29:23), "A man's haughtiness will bring him down" applies to Amalek who behaved arrogantly towards God. Haman, too, showed this arrogance. Despite his lowly beginnings and indebtedness to Mordekhai (see n.81), he wanted to be worshipped as a god and sought to gain prominence in order to annihilate the Jewish people, especially Mordekhai.

LIKUTEY MOHARAN #10:10,11

וְהִנֵּה, כְּלַל הַדְּבָרִים אֵלּוּ, שֶׁעַל־יְדֵי הַצַּדִּיק, שֶׁהוּא בְּחִינַת הָרוּחַ, אִתְעַבֵּר אֵל אַחֵר, כְּפִירוֹת, וְעַל־יְדֵי הָרוּחַ בָּאִים רְקוּדִין וְהַמְחָאַת כַּף, כִּי עַל־יְדֵי הַצַּדִּיק שֶׁהוּא בְּחִינַת הָרוּחַ נִתְעַלּוּ הָרַגְלַיִן, וְנִתְגַּלָּה הֶאָרַת הַיָּדַיִם, וְנִתְרַבָּה הָאֱמוּנָה, כַּמְבֹאָר לְמַעְלָה. וְעַל כֵּן כְּתִיב בְּיוֹסֵף, שֶׁהוּא בְּחִינַת הַצַּדִּיק (בְּרֵאשִׁית מ"א): "וּבִלְעָדֶיךָ לֹא יָרִים אִישׁ אֶת יָדוֹ וְאֶת רַגְלוֹ", כִּי בִּלְעֲדֵי בְּחִינַת יוֹסֵף, שֶׁהוּא בְּחִינַת הַצַּדִּיק, אִי אֶפְשָׁר לְהַעֲלוֹת וּלְהָרִים הַיָּדַיִם וְהָרַגְלַיִם כַּנַּ"ל.

וְהִנֵּה, מִכְּלַל הַדְּבָרִים אַתָּה שׁוֹמֵעַ, שֶׁנִּגְלֶה הוּא בְּחִינַת יָדַיִם, וְנִסְתָּר הוּא בְּחִינַת רַגְלַיִן, בְּחִינַת מָרְדְּכַי וְאֶסְתֵּר; וְאַף שֶׁנִּסְתָּר הוּא לְמַעְלָה מִנִּגְלֶה, עִם כָּל זֶה הִתְגַּלּוּת הַנִּגְלֶה הוּא בְּמָקוֹם גָּבוֹהַּ, דְּהַיְנוּ הַיָּדַיִם, וְהַנִּסְתָּר – בָּרַגְלַיִן, שֶׁהִיא לְמַטָּה מִיָּדַיִם. וְהָעִנְיָן עָמֹק, אַךְ הוּא עִנְיָן שֶׁכָּתוּב בַּזֹּהַר, תַּנָּאִים בַּשּׁוֹקַיִן וְאָמוֹרָאִים בַּיָּדִין. וְאַף שֶׁהַתַּנָּאִים לְמַעְלָה מֵאָמוֹרָאִים, מִכָּל מָקוֹם הֵם בְּמָקוֹם שֶׁהוּא לְמַטָּה מִמְּקוֹם הָאָמוֹרָאִים, וְכֵן נְבִיאִים וּכְתוּבִים, וּכְבָר מְבֹאָר עַל זֶה תֵּרוּץ.

יא. (עוֹד רְאֵה זֶה מָצָאתִי מִכְּתַב־יַד רַבֵּנוּ, זִכְרוֹנָם לִבְרָכָה, בְּעַצְמוֹ מֵעִנְיָן הַתּוֹרָה הַנַּ"ל, וְזֶהוּ:)
וְאֵלֶּה הַמִּשְׁפָּטִים אֲשֶׁר תָּשִׂים לִפְנֵיהֶם וְכוּ'. גֵּאוּת – מוֹדַעַת זֹאת

---

already mentioned in the lesson (§4 end) that Yosef represents the aspect of making amends. This explains why without him it is impossible to raise up the hands and feet in order to nullify decrees.

Elsewhere, Rebbe Nachman explains that Egypt is not the place of prayer (see *Likutey Moharan* I, 7:1 and 9:5). This implies that Yosef's descent into Egypt was a supreme test. Nevertheless, we see that he succeeded in achieving his appropriate level of *ruach*, subduing his adversaries and becoming viceroy over the entire land (*ibid.*, 8:5).

132. **An answer...already been given.** This same passage in the *Zohar* states that the Books of the Prophets correspond to the feet and the Sacred Writings (Hagiographa) to the hands. Thus, the question can be asked here as well: How is it possible for that which is more exalted to correspond to a lower position? An anonymous teaching printed at the end of the *Tikkuney Zohar* provides us with an answer. It is explained that the Prophets and the *Tannaim* appear in the position of the feet of the Divine persona of *Z'er Anpin*, the masculine principle, whereas the Hagiographa and the *Amoraim*, though they appear in the higher

Now, the sum of all this is as follows: Through the tzaddik, who corresponds to *ruach*, [belief in an] "other god" <and> atheism disappear. And, as a result of the *ruach*, there is dancing and hand-clapping. As explained above, this is because through the tzaddik/the *ruach*, the feet are lifted up, the emanation of the hands is revealed, and faith increases.[130] This is why of Yosef, who is the aspect of tzaddik, it is written (Genesis 41:44), "Without your permission, no man will lift up his hand or foot [in all of Egypt]." For without the aspect of Yosef, the tzaddik, it is impossible to lift up or raise either the hands or the feet.[131]

And so, from all of this you can understand that revealed [Torah] corresponds to the hands, and hidden [Torah] corresponds to the feet—corresponding to Mordekhai and Esther. And even though the hidden is more exalted than the revealed, still, the revealed manifests in a higher position, i.e., the hands, whereas the hidden is in the feet, which are lower than the hands. This matter is complex, yet aligns with that which is written in the *Zohar* (II, 258a): The *Tannaim* (early Sages) are in the thighs and the *Amoraim* (later Sages) in the hands. Although the *Tannaim* are more exalted than the *Amoraim*, nevertheless, their position is lower than the position of the *Amoraim*. The same is true of the Books of the Prophets vis-a-vis the Sacred Writings. An answer for this has already been given.[132]

11. From a manuscript written by Rebbe Nachman relating to this lesson:
And these are the laws that you must place before them:

---

addition to what went first, i.e., there is haughtiness in the world; the rectification comes through **the laws** — by being bound to the *ruach*, the tzaddik, who can subdue these idolators. Then one can merit to **that you shall place before them: Woman is equated with man** — with haughtiness and idolatry eliminated, one can bring about a unification of the Holy One and His *Shekhinah* and thus nullify all decrees.

130. **faith increases.** When a person draws closer to the tzaddik, his haughtiness decreases and he is open to receiving more of the tzaddik's *ruach*: faith. This is likewise accomplished through Torah study, which itself corresponds to the *ruach* (*Mai HaNachal*).

131. **Yosef, the tzaddik....** In the language of the Kabbalah, Yosef corresponds to the *sefirah* of *Yesod* (see Appendix: The Seven Supernal Shepherds). This makes him synonymous with the quality of tzaddik, as the *Zohar* (I, 59b) teaches: Only someone who guards the sign of the Covenant (*Yesod*) is entitled to be called tzaddik. Rebbe Nachman has

LIKUTEY MOHARAN #10:11

בְּכָל הָאָרֶץ שֶׁהִיא מִדָּה מְגֻנָּה וְצָרִיךְ לִבְרֹחַ מִמֶּנָּה, אֲבָל יֵשׁ בְּנֵי־אָדָם שֶׁרוֹדְפִים אַחַר כָּבוֹד וְרוֹצִים לִמְלֹךְ וּלְהַנְהִיג אֶת הָעוֹלָם, וְאוֹמְרִים שֶׁיֵּשׁ לְאֵל יָדָם לַעֲשׂוֹת פִּדְיוֹנוֹת וּלְהִתְפַּלֵּל תְּפִלּוֹת; וַעֲלֵיהֶם נֶאֱמַר: "הָשֵׁב אֵשֶׁת הָאִישׁ כִּי נָבִיא הוּא וְיִתְפַּלֵּל בַּעַדְךָ וֶחְיֵה".

כִּי זֶה יָדוּעַ שֶׁהַקָּדוֹשׁ־בָּרוּךְ־הוּא [חָסֵר, וְכָךְ צָרִיךְ לוֹמַר: שֶׁהַקָּדוֹשׁ־בָּרוּךְ־הוּא מִתְאַוֶּה לִתְפִלָּתָן שֶׁל צַדִּיקִים, וְצָרִיךְ לֵילֵךְ אֶצְלָם שֶׁיִּתְפַּלְלוּ עָלָיו] עֲלֵיהֶם. אֲבָל בַּעֲלֵי־גַּאֲוָה אֵין הוֹלְכִים אֶל צַדִּיקִים לְבַקְּשָׁם שֶׁיִּתְפַּלְלוּ עֲלֵיהֶם, וְגַם אֵין מַנִּיחִים שְׁאָר בְּנֵי־אָדָם שֶׁיֵּלְכוּ אֵצֶל צַדִּיקִים שֶׁיִּתְפַּלְלוּ עֲלֵיהֶם, כִּי אָמְרוּ אֵלּוּ בַּעֲלֵי־גַּאֲוָה, שֶׁגַּם הֵם צַדִּיקִים וִיכוֹלִים לְהִתְפַּלֵּל, וְאֵין צַדִּיק בָּאָרֶץ יוֹתֵר מֵהֶם. וּבְזֶה הֵם נִקְרָאִים בְּשֵׁם אֲבִימֶלֶךְ – אָבִי לְשׁוֹן רָצוֹן, כְּמוֹ "וְלֹא אָבָה ה' אֱלֹקֶיךָ" וְכוּ':

To briefly summarize, every person has an obligation to reveal God's glory for all to see. This goal is most perfectly fulfilled when gentiles and those distant from God recognize His greatness. This is achieved through proper prayer, by bringing prayer into every detail of our lives. However, to be effective, the prayer must be pure; something which can really only be accomplished by the true tzaddik. Indeed, whenever a person experiences suffering in his life, he should turn to the tzaddikim and ask them to pray on his behalf. For God desires and has pleasure from their prayers. Unfortunately, this, too, is no simple matter. There are false and haughty leaders who mislead people, preventing them from turning to the true tzaddik for help. As long as these haughty individuals, who are likened to idolators, continue to plague the world, God's anger prevails. As a result, the world is subject to the Divine judgment which comes from His "turning away" and which gives the forces of evil free reign. This is then manifested in the suffering brought on by what appears to us as the decrees of human origin and natural causes. In fact, the only way to mitigate and nullify these decrees is by focusing on their true origin and cause. And this requires our binding ourselves to the true tzaddikim. Attaching oneself to them and to the Torah eliminates haughtiness—idolatry and self-worship—and brings an increase of faith into the world. This, in turn, provides the *ruach* which counters all heresy and false beliefs, and gives rise to a spirit of holiness and great joy. With this joy in his heart, a person will feel moved to clap and dance. Not only does this nullify all decrees, it also brings wisdom, length of days, and an understanding of Torah— both revealed and hidden.

LIKUTEY MOHARAN #10:11

{"Sing to God, for He has done *gei'ut* (glorious things); this is known in all the earth" (Isaiah 12:5).}

"This is known in all the earth," that *gei'ut* (haughtiness) is a despicable quality, one from which a person must flee.[133] Yet, there are people who run after honor. They desire to rule and direct everything. They claim to have the "power in their hands"[134] to perform redemptions and pray [effective] prayers. Of such individuals it is said, "return the man's wife, for he is a prophet. He will pray for you, and you will live."

For this is known: The Holy One {desires the prayers of the tzaddikim. A person must turn to them, so that they will pray for him}. But the haughty people do not turn to the tzaddikim to request that they pray on their behalf. What is more, they also prevent others from going to the tzaddikim to enlist their prayers. For these haughty individuals claim that they, too, are tzaddikim capable of praying, and that there is no one more righteous than they in the world. This has earned them the title "Avimelekh": *AVi* connotes "desire," as in (Deuteronomy 23:6), "But God your Lord did not *AVa* (desire) to pay heed to Bilaam."[135]

position, the hands, this refers to the hands of the Divine persona of *Malkhut,* or *Nukva,* the feminine principle. According to the Kabbalah, *Z'er Anpin* is above *Nukva* in the hierarchy of the Divine personas (see Appendix: The Divine Persona). As such, even though the Hagiographa/*Amoraim* appear in a higher position, relative to the larger picture — the entire hierarchy of the personas — this is actually on a lower level. This commentary further states that when the two personas are united, then "man and woman" — *Z'er Anpin* and *Nukva* — appear equal. And when this is the case, the Hagiographa/*Amoraim* are in their position corresponding to the hands, while the Prophets/*Tannaim* are in their position corresponding to the feet. Thus the more exalted appear to be in a lower position.

133. **haughtiness . . . .** The verse quoted from Isaiah refers to the glorious things which God has done, for His deeds are to be publicized and made "known in all the earth." Thus we see that the Jews sang the Song of the Sea extolling God's glory for having delivered them at the Red Sea (Exodus 15) and they will sing of His glory when the son of David arrives (Psalms 93). But when a person takes the glory for himself, it is a sign of haughtiness. This, too, is "known in all the earth."

134. **power in their hands.** This is a paraphrase of what Lavan said to Yaakov (Genesis 31:29) and implies a false sense of power and control which the wicked possess.

135. **AVi . . . AVa . . . .** All this appears in detail in section 4.

LIKUTEY MOHARAN #11:1

ליקוטי מוהר"ן סימן י"א

אֲנִי ה' הוּא שְׁמִי וּכְבוֹדִי לְאַחֵר לֹא אֶתֵּן וּתְהִלָּתִי לַפְּסִילִים (יְשַׁעְיָהוּ מ"ב):

א. כִּי יֵשׁ יְחוּדָא עִלָּאָה וְיִחוּדָא תַּתָּאָה, הַיְנוּ: שְׁמַע יִשְׂרָאֵל, וּבָרוּךְ שֵׁם כְּבוֹד מַלְכוּתוֹ לְעוֹלָם וָעֶד (זֹהַר בְּרֵאשִׁית יח:), וְכָל אֶחָד מִיִּשְׂרָאֵל צָרִיךְ שֶׁיִּהְיֶה נַעֲשֶׂה זֹאת עַל־יָדוֹ, עַל־יְדֵי־זֶה יָכוֹל לָבוֹא לִתְבוּנוֹת הַתּוֹרָה לְעָמְקָהּ;

name of God, *YHVH*, the upper unification, the transcendant, corresponds to the first two letters of God's name: *Yod Heh* (יה); the lower unification, the immanent, corresponds to the last two letters of God's name: *Vav Heh* (וה). Through his actions, man has the ability to unite these letters and the Divine influences which they represent. And, in so doing, he also creates a degree of union and oneness between himself and the One Above.

This *yichud* of God's name is alluded to in the verse, "And it will come to pass that *YHVH* will be king of all the world, on that day God and His name *YiHiYeH* (will be) one" (Zekhariah 14:9). The Ari explains that presently there is a distinction: an upper unification and a lower unification. But "on that day" when *YHVH* will be universally recognized as king, the lower unification (*VH*) will be elevated to the level of upper unification (*YH*); making God and His name one—*YHYH* (*Shaar HaPesukim*, loc. cit.).

At this stage in the lesson, Rebbe Nachman focuses on the *Shema* prayer which we recite at least twice daily. It will soon become clear that by reciting the *Shema* with concentration one can achieve guarding the *brit* (sign of the Covenant; see n.29), Torah study, and eliminating his own haughtiness while elevating the glory of God. For, when one fully appreciates that God is One and that there is nothing else, as the *Shema* prayer proclaims, then he brings about an upper unification. When he then recites the *Barukh shem kavod malkhuto...*, accepting the Kingship of God and the all-encompassing influence of His Divine Providence, he brings about a lower unification.

The Talmud teaches: No one can match the level of the martyrs who give their lives sanctifying God's name (cf. *Pesachim* 50a). In the annals of Jewish martyrdom (the Crusades, Inquisition, Cossack pogroms, the Holocaust, etc.) it was always the *Shema* prayer—the declaration of God's unity—which was on the martyr's lips before he returned his soul to its Creator. This is the very same *Shema* which we recite daily, extolling God's greatness, which has the power to bring about an upper unification of His holy name. By giving their lives to sanctify God's name, these martyred Jews also created this upper unification and thus earned themselves the highest place in Gan Eden. (Elsewhere, Rebbe Nachman explains that it is possible for one to come to this level of self-sacrifice and martyrdom in thought alone. This can be achieved through deep and total concentration, and can even bring a person to actually feel the pain of death; see *Likutey Moharan* I, 193.)

6. **deep Torah understanding.** Rebbe Nachman will later explain (see §§6,7) that there are various levels of Torah: Halakhah and Kabbalah (revealed and hidden), the concepts of

LIKUTEY MOHARAN #11[1]

"*Ani YHVH* (I am God), that is My name. My glory I shall not give to another, nor My praise to idols."

(Isaiah 42:8)

There is an upper unification and a lower unification: *Shema Yisrael*[2] and *Barukh shem kvod malkhuto l'olam va'ed* (Blessed be the name of His glorious Kingdom forever more) (*Zohar* I, 18b).[3] Each and every Jew[4] should make certain to bring about [these unifications].[5] By doing so, one can come to deep Torah understanding.[6]

1. **Likutey Moharan #11.** The only information which has been passed down regarding this lesson is that it was given on Shavuot, 5563 (May 26, 1803), in Breslov. Nothing else has been recorded regarding the circumstances surrounding the teaching. When Rebbe Nachman mentioned the words "deep Torah understanding," he said that these were three separate levels: deep, Torah and understanding. He did not, however, explain this (*Parparaot LeChokhmah*).

2. **upper unification...Shema.** The upper unification is the *Shema Yisrael*: Hear O Israel, *YHVH* is our Lord, *YHVH* is One. It is a statement of belief in God's oneness— i.e., He is the One and Only. For in truth, the creation in its totality is naught, even non-existent, when measured against God. On the level of upper unification everything is just as it was prior to Creation when there was only God (*Rabbi Shmuel Moshe Kramer*). It is thus the level of the transcendant. For a fuller explanation see below, note 95.

3. **lower unification...Kingdom....** The lower unification is the *Barukh shem*: Blessed be the name of His glorious Kingdom forever more (recited in the prayers immediately after the *Shema*). It is a statement of belief in God's absolute Kingship. For in truth, He rules over and sustains everything according to His will. The lower unification is, in fact, a proclamation of the *raison d'etre* of creation and the essence of His glory: the recognition of His Kingship, His sovereignty, over all parts of creation—now and forever more (*Rabbi Shmuel Moshe Kramer*). It is thus the level of the immanent. For a fuller explanation see below, note 95.

4. **every Jew.** This indicates Rebbe Nachman's conviction that every Jew can bring about these exalted unifications, though, as he goes on to explain, this requires our emerging from our low spiritual levels (*Mabuey HaNachal*). See also *Likutey Moharan* I, 9, notes 14 and 20.

5. **these unifications....** Rabbi Nachman Goldstein, author of the commentary *Parparaot LeChokhmah* on the *Likutey Moharan,* states that these concepts of upper unification and lower unification contain many deep and difficult mysteries, and therefore very little may be openly said or written about them (*Yerach HaEitanim*). As such, the explanation which follows is only intended to provide the reader with the general keys for some understanding of Rebbe Nachman's lesson. It is in no way meant to be a thorough discussion of these concepts.

In the language of the Kabbalah, the term *yichud* (unification) applies to the uniting of the letters of God's holy names; be it the joining of the letters of one particular name with each other, or the letters of one holy name with those of another. These unifications, which are achieved through knowledge of the Torah and the fulfillment of its mitzvot, are the union of the transcendant and immanent aspects of Divine influence. For example, in the ineffable

LIKUTEY MOHARAN #11:1

כִּי מִי שֶׁהוּא בְּמַדְרֵגָה פְּחוּתָה, הוּא עֲדַיִן רָחוֹק מִתְּבוּנוֹת הַתּוֹרָה,
רַק עַל־יְדֵי אֶמְצָעוּת הַדִּבּוּר יָכוֹל לָבוֹא לִתְבוּנוֹת הַתּוֹרָה לְעָמְקָהּ,
הַיְנוּ עַל־יְדֵי שֶׁהוּא מְדַבֵּר בְּהַתּוֹרָה בְּדִבּוּרִים, כְּמוֹ שֶׁכָּתוּב (מִשְׁלֵי
ד): "כִּי חַיִּים הֵם לְמוֹצְאֵיהֶם" – 'לְמוֹצִיאֵיהֶם בַּפֶּה'.
מֵאִיר לוֹ הַדִּבּוּר בְּכָל הַמְּקוֹמוֹת שֶׁצָּרִיךְ לַעֲשׂוֹת תְּשׁוּבָה, כְּמוֹ
שֶׁאָמְרוּ רַבּוֹתֵינוּ, זִכְרוֹנָם לִבְרָכָה (בְּרָכוֹת כב.): 'פְּתַח פִּיךָ וְיָאִירוּ
דְבָרֶיךָ'. וּבְכָל פַּעַם וּפַעַם, עַל־יְדֵי כָּל תְּשׁוּבָה וּתְשׁוּבָה, הוּא הוֹלֵךְ
מִמַּדְרֵגָה לְמַדְרֵגָה, עַד שֶׁיּוֹצֵא מִמַּדְרֵגָה פְּחוּתָה וּבָא לִתְבוּנוֹת
הַתּוֹרָה לְעָמְקָהּ.

means for recognizing Him as Ruler. Hence, enunciating the words of Torah is itself an expression of one's acceptance of God's Kingship.

The Talmud (*Eruvin, loc. cit.*) further relates that Bruryah, Rabbi Meir's wife, came across a student studying quietly. She rebuked him saying, "Only when the Torah permeates all 248 limbs will it remain with the person." And Rabbi Eliezer ben Yaakov had a student who studied quietly for three years and then forgot all his learning (*ibid.*). The spoken words of Torah have the power to reverberate, as it were, through the entire body, to reveal and bestow God's Kingship upon "those who express them." They become an integral part of the speaker himself. However, when one does not speak the words of Torah, he is not revealing God's Kingship and can even come to forget the King.

9. **Open your mouth....** The Talmud relates: Rabbi Yehudah ben B'teirah had a student who mumbled the words of Torah he was studying. Rabbi Yehudah said to him: "Open your mouth..." Rashi explains that this student had had a nocturnal emission, and therefore mumbled his words as he was afraid to enunciate them while impure. Rabbi Yehudah told the student to open his mouth, to enunciate his words clearly so that they would enlighten him.

Actually, this Talmudic passage is meant to be more than just a proof to support the Rebbe's contention that speech enlightens. Further on in the lesson (§§3-5), Rebbe Nachman introduces the importance of guarding the Covenant and ties it into the concept of upper and lower unifications, speech and glory (discussed in §2). Even so, with this story about the impure student Rebbe Nachman is already alluding to these connections. The student did not guard the Covenant and his speech was garbled. Because of this, his Torah study was impaired and he was on a low spiritual level. Rabbi Yehudah tried to elevate him by getting him to enunciate clearly. The Torah would then enlighten him regarding all the areas where he must repent, and he would thereby be brought to the upper levels of spirituality (*Mabuey HaNachal*).

10. **every time...every repentance....** For each bit of Torah study is yet another revelation of God's Kingship, which, when internalized, elevates the student still further. Eventually, the speaking itself will bring him to the stages of repentance necessary for the comprehension of the Torah's profound insights.

LIKUTEY MOHARAN #11:1

When a person is on a low spiritual level, he is still very far from Torah understanding. Only through speech[7] will he be able to come to deep Torah understanding—i.e., by verbalizing the words of Torah. As it is written (Proverbs 4:22), "For they are life *l'motzA'eihem* (to those who find them)"—[and our Sages taught: Read this] *l'motzI'eihem* (to those who express them) verbally (Eruvin 54a).[8]

Speech enlightens a person regarding all the areas in which he needs to repent. As our Sages taught: Open your mouth and your speech will enlighten (Berakhot 22a).[9] And each and every time, because of each and every repentance, he moves from level to level until he emerges from his low spiritual level and comes to deep Torah understanding.[10]

---

secrets and deep secrets. Through repentance, it is possible to emerge from our low spiritual levels and achieve deep insights into the Torah.

This was actually God's purpose in redeeming the Jews from Egypt. As He told Moshe (Exodus 3:12), "When you get the Jews out of Egypt, all of you will then become God's servants on this mountain" (*Mai HaNachal*). For this was His intention all along: To make them His servants by presenting the descendants of His beloved Avraham, Yitzchak and Yaakov with the greatest treasure imaginable—the Torah. As the blueprint of creation and the key to all existence, the Torah affords those who possess it with an intimate knowledge of God. Its deep insights provide man with all he will ever need in life, because the Torah itself is "the Tree of Life for those who take hold of it." And since Mt. Sinai, the Divine plan has unswervingly remained for the Jewish people to attain ever higher levels of Torah knowledge, i.e., knowledge of God and of the upper and lower unifications. Thus, even in the present exile one must strive for as much Torah knowledge as possible, for this is the key to redemption—personal and universal. This, in turn, ties in with the end of the lesson where Rebbe Nachman discusses exile's causes and the means for undoing them.

7. **Only through speech.** This is because speech is that faculty which reveals. *Dibbur* (speech) emanates from the lowest *sefirah,* which is *Malkhut* (Kingship). Speech is therefore the means of revelation of God's Kingship, through which one proclaims his acceptance of God's all-pervading sovereignty.

Rebbe Nachman often emphasized the very important role which speech plays in the life of a Jew. He said, "Speech has tremendous power. Speak many words of Torah, recite many prayers, and make all kinds of appeals and entreaties to God. More than anything else, talk to God in your own language. If you are determined and make a practice of this every day of your life, you will certainly attain the ultimate good both in this world and in the world to come" (*Advice,* Speech 20). Here, the speech Rebbe Nachman refers to is specifically words of Torah. However, later on in the lesson we will see that the type of speech which enlightens a person also includes the words of prayer (see below nn.64,80).

8. **who expresses them verbally.** The Torah brings life, "For it is your life" (Deuteronomy 30:20), but only when its teachings are revealed. This is the reason one must pronounce the words as he studies. Through Torah we acquire knowledge of God and therefore have the

LIKUTEY MOHARAN #11:1 164

וְזֶה שֶׁשָּׁאֲלוּ יוֹחָנִי וּמַמְרֵא לְמֹשֶׁה (מְנָחוֹת פה.): 'תֶּבֶן אַתָּה מַכְנִיס לַעֲפָרַיִם? הֵשִׁיב לָהֶם: אָמְרֵי אֱנָשֵׁי, לְמָתָא יַרְקָא, יַרְקָא שְׁקַל'. 'תֶּבֶן' – זֶה בְּחִינַת תְּבוּנָה, כְּמוֹ שֶׁכָּתוּב (מִשְׁלֵי ב): "תְּבוּנָה תִּנְצְרֶךָּ", שֶׁהֵם הֵבִינוּ שֶׁמֹּשֶׁה רוֹצֶה לְהַכְנִיס תְּבוּנוֹת הַתּוֹרָה בְּיִשְׂרָאֵל, וְעַל כֵּן שָׁאֲלוּ, כִּי בִּזְמַן שֶׁאֵין יִשְׂרָאֵל עוֹשִׂין רְצוֹנוֹ שֶׁל מָקוֹם הֵם מְשׁוּלִים לְעָפָר: וְאֵיךְ יוּכַל לַהֲבִיאָם לְמַדְרֵגָה גְּבוֹהָה, לִתְבוּנוֹת הַתּוֹרָה?

וְזֶה: 'תֶּבֶן' – לְשׁוֹן תְּבוּנוֹת הַתּוֹרָה, 'אַתָּה מַכְנִיס לַעֲפָרִים' – זֶה בְּחִינַת עָפָר, הַיְנוּ מַדְרֵגָה פְּחוּתָה. 'הֵשִׁיב לָהֶם: אָמְרֵי אֱנָשֵׁי', הַיְנוּ עַל-יְדֵי הָאֲמִירוֹת, עַל-יְדֵי הַדִּבּוּר שֶׁל אִישׁ הַיִּשְׂרְאֵלִי, הוּא מֵאִיר לוֹ לְכָל הַמְּקוֹמוֹת שֶׁצָּרִיךְ לַעֲשׂוֹת תְּשׁוּבָה. וְזֶהוּ: 'לְמָתָא יַרְקָא' – לַמְּקוֹמוֹת שֶׁצָּרִיךְ לַעֲשׂוֹת תְּשׁוּבָה. 'יַרְקָא' – הוּא בְּחִינַת תְּשׁוּבָה, כְּמוֹ שֶׁאָמְרוּ בַּמִּדְרָשׁ (בְּרֵאשִׁית רַבָּה פָּרָשָׁה מג): "וַיָּרֶק אֶת חֲנִיכָו" – אוֹרִיקָן בְּפָרָשַׁת שׁוֹפְטִים, הַיְנוּ שֶׁזֵּרְזָם לַעֲשׂוֹת תְּשׁוּבָה, כִּי פָּרָשַׁת שׁוֹפְטִים נֶאֱמַר עַל תְּשׁוּבָה: "מִי הָאִישׁ הַיָּרֵא וְרַךְ הַלֵּבָב" – 'הַיָּרֵא מֵעֲבֵרוֹת שֶׁבְּיָדוֹ'.

Talmudic passage. Rather than say that Pharaoh's magicians were alluding to Moshe's bringing sorcery into Egypt, Rebbe Nachman focuses on the word *teven/tevunah*, suggesting that they could not comprehend Moshe's bringing understanding into the Jews. How could Moshe expect to bring them to deep understanding in Egypt when they had not yet received the Torah? How could they be expected to rise to great spiritual levels when, without the Torah, they are likened to the dust of the earth?

14. **needs to repent.** In Egypt, speech itself was in exile. The Jews never had the time to speak to God or pray to Him (see *The Breslov Haggadah*, p.66). A close examination of God's directive that Moshe redeem the Jews (Exodus 3) shows that even before presenting their demand to Pharaoh, Moshe and Aharon went to *speak* to the Jews. The Torah tells us that "the people believed...and they bowed their heads and prostrated themselves" (Exodus 4:29-30). The words of God had moved them to repent and they experienced the first glimmer of salvation. Only afterwards, Moshe and Aharon went to Pharaoh (Exodus 5). By then, the Jews had already begun to speak, sigh and pray to God.

15. **Shoftim...repentance...committed.** The Midrash (*loc. cit.*) explains that Avraham spoke to his servants, cajoled and bribed them to join him in waging war against the Four Kings (Genesis 14). But they were frightened and argued that they feared being killed in battle. Avraham replied: "Even if we lose our lives, it will be in sanctifying God's name." (This is

LIKUTEY MOHARAN #11:1

This is what Yochni and Mamrei asked Moshe: "You're bringing *teven* (straw) into Apharayim?" To which he answered, "People say, 'To the vegetable market, take vegetables [to sell]' " *(Menachot 85a)*.[11] *TeVeN* corresponds to *TeVuNah* (understanding) < of Torah >, as is written *(Proverbs 2:11)*, "understanding will preserve you."[12] [Yochni and Mamrei] understood that Moshe wanted to bring Torah understanding into the Jewish people. This is why they asked, because when the Jews do not carry out God's will, they are likened to *aphar* (dust). How could he bring them to a high level, to Torah understanding?[13]

Thus: "*Teven*" connotes *tevunot* of Torah. "You're bringing into Apharayim?" alludes to *aphar*, i.e., a low spiritual level. He answered them, "People say"—in other words, through speaking; the speech of a Jewish person directs him to all the areas in which he needs to repent.[14] This is, "To a place of *yarka* (vegetables)"—the areas in which he should repent. *YaRKa* corresponds to repentance, as the *Midrash* comments: "*vaYaReK* (he called out) his trained servants" *(Genesis 14:14)*—[Avraham] enlightened them by reciting the Chapter of Shoftim *(Bereishit Rabbah 43:2)*. In other words, he encouraged them to repent. For the Chapter of Shoftim deals with repentance, [as our Sages taught:] "Is there any among you who is afraid or fainthearted" *(Deuteronomy 20:8)*—he fears because of the sins he committed *(Sotah 43a)*.[15]

---

11. **Yochni and Mamrei....** These were Pharaoh's magicians who challenged Moshe when he performed the miracles in Egypt. The Talmud teaches *(Sanhedrin 67b)*: Why are magicians called *MeKhaShPhiM*? It is because they are *MeKhasheiSh PaMaliah shel maalah* (they weaken the heavenly hosts). That is, the existence of sorcery and magic confound one's ability to believe in God. Yochni and Mamrei were really asking, "Seeing that Egypt is *the* place of sorcery, why are you bringing your sorcery here? Isn't there enough magic here, making your powers unnecessary?!" (In other words, "Why are you bringing coals to Newcastle?") Moshe answered, "People bring vegetables specifically to a vegetable market. This is because the connoisseurs shop there, and they know which are quality vegetables and which are not." In other words, Moshe wanted to emphasize that people would be able to tell which supernatural act was a result of sorcery and which was produced by the word of God.

12. **preserve you.** *Tevunah* (Torah understanding) preserves and protects spiritually, much as *teven* (straw) protects and preserves physically. The understanding of Torah which one possesses protects and keeps him even when he cannot study *(Sotah 21a)*. Thus the verse reads, "*understanding* will preserve you" *(MaBuey HaNachal)*.

13. **dust...high level....** "When the Jewish people keep the Torah, they are likened to the stars—no one can reach them. However, when they fail to fulfill the word of God, they are likened to dust [of the earth]—easily trodden upon and on the lowest of levels" *(Megillah 16a)*.

Thus, within the context of the lesson, we have a more literal interpretation of this

LIKUTEY MOHARAN #11:1,2 166

וְזֶהוּ: 'אָמְרֵי אֱנָשֵׁי, לְמָתָא יַרְקָא', הַיְנוּ עַל־יְדֵי הָאֲמִירוֹת וְהַדִּבּוּר
שֶׁל אִישׁ הַיִּשְׂרְאֵלִי, 'לְמָתָא יַרְקָא' – לַמְּקוֹמוֹת שֶׁצָּרִיךְ לַעֲשׂוֹת
תְּשׁוּבָה יָאִיר לוֹ הַדִּבּוּר, שֶׁיּוּכַל לַעֲשׂוֹת תְּשׁוּבָה. וְזֶה: 'יַרְקָא שְׁקַל'
– בְּחִינַת תְּשׁוּבַת הַמִּשְׁקָל, שֶׁהַדִּבּוּר יָאִיר לוֹ שֶׁיּוּכַל לַעֲשׂוֹת
תְּשׁוּבַת הַמִּשְׁקָל מַמָּשׁ:

ב. אַךְ לַדִּבּוּר שֶׁיָּאִיר לוֹ אִי אֶפְשָׁר לִזְכּוֹת, כִּי אִם עַל־יְדֵי כָּבוֹד,
הַיְנוּ שֶׁיִּרְאֶה שֶׁיִּהְיֶה כְּבוֹד הַשֵּׁם יִתְבָּרַךְ בִּשְׁלֵמוּת, שֶׁיִּהְיֶה כְּבוֹדוֹ
לְאֵין נֶגֶד כְּבוֹד הַשֵּׁם יִתְבָּרַךְ, הַיְנוּ עַל־יְדֵי עֲנָוָה וְקַטְנוּת. כִּי עִקַּר
בְּחִינַת הַדִּבּוּר הוּא מְכֻבָּד, כְּמוֹ שֶׁכָּתוּב (תְּהִלִּים כ"ד): "מִי הוּא זֶה
מֶלֶךְ הַכָּבוֹד", הַיְנוּ מַלְכוּת פֶּה.

כִּי כְּשֶׁהַתּוֹרָה בָּאָה לְתוֹךְ דִּבּוּרִים פְּגוּמִים, לְפֶה פָּגוּם, לֹא דַי שֶׁאֵין
דִּבּוּרֵי הַתּוֹרָה מְאִירִים לוֹ, כִּי אִם גַּם הַתּוֹרָה עַצְמָהּ נִתְגַּשֵּׁם

that bestows glory upon those who fear him? "The God of Hosts is the king of glory, evermore" (Psalms, *ibid.*). In each of the next two explanations which the Midrash offers we find that this glory or honor which God's bestows has to do with speech. God bestowed glory and honor upon Miriam by having the Jewish people wait for her while she repented for having spoken slanderously of her brother (Numbers 12; see n.79 below). The next explanation depicts the glory which God bestowed upon Moshe in that, as the Torah tells us, it was not God who spoke and Moshe who answered, but the reverse: "Moshe spoke, and God answered with a voice" (Exodus 19:19).

18. **Malkhut is mouth.** Of the ten *sefirot*, *Malkhut* is likened to the mouth, the power of speech (*Tikkuney Zohar, Introduction*). This is so because the mouth—speech—gives vent to one's inner feelings, much as the function of *Malkhut* is to "reveal" by being the channel through which the hidden influences of the upper *sefirot* are brought out into this world. The *Mai HaNachal* adds that it is therefore one's speech which will reveal whether one accepts God's *Malkhut* (Kingship). When he does, his mouth actually becomes a holy mouth—a mouth suitable for holiness, Torah and prayer.

19. **corporal and blackened....** Torah is spiritual. However, when one's mouth is foul, the words of Torah he speaks lose their spirituality. They take on, as it were, a degree of physicality and crassness. The Torah's light becomes dimmed. Elsewhere, Rebbe Nachman taught that when one transcends earthly interests and attachments, he can grasp the entire Torah. He will not forget what he has learned because his incorporeality enables him to encompass the limitless spirituality of the Torah. But when one brings corporeality to the words of Torah and causes them to take on c, he will only be able to grasp certain aspects of the Torah, never its entirety. If he attempts to absorb new understanding in

LIKUTEY MOHARAN #11:1,2

This is the meaning of "People say, 'To the vegetable market' "—i.e., through the reciting and speaking of a Jewish person; "to the vegetable market"—[he is directed] to the areas in which he needs to repent. Speech directs him so that he can repent. And this is "*yarka Sh'KuL* (take vegetables)," corresponding to *teshuvat hamiShKaL* (fitting repentance). Speech will enlighten him so that he will be able to repent precisely commensurate with his sins.[16]

2. However, it is impossible for a person to merit having his speech enlighten him except through glory. That is, he should see to it that the Holy One's glory is complete; his own glory should be non-existent in relationship to the Holy One's glory. [This is achieved] by means of humility and humbleness. For the essence of speech comes from glory, as is written (Psalms 24:10), "Who is this *MeLeKh* (king) of glory?"[17]—i.e., "*MaLKhut* (Kingship) is mouth" (*Tikkuney Zohar*, Second Introduction).[18]

For when the Torah comes into tarnished speech—a foul mouth—not only do the words of Torah not enlighten him, but the Torah itself becomes corporal and blackened there in his mouth.[19] As is written

---

connected to reciting the *Shema*, as above.) Avraham called out to his trained servants with the words from the Biblical portion of Shoftim, saying, "Is there any among you who is afraid and faint-hearted? Let him return home." In the end, as our Sages taught, those who did not take up arms were those who feared being punished for the sins which they had committed and for which they had not repented (*Sotah, loc. cit.*). Avraham's senior servant, Eliezer, did go with him. Further in the lesson (§5), Rebbe Nachman explains that guarding the *brit* has an upper and lower level, and elsewhere (*Likutey Moharan* I, 31:5), we find that the Rebbe associates Avraham with the upper *brit* and Eliezer with the lower *brit*.

16. **fitting repentance....** Literally, *teshuvat hamishkal* is balanced repentance. This implies that person who has transgressed God's word willingly endures suffering commensurate with the pleasure he experienced in committing the sin. This is obviously extremely difficult. However, Rebbe Nachman is quite explicit in his insistence that through speech which enlightens, it is even possible to achieve this ultimate level of repentance.

In review: To attain understanding of the Torah's depths, which requires bringing about an upper and lower unification, one must achieve enlightened speech, speech which guides him to his appropriate path of repentance .

17. **speech comes from glory....** Simply, by making certain that God's glory is complete—taking none of it for himself—a person comes to a pure mouth, as will be explained. When this happens, his words of Torah have the power to enlighten him regarding the particular areas where he has to repent. The Midrash (*Shocher Tov* #24) on the verse which Rebbe Nachman quotes to show the relationship between speech and glory teaches: Who is the king

LIKUTEY MOHARAN #11:2

168

וְנִתְחַשֵּׁךְ שָׁם מִפִּיו, כְּמוֹ שֶׁכָּתוּב (יְהוֹשֻׁעַ א): "לֹא יָמוּשׁ סֵפֶר הַתּוֹרָה הַזֶּה מִפִּיךָ", בְּחִינַת "וְיָמֵשׁ חֹשֶׁךְ" (שְׁמוֹת י), הַיְנוּ שֶׁלֹּא יִתְגַּשְּׁמוּ וְיִתְחַשְּׁכוּ מִפִּיךָ, כִּי עַל-יְדֵי שֶׁאֵין מַשְׁגִּיחִין שֶׁיִּהְיֶה כְּבוֹד הַשֵּׁם יִתְבָּרַךְ בִּשְׁלֵמוּת, הַיְנוּ עַל-יְדֵי גַּדְלוּת, עַל-יְדֵי-זֶה אֵין יְכוֹלִין לִפְתֹּחַ פֶּה, בִּבְחִינַת (תְּהִלִּים י"ז): "סָגְרוּ פִּימוֹ דִּבְּרוּ בְגֵאוּת"; כְּמַעֲשֶׂה דְּלֵוִי בַּר סִיסָא, שֶׁהֶעֱלוּהוּ לַבִּימָה, וְטָפַת רוּחוֹ עָלָיו, וְלֹא אֲנִיבוֹן.

כִּי עַל-יְדֵי הַגֵּאוּת, הוּא בְּחִינַת עֲבוֹדַת אֱלִילִים: וּבַעֲבוֹדַת אֱלִילִים כְּתִיב: "פְּסִילֵי אֱלֹהֵיהֶם תִּשְׂרְפוּן בָּאֵשׁ" (דְּבָרִים ז), 'וְכָל הָעוֹמֵד לִשְׂרֹף כְּשָׂרוּף דָּמֵי, וְכִתוּתֵי מִכְתָּת שְׁעוּרֵהּ', כַּמּוּבָא בַּגְּמָרָא (רֹאשׁ-הַשָּׁנָה כח.) לְעִנְיַן שׁוֹפָר שֶׁל עֲבוֹדַת אֱלִילִים; וְכֵיוָן שֶׁמְּכַתָּת כָּתִית שְׁעוּרֵהּ, אֵין לוֹ כְּלֵי הַדִּבּוּר לְדַבֵּר עִמָּהֶם.

אַךְ כְּשֶׁהוּא נִזְהָר וְשׁוֹמֵר כְּבוֹד הַשֵּׁם שֶׁיִּהְיֶה בִּשְׁלֵמוּת, שֶׁהוּא נִבְזֶה

---

21. **closed up....** And even if the haughty man continues speaking, his words will neither enlighten nor have any positive influence. In addition, this can be seen as very good advice: "When feeling haughty and proud, close your mouth!" (*Mabuey HaNachal*).

22. **Levi bar Sisa.** He was a tzaddik and therefore, when he felt the words of Torah "blackening," he did not talk. Most people, however, are not so spiritually sensitive and are unaware of the way their haughty feelings blemish their words. They must be especially careful with the power of speech and the Torah they might wish to speak. Yet, the question arises: If one should not speak unless he is pure, how then can those on the lower levels ever hope to achieve "enlightened speech"? Even so, the Talmud teaches: One should always study Torah, even if not for its own sake; for by studying even for the wrong reasons, one can come to studying for the right reasons (*Pesachim* 50b). The same is true for the person who is on the lowest of spiritual levels. Provided he sincerely tries to conduct himself properly and without arrogance, he has the ability to eventually rise above his haughtiness and reach even the highest of levels (*Mabuey HaNachal*).

23. **shofar used for idolatry...with which to speak.** This Talmudic discussion takes up the issue of fulfilling the mitzvah of shofar when the shofar in question has been used for some idolatrous practice. The law requires the shofar be of a minimum size. It also requires an object used for idol worship to be destroyed by fire. Such an object is considered destroyed even before it has been burned and therefore is legally non-existent. Thus, the shofar in question may not be used to fulfill the mitzvah of blowing the shofar on Rosh HaShanah.

After establishing the connection between haughtiness and idolatry, Rebbe Nachman incorporates this Talmudic passage to show that any sounds emanating from idolatry—

In Mitzrayim

(Joshua 1:8), "This Book of Torah should not *YaMuSh* (depart) from your mouth," corresponding to (Exodus 10:21), "darkness *YaMaSh* (that was tangible)." In other words, [the words of Torah] should not become corporal and blackened by your mouth. By failing to make certain that the Holy One's glory is complete—i.e., by being haughty[20]—a person cannot open his mouth, as in (Psalms 17:10), "Their mouth closed up, [for] they spoke haughtily."[21] This resembles the story of Levi bar Sisa. He was called up to the podium, but his spirit grew haughty and he was unable to speak (*Yerushalmi, Yevamot* chap. 12).[22]

As a result of haughtiness, a person is in an aspect of idolatry. Concerning the worship of idols [it is written] (Deuteronomy 7:5), "the images of their gods destroy by fire." In connection to a shofar used for idolatry, the Talmud teaches: Anything about to be destroyed by fire is already considered destroyed and utterly reduced in size (*Rosh HaShanah* 28a). And, since his size has been utterly reduced, he no longer has a voice with which to speak.[23]

However, when a person is careful and makes certain that God's glory is complete—he is "lowly, and in his own eyes repulsive" (Psalms

---

his limited mind, he will find that it responds the way anything physical would when full: the old is removed, forgotten in favor of the new (*Likutey Moharan* I, 110).

The verse, "This Book of Torah should not *yamush* from your mouth," was said to Yehoshua when he was appointed leader of the Jewish people following Moshe's passing. The *Mai HaNachal* explains that God's intent was to warn him against taking the glory and honor which accompanies leadership for himself. For if he did, the words of Torah would become corporeal in his mouth. But, if Yehoshua heeded the warning, God indicated that the Torah would enlighten him and make him successful in his new role. This can be seen as a timeless warning to the leaders of the Jewish people. Far more than the common person, it is the leader who must guard against arrogance and haughtiness, and the excesses of power and authority.

Thus the Torah tells us that Moshe was the most humble of all men (Numbers 12:3). And, because he achieved the greatest level of humility, he was considered worthy and qualified to lead God's chosen people out of exile, bring them the Torah and guide them to the Holy Land. Moshe could descend to those on the lowest spiritual levels, the *aphar* (dust), and elevate them with his speech. However, when leaders do not have this quality of proper humility, they lengthen the exile, as we find in Rebbe Nachman's explanation of Rabbah bar bar Chanah's story, below.

20. **haughty.** When a person is haughty, God says: "I will not dwell in the same world with him" (*Sotah* 5a). By taking for oneself the credit which accompanies one's achievements, a person reveals that he does not fully recognize God and His all-pervading Divine providence. In the hands of God, as it were, the translation of the Hebrew word *kavod* is glory—God's glory. But in the hands of man, that same *kavod* becomes haughtiness and self-importance, making God's glory incomplete.

LIKUTEY MOHARAN #11:2,3

בְּעֵינָיו נִמְאָס, עַל־יְדֵי־זֶה יוּכַל לְדַבֵּר דִּבּוּרִים הַמְּאִירִים, בִּבְחִינַת
(יְחֶזְקֵאל מ"ג): "וְהָאָרֶץ הֵאִירָה מִכְּבוֹדוֹ", וְהֵם מְאִירִים לוֹ
לִתְשׁוּבָה, וְיָכוֹל לָבוֹא לִתְבוּנוֹת הַתּוֹרָה לְעָמְקָהּ כַּנַּ"ל:

ג. וְכָבוֹד בִּשְׁלֵמוּת, אֵינוֹ כִּי אִם עַל־יְדֵי וָא"ו שֶׁיַּמְשִׁיךְ לְתוֹכָהּ, כִּי
בְּלֹא וָא"ו נִשְׁאָר כְּבַד פֶּה, וְעַל־יְדֵי וָא"ו הוּא בִּבְחִינַת (תְּהִלִּים ל):
"כָּבוֹד וְלֹא יִדֹּם";

כִּי כָּל מָקוֹם שֶׁנֶּאֱמַר וָא"ו, הוּא מוֹסִיף (פְּסָחִים ה.), הַיְנוּ בְּחִינַת
תּוֹסְפוֹת קְדֻשָּׁה, הַיְנוּ שְׁמִירַת הַבְּרִית, כְּמַאֲמַר חֲכָמֵינוּ, זִכְרוֹנָם
לִבְרָכָה: 'כָּל מָקוֹם שֶׁאַתָּה מוֹצֵא גֶדֶר עֶרְוָה, אַתָּה מוֹצֵא קְדֻשָּׁה'
(וַיִּקְרָא רַבָּה כ"ה, הוּבָא בְּרַשִׁ"י), כִּי זֶה תָּלוּי בָּזֶה, גֵּאוּת וְנִאוּף, כְּמוֹ

The *Mai HaNachal* points out that Moshe, when told by God to redeem the Jewish people, said, "But I am *k'vad peh*" (Exodus 4:10). He did not see himself as having properly guarded the *brit* and therefore considered himself unworthy and incapable of bringing the Jews to "enlightened speech" and to deep Torah understanding. God told Moshe that He would be with him and said, "I will be with your mouth..." (Exodus 4:15), for in God's eyes Moshe had indeed been found worthy (see below n.38).

28. **to add.** In Hebrew, the letter *vav* at the beginning of a word is used as a conjunction, almost always as the word "and." The Talmud tells us that wherever the *vav* appears, it also serves to *add* something which is not obvious, something beyond the simple meaning of the word. Rebbe Nachman teaches that, when the letter *vav* is placed inside *kavOd*, it indicates the additional or extra holiness which enables one to speak. The *Zohar* (III, 2a) states that "the letter *vav* is called the letter of truth." As such, when the *vav* is part of his speech, so that *k'vad peh* becomes *kavOd*, then his speech has the power to enlighten. A further connection which truth has with this lesson will be explained later on (n.83).

29. **addition of holiness...brit.** The *brit* (Covenant) which God made with Avraham and his descendants after him is sealed through the circumcision of the foreskin. This is the sign of the Covenant (Genesis 17). As such, the Jewish people's covenant with God is centered on sexual purity. Guarding the *brit*—the Covenant or, alternatively, the organ of procreation— thus implies a high standard of moral behavior in thought, word and deed. The *Mai HaNachal* points out that every day one should see to strive for additional holiness of the *brit*. That is, by striving for more holiness, one can actually achieve greater and greater levels daily.

In the language of the Kabbalah, the letter *vav*, with its numerical value of six, symbolizes the persona of *Z'er Anpin* which encompasses the six *sefirot*: Chesed, Gevurah, Tiferet, Netzach, Hod, Yesod (see Lesson #12, n.41; see Appendix: The Divine Persona). In Primordial Man, *Yesod* (Foundation) corresponds to *brit* (see Appendix: The Sefirot and Man). Therefore, where the letter *vav* is used, it generally denotes increased sexual purity— i.e., additional holiness in guarding the *brit*, the sign of the Covenant.

LIKUTEY MOHARAN #11:2,3

15:4)[24]—this enables him to speak words which enlighten. As is written (Ezekiel 43:2), "And the earth shone with His glory."[25] [His words] enlighten him to repentance, and he can then come to deep Torah understanding.[26]

3. *KaVoD* (glory) is only complete when it has the letter *vav* drawn into it. Without the *vav* he remains "*K'VaD* (heavy) of tongue" (Exodus 4:10). But with the *vav* he is in the aspect of (Psalms 30:13), "...*kavOd*, and not remain silent."[27]

This is because wherever the letter *vav* is used, it comes to add (*Pesachim* 5a).[28] In other words, there is an addition of holiness: guarding the *brit* (the Covenant).[29] As our Sages taught: Wherever you find protective measures against immorality, there you will find holiness (*Vayikra Rabbah* 24:6). For one is contingent upon the other,

haughtiness—should be considered as nothing, since their source is considered naught. Just as the shofar of idolatry cannot be sounded, the man who is haughty cannot speak.

24. ...repulsive. That is, he negates his own self-importance and pride completely, and defers totally to God.

25. earth shone with His glory. The earth is *aphar*, the lowest level. Yet we see that it shines with God's glory. The same is true of the person who achieves true humility. His lowliness should not be misunderstood as a low spiritual level. On the contrary, he is likened to the earth and likewise shines—his words enlighten—with God's glory.

The earth is also synonymous with *Malkhut*. Just as *Malkhut* is the lowest of the *sefirot*, so too, the earth is a symbol of lowliness and humility. And, as explained above (see n.18), *Malkhut* is the mouth. See also *Likutey Moharan* I, 12:1 where Rebbe Nachman quotes the *Tikkuney Zohar* (Introduction) that the *peh* (mouth) also symbolizes the Oral Law. He explains that the Oral Law is the source of the speaking spirit—man's living soul—as in (Genesis 2:7), "The *earth* shall bring forth a living soul" (*Mai HaNachal*).

26. deep Torah understanding. In review: To attain understanding of the Torah's depths, which requires bringing about an upper and lower unification, one must achieve enlightened speech, speech which guides him to his appropriate path of repentance (§1). To achieve this level of speech one must eliminate his haughtiness and idolatrous self-importance, as otherwise the words of Torah are corrupted in his mouth. By doing so, God's glory is complete and so one's words shine with His glory (§2).

27. KaVoD...K'VaD...silent. *Kavod* (glory) can be written with or without the letter *vav*. When spelled with a *vav*, *kavOd* (כבוד) has a numerical value of 32. This refers to the Thirty-Two Paths of Wisdom (*Sefer Yetzirah* 1:1), the source of deep Torah understanding. These thirty-two paths correspond to the thirty-two teeth of the mouth, *Malkhut* is *peh*, from which speech emanates. When *kavOd* is complete—with its *vav*—it is "So that glory may sing praise to You, and not remain silent." Otherwise, when *kavod* is without the *vav* (כבד), the Thirty-Two Paths of Wisdom are incomplete. This is *k'vad peh*, faltering speech and a foul mouth.

LIKUTEY MOHARAN #11:3

172

שֶׁאָמְרוּ חֲכָמֵינוּ, זִכְרוֹנָם לִבְרָכָה (סוֹטָה ד:) עַל פָּסוּק (מִשְׁלֵי ו):
"וְאֵשֶׁת אִישׁ נֶפֶשׁ יְקָרָה תָצוּד".

וְעַל כֵּן בְּרִית מְכֻנֶּה בְּשֵׁם שַׁדַּ"י, כְּמוֹ שֶׁכָּתוּב (בְּרֵאשִׁית ל"ה): "אֲנִי
אֵל שַׁדַּי פְּרֵה וּרְבֵה", כִּי שַׁדַּי הוּא בְּחִינַת 'שֶׁיֵּשׁ דַּי בֶּאֱלֹקוּתִי לְכָל
בְּרִיָּה' (כַּמּוּבָא בְּפֵירַשְׁ"י לֶךְ-לְךָ יז). וּכְשֶׁאֵינוּ שׁוֹמֵר הַבְּרִית, הַיְנוּ עַל-
יְדֵי גַאֲוָת, הוּא עוֹשֶׂה לְעַצְמוֹ עֲבוֹדַת אֱלִילִים, הוּא מַרְאֶה שֶׁאֵין דַּי
לוֹ בֶּאֱלֹקוּתוֹ, עַד שֶׁצָּרִיךְ עֲבוֹדַת אֱלִילִים, וְעַל כֵּן פּוֹגֵם בְּשַׁדַּי,
שֶׁיֵּשׁ דַּי בֶּאֱלֹקוּתוֹ לְכָל בְּרִיָּה; וּכְשֶׁשּׁוֹמֵר הַבְּרִית, הוּא זוֹכֶה לָאוֹר

must also see to study and comply with Torah law.

30. **adulteress...haughty soul.** The Talmud teaches (*loc. cit.*): Whoever is haughty will in the end succumb to immorality. The equation is thus complete: The adulteress traps the haughty and the haughty succumb to immorality. One is contingent upon the other. Our Sages also taught (*loc. cit.*) that even if one is learned in Torah, he can still succumb to temptation. This harks back to the previous note in that one must see to adhere to Torah. Knowledge alone is not enough. However, with ongoing study and practice, the Torah will protect him from sin.

31. **fruitful....** When God blessed Yaakov that he would be fruitful and multiply, He used His holy name Shadai. Thus, Shadai and the *brit* are interrelated, the sign of the *brit* being the reproductive organ.

32. **yeSh DaI...** As explained earlier, the *shefa* from Above descends through the upper *sefirot* and then through *Z'er Anpin*. The last of these six *sefirot, Yesod,* corresponds to the *brit*. From there the *shefa* emanates to this world, *Malkhut*. Thus, it is in *Shadai/Yesod*—the seat of distribution of *shefa*—that we ascertain that there is *enough* for all of creation (see Appendix: Sefirot and Associated Names of God).

The *Mai HaNachal* points out that when God again addressed Moshe after he and Aharon had gone to Pharaoh the first time, He said: "I revealed Myself to the Patriarchs as *El Shadai,* but did not allow them to know Me by My name *YHVH*" (Exodus 6:3). This was because the earlier generations had not yet reached a level of guarding the Covenant completely, the upper and lower unifications, because they had not yet received the Torah. However, because Moshe had already spoken to the Jews and enlightened them with his speech, and because he was destined to receive the Torah, God revealed Himself more completely, with both unifications—"My name" and "*YHVH*."

33. **fails to guard....** Guarding the Covenant on both levels of unification (as we shall see in §§5 and 6) corresponds to the *Shema* and the *Barukh shem*, which denote unity and pure faith. Conversely, by not guarding the Covenant on these two levels one negates faith and thereby enforces idolatry (*Mai HaNachal*). Furthermore, because haughtiness is akin to immorality, one's pride and self-importance are also a breach of the covenant. Therefore, failing to guard the *brit* leads to a person making a god of himself, as our Sages taught: When a person is haughty, it is as if he worshipped idolatry (*Sotah* 4b).

haughtiness and immorality, as our Sages said of the verse (Proverbs 6:26), "The adulteress traps the haughty soul" (Sotah 4b).[30]

opposite of avodah zara

This is why the *brit* is referred to by the holy name *Shadai*, as is written (Genesis 35:11), "I am the Omnipotent *Shadai*; be fruitful and multiply."[31] For *ShaDaI* indicates "that *yeSh DaI* (there is enough) of My Godliness for every creation" (Rashi, Genesis 17:1).[32] But when a person—because of haughtiness—fails to guard the *brit*, he makes a god of himself. He makes it appear as though there *is not* enough in His Godliness for him, so that he requires idol worship. And thus he blemishes the name *Shadai*; for there *is* enough of His Godliness for every creation.[33] Whereas, by guarding the *brit*, he is rewarded with a

---

With the keys provided in the lesson to this point, the following elucidation is in order: God is continuously sending *shefa* (a benevolent influx of spiritual energy) to this world. The Kabbalistic teachings explain that this *shefa* is systematically channeled into the world by means of the *sefirot* (Divine emanations) which act, so to speak, as vessels for receiving and then passing the influx onward. The process begins with the upper *sefirot* receiving this abundance (see Appendix: The Structure of the Sefirot): *Keter* receives the *shefa* from Above and passes it on to *Chokhmah* which then channels it to the third *sefirah*, *Binah*. It then filters the influx down through the six lower *sefirot*, known collectively as *Z'er Anpin*, from where it is then given over to the lowest *sefirah*, *Malkhut*, symbolic of this world. Because of the gradual and gradated nature of this process, the amount of this abundant influx which each level receives is commensurate with the "vessel's" ability to maintain it. The same may be said of the recipients of this *shefa*. Each order of creation receives in accordance with its ability to receive. And even within the specific orders there are distinctions. Thus, all men are not equal; each one reaps only as much as his spiritual development allows. Nevertheless, in our lesson, Rebbe Nachman gives us to understand that everyone has some role to play in the process of bringing *shefa* to the world and anyone can, by emerging from his low spiritual level, increase that participation immeasurably (see n.4 above).

The Ari explains that *tevunah* (deep Torah understanding) is rooted in the *sefirah* of *Binah* (Understanding), Torah is associated with *Z'er Anpin*, and *Malkhut* is the mouth, the power of speech. When one purifies his speech, his Torah study has the power to draw an abundant influx from God (see above, §1 and nn.7-10). However, this can only be accomplished by purifying one's *brit*. For then, after one channels the *shefa* from *Binah* (Understanding) to *Z'er Anpin* (Torah), it can then be filtered down to *Malkhut* (mouth) in holiness and enlighten his speech, eventually bringing him to repent fully. This can be further understood in light of the fact that *teshuvah* (repentance) has its source in *Binah*. Torah law unequivocally dictates that the sinner must be punished for his sins. However, because *teshuvah* is rooted in an even higher source than Torah law, for *Binah* is above *Z'er Anpin*, one has recourse to repent and draw *shefa* from there. By evoking God's forgiveness, this *teshuvah* will provide him with a pardon which overrides the law calling for punishment. And, as Rebbe Nachman has shown, this exalted level of full repentance is achieved through "enlightened speech." Even so, it must be understood that ultimately *teshuvah* as well as all *shefa* must, in any case, pass through the channel of *Z'er Anpin*—Torah. In other words, in the normal working of the process of Divine influences, repentance without Torah is an impossibility. Therefore, one

LIKUTEY MOHARAN #11:3,4 — 174

הַמֵּאִיר לוֹ לִתְשׁוּבָה כַּנַּ"ל:

ד. וְאוֹר הַזֶּה הוּא בְּחִינַת טַל אוֹרוֹת: הַכְּלוּלִים בַּנָּאוּ שֶׁל כָּבוֹד,
בִּבְחִינַת (אִיּוֹב ל"ג): "הֶן כָּל אֵלֶּה יִפְעַל אֵל פַּעֲמַיִם שָׁלוֹשׁ עִם
גָּבֶר". 'פַּעֲמַיִם שָׁלוֹשׁ' – הֵם בְּחִינַת טַל אוֹרוֹת שֶׁל מִלּוּי שָׁלֹשׁ
אוֹתִיּוֹת רִאשׁוֹנוֹת (פֵּרוּשׁ, כִּי שָׁלֹשׁ אוֹתִיּוֹת רִאשׁוֹנוֹת שֶׁל שֵׁם הֲוָיָה
בְּמִלּוּי אַלְפִּין הֵם בְּגִימַטְרִיָּא טַ"ל, וְהֵם בְּחִינַת טַל אוֹרוֹת, וְהֵם
כְּלוּלִים בְּהַוָא"ו שֶׁל הַשֵּׁם). 'עִם גָּבֶר' – שֶׁהֵם כְּלוּלִים בַּבְּרִית, כִּי

things... *three times*..."—we again have a total of 39 (*VAV*x3 = 39). Thus, the thirty-nine-lights are encompassed in the *vav* itself.

Alternatively, this can be understood by applying Kabbalistic principles for aligning the four letters of God's ineffable name with the ten Divine emanations. In this arrangement, the *sefirah* of *Keter* (Crown), because of its absolutely transcending nature, has no complement in one of the four letters but is merely associated with the apex of the first letter, the point of the *yod* (י). Of the remaining *sefirot, Chokhmah* (Wisdom) corresponds to *yod* itself; *Binah* (Understanding) to the first *heh*; the six *sefirot* of *Z'er Anpin* to the *vav*; and *Malkhut* to the final *heh* (see Appendix: Levels of Existence). As mentioned earlier (n.32), the *shefa* flows down through the *sefirah* hierarchy, comes together in *Yesod* and from there is distributed to *Malkhut*. When seen in terms of the Tetragrammaton, the *shefa*/thirty-nine-lights/dew passes through the *Y* and the *H*, and then comes together in the *V* from where it is distributed to the symbol of this world, the final *H*. This explains how the thirty-nine-lights are encompassed in the *vav* of God's name. It also helps us to understand Rebbe Nachman's earlier statement that the thirty-nine-lights are encompassed in the *vav* of *kavOd*, for, as we've seen (n.29), this *vav* alludes to the additional degree of holiness required for guarding the *brit* which is *Yesod*. Moreover, when one accomplishes bringing the *vav* into *kavOd* by guarding the *brit*, in which the thirty-nine-lights are encompassed, he merits the "enlightening" light of repentance and can come to a deep understanding of the Torah.

38. strength. "Who is a *gibor*, a strong person? One who conquers his inclination" (*Avot* 4:1). In Torah and Rabbinic literature, the quality of *gevurah* (strength) is commonly attributed to the person who controls his sexual urge. Such a person is called a man (*gever*). When one controls his desires, he can then draw the *shefa* from *Yesod*/*brit* to *Malkhut*. This is the meaning of the verse quoted from Judges (*loc. cit.*), "For as a man is, so is his *gevurah*"—his ability to draw down the *shefa* and illumine the lower levels is commensurate with his degree of sexual purity. This is the reason why Moshe, having reached the highest level of sexual purity humanly possible, was able to bring down the entire Torah and enlighten the Jewish people with speech that shines. (See above n.29 that Torah corresponds to *Z'er Anpin*/the *vav*—the revelation of the lights.)

It is interesting to note that when the Jewish people stood at Mt. Sinai to witness the Torah's revelation, they heard God's first two commandments: "I am your God...Do not have any other gods...," and passed away. Their corporeality, even with purification, was incapable of containing the great influx of heavenly light which they experienced. The

175   *LIKUTEY MOHARAN #11:3,4*

light that directs him to repentance, as above.[34]

4. And, this light [which leads him to repent] corresponds to the thirty-nine-lights[35] which are encompassed in the *vav* of *kavOd*. This is alluded to in (Job 33:29), "God does all these things twice or three times with a man." " Three times " corresponds to the thirty-nine-lights of the expanded first three letters < of the Tetragrammaton >. {To explain: The first three letters of the *YHVH*, when spelled out using the letter *alef*, have a numerical value of thirty-nine, corresponding to the thirty-nine-lights.[36] They are thus encompassed in the *VAV* of God's name.[37]} "With a man"—for [these lights] are included in the *brit*, [as in,] "For as a man is, so is his strength" (Judges

The Maharsha comments on this passage in the Talmud that man is composed of two spirits: one of purity, one of impurity. The spirit of purity is akin to humility and recognizing God. The spirit of impurity, on the other hand, is akin to haughtiness and falsehood.

34. **repentance, as above.** See above note 29, "The Ari explains...."

In review: To attain understanding of the Torah's depths, which requires bringing about an upper and lower unification, one must achieve enlightened speech, speech which guides him to his appropriate path of repentance (§1). To achieve this level of speech one must eliminate his haughtiness and idolatrous self-importance, as otherwise the words of Torah are corrupted in his mouth. By doing so, God's glory is complete and so one's words shine with His glory (§2). Haughtiness and immorality are contingent one upon the other. Nullifying one's haughtiness completely therefore requires guarding the *brit*. Through this high standard of moral behavior one merits to the light of repentance (§3).

35. **thirty-nine-lights.** According to Hebrew alphabetical-numerology, known as *gematria*, thirty-nine is *Lamed* (ל = 30) and *Tet* (ט = 9). *TaL* (טל) is also Hebrew for "dew." Dew was given a special blessing in that unlike other forms of precipitation, it never fails to descend upon the earth (*Rashi*, Judges 6:38). Dew thus corresponds to the *shefa* referred to previously, for it also never ceases descending to this world.

36. **three letters...value...thirty-nine-lights.** "Expansion" of the Tetragrammaton is done in four different ways, the changes being in the different ways to spell out the last three letters (ההה). For example, the letter *heh* (ה) can be spelled *heh yod* (הי), *heh alef* (הא), or *heh heh* (הה). The same applies to the letter *vav* (ויו, ואו, וו). Thus, if the first three letters of *YHVH* are spelled out with both *heh* and *vav* expanded with an *alef*, then *yod* = יוד = 20, *heh* = הא = 6, *vav* = ואו = 13 — for a total of 39, corresponding to the thirty-nine-lights. Adding the second *heh* similarly expanded, the *YHVH* has a value of 45, the equivalent of *ADaM* (man, אדם); the significance of this will be explained shortly (see Appendix: Expansions of the Holy Names of God).

37. **VAV of God's name.** Again employing expansion and *gematria*, this can be understood as follows: Using the *alef* to expand the letter *VAV* (ואו) we find that *vav* has a value of 13 (ואו = 6 + 1 + 6 = 13). When the verse quoted by Rebbe Nachman is applied — "God does these

LIKUTEY MOHARAN #11:4

176

כְּאִישׁ גְּבוּרָתוֹ. וְעַל שֵׁם זֶה נִקְרָא בְּרִית בֹּעַז (תִּקּוּן לֹא) – בּוֹ עֹז, בּוֹ תָּקְפָּא.

אֲבָל כְּשֶׁאֵינוּ שׁוֹמֵר הַבְּרִית, הוּא מְקַלְקֵל הַטַּ"ל אוֹרוֹת וּמַמְשִׁיךְ עַל עַצְמוֹ עַל הַפַּרְנָסָה, הַיְנוּ טַ"ל מְלָאכוֹת, כַּמּוּבָא בַּזֹּהַר (ח"ג רמד.): 'מָאן דְּזָרֵק פֵּרוּרִין דְּנַהֲמָא, עֲנִיּוּת רָדֵף אַבַּתְרֵהּ, כָּל־שֶׁכֵּן מָאן דְּזָרֵק פֵּרוּרִין דְּמֹחָא'.

Himself. Therefore, when a person belittles bread, [even crumbs,] it is as if he directly belittles and shows disrespect for God. As punishment for this, he will derive no pleasure from that which he disparaged and poverty will be his lot. Regarding the great significance of bread and the grains used in making it, the *Zohar Chadash* (8b) teaches that there exists lower realms of creation inhabited by life forms very different from those known to man. Though we do not know where these lower realms are and have very little information about them (they were known to the Talmudic Sages) we do know, based on this passage in the *Zohar Chadash,* that these forms of life are far less intelligent than those of our world. This inferior intellectual capability is attributed to the absence of grain in those realms. This relates to our lesson. Rebbe Nachman teaches that one must strive for deep Torah understanding which, without the benefit of grains/bread, one cannot hope to achieve. Similarly, our Sages taught: An infant cannot call his father or mother until he tastes grain (*Sanhedrin* 70b).

42. **crumbs of the mind.** The *Zohar* (*loc. cit.*) offers a number of explanations, all of which indicate a casting off of the wisdom and intellect—the "bread" of the mind.

The explanation which immediately reflects Rebbe Nachman's intent at this point is that the crumbs refer to drops of semen which, as we've seen elsewhere (*Likutey Moharan* I, 7:3, excerpts and notes), are the drops of intellect which emanate from the mind. The *Zohar* mentions various ways which these drops of seed are thrown away and wasted: 1) having sexual relations with a *niddah* (any woman, even one's own wife, who has not fulfilled the requirements associated with immersing in a *mikvah* after menstruation); 2) having relations with a non-Jewess; 3) having relations with a woman whom one is forbidden to marry (e.g., a *kohein*, a priest, who marries a divorcee, etc.). Also included are all forms of homosexuality and the most severe example of throwing away "the crumbs of the mind," the wasting of seed through masturbation. This was the sin of the Generation of the Flood.

Thus, Rebbe Nachman tells us that when one fails to guard the *brit,* as in any of the previously mentioned examples, he exchanges, as it were, the thirty-nine-lights for thirty-nine-works. And, because of this, as the *Zohar* teaches: Poverty chases after him. He will therefore experience the burdens of earning a living.

Further explanations for "crumbs of the mind" offered by the *Zohar* include those who belittle the "crumbs" of Torah—the tips and crowns of the Torah letters; and even worse, those who throw away the Torah's mysteries and deep secrets by revealing them to undeserving and unrighteous individuals. This, too, ties in with our lesson, the theme of which is the achieving of deep Torah understanding (see also §7 where Rebbe Nachman discusses Kabbalah and deep secrets). Thus, Rebbe Nachman tells us that to achieve such insights one must purify his speech through the elimination of his own haughtiness. This

LIKUTEY MOHARAN #11:4

8:21).[38] It is for this reason that the *brit* is referred to as Boaz: *bo oz*—in him, there is strength (*Tikkuney Zohar* #31).[39]

But when a person does not guard the *brit*, he damages the thirty-nine-lights and draws upon himself the yoke of earning a living—i.e., the thirty-nine-works.[40] As is taught in the *Zohar* (III, 244a): One who throws away crumbs of bread is pursued by poverty.[41] All the more so someone who throws away the "crumbs" of the mind.[42]

Talmud tells us that they were revived with *tal* (dew), the same dew that will be used to revive to dead at the time of the Resurrection (*Shabbat* 88b). The word Torah (תורה) has a numerical value of 611. Together with the first two mitzvot heard directly from God, these are the 613 Divine commandments of the Torah. In fact, these two mitzvot which the Jewish people heard directly from God are synonymous with the two unifications which Rebbe Nachman mentions in the lesson. "I am your God..." corresponds to the *Shema*, believing in God's oneness (cf. *Sefer HaMitzvot*, Positive Commandment 1), whereas "Do not have any other gods..." corresponds to the *Barukh Shem*, believing in God's absolute Kingship and thus not making a god of oneself or of one's accomplishments (see n.33; cf. *Sefer HaMitzvot*, Prohibitive Commandment 2). Fulfilling these two mitzvot enables one to successfully carry out the other 611 mitzvot—the Torah, through which the *tal*-lights can be revealed (*Mai HaNachal*). With this, we can understand another Talmudic teaching, Whoever partakes of the *tal* of Torah, the *tal* of Torah will resurrect him (*Ketuvot* 111b). This is generally explained as referring to the period following the coming of Mashiach. However, from Rebbe Nachman's lesson we learn that through Torah study which leads to "enlightened speech" (see above nn.8,9), this can take place right here and now! Torah study will bring a person to repentance—"resurrection"—even in this world.

39. **Boaz, bo oz....** In the Book of Ruth (chap. 3) we find that God put Boaz through a very trying test in guarding the *brit*. Our Sages comment that this test was even greater and more difficult than the one Yosef underwent in Egypt (*Sanhedrin* 19b). Because he did not succumb, Boaz merited being called the "strong one," for he successfully controlled his inclination and overcame temptation.

40. **thirty-nine-works.** The concept of the thirty-nine-works which counter the thirty-nine-lights will be made clear within the text. One who fails to guard the *brit* loses the light of spirituality which—with regard to receiving God's *shefa*—could put him above the dictates of nature. He is instead made subject to the (often times bitter) *work*ings of this world.

As previously explained (n.29), *shefa* constantly fills the world. The obvious question is, where is it? Woven into the tapestry of his lesson is Rebbe Nachman's deep and poignant answer. There are those who guard the Almighty's Covenant by guarding its sign and insignia, the *brit*. For them, there is always *dai* (enough). They are satisfied with their lot and feel they have sufficient *shefa*. This, however, is not the case for those who fail to guard the Covenant and succumb to temptation. For them, there is never *dai*. They constantly feel the yoke of earning a living, having to always work for more because they never feel they have enough. Such people are truly suffering under the yoke of the thirty-nine works and will never feel satisfied no matter how much *shefa* fills the world. They will always desire more.

41. **crumbs of bread...poverty.** The *Zohar* (*loc. cit.*) states that everything in creation has an angel governing it. Grains used for bread, however, are under the direct auspices of God

LIKUTEY MOHARAN #11:4

178

וְזֶה: בּוֹ עַז, בּוֹ כָּלוּל שְׁנֵי הַבְּחִינוֹת, הַיְנוּ ל"ט אוֹרוֹת – מִי
שֶׁשּׁוֹמֵר הַבְּרִית, וְל"ט מְלָאכוֹת – מִי שֶׁפּוֹגֵם בּוֹ; כִּי עַז עִם
הַכּוֹלֵל – שְׁתֵּי פְּעָמִים טַל:

וְזֶה: "מִשְׁכָּן מִשְׁכָּן" שְׁתֵּי פְּעָמִים – שְׁתֵּי פְּעָמִים ל"ט, כִּי ל"ט
מְלָאכוֹת גָּמְרִינַן מִמִּשְׁכָּן (כְּמוֹ שֶׁאָמְרוּ חֲכָמֵינוּ, זִכְרוֹנָם לִבְרָכָה, שַׁבָּת
מט:). וּמִי שֶׁשּׁוֹמֵר אֶת בְּרִיתוֹ, אַף-עַל-פִּי שֶׁהוּא עוֹשֶׂה הַל"ט
מְלָאכוֹת – הֵם בִּבְחִינַת מְלֶאכֶת הַמִּשְׁכָּן, הַיְנוּ מִשְׁכָּן בְּבִנְיָנָהּ,
בְּחִינַת ל"ט אוֹרוֹת; אַךְ מִי שֶׁפּוֹגֵם בַּבְּרִית – הַמְּלָאכוֹת שֶׁלּוֹ הֵם
בִּבְחִינַת מִשְׁכָּן בְּחָרְבָּנָהּ, בִּבְחִינַת ל"ט מַלְקוֹת (תִּקּוּן מח), בְּחִינַת

the *gevurot* sweetens the stern judgments and decrees (see *Likutey Moharan* I, 10 and nn.2, 63) which are an inevitable aspect of our lives. And so, by adding holiness, the *vav* of *kavod*, to all aspects of guarding the *brit*, man can even sweeten the thirty-nine-works which he finds himself obliged to perform.

45. **Tabernacle...thirty-nine-works....** On Shabbat, the Day of Rest, it is forbidden to work. The term "work" should not be thought of as labor and strenuous activity, implying that only such labor is prohibited; rather, as our Sages taught, work which is forbidden on Shabbat consists of those activities which were necessary for building the Tabernacle. These activities and their derivatives are considered creative acts and are therefore proscribed on the day which God rests, as it were, from His creating the world. The Mishnah (*Shabbat* 73a) enumerates "40 less one," or 39 such works.

46. **Tabernacle...thirty-nine-lights.** Even though he is obliged to "work," he knows that, in truth, it is God and not the labor of his hands that provides. He trusts that God will give him *dai* (enough) and therefore every work he performs is likened to building the Tabernacle and drawing the *shefa* to the world. It is worth noting that the Tabernacle (where Moshe spoke with God) and later the Holy Temple (where the Sanhedrin held court) were where the Jewish people came to seek the word of God—to gain understanding of His holy Torah. In the context of our lesson, by guarding the Covenant, one's works are transformed; no longer the yoke of earning a living, they are the works of building the Tabernacle, the attaining of deep Torah understanding.

It should be pointed out that building the Tabernacle does not override Shabbat. Thus, even when one's acts are pure and correspond to the thirty-nine-lights, it is still forbidden to work on Shabbat. The relationship between these works and Shabbat will be dealt with in section 5.

47. **Tabernacle when destroyed.** Even though it appears that this person is contributing to society—that his work is productive—the truth is that his so called achievements are spiritually bereft of value and accomplish nothing. Compare above, section 2 and note 23.

48. **thirty-nine-lashes.** The *Tikkuney Zohar* (*loc. cit.*) associates the thirty-nine-lashes with the thirty-nine-works which are prohibited on Shabbat, saying that one who observes Shabbat is spared this punishment. When one abstains from work on Shabbat and enjoys *ONeG* Shabbat (the delight of Shabbat), he merits the thirty-nine-lights of Resurrection. However,

LIKUTEY MOHARAN #11:4

This is *bo oz*: *Bo* (in him) there are incorporated two aspects.[43] There are the thirty-nine-lights <for> someone who guards the *brit*; and there are the thirty-nine-works <for> someone who defiles it. For <the numerical value of> *oz*, counting the word itself, is twice thirty-nine.[44]

And this is the reason for the repetition in (Exodus 38:21), "[These are the accounts of the] Tabernacle, the Tabernacle...." Twice thirty-nine, because the thirty-nine-works are deduced from [the construction of] the Tabernacle (*Shabbat* 49b).[45] Thus, someone who guards his *brit*, even though he engages in the thirty-nine-works, [his works] are an aspect of the works of the Tabernacle—i.e., the Tabernacle when built up, corresponding to the thirty-nine-lights.[46] However, someone who defiles the *brit*, the work he does is an aspect of the Tabernacle when destroyed.[47] This corresponds to the thirty-nine-lashes[48]

---

implies the controlling of one's speech by revealing to others only that which is appropriate and no more. Revealing too much indicates a sense of arrogance and haughtiness ("see how much I know!"), which, as the *Zohar* teaches, associates the revealer with immorality. For haughtiness and immorality are contingent upon one another (see n.30 above).

43. **two aspects.** The potential for both exists in all men, and at all times. One can strive for purity in certain areas only to be lax in others. Therefore, each person must focus his energies on both aspects: seeking additional holiness in matters concerning the *brit* and, at the same time, making sure to guard against those things that defile. This was the tzaddik Boaz—in him there is twice thirty-nine.

44. **twice thirty-nine.** The word *oz* (עז) plus 1, added for the word itself, has a numerical value of 78. The Hebrew word for bread, *LeCheM* (לחם) also equals 78 (*Mabuey HaNachal*). See note 41 above, concerning the significance of bread. The Ari teaches that *lechem* is equal to three times the name *YHVH* (3x26), for bread—i.e., the *shefa* of food—is brought into this world by means of the three *YHVH* present in three *chasadim* (benevolences). Furthermore, it is necessary to dip one's bread in salt at the beginning of the meal. Salt in Hebrew is *MeLaCh* (מלח), also 78. However, unlike the bread which stems from Divine benevolence, salt is derived from the three *YHVH* present in three *gevurot* (severities) (*Shaar HaMitzvot*, Ekev p. 41).

Taken further, this can be applied to the concept of *Malkhut* is *peh* with its "thirty-two teeth" of wisdom (see n.27). The Ari states that the thirty-two teeth are what grind (prepare) the bread, which is manna for the tzaddikim (*ibid.*). This manna corresponds to what Rebbe Nachman calls the thirty-nine-lights. But there are also the thirty-nine-works—the bitter way to earn one's living, much as salt is brackish to the taste. Those who guard the Covenant and thereby attain *kavod*/the thirty-two teeth of wisdom, are given the thirty-nine-lights. Their *shefa* from heaven descends as manna. Their livelihood comes easily and is always sweet. But those who defile the Covenant and thereby remain with their haughtiness are given the thirty-nine-works. Their *shefa* descends from heaven as "salt." Their livelihood comes with difficulty and is always bitter. Even so, one must always see to dip his bread in salt: not to make bitter that which is sweet, but to sweeten that which is bitter. Joining the *chasadim* with

LIKUTEY MOHARAN #11:4,5

180

(דְּבָרִים כ"ה): "אַרְבָּעִים יַכֶּנּוּ וְלֹא יוֹסִיף", הַיְנוּ בְּחִינַת פְּגַם הַבְּרִית, שֶׁהוּא בְּחִינַת תּוֹסָפוֹת כַּנַּ"ל:

ה. וּשְׁמִירַת הַבְּרִית יֵשׁ בּוֹ שְׁנֵי בְּחִינוֹת: יֵשׁ מִי שֶׁזִּוּוּגוֹ בְּשֵׁשֶׁת יְמֵי הַחֹל, וְאַף־עַל־פִּי־כֵן הוּא שׁוֹמֵר אֶת בְּרִיתוֹ עַל־פִּי הַתּוֹרָה, שֶׁאֵינוֹ יוֹצֵא מִדִּינֵי הַתּוֹרָה; וְיֵשׁ מִי שֶׁהוּא שׁוֹמֵר הַבְּרִית, שֶׁזִּוּוּגוֹ מִשַּׁבָּת לְשַׁבָּת.

וְהוּא בְּחִינַת יִחוּדָא עִלָּאָה וְיִחוּדָא תַּתָּאָה. וְזֶה בְּחִינַת שַׁדַּי שֶׁל שַׁבָּת, שֶׁאָמַר לְעוֹלָמוֹ דַּי (בְּרֵאשִׁית־רַבָּה מו, חֲגִיגָה יב), שֶׁצִּמְצֵם אֶת עַצְמוֹ מִכָּל הַמְּלָאכוֹת, וְזֶה בְּחִינַת יִחוּדָא עִלָּאָה.

וְיֵשׁ בְּחִינַת שַׁדַּי שֶׁל חֹל, שֶׁגַּם בְּחֹל יֵשׁ צְמְצוּמִים מִמְּלָאכָה לַחֲבֶרְתָּהּ, וְזֶה בְּחִינַת מט"ט, שֶׁשִּׁלְטָנוּתֵהּ שֵׁשֶׁת יְמֵי הַחֹל, בְּחִינַת

the *brit* one draws upon himself the yoke of livelihood, the thirty-nine-works, corresponding to the thirty-nine-lashes (§4).

51. **two levels.** In sum, Rebbe Nachman has taught that one should strive to achieve enlightened speech, for through it he can come to deep Torah understanding. Such speech is attained when one is humble and has no self-importance. Only then is God's glory complete. Nullifying one's haughtiness completely requires guarding the *brit*. With a high standard of moral behavior one merits the thirty-nine-lights. Conversely, by not guarding the *brit*, one defiles himself with the thirty-nine-works, the thirty-nine-lashes. Now, Rebbe Nachman introduces the next phase of the lesson which details the various levels of guarding the *brit*, explaining how this directly ties in with enlightened speech.

52. **weekdays...Shabbat.** The Talmud lists the number of times in a week a man must fulfill his conjugal obligation (*Ketuvot* 61b). This law applies to the average person. The conjugal obligation of a Torah scholar, on the other hand, should be fulfilled on Friday nights (*ibid.*, 62b). Even those whose marital relations are during the week must see to adhere to that which is permitted by the Torah and guard against that which has been proscribed. And the Torah scholar, whose level is synonymous with the upper unification, as Rebbe Nachman will next show, must be especially careful.

53. **...unification.** Man's actions in this physical world produce corresponding "actions" in the spiritual worlds Above. Thus, a union between husband and wife in this world brings about a unification in the transcendant worlds. These unifications build the supernal Tabernacle and bring the thirty-nine-lights, the abundant influx of *tal* into the world. However, engaging in immoral or prohibited unions causes sparks of holiness to be ensnared by the Other Side. This is the destruction of the Tabernacle, the thirty-nine-works/lashes.

54. **work to the next.** This is because not all acts can be performed at once.

(Tikkuney Zohar, Introduction, p.12b), as in (Deuteronomy 25:3), "Forty lashes he may give him and not exceed."[49] This alludes to defiling the *brit,* which is an aspect of excesses, as explained.[50]

5. Guarding the *brit* has two levels.[51] There is the person whose marital relations are during the six days of the week. Even so, he guards his *brit* as the Torah requires, because he does not transgress the Torah's laws. And there is the person who guards the *brit* in that his marital relations are [only] from Shabbat to Shabbat.[52]

These [two levels] correspond to the upper unification and the lower unification.[53] There is the aspect of *Shadai* of Shabbat: [When God reached the Shabbat of Creation,] He said to His world, "*Dai!* (Enough!)" *(Chagigah* 12a), restricting Himself from all works. This corresponds to the upper unification.

There is also the aspect of *Shadai* of the weekdays. For even on the weekdays there are restrictions, from one work to the next.[54] This corresponds to Metat, whose rule is the six days of the week,

those who do not observe Shabbat are smitten with the thirty-nine-lashes, turning *ONeG* (ענג) into *NeGA* (נגע, leprosy; cf. n.79 below). Furthermore, the *Tikkuney Zohar* (#48, p.85) connects the punishment of thirty-nine-lashes with the thirty-nine-curses placed upon Adam (10), Chavah (10), the Serpent (10) and the earth (9), when Adam ate from the Tree of Knowledge (see Genesis 3:14-21). Analysis of these thirty-nine-curses reveals that in one form or another they all pertain to hard work, so that here again the thirty-nine-works are synonymous with the hardships and suffering of the thirty-nine-lashes.

49. **Forty...not exceed.** While the verse mentions the figure forty, the Mishnah and ensuing Talmudic discussion conclude that the wording of the verse implies the number near forty: hence thirty-nine *(Makkot* 22a).

50. **excesses, as explained.** As explained above (see n.29), every day one should see to strive for additional holiness of the *brit,* increased sexual purity through which the thirty-nine-lights are attained. Conversely, when one is always unsatisfied, when he never has enough, he craves excesses (see n.40). This is the category of the thirty-nine-works, the thirty-nine-lashes. This is the meaning of "Forty lashes...not exceed." Because he did not strive for additional holiness, for increased purity in thought, word and deed, he received the thirty-nine-lashes.

In review: To attain understanding of the Torah's depths, one must achieve enlightened speech, speech which guides him to his appropriate path of repentance (§1). To achieve this level of speech one must eliminate his haughtiness and idolatrous self-importance, as otherwise the words of Torah are corrupted in his mouth. By doing so, God's glory is complete and so one's words shine with His glory (§2). Haughtiness and immorality are contingent one upon the other. Nullifying one's haughtiness completely therefore requires guarding the *brit.* Through this high standard of moral behavior one merits to the light of repentance (§3). This light corresponds to the thirty-nine-lights. Conversely, by not guarding

LIKUTEY MOHARAN #11:5,6 — 182

שִׁשָּׁה סִדְרֵי מִשְׁנָה (כַּמּוּבָא בַּזֹּהַר הַקָּדוֹשׁ וּבְכִתְבֵי הָאֲרִיזַ"ל), שֶׁשְׁמוֹ כְּשֵׁם רַבּוֹ, כְּמוֹ שֶׁכָּתוּב (שְׁמוֹת כ"ג): "כִּי שְׁמִי בְּקִרְבּוֹ" (כַּמּוּבָא בְּפֵירַשְׁ"י שָׁם); וְזֶה בְּחִינַת יִחוּדָא תַּתָּאָה, הַיְנוּ שֶׁהַקָּדוֹשׁ־בָּרוּךְ־הוּא מַלְבִּישׁ אֶת עַצְמוֹ בְּמט"ט בְּשֵׁשֶׁת יְמֵי הַחֹל וּמַנְהִיג הָעוֹלָם עַל־ יָדוֹ:

ו. וְזֶה בְּחִינַת הֲלָכָה וְקַבָּלָה. קַבָּלָה הִיא בְּחִינַת (תְּהִלִּים כ"ט): "הִשְׁתַּחֲווּ לַה' בְּהַדְרַת קֹדֶשׁ" – רָאשֵׁי־תֵבוֹת קַבָּלָה; וַהֲלָכָה הִיא בְּחִינַת (שָׁם ק): "הָרִיעוּ לַה' כָּל הָאָרֶץ" – רָאשֵׁי־תֵבוֹת הֲלָכָה, כַּמּוּבָא בַּכַּוָּנוֹת.

"הִשְׁתַּחֲווּ לַה' בְּהַדְרַת קֹדֶשׁ" – זֶה בְּחִינַת יִחוּדָא עִלָּאָה, הַיְנוּ זִוּוּג שֶׁל שַׁבָּת, וְזֶה בְּחִינַת בְּרִית עִלָּאָה, שֶׁשָּׁם עִקַּר הַהִשְׁתַּחֲוָיָה, בִּבְחִינַת (בְּרֵאשִׁית מ"ב): "וַיָּבֹאוּ אֲחֵי יוֹסֵף וַיִּשְׁתַּחֲווּ לוֹ", וְהוּא

In review: To attain understanding of the Torah's depths, one must achieve enlightened speech, speech which guides him to repentance (§1). For this level of speech one must eliminate his haughtiness, as otherwise the words of Torah are corrupted in his mouth. By doing so, one's words shine with His glory (§2). Haughtiness and immorality are contingent one upon the other. Nullifying one's haughtiness completely therefore requires guarding the *brit*. Through this high standard of moral behavior one merits to the light of repentance (§3). This light corresponds to the thirty-nine-lights. Conversely, by not guarding the *brit* one draws upon himself the yoke of livelihood, the thirty-nine-works, corresponding to the thirty-nine-lashes (§4). There are two levels in guarding the *brit*, corresponding to the holiness of the weekdays, the lower unification, and the higher holiness of Shabbat, the upper unification (§5).

58. **KaBbaLaH.** For few are those who merit "the grandeur of holiness." This verse which Rebbe Nachman quotes from Psalm 29 is particularly appropriate to the lesson in that it begins, "Give to God the *glory* due His name...."

59. **all the earth...HaLaKhaH.** Halakhah, on the other hand, pertains to and is pertinent to all.

60. **bowing down.** In the terminology of the Kabbalah, the upper *brit*/Yesod of the persona *Abba* is the vehicle through which *shefa* fills the world/*Malkhut*. This implies a "bowing down" from above.

61. **before him.** To reach the level of the upper unification, the *brit* of Shabbat, one must completely subdue his own haughtiness and merit enlightened speech. Our Sages taught that whoever runs away from glory will find it running after him (*Eruvin* 13b), and the Midrash teaches: When one adds to the glory of Heaven and decreases his own importance, not only is God's glory increased, but so is his (*Bamidbar Rabbah* 2). This was Yosef. He attained the highest level of guarding of the *brit* and as a result came to be seen as the personification of *Yesod,* the tzaddik. Eventually, Yosef's brothers realized this greatness and recognized his

LIKUTEY MOHARAN #11:5,6

corresponding to the six orders of the *Mishnah* (*Tikkuney Zohar* #18).[55] For [Metat's] name is like that of his Master's, as is written (Exodus 23:21), "because My name is in him."[56] This is the lower unification. In other words, the Holy One, blessed-be-He, clothes Himself in Metat during the six days of the week and rules the world through him.[57]

6. This also corresponds to Halakhah (the law) and Kabbalah (the mystical tradition). As we find in the *Kavanot* (*Shulchan Arukh HaAri, Shacharit shel Shabbat* 4): Kabbalah is an aspect of *"Hishtachavu L'hashem B'hadrat Kodesh"* ("Bow down to God in the grandeur of holiness") (Psalms 29:2), the initial letters of which spell *KaBbaLaH*.[58] Halakhah is an aspect of *"Hareeu L'hashem Kol Haaretz"* ("Sound a joyful note to God, all the earth") (Psalms 100:1), the initial letters of which spell *HaLaKhaH*.[59]

Hishtachavu l'Hashem b'hadrat kodesh corresponds to the upper unification/marital relations of Shabbat. This is the upper *brit,* which contains the primary [expression] of bowing down,[60] as in (Genesis 42:6), "Yosef's brothers came and bowed themselves before him."[61] [Yosef]

---

55. **six days of the week . . . orders of the Mishnah.** Rabbi Chaim Vital writes of his teacher, the holy Ari, that when he would study the Torah law and the Mishnah from which it is derived, he would review the law six times, corresponding to the six days of the week. The Ari would review his studies a seventh time, according to its esoteric meaning (see §7), corresponding to the Shabbat (*Shaar HaMitzvot, V'Etchanan*). See note 57 and section 6 below for the connection which this has to the angel Metat.

56. **My name is in him.** See Rashi (*loc. cit.*) that the angel's [full] name, MeTaTRON (מטטרון), has the same numerical value (314) as *ShaDaI* (שדי) (see Appendix: Gematria Chart).

57. **through him.** Shabbat is on a much higher level of holiness than the weekdays. It is completely holy, with the negative forces and qualities of bad, evil, falsehood, etc., having no place therein. This is not true of the weekdays. During the six days of the week, a mixture of good and evil, false and true, etc., predominates. Similarly, God is, so to speak, completely holy. Rulership of the world on Shabbat is entirely under His personal jurisdiction and domain. However, during the weekdays God clothes Himself in the angel Metat (*Yevamot* 16b, *Tosafot*; *Zohar* I, 126a). Through him God rules the world, not directly and openly, but indirectly through a veil. This distancing from absolute holiness allows for the appearance of a creation separate from and even devoid of God, which is ultimately what provides man the maximum free will to serve God of his own volition. See *Mayim* (pp.55-58, Breslov Research, 1987).

ShaBbaT (שבת) corresponds with *TaShuV* (תשב, repentance). On Shabbat, one is not to engage in any work at all. His mind is then free to seek holiness and his heart open to yearn for God. No longer under the jurisdiction of the thirty-nine-works, it is automatically easier for him to repent. This is why even building the Tabernacle is forbidden on Shabbat. Though an act of holiness, this building nonetheless involves the thirty-nine-works, from whose domain he has entirely been released (cf. n.7 above).

בְּחִינַת הֲדָרַת קֹדֶשׁ, בִּבְחִינַת (דְּבָרִים ל"ג): "בְּכוֹר שׁוֹרוֹ הָדָר לוֹ".

"הָרִיעוּ לַה' כָּל הָאָרֶץ" – זֶה בְּחִינַת יְחוּדָא תַּתָּאָה, הַיְנוּ זִוּוּג שֶׁל
חֹל, שֶׁהוּא בִּבְחִינַת מט"ט, שֶׁשָּׁלְטָנוּתֵהּ שֵׁשֶׁת יְמֵי הַחֹל, שִׁשָּׁה
סִדְרֵי מִשְׁנָה. וְזֶה: 'הָרִיעוּ' (לְשׁוֹן תְּרוּעָה וְזִמְרָה), בִּבְחִינַת (יְשַׁעְיָהוּ
כ"ד): "מִכְּנַף הָאָרֶץ זְמִרֹת שָׁמַעְנוּ", כִּי מט"ט הוּא בִּבְחִינַת כָּנָף,
לְשׁוֹן "וְלֹא יִכָּנֵף עוֹד מוֹרֶיךָ" (שָׁם ל), כִּי בּוֹ מִתְלַבֵּשׁ הַקָּדוֹשׁ־
בָּרוּךְ־הוּא בְּשֵׁשֶׁת יְמֵי הַחֹל כַּיָּדוּעַ:

ז. וְזֶה בְּחִינַת רָזִין, וְרָזִין דְּרָזִין. רָזִין – הוּא בְּחִינַת הֲלָכָה, רָזִין

further developed at the end of the lesson in the *Mai HaNachal's* summation.

65. **Metat...KaNaF.** The Hebrew word *k'naf,* corner, also means wing. It is thus an allusion to the angels who, when they appear to man, have wings (Isaiah 6). In particular this refers to Metat, the *sar haolam* (ministering angel) in charge of all the angels.

66. **teacher....** As mentioned, Metat corresponds to the Mishnah. He is known as the Master of Mishnah and those who wish to study and draw from the "six orders" must learn from him.

67. **Holy One...as is known.** In truth, "Your teacher" refers to God, for He alone is the source of everything. However, when the Infinite One veils Himself in His ministering angel—corresponding to the lower unification/thirty-nine-works/weekday *brit*/Halakhah—it appears as if everything is under the jurisdiction of Metat. In the future, however, all these lower levels will be elevated. Thus, "Your teacher will not distance himself anymore" applies to the Future, the time of the ultimate Shabbat. In the context of the lesson, the verse would then be, "Your Teacher [God], will not veil Himself in Metat anymore." For then, God's Oneness—corresponding to the upper unification/thirty-nine-lights/Shabbat *brit*/Kabbalah—will be revealed to the world.

In review: To attain understanding of the Torah's depths, one must achieve enlightened speech, speech which guides him to repentance (§1). For this level of speech one must eliminate his haughtiness, as otherwise the words of Torah are corrupted in his mouth. By doing so, one's words shine with His glory (§2). Because haughtiness and immorality are contingent one upon the other, nullifying haughtiness requires guarding the *brit*. Through this high standard of moral behavior one merits to the light of repentance (§3). This light corresponds to the thirty-nine-lights. Conversely, by not guarding the *brit* one draws upon himself the yoke of livelihood, the thirty-nine-works, corresponding to the thirty-nine-lashes (§4). There are two levels in guarding the *brit*, corresponding to the holiness of the weekdays, the lower unification, and the higher holiness of Shabbat, the upper unification (§5). The lower level, the weekdays, corresponds to Halakhah; the upper level, Shabbat, corresponds to Kabbalah (§6).

68. **Razin corresponds to Halakhah.** Although the Halakhah is generally thought of as the revealed aspect of the Torah, Rabbi Chaim Vital explains that there can be no doubt that when any of the Talmudic Sages posited a *halakhah,* he did so in concordance with the

LIKUTEY MOHARAN #11:6,7

himself is "the grandeur of holiness," as in (Deuteronomy 33:17), "His grandeur is like a firstborn ox."[62]

Hareeu l'Hashem kol haaretz corresponds to the lower unification/marital relations of the weekdays. This is Metat whose rule is the six days of the week/the six orders of the Mishnah.[63] This is *hareeu* {which connotes sounding a note and song[64]}, as in (Isaiah 24:16), "From the *k'naf* (distant corner) of the earth we heard songs." For Metat corresponds to *KaNaF*,[65] similar to (Isaiah 30:2), "Your teacher will not *yeKaNeF* (distance himself) anymore."[66] This is because the Holy One clothes Himself in him during the six days of the week, as is known.[67]

7. {"From the distant corner of the earth we heard songs, *tzvi latzaddik* (glory to the righteous). But I said, '*Razi li* (A secret to me), *razi li* (a secret to me)!' " (Isaiah 24:16).}

This also the aspect of secrets and deep secrets. *Razin* (secrets) corresponds to Halakhah.[68] *Razin d'razin* (deep secrets) corresponds

---

superiority. Yosef had increased God's glory and had been rewarded in kind. His brothers, therefore, "came and bowed themselves before him" (*Mai HaNachal*).

62. His grandeur.... This appears as part of Moshe Rabbeinu's blessing to the tribe of Yosef. The Hebrew word *b'khor* (firstborn) also means greatness. Greatness and grandeur is Yosef's because he merited guarding the *brit* with abundant and additional holiness.

Rashi (*loc. cit.*) explains that Moshe's words were an allusion to Yehoshua, Yosef's descendant, who would go on to defeat many kings during his conquest of the Holy Land. Prior to the conclusion of his lesson, Rebbe Nachman explains that the quality of haughtiness—the desire for grandeur—is responsible for delaying the Jewish people's return to the Holy Land. Conversely, humility and the elimination of self-importance are the keys for entry into the Land of Israel. And so, after Moshe's passing (Deuteronomy 31), it was Yehoshua who was charged with bringing the Jews into the Holy Land. He had already defeated Amalek (Exodus 17), and was now told (Joshua 1:8), "This Book of Torah shall not depart out of your mouth" (see n.19 above). The nation of Amalek was known for its immorality (see *Rashi,* Deuteronomy 25:18) and only one who guarded the *brit* completely, as Yehoshua did, could defeat them. Yehoshua was also very modest; his words were thus enlightened speech and had the power to bring others to understand the Torah. When he assumed the mantle of leadership, the Jews "bowed" or submitted to his authority (he had attained the higher level of *brit,* the upper unification). The verse thus states: "Whoever shall rebel against your mouth..." (Joshua 1:18). Yehoshua had achieved the level of enlightened speech and was therefore able to elevate all the Jews and lead them into the Holy Land.

63. six...six.... As mentioned earlier, the Mishnah is the source from which the law—the body of Halakhah— is derived (see notes 55 and 57 above). See also *Likutey Moharan* I, 79 that Metat is the Mishnah/the weekdays which comprise the six aspects kosher and unkosher, pure and impure, permitted and prohibited.

64. song. In his commentary to this lesson, the *Mai HaNachal* suggests that in introducing the aspect of *hareeu,* Rebbe Nachman teaches that even song and prayer can bring a person to the enlightened speech which leads to deep Torah understanding. This connection will be

LIKUTEY MOHARAN #11:7

186

הְרָזִין – הוּא בְּחִינַת קַבָּלָה; הִתְלַבְּשׁוּת הַקַּבָּלָה בַּהֲלָכָה – הוּא
בְּחִינַת הַנְהָגַת הַקָּדוֹשׁ-בָּרוּךְ-הוּא בְּשֵׁשֶׁת יְמֵי הַחֹל, שֶׁהוּא בְּחִינַת
יְחוּדָא תַּתָּאָה.

וְזֶה בְּחִינַת: (סִיּוּם הַפָּסוּק מִכְּנַף הָאָרֶץ הַנַּ"ל) "צְבִי לַצַּדִּיק רָזִי-לִי
רָזִי-לִי". 'צְבִי לַצַּדִּיק' – הַיְנוּ בְּחִינַת קְדֻשַּׁת הַזִּוּוּג, יֵשׁ בּוֹ שְׁנֵי
רָזִין, הַיְנוּ יְחוּדָא עִלָּאָה וְיְחוּדָא תַּתָּאָה, שֶׁהֵם בְּחִינַת הֲלָכָה
וְקַבָּלָה, בְּחִינַת רָזִין וְרָזִין דְּרָזִין:

וְזֶה שֶׁאָמְרוּ חֲכָמֵינוּ, זִכְרוֹנָם לִבְרָכָה (חֻלִּין ס.): "יְהִי כְבוֹד ה'
לְעוֹלָם", שַׂר הָעוֹלָם אֲמָרוֹ. בְּשָׁעָה שֶׁאָמַר הַקָּדוֹשׁ-בָּרוּךְ-הוּא
לָאִילָנוֹת לְמִינֵהוּ, נָשְׂאוּ דְשָׁאִים קַל-וָחֹמֶר בְּעַצְמָן: מָה אִילָנוֹת,
שֶׁהֵם גְּבוֹהִים וְאֵינָם תְּכוּפִים, אָמַר הַקָּדוֹשׁ-בָּרוּךְ-הוּא לְמִינֵהוּ, כָּל
שֶׁכֵּן אָנוּ, שֶׁאָנוּ קְטַנִּים וּתְכוּפִים, שֶׁצְּרִיכִים לָצֵאת לְמִינֵהוּ. פָּתַח
שַׂר הָעוֹלָם וְאָמַר: "יְהִי כְבוֹד ה' לְעוֹלָם".

כִּי בֶּאֱמֶת גַּם הַגְּדוֹלִים, שֶׁזִּוּוּגָן אֵינָם תְּכוּפִים, רַק מִשַּׁבָּת לְשַׁבָּת, גַּם
לָהֶם הַזְהִירָה הַתּוֹרָה עַל שְׁמִירַת הַבְּרִית, שֶׁיִּשְׁמְרוּ אֶת עַצְמָן, כְּמוֹ
שֶׁכָּתוּב (שְׁמוֹת ל"א): "וְשָׁמְרוּ בְנֵי יִשְׂרָאֵל אֶת הַשַּׁבָּת" – רָאשֵׁי-תֵּבוֹת
בִּיאָה, כַּמּוּבָא בַּכַּוָּנוֹת; הַיְנוּ אַף-עַל-פִּי שֶׁזִּוּוּגוֹ הוּא רַק מִשַּׁבָּת
לְשַׁבָּת, אַף-עַל-פִּי-כֵן צָרִיךְ שְׁמִירָה גְדוֹלָה, בְּחִינַת וְשָׁמְרוּ וְכוּ';

Tzvi, which in Hebrew means glory and splendor, in Aramaic means to find pleasure in and desire (cf. Proverbs 3:31, *Targum*). The desire of the tzaddik is for the holy unifications, lower and upper, which correspond to Halakhah and Kabbalah, secrets and deep secrets.

71. **Our Sages...in His works.** This took place on the third day of Creation, see also Rashi on Genesis 1:12. The trees allude to the tzaddikim—tall in stature and few and far between. The fulfillment of his conjugal obligations are not carried out in close proximity. The grass, on the other hand, implies the ordinary man—lower in stature and much more common. The fulfillment of his conjugal obligations are carried out in close proximity.

72. **BYAH.** From this verse we learn that guarding the Shabbat is achieved in part by guarding the *brit* through engaging in marital relations with holiness. As the Ari explains, Shabbat (Friday night) is a particularly propitious time for these relations because this is when the upper unifications take place in the transcendant worlds.

73. **v'ShaMRu.** That is, having reached this higher level, he should take care not to descend to the level of weekday relations, the lower unification, and certainly to never fall beneath this.

LIKUTEY MOHARAN #11:7

to Kabbalah. The encompassing of the Kabbalah within the Halakhah is similar to the Holy One's conduct during the six days of the week—the lower unification.[69]

This is alluded to in, "...*tzvi latzaddik...razi li, razi li*." The words *tzvi latzaddik* refers to the holiness of marital relations, of which there are two *razin*: the upper unification and the lower unification. These correspond to Halakhah and Kabbalah, secrets and deep secrets.[70]

And this is what our Sages taught: "May God's glory be forever" (Psalms 104:31)—the ministering angel of the world said this. When the Holy One commanded the trees [to yield fruit] after their own kind, the grasses drew an inference with regard to themselves: If the trees— which are large and do not [reproduce] in close proximity—were commanded by the Holy One "after its own kind" (Genesis 1:11), then all the more so we—who are small and do [reproduce] in close proximity—must bring forth [only] "after its own kind." The ministering angel of the world spoke up and said, "May God's glory be forever; [God shall rejoice in His works]" (Chullin 60a, cf. Rashi).[71]

For in truth, even the great ones—whose marital relations are not in close proximity, but from one Shabbat to the next—are also warned by the Torah concerning guarding the *brit*. They must guard themselves. As is brought in the *Kavanot* (Pri Etz Chaim, Shaar HaShabbat 18): It is written (Exodus 31:16), "*v'shamru B'nei Yisrael Æt Hashabbat* (the Children of Israel shall keep the Shabbat)"—the first letters of which spell *BYAH* (sexual relations).[72] In other words, even though his marital relations are only from Shabbat to Shabbat, he still must exercise great *ShMiRah* (guarding). This is "*v'ShaMRu....*"[73]

"secret" of the law—in accord with the Kabbalistic interpretation (*Etz Chaim*, Introduction). As a result, the secrets of Torah are unquestionably found in the Halakhah, albeit in a hidden manner, much as God veils Himself in Metat during the weekdays.

Rebbe Nachman himself said that in his youth he studied the entire Codes three separate times. The first time, he studied the material simply, in order to become acquainted with the particulars of the law. The second time he studied the Codes he traced each law back to its Talmudic source. The third time he understood the Kabbalistic significance of each law and its relationship to the transcendental worlds (*Rabbi Nachman's Wisdom* #76).

69. **lower unification.** By guarding the Covenant on the lower level—having marital relations during the weekdays but being careful to keep within the parameters of the Halakhah—one will merit deep Torah understanding in Halakhah. Yet, the deep secrets will remain hidden from him. Only the one whose guarding the Covenant is on the higher level—limiting marital relations to Shabbat and with the additional aspects of holiness—will merit deep Torah understanding in the Kabbalah (*Mai HaNachal*).

70. **holiness of marital relations....** The tzaddik is the guardian of the Covenant incarnate.

LIKUTEY MOHARAN #11:7,8 — 188

כָּל שֶׁכֵּן הַקְּטַנִּים, שֶׁהֵם בְּחִינַת דְּשָׁאִין, שֶׁזִּוּוּגָם תְּכוּפִים, גַּם בְּשֵׁשֶׁת יְמֵי הַחֹל, מִכָּל שֶׁכֵּן שֶׁצְּרִיכִים שְׁמִירָה גְּדוֹלָה לִשְׁמֹר אֶת בְּרִיתָם, שֶׁיִּשְׁמְרוּ אֶת עַצְמָם עַל־פִּי הַתּוֹרָה, בִּבְחִינַת לְמִינֵיהֶם. מִיָּד כְּשֶׁשָּׁמַע שַׂר הָעוֹלָם – שֶׁהוּא מט״ט, שֶׁשֶּׁלְטָנוּתֵהּ שֵׁשֶׁת יְמֵי הַחֹל, בְּחִינַת דְּשָׁאִים, בְּחִינַת יְחוּדָא תַּתָּאָה; פָּתַח וְאָמַר: "יְהִי כְבוֹד ה'" – כְּבוֹד דַּיְקָא, כִּי עַל־יְדֵי שְׁמִירַת הַבְּרִית בִּשְׁנֵי הַבְּחִינוֹת הַנַּ״ל, הַכָּבוֹד בִּשְׁלֵמוּת כַּנַּ״ל.

נִמְצָא, שֶׁעַל־יְדֵי שְׁמִירַת הַבְּרִית בִּשְׁנֵי הַבְּחִינוֹת הַנַּ״ל, שֶׁהוּא בְּחִינַת יְחוּדָא עִלָּאָה וְיִחוּדָא תַּתָּאָה, הַיְנוּ מֵאִילָנוֹת וּדְשָׁאִים, גְּדוֹלִים וּקְטַנִּים, זִוּוּג שֶׁל שַׁבָּת וְזִוּוּג שֶׁל חֹל, בְּחִינַת הֲלָכָה וְקַבָּלָה, רָזִין וְרָזִין דְּרָזִין – אֲזַי הַכָּבוֹד בִּשְׁלֵמוּת כַּנַּ״ל; וְעַל־יְדֵי הַכָּבוֹד זוֹכֶה לְדִבּוּר הַמֵּאִיר, וְעַל־יְדֵי הַדִּבּוּר יָכוֹל לָבוֹא לִתְבוּנוֹת הַתּוֹרָה לְעָמְקָהּ כַּנַּ״ל:

ח. וְזֶה שֶׁאָמַר רַבָּה בַּר בַּר־חָנָה: זִמְנָא חֲדָא הֲוֵי אָזְלִינַן בִּסְפִינְתָּא, וַחֲזָאי לְהַאי צְפַרְתָּא, דְּהֲוֵי קָאי עַד קַרְסֻלֵּהּ בְּמַיָּא, וְרֵישֵׁהּ בְּרָקִיעַ. וְאָמְרִינַן: לֵית מַיָּא, וּבְעֵינַן לְמֵיחַת לַאֲקוּרֵי נַפְשִׁין. נְפַק בְּרַת־קָלָא וְאָמַר לָן: לָא תֵּחוּתוּ לְהָכָא, דְּנְפַלָא לֵהּ חַצִּינָא לְבַר־נַגָּרָא הָכָא הָא שְׁבַע שְׁנִין, וְלָא מָטֵי לְאַרְעָא. וְלָא מִשּׁוּם דִּנְפִישָׁא מַיָּא, אֶלָּא מִשּׁוּם

רַשְׁבַּ״ם:

וַחֲזֵינַן לְהַאי צְפַרְתָּא וְכוּ' – הָכֵי גַּרְסִינַן. וְאָמְרִינַן לֵיכָּא מַיָּא – הָיִינוּ סְבוּרִין שֶׁאֵינָן עֲמֻקִּין, הוֹאִיל וְלָא קָאי בַּמַּיִם אֶלָּא עַד קַרְסוּלֵיהּ. חֲצִינָא – גַּרְזֶן אוֹ מַעֲצָד לְבַר נַגָּרָא – חָרַשׁ עֵצִים. וְלָא מִשּׁוּם דַּעֲמִיקָא מַיָּא – מַהֲלַךְ שֶׁבַע שָׁנִים לֹא הִגִּיעַ הַחֲצִינָא לַקַּרְקַע. אֶלָּא מִשּׁוּם דִּרְדִיפֵי

world "Dai!" For 6,000 years the world would exist as it is, with the angel Metat allowed to rule during the 6 days of the week (the "day" of God being equal to 1,000 years). But then, "Dai!" Then, with the advent of the seven thousandth year—the ultimate Shabbat—God's rule will be openly revealed, no longer veiled in the hands of His ministering angel.

76. speech...to deep Torah understanding. In review: To attain understanding of the Torah's depths, one must achieve enlightened speech, speech which guides him to repentance (§1). For

189   *LIKUTEY MOHARAN #11:7,8*

All the more so the small ones, who correspond to the grasses. Their marital relations, which also take place during the weekdays, are in close proximity. They must certainly exercise great caution in guarding their *brit*. They must guard themselves in accordance with the Torah, in the aspect of "after its own kind."[74]

As soon as the ministering angel of the world—this is Metat[75] whose rule is the six weekdays, corresponding to the grasses/the lower unification—heard this, he spoke up and said, "May God's glory be [forever]." Specifically "glory," because, as explained, by guarding the *brit* on both levels glory is complete.

Thus, by guarding the *brit* on the two levels mentioned— corresponding to the upper and lower unifications/trees and grasses/great ones and small ones/marital relations of Shabbat and of weekdays/Halakhah and Kabbalah/secrets and deep secrets—glory is then complete. And through glory a person merits speech which enlightens; and through speech he can come to deep Torah understanding.[76]

---

8. This is what Rabbah bar bar Chanah recounted: We were once travelling in a ship. We saw this bird which was standing up to its ankles in water, and its head was in the firmament. We concluded that there wasn't [much] water and wanted to go down into it *l'okurei nafshin* (to cool ourselves). A heavenly voice called out to us, "Do not go down into here. A carpenter's *chatzina* (axe) fell in here seven years ago, and it has not yet reached the ground. Not [only] because the water is abundant, but because the water runs so

Rashbam:

We saw this bird - this is the correct reading of the text: We concluded that there wasn't much water - we figured that it wasn't very deep, because it was only standing in the water up to its ankles: axe - a pick-axe or adze: carpenter - a woodcutter: Not only because the water is abundant - it went for seven years, and the axe did not reach the ground: but because the water runs so rapidly -

---

74. **own kind.** Rashi (*loc. cit.*) adds that the grasses realized that if they were not sufficiently careful to avoid intermingling, there would be no way to tell them apart. Each one therefore reproduced "after its own kind." Implied by this is that the "small ones" must be careful to avoid indulging in excesses (see above, n.50), as this can lead one completely astray—the loss of one's "root" and identity. Whether on a higher or lower level, one must always look to ascend to ever higher degrees in guarding the Covenant (see above, §3, n.28).

75. **Metat.** The Maharsha (*loc. cit.*) comments that the ministering angel of the world is Metatron. As mentioned in note 56, both Metatron and God's name *Shadai* have the numerical value of 314. The Maharsha explains: God is called *Shadai* because He said to His

LIKUTEY MOHARAN #11:8 190

דִּרְדִיפָא מַיָּא. אָמַר רַב אָשֵׁי: מַיָּא – מִתּוֹךְ חֲרִיפוּת הַנָּהָר לֹא הָיָה
הַאי, זִיז שָׂדַי הוּא, דִּכְתִיב: נִצְלָל עֲדַיִן, וְלֹא מֵחֲמַת הָעֹמֶק בִּלְבָד.
"וְזִיז שָׂדַי עִמָּדִי": וְזִיז שָׂדַי עִמָּדִי – רֹאשׁוֹ מַגִּיעַ לָרָקִיעַ:

צְפַרְתָּא – זֶה בְּחִינַת הַדִּבּוּר, שֶׁהוּא אֶמְצָעִי בֵּין הָאָדָם, שֶׁהוּא
נִתְהַוֶּה מִפַּמְיִין דּוּכְרִין וְנוּקְבִין, וּבֵין הַשָּׁמַיִם, שֶׁהוּא בְּחִינַת תְּבוּנוֹת
הַתּוֹרָה, כַּמּוּבָא (וַיִּקְרָא רַבָּה ט״ז וּבְעֲרָכִין טז:) עַל מְצֹרָע שֶׁצָּרִיךְ
לְהָבִיא שְׁתֵּי צִפֳּרִים: ׳יָבוֹא פַּטָטַיָּא וִיכַפֵּר עַל פַּטָטַיָּא׳. וְזֶהוּ:

דְּקָאֵי עַד קַרְסֻלֵּהּ בְּמַיָּא – כִּי מֵאַחַר שֶׁהַדִּבּוּר צָרִיךְ לְהָאִיר לוֹ בְּכָל
הַמְּקוֹמוֹת שֶׁצָּרִיךְ לַעֲשׂוֹת שָׁם תְּשׁוּבָה, הוּא לִפְעָמִים בִּבְחִינַת (רוּת
ג:): "וַתִּגַל מַרְגְּלֹתָיו: וַתִּשְׁכָּב", שֶׁהַדִּבּוּר צָרִיךְ לְהָאִיר בָּאָדָם,
שֶׁהוּא לְמַטָּה בְּמַדְרֵגָה פְּחוּתָה. וְעַל כֵּן נִקְרָא הַדִּבּוּר צְפַרְתָּא דְּקָאֵי

---

79. **chatterer.** The bird in Rabbah bar bar Chanah's story alludes to speech. The Torah
(Leviticus 14) tells us that the purification of the leper requires his bringing two birds to the
priest. The Midrash (*loc. cit.*) teaches: Why is the purification of the leper dependent upon
two, live, kosher birds? Let the chatterer [the chirping bird] come and atone for the chatterer
[the one who speaks slanderously of others]. As Rabbi Yochanan said in the name of Rabbi
Yosi, "Whoever slanders will be stricken with leprosy."

Rebbe Nachman contrasts slander with enlightened speech, indicating that only
enlightened speech—symbolized by the bird—can atone for the slanderer—the chatterer.
Hence the connection between enlightened speech and repentance mentioned earlier (§1 and
nn.9,14,16).

See also note 48 above for the *Tikkuney Zohar's* teaching about how not delighting in
Shabbat turns *ONeG* to *NeGA* (leprosy). The *Kisey Melekh* (*loc. cit.*) comments that in the
time of the Temple, leprosy was the punishment for not partaking of *oneg* Shabbat. Today,
the punishment is poverty (cf. n.42). Conversely, the Talmud teaches: What makes the
wealthy deserving of their riches? they honor the Shabbat (*Shabbat* 119a).

80. **She...lay down.** This refers to Ruth, who lay down at the feet of Boaz (cf. *Likutey
Moharan* I, 7, n.77). As explained earlier (§4), Boaz represents the tzaddik, the guardian of
the *brit*, who can elevate speech to the level of enlightened speech. Ruth represents the power
of speech, as our Sages taught: She was called Ruth (רות) because it would one day be said of
her descendant King David that he *ravah* (רוה, satiated) God with song and prayers of praise
(*Berakhot* 7b). The *Mai HaNachal* adds: From this we can see that it is not only Torah study,
but also prayer, which can lead to enlightened speech. This is also a reason why we read the
Book of Ruth on Shavuot, the holiday marking the receiving of the Torah, because Torah
and prayer enhance and are bound to one another.

LIKUTEY MOHARAN #11:8

rapidly." Rav Ashi said, "This bird was *Ziz Sadai*, as is written (Psalms 50:11), **'And the *ziz sadai* is with me' "** (*Bava Batra* 73b).

because of the quickness of the river, it hadn't yet settled; and not only because of its depth: **And *ziz sadai* (the bird of the field) is with me** - his head reaching the firmament:

this bird — This alludes to speech which is a bridge between man—who is formed from the masculine waters and the feminine waters[77]—and the heavens—which corresponds to Torah understanding.[78] As is taught concerning a leper: He must bring two birds.... Let the chatterer come and atone for the chatterer (*Vayikra Rabbah* 16:7; *Erkhin* 16b).[79] And this is:

which was standing up to its ankles in water — Now that speech should enlighten him regarding all the areas in which he needs to repent, he is sometimes in the aspect of, "She uncovered his feet and lay down" (Ruth 3:14; *Tikkuney Zohar* #21, p.50a).[80] That is, speech must show a person

this level of speech one must eliminate his haughtiness, as otherwise the words of Torah are corrupted in his mouth. By doing so, one's words shine with His glory (§2). Because haughtiness and immorality are contingent one upon the other, nullifying haughtiness requires guarding the *brit*. Through this high standard of moral behavior one merits to the light of repentance (§3). This light corresponds to the thirty-nine-lights. Conversely, by not guarding the *brit* one draws upon himself the yoke of livelihood, the thirty-nine-works, corresponding to the thirty-nine-lashes (§4). There are two levels in guarding the *brit*, corresponding to the holiness of the weekdays, the lower unification, and the higher holiness of Shabbat, the upper unification (§5). The lower level, the weekdays, corresponds to Halakhah; the upper level, Shabbat, corresponds to Kabbalah (§6). Halakhah is the Torah's secrets; Kabbalah is the Torah's deep secrets. By guarding the *brit* on both levels, God's glory is complete. The humble person then merits speech that enlightens and deep Torah understanding (§7).

77. **masculine...feminine waters.** "Masculine waters" is the Kabbalistic term for spiritual energy which descends from Above. It symbolizes the flow of *shefa* which God benevolently provides for man. "Feminine waters," conversely, is spiritual energy ascending from below. It is symbolic of the man's fulfillment of the Divine will. Just as in the physical, conception occurs through a combining of male and female "fluids," so too, as it were, in the spiritual. Creation occurs through a supernal coupling which unites the masculine and feminine waters, i.e., the unification of the various energies and their corresponding *sefirot* that represent the male and female characteristics. At the time of Creation, man was formed from a unification of these forces.

78. **heavens...Torah understanding.** Because deep Torah understanding, whether in Halakhah or Kabbalah, is such a lofty concept, it is likened to the heavens (*Parparaot LeChokhmah*).

LIKUTEY MOHARAN #11:8

עַד קַרְסָלֵּהּ בְּמַיָּא.

מַיָּא – הוּא בְּחִינַת הָאָדָם, שֶׁנִּתְהַוָּה מִמַּיִּין דּוּכְרִין וּמַיִּין נוּקְבִין כַּיָּדוּעַ, וְהַדִּבּוּר, שֶׁהוּא בְּחִינַת צַפַּרְתָּא קָאֵי עַד קַרְסָלֵּהּ, אֵצֶל הָאָדָם שֶׁהוּא בְּמַדְרֵגָה פְּחוּתָה, כְּדֵי לְהָאִיר לוֹ, בִּבְחִינַת וַתִּגַּל מַרְגְּלֹתָיו וְכוּ' כַּנַּ"ל, וְזֶהוּ דְּקָאֵי עַד קַרְסָלֵּהּ בְּמַיָּא כַּנַּ"ל.

וְאָמְרִינַן לֵית מַיָּא – הַיְנוּ שֶׁהֱבִינוּ שֶׁאִי אֶפְשָׁר לִזְכּוֹת לְדִבּוּר אֶלָּא עַל-יְדֵי כָּבוֹד בִּשְׁלֵמוּת, שֶׁיִּהְיֶה הָאָדָם בְּעֵינָיו אֶפֶס וָאַיִן. וְזֶהוּ: לֵית מַיָּא, שֶׁהָאָדָם יַחֲזִיק עַצְמוֹ לְאַיִן.

וּבְעֵינַן לְנַחוּתֵי – לְשׁוֹן שִׁפְלוּת, הַיְנוּ לִהְיוֹת שָׁפָל וְעָנָו; אַךְ שֶׁהָיָה לְאוֹקוּרֵי נַפְשִׁין – לְשׁוֹן (יְשַׁעְיָהוּ י"ג): "אוֹקִיר אֱנוֹשׁ מִפָּז", הַיְנוּ שֶׁהָיָה הָעֲנָוָה בִּשְׁבִיל גַּדְלוּת, כְּדֵי לְהִתְכַּבֵּד וּלְהִתְיַקֵּר; כִּי מֵחֲמַת שֶׁיּוֹדְעִין גֹּדֶל בִּזּוּי הַגַּדְלוּת, עַל כֵּן הֵם עֲנָוִים, בִּשְׁבִיל לְהִתְכַּבֵּד וּלְהִתְיַקֵּר עַל-יְדֵי הָעֲנָוָה, וְזֶהוּ בְּחִינַת עֲנִיווּת שֶׁהוּא תַּכְלִית הַגַּדְלוּת.

וְזֶהוּ: וּבְעֵינַן לְנַחוּתֵי – לִהְיוֹת שְׁפָלִים וַעֲנָוִים, לְאוֹקוּרֵי נַפְשִׁין – כְּדֵי שֶׁעַל-יְדֵי-זֶה נִהְיֶה יְקָרִים וַחֲשׁוּבִים, כִּי הַגַּאֲוָה מְבֻזָּה מְאֹד.

נְפַק בְּרַת-קָלָא וְאָמַר, לָא תְּחוּתוּ לְהָכָא – לָא תְּחוּתוּ לִהְיוֹת שְׁפָלִים בִּשְׁבִיל זֶה, בִּשְׁבִיל לְאוֹקוּרֵי נַפְשִׁין; שֶׁהִזְהִירָם הַבַּת-קוֹל שֶׁלֹּא יִהְיוּ עֲנָוִים בִּשְׁבִיל לְהִתְיַקֵּר וּלְהִתְכַּבֵּד, כִּי זֶה עֲנִיווּת הִיא תַּכְלִית הַגַּדְלוּת.

דְּנִפְלָה חֲצִינָא לְבַר-נַגָּרָא הָא שְׁבַע שְׁנִין, וְלָא מָטְיָא לְאַרְעָא –

---

83. **humility that is...haughtiness.** See above note 28 where the concept of truth is mentioned. Although Rebbe Nachman has not referred to truth directly, it is an integral aspect of this lesson, as it is in many of the Rebbe's teachings. In the context of this lesson, anyone can claim to be truly humble and, more likely, act the part. However, only the person who is completely honest with himself will be capable of recognizing the real motivations for his actions: is he truly humble or is his humility motivated by haughtiness and a desire for recognition and esteem?

LIKUTEY MOHARAN #11:8

that he is down on a low spiritual level. This is the reason why speech is called **a bird which was standing up to its ankles in water**.[81]

water — This alludes to man. He is formed from [a combination of] the masculine waters and the feminine waters, as is known. Thus, speech, which is likened to **a bird**, is **standing up to his ankles**—with the man who is on a low level. This, in order to enlighten him, as in, "She uncovered his feet...." This is, **which was standing up to its ankles in water**.[82]

We concluded that there wasn't water — That is, we understood that it is impossible to merit speech unless glory is complete. A person should view himself as absolutely nothing. This is the meaning of **there wasn't water**: A man should consider himself as non-existent.

and we wanted to go down into it — [To **go down**] indicates lowliness, being lowly and humble. But it was:

l'OKuRei nafshin (to cool ourselves) — This is similar to (Isaiah 13:12), "*OKiR enosh* (I will make man more prominent) than fine gold." That is, his humbleness was egotistical—so as to gain glory and *yaKaR* (prominence). Because people know just how despicable haughtiness is, they act humbly, in order to acquire glory and prominence through humility. This is the concept of humility that is the ultimate degree of haughtiness.[83]

This is the meaning of **and we wanted to go down into it**—to be lowly and humble. **L'okurei nafshin**—so that by doing this we would be prominent and important, because haughtiness is very despicable.

A heavenly voice called out, Do not go down into here — [In other words,] **do not go down** to act lowly for this reason—in order to *okurei nafshin*. The heavenly voice warned them not to be humble so as to gain prominence and glory. For this humility is actually the ultimate degree of haughtiness.

A carpenter's axe fell in here seven years ago, and it has not yet reached

---

81. **ankles in water.** The ankles allude to a low level.

82. **ankles in water.** That is, the bird (speech) was standing up to its ankles (a low level) in water (man). In other words, speech had reached down to the lower levels.

LIKUTEY MOHARAN #11:8   194

שֶׁהַבַּת־קוֹל הוֹדִיעָה לָהֶם שֹׁרֶשׁ הַגַּדְלוּת, כְּדֵי שֶׁיִּתְרַחֲקוּ עַד קָצֶה
אַחֲרוֹן, וְלֹא יָחוּתוּ לְהָכָא, שֶׁלֹּא יִהְיוּ עֲנָוִים בִּשְׁבִיל גַּדְלוּת,
כְּמַאֲמַר חֲכָמֵינוּ, זִכְרוֹנָם לִבְרָכָה (אָבוֹת פֶּרֶק ד): 'מְאֹד מְאֹד הֱוֵי
שְׁפַל־רוּחַ', הַיְנוּ שֶׁהוֹדִיעָה לָהֶם, שֶׁהַגַּדְלוּת הוּא מַנְפִּילוֹת
הַהִתְפָּאֲרוּת וְהַגַּאֲוָה שֶׁל הַקָּדוֹשׁ־בָּרוּךְ־הוּא, שֶׁהוּא לְבוּשׁוֹ, כְּמוֹ
שֶׁכָּתוּב (תְּהִלִּים צג): ה' מָלָךְ גֵּאוּת לָבֵשׁ. וְזֶה:
דִּנְפַלָּא חֲצִינָא – בְּחִינַת לְבוּשׁ, כְּמוֹ שֶׁכָּתוּב (שָׁם קכ"ט): "וְחִצְנוֹ
מְעַמֵּר".

בַּר נַגָּרָא – זֶה הַקָּדוֹשׁ־בָּרוּךְ־הוּא, כְּמוֹ שֶׁכָּתוּב (שָׁם ק"ד):
"הַמְקָרֶה בַמַּיִם עֲלִיּוֹתָיו", וּכְמַאֲמַר (חֻלִּין ס.): 'אֱלֹקֵיכֶם נַגָּר הוּא';
מִנְפִּילַת הַלְּבוּשׁ הַזֶּה נִתְהַנָּה הַגַּדְלוּת, שֶׁהוּא בְּחִינַת שֶׁבַע בָּתֵּי
עֲכוּ"ם, שֶׁעַל־יְדֵי־זֶה גָּלוּ יִשְׂרָאֵל מֵאַרְצָם, כְּמַאֲמַר חֲכָמֵינוּ, זִכְרוֹנָם
לִבְרָכָה (גִּטִּין פח.): לֹא גָּלוּ יִשְׂרָאֵל עַד שֶׁעָבְדוּ בָהּ שֶׁבַע בָּתֵּי
עֲכוּ"ם. וּבִשְׁבִיל זֶה נִקְרָא עֲכוּ"ם בִּלְשׁוֹן תִּפְאֶרֶת, כְּמוֹ שֶׁכָּתוּב
(יְשַׁעְיָהוּ מ"ד): "כְּתִפְאֶרֶת אָדָם לָשֶׁבֶת בָּיִת", כִּי הָעֲבוֹדָה זָרָה,
שֶׁהוּא הַגַּדְלוּת, הוּא מַנְפִּילַת הִתְפָּאֲרוּתוֹ. וְזֶהוּ:

---

86. **seven royal houses....** These were the seven kings of the Ten Tribes who forcefully introduced idolatry into Israel. This ultimately led to their exile by Sennacherib the Assyrian king. They were: 1) Yeravam ben N'vat; 2) Basha ben Achiya; 3) Achav ben Omri; 4) Yehu ben Nimshi; 5) Pekach ben Rimalyahu; 6) Menachem ben G'di; 7) Hoshea ben Ailah (Kings 1 and 2).

87. **splendor...in the house.** This refers to an exotic, carved wooden idol, in the form of a man. Within the context of the lesson, it refers to how—through haughtiness, the misuse of splendor—man can easily bring this idolatry into his own house.

88. **...His splendor.** Thus, Rabbah bar bar Chanah's story to this point reads as follows: There is a type of speech which can reach down to and elevate a person who is on the lowest levels. Yet, this can only be accomplished when the person totally negates his own self-importance, thereby making God's glory complete. If, however, his humility is for the sake of haughtiness, then such speech is unattainable. This is why heaven warns against such "humility." Instead of ascribing the glory to God, it indicates a debasement of the Holy One's splendor and majesty, and is akin to idolatry.

LIKUTEY MOHARAN #11:8

the ground — The heavenly voice informed them of the root of haughtiness, so that they should distance themselves [from it] to the utmost. They should **not go down into here**—they should not act humbly in order to gain acclaim, as our Sages taught: Be very, very humble (Avot 4:4). That is, [the heavenly voice] informed them that haughtiness stems from a debasement of the Holy One's splendor and majesty. These [qualities] are His garment, as is written (Psalms 93:1), "God reigns, He is clothed in majesty."[84] And thus:

ChatZiNa (axe) fell — This alludes to a garment, as is written (Psalms 129:7), "[The harvester did not fill his hand, nor put] bound sheaves into *ChitZNo* (his garment corner)."

a carpenter — This is the Holy One, as is written (Psalms 104:3), "Who lays the beams of His upper chambers in the waters." This is also [as our Sages] taught: Your God is a carpenter (*Chullin* 60a).[85] The debasement of this garment produces haughtiness, which corresponds to the seven [royal] houses of idolatry. Because of this [idolatry], the Jewish people were exiled from their land, as our Sages taught: Israel was not exiled until the seven [royal] houses had worshipped idolatry (*Gittin* 88a).[86] And this is the reason why idolatry is called splendor, as in (Isaiah 44:13), "...like the splendor of a man, to sit in the house."[87] For idolatry, which is haughtiness, comes from a debasement of His

---

84. **He is clothed in majesty.** God cloaks and veils Himself in Metat, the lower unification of God's immanent rulership over the world. This is His garment of splendor and majesty. Glory is His. But when man takes the qualities of splendor and majesty for himself, this is haughtiness. He has debased the King's garment and diminished His glory (see §2).

85. **carpenter.** The Talmud (*loc. cit.*) relates the following story: The emperor's daughter once remarked to Rabbi Yehoshua that the God of the Jews must be a carpenter, for the verse states, "Who lays beams...." This being the case, she mockingly (haughtily) requested that God give her a spinning wheel. Rabbi Yehoshua agreed and prayed, and she became a leper. It was the custom in Rome for a leper to be brought into the marketplace and given a spinning wheel. One day, Rabbi Yehoshua passed by the marketplace and found her there. She had been given the spinning wheel which she requested.

Thus, this passage from the Talmud is in line with what has been explained earlier. Slander, as a manifestation of haughtiness and an indication for a desire to increase one's own importance, is the antithesis of enlightened speech. The punishment of leprosy is a sign of how removed the slanderer is from anything holy (see *Aleph-Bet Book*, Translator's Introduction). The banishment which the slanderer must undergo can be likened to exile, which Rebbe Nachman discusses next.

LIKUTEY MOHARAN #11:8

הָא שֶׁבַע שְׁנִין – זֶה בְּחִינַת הַגַּדְלוּת, שֶׁהוּא בְּחִינַת שֶׁבַע בָּתֵּי עֲבוֹדָה זָרָה כַּנַּ״ל.

וְזֶהוּ: וְלָא מְטֵי לְאַרְעָא – הַיְנוּ שֶׁעַל־יְדֵי הֶעָווֹן הַזֶּה עֲדַיִן לֹא חָזַרְנוּ לְאַרְצֵנוּ, כִּי עַל־יְדֵי הֶעָווֹן הַזֶּה שֶׁהוּא הַגַּדְלוּת, שֶׁהוּא כְּעוֹבֵד עֲבוֹדָה זָרָה, בְּחִינַת שֶׁבַע בָּתֵּי עֲבוֹדָה זָרָה, עַל־יְדֵי־זֶה גָּלִינוּ מֵאַרְצֵנוּ כַּנַּ״ל, וְעַל־יְדֵי־זֶה עֲדַיִן לֹא חָזַרְנוּ לְאַרְצֵנוּ – הַכֹּל עַל־יְדֵי הֶעָווֹן הַזֶּה שֶׁל הַגַּדְלוּת, שֶׁהוּא בְּחִינַת עֲבוֹדָה זָרָה כַּנַּ״ל. וְזֶהוּ:

וְלָא מִשּׁוּם דְּנְפִישֵׁי מַיָּא – הַיְנוּ, לֹא תֹאמַר שֶׁבִּשְׁבִיל זֶה לָא מְטֵי לְאַרְעָא, דְּהַיְנוּ שֶׁאֵין יְכוֹלִין לְהַגִּיעַ וְלָשׁוּב לְאֶרֶץ־יִשְׂרָאֵל מִשּׁוּם דְּנְפִישֵׁי מַיָּא, מֵחֲמַת שֶׁהָעַכּוּ״ם הֵם רַבִּים, בְּחִינַת ״רַבִּים הַגּוֹיִם הָאֵלֶּה״ (דְּבָרִים ז), שֶׁהֵם בְּחִינַת מַיִם רַבִּים;

אֶלָּא מִשּׁוּם דִּרְדִיפֵי מַיָּא – שֶׁהֵם רוֹדְפִים אַחַר הַכָּבוֹד שֶׁהוּא בְּחִינַת מַיִם, בְּחִינַת ״אֵל הַכָּבוֹד הִרְעִים, ה׳ עַל מַיִם רַבִּים״ (תְּהִלִּים כ״ט), עַל־יְדֵי־זֶה אֵין יְכוֹלִין לְהַגִּיעַ וְלַחֲזֹר לְאֶרֶץ־יִשְׂרָאֵל, הַיְנוּ עַל־יְדֵי רְדִיפַת הַכָּבוֹד וְהַגַּדְלוּת, כִּי עִקַּר אֲרִיכַת הַגָּלוּת שֶׁאֵין יְכוֹלִין לָשׁוּב לְאַרְצֵנוּ הוּא רַק מֵחֲמַת עֲווֹן הַגַּדְלוּת וּרְדִיפַת הַכָּבוֹד כַּנַּ״ל.

כָּל זֶה הוֹדִיעָה לָהֶם הַבַּת־קוֹל גֹּדֶל בִּזּוּי הַגַּדְלוּת, כְּדֵי שֶׁיִּתְרַחֲקוּ מֵהַגַּדְלוּת עַד קָצֶה אַחֲרוֹן כַּנַּ״ל, וְאָז כְּבוֹד הַשֵּׁם יִתְבָּרַךְ בִּשְׁלֵמוּת כַּנַּ״ל, וְאָז זוֹכִין לַדִּבּוּר הַמֵּאִיר, שֶׁהוּא בְּחִינַת צַפַּרְתָּא הַנַּ״ל כַּנַּ״ל. אֲבָל אֵיךְ זוֹכִין לָזֶה, לְשַׁבֵּר הַגַּדְלוּת וְהַכָּבוֹד שֶׁל עַצְמוֹ לְגַמְרֵי, וְשֶׁיִּהְיֶה כְּבוֹד הַשֵּׁם יִתְבָּרַךְ בִּשְׁלֵמוּת – הוּא עַל־יְדֵי שְׁמִירַת

---

91. **upon many waters.** This is because God's glory is revealed through water and rain. Through water, as at the splitting of the Red Sea (Exodus 14). And through rain, as our Sages taught: As great as the day heaven and earth were created is the day on which it rains, as in (Job 9:10), "He does great things which are unfathomable" (*Taanit* 9b; cf. *Parparaot LeChokhmah*).

LIKUTEY MOHARAN #11:8

splendor.[88] And this is:

seven years ago — This corresponds to haughtiness, the seven houses of idolatry mentioned above.

and it has not yet reached the ground — That is, because of this sin we have still not returned to our land. As a result of this sin of haughtiness—which is likened to serving idolatry/the seven [royal] houses of idolatry—we were exiled from our land. And this is why we have not yet returned to our land; all because of this sin of haughtiness, which is synonymous with idol worship. And this is:

Not only because the water is abundant — Do not say that it is because of this that **it has not yet reached the ground**. In other words, that we cannot approach and return to the Land of Israel **because the water is abundant**—because the idolatrous nations are many,[89] as in (Deuteronomy 7:17), "Many are these nations." They are an aspect of "many waters" (Song of Songs 8:7).[90]

but because the water runs so rapidly — because they run after glory. For [glory] corresponds to water, as in (Psalms 29:3), "The God of glory thunders, God is upon many waters."[91] This is why we cannot approach and return to the Land of Israel—i.e., because of the running after glory and the haughtiness. For the main cause of this lengthy exile which prevents us from returning to our land is only the sin of haughtiness and the running after glory, as explained.

The heavenly voice informed them of all this; just how repulsive haughtiness is, so that they would distance themselves from haughtiness to the utmost. Then, God's glory is complete and one merits speech which enlightens/the bird, as explained above. But how does one achieve this, to utterly break one's own haughtiness and glory so that the glory of God is complete? This happens by guarding

---

89. **nations are many.** The Jewish people might mistakenly attribute their extended exile to the abundant strength and great numbers of the idolatrous gentile nations. The heavenly voice therefore informs them that it is not so. For in truth, their own haughtiness has brought this about. Haughtiness and self-importance is the idolatry. In the time of Moshe and Yehoshua were the nations not idolators? And yet, the Jewish people were able to conquer them and enter the Holy Land. The same holds true today. Only through the total elimination of haughtiness—the subduing of our own idolatry—will we be able to return to our land.

90. **many waters.** "Many waters cannot extinguish the love." Rashi (*loc. cit.*) explains that the many nations are incapable of undoing God's love for His chosen people.

LIKUTEY MOHARAN #11:8 198

הַבְּרִית בִּשְׁתֵּי בְּחִינוֹת הַנַּ"ל, שֶׁהֵם בְּחִינַת יִחוּדָא עִלָּאָה וְיִחוּדָא תַּתָּאָה.

שֶׁאָמַר רַב אַשֵׁי: הַאי זִיז שָׂדַי הוּא – הַיְנוּ בְּחִינַת יִחוּדָא עִלָּאָה וְיִחוּדָא תַּתָּאָה, שֶׁעַל־יְדֵי יִחוּדָא עִלָּאָה וְיִחוּדָא תַּתָּאָה, שֶׁהֵם בְּחִינַת שְׁמִירַת הַבְּרִית בִּשְׁתֵּי בְּחִינוֹת כַּנַּ"ל, עַל־יְדֵי־זֶה הַכָּבוֹד בִּשְׁלֵמוּת, וְעַל־יְדֵי כָּבוֹד בִּשְׁלֵמוּת זוֹכִין לְצִפַּרְתָּא, שֶׁהוּא הַדִּבּוּר, שֶׁהוּא אֶמְצָעִי בֵּין מַיָּא לָרָקִיעַ כַּנַּ"ל, כִּי זִיז הוּא בְּחִינַת יִחוּדָא תַּתָּאָה, בְּחִינַת מט"ט, בְּחִינַת מִכְּנַף הָאָרֶץ כַּנַּ"ל. כִּי אִיתָא בְּמִדְרָשׁ־רַבָּה (בְּרֵאשִׁית־רַבָּה יט, וַיִּקְרָא רַבָּה כב): 'עוֹף אֶחָד יֵשׁ, בְּשָׁעָה שֶׁמַּפְרִישׂ אֶת כְּנָפָיו הוּא מַחֲשִׁיךְ אֶת הַשֶּׁמֶשׁ, וְזִיז שְׁמוֹ'; וְזֶה בְּחִינַת יִחוּדָא תַּתָּאָה, בְּחִינַת מט"ט, בְּחִינַת מִכְּנַף הָאָרֶץ, שֶׁבּוֹ מִתְלַבֵּשׁ בְּרִית עִלָּאָה, שֶׁהוּא בְּחִינַת הַשֶּׁמֶשׁ שָׁדַי – זֶה בְּחִינַת יִחוּדָא עִלָּאָה כַּנַּ"ל:

lesson, the following commentary by Rabbi Shmuel Moshe Kramer (which appears in *Mabuey HaNachal*, vol. 3) seems in order: Rebbe Nachman's explanation of Rabbah bar bar Chanah's story needs to be studied more closely. Although on a simple level he seems to be saying that heaven warns against the false humility which is really intended to increase one's self-importance, this is actually very hard to understand. Are we not talking about a person who has already reached the level of understanding where he knows that it is impossible to achieve enlightened speech except when the glory of God is complete? Have we not been told that in order to achieve this, a person has to totally eliminate whatever modicum of haughtiness he has inside himself? How then can we say that his humility was for the sake of achieving prominence? Furthermore, from the warning of the heavenly voice, it would seem that he had already achieved some degree of humility and was now being told to go even further in subduing his self-importance. This would hardly be the case if all his humility had only been self-serving. In fact, he would not have eliminated haughtiness, but increased it!

It therefore seems likely that when Rebbe Nachman says, "Because people know just how despicable haughtiness is, they act humbly..." he is not referring to someone who understands that people find haughtiness despicable and so he acts humbly in order to win prominence and gain their respect. Rather, Rebbe Nachman must be referring to someone who truly understands that haughtiness is in itself despicable. He realizes that it would be most appropriate for him to distance himself from such a undesirable quality, a quality which logic and reason behoove all men to disavow. And he knows that humility and unpretentiousness, on the other hand, are truly valuable characteristics—fitting glory for the soul. In other words, the inappropriateness of self-importance is appreciated from a perspective of moral rectitude and justness.

199   *LIKUTEY MOHARAN #11:8*

the two levels of *brit*: the upper unification and lower unification. And this is what Rav Ashi said:

This bird was Ziz Sadai — This implies the upper and lower unifications. Through the upper unification and the lower unification—the guarding of the *brit* on both levels—glory is complete. And when glory is complete, one merits to the bird/speech, which is a bridge [standing] between the water and the firmament, as above. For the Ziz corresponds to the lower unification/Metat/"from the distant corner of the earth."[92] As we find in the *Midrash Rabbah*: There is one bird which, when it spreads out *K'NaFav* (its wings), it blackens [or blocks out] the sun. Its name is Ziz (*Bereishit* 19:6; *Vayikra* 22:7).[93] This corresponds to the lower unification/Metat/"from the *K'Naf* of the earth," in which the upper *brit*/the sun is clothed.[94] [Thus,] **Sadai** alludes to the upper unification, as explained.[95]

---

92. **Ziz...corner....** This has been explained above in section 6: Metat corresponds to the lower unification, the lower concept of *brit*, the six weekdays and the six orders of the Mishnah. He is also referred to as *kanaf*, the winged one.

93. **K'NaFav...Ziz.** Thus, we see the connection between Ziz, the bird/speech and *kanaf*, which is Metat. That is, even achieving the level of the lower unification/guarding the *brit* on the weekdays, one can achieve enlightened speech.

94. **upper brit/sun is clothed.** This is the first time the sun is mentioned. The *Zohar* (II, 3b) teaches that the sun symbolizes guarding the Covenant. Just as the sun "enlightens" the world (see *Likutey Moharan* I, 1:1 that the sun is synonymous with the Torah), so too, the *brit* "enlightens" the body. This corresponds to the higher concept of guarding the *brit*, as we see here. The Ziz/the lower level blocks out the light of the sun/the higher level: Metat/the lower unification veils and hides, so to speak, his Master/the upper unification. (This is the mistake which Acher made when he entered Paradise; see *Mayim*, Breslov Research Inst.) And because the light of the "sun" is blocked out, those on the lower level cannot perceive it. Even so, speech descends to show man how to repent, and it is possible to achieve enlightened speech on this level as well. And, having achieved it, he will want to strive for the higher levels/the upper unification/the light of the sun.

95. **as explained.** This has been explained in section 5: The Holy One/the upper *brit*/the *Shadai* of Shabbat is clothed in Metat/the lower *brit*/the *Shadai* of the weekdays and through him rules the world. The conclusion of the story would then be: Having not heeded the heavenly warning, we were forced into exile because of our haughtiness. So serious is this sin that, even after two millenia, we still cannot return to the Holy Land. Nevertheless, there is a solution. By guarding the *brit* we can break our own idolatrous self-importance and return the glory to its rightful Owner. This will lead to enlightened speech which, in turn, will enable us to come to deep Torah understanding. And with our idolatry removed, we will finally be able to return to the Land of Israel.

Before going on to Rebbe Nachman's explanation of how the opening verse ties into the

LIKUTEY MOHARAN #11:9

200

ט. וְזֶה: אֲנִי ה׳ – יְחוּדָא עִלָּאָה,

הוּא שְׁמִי – יְחוּדָא תַּתָּאָה;

וּכְבוֹדִי לְאַחֵר לֹא אֶתֵּן – זֶה בְּחִינַת כָּבוֹד בִּשְׁלֵמוּת,

וּתְהִלָּתִי לַפְּסִילִים – זֶה בְּחִינַת הַדִּבּוּר, כְּמוֹ שֶׁכָּתוּב: "תְּהִלַּת ה׳

יְדַבֶּר פִּי" – הַכֹּל כַּנַּ"ל:

Divine benevolence. God gave him this virtue or eminence so that he should realize that there is none and nothing besides Him, and so that he should be nothing and naught in his own eyes. Yet, he corrupts its purpose, using these qualities for his own glory and honor. This then is why Rebbe Nachman tells us that haughtiness stems from a debasement of the Holy One's garment—His splendor and majesty.

Understanding this, a person can hope to achieve genuine and inner humility. He will realize the truth: that he is nothing and that all glory and greatness belong only to God.

96. **speak God's praise.** This denotes prayer which, as explained in note 80 above, combines with Torah study to bring a person to deep understanding (*Mai HaNachal*).

97. **has all been explained.** The *Mai HaNachal* reviews the lesson as follows: By striving for the level of complete faith embodied in the concepts of the upper and lower unification, each and every Jew can attain deep Torah understanding. How does this come about? The answer is that deep Torah understanding is the result of having achieved a level of enlightened speech (§1). Yet, in order to achieve such speech, it is first necessary to eliminate one's own idolatrous self-importance. Haughtiness is akin to idolatry and unless one removes it entirely from his inner being, there is no way he can come to complete faith (§2). And to acquire such humility it is necessary to guard the *brit* (§3). This maintaining of a high moral standard has two levels, corresponding to the holiness of the weekdays and the higher holiness of Shabbat (§5). By guarding the *brit*, a person can come to true humility and thereby make God's glory complete (§7). Then his enlightened speech—words of Torah and prayer— will direct him to those areas where he needs to repent. And, by repenting time and again, a person is able to emerge from his low spiritual level. Having eliminated his personal idolatry, his faith will increase and ascend level after level, so that he will believe in and understand the unity of God, the *Shema*, and His absolute Kingship, the *Barukh shem*. He will be capable of bringing about the lower and then the upper unification, and this, in turn, will lead him to deep Torah understanding—on the levels of both Halakhah/the weekdays and Kabbalah/Shabbat (§§1,6).

201   *LIKUTEY MOHARAN #11:9*

9. And this is [the explanation of the opening verse]:
{"*Ani YHVH* (I am God), that is My name. My glory I shall not give to another, nor My praise to idols."}

Ani YHVH — ["*YHVH*" is] the upper unification.

that is My name — ["My name" is] the lower unification.

My glory I shall not give to another — This corresponds to glory that is complete.

nor My praise to idols — This corresponds to speech. As is written (Psalms 145:21), "My mouth will speak God's praise."[96] This has all been explained.[97]

Now, there can be no doubt that someone who has attained this has certainly attained a valuable quality. He has also certainly succeeded in distancing himself from haughtiness to some degree. Even so, he has not gotten anywhere near the quality of true humility. Indeed, vis-a-vis inner and genuine humility, his level can be seen as "humility which is the ultimate degree of haughtiness." This is because his humility stems from a personal desire to be truly virtuous. Yet, true humility requires a person being nothing and non-existent in his own eyes (and not as a result of a feeling that it is only right that one's soul be humble). And this cannot be achieved by means of a logical understanding based upon moral rectitude that haughtiness is despicable. Rather, to achieve true humility, it is necessary to achieve a deep understanding of the very root and essence from which human haughtiness stems—the Holy One's garment of splendor and majesty, as Rebbe Nachman has explained.

This can be further understood in light of the major theme of this lesson: the upper and lower unification. In brief, this entails believing and knowing clearly that God is the Lord and there is none other. It involves comprehending that the ultimate purpose of all the worlds and everything in them is to serve as a garment, a contraction and a vehicle for attaining the knowledge that God is the One and Only. That is, in and of itself, the creation is nothing and naught. Its value stems from creation's being the specific means, the tool, through which to achieve the awareness that there is none and nothing other than God. Consequently, any force or *shefa* in the world, which in any case exists solely from the perspective of the creation and the created, is only a vehicle and garment through which to perceive and appreciate God's exaltedness and greatness—that He alone rules in the heavens above and on the earth below. Therefore, when God benevolently provides man with some benefit such as wisdom, power or wealth, it is only so that he should come to understand God's greatness and his own inconsequentiality. This is because, in essence, wisdom, power and wealth are manifestations of God's garment, as it were. They are the means for man's coming to know Him. As a result, any virtue and eminence which a person does have, is only so that he might achieve true humility through them. This is their sole purpose. But if a person prides himself in the special qualities with which God has graced him, then he has completely perverted the intent of this

LIKUTEY MOHARAN #12:1

ליקוטי מוהר"ן סימן י"ב

תְּהִלָּה לְדָוִד אֲרוֹמִמְךָ אֱלֹהַי וְכוּ׳ (תְּהִלִּים קמ"ה):

לְשׁוֹן רַבֵּנוּ, זִכְרוֹנוֹ לִבְרָכָה

א. מַה שֶּׁאָנוּ רוֹאִים, שֶׁעַל־פִּי הָרֹב הַלּוֹמְדִים חוֹלְקִים עַל
הַצַּדִּיקִים, וְדוֹבְרִים עַל הַצַּדִּיק עָתָק בְּגַאֲוָה וָבוּז, זֶהוּ מְכֻוָּן גָּדוֹל
מֵאֵת הַשֵּׁם יִתְבָּרַךְ.

כִּי יֵשׁ בְּחִינַת יַעֲקֹב וְלָבָן: יַעֲקֹב הוּא הַצַּדִּיק הַמְחַדֵּשׁ חִדּוּשִׁין
דְּאוֹרַיְתָא וְלוֹמֵד תּוֹרָתוֹ לִשְׁמָהּ, וְטוּבוֹ גָּנוּז וְשָׁמוּר וְצָפוּן לֶעָתִיד,

many scholars who study the Word of God as a scholarly pursuit, not at all intending to use their wisdom to serve Him. Resh Lakish describes how the Talmud encompasses all facets of life, yet, "the fear of God is man's treasure" (*Shabbat* 31a). King David tells us, "The beginning of wisdom is the fear of God" (Psalms 111:10). Thus, the Torah contains all the necessary ingredients for achieving great knowledge of God and all that He created. Nevertheless, the first step must be the fear of God.

3. **contemptuously.** Questions raised about the tzaddik's actions which stem from a serious desire to understand the ways of "God's anointed" are not only not frowned upon, they are most welcome. However, if the same questions were raised to ridicule the tzaddik and undermine his position as a beloved leader of his followers, they would be contemptible. Yet, often times it may be hard to distinguish the true intention of the questioner. The key to this lies in listening to how a person presents his question. Even when contempt for the tzaddik is well hidden in the proud man's heart, words of arrogance will inevitably escape from his lips. One only has to pay close attention to what he says and how he says it. For such is the nature of speech, *Malkhut*—it reveals that which is hidden from the eyes of men (see Lesson #11, n.7; cf. n.14 below).

4. **originates Torah insights.** This can be understood in two ways:
  1) Originating new concepts and understanding in matters of Torah.
  2) Continuously generating new feelings in and for the Torah. That is, he never feels "old" about the Torah he has already studied. His yearning to come close to God is as vibrant and alive as it was when it originated.

5. **purely for its own sake.** The *Tikkuney Zohar* (Introduction, p.2a) teaches that *LiShMaH*, studying Torah purely for its own sake, is *L'SheiM Heh*, purely for the sake of the *Heh*. The letter *Heh* referred to is the last letter of the Tetragrammaton (*YHVH*), and is a reference to the *Shekhinah* (Divine Presence). Those who study the Torah purely for its own sake merit tasting the Torah's sweetness, for the Torah is entirely comprised of the names of God (*Zohar* III, 72a).

LIKUTEY MOIIARAN #12[1]

"Tehillah l'David (A psalm of David): I will exalt You, my Lord, the King; and I will bless Your name for ever and ever."

(Psalms 145:1)

This that we see that, generally, the learned[2] oppose the tzaddikim and "speak arrogant words, proudly and contemptuously,[3] against the righteous" (cf. Psalms 31:19)—this is precisely the way God intends it.

For there are the aspects of Yaakov and Lavan. Yaakov is the tzaddik who originates Torah insights[4] and studies Torah *lishmah* (purely for its own sake).[5] The good which is his is stored, guarded

---

1. **Likutey Moharan #12.** This lesson was taught on Shabbat Nachamu, the Shabbat after Tisha B'Av, 5563 (July 30, 1803). While teaching the lesson, Rebbe Nachman quoted the verse *"Nachamu, nachamu* (Be consoled) my people..." (Isaiah 40:1) and explained its connection to the other topics mentioned here. However, when he gave over the lesson to be copied, he intentionally omitted this explanation from the final version (*Parparaot LeChokhmah*). This entire lesson is *leshon Rabbeinu z'l.* See Lesson #7 note 1, where this terminology has been explained.

The reader will find woven into this lesson much material concerning the unification of the Divine personas, a subject which involves some of the deepest and most difficult secrets of the Kabbalah. Indeed, because of its extremely complex nature, many of the Breslover Chassidim living in Uman would gloss over the lesson (though never skip it entirely, because there are also sections which offer simple and straightforward advice on how to serve God). It should therefore be made clear that the sole intention in explaining the Kabbalistic concepts in footnotes is to assist the reader in understanding these ideas within the context of Rebbe Nachman's words. Thus, emphasis has been placed on developing the esoteric concepts as they specifically relate to the lesson. Neither in this lesson, nor in any of the others in which Kabbalistic terminology appears, has there been an attempt to fully explain the Kabbalah and its significance. (See Lesson #11, n.42 end, for the *Zohar's* warning against revealing the hidden teachings of the Torah.) Whether the subject matter is Divine personas, the different formations of the holy names or the *sefirot,* the objective is to clarify its relationship to themes of Rebbe Nachman's teaching.

Perhaps even more importantly, the footnotes on these difficult topics seek to point out the practical, the advice which the lesson offers concerning everyday existence. An effort has also been made to occasionally show how the lesson's themes connect with material from the Torah in general. Seen from Rebbe Nachman's perspective, passages—in all the different branches of Torah—take on whole new meaning and open the reader to aspects of Torah he never imagined existed.

2. **learned.** This refers to those who, though erudite in Torah, lack the fear of God. There are

LIKUTEY MOHARAN #12:1

כְּמוֹ שֶׁאָמְרוּ רַבּוֹתֵינוּ, זִכְרוֹנָם לִבְרָכָה: 'לְמָחָר לְקַבֵּל שְׂכָרָם'
(עֵרוּבִין כב.).; וְעַל שֵׁם שֶׁשָּׂכְרוּ לְבַסּוֹף, עַל שֵׁם זֶה נִקְרָא יַעֲקֹב –
לְשׁוֹן עָקֵב וָסוֹף, שְׂכָרוֹ לְבַסּוֹף.

וְלָבָן הוּא תַּלְמִיד־חָכָם, שֵׁ"ד יְהוּדִי, שֶׁתּוֹרָתוֹ לְהִתְיַהֵר וּלְקַנְטֵר,
וְתַלְמִיד־חָכָם כָּזֶה, נְבֵלָה טוֹבָה הֵימֶנּוּ.

וְזֶה יָדוּעַ, שֶׁאֵינוֹ נִקְרָא תַּלְמִיד־חָכָם אֶלָּא עַל־יְדֵי תּוֹרָה שֶׁבְּעַל־
פֶּה, כִּי זֶה שֶׁיּוֹדֵעַ לִלְמֹד חָמֵשׁ אֵינוֹ נִקְרָא תַּלְמִיד־חָכָם, אֶלָּא זֶה
שֶׁהוּא בָּקִי בִּגְמָרָא וּפוֹסְקִים. וּכְשֶׁלּוֹמֵד בְּלֹא דַּעַת, נִקְרָא לָבָן, עַל
שֵׁם עַרְמִימִיּוּת שֶׁנִּכְנָס בּוֹ, וְשׂוֹנֵא וְרוֹדֵף אֶת הַצַּדִּיקִים, צַדִּיק עֶלְיוֹן

---

than a dead animal is because the animal, in dying, has descended from animate to inanimate. But the human scholar who is devoid of decency has descended from the higher level of "speaker." Concerning the verse (Isaiah 26:19), "The dead shall live, my corpse shall rise...," the *Iyun Yaakov* (*Ketuvot* 111b) explains that this refers to someone who engages in Torah study. His corpse will rise in the time of the Resurrection. However, the corpse of the scholar-demon will not rise because *his* Torah is not the Torah of which it is said, "She is a tree of life for those who cling to her" (Proverbs 3:18).

11. **daat.** Generally, *daat* is translated as knowledge, something which this scholar-demon might have in abundance. However, acquiring true *daat* implies much more than the expansion of one's mental capacities. As explained in the previous note, the scholar must couple his knowledge with common decency and respect. As our Sages taught: Without decency and respect there is no Torah knowledge (*Avot* 3:21).

12. **Lavan...cunning....** As in the Talmudic passage which Rebbe Nachman later quotes (§2): When a person studies Torah, he acquires cunning. Cunning in itself is neutral. The Torah scholar who fears God will use this cunning to further his service of God and to benefit others. Not so the scholar who lacks common decency and fear of God. He will use his cunning in a negative way, to transgress the will of God or to provoke and harass others. This is Lavan the Aramaean who, in his desire to "uproot the entire Jewish nation," attempted to deceive Yaakov, the "*ish tam,*" in every way (see *The Breslov Haggadah*, p.59). The *Mai HaNachal* points out that *LaVaN* and *NaVaL*, Hebrew for carcass or something disgusting, share the same letters as well as the same qualities.

Interestingly, the Ari points out that Naval the Karmelite (1 Samuel, 25) was a reincarnation of Bilaam (cf. n.105 below), himself a reincarnation of Lavan. LaVaN (לבן), as primogenitor of this line, is therefore an acrostic for Lavan (לבן), Bilaam (בלעם), Naval (נבל) (*Shaar HaGilgulim* #22). Furthermore, just as Lavan attempted to uproot Yaakov, so too, Bilaam sought to destroy Moshe, and Naval hoped to defeat King David. And, as the Rebbe explains at the end of the lesson, King David is synonymous with the Oral Law, which Naval, the scholar-demon, seeks to control.

13. **upper...lower tzaddik.** The upper tzaddik refers to the Divine persona of *Z'er Anpin* (see n.41 below). The lower tzaddik refers to the tzaddikim in this world who study the Torah.

LIKUTEY MOHARAN #12:1

and hidden away for the Future,[6] as our Sages taught: ...tomorrow, to receive their reward (*Eruvin* 22a).[7] It is because his reward comes at the end that he is called *yaAKoV*, which connotes *AKeV* (heel) and end. His reward comes at the end.

But Lavan is a scholar-demon.[8] He studies Torah in order to show off and criticize.[9] And such a Torah scholar, "a carcass is better than he" (*Vayikra Rabbah* 1:15).[10]

It is common knowledge that a person is only called a scholar [when versed] in the Oral Law. Someone who knows how to study the Five Books of the Torah is not called a scholar; only one who is knowledgeable in the Talmud and Codifiers. When such a person studies Torah without *daat*,[11] <i.e., not *lishmah*,> he is called Lavan—because of the cunning which he acquires.[12] He despises and persecutes the tzaddikim: the upper tzaddik and the lower tzaddik.[13]

6. **for the Future.** Even in this physical world, his studying of the Torah is for the spirituality which it contains. This being so, the reward for his study is reserved for the World to Come, which is totally spiritual (*Biur HaLikutim*).

7. **tomorrow...reward.** The verse reads (Deuteronomy 7:11), "Safeguard the commandments...*today*, to fulfill them." Our Sages explain (*Eruvin, loc. cit.*): Today (this world) to fulfill them, not tomorrow (the World to Come) to fulfill them. Today to fulfill them, tomorrow to receive their reward—i.e., the spiritual reward.

8. **scholar-demon.** This is a shortened version of "Torah-scholar-Jewish-demon." The *Zohar* (III, 253a) states that those who only study the revealed Torah (Mishnah) eat from the Tree of Knowledge. This "food" also contains worthless matter which must be removed. Because "waste" is the property of the Other Side, this worthless matter is given over to the demons who serve these students of Mishnah. Thus, among the destructive demons there are those that are "Jewish" and learned, such as Ashmadai. This king of the demons, who was recognized for his cleverness, once banished King Solomon and took his place on the throne (*Gittin* 68a; *Ruth Rabbah* 5:6). Though one studies Torah, he may fall into the trap of being a scholar-demon. Why this happens is explained in the following note and made clearer in section 3 below.

9. **show off and criticize.** The Talmud teaches: When someone studies Torah not purely for its own sake, the Torah becomes his potion of death (*Taanit* 7a). "Whoever fulfills Torah and mitzvot not for their own sake, it would have been better were he never created" (*Berakhot* 17a). Conversely, our Sages taught: A person should always study Torah, even if not for its own sake. For by doing so, he will come to study purely for its own sake (*Sotah* 23b). Tosafot (*ibid., s.v. l'olam; Nazir* 23b, *s.v. shemitokh*) explains the contradiction: Study not for its own sake is also permitted (even encouraged) when its goals are rewards and honor etc. However, study not for its own sake, but to transgress the will of God or to provoke and harass others, is despicable. His knowledge is deadly, and such a *lamdan* (scholar) is akin to a Torah-scholar-Jewish-demon.

10. **a carcass is better....** The Midrash (*loc. cit.*) states: A scholar who has no *daat*, a carcass is better than he. Here, *daat* implies common decency and respect. The reason he is worse

LIKUTEY MOHARAN #12:1

206

וְצַדִּיק תַּחְתּוֹן, כִּי שְׁכִינְתָּא בֵּין תְּרֵין צַדִּיקַיָּא יָתְבָא, כְּמוֹ שֶׁכָּתוּב בַּזֹּהַר (וַיֵּצֵא קנג:, וַיְחִי רמה:): צַדִּיקִים יִרְשׁוּ אָרֶץ – צַדִּיקִים תְּרֵי מַשְׁמַע. וּשְׁנֵי צַדִּיקִים אֵלּוּ הֵם: זֶה הַצַּדִּיק שֶׁחִדֵּשׁ זֹאת הַתּוֹרָה שֶׁבְּעַל־פֶּה, זֶה צַדִּיק עֶלְיוֹן; וְצַדִּיק הַתַּחְתּוֹן, זֶה שֶׁלּוֹמֵד הַחִדּוּשִׁין; וְתוֹרָה שֶׁבְּעַל־פֶּה הַיְנוּ שְׁכִינְתָּא, כְּמוֹ שֶׁכָּתוּב: 'מַלְכוּת פֶּה, וְתוֹרָה שֶׁבְּעַל־פֶּה קָרִינַן לַהּ'. וּכְשֶׁהַשְּׁכִינָה הַנִּקְרָא תּוֹרָה שֶׁבְּעַל־פֶּה בָּאָה בְּתוֹךְ תַּלְמִיד־חָכָם שֵׁד יְהוּדִי, זֶה נִקְרָא גָּלוּת הַשְּׁכִינָה, וְאָז יֵשׁ לוֹ פֶּה לְדַבֵּר עַל צַדִּיק עָתָק וְכוּ'.

וּכְשֶׁהָאָדָם לוֹמֵד בִּקְדֻשָּׁה וּבְטָהֳרָה אֵיזֶה דִּין וּפְסָק, שֶׁחִדֵּשׁ אֵיזֶה תַּנָּא אוֹ צַדִּיק אַחֵר, עַל־יְדֵי־זֶה נַעֲשָׂה בְּחִינַת נְשִׁיקִין (ב). וּנְשִׁיקִין

in the Written Law, the sources for the principles. The thoughts that one generates in attempting to locate these sources can therefore be considered "original" insights.

16. Malkhut is peh...Oral Law. *Malkhut* is *peh,* for by proclaiming God's sovereignty, His Kingship is recognized. Furthermore, while the Written Law can be studied on one's own, the *Torah shebe'al peh* requires the transmission of an oral tradition received from a teacher.

17. in exile...against the tzaddik. Instead of teaching the Torah and speaking to people about devoting themselves to God, thereby bringing Mashiach and the rebuilding of the Temple closer, the mouth of the scholar-demon is preoccupied with its own verbal attack upon the tzaddik. In this sense, the learned individual is the captor of *Malkhut,* delaying the *shefa* from properly descending, prolonging the Divine Presence's exile. And, keeping the Divine Presence in exile gives the scholar-demon the power to provoke and persecute the tzaddik in this world, for he receives this *shefa* from the upper tzaddik and uses it incorrectly.

18. Tanna. *Tanna* is the term used for a scholar whose original insights are quoted in the Mishnah, the earlier section of the Oral Law. It is not clear why Rebbe Nachman used the word *Tanna* to describe the tzaddikim who revealed Torah. Compounding the question is his statement towards the end of the section that "even tzaddikim who have already passed away...," as obviously all the *Tannaim* have long since passed away. It would seem that because original Torah insights have their root in the Oral Law, which is Mishnah, the Rebbe refers to all the tzaddikim as *Tanna.*

19. neshikin...spirit with spirit. Man's actions in this physical world both mirror and give rise to corresponding spiritual "actions" in the transcendant worlds Above (cf. Lesson #11, n.53). Thus, when a person uses his mouth, the source of *ruach* (spirit; *Zohar* II, 224b), to study the "Oral Law" which the *Tanna* or some other tzaddik initiated through his mouth, this is *neshikin*—the joining of spirit with spirit. Though he is here in this world, his spirit kisses the spirit of the tzaddik who has long since departed.

LIKUTEY MOHARAN #12:1

As is written in the *Zohar* (I, 153b): The Divine Presence resides between two tzaddikim, as in (Psalms 37:29), "Tzaddikim will inherit the earth"—[the plural,] *tzaddikim,* indicating two.[14] These are the two tzaddikim: the tzaddik who originated this teaching of Oral Law is the upper tzaddik, and the lower tzaddik is the one who studies these original insights.[15]

And Oral Law is the Divine Presence. As < Eliyahu taught > : *Malkhut* (Kingship) is *peh* (mouth)—she is called *Torah shebe'al peh* (Oral Law) (*Tikkuney Zohar,* Introduction).[16] When the Divine Presence, which is known as the Oral Law, comes into the scholar-demon, it is referred to as the Divine Presence in exile. < From this > [the scholar] has the mouth to "speak arrogant words, proudly and contemptuously, against the tzaddik."[17]

But when, with holiness and purity, a person studies some law or legal decision which a *Tanna*[18] or some other tzaddik originated, this brings about the aspect of *neshikin* (kisses). *Neshikin* is the binding of spirit with spirit.[19] For this legal decision was spoken by the *Tanna,*

---

14. between two tzaddikim...the earth.... The earth is the concept of *Malkhut,* for this is where the Kingship of God is revealed. *Malkhut* is also synonymous with the Divine Presence and the Oral Law. Thus, the earth/*Malkhut* which the tzaddikim will inherit is the Divine Presence, the Oral Law (see Appendix: The Divine Persona, Alternate Names).

This point that the Divine Presence resides between two tzaddikim is integral to the entire lesson. The *Zohar* (*loc. cit.*) states that Rachel, symbolic of the Divine Presence (cf. *Tzaddik* #563, n.27 below), gave birth to two tzaddikim—Yosef and Binyamin. Rachel/the Divine Presence is therefore situated between these two tzaddikim. Yosef symbolizes the upper tzaddik from whom great spiritual light radiates. Binyamin symbolizes the lower tzaddik, the tzaddikim of this world. By virtue of his desire to ascend, he reflects the great light and receives more of it. Thus, when the "earth" corresponds to the Divine Presence/Rachel, it is inherited by these two tzaddikim, "Yosef" and "Binyamin."

15. ...original insight. Rebbe Nachman now redefines this statement, with "earth" representing the Oral Law. It is situated between the upper tzaddik/Yaakov—the Written Law—above, and the lower tzaddik—the tzaddikim in this world who study the Torah— below. (Yaakov and Yosef are considered as one; *Zohar* I, 182b).

Every Torah concept has its origin in the Written Law (*Likutey Halakhot, Reishit Hagez* 5:16). This being the case, how can it be said that one originates Torah thoughts? To answer this, let us consider the following contradictory statements. The Talmud teaches: Whatever a worthy student will originate in Oral Law has already been given over to Moshe (*Yerushalmi, Peah* 2:4). Yet we find that: Particulars not revealed to Moshe Rabbeinu were revealed to Rabbi Akiva and his friends (*Bamidbar Rabbah* 19:6). The *Anaf Yosef* (*Shabbat* 119b) states that whereas every principle of Torah, without exception, was revealed to Moshe, its source in the Written Law was not revealed to him. Moshe had no need for this, because he had heard the entire Torah directly from God. However, we are enjoined in Torah study to find,

LIKUTEY MOHARAN #12:1

זֶה בְּחִינַת הִתְדַּבְּקוּת רוּחָא בְּרוּחָא; כִּי הַפֶּסֶק הַזֶּה הוּא דִּבּוּרוֹ שֶׁל הַתַּנָּא, וְדִבּוּר הוּא הַחִיּוּת, כְּמוֹ שֶׁכָּתוּב (בְּרֵאשִׁית ב): "לְנֶפֶשׁ חַיָּה", וְתַרְגּוּמוֹ: 'לְרוּחַ מְמַלְּלָא'.

וְרוּחַ מְמַלְּלָא, הַיְנוּ הַנֶּפֶשׁ חַיָּה, הִיא בָּאָה מִתּוֹרָה שֶׁבְּעַל־פֶּה, כְּמוֹ שֶׁכָּתוּב (שָׁם א): "תּוֹצֵא הָאָרֶץ נֶפֶשׁ חַיָּה". נִמְצָא, בְּשָׁעָה שֶׁמְּחַדֵּשׁ הַתַּנָּא אֵיזֶה חִדּוּשׁ וּמְדַבֵּר זֶה הַחִדּוּשׁ, זֶה הַדִּבּוּר בְּעַצְמוֹ הִיא בְּחִינַת הַתּוֹרָה שֶׁבְּעַל־פֶּה שֶׁחִדֵּשׁ, כִּי מִשָּׁם מוֹצָאָהּ, כְּמוֹ שֶׁכָּתוּב: "תּוֹצֵא הָאָרֶץ נֶפֶשׁ חַיָּה". נִמְצָא, עַכְשָׁו כְּשֶׁלּוֹמְדִים אֶת הַחִדּוּשׁ הַזֶּה, וּכְשֶׁמַּכְנִיסִין הַלִּמּוּד וְהַחִדּוּשׁ בְּתוֹךְ פֶּה, נִמְצָא שֶׁמִּדַּבְּקִין רוּחַ הַצַּדִּיק שֶׁחִדֵּשׁ זֶה הַחִדּוּשׁ עִם רוּחַ מְמַלְּלָא, הַיְנוּ עִם הַדִּבּוּר הַלּוֹמֵד זֶה הַחִדּוּשׁ עַכְשָׁו. וְזֹאת הַהִתְדַּבְּקוּת רוּחָא בְּרוּחָא נִקְרָא נְשִׁיקִין.

נִמְצָא, כְּשֶׁלּוֹמְדִין אֵיזֶה הֲלָכָה שֶׁחִדְּשׁוּ הַתַּנָּאִים, עַל־יְדֵי־זֶה נִתְדַּבֵּק רוּחַ הַתַּנָּא עִם רוּחַ הַלּוֹמֵד, וְדוֹמֶה כְּאִלּוּ נוֹשֵׁק אֶת עַצְמוֹ עִם הַתַּנָּא. אֲבָל תַּלְמִיד־חָכָם שֵׁד יְהוּדִי, כְּשֶׁלּוֹמֵד גְּמָרָא אוֹ פְּסַק־דִּין, עָלָיו כָּתוּב (מִשְׁלֵי כ"ז): "נֶעְתָּרוֹת נְשִׁיקוֹת שׂוֹנֵא", כִּי הַתַּנָּא אֵינוֹ יָכוֹל לִסְבֹּל רוּחוֹ שֶׁל תַּלְמִיד־חָכָם שֵׁד יְהוּדָאִין, כִּי מִי יָכוֹל לִסְבֹּל לְנַשֵּׁק אֶת עַצְמוֹ עִם נְבֵלָה, כָּל שֶׁכֵּן שֶׁנְּבֵלָה טוֹבָה הֵימֶנּוּ.

וַאֲפִלּוּ צַדִּיקִים שֶׁכְּבָר הָלְכוּ לְעוֹלָמָם, וּכְשֶׁאָנוּ לוֹמְדִין תּוֹרוֹתֵיהֶן, עַל־יְדֵי־זֶה נִתְדַּבֵּק רוּחָם בְּרוּחֵנוּ, כְּמוֹ שֶׁאָמְרוּ חֲכָמֵינוּ, זִכְרוֹנָם לִבְרָכָה (יְבָמוֹת צז): 'שִׂפְתוֹתֵיהֶם דּוֹבְבוֹת בַּקֶּבֶר', וְזֶה עַל־יְדֵי בְּחִינַת נְשִׁיקָה:

---

24. **profuse.** Though they are many, they are unwanted, even despised.

25. **carcass is better than he.** "The tzaddikim, even after their passing, are considered alive...[but] the wicked, even when alive, are considered dead" (*Berakhot* 18a,b). Thus, the scholar-demon is considered dead, a living corpse, and even lower than a corpse (n.10 above).

26. **their lips move....** King David prayed, "Let me dwell in Your tent *olamim* (forever)" (Psalms 61:5). The plural "*olamim*" indicates two worlds. The Talmud asks: Can one dwell in two worlds at one time? Our Sages answer: King David prayed that people repeat his teachings, quoting him in this world, so that it would always be as if he were still alive

LIKUTEY MOHARAN #12:1

and speech is the life-force, as is written (Genesis 2:7), "[Man] became a living soul," which Onkelos renders, "a speaking spirit."[20]

Now, the "speaking spirit"—the "living soul"—comes from the Oral Law, as is written (Genesis 1:24), "Let the earth bring forth a living soul."[21] Consequently, when the *Tanna* originates some insight and verbalizes this insight, the speaking itself is an aspect of Oral Law which he originated. For that is where he drew it from,[22] as in, "Let the earth bring forth a living soul." So that now, when one studies this insight and brings the learning and insight into his mouth, the result is that the spirit of the tzaddik who originated this insight binds itself with the "speaking spirit"—with the words of the one who is now studying the insight.[23] This binding of spirit with spirit is called *neshikin*.

We find then that when a person studies < *lishmah* > a law which the *Tannaim* instituted, through this the spirit of the *Tanna* binds itself with the spirit of the one studying. It is as if he exchanges kisses with the *Tanna*. However, of the scholar-demon who studies the Talmud or a legal decision it is written (Proverbs 27:6), "The kisses of an enemy are profuse."[24] This is because the *Tanna* cannot tolerate the spirit of a scholar-demon. For who could stomach exchanging kisses with a carcass, especially when "a carcass is better than he"?[25]

And even tzaddikim who have already passed away, by studying their teachings, their spirit becomes bound with ours < in the aspect of *neshikin* >. As our Sages taught: [When a person quotes the sages in this world,] their lips move in the grave (*Yevamot* 97a).[26] This is a result of the aspect of *neshikin*.

---

20. **speaking spirit.** Speech is unique to man, the quality which distinguishes him from the other forms of creation (mineral, vegetable, animal). As Onkelos indicates, the living-soul in man is his speaking spirit. Speech is his life.

21. **earth...living soul.** As we've seen, the earth is *Malkhut,* the Oral Law (*Mai HaNachal*). Thus, this verse from the beginning of Genesis which Rebbe Nachman quotes to show the root of man's living soul now reads, "Let the *Oral Law* bring forth a *speaking spirit.*"

22. **where he drew it from.** Just as speech/the speaking spirit has its root in the Oral Law, so too the insight which the upper tzaddik originates. Thus, when he reveals this insight of Oral Law with his mouth, the tzaddik's speech, his spirit, remains bound with it.

23. **one who is now studying....** The lower tzaddik, the individual actually studying, repeats the words of the upper tzaddik. In enunciating the teaching (see Lesson #11:1 and n.8), he attaches himself to its quality of speech which, in turn, is still bound to its source, the upper tzaddik. This binding brings them together (*Mabuey HaNachal*).

LIKUTEY MOHARAN #12:1

210

וְזֶה בְּחִינַת: (בְּרֵאשִׁית כ"ט) וַיִּשַּׁק יַעֲקֹב לְרָחֵל, וַיִּשָּׂא קֹלוֹ וַיֵּבְךְּ,
פֵּרֵשׁ רַשִׁ"י: 'שֶׁצָּפָה בְּרוּחַ־הַקֹּדֶשׁ שֶׁאֵינָהּ נִכְנֶסֶת עִמּוֹ לִקְבוּרָה'.
רָחֵל – בְּחִינַת תּוֹרָה שֶׁבְּעַל־פֶּה, שֶׁהִיא כְּרָחֵל לִפְנֵי גוֹזְזֶיהָ, שֶׁהַכֹּל
גּוֹזְזִין וּפוֹסְקִין מִמֶּנָּה הֲלָכוֹת, וְהֵם נַעֲשִׂים לְבוּשִׁין, כְּמוֹ שֶׁכָּתוּב
(מִשְׁלֵי כ"ז): "כְּבָשִׂים לִלְבוּשֶׁךָ", כְּמוֹ שֶׁכָּתוּב (יְשַׁעְיָהוּ ג): "שִׂמְלָה
לְכָה קָצִין תִּהְיֶה לָנוּ". כְּשֶׁאָדָם כָּשֵׁר לוֹמֵד תּוֹרַת הַתַּנָּא, אֲזַי הַתַּנָּא
נוֹשֵׁק אוֹתוֹ וְהוּא נוֹשֵׁק הַתַּנָּא, וְגוֹרֵם תַּעֲנוּג גָּדוֹל לְהַתַּנָּא, כְּמוֹ
שֶׁכָּתוּב: 'שִׂפְתוֹתָיו דּוֹבְבוֹת בַּקֶּבֶר' וְכוּ'.

וְזֶה בְּחִינַת: וַיִּשַּׁק יַעֲקֹב – הוּא הַתַּנָּא, לְרָחֵל – הִיא הַתּוֹרָה
שֶׁבְּעַל־פֶּה שֶׁחִדֵּשׁ, שֶׁנִּשֵּׁק וְדִבֵּק אֶת רוּחוֹ בְּרוּחַ־הַקֹּדֶשׁ שֶׁבַּשְּׁכִינָה.

relationships established by the following passage from the *Zohar* (II, 29b) should be kept in mind. The verse reads (*loc. cit.*), " 'As a *rachel* before her shearers is silent....' Why silent? Rachel is *Malkhut*, speech. Yaakov is *Z'er Anpin*, the voice. When the Divine Presence, *Malkhut,* is in exile, its voice disappears and it falls silent." Rachel/the Oral Law is attached to Yaakov/the *Tanna* who originated the law. When, however, the Oral Law falls into exile in the mouth of Lavan/the scholar-demon it is held captive there, just as speech was held captive in Egypt (*Rabbi Nachman's Wisdom* #88).

28. **Sheep...garments.** Just as the shorn wool is made into garments, the Oral Law, the teachings of the tzaddikim, becomes the garments for one's soul. Rebbe Nachman thus taught that after a person passes away, the tzaddik has the power to give this person one of the tzaddik's own "garments" with which to clothe his soul (*Tzaddik* #228).

The Talmud (*Chagigah* 13a) often refers to things which are *kavush* (veiled and preserved) with God, hidden from and unknown to man. KeVeS (כבש, sheep) is similar to KaVuSh (כבוש). Similarly, the Oral Law is "dressed" within the Written Law, hidden and unknown. The tzaddik, however, reveals and originates this source. It becomes his garment and he can share it with others—with those who repeat his teachings. It then becomes their garment, for their soul, because they dress their souls with the garment of Torah. See above, note 15.

29. **garments...be our leader.** The Talmud (*Shabbat* 119b) explains: When one has attained Torah wisdom, he is worthy of becoming a leader (*Mai HaNachal*). In the context of the lesson, this relates to the garment which the upper tzaddik attains and gives over to his followers, the concept of the lower tzaddik.

30. **virtuous individual.** Until now, Rebbe Nachman has referred only to the tzaddik who studies Torah as "the lower tzaddik." Now, he has broadened this category to include all people—just as long as they are virtuous. As to who this is, see note 9 above.

31. **great delight....** See above, note 26, that his studying of the *Tanna's*/the tzaddik's teachings causes this upper tzaddik to be in both worlds—this lower one as well.

LIKUTEY MOHARAN #12:1

{"Yaakov kissed Rachel and he wept aloud. Yaakov told Rachel that he was her father's relative, that he was Rivkah's son. She ran and told her father. When Lavan heard the name of Yaakov, his sister's son, he ran to greet him. He embraced and kissed him, and brought him into his home. And *yesaper* ([Yaakov] told) Lavan all that had happened. Lavan said to him, 'Yes, indeed, you are my own flesh and blood.' And he *yeshev* (dwelled) with him for *chodesh yamim* (a month's time). Lavan then said to Yaakov, 'You are my brother...' " (Genesis 29:11-15).}

This corresponds to "Yaakov kissed Rachel and wept aloud." Rashi explains: "he foresaw with the holy spirit that she would not be buried with him." "Rachel" alludes to the Oral Law, < for she corresponds to speech, to the Divine Presence >. She is "as a *rachel* (lamb) before her shearers" (Isaiah 53:7).[27] Everyone shears and extracts laws from her (*Tikkuney Zohar* #21, p.46b). [The laws] become garments, as is written (Proverbs 27:26), "Sheep shall provide your garments,"[28] and as in (Isaiah 3:6), "You have garments, you will be our leader."[29] When a virtuous individual[30] studies the *Tanna's* teaching, the *Tanna* kisses him. And he kisses the *Tanna* and brings the *Tanna* great delight, as in, "his lips move in the grave."[31]

This is the meaning of "Yaakov kissed"—he is the *Tanna*; "Rachel"—she is the Oral Law which he originated. He kissed and bound his spirit with the holy spirit in the Divine Presence. "And he

(*Yevamot* 97a). Tosafot (*s.v. agura*) explains that while one's soul is in the House of Study above, in this world his lips are moving in the grave, as though he were speaking. In this sense, he is in both worlds at once. The Maharsha explains that speech is the soul's manifestation in the body (as above and nn. 20,21). Because the spirit is eternal, it can still affect the body even though they are no longer bound together as one. This occurs when someone alive in this world repeats the Torah which this person had revealed (*Kuntres Acharon, s.v. siftotav*). Furthermore, because the Oral Law is the root of speech, it becomes possible to revive the power of speech whenever the Oral Law is repeated (*Mabuey HaNachal*). Thus, by repeating the tzaddik's lessons, his original insights, a person can still bind himself to the tzaddik even though the tzaddik has long since passed away.

The Talmud compares this to someone who drinks a very old, fine wine. Even though the wine has been drunk, its taste lingers on the lips. So, too, the one who has originated Torah insights. Though he has departed from the world, his power of speech lingers on his lips, and [by the repetition of his words] is aroused (*Yerushalmi, Berakhot* 2). (This analogy to wine takes on further significance in section 4, where Rebbe Nachman incorporates the concept of wine within the lesson.)

The *B'er HaGolah*, a commentary on the *Shulchan Arukh*, lists all the sources (from the Talmud and Codifiers) for the laws cited. Based upon this lesson, it is clearly advisable to include this commentary when studying the *Shulchan Arukh*.

27. **her shearers.** Just as a lamb is sheared, yet the wool grows back, one can keep reviewing the Oral Law and constantly find new and original thoughts therein.

To better understand the direction which Rebbe Nachman's lesson now takes, the

LIKUTEY MOHARAN #12:1,2 212

וַיֵּבְךְּ – שֶׁצָּפָה בְרוּחַ-הַקֹּדֶשׁ שֶׁלּוֹ, שֶׁהוֹצִיא מִפִּיו וְהִכְנִיס בְּתוֹךְ הַתּוֹרָה שֶׁבְּעַל-פֶּה, וְרָאָה שֶׁבַּגָּלוּת הַזֶּה עַל-פִּי הָרֹב הַלּוֹמְדִים אֵינָם הֲגוּנִים; נִמְצָא שֶׁעַל-יְדֵי לְמוּדָם שֶׁיִּלְמְדוּ לֹא תִּכָּנֵס רוּחַ-הַקֹּדֶשׁ שֶׁל רָחֵל, שֶׁל תּוֹרָה שֶׁבְּעַל-פֶּה, לִקְבוּרָה, שֶׁאֵין שְׂפָתוֹתָיו דּוֹבְבוֹת בַּקֶּבֶר עַל-יְדֵי לְמוּדוֹ שֶׁל רָשָׁע, וְעַל-יְדֵי-זֶה וַיֵּבְךְּ עַל גָּלוּתוֹ.

וְעוֹד, שֶׁלִּפְעָמִים הַלַּמְדָן אוֹמֵר אֵיזֶה חִדּוּשׁ בְּשֵׁם עַצְמוֹ וְלֹא בְּשֵׁם הַתַּנָּא, נִמְצָא שֶׁעַל-יְדֵי-זֶה אֵינוֹ נִכְנָס עִם הַתַּנָּא לִקְבוּרָה, כִּי אֵין אוֹמֵר בְּשֵׁם אוֹמְרוֹ.

ב. וְאִם יִקְשֶׁה לְךְ: הֲלֹא תֵּכֶף כְּשֶׁלּוֹמֵד הַלַּמְדָן הַחִדּוּשׁ שֶׁל הַצַּדִּיק, הָיָה לוֹ לַחֲזֹר בִּתְשׁוּבָה, וְאֵיךְ מַנִּיחַ הַתּוֹרָה שֶׁבְּעַל-פֶּה אֶת הַלַּמְדָן

of the Oral Law's fall to the lower levels of the unworthy scholar. He proudly shows off his knowledge—"on the road." Yet, despite this, all is not lost. Precisely because Rachel was buried on the road, access to her grave was made that much easier. Many years later, when the Jewish people were sent into exile, they passed through Bet Lechem and stopped at Rachel's Tomb, the site which Yaakov intentionally chose. They wept and prayed there (*Rashi,* Genesis 48:7). Rachel herself was aroused to pray on behalf of the Jews, and God promised her to return the exiles in her merit (Jeremiah 31:14-16). This corresponds to the *Tanna's* weeping over *his* exile, because his teachings have become captive in the mouth of the scholar-demon.

34. in his own name.... His desire for acclaim is so great that he will even stoop to "taking" what is not his. Such haughtiness is the telling trait of the one who studies Torah not for its sake. See Lesson #11, in which Rebbe Nachman speaks about those whose humility is only for the sake of haughtiness. For even if such a scholar-demon conducts himself humbly, it is only to increase his own self-importance.

35. who first said it. For the *Tanna's* lips will not move in the grave. Furthermore, our Sages tell us that repeating something in the name of the one who said it brings redemption to the world, as in (Esther 2:22), "Esther told the king in Mordekhai's name" (*Megillah* 15a). The *Etz Yosef* adds that we can presume that Mordekhai had expected Esther to disclose the plot against Achashveirosh's life in her own name. He hoped that by doing so, she would win even more favor from the king. Otherwise, why didn't Mordekhai himself tell Achashveirosh what he had overheard? But Esther refused to take the credit which rightfully belonged to someone else. She could not bring herself to such arrogance. It was therefore the quality of humility which brought redemption to the Jews. And this will likewise be the quality of the Mashiach. He will be humble and lowly in his own eyes—"a poor man riding on a donkey" (Zakhariah 9:9).

In review: It is by Divine design that learned scholars are wont to oppose the tzaddikim. When that which the upper tzaddik originates, the Oral Law, is studied by a righteous person

LIKUTEY MOHARAN #12:1,2

wept"—He foresaw with his holy spirit, which he took from his mouth and put into the Oral Law, and saw that in this exile the learned are generally unworthy people. Consequently, the studying in which they engage[32] causes the holy spirit of Rachel/Oral Law not to enter the grave.[33] For [the *Tanna's*] lips do not move in the grave from the wicked man's studying. And because of this, "he wept" over his exile.

Furthermore, there are even times when the learned individual will teach an original insight in his own name instead of crediting the *Tanna*.[34] As a result, he does not enter the grave with the *Tanna*. For he does not say it in the name of the one who [first] said it.[35]

2. Should you wonder: Why isn't it that as soon as the learned individual studies the tzaddik's insight, he repents? And how is it that the Oral Law allows the learned individual to continue with his

---

32. **learned...unworthy...in which they engage.** Rebbe Nachman taught: In earlier generations, Torah study even had the power to protect people from death (as it did for King David; *Shabbat* 30a,b), yet now we find that people pass away while they are studying. "Know," he said, "even today, if Torah study is conducted properly, it still has its great protective powers. But, if not, if a person does not study as he should, God forbid, then his studying only serves to strengthen the Other Side. This is especially the case when that which he studies is the Talmud. This is because Talmud (תלמוד) has the same numerical value as the *kelipah* (evil force) known as Lilit (לילית), 480 (see Appendix: Gematria Chart). Thus, Talmud can either subdue the *kelipah,* or cause the person to be subdued by it" (*Likutey Moharan I,* 214).

The Midrash (*Eikhah Rabbah* 2:4) teaches that prior to the destruction of the Second Temple, there were 481 study houses in Jerusalem. The Torah's "outnumbering" the *kelipah* (Lilit) alludes to the power which holiness had to subdue the evil forces.

33. **the grave.** The Ari explains: Conceptually, death and burial indicate a descent to a lower spiritual level. "The grave" thus implies being hidden in a level which is lower than one's rightful level. Had Rachel's soul not left her during childbirth, she might have been able to ascend to the level of Yaakov and then merit being buried together with him. But, because it did, she was not buried next to him (inside the Tomb of the Patriarchs, in Hebron). Rather, after giving birth to Binyamin, she was buried on the road, in Bet Lechem (*Shaar HaHakdamot* p.86).

In our lesson, Binyamin corresponds to the lower tzaddik (above, n.14), the one who studies the Oral Law. Yet, on this lower level, there exists a danger of falling into the trap of the Other Side. The scholar may misuse his knowledge and become the scholar-demon. And, whereas "Binyamin" as the lower tzaddik strives to reach ever higher levels of holiness, this is not true of the haughty scholar. His mastery of the Oral Law becomes a weapon, a means for showing off and criticizing others (n.9 above). The Oral Law itself is transformed into "arrogant words" and corrupted letter-combinations (see §4). And this is why Rachel's soul left her, why the Divine Presence is in exile. Her being buried alongside the road is symbolic

LIKUTEY MOHARAN #12:2

214

לֵילֵךְ בְּרִשְׁעָתוֹ? תְּשׁוּבָה עַל זֶה: וַיַּגֵּד יַעֲקֹב לְרָחֵל כִּי אֲחִי אָבִיהָ
הוּא וְכִי בֶן־רִבְקָה הוּא – פֵּרוּשׁ: בְּשָׁעָה שֶׁהִגִּיד הַצַּדִּיק הַתּוֹרָה
שֶׁבְּעַל־פֶּה, הִגִּיד אוֹתָהּ בִּבְחִינוֹת (הוֹשֵׁעַ י"ד): "צַדִּיקִים יֵלְכוּ בָם
וּפשְׁעִים יִכָּשְׁלוּ בָם".

וְזֶה: "כִּי אֲחִי אָבִיהָ הוּא" בְּרַמָּאוּת, בִּבְחִינַת "וּפשְׁעִים יִכָּשְׁלוּ
בָם"; "וְכִי בֶן־רִבְקָה הוּא" הַכְּשֵׁרָה, וְזֶה בְּחִינַת "צַדִּיקִים יֵלְכוּ
בָם".

וְלֹא עוֹד, וַתָּרָץ וַתַּגֵּד לְאָבִיהָ – הַיְנוּ זֹאת הַבְּחִינָה שֶׁל "וּפשְׁעִים
יִכָּשְׁלוּ בָם" בָּא לוֹ בְּנָקֵל יוֹתֵר, כְּמוֹ שֶׁאָמְרוּ חֲכָמֵינוּ, זִכְרוֹנָם
לִבְרָכָה (סוֹטָה כא:): 'אֲנִי חָכְמָה שָׁכַנְתִּי עָרְמָה', כִּי כְּשֶׁאָדָם לוֹמֵד
תּוֹרָה, נִכְנָס בּוֹ עַרְמִימִיּוּת. וְזֶה: "וַתָּרָץ" – כְּאָדָם שֶׁרָץ בִּמְהִירוּת
וּבְנָקֵל; וַתַּגֵּד לְאָבִיהָ – שֶׁהַתּוֹרָה הִיא מַגֶּדֶת לְהַלַּמְדָן עַרְמִימִיּוּת.
(וְזֶהוּ: וַתָּרָץ וַתַּגֵּד) לְאָבִיהָ, שֶׁהָעַרְמִימִיּוּת בָּא בְּנָקֵל וּבִמְהִירוּת
יוֹתֵר לָאָדָם, כִּי הַקְּדֻשָּׁה צָרִיךְ סִיּוּעַ מִלְעֵלָּא, כְּמוֹ שֶׁאָמְרוּ (יוֹמָא לח;
עֲבוֹדָה זָרָה נה): 'הַבָּא לְטַהֵר, מְסַיְּעִין לוֹ', אֲבָל הָעַרְמִימִיּוּת
פּוֹתְחִין, יֵשׁ לוֹ פְּתָחִים הַרְבֵּה, וּבָא לוֹ בְּנָקֵל:

not, however, true of holiness and true wisdom. One who seeks qualities of virtue must strive
for them and then patiently await their actualization. He requires help. This Divine assistance
will be forthcoming, but not immediately. Rebbe Nachman thus tells us that cunning comes
very easily to a person, almost naturally. One must therefore be very careful and constantly
seek proper guidance from the true tzaddik or teacher. Because the "openings," the pitfalls,
are many, it is not only foolish, but dangerous, to rely on personal insight and inclination.
Interestingly, the Talmud (loc. cit.) bases this teaching on the verse (Proverbs 3:34), "If he
joins the scorners, he too will become one; but if he joins the humble, he will be granted
grace." This ties in with what Rebbe Nachman taught earlier, that the virtuous individual
displays the quality of humility, whereas the haughty scholar scorns and derides the righteous.

In review: It is by Divine design that learned scholars are wont to oppose the tzaddikim.
When that which the upper tzaddik originates, the Oral Law, is studied by a righteous person
in this world, the lower tzaddik, there is a binding of spirit between them. However, when
someone who lacks decency and respect studies the upper tzaddik's teachings, he causes the
Oral Law/the Divine Presence to descend into exile. This teaching then becomes a weapon in
the mouth of the scholar-demon with which he persecutes the lower tzaddik (§1). This is
possible because the nature of Torah is twofold: life-giving in the hands of the lower tzaddik,
poisonous in the hands of the scholar-demon (§2).

215   *LIKUTEY MOHARAN #12:2*

wickedness?[36] The answer is: "He told her that he was her father's relative, that he was Rivkah's son." This means that when the tzaddik said the Oral Law, he said it in the aspect of (Hosea 14:10), "Tzaddikim will walk in them, but sinners will stumble in them."[37]

And this is, "that he was her father's relative"—in deceit. This is the aspect of "but sinners will stumble in them." "That he was Rivkah's son"—the virtuous one.[38] This is the aspect of "Tzaddikim will walk in them."

Not only this, but, "She ran and told her father." In other words, this aspect of "but sinners will stumble in them" comes to him more easily. As our Sages taught (Proverbs 8:12), "I, wisdom, dwell with cunning"—<once a> person studies Torah, he acquires cunning (*Sotah* 21b). And this is, "She ran"—it is like a person who runs swiftly and easily; "and told her father"—for the Torah teaches cunning to the learned. And so, "She ran and told her father"—cunning comes more easily and swiftly to a person.[39] This is because holiness requires [waiting for] assistance from Above, as our Sages taught: Someone who comes to purify himself, he receives assistance (*Shabbat* 104a). But cunning is made open—it has many openings (*ibid., Tosafot s.v. iss d'garsy*)—and comes to him easily.[40]

in this world, the lower tzaddik, there is a binding of spirit between them. However, when someone who lacks decency and respect studies the upper tzaddik's teachings, he causes the Oral Law/the Divine Presence to descend into exile. This teaching then becomes a weapon in the mouth of the scholar-demon with which he persecutes the lower tzaddik.

36. Should you wonder.... The root of the word Torah is *horaah* (to teach). The question then is, if the Torah itself is a teacher, why isn't it that...he repents...?

37. tzaddikim...sinners.... "This is the Torah that Moshe *sam* (presented) before the Jewish people" (Deuteronomy 4:44). The Torah is a *sam* (elixir). Studied properly, it is an elixir of life. Studied improperly, it can be a deadly poison (*Yoma* 72b; cf. *Mabuey HaNachal*). See below section 3.

38. in deceit...the virtuous one. Yaakov told Rachel, "If he, [Lavan,] acts with deceit, I am his brother in deceit; but if he is virtuous, I too [will be, for] I am the son of Rivkah, his virtuous sister" (*Rashi*, Genesis 29:12).

39. father...easily and swiftly to a person. See *Likutey Moharan* 10:4 that "father indicates wisdom" (*Megillah* 13a). In this case, the father—Lavan/the scholar-demon—uses his wisdom in order to deceive. This quality of cunning "runs" to a person, it is only too easy to fall into its trap.

40. many openings...comes to him easily. A person inclined toward any aspect of impurity and immorality will find relatively few barriers in his way: one only has to begin seeking the means for achieving his goal and he will find the path open. Such is the nature of this world. This is

LIKUTEY MOHARAN #12:3

ג. וְאִם יִקְשֶׁה לְךָ: אִם הַתַּנָּא הָיָה צַדִּיק גָּמוּר, אֵיךְ בָּא זֶה הַדָּבָר,
שֶׁאוֹמֵר תּוֹרָתוֹ שֶׁיָּכוֹל לִסְבֹּל שְׁנֵי מַשְׁמָעוּת: מַשְׁמָעוּת טוֹב, דְּהַיְנוּ
'צַדִּיקִים יֵלְכוּ בָם' וּמַשְׁמָעוּת לְהִפּוּךְ, דְּהַיְנוּ 'וּפשְׁעִים יִכָּשְׁלוּ בָם'.

אֲבָל דַּע, שֶׁהַתַּנָּא הָיָה צַדִּיק גָּמוּר, וְתוֹרָתוֹ זַכָּה מִבְּלִי פְּסֹלֶת; וּמַה
שֶּׁנִּרְאָה בָּהּ מַשְׁמָעוּת עַרְמוּמִיּוּת, זֶה, כִּי כָּל הָעוֹלָם מְקַבְּלִים
פַּרְנָסָתָם מִשְּׂמֹאלָהּ, כְּמוֹ שֶׁכָּתוּב (מִשְׁלֵי ג): "מִשְּׂמֹאלָהּ עשֶׁר
וְכָבוֹד" – בִּשְׁבִיל זֶה נָפַל הַתַּנָּא בִּשְׁעַת אֲמִירַת תּוֹרָתוֹ לְאֵיזֶה
שְׁגִיאָה דַּקָּה כְּחוּט הַשַּׂעֲרָה, לִבְחִינַת שְׂמֹאלָהּ, כְּדֵי שֶׁעַל-יְדֵי זֶה
בְּחִינַת שְׂמֹאלָהּ יְקַבֵּל שֶׁפַע וּפַרְנָסָתוֹ לְעוֹלָם, וּלְהַמְשִׁיךְ לָהֶם עשֶׁר
וְכָבוֹד, כְּמוֹ שֶׁכָּתוּב: "מִשְּׂמֹאלָהּ עשֶׁר וְכָבוֹד"; אֲבָל מִצַּד הַתַּנָּא

In Kabbalistic terminology, the right always denotes *Chesed* (Lovingkindness) and the left *Gevurah* (Strength). Jews receive their *shefa* from the right, non-Jews from the left. However, during the exile, instead of the *shefa* coming directly to the Jews, it first descends to the gentiles and the Jews receive only the residue (*Zohar* II, 152b).

One who is attached to Torah is attached to the Source of everything—God (above, n.5). It therefore follows that one who studies Torah should have everything good: long life, wealth, glory, health etc., for God is constantly sending *shefa,* abundance. The Talmud therefore asks: Why is long life only on the right side...? It answers: The right, *lishmah,* gets both; the left, only riches and glory.

Long life refers to the World to Come, the spiritual. Obviously, one who studies *lishmah* is interested only in the spiritual aspect of Torah and his outlook is only for the future, as above in note 6. Thus, even though the tzaddik does not seek them, riches and glory descend to the world. However, now that we are in exile, we do not have direct *shefa.* For the Jews to receive any *shefa* at all, we must receive it through the left side. Therefore, the tzaddik must fall to the "left side" to draw *shefa* from there. The fact that the Talmud asks the question "Long life and not riches?" is in itself an aspect of "falling to the left side," the side of only riches and glory, to bring this *shefa.* This question is also the concept of questions that are raised about the tzaddikim. With this introduction, we can now proceed.

42. **the left side.** With the destruction of the Holy Temple, the Jewish people lost the means for receiving their *shefa* of Divine blessing from the right side. Rather, the entire influx of benevolent spiritual energy which descends must be drawn via the less exalted path of the left. In conjunction with this, Rebbe Nachman taught that as long as the Jews are in exile, it is all but impossible for a virtuous person to possess great wealth. It is written (Lamentations 1:9), "And she fell *pla'im* (incredibly)." Rearranged, the letters of *PLA'iM* spell *ALaPhiM* (thousands). We then read the verse, "And the thousands fell." The thousands of wealth have fallen so incredibly...someone who desires them must also fall (*Rabbi Nachman's Wisdom* #4). The *Parparaot LeChokhmah* adds that this is because the *shefa* of wealth has descended into the left of the Other Side.

43. **bring blessing...riches and glory.** Certainly, the right also contains the *shefa* of wealth and

217 **LIKUTEY MOHARAN #12:3**

3. And should you wonder:[41] If the *Tanna* was a perfect tzaddik, how is it possible that he teaches Torah capable of carrying a double entendre—a positive connotation, that the "tzaddikim will walk in them," and an opposite connotation, that "sinners will stumble in them"?

But know! the *Tanna* was a perfect tzaddik. His Torah was pure, without deficiency. That it appears to have in it this sense of cunning, this is [only] because all people receive < livelihood from the left side >.[42] As it is written (Proverbs 3:16), "[Length of days in her right hand,] and in her left hand are riches and glory." This is why the *Tanna* lapsed into some minute and miniscule oversight—corresponding to the left—while relating his teaching; so that < he would be able to bring down blessing > for the world and draw riches and glory to them. As is written, from "her left hand are riches and glory."[43]

---

41. **And should you wonder.** This section will discuss the following verse and the Talmudic teaching concerning it. The verse, referring to Torah, reads, "Length of days is in her right hand, and in her left hand are riches and glory" (Proverbs 3:16). Our Sages ask: Is there only long life in the right? Are there no riches and glory as well? They answer: In the right, there is long life; all the more so riches and glory. But in the left, there is only riches and glory (*Shabbat* 63a). The right means studying *lishmah,* for its own sake; the left, not for its own sake (*Rashi, s.v. l'masmi'ilim bo*).

God is continuously sending *shefa* to this world. The Kabbalistic teachings explain that this *shefa* is systematically channeled into the world by means of the *sefirot* (Divine emanations) which act, so to speak, as vessels for receiving and then passing the influx onward. The process begins with the upper *sefirot* receiving this abundance (see Appendix: The Structure of the Sefirot): *Keter* receives the *shefa* from Above and passes it on to *Chokhmah,* which then channels it to the third *sefirah, Binah.* It filters the influx down through the six lower *sefirot,* known collectively as *Z'er Anpin,* from where it is then given over to the lowest *sefirah, Malkhut,* symbolic of this world.

There are five Divine personas, corresponding to the Ten *Sefirot: Arikh Anpin* to *Keter; Abba* to *Chokhmah; Imma* to *Binah; Z'er Anpin* to *Chesed, Gevurah, Tiferet, Netzach, Hod, Yesod;* and *Nukva* of *Z'er Anpin* to *Malkhut* (see Appendix: The Divine Persona). *Arikh Anpin* is a concept of long life and is inclusive of male/female characteristics. The other four are clearly identified as male (*Abba, Z'er Anpin*) or female (*Imma, Malkhut*) personas. These Divine personas all have defined sides, right (male aspect), left (female aspect) and center (combined aspects). Thus, each concept maintains within it an aspect of the other concepts.

Above these personas is an even higher concept, *Atik,* the Ancient One. *Atik* is so exalted that it cannot be said to have sides. This is the meaning of, "In *Atik* there is no left, in *Atik* all is right" (*Zohar* III, 129a). This indicates that as there are no sides at all, everything is a unity; a singular concept, that concept being entirely kindness and good.

All *shefa* descends from God in the form of "spiritual lights," through the upper levels to the lower, until it reaches this physical world. Each *sefirah* channels these "lights" with less intensity than its predecessor. After the *shefa* reaches the bottom level, it ascends back, seeking to return to its Source (see above, n.14).

LIKUTEY MOHARAN #12:3

אֵין נִפְתָּל וְעִקֵּשׁ.

וְעַל זֶה צָרִיךְ הַלַּמְדָן לֵידַע קֹדֶם לִמּוּדוֹ, שֶׁבְּשָׁעָה שֶׁיּוֹשֵׁב לִלְמֹד, הַצַּדִּיק שֶׁבְּגַן־עֵדֶן צַיֵּת לְקָלָהּ, כְּמוֹ שֶׁכָּתוּב (שִׁיר־הַשִּׁירִים ח): "הַיּוֹשֶׁבֶת בַּגַּנִּים חֲבֵרִים מַקְשִׁיבִים לְקוֹלֵךְ".

וְזֶה: וַיְהִי כִשְׁמֹעַ לָבָן אֶת שֵׁמַע יַעֲקֹב בֶּן אֲחֹתוֹ – הַיְנוּ, כְּשֶׁהַלַּמְדָן יוֹדֵעַ שֵׁמַע יַעֲקֹב, שֶׁיַּעֲקֹב בֶּן אֲחֹתוֹ, בְּחִינַת כַּשְׁרוּת, שֶׁלָּמַד וְאָמַר זֹאת הַתּוֹרָה בְּכַשְׁרוּת לִשְׁמָהּ, וְיַעֲקֹב, הַיְנוּ הַתַּנָּא, צַיֵּת לְקָלָהּ. וַיָּרָץ לִקְרָאתוֹ וַיְחַבֶּק וַיְנַשֶּׁק לוֹ, הַיְנוּ שֶׁעַל־יְדֵי לִמּוּדוֹ מִתְדַּבֵּק רוּחַ הַתַּנָּא בְּרוּחוֹ, זֶה בְּחִינַת נְשִׁיקִין; וַיְבִיאֵהוּ אֶל בֵּיתוֹ – שֶׁמֵּבִיא אֶת רוּחַ הַתַּנָּא לְתוֹךְ הַתּוֹרָה שֶׁלּוֹמֵד עַכְשָׁו, כִּי שָׁם בֵּיתוֹ, כְּמוֹ שֶׁכָּתוּב: "תּוֹצֵא הָאָרֶץ נֶפֶשׁ חַיָּה".

and the *shefa* can properly descend (*Likutey Halakhot, Talmud Torah* 3:5).

It is worth noting that the term here translated as "oversight" is *shegiah* (שגיאה). A *shegiah* is by definition unintentional; it is the type of mistake or blunder committed due to human fallibility, from which even the tzaddik is not immune. Thus, the only way to avoid unintentional error and sin is through Divine assistance. In the case of the perfect tzaddik, the one in whom there is no crookedness, this assistance is always forthcoming. Yet, occasionally, God withholds His assistance so that through the tzaddik's very minor oversight, material sustenance is drawn to the world.

45. **hearken to your voice.** When a person studies Torah, and all the more so when he rises at midnight to study Torah, the Holy One and the tzaddikim in the Garden of Eden hearken to his voice (*Zohar* III, 213a). At midnight, the northern wind of *Gevurah* (from the left side) is mitigated by a southern force of *Chesed* (from the right). When this happens, the Holy One delights with the tzaddikim. Anyone who studies Torah at this time...a benevolent *shefa* begins to descend (*Zohar* I, 92b). *Shefa* is thus associated with Torah and the right side, but now must also come from the left. In the terminology of the Kabbalah, this is symbolized in the preparation for the unification of the Divine persona *Z'er Anpin*/Yaakov with *Malkhut*/Rachel, which begins to take place after midnight (*Pri Etz Chaim, Shaar HaTefillin* 7; see Appendix: The Divine Persona, Alternate Names).

46. **...his home is.** This refers to the learned individual who, unlike the scholar-demon, "knows Yaakov's name"—he studies Torah purely for its own sake. He is the lower tzaddik, corresponding to Binyamin (above, n.14 and 33). After he passes away, the tzaddik returns to the places in this world where he originated Torah insights. This is especially true when others who follow after him speak words of Torah in the same place (*Zohar* III, 220a). Thus, the tzaddik's home can be anywhere, particularly where his teachings are repeated.

47. **earth...living soul.** As explained above in section 1 and notes 20 and 21, the earth is *Malkhut*, the Oral Law, the source of speech. They all correspond to the feminine aspect and therefore to the concept of home, as our Sages taught: A man's home is his wife (*Yoma* 2a).

LIKUTEY MOHARAN #12:3

However, from the *Tanna's* side, there is no crookedness and perversion <whatsoever>.[44]

And in this regard, prior to his studying the learned individual must know that when he sits down to study, the tzaddik, who is in the Garden of Eden, pays heed to his voice. As it is written (Song of Songs 8:13), "You who dwell in the gardens, companions hearken to your voice."[45]

This is, "When Lavan heard the name of Yaakov, his sister's son...." In other words, this is when the learned individual knows of Yaakov's name—that Yaakov is "his sister's son," the aspect of virtuousness—because he <studies> this teaching with virtue and for its own sake. Thus Yaakov—i.e., the *Tanna*—pays heed to his voice.

And "he ran to greet him," embracing and kissing him. That is, through his <proper> studying, the spirit of the *Tanna* becomes bound with his spirit. This is the aspect of *neshikin*. "And brought him into his home"—he brings the spirit of the *Tanna* into the Torah he is now studying. For that is where his home is,[46] as in, "Let the earth bring forth a living soul."[47]

glory, and the tzaddik himself is capable of drawing it down. But, as the *Parparaot LeChokhmah* explains, when one has attained the spiritual level of the right side, it does not even dawn upon him to concern himself with physical sustenance. On the contrary, any physical *shefa* he does receive, he converts to an influx of spirituality. Therefore, he must fall to "the left" to draw material *shefa*.

Elsewhere, Rebbe Nachman taught that establishing supportive proofs from the Torah for rabbinical enactments brings a *shefa* of abundant livelihood to the world. This is because a number of teachings have no apparent source in Scripture and the rabbis labored to find some supporting reference (*Aleph-Bet Book,* Original Torah Insights 2). Furthermore, the *Tikkuney Zohar* (Addendum #6) explains that "from the right side, the Written Law was given, and from the left side, the Oral Law." Thus, the benefits and blessings which should descend from the right, instead descend from the left.

44. **the Tanna's side....** Reb Noson explains that ultimately, the essential source of the *shefa* for wealth is even higher than the left side. It descends from the level of *Atik,* which is called *Mazal* and which is above the distinction between right and left. At this level, *shefa* is unified and without differentiation or form. The benevolent influx of spiritual energy is therefore likened to an absolutely purified light. It is only once the Divine *shefa* descends through the transcendant worlds and reaches this world that it assumes form and corporeality. Thus, as it descends to the levels where right and left exist, it takes on the distinctions of the right side (long life) and the left side (riches and glory). Consequently, the tzaddik must fall to the left to draw *shefa* from there. Yet, when he does this, the tzaddik must be careful not to get caught there. Though he himself is pure, the forces of the Other Side can attempt to overpower him and seize the *shefa* for themselves. This is why the tzaddik, after entering these lower levels of the left, must immediately leap back to the right side. This way, the left is joined with the right

LIKUTEY MOHARAN #12:3   220

וַיְסַפֵּר לְלָבָן – לְשׁוֹן סַפִּיר וָאוֹר, שֶׁרוּחַ הַתַּנָּא מֵאִיר לְהַלַּמְדָן
וּמְבָאֵר לוֹ אֶת הַדְּבָרִים הָאֵלֶּה – פֵּרֵשׁ רַשַׁ"י: שֶׁלֹּא בָא אֶלָּא מִתּוֹךְ
אֹנֶס אָחִיו, שֶׁנָּטַל מִמֶּנּוּ מָמוֹנוֹ; פֵּרוּשׁ, שֶׁרוּחַ הַתַּנָּא מוֹדִיעַ
לְהַלַּמְדָן, שֶׁלֹּא בָא הַתַּנָּא לִבְחִינָה הַזֹּאת, שֶׁיְּסַבֵּל תּוֹרָתוֹ מַשְׁמָעוּת
עַרְמִימִיּוּת, אֶלָּא מִתּוֹךְ אֹנֶס אָחִיו שֶׁנָּטַל מָמוֹנוֹ, כְּדֵי 'בִּשְׂמֹאלָהּ
עֹשֶׁר וְכָבוֹד', כְּדֵי לְהַמְשִׁיךְ לָהֶם שֶׁפַע גַּשְׁמִיּוּת.
כְּשֶׁיֵּדַע הַלַּמְדָן כָּל זֶה, יֹאמַר לָבָן: אַךְ עַצְמִי וּבְשָׂרִי אָתָּה, דְּהַיְנוּ
שֶׁיִּתְקַשֵּׁר הַלַּמְדָן עִם הַתַּנָּא בְּהִתְקַשְׁרוּת גָּדוֹל.

וַיֵּשֶׁב עִמּוֹ חֹדֶשׁ יָמִים – וְיִתְיַשֵּׁב בַּדָּבָר עִם רוּחַ הַתַּנָּא, אֵיךְ לַחֲזֹר
בִּתְשׁוּבָה, לְחַדֵּשׁ יָמָיו שֶׁעָבְרוּ בַּחֹשֶׁךְ, בִּבְחִינַת (תְּהִלִּים ק"ג):
"תִּתְחַדֵּשׁ כַּנֶּשֶׁר נְעוּרָיְכִי".
אֲבָל תַּלְמִיד-חָכָם, שֵׁד יְהוּדִי, אֵינוּ רוֹאֶה כָּל אֵלֶּה וְאֵינוּ שׁוֹמֵעַ
שֶׁמַע בֶּן-אֲחוֹתוֹ;
"וַיֹּאמֶר לוֹ אָחִי אַתָּה" – שֶׁלָּבָן חוֹשֵׁב וְאוֹמֵר, שֶׁגַּם הַתַּנָּא לֹא
אָמַר תּוֹרָתוֹ אֶלָּא בְּעַרְמִימִיּוּת, וְאֵין בָּהּ שׁוּם צַד כַּשְׁרוּת, וְחוֹשֵׁב
שֶׁהוּא אָחִיו בְּרַמָּאוּת, שֶׁכֻּלּוֹ רַמָּאוּת, חַס וְשָׁלוֹם, וְאֵינוֹ רוֹצֶה

---

50. **darkness.** Darkness represents the Other Side. This refers to the days during which he failed to serve God. They remain dark. One must see to renew these days and fill them with spiritual light (*Likutey Moharan* I, 179).

51. **renewed like that of the eagle.** Rashi explains that there is a species of eagle which constantly renews itself. He also quotes the Midrash that there is an eagle which lives for many years and then rejuvinates itself (cf. *Bereishit Rabbah* 19:5; *Tzaddik* #425 and note).

52. **sister's son.** Until this point in the section, Rebbe Nachman has been discussing the scholar who studies the *Tanna's* teaching and is willing to repent. Even so, he is referred to as Lavan. This is because, despite his study of the Torah, the possibility of his becoming a scholar-demon still exists. The Torah can provide him with either wisdom or cunning. Thus, Lavan, which in Hebrew means white, indicates either the cleansing "white" of repentance or the deceiving "white" of the impostor. "When Lavan heard the name of Yaakov, his sister's son..." refers to the virtuous scholar who looks to find Rivkah's quality of vituousness. The scholar-demon, however, does not recognize this quality. When he hears the name of Yaakov, he says, "You are *my* brother..."—cunning and deceitful, just as he himself is.

LIKUTEY MOHARAN #12:3

And "*yeSaPeR* (he told) Lavan.*" This is similar to *SaPiR* (shining) and light. The spirit of the *Tanna* shines to the learned individual and enlightens him on "all that had happened." Rashi explains that [Yaakov told Lavan that] he had not come [bearing gifts] but after having been robbed by his brother who had taken away his money.[48] The meaning is: The *Tanna's* spirit informs the learned individual that the *Tanna* comes to this aspect whereby his teaching carries a sense of cunning only after having been robbed by his brother who has taken his money. This is so that "in her left hand are riches and glory"—in order to draw upon them material blessing.

When the learned individual knows all this, [then] Lavan says, "Yes, indeed, you are my own flesh and blood"—i.e., so that the learned individual should bind himself to the *Tanna* with a very strong attachment. "And he *yeSheV* (dwelled) with him for a *ChoDeSh YaMim* (month's time)." He *yityaSheV* (dwelled) on the matter with the spirit of the *Tanna*,[49] [to determine] how to repent <and> *ChaDeSh YaMav* (renew his days) spent in darkness.[50] This corresponds to (Psalms 103:5), "Your youth is renewed like that of the eagle."[51]

But the scholar-demon does not see all this and does not hear of the name of "his sister's son."[52]

He said to him, "You are my brother." Lavan thinks and says that the *Tanna* also only delivers his teaching with craftiness, and that it hasn't any virtuous aspect. He thinks that [the *Tanna*] is "his brother" in deceit; that everything is deception, God forbid. He does not want

---

48. **robbed...took his money.** When Esav discovered that his brother had made off with the blessings, he decided to kill Yaakov. Their mother, Rivkah, knew of her older son's plan and sent Yaakov away. When he fled, Yaakov took with him money, gold and jewelry. Esav ordered his son to chase after Yaakov and kill him. When Eliphaz caught up with his uncle, Yaakov pleaded with him to spare his life. "A poor man is considered dead" (*Nedarim* 64b), Yaakov told him. Eliphaz consented and took all of Yaakov's wealth instead. In Rebbe Nachman's lesson, this relates to when the Jewish people descend into exile and the *shefa* is first directed to non-Jews, the left side. Because of this, the tzaddik must now fall to the left to bring *shefa*. The *Parparaot LeChokhmah* places particular emphasis on Rebbe Nachman's quoting of Rashi's comment: "...having been robbed...who had taken away *his* money." The tzaddik's temporary descent into the left is to take back what is rightfully his—the *shefa* which should descend to the Jewish people from the right.

49. **bind himself...with the spirit of the Tanna.** Through the concept of *neshikin*, which is as if he were talking with the *Tanna* (as above §1 and nn. 19,23).

LIKUTEY MOHARAN #12:3,4

לַחֲזֹר בִּתְשׁוּבָה, וְדוֹבֵר עַל צַדִּיק עָתָק בְּגַאֲוָה וָבוּז:

ד. וְדַע, שֶׁזֶּה מְכֻוָּן מֵאֵת הַשֵּׁם יִתְבָּרַךְ, שֶׁהַקָּדוֹשׁ־בָּרוּךְ־הוּא מַפִּיל אֵיזֶה צַדִּיק גָּדוֹל בְּפִיו שֶׁל הַלַּמְדָן; הַיְנוּ הַלַּמְדָן דּוֹבֵר רָעוֹת עַל הַצַּדִּיק, כְּדֵי שֶׁהַצַּדִּיק יִקַּח הַתּוֹרָה שֶׁבְּעַל־פֶּה, הַיְנוּ הַשְּׁכִינָה, מֵהַגָּלוּת שֶׁבְּפֶה הַלַּמְדָן, וּמַעֲלֶה אוֹתָהּ לְשָׁרְשָׁהּ מִמַּדְרֵגָה לְמַדְרֵגָה: מִתְּחִלָּה לִבְחִינַת חִבּוּק, וְאַחַר־כָּךְ לִבְחִינַת נְשׁוּק, וְאַחַר־כָּךְ לִבְחִינַת זִוּוּג.

כְּמוֹ שֶׁכָּתוּב (שִׁיר־הַשִּׁירִים ב): "אֲנִי חֲבַצֶּלֶת הַשָּׁרוֹן" – בַּתְּחִלָּה הִיא יְרֻקָּה כַּחֲבַצֶּלֶת, כְּמוֹ שֶׁאָמְרוּ (מְגִלָּה יג): 'אֶסְתֵּר יְרַקְרֹקֶת הָיְתָה'.

---

55. **chibuk...neshuk...zivvug.** As explained above (n.19), man's actions in this physical world both mirror and give rise to corresponding spiritual "actions" in the transcendant worlds. Rebbe Nachman now introduces the Kabbalistic principles of *chibuk, neshuk* and *zivvug*. These are spiritual concepts which precede and give rise to a unification between the Divine personas of *Z'er Anpin* and *Malkhut*. However, before such a unification can take place, it is necessary to gradually elevate *Malkhut* from level to level, from "immaturity" and incompleteness to "maturity" and completeness. This is the building up of *Malkhut* which Rebbe Nachman mentions further on in this section and at the end of the lesson.

At this point, it must be made perfectly clear that **there is absolutely nothing physical nor is there any aspect of corporeality in the transcendant worlds!** This cannot be stressed enough. Any analogy, comparison, or use of terminology such as persona, male, female, right and left etc., is only a means through which the serious student of the Kabbalah can hope to achieve even the minutest grasp of the spiritual realm. As Eliyahu the Prophet warned, **"There exists neither form, nor shape, nor any figure whatsoever, for all is spiritual."** If one is not capable of accepting and believing this, then one should not proceed (see Rabbi Chaim Vital's introduction to *Etz Chaim*). Rather, the reader is advised to skip the footnotes and simply read the text. For Rebbe Nachman's words are filled with *yirat shamayim* (fear of God) and are therefore beneficial even when not understood intellectually. As the Talmud teaches (*Pesachim* 22b): A person should say, "Just as I am rewarded for my study, so shall I be rewarded for not studying [that which is beyond my comprehension]."

56. **rose of Sharon.** The *Shekhinah* (Divine Presence), which is also *Malkhut*/the Oral Law/ Rachel, is likened to the *chavatzelet haSharon* (rose of Sharon). *ShaRon* resembles the word *ShiR* (song), implying that the Divine Presence constantly sings the praise of God. Rebbe Nachman will soon quote the remainder of this verse to show that the Divine Presence is likened to the *shoshanat haamakim* (rose of the valley). Rashi (*loc. cit.*) comments that *chavatzelet* and *shoshanah* are one and the same. This is in agreement with the Midrash that teaches: Is not *chavatzelet* the same as *shoshanah*? While it is yet small it is called *chavatzelet*, but when it is fully grown it is called *shoshanah*. The significance of this distinction will become clearer as the lesson develops.

The Divine Presence is also known as *Knesset Yisrael*—the collective entity of the Jewish

LIKUTEY MOHARAN #12:3,4

to repent and "speaks arrogant words, proudly and contemptuously, against the tzaddik."[53]

4. And know! this is precisely as God intends it. The Holy One causes some great tzaddik to fall into the mouth of the learned individual— i.e., the learned individual speaks wickedly of the tzaddik. This is so that the tzaddik can then free the Oral Law, the Divine Presence, from being exiled in the mouth of the learned.[54] He then elevates her to her Source, from level to level: first to the aspect of *chibuk* (embracing), afterwards to aspect of *neshuk* (kissing), and finally to the aspect of *zivvug* (intimacy).[55]

As it is written (Song of Songs 2:1), "I am the rose of Sharon"[56]—at first she is green like a rose (*Zohar* I, 221a).[57] As [our Sages] taught:

---

53. **speaks arrogant...against the tzaddik.** As explained above (n.37), the Torah is an elixir which Moshe presented before the Jewish people. When it fills the mouth of the virtuous scholar, it causes him to repent. However, when it fills the scholar-demon's mouth, it becomes a deadly poison of arrogant and evil speech.

When Lavan saw Yaakov, he ran to him and hugged and kissed him. This corresponds to the concepts of *chibuk* and *neshuk,* mentioned in the next section. Rashi (Genesis 29:13) explains: Lavan assumed that Yaakov would be bringing great riches. Hadn't Eliezer arrived bearing expensive gifts when he came looking for a wife for Yaakov's father, Yitzchak? And so Lavan ran out to greet his nephew. When he saw no obvious signs of this wealth, he presumed that Yaakov was carrying gold on his person. Lavan hugged his guest, but was again disappointed. Finding nothing hidden there, it occurred to him that perhaps Yaakov had jewels in his mouth and Lavan kissed him. The scholar-demon presumes that the *Tanna* is just like him, hungry for wealth and glory. He further assumes that everything the *Tanna* teaches is only for riches, the left side (*Rabbi Zvi Cheshin*).

In review: It is by Divine design that learned scholars are wont to oppose the tzaddikim. When that which the upper tzaddik originates, the Oral Law, is studied by a righteous person in this world, the lower tzaddik, there is a binding of spirit between them. However, when someone who lacks decency and respect studies the upper tzaddik's teachings, he causes the Oral Law/the Divine Presence to descend into exile. This teaching then becomes a weapon in the mouth of the scholar-demon with which he persecutes the lower tzaddik (§1). This is possible because the nature of Torah is twofold: life-giving in the hands of the lower tzaddik, poisonous in the hands of the scholar-demon (§2). Thus, despite the tzaddik's personal level of righteousness, which he certainly invests into his teaching, an unworthy person can take improper guidance from that teaching of Oral Law. This is because in order to bring livelihood to the world, the tzaddik includes the quality of the left side, which is the aspect of "sinners will stumble in them." This study of Torah not purely for its own sake is used by the scholar-demon to arrogantly oppose the tzaddikim (§3).

54. **from being exiled....** As above in section 1, the Divine Presence/the Oral Law is in exile in the scholar-demon's mouth.

LIKUTEY MOHARAN #12:4 224

וְזֶה בְּחִינַת חִבּוּק – "וִימִינוֹ תְּחַבְּקֵנִי".

כִּי הַשִּׂמְחָה בָּא מֵהַלֵּב, כְּמוֹ שֶׁכָּתוּב (תְּהִלִּים ד): "נָתַתָּה שִׂמְחָה
בְלִבִּי", וְהַלֵּב הוּא בִּינָה, שֶׁשָּׁם יַיִן הַמְשַׂמֵּחַ, שֶׁהוּא עָלְמָא סְתִימָא,
בְּחִינַת (שָׁם קד): "וְיַיִן יְשַׂמַּח לְבַב".

וְהַצַּדִּיק שֶׁנּוֹפֵל לְתוֹךְ פִּי הַלַּמְדָן, שֶׁהַלַּמְדָן דוֹבֵר עָלָיו עָתָק, וְהוּא
מֵבִין שֶׁאֵלּוּ הַדְּבָרִים שֶׁהַלַּמְדָן דוֹבֵר עָלָיו הֵם צְרוּפִים מֵאוֹתִיּוֹת
שֶׁבַּתּוֹרָה שֶׁבְּעַל-פֶּה, וּמֵבִין מֵאֵיזֶה הֲלָכוֹת נַעֲשׂוֹ הַדִּבּוּרִים אֵלּוּ,

62. **wine of joy.** The wine of joy also corresponds to *Binah*. The wine of joy which the *Zohar* (*loc. cit.*) mentions refers to the light of the *chasadim* from *Chokhmah* which passes through *Binah* bringing *shefa* to *Z'er Anpin* and eventually *Malkhut*.

63. **hidden world.** Being one of the three upper *sefirot*, *Binah* itself is part of the hidden world, which allows no revelation of the transcending lights. Yet, there is an aspect of *Binah* which lowers itself, as it were, in order to transport the *shefa* to the lower *sefirot* and particularly to *Malkhut*, the revealed world (cf. *Etz Chaim, Shaar HaKlallim* 11). It is thus taught in the writings of the Ari that *Binah* is the heart, because the heart's understanding is what gives formation and expression to the abstract wisdom of *Chokhmah* (cf. *ibid., Shaar* 31:4; see Appendix: The Sefirot and Man).

As a result of *Binah* lowering itself, a division of sorts is created in the Divine Presence. From the *Zohar* and the Ari's writings we find that the lower of these levels in *Malkhut* retains the name Rachel, whereas the upper, more hidden level, is called Leah (cf. *Etz Chaim* 37:4) or *Tevunah*. Corresponding to these two levels in the Divine Presence, *Z'er Anpin* is also divided into two levels, *Yisrael Sabba* and *Yaakov*. Thus, the Torah (Genesis 32:29) tells us that Yaakov—after having achieved a higher spiritual level—was given a second name. He was called Yisrael. And, as the personification of *Z'er Anpin*, he married two sisters, Leah and Rachel.

The unification of *Yisrael Sabba* and *Tevunah* (Yisrael and Leah) is referred to as the hidden world, whereas that of Yaakov and Rachel is referred to as the revealed world. Accordingly, we find that Rachel was buried along the "open" road, while Leah was buried "inside" the Cave of Makhpelah (*Shaar HaHakdamot* p.374; see above, n.33).

64. **wine that makes the heart rejoice.** With this verse, Rebbe Nachman joins the concepts of wine, joy and heart, all of which are synonymous with *Binah*. Note the order: first *chibuk*, then *Binah*.

65. **tzaddik...understands....** Rebbe Nachman now relates the first part of the lesson to the concepts introduced in this section. The understanding which the tzaddik achieves is also an aspect of *Binah* (*Parparaot LeChokhmah*).

66. **permutations...the Oral Law.** When God decided to create the world, He looked into a blueprint—the Torah—and then permuted creation's building blocks—the Hebrew *aleph-bet*—with which He then gave form to all existence (*Bereishit Rabbah* 1:1; *ibid.*, 18:4). (The Ari teaches that the formation of the letters of the *aleph-bet* took place in *Binah*; *Shaar Maamarei Rashbi* p.135). Because each thing owes its existence to the Torah, it must be in some way referred to in the Book of Torah. This includes even the words of the scholar-

LIKUTEY MOHARAN #12:4

225

Esther was of a greenish complexion *(Megillah 13a).*[58] And this is the aspect of *chibuk*[59]: "His right hand embraces me" *(Song of Songs 2:6).*[60]

For joy comes from the heart, as is written *(Psalms 4:8)*, "You put joy in my heart." And the heart is *Binah* (understanding) *(Tikkuney Zohar, Introduction).*[61] There, [one finds] the wine of joy *(Zohar III, 127a)*[62]—the hidden world[63]—corresponding to *(Psalms 104:15)*, "Wine that makes the heart rejoice."[64]

Now, this tzaddik, [although] he has fallen into the mouth of the learned individual who speaks arrogantly against him, he understands[65] that the things which the learned individual says of him are really permutations of the letters of the Oral Law.[66] He also understands from which particular laws these words originate. He

---

people. The relationship which *Knesset Yisrael/Malkhut* has with the Holy King/*Z'er Anpin* is that of a bride and groom. Thus, it is generally *Z'er Anpin* which provides for *Malkhut*. Yet, before the groom can give to his bride, she must first become "fully-grown." Primarily, this is achieved through *Binah* (*Imma*, mother) and *Chokhmah* (*Abba*, father). *Binah* raises *Malkhut* by directly providing it with the so-called spiritual energy needed for growth. Even so, it is *Chokhmah* that is *Malkhut's* root—the fundamental source of its light, as in, "*Abba* established the daughter" (*Zohar* III, 288a). It is to these different stages of *Malkhut's* development that the lesson now turns.

57. **green....** There are times when the rose/*Malkhut* is green and is called *chavatzelet*. This is when it receives from *Binah* which is *yarok*, the green line. When fully grown, the rose/*Malkhut* is red and has six petals. This is when *Malkhut* receives from all six *sefirot* of *Z'er Anpin*. At this point it is called *ShoShanah* (שושנה), which connotes *SheSh* (שש, six). When likened to a *chavatzelet*, the Divine Presence is receiving *chasadim* (benevolences) from *Binah*. This is the *chibuk*, and through it *Malkhut* is built up. It becomes *shoshanat haamakim* when it receives the *gevurot* (severities) from *Z'er Anpin*. And, as explained above (n.44), when benevolences and severities (*chasadim* and *gevurot*, right and left) are joined, the *shefa* can properly descend.

58. **Esther...complexion.** Esther is also compared to *Malkhut* (see Lesson #10, n.96). The name eSTheR carries the connotation haSTeR which means hidden (*Chullin* 139a), alluding to the Divine Presence being hidden and concealed from man.

Thus, "Esther was of a greenish complexion" alludes to those times when *Malkhut* directly receives *chasadim* from *Binah*.

59. **chibuk.** The concept of *chibuk* is manifested when *Malkhut* is "embraced" by and receiving from *Binah*, as will be explained.

60. **right hand embraces me.** Because the *shefa* has fallen to the left side, a rectification will necessitate the presence of an aspect of the right side. When their forces fuse, the influx can descend (see above, nn.44,57).

61. **the heart is Binah.** The exact language of this *Tikkuney Zohar* reads: *Binah* (בינה) is the heart, and with it the heart understands (מבין). From this we can conclude that because the seat of joy is in the heart, joy, heart and *Binah* are one concept.

LIKUTEY MOHARAN #12:4

וּמְקַבֵּל אוֹתָם בְּשִׂמְחָה וּבְאַהֲבָה, כְּמוֹ שֶׁאָמְרוּ חֲכָמֵינוּ, זִכְרוֹנָם לִבְרָכָה (שַׁבָּת פח:): 'הַנֶּעֱלָבִים וְכוּ', שְׂמֵחִים בְּיִסּוּרִים וְעוֹשִׂים מֵאַהֲבָה'. וְאַהֲבָה, שֶׁהַצַּדִּיק מְקַבֵּל אֶת הַחֶרְפָּה בְּאַהֲבָה, זֶה בְּחִינַת חִבּוּק, "וִימִינוֹ תְּחַבְּקֵנִי"; וְעַל-יְדֵי הַשִּׂמְחָה שֶׁשָּׂמֵחַ בַּיִּסּוּרִין [הוּא] מַעֲלֶה לִבְחִינַת "אֲנִי חֲבַצֶּלֶת הַשָּׁרוֹן", לִבְחִינַת לֵב, כְּמוֹ שֶׁכָּתוּב: "נָתַתָּה שִׂמְחָה בְלִבִּי"; וְאָז הוּא בִּבְחִינַת (תְּהִלִּים ע"ג): "צוּר לְבָבִי", שֶׁבִּבְחִינַת תּוֹרָה שֶׁבְּעַל-פֶּה הַנִּקְרֵאת צוּר, כַּמּוּבָא בַּתִּקּוּנִים (תִּקּוּן כ"א מג.): 'אִלְמָלֵא לֹא הִכָּה מֹשֶׁה רַבֵּנוּ, עָלָיו הַשָּׁלוֹם, אֶת הַצּוּר, לֹא הָיוּ צְרִיכִין לִטְרֹחַ כָּל-כָּךְ בַּתּוֹרָה שֶׁבְּעַל-פֶּה'.

וְזֶה בְּחִינַת (בְּרֵאשִׁית י"ד): "וַיָּרֶק אֶת חֲנִיכָיו", שֶׁאַבְרָהָם הוּא בְּחִינַת יָמִין, בְּחִינַת חִבּוּק; 'וַיָּרֶק' – זֶה בְּחִינַת קַו הַיָּרֹק, שֶׁנִּמְשָׁךְ

Reb Noson explains: King David epitomizes *Malkhut* (Kingship) and is therefore synonymous with the Oral Law (see end of lesson and n.12 above). Rebbe Nachman calls the tzaddik who reveals Torah insights a "wall" (below, commentary on Rabbah bar bar Chanah). Thus, because he was the Torah-teaching-tzaddik who fell to the left side in order to deliver riches to the world, King David was actually the source of Naval's great wealth. Naval, on the other hand, was the Jewish scholar-demon who demeans the tzaddik, the one who studies the Oral Law *lishmah*. Naval displayed this arrogance precisely when he was shearing his sheep— i.e., studying the Oral Law. He did not study purely for its own sake and, as a result, had been unable to clarify the law at its root and elevate it to the right side. He therefore perverted the law and made false accusations against King David. His riches remained attached to the left side and Naval became an opponent to the true tzaddik (*Likutey Halakhot, Reishit HaGez* 5:2).

We can take this even further. After refusing to help King David, Naval made a big feast. During the festivities he became drunk. Later, when he discovered that his wife had given supplies to King David and his men, the verse (37) states, "His heart died within him, and he became like an *evan* (stone)." The wine which Naval had drunk was not the wine of joy. On the contrary, it was the wine of drunkenness, and it brought him to depression. "His heart," the seat of joy, "died within him." We are further told that "he became like a stone," that is, even the Torah knowledge he had acquired died. Rather than a *tsur* (rock), the Oral Law which can be elevated to the heart, he was left like an *evan* (stone). As Rebbe Nachman points out at the end of the lesson, the tzaddik ultimately removes whatever sparks of holiness the scholar-demon has and by doing so, puts him to death. This is as the Ari teaches: Naval was reincarnated as a stone (*Shaar HaGilgulim* 22).

71. **This also.** Here, Rebbe Nachman resumes building the connections between the various concepts, tying *chibuk/yemin* (the right side) to *Binah*/green.

72. **Avraham...right...chibuk.** Avraham is known as (Isaiah 41:8), "Avraham my beloved." He is *Chesed*, Lovingkindness incarnate. Avraham is therefore symbolic of the right, and the right side is *chibuk*, as in, "His right hand embraces me."

227   *LIKUTEY MOHARAN #12:4*

accepts [the scholar-demons arrogant words] joyously and with love, as our Sages taught: Those who are insulted...rejoice in their suffering and act out of love (*Shabbat* 88b).

And <this> love, that the tzaddik accepts humiliation with love, is the aspect of *chibuk*: "His right hand embraces me."[67] By means of the joy that results from his rejoicing in the suffering, he elevates [the Divine Presence], the aspect of "I am the rose of Sharon," to the aspect of heart, as in, "You put joy in my heart."[68] Then he is in the aspect of "rock of my heart" (Psalms 73:26), corresponding to the Oral Law, which is called a rock.[69] As is brought in the *Tikkuney Zohar* (#21, p.43a): Had Moshe Rabbeinu, of blessed memory, not hit the rock, we would not have to labor so hard in the Oral Law.[70]

This also[71] corresponds to (Genesis 14:14), "And [Avraham] *yarek* (called out) *et chanikhav* (his trained servants)." Avraham is the aspect of right, corresponding to *chibuk*.[72] The word "*YaReK*"

---

demon. They, too, are rooted in the Torah, in the permutations of the Oral Torah. Recognizing that root, the tzaddik is able to elevate the scholar-demon's corrupted permutations and, by connecting them to their origin, rectify them.

67. **love...chibuk...embraces me.** An embrace is a sign of love. It is performed by the right hand, the side of *Chesed* (Lovingkindness) (*Parparaot LeChokhmah*). This will soon be connected to *yemin* (the right side) and to Avraham whose quality is love.

68. **joy in my heart.** By rejoicing in his suffering, the tzaddik elevates the Divine Presence which, through the right handed *chibuk,* is brought to the level of *Binah.* This is bringing joy into the heart.

69. **Oral Law...rock.** The Oral Law/*Malkhut,* synonymous with "rock," is elevated to the heart, the concept of *Binah.* The Hebrew for heart is *lev* (לב). The Written Law, which is the root of the Oral Law, starts with a *Bet* (ב) and ends with a *Lamed* (ל), alluding to the Oral Law being elevated to the *lev.*

70. **Moshe...hit the rock....** This corresponds to what Rebbe Nachman taught earlier that the tzaddik falls to the left side in order to draw *shefa.* However, he must take care to immediately return to the right side (see above n.44). Moshe fell to the left side to bring the Jews water in the desert. But, instead of speaking to the *tsur* (rock), he *struck* it twice (Numbers 20:7-14). Though sufficient water (*shefa*) proceeded to flow from it, his action was one of falling to the left side and not returning immediately. As a result, to this very day, all those who study the Oral Law/the rock, must labor to understand it (*Mabuey HaNachal*).

Reb Noson shows how this is connected to the story of King David and Naval (1 Samuel 25). Prior to becoming king, David and his men protected Naval's flocks. Once, at a time when these sheep were being sheared, he requested that the wealthy Naval provide him and his men with some food and drink. Naval arrogantly refused, demeaning King David in the process. However, one of the shepherds presented King David's request to Naval's wife, Avigayil, saying (v.16), "They were a wall for us...." Avigayil herself then brought supplies to King David.

LIKUTEY MOHARAN #12:4

228

מְבִינָה וּמַקִּיף אֶת כָּל הָעוֹלָם. וַחֲנִיכָיו זֶה בְּחִינַת חֲסָדִים, כַּמּוּבָא
בַּמִּדְרָשׁ (בְּרֵאשִׁית רַבָּה מג), לְשׁוֹן חֲנִיכָתוֹ, שֶׁשְּׁמָן אַבְרָהָם כִּשְׁמוֹ;
הַיְנוּ שֶׁקַּו הַיָּרֹק מִבְּחִינַת אֲנִי חֲבַצֶּלֶת, בְּחִינַת אֶסְתֵּר יְרַקְרֹקֶת, זֹאת
עָלֶיהָ יֵשׁ לַשְּׁכִינָה עַל־יְדֵי חִבּוּק יָמִין.

וְעִקָּר בִּנְיָנָהּ עַל־יְדֵי חָכְמָה, שֶׁאָז רְאוּיָהּ לְזִוּוּג, כְּמוֹ שֶׁכָּתוּב
(בְּרֵאשִׁית כ): "וְגַם אָמְנָה אֲחוֹתִי בַת אָבִי אַךְ לֹא בַת אִמִּי" וְכוּ',
וְאָז: "וַתְּהִי לִי לְאִשָּׁה", שֶׁאָז הִיא רְאוּיָה לְזִוּוּג (כַּמּוּבָא בַּזֹּהַר אֱמֹר ק:
רַבִּי אַבָּא שָׁלַח לֵהּ לְרַבִּי שִׁמְעוֹן, אָמַר: אֵימָתַי זִוּוּגָא דִּכְנֶסֶת־יִשְׂרָאֵל בְּמַלְכָּא
קַדִּישָׁא? שָׁלַח לֵהּ: וְגַם אָמְנָה וְכוּ' עַיֵּן שָׁם).
וְאִיתָא בְּפֵרוּשׁ סִפְרָא דִּצְנִיעוּתָא, שֶׁהַנְּשִׁיקִין הִיא עַל־יְדֵי הַחָכְמָה,
כְּשֶׁנִּתְעוֹרְרִים הַשְּׂפָתַיִם עֶלְיוֹנִים, שֶׁהֵן נֶצַח וָהוֹד עֶלְיוֹנִים, לִבְחִינַת

The *Parparaot LeChokhmah* adds that this verse, "He called out his trained servants," was said of Avraham when he went into battle against the Four Kings, who had taken his nephew Lot captive. In rescuing Lot, Avraham was in essence saving all of Lot's descendants and particularly King David—the personification of *Malkhut*/the Oral Law (end of lesson and n.12 above). Through the power of the right side/Avraham/*Chesed, Malkhut* was freed and elevated to *Binah*.

75. **rose of Sharon/Esther....** See above notes 58-59, that this refers to the Divine Presence, *Malkhut*.

76. **chibuk from the right.** As explained, with the power of the right side, *Binah* encircles everything below it, including *Malkhut*—the Divine Presence.

77. **daughter of my father...not...mother.** See Genesis (*loc. cit.*) that this was Avraham's explanation to Avimelekh for why he had called his wife Sarah, "my sister." In fact, Sarah was Avraham's father's granddaughter and Avraham's niece, the daughter of his half-brother Haran. However, as Rashi explains, grandparent's consider their children's children as their own. Thus, Avraham could call her his sister and yet take her for his wife. In terms of the lesson, see note 56 that the Divine Presence/*Malkhut* is actually rooted in the persona of *Abba*/*Chokhmah*. The "daughter" therefore gravitates, as it were, to the "father"—*Malkhut* to *Chokhmah*—in order to receive the light as directly as possible (cf. *Likutey Moharan* I, 1). Thus, when *Binah* has embraced and elevated *Malkhut*, the Divine Presence is that much closer to *Chokhmah* and is therefore more prepared for unification (see next note).

78. **Knesset Yisrael with the Holy King.** See above note 56 that this refers to the *zivvug* which unites the Divine Presence/*Malkhut* with the Holy One/*Z'er Anpin*. This process is begun when *Chokhmah*, the provider of the *chasadim*, channels these benevolences into *Binah*. From there, the *chasadim* descend to *Malkhut* and bring about a unification between the Holy King and Knesset Yisrael. This is the meaning of the Divine Presence being the father's daughter— the *shefa* descends from *Chokhmah*—but not the mother's daughter—because *Binah* is merely the channel for the light of the *chasadim* and not its source.

LIKUTEY MOHARAN #12:4

alludes to the line of *YaRoK* (green) which is drawn from *Binah* and encircles the entire world (cf. *Chagigah* 12a).[73] "*ChaNiKhav*" alludes to benevolences, as the Midrash comments: It is similar to *ChaNiKhato* (his surname) in that all of them were named Avraham after him (*Bereishit Rabbah* 43:2).[74] In other words, this green line, which corresponds to "the rose of Sharon"/"Esther was of a greenish complexion,"[75] is the elevation which the Divine Presence has through *chibuk* from the right.[76]

{"In any case, she really is my sister; the daughter of my father, but not the daughter of my mother. She [later] became my wife" (Genesis 20:12).}

Now, [the Divine Presence] is essentially built up through *Chokhmah* (Wisdom). Then she is suitable for *zivvug*, as is written, "In any case, she really is my sister; the daughter of my father, but not the daughter of my mother."[77] And then, "she became my wife"—for then [the Divine Presence] is suitable for intimacy. {As is brought in the *Zohar* (III, 100b): Rabbi Abba sent to Rabbi Shimon, saying, "When is the *zivvug* of *Knesset Yisrael* with the Holy King?"[78] His reply was, "In any case, she really is my sister...."}

73. **line of YaRoK, green....** This line is what brings darkness to the world (*Chagigah* 12a). The Maharsha (*loc. cit.*) explains that this is the heavenly force which causes darkness to descend at nightfall and the *Tikkuney Zohar* (#18, p.36a) relates this to the *tohu* which existed at the beginning of creation. The sources also relate the line of green to *Binah* (*Tikkuney Zohar*, Introduction; *Etz Chaim* 39:10). As the persona of *Imma*, *Binah* is "the mother sitting on the chicks" (Deuteronomy 22:6) and thus encircles the seven lower *sefirot* (for each *sefirah* encompasses that which is below it). The encircling of *Z'er Anpin* and *Malkhut* by *Binah* indicates the concept of embracing (*Parparaot LeChokhmah*).

Within the context of our lesson, this relates to Yaakov/*Z'er Anpin* working seven years in order to wed Rachel/*Malkhut*. And Yaakov as the upper tzaddik labored at tending the sheep, symbolic of the Oral Law itself (above §1). The Torah (Genesis 29:20) tells us that for Yaakov the seven years "seemed like *yamim aChaDim* (a few days)"; which the *Zohar* (I, 153b) explains as "unified days" because Yaakov unified the seven years—the seven *sefirot*—as *eChaD* (one). The *Biur HaLikutim* adds that although Yaakov worked for Rachel/*Malkhut*, the revealed world, he first married Leah/*Binah*, the hidden world (Leah is both lower *Binah* and upper *Malkhut*; cf. n.63). This was because he first had to ascend to *Binah*, the source of *chibuk*, so as to be able to bind everything together.

74. **named Avraham after him.** Avraham's *chanikhav* (trained servants) were people whom he had taught and "trained" to believe in the One God. Because he had converted them, his servants all took the name Avraham (as is now customary for converts to do). The *Matnat Kehunah* (*loc. cit.*) points out that the word *chaNIKhaV* resembles *KINuyaV* (name, nickname), indicating that they were all named after him. Rebbe Nachman takes this even further to show that they also took Avraham's quality of lovingkindness. Thus, the *chibuk* from the right side, from Avraham, denotes encircling the *Malkhut* with *chasadim* (benevolences), so that it may ascend to *Binah* (*Parparaot LeChokhmah*). See above note 57.

LIKUTEY MOHARAN #12:4

230

זִוּוּג, לִבְחִינַת הִתְדַּבְּקוּת רוּחָא בְּרוּחָא, אֲזַי נִתְעוֹרְרִין נֶצַח וָהוֹד
תַּחְתּוֹנִים לְזִוּוּג, לְאִתְדַּבְּקָא גוּפָא בְּגוּפָא.

נִמְצָא, כְּשֶׁהַצַּדִּיק מַשְׂכִּיל בְּחָכְמָתוֹ וְיוֹדֵעַ מֵאֵיזֶה צֵרוּפִין שֶׁל תּוֹרָה
שֶׁבְּעַל-פֶּה נַעֲשָׂה אֵלוּ הַצֵּרוּפִין שֶׁהַהַלְמְדָן דּוֹבֵר עָלָיו, וְהַצַּדִּיק
לוֹמֵד אֵלוּ הַצֵּרוּפִין וְעוֹשֶׂה מֵהֶם צֵרוּף הֲלָכָה שֶׁהָיָה מִקֹּדֶם
שֶׁנִּתְקַלְקֵל – כְּשֶׁיֵּשׁ לוֹ זֹאת הַחָכְמָה, אֲזַי עַל-יְדֵי הַחָכְמָה הַזֹּאת
הַשְּׁכִינָה הִיא מִבְּחִינוֹת (שִׁיר-הַשִּׁירִים ב): "שׁוֹשַׁנַּת הָעֲמָקִים",
מִבְּחִינַת נְשִׁיקִין, בְּחִינַת "שִׂפְתוֹתָיו שׁוֹשַׁנִּים", בְּחִינַת אִתְדַּבְּקוּת
רוּחָא בְּרוּחָא, וְאָז מִתְעוֹרֵר זִוּוּגָא דְּגוּפָא בְּגוּפָא,
שֶׁהַשְּׁכִינָה בֵּין תְּרֵין צַדִּיקַיָּא יָתְבָא, בֵּין צַדִּיק עֶלְיוֹן, שֶׁהוּא הַתַּנָּא
שֶׁחִדֵּשׁ זֹאת הַתּוֹרָה וְעַכְשָׁו מַשְׁפִּיעַ בָּהּ, וּבֵין צַדִּיק הַתַּחְתּוֹן,

point, the building up of *Malkhut* is complete. The rose can now be called a *shoshanah*. Its petals are now six and the *gevurot* it has received have turned it red. *Malkhut*/Rachel is now ready to be truly united with *Z'er Anpin*/Yaakov. Thus, the *zivvug* of the upper lips which binds spirit with spirit has initiated a *zivvug* of the lower *Netzach* and *Hod* which, together with *Yesod*, bring about the "maturing" of *Malkhut*. The unification of the Holy King and *Knesset Yisrael* for the transference of *shefa* can now take place.

It is vis-a-vis the unification of the upper *Netzach* and *Hod* of *Chokhmah* that the unification of *Z'er Anpin* and *Malkhut* is referred to as the binding of body with body.

82. **his wisdom.** This indicates *Chokhmah*, unlike Rebbe Nachman's previous mention of the tzaddik's understanding the letter permutations (above, n.66), which corresponds to *Binah*. Thus, as opposed to the earlier process of *chibuk*, we now have the *neshikin* which the tzaddik awakens through his wisdom (*Mabuey HaNachal*).

83. **words...originate.** That is, he locates the source of these arrogant words in the Oral Torah. See above, note 66.

84. **rose of the valleys.** As explained, this is when the rose has fully matured, when *Malkhut* is ready to unite with *Z'er Anpin*, something which can only occur after the "lower three" have been roused through the *neshikin*.

85. **lips like roses.** That is, the Divine Presence/the rose is likened to the upper lips which, through *neshikin*, are roused to unification.

86. **resides between two tzaddikim.** Rebbe Nachman now connects this entire structure to the very beginning of the lesson. As we've seen, the upper tzaddik/*Z'er Anpin* is the origin of the Oral Law/the Divine Presence. The lower tzaddik, who with his study has used his wisdom and understanding to rouse the origin of this teaching of Oral Law, elevates the Oral Law/the Divine Presence back to its source and thereby brings about the unification (*Parparaot LeChokhmah*).

231 *LIKUTEY MOHARAN #12:4*

We also find in a commentary to *Sifra De'Tzniuta*[79] that *neshikin* is the result of *Chokhmah*.[80] When the upper lips, which are the upper *Netzach* (Victory) and *Hod* (Splendor), are roused to the aspect of *zivvug*—to the binding of spirit with spirit—then the lower *Netzach* and *Hod* are roused to *zivvug*—to binding body with body.[81]

Consequently, when the tzaddik applies his wisdom[82] and determines from which sets of letters of the Oral Law these <words> which the learned individual speaks against him originate,[83] and the tzaddik studies these letter permutations and makes of them the letter permutations of law which they had been <previously, before> they were corrupted; then, when [the tzaddik] has this wisdom, this wisdom causes the Divine Presence to be in the aspect of "the rose of the valleys" (Song of Songs 2:1).[84] This is the aspect of *neshikin,* as in (Songs 5:13), "his lips like roses."[85] It is the binding of spirit with spirit, which then gives rise to a *zivvug* of body with body.

For "the Divine Presence resides between two tzaddikim"[86]: between the upper tzaddik—the *Tanna* who originated this teaching and now [continues to] fill it with an influx, and the lower tzaddik—

---

79. **Sifra De'Tzniuta.** Literally, "The Book of the Hidden," it appears as part of the *Zohar* (II, 176ff) and is divided into "five books" paralleling the Five Books of the Torah. Encompassing some of the deepest mysteries of the Kabbalah, there are those who attribute this esoteric teaching to the Patriarch Yaakov. The commentary to *Sifra De'Tzniuta* referred to here is *Shaar Maamarei Rashbi,* one of the *Shmonah Shaarim* (Eight Gates) of the teachings of the Ari which were collated and written by Rabbi Chaim Vital.

80. **neshikin...Chokhmah.** *Neshikin,* the binding of spirit with spirit, can only take place when some aspect of *Chokhmah* itself descends to *Malkhut*. This will be made clear in the following note.

81. **upper lips...body to body.** Here, Rebbe Nachman incorporates the explanation of the abovementioned section of the *Zohar* in which the Ari speaks about the rose of Sharon, the rose of the valley, *chibuk, neshuk, zivvug,* etc. (*Shaar Maamarei Rashbi,* p.32). Very briefly, when *Malkhut* receives from *Binah,* the light of the *chasadim* is transferred to *Malkhut* via *Chesed, Gevurah* and *Tiferet* (referred to here as the "upper three"). These three correspond to the upper part of the torso and the two hands with which *chibuk* is achieved, as in, "His left hand is under my head and his right hand embraces me." However, *Malkhut/chavatzelet* remains incomplete. It is green and does not yet have all six petals that will grace it when it is fully mature and called "*shoshanah*" (see n.56). To achieve *Malkhut's* completion, there must first be a process of *neshikin*. This occurs when the "upper lips" (*Netzach* and *Hod* of *Chokhmah*) are awakened to bind spirit with spirit. And this union of the upper *Netzach* and *Hod* rouses the lower *Netzach* and *Hod*. In the unification which follows, *Malkhut* receives the light of the *gevurot* from *Z'er Anpin*. It is transferred through *Netzach, Hod, Yesod* (referred to here as the "lower three"; see Appendix: The Structure of the Sefirot). At this

LIKUTEY MOHARAN #12:4,5

הַלּוֹמֵד לְהַתּוֹרָה וּמַעֲלֶה לְהַשְּׁכִינָה מַיִּין נוּקְבִין כְּדֵי שֶׁתִּתְדַּבֵּק.
וְזֶה: "שִׂפְתוֹתָיו שׁוֹשַׁנִּים", עַל־יְדֵי בְּחִינַת נְשִׁיקִין; "נֹטְפוֹת מוֹר
עֹבֵר" – לָשׁוֹן מֵעֵבֶר לְעֵבֶר, הַיְנוּ שֶׁנּוֹטֵף לְהַשְּׁכִינָה רֵיחַ טוֹב מִשְּׁנֵי
עֲבָרִים, מִצַּדִּיק עֶלְיוֹן וּמִצַּדִּיק תַּחְתּוֹן, וְזֶה: 'הַדּוּדָאִים נָתְנוּ רֵיחַ',
שֶׁשְּׁנֵי דוֹדִים, הַיְנוּ שְׁנֵי הַצַּדִּיקִים, נָתְנוּ רֵיחַ:

ה. וְזֶה שֶׁאָמַר רַבָּה בַּר בַּר־חָנָה: לְדִידִי חֲזֵי לִי הוּרְמִיז בַּר לִילִיתָא, דַּהֲוָה קָא רָהֵט אַקּוּפָא דְשׁוּרָא דְּמָחוֹזָא, וּרְהֵט פָּרָשָׁא כִּי רָכֵב סוּסְיָא מִתַּתָּאֵי, וְלָא יָכֵיל לֵהּ. זִמְנָא חֲדָא הֲוֵי מְסָרְגִין לֵהּ תַּרְתֵּי חֵיוָתָא וְקָיְמִין אַתְּרֵי גִּשְׁרֵי דְּדוֹנַג, וְשַׁוֵּר מֵהַאי לְהַאי וּמֵהַאי לְהַאי, וּנְקַט תְּרֵי כָּסָא דְּחַמְרָא בִּידֵהּ וּמוֹרֵק מֵהַאי לְהַאי, וְלָא נָטְפֵי מִנַּיְהוּ נִטְפָא לְאַרְעָא. וְאוֹתוֹ הַיּוֹם יַעֲלוּ שָׁמַיִם

רַשְׁבַּ"ם:

הוּרְמִיז – שֵׁד הוּא, כְּדְאָמְרִינָן בְּסַנְהֶדְרִין: מִפַּלְגָּךְ לְתַתָּאֵי דְּהוּרְמִיז. אַקּוּפָא דְּשׁוּרָא – עַל שְׁנֵי הַחוֹמָה; וְהַאי עֲבְדָא, לְהוֹדִיעַ צִדְקוֹתָיו שֶׁל הַקָּדוֹשׁ־בָּרוּךְ־הוּא, שֶׁמְּרַחֵם עַל בְּרִיּוֹתָיו וְאֵינוּ נוֹתֵן רְשׁוּת לְאֵלּוּ לְהַזִּיק, וְגַם שֶׁלֹּא לָצֵאת בַּדֶּרֶךְ יְחִידִי. וּרְהֵט פָּרָשָׁא – לְפִי תֻּמּוֹ. וְלָא יָכֵיל לֵהּ – שֶׁהָיָה הַשֵּׁד רָץ בְּיוֹתֵר. וּמִיהוּ, הַפָּרָשׁ לֹא הָיָה מִתְכַּוֵּן לְכָךְ. מְסָרְגִין – שֶׁהָיָה אָכַף וְסַרְגָּא נְתוּנִין עַל הַפְּרָדוֹת. אַתְּרֵי גִּשְׁרֵי דְּדוֹנַג – שָׁם אוֹתוֹ נָהָר, וְהָיוּ רְחוֹקִים זֶה מִזֶּה, וְהַשֵּׁד מְדַלֵּג מִפְּרִדָה זוֹ לְפִרִדָה זוֹ. תַּרְתֵּי כָּסֵי דְּחַמְרָא – שְׁנֵיהֶם מְלֵאִים יַיִן. וַהֲוָה מוֹרֵק – תַּרְוַיְהוּ בְּיַחַד, זֶה בְּתוֹךְ זֶה, בַּהֲדֵי דְּקָא מְשַׁוֵּר, וְאֵין נִשְׁפָּךְ אֲפִלּוּ טִפָּה אַחַת, וְאַף־עַל־פִּי שֶׁהָיָה אוֹתוֹ הַיּוֹם רוּחַ־סְעָרָה, שֶׁהָיוּ עוֹלִים יוֹרְדֵי הַיָּם בָּאֲנִיּוֹת עַד לֵב הַשָּׁמַיִם וְיוֹרְדִים עַד תְּהוֹמוֹת מִכֹּחַ הָרוּחַ, וְאַף־עַל־פִּי־כֵן לֹא נָפְלָה טִפָּה לָאָרֶץ. יַעֲלוּ שָׁמַיִם וְגוֹ' – פָּסוּק הוּא גַּבֵּי

---

with levels higher than it. This motivates the higher levels to send even more *shefa* (cf. Lesson #11, n.77).

88. **side to side.** The Hebrew for "flowing," *over* (עובר), also connotes from side to side, *m'eiver l'eiver* (מעבר לעבר).

89. **gave fragrance to the Divine Presence.** As opposed to the scholar-demon who is worse than a carcass and gives off foul odors (*Mabuey HaNachal*). Cf. *Likutey Moharan* I, 2 end.

In review: When the Oral Law which upper tzaddik originates is studied by a righteous person—i.e., the lower tzaddik—there is a binding of spirit between them. However, when

233   LIKUTEY MOHARAN #12:4,5

who studies this teaching and raises < [the Divine Presence] in order to bring > feminine waters[87] so that she will bind herself [with the Holy King].

And this is the meaning of "his lips like roses"—through the aspect of *neshikin*; "they drip flowing myrrh" (Song of Songs 5:13)—[flowing] from side to side.[88] In other words, a pleasant fragrance drips on the Divine Presence from both sides, from the upper tzaddik and from the lower tzaddik. And thus, "the *DuDa'im* (mandrakes) gave fragrance" (Songs 7:14). The two *DoDim* (beloveds), i.e., the two tzaddikim, "gave fragrance" [to the Divine Presence].[89]

5. This is what Rabbah bar bar Chanah recounted: I myself saw Hurmiz the son of Lilit. He was running along the top of the wall of Machoza. A *parasha* (cavalryman) moving swiftly on a horse down below could not overtake him. Once, two mules were saddled for him. They stood on two bridges of the Donag. He leaped back and forth from one to the other, holding two cups of wine in his hands. And he *morek* (poured) from one cup to the other, without dripping any of it on the ground, though it was a day of "rising up to the sky and

Rashbam:

Hurmiz - a demon. As is taught in *Sanhedrin* (39a), From your waist down belongs to Hurmiz: **along the top of the wall** - on the edge of the wall. This incident points to God's righteousness. He has mercy on His creations. He does not allow these demons to do harm and advises against traveling on the road alone: **a cavalryman moving swiftly** - he did so unintentionally: **could not overtake him** - because the demon ran much faster; though the cavalryman was not thinking about this: **were saddled** - a saddle and strap had been placed on the mules: **on two bridges of the Donag** - this was the name of the river. The bridges were distant from each other, yet the demon would leap from one mule to the other: **two cups of wine** - both were filled with wine: **And he poured** - both of them at once, one into the other, while leaping. Yet, not even a single drop spilled, despite the fact that on that day it was so stormy that anyone who was travelling by ship was tossed up to the sky and then down to the depths by the strong winds. Even so, not a drop fell to the ground: **rising up to the sky -**

---

87. **feminine waters.** "Feminine waters" is the spiritual energy which ascends from below and is symbolic of man's fulfillment of the Divine will. This is in contrast to "masculine waters," which is the Kabbalistic term for spiritual energy which descends from Above and symbolizes the flow of *shefa* which God benevolently provides for man.

The studying of Oral Law which the lower tzaddik engages in, specifically the rectification of the scholar-demon's evil speech, raises the Divine Presence to be unified

יֵרְדוּ תְהוֹמוֹת הֲוָה, וְשִׁמְעַת יוֹרְדֵי הַיָּם בִּתְהִלִּים. שִׁמְעַת בֵּי מַלְכוּתָא וּקְטַלֵּהּ. מַלְכָּא וּקְטַלֵּהּ – מַלְכָּא דְּשִׁידָא, שֶׁאֵין דַּרְכּוֹ שֶׁל שֵׁד לְהֵרָאוֹת לִבְנֵי־

אָדָם, וַהֲרָגוּהוּ מִפְּנֵי שֶׁהָיָה מְגַלֶּה סוֹדָם. וְאִית דְּאָמְרֵי: בֵּי מַלְכָּא – קֵיסָר, שֶׁהָיָה יָרֵא שֶׁלֹּא יִטֹּל מַלְכוּתוֹ, שֶׁהָיָה אוֹתוֹ שֵׁד מֵאָדָם שֶׁבָּא עַל שֵׁדָה, וְהָיָה דָר בֵּין הָאֲנָשִׁים.

לְדִידִי חֲזֵי לִי הוֹרְמִיז – פֵּרֵשׁ רַבֵּנוּ שְׁמוּאֵל: שֵׁד הוּא.

בַּר לִילִיתָא – זֶה תַּלְמִיד־חָכָם, שֵׁד יְהוּדָאִין, וְזֶה: 'בַּר לִילִיתָא', כַּמּוּבָא בַּמִּדְרָשׁ (שׁוֹחֵר־טוֹב תְּהִלִּים יט): 'אֵיךְ יָדַע מֹשֶׁה בֵּין יוֹם לְלַיְלָה כְּשֶׁהָיָה בָּרָקִיעַ? וּמוּבָא, כְּשֶׁלָּמַד עִמּוֹ תּוֹרָה שֶׁבְּעַל־פֶּה, יָדַע שֶׁהוּא לַיְלָה', וְזֶה בַּר לִילִיתָא, שֶׁעִקָּר הַלִּמּוּדָן מִתּוֹרָה שֶׁבְּעַל־ פֶּה.

וַהֲוָה רָהֵט אַקּוֹפָא דְּשׁוּרָא – זֶה צַדִּיק הַדּוֹר, שֶׁתַּלְמִיד־חָכָם, שֵׁד יְהוּדָאִין, רוֹדֵף אֶת הַצַּדִּיק הַדּוֹר שֶׁנִּמְשַׁל לְחוֹמָה, כְּמַאֲמַר חֲכָמֵינוּ, זִכְרוֹנוֹ לִבְרָכָה (בָּבָא בַּתְרָא ז:): 'תַּלְמִיד־חָכָם אֵין צָרִיךְ לִנְטִירוּתָא', עַיֵּן שָׁם.

וּרְהֵט פַּרְשָׁא – פֵּרֵשׁ רַבֵּנוּ שְׁמוּאֵל: 'לְפִי תֻּמּוֹ'. פָּרְשָׁא – זֶה הַתַּנָּא, שֶׁחִדֵּשׁ זֹאת הַתּוֹרָה וּפֵרְשָׁהּ אוֹתָהּ יָפֶה וְהוֹצִיא לָאוֹר

back to its source, binding his spirit with that of the upper tzaddik—the *neshuk*. This, in turn, gives rise to a complete union, *zivvug*. It is thus God's will that learned scholars oppose the tzaddikim. As a result, the construction of the Divine Presence is completed—her exile is brought to an end (§4).

90. day and night. During the forty days he spent in heaven, Moshe did not eat or drink. This implies his attaching himself to the right side, the spiritual realm. He was therefore made to study "at night," corresponding to the left side, in order that he fall to the left and bring *shefa* to the world (cf. *Biur HaLikutim; Mabuey HaNachal*).

91. wall...Torah scholar.... The Talmud (*loc. cit.*) teaches that because his merit is so outstanding, not only does the tzaddik not require protection, but he himself protects the city in which he resides and its inhabitants. Furthermore, in accepting abuse and elevating it to its source, the tzaddik serves as a wall for the average person by protecting him from persecution at the hands of the scholar-demon (*Mabuey HaNachal*).

LIKUTEY MOHARAN #12:5

going down to the deeps." The *malkhut* **(government) heard about this and put him to death** (*Bava Batra* 73a). this verse appears in Psalms (107:26), in relation to seafarers: **The government heard about this and put him to death** - this refers to the king of the demons. It is not the way of demons to reveal themselves to humans, and he was executed for having revealed their secret. Another interpretation is that "the government" refers to the king, who feared that Hurmiz might usurp the throne. This was because this particular demon was fathered by a human who had had relations with a female demon, and he lived amongst humans:

I myself saw Hurmiz — Rashbam explains that this is a demon.

the son of Lilit — A reference to the scholar-demon. This is the meaning of **the son of Lilit**. As the Midrash comments: When Moshe was in heaven, how did he differentiate between day and night?[90] < The answer is > that when he was taught the Oral Law, he knew it was *LayLah* (night) (*Shochar Tov* 19). Hence he is **the son of LiLit**. For, essentially, a person is called a scholar due to [his knowledge of] the Oral Law.

He was running along the top of the wall — This alludes to the tzaddik of the generation. The scholar-demon persecutes the tzaddik of the generation, who is likened to a wall, as our Sages taught: A [true] Torah scholar needs no protection (*Bava Batra* 7b). See there.[91]

A parasha (cavalryman) moving swiftly — Rashbam explains that he did so unintentionally. This *PaRaSha* is the *Tanna* who originated the teaching and *PeRShah* (explained) it < with his lips >. He clarified its

---

someone who lacks decency and respect studies the upper tzaddik's teachings, he causes the Oral Law/the Divine Presence to descend into exile. This teaching then becomes a weapon in the mouth of the scholar-demon with which he persecutes the lower tzaddik (§1). This is possible because the nature of Torah is twofold: life-giving in the hands of the lower tzaddik, poisonous in the hands of the scholar-demon (§2). Thus, despite the tzaddik's personal level of righteousness, an unworthy person can take improper guidance from that teaching of Oral Law. This is because in order to bring livelihood to the world, the tzaddik includes the quality of the left side. This study of Torah not purely for its own sake is used by the scholar-demon to arrogantly oppose the tzaddikim (§3). However, by rectifying the left side through the right-handed *chibuk*, i.e., the benevolences of lovingkindness, the corruption of the Oral Law and the captivity of the Divine Presence/*Malkhut* can be undone. This is achieved through the lower tzaddik. When he accepts the persecution of the scholar-demon with love, this *chibuk* initiates the process of building up the *Malkhut*. Then, by studying the letter permutation of that teaching of Oral Law from which the scholar-demon draws, he elevates the teaching

LIKUTEY MOHARAN #12:5

תַּעֲלוּמָה, גַּם אוֹתוֹ רוֹדֵף, אֲבָל לְפִי תֻּמּוֹ, כִּי תַּלְמִיד־חָכָם, שֵׁד
יְהוּדִי, אֵינוֹ מְכַוֵּן לִרְדֹּף אֶת הַתַּנָּא, וְזֹאת הָרְדִיפָה נַעֲשֶׂה מִמֵּילָא.

כִּי רָכֵב סוּסְיָא מְתַתָּאֵי – כִּי הַלַּמְדָן, עַל־יְדֵי שֶׁלּוֹמֵד תּוֹרַת הַתַּנָּא,
עַל־יְדֵי־זֶה מַחֲזִיר נַפְשׁוֹ שֶׁל הַתַּנָּא לְתוֹךְ גּוּפוֹ שֶׁל הַתַּנָּא; הַחֲזָרַת
נֶפֶשׁ לַגּוּף, כְּמוֹ רְכִיבַת הַסּוּס, שֶׁהַסּוּס טְפֵלָה לוֹ: וְזֶה מְתַתָּאֵי, כִּי
הַתַּחְתּוֹנִים גּוֹרְמִים בְּלִמּוּדָם לְהַרְכִּיב נֶפֶשׁ הַתַּנָּא עַל סוּסוֹ, עַל
גּוּפוֹ, כְּמוֹ שֶׁכָּתוּב: "שִׂפְתוֹתָיו דּוֹבְבוֹת" וְכוּ'. אֲבָל
'וְלֹא יָכִיל לוֹ' – שֶׁהַתַּנָּא לֹא יָכוֹל לִסְבֹּל נְשִׁיקָתוֹ, כִּי נְבֵלָה טוֹבָה
הֵימֶנּוּ, וְנֶעְתָּרוֹת נְשִׁיקוֹת שׂוֹנֵא, וְהַתַּנָּא בּוֹרֵחַ מִמֶּנּוּ. וְאִם יִקְשֶׁה
לְךָ: אֵיךְ הוּא אֵינוֹ מַחֲזִיר תּוֹרָתוֹ שֶׁל הַתַּנָּא לַלַּמְדָן לְמוּטָב,
וְאַדְּרַבָּא, שֶׁנִּתּוֹסֵף לוֹ גַּדְלוּת בְּיוֹתֵר, וְאֵיךְ בָּא זֶה, שֶׁמְּתּוֹרָה
הַקְּדוֹשָׁה שֶׁל הַתַּנָּא יָכוֹל הַלַּמְדָן לְהִכָּשֵׁל. וְתָרֵץ עַל זֶה:
זִמְנָא חֲדָא הֲוֵי מְסָרְגִין לֵהּ תַּרְתֵּי חַיּוּתָא – כִּי לִפְעָמִים הַתַּנָּא נוֹפֵל
לְאֵיזֶה שְׁגִיאָה דַּקָּה מִן הַדַּקָּה, כְּדֵי שֶׁעַל־יְדֵי־זֶה יַמְשִׁיךְ לָעוֹלָם
תַּרְתֵּי חַיּוּתָא; כִּי יֵשׁ שְׁנֵי מִינֵי חַיּוּת: חַיּוּת רוּחָנִי – אֹרֶךְ יָמִים
בִּימִינָה, וְחַיּוּת גַּשְׁמִי – "בִּשְׂמֹאלָהּ עֹשֶׁר וְכָבוֹד"; וְהַתַּנָּא מֵחֲמַת
דְּבֵקוּתוֹ הָעֲצוּמָה בַּחַיּוּת הָרוּחָנִי, אֵינוֹ מַתִּיר אֶת עַצְמוֹ, חַס
וְשָׁלוֹם, מִכָּל וָכֹל מֵחַיּוּת הָרוּחָנִי, וּמֵחֲמַת שֶׁהוּא נָפַל לִבְחִינַת
הַלִּמּוּד [שֶׁלֹּא לִשְׁמָהּ] בִּשְׁבִיל חַיּוּת גַּשְׁמִי.

קָיְמִין אַתְרֵי גִּשְׁרֵי דְּדוֹנַג, וְשַׁוֵּר מֵהַאי לְהַאי – כְּמוֹ אָדָם שֶׁעוֹמֵד
עַל גֶּשֶׁר שֶׁל שַׁעֲוָה וְאֵינוֹ יָכוֹל לַעֲמֹד – קוֹפֵץ עַל גֶּשֶׁר הַשֵּׁנִי;

---

95. **runs away from him.** This indicates why Yaakov ran away from Lavan after working for him for 20 years. Yaakov could no longer bear his "kisses." And so, when Lavan went to shear his sheep—the studying of the Oral Torah by the scholar-demon—he made his escape. And this explains why, when Lavan caught up with Yaakov, he said to him (Genesis 31:28), "Why did you not let me *kiss* my children?" (*Mabuey HaNachal; Likutey Halakhot, Reishit HaGez* 5:3).

96. **even more haughty.** See note 34 above.

LIKUTEY MOHARAN #12:5

obscurities. He, too, is persecuted, though unintentionally. For the scholar-demon does not intend to run after the *Tanna*. This persecution happens automatically.[92]

mounted on a horse down below — By studying of the *Tanna's* teaching, the learned individual causes the *Tanna's* soul to return to his body. This return of soul to body is similar to one's being mounted on a horse: the horse is secondary to <the rider>.[93] And this is the aspect of **down below**. Through their studying, those from below cause the *Tanna's* soul to mounted upon his horse—his body, as in, "His lips move in the grave."[94] But:

could not overtake him — For the *Tanna* cannot take his kisses, because "A carcass is better than he," and, "The kisses of an enemy are profuse." Thus the *Tanna* runs away from him.[95] And should you wonder: How is it that the *Tanna's* teaching not only fails to bring the learned individual to repent, but on the contrary, he becomes even more haughty?[96] And how does it happen that from the holy teaching of the *Tanna,* the learned individual is able to stumble? The answer is:

Once, two mules were saddled for him — There are times when the *Tanna* lapses into some extremely minute oversight so that through it he can draw a twofold life-force to the world.

For there are two types of life-force: spiritual life-force, which is "Length of days in her right hand"; and material life-force, which is "in her left hand are riches and glory." The *Tanna,* because of his resolute cleaving to the spiritual life-force, does not, God forbid, detach himself from the spiritual vitality. But, as a result of his lapsing into <an aspect of oversight> for material life-force:

They stood on two bridges of the Donag (wax). He leaped back and forth from one to the other — He is like a man standing on a bridge made of wax. It is impossible for him to remain there. He leaps over

---

92. **though unintentionally....** The scholar-demon's intention is to persecute, to ridicule and debase the lower tzaddik.

93. **secondary to the rider.** As the *Zohar* (II, p.260a) explains, the relationship between higher and lower aspects resembles the relationship between the rider and his horse. And just as the rider is mounted on the horse, the soul is mounted on the body. Just as the horse serves the rider, the body serves the soul (cf. *Zohar* III, 228b).

94. **his lips move....** As explained above, section 1 and note 26.

LIKUTEY MOHARAN #12:5 238

וּמֵחֲמַת שֶׁגַּם הַשֵּׁנִי שֶׁל שַׁעֲוָה, קוֹפֵץ עַל הָרִאשׁוֹנָה, קוֹפֵץ מֵהַאי לְהַאי. כֵּן הַתַּנָּא – עִקָּר לִמּוּדוֹ תָּמִיד לִשְׁמָהּ, וּמֵחֲמַת שֶׁצָּרִיךְ לְהַמְשִׁיךְ חִיּוּת גַּשְׁמִי לָעוֹלָם, מַפִּילִין אוֹתוֹ לִלְמוֹד שֶׁלֹּא לִשְׁמָהּ, אֲזַי נוֹטְלִין מִמֶּנּוּ לִמּוּד בְּחִינַת לִשְׁמָהּ, וְשׁוֹוֵר מִלִּשְׁמָהּ לְשֶׁלֹּא לִשְׁמָהּ; וּמֵחֲמַת קְדֻשָּׁתוֹ וּפְרִישׁוּתוֹ, שׁוֹוֵר וְקוֹפֵץ מִשֶּׁלֹּא לִשְׁמָהּ לְלִשְׁמָהּ, כִּי זֹאת הַבְּחִינָה אֶצְלוֹ כְּמוֹ גֶּשֶׁר שֶׁל דּוֹנַג, שֶׁאֵין יְכוֹלִים לַעֲמֹד עָלָיו. שׁוֹוֵר לְתוֹךְ לִשְׁמָהּ, וּמִלִּשְׁמָהּ – מֵחֲמַת הֶכְרֵחַ לְטוֹבַת הָעוֹלָם – שׁוֹוֵר מֵהַגֶּשֶׁר הַזֹּאת, שֶׁהוּא אֶצְלוֹ עַכְשָׁו כְּמוֹ גֶּשֶׁר שֶׁל דּוֹנַג, וְשׁוֹוֵר מִזֶּה לָזֶה וּמִזֶּה לָזֶה, וְעַל-יְדֵי-זֶה יֵשׁ בְּתוֹרָתוֹ בְּחִינַת "וּפשְׁעִים יִכָּשְׁלוּ בָם". הַתִּקּוּן לְכָל הַנַּ"ל.

וְנָקִיט תְּרֵי כָּסָא דְּחַמְרָא בִּידֵהּ – כִּי יֵשׁ שְׁנֵי בְּחִינַת יַיִן, בְּחִינַת תּוֹרָה שֶׁבְּעַל-פֶּה, בְּחִינַת יֵין מַלְכוּת רַב (אֶסְתֵּר א), וּבְחִינַת בִּינָה לִבָּא, שִׂמְחַת הַלֵּב, "וְיַיִן יְשַׂמַּח לְבַב", גַּם הוּא בְּחִינַת יַיִן.

וּמוֹרֵק מֵהַאי לְהַאי – שֶׁיַּמְשִׁיךְ קַו יָרֹק מֵהַאי, בִּבְחִינַת "וַיָּרֶק אֶת חֲנִיכָיו" כַּנַּ"ל. וְזֶה חִבּוּק, שֶׁיְּקַבֵּל בְּאַהֲבָה אֶת הָרְדִיפָה וְיִשְׂמַח בְּיִסּוּרִין, עַל-יְדֵי-זֶה הַשְּׁכִינָה, שֶׁהוּא תּוֹרָה שֶׁבְּעַל-פֶּה, הִיא בְּחִינַת חִבּוּק, בִּבְחִינַת "אֲנִי חֲבַצֶּלֶת", יָרֹק כַּחֲבַצֶּלֶת, שֶׁיִּהְיֶה הַחִבּוּק בִּשְׁלֵמוּת. וְזֶה:

tzaddik himself. Although he himself has no desire or connection to the left side and, in fact, his falling to there is both positive and necessary—so as to bring material prosperity to the world—even so, the tzaddik has had to descend from his level of *lishmah*. His leaping back, however, is a rectification for this as well.

99. **wine of Malkhut.** The Hebrew word for abundance, *rav*, also means rabbi and scholar. This could therefore be a reference to the title "Rav," which is only earned when one has mastery of the Oral Law, as above in section 1.

100. **Binah...joy....** As above in section 4 and notes 62 and 64.

101. **YaRoK from the aspect of Binah....** From *Binah* to *Malkhut*, encircling the Divine Presence/*chavatzelet* with a *chibuk* (embrace) from the right side.

239   *LIKUTEY MOHARAN #12:5*

to the second bridge. But, because the second bridge is also made of wax, he has to leap to the first one—leaping back and forth. So, too, the *Tanna*. Primarily, his study is always for its own sake. However, because it is up to him to draw material life-force to the world, he is made to lapse into study that is not purely for its own sake. The aspect of *lishmah* is <taken> from him, and he leaps from purely- to not-purely-for-its-own-sake. Yet, due to his holiness, <he cannot bear the non-*lishmah* and so again> jumps to *lishmah*. This is because, for him, the aspect [not-purely-for-its-own-sake] is like the bridge of *donag*, which cannot be stood upon. So he leaps into purely-for-its-own-sake, <but> because there is a need to benefit the world he leaps from this bridge, which for him—at that particular moment—is like a bridge of wax. And **he leaped back and forth from one to the other.**[97] As a result, his teachings have the aspect of "but the sinners will stumble in them." [This leaping back and forth is thus] the rectification for all the above.[98]

holding two cups of wine in his hands — There are two aspects of wine: the aspect of Oral Law, which is "wine of *Malkhut*[99] in abundance" (Esther 1:7); and the aspect of *Binah*/heart, the joy of the heart—"wine that makes the heart rejoice."[100]

And he moReK (poured) from one cup to the other — He should draw out the line of *YaRoK* from <the aspect of *Binah*>...,[101] as in, "And he *YaReK* his trained servants." This is *chibuk*—accepting the persecution with love and rejoicing in the suffering. As a result, the Divine Presence/the Oral Law is in the aspect of *chibuk,* corresponding to, "I am the rose"—"*YaRuKah* (green) like a rose." The *chibuk* is thus complete. And this is:

---

97. **leaped back and forth....** Our Sages taught: A person should always study Torah, even if not for its own sake. For by doing so, he will come to study purely for its own sake (see n.9 above). Because the upper tzaddik, the origin/originator of the Oral Law, goes back and forth between study for its own sake and study not for its sake, he places that very same quality in the teaching he originates. Therefore, those who study his laws and teachings in this world should see to always study Torah, even if they can only study not for its own sake—i.e., their motivation for study is something other than *lishmah*. Because the potential for *lishmah* exists in the tzaddik's teaching, through their study of that teaching they will also have this quality of Torah purely-for-its-own-sake drawn to them (*Mabuey HaNachal*).

98. **rectification for all the above.** This leaping back and forth is a rectification for the scholar-demon, the one who speaks against the tzaddik. It is also, so to speak, a rectification for the

LIKUTEY MOHARAN #12:5

240

וְלֹא נָטְפָא מִנַּיְהוּ לְאַרְעָא; וְאוֹתוֹ הַיּוֹם יַעֲלוּ שָׁמַיִם יֵרְדוּ תְהוֹמוֹת
הֲוָה – הַיְנוּ, שֶׁהַשְּׁכִינָה יָשְׁבָה בֵּין תְּרֵין צַדִּיקַיָּא: צַדִּיק עֶלְיוֹן –
זֶה בְּחִינַת "יַעֲלוּ שָׁמַיִם"; "יֵרְדוּ תְהוֹמוֹת" – זֶה בְּחִינַת צַדִּיק
תַּחְתּוֹן, זֶה בְּחִינַת נְשִׁיקִין, בְּחִינַת "נֹטְפוֹת מוֹר עֹבֵר" כַּנַּ"ל; וְעַל־
יְדֵי מַה נַּעֲשֵׂית בְּחִינַת נְשִׁיקִין, בְּחִינַת "נֹטְפוֹת מוֹר עֹבֵר"? עַל־יְדֵי
הַחָכְמָה כַּנַּ"ל. וְזֶה:

וּשְׁמַע מַלְכוּתָא וּקְטָלֵהּ – הַיְנוּ שֶׁיַּשְׂכִּיל וְיִשְׁמַע אֶת הַתּוֹרָה
שֶׁבְּעַל־פֶּה, הַנִּקְרָא מַלְכוּת־פֶּה, וְיַשְׂכִּיל מִצֵּרוּפָיו הַיּוֹצְאִים
מִתַּלְמִיד־חָכָם, שֵׁד יְהוּדִי, יִשְׁמַע וְיַשְׂכִּיל בְּשָׁעָה שֶׁשּׁוֹמֵעַ
הַחֵרוּפִין וְהַגִּדּוּפִים הַיּוֹצְאִים מִפֶּה תַּלְמִיד־חָכָם שֵׁד יְהוּדִי,
יִשְׁמַע תּוֹרָה שֶׁבְּעַל־פֶּה, עַל־יְדֵי־זֶה

קְטָלֵהּ – כִּי עִקַּר חִיּוּת שֶׁל הַקְּלִפּוֹת וְהַשֵּׁדִין אֵינָם אֶלָּא מִנִּיצוֹצֵי
הַשְּׁכִינָה, כָּל זְמַן שֶׁהִיא אֵינָהּ בִּשְׁלֵמוּת וְיֵשׁ לָהּ אֵיזֶה חִסָּרוֹן, אֲזַי
יֵשׁ לָהֶם חִיּוּת. כְּשֶׁמַּעֲלִין אוֹתָהּ לִבְחִינַת חָכְמָה, שֶׁשָּׁם עִקַּר בִּנְיָנָהּ,
וּכְשֶׁנִּבְנֵית בִּשְׁלֵמוּת – עַל־יְדֵי־זֶה וּקְטָלֵהּ לְשֵׁד יְהוּדִי:

Having seen the Jewish nation use the power of the sword to utterly destroy the mighty warriors Sichon and Og, Balak reasoned that his only recourse was to fight them with the strength from the right, the power of the mouth. That is, he wanted to attack them at the root of their strength, the Oral Law/*Malkhut*, in order to subdue them. Only because Moshe was a great tzaddik, was he able to counteract Bilaam's "mouth." We find, therefore, that for his services, Bilaam sought great wealth from Balak. Though he was to make use of the power of the right side, in essence, his true desire was only the left side, the riches and glory.

Furthermore, the Hebrew for donkey, *AToN* (אתון), suggests the converse relationship it has with the *TaNnA* (תנא), the tzaddik who reveals Torah. Rather than binding his spirit with the *Tanna*, the scholar-demon Bilaam had committed bestiality with his donkey. When the angel blocked the road so that he could not pass, Bilaam began to debate with his donkey. Balak's messengers who were accompanying Bilaam ridiculed him for this. "You are trying to destroy an entire nation with your mouth and you cannot even successfully debate with your donkey" (*Sanhedrin* 105b). Bilaam was totally impure. He engaged in *chibuk, neshuk* and *zivvug* with an animal. Moshe, conversely, was totally pure and was able to bring about the unification by elevating the Torah to its source. And it was this purity which enabled Moshe to counteract Bilaam's bestial act and ultimately defeat and destroy him.

241   *LIKUTEY MOHARAN #12:5*

without dripping any of it on the ground, though it was a day of rising up to the sky and going down to the deeps — This alludes to the Divine Presence residing between the two tzaddikim. The upper tzaddik corresponds to **rising up to the sky**; < the lower tzaddik corresponds to **going down to the deeps** >. This is the aspect of *neshikin*, corresponding to, "they drip flowing myrrh." How is *neshikin*/"they drip flowing myrrh" achieved? Through *Chokhmah*, as mentioned above.[102] And thus:

The malkhut (government) heard about this and put him to death — In other words, he will comprehend and hear the Oral Law—known as "*Malkhut peh*"[103]—acquiring wisdom from the letter permutations coming from the scholar-demon. < That is, he will make permutations out of the abuse and insults, and turn them back into the permutations of law which they had previously been. > As a result:

put him to death — For the main life-force of the evil forces and demons comes only from the sparks of the Divine Presence. As long as she is incomplete and has some lack, then they have life-force.[104] < But, > when she is elevated to the aspect of *Chokhmah*—which is primarily where she is built up—and she is built up completely, through this the scholar-demon is **put to death**.[105]

---

102. **as mentioned above.** See end of section 4 and note 81.

103. **Malkhut peh.** See section 1 and note 16 above.

104. **incomplete...life-force.** For they draw their vitality, their *shefa*, from the "immaturity" of the *Malkhut*. And only by raising these fallen sparks will the Divine Presence be made complete (see n.55 above).

105. **scholar-demon is put to death.** Reb Noson relates this to the episode of Bilaam (Numbers 22-25). He writes (*Likutey Halakhot, Reishit HaGez* 5): Torah is the source of everything: "Length of days is in her right hand, and in her left hand are riches and glory." As we've seen, the Jews draw from the right, the nations from the left. Thus, whereas the Jewish strength lies in their voices, their prayer, which comes from the right, the strength of the nations lies in their might and the sword, which come from the left. Now, Moshe was the holy and pure tzaddik whom Rebbe Nachman mentions in the lesson. Though he received from the left side, thereby assuring that the Jewish people would receive proper sustenance, he was able to immediately return to the right. And, by doing so, even the qualities of the left were drawn into the right side. Thus, the power of the sword, the prowess to engage in battle, was also given to the Jews.

    The Torah tells us that Bilaam was hired by Balak, King of Moab, to curse the Jews.

LIKUTEY MOHARAN #12:6

ו. וְזֶה פֵּרוּשׁ: תְּהִלָּה לְדָוִד, תְּהִלָּה – לְשׁוֹן עִרְבּוּב, כְּמוֹ שֶׁכָּתוּב
(איוב ד): "וּבְמַלְאָכָיו יָשִׂים תָּהֳלָה".

דָּוִד – זֶה בְּחִינַת תּוֹרָה שֶׁבְּעַל־פֶּה; הַיְנוּ כְּשֶׁהַתּוֹרָה שֶׁבְּעַל־פֶּה
נוֹפֶלֶת וְנִתְעַרְבֵּב לְצֵרוּפִים אֲחֵרִים כַּנַּ"ל.

אֲרוֹמִמְךָ אֱלֹקַי הַמֶּלֶךְ – הִתְרוֹמְמוּת שֶׁלָּהּ עַל־יְדֵי אֱלֹקַי, בְּחִינַת
חֶסֶד אֵל כָּל הַיּוֹם.

הַמֶּלֶךְ – לִבְחִינַת בִּינָה לִבָּא, שֶׁהַלֵּב בַּנֶּפֶשׁ כַּמֶּלֶךְ בַּמִּלְחָמָה.

וַאֲבָרְכָה שִׁמְךָ – הַיְנוּ אַחַר־כָּךְ מַעֲלֶה אֶת הַתּוֹרָה שֶׁבְּעַל־פֶּה
לִבְחִינַת חָכְמָה כַּנַּ"ל, הַנִּקְרָא בָּרוּךְ עַל שֵׁם רִבּוּי דְּבִרְכָאָן, כִּי
הַחָכְמָה הִיא מְקוֹר הַבְּרָכָה.

In this vein Reb Noson writes: Examining the history of our Oral Law, we find that in the approximately 100 years prior to the destruction of the Second Temple there were only three points of contention between the contemporary major Torah scholars, Shamai and Hillel. Later, with the proliferation of students who had not properly mastered their studies, disputes became more common. This was a necessary development, so as to draw increased *shefa* to the world. Even so, their disagreements were limited and contained within the confines of the Torah. These scholars soon returned to the right side, accord and agreement. There were divergent opinions concerning the correct application of the Oral Law, but even so all the parties involved continued to maintain good relations and even united their families in marriage. However, in our time, the rampant strife has nothing to do with Torah or religious matters. Rather, it is a manifestation of the left side, the work of the scholar-demon. No longer purely for the sake of Torah, all dispute and disagreement, even when couched in Torah language, is the result of the hunger for glory and riches (*Likutey Halakhot, Talmud Torah* 3:2). Compare to note 32, above.

108. **other letter permutations....** This happens when the Oral Law falls into the mouth of the scholar-demon.

109. **Elohai...is always.** The *Parparaot LeChokhmah* explains that the holy name *El* has its source in *Binah* and brings down *chasadim* to the letters *Vav-Heh*, the last two letters of the Tetragrammaton. In the terminology of the lesson, this refers to the channeling of *shefa* to *Z'er Anpin*, the *vav*, and to *Malkhut*, the *heh* (see Appendix: Levels of Existence). Cf. Lesson #11, note 5.

110. **heart...melekh engaged in battle.** Kingship is thus connected to *Binah*, the heart.

111. **...source of blessing.** Thus, the verse which opens the lesson now reads: **Tehillah l'David** — if there is confusion in the Oral Law and its letter permutations have been corrupted; **I will exalt You, ELohai, haMelekh** — this can be rectified by drawing *chasadim/shefa* from *Binah* to *Malkhut* and elevating *Malkhut* to *Binah*; **and I will bless Your name for ever and ever** — there

243   *LIKUTEY MOHARAN #12:6*

6. And this is the explanation [of the opening verse]:
"Tehillah l'David **(A psalm of David): [I will exalt You,** *ELohai* **(my Lord),** *haMelekh* **(the King); and I will bless Your name for ever and ever]."**

TeHiLlaH — This connotes confusion and mixture, as in (Job 4:18), "And in His angels He places *T'HoLlaH* (confusion)."[106]

David — <He> corresponds to the Oral Law, <to *"Malkhut peh"*>.[107] In other words, when the Oral Law falls and becomes confused and mixed into other letter-permutations....[108]

I will exalt You, ELohai, haMelekh — [The Oral Law/*Malkhut*] is exalted through *ELohai*, as in (Psalms 52:3), "The lovingkindness of *EL* (the Omnipotent One) is always."[109]

haMelekh — [She is exalted and elevated] to *Binah*/heart, for "the heart in the soul is like a *melekh* (king) engaged in battle" (*Sefer Yetzirah,* chap. 6).[110]

and I will bless Your name — That is, afterwards, he elevates the Oral Law to the aspect of *Chokhmah* (Wisdom), which is called "blessed" due to its abundance of blessings. For *Chokhmah* is the source of blessing.[111]

---

106. **T'HoLlaH.** *Tehillah* (a psalm, תהלה) and *t'hollah* (confusion, תהלה) have the same letters. This can be understood as an allusion to prayer, a subject which commands a major position in Rebbe Nachman's teachings. There is much confusion as to who is the true tzaddik and who is the scholar-demon. Obviously, no one will readily admit that his Torah study is, by nature, not purely for its own sake. The only way to come to some clarity and remove the confusion is by constantly praying to God for truth and guidance. He then leads a person on the proper path and directs him to the true tzaddik.

107. **David...Oral Law...Malkhut peh.** King David is the symbol of *Malkhut* (cf. nn.12,16) which, in turn, corresponds to the Oral Law. This explains why, of all the leaders of the Jewish people, it was King David who suffered almost incessantly throughout his life. First, he was suspected of being illegitimate and thus unfit to marry within the Jewish community. As a young man, he was tormented and persecuted by King Shaul. Even after ascending the throne he knew little peace. He was forced into battle against the Philistines, Amalek, Edom, and others. His son Avshalom rebelled against him. He was cursed by Shim'iy ben Geira, the Chief Justice of the Sanhedrin, and suffered many other indignities. In all of this, King David symbolized the Oral Law in exile. It, too, has been assailed by constant denunciation and ridicule. However, King David will reign again. This will be in the time of the Mashiach. And then, the Oral Law will likewise be redeemed. The great tzaddikim, those who constantly seek to elevate the Torah, will free it from exile.

LIKUTEY MOHARAN #12:6

very important and relevant piece of advice for this day and age, precisely because the Other Side, the left side, predominates in our world. The only way to successfully guard oneself from being taken in is by beseeching God to show one the truth, again and again.

When teaching this lesson, Rebbe Nachman quoted the verse "*Nachamu, nachamu* (Be consoled) my people...." He said: "*Nachamu, nachamu,* referring to the upper and lower tzaddik." Yet, when he gave over the lesson to be copied, he deleted all mention of this from the final version (see above, n.1). In his work *Likutey Halakhot,* Reb Noson quotes this verse from Isaiah, noting that ever since the destruction of the Temple the primary mission of the tzaddikim is to elevate the Oral Law. This elevation of the Oral Law will be the true consolation. And then, as this passage from Isaiah goes on to say, "A voice cries in the wilderness, prepare a path for God...the crooked made straight...and the glory of God shall be revealed, for the mouth of God spoke" (v.3-5). That is, now that the tzaddik has elevated the evil words of the scholar-demon, we will understand that all crookedness actually has its source in the Word of God. This, Reb Noson tells us, will only take place once Eliyahu the Prophet has brought peace to the world. He will eliminate the strife and disagreement which results from the study of Torah not purely for its own sake—the cause of all destruction— and reveal the truth and the greatness of the true tzaddik, speedily in our time, Amen (*Reishit HaGez* 5:20).

LIKUTEY MOHARAN #12:6

will be an abundance of blessing emanating from *Chokhmah*. By elevating *Malkhut* still further, *Chokhmah* illuminates *Malkhut* whose structure is then complete. All the evil forces are eliminated and the unification which follows brings a blessing of *shefa* into the world.

* * *

A primary objective of the lesson is to point out the importance of studying Torah *lishmah*. Such Torah study has a most positive influence on the person. It binds him to the upper tzaddik who revealed the teaching and creates great unifications Above, ultimately leading to the end of exile, as explained in section 4.

When this level of Torah study is impossible to reach, as is the case with the vast majority of people, then one should try his best to study as much Torah as possible. One should keep in mind even when studying not purely for its own sake that he at least *wants* to walk on the right side, he at least *wants* to follow the correct path in his studies and actions. By doing so, he will still be able to bind his spirit with the *Tanna's* so that the *Tanna's* Torah can guide him to true repentance. And even if one falls to the left side, to a desire for riches and glory, he can still leap back. For the *Tanna* must also fall to the left side to draw *shefa* for the world, as in section 3.

Nevertheless, one must be extremely wary of anyone, even someone who appears very learned, who uses his Torah expertise to belittle others and demean the tzaddikim. This is a

LIKUTEY MOHARAN #13:1

246

לִיקוּטֵי מוֹהֲרַ"ן סִימָן י"ג

אַשְׁרֵי הָעָם יֹדְעֵי תְרוּעָה ה' וְכוּ' (תְּהִלִּים פ"ט).

א. לְהַמְשִׁיךְ הַשְׁגָּחָה שְׁלֵמָה אִי אֶפְשָׁר, אֶלָּא עַד שֶׁיִּשַׁבֵּר תַּאֲוַת מָמוֹן, וּשְׁבִירָתָהּ הוּא עַל־יְדֵי צְדָקָה.

כִּי אִיתָא בַּזֹּהַר (פִּינְחָס רכד.): 'רוּחָא נָחַת לְשַׁכֵּךְ חֲמִימָא דְלִבָּא, וְכַד נָחֵת רוּחָא, לִבָּא מְקַבֵּל לֵהּ בְּחֶדְוָה דְּנִגּוּנָא דְּלֵיוָאֵי'.

6. **ruach...Levitical song.** This passage from the *Zohar* (*loc. cit.*) discusses the daily burnt offering in the Temple whose fragrance would ascend while the Levites played their instruments and sang. Rabbi Yehudah said, "A sacrifice has both *ashan* (smoke) and *reiach nichoach* (pleasant aroma)." These refer, respectively, to the left and right, the *sefirot* of *Binah/Gevurah/Hod* (Understanding/Strength/Splendor) and *Chokhmah/Chesed/Netzach* (Wisdom/Lovingkindness/Victory) (see Appendix: The Structure of the Sefirot). Similarly, there are two apertures in the *af* (nose), the right nostril for receiving the pleasant aroma, the left nostril for receiving the smoke. Thus, of the *ashan* it is written (Deuteronomy 29:19), "God's *af* (nose, anger) will smoke against that person," and (Psalms 18:9), "An *ashan* arose in His nose." In contrast, we find about the *reiach nichoach* that "the *reiach* of your *af* is like [fragrant] apples" (Song of Songs 7:9).

Rebbe Nachman will explain that, when bound together, the *reiach nichoach* and the *ashan*—a mixture of the qualities of *chesed* and *din*—become a true (tempered) judgment or *daat* (holy knowledge). This binding corresponds to the incense offering in the Temple (see n.14) and is brought about by two *ruchot*. One *ruach*, the *ruach* of the heart, rises from the left side (*Binah*) with *gevurot* (severities). These *gevurot* are likened to a fire, hot and burning. The second *ruach* then descends from the right side (*Chokhmah*) with *chasadim* (benevolences). These *chasadim* from the mind are likened to the coolness of water, with the power to douse the burning flame of the *dinim*.

In explaining this process in which the *chasadim* of *Chokhmah*, the mind, mitigate the *dinim* (stern judgments or *gevurot*) of *Binah*, the heart, the *Zohar* quotes the Talmudic teaching: Someone who wants to become wise should face south, and someone who wants to become wealthy should face north (*Bava Batra* 25b). The entrance to the Holy Temple is on the east side. Therefore, when entering, one is facing west, towards the Holy of Holies. On his right is the Showbread, symbolic of prosperity. Its position is on the Table, to the north. On his left is the Menorah, symbolic of wisdom. Its position is to the south of the entrance of the Holy of Holies. Our Sages therefore taught that a person wanting riches and prosperity should favor north when praying; the person wanting wisdom should favor south.

This passage from the *Zohar* has been cited at length because it is fundamental to proper understanding of section 1 of this lesson. As we shall see, *ruach* corresponds to charity; burning to desire; cooling to breaking the desire; the Levitical song to business; heart to joy and incense; smoke to idolatry; the burnt offering to *daat* and the Holy Temple rebuilt.

LIKUTEY MOHARAN #13[1]

"*Ashrei haam* (Happy is the people) that knows the shofar's blast; God, in the light of Your countenance they shall go."

(Psalms 89:16)

bracha

Drawing complete Divine providence[2] is impossible, unless one first shatters the desire for money.[3] Its shattering is achieved through charity.[4] *which are not being used for mitzvot.*

For it is taught in the *Zohar* (III, 224a): A *ruach*[5] descends to allay the burning of the heart. When the *ruach* (wind) descends, the heart receives it with the rejoicing of the Levitical song.[6]

---

1. **Likutey Moharan #13.** This lesson was taught on Shabbat, Rosh HaShanah 5564 (September 17, 1803). No other details are extant regarding the revealing of this lesson (*Parparaot LeChokhmah*).

2. **Divine providence.** In section 4, Rebbe Nachman explains the inner concept of Divine providence as related to and in the terminology of this lesson. However, generally, Divine providence is God's overseeing every single aspect of His creation. This applies equally to all levels: mineral, vegetable, animal and human. Every part of creation receives its sustenance according to God's will. In terms of man, this implies the continuous role which Divine providence plays in his life, providing him with the necessary tools to carry out the mission for which he was created.

3. **desire for money.** Man's livelihood is arguably the area in which Divine providence is most apparent. A person who believes that it is only God who provides will not choose an excrutiatingly long workday as his means of income. Rather, he will perform his job honestly and make sure to set aside time for Torah study, prayer and the mitzvot. He *knows* that God will provide for him even if he is not a workaholic. By shattering the desire for money, his faith in God is intact. Therefore, by relying only on God for livelihood, one attains Divine providence.

4. **charity.** By willingly giving of one's possessions to those less fortunate, a person proves his faith in God. The person who gives charity understands that God alone provides and that he is but the Almighty's agent; having himself received so that he might pass this kindness on to others. Rebbe Nachman explains that giving charity is comparable to passing judgment: the giver "impoverishes" himself and makes the poor person "rich." In this sense, he can be likened to a judge—i.e., God (*Likutey Moharan* I, 2:4; also see end of lesson). This is actually the concept of Divine providence: the providing for others.

5. **ruach.** The Hebrew word *ruach* carries three different but interrelated meanings: wind; breath; spirit. All three meanings are used in our text.

LIKUTEY MOHARAN #13:1 248

'רוּחָא' – זֶה בְּחִינַת צְדָקָה, שֶׁהוּא רוּחַ נְדִיבָה, עַל־יָדוֹ מְקָרְרִין חֲמִימוּת תַּאֲוַת מָמוֹן. וְזֶה בְּחִינַת (תְּהִלִּים ע"ו): "יִבְצֹר רוּחַ נְגִידִים" – שֶׁהָרוּחַ מְמַעֵט תַּאֲוַת הַנְּגִידוּת וְהָעֲשִׁירוּת.

'נְגוּנָא דִּלְיָוָאֵי' – זֶה בְּחִינַת מַשָּׂא וּמַתָּן בֶּאֱמוּנָה, שֶׁשָּׂמֵחַ בְּחֶלְקוֹ וְאֵינוֹ אָץ לְהַעֲשִׁיר. כִּי הַנְּגִינָה זֶה הַמַּשָּׂא וּמַתָּן, כְּמוֹ שֶׁכָּתוּב (שָׁם פ"א): "שְׂאוּ זִמְרָה וּתְנוּ תֹף". 'חֶדְוָה' – זֶה שֶׁשָּׂמֵחַ בְּחֶלְקוֹ, וְזֶה בְּחִינַת קְטֹרֶת, שֶׁמְּקַשֵּׁר חֲמוּם הַלֵּב עִם הָרוּחַ, וְזֶה (מִשְׁלֵי כ"ז): "קְטֹרֶת יְשַׂמַּח לֵב", וְזֶה בְּחִינַת (דְּבָרִים ל"ג): "יָשִׂימוּ קְטוֹרָה

or without faith. The Torah encourages the honest pursuit of one's livelihood, as in, "Someone who wants to become wealthy should face north." Honesty in this area is itself an expression of one's faith. And if, while earning his living, he maintains his involvement in Torah study and mitzvot, the wealth and prosperity he attains can be a source of great benefit for himself and for the world. The reverse of this is engaging in business without faith— dishonestly. One who pursues his livelihood by such means indicates his dissatisfaction and lack of appreciation for what he has. Instead, he is overcome by a burning and insatiable desire to attain more and more wealth, even if this requires his using unscrupulous means to get it. In *Likutey Moharan* I, 54, Rebbe Nachman details the connections between business and song, and the benefits they can bring to the world (*Parparaot LeChokhmah*).

11. **does not run....** Because he has faith, he feels secure that God will provide him with all his needs.

12. **song...give-and-take....** Thus, song and business are similar in that they are both a process of give-and-take. Cf. *Rabbi Nachman's Tikkun* pp.56-59.

13. **...happy with his lot.** Thus, the Levitical song implies engaging in business (give-and-take) honestly and with faith (being happy with one's lot). The passage from the *Zohar* which Rebbe Nachman quoted above can therefore be understood as follows: The *ruach* (charity) cools the desire to attain great wealth. This is because the person engages in business honestly and is happy with his lot.

14. **incense...heart's burning...ruach.** That is, the burning desire of the heart becomes bound to the cooling quality of the *ruach*—this is the *ketoret* (incense offering). As the *Zohar* (*ibid.*) points out, the Aramaic translation of *kesher* (binding) is *k'ter*. The *Zohar* also teaches that there is nothing in the world as effective for mitigating harsh decrees as the *ketoret*. This is because the incense offering binds the *dinim* with mercy, the *ashan* with the *reiach nichoach* in the *af*.

The *Parparaot LeChokhmah* points out that there is a positive aspect to the desire for wealth. The Ari explains that when a person pursues his livelihood honestly and with faith, great rectifications are achieved. Yet, without this urge there would be nothing to motivate an individual to engage in the give-and-take of business. The desire for wealth is therefore a necessary aspect of man's nature. Thus, man's objective must be to cool the desire by binding it with the *ruach*, rather than extinguishing it altogether.

249 *LIKUTEY MOHARAN #13:1*

"*Ruach*" corresponds to [giving] charity, which is [indicative of] a "generous *ruach* (spirit)."[7] With this [*ruach*], the burning desire for money is cooled.[8] This corresponds to (Psalms 76:13), "He shall cut off the *ruach* of the noblemen"—because the *ruach* lessens the desire for nobility and wealth.[9]

"The Levitical song" corresponds to engaging honestly in the give-and-take of business.[10] He is happy with his lot and does not run to get rich.[11] This is because song corresponds to the give-and-take, as is written, "Take up a song and give a timbrel" (Psalms 81:3).[12] [And] "rejoicing" refers to the one who is happy with his lot.[13]

And this is the aspect of the incense, it binds the heart's burning with the *ruach*.[14] This is the meaning of, "Incense makes the heart rejoice" (Proverbs 27:9).[15] It also corresponds to (Deuteronomy 33:10), "They

---

7. **generous spirit.** This phrase appears in Psalms (51:14), "Return to me the joy of Your salvation and support me with a generous *ruach*." This *RuACh*, which corresponds to charity and acts of kindness, is like the *ReiACh*, the pleasant aroma corresponding to *chesed*.

8. **burning...is cooled.** Rebbe Nachman connects this teaching from the *Zohar* (*ibid.*) to the opening theme of his lesson: shattering one's desire for money. When a person has a strong desire for wealth, the *ashan* from the side of the heart rises to the nose, as in, "An *ashan* arose in His nose"—and because of this "God's *af* (Divine anger) will smoke against that person." But then a *ruach/chasadim* descends from *Chokhmah*, the mind, in order to allay this passion. The *Parparaot LeChokhmah* adds that the primary purpose of the *ruach* is to cool this burning, because avarice is an aspect of idolatry, as will be explained shortly.

9. **ruach lessens....** This verse therefore alludes to the second *ruach* which cuts off the *ruach* for wealth. This second *ruach* is charity, through which the burning desire for money is cooled.

The role which charity plays in bringing the *ruach* to allay avarice can be illustrated with the following teaching from the *Zohar* (III, 195a): There are three types of prayer offered by man: a prayer of Moshe (Psalms 90:1); a prayer of David (Psalms 86:1); a prayer of the poor man (Psalms 102:1). There has never been a human being who could match Moshe Rabbeinu. There has never been a king who could match King David. There has never been a broken heart that could match the broken heart of the poor man. And the prayer of the poor man is far greater than the other two.

Through his suffering, the poor man awakens Divine compassion. Even so, because his affliction is an indication that his fellow man has not cared for him, it also arouses Divine anger. Thus, the poor person's plight causes God's *af* to smoke and gives rise to *dinim* in the world. However, an act of *chesed*—giving charity—has the power to cool the burning and mitigate the Divine decrees which come in its wake. See Lesson #10 and note 2. On another level, this blend of Divine anger with Divine compassion is also essential to the inner development of man himself. This will be better understood further on in the lesson (§5 and n.81). There, Rebbe Nachman talks about the "wealthy and impoverished" and how *adam* (man) is actually a combination of these two, which correspond to the burning and the *ruach*.

10. **give-and-take of business.** There are two ways of engaging in business matters—with faith

LIKUTEY MOHARAN #13:1

250

בְּאַפֶּךּ", שֶׁעַל־יְדֵי בְּחִינַת קְטֹרֶת הַנַּ״ל נִתְבַּטֵּל בְּחִינַת (בְּרֵאשִׁית ג):
"בְּזֵעַת אַפֶּךָ תֹּאכַל".

וְזֶה בְּחִינַת הִתְגַּלּוּת מָשִׁיחַ, שֶׁאֲזַי יִתְבַּטֵּל חֶמְדַּת הַמָּמוֹן, כְּמוֹ
שֶׁכָּתוּב (יְשַׁעְיָהוּ ב): "בַּיּוֹם הַהוּא יַשְׁלִיךְ הָאָדָם אֶת אֱלִילֵי כַסְפּוֹ
וֶאֱלִילֵי זְהָבוֹ". וְזֶה בְּחִינַת (אֵיכָה ד): "רוּחַ אַפֵּינוּ מְשִׁיחַ ה׳".

'וְכָל זְמַן שֶׁיֵּשׁ עֲבוֹדָה זָרָה זֹאת שֶׁל מָמוֹן בָּעוֹלָם, חֲרוֹן־אַף
בָּעוֹלָם'; וּכְפִי הַבִּטּוּל שֶׁל עֲבוֹדָה זָרָה זֹאת – כֵּן נִתְבַּטֵּל הַחֲרוֹן־
אַף, בִּבְחִינַת "רוּחַ אַפֵּינוּ מְשִׁיחַ ה׳", וְנִתְמַשֵּׁךְ חֶסֶד בָּעוֹלָם,

smoke corresponds to *dinim*, the stern, untempered judgments and decrees which descend upon the world. The solution is to temper these *dinim* with *chesed*, the concept of the incense offering. The incense is synonymous with being happy and content, the very opposite of anger. Thus, by breaking the desire for money, one sweetens the decrees and is protected from *dinim* (*Mai HaNachal*).

This teaching in the *Sifri* (*loc. cit.*) is brought in reference to the laws concerning a Condemned City (Deuteronomy 13:13-19). If the majority of a city's inhabitants serve idols, then all the inhabitants are put to death and their possessions are incinerated so that nothing remains of idolatry. The statement "As long as there is this worshipping of money in the world...," refers to an object which has been stolen from the condemned possessions before they could be destroyed. Even though he knows that the object is tainted with idolatry, the thief will still not give it up. In terms of our lesson, this is akin to those people who, though they know that God alone provides, still entertain the notion that by working harder they just might profit a bit more. This notion is analogous to idolatry.

The Condemned City has a further connection with the lesson: "Gather all [the city's] possessions to its central square, and burn the city along with all its goods, [almost] like a sacrifice to God your Lord" (Deuteronomy 13:17). In this sense, the Condemned City resembles the daily sacrifice; both are a "burnt offering to God." Yet there is an essential difference between them. The sacrifice exemplified a "generous spirit," an offering funded by the contributions which the Jews voluntarily gave to the Temple. Not so the possessions of the Condemned City. While everything must be burnt "like a sacrifice to God," in no way can it be seen as an act of charity. Quite the contrary, the burning of the city and all its goods points to the negative aspect of wealth—its connection to idolatry. What is true is that in either case, the offering is given to God. In a similar vein, the Talmud teaches: Just as a person's yearly earnings are decreed on Rosh HaShanah, so too are the losses he will incur. If he is deserving, his "losses" will be through the charity he gives (*Bava Batra* 10a). In other words, a deserving person, someone whose belief in Divine providence brings him to give charity, will "lose" his money to mitzvot and be rewarded. The individual who lacks this belief will also incur losses. However, his losses will earn him no reward.

LIKUTEY MOHARAN #13:1

shall place incense in Your *af* (nostrils)," because the aspect of incense nullifies the [curse]: "By the sweat of your *af* you will eat [bread]" (Genesis 3:19).[16]

This likewise corresponds to the revelation of Mashiach, at which time the lust for money will be eliminated. As it is written (Isaiah 2:20), "On that day, man will throw off his idols of silver and his idols of gold."[17] It is also (Lamentations 4:20), "The *ruach* (breath) of our *af*, the *mashiach* (anointed) of God."[18]

And, as long as there is this worshipping of money in the world, there is *charon af* (burning anger) in the world (cf. *Sifri* 13:18).[19] But, to the extent that this form of idolatry is nullified, so is the burning anger eliminated, as in, "The *ruach* of our *af*, the anointed of God."

---

15. **Incense makes the heart rejoice.** This incense, which is the binding of the heart's burning/*ashan* with the *ruach*/*reiach nichoach*, is synonymous with being "happy with one's lot." The Talmud teaches that the incense brings great wealth to the one who offers it on the altar (*Yoma* 26a). As explained in the lesson, wealth is being satisfied with one's lot—the greatest wealth of all. This is the quality of the incense: it makes one happy for he becomes content with what he has.

16. **Your af...sweat of your af....** Adam was told that he would earn his livelihood "by the sweat of your *af* (brow)." He was no longer going to be satisfied with what he had and would feel obliged to constantly toil for more. This was his punishment for having eaten from the Tree of Knowledge. He had been dishonest in taking that which was not his to take. But when one conducts himself honestly and with faith, then the concept of *af*/incense brings him contentment (*Mai HaNachal*).

The verse which Rebbe Nachman has quoted from Deuteronomy is part of the blessing which Moshe gave to the tribe of Levi before he passed away. The passage reads: "They shall teach Your judgments to Yaakov, and Your Torah to Israel. They shall place incense in Your nostrils and burnt offerings upon Your altar. May God bless his wealth and favor the work of his hands." How will the tribe of Levi merit to teach—to bring *daat* (holy knowledge) to the Jews? The Levites will achieve this through the incense, the quality of contentment. And, because of this, God will bring them prosperity from their possessions and their efforts in earning a living (*Mai HaNachal*). The lesson will soon focus on the connection which *daat*—Torah wisdom—has with the previously mentioned concepts.

17. **idols of gold.** Man will throw off the idolatry, not the silver and gold (*Rabbi Eliyahu Chaim Rosen*).

18. **ruach...af...mashiach of God.** Here, Rebbe Nachman points to the connection between *ruach*/charity and *af*/incense/contentment. That is, when one is truly content with what he has, which is attained by giving charity, then he has a sense of what life will be when Mashiach comes. For then, everyone will be content. See also *Likutey Moharan* I, 2:1 that the basic weapon of the Mashiach, prayer, corresponds to the restraining of Divine anger and the *ruach* of the fear of God.

19. **charon af in the world.** This is the Divine anger/*ashan* mentioned above in note 6. This

בִּבְחִינַת (תְּהִלִּים י״ח): "וְעוֹשֶׂה חֶסֶד לִמְשִׁיחוֹ".

וּכְשֶׁיִּתְגַּלֶּה חֶסֶד הַזֶּה, יִתְמַשֵּׁךְ הַדַּעַת, שֶׁהִיא בִּנְיַן הַבַּיִת, בִּבְחִינַת (שָׁם ה): "וַאֲנִי בְּרֹב חַסְדְּךָ אָבוֹא בֵיתֶךָ", כְּמוֹ שֶׁכָּתוּב בַּזֹּהַר (פִּינְחָס רכ:): 'וְיִמִּינָא דָּא זָמִין לְמִבְנָא בֵּי-מַקְדְּשָׁא – כִּי הַדַּעַת הוּא בְּחִינַת בַּיִת, כְּמַאֲמַר חֲכָמֵינוּ, זִכְרוֹנָם לִבְרָכָה (בְּרָכוֹת לג): 'מִי שֶׁיֵּשׁ בּוֹ דֵעָה, כְּאִלּוּ נִבְנָה בֵּית-הַמִּקְדָּשׁ' וְכוּ':

ב. וְזֶה בְּחִינוֹת הִתְגַּלּוּת הַתּוֹרָה שֶׁל לֶעָתִיד לָבוֹא, כַּמּוּבָא בַּזֹּהַר:

said, "it is as if the Holy Temple was built in his day"—as far as he is concerned, it *is* built!

This shows the importance of reciting chapters which deal with the daily burnt offering and the incense offering (cf. *Shulchan Arukh, Orach Chaim* 1:9). We also can understand why we are advised to give charity before praying (*ibid.*, 92:10; *Bava Batra* 10a). Giving charity corresponds to the burnt offering, to uniting the contrasting forces of *chesed* and *din*. The incense offering binds them together bringing about tempered judgment. This corresponds to breaking the desire for money and eliciting Divine providence, thereby providing contentment in one's life.

Today, one can attain this contentment through the daily prayers, as in, "Let our lips (prayers) be in place of the sacrifices" (Hosea 14:3). Though presently there is no way for us to bring the sacrifices, we can, by reciting the corresponding prayers, achieve the same end (*Likutey Halakhot, Tefillah* 4:15-17). And where is it that today's sacrifices are offered? Rebbe Nachman has already given us the answer. When a person achieves the level of *daat*, it is as if the Holy Temple were built. Therefore, he *himself* is the Holy Temple, as it were.

Reb Noson adds that the section of the Morning Prayer known as *Pesukey d'Zimra* (the psalms and songs recited immediately after the sacrifices) corresponds to the "Song of the Levites," the melodies sung while the sacrifices were being offered (*Likutey Halakhot, Tefillah* 4:19).

In review: To draw Divine providence one should give charity. Giving charity breaks one's desire for money, as a result of which one experiences joy and contentment. Charity is also an aspect of the revelation of Mashiach, when the idolatrous worship of money is nullified. Divine anger is thus eliminated, lovingkindness is revealed, and it is as if one built the Holy Temple—synonymous with *daat*.

24. **A wise man....** The angels are known as "the strong ones" (cf. Psalms 103:20). Rashi explains "A wise man..." as follows: Moshe is the wise man. He ascended to heaven, the city of the strong (the angels), and brought down the Torah [which the angels had assumed would stay with them].

25. **this is the aspect of...Future.** This attainment of *daat* through which the Holy Temple is built corresponds to the deep level of Torah understanding that will only be openly revealed in the Future, in the World to Come.

26. **Torah of the Hidden Ancient One....** "Woe to the person who thinks that the stories in the Torah are mere stories!... When the exalted teachings of the Torah descend to this world, they are clothed in forms which enable them to be understood. The Torah's accounts can be likened to a garment which clothes the *neshamah* (soul), the inner depths of the teaching. A

253 LIKUTEY MOHARAN #13:1,2

Lovingkindness is then drawn down into the world, as in (Psalms 18:51), "He does *chesed* (lovingkindness) for His anointed."[20]

When this *chesed* is revealed, *daat* (holy knowledge)—through which the House is built[21]—is drawn down. This corresponds to (Psalms 5:8), "But as for me, with an abundance of Your lovingkindness will I come to Your House." As it is written in the *Zohar* (III, 220b): And the right side...it has been readied for building the Holy Temple.[22] This is because knowledge is the aspect of House, as our Sages taught: When someone has *daat*, it is as if the Holy Temple was built... (*Berakhot* 33a).[23]

2. {"A wise man ascends the city of the strong, and brings down the mighty in which it trusts" (Proverbs 21:22).}[24]

And, this is the aspect of Torah revelation of the Future.[25] It is brought in the *Zohar* (III, 152a) that in the Future, the Torah of the Hidden Ancient One will be revealed.[26] This is because the essence of

---

20. **lovingkindness for his anointed.** Through the contentment which Mashiach will bring to the world, all idolatry will be nullified and eliminated. The ensuing appeasement of Divine anger will induce the flow of *chesed* (lovingkindness) from Above.

21. **the House is built.** This is a reference to the Holy Temple, which will be rebuilt only once Mashiach arrives. As Rebbe Nachman soon shows, its construction is dependent upon *daat*.

22. **right...building the Holy Temple.** The *sefirah* of *Chesed* is on the right side. As mentioned in note 6, there is a *ruach* which descends from the right side, from *Chokhmah* (Wisdom), with *chasadim*. These benevolences are the lovingkindness which is revealed when the idolatrous worship of money is nullified. The passage which Rebbe Nachman quotes tells us that the *chasadim* of the right side are already in place—waiting only for us to draw them down. And with their revelation, the Holy Temple will be built.

23. **knowledge...as if the Holy Temple....** This passage from the Talmud (*loc. cit.*) reads as follows: Great is *daat* for it appears between two names of God, as in, "For the Lord of knowledge is God" (1 Samuel 2:3).... Great is the Holy Temple for it appears between two names of God, as in, "...Your accomplishment, God; the Temple of God Your hands have founded." And Rabbi Eliezer said, "When someone has *daat*, it is as if the Holy Temple was built in his day." The *Maharsha* (*s.v. g'dolah*) explains that the two holy names surrounding the word "*daat*" are the name of mercy on its right side and the name of judgment on its left side. *Daat* is the ability to permute and combine the letters of these names. The person who can do this can also permute the letters with which heaven and earth were created and he can combine right and left to build the Holy Temple. Thus, when one breaks his lust for money, he achieves for himself the nullification of idolatry and the revelation of lovingkindness. In drawing the *ruach* from *Chokhmah* to cool the burning desire of the *gevurot*, he unites them as the incense/*af* and has contentment. This unity of right and left is the creation of *daat* (for *daat* is the combination of the *chasadim* of *Chokhmah* with the *gevurot* of *Binah*). With this holy knowledge, he already possesses the type of awareness that will prevail in the messianic era, when the Temple will again stand. His personal contribution to its building is complete. As Rabbi Eliezer

LIKUTEY MOHARAN #13:2,3 254

שֶׁלֶּעָתִיד יִתְגַּלֶּה אוֹרַיְתָא דְּעַתִּיקָא סָתִימָאָה; כִּי עִקַּר קַבָּלַת הַתּוֹרָה עַל־יְדֵי הַשֵּׂכֶל, שֶׁהוּא משֶׁה־מָשִׁיחַ, כְּמוֹ שֶׁכָּתוּב (מִשְׁלֵי כא): "עִיר גִּבֹּרִים עָלָה חָכָם".

וּמִי שֶׁיֵּשׁ לוֹ בְּחִינַת משֶׁה־מָשִׁיחַ, יוּכַל לְקַבֵּל תּוֹרָה, וְיָכוֹל לְהַמְשִׁיךְ הֶאָרַת הַתּוֹרָה לְלַמֵּד שְׁאָר בְּנֵי־אָדָם; כִּי הִתְגַּלּוּת הַתּוֹרָה בָּא מִיְּחוּדָא דְּקֻדְשָׁא־בְּרִיךְ־הוּא וּשְׁכִינְתֵּהּ, כְּמוֹ שֶׁכָּתוּב (שָׁם א): "שְׁמַע בְּנִי מוּסַר אָבִיךְ" וְכוּ' – 'אָבִיךְ' דָּא קֻדְשָׁא־בְּרִיךְ־הוּא, 'וְאִמֶּךְ' דָּא כְּנֶסֶת־יִשְׂרָאֵל:

וְיִחוּדָם – עַל־יְדֵי הַעֲלָאַת נַפְשׁוֹת יִשְׂרָאֵל בִּבְחִינַת מַיִּן נוּקְבִין, וְהֶחָכָם יָכוֹל לִקַּח הַנְּפָשׁוֹת וּלְהַעֲלוֹתָם בִּבְחִינַת מַיִּן נוּקְבִין, בִּבְחִינַת (שָׁם יא): "וְלֹקֵחַ נְפָשׁוֹת חָכָם", וְעַל־יְדֵי הַיִּחוּד הַזֶּה נוֹלָד הַתּוֹרָה; וּכְשֶׁעוֹלֶה הֶחָכָם עִם הַנְּפָשׁוֹת, בִּבְחִינַת עִיר גִּבֹּרִים עָלָה חָכָם, עַל־יְדֵי זֶה – "וַיֹּרֶד עֹז מִבְטֶחָה":

---

principle. *Knesset Yisrael*, which is another name for the Divine Presence (embodied in the collective entity of the Jewish people), alludes to *Malkhut*. See Lesson #12, note 78.

31. **feminine waters.** This Kabbalistic principle known as *mayin nukvin* applies to the ascending of spiritual energy from below. This occurs through man's fulfillment of the Divine will. More specifically, the souls of the tzaddikim labor to reach the level where they can raise *mayin nukvin* and thereby bring about the unifications Above.

32. **takes souls is wise.** The entire verse reads, "The fruits of the tzaddik are as a tree of life; and he that takes souls is wise." The *Metzudat David* (op. cit.) explains that the tzaddik's deeds are like a tree of life, they bring life to people in this world. And the wise man, by teaching others, "takes" them unto himself; he acquires them, for they will be devoted to him. In terms of our lesson, the wise man is the tzaddik. He is totally devoted to helping others improve themselves and rectify their souls.

There is a manuscript which varies somewhat from the printed text (see end of lesson). It includes the following explanation for the opening part of the verse. "The fruits of the tzaddik" allude to the unifications brought about by the tzaddik; "are as a tree of life," the Torah, which is compared to the Tree of Life. In other words, the unification which the wise man/the tzaddik brings about by elevating the souls as *mayin nukvin*, causes Torah to be revealed (*Mabuey HaNachal*).

33. **Torah is born.** This is a sign that the efforts of the tzaddikim bear fruit. Because these souls are devoted to him, the tzaddik is able to raise their souls as *mayin nukvin*. This, in turn, brings about the unification through which Torah insights are born.

34. **wise man ascends...it trusts.** The Midrash (*Tanchuma, Noach* 2) relates this verse to "a

LIKUTEY MOHARAN #13:2,3

receiving the Torah is through the intellect—which is Moshe-Mashiach,[27] as in, "A wise man ascends the city of the strong."[28]

A person possessing the aspect of Moshe-Mashiach is capable of receiving the Torah and can draw down the Torah's emanating light in order to teach other people.[29] For the revelation of the Torah comes from a unification of the Holy One and His Divine Presence. As it is written (Proverbs 1:8), "Hear my son the instruction of your father, and do not forsake the Torah of your mother." [And it is taught:] "Your father" alludes to the Holy One, and "your mother" alludes to *Knesset Yisrael* (Zohar II, 85a).[30]

Their unification is brought about through the elevation of the Jewish souls in the aspect of feminine waters.[31] The wise man can take the souls and elevate them in the aspect of feminine waters, as in (Proverbs 11:30), "He that takes souls is wise."[32] And through this unification, the Torah is born.[33] Thus, when the wise man ascends with the souls—this being "A wise man ascends the city of the strong"—through this [he] "brings down the mighty in which it trusts."[34]

---

fool is impressed with the outer garment and seeks no deeper. He fails to recognize that the words of Torah are merely its body, a cloak, and that there is a depth to Torah, a *neshamah* hidden within which must be sought after. Furthermore, there exists an even higher level, that of *neshamah* of the *neshamah*. This innermost level of Torah will only be revealed in the Future" (*Zohar, loc. cit.*). In the terminology of the Kabbalah, the garment of the Torah, its revealed form, corresponds to *Malkhut*. The *neshamah*, the soul within the body, corresponds to the Divine persona *Z'er Anpin*. The *neshamah* of the *neshamah*, the insights of Torah which will be revealed when Mashiach comes, is known as the Torah of *Atik*, the Hidden Ancient One.

27. **Moshe-Mashiach.** Mashiach is also known as Shiloh (Genesis 49:10). Both Shilo (שילה) and Moshe (משה) have a numerical value of 345 (see Appendix: Gematria Chart). Moshe thus implies the Mashiach (cf. Lesson #9, n.52). Furthermore, Moshe is sometimes associated with the aspect of *daat* and the *sefirah* of *Daat*, the combination of the elements of *Chokhmah* and *Binah*. This is the holy knowledge that brings the revelation of Mashiach mentioned above (§1). The *Mabuey HaNachal* adds: From this we see that just as the Torah's revelation at Sinai came through Moshe, so too in the Future, the revelation of the Torah of the Ancient One will come through Moshe.

28. **city of the strong.** Moshe, the personification of *daat*, is the wise man who can ascend to heaven.

29. **to teach other people.** With this holy knowledge one can receive the Torah, just as Moshe did; and he can teach the Torah to others, just as Moshe did.

30. **Holy One...Knesset Yisrael.** The Holy One alludes to *Z'er Anpin*, the masculine

LIKUTEY MOHARAN #13:3

256

ג. וְנֶפֶשׁ – זֶה בְּחִינַת רָצוֹן,

שֶׁכָּל אֵלּוּ בְּנֵי־אָדָם הַבָּאִים לַחֲכַם־הַדּוֹר, כָּל אֶחָד וְאֶחָד יֵשׁ לוֹ
אֵיזֶהוּ רָצוֹן, וְהַצַּדִּיק לוֹקֵחַ כָּל הָרְצוֹנוֹת וְעוֹלֶה עִמָּהֶם, וְאַחַר־כָּךְ
– "וַיֵּרֶד עֹז מִבְטָחָה", בִּבְחִינַת (יְחֶזְקֵאל א): "וְהַחַיּוֹת רָצוֹא
וָשׁוֹב"; 'רָצוֹא' – בַּעֲלִיּוֹת הַנְּפָשׁוֹת, 'וָשׁוֹב' – בַּחֲזָרַת הַנְּפָשׁוֹת,
עִם הִתְגַּלּוּת הַתּוֹרָה.

וְזֶה שֶׁמּוּבָא בְּתִקּוּנֵי־זֹהַר (תִּקּוּן ע, קט.): 'רָצוֹא' – דָּא נוּרִיאֵל,
'וָשׁוֹב' – דָּא מְטַ"ט שַׂר הַפָּנִים; נוּרִיאֵל – דָּא נוּר דָּלוּק (זֹהַר
בְּרֵאשִׁית כג: וּבְתִקּוּנָא שְׁבְעִין) בַּחֲמִימוּת תַּאֲוַת מָמוֹן, וָשׁוֹב – דָּא

Talmud teaches: One may not even reveal [the mysteries of] the Chariot to a learned person unless he can understand it on his own (*Chagigah* 11b). It should, however, be understood that even though one may not be capable of understanding the secrets and profundities of the *Merkavah* vision (as well as other Kabbalistic teachings), there is still a great deal of wisdom and moral advice which can be gleaned from these concepts. This explains why they are spoken about openly in various texts. This is essentially what Rebbe Nachman has done in *Likutey Moharan*; he took the loftiest concepts and deepest mysteries and related them to everyday life in order to help man serve God.

40. **Ratzo is...Nuriel.** Both *RatZO* (רצוא) and NURIEL (נוריאל) have a numerical value of 297 (see Appendix: Gematria Chart). Conceptually, the angel Nuriel implies running, going forth or up. In our context, this is the wise man raising up the souls (*Mabuey HaNachal*). Rebbe Nachman will shortly associate Nuriel with the concept of "burning" desires, *nur* in Aramaic meaning fire. This signifies the desires and wills which people bring to the tzaddik for him to raise.

41. **vashov is...MeTaT....** Both *VaShOV* (ושוב) and MeTaTRON (מטטרון) have a numerical value of 314. The angel Metatron (abbreviated as Metat) is known as the Minister of the Countenance. In Hebrew this is "*Metatron Sar Hapanim*" (מטט שר הפנים), the first letters of which spell Moshe (משה). This is because like Moshe, Metat is *vashov*—i.e., like the wise man who returns from Above with Torah.

42. **burning...desire for money.** To understand this better, we must first introduce the Ari's teaching that the name MeTaTRON (מטטרון) is comprised of two words: RiMON (רמן) and TaT (טט). *TaT* is equivalent to 18 and thus alludes to *chai* (חי) which means life. This implies that the *dinim* and *kelipot* (forces of evil) have no hold over him. The second word, RiMON, has a numerical value of 296, so that when one is added for the word itself, it has the same *gematria* as the name Nuriel. From this we see that Nuriel is included in Metatron, though because it lacks the 18 of life, at Nuriel's level the possibility for the evil forces to take hold still exists. In the same vein, the words *tov v'ra* (good and evil) also have a numerical value of 296, when the two words individually and their combination are also taken into account (*Shaar HaHakdamot* p. 394; *Likutey Torah*, Ezekiel 1).

LIKUTEY MOHARAN #13:3

3. Now, the soul is the aspect of will.[35]

For each and every one of these people who comes to the wise man of the generation has some [good] will.[36] The tzaddik takes all the wills and ascends with them.[37] And afterwards, [he] "brings down the mighty in which it trusts."[38] This corresponds to (Ezekiel 1:14), "And the living creatures *ratzo vashov* (run and return)"—"*ratzo*" in the elevation of the souls, "and *shov*" in the return of the souls with a revelation of Torah.[39]

This is what is brought in the *Tikkuney Zohar* (Tikkun #70, p.109a): *Ratzo* is Nuriel,[40] *vashov* is Metat, the Minister of the Countenance.[41] Nuriel is a *nur* (candle) that is lit (Zohar I, 23b)—burning with a desire for money.[42] *Vashov* is Metat, *Sar Hapanim* (Minister of the

wise man" who gives charity. As we have seen, giving charity breaks the desire for money, sweetens the severities and draws *chasadim*—the benevolences which create the proper *daat* for elevating souls. Furthermore, Torah observance itself is likened to *tzedakah* (charity), as is written (Deuteronomy 6:25), "It shall be our *tzedakah* that we keep all these commandments...." Through the Torah, we draw Divine providence upon ourselves. The joy and faith which this imparts encourages the giving of more charity, which brings yet more blessings... (*Mai HaNachal*).

In review: To draw Divine providence one should give charity. Giving charity breaks one's desire for money, as a result of which one experiences joy and contentment. Charity is also an aspect of the revelation of Mashiach, when the idolatrous worship of money is nullified. Divine anger is thus eliminated, lovingkindness is revealed, and it is as if one built the Holy Temple—synonymous with *daat* (§1). *Daat*, the deeper knowledge required to understand the Torah's mysteries, is what enables one to receive Torah insights and teach them to others. Doing so attracts their souls, which he then elevates to create a unification. As a result (and provided he has divested himself totally of the desire for money), new Torah insights are revealed (§2).

35. **soul is...will.** As in the verse (Genesis 23:7), "If it be your *nefesh*"— your will—"to help me...." Thus, the *nefesh*, the general term for man's soul, corresponds to [and is the seat of] his will (*Parparaot LeChokhmah*).

36. **some good will.** The very fact that a person comes to the tzaddik is an indication of his desire for holiness. However, as we shall see later on in the lesson, even though a person's will is to get closer to God, he still has his desires for the things which draw him away from holiness and so need a *tikkun* (rectification).

37. **takes all the wills....** In other words, he purifies the desires of men by teaching them how to properly serve God.

38. **brings down.....** As mentioned, the tzaddik descends with new Torah insights which have been revealed because of his raising *mayin nukvin*.

39. **And the living creatures....** Rebbe Nachman is quoting from Yechezkel's vision of the *Merkavah* (Divine Chariot). He goes on to discuss these points in greater detail in section 5; see notes 61 and 62. The mystery of the *Merkavah* is such a profound secret of Torah that the

LIKUTEY MOHARAN #13:3,4

258

מְטַ"ט שַׂר הַפָּנִים, דְּאִיהוּ רָשִׁים בְּשֵׁם מֹשֶׁ"ה, דְּאִיהוּ מָשִׁיחַ;
שֶׁהוּא "רוּחַ אַפֵּינוּ", שֶׁעַל־יָדוֹ נִשְׁתַּכֵּךְ הַחֲמִימוּת.
וְזֶה: שָׁכְכָה – גִּימַטְרִיָּא מֹשֶׁה, שֶׁהוּא מְשַׁכֵּךְ אֱלִילֵי כֶסֶף וְזָהָב;
רָצוֹא – דָּא רָצוֹן, שֶׁהוּא הַנֶּפֶשׁ, וָשׁוֹב – דָּא מֹשֶׁה – שֶׁמְּקַבֵּל
הַתּוֹרָה:

ד. וְעַל־יְדֵי הַמְשָׁכַת הַתּוֹרָה נִמְשָׁךְ הַשְׁגָּחָה, כִּי הַתּוֹרָה הִיא

leads the *Zohar* to interchange the two, so that the verse from Psalms (144:15) now reads: "Happy is the people *that Moshe is* for them." This is said in praise of Moshe, the tzaddik, who has the power to set things right for the Jewish people.

45. idols of silver and gold. The *Mai HaNachal* reviews this concept in the context of the Purim story. Haman hung an idol from his neck and insisted that everyone bow before him (*Esther Rabbah* 2:5). The Midrash also tells us that he was extremely desirous of money (*Kohelet Rabbah* 2:26). In contrast, Mordekhai and Esther, who possessed the holy spirit (*Megillah* 7a), were able to use their *ruach* (generous spirit) to overcome Haman. This explains the custom of giving charity freely on Purim (*Orach Chaim* 695), because the nullification of Haman and his power (lust for money) is achieved by means of charity. The Talmud also tells us that on Purim, the Jews received the Torah anew (*Shabbat* 88a). This corresponds to receiving the Torah of the Future. Therefore, the account of Purim's events is called the *megillah,* for it resembles the Torah of the Future being *megaleh* (revealed). "The king's anger was allayed" refers not only to King Achashveirosh who, despite his great wealth, was steeped in the desire for money and had to be calmed, but also to the King of the world (God), whose anger, *charon af,* was assuaged through the elimination of idolatry—symbolized by Haman's being hanged.

46. who receives the Torah. We therefore find that *ratzo v'shov* (רצוא ושוב) has the same numerical value of 611 as *Torah* (תורה) (*Mabuey HaNachal*).

In review: Giving charity breaks one's desire for money, as a result of which one draws Divine providence and experiences joy and contentment. Charity is also an aspect of the revelation of Mashiach, when the idolatrous worship of money is nullified. Divine anger is thus eliminated, lovingkindness is revealed, and it is as if one built the Holy Temple—synonymous with *daat* (§1). *Daat,* the deeper knowledge required to understand the Torah's mysteries, is what enables one to receive Torah insights and teach them to others. Doing so attracts their souls, which he then elevates to create a unification. As a result (and provided he has divested himself totally of the desire for money), new Torah insights are revealed (§2). When people bring their will/soul to the wise man, the tzaddik purifies their desires and "runs"/ascends with them. Later, when he "returns" with the souls, he also brings a revelation of Torah to the world (§3).

47. Divine providence.... Here Rebbe Nachman returns to the lesson's opening theme and explains what is meant by Divine providence.

259   *LIKUTEY MOHARAN #13:3,4*

Countenance). He is hinted to in the name MoShE, who is himself Mashiach/the "*ruach* of our nostrils" through which the burning [desire] is allayed.[43]

{"Happy is the people *shekakhah* (that such is the case) for them" (Psalms 144:15).}

And this is: "*SheKaKhaH*" has the same numerical value as MoShE (*Zohar* III, 111b).[44] He *m'ShaKeKh* (allays) the [desire for] "idols of silver and gold."[45]

RatZO is *RatZOn* (will), which is the soul. *Vashov* is Moshe, who receives the Torah.[46]

4. And, by drawing down Torah, Divine providence is drawn down [to the world].[47] This is because the Torah consists of *T-N-T-A*: {*Te'amim*

The *Parparaot LeChokhmah* asks, How is it that Rebbe Nachman associates the concept of running/the holy angel Nuriel with the burning desire for money? He answers that all "burning" emanates from the heart, from the *gevurot* in *Binah*, at which point the desire is entirely pure. Yet, even though at its root the desire which a person has for money is an expression of his inner "will" to use the money only for the service of God, as this burning desire "materializes" in this world, the potential for its falling into an evil desire and descending to the level of idolatry/*charon af* predominates. And this is corrected through the "returning"/Metat, as Rebbe Nachman will next explain.

43. ...**burning desire is allayed.** Because Metatron, the angel who is known as the Minister of the Countenance, corresponds to Moshe, he is the *ruach* of our *af*/Mashiach who nullifies the desire for money (as explained above in §1). With this *ruach* of the *chasadim*, the *kelipot* cannot gain a hold on the burning desire. Rather, the burning desire becomes attached to the "generous spirit"/charity, which promotes Levitical song/faith and joy/contentment in one's life (*Parparaot LeChokhmah*).

Examining his words closely, it is clear that there is an even deeper implication to Rebbe Nachman's teaching that one can give charity and thereby elicit Divine providence. While it is true that one's giving charity will evoke a degree of providence, the truly complete level of this rectification can only be achieved by first bringing one's desires to the tzaddik. The reason for this is that if one has already experienced this burning desire for money, then even his giving charity cannot be done with a full heart. He may succeed in subduing his desire, however, as Rebbe Nachman alluded to earlier, the quality of a "generous spirit" requires more than just the giving—it must be given benevolently and without reservation (n.19). But, by coming to the tzaddik with this desire, the tzaddik elevates the person to the level where his desire for money is itself broken (*Mabuey HaNachal*).

The Hebrew for allayed is *shakhakhah*, as in (Esther 7:10), "The king's anger was allayed." *Shakhakhah* is therefore a reference to Moshe, for he is the tzaddik who allays "the King's (God's) anger" by nullifying the idolatrous desire for money (*Parparaot LeChokhmah*).

44. **SheKaKhaH...numerical value as MoShE.** The *Zohar* (*loc. cit.*) teaches that *shekakhah* (שככה) and Moshe (משה) have the same *gematria*, 345 (See Appendix: Gematria Chart). This

LIKUTEY MOHARAN #13:4

טַנְתָּ"א (טְעָמִים, נְקוּדוֹת, תַּגִּין, אוֹתִיּוֹת), שֶׁהֵם תְּלָת גְּוָנִין דְּעֵינָא, וּבַת־עַיִן.

וְזֶה שֶׁמַּתְחֶלֶת הַתּוֹרָה בִּ'בְרֵאשִׁית' (תִּקּוּנֵי זֹהַר דַּף יח:): תַּמָּן רָאשֵׁי, תַּמָּן בַּת. רָאשֵׁי – "אֵלֶּה רָאשֵׁי בֵית אֲבֹתָם" (שמות ו), שֶׁהָאָבוֹת הֵם תְּלָת גְּוָנִין דְּעֵינָא; תַּמָּן בַּת – דָּא בַּת־עַיִן.

נִמְצָא, כְּשֶׁחָכָם מֵבִיא תּוֹרָה כַּנַּ"ל, נִמְצָא שֶׁמֵּבִיא כֹּחַ הָרְאוּת שֶׁל הַשְׁגָּחַת הַשֵּׁם יִתְבָּרַךְ עָלֵינוּ; וְכָל אֶחָד, כְּפִי קְרוּבוֹ אֶל הַתּוֹרָה, כֵּן הַשְׁגָּחַת הַשֵּׁם יִתְבָּרַךְ עָלָיו.

כִּי עִקַּר כֹּחַ הָרְאוּת, מֵחֲמַת שֶׁמַּכֶּה בַּדָּבָר הַנִּרְאֶה, וְחוֹזֵר כֹּחַ הָרְאוּת מֵחֲמַת הַהַכָּאָה הַהוּא לָעֵינַיִם, וְנִצְטַיֵּר הַדָּבָר הַנִּרְאֶה בָּעֵינַיִם, וְאָז

---

51. **Rashei...patriarchs....** Thus, the three heads, *Chesed, Gevurah, Tiferet*, correspond to the three patriarchs, Avraham, Yitzchak, Yaakov (see Appendix: The Seven Supernal Shepherds). The Patriarchs are the heads of the Community or House of Israel—*Malkhut*.

This verse, "These are the heads...," specifically applies to the three tribes of Reuven, Shimon and Levi. For although this chapter in the Torah seems ready to provide a geneological accounting of the heads of *all* the tribes, it stops after listing the family heads of Levi and mentioning that the tribe's most distinguished leaders, Moshe and Aharon. Rather than carrying on with this listing, the Torah goes on to describe all the events leading up the Exodus of the Jews from Egypt, including a detailed account of the plagues, and then Moshe's bringing down the Torah at Mount Sinai. A completion of this geneological accounting never appears. This indicates that "These are the heads" refers exclusively to the first three tribes. In the context of our lesson, they are the souls who are elevated in the aspect of "pregnancy" (see below, n.78) through which new Torah insights are born (*Mai HaNachal*).

52. **bat of the eye.** *Bat*, which literally means daughter, refers to the pupil of the eye—*Malkhut*. As the focal point and the "apple" of the eye, the pupil is synonymous with *Malkhut* into which all the upper lights converge and through which they are perceived (cf. *Zohar* II, 204a). *Malkhut* also corresponds to the central point and foundation of everything holy, faith in God.

53. **Torah...vision...providence upon him.** The theme of the wise man bringing Torah has been explained in section 2. Wisdom also corresponds to the eyes, as is written (Genesis 3:7), "And the eyes of both of them were opened." Rashi explains they "opened" with wisdom. It is the seeing of the mind's eye. Wisdom is therefore an aspect of sight—insight. And, because the wisdom which the wise man brings is Torah wisdom, it corresponds to Divine providence, the "seeing eye of God." As explained earlier, the Torah is comprised of *T-N-T-A*, which emanates from the eyes. Thus, the closer one is to Torah, the more he draws Divine providence upon himself.

261   *LIKUTEY MOHARAN #13:4*

(cantillations), *Nekudot* (vowel points), *Tagin* (crowns) and *Aotiyot* (letters)}.[48] These are the three colors of the eye and the pupil.[49]

This is why the Torah begins with the word *BeRAiShIT: RAShel* is there, *BaT* is there *(Tikkuney Zohar #4, p.18a)*.[50] "*Rashei*" is "These are the *rashei* (heads) of their fathers' houses" *(Exodus 6:14)*, for the [three] patriarchs correspond to the three colors of the eye.[51] "*Bat* is there" refers to the *bat* (pupil) of the eye.[52]

We find therefore that as a result of the wise man's bringing Torah, he brings the power-of-vision of the Holy One's providence upon us. And each person, to the extent that he is close to the Torah, accordingly has God's providence upon him.[53]

This is because the faculty of visual perception primarily [operates as follows]: As a result of its striking the object being observed, the power-of-vision ricochets to the eyes and the sighted object is then

---

48. **T-N-T-A....** The letters *T-N-T-A* (ת-נ-ט-א) are an acrostic for the four elements which make up the "written language" of the Torah: cantillation marks (טעמים), vowel points (נקדות), crowns or letter decorations (תגין) and the letters themselves (אותיות). Each of these elements plays a distinctive role in the Torah's written composition. The letters of the Torah are the building blocks of creation itself (see Lesson #12, n.66). The tops of some letters are adorned with small markings which give the appearance of crowns. The vowels and cantillations, though not actually in the Torah scroll, are pronounced and sung. Without them, the letters themselves would be expressionless shapes. *T-N-T-A* is therefore the Torah; it is what is "returned" by the wise man when he, together with the souls which he had elevated, comes back to this world.

T-N-T-A is also the term for one of the deepest mysteries in Kabbalah, referring to the spiritual lights which emanated from within *Adam Kadmon* (Primordial Man) at the very beginning of Creation (see Appendix: Levels of Existence). These lights, which preceded all creation, are different expansions of the Tetragrammaton used by God in the formation of each thing that exists (*Etz Chaim, Heichal Adam Kadmon, Shaar T-N-T-A; ibid., Heichal HaNekudim, Shaar Drushei HaNekudot* 1).

More specifically, *T-N-T-A*, as it relates to our context, corresponds to Divine providence. These lights, which were used to construct the uppermost world of *Atzilut* and then filtered into the worlds below, emanated from the "eyes" of *Adam Kadmon*. This connection will become clearer as the lesson unfolds.

49. **the eye and the pupil.** The eye consists of three basic colors: the white of the sclera; the red of the exterior muscle; the iris (colored). These correspond to *Chesed, Gevurah* and *Tiferet*, respectively. The pupil of the eye, which is black, corresponds to *Malkhut*. They also align with the four elements of *T-N-T-A*.

50. **BeRAiShIT....** The letters of the word *beraishit* (בראשית) form the words *RAShel* (ראש), and *BaT* (בת), referring to *Chesed, Gevurah, Tiferet* and *Malkhut*. (The Divine persona of *Z'er Anpin* consists of six *sefirot* divided into two groups. The Divine emanations in the lower group, *Netzach, Hod, Yesod*, are considered an extension of and are embodied in the upper three, *Chesed, Gevurah, Tiferet*.)

LIKUTEY MOHARAN #13:4

הָעֵינַיִם רוֹאִים אֶת הַדָּבָר הַנִּרְאֶה, כִּי הָרְאוּת מֵבִיא אֶת הַדָּבָר לְתוֹךְ הָעֵינַיִם.

אֲבָל כְּשֶׁהַדָּבָר הַנִּרְאֶה הוּא רָחוֹק, אָז קֹדֶם שֶׁיַּגִּיעַ כֹּחַ הָרְאוּת לְהַדָּבָר הַנִּרְאֶה, מִתְפַּזֵּר בְּתוֹךְ הָאֲוִיר וְנִתְעַכֵּר, וְאֵין מַגִּיעַ בְּהַכָּאָה עַל הַדָּבָר, וְעַל־יְדֵי־זֶה אֵין חוֹזֵר הָרְאוּת לָעֵינַיִם, וְאָז אֵין הָעֵינַיִם רוֹאִין, כִּי עִקַּר הָרְאוּת הוּא מֵחֲמַת הַהַכָּאָה. וְזֶה (תְּהִלִּים פ): "שׁוּב נָא הַבֵּט מִשָּׁמַיִם וּרְאֵה" – שֶׁיָּשׁוּב הַבָּטָה שֶׁמַּבִּיט מִשָּׁמַיִם עָלֵינוּ, יָשׁוּב עַל־יְדֵי הַהַכָּאָה, יָשׁוּב הָרְאוּת לְעֵינָיו, וְאָז: 'וּרְאֵה', כִּי הָרְאִיָּה עַל־יְדֵי הֲשָׁבַת הַהַבָּטָה.

וְזֶה בְּחִינַת: "וְהַחַיּוֹת רָצוֹא וָשׁוֹב"; וְהַחַיּוֹת – הַיְנוּ הַתּוֹרָה, שֶׁהִיא הַחַיִּים, 'רָצוֹא' – בִּבְחִינַת הַבָּטָה מֵעֵלָּא לְתַתָּא, 'וָשׁוֹב' – בְּחִינַת הַכָּאַת הָרְאוּת בַּדָּבָר הַנִּרְאֶה, וְנֶחֱזָר לָעֵינַיִם וְנִצְטַיֵּר בָּעֵינַיִם, כִּי הָעֵינַיִם הֵם כְּמַרְאָה לְטוּשָׁה, שֶׁנִּתְרָאֶה בָּהֶם כָּל דָּבָר שֶׁעוֹמֵד כְּנֶגְדּוֹ.

וְעַל־יְדֵי שֶׁאֲנַחְנוּ קְרוּבִים אֶל הַתּוֹרָה, נִמְצָא שֶׁאֲנַחְנוּ קְרוּבִים אֶל הָרְאוּת, וְעַל־יְדֵי זֶה כֹּחַ הָרְאוּת נֶחֱזָר לְעֵינָיו, וְנִתְרָאִים וְנִצְטַיְּרִים

One who has Torah, has life; he is likened to the "living creatures" of Yechezkel's prophetic vision.

58. **Run...return....** Looking down from Above refers to the "seeing eye of God" looking down upon man. It "returns" with the Torah drawn by the tzaddik, as the Torah, too, is synonymous with vision, "seeing." Therefore, the person who fixes his gaze upon life, the Torah, will elicit God's "seeing eye" of providence.

59. **partial seeing.** Because they are distant from the Torah, they cannot focus. They are only focused upon, and their own seeing—the Divine providence which they elicit—is therefore incomplete.

"Seeing" and "partial seeing" correspond to the concepts of Divine providence and nature, respectively. God, who created everything, oversees His creation. Believing and accepting this brings one under the direct governance of Divine providence. However, to the extent that one's belief in or acceptance of God's omniscience and omnipotence is lacking, he receives an inadvertent providence—only partial seeing. The events of his life will be governed by natural causes and not directly by God. This in itself raises a question: God, who oversees all of His creations, must also oversee nature. This being the case, what then is the actual difference between Divine providence and nature?

The answer is that God does oversee everything. When a person acts properly and

LIKUTEY MOHARAN #13:4

pictured in the eyes. The eyes thus see the observed object, because the faculty of sight brings the object into the eyes.[54]

If, however, the object being observed is distant, then before the power-of-vision reaches the object it becomes diffused in the atmosphere and obscured. It does not reach the object being observed with any force, and consequently the power-of-vision does not ricochet to the eyes. And so the eyes do not see.[55]

This is because seeing essentially depends upon the striking, as in (Psalms 80:15), "O return, look from heaven and see." The look with which we are looked upon from heaven should return; it should return by means of the striking. The power-of-vision should return to His eyes. And then, "and see"—for the seeing comes from a return of the looking.[56]

This corresponds to "And the living creatures run and return." "And the living creatures" alludes to the Torah, which is life.[57] "Run" is the aspect of looking down from Above; "and return" is the power-of-vision striking the observed object, ricocheting to the eyes, and being pictured in the eyes.[58] For the eyes are like a polished mirror in which is reflected whatever stands opposite it.

Thus, by virtue of our being close to the Torah, we are close to the power-of-vision. Because of this, the power-of-vision returns to His eyes and we are reflected and pictured in His eyes. But the gentiles, by virtue of their being distant from the Torah, are distant from His providence and His providence does not reach them with force. Consequently, His providence upon the gentile nations is with [only] partial seeing,[59] corresponding to "run," whereas His providence

---

54. **faculty of sight...into the eyes.** When the power-of-vision is reflected back to the eyes, it is the pupil which allows in the light. The diffused light converges in the pupil so that the eye sees. Similarly, within the context of the lesson, the great light of Torah, which is *daat* (a combination of forces from *Chokhmah* and *Binah*), only becomes apparent when it emerges through *Malkhut*. By virtue of *Malkhut* being symbolic of faith, this indicates the importance of trusting in God and being content with one's lot, a recognition of Divine providence. Thus, to receive and reveal the Torah, one must first possess the faith through which these insights are processed.

55. **the eyes do not see.** Without faith one is incapable of focusing on the Torah and hence cannot receive its "lights." It is as if he were distant from the object he wishes to focus on. The reason for this is that a person without faith is distant from Divine providence.

56. **return of the looking.** But when one is not within range, that is, distant from the Torah (*T-N-T-A*), there is no return sight.

57. **Torah, which is life.** Of the Torah it is said, "For it is your life..." (Deuteronomy 30:20).

LIKUTEY MOHARAN #13:4,5   264

אֲנַחְנוּ בְּעֵינָיו. אֲבָל הָעַכּוּ״ם, מֵחֲמַת שֶׁהֵם רְחוֹקִים מֵהַתּוֹרָה, הֵם
רְחוֹקִים מֵהַשְׁגָּחָתוֹ, וְהַשְׁגָּחָתוֹ אֵין מַגִּיעַ עֲלֵיהֶם בְּהַכָּאָה. נִמְצָא
הַשְׁגָּחָתוֹ עַל הָעַכּוּ״ם בַּחֲצִי הָרְאוּת, בִּבְחִינַת רָצוֹא, וְעָלֵינוּ
הַשְׁגָּחָתוֹ בִּשְׁלֵמוּת:

ה. וְזֶהוּ בְּחִינַת תִּקּוּנָא דִּמְרַכַּבְתָּא עִלָּאָה וּמְרַכַּבְתָּא תַּתָּאָה –

In review: Giving charity breaks one's desire for money, as a result of which one draws
Divine providence and experiences joy and contentment. Charity is also an aspect of the
revelation of Mashiach, when the idolatrous worship of money is nullified. Divine anger is
thus eliminated, lovingkindness is revealed, and it is as if one built the Holy Temple—
synonymous with *daat* (§1). *Daat,* the deeper knowledge required to understand the Torah's
mysteries, is what enables one to receive Torah insights and teach them to others. Doing so
attracts their souls, which he then elevates to create a unification. As a result, (and provided
he has divested himself totally of the desire for money,) new Torah insights are revealed (§2).
When people bring their will/soul to the wise man, the tzaddik purifies their desires and
"runs"/ascends with them. Later, when he "returns" with the souls, he also brings a
revelation of Torah to the world (§3). This drawing of new Torah insights elicits Divine
providence, Heaven's power-of-vision. Those close to Torah are completely reflected in His
eyes, whereas the gentiles and those distant from Torah receive only a partial seeing (§4).

61. **Ezekiel 1.** Yechezkel's prophesy took place in exile, in Babylon. He was shown the Divine
Chariot and was then able to described it in detail (see above, n.39). Reb Noson points out
that the first letters of the opening words, "*Niftchu Hashamayim V'ereh Marot Elohim* (The
heavens were opened...)," form the Hebrew word for faith, *EMUNaH* (*Likutey Halakhot,
Even HaEzer,* Appendix). This can be understood as alluding to the fact that presently, the
way to become worthy of heavenly revelations is through the perfection of one's faith. This
relates to our lesson from which we've seen that in order to break bad desires one must give
charity, an aspect of faith. By doing so, even in this exile one can merit truly exalted levels.

It must be made perfectly clear that **there is absolutely nothing physical nor is there any
aspect of corporeality in the transcendant worlds!** This cannot be stressed enough. Any
analogy, use of terminology, or comparison to anything physical in Yechezkel's vision of the
Chariot is only a means through which the serious student of the Kabbalah can hope to
achieve even the minutest grasp of the spiritual realm. As Eliyahu the Prophet warned,
"There exists neither form, nor shape, nor any figure whatsoever, for all is spiritual." See
Lesson #12, note 55.

62. **Upper...Lower Chariot.** In an ancient (first century) esoteric text known as the *Hekhalot
Rabbati* (Greater Chambers), we find a description of the methods used for ascending
spiritually, mentally, through the seven chambers which lead to the Throne of Glory. During
this mystical experience, which is known as *Merkavah* (Chariot), one is, as it were, placed in a
karon (chariot) which serves as his spiritual vehicle for ascent. Opposite the door of the
seventh and uppermost chamber the initiate encounters the four living creatures with the face

LIKUTEY MOHARAN #13:4,5

upon us is complete.[60]

5. {"Now it came to pass. . .that the heavens were opened and I saw visions of God. . . . Also out of the midst of it came the likeness of four living creatures. . . . They had the face of an *adam* (man), the face of an *aryeh* (lion). . .the face of a *shor* (ox). . .and the face of a *nesher* (eagle). . . . And the living creatures run and return. . . . And when the living creatures move, the *ofanim* (wheels) go. . .for the spirit of the living creatures is in the wheels. . . . And above the firmament that is over their heads is the likeness of a *kisay* (throne), in appearance like a sapphire stone. And upon the likeness of the throne is a likeness, in appearance like an *adam*, up above it" (Ezekiel 1).[61]}

Now, this is the *tikkun* (rectification) of the Upper Chariot and the Lower Chariot.[62] Through the wise man who takes the souls and

refrains from transgressing God's will, he becomes worthy of receiving Divine providence directly. However, the person who sins may no longer deserve to be given anything, including life itself. Yet, *shefa* (an influx of blessing) is always descending, even to the undeserving. Because of this, another means for transferring the *shefa* to man is required. To this end, God created nature. It serves as a buffer, so that even though a person is undeserving of any good, he is still able to benefit from the influx of blessing which comes to the world and its inhabitants naturally. Even so, one must never be satisfied with such a level, receiving Divine providence indirectly. Rather, a person should always strive to better himself and attain true faith, thereby drawing upon himself direct Divine providence.

In Hebrew, nature is *hateva* (הטבע). This word is the numerical equivalent of God's name *Elohim* (אלהים), 86. In other words, even nature is actually Godliness, just in a hidden (partial seeing) form (*Mabuey HaNachal*).

60. **upon us is complete.** Rebbe Nachman has applied this verse about the living creatures running and returning to a number of different aspects of the lesson. We have seen that "run" is Nuriel/the burning desire which is allayed by "return"/MeTaT/Moshe, who cools off this desire and elicits *chesed* and *daat* to draw the souls. He has also explained running as the will of the people who come to the tzaddik and returning as the wise man who brings down Torah. Finally, he has shown that running is looking down and returning is looking up—a reference to complete seeing. As such, all these concepts are encompassed in the vision of the Chariot (*Mai HaNachal*). In the next section (5), Rebbe Nachman will explain how the specific details of this prophetic vision relate to each individual as well as to the themes of his lesson.

It is worth noting that the one time in the year when this chapter of the Chariot is read publicly, is on the holiday of Shavuot. This is the day the Jewish people received the Torah and, as we've seen from the lesson, Yechezkel's vision and receiving the Torah are conceptually the same. This is also why it was only after having been enslaved in and redeemed from Egypt—a land of idolatry, filled with the desire for money (see *Rabbi Nachman's Stories* #12)—that the Jews were able to receive the Torah. And, when Mashiach comes and the idolatry of money will be destroyed completely, then we will again receive the Torah—the Torah of the Future (as above, §2). In addition, by going to the true tzaddik, one can, even now, be part of the Torah's revelation. Like Moshe, the tzaddik has the power to elevate those dependent upon him, so that when he gives a Torah lesson their souls play an integral part in the insights the tzaddik reveals. Not only this! From the lesson we can likewise understand that by going to the tzaddik, one comes under the direct and caring Divine providence of God's "seeing eye" (*Mai HaNachal*).

LIKUTEY MOHARAN #13:5   266

שֶׁעַל־יְדֵי הֶחָכָם שֶׁלּוֹקֵחַ הַנְּפָשׁוֹת וְעוֹלֶה עִמָּהֶם, וְיֵרֵד עֹז מִבְטָחָה, נִתְתַּקְנוּ שְׁנֵי הַמֶּרְכָּבוֹת.

כִּי יֵשׁ אַרְבַּע חַיּוֹת בִּבְחִינַת נֶפֶשׁ, וְכִסֵּא, וְיוֹשֵׁב עַל הַכִּסֵּא. אַרְיֵה שֶׁבִּבְחִינַת נֶפֶשׁ – זֶה בְּחִינַת (שִׁיר־הַשִּׁירִים ה): "אָרִיתִי מוֹרִי עִם בְּשָׂמִי"; 'מוֹרִי' – זֶה בְּחִינַת "מָרַת נָפֶשׁ" (שְׁמוּאֵל־א א), בְּחִינַת (מְלָכִים־ב ד): "וְנַפְשָׁהּ מָרָה לָהּ", זֶה בְּחִינוֹת פְּגַם הַנֶּפֶשׁ, פְּגַם הָרָצוֹן; כְּשֶׁרוֹצֶה דְּבַר־תַּאֲוָה זֶה הָרָצוֹן, הוּא פְּגַם וּמָרָה לַנֶּפֶשׁ. וְעַכְשָׁו כְּשֶׁבָּא זֶה הָאָדָם לַחֲכַם־הַדּוֹר עִם נַפְשׁוֹ וּרְצוֹנוֹ, וַחֲכַם־הַדּוֹר לוֹקֵחַ כָּל הָרְצוֹנוֹת וְלוֹקֵט אוֹתָם אֶחָד לְאֶחָד, כְּדֵי לְהַעֲלוֹת אוֹתָם כַּנַּ"ל, וְאָז מְלַקֵּט גַּם כָּל הָרְצוֹנוֹת וְהַנְּפָשׁוֹת שֶׁנָּפְלוּ. וְזֶהוּ בְּחִינַת: 'אַרְיֵה' – לְשׁוֹן לֶקֶט, שֶׁמְּלַקֵּט מָרַת הַנֶּפֶשׁ, הַיְנוּ פְּגַם

resin with a bitter taste, alludes to *morat,* the bitterness of a blemished soul. The fragrant spice mentioned in the verse implies the holy desires of a pure soul.

66. **as above.** See section 3.

67. **all... which have fallen.** This refers to the previous desires which this person had, before he decided to go to the tzaddik for rectification (*Parparaot LeChokhmah*).

68. **gathers... the blemish of the soul.** The *Parparaot LeChokhmah* explains: The very fact that a person comes to the tzaddik for a *tikkun* is in itself an indication of his good desire and will to get closer to God. Even so, he no doubt has other wills, lusts and desires which turn him away from holiness. These are very bitter for the soul to bear and require a *tikkun*. Therefore, together with the good, the tzaddik must also "gather" these evil desires. They, too, must be elevated, otherwise the soul of this person remains blemished and cannot be raised up. Now, by coming to the tzaddik, the process of rectification is begun. In working to elevate this person's soul, the tzaddik brings him to experience feelings of bitterness and remorse over his previous sins and blemishes. It might even be that the person himself is not aware of his own evil desires, the bitterness which his soul experiences. Yet now, by coming to the wise man, the tzaddik sensitizes him to the inner workings of his soul so that he is worthy of realizing his mistakes and repenting. And, by repenting, the person who has come to the tzaddik becomes even more aware of his past desires. He feels even more bitterness and remorse, and continues to repent. The tzaddik also takes these desires, this bitterness of the soul, and elevates them as *mayin nukvin*. This, in turn, brings further Torah revelations, which lead to still more holy desires, and so on. Thus, even a person steeped in evil desires has a way to improve and rectify himself. He can come to the tzaddik. This one straightforward act, because it is an expression of a holy desire, will begin a process through which his soul as well can reach its perfection.

The *Mabuey HaNachal* adds: At its root, all desire is the burning of the transcendant "heart." It is from this exalted level that yearning and longing for God stems. However, as it

LIKUTEY MOHARAN #13:5

ascends with them "and brings down the mighty in which it trusts," the two Chariots are rectified.

For in the aspect of soul, there are four living creatures, a throne and one who sits on the throne.[63]

ARYeh (lion) in the aspect of soul corresponds to (Song of Songs 5:1), "*ARYsy mory* (I gathered my myrrh) with my spice."[64] "*MoRy*" corresponds to "*MaRat* (bitterness of) soul" (1 Samuel 1:10), as in, "For her soul is bitter within her" (2 Kings 4:27). This indicates a blemish of the soul, a flaw of the will. When a person wants some object of desire, this will is a flaw and is bitter for the soul.[65]

And now, when this person comes with his soul and his will to the wise man of the generation, and the wise man of the generation takes all the wills and gathers them together one with another in order to elevate them as above,[66] then he also gathers together all the wills and souls which have fallen.[67] This is the aspect of *aryeh*: it connotes of gathering; he gathers together the bitterness of the soul—i.e., the blemish of the soul.[68] [And this is] "with my spice"—with the good

---

of a man, a lion, an ox and an eagle. And when he finally merits standing before the Throne of Glory, it begins to sing.

In the terminology of the *Zohar* and the teachings of the Ari, the Upper and Lower Chariots correspond to the different *sefirot*. The difference between upper and lower aligns with the abovementioned distinction between the three colors of the eye and the pupil (notes 50-52), with the Upper Chariot corresponding to *Chesed, Gevurah* and *Tiferet* as they relate to *Malkhut*, and the Lower Chariot being *Malkhut* itself (*Sulam, Zohar* I, 196b). This *Zohar* explains that Yosef's being put in charge of Egypt's sustenance and riding in Pharaoh's second royal chariot alludes to the rule of the tzaddik/*Yesod* who brings *shefa* to *Malkhut*.

In explaining the two Chariots in terms of the lesson, the *Mai HaNachal* says that the Upper Chariot alludes to the raising up of the souls, the souls themselves corresponding to the Lower Chariot, while the Lower Chariot alludes to the bringing down of Torah, which itself corresponds to the Upper Chariot.

63. **creatures...throne...one who sits on the throne.** Rebbe Nachman will now explain the different elements in Yechezkel's vision, first as they apply to the elevation of souls performed by the wise man, and then as they apply to the Torah with which he descends.

The initial part of this process, the "elevating," is the rectification which the tzaddik brings to the Lower Chariot/the souls. The second half of the process, the "descending," is the *tikkun* which the tzaddik brings to the Upper Chariot/the Torah.

64. **ARYeh....** Of the four faces of the living creatures, the *aryeh* alludes to the process of gathering.

65. **MoRy...MaRat...bitter for the soul.** One's will and desires are directly linked to his soul (as above, §3 and n.35). By virtue of this relationship, the evil desires which a person has are capable of blemishing his soul. In contrast, holy desires cause his soul to give off a "pleasant fragrance." Both are included in the verse, "I gathered...." Myrrh, which is an aromatic

LIKUTEY MOHARAN #13:5   268

הַנֶּפֶשׁ; "עִם בְּשָׂמִי" – עִם הָרָצוֹן הַטּוֹב שֶׁמַּעֲלֶה רֵיחַ טוֹב.

וּבְחִינַת שׁוֹר שֶׁבַּנֶּפֶשׁ – זֶה הָאוֹר הַמִּצְחָצָח שֶׁנִּתּוֹסֵף בַּנֶּפֶשׁ מֵחֲמַת הַקִּבּוּץ, שֶׁנִּתְקַבֵּץ פִּזּוּרֵי הַנֶּפֶשׁ, וְאָז מֵאִיר הַנֶּפֶשׁ בְּיוֹתֵר, כִּי כְּשֶׁהָרָצוֹן אֵין מֵאִיר, אָז הַנֶּפֶשׁ בִּבְחִינַת וְנֶפֶשׁ רְעֵבָה, כִּי עִקָּר הָרָעָב מֵחֲמַת הֶעְדֵּר הָאוֹר, כְּמוֹ שֶׁאָמְרוּ חֲכָמֵינוּ, זִכְרוֹנָם לִבְרָכָה (יוֹמָא עד:): "וַיְעַנְּךָ וַיַּרְעִיבֶךָ וַיַּאֲכִילְךָ אֶת הַמָּן" – 'מִכָּאן שֶׁהַסּוּמָא אֵינוֹ שָׂבֵעַ', כִּי עִקָּר הַשּׂבַע מֵחֲמַת הָאוֹר שֶׁיִּרְאֶה בְּעֵינָיו, וְעַל-יְדֵי שֶׁאֵינוֹ רוֹאֶה, אֵין נִתְמַלֵּא נַפְשׁוֹ, הַיְנוּ רְצוֹנוֹ, כִּי "טוֹב מַרְאֵה עֵינַיִם מֵהֲלָךְ-נָפֶשׁ" (קֹהֶלֶת ו);

וּכְשֶׁמְּצַחְצֵחַ נַפְשׁוֹ בְּצַחְצָחוֹת הָאוֹר, אֲזַי "וְנֶפֶשׁ רְעֵבָה מִלֵּא טוֹב" (תְּהִלִּים ק"ז), בִּבְחִינַת (יְשַׁעְיָהוּ נ"ח): "וְהִשְׂבִּיעַ בְּצַחְצָחוֹת נַפְשֶׁךָ".

money spread out represents a soul that is spread out. And, just as a torch shines more brightly that an equivalent amount of individual candles, a soul united is brighter than one which is fragmented.

71. **the will does not shine....** Even when a person hungers to serve God, if his will is fragmented—splintered by good and evil desires—it cannot shine.

72. **never satiated.** A blind man, because he cannot see what he is eating, may feel full, but is never satiated. He does not *know* what he ate. In the desert the Jews ate the manna. It was a heavenly food and bore no resemblance to any food known to man. Therefore, though they consumed it, they never felt as if they had eaten (for what in fact was it that they had eaten?). This is the meaning of, "He made you suffer...go hungry and He fed you the manna." The question is asked, Why were the Jews not satiated by the manna? The answer is that Torah can only be attained by one who has a minimum attachment to pleasure (*Avot* 6:5). Thus, the Jews were made to suffer by going hungry. They were being prepared for receiving the Torah (*Iyun Yaakov, Yoma* 74b). This relates to our lesson, because contentment with one's lot is one of the necessities for acquiring Torah (*Avot* 6:4). By achieving this level, one can attain *daat*, which enables him to reveal the Torah of the Future (as above, §1 and 2).

73. **satiation...that one sees with his eyes.** If the fragments of his soul have been united, his soul will shine brightly. He will be satiated and content with what he has in life.

74. **the wandering of the soul.** The Talmud (*Yoma* 74b) continues: Because the blind are never satiated, one should always eat his sumptuous meals by the light of day, as it is written, "Better is the sight...." Thus we see that light and sight are synonymous. It is therefore better to have sight, the united light of the soul, rather than a wandering of the soul, which is fragmentation and emptiness.

75. **satiate your soul with clearness.** Clearness also indicates a unification of the soul, when it is neither splintered nor fragmented. The verse which precedes this one states that if one "draws out his soul" and feeds the hungry (i.e., gives charity), his light will shine in the darkness. In

LIKUTEY MOHARAN #13:5

269

will, which gives off a pleasant fragrance.[69]

Shor (ox) in the aspect of soul is the clear light added to the soul because of the coming together, the uniting of the soul's fragments.[70] Then, the soul shines even more. For when the will does not shine, then the soul is in the aspect of "the soul hungers" (Psalms 107:9).[71]

The essence of the hunger [that a person feels] stems from a lack of light. As our Sages taught: "He made you suffer and let you go hungry, and He fed you the manna" (Deuteronomy 8:3)—from here we learn that a blind man is never satiated (*Yoma* 74b).[72] This is because satiation essentially comes from the light that one sees with his eyes.[73] But, because he does not see, his soul—his will—is never fulfilled, for "Better is the sight of the eyes than the wandering of the soul" (Ecclesiastes 6:9).[74]

However, when he purifies his soul with the clearness of the light, then, "[He has satisfied the longing soul] and the hungry soul He has filled with goodness" (Psalms, *ibid.*). This corresponds to (Isaiah 58:11), "And He will satiate your soul with clearness."[75] This is the aspect of

---

descends and becomes enveloped in this world, desire is transformed into the source of all vanity and lust through which man blemishes his soul. But, by bringing these fallen desires and wills to the tzaddik, they can be rectified and returned to their root. The tzaddik elevates the person's will so that all his desires are directed towards an increase of holiness and a yearning for closeness to God.

69. **pleasant fragrance.** The verse thus reads: The wise man says, "I gathered the blemishes and bitterness of the souls together with their good desires." This is the concept of *aryeh* (gathering) in the aspect of soul: the tzaddik *gathers* a person's evil desires together with the pleasant fragrances stemming from his desire to serve God (*Parparaot LeChokhmah*).

Rashi (*loc. cit.*) applies this verse to the offering of incense brought by the leaders of the tribes at the consecration of the Tabernacle (Numbers 7). Seen within the context of our lesson, the leaders are synonymous with the wise man/the tzaddik; the incense, which corresponds to the binding (above §1), is the gathering of the souls; the Tabernacle represents the Holy Temple, the concept of *daat*. Furthermore, the Midrash (*Bamidbar Rabbah* 13:14) points out that each leader brought his offering in accordance with the needs and wants of his own tribe. In other words, he was able to elevate them according to their desires.

70. **Shor...clear light....** After the *aryeh*/the gathering of the desires, the *shor* in the Chariot alludes to a second element in the aspect of soul: the uniting of the soul's fragments. This refers to breaking one's desire for money, a desire which causes the splintering of the soul/the will into different interests and concerns. (A person seeking wealth spreads himself out through diversified investments.) In gathering a person's evil desires, the tzaddik halts this splintering and unites that which was fragmented (*Parparaot LeChokhmah*).

Elsewhere, Rebbe Nachman explains that the soul and money are rooted in the same transcendant source (*Likutey Moharan* I, 68, 69). (This explains why the desire for money seems to be a part of human nature. This is the soul seeking to return to its source.) Thus,

LIKUTEY MOHARAN #13:5 — 270

וְזֶה בְּחִינַת שׁוֹר, לְשׁוֹן הִסְתַּכְּלוּת, בְּחִינַת מַרְאֵה עֵינַיִם מְהַלֵּךְ־נֶפֶשׁ.

וְנֶשֶׁר שֶׁבִּבְחִינַת נֶפֶשׁ – זֶה הַחִדּוּשׁ שֶׁנִּתְחַדֵּשׁ הַנֶּפֶשׁ בַּעֲלִיָּתָהּ בִּבְחִינַת עִבּוּר. וְזֶה בְּחִינַת נֶשֶׁר – "תִּתְחַדֵּשׁ כַּנֶּשֶׁר נְעוּרָיְכִי" (תְּהִלִּים ק"ג).

וְאָדָם שֶׁבַּנֶּפֶשׁ – זֶה בְּחִינַת (בְּרֵאשִׁית ב) : "וַיְהִי הָאָדָם לְנֶפֶשׁ חַיָּה", כִּי הָאָדָם בְּחִינוֹת מִסְכֵּנֵי וַעֲתִּירֵי, כְּמוֹ שֶׁכָּתוּב (בְּהַקְדָּמַת הַזֹּהַר יג:) : "נַעֲשֶׂה אָדָם בְּצַלְמֵנוּ" – עֲתִּירֵי, "כִּדְמוּתֵנוּ" – מִסְכְּנֵי. וּכְשֶׁנִּתְלַקְּטוּ הַנְּפָשׁוֹת, אֲזַי הֵם בִּבְחִינַת אָדָם, נְפָשׁוֹת גְּדוֹלוֹת וּקְטַנּוֹת, בִּבְחִינַת מִסְכְּנֵי וַעֲתִּירֵי.

וְאוֹפַנִּים – הֵן הַגּוּפִין, כִּי עִקַּר פְּעֻלּוֹתֵיהֶן שֶׁל הַגּוּפִין אֵינוֹ אֶלָּא מִן הַחִיּוּת שֶׁבַּנֶּפֶשׁ, שֶׁהַנֶּפֶשׁ מַרְאָה פְּעֻלּוֹתֶיהָ עַל־יְדֵי אֵיבְרֵי הַגּוּף, וְאֵין לַגּוּף שׁוּם תְּנוּעָה עַצְמִית, וְהַכֹּל עַל־יְדֵי כֹּחוֹת הַנֶּפֶשׁ.

---

teaches: When a non-Jew converts, he is like a new-born child (*Yevamot* 22a). Many commentaries point out that this is equally applicable to a Jew who repents. He, too, is starting his life anew.

80. **adam...living soul.** The *adam* in the Chariot alludes to a fourth element in the aspect of soul: the "living soul." When one comes to the wise man and his soul is renewed through the aspect of pregnancy, he matures into a "living soul"—the living creatures of the Chariot who run and return.

81. **wealthy...impoverished.** This passage from the *Zohar* (*loc. cit.*) explains that men are created rich and poor to facilitate the performance of the mitzvah of *tzedakah* (charity). By helping others, man unites with his fellow man. This ties in very well with the lesson. Through performing the mitzvah of charity, one attains *daat* (the combination of *ashan* and *ruach*, *gevurot* and *chasadim*) which then allows for the rejuvination of the soul, as in, "Let us make *adam*...."

82. **Ofanim are the bodies.** "For the spirit of the living creature was in the wheel" (Ezekiel 1:20). In other words, the spirit/the will of the creature descended into the wheel, making it go wherever the creature wanted it to. In the context of our lesson, this relates to the will of the soul over the body; the will of the soul ruling the body, rather than the body's desires ruling the soul. This distinction is likewise applicable to the tzaddik and his followers. His soul, vis-a-vis those of his followers, is like the soul vis-a-vis the body. The tzaddik's living spirit enters into and directs the body, and not the reverse.

LIKUTEY MOHARAN #13:5

ShoR: it connotes gazing,[76] corresponding to "...the sight of the eyes than the wandering of the soul."[77]

Nesher (eagle) in the aspect of soul is the renewal which the soul experiences when it ascends in the aspect of *eybur* (pregnancy).[78] This is the aspect of *nesher*: "Your youth is renewed like that of the eagle" (Psalms 103:5).[79]

Adam (man) in the aspect of soul corresponds to (Genesis 2:7), "And the *adam* became a living soul."[80] For "the *adam*" indicates impoverished and wealthy, as is written (Genesis 1:26), "Let us make man in our image"—wealthy; "in our likeness"—impoverished (*Zohar*, Introduction p.13b).[81]

Now, when the souls come together, they are then in the aspect of *adam*; souls great and small, corresponding to impoverished and wealthy.

Ofanim (wheels) are the bodies.[82] For the body's main functioning comes only from the life-force in the soul. The soul exhibits its functioning through the limbs of the body, whereas the body has no movement of its own. Everything happens because of the soul's powers.

---

other words, the person who breaks his desire for money by giving to the poor is rewarded with unity of the soul, which enables it to shine.

In Hebrew, clearness is *tzachtzachot*. The Ari explains that *tzachtzachot* is also the term used for the heavenly lights which existed at the very earliest point of Creation. These transcendant lights are therefore similar to *T-N-T-A*, the elements of Torah mentioned above (§4). Thus, by uniting his soul, one can also acquire Torah (as in n.70). See below, note 108.

76. **ShoR...gazing.** This is as in the verse (Numbers 24:17), "*aShuRenu* (I gazed upon it), but it was not near."

77. **of the soul.** Thus, *shor* (ox) in the aspect of soul alludes to the soul's clear light which predominates when the soul itself is united.

78. **nesher...renewal....** The *nesher* in Yechezkel's vision alludes to the third element in the aspect of soul: the concept known as pregnancy. Just as in pregnancy the fetus develops and grows to maturity, the Kabbalistic *eybur* applies to the spiritual growth of something that begins small and develops. Earlier in the lesson (§2), Rebbe Nachman discussed the unification of the Holy One and His Divine Presence which is brought about by the elevation of the Jewish souls in the aspect of feminine waters. This elevation of the soul is its *eybur*, as the wise man raises it up to be renewed.

79. **renewed like that of the eagle.** Rashi explains that there is a species of eagle which constantly renews itself. He also quotes the Midrash that there is an eagle which lives for many years and then rejuvinates itself (cf. *Bereishit Rabbah* 19:5; *Tzaddik* #425 and note). Here we see that when renewal occurs, it is as if the soul begins life anew. The Talmud

LIKUTEY MOHARAN #13:5 272

וְכִסֵּא שֶׁבִּבְחִינַת נֶפֶשׁ – הוּא נֶפֶשׁ הֶחָכָם שֶׁנִּתְכַּסֶּה, בִּבְחִינַת (מִשְׁלֵי
ג): "יְקָרָה הִיא מִפְּנִינִים" [כְּמוֹ שֶׁדָּרְשׁוּ רַבּוֹתֵינוּ, זִכְרוֹנָם לִבְרָכָה
(סוֹטָה ד:) מִכֹּהֵן גָּדוֹל שֶׁנִּכְנָס לִפְנַי וְלִפְנִים], כִּי מֵחֲמַת שֶׁנֶּפֶשׁ
הֶחָכָם הוּא יָקָר, הוּא נִתְכַּסֶּה לִפְנַי וְלִפְנִים, וְכָל הַנְּפָשׁוֹת נַעֲשִׂין
לְבוּשִׁין אֶצְלָהּ.

וְהָאָדָם הַיּוֹשֵׁב עַל הַכִּסֵּא – הוּא דַּעְתּוֹ שֶׁל הֶחָכָם, כִּי "גַּם בְּלֹא
דַעַת נֶפֶשׁ לֹא טוֹב" (מִשְׁלֵי י"ט).

וְיֵשׁ אַרְבַּע חַיּוֹת בַּתּוֹרָה: אַרְיֵה שֶׁבַּתּוֹרָה, כִּי הַתּוֹרָה נִקְרָא עֹז –
"וּמָה עַז מֵאֲרִי" (שׁוֹפְטִים י"ד); וְשׁוֹר שֶׁבַּתּוֹרָה – זֶה בְּחִינַת (מִשְׁלֵי
ח): "בִּי שָׂרִים יָשֹׂרוּ"; וְנֶשֶׁר שֶׁבַּתּוֹרָה – זֶה בְּחִינַת חִדּוּשִׁין
דְּאוֹרַיְתָא, בִּבְחִינַת "תִּתְחַדֵּשׁ כַּנֶּשֶׁר". וְאָדָם שֶׁבַּתּוֹרָה – זֶה בְּחִינַת
(בְּמִדְבַּר י"ט): "זֹאת הַתּוֹרָה אָדָם", וְיֵשׁ בָּהּ קַלּוֹת וַחֲמוּרוֹת, שֶׁהֵם
בְּחִינַת מִסְכְּנֵי וְעַתִּירֵי;

וְכִסֵּא שֶׁבִּבְחִינַת תּוֹרָה – הֵם דְּבָרִים שֶׁכִּסָּה עַתִּיק-יוֹמִין (פְּסָחִים

---

88. **Torah is called might.** "God will give might to His nation" (Psalms 29:11). Rashi explains that this might is Torah. Also see *Shir HaShirim Rabbah* 2:3.

89. **mightier than a lion.** This was the answer to the riddle which Shimshon presented to the Philistines: What is it, that "...out of the mighty came sweetness"? This relates to the sweetening and allaying of the burning desires.

90. **sarim yaSoRu.** In this verse from Proverbs, "me" is the Torah, through which one's rule is established (*Metzudat Tzion, loc. cit.*). This is the implication of the *shor*, as the Talmud teaches (*Chagigah* 13b): The king (ruler) of the domestic animals is the ox (*Parparaot LeChokhmah*).

91. **new Torah insights.** As in the soul, *nesher* alludes to the birth of something new. In terms of the Torah, this is the revelation of original Torah insights, as mentioned above in section 2.

92. **Ancient of Days....** This passage in *Pesachim* (*loc. cit.*) defines two categories of the teachings of the Ancient of Days: concepts that were concealed and are to remain concealed, and concepts that were concealed and should be revealed. Those that are not meant to be revealed remain hidden. However, those that should be revealed, are made known when the wise man elevates the souls of his followers and then returns with new Torah insights. These revelations, as Rebbe Nachman tells us, are from the Torah of the Future—that which the Ancient of Days concealed. See note 26 that these new insights already exist in the Torah, but they are concealed within garments, the sagas which the Torah records.

LIKUTEY MOHARAN #13:5

KiSay (throne) in the aspect of soul is the wise man's soul, which is *nitKaSeh* (concealed).[83] This corresponds to (Proverbs 3:15), "[The wise man's soul] is more precious than *PNiNiM* (pearls)," {about which our Sages expounded: More precious than the High Priest who entered *liPhNi v'liPhNiM* (the innermost sanctum) (Sotah 4b).}[84] Because the soul of the wise man is so precious, it is concealed in the innermost sanctum and all the souls become her garb.[85] And, [finally,] the *adam* who sits on the throne is the knowledge of the wise man, for "Also, that the soul be without *daat* is not good" (Proverbs 19:2).[86]

There are also the four living creatures in [the aspect of] Torah.[87] *Aryeh* [is] in the Torah, for the Torah is called "might,"[88] and "what is mightier than a lion?" (Judges 14:18).[89] *ShoR* in the Torah is alluded to in (Proverbs 8:16), "By me *sarim yaSoRu* (rulers rule)."[90] *Nesher* in the Torah is the aspect of new Torah insights,[91] as alluded in, "...renewed like that of the eagle." *Adam* in the Torah is alluded to in (Numbers 19:14), "This is the Torah: a man!" The [Torah] has lenient and strict applications, corresponding to "impoverished" and "wealthy."

Kisay in the aspect of Torah are those things which the Ancient of Days *kisah* (Pesachim 119a)[92]—they conceal themselves within the stories

83. **concealed.** The *kisay* of Yechezkel's vision alludes to the hidden and concealed nature of the tzaddik's own soul. Rebbe Nachman is pointing out the greatness of the true tzaddikim (those who labor to rectify the souls of their fellow Jews) and their followers. The tzaddik is likened to the throne of the Chariot and the souls close to him are likened to its wheels! (*Mai HaNachal*).

84. **High Priest....** This passage from the Talmud (*loc. cit.*) points out the greatness of one who studies Torah/the wise man/the tzaddik. He is greater in stature than even a High Priest, who is the only one permitted to enter the Holy of Holies and then, only on Yom Kippur. This is an indication that Torah knowledge is actually more exalted than even the holiest and innermost sanctum of this world.

85. **concealed in the innermost...garb.** Just as the High Priest was able to elicit forgiveness for sin and a purification of the soul by entering the Holy of Holies, *LiPhNi v'liPhNiM* (לפני ולפנים), the wise man, whose soul is likened to *PNiNiM* (פנינים, pearls), is able to elicit repentance and the renewal of the soul.

86. **...without daat is not good.** One's will and desires are directly linked to his soul (as above, §3 and n.35). With *daat,* his will is for that which is good, his desire is for holiness. However, without *daat,* his will and desire are not for that which is good or holy, and this is not good for his soul. Therefore, the *adam* sits *on* the throne—the wise man's holy knowledge must sit *on* the soul—to control it.

87. **four living creatures in Torah.** Having explained how the different elements in Yechezkel's vision apply to the soul—the Lower Chariot, Rebbe Nachman now focuses on how they apply to the Torah—the Upper Chariot.

LIKUTEY MOHARAN #13:5

קיט. וְעַיֵּן זֹהַר בְּהַעֲלֹתְךָ קנב.), וְהֵם מְכַסִּים אֶת עַצְמָן בְּסִפּוּרֵי הַתּוֹרָה; וְיוֹשֵׁב עַל הַכִּסֵּא – הוּא עַתִּיק-יוֹמִין, בִּבְחִינַת (דָּנִיֵּאל ז): "וְעַתִּיק יוֹמִין יְתִב"; וְאוֹפַנִּים שֶׁבַּתּוֹרָה – הֵן הֵן גּוּפֵי הַלְכוֹת.

וְזֶה שֶׁמֵּבִיא בְּתַעֲנִית (כג:): מַעֲשֶׂה דְּרַבִּי יוֹנָה: כַּד הֲוָה אִצְטְרִיךְ עָלְמָא לְמִטְרָא, אָמַר: אֵזִיל וְאַיְתֵי בְּזוּזָא עֲבוּרָא; וַהֲוֵי קָאֵי בְּאַתְרָא עֲמִיקֵי, בְּאַתְרָא צְנִיעָא מִכְסֵי שַׁקָּא, וְעַל-יְדֵי-זֶה וְאָתֵי מִטְרָא. כַּד הֲוָה מִצְטְרִיךְ עָלְמָא לְמִטְרָא – הַיְנוּ לַתּוֹרָה, כְּמוֹ שֶׁכָּתוּב (דְּבָרִים ל"ב): "יַעֲרֹף כַּמָּטָר לִקְחִי".

אָמַר, אֵזִיל וְאַיְתֵי בְּזוּזָא עֲבוּרָא. עֲבוּר – זֶה בְּחִינַת ע"ב רי"ו; ע"ב הוּא שָׁכוּךְ, רי"ו – זֶה בְּחִינַת חֲמִימוּת. בְּזוּזָא – זֶה בְּחִינַת תַּאֲוַת מָמוֹן, הַיְנוּ דַּאֲזַל לְשַׁכֵּךְ תַּאֲוַת מָמוֹן כַּנַּ"ל. וַהֲוָה קָאֵי בְּאַתְרָא עֲמִיקֵי – עַל-יְדֵי שֶׁשִּׁכֵּךְ תַּאֲוַת מָמוֹן זָכָה לְאַתְרָא עֲמִיקֵי, שֶׁהוּא בְּחִינַת חֶסֶד, כְּמַרְאֵה הַחַמָּה עֲמֻקָה מִן הַצֵּל (שְׁבוּעוֹת ו:), וְחֶסֶד הוּא אוֹר יוֹם, כְּמוֹ שֶׁכָּתוּב (תְּהִלִּים מ"ב): "יוֹמָם

(severities) and *dinim* (stern judgments) that give rise to the burning (*Parparaot LeChokhmah*). See above, note 6.

101. **zuza.** The *zuza* (often referred to as *zuz*), a silver coin in Aramaic, represents the evil desire for money. As mentioned above (nn.10,42), there is a burning which is pure. (See also n.68 concerning the desire and yearning to come closer to God.) This is referred to here as *rayu*. However, when this burning "materializes" as an evil desire, it is known as *zuza*—the desire for money. Rabbi Yonah went to cool the burning desire, the idolatry of money, in order to reveal new Torah insights.

102. **went to allay....** Rabbi Yonah went to combine *EB* and *RaYU*, *chesed* and *gevurah*, so that there would be an *EYBUR* for the renewal of the souls. This is how he hoped to bring Torah into the world (*Parparaot LeChokhmah*).

103. **sun-lit...shaded spots.** This refers to the leprosy of *baheret*, in which a white spot appears on the body (Leviticus 13:2). It is the whitest (brightest) of all the various types of leprosy (*Nega'im* 1:1). The Talmud (*loc. cit.*), when explaining the nature of this whiteness, compares it to "a sun-lit spot which appears recessed within a shaded area." It therefore appears deeper (more set back) than the surrounding skin.

104. **in the daytime.** In order to show that the "deep place" to which Rabbi Yonah merited is *chesed*, Rebbe Nachman quotes the verse from Psalms that *chesed* is synonymous with the daytime/*sun-lit* area. These sun-lit or brighter areas, as the Talmud (*Shavuot* 6b) teaches,

LIKUTEY MOHARAN #13:5

of the Torah. The one who sits on the throne is the Ancient of Days [Himself], as in (Daniel 7:9), "The Ancient of Days did sit."[93] [Finally,] *ofanim* in Torah are themselves the bodies of law.[94]

And this is the story brought in *Taanit* **(23b) about Rabbi Yonah:[95] When the world was in need of rain, he said, "I will go and purchase a** *zuz* **worth of** *eybura* **(grain)." [Instead,] he would stand in a deep place, a concealed place, covered in sackcloth. This would cause the rains to come.**

When the world was in need of rain — In other words, [in need] of Torah, as in (Deuteronomy 32:2), "My teaching shall drop like rain."[96]

He said, I will go and purchase a zuz worth of eybura (grain) — *EYBUR*[97] corresponds to *EB RaYU*.[98] *Eb* alludes to allaying[99]; *rayu* is the aspect of burning[100]; *zuza*[101] corresponds to the desire for money. In other words, he went to allay the [burning] desire for money.[102]

he would stand in a deep place — Having allayed the desire for money, he merited a "deep place." This is the aspect of lovingkindness, as in the way "the sun-lit spots appear deeper than the shaded spots" (*Shavuot* 6b).[103] And lovingkindness is the light of day, as is written (Psalms 42:9), "God will command His lovingkindness in the daytime."[104] And

---

93. **Ancient of Days did sit.** This corresponds to *daat*, the Torah knowledge of the wise man which "sits" on the throne of the Lower Chariot.

94. **bodies of law.** See above (n.82) that the *ofanim* (wheels) allude to the body. And, just as the body is a garment for the soul, the bodies of law of the Torah are garments for the Torah's inner meaning.

95. **story...Rabbi Yonah.** Rebbe Nachman will now review the lesson to this point, summarizing the different themes within this story. This in itself is an example of how the revelations of the Ancient of Days are cloaked within stories of Torah (as in nn.26,92).

96. **My teaching...rain.** "Just as rain brings life to the world, so too My Torah" (*Sifrei, loc. cit.*). See above, section 4.

97. **EYBUR.** The way to draw the Torah which the world requires is to elevate the souls in the concept of *eybur* (pregnancy).

98. **EB RaYU.** In Hebrew, *EB RaYU* (עב ריו) has the same letters as *eybur* (עיבור). In other words, the way to bring about this pregnancy is through *eb rayu*. The letters *EB* (עב) have a numerical value of 72, corresponding to *CheSeD* (חסד). The *gematria* of the letters *RaYU* (ריו) is 216, corresponding to *GeVURaH* (גבורה) (*Parparaot LeChokhmah*; see Appendix: Gematria Chart).

99. **EB...allaying.** Because it corresponds to *chesed*, *eb* alludes to the *chasadim* (benevolences) that cool the burning arising from the severities (*Parparaot LeChokhmah*). See above, note 6.

100. **rayu...burning.** Because it corresponds to *gevurah*, *rayu* alludes to the *gevurot*

LIKUTEY MOHARAN #13:5,6 276

יְצַוֶּה ה' חַסְדּוֹ"; וְעַל־יְדֵי הַחֶסֶד זָכָה לְבִנְיַן הַבַּיִת, לִבְחִינַת שֵׂכֶל
כַּנַּ"ל.

וְזֶה: אַתְרָא צְנִיעָא — שֶׁהוּא בֵּית־הַמִּקְדָּשׁ, שֶׁהוּא הַשֵּׂכֶל, כְּמוֹ
שֶׁכָּתוּב (מִשְׁלֵי י"א): "וְאֶת צְנוּעִים חָכְמָה".
וַהֲוָה מִכַּסֵּי שָׁקָא — זֶה בְּחִינַת לְקִיחַת הַנְּפָשׁוֹת לְהַעֲלוֹת אוֹתָם,
כַּנַּ"ל: "וְלִקַּח נְפָשׁוֹת חָכָם", וּכְלָלִיּוּת הַנְּפָשׁוֹת הֵם מְכֻנִּים בְּשֵׁם
שָׂק, כִּי הֵם מִתְעַדְּנִים מִשַּׁקְיָא דְּנַחֲלָא, בִּבְחִינַת "וְהִשְׂבִּיעַ
בְּצַחְצָחוֹת נַפְשֶׁךָ", וְעַל־יְדֵי־זֶה:
וְאָתֵי מִטְרָא — שֶׁהַמָּשִׁיךְ תּוֹרָה, בִּבְחִינַת "וַיֵּרֶד עֹז מִבְטָחָה":

ו. אַךְ צָרִיךְ לְבַקֵּשׁ מְאֹד וְלַחֲזֹר אַחַר חָכָם כָּזֶה, וּלְבַקֵּשׁ מֵהַשֵּׁם
יִתְבָּרַךְ, שֶׁיִּזְכֶּה לִמְצֹא חָכָם כָּזֶה, שֶׁיְּקַבֵּץ הַנְּפָשׁוֹת, בִּבְחִינַת:
"וְלִקַּח נְפָשׁוֹת חָכָם", וְיַעֲלֶה אוֹתָם וְיוֹרֵד עִמָּהֶם תּוֹרָה. כִּי גַם
הֶחָכָם בְּעַצְמוֹ אִי אֶפְשָׁר שֶׁיַּעֲשֶׂה זֹאת בְּשֵׂכֶל אֶחָד, כִּי הֵם שְׁנֵי
שְׂכָלִיִּים: מַה שֶּׁמְּקַבֵּץ הַנְּפָשׁוֹת הוּא שֵׂכֶל אֶחָד, וּמַה שֶּׁמַּעֲלֶה

In review: Giving charity breaks one's desire for money, as a result of which one draws Divine
providence and experiences joy and contentment. Charity is also an aspect of the revelation of
Mashiach, when the idolatrous worship of money is nullified. Divine anger is thus eliminated,
lovingkindness is revealed, and it is as if one built the Holy Temple—synonymous with *daat*
(§1). This deeper knowledge, required to understand the Torah's mysteries, enables one to
receive Torah insights and teach them to others. Doing so attracts their souls, which he then
elevates to create a unification. As a result, new Torah insights are revealed (§2). When people
bring their will/soul to the wise man, the tzaddik purifies their desires and "runs"/ascends with
them. Later, when he "returns" with the souls, he also brings a revelation of Torah to the
world (§3). This drawing of new Torah insights elicits Divine providence, Heaven's power-of-
vision. Those close to Torah are completely reflected in His eyes, whereas the gentiles and
those distant from Torah receive only a partial seeing (§4). The wise man who ascends and
descends with the souls also gathers, satiates, renews and rejuvinates all the fallen wills/souls.
This is a rectification of the Upper and Lower Chariots (§5).

110. **merit finding such a wise man....** Such a wise man/tzaddik is on the level of Moshe
Rabbeinu—the one who ascended and then brought down the Torah. However, finding him
does not come easy. These tzaddikim are few and far between. Rabbi Shimon bar Yochai
said: "I saw the *b'nei aliyah* (those who have attained an exceptionally high spiritual plane)
and they are few" (*Sukkah* 45b). This remark appears in the Talmud in relation to those who
merit seeing the Divine Presence. Rashi (*s.v. aspaklarya*) comments that there are tzaddikim

277   *LIKUTEY MOHARAN #13:5,6*

through the lovingkindness he was worthy of building the House, the aspect of intellect, as above.[105] And this is:

a concealed place — This refers to the Holy Temple, which is the intellect, as is written (Proverbs 11:2), "But with the concealed (modest) is wisdom."[106]

covered in a sackcloth — This alludes to taking the souls in order to elevate them, as mentioned above: "He that takes souls is wise."[107] The encompassing of the souls is known as a *SaK* (sack), for "they delight in the *ShaKya* (drink) of the brook." This corresponds to, "And He shall satiate your soul with clearness."[108] And through this:

the rains to come — He drew down Torah, as in, "...and brings down the mighty in which it trusts."[109]

6. However, a person must continuously ask for and seek out a wise man such as this. And he should ask of God that he merit finding such a wise man who will gather together the souls[110]—as in, "He that takes souls is wise"—and elevate them, and then bring them down with Torah. For even the wise man himself cannot do this with one intellect. These are two [separate] intellects: gathering the souls is one

---

appear *deeper.* Thus, in allaying the desire for money, which comes from the *gevurot*/the left side, Rabbi Yonah merited a "deep place" of lovingkindness, from the right.

105. **as above.** See end of section 1. When the *chasadim* overpower *dinim,* one merits *daat* (holy knowledge/intellect)—the concept of the Holy Temple.

106. **Holy Temple...concealed is wisdom.** Thus, Rabbi Yonah attained the level of the Holy Temple. First he achieved the level of *chesed,* a deep place. In this merit he came to the concealed place, the Temple—*daat.*

107. **sackcloth...wise man.** For the souls are his garment, as above note 85.

108. **ShaKya of the brook.** Rebbe Nachman is referring to the passage in the *Zohar* (III, 67b) that teaches: Those who delight in the Torah will merit to drink from the brook, as is written, "He will satiate your soul with clearness" (see n.75). The "brook" is part of the reward that will be given to the tzaddikim who study Torah. In our context, this relates to the souls that attach themselves to the tzaddik. Rabbi Yonah was "covered in a *sak*"—the souls he sought to elevate became the garment of his soul—so that he could raise them up and then descend with new Torah insights. And, by virtue of their attachment to him, they would receive a share of his reward. They, too, would drink from the brook and satiate their souls with the *tzachtzachot* (clearness).

109. **brings down the mighty....** Just as the rains are called mighty (*Taanit* 2a), so too the Torah (n.88 above). The verse thus refers to the revealing of new Torah insights, as above in section 2.

אוֹתָם וּמוֹרִיד עֹז מִבְטָחָה הוּא שֵׂכֶל אַחֵר. וְזֶה בְּחִינַת שִׁין שֶׁל שְׁלֹשָׁה רָאשִׁים וְשִׁין שֶׁל אַרְבָּעָה רָאשִׁים, שֶׁהַשְּׁנֵי שִׁינִין הֵם הַשְּׁנֵי שְׂכָלִים:

וְזֶה פֵּרוּשׁ:

אָמַר רַבָּה בַּר בַּר־חָנָה: אִשְׁתָּעוּ לִי נָחוּתֵי יַמָּא: בֵּין גַּלָּא לְגַלָּא תְּלַת מְאָה פַּרְסֵי, וְרוּמְיָא דְּגַלָּא תְּלַת מְאָה פַּרְסֵי. זִמְנָא חֲדָא הֲוֵי אָזְלִינַן בְּאָרְחָא, וּדְלִינַן גַּלָּא, עַד דַּחֲזֵינַן בֵּי מַרְבַּעְתָּא דְּכוֹכָבָא זוּטָא, דַּהֲוֵי כְּמִבְזַר אַרְבְּעִין גְּרִיוָא בִּזְרָא דְחַרְדְּלָא; וְאִי דְּלִינַן טְפֵי, הֲוָה מַקְלִינַן מֵהַבְלָא. וְרָמְיָא לָהּ גַּלָּא קָלָא לַחֲבֶרְתָּהּ וְאָמְרָה לָהּ: חֲבֶרְתִּי מִי שַׁבְקִית מִידֵי בְּעָלְמָא דְּלָא שַׁטְפִית, וְנֵיתֵי אֲנָא וְנַחְרְבֵהּ. אָמְרָה לָהּ: פּוּק חֲזִי גְּבוּרְתָּא

רַשְׁבַּ"ם:

בֵּין גַּלָּא לְגַלָּא וְכוּ' – מִשּׁוּם דְּקָאָמְרִינַן בִּסְמוּךְ, 'וְרָמָא גַּלָּא קָלָא לַחֲבֶרְהּ', אִצְטְרִיךְ לְאַשְׁמְעִינַן דְּמִשְּׁלֹשׁ־מֵאוֹת פַּרְסֵי שָׁמַע קוֹלוֹ שֶׁל חֲבֵרוֹ. דְּלֵינַן גַּלָּא – יוֹתֵר מִשְּׁעוּר גָּבְהוֹ הִשְׁלִיכָנוּ לְמַעְלָה עַד לָרָקִיעַ; אִי נָמֵי, הַבְלָא דְּרָקִיעַ נָפִישׁ עַד מַהֲלָךְ קָרוֹב לְת"ק שָׁנָה שֶׁיֵּשׁ מִן הָרָקִיעַ לָאָרֶץ. מַרְבַּעְתָּא – שְׁכִיבָא. דְּכוֹכָבָא זוּטָא – כּוֹכָב קָטָן שֶׁבְּקְטַנִּים. בִּזְרָא – בֵּית זֶרַע אַרְבָּעִים כּוֹר שֶׁל חַרְדָּל, דִּנְפִישֵׁי מִכָּל שְׁאָר זְרָעִים. מַקְלִינַן מֵהַבְלָא – נִשְׂרָפִין מֵחֹם הַכּוֹכָב. וְרָמָא לַהּ גַּלָּא – נָתַן קוֹלוֹ, כְּלוֹמַר, צָעַק, כְּדִגְמַת תְּהוֹם אֶל תְּהוֹם קוֹרֵא

לְקוֹל וְגוֹ', וְשֶׁמָּא הַמַּלְאָכִים הַמְמֻנִּים עֲלֵיהֶם הֵם. שַׁבְקִית מִידֵי בְּעָלְמָא וְכוּ' – מִפְּנֵי שֶׁהִגְבִּיהָּ כָּל כָּךְ, הָיָה סָבוּר שֶׁיָּצָא חוּץ לִשְׂפַת הַיָּם וְשָׁטַף אֶת הָעוֹלָם. וְנַחְרְבֵהּ – מִפְּנֵי עֲווֹן הַדּוֹר. אָמַר לֵהּ – גַּלָּא לְחַבְרֵהּ. פּוּק חֲזִי גְּבוּרְתָּא דְּמָרָךְ

112. **elevating...bringing down...another intellect.** As in, "A wise man ascends the city of the strong, and brings down the mighty in which it trusts." These are two separate concepts, first taking the soul and then ascending and descending with it... (*Parparaot LeChokhmah*).

113. **shin of three heads...four heads.** The *bayit* (house) of the head *tefillin* has the letter *shin* embossed on either side. On the right side the *shin* (ש) is regular, with three stems coming out of the base. On the left side, however, the *shin* has four stems coming out of the base. In the Kabbalah, *tefillin* represents *mochin* (intellect). The two forms of the *shin* apply to different *mochin*. The three-stemmed *shin* refers to the *mochin* which correspond to the *sefirot* of *Chokhmah*, *Binah* and *Daat*. The four-stemmed *shin* refers to the *mochin* which correspond to

LIKUTEY MOHARAN #13:6

intellect,[111] < bringing down Torah > is another intellect.[112] This corresponds to the *shin* of three heads and the *shin* of four heads.[113] The two [forms of the] *shin* are the two intellects.

This is the explanation:

Rabbah bar bar Chanah recounted: Seafarers told me that between one wave and another there are three hundred miles, and the height of each *gal* (wave) is three hundred miles. Once, we were traveling on the *orcha* (way), when a wave lifted us up until we saw the *marvata* (resting place) of a small star. It was equivalent to the area needed to plant forty measures of mustard *bizra* (seed). Had we been lifted up any higher, we would have been *kalah* (consumed) by the *hevel* (vapor). One wave called out to its neighbor, saying: "Perhaps you left over *meeday* (something) in this world which you have not flooded? I will come and destroy it." Said the other, "Go, see the great power of your Master.

Rashbam: **between one wave and another -** because we will soon be told that one wave called out to its neighbor, we are now informed that it was from a distance of three hundred miles that it heard its neighbor's call: **a wave lifted us up** - higher than its own height, it threw us up to the heavens; or alternatively, the vapor of the heavens was so great that it extended nearly the full five hundred years which separate the heavens from the earth: **the resting place** - a lying position: **of a small star** - the smallest of the small stars: **seed** - the *bet zera* (seeded area) of 40 measures of mustard, which is more abundant than all other seeds: **consumed by the vapor** - burnt by the heat of the star: **One wave called out** - it raised its voice, that is, it cried out; similar to "deep calls to deep, to the voice...." It seems this refers to those angels in charge of [the waves]: **Perhaps you left over something of this world** - because it had risen up so high, it seemed as though it had gone past the seashore and flooded the world: **and destroy it** - because of the generation's sins: **Said the other** - one wave to its

who cannot see clearly, and some, though they are righteous, who do not even see at all. *Aliyah* has the connotation of elevating and ascending. Thus, within the context of the lesson, *b'nei aliyah* refers to the tzaddikim who have the "intellects" to gather the souls, elevate them and bring down Torah. If already in his generation (and for all time) Rabbi Shimon bar Yochai said that there were few, how many of these tzaddikim exist nowadays who can readily perform this *tikkun*? Therefore, Rebbe Nachman advises us to seek and search for such a wise man. We must pray for this constantly, beseeching and pleading with God that we merit being attached to just such a tzaddik. See also *Tzaddik #602*, regarding Rabbi Yochanan ben Zakkai.

111. **gathering...is one intellect.** As in, "And he that takes souls is wise" (*Parparaot LeChokhmah*).

LIKUTEY MOHARAN #13:6

280

דְּמָרָךְ, דַּאֲפִלּוּ כִּמְלֹא חוּטָא דְּחָלָא לֵית דְּעָבַר, וְכוּ' – כְּלוֹמַר, אֵין
שֶׁנֶּאֱמַר: "הַאוֹתִי לֹא תִירָאוּ נְאָם ה'" וְכוּ': לִי רְשׁוּת לָצֵאת.
כִּמְלֹא חוּטָא דְּחָלָא

– כִּמְלֹא רֹחַב הַחוּט אֵינִי יָכוֹל לָצֵאת חוּץ מִן הַחוֹל. שֶׁנֶּאֱמַר הַאוֹתִי לֹא תִירָאוּ
– תַּלְמוּדָא קָאָמַר לַהּ.

נְחוּתֵי יַמָּא – הַיְנוּ מַמְשִׁיכֵי יַמָּא דְּאוֹרַיְתָא לָזֶה הָעוֹלָם.

בֵּין גַּלָּא לְגַלָּא תְּלָת מֵאָה פַּרְסֵי – שֶׁהוּא בְּחִינַת שִׁין הַנַּ"ל.

וְרוּמְיָא דְּגַלָּא תְּלָת מֵאָה פַּרְסֵי – שֶׁהוּא בְּחִינַת שִׁין שְׁנִיָּה הַנַּ"ל
(הַיְנוּ בְּחִינַת שְׁנֵי הַשְּׂכָלִיִּים הַנַּ"ל, שֶׁהוּא הַשֵּׂכֶל שֶׁל קִבּוּץ
הַנְּפָשׁוֹת, וְהַשֵּׂכֶל שֶׁל הַעֲלָאַת הַנְּפָשׁוֹת לְהַמְשִׁיךְ תּוֹרָה, שֶׁאֵלּוּ שְׁנֵי
הַשְּׂכָלִיִּים שֶׁל הַצַּדִּיק שֶׁהוּא חָכָם הָאֱמֶת הֵם בְּחִינַת שְׁנֵי שִׁינִין
כַּנַּ"ל). וְהַגַּלִּים הֵם הַנְּפָשׁוֹת, בִּבְחִינַת צַהֲלִי קוֹלֵךְ בַּת גַּלִּים, שֶׁהִיא
בַּת אֲבָהָן.

בֵּין גַּלָּא לְגַלָּא – אֵלּוּ הַחֲכָמִים שֶׁהֵם בֵּין גַּלָּא לְגַלָּא, הַיְנוּ
מְחַבְּרִים כָּל הַנְּפָשׁוֹת, בִּבְחִינַת "וְלָקַח נַפְשׁוֹת חָכָם".

תְּלָת מֵאָה פַּרְסֵי – שֶׁהִיא בְּחִינַת שִׁין אַחַת.

וְרוּמְיָא דְּגַלָּא תְּלָת מֵאָה פַּרְסֵי – הַיְנוּ לְהַעֲלוֹת הַנְּפָשׁוֹת, זֶה
בְּחִינַת שִׁין אַחֶרֶת.

---

presence? [For it is] I who have placed the sand as the boundary of the sea...though its
waves toss themselves...they cannot pass over it."

115. **shin, three hundred....** The *shin,* with a numerical value of 300, corresponds to the three
hundred miles between the waves.

116. **Batgallim...bat of the patriarchs.** The Jewish people are the *bat* (daughter) and they are
the *bat ayin* (apple of God's eye), corresponding to the Community of Israel/*Malkhut,* as
above (§4 and nn.51,52). Thus, *Batgallim* (daughter of the waves) alludes to the souls of the
Jewish people which are lifted up.

117. **between one wave...one shin.** The gathering of the souls, uniting them together.

118. **height of each wave...other shin.** The elevating, height, of the souls.

281   *LIKUTEY MOHARAN #13:6*

Even a hairsbreadth of the *chol* (sand) cannot be *e'var* (crossed over)." As is written (Jeremiah 5:22), **"Do you not fear Me? says God. . ."** (*Bava Batra* 73a).[114] neighbor: Go, see the great power of your Master - In other words, I do not have permission to go beyond: **Even a hairsbreadth of the sand** - I cannot go past the sand's shoreline even the width of a strand's worth: **As is written, Do you not fear Me?** - the Talmud made this remark [and not Rabbah bar bar Chanah]:

Seafarers — This alludes to those who draw the sea of Torah to this world.

Between one wave and another there are < shin > (three hundred) miles — This corresponds to the abovementioned **shin.**[115]

and the height of each *gal* (wave) is < shin > (three hundred) miles — This is the second *shin* mentioned above.

{In other words, the two intellects: the intellect of gathering the souls, and the intellect of elevating the souls in order to drawn down Torah. These two intellects of the tzaddik, he being the true wise man, correspond to the two [forms of the] *shin*.} The **gallim** (waves) are the souls, as alluded in (Isaiah 10:30), "Lift up your voice, Batgallim"—she is the *bat* (daughter) of the patriarchs (*Sanhedrin* 94b).[116]

Between one wave and another — These are the wise men, who are **between one wave and another**. That is, they unite all the souls, as in, "He that takes souls is wise."

three hundred miles — This corresponds to one *shin*.[117]

and the height of each wave is three hundred miles — In other words, to elevate the souls. This corresponds to the other *shin*.[118]

Chokhmah, Binah, Chesed and *Gevurah* (*Mai HaNachal*; also see *Pri Etz Chaim, Shaar HaTefillin*). This is discussed at length in the writings of the Ari. In our context, the sets of *mochin* alluded to by the two forms of the *shin* indicate the combinations of forces through which the stern judgments are mitigated—i.e., the combining of *chasadim* and *gevurot* to form *daat*.

In addition, the *Zohar* (I, 129b) relates the two forms of the *shin* to the two Chariots, upper and lower. Thus, by putting on *tefillin* daily, with intent to fulfill the mitzvah properly, one draws upon himself the holiness of the two Chariots. As explained above in section 5, this elevates our desires and draws down new Torah insights. Yet, quintessentially, this also requires being bound to the tzaddik. He is the wise man—corresponding to the *mochin*, the two *shin* of the *tefillin*, the two intellects necessary to gather and elevate the souls/the desires in order to reveal new Torah insights.

114. **Do you not fear Me? says God.** The verse continues: "Will you not tremble at My

LIKUTEY MOHARAN #13:6

זִמְנָא חֲדָא אַזְלִינַן בְּאָרְחָא – הַיְנוּ שֶׁאֲנַחְנוּ נִכְנַסְנוּ לְעוֹרֵר זִוּוּג,
הַנִּקְרָא אֹרַח, כְּמוֹ שֶׁכָּתוּב (תְּהִלִּים קל"ט): "אָרְחִי וְרִבְעִי".
וּדְלֵינַן גַּלָּא – הַיְנוּ שֶׁדְּלֵינַן הַנְּפָשׁוֹת לְמַעְלָה, בִּבְחִינַת עִיר גִּבֹּרִים
עָלָה חָכָם.

עַד דַּחֲזֵינַן בֵּי מַרְבַּעְתָּא דְּכוֹכָבָא זוּטָא – הַיְנוּ שֶׁגֵּרַמְנוּ זִוּוּגָא
עִלָּאָה. מַרְבַּעְתָּא – זֶה בְּחִינַת זִוּוּג, כְּמוֹ שֶׁכָּתוּב: "אָרְחִי וְרִבְעִי".
שְׁכִינְתָּא נִקְרֵאת בִּשְׁעַת זִוּוּג כּוֹכָבָא זוּטָא, כַּמּוּבָא בַּזֹּהַר (בָּלָק
קצ"א.), 'אִתְעֲבִידַת נְקֻדָּה זְעֵירָא מִגּוֹ רְחִימְתָּא, כְּדֵין אִתְחַבְּרָא
בְּבַעְלָהּ', עַיֵּן שָׁם.

וַהֲוָה כְּמִבְזַר אַרְבְּעִין גְּרִיעָא בְּזַרְעָא דְּחַרְדְּלָא – כַּמּוּבָא בַּזֹּהַר (פִּינְחָס
רמ"ט:): 'הַאי חַיָּה כַּד אִתְעַבְּרָא, אִסְתַּתְּמַת וְלָא יְכִילַת לְאוֹלָדָא, עַד
דְּאַתְיָא נָחָשׁ וְנָשֵׁךְ בְּעֶרְיָתָא, כְּדֵין אִתְפַּתְּחַת וְנָפֵק מִנַּהּ דְּמָא, וְהִיא
שָׁתִית לְדָמָא'. וְזֶה בְּחִינַת 'בְּזַרְעָא דְּחַרְדְּלָא', הַיְנוּ בְּחִינַת טִפַּת דָּם
כְּחַרְדָּל, דְּנָפֵק מִנַּהּ מֵחֲמַת הַנְּשִׁיכָה בְּבֵית הַזֶּרַע. 'בְּזַרְעָא' – פֵּרֵשׁ
רַבֵּינוּ שְׁמוּאֵל: 'בֵּית זֶרַע'. וְאַחַר־כָּךְ אוֹלִידַת, וְהַתּוֹלָדָה הַזֹּאת הִיא
הַתּוֹרָה כַּנַּ"ל, וְהַתּוֹרָה הַזֹּאת הִיא הוֹלֶכֶת דֶּרֶךְ אַרְבָּעִים יוֹם, הַיְנוּ
בְּחִינַת שְׁאָר חַיָּתָא שֶׁהֵם אַרְבָּעִים, עֲשָׂרָה לְכָל סְטַר, כַּמּוּבָא שָׁם

Malkhut is a sign of modesty, as will be explained shortly. Because of their modesty and
humbleness, the Jewish people—the Community of Israel—are beloved in God's eyes, and
He brings the apple of His eye closer to Him.

122. **That creature...drinks the blood.** The entire passage in the *Zohar* about this creature is
actually an allusion to *Malkhut*/the Divine Presence which is about to "give birth" to new
souls. Thus, "when becoming pregnant" refers to the elevation of the souls in the aspect of
eybur, and "blood emerges" indicates the birth of new Torah insights.

123. **mustard seed...bet zera.** "A drop of blood the size of a mustard seed" is an expression
which appears in the Talmud (*Niddah* 66a) in connection to blood which exits from the
womb.

124. **Torah, as mentioned earlier.** In section 2. That is, *Malkhut*, by uniting with *Z'er Anpin*,
gives birth to, reveals, new Torah insights.

125. **forty days...creatures...forty, ten on each side....** The four creatures in Yechezkel's
vision of the Chariot correspond to the four sides of the world. Each of the four sides is a
complete structure of ten *sefirot*. These are the forty creatures. Thus, there is a concept of

LIKUTEY MOHARAN #13:6

Once, we were traveling on the orcha (way) — That is, we went in to rouse a unification, which is called *ORaCh*, as in (Psalms 139:3), "...*ORChi* (my going on the way) and my laying down."[119]

when a wave lifted us up — In other words, they **lifted up** the souls Above, corresponding to, "A wise man ascends the city of the strong."

until we saw the marvata (resting place) of a small star — That is, we brought about an upper unification. [The word] **maRVata** alludes to unification, as in, "...my going on the way and *RiV'ee* (my laying down)."[120] At the time of unification, the Divine Presence is called **a small star**. As is brought in the *Zohar* (III, 191a): Out of love, [the Divine Presence] becomes a small point, and in so doing unites with her husband. See there.[121]

It was equivalent to the area needed to plant forty measures of mustard bizra (seed) — As is brought in the *Zohar* (III, 249b): That creature, when she becomes pregnant, she closes up. She is unable to give birth, until a snake comes and bites her pudendum. This causes it to open and blood emerges. And [the snake] drinks the blood.[122] This is the aspect of the **mustard seed**—i.e., "a drop of blood the size of a mustard seed" that emerges from her because of the bite in the *bet zera* (womb).[123] Thus, Rashbam explains *BiZRa* as *Bet ZeRa*. Afterwards, she gives birth. This < birth is an aspect of bringing down > the Torah, as mentioned earlier.[124] This Torah then travels for forty days. This corresponds to "the other creatures which total forty," ten on each side, as explained there (*ibid.*).[125] This is the aspect of **forty measures,**

---

119. **ORChi, my going on the way....** The Talmud explains that both *orchi* and *riv'ee* are references to marital relations (*Niddah* 31a). Here, "my going on the way" alludes to the going to rouse a holy unification in the transcendant worlds, as above in section 2.

120. **RiV'ee, my laying down.** Previously, Rebbe Nachman emphasized the word *orchi*, because the process leading to union had begun but had not yet been completed. But now, he focuses on the second word, *riv'ee* (laying down). This is because after the "wave had lifted them up," the unification through which new Torah insights are revealed had been accomplished.

121. **See there.** The *Zohar* explains that the small point is reflected in the letter *yud*, which is essentially no more than a black dot. In other words, *Malkhut* reduces itself and becomes a mere point. Her "husband," *Z'er Anpin*, then builds and raises her up gradually, until she is ready for union. This, the *Zohar* explains, is the meaning of the verse (Song of Songs 1:5), "I am black, but comely, daughters of Jerusalem." Within the context of our lesson, *Malkhut*/the Divine Presence refers to the *bat ayin*, as the pupil is also a black dot. The "shrinking" of

LIKUTEY MOHARAN #13:6

(כַּזֹּהַר הַנַּ"ל), וְזֶה בְּחִינַת אַרְבְּעִין גְּרִיעָא, בְּחִינַת אַרְבְּעִין חַיָּתָא, שֶׁהֵם אַרְבָּעִים יוֹם שֶׁל הַתּוֹרָה:

וְאִי דְּלֵינָן טְפֵי, הֲוָה מַקְלִינָן מֵהַבְלָא – כִּי (קֹהֶלֶת ח): "יֵשׁ הֶבֶל אֲשֶׁר נַעֲשָׂה עַל הָאָרֶץ, אֲשֶׁר יֵשׁ צַדִּיקִים אֲשֶׁר מַגִּיעַ אֲלֵהֶם כְּמַעֲשֵׂה הָרְשָׁעִים" וְכוּ', וְעַל-יְדֵי הַהֶבֶל הַזֶּה רַבִּים נִתְפַּקְרוּ, שֶׁרוֹאִים "צַדִּיק וְרַע לוֹ, רָשָׁע וְטוֹב לוֹ". וְאִי דְּלֵינָן הַרְבֵּה נַפָשׁוֹת, אֲזַי בְּוַדַּאי הֲוָה מַקְלִינָן – לְשׁוֹן קוּלָא, 'מֵהַבְלָא' – מֵהֶבֶל הַזֶּה, וְלֹא הָיָה הֶבֶל הַזֶּה כָּל-כָּךְ קָשֶׁה עַל הָעוֹלָם.

Although Rebbe Nachman has explained these points as they relate to the individual, the influence of Divine providence and the forces of nature are primarily evident in the way they affect the world at large. Our Sages taught: The world is judged according to the majority (*Kiddushin* 40b). Thus, if most people are not as they should be, Divine providence would dictate that the world be destroyed because of their actions, God forbid. At such a time, the tzaddikim would also be in danger, as when Noach was forced to take refuge in the ark because of the generation's sins. Therefore, God allows the world to be governed by nature, His hidden providence, so that the world can continue to exist. This is a sign of the great mercy with which He rules His creation. However, in permitting this, "A *hevel* transpires": the righteous suffer, the wicked prosper. As for the tzaddikim themselves, because of their true righteousness, they are willing to endure the suffering so that the world at large can continue to exist (*Parparaot LeChokhmah*).

The *Biur HaLikutim* interprets this *hevel* as a person's jealousy, the pointless and empty envy which leads to the burning desire for money. This brings to a less than total honesty in business, which in turn leads to the casting off of one's faith (as explained above, §1). The *Mabuey HaNachal* explains this as one and the same: The burning desire for money is, in effect, a denial of Divine providence.

129. **KuLa, made easier.** The greater the amount of holy desires brought to the tzaddik, the more souls he is able to elevate and the greater the unification made Above. As a result, the Torah insights which the tzaddik reveals increases, as does the Divine providence which is drawn into the world along with them. Were this to happen so totally that the world becomes governed directly by "God's seeing eye," the tzaddikim would prosper and the wicked would receive what they deserve. The evil and unholy desires, the vapor/vanity, would then not be so troublesome for the world (*Parparaot LeChokhmah*).

130. **vanity...not so difficult....** Rebbe Nachman opened the lesson with, "To draw complete Divine providence...." In section 4, the Rebbe explains the concept of Divine providence, i.e., complete seeing, as opposed to partial seeing. The closer one is to Torah, the more he draws Divine providence upon himself. Drawing Torah is possible by elevating the souls. Thus, had many souls been lifted, it would not be so difficult...because then more people would be closer to Torah, drawing Divine providence upon the world (*Parparaot LeChokhmah*).

LIKUTEY MOHARAN #13:6

corresponding to the forty creatures, which are the forty days of the Torah.[126]

Had we been lifted up any higher, we would have been kalah (consumed) by the hevel (vapor) — For, "There is a *hevel* (vanity) which transpires on earth: there are tzaddikim who receive according to the deeds of the wicked..." (Ecclesiastes 8:14).[127] Because of this *hevel,* many have cast off religion; they see that "the righteous man has it bad and the wicked man has it good" (Berakhot 7a).[128] But, if many souls would have **been lifted up,** then certainly **we would have been KaLa**—similar to *KuLa* (made easier)[129]—**from the vapor**—from this *hevel.* Then this vanity would not be so troublesome for [the peoples of] the world.[130]

forty in the Chariot (*Sulam, Zohar, loc. cit.*). The fact that the four creatures appear in the four corners of the earth is an indication that all souls, no matter where they are—to wherever they have strayed—can still receive a *tikkun.*

126. ...**forty days of the Torah.** The forty measures of seed and the forty creatures allude to the forty days which Moshe remained on the mountain receiving the Torah (Exodus 24:18).

127. **hevel...tzaddikim...wicked.** The word *hevel* means vapor, and also connotes vanity, something which is empty and pointless. Rebbe Nachman taught that a person's desires resemble *hevel.* Thus, if he desires that which is good and holy, the "good vapors" which are created bring *tikkunim* to the world. However, if, God forbid, he desires that which is evil and unholy, the "empty vapors" dominate (*Likutey Moharan* I, 31:appendix; *ibid.,* 109).

128. **righteous man has it bad...wicked man has it good.** Because of the empty *hevel* which exists, many have spurned faith and turned away from God. Religion seems pointless if the righteous are made to suffer while the wicked prosper. In the words of the Midrash (*Vayikra Rabbah* 28:1): It seems as if there is no judgment and no Judge, God forbid. The *Parparaot LeChokhmah* rephrases this in the context of our lesson: If everything is governed by Divine providence, the tzaddik should experience nothing but good, and the wicked man nothing but bad. He states, however, that it is impossible for the human mind to understand God's greatness or grasp the ways of His judgment.

The *Parparaot LeChokhmah* points out the affect which Divine providence and the forces of nature do have. As mentioned earlier (n.59), nature is Divine providence in disguise. Quoting *Likutey Moharan* II, 17, he explains that man is fortunate that he is alternatively influenced by these two heavenly forces. When man is as he should be, his life and all he receives are governed by God's direct seeing—Divine providence. What would happen, however, if man did not behave as God wants him to? If only Divine providence ruled his existence, man would receive nothing, for he would be deemed undeserving of the benefits of "God's seeing eye." But, because one's life can be given over to the forces of nature, he has a possibility of receiving good. Yet, as a result, "There is a vanity which transpires on earth: there are tzaddikim who receive according to the deeds of the wicked...." This vanity results from the allowance made for the natural forces to operate. The person who sins has a "buffer." Despite his actions he receives good, even though he has aroused stern judgment upon himself and the world.

LIKUTEY MOHARAN #13:6

286

וְרָמְיָא גַּלָּא קָלָא לַחֲבֶרְתָּהּ: חֲבֶרְתִּי, מִי שַׁבְקִית מִידֵי בְּעָלְמָא דְּלָא
שְׁטַפִיתֵהּ, וְגֵיתֵי אֲנָא וְנַחַרְבֵהּ – הַיְנוּ, כְּשֶׁאַחַר-כָּךְ, כְּשֶׁכָּל אֵלּוּ
הַנְּפָשׁוֹת חוֹזְרִים מֵעֲבוּר הַנַּ"ל, וְעַל-יְדֵי הַכְּלָלִיּוּת נִתּוֹסֵף בָּהֶם
אַהֲבָה זֶה לָזֶה, וְאָז מְעוֹרְרִין אֵלּוּ לְאֵלּוּ וְאוֹמְרִים זֶה לָזֶה וּמַזְכִּירִין
זֶה אֶת זֶה: אָחִי, שֶׁמָּא שָׁבַקְתָּ אֵיזֶה מִדָּה בָּעוֹלָם הַזֶּה, שֶׁעֲדַיִן הִיא
מוֹשֶׁלֶת עָלֶיךָ וְאֵין אַתָּה יָכוֹל לְהִתְגַּבֵּר עָלֶיהָ.

וְגֵיתֵי אֲנָא וְנַחַרְבֵהּ – הַיְנוּ אֲסַיֵּיע לְךָ לְכַלּוֹת אֶת הַמִּדָּה הַזֹּאת מִמְּךָ.
וְהֵשִׁיב לוֹ:

פּוּק חֲזִי גְבוּרְתָּא דְמָרָךְ, שֶׁהוּא הֶחָכָם הַנַּ"ל;

רְאֵה כַּמָּה כֹּחוֹ גָדוֹל, דַּאֲפִלּוּ כִּמְלֹא חוּטָא דְחָלָא לֵית דְּעָבַר –
פֵּרֵשׁ רַבֵּנוּ שְׁמוּאֵל: אֲפִלּוּ כִּמְלֹא רֹחַב הַחוּט לֹא יָכֹלְתִּי לָצֵאת חוּץ
מִן הַחוֹל; פֵּרוּשׁ: אַתְּ שׁוֹאֶלֶת אוֹתִי, שֶׁמָּא שָׁבַקְתִּי מִדָּה בָּעוֹלָם
שֶׁעֲדַיִן לֹא תִּקַּנְתִּי אוֹתָהּ – תֵּדַע חֲבֶרְתִּי, שֶׁעֲדַיִן אֲנִי מְשֻׁקָּע בְּכָל
הַתַּאֲווֹת, וַעֲדַיִן לֹא יָצָאתִי מִן הַחוֹל אֶל הַקֹּדֶשׁ אֲפִלּוּ כִּמְלֹא חוּט,
וּבְוַדַּאי מִי שֶׁהוּא בְּמַדְרֵגָה כָּזֹאת, בְּוַדַּאי

לֵית דְּעָבַר – הַיְנוּ שֶׁאִי אֶפְשָׁר לוֹ לָבוֹא לִבְחִינוֹת עֲבוּר הַנַּ"ל:

---

inspiring one another to serve God. This is an accurate measure of their true intentions in visiting the tzaddik and improving their ways.

This love between friends also connects to Purim. The Jewish people then received the Torah anew (above, n.45), corresponding to the uniting of souls and the bringing down of Torah insights. On Purim, one is required to send gifts of food to a friend (*Orach Chaim* 694:1). This is synonymous with the love that exists between the followers of the true tzaddik, for they are true friends (*Mai HaNachal*).

134. **even a hairsbreadth...into holiness.** *Chol* is the Hebrew term for both sand (חול) and profane or secular (חל). A person who is honest with himself will recognize just how much he is immersed in the *chol* and physicality of this world. It is precisely this honesty which allows him to admit his faults and seek a tzaddik that will rectify his soul.

135. **E'VaR...EyBuR, pregnancy.** *E'var* (עבר) is similar to *eybur* (עיבור; the letters *b* and *v* being interchangeable).

Under normal circumstances, there is no way for the soul of someone so steeped in physicality to be elevated.

LIKUTEY MOHARAN #13:6

One wave called out to its neighbor: My friend, perhaps you left over MeeDay (something) of this world which you have not flooded? I will come and destroy it — In other words, later on, when all these souls return from "pregnancy"[131]—and, because they were united, the < abudant > love between them grew[132]—they inspire each other, and say to one another, and remind one another: "My brother, **perhaps you left over** some < bad > *MeeDah* (character trait) which still rules over you and that you cannot overcome?"[133]

I will come and destroy it — That is, "I will assist you in ridding yourself of it." And he answered him:

Go, see the great power of your master — This is the wise man, as mentioned above. **See the great power** he has.

Even a hairsbreadth of the chol (sand) cannot be crossed over — Rashbam explains: "I cannot go past the sand's shoreline even the width of a strand's worth." This means as follows: "You ask me if I have perhaps left over < some bad > character trait of this world which I've not yet rectified. You should know, my friend, that I am still immersed in all the < evil > desires and have not yet gone **even a hairsbreadth** out **of the chol** (profane) into holiness."[134] And certainly, someone who is on a spiritual level such as this:

cannot be E'VaR (crossed over) — In other words, it is impossible for him to attain the abovementioned aspect of *EyBuR* (pregnancy).[135]

---

131. **souls return....** After they have been elevated, they return renewed, revealing new Torah insights.

132. **love between them grew.** As we've seen, uniting the soul's fragments causes it to shine more brightly (§5). The uniting of many souls produces even greater brightness (n.70). Brightness is light, *chesed* (n.104), and *chesed* (lovingkindness) is akin to *ahavah* (love). Thus, when the souls are elevated, the love between them automatically grows.

    See *Tzaddik* #292 and #471 concerning the love which the tzaddik has for his followers and that which exists between the followers themselves.

133. **inspire...say...remind....** When one feels true love for his fellow man, he can speak openly and point out his friend's faults. His friend will sense the love and know that the one advising him is only seeking his benefit. Conversely, when one is drawn by worldly desires and feelings, then anything he says that has a negative connotation is taken as an affront by the one spoken to. The *Mai HaNachal* adds: From this we can understand that there should be great love between the followers of the true tzaddik. They should always be reminding and

LIKUTEY MOHARAN #13:6,7

וְאַף־עַל־פִּי־כֵן,

פּוּק חֲזִי גְּבוּרְתָּא דְּמָרָךְ – הַיְנוּ כֹּחַ הֶחָכָם, שֶׁכָּל כָּךְ כֹּחוֹ חָזָק, שֶׁאֲפִלּוּ נֶפֶשׁ שֶׁלִּי הֶעֱלָה בַּעֲבוּר:

ז. וְזֶה פֵּרוּשׁ: אַשְׁרֵי הָעָם – זֶה בְּחִינַת הַשְׁגָּחָה,

יֹדְעֵי תְרוּעָה – זֶה בְּחִינַת יַעֲקֹב, שֶׁהוּא בְּחִינַת צְדָקָה, כְּמוֹ שֶׁכָּתוּב (תְּהִלִּים צ"ט): "מִשְׁפָּט וּצְדָקָה בְּיַעֲקֹב אַתָּה עָשִׂיתָ".

ה' – זֶה בְּחִינַת הַוָיוֹת, בְּחִינַת חֲסָדִים.

בְּאוֹר פָּנֶיךָ – זֶה בְּחִינַת הַשֵּׂכֶל, כְּמוֹ שֶׁכָּתוּב (קֹהֶלֶת ח): "חָכְמַת אָדָם תָּאִיר פָּנָיו".

יְהַלֵּכוּן – אֵלּוּ הַנְּפָשׁוֹת, בְּחִינַת מַהֲלַךְ־נָפֶשׁ.

(עוֹד מָצָאתִי כְּתַב־יַד רַבֵּנוּ, זִכְרוֹנוֹ לִבְרָכָה, שֶׁשַּׁיָּךְ לְהַתּוֹרָה הַנַּ"ל, אַךְ מָצָאתִי רַק קְצָה הַנְּיָר, וְלֹא נִכְתַּב שָׁם רַק סוֹפוֹ שֶׁל עִנְיָן, וְחָסֵר הַתְחָלַת הָעִנְיָן, וְזֶהוּ:)

הַתּוֹרָה, שֶׁהִיא בְּחִינַת רְאִיָּה, טַנְתָּ"א כַּנַּ"ל, "כָּל בָּשָׂר יַחְדָּו" – זֶה בְּחִינַת לְקִיטַת הַנְּפָשׁוֹת כֻּלָּם, בִּבְחִינַת לִקַּח נְפָשׁוֹת חָכָם כַּנַּ"ל; כִּי

138. **teruah...Yaakov.** The three sounds of the shofar are: *teki'ah, shevarim, teruah.* These three correspond to *Chesed, Gevurah, Tiferet* and to Avraham, Yitzchak and Yaakov, respectively (*Tikkuney Zohar* #55).

139. **charity in Yaakov.** Yaakov is compared to both charity and *teruah,* so that knowing "the shofar's blast" corresponds to giving charity. The attainment of Divine providence comes through charity (above, §1).

140. **YHVH...benevolences.** For the holy name YHVH always denotes *chesed* (*Mai HaNachal*). By giving charity, one breaks the idolatry of money and sweetens the judgments, the *charon af.* This drawing of *chasadim* (benevolences) into the world is, in essence, the function of the Mashiach (above, §1).

141. **countenance...intellect....** Through *chesed* one merits *daat,* the concept of the Holy Temple.

142. **the going of the soul.** See above, section 5 and note 72. Acquiring holy knowledge enables one to draw and reveal new Torah insights. This is achieved by gathering the souls and elevating them. Through this, Divine providence is brought upon the world. Thus, the entire lesson is summed up in this verse.

289   *LIKUTEY MOHARAN #13:6,7*

Yet, despite this, **Go, see the great power of your master**. This is the power of the wise man. His power is so great that he even lifted up my soul in [the aspect of] pregnancy.[136]

7. And this is the explanation [of the opening verse]:
{*"Ashrei haam* (Happy is the people) that knows *teruah* (the shofar's blast); *YHVH* (God), in the light of Your countenance they shall go."}

AShRei haam — This alludes to Divine providence, < in that it is similar to *AShuRenu* > .[137]

that knows teruah (the shofar's blast) — This [*teruah*] corresponds to Yaakov,[138] who is an aspect of charity, as in (Psalms 99:4), "You execute justice and charity in Yaakov."[139]

YHVH — This is the aspect of the *HaVaYaH,* the aspect of benevolences.[140]
Chesed

in the light of Your countenance — This is the intellect, as is written (Ecclesiastes 8:1), "A man's wisdom causes his face to shine."[141]

they shall go — These are the souls, corresponding to "the going of the soul."[142]

[Reb Noson writes:]
In addition to the above, I've found a manuscript of the Rebbe's relating to this lesson. However, all that I found was a piece of the page and only the conclusion

136. **Go, see the great power....** Reb Alter Tepliker (d. 1919), author of the *Mabuey HaNachal,* writes that he had heard from some Breslover Chassidim that when Rebbe Nachman gave this lesson, he said: "If one has broken all the evil desires and negative traits save one, and of that one all that remains to correct is but a hairsbreadth before he crosses over completely into holiness, even such a soul cannot be elevated in the aspect of *eybur.* How much more so, one who has not taken even a hairsbreadth of a step from the physical to the spiritual. Nevertheless, **Go, see the great power of your master**—the great and true tzaddik. Even such a soul, though steeped in the physical, can be raised up by the tzaddik" (*Mai HaNachal*).

137. **Ashrei....** The word *ashrei* (אשרי, happy) is similar to *ashurenu (*אשורנו), which, as explained, indicates gazing and seeing. Thus, this alludes to Divine providence, the "seeing eye of God" (see above, §4; above, n.76).
     The *Mai HaNachal* adds: Above (§3, n.44), Rebbe Nachman taught that the word *shekakhah*—from the verse "*Ashrei haam shekakhah...*"—alludes to Moshe. Here we see that "*Ashrei haam yodei...*" alludes to Divine providence. From this we can conclude that the way to achieve Divine providence is by being attached to the tzaddik.

LIKUTEY MOHARAN #13:7

פִּי ה' דִּבֵּר – כָּל זֶה נַעֲשֶׂה עַל־יְדֵי רוּחַ נְדִיבָה כַּנַּ"ל, שֶׁהוּא פִּי ה',
כְּמוֹ שֶׁאָמְרוּ חַזַ"ל: בְּפִיךָ זוֹ צְדָקָה (עַד כָּאן לְשׁוֹנוֹ זַ"ל).
וּמוּבָן הַדָּבָר, שֶׁמֵּבִיא הַמִּקְרָא: "וְנִגְלָה כְבוֹד ה' וְרָאוּ כָל בָּשָׂר
יַחְדָּו כִּי פִּי ה' דִּבֵּר" וּמְבָאֵר כָּל הַמַּאֲמָר הַנַּ"ל, שֶׁהוּא מְפֹרָשׁ
בְּפָסוּק זֶה, אַךְ בַּעֲווֹנוֹתֵינוּ הָרַבִּים חָסֵר פֵּרוּשׁ רֵישֵׁהּ דִּקְרָא.

The *Parparaot LeChokhmah* points out that both versions of this lesson are Rebbe Nachman's, that is, both are his own written version (see Lesson #7, n.1). He also explains that the *Likutey Moharan* has some lessons written by the Rebbe himself (see *Tzaddik* #362) and others written by Reb Noson and then reviewed by Rebbe Nachman prior to their being released for copying and publication (see *Until The Mashiach*, p.287). Rebbe Nachman would hand over to Reb Noson only the version he wanted released. For reasons known only to himself, there were times when the Rebbe saw fit to delete certain sections from the text though they had been in the original version and been part of his oral discourse.

Apparently, this manuscript was found intact quite some time after Rebbe Nachman passed away, and was not widely circulated. It is clear that more than one hundred years later Reb Alter Tepliker had not seen it, because he offers his own interpretation of the verse based on this lesson, making no reference whatsoever to Rebbe Nachman's explanation.

145. **wise...glory.** Our Sages taught: The only glory is Torah (*Avot* 6:3).

146. **Temple.** The Temple, which is built through the drawing of *chasadim* from *Chokhmah* (Wisdom) and acquiring *daat*, is related to the beginning. Beginning is *reishit* which indicates wisdom, as in (Psalms 111:10), "The beginning is wisdom."

147. **Torah...sight/T-N-T-A, as above.** From here to the end is the segment of the handwritten manuscript which Reb Noson found, and therefore was printed in all subsequent editions. The connection between Torah, sight and *T-N-T-A* has been explained in section 4.

148. **gathering...mentioned above.** This appears in section 3. All flesh refers to the souls, for they are like bodies to the wise man (above, §5, nn.82,94).

149. **mouth...is charity.** Once a person has verbally pledged to give charity, he must fulfill his commitment (*Nedarim* 7a). The Talmud also says that even greater than the financial support which the poor man receives is the emotional succor he is given by the person who empathizes with his plight (*Bava Batra* 9b).

The verse now reads: **And the glory of God will be revealed** — to draw Divine providence, one must first attain wisdom or *daat*, the concept of the Holy Temple. **All flesh will see it together** — when one attains this level, he is the wise man who can draw down Torah by gathering the souls. This brings Divine providence, the concept of seeing. How can this be achieved? **For the mouth of God has spoken** — by giving charity.

* * *

Reb Noson writes that even now, even after the very great tzaddikim have passed away, through their merit our souls can still be elevated by our Torah study. "...in the night, her

291   *LIKUTEY MOHARAN #13:7*

appears there. The opening of the lesson is missing. This is [what was found]:

...the Torah, which is an aspect of sight/*T-N-T-A,* as above.[143] "All flesh...together" corresponds to the gathering of the souls, all of them, as in, "He that takes souls is wise." [This as been] mentioned above. "For the mouth of God has spoken"—all this is accomplished through the generous spirit. This is "the mouth of God," as our Sages taught: "In your mouth" (Deuteronomy 23:24)—this is charity (*Rosh HaShanah* 6a). {End of fragment.}

It is clear that he brought the verse (Isaiah 40:5), "And the glory of God will be revealed, and all flesh will see it together; for the mouth of God has spoken," and then taught the above discourse as an explanation of this verse. But, because of our many sins, the explanation of the opening part of the verse is missing.[144]

* * *

"And the glory of God will be revealed, all flesh will see it together; for the mouth of God has spoken" (Isaiah 40:5).

And the glory of God — This is wisdom, as in (Proverbs 3:35), "The wise will inherit glory."[145] This corresponds to the Holy Temple, as is written (Jeremiah 17:12), "The glorious throne, exalted from the beginning, is the place of our Temple."[146] And through this:

all flesh will see it together — "See it" alludes to drawing down of the Torah, which is an aspect of sight/*T-N-T-A,* as above.[147] "All flesh...together" corresponds to the gathering of the souls, all of them, as in, "He that takes souls is wise." [This has been] mentioned above.[148]

for the mouth of God has spoken — All this is accomplished through the generous spirit. This is "the mouth of God," as our Sages taught: "In your mouth"—this is charity (*Rosh HaShanah* 6a).[149]

---

143. **Torah...sight/T-N-T-A, as above.** See section 4.

144. **is missing.** The entire manuscript was eventually found and now appears as an addendum in some editions of the *Likutey Moharan.* This version does contain the explanation of the entire verse which Reb Noson mentions. Its translation follows. There are also some minor variations in the text itself, none of which change the points of the lesson. To point them out, however, would require many explanatory notes regarding these differences and, because that would interrupt the flow of the lesson, the text here is the one common to all editions of *Likutey Moharan.*

LIKUTEY MOHARAN #13:7

Today, the great *tikkun* explained in this lesson can be achieved by studying the works of the true tzaddik and by making a pilgrimage to his gravesite, praying there together with his other followers to come closer to God and to fulfill His will. This is especially true for those who come to Rebbe Nachman's gravesite before Rosh HaShanah for the *kibutz* (gathering). Even now, Rebbe Nachman is working on behalf of the fallen souls. He raises them up and elevates them, even more so than during his lifetime, because "tzaddikim are greater after death than when they were alive" (*Chullin* 7b). And we see clearly the love and affection the chassidim have for each other, how they strive to renew themselves and encourage each other in the service God. By uniting his soul with the others who join this *kibutz,* by praying and beseeching God to bring him closer, a person can even now draw upon himself the power which the tzaddik has to renew and rectify his soul (*Parparaot LeChokhmah*).

LIKUTEY MOHARAN #13:7

candle will not be extinguished" (Proverbs 31:18). That is, even in the night, after the tzaddik's passing, the light which he drew into the world remains. Furthermore, the verse tells us that God made His covenant "...both with those who are standing here with us today...and those who are not here with us today" (Deuteronomy 29:14). As Rashi explains, "those who are not here" refers to all future generations. In other words, these great tzaddikim were capable of ascending to such great heights, elevating the souls of their followers with them, that they were able to draw down the most exalted Torah insights. These revelations forever have the power to rectify and elevate all those who study their teachings...those who were there and those of future generations. And the primary means for receiving this great light is by being forever firm in one's desire to come closer to God, for the soul corresponds to the will...(*Likutey Halakhot, Aveidah u'Metziah* 3:5).

ליקוטי מוהר"ן סימן י"ד

תִּקְעוּ בַחֹדֶשׁ שׁוֹפָר בַּכֶּסֶה וְכוּ' (תְּהִלִּים פ"א).

א. לְהַמְשִׁיךְ שָׁלוֹם בָּעוֹלָם, צָרִיךְ לְהַעֲלוֹת כְּבוֹד הַקָּדוֹשׁ־בָּרוּךְ־הוּא לְשָׁרְשׁוֹ, הַיְנוּ לַיִּרְאָה, כְּמוֹ שֶׁכָּתוּב (דְּבָרִים כ"ח): "לְיִרְאָה אֶת הַשֵּׁם הַנִּכְבָּד".

ב. וְאִי אֶפְשָׁר לְהַעֲלוֹת אֶת הַכָּבוֹד אֶלָּא עַל־יְדֵי תּוֹרַת חֶסֶד; "וְתוֹרַת חֶסֶד" – אָמְרוּ חֲכָמֵינוּ, זִכְרוֹנָם לִבְרָכָה (סֻכָּה מט:): 'זֶהוּ הַלּוֹמֵד תּוֹרָה עַל־מְנָת לְלַמְּדָהּ', כִּי זֶה עִקַּר כְּבוֹדוֹ, כַּמּוּבָא בַּזֹּהַר (יִתְרוֹ סט.): 'בְּשַׁעֲתָא דִּשְׁאָר עַכּוּ"ם אָתְיָן וְאוֹדָן לְקֻדְשָׁא־בְּרִיךְ־הוּא, כְּדֵין אִסְתַּלֵּק וְאִתְיַקַּר שְׁמָא דְּקֻדְשָׁא־בְּרִיךְ־הוּא עֵלָּא וְתַתָּא, כְּמוֹ גַּבֵּי יִתְרוֹ: בְּשַׁעֲתָא דְּאָמַר יִתְרוֹ: "עַתָּה יָדַעְתִּי כִּי גָדוֹל ה' מִכָּל הָאֱלֹהִים", כְּדֵין אִסְתַּלֵּק וְאִתְיַקַּר שְׁמָא דְּקֻדְשָׁא־בְּרִיךְ־הוּא'. נִמְצָא, זֶהוּ כְּבוֹדוֹ, כְּשֶׁבְּנֵי־אָדָם שֶׁהֵם מִחוּץ לַקְּדֻשָּׁה מְקָרְבִין אֶת

---

especially that commandment which advises him to teach the Torah's rules and laws (cf. Deuteronomy 4:24). (Naturally, this refers to one who is capable of teaching but fails to do so, and not to a person who cannot teach.) We see therefore that teaching others, sharing with them, is an act of kindness. Conversely, not teaching others is tantamount to despising God's word—not elevating the glory of God to its source.

4. above and below. When those who are "outside" the realm of holiness come "within," then there is an increased or additional revelation of His glory. God's glory is elevated. Thus, by teaching others about God—by making His name known—one elevates His glory. Compare Lesson #11, notes 7 and 17, where glory is connected to speech—the means through which the word of God is transmitted to others.

5. Yitro...glorified. Yitro (Jethro) was a high priest and engaged in every known form of contemporary idol worship (*Rashi*, Exodus 18:11). After hearing of the wondrous miracles which had been performed on behalf of the Jews, he gave praise to God, saying, "Now [even] *I* know...." When someone who is close to God recognizes Him, it is natural and to be expected. But when a "Yitro"—who is very distant from holiness—comes to praise God, it produces a manifestation of God's glory which is revealed to even the lowest and outermost levels.

295   *LIKUTEY MOHARAN #14:1,2*

LIKUTEY MOHARAN #14[1]

"Blow a shofar at the New Moon; at the appointed time for the day of our festival."

(Psalms 81:4)

L'hamshikh shalom (To draw peace) into the world it is necessary to elevate the Holy One's glory to its source—i.e., to fear. As it is written (Deuteronomy 28:58), "To fear the glorious name."[2]

2. Yet, it is impossible to elevate the glory except through the Torah of lovingkindness. And of the Torah of lovingkindness our Sages taught: This is the one who studies Torah in order to teach it (*Sukkah* 49b).[3] For this is the essence of His glory, as is brought in the *Zohar* (II, 69a): When the other nations come and recognize the Holy One, then the name of God ascends and is glorified above and below.[4] This was the case with Yitro. When Yitro said (Exodus 18:11), "Now I know that God is greater than all gods," with this God's name ascended and was glorified.[5]

We find, therefore, that this is His glory—when people who are outside holiness draw closer, <to within> the [realm of] holiness.

---

1. **Likutey Moharan #14.** This lesson was taught on Shabbat Chanukah, 29 Kislev, 5564 (December 14, 1803). This was just after Rabbi Gedaliah of Linitz passed away. Rabbi Gedaliah, who was a disciple of Rabbi Yaakov Yosef of Polonnoye, the author of *Toldot Yaakov Yosef*, was credited by Rebbe Nachman with the compilation of the *Shevachey Baal Shem Tov*. In the lesson, Rebbe Nachman alludes to Rabbi Gedaliah's passing, quoting the *Shulchan Arukh* (*Orach Chaim* 670:1) that it is forbidden to eulogize on Chanukah (see §13 of text). The Rebbe also said: "It is difficult now to reveal Torah. For every tzaddik has a portion of Torah, and when that tzaddik leaves this world, his portion of Torah leaves with him" (*Parparaot LeChokhmah; Until the Mashiach,* p.102).

2. **the glorious name.** In the context of our lesson, the verse should be read, "To [attain] fear, glorify the name of God." This is the major theme of Rebbe Nachman's teaching: To attain peace one has to be able to elevate the glory of God/His name to its source, which is fear. Fear itself is associated with the *sefirah* of *Gevurah* (Strength) and *gevurot* (severities) (cf. Lesson #15 §2).

3. **in order to teach it.** This is the quality of *chesed* (lovingkindness). He learns Torah in order to share it with others. The Talmud teaches (*Sanhedrin* 99a): "For he denigrated the word of God" (Numbers 15:31)—this is one who studies the word of God, the Torah, but does not teach it to others. In keeping the Torah's knowledge from others he denigrates God's word,

LIKUTEY MOHARAN #14:2,3

עַצְמָן לִפְנִים מֵהַקְּדֻשָּׁה – הֵן גֵּרִים שֶׁמִּתְגַּיְּרִין, הֵן בַּעֲלֵי־תְּשׁוּבָה, שֶׁגַּם הֵם הָיוּ מִבַּחוּץ – וּכְשֶׁמְּקָרְבִין וּמַכְנִיסִים אוֹתָם לִפְנִים, זֶהוּ כְּבוֹדוֹ:

וְעַכְשָׁו הַכָּבוֹד בַּגָּלוּת, כִּי עִקַּר הַכָּבוֹד אֵצֶל הָעַכּוּ"ם, וַאֲנַחְנוּ בְּנֵי־יִשְׂרָאֵל שְׁפָלִים וְנִבְזִים. וְלֶעָתִיד לָבוֹא, שֶׁיִּתְגַּלֶּה כְּבוֹדוֹ מִבֵּין הַחֹשֶׁךְ, כְּמוֹ שֶׁכָּתוּב (יְשַׁעְיָהוּ מ): "וְנִגְלָה כְּבוֹד ה'" וְכוּ', כִּי "אָז יַטּוּ כֻלָּם לְעָבְדוֹ שְׁכֶם אֶחָד", "אָז יֹאמְרוּ בַגּוֹיִם לְכוּ וְנֵלְכָה בְּאוֹר ה'" (שָׁם ב). וְכָבוֹד נִקְרָא אוֹר, כְּמוֹ שֶׁכָּתוּב (יְחֶזְקֵאל מ"ג): "וְהָאָרֶץ הֵאִירָה מִכְּבֹדוֹ":

ג. וְאִי אֶפְשָׁר לְקָרֵב אֶת הַגֵּרִים עִם בַּעֲלֵי הַתְּשׁוּבָה, אֶלָּא עַל־יְדֵי תּוֹרָה, כְּמוֹ שֶׁכָּתוּב (מִשְׁלֵי ה): "יָפוּצוּ מַעְיְנוֹתֶיךָ חוּצָה", שֶׁצָּרִיךְ לְהַשְׁקוֹת אוֹתָם שֶׁהֵם מִבַּחוּץ, לְהוֹדִיעַ לָהֶם הַדֶּרֶךְ יֵלְכוּ בָהּ.

וְזֶה שֶׁאָמְרוּ חֲכָמֵינוּ, זִכְרוֹנָם לִבְרָכָה (אָבוֹת ו): 'אֵין כָּבוֹד אֶלָּא תּוֹרָה'. וְזֶהוּ (יִרְמְיָה ט"ו): "אִם תּוֹצִיא יָקָר מִזּוֹלֵל", וְאָמְרוּ חֲכָמֵינוּ,

In review: To promote peace in the world one must elevate God's glory to its source: fear (§1). This can only be accomplished through the Torah—teaching it to others and bringing them to recognize God. God's glory is thus elevated from darkness and exile (§2).

11. **outside...given to drink....** The Torah is likened to a spring whose waters have the power to sustain even those on the outside. It must, however, be the Torah of *chesed,* teaching others (*Mai HaNachal*).

12. **glory other than Torah.** Thus, for there to be glory there must be Torah. It is not possible to attain glory and elevate it unless one first has acquired Torah.

13. **take out the precious....** This Talmudic passage (*loc. cit.*) explains "take out the precious" as referring to the taking out of God's chosen ones "from the vile" of their sins; repentance of those who are on the outside is the theme of this part of the lesson.

14. **the lowliness of exile.** Bringing people back to God is likened to glory, for through this act, the glory of God is revealed—elevated from exile.

This same Talmudic passage (*Bava Metzia* 85a) quotes the remainder of the verse, "...you will be like My mouth." In other words, whoever brings back people to God is given the ability to repeal and nullify a harsh decree proclaimed by heaven! Such is the power of the mitzvah of bringing people back to God.

Guiding and helping one's fellow Jews back to God is a major theme here and indeed throughout Rebbe Nachman's writings. See *Tzaddik* #304, #310, #325; *The Aleph-Bet Book,*

Zohar, Kiruv considered holy of holies

LIKUTEY MOHARAN #14:2,3

This applies equally to converts who convert and to *baaley teshuvah* (repentant Jews), for they were also on the outside.[6] And when [the converts and the *baaley teshuvah*] are drawn closer and brought inside, this is His glory.

But now, the glory is <itself> in exile. For the main glory is [currently] with the gentiles, whereas we, the Jewish people, are lowly and disgraced.[7] But in the Future,[8] when His glory will be revealed from out of the darkness, as in (Isaiah 40:5), "And the glory of God will be revealed, and all flesh shall see it"—for at that time they will all incline together "to serve Him with one consent" (Zephaniah 3:9)—then the nations will say (Isaiah 2:5), "Come, let us walk in the light of God."[9] And glory is called light, as is written (Ezekiel 43:2), "The earth was illuminated by His glory."[10]

3. Now, the only way to attract converts and *baaley teshuvah* is through Torah, as it is written (Proverbs 5:16), "Your wellsprings shall spread outward." For those who are on the outside must be given to drink—they must be informed of the path they are to follow.[11]

This is what our Sages taught: There is no glory other than Torah (*Avot* 6:3).[12] And, concerning "If you take out the precious from the vile" (Jeremiah 15:19), our Sages taught: This refers to those who draw people to the service of God (*Bava Metzia* 85a).[13] For this is called "taking out the precious"—i.e., glory—"from the vile"—from the lowliness of exile.[14]

---

6. **converts...baaley teshuvah....** A Jew who repents can be likened to a convert, as he too was on the outside before entering the realm of holiness.

   This is a general rule in Rebbe Nachman's teachings: Wherever he speaks about converts, he is also speaking about *baaley teshuvah* (*Rabbi Eliyahu Chaim Rosen*).

7. **Jewish people...disgraced.** Here, Rebbe Nachman indicates that the glory belongs to the Jews, whereas previously he stated that the glory is God's. This, however, is no contradiction, because the Jewish soul is itself a "Godly portion." Thus, the glory of the Jewish people is bound with God's glory and when His glory will be revealed, so will theirs (*Mabuey HaNachal*).

8. **in the Future.** This refers to when the Mashiach comes.

9. **to serve Him...in the light of God.** When the nations of the world recognize and accept the need for serving God, they will say, "Come, let us walk in the light." This, as opposed to the darkness ("outside") of idolatry. Then the glory of the Jewish people will also be elevated, as the nations will turn to them for guidance in following God's light (*Mabuey HaNachal*).

10. **illuminated by His glory.** When glory is revealed it shines brightly and is recognized. Furthermore, the earth, which is trod upon by all, corresponds to the lowest levels mentioned previously in the text. Thus, the verse can be read as follows: **The earth...** — even the lowest levels/darkness shall shine brightly when God's glory is revealed. As explained above, this is what happened with Yitro (*Mabuey HaNachal*).

LIKUTEY MOHARAN #14:3

זִכְרוֹנָם לִבְרָכָה (בָּבָא מְצִיעָא פה.): 'אֵלּוּ שֶׁמְּקָרְבִין בְּנֵי־אָדָם לַעֲבוֹדַת הַשֵּׁם יִתְבָּרַךְ'; כִּי זֶהוּ נִקְרָא "מוֹצִיא יָקָר", הַיְנוּ כָּבוֹד, "מְזוֹלֵל" – מִזִּילוּתָא דְּגָלוּתָא.

וְזֶה (תְּהִלִּים קי"ג): "רָם עַל כָּל גּוֹיִם ה'", הַיְנוּ כְּשֶׁהָעַכּוּ"ם מוֹדִין וּמְשַׁבְּחִין לֵהּ, אֲזַי "עַל הַשָּׁמַיִם כְּבוֹדוֹ", אֲזַי נִתְעַלֶּה הַכָּבוֹד מֵהַחֹשֶׁךְ.

וְאִי אֶפְשָׁר לָבוֹא לְהִתְעוֹרְרוּת הַתְּשׁוּבָה – הֵן לְרִשְׁעֵי יִשְׂרָאֵל, הֵן לַגֵּרִים – אֶלָּא עַל־יְדֵי הַתּוֹרָה שֶׁמְּאִירִין לָהֶם אֶל מָקוֹם שֶׁהֵם שָׁם, כְּמוֹ שֶׁכָּתוּב: "יָפוּצוּ וְכוּ' חוּצָה" – 'חוּצָה' דַּיְקָא; כִּי הַתּוֹרָה הֵם שִׁשִּׁים רִבּוֹא אוֹתִיּוֹת, כְּנֶגֶד שִׁשִּׁים רִבּוֹא נְשָׁמוֹת, וְיֵשׁ לְכָל הַנְּשָׁמוֹת שֹׁרֶשׁ לְמַעְלָה בְּמַחֲשָׁבָה דְקֻדְשָׁא־בְּרִיךְ־הוּא, כִּי 'יִשְׂרָאֵל עָלוּ בַּמַּחֲשָׁבָה תְּחִלָּה'.

וְעַל־יְדֵי זִוּוּג הַנְּשָׁמוֹת נִבְרָאִים נְשָׁמוֹת גֵּרִים: וּכְשֶׁנִּתְעוֹרְרִים הַנְּשָׁמוֹת עַל־יְדֵי אוֹתִיּוֹת הַתּוֹרָה שֶׁהוֹצִיא מִפִּיו וּמִתְנוֹצְצִים זֶה לָזֶה – זֶה בְּחִינַת זִוּוּג, שֶׁזֶּה מְקַבֵּל הָאָרָה מִזֶּה; וְעַל־יְדֵי הַזִּוּוּג שֶׁל הִתְנוֹצְצוּת הַנְּשָׁמוֹת שֶׁבַּמַּחֲשָׁבָה נִבְרָאִים נְשָׁמוֹת גֵּרִים.

count them, he would find no more than some 304,000 letters. The commentaries offer various explanations for this (see *The Breslov Haggadah* p. 62), though all accept that there are 600,000 letters.

18. **six hundred thousand souls.** This refers to the 600,000 Jewish souls mentioned in Exodus 12:37, those who left Egypt and received the Torah. They correspond to the equivalent number of letters of the Torah (*Zohar Chadash, ibid.*). There are also times when these 600,000 letters are encompassed in an individual Jewish soul; see below note 71.

19. **Israel arose first....** At the time of Creation, "Israel arose first in thought." Everything God created was for the sake of the Jewish people. It was also for the sake of Torah (*Bereishit Rabbah, op. cit.*). This shared quality of the Torah and the Jewish souls indicates that they both have their source in the Holy One's thought.

20. **souls of the converts are created.** Just as a physical union creates the body, a spiritual union between the souls of the tzaddikim creates the soul. These souls are the souls of converts, for the Jewish souls were made at the time of Creation. That is why Rebbe Nachman discusses the souls of converts and of *baaley teshuvah* separately. (See *Zohar* III, 168a.)

21. **receives light from the other.** Torah is glory, light, as above. When the letters of the Torah are pronounced, the light they generate from one to the other forms a word. So too when the

299   *LIKUTEY MOHARAN #14:3*

And this is (Psalms 113:4): "God is high above all nations, [His glory is above the heavens]." That is, when the gentiles acknowledge and praise Him, then "His glory is above the heavens"—<i.e.,> the glory then ascends from the darkness.[15]

Yet, it is impossible for either Jewish sinners or converts to come to an awakening of repentance except through the Torah, which shines to them wherever they are,[16] as in, "Your wellsprings shall spread outward." Specifically "outward," because the Torah is comprised of 600,000 letters,[17] corresponding to the 600,000 [Jewish] souls.[18] And each soul has its own source Above, in the Divine thought of the Holy One, for "Israel arose first in thought" (*Bereishit Rabbah* 1:5).[19]

And through a union of souls, the souls of the converts are created.[20] When the souls are aroused through the letters of Torah that a person recites, and they shine to one another, this is the concept of union—each one receives light from the other.[21] And, by means of the union of the souls' shining within <the Holy One's> thought, the souls of converts are created.

Repentance 34, 36-38, 54. Concerning this great mitzvah the *Zohar* (II, 128b) teaches: One should run after his fellow Jew who has sinned in order to remove from him the filth and subdue the Other Side.... By doing so, it is as if he gave birth to him (for the penitent is like a new-born person). This is a very great tribute which causes God's glory to be elevated more than any other tribute. Whoever engages in this is like Aharon, of whom it is written (Malakhi 2:6), "He brought many back from sin." The person who brings the sinners back to God surpasses all others in three aspects: 1) in the way he subdues the Other Side; 2) in the way he elevates the glory of God; 3) in the way he causes the entire world to be preserved, above and below. About this person the verse says (Malakhi 2:5), "My covenant is with him, life and peace.... He will merit seeing children and grandchildren, rewarded with this world and the next. His enemies will be incapable of standing up against him. He will ascend through the Twelve Gates in heaven (corresponding to the Twelve Tribes) and no one can stand in his way."

15. **glory then ascends from the darkness.** In contrast to the earth, which is compared to darkness (above n.10), heaven is associated with light. In the context of our lesson, this verse from Psalms (*loc. cit.*) reads: When it is recognized that **God is high above all nations**, then, **His glory is above the heavens**—His glory is elevated from the darkness of exile and shines brightly (*Mabuey HaNachal*).

16. **Torah...wherever they are.** After providing a general picture of how converts and *baaley teshuvah* are associated with Torah, light and the elevation of glory, Rebbe Nachman now goes on to explain, in detail, the process through which this connection comes about.

17. **six hundred thousand letters.** The *Zohar Chadash* (*Shir HaShirim* 91a) teaches that there are 600,000 letters in the Five Books of Moshe. The word *Bereishit* (בראשית) is an acrostic for "There are 600,000 letters in Torah" (יש ששים רבוא אותיות בתורה). Yet, if one were to actually

גַּם הַפּוֹשְׁעֵי־יִשְׂרָאֵל, כָּל זְמַן שֶׁשֵּׁם יִשְׂרָאֵל נִקְרָא עָלָיו (כִּי נִקְרָא
'פּוֹשְׁעֵי־יִשְׂרָאֵל', נִמְצָא שֶׁשֵּׁם יִשְׂרָאֵל נִקְרָא עַל־כָּל־פָּנִים עָלָיו
עֲדַיִן, מֵאַחַר שֶׁנִּקְרָא פּוֹשְׁעֵי יִשְׂרָאֵל), 'אַף־עַל־פִּי שֶׁחָטָא, יִשְׂרָאֵל
הוּא' (סַנְהֶדְרִין מד.), יֵשׁ לוֹ אֲחִיזָה וְשֹׁרֶשׁ בְּמַחֲשָׁבָה עֶלְיוֹנָה, וְעַל־
יְדֵי הַהִתְנוֹצְצוּת הַתְנוֹצֵץ גַּם שֹׁרֶשׁ נִשְׁמָתוֹ בֵּין שְׁאָר הַשָּׁרָשִׁים,
וּמַגִּיעַ הָאָרָה לָזֶה הַפּוֹשְׁעֵי־יִשְׂרָאֵל מִשֹּׁרֶשׁ נִשְׁמָתוֹ, וְעַל־יְדֵי הָאָרָה
הַזֹּאת חוֹזֵר בִּתְשׁוּבָה.

ד. וְזֶה שֶׁאָמְרוּ חֲכָמֵינוּ, זִכְרוֹנָם לִבְרָכָה (נְדָרִים פא.): 'מִפְּנֵי מָה
תַּלְמִידֵי־חֲכָמִים אֵין בְּנֵיהֶם תַּלְמִידֵי־חֲכָמִים? מִפְּנֵי שֶׁלֹא בֵּרְכוּ
בַּתּוֹרָה תְּחִלָּה' – שֶׁצָּרִיךְ כָּל אָדָם, וּבִכְפָרט תַּלְמִיד־חָכָם, לְבָרֵךְ
וּלְהָאִיר בְּלִמּוּד תּוֹרָתוֹ בְּשֹׁרֶשׁ הַנְּשָׁמוֹת, הַיְנוּ בְּמַחֲשָׁבָה תְּחִלָּה, כִּי
שָׁם שָׁרְשֵׁנוּ.

נִמְצָא, כְּשֶׁמֵּבִיא הָאָרָה וּבְרָכָה לְתוֹךְ תְּחִלַּת הַמַּחֲשָׁבָה, וְעַל־יָדוֹ

to recognize God. God's glory is thus elevated from darkness and exile (§2). Specifically this requires spreading the Torah outward, to inspire *baaley teshuvah* and converts (§3).

25. **blessing for Torah first....** The simple meaning of this Talmudic passage (*loc. cit.*) is as follows: How can it be that a Torah scholar's son does not himself develop into a scholar? This happens because, before studying, the Torah scholar did not first recite the daily Torah blessings, thanking God for the Torah. The commentaries explain that he studied Torah as a wisdom, not as the word of God through which man can come closer to Him and know His ways. This is very different than Rebbe Nachman's interpretation, which follows (see next note).

26. **first in thought...source is.** Rebbe Nachman explains the above Talmudic passage as follows: What does it mean that the scholars did not bless "first"? They did not look to awaken the beginning of the Torah—i.e., its source in upper thought. Having failed to illuminate the source, it did not shine brightly from the start. Without this proper beginning, their children do not become scholars. Indeed, because these Torah scholars did not awaken the source from where the souls of their offspring were drawn, those souls came down darkened and dulled, unable to illuminate in Torah.

The *Mai HaNachal* adds that reciting the blessings over the Torah, that is, thanking God for the Torah and praising Him for it, affords one's Torah study this very power to bless and illuminate its beginning, its source. It is therefore interesting to note that the *Shulchan Arukh* (*Orach Chaim* 47:1) states: "One must be extremely vigilant in reciting the Torah Blessings." Such a stringent tone regarding the reciting of a blessing has no parallel anywhere else in the Codes. Yet, with what Rebbe Nachman has just explained, the need for this vigilance is quite understandable.

We find in the Torah Blessings the words, "He has chosen us from all the nations and

LIKUTEY MOHARAN #14:3,4

So, too, the Jewish sinner. As long as he is called a Jew {for we refer to him as a "Jewish sinner," therefore the name "Jew" still applies to him,[22]} even though he has sinned, he is a Jew (*Sanhedrin* 44a). He <also> has a hold and a source in upper thought.[23] As a result of the shining, the source of his soul shines together with the other sources, so that an illumination reaches this Jewish sinner from his soul's source. And, by virtue of this illumination, he returns in repentance.[24]

4. This is what our Sages taught: Why do Torah scholars not have sons who are Torah scholars? Because they did not recite the blessing for Torah first (*Nedarim* 81a).[25] Every person, and especially the Torah scholar, must bless <the Torah first. That is,> through his Torah study, <he must bless> and illuminate the source of the souls—i.e., the "first in thought." For that is where our source is.[26]

We find, therefore, when a person brings illumination and blessing into the first thought, and through this the souls shine and are blessed, then when he draws down a soul for his son, he certainly

souls are aroused, one soul illuminates the next. Conceptually, this is a form of union. Speaking is important in that, just as in the mundane when one speaks he awakens thoughts in his mind, by speaking words of Torah, the spiritual, he awakens the Divine thought/the source of the souls.

22. **Jewish sinner....** Though he may be very distant from God and His Torah, as long as he has even a minute amount of belief he is still considered a Jew (*Mabuey HaNachal*).

23. **upper thought.** This is because Divine thought has been the source of his soul ever since the time of Creation.

24. **through the shining...repentance.** This arousal or awakening of the Torah letters/souls at their source initiates a union which causes other letters/souls to begin to shine. That is, there are 600,000 letters and souls corresponding to one another. Each has a place in the "thought of God," which is its source. When reciting Torah, one illuminates the letters at their source. Not only does he cause his own soul to shine, he even causes the soul of a wicked person to be illuminated and brought to repentance; all through his Torah study.

The obvious question is: What happens if the soul has its source in a letter in Genesis and the person now studying Torah is reading a chapter in Numbers? To this, Rebbe Nachman answers that when one letter begins to shine, it illuminates its source. Once the light begins to shine at its source, its light is reflected to other souls causing their lights to begin to shine. A chain reaction occurs. This is true for every area of Torah study, such as Mishnah, Talmud, etc. All parts of the Torah have their source in the Written Law, the Five Books of Moshe (cf. Lesson #12, n.15). We therefore see that by studying Torah, no matter where one is (wherever in the world or whatever spiritual level one is on), he can awaken his and other souls to repent (*Mai HaNachal*).

In review: To promote peace in the world one must elevate God's glory to its source: fear (§1). This can only be accomplished through the Torah—teaching it to others and bringing them

LIKUTEY MOHARAN #14:4,5

מִתְנוֹצְצִין וּמִתְבָּרְכִין הַנְּשָׁמוֹת, נִמְצָא כְּשֶׁמַּמְשִׁיךְ נְשָׁמָה לִבְנוֹ,
בְּוַדַּאי הוּא מַמְשִׁיךְ נְשָׁמָה בְּהִירָה וְזַכָּה, וְעַל־יְדֵי־זֶה גַּם בְּנוֹ יִהְיֶה
תַּלְמִיד־חָכָם;

אֲבָל כְּשֶׁאֵין מֵאִיר וּמְבָרֵךְ אֶת הַתְּחִלָּה עַל־יְדֵי לִמּוּדוֹ, אָז
כְּשֶׁמַּמְשִׁיךְ נְשָׁמָה לִבְנוֹ, הַנְּשָׁמָה הִיא בִּבְחִינַת (שִׁיר־הַשִּׁירִים ה):
"אֲנִי יְשֵׁנָה", וְאֵינָהּ מְאִירָה – מִפְּנֵי זֶה לֹא יִהְיֶה בְּנוֹ תַּלְמִיד־חָכָם,
וְזֶה מִפְּנֵי שֶׁלֹּא בֵּרְכוּ בַּתּוֹרָה תְּחִלָּה, הַיְנוּ שֹׁרֶשׁ הַנְּשָׁמוֹת, בִּבְחִינַת
יִשְׂרָאֵל עָלָה בְּמַחֲשָׁבָה תְּחִלָּה:

ה. וְאֵין אָדָם זוֹכֶה לְתוֹרָה, אֶלָּא עַל־יְדֵי שִׁפְלוּת, כְּמוֹ שֶׁאָמְרוּ
חַזַ"ל (עֵרוּבִין נד): "וּמִמִּדְבָּר מַתָּנָה", שֶׁיְּשַׁבֵּר גַּאֲוָתוֹ מֵאַרְבַּע
בְּחִינוֹת שִׁפְלוּת. כִּי צָרִיךְ הָאָדָם לְהַקְטִין אֶת עַצְמוֹ לִפְנֵי גְּדוֹלִים
מִמֶּנּוּ, וְלִפְנֵי בְּנֵי־אָדָם כְּעֶרְכּוֹ, וְלִפְנֵי קְטַנִּים מִמֶּנּוּ, וְלִפְעָמִים,
שֶׁהוּא בְּעַצְמוֹ קָטָן שֶׁבִּקְטַנִּים – וְצָרִיךְ לְהַקְטִין אֶת עַצְמוֹ כְּנֶגֶד

to be tread upon (i.e., he is humble), then the Torah is given to him as a present, *matanah* (*Eruvin* 54a). From here we see that one merits Torah through humility.

30. **greater...equals...lesser than he.** If one is haughty, he will consider himself above even those whom he begrudgingly admits are greater than himself. To acquire the Torah he must break this haughtiness. But not only this. When he considers himself equal to someone on his own level, this also indicates a degree of arrogance which must be broken. And even in relationship to someone lesser than himself, it is also a sign of haughtiness to think of oneself as being greater. Thus, the person who wants to acquire Torah must eliminate any vestige of haughtiness which he may possess. Even if he is truly worthy, he should not pride himself as such. For the more he lowers himself and limits his own self-importance, the more room, so to speak, there is for the revelation of God's glory in the world (cf. *Likutey Moharan* 6:1, 11:2).

31. **smallest of the small.** The *Biur HaLikutim* comments: This fourth aspect of humility which Rebbe Nachman mentions, the humility required of someone who is the smallest of the small, would seem to pose a number of difficulties. Firstly, who is this referring to? Who is it that is on a lower level than anyone else around him? Does this apply to any more than one person in perhaps hundreds of thousands? And even then, for someone on this level what four aspects of humility are there? Because he is already lesser than the rest, there really exists only two categories in which he might exhibit haughtiness: in relationship to those greater than himself and to those who are his equal. The third and fourth aspects of humility do not seem to apply. However, the answer to both these questions [which Rebbe Nachman has already discussed at length in *Likutey Moharan* I, 6:3] is that one must constantly increase his own level of humility. Then, as he continually humbles himself, he attains ever greater levels of

LIKUTEY MOHARAN #14:4,5

draws a pure and clear soul. As a result, his son will also be a Torah scholar.[27]

However, when he does not illuminate and bless the "first" through his study of Torah, then, when he draws a soul for his son, this soul is in the aspect of "I am asleep" (Song of Songs 5:2). It does not shine. This is why his son will not be a Torah scholar. And this is: "Because they did not recite the blessing for Torah first"—i.e., the source of the souls, as in, "Israel arose first in thought."[28]

5. Now, a person can only merit Torah through humility, as our Sages taught (Eruvin 54a): "And from the wilderness to Matanah" (Numbers 21:18).[29] He has to break his haughtiness, [drawing] from the four aspects of humility. For a person has to humble himself <in four aspects. The first is> before those greater than he. <The second is> before his equals. <The third is> before those lesser than he.[30] <The fourth aspect is> that he himself is sometimes the smallest of the small[31] and must <then> humble himself relative to his own level. He

---

given us His Torah...." The *Mabuey HaNachal* explains that this alludes to faith in God and the Torah. We trust that God has chosen and prepared our souls to be at the source—God's thought—and we believe that the Torah has the power to awaken our souls and direct us to repent. In this sense, the Torah is unique. No wisdom, no matter how deeply it is studied, has the power to inspire or connect to man's upper soul. The *Mabuey HaNachal* also mentions that this blessing and illuminating of the source through one's Torah study is in essence the concept of *lishmah,* the studying of Torah for its own sake (cf. Lesson #12, nn.5,9).

27. **his son...scholar.** This is because he illuminated this particular soul at its source.

Elsewhere, Rebbe Nachman explains this in greater detail. He mentions that everything a person does influences and has a part in the "beginning" and affects the source. Thus, for example, "when a child is conceived, his conception is affected by the food previously eaten by his parents. They must sanctify and bless this beginning, i.e., the things that precede conception, such as eating." Thus, a person who is careful about everything he does in the "beginning" assures a luminous and pure soul for his child. This is because he is careful that *all* the "beginnings" were as proper and as pure as possible (*Rabbi Nachman's Wisdom* #132).

28. **asleep...in thought.** This is in contrast to the aroused and awakened soul mentioned above. By not blessing the "first," the soul drawn into this world is asleep. It does not shine and will have great difficulty becoming a scholar.

In review: To promote peace in the world one must elevate God's glory to its source: fear (§1). This can only be accomplished through the Torah—teaching it to others and bringing them to recognize God. God's glory is thus elevated from darkness and exile (§2). Specifically this requires spreading the Torah outward, to inspire *baaley teshuvah* and converts (§3). This entails bringing illumination and blessing into the "first" of thought, causing the souls to shine (§4).

29. **wilderness to Matanah....** Our Sages taught: If one allows himself to be as a wilderness

LIKUTEY MOHARAN #14:5   304

מַדְרֵגַת עַצְמוֹ, וְיִדַמֶּה בְּעֵינָיו שֶׁהוּא לְמַטָּה מִמַּדְרֵגָתוֹ, בִּבְחִינַת
(שְׁמוֹת ט"ז): "שְׁבוּ אִישׁ תַּחְתָּיו":

וְזֶה שֶׁאָמַר רַבָּה בַּר בַּר-חָנָה:
לְדִידִי חָזֵי לִי הַאי אוּרְזִילָא בַּר-
יוֹמָא, דַּהֲוֵי כְּהַר-תָּבוֹר. וְהַר-תָּבוֹר
כַּמָּה הֲוֵי? אַרְבָּעָה פַּרְסֵי. וּבֵי
מַשְׁכָא דְּצַוְּארֵהּ – תְּלָתָא פַּרְסֵי,
וּבֵי מַרְבַּעְתָּא דְּרֵישֵׁהּ – פַּרְסָא
וּפַלְגָּא. וּרְמָא כּוּפְתָּא, וְסָכְרָא
לְיַרְדְּנָא.

רַשְׁבַּ"ם:

אוּרְזִילָא בַּר-יוֹמָא – רְאֵם בֶּן יוֹם
אֶחָד, דְּאוֹתוֹ הַיּוֹם נוֹלָד: כְּהַר-
תָּבוֹר – כֵּן הָיָה גָּדוֹל. בֵּי מַרְבַּעְתָּא
דְּרֵישֵׁהּ – מָקוֹם הַנַּחַת רֹאשׁוֹ
כְּשֶׁשּׁוֹכֵב עַל הַקַּרְקַע. רְמָא כּוּפְתָּא
– הִטִּיל רְעִי. סָכְרָא – הָרְעִי
לְיַרְדְּנָא לְפִי שָׁעָה, עַד שֶׁמִּסְמְסוּהוּ
הַמַּיִם מְעַט מְעַט.

אוּרְזִילָא בַּר-יוֹמָא – הַיְנוּ בְּחִינַת כָּבוֹד, שֶׁהוּא בָּעֲכוּ"ם, בִּזְלוּתָא.
וְזֶה: אוּר זִילָא. אוּר – הַיְנוּ בְּחִינַת כָּבוֹד, כְּמוֹ שֶׁכָּתוּב: "וְהָאָרֶץ
הֵאִירָה מִכְּבוֹדוֹ". וְלָמָּה נִקְרָא בַּר-יוֹמָא – כִּי לֹא יִתְגַּלֶּה הַכָּבוֹד
אֶלָּא בְּבִיאַת מְשִׁיחֵנוּ; וּכְתִיב בֵּהּ: אֵימָתַי יָבוֹא מַר? הַיּוֹם –

restricting his haughtiness and self-importance in all areas. A further connection can be made to that which the Talmud teaches (*Berakhot* 8a): God only seeks the four cubits of Halakhah—i.e., the study of Torah (cf. *Likutey Halakhot, B'tziat HaPat* 5:35). Thus, these four cubits, the four borders or limitations, the four aspects of humility, enable one to acquire Torah. (The relationship which this has to manna will be further developed in §9 and n.71).

33. **illuminated by His glory.** As mentioned above in section 2 and note 10.

34. **Today...hearken to His voice.** Rabbi Yehoshua ben Levi asked the Mashiach when he would come to redeem the world. The Mashiach replied, "Today!" When he did not arrive, Rabbi Yehoshua was disappointed and turned to Eliyahu HaNavi for an explanation. Eliyahu responded with the verse (Psalms 95:7), "Today! If you will hearken to [God's] voice!" In other words, from this Talmudic passage we can understand that Mashiach is already here, waiting to reveal himself. The fact that he has not yet done so is because our service of God is lacking. However, were we to listen to God and serve Him, His glory would be revealed through *our* actions. God's glory would be elevated to the level necessary for bringing the full redemption—only one day is needed!

With this, the *Mabuey HaNachal* answers an apparent contradiction in the text. Later on (§6), Rebbe Nachman writes that everyone can, and must, elevate the glory. Yet, here we are told that the full revelation of God's glory will only take place when the Mashiach comes. This is resolved as follows: Each day is elevated and rectified to the degree that one elevates

LIKUTEY MOHARAN #14:5

305

should imagine himself lower than he [really] is, corresponding to (Exodus 16:29), "Every person must sit beneath his place."[32]

This is what Rabbah bar bar Chanah recounted: I once saw a one-day-old *urzila* **(mountain goat) which was as big as Mount Tabor. And how large was** *Har* **(Mount) Tabor? Four miles. The length of its outstretched neck was three miles and the length of its head's** *marvata* **(resting place) was a mile and a half. It cast a ball of dung which obstructed the Jordan River** (*Bava Batra* 73b).

Rashbam:

a one-day-old urzila - a newborn mountain goat which had been born that very day: **as Mount Tabor** - that is how big it was: **the length of its head's marvata** - the place upon which it laid its head while lying on the ground: **cast a ball of dung** - it excreted: **which obstructed** - the dung temporarily blocked the Jordan's flow, until the water gradually dissolved it:

a one-day-old urzila (mountain goat) — This alludes to the aspect of glory, which is < in exile > *b'ZiLuta* (in disgrace). This is **ur-ZiLa**. *Ur* (illumination) corresponds to glory, as in, "The earth was illuminated by His glory."[33] And why was it called **one-day-old**? because the glory will not be revealed until the arrival of our Mashiach. Of him it is written (*Sanhedrin* 98a): [When asked,] "When will my master arrive?" < he answered, > "Today!" < And Eliyahu, of blessed memory, explained: > "Today! If you will hearken to His voice."[34] Each day,

humility, reaching the level of the "smallest of the small." Yet, even here, he must humble himself still further, until he feels himself as naught.

This exceptional level of humility was achieved by Moshe and Aharon, who considered themselves as naught (Exodus 16:7). Thus, Moshe received the Torah and Aharon brought people back to God (above, n.14)—precisely because of their humbleness.

32. **beneath his place.** Whatever your level, "sit" beneath it—be even more humble than that.

In Scripture, this verse refers to every person remaining (sitting) "in his designated place" and "not leaving his encampment on Shabbat" in order to collect the daily allotment of manna (a double portion fell on Friday). From this command our Sages deduce the laws of *techumin* (boundaries), the limited distance one can go beyond the city borders on Shabbat (*Eruvin* 17b). In addition, from this verse the Talmud derives the exact limited distance one may carry on Shabbat in a public domain, this being four cubits (approx. 6 feet). This is inferred in "every person...in his designated place"—man's height is generally three cubits and a fourth cubit is added to allow for the expanse of his hands and legs (*ibid.*, 48a). Within the context of the lesson, the three cubits correspond to the three aspects of humility: in relationship to those greater, the same as and lower than himself. The fourth cubit corresponds to that level of the smallest of the small. These limitations and restrictions in how far one may expand himself, so to speak, allude to the need for man's limiting and

LIKUTEY MOHARAN #14:5

306

"הַיּוֹם אִם בְּקֹלוֹ תִשְׁמָעוּ" (כְּמוֹ שֶׁאָמְרוּ רַבּוֹתֵינוּ, זִכְרוֹנָם לִבְרָכָה סַנְהֶדְרִין צח.), וּבְכָל יוֹם מוּכָן הַכָּבוֹד לָצֵאת מִזִּילוּתָא.

וַהֲוָה כְּהַר־תָּבוֹר – שֶׁרָאָה שֶׁהַעֲלָאַת הַכָּבוֹד תָּלוּי בָּזֶה שֶׁאָדָם מְשַׁבֵּר גַּאֲוָתוֹ – כְּפִי הִשְׁתַּבְּרוּת גַּאֲוָתוֹ, כֵּן הוּא הַעֲלָאַת הַכָּבוֹד, כִּי כְּבוֹדוֹ נִתְעַלֶּה עַל־יְדֵי הַתּוֹרָה כַּנַּ"ל, וְאֵין אָדָם זוֹכֶה לַתּוֹרָה אֶלָּא עַל־יְדֵי שִׁפְלוּת, כְּמוֹ שֶׁאָמְרוּ חֲזַ"ל: "וּמִמִּדְבָּר מַתָּנָה". וְזֶה: הַר תָּבוֹר; הַר – לְשׁוֹן גַּדְלוּת, כְּמוֹ שֶׁכָּתוּב (תְּהִלִּים ל): "הֶעֱמַדְתָּ לְהַרְרִי עֹז", וְתָבוֹר – לְשׁוֹן שְׁבִירָה.

וְהַר־תָּבוֹר כַּמָּה הֲוָה, אַרְבַּע פַּרְסֵי – הַיְנוּ אַרְבַּע בְּחִינוֹת שִׁפְלוּת הַנַּ"ל שֶׁצָּרִיךְ לְהַקְטִין: לִפְנֵי צַדִּיקִים, בֵּינוֹנִים, רְשָׁעִים, וְלִפְנֵי מַדְרֵגַת עַצְמוֹ, וְשֶׁיְּדַמֶּה בְּעֵינָיו כְּאִלּוּ לֹא בָּא עֲדַיִן לִפְנֵי מַדְרֵגָתוֹ שֶׁהוּא בָהּ. וְזֶה: הַר־תָּבוֹר אַרְבַּע פַּרְסֵי – שֶׁשְּׁבִירַת הַגַּדְלוּת הֵם בְּאַרְבַּע בְּחִינוֹת הַנַּ"ל.

וּמַשְׁכָא דְצַוָּארֵהּ תְּלָתָא פַּרְסֵי – זֶה בְּחִינַת הַדְּבָרִים שֶׁדֶּרֶךְ בְּנֵי־אָדָם לְהִתְגַּדֵּל בָּהֶם, הֵם שְׁלֹשָׁה דְּבָרִים, וְצָרִיךְ לִשְׁמֹר אֶת עַצְמוֹ מֵהֶם, כְּמוֹ שֶׁכָּתוּב (יִרְמְיָה ט): אַל יִתְהַלֵּל חָכָם בְּחָכְמָתוֹ וְכוּ', וְהֵם שָׁלֹשׁ בְּחִינוֹת: חָכָם, גִּבּוֹר, עָשִׁיר. וְהַגַּדְלוּת נִקְרָא מַשְׁכָא דְצַוָּארָא, בִּבְחִינַת (תְּהִלִּים ע"ה): "תְּדַבְּרוּ בְצַוָּאר עָתָק".

---

merits arousing the souls to repentance (§3). And through repentance, they recognize God's glory (§2).

37. **my har...shebirah, breaking.** The very appearance of a tall *har* (mountain) suggests arrogance and haughtiness. In Aramaic, *t'bar* means to break. Thus, Har Tabor connotes the breaking of haughtiness.

38. **three aspects...haughty neck.** This refers to the *urzila*, the glory (*ur*) in exile (*b'ziluta*). Fundamentally, there are three elements that promote haughtiness in a person: wisdom, might, and wealth. We find that when speaking arrogantly or boasting about one's attributes, a person will cock his head and hold his neck erect.

39. **union...Divine thought.** As explained above in section 3.

LIKUTEY MOHARAN #14:5

the glory is <capable> of emerging from its disgrace. <This is the meaning of **one-day-old**. >

which was as big as Har (Mount) Tabor — [Rabbah bar bar Chanah] saw that the elevation of glory depends upon a person breaking his haughtiness.[35] Glory ascends in proportion to the extent one breaks one's haughtiness, because His glory is elevated through Torah, as above. And, a person can only merit Torah through humility, as our Sages taught: "And from the wilderness to Matanah."[36] This is **Har Tabor**. *Har* denotes arrogance, as in (Psalms 30:8), "You have made my *har* stand proud"; and *taBoR* indicates *sheBiRah* (breaking).[37] <Thus, **Har Tabor** alludes to breaking haughtiness. >

And how large was Mount Tabor? Four miles — This alludes to the four aspects of humility mentioned above. A person must humble <himself> before the righteous, the ordinary people, the wicked and before his own level. He should see himself as if he has not yet attained [even] the level which he is on. This is **Mount Tabor, four miles**. The breaking of haughtiness is in four aspects.

The length of its neck when outstretched was three miles — This corresponds to the things which people tend to be haughty about, of which there are three. A person must guard himself against them, as is written (Jeremiah 9:22), "Let not the wise man glory in his wisdom, nor the mighty man in his might, nor the rich man in his wealth." They are three aspects: wise, mighty, wealthy. And haughtiness is called an **outstretched neck**, corresponding to (Psalms 75:6), "Speak [not] with a haughty neck."[38]

---

the glory by drawing himself and others closer to God. The day everyone turns to Him will be the day when all the components of God's glory will be elevated, and on that day Mashiach will come.

35. **Mount Tabor...haughtiness.** Mount Tabor, as well as a number of other mountains, requested of God that He give the Torah on it. God refused, insisting that each of these mountains was unfit. Each mountain possessed a degree of haughtiness, presuming that due to its beauty or great height it was deserving of this honor and glory. Only Mount Sinai remained silent and made no claim. Because of this display of humility, God elected to give the Torah on it (*Sotah* 5a, *Rashi, s.v. kol harim*; also see *Megillah* 29a). Thus, Rebbe Nachman will soon explain that Mount Tabor alludes to haughtiness.

36. **...Matanah.** As we've seen, through humility one merits Torah (§5). Through Torah one

LIKUTEY MOHARAN #14:5 — 308

וּמַרְבְּעָתָא דְּרֵישֵׁהּ פַּרְסָא וּפַלְגָּא – זֶה בְּחִינַת זִוּוּג הַנַּעֲשֶׂה בְּרֵאשִׁית הַמַּחֲשָׁבָה; מַרְבְּעָתָא – לְשׁוֹן זִוּוּג, כְּמוֹ שֶׁכָּתוּב (שָׁם קלט): "אָרְחִי וְרִבְעִי". וְעַל־יְדֵי הַזֶּה זִוּוּג נַעֲשֶׂה פַּרְסָא וּפַלְגָּא: פַּרְסָא – זֶה רֶמֶז עַל הַמְשָׁכַת הַנְּשָׁמוֹת לִבְנֵיהֶם, זֶה מְכֻנֶּה בְּשֵׁם פַּרְסָה שְׁלֵמָה; וְהִתְנוֹצְצוּת שֶׁהַנְּשָׁמוֹת מִתְנוֹצְצִין וּמְאִירִין וּמְעוֹרְרִין אֶת הַפּוֹשְׁעֵי־יִשְׂרָאֵל בִּתְשׁוּבָה וּמוֹלִידִין נִשְׁמוֹת גֵּרִים – זֶה מְכֻנֶּה בְּשֵׁם פַּלְגָּא,

כִּי עֲדַיִן רְחוֹקִים מֵהַקְּדֻשָּׁה מְאֹד וְיָכוֹל לִהְיוֹת לָהֶם מְנִיעוֹת רַבּוֹת, וְצָרִיךְ לָהֶם יְגִיעוֹת רַבּוֹת כְּדֵי לְהַפְשִׁיט מֵהֶם הַבְּגָדִים צוֹאִים שֶׁהִלְבִּישׁוּ, כְּמוֹ שֶׁכָּתוּב (זְכַרְיָה ג): "הָסִירוּ הַבְּגָדִים הַצֹּאִים", כִּי אֵלּוּ הַבְּגָדִים הַצּוֹאִים הֵם מוֹנְעִים אוֹתָם מִלַּחֲזֹר לַקָּדוֹשׁ־בָּרוּךְ־הוּא, וְהֵם מַפְסִיקִים כְּמוֹ נָהָר הַמַּפְסִיק, שֶׁאִי אֶפְשָׁר לַהֲלֹךְ דֶּרֶךְ אוֹתוֹ הַנָּהָר, וְצָרִיךְ לְהַשְׁלִיךְ הַבְּגָדִים הַצּוֹאִים. וְזֶה: רְמָא כּוּפְתָּא וְסַכְרָא לְיַרְדְּנָא – עַל־יְדֵי שֶׁמַּפְשִׁיטִין וּמַשְׁלִיכִין מֵעֲלֵיהֶם הַבְּגָדִים הַצּוֹאִים, נִתְבַּטְּלִים כָּל הַמְנִיעוֹת וְהַמָּסַכִים הַמַּבְדִּילִים בֵּינָם לְבֵין הַקְּדֻשָּׁה. וְזֶה: וְסַכְרָא לְיַרְדְּנָא – כִּי הַיַּרְדֵּן מַפְסִיק בֵּין קְדֻשַּׁת אֶרֶץ־יִשְׂרָאֵל לְחוּץ־לָאָרֶץ. וּבִשְׁבִיל זֶה נִקְרָאִים בְּשֵׁם פַּלְגָּא, כִּי עֲדַיִן צָרִיךְ לְהַשְׁלִיךְ מֵהֶם הַבְּגָדִים הַצּוֹאִים, כְּדֵי לְהָסִיר הַמַּפְסִיקִים וְהַמּוֹנְעִים

lesson, this indicates more than that one's sins are soiled garments which block one's admission to the side of holiness. In addition, the soiled garments apply to the barriers to holiness which a person encounters as a result of his "beginning," a soul unblessed and unillumined at the time of conception. Thus, even before he transgresses, a person starts his life with these "soiled garments" and must work very, very hard to shed them.

This concept that desires and bad traits are with a person from the time of his birth has also been explained above in Lesson #10 (§4 and n.35). There we see that parents' thoughts during cohabitation play a major role in the physical, emotional and spiritual development of their child.

44. Jordan...separating them from holiness. Although Rebbe Nachman has not previously mentioned the Holy Land directly, it is alluded to in section 2 where he says that the glory is now with the non-Jews. The glory "left the Holy Land" when the Jews sinned and were exiled. Even so, when they repent and recognize God's glory, it will return with them at the

309   *LIKUTEY MOHARAN #14:5*

and the length of its head's marvata (resting place) was a mile and a half — This alludes to the union which takes place in the beginning of Divine thought.[39] [The word] **maRVata** connotes union, as in (Psalms 139:3), "...my way and my *RiV'ee* (laying down)."[40] And through this union, there is **a mile and a half**. "A mile" hints to the drawing of souls to their sons, which is termed "a whole mile,"[41] whereas the shining [by] which the souls shine, illuminate and arouse the Jewish sinners to repentance and give birth to the souls of converts is termed "half."[42]

The reason for this is that [these *baaley teshuvah* and converts] are still very far from holiness, and are likely to encounter many obstacles. One has to expend great effort in order to strip them of the soiled garments which they put on, as in (Zekhariah 3:4), "Remove the soiled garments." For it is these soiled garments that prevent them from returning to the Holy One. They are barriers, just as a river bars passage and makes it impossible to journey on in the direction of that river. These soiled garments are barriers that must be thrown off.[43] And this is:

It cast a ball of dung which obstructed the Jordan River — By stripping and throwing off the soiled garments from them, all the obstacles and partitions separating them from holiness are eliminated.

obstructed the Jordan River — This is because the Jordan separates between the holiness of the Land of Israel and the Diaspora. And this is the reason they are called "half," for one still has to throw off the soiled garments from them in order to remove the barriers, obstacles and partitions separating them from holiness.[44] But these souls which

---

40. **my way and RiV'ee.** This verse is explained in the Talmud as referring to marital relations (*Niddah* 31a). See Lesson #13, note 120, where Rebbe Nachman also applies this to the arousal of a holy unification in the transcendant worlds.

41. **a complete mile.** As explained above in section 4. The soul is drawn directly from its source, Divine thought.

42. **half.** For this soul is only drawn through the awakening that takes place in Divine thought, which is initiated by another person. See above section 3.

43. **soiled garments...thrown off.** Yehoshua ben Yehotzadak was the High Priest during the early years of the Second Temple. Although he himself was a complete tzaddik, Yehoshua's children had intermarried. A condition for his being appointed to the head of the priesthood was that his sons divorce their non-Jewish wives. They, because of their sins, were referred to as "soiled garments." Only after they complied was he pure enough to make his entrance to the Temple, referred to in later verses as wearing "clean garments." Within the context of our

LIKUTEY MOHARAN #14:5　　　310

וְהַמָּסַכִּים הַמַּבְדִּילִים בֵּינָם לְבֵין הַקְּדֻשָּׁה. אֲבָל, אֵלוּ הַנְּשָׁמוֹת
שֶׁתַּלְמִידֵי־חֲכָמִים מַמְשִׁיכִין לִבְנֵיהֶם כַּנַּ״ל – זֶה מְכֻנֶּה בְּשֵׁם פַּרְסָה
שְׁלֵמָה, כִּי אֵין לָהֶם מָסַכִּים הַמַּבְדִּילִים.

וְזֶה: 'וְכִבַּדְתּוֹ – כַּבְּדֵהוּ בִּכְסוּת נָקִי', כְּמוֹ שֶׁדָּרְשׁוּ רַבּוֹתֵינוּ,
זִכְרוֹנָם לִבְרָכָה עַל פָּסוּק: וְלִקְדוֹשׁ ה' מְכוּבָּד וְכוּ', שַׁבָּת קיט.).
'כְּסוּת נָקִי' – הַיְנוּ לְהַשְׁלִיךְ הַבְּגָדִים הַצּוֹאִים, כִּי זֶה עִקַּר כְּבוֹד
הַשֵּׁם יִתְבָּרַךְ, "אִם תּוֹצִיא יָקָר מִזּוֹלֵל", לְהַחֲזִיר בְּנֵי־אָדָם
בִּתְשׁוּבָה וּלְהַמְשִׁיךְ נִשְׁמוֹת הַגֵּרִים.

וְגֵרִים שֶׁמִּתְגַּיְּרִין, הֵם בָּאִים תַּחַת כַּנְפֵי הַשְּׁכִינָה, וּבִשְׁבִיל זֶה נִקְרָא
גֵּר־צֶדֶק (כַּמּוּבָא בְּהַקְדָּמַת הַזֹּהַר ו). וְזֶה שֶׁמּוּבָא בַּזֹּהַר (יִתְרוֹ בר״מ צג.):
'כְּסוּת נָקִי, דָּא כַּנְפֵי מִצְוָה' – הַיְנוּ שְׁכִינָה הַנִּקְרָאת מִצְוָה,
בִּבְחִינוֹת (תְּהִלִּים קיט): "כָּל מִצְוֹתֶיךָ צֶדֶק". וְזֶהוּ: 'וְכִבַּדְתּוֹ', שֶׁזֶּה

---

for repentance, a person tries to shed his attachment to corporeality. This is why the physical pleasures of eating, drinking, etc. are prohibited. Thus, to honor Yom Kippur we wear clean garments. This applies to those who must repent, those who are called "half." Similarly, to honor God—to reveal His glory—we must shed physicality and wear "clean garments." And Shabbat, too, corresponds to repentance; hence *ShaBbaT* (שבת) and *TaShuV* (תשב, return) have the same letters. Nevertheless, the level of Shabbat generally refers to those who are called "complete"—their garments are already clean. Those on this level are not only permitted to eat, but are enjoined to delight in good food and drink. The concept of Shabbat as it relates to humility and Torah has been explained above in section 4 and note 32.

46. **under the wings....** The place of converts is under the wings of the *Shekhinah*. The place of the Jews is above the wings (*Biur HaLikutim*).

Rebbe Nachman will now explain that a convert is called righteous by virtue of his being brought under the wings of the Divine Presence.

47. **Shekhinah...mitzvah.** The *Zohar* (II, 93a) explains: "Honor...your mother" (Exodus 20:12)—this alludes to the Divine Presence, *Malkhut*. Honor her with clean garments, *kanfey mitzvah*. This *kanfey* (corners of) *mitzvah* refers to the four-cornered garment, the *tallit* (*Sulam, loc. cit.*). Thus the Talmud relates that to honor the Shabbat, Rabbi Yehudah bar Ilai would bathe himself and then adorn a special fringed cloak (*Shabbat* 25b). It is also known that on Friday afternoon right before sunset, the holy Ari and his disciples would put on their *talleitim* (prayer shawls) and go out into the orchards of Safed to greet the Divine Presence/ Shabbat.

The Ari (*Shaar HaGilgulim* 11) teaches that the mitzvot correspond to the level of *nefesh*, the lower soul which is synonymous with *Malkhut*. Thus, as Rebbe Nachman points out, the *Shekhinah*, which is also *Malkhut*, corresponds to mitzvah.

LIKUTEY MOHARAN #14:5

the Torah scholars draw down to their sons are termed "a whole mile," for they have no separating partitions. *Shabbos*

This is the meaning of "and you shall honor it" (Isaiah 58:13)—honor it with clean garments! (*Shabbat* 119a).[45] "Clean garments" alludes to throwing off the soiled garments. For this is the essence of God's glory: "If you take out the precious from the vile"—to induce people to repent and to draw down the souls of converts.

And when converts convert, they come under the wings of the *Shekhinah* (Divine Presence) (*Sanhedrin* 96b). This is why [the convert] is called a *ger tzedek* (righteous convert) (*Zohar*, Introduction p.13).[46] As is brought in the *Zohar* (II, 93a): "Clean garments" is *kanfey* (garment corners of) mitzvah. This alludes to the *Shekhinah*, which is known as "mitzvah,"[47] as in (Psalms 119:172), "All Your mitzvot are righteousness." And this is the meaning of "and you shall honor it." For

time of redemption. This is the function of the Jordan River: it separates the Land of Israel, the revelation of God's glory, from the Diaspora, the darkening and exile of His glory (*Biur HaLikutim*).

In our lesson, Rebbe Nachman relates this role of the Jordan to the obstacles one faces when trying to return to God. In actuality, this "crossing the Jordan" is necessary at every level. Even when one enters the realm of the holy, he faces obstacles and barriers at each and every stage of his spiritual development. This is actually for one's benefit. Just as dross is removed from gold by subjecting it to increasingly higher temperatures, so, too, by dealing with *m'niot* (obstacles) at each higher level one becomes purer and purer. This cleansing process is what enables a person to truly taste spirituality. His *M'NIOT* are transformed into *N'IMOT* (great pleasures). For only by overcoming these obstacles can a person partake of the great spiritual pleasures which await those who come closer to God (*Mabuey HaNachal*).

Similarly, our Sages taught: The Jews were only exiled among the nations so as to enable non-Jews to convert (*Pesachim* 87b). Indeed, had the exile been intended only as a form of punishment, there were many other ways through which God could have achieved this aim. We must therefore conclude that the Jewish people's being sent out of the Holy Land was for the purpose of revealing God to the nations (*Maharsha, s.v. lo*). Thus, even though the Jewish people sinned and God's glory became concealed in exile, this concealment is actually the very means through which the glory will be revealed to the utmost.

45. **honor it...clean garments.** This refers to the honoring of Shabbat. Commenting on this verse from Isaiah: "And call the Shabbat a delight, the holy day of God [call] honorable; and you shall honor it...," our Sages asked: If Shabbat is mentioned, what "holy day" are we to call honorable? They answered that this holy day is Yom Kippur, on which there is no eating or drinking, and which we honor with clean garments. As for the Shabbat, the Talmud tells us that "you shall honor it" with good food...(see *Shabbat* 119a). It might therefore seem surprising that Rebbe Nachman associates "you shall honor it," a reference to Shabbat, with clean garments, which the Talmud associates with Yom Kippur.

However, in light of the lesson, this is not inconsistent. On Yom Kippur, which is a time

LIKUTEY MOHARAN #14:5-7 312

עִקַּר כְּבוֹדוֹ, שֶׁיַּכְנִיס גֵּרִים תַּחַת כַּנְפֵי הַשְּׁכִינָה כַּנַּ"ל:

ו. וְכָל אֶחָד לְפִי בְּחִינָתוֹ יָכוֹל לֵידַע הַעֲלָאַת הַכָּבוֹד לְשָׁרֶשׁ הַיִּרְאָה; לְפִי הַכָּבוֹד שֶׁמְּכַבֵּד אֶת יִרְאֵי־הַשֵּׁם, כֵּן עָלָה הַכָּבוֹד לְשָׁרְשׁוֹ, כִּי שָׁם שֹׁרֶשׁ הַכָּבוֹד, בִּבְחִינַת (שָׁם טו): "וְאֶת יִרְאֵי ה' יְכַבֵּד". כִּי כָּל זְמַן שֶׁהַכָּבוֹד הוּא בַּגָּלוּת, כָּל אֶחָד לְפִי בְּחִינָתוֹ הוּא מְזַלְזֵל בְּיִרְאֵי־ הַשֵּׁם, וְכָל אֶחָד לְפִי תִּקּוּנוֹ אֶת הַכָּבוֹד, כֵּן הוּא מְכַבֵּד יִרְאֵי־הַשֵּׁם:

ז. וְעִקַּר הַדָּבָר – שֶׁיְּכַבֵּד יִרְאֵי־הַשֵּׁם בְּלֵב שָׁלֵם, כְּמוֹ שֶׁאָמְרוּ חֲכָמֵינוּ, זִכְרוֹנָם לִבְרָכָה (קִדּוּשִׁין לב:): 'דָּבָר הַמָּסוּר לַלֵּב, נֶאֱמַר בּוֹ

situation in which those who truly fear God and conduct their lives accordingly are looked down upon and sometimes even despised. Rather than respecting and giving honor to the rabbi of one's community and other learned people, the glory and reverence are reserved for those who have affluence, influence or power. Exile dictates that glory be humbled. However, man's mission is to elevate it, by choosing to honor righteous people.

The verses (Psalms 15:3-4) read, "He did not slander...is humble, despises wickedness, and gives glory/honor to those that fear God...." All this ties in with Rebbe Nachman's opening statement, "To achieve peace...." Those who seek strife will slander others and not despise wickedness, they do not want peace. However, those who do truly wish for peace are humble, seek God's glory and respect those who are deserving of honor (*Mai HaNachal*).

52. **to the heart...fear your Lord.** There are certain mitzvot, injunctions as well prohibitions, that are "given over to the heart"—that only God knows the true intentions of one's behavior. Others have no way of knowing whether his failure to carry out a positive command or his transgressing a negative one was intentional or not. Thus, for example, a Jew is commanded "not to put a stumbling block [i.e., give bad advice] before the [conceptually] blind...," and "to stand up and give honor to a sage..." (Leviticus 19:14,32). Because these involve matters which are hidden in the heart, one can claim to be innocent of any wrongdoing. After giving bad advice and causing his friend, who did not know any better, to stumble in some matter, he can claim he was not aware that there was anything wrong with his suggestion. He can say, "I didn't realize!" and no one—other than God—will ever know. Likewise, he can fail to rise when he sees a sage approaching and then claim, "I didn't see him coming." Who—other than God—will ever know? Therefore, immediately following these commandments the Torah warns, "And you shall fear your Lord!" Thus, the Talmud emphasizes that anything "given over to other heart" requires that we fear God. We must remember that God knows even our hidden thoughts and though we may be capable of deceiving our fellow man, we cannot fool Him (*Kiddushin* 32a).

At the outset of the lesson Rebbe Nachman states that the source of glory is in fear. God's *kavod* (glory) corresponds to the *sefirah* of *Malkhut*, hence God's Kingship (the literal meaning of *Malkhut*) is revealed when His glory is elevated (cf. Lesson #11, n.18; Lesson #12, nn.14,16). The Ari explains that the building up, the elevation, of *Malkhut* requires its receiving the *gevurot* (severities) whose source is in *Binah* (*Parparaot LeChokhmah*; cf. Lesson

313   *LIKUTEY MOHARAN #14:5-7*

this is the essence of His glory: to bring converts under the *kanfey* (wings) of the *Shekhinah*.[48]

6. Each person, according to his level, can be aware of glory's elevation to the source of fear.[49] To that degree that he honors those who fear God, the glory [i.e., God's honor,] ascends to its source—the source of glory being there [in fear]. This corresponds to (Psalms 15:4), "He honors to those who fear God."[50] Because, as long as the glory is in exile, each person, in his own way, disgraces those who are God-fearing; whereas, to the degree that he rectifies the glory, he correspondingly honors those who fear God.[51]

7. And the essential thing is that a person sincerely honor those who fear God. As our Sages taught: Of those things which are given over to [i.e., hidden in] the heart, it is said, "And you shall fear your Lord!" (*Kiddushin* 32b).[52] Therein lies the essence of glory, as in (Isaiah 29:13),

---

48. **mitzvot are righteousness...wings of the Shekhinah.** From this verse in Psalms we see that the mitzvot correspond to *tzedek* (righteousness). In addition, we've just seen that *kanfey* is "clean garments," and that mitzvah is synonymous with the *Shekhinah*. In that case, the *Shekhinah* itself corresponds to *tzedek*. Because of this, the convert who sheds his "soiled garments" and dons "clean garments"/the mitzvot, can come close to the Divine Presence (*Mabuey HaNachal*). Thus, his adorning of the *kanfey mitzvah* brings him under the *kanfey* (wings) of the *Shekhinah*.

In review: To promote peace in the world one must elevate God's glory to its source: fear (§1). This can only be accomplished through the Torah—teaching it to others and bringing them to recognize God. God's glory is thus elevated from darkness and exile (§2). Specifically this requires spreading the Torah outward, to inspire *baaley teshuvah* and converts (§3). This entails bringing illumination and blessing into the "first" of thought, causing the souls to shine (§4). But to acquire Torah so that one can share it, one must be humble. One can then help those distant from holiness to shed their "soiled garments" and come under the wings of the *Shekhinah*—the greatest elevation of God's glory (§5).

49. **glory's elevation to the source of fear.** After explaining how one can elevate God's glory, Rebbe Nachman returns to his opening statement, "It is necessary to elevate...to fear" and explains how one can know whether that glory is truly being elevated to its source in fear or not. Often times, one thinks he is doing the right thing but is mistaken. The Rebbe therefore offers a barometer with which one can measure: one can look at the way he himself honors and gives respect to those who are truly God-fearing. With this test, he can know if his teaching others and his other apparently righteous deeds are having the desired affect. Will he ultimately elevate God's glory and not his own?

50. **honors those....** Whereas Rebbe Nachman began the lesson with what for most people appears to be a purely abstract suggestion, telling us to elevate God's glory to fear (see n.2), he now offers a very practical way to apply this: by honoring those who are God-fearing. This display of honor for those who fear God is the elevation of glory to its source, to fear.

51. **disgraces...honors those who fear God.** Rebbe Nachman is referring to the very prevalent

LIKUTEY MOHARAN #14:7,8

וְיָרֵאתָ מֵאֱלֹקֶיךָ', וְשָׁם עִקַּר הַכָּבוֹד, כְּמוֹ שֶׁכָּתוּב (יְשַׁעְיָהוּ כ"ט): "בִּשְׂפָתָיו כִּבְּדוּנִי וְלִבּוֹ רִחַק מִמֶּנִּי":

ח. כְּשֶׁמַּחֲזִיר הַכָּבוֹד לְשָׁרְשׁוֹ, הַיְנוּ לַיִּרְאָה כַּנַּ"ל, וְאָז נִשְׁלָם פְּגָמֵי הַיִּרְאָה, וְאָז זוֹכֶה לְשָׁלוֹם.

וְיֵשׁ שְׁנֵי מִינֵי שָׁלוֹם: יֵשׁ שָׁלוֹם בַּעֲצָמָיו, כִּי תְּחִלָּה צָרִיךְ אָדָם לִרְאוֹת שֶׁיִּהְיֶה שָׁלוֹם בַּעֲצָמָיו, כִּי לִפְעָמִים אֵין שָׁלוֹם, כְּמוֹ שֶׁכָּתוּב (תְּהִלִּים ל"ח): "אֵין שָׁלוֹם בַּעֲצָמַי מִפְּנֵי חַטָּאתִי". וְעַל-יְדֵי הַיִּרְאָה, זוֹכֶה לְשָׁלוֹם בַּעֲצָמָיו, כְּמוֹ שֶׁכָּתוּב בַּזֹּהַר (יִתְרוֹ עט.): בְּאַתְרָא דְּאִית דְּחִילָא, תַּמָּן תִּשְׁתַּכַּח שְׁלִמְתָא, כְּמוֹ שֶׁכָּתוּב (שָׁם לד): "כִּי אֵין מַחְסוֹר לִירֵאָיו".

and perishing from the earth. This we see from the verses in Isaiah, "... with their lips they honor Me, but their hearts are distanced from Me, their fear of Me is like a habit. Therefore, the wisdom of the wise"—the ones who can bring forth Torah to elevate God's glory—"shall perish." There will be concealment of the Torah rather than illumination.

54. **peace.** In contrast to a lack of peace, which denotes fragmentation, peace, conceptually, is a whole. When blemished (fragmented) fear is made complete, peace is automatic. Rebbe Nachman will next connect the previous two sections (6 and 7) to his opening statement: "To draw peace into the world...."

55. **peace in one's bones...inner peace.** This implies peace between the soul and the body. The body listens to and obeys the soul, through which fear is complete (*Parparaot LeChokhmah*).

56. **no inner peace...sin.** This is because sin causes blemish, a concept of fragmentation.

This is connected to the previous sections and in particular to the verses quoted in note 51: "He did not slander...is humble, despises wickedness, and gives glory/honor to those that fear God...." Just as between people there are slanderers and strife-seeking individuals, so too, in the spiritual, there are prosecuting angels who use the powers given them by one's sins to oppose that person's service of God. As a result, the body creates obstacles and stumbling blocks for the soul and the person consequently has no inner peace. One then has to attempt to bring himself back to the spiritual. This in itself is a concept of bringing others to serve God—he is bringing his own body, which now is acting like "others," back to spiritual desires (*Mai HaNachal*).

57. **completeness...lack nothing.** This state of completeness and lacking nothing is synonymous with peace. The *Zohar* (*loc. cit.*) emphasizes the need for fear in order to achieve this. In contrast, a person only sins because he lacks fear. As a result, he becomes fragmented, with no inner peace. However, when he repents—*teshuvah*'s source being in *Binah* (cf. n.52)—he attains fear.

315   *LIKUTEY MOHARAN #14:7,8*

"With their lips they honor Me, but their hearts they have distanced from Me."[53]

8. When a person returns the glory to its source, i.e., to fear, and thus completes that which is lacking in fear, he then merits peace.[54]

There are two types of peace. There is the peace in one's bones, for a person must first see to it that he has inner peace.[55] Because, at times, there is no peace, as in (Psalms 38:4), "There is no inner peace because of my sin."[56] But through the fear, a person merits peace in his bones. As is brought in the *Zohar* (II, 79a): In the place where there is fear, there you will find wholeness, as in (Psalms 34:10), "For those who fear Him lack nothing."[57]

#12, n.81). Fear is a quality associated with the *gevurot* and the *sefirah* of *Gevurah*, whereas *Binah*, the seat of the *gevurot*, is in the heart. Thus, within our context, we see that the elevation of glory (*Malkhut*) is to its source in fear (the *gevurot*). This glory can be elevated when one fears with a "whole heart" (*Binah*).

53. **lips they honor Me...hearts they have distanced from Me.** One can give honor with his lips. It is known as "lip service." In reality, the things he says or does are very distant from his true thoughts and feelings. Yet, on the outside it appears as if he really means to honor or show respect for someone or something. This "lip service" is possible, because honor is essentially something which is "given over to the heart," as in the previous note.

The verses in Isaiah (29:13-14) read "...with their lips they honor Me, but their hearts they have distanced from Me, their fear of Me is like a habit.... Therefore, the wisdom of the wise shall perish..." Honor should be in the heart. When it becomes habitual, respect is lacking and glory cannot be elevated (*Mabuey HaNachal*).

When Rebbe Nachman taught this lesson he said that when a tzaddik passes away it is difficult to reveal new Torah insights. This is because when a tzaddik leaves this world his portion of the Torah leaves with him, thus making it hard for the remaining tzaddikim to originate new ideas (see above, n.1). This ties in with the remainder of the verse, "the wisdom of the wise shall perish." As our Sages explain: This refers to the passing away of tzaddikim (*Eikhah Rabbah* 1:39). In section 3, Rebbe Nachman explained that the Torah has its source in Divine thought. Accordingly, whatever aspects of Torah a particular tzaddik illuminates during his lifetime is his "share" and "portion" of Divine thought. Thus, when a tzaddik passes on, the letters/souls which are "his," no longer shine. This is what makes it difficult for another tzaddik to reveal Torah (*Mabuey HaNachal*).

We can now take this further. Rebbe Nachman has told us that without the fear of God in one's heart, one does not fear or have true respect for those who do fear Him. The verse thus tells us that as a result, "the wisdom of the wise shall perish." When the God-fearing are not respected, it is because there is no fear of God in people's hearts. Their hearts are therefore incapable of acquiring Torah, the "wisdom of the wise," which is a necessary ingredient for elevating glory to fear. Lacking fear, there can be no Torah with which to elevate God's glory. But not only this! Because they lack fear and fail to honor those who truly deserve it, these people are ultimately held responsible for the tzaddik's passing away

LIKUTEY MOHARAN #14:8

316

כְּשֶׁיֵּשׁ שָׁלוֹם בַּעֲצָמָיו, אָז יָכוֹל לְהִתְפַּלֵּל. כִּי עִקַּר הַתְּפִלָּה עַל־יְדֵי הַיִּרְאָה, בִּבְחִינַת (מִשְׁלֵי ל"א): "אִשָּׁה יִרְאַת ה' הִיא תִתְהַלָּל", כִּי הַתְּפִלָּה בִּמְקוֹם קָרְבָּן, וּבְקָרְבָּן כְּתִיב בֵּהּ: "כֹּל אֲשֶׁר בּוֹ מוּם לֹא יִקְרָב"; וּכְשֶׁאֵין בּוֹ מוּם, הַיְנוּ בְּאַתְרָא דְּאִית דְּחִילָא, אֲזַי יָקְרַב לַעֲבֹד עֲבוֹדָתוֹ תַּמָּה.

וְזֶה שֶׁכָּתוּב בְּחַנָּה (שְׁמוּאֵל־א א): "וְחַנָּה מְדַבֶּרֶת עַל לִבָּהּ" – עַל־ יְדֵי הַיִּרְאָה זָכְתָה לִתְפִלָּה, כִּי עִקַּר הַיִּרְאָה הוּא בַּלֵּב כַּנַּ"ל, וְעַל־יְדֵי תְּפִלָּה זוֹכֶה לַשָּׁלוֹם הַכְּלָלִי, הַיְנוּ שְׁלֵמוּת הָעוֹלָמוֹת, כִּי עַל שֵׁם זֶה תְּפִלָּה נִקְרָא קָרְבָּן, עַל שֵׁם קֵרוּב הָעוֹלָמוֹת לִשְׁלֵמוּתָן:

---

62. perfection of the worlds. This not only connotes peace in the spiritual universes Above, but also peace in the home, between friends, and between enemies and opposing forces such as the realms of the physical and the spiritual. These, too, are "worlds" in need of perfect peace and harmony. In fact, the universal peace that will exist in this lower world—when everyone will recognize and serve God "with one consent"—will cause all the upper worlds to be drawn closer together. *Shefa* (great abundance and blessing) can then descend from Above and each world, the one we are in and those higher than it, will have what it uniquely needs to perfect its service of the Holy One.

63. KoRBan...the worlds KeiRuV.... The sacrifice (קרבן) corresponds to both the drawing closer (קרוב) of the worlds to a universal peace and bringing people closer (קירוב) to God. Thus (*Sifra* 13), "Each and every sacrifice brings peace to the world" (*Parparaot LeChokhmah*).

Although we see that one who is blemished may not offer a sacrifice, we must not conclude that we, who lack completeness, ought not to pray, God forbid. This teaching that each and every sacrifice adds to the peace in the world shows that a person must always try his best, even though he has not yet put on "clean garments." Even the little bit that a person tries to correct in himself brings him closer to true fear. The little that he sacrifices to elevate himself also serves to elevate the glory of the Holy One (*Mabuey HaNachal*).

In review: To promote peace in the world one must elevate God's glory to its source: fear (§1). This can only be accomplished through the Torah—teaching it to others and bringing them to recognize God. God's glory is thus elevated from darkness and exile (§2). Specifically this requires spreading the Torah outward, to inspire *baaley teshuvah* and converts (§3). This entails bringing illumination and blessing into the "first" of thought, causing the souls to shine (§4). But to acquire Torah so that one can share it, one must be humble. One can then help those distant from holiness to shed their "soiled garments" and come under the wings of the *Shekhinah*—the greatest elevation of God's glory (§5). The degree to which a person honors those who fear God is indicative of how much he elevates God's glory to its source in fear (§6). Because this honor/glory is hidden in the heart, its sincerity must be governed by fear of God (§7). Returning glory to its source completes fear. With this completeness, sin is eliminated, resulting in inner peace; and prayer is enhanced, resulting in universal peace (§8).

LIKUTEY MOHARAN #14:8

<And> when a person has inner peace, he is then able to pray. For the essence of [praising God in] prayer is achieved through fear, corresponding to (Proverbs 31:30), "A woman who fears God, she shall be praised."[58] This is because prayer is in place of the *KoRBan* (sacrifice),[59] and of the sacrifice it is written (Leviticus 21:18), "Any man who is blemished shall not *yiKRaV* (draw close)."[60] But when he is not blemished—that is, "In a place where there is fear"—he can then draw close to perform a complete service.

And this is what is written of Chanah (1 Samuel 1:13), "Now, Chanah was speaking to her heart"—<i.e.,> through fear she merited to prayer, for the essence of fear is in the heart.[61]

And through prayer, a person merits universal peace—i.e., perfection of the worlds.[62] This is the reason why prayer is called a *KoRBan*, by virtue of its bringing the worlds *KeiRuV* (closer) to their perfection.[63]

---

58. **a woman who fears....** As we've seen, glory and fear are associated with *Gevurah* and *Binah*. Both these Divine emanations are from the left side of the *sefirah* hierarchy and correspond to the feminine principle. Thus, it is the woman who fears. And when there is fear, then there can be the raising up, the expression, of God's glory—prayer.

59. **in place of the sacrifice.** The prayers were arranged corresponding to the daily sacrifices (*Berakhot* 26b).

60. **blemished shall not yiKRaV.** In this verse from Leviticus, the word *yikrav* (יקרב) indicates both the offering of a sacrifice (קרבן) and "drawing close." See also note 63.

Just as it is forbidden to offer a blemished animal as a sacrifice, it is forbidden for one who is blemished to present the offering to God. Similarly, in offering one's prayers, one must strive to be a proper vehicle. This can be achieved through fear, which affords one completeness and the ability to pray (*Parparaot LeChokhmah*).

61. **Chanah....** This happened when Chanah came to the Tabernacle to pray for children. She "spoke to her heart." That is, through the fear that was embedded in her heart (as above, §§6,7), she merited prayer.

The Talmud teaches that Chanah was one of seven prophetesses, and her husband Elkanah one of the prophets (*Megillah* 14a). Before each festival, Elkanah would begin his pilgrimage to the Tabernacle in Shilo. Every holiday he traveled a different route in order to encourage as many people as possible to join him. Each year he would bring more and more people with him (*Rashi,* 1 Samuel 1:3). This relates to the teaching of Torah and the elevation of God's glory mentioned in the lesson. As for Chanah, she was outstanding in her respect for those who fear God. Because of this, she did not respond disrespectfully when Eli, the High Priest, mistakenly accused her of entering the Tabernacle while drunk (1 Samuel 1:14-16). In the merit of her prayers she was blessed with a son, Shmuel, whose greatness is likened to that of Moshe and Aharon (Psalms 99:6). Our Sages point out that many of the laws of prayer are learned from the way Chanah prayed (*Berakhot* 31a,b).

LIKUTEY MOHARAN #14:9
318

ט. וְזֶה שֶׁאָמַר רַבָּה בַּר בַּר־חָנָה:

אָמַר לִי הַהוּא טַיָּעָא: תָּא וְאַחֲוֵי
לָךְ הֵיכֵי דְּנָשְׁקֵי אַרְעָא וּרְקִיעַ
בַּהֲדָדֵי. אֲזַלִי וַחֲזַאי, דְּעָבִיד כּוּי
כּוּי. שְׁקַלִית לְסַלְתָּאי וְאַנַּחְתֵּיהּ
בְּכַוְּתָא דִּרְקִיעָא. בַּהֲדֵי דִּמְצַלֵּינָא
בָּעוּתָא, וְלֹא אַשְׁכְּחִיתָהּ. אָמְרִי:
אִיכָּא גַּנְבֵי הָכָא. אָמַר לִי: גַּלְגַּלָּא
דִּרְקִיעַ הוּא דְּהָדַר. נְטַר עַד
לִמְחָר כִּי הַשְׁתָּא, וּמַשְׁכַּח לַהּ.

רַשְׁבַּ"ם:

הֵיכָא דְּנָשְׁקֵי אַרְעָא וּרְקִיעָא –
מָקוֹם גָּבוֹהַּ הָיָה שָׁם, שֶׁנּוֹשְׁקִים
יַחַד זֶה לָזֶה. וְלָאו הַיְנוּ סוֹף הָעוֹלָם,
דְּהָא מַהֲלַךְ הָעוֹלָם ת"ק שָׁנָה הֲוֵי,
וְאֶרֶץ־יִשְׂרָאֵל אֶמְצָעִיתוֹ שֶׁל הָעוֹלָם
הִיא, דִּכְתִיב: יֹשְׁבֵי עַל טַבּוּר הָאָרֶץ,
וְהַיְנוּ מְקוֹמוֹ שֶׁל רַבָּה בַּר בַּר־חָנָה.
סַלְתָּאי – סַל לֶחֶם שֶׁלִּי. דְּהָדַר –
חוֹזֵר, כִּדְאָמְרִינַן בִּפְסָחִים: גַּלְגַּל
חוֹזֵר וּמַזָּלוֹת קְבוּעִים.

דְּנָשְׁקֵי אַרְעָא וּרְקִיעָא – זֶה בְּחִינַת שָׁלוֹם בְּעַצְמָיו. אַרְעָא – זֶה
בְּחִינַת גּוּף, רְקִיעָא – זֶה בְּחִינַת נְשָׁמָה, כְּמוֹ שֶׁכָּתוּב (תְּהִלִּים נ):
"יִקְרָא אֶל הַשָּׁמַיִם מֵעַל" – זֶה הַנְּשָׁמָה, "וְאֶל הָאָרֶץ" – זֶה הַגּוּף
(סַנְהֶדְרִין צא:). וּכְשֶׁיֵּשׁ בֵּינֵיהֶם שָׁלוֹם, עַל־יְדֵי־זֶה

עֲבִידֵי כּוּי – עַל־יְדֵי־זֶה נַעֲשֶׂה תְּפִלָּה, כַּנַּ"ל, בִּבְחִינַת (דָּנִיֵּאל ו):
"וְכַוִּין פְּתִיחָן לֵהּ בְּעִלִּיתֵהּ".

וְשָׁקַלִית לְסַלְתָּאי וְאַנַּחְתֵּיהּ בְּכַוְּתָא דִּרְקִיעַ. סַלְתָּא – זֶה פַּרְנָסָה,
כְּמוֹ 'מִי שֶׁיֵּשׁ לוֹ פַת בְּסַלּוֹ' (יוֹמָא עד:),

הַיְנוּ שֶׁלֹּא רָצָה לַעֲסֹק בְּשׁוּם עֵסֶק מֵעִסְקֵי עוֹלָם הַזֶּה, רַק בִּשְׁבִיל

---

65. **windows...and he prayed.** The Talmud (*Berakhot* 31a) teaches that a person should try to
pray in a room which has windows. This we learn from Daniel who, when he wanted to pray
to God despite the king's decree against this, chose a room with windows. Thus windows are
associated with prayer.

66. **bread in his basket.** Bread is used as a general term to denote livelihood. The Talmud (*loc.
cit.*) states that one who has bread in his basket cannot be compared to one who does not.
Rashi explains that the latter has eaten what he has and must now worry about provisions for
the next day.

LIKUTEY MOHARAN #14:9

9. This is what Rabbah bar bar Chanah recounted: This merchant said to me, "Come, I will show you the place where earth and heaven kiss." I went and saw that many windows had been created. I took my basket and placed it in the window of heaven. After I finished praying, I wanted to take [my basket] but could not find it. "Are there thieves here?" I asked. The merchant said to me, "It is the *galgala* (sphere) of heaven which turned. Wait until this time tomorrow and you will find it" (*Bava Batra* 74a).

Rashbam:

where earth and heaven kiss - there was a high place there where one meets the other; though this was not the end of the universe, for the universe extends a distance of five hundred years. And the Land of Israel, which is where Rabbah bar bar Chanah was, is the middle of the universe, as in (Ezekiel 38:12), "They live at the center of the earth": **my basket** - my bread basket: **which turned** - it turns around, as is taught in *Pesachim* (94b): It is the sphere of heaven which rotates and the constellations which are stationary:

where earth and heaven kiss — This alludes to inner peace. "Earth" corresponds to the body; "heaven" corresponds to the soul. < As our Sages taught: > It is written (Psalms 50:4), "He calls to the heavens above..."—this is the soul; "...and to the earth"—this is the body (*Sanhedrin* 91b). And when there is peace between them,[64] then through this:

windows had been created — < That is, > prayer is created, as in (Daniel 6:11), "The windows of his upper room were directed [towards Jerusalem...and he prayed]."[65]

I took my basket and placed it in the window of heaven — "Basket" denotes livelihood, as in [the expression]: "One who has bread in his basket..." (*Yoma* 74b).[66]

In other words, [Rabbah bar bar Chanah] did not want to engage in any of the mundane endeavors of this world, but only for [the

---

64. **peace between them.** The Talmud (*loc. cit.*) applies this teaching to explain how the soul and the body are judged after one's passing. The soul claims that the body is the guilty one, arguing that ever since being separated from the body it, the soul, has not sinned. Likewise, the body claims that the soul, not it, deserves to be judged, supporting its argument by showing that since the soul has left it, the body itself has been no more than stone, incapable of any movement. After hearing their claims, God puts the soul back into the body and then issues a verdict and exacts punishment from both.

From our text we see that when earth and heaven, the body and the soul, kiss, there is peace between two opposites. And when this peace exists, there is no sin. Then one can pray.

LIKUTEY MOHARAN #14:9

נִשְׁמָתוֹ. גַּם כָּל תְּפִלּוֹתָיו לֹא הָיוּ אֶלָּא בִּשְׁבִיל לְקַשֵּׁר נִשְׁמָתוֹ;
אֲפִלּוּ אֵלּוּ תְּפִלּוֹת הַמְפֹרָשִׁים בַּתְּפִלָּה שֶׁהֵם לְצֹרֶךְ הַגּוּף, כְּגוֹן
"רְפָאֵינוּ" וּ"בָרֵךְ עָלֵינוּ" וּשְׁאָר צָרְכֵי הַגּוּף, לֹא הָיָה כַּוָּנָתוֹ שֶׁל
רַבָּה בַּר בַּר־חָנָה בִּשְׁבִיל גּוּפוֹ, אֶלָּא בִּשְׁבִיל נִשְׁמָתוֹ, שֶׁהָיָה מְכֻוָּן
לְפַרְנָסַת נִשְׁמָתוֹ וְלִרְפוּאָתָהּ. וְזֶה:

וְשַׁקְלֵית לְסַלְתָּאִי וְאַנַּחְתֵּיהּ בְּכַוְתָא דִּרְקִיעָ. – שֶׁשָּׁקַל לַתְּפִלָּה
שֶׁהוּא לְצֹרֶךְ הַגּוּף, וְאַנַּחְהָ בִּתְפִלָּה, הַכֹּל לְצֹרֶךְ נִשְׁמָתוֹ, כִּי מִמֵּילָא
כְּשֶׁנִּתְקָן שָׁם בְּרוּחָנִיּוּת, נִתְקָן גַּם בְּגַשְׁמִיּוּת.

וְעַד דִּמְצַלֵּינָא בָּעוּתִי, לָא אַשְׁכָּחָה – הַיְנוּ אַחַר־כָּךְ לֹא מָצָא כְּדֵי
פַּרְנָסָתוֹ, אַף־עַל־פִּי שֶׁתִּקֵּן בְּרוּחָנִיּוּת, אַף־עַל־פִּי־כֵן לֹא נִמְשַׁךְ לוֹ
שֶׁפַע בְּגַשְׁמִיּוּת.

אָמַר: אִיכָּא גַּנְבָא הָכָא, שֶׁגּוֹנְבִים הַשֶּׁפַע שֶׁלִּי. הֵשִׁיב לוֹ:
גַּלְגַּלָּא דִרְקִיעָא דְּהַדְרָא – הַיְנוּ גִּלְגּוּלִין דְּנִשְׁמָתִין, הִיא הַגּוֹרֶמֶת
שֶׁאֵין לַצַּדִּיק כְּדֵי פַרְנָסָתוֹ, כְּמוֹ שֶׁכָּתוּב גַּבֵּי רַבִּי פְּדָת (תַּעֲנִית כה.)
'אִי בָּעִית דְּאַחֲרוּב עָלְמָא, וְאֶפְשָׁר דְּאִיבְּרֵית בְּשַׁעֲתָא דִּמְזוֹנָא'.

the world. Each person receives all that he needs. Rabbah bar bar Chanah therefore wondered if perhaps someone had come and stolen the blessing he should have received by virtue of his having elevated God's glory to its source. He had achieved inner peace and had been able to pray. He had also rectified *Malkhut*, which was receiving from *Binah*, the heart, the home of all *shefa* before it descends to this lower world. Where then was his rightful share? (For the connection between *Malkhut, Binah* and the flow of *shefa*, see Lesson #12:4, also n.52 above.)

70. **reincarnation of souls.** Even though one may have attained perfection in his present incarnation, it is possible that in previous lives he committed various acts that he has yet to rectify. Therefore, he cannot now receive his full measure of *shefa*. Similarly, in the more general sense, full blessing for all the worlds will only be achieved when Mashiach comes, as mentioned above in section 2. Only then will the complete rectification be made.

71. **Rabbi P'dat....** The two versions of this story, in the Talmud (*Taanit* 25a) and in the *Tikkuney Zohar* (#69, p.100a), differ slightly. Rabbi P'dat was extremely poor and languished in abject poverty for many years. Once, he fainted and God came to him in a vision. "If you so desire, the world will be overturned and recreated. Perhaps in the next *gilgul* (incarnation) you will be born at a time when the constellation of material prosperity is ascendant." Thus, even though he was great enough to have God directly speak to him (in a vision), this did not ensure that his material needs would be taken care of.

LIKUTEY MOHARAN #14:9

spiritual growth of] his soul. Even all his prayers were solely to bind his soul < to its source > . Even those prayers specified in the *Amidah* that are for one's material needs—such as "Heal us" and "Bless us [for this year and its livelihood]," as well as the other requests for the material necessities—[when he recited them,] Rabbah bar bar Chanah's intention was not for his body but for his soul. What he had in mind was his soul's livelihood and healing.

And this is: **I took my basket and placed it in the window of heaven.** He took the prayer that is for the needs of the body and "placed it" entirely for the needs of his soul.[67] For it automatically follows that when there is a rectification in the spiritual, the physical is also rectified.

After I finished praying, I wanted to take [my basket] but could not find it — In other words, he did not afterwards have enough for his livelihood. Though he had rectified the spiritual, even so, abundant material blessing had not come to him.[68]

Are there thieves here? I asked — [Thieves] who have stolen my blessing of abundance.[69] [The merchant] answered him:

It is the GaLGaLa (sphere) of heaven which turned — This has to do with the *GiLGuL* (reincarnation) of souls,[70] which is what causes the righteous to have insufficient livelihood. < As our Sages taught > concerning Rabbi P'dat: "If you so desire, the world shall be destroyed and perhaps you will be reborn in a time of material prosperity" (*Taanit 25a; Tikkuney Zohar #69*).[71]

[Handwritten margin note: gashmius should come automatically if brochos are centered on neshama]

---

67. **the window of heaven...needs of his soul.** This translates in our text as follows: Having achieved an inner peace between body and soul, Rabbah bar bar Chanah placed the basket, the material, aside and prayed only for the spiritual, the "window of heaven." Once a person attains such peace all the worlds are brought together and *shefa* can descend. He no longer has a need to pray for the material, for his livelihood will descend to him automatically (*Parparaot LeChokhmah; Mai HaNachal*).

This ties in with the concept of the manna, livelihood (n.32). The manna descended to each person according to his needs, without his having to ask/pray for it. The Jews who received the Torah at Mount Sinai were at peace with each other and unified in heart (*Rashi, Exodus 19:2*). They had achieved the inner peace which enables one to pray. However, they only had to pray for the spiritual, their material livelihood was "guaranteed."

68. **abundant material blessing....** Having rectified the spiritual, he was certain that he would find his material needs taken care of. However, when he finished praying, his basket, his livelihood, was nowhere to be found.

69. **stolen my blessing of abundance.** When *Malkhut* is rectified, then all *shefa* descends directly to

LIKUTEY MOHARAN #14:9

וְזֶה (בְּרֵאשִׁית וֹ): "קַנִּים תַּעֲשֶׂה לַתֵּבָה" – אִיתָא בַּמִּדְרָשׁ (בְּרֵאשִׁית רַבָּה לֹא): 'מַה קַנִּים מְטַהֲרִין אֶת הַמְצֹרָע, אַף תֵּבָתְךָ מְטַהַרְתְּךָ'. 'הַמְצֹרָע' – זֶה נִרְגָּן מַפְרִיד אַלּוּף (מִשְׁלֵי טז), וּמַפְרִיד בֵּין אִישׁ וְאִשְׁתּוֹ, וְעַל־יָדֵי־זֶה: בָּדָד יֵשֵׁב (עֲרָכִין טז.); וְקַנִּים מְטַהֲרִים אוֹתוֹ, אַף תֵּבָתְךָ, הַיְנוּ תֵּבַת הַתְּפִלָּה, מְתַקְּנִין אֶת הַמַּחֲלֹקֶת וְעוֹשֶׂה שָׁלוֹם הַכְּלָלִי, שָׁלוֹם כָּל הָעוֹלָמוֹת. וְזֶה שֶׁמְּסַיְּמִין הַתְּפִלָּה בְּשָׁלוֹם:

With these manifest and recondite teachings, we can better understand the question which Rebbe Nachman addresses in his lesson: How is it that the tzaddik who has attained exalted spiritual levels is left without the material sustenance which he requires? What happened to Rabbah bar bar Chanah's basket? Where was the *shefa* that he should have automatically received by virtue of his righteousness? Rabbi P'dat (as well as Rabbah bar bar Chanah) prayed only for spirituality, the needs of his soul. He elevated God's glory, achieved completeness through fear, came to inner peace, was able to pray.... And though he had no interest in and did not ask for his material needs, he should have been given *shefa* directly. Where was his manna? Where was his livelihood? To this Rebbe Nachman answers that, in fact, the *shefa* from the Upper Mazal had descended. The reason neither of these tzaddikim, Rabbah bar bar Chanah or Rabbi P'dat, received it has to do with the mystery of *gilgulim* of the soul. Because of the various reincarnations through which one's soul passes, there can be no guarantee of prosperity even for the truly righteous. It is always possible that he is presently undergoing the hardships of poverty in order to rectify some transgression performed during a previous *gilgul*. Also implied in the lesson is the *gilgulim* (revolving) of the *galgalim* (*mazalot*). These upper worlds are in constant motion and not always are they completely aligned to facilitate the direct transference of *shefa* down to *Malkhut*/earth. Because of this, even when the tzaddik has completely rectified his personal level, his lot may nevertheless be one of poverty.

The *Mabuey HaNachal* adds that the true tzaddik can easily change his lot and with but little effort obtain this *shefa* just by praying for it. He is a Master of Prayer and can align the worlds so as to provide for all his needs. However, the tzaddik puts his basket in the window of heaven. When he comes to pray he divests himself of all corporeality. Hence, instead of praying for his material prosperity, he beseeches God for the needs of his soul.

72. kinim purifies the leper.... The word *kinim* may mean compartments, rooms, or nests. It is also the name of a bird offering brought by a leper (Leviticus 12). Rebbe Nachman here introduces the concept of slanderers and others who promote strife, opponents of peace, for whom the punishment is leprosy. (This is actually alluded to earlier in §8, in the verse, "There is no peace in my bones because of my sin." See nn. 51 and 56 for the connection to slanderers.)

73. separates husband and wife. Conceptually, husband and wife allude to God and the Community of Israel. Thus, by speaking slander, one separates God and the Jewish people. This is the concept of exile, the negation of God's glory.

74. he sits alone. This refers to the exile, as in (Lamentations 1:1), "How does [Jerusalem] sit alone, the city that was full of people! She has become like a widow!"

75. prayer rectifies...peace. Inner peace joins the physical and spiritual together, in contrast to the leper who separates them. This peace can be achieved only by bringing back those who

LIKUTEY MOHARAN #14:9

And this is: "Make *kinim* (compartments) for the ark " (Genesis 6:14). In the Midrash we find: Just as the *kinim* (bird offering) purifies the leper, so, too, your ark is your purification (*Bereishit Rabbah* 31:9).[72] The leper is "the whisperer who separates close friends" (Proverbs 16:28). He separates husband and wife (*Erkhin* 16b),[73] because of which "he sits alone" (Leviticus 13:46).[74] Yet, the bird offering purifies him. "So, too, *TeyVaTkha* (your ark)...."—i.e., *TeyVaT* (the word of) prayer rectifies the strife and creates universal peace, the peace of all the worlds. And this is why the *Amidah* concludes with [the blessing for] peace.[75] *This is what tefillah is able to correct ie a blemish of peace (in all the worlds)*

Thus Kohelet says, "A generation goes and a generation comes, but the earth stands forever" (Ecclesiastes 1:4). The *Tikkuney Zohar* explains this to mean that a generation that goes, comes back in *gilgul* (a generation being 600,000 souls). "The earth" refers to *Malkhut*, the manifestation of His Kingdom in this world. Hence, all *shefa* (the forces which provide blessing and prosperity) which descends to this world must first pass through *Malkhut*. As a result, this *shefa*, though it has its source in the Upper Mazal, must nevertheless be "processed" by the twelve *mazalot* (constellations) which correspond to *Malkhut*. The particular alignment of these *mazalot* dictates each generation's prosperity. If *Malkhut* is complete and every level Above is in its proper place for the transference of the *shefa*, then one can expect abundance in livelihood. But if the levels above *Malkhut* are misaligned, then *Malkhut* does not receive full *shefa*. The *shefa* the world at large does receive is therefore indirect and only semi-potent.

The Talmud (see *Shabbat* 156a), however, teaches that the Jewish people are above the dictates of the zodiac. As Rashi explains, through prayer, charity and other deeds, a Jew can change his *mazal* for the better. This is because the Jewish people have their source in *Chokhmah* (Wisdom)—Divine thought—as it relates to *Keter* (Crown). Because of this, the livelihood of a Jew who is worthy is governed by the Upper Mazal, the level of the Divine persona *Atik/Keter* (see Appendix: The Divine Persona). His righteousness gives him the power to draw a *shefa* which is both direct and potent, without having to concern himself with the alignment of the constellations (though even in his case the *shefa* passes through *Malkhut*). (All this is explained in greater detail in the *Tikkuney Zohar* #69, and in the commentary of the *Kisey Melekh, loc. cit.*).

In the context of our lesson, this relates to what Rebbe Nachman mentioned (§3) about the 600,000 souls (a generation) which are in Divine thought. These 600,000 souls are the Torah which, when illuminated, elevate God's glory/*Malkhut* (n.52 above). By elevating God's glory one merits peace, through which one can pray and bring an all-encompassing, universal peace (§8). His soul, like that of Moshe Rabbeinu, has the power to encompass the souls of the entire generation—all 600,000 (cf. *Shaar HaPesukim, BeHaalotekha*). Thus, when one can ascend to Divine thought, which is bound to *Keter*, one can unite all the worlds and draw direct and bountiful *shefa* for everyone. As explained (n.67), the relationship which the spiritual has to the physical with regard to one's livelihood was exemplified in the manna. Our Sages taught: Torah was given only to those who ate the manna (*Mekhilta, BeShalach* 17). That is, when one merits Torah in a way that awakens the souls, he merits receiving his livelihood in the same fashion as the Jewish people received the manna in the desert—directly and in abundance.

LIKUTEY MOHARAN #14:10

324

י. וְזֶה פֵּרוּשׁ: תִּקְעוּ – לְשׁוֹן שָׁלוֹם, כְּמוֹ שֶׁכָּתוּב (יְשַׁעְיָהוּ כב):
"וּתְקַעְתִּיו יָתֵד בְּמָקוֹם נֶאֱמָן".

בַּחֹדֶשׁ שׁוֹפָר – בְּהִתְפָּאֲרוּת חָדָשׁ, הַיְנוּ הִתְעַלּוּת כְּבוֹדוֹ עַל-יְדֵי
הִתְקָרְבוּת הַגֵּרִים אוֹ בַּעֲלֵי-תְּשׁוּבָה.

בַּכֶּסֶה – זֶה בְּחִינַת יִרְאָה, שֶׁהוּא שֹׁרֶשׁ הַכָּבוֹד; וְכֶסֶה – לְשׁוֹן
הִתְכַּסְיָא, שֶׁזֶּה בְּחִינַת: 'דָּבָר הַמָּסוּר לַלֵּב, נֶאֱמַר בּוֹ וְיָרֵאתָ
מֵאֱלֹקֶיךָ', שֶׁזֶּה הַדָּבָר מְכֻסֶּה מֵעֵין כֹּל.

לַיּוֹם – זֶה בְּחִינַת שָׁלוֹם בַּיִת, כִּי יוֹם הוּא בְּחִינַת אוֹר, כְּמוֹ
שֶׁכָּתוּב (בְּרֵאשִׁית א): "וַיִּקְרָא אֱלֹקִים לָאוֹר יוֹם", וְאוֹר הוּא שָׁלוֹם
בַּיִת, כְּמוֹ שֶׁאָמְרוּ חֲכָמֵינוּ, זִכְרוֹנָם לִבְרָכָה (שַׁבָּת כג:): 'נֵר-שַׁבָּת
קוֹדֶם לְקִדּוּשׁ הַיּוֹם', כִּי שָׁלוֹם בַּיִת קוֹדֶם.

חַגֵּנוּ – זֶה בְּחִינַת תְּפִלָּה, עֲבוֹדָה, כְּמוֹ שֶׁאָמְרוּ חֲכָמֵינוּ, זִכְרוֹנָם
לִבְרָכָה (פְּסָחִים קיח.): 'לָמָּה נִסְמְכָה פָּרָשַׁת עַכּוּ"ם לְמוֹעֲדִים?
לוֹמַר, כָּל הַמְבַזֶּה אֶת הַמּוֹעֲדוֹת, כְּאִלּוּ עוֹבֵד עֲבוֹדַת אֱלִילִים'.

79. **light, Day.** This alludes to the light that shines when the glory is revealed (above §2, nn.9,10).

80. **peace in the home comes first.** Our Sages taught (*Shabbat* 23b): If one has only enough money to purchase either Shabbat candles or wine for the *Kiddush,* let him purchase the candles for Friday evening. Sitting with his family in darkness could lead to strife. He should therefore make certain to have the Shabbat candles, for this brings peace to the home. Thus, day/light is synonymous with peace in the home.

81. **chapter on idolatry...festivals.** These both appear in Exodus 34.

82. **disgraces the festivals....** As mentioned earlier (n.45), honoring the holy days and Shabbat entails wearing clean clothing. In the context of the lesson, this implies the donning of "clean garments" by those who return to God. This brings about the elevation of His glory. However, by failing to shed their "soiled garments," by not repenting, they are considered as having disgraced the festivals—thereby concealing God's glory and extending the exile.

The *Mai HaNachal* points out that this is why the festivals are also called *regalim:* to allude to the elevation of the glory to fear and thereby achieve prayer, which then brings to universal peace. *Regel* means foot, a reference to the pilgrimage, and, as the lowest part of the body, refers to the lowest spiritual levels. Thus, the festivals are meant to elevate these lowly levels, by bringing them up into holiness. We therefore find that on the holidays we are commanded to "divide the day," giving half to God (in prayer, Torah study, etc.) and

10. This is the explanation [of the opening verse]:

{*"Tik'u* (Blow) a shofar *hachodosh* (at the New Moon); *bakeseh* (at the appointed time) for the day of our festival."}

TiK'u — This connotes peace, as in (Isaiah 22:23), "And *TeKativ* (I will affix him) as a stake in a <u>secure place</u>."[76]

baChoDeSh shoFaR — With a *hitPaRut ChaDaSh* (new glory)—i.e., the elevation of His glory by drawing close the converts or *baaley teshuvah*.[77]

bakeseh — This is the aspect of fear, which is the source of glory. *KeSeh* is similar to *hitKaSyah* (hidden). This corresponds to, "Of those things which are given over to [i.e., hidden in] the heart, it is said, 'And you shall fear your Lord!'"—for [fear] is a thing which is hidden from all eyes.[78]

for the day of — This alludes to peace in the home. For "day" is an aspect of light, as is written (Genesis 1:5), "And the Lord named the light 'Day.'"[79] And light denotes peace in the home, as our Sages taught: The Shabbat lights take precedence over the *Kiddush* of the day—because peace in the home comes first (Shabbat 23b).[80]

our festival — This corresponds to prayer, Divine service. As our Sages taught: Why is the Torah chapter on idolatry adjacent to that of the festivals?[81] This is to teach that anyone who disgraces the festivals, it is as though he serves idolatry (Pesachim 118a).[82] We see,

are distant from God and thereby elevating His glory. Then one attains true fear, a level of completeness. This completeness or inner peace enables him to pray and through prayer he rectifies strife and promotes universal peace (cf. above, §8).

76. **And TeKativ...in a secure place.** Rashi reads this as, "I will plant him firmly in the place...." The word "firmly" refers to something that is lasting and complete—the permanent peace that will reign when God brings back the exiled.

The conclusion of the verse reads, "...and he will be a throne of glory to his father's house." This also alludes to our text in that peace can only come by bringing those on the outside back to God and thereby elevating the Holy One's glory (*Parparaot LeChokhmah*).

77. **baChoDeSh shoFaR....** The word *chadesh* means renewal. *ShoFaR* (שופר) is similar to the Aramaic for beauty, *ShuFRa* (שופרא). It thus suggests *Pe'eR* (פאר, glory and magnificence). Thus, when is it that peace (*tik'u*) is achieved? When this new beauty is manifest—when God's glory is revealed by the renewed *baaley teshuvah* and the new converts who have now been brought to devote themselves to God.

78. **...hidden from all eyes.** This refers to one's thoughts, which are hidden and thus correspond to the heart (see above, §7 and n.52). The seat of the glory is also in the heart, the place in which fear is hidden.

LIKUTEY MOHARAN #14:10,11 326

נִמְצָא – שְׁמִירַת הַמּוֹעֵד זֶה בְּחִינַת עֲבוֹדָה תַּמָּה, 'וְאֵין עֲבוֹדָה אֶלָּא תְפִלָּה' (ספרי פ' עקב: עיין ב"ר פ' ל"ג): וְעַל־יְדֵי תְּפִלָּה יָבוֹא לְשָׁלוֹם הַכְּלָלִי כַּנַּ"ל.

נִמְצָא מִי שֶׁרוֹצֶה לְהַמְשִׁיךְ שָׁלוֹם הַכְּלָלִי, צָרִיךְ לְהַעֲלוֹת הַכָּבוֹד לְשָׁרְשׁוֹ, הַיְנוּ לַיִּרְאָה, וְעַל־יְדֵי הַיִּרְאָה הוּא זוֹכֶה לְשָׁלוֹם־בַּיִת, וְעַל־יְדֵי שָׁלוֹם־בַּיִת הוּא זוֹכֶה לִתְפִלָּה, וְעַל־יְדֵי תְּפִלָּה הוּא זוֹכֶה לְשָׁלוֹם הַכְּלָלִי:

יא. זֹאת הַתּוֹרָה שַׁיָּךְ עַל פְּסוּקִים אֵלּוּ (תְּהִלִּים קמ"ה): "טוֹב ה' לַכֹּל וְרַחֲמָיו עַל כָּל מַעֲשָׂיו" וְכוּ'.

"טוֹב ה' לַכֹּל" – זֶה בְּחִינַת תְּפִלָּה, שֶׁמַּאֲמִין בָּהּ', שֶׁהַקָּדוֹשׁ־בָּרוּךְ־הוּא טוֹב לַכֹּל – הֵן לִרְפוּאָה, הֵן לְפַרְנָסָה, הֵן לְכָל הַדְּבָרִים. כְּשֶׁמַּאֲמִין כָּךְ, בְּוַדַּאי יִהְיֶה עִקַּר הִשְׁתַּדְּלוּתוֹ בָּתַר קֻדְשָׁא־בְּרִיךְ־הוּא, וְלֹא יִרְדֹּף אַחַר תַּחְבּוּלוֹת רַבּוֹת; כִּי מִי שֶׁאֵין מַאֲמִין בְּהַקָּדוֹשׁ־בָּרוּךְ־הוּא, צָרִיךְ לְהִשְׁתַּדֵּל אַחַר תַּחְבּוּלוֹת רַבּוֹת. לְמָשָׁל, כְּשֶׁצָּרִיךְ לִרְפוּאָה – צָרִיךְ לְהִשְׁתַּדֵּל אַחַר עֲשָׂבִים רַבִּים, וְלִפְעָמִים אֵלּוּ עֲשָׂבִים הַצְּרִיכִים לוֹ אֵינָם בַּנִּמְצָא בִּמְדִינָתוֹ, וְהָעֲשָׂבִים הַנִּמְצָאִים אֵינָם טוֹבִים לְמַכָּתוֹ. אֲבָל הַקָּדוֹשׁ־בָּרוּךְ־הוּא טוֹב לְכָל הַמַּכּוֹת לְרַפְאוֹתָם, וְהוּא בַּנִּמְצָא תָּמִיד, כְּמוֹ שֶׁכָּתוּב (דְּבָרִים ד): "מִי כַּה' אֱלֹקֵינוּ בְּכָל קָרְאֵנוּ אֵלָיו".

וְעַל־יְדֵי הַתְּפִלָּה זוֹכֶה לְשָׁלוֹם הַכְּלָלִי. וְזֶה: "וְרַחֲמָיו עַל כָּל

---

attained this peace, **of our festival** — he merits prayer, the concept of the festivals, which then brings to the encompassing, universal peace.

84. **are not available....** When this is the case, such a person will go to great lengths and extend himself in every which way to find that which he seeks (as opposed, for example, to the manna which came to the Jews without their having to go look for it).

85. **whenever we pray to Him.** God is always within reach and one never needs to go to great lengths to find that which he seeks.

86. **mercies are upon all His works.** After showing how "God is good for everything" and those who trust in Him have no need to turn anywhere in times of need but to Him, Rebbe Nachman now returns to the opening verse of this section.

327   LIKUTEY MOHARAN #14:10,11

therefore, that keeping the festival is an aspect of a complete service. And what is service if not prayer (*Sifri* 102)? And through prayer one comes to universal peace, as above.[83]

We see, therefore, that someone who wants to draw universal peace has to elevate the glory to its source—i.e., to fear. And through fear, he merits peace in the home. Through peace in the home he then merits prayer. And through prayer, he merits universal peace.

11. This lesson applies to the following verses:
"God is good for all, and His mercies are upon all His works. All Your works will praise You, God; Your pious ones will bless You. They will speak of the glory of Your Kingdom and talk of Your might" (Psalms 145:9-11).

"God is good for all." This is the aspect of prayer; that the person believes in God, that the Holy One is good for all: for health, for livelihood, for all things [a person needs]. When a person believes this, then the main focus of his efforts will certainly be for the Holy One, rather than pursuing all kinds of strategies. This is because when one does not believe in the Holy One, he must work at all kinds of strategies. For example: If he is sick, he must work at getting all sorts of medicines. And there are times when the particular medicines he needs are not available in his country, whereas those medicines that are available are useless for his illness.[84] The Holy One, however, "is good for all" illnesses—to heal them. He is also always available, as is written (Deuteronomy 4:7), "Who is. . .like God our Lord is, whenever we pray to Him!"[85]

And through prayer, a person merits universal peace. This is the meaning of, "His mercies are upon all His works."[86] In other words,

---

keeping half for man (delighting in the physical pleasures of the holiday) (*Orach Chaim* 529:1). In other words, we are directed to join the physical and the spiritual, the concept of peace in the home that one attains when he elevates glory to fear by bringing those on the outside closer to God.

83. . . .**universal peace, as above.** See above section 8 and note 60 for the connection between prayer and complete service. Here we see that the festivals, by virtue of their being a manifestation of God's will and miracles, and thus a denial of nature and the forces of idolatry, are also a complete service.

We now have a deeper understanding of the lesson's opening verse: Tik'u — to attain peace, **bachodesh shofar** — one must cause new revelations of God's glory. That is, he must teach Torah to others and bring them to serve God. This can be accomplished **bakeseh** — by raising this glory to its source, fear, which belongs in the heart. By doing so, then: **for the day** — one merits inner peace, peace in the home, which is compared to light. And, having

LIKUTEY MOHARAN #14:11

מַעֲשָׂיו" – הַיְנוּ שֶׁרַחֲמֵי הַשֵּׁם יִתְבָּרַךְ יִתְמַשֵּׁךְ עַל כָּל הַבְּרוּאִים,
וְכָל הַבְּרוּאִים יְרַחֲמוּ אֶחָד עַל חֲבֵרוֹ וְיִהְיֶה שָׁלוֹם בֵּינֵיהֶם, כְּמוֹ
שֶׁכָּתוּב (יְשַׁעְיָהוּ י"א): "וְגָר זְאֵב עִם כֶּבֶשׂ וְנָמֵר עִם גְּדִי וְכוּ', לֹא
יָרֵעוּ וְלֹא יַשְׁחִיתוּ", כִּי יִהְיֶה שָׁלוֹם בֵּינֵיהֶם. וְזֶה: "וְרַחֲמָיו עַל כָּל
מַעֲשָׂיו", כְּמוֹ שֶׁאָמְרוּ חֲכָמֵינוּ, זִכְרוֹנָם לִבְרָכָה (שַׁבָּת קנא:): 'כָּל
הַמְרַחֵם עַל הַבְּרִיּוֹת, מְרַחֲמִין עָלָיו מִן הַשָּׁמַיִם', כְּמוֹ שֶׁכָּתוּב:
"וְנָתַן לְךָ רַחֲמִים וְרִחַמֶךָ".

וְאַחַר־כָּךְ מְפָרֵשׁ הַפָּסוּק אֵיךְ יִזְכֶּה לִתְפִלָּה, עַל־יְדֵי שָׁלוֹם־בַּיִת
יְהֵא שָׁלוֹם בַּעֲצָמָיו, בֵּין גּוּפוֹ וְנַפְשׁוֹ כַּנַּ"ל. וְזֶה: "יוֹדוּךְ כָּל
מַעֲשֶׂיךָ" – 'מַעֲשֶׂיךָ' – זֶה בְּחִינַת עֲשִׂיָּה, בְּחִינַת גּוּף;
"וַחֲסִידֶיךָ יְבָרְכוּכָה" – 'חֲסִידֶיךָ', זֶה בְּחִינַת נֶפֶשׁ, כְּמוֹ שֶׁכָּתוּב
(מִשְׁלֵי י"א): "גֹּמֵל נַפְשׁוֹ אִישׁ חָסֶד".

וְאַחַר־כָּךְ מְפָרֵשׁ הַפָּסוּק, אֵיךְ יִזְכֶּה לְשָׁלוֹם־בַּיִת – עַל־יְדֵי שֶׁיַּעֲלֶה
כְּבוֹד הַשֵּׁם יִתְבָּרַךְ לְשָׁרֶשׁ הַיִּרְאָה, הַנִּקְרָאִים גְּבוּרוֹת. וְזֶהוּ: "כְּבוֹד
מַלְכוּתְךָ יֹאמֵרוּ" – שֶׁיִּתְגַּלֶּה כְּבוֹדוֹ וְיִתְעַלֶּה לְשָׁרְשׁוֹ; וְזֶהוּ:
"וּגְבוּרָתְךָ יְדַבֵּרוּ" – 'וּגְבוּרָה' זֶה בְּחִינַת יִרְאָה, כְּמוֹ שֶׁאָמְרוּ
חֲכָמֵינוּ, זִכְרוֹנָם לִבְרָכָה (בְּרָכוֹת נט.): "וֶאֱלֹקִים עָשָׂה שֶׁיִּירְאוּ
מִלְּפָנָיו" – 'אֵלּוּ רְעָמִים', וּכְתִיב (אִיּוֹב כ"ו): "וְרַעַם גְּבוּרוֹתָיו מִי
יִתְבּוֹנָן":

---

89. **give you mercy....** That is, His mercy will be given over to you—it will be within you—
for you to extend.

90. **Asiyah, the body.** The spiritual world known as Asiyah corresponds to the lowest world,
the physical (see Appendix: Levels of Existence).

91. **man of kindness, piety...soul.** A pious man is known as a *ChaSiD* (חסיד) because he is
beneficent to and shows kindness (*CheSeD*, חסד) for—not his body, but—his soul.

92. **speak of the glory....** That is, we know the glory is elevated because we are speaking
about it, recognizing it. See above, note 5.

93. **fear...thunder of His might.** Thunder was created in order to bring fear into the hearts of
men. Thus thunder, which corresponds to fear, is associated with the *sefirah* of *Gevurah* and

LIKUTEY MOHARAN #14:11

329

God's mercies are drawn upon all created beings.[87] The created beings will have mercy for one another,[88] and there will be peace between them. As it is written (Isaiah 11:6,9), "And the wolf shall dwell with the lamb, and the leopard shall lie down with the kid...they shall not harm or destroy"—for there will be peace between them. This is: "His mercies are upon all His works." As our Sages taught: Whoever has mercy on [God's] creations, Heaven has mercy upon him, as is written (Deuteronomy 13:18), "And He will give you mercy and have mercy upon you" (*Shabbat* 151b).[89]

Afterwards, the verse explains how to merit prayer, [in that] through peace in the home one achieves inner peace—between his body and soul, as above. And this is: "All *maaseykha* (Your works) will praise You." [The word] *maASeYkha* corresponds to *ASiYah*, the body.[90]

"And *chasidekha* (Your pious ones) will bless You." *ChaSiDekha* alludes to the soul, as in (Proverbs 11:17), "The man of *CheSeD* (kindness, piety) is beneficent to his own soul."[91]

Then the verse explains how to merit peace in the home: by elevating the glory of the Holy One to the source of fear, which is called "mighty." This is: "They will speak of the glory of Your Kingdom"—His glory will be revealed and ascend to its source.[92] And thus, "...and talk of Your might"—"might" corresponds to fear. As our Sages taught: "And the Lord does it so that they should fear Him" (Proverbs 3:14)—this refers to thunder (*Berakhot* 59a); and it is written (Job 26:14), "But who can understand the thunder of His might?"[93]

---

87. ...**all created beings.** The verse thus reads: When prayer is offered, **God is good for everything**; and then **His mercies are upon all** — *all* created beings will receive His mercy, for they will all be united and there will be an all-encompassing peace throughout the world.

88. **mercy for one another.** Rebbe Nachman takes this verse one step beyond its simple meaning. Not only will God be merciful upon all that He created, but as the Midrash (*Bereishit Rabbah* 33:3) explains, His mercies will be drawn into the people. Man will feel compassion and mercy for his fellow man. Rebbe Nachman uses this to introduce a further aspect of the encompassing, universal peace. Above, we were told that the universal peace denotes a perfection of all the worlds (§8), with each of the worlds having what it uniquely requires in order to perfect its service of the Holy One (n.62). From this teaching we see that the all-encompassing peace implies not just a perfected co-existence but, more importantly, a perfected state of interaction between all the different worlds. The "mercies" which God will put into His creations will be manifested between themselves. Thus, for example, whatever one person has he will gladly share with another. As Rebbe Nachman taught in section 2, the Torah needed for elevating the glory to fear must be the Torah of lovingkindness.

LIKUTEY MOHARAN #14:12

330

(מִסִּימָן יב עַד כָּאן – לְשׁוֹנוֹ, זִכְרוֹנוֹ לִבְרָכָה)

יב. וְזֶה בְּחִינַת מִצְוַת נֵר־חֲנֻכָּה, שֶׁמִּצְוָתָהּ לְהַדְלִיק סָמוּךְ לְפֶתַח הַבַּיִת. כִּי הַדְלָקַת הַנֵּר הוּא בְּחִינַת הֶאָרַת הַכָּבוֹד, בְּחִינַת "וְהָאָרֶץ הֵאִירָה מִכְּבוֹדוֹ", כַּנַּ"ל, וְעַל כֵּן מִצְוָתָהּ לְהַדְלִיק סָמוּךְ לְפֶתַח הַבַּיִת – דָּא פִּתְחָא עִלָּאָה, בְּחִינַת יִרְאָה, הַיְנוּ לְהַחֲזִיר הַכָּבוֹד לְשָׁרְשׁוֹ, דְּהַיְנוּ לַיִּרְאָה כַּנַּ"ל.

וְאֵימָתַי עוֹלֶה הַכָּבוֹד? כְּשֶׁמַּחֲזִירִין בְּנֵי־אָדָם בִּתְשׁוּבָה וְעוֹשִׂין בַּעֲלֵי־תְשׁוּבָה וְגֵרִים, שֶׁזֶּה עִקַּר כְּבוֹדוֹ כַּנַּ"ל.

וְזֶהוּ שֶׁזְּמַן הַדְלָקַת נֵר־חֲנֻכָּה, שֶׁהוּא הֶאָרַת הַכָּבוֹד, הוּא 'מִשְּׁעַת יְצִיאַת הַכּוֹכָבִים, עַד שֶׁתִּכְלֶה רֶגֶל מִן הַשּׁוּק' (שַׁבָּת כא: וּבְשֻׁלְחָן־עָרוּךְ סִימָן תרע"ב). 'יְצִיאַת הַכּוֹכָבִים' – זֶה בְּחִינַת (דָּנִיֵּאל יב): "מַצְדִּיקֵי הָרַבִּים כַּכּוֹכָבִים", דְּהַיְנוּ שֶׁהֵם מַצְדִּיקֵי הָרַבִּים, וְעוֹשִׂין בַּעֲלֵי־תְשׁוּבָה וְגֵרִים, שֶׁעַל־יְדֵי־זֶה מֵאִיר הַכָּבוֹד וְחוֹזֵר לְשָׁרְשׁוֹ שֶׁהוּא הַיִּרְאָה כַּנַּ"ל, וְעַל־יְדֵי־זֶה זוֹכִין לְשָׁלוֹם, וְנִתְבַּטֵּל הַמַּחֲלֹקֶת כַּנַּ"ל.

וְזֶהוּ: 'עַד שֶׁתִּכְלֶה רֶגֶל מִן הַשּׁוּק' (הַשּׁוּק הוּא מְקוֹמוֹת

---

light into the lowest of levels. When this happens, the glory of His Kingdom/*Malkhut*, the lowest of the ten *sefirot*, is revealed; hence the earth is "illuminated with His glory."

96. the supernal entrance...fear. "Fear of God is the very first step and the foundation upon which all Godly service can be performed. Without this fear one cannot enter" (*Zohar Chadash, Ki Tisa, s.v. yirat*). Thus, elevating God's glory to its source corresponds to putting the lit menorah/the glory "next to the entrance"/fear so that the earth/God's Kingdom will be illuminated and revealed.

97. stars come out...street. Ideally, the candles are to be lit in a place where they can be clearly seen by passersby in the street. This is in order to publicize the great miracle which Chanukah commemorates. For this reason, the candle-lighting should take place from dusk (when the flame of the candles can first be observed), and the lights should continue burning until people stop walking about in the street (when one can no longer make known this miracle to others). (As to how this mitzvah is performed in our modern, street-lit and late-night society, see *The Laws of Chanukah* by Rabbi Shimon Eider.)

98. turn the many to righteousness.... The Talmud interprets this verse as referring to those who teach others to go in the right way (*Bava Batra* 8b; *Rashi, s.v. m'lamdei tinokot*).

LIKUTEY MOHARAN #14:12

12. And this corresponds to the mitzvah of the Chanukah candle.[94] There is a requirement to light it next to the entrance of the house (*Orach Chaim* 671:5). This is because lighting the candle corresponds to the illumination of the glory, as in, "The earth was illuminated by His glory."[95] The mitzvah, therefore, is to light it next to the entrance of the house: this is the supernal entrance, corresponding to fear[96]—i.e., the returning of the glory to its source, which is fear, as mentioned above.

And when is it that the glory ascends? when we bring people to return in repentance and make *baaley teshuvah* and converts. For this is His main glory, as above.

This is why the time for lighting the Chanukah candle, which is the illumination of the glory, is from the time the stars come out until people stop walking about in the street (*Orach Chaim* 672:1).[97] "From the time the stars come out" corresponds to "...and those who turn the many to righteousness like the stars" (Daniel 12:3)—i.e., they turn the many to righteousness and make *baaley teshuvah* and converts.[98] For it is through this that the glory shines and returns to it source, which is fear. As a result, one merits peace and strife is eliminated, as explained.

And this is the meaning of "until people stop walking about in the street." {The street is the place of the external forces (*Pri Etz Chaim*,

---

the *gevurot* (severities) which ascend to the *sefirah* of *Binah*, the heart (see n.52; cf. *Likutey Moharan* I, 5:3).

We can now understand these verses quoted from Psalms as follows: **God is good for everything** — when prayer is offered, **His mercies are upon all His works** — mercy is put into and given over to all the worlds. His mercies are thus manifested and shared, bringing universal peace. And how does one come to offer prayer such as this? It can only come about when **All Your works** — the body — **will praise You, God; and Your pious ones** — the soul — **will bless You.** This is when there is peace in the home, peace in one's bones, between body and soul. It is the inner peace which results from: **They will speak of the glory of Your kingdom and talk of Your might** — the elevation of glory/Malkhut to its source, fear.

The lesson to this point is *leshon Rabbeinu z'l*. See note 1 to Lesson #7.

94. **Chanukah candle.** Rebbe Nachman next shows how the concepts presented in this lesson connect with the laws of Chanukah.

95. **candle...earth was illuminated....** The menorah should be placed within 10 handbreadths (approx. 30 inches) from the ground (*Orach Chaim* 671:6). This requirement of positioning the Chanukah candles close to the earth is symbolic of the need for bringing

LIKUTEY MOHARAN #14:12 332

הַחִיצוֹנִים); 'רֶגֶל' – זֶה בְּחִינַת "נִרְגָּן מַפְרִיד אַלּוּף" הַנַּ"ל, דְּהַיְנוּ בַּעֲלֵי לָשׁוֹן הָרָע וּמַחֲלֹקֶת, הַהוֹלְכִים וּמְרַגְּלִים וּמְדַבְּרִים רְכִילוּת וְלָשׁוֹן הָרָע וְעוֹשִׂין מְרִיבָה וּמַחֲלֹקֶת בֵּין אָדָם לַחֲבֵרוֹ וּבֵין אִישׁ לְאִשְׁתּוֹ, בְּחִינַת (תְּהִלִּים ט"ו): "לֹא רָגַל עַל לְשׁוֹנוֹ".

וְזֶהוּ שֶׁצְּרִיכִין לְהָאִיר וּלְהַדְלִיק נֵר־חֲנֻכָּה סָמוּךְ לַפֶּתַח, דְּהַיְנוּ לְהָאִיר הַכָּבוֹד וּלְהַחֲזִירוֹ לְשָׁרְשׁ הַיִּרְאָה כַּנַּ"ל, עַד שֶׁיִּזְכֶּה לְשָׁלוֹם וִיבַטֵּל וִיכַלֶּה הַנִּרְגָּן מַפְרִיד אַלּוּף. וְזֶהוּ: 'עַד שֶׁתִּכְלֶה רֶגֶל מִן הַשּׁוּק' – שֶׁיִּתְבַּטֵּל בַּעֲלֵי לָשׁוֹן הָרָע וּרְכִילוּת אֲשֶׁר רָגַל עַל לְשׁוֹנָם, וְיִתְרַבֶּה הַשָּׁלוֹם בָּעוֹלָם.

וְעַל־יְדֵי הַשָּׁלוֹם זוֹכִין לִתְפִלָּה, וְעַל־יְדֵי־זֶה זוֹכִין לַשָּׁלוֹם הַכְּלָלִי, שָׁלוֹם בְּכָל הָעוֹלָמוֹת. וַאֲזַי כְּשֶׁזּוֹכִין לַשָּׁלוֹם הַכְּלָלִי, אֲזַי יִתְבַּטֵּל כָּל הַמַּשָּׂא וּמַתָּן מִן הָעוֹלָם, כִּי כָּל הַמַּשָּׂא וּמַתָּן שֶׁבָּעוֹלָם הוּא מֵהֶעְדֵּר הַשָּׁלוֹם, כִּי אִי אֶפְשָׁר שֶׁיִּהְיֶה רְצוֹן הַמּוֹכֵר וְהַקּוֹנֶה שָׁוֶה, כִּי זֶה רוֹצֶה לִמְכֹּר וְזֶה רוֹצֶה לִקְנוֹת; וְאִם הָיָה רְצוֹנָם שָׁוֶה – לֹא הָיָה אֶפְשָׁר שֶׁיִּהְיֶה נַעֲשֶׂה שׁוּם מַשָּׂא וּמַתָּן.

נִמְצָא, שֶׁכָּל הַמַּשָּׂא וּמַתָּן וְהַסְּחוֹרוֹת הוּא רַק עַל־יְדֵי בְּחִינַת מַחֲלֹקֶת, שֶׁאֵין שָׁלוֹם בֵּין הָרְצוֹנוֹת. וְזֶה בְּחִינַת (בְּרֵאשִׁית י"ג):

Rebbe Nachman develops this idea further, adding that not only are we not to speak badly of others, we are not even permitted to "slander" ourselves. Rather, we are to *always* look for the good points, in ourselves and in others. Focusing on a person's good points has the power to elevate even a wicked person to a level of merit. This is the concept of bringing others, as well as oneself, to serve God (as above, n.56). (Lesson #282 has been published separately as *Azamra*, Breslov Research Institute, 1984).

102. **business activity...eliminated from the world.** This is because everyone will then receive their *shefa* directly. See above, notes 69 and 71.

103. **concept of strife.** Even after one has attained the great level of inner peace and has merited to pray properly, until there is an all-encompassing peace in the world the concept of strife and business activity will continue to exist.

104. **wills.** When the will to serve God is universal, *shefa* descends directly and potently for

LIKUTEY MOHARAN #14:12

Chanukah).[99]} *ReGeL* (walking about) alludes to "the whisperer who separates close friends"—i.e., those who engage in slander and strife. These people *m'RaGeL* (go about snooping) and speaking gossip and slander, inciting strife and friction between friends and between husband and wife. This corresponds to (Psalms 15:2), "He that does not *RoGaL* (slander) with his mouth."[100]

This is why it is necessary to illuminate and light the Chanukah candle next to the entrance—i.e., illuminate the glory and return it to the source of fear until peace is merited and "the whisperer who separates close friends" is eliminated and destroyed. And this is: "until people stop walking about in the street." Those who engage in slander and gossip, who slander with their mouths, are [stopped and] eliminated; and peace is increased in the world.[101]

And through peace people merit prayer, through which they then merit universal peace, peace in all the worlds. And then, when they will merit universal peace, all business activity will be eliminated from the world.[102] This is because all business activity in the world stems from a lack of peace. For it is impossible for the will of the seller and the buyer to be the same; this one wants to sell while the other one wants to buy. If their wants were the same, it would be impossible to transact any business.

We see, therefore, that all business activity and trade come only through the concept of strife,[103] when there is no peace between the

---

99. **place of the external forces.** This is the place of the Other Side. In the context of the lesson, it relates to those who have fallen away from God or who were never previously within the realm of holiness.

100. **...does not slander with his mouth.** The foot (רגל) implies those who go walking about snooping (מרגל), spreading gossip and slander (רוגל).

Thus, **One must light the candles** — glory — **next to the door** — thus elevating the glory to its source, fear. **He must do this until the regel ceases from the outside** — slanderers cease to exist — **so that one can publicize the miracle** — bringing others to recognize and serve God.

As explained above (§§3,4), Torah study awakens the souls and awakening the souls enables one to draw down a pure soul for one's child. The light of Chanukah corresponds to the light of Torah, so that lighting the Chanukah lights can also bring an awakening to the souls and therefore ensure a pure soul for one's child. This is alluded to in the Talmudic teaching (*Shabbat* 23b): Whoever is fastidious in lighting the candles of Shabbat and Chanukah will have children who are Torah scholars (*Mai HaNachal*).

101. **peace is increased in the world.** Rebbe Nachman thus indicates that by not gossiping and slandering others we are bringing peace to the world. Elsewhere (*Likutey Moharan* I, 282),

LIKUTEY MOHARAN #14:12,13

334

"וַיְהִי רִיב בֵּין רֹעֵי מִקְנֵה אַבְרָם וּבֵין רֹעֵי מִקְנֵה לוֹט, וְהַכְּנַעֲנִי אָז
בָּאָרֶץ"; 'כְּנַעֲנִי' – זֶה בְּחִינַת סוֹחֵר, כְּמוֹ שֶׁפֵּרֵשׁ רַשַׁ"י עַל פָּסוּק
(הוֹשֵׁעַ י"ב): "כְּנַעַן בְּיָדוֹ" וְכוּ', הַיְנוּ עַל־יְדֵי בְּחִינַת רִיב וּמַחֲלֹקֶת,
בְּחִינַת "וַיְהִי רִיב" וְכוּ', עַל־יְדֵי־זֶה: "וְהַכְּנַעֲנִי אָז בָּאָרֶץ", עַל־
יְדֵי־זֶה יֵשׁ סוֹחֲרִים וּמַשָּׂא וּמַתָּן בָּעוֹלָם;
אֲבָל, לֶעָתִיד לָבוֹא, שֶׁיִּהְיֶה הַשָּׁלוֹם הַמֻּפְלָא בָּעוֹלָם, כְּמוֹ שֶׁכָּתוּב:
"וְגָר זְאֵב עִם כֶּבֶשׂ וְנָמֵר עִם גְּדִי", אֲזַי יִתְבַּטֵּל הַמַּשָּׂא וּמַתָּן, כְּמוֹ
שֶׁכָּתוּב (זְכַרְיָה י"ד): "וְלֹא יִהְיֶה כְּנַעֲנִי עוֹד" כַּנַּ"ל.
וְזֶהוּ גַּם כֵּן בְּחִינַת 'עַד שֶׁתִּכְלֶה רֶגֶל מִן הַשּׁוּק', הַיְנוּ שֶׁמִּצְוָה
לְהַדְלִיק נֵר־חֲנֻכָּה עַד שֶׁתִּכְלֶה רֶגֶל מִן הַשּׁוּק, הַיְנוּ בְּחִינַת שָׁלוֹם,
שֶׁנַּעֲשֶׂה עַל־יְדֵי הַחֲזָרַת הַכָּבוֹד כַּנַּ"ל, עַד שֶׁיִּתְבַּטֵּל כָּל הַמַּשָּׂא
וּמַתָּן כַּנַּ"ל. וְזֶהוּ: 'עַד שֶׁתִּכְלֶה רֶגֶל מִן הַשּׁוּק' – שֶׁלֹּא יִשָּׁאֵר שׁוּם
רֶגֶל בַּשּׁוּק, כִּי יִתְבַּטֵּל כָּל הַמַּשָּׂא־וּמַתָּן עַל־יְדֵי הַשָּׁלוֹם כַּנַּ"ל:

יג. (שַׁיָּךְ לְעֵיל) לְפִי הַכָּבוֹד שֶׁמְּכַבֵּד יְרְאֵי־הַשֵּׁם, כֵּן עָלָה הַכָּבוֹד
לְשָׁרְשׁוֹ. כִּי כָּל זְמַן שֶׁהַכָּבוֹד הוּא בְּגָלוּת – כָּל אֶחָד לְפִי בְּחִינָתוֹ,
כֵּן הוּא מְזַלְזֵל בְּיִרְאֵי־הַשֵּׁם, וְכָל אֶחָד לְפִי תִּקּוּנוֹ אֶת הַכָּבוֹד, כֵּן
הוּא מְכַבֵּד יִרְאֵי־הַשֵּׁם וְכוּ'. וְעַל־יְדֵי זֶה, הַיְנוּ עַל־יְדֵי הַכָּבוֹד
שֶׁמְּכַבֵּד יִרְאֵי־הַשֵּׁם, שֶׁהוּא בְּחִינַת הַחֲזָרַת הַכָּבוֹד לְשָׁרְשׁוֹ, דְּהַיְנוּ
לַיִּרְאָה, עַל־יְדֵי־זֶה זוֹכִין לְשָׁלוֹם, כַּמְבֹאָר לְעֵיל הֵיטֵב.

---

106. **Kanaan....** Rashi explains that they were merchants, i.e., businessmen.

107. **wondrous peace in the world.** Neither the wolf nor the leopard will alter its nature nor change into a lamb or kid. Rather, each will retain its own identity, its own distinctive powers, and despite this, a wondrous, universal peace will be maintained. Similarly, in the time of the Mashiach, man will not change into an angelic being. Rather, he will remain physically the same, and even so will recognize and serve God, and peace will reign.

108. **all business...eliminated....** The light of Chanukah will enlighten man to the point where his only desire and prayer will be for spiritual improvement (as was the case with Rabbah bar bar Chanah). Through his prayers, man will bring about the all-encompassing peace. The world will then be free of strife and the marketplace will then be empty, devoid of all wheeling and dealing.

109. **taught above.** This already appears in the lesson as part of section 6.

LIKUTEY MOHARAN #14:12,13

wills.[104] This is alluded in (Genesis 13:7), "Friction existed between the shepherds of Avram's flocks and the shepherds of Lot's flocks; and the Kanaanites were then living in the land."[105] "Kanaan" alludes to a trader, as in Rashi's explanation of the verse (Hosea 12:8), "As for Kanaan, the balances of deceit are in his hand."[106] In other words, due to the aspect of friction and strife—corresponding to "Friction existed..."—through this, "the Kanaanites were then living in the land"—there are traders and business activity in the world.

But in the Future, when there will be the wondrous peace in the world[107]—as in, "And the wolf shall dwell with the lamb, and the leopard shall lie down with the kid..."—then all business activity will be eliminated. As is written (Zekhariah 14:21), "And the Kanaanites will be no more."

And this is also the aspect of "until people stop walking about in the street" [literally, "until there is not a *regel* (foot) in the marketplace"]. In other words, the mitzvah of lighting the Chanukah candle until people stop walking about in the marketplace corresponds to peace, which comes about through returning the glory until such time as all business activity is eliminated. Thus, "until people stop walking about in the street" indicates that there will not remain a *regel* in the marketplace; because of the peace, all business activity will have been eliminated, as mentioned above.[108]

13. The following piece applies to what was taught above[109]:

To that degree that he honors those who fear God, the glory [God's honor] ascends to its source.... Because, as long as the glory is in exile, each person, in his own way, disgraces those who are God-fearing; whereas, to the degree that he rectifies the glory, he correspondingly honors those who fear God.

Now, through this—i.e., through the honor shown for those who fear God, which is the concept of returning the glory to its source, to fear—we merit peace, as has been thoroughly explained.

---

all. Conversely, as long as there is a will for money, business interests shall continue to occupy people's lives and they cannot receive their material needs as the Jews received the manna.

105. **Friction existed....** Avraham is known as an *ish chesed* (man of lovingkindness). He shared his Torah with others and converted many to belief in God. We are therefore told that when God commanded him to leave his birthplace and his father's house, he took along all the people he had gathered (literally, all the souls he had made; Genesis 12:5). Avraham's nephew Lot joined him and was also converted to God's cause. However, Lot remained tied to his desire for money. His will to serve God was not complete and therefore his shepherds, whose hearts were like their master's, were in conflict with Avraham's shepherds, whose hearts were like their master's.

LIKUTEY MOHARAN #14:13

וְזֶהוּ שֶׁאָמְרוּ רַבּוֹתֵינוּ, זִכְרוֹנָם לִבְרָכָה (שַׁבָּת קיט:): 'הַמְבַזֶּה
תַּלְמִיד־חָכָם, אֵין רְפוּאָה לְמַכָּתוֹ', כִּי הַמְבַזֶּה תַּלְמִיד־חָכָם וּמְזַלְזֵל
יִרְאֵי־הַשֵּׁם, נִמְצָא שֶׁפּוֹגֵם בַּכָּבוֹד, וְאֵינוּ מַחֲזִירוֹ לְשֹׁרֶשׁ הַיִּרְאָה,
וַאֲזַי אֵין זוֹכֶה לְשָׁלוֹם, וְעַל כֵּן אֵין רְפוּאָה לְמַכָּתוֹ,
כִּי כָּל הַחוֹלַאַת בָּאִין עַל־יְדֵי בְחִינַת מַחֲלֹקֶת, כִּי כָּל הַחוֹלַאַת הֵם
בְּחִינַת מַחֲלֹקֶת, שֶׁאֵין שָׁלוֹם בַּעֲצָמָיו, וְהַיְסוֹדוֹת מִתְגַּבְּרִין זֶה עַל
זֶה וְאֵין מִתְנַהֲגִים בְּשָׁלוֹם, בַּמֶּזֶג הַשָּׁוֶה, וְעַל־יְדֵי־זֶה בָּא חוֹלַאַת
כַּיָּדוּעַ.

וְעַל כֵּן כְּשֶׁמְּבַזֶּה תַּלְמִיד־חָכָם וּפוֹגֵם בַּשָּׁלוֹם, עַל כֵּן אֵין רְפוּאָה
לְמַכָּתוֹ כַּנַּ״ל, כִּי עִקַּר הָרְפוּאָה עַל־יְדֵי הַשָּׁלוֹם כַּנַּ״ל, בִּבְחִינַת:
"שָׁלוֹם שָׁלוֹם לָרָחוֹק וְלַקָּרוֹב אָמַר ה' וּרְפָאתִיו" (יְשַׁעְיָהוּ נ״ז):

גַּם בְּעֵת אֲמִירַת הַתּוֹרָה הַנַּ״ל הִזְכִּיר רַבֵּנוּ, זִכְרוֹנוֹ לִבְרָכָה, מַאֲמַר
רַבּוֹתֵינוּ, זִכְרוֹנָם לִבְרָכָה: 'אֵין מַסְפִּידִין בַּחֲנֻכָּה' (שַׁבָּת כא: וּבְשֻׁלְחָן־
עָרוּךְ סִימָן תר״ע), וְאֵינִי זוֹכֵר מַה שֶּׁפֵּרֵשׁ בּוֹ. (וְהַנִּרְאָה לַעֲנִיּוּת דַּעְתִּי,
כִּי הַהֶסְפֵּד הוּא בִּשְׁבִיל לְתַקֵּן הִסְתַּלְּקוּת הַכָּבוֹד, שֶׁנִּפְגַּם עַל־יְדֵי
הִסְתַּלְּקוּת הַצַּדִּיק הַזֶּה, שֶׁהָיָה מַצְדִּיק אֶת הָרַבִּים, שֶׁעַל־יְדֵי־זֶה
עִקַּר הֶאָרַת הַכָּבוֹד כַּנַּ״ל, וּכְמוֹ שֶׁאָמְרוּ רַבּוֹתֵינוּ, זִכְרוֹנָם לִבְרָכָה:
'הֶסְפֵּדָא יְקָרָא דְחַיֵּי אוֹ יְקָרָא דְשָׁכְבֵי' (סַנְהֶדְרִין מו:). וְעַל כֵּן בַּחֲנֻכָּה
אֵין מַסְפִּידִין בּוֹ, כִּי אָז מֵאִיר הַכָּבוֹד עַל־יְדֵי נֵר־חֲנֻכָּה כַּנַּ״ל).

לְעֵיל. וְזֶהוּ: וְלִפְנֵי כָבוֹד עֲנָוָה (מִשְׁלֵי טו), כִּי עַל־יְדֵי עֲנָוָה זוֹכִין

---

between the passing of a tzaddik, Chanukah and eulogies. The *tZaDdiK* is so called because
he is *matZDiK* (brings merit to) others. In the context of the lesson, what he is doing is
elevating God's glory. However, when he passes on, his work stops. In this light, we can
appreciate an even deeper understanding of the question which our Sages raise (*loc. cit.*). In
asking whether a eulogy is in honor/glory of the living or the dead, the implication is that the
reason for the eulogy is to enhance the glory not *of* the deceased but the glory which the
deceased could have elevated—God's glory—had he remained alive. However, because
Chanukah itself elevates the glory, no eulogies are necessary.

LIKUTEY MOHARAN #14:13

And this is as our Sages taught: Anyone who disgraces a Torah scholar is afflicted with an incurable ailment (Shabbat 119b). For when a person disgraces a Torah scholar or ridicules those who fear God, he blemishes the glory and does not return it to the source of fear. As a result, he does not merit peace, and so his ailment remains incurable.

This is because all illnesses stem from the aspect of strife. For all illnesses correspond to strife in that there is no peace in his bones. The *yesodot* (elements) are in conflict with one another and do not function peacefully and in proper balance.[110] As a result, he suffers illness, as is known.

Therefore, when he disgraces a Torah scholar and blemishes the peace, his ailment is incurable.[111] For the essence of healing comes through peace, as mentioned above. This corresponds to (Isaiah 57:19), "Peace, peace, for both far and near, says God; and I will heal him."[112]

When this lesson was given, Rabbeinu z'l also mentioned the teaching of our Sages: No eulogies are made during Chanukah (*Shabbat* 21b; *Orach Chaim* 670). However, I do not recall his explanation of this. {Based on my limited knowledge, it seems that the eulogy is meant to rectify the departure of the glory. The [glory] was blemished by the passing of this tzaddik, whose "turning the many to righteousness" brought about the main illumination of the glory. This is similar to what our Sages taught: A eulogy: Is it to honor the living or to honor the dead (*Sanhedrin* 46b)? This is why during Chanukah no eulogies are made. For then, the glory shines due to the Chanukah candle, as mentioned above.[113]}

See [sections 2-5] above. This is the meaning of "And humility precedes glory" (Proverbs 15:33)—for it is through humility that one

---

110. **do not function peacefully....** See above, section 8 and note 55, that there is no inner peace—literally, no peace in his bones. The elements which Rebbe Nachman refers to are four: fire, air, water and earth (cf. Lesson #8:5).

111. **incurable.** This person can never attain the balance between body and soul required for inner peace.

112. **I will heal him.** It must be pointed out that no matter what a person has done, no matter how grave his sin, repentance always helps. Thus, Rebbe Nachman concludes with the verse "Peace, peace, for both far and near...." The Talmud explains this as referring to one who was distant, but who is now near. Because he repented, God says, "I will heal him" (cf. *Berakhot* 34b).

113. **No eulogies are made during Chanukah....** Cf. notes 1 and 53 for the connection

LIKUTEY MOHARAN #14:13

לְכָבוֹד, כַּמְבֹאָר לְעֵיל, שֶׁעִקַּר הִתְעַלּוּת הַכָּבוֹד הוּא עַל־יְדֵי גֵּרִים
וּבַעֲלֵי־תְּשׁוּבָה שֶׁעוֹשִׂין, וְזֶה זוֹכִין עַל־יְדֵי תּוֹרַת חֶסֶד וְכוּ';
וְלַתּוֹרָה אִי אֶפְשָׁר לִזְכּוֹת, כִּי אִם עַל־יְדֵי עֲנָוָה וְכוּ', כַּמְבֹאָר לְעֵיל.
נִמְצָא שֶׁאִי אֶפְשָׁר לִזְכּוֹת לְכָבוֹד דִּקְדֻשָּׁה, כִּי אִם עַל־יְדֵי עֲנָוָה,
וְזֶהוּ: "וְלִפְנֵי כָבוֹד עֲנָוָה", כַּנַּ"ל:

יְסוֹד הָעִנְיָן חֲמִשָּׁה דְּבָרִים: לְהַחֲזִיר כָּבוֹד לַיִּרְאָה, וְיִרְאָה אֶל הַלֵּב,
וְשָׁלוֹם הַכְּלָלִי, וְשָׁלוֹם הַפְּרָטִי. לְהַחֲזִיר בְּנֵי־אָדָם בִּתְשׁוּבָה, שֶׁזֶּה
בְּחִינַת אִם תּוֹצִיא יָקָר מִזּוֹלֵל כַּנַּ"ל, הוּא תִּקּוּן קְרִי – אַתְוָן דְּדֵין
כְּאַתְוָן דְּדֵין.

they remained firm in their faith and united under the leadership of Matityahu the High Priest and his sons. The *kohanim* (priests), and particularly the *kohein gadol* (high priest), are symbolic of the tzaddikim of each generation to whom we must turn for guidance in "repelling" the invaders and purifying ourselves. Just as the *kohanim* wore special vestments in order to perform the service in the Holy Temple, the place of God's glory, the tzaddik is the one whose "garments are clean" and he can therefore elevate God's glory to its fullest.

After successfully vanquishing their enemies, chasing them from the Holy Land, the Jews entered the Temple to cleanse it of all traces of idolatry. They stripped themselves of the "soiled garments" and began to purify the Holy Temple—to reveal God's hidden glory. This was achieved through the small measure of pure, uncontaminated menorah oil which they found. Kindling the lights of the menorah, they reconsecrated the Temple. Similarly, the great tzaddikim are constantly revealing Torah—the light which awakens the souls at their source.

The Talmud teaches that today, while we are in exile, our synagogues and study houses serve as the Holy Temple (*Megillah* 29a). Thus, one's synagogue affiliation should afford him the opportunity to participate in daily Torah study groups and prayer. The strength of the group will certainly facilitate the arousal of his soul's illumination at its source. Attaching himself to the tzaddik and his followers is therefore most important. At the very least, a person should not disassociate himself from them. The battle to remove the "soiled garments" is constant, the tzaddik's efforts to reveal Torah unending. Thus, we celebrate Chanukah every year, lighting one candle the first night and adding one each additional night. This is symbolic of our ongoing struggle and of the ever increasing awareness of the Torah, the tzaddik's teachings and God's glory. Ultimately, whoever makes the effort to attach himself to the tzaddik will be able to attain his rectification (*Likutey Halakhot, B'tziat HaPat* 5:13-17).

* * *

Reb Noson also points out the connections which this lesson has with Yosef and his brothers (the weekly Torah portions which record the events of their lives are read during the Chanukah season).

339 LIKUTEY MOHARAN #14:13

merits glory. As was mentioned above, the main elevation of the glory comes through the making of *baaley teshuvah* and converts, which can only be achieved by means of the Torah of lovingkindness, etc. And it is impossible to merit Torah, except through humility, as explained earlier. We find, therefore, that it is impossible to merit glory in holiness except by means of humility. This is: "And humility precedes glory."

<The general principles> of the lesson are five: returning the glory to fear; [returning] fear to the heart; universal peace; peace on a personal level; and getting people to repent, which corresponds to "If you take out the *YaKaR* (precious) from the vile." This is the rectification for *KeRY* (wasting seed), as their letters are the same.[114]

114. **YaKaR...KeRY....** Rebbe Nachman brings these last few words to show the connection which this lesson has with guarding the Covenant. The Talmud (*Eruvin* 18b) teaches that during the 130 years that Adam abstained from marital relations after his expulsion from the Garden of Eden, he experienced *kery* (wasted seed). Rather than becoming proper flesh and blood children, his offspring became the demons and forces of the Other Side which stand ready to punish whoever strays from the proper path (*Zohar* I, 169b; also see *Rashi*, 2 Samuel 7:14). Above (n.56), we've seen that the opposing forces which hinder man's service of God are the outcome of his own sins, similar to what has been taught about Adam. Thus, the person who blemishes the Covenant has created his own opposition—his own "Jordan River," his own "soiled garments"—which interfere with his devotion to God.

Furthermore, the Ari teaches that wasted seed results in exile. The sparks of souls are dispersed throughout the world, held in captivity by the lower forces, and must be elevated (*Shaar HaPesukim, Shemot*). This corresponds to the *urZiLa* of Rabbah bar bar Chanah's story (§5) and the lowering and lessening of God's glory (as in n.44).

Conversely, by guarding the Covenant, one "takes out the precious from the vile" (cf. n.13; *Bava Metzia* 85a). This gathering of the sparks from exile is their elevation, the elevation of God's glory. And, whereas the wasting of seed leads to exile and distances one from God, repentance draws one closer to the Holy One and elevates His glory.

* * *

In this lesson, Rebbe Nachman has woven together a number of different topics including God's glory, the negating of idolatry, Torah study, Shabbat and the Covenant. Reb Noson shows how these and other points mentioned are all tied to the festival of Chanukah, which also appears in Rebbe Nachman's teaching.

When the Greeks invaded the Holy Land, they desecrated the Holy Temple and filled it with idolatry. They also issued harsh, evil decrees against the Jews, prohibiting circumcision of children (the Covenant), the observance of Shabbat, and the study of Torah. There was even a decree forcing the Jews to renounce their acceptance of God (a negation of His glory). As such, the Greeks are the paradigm of the alien weltanschauung and wisdom that invades the Holy Land, the concept of the "soiled garments" that separate one from holiness. It is difficult to shed these garments—the Jews suffered unspeakable horrors for twenty years. But even sleeping souls at their source. He accurately interpreted dreams for others, indicating his ability to bring souls to their correct paths. This eventually led to his meeting with Pharaoh, who recognized Yosef's greatness and elevated him to the position of viceroy. Pharaoh's acknowledgement of Yosef's wisdom and his dressing him in royal garments signify that indeed Yosef never soiled his garments.

Even in Egypt, a deep and lonely exile, Yosef was able to retain his attachment to Torah. Yosef was tested and proven worthy of Yaakov's confidence in him. He had shown that he was still attached to the tzaddik, Yaakov, and worthy of the "clean garments" that Yaakov bestowed upon him. Therefore, Yosef's descent to Egypt prepared the means of sustenance for all Israel during their later sojourn there (*Likutey Halakhot, B'tziat HaPat* 5:40-41).

Also, as viceroy, Yosef was able to order the Egyptians to circumcise themselves. This is a concept of guarding the Covenant to rectify *kery*, the "taking out of the precious from the vile" (see beginning of this note; *The Breslov Haggadah*, Appendix A, p.3).

LIKUTEY MOHARAN #14:13

Yosef was Yaakov's favorite son. Yaakov appreciated Yosef's righteousness and judged his son worthy of receiving both his Torah knowledge and the multi-colored cloak which he gave him. However, our Sages taught: The giving of the cloak aroused the jealousy of the brothers and brought about our forefather's descent to Egypt (*Shabbat 10b*). They sold him into slavery and dipped his cloak in blood in order to deceive Yaakov into thinking that wild animals had devoured Yosef. Yosef was seventeen at the time and his brothers thought him untried in guarding the "clean garments." They dipped his cloak in blood to allude to this fact. Yaakov began to cry, suspecting that perhaps Yosef had fallen prey to "wild animals"—i.e., the ensarement of the "soiled garments" of immorality and non-Jewish ways.

In fact, however, Yosef was truly worthy of all that Yaakov had given him. He was bought by Potifar, an Egyptian minister, whose wife attempted to seduce Yosef. She grabbed him, but he shed his garment and fled, keeping himself and his garment pure. He was captured and imprisoned. Yet, while in prison, his Torah study was so pure that it illumined

LIKUTEY MOHARAN #15:1,2 — 342

ליקוטי מוהר"ן סימן ט"ו

וְאַתֶּם תִּהְיוּ לִי מַמְלֶכֶת כֹּהֲנִים וְכוּ' (שְׁמוֹת יט):

לְשׁוֹן רַבֵּנוּ, זִכְרוֹנוֹ לִבְרָכָה

א. מִישֶׁרוֹצֶה לִטְעֹם טַעַם אוֹר הַגָּנוּז, הַיְנוּ סוֹדוֹת הַתּוֹרָה שֶׁיִּתְגַּלֶּה
לֶעָתִיד, צָרִיךְ לְהַעֲלוֹת מִדַּת הַיִּרְאָה לְשָׁרְשָׁהּ:

ב. וּבַמֶּהמַעֲלִין אֶת הַיִּרְאָה? בִּבְחִינַת מִשְׁפָּט, כְּמוֹ שֶׁכָּתוּב (מִשְׁלֵי
כט): "מֶלֶךְ בְּמִשְׁפָּט יַעֲמִיד אָרֶץ", וְאָרֶץ הוּא בְּחִינַת יִרְאָה, כְּמוֹ
שֶׁכָּתוּב (תְּהִלִּים ע"ו): "אֶרֶץ יָרְאָה", הַיְנוּ שֶׁיִּשְׁפֹּט אֶת כָּל עֲסָקָיו,
כְּמוֹ שֶׁכָּתוּב (שָׁם קי"ב): "יְכַלְכֵּל דְּבָרָיו בַּמִּשְׁפָּט", הַיְנוּ שֶׁיִּשְׁפֹּט
וְיָדִין בְּעַצְמוֹ כָּל עֲסָקָיו,

2. Or HaGanuz, Hidden Light. Reb Noson said: "Rebbe Nachman is the 'Or HaGanuz.' Whoever wants to taste him must have a lot of *hitbodedut* (secluded prayer)" (*Aveneha Barzel*, p.69, #47). This will become clearer in section 2 of the lesson.

3. mysteries of the Torah.... The Light of Creation was so bright that with it, one could see from one end of the world to the other. But God saw that man, because he would sin, would be unworthy of this powerful light, so He hid it away to give to the tzaddikim in the Future (*Bereishit Rabbah* 12:6; *Zohar* I, 30b). Where did God hide this light? From the *Zohar Chadash* (7a) we see that "the *Or HaGanuz* is hidden in the letter *vav*." This alludes to the Torah. The letter *vav*, which has a numerical value of six, corresponds to the Torah, about which we are taught that "the Tablets that Moshe brought down from heaven were six cubits by six cubits" (*Bava Batra* 14a). Thus, the Hidden Light refers to the mysteries of the Torah that will only be revealed in the Future. However, Rebbe Nachman tells us here that one can, even now, have a taste of this Hidden Light.

4. judgment...land/earth...feared. Literally, this verse reads, "With judgment, the king will *make stand* the earth." Thus, it is judgment which elevates the earth, and from the verse which Rebbe Nachman quotes from Psalms we see that the earth is synonymous with fear. Therefore, what is needed to elevate fear, to make the earth stand, is the practice of judgment.

This elevation and enhancement of fear due to judgment can be empirically verified as well. When judgment is enacted, others who see it have respect for the righteousness of the law and fear it, lest they too fall victim to this judgment.

5. all his actions. Rebbe Nachman now explains how one can constantly enact judgment and thereby always elevate fear to its source.

6. evaluate all his actions. This is Rebbe Nachman's advice of *hitbodedut*, the secluded prayer and meditation that one should practice daily. Throughout the Rebbe's writings one sees the importance of *hitbodedut*. *Outpouring of the Soul* (Breslov Research Institute, 1980), by Reb

LIKUTEY MOHARAN #15[1]

"You will be to Me a kingdom of priests and a holy nation. These are the words that you should speak to the Children of Israel."

(Exodus 19:6)

Anyone who wants to experience a taste of the *Or HaGanuz* (Hidden Light)[2]—i.e., the mysteries of the Torah that will be revealed in the Future[3]—must elevate the aspect of fear to its source.

2. And with what is fear elevated? With the aspect of judgment. As it is written (Proverbs 29:4), "Through judgment, the king will establish the land." And land corresponds to fear, as in (Psalms 76:9), "The earth feared."[4] That is, a person should judge all his actions,[5] as is written (Psalms 112:5), "He conducts his affairs with judgment"—i.e., he should himself judge and evaluate all his actions.[6]

---

1. **Likutey Moharan #15.** This lesson was taught in Zlatipolia, most likely on Shabbat Yitro, 20 Shevat 5562 (January 23, 1802).

One of Rebbe Nachman's closest followers, the Terhovitza Magid, had a son-in-law whose name was Reb Yitzchak Isaac. Reb Yitzchak Isaac was a very learned man, and a follower of Rebbe Zusia of Anipoli. When his mentor passed away, the Terhovitza Magid wanted his son-in-law to join Rebbe Nachman's following. At first, Reb Yitzchak Isaac was skeptical. When he finally did visit Rebbe Nachman, the Rebbe spoke to him about fear of Heaven and how if one truly fears God he can taste the Hidden Light of the Torah, a light that will only be revealed in the Future. Rebbe Nachman then said: "I am a treasure-house of *yirat shamayim* (fear of Heaven)." Suddenly experiencing tremendous fear, Reb Yitzchak Isaac fainted. When he came to, Rebbe Nachman said, "I just wanted you to taste a bit of the Hidden Light!" The Rebbe then spoke to him about the Holy Temple, intense prayer and humility. Reb Yitzchak Isaac was so astounded, he became a devoted follower of Rebbe Nachman, exclaiming, "I don't know how anyone can study Torah or pray without the Rebbe's guidance! All my days, I will regret that it took me so long to visit Rebbe Nachman." Shortly afterwards, the Terhovitza Magid visited Rebbe Nachman and heard this lesson in which all these concepts are discussed (*Tovot Zikhronot* p. 119-121; also see *Until the Mashiach*, p. 69).

This lesson, which is *leshon Rabbeinu z'l* (see Lesson #7, n.1), is the final one in which Rebbe Nachman expounds on the fantastic stories of Rabbah bar bar Chanah (they are recorded in *Bava Batra* 73b-74b). The Rebbe said that he had actually given these lessons in the name of Rabbah bar bar Chanah himself. When he first started revealing these teachings Rebbe Nachman disclosed that Rabbah bar bar Chanah had come to him, saying, "Why don't you pay attention to my stories? If you do so, I will reveal to you the most awesome and wonderful new insights" (*Tzaddik* #131). (The amazing story which appears in this lesson is also explained in *Likutey Moharan* I, 3, but in an entirely different manner.)

LIKUTEY MOHARAN #15:2

וּבָזֶה יָסִיר מֵעָלָיו כָּל הַפְּחָדִים, וְיַעֲלֶה בְּחִינַת יִרְאָה בָּרָה וּנְקִיָּה,
וְתִשָּׁאֵר אַךְ יִרְאַת־הַשֵּׁם וְלֹא יִרְאָה אַחֶרֶת. כִּי כְּשֶׁאֵין אָדָם דָּן
וְשׁוֹפֵט אֶת עַצְמוֹ, אֲזַי דָּנִין וְשׁוֹפְטִין אוֹתוֹ לְמַעְלָה, כִּי 'אִם אֵין דִּין
לְמַטָּה – יֵשׁ דִּין לְמַעְלָה' (דְּבָרִים רַבָּה ה); וּכְשֶׁשּׁוֹפְטִין אֶת הָאָדָם
בְּמִשְׁפָּט דִּלְעֵלָּא, אֲזַי הַדִּין נִתְלַבֵּשׁ בְּכָל הַדְּבָרִים, וְכָל הַדְּבָרִים
נַעֲשִׂים שְׁלוּחִים לַמָּקוֹם לַעֲשׂוֹת בָּזֶה הָאִישׁ מִשְׁפָּט כָּתוּב, כְּמוֹ
שֶׁאָמְרוּ חֲכָמֵינוּ, זִכְרוֹנָם לִבְרָכָה (נְדָרִים מא): '"לְמִשְׁפָּטֶיךָ עָמְדוּ",
אֲזַי "הַכֹּל עֲבָדֶיךָ" – לַעֲשׂוֹת דִּין בָּזֶה הָאָדָם'.
אֲבָל כְּשֶׁשּׁוֹפֵט אֶת עַצְמוֹ, וּכְשֶׁיֵּשׁ דִּין לְמַטָּה אֵין דִּין לְמַעְלָה, וְאֵין
הַיִּרְאָה מִתְלַבֵּשׁ בְּשׁוּם דָּבָר לְעוֹרֵר אֶת הָאָדָם, כִּי הוּא בְּעַצְמוֹ
נִתְעוֹרֵר. וְזֶהוּ (תְּהִלִּים נ): "וְשָׂם דֶּרֶךְ" – מִי שֶׁשָּׂם אָרְחוֹתָיו (כְּמוֹ
שֶׁדָּרְשׁוּ רַבּוֹתֵינוּ, זִכְרוֹנָם לִבְרָכָה סוֹטָה ה:), הַיְנוּ שֶׁשּׁוֹפֵט אָרְחוֹתָיו, כְּמוֹ

---

certain punitive measures, this punishment is carried out in a prescribed manner. Even if there are variables which affect the actual execution, the general categories of fines, incarceration, capital punishment etc., all fall within given parameters. However, when God decrees correctional measures, punishment may come in any number of forms and different combinations because "*all* are Your servants" to execute justice. Thus, monetary losses (business/home/automobile, etc.) are but different forms of heavenly fines, and illnesses or accidents which keep one tied down are just other forms of incarceration. The Talmud teaches: Even though capital punishment has been abolished, the laws of capital punishment remain in effect. Thus, if one commits a sin for which the punishment is stoning (which in part entails being thrown down from a height of two stories), then he may "accidentally" fall off a roof or die a similarly violent death. If one commits a sin for which the punishment is strangulation, then he may be punished by drowning or another form of asphyxiation (*Ketuvot* 30a,b). These are just some of the "messengers" available to God for executing justice.

10. **he has roused himself.** Through constant self-judgment, one draws upon oneself the fear of Heaven. Because judgment is an extension of fear, by executing self-judgment one obviates the need for Heaven to instill fear in him. Therefore, he fears no one and nothing but God Himself.

11. **judges the way he acts.** Our Sages taught: "And *sam* the way..."—do not read *v'SaM*, but rather *v'ShaM* (he appraises). This refers to someone who evaluates and judges all his actions. Likewise, the Maharsha (*Moed Katan* 5a, *s.v. al*) explains that *sham orchotav* (appraises his ways) is the concept of judging oneself. On the Talmudic passage quoted in our text (*loc. cit.*), the *Iyun Yaakov* comments that this refers to one who is "hidden" (modest and humble) in his ways. He will merit seeing the hidden treasures of God. This ties in perfectly with our lesson, referring to one who, by practicing the hidden/secluded prayer, will merit seeing the Hidden Light.

LIKUTEY MOHARAN #15:2

By doing this, all fright is removed from him and an aspect of a clear and pure fear emerges. Only fear of God remains, no other fear.[7] For when a person does not evaluate and judge himself, he is then evaluated and judged from Above. This is because "when there is no judgment below, there is judgment Above" (*Devarim Rabbah* 5:4).[8] And when a man is judged with the judgment of heaven, then justice becomes clothed in all things and all things become God's messengers for executing "the written judgment" (Psalms 149:9) upon this man. As our Sages taught: "To Your judgments they were steadfast...," and thus "all are Your servants" (Psalms 119:91)—so as to execute justice upon this man (*Nedarim* 41a).[9]

{"And he that puts right the way, to him I will show the salvation of the Lord" (Psalms 50:23).}

However, when a person judges himself, when there is judgment below [so that] there is no judgment Above, then fear does not clothe itself in anything in order to rouse the person. This is because he has roused himself.[10] This is the meaning of, "And *sam* (he puts right) the way..."—someone who evaluates his ways (*Sotah* 5b). In other words, he judges the way he acts,[11] as in (Exodus 21:1), "These are the

Alter Tepliker (author of the *Mai HaNachal*; d. 1919) deals entirely with this indispensable tool for our spiritual development. Here, Rebbe Nachman says that a person should judge each and every one of his actions. This includes evaluating relationships with family and friends, his business practices, and especially his service and dedication to God. He should examine all his past actions to determine whether they were carried out properly, with truth and sincerity, or if there was something lacking that needs to be corrected. One should also evaluate his plans and intentions to verify if they are indeed appropriate. By judging and passing judgment on himself a person elevates his fear of Heaven, as Rebbe Nachman will now explain.

7. **fear of God...no other....** As Rebbe Nachman explains further on (see §3:end and n.21), all fear stems from the uppermost fear—the true root of fear—fear of God Himself. As the quality of fear descends into this world, it can be manifested in many different forms. Because of this, man believes that his feelings of fear and anxiety have really to do with the object of his fear, whether it is, for example, one's employer, a domineering parent or spouse, or public exposure. However, when one elevates fear to its source, then all that remains is the fear of God. All other fears fall away. The *Zohar* (III, 67b) teaches: Whoever delights in the Torah will not fear anything. This is connected to what Rebbe Nachman discusses further on in the lesson regarding the revealed and hidden Torah.

8. **no judgment below....** When justice is executed by judges in this world, there is no need for a heavenly judgment. But when justice is not executed below, so that justice is lacking, then a heavenly judgment must be carried out (*Devarim Rabbah* 5:5). Rebbe Nachman therefore advises a person to judge himself daily, as this enables him to postpone the heavenly judgment he might otherwise receive.

9. **God's messengers...execute justice upon this man.** When a judge issues a verdict calling for

LIKUTEY MOHARAN #15:2,3

346

שֶׁכָּתוּב (שְׁמוֹת כ״א): "וְאֵלֶּה הַמִּשְׁפָּטִים אֲשֶׁר תָּשִׂים":
עַל־יְדֵי־זֶה "אַרְאֶנּוּ בְּיֵשַׁע אֱלֹקִים" – זֶה בְּחִינַת יִרְאָה, כְּמוֹ
שֶׁכָּתוּב (קֹהֶלֶת י״ב): "אֶת הָאֱלֹקִים יְרָא"; הַיְנוּ בְּחִינַת יִרְאָה עוֹלָה
מֵהַקְּלִפָּה וּמֵהָאֱמוֹת עַל־יְדֵי מִשְׁפָּט, כִּי מִתְּחִלָּה הָיְתָה נִתְלַבֵּשׁ
בַּקְּלִפָּה. וְזֶהוּ שֶׁהָאָדָם מְפַחֵד אֶת עַצְמוֹ מֵאֵיזֶה דָבָר, מְשׁוֹר אוֹ
מִגַּנָּבִים וּשְׁאָר פְּחָדִים – זֶה הוּא שֶׁהַיִּרְאָה נִתְלַבֵּשׁ בְּזֶה הַדָּבָר, כִּי
אִם לֹא הָיָה נִתְלַבֵּשׁ הַיִּרְאָה בְּזֶה הַדָּבָר, לֹא הָיָה כֹּחַ בְּזֶה הַדָּבָר
לְהַפְחִיד אֶת הָאָדָם:

ג. וְשֹׁרֶשׁ הַיִּרְאָה הוּא דַעַת, כְּמוֹ שֶׁכָּתוּב בְּעֵץ־הַחַיִּים, שֶׁמַּנְצְפַּ״ךְ
הוּא בְּדַעַת דִּזְעֵיר־אַנְפִּין, כְּמוֹ שֶׁכָּתוּב (מִשְׁלֵי ב): "אָז תָּבִין יִרְאַת
ה' וְדַעַת אֱלֹקִים תִּמְצָא". וְעִקַּר הַדַּעַת הוּא בַּלֵּב, כְּמוֹ שֶׁכָּתוּב
(דְּבָרִים כ״ט): "וְלֹא נָתַן לָכֶם לֵב לָדַעַת". גַּם שָׁם עִקַּר הַיִּרְאָה, כְּמוֹ

word and close it. This alludes to the *gevurot*, which remain contained in the *Daat* of *Z'er Anpin* (cf. *Etz Chaim, Shaar Drushei HaTzelem* 25:2).

These *gevurot* (severities) correspond to fear, fear in the form of decrees/judgments that can be put into this world to mete out punishment. Therefore Rebbe Nachman states that the source of fear is *daat*, referring to the *gevurot*. And although *daat* also consists of *chasadim*, Rebbe Nachman is presently concerned with elevating fear to its source and accordingly focuses only on the *gevurot*. Further on in the lesson he will incorporate the concept of the *chasadim* as well.

It is worth noting that Moshe Rabbeinu was so great, that in the profound teachings of the holy Ari he is equated with "*Daat* of *Z'er Anpin*" (*Etz Chaim* 32:1). This ties in with the Midrash mentioned in the previous note which associates the five end-letters with Moshe's greatness. This theme will be further developed in the course of the lesson.

17. **understand...daat....** In the context of the lesson, the second half of this verse reads: "...and *daat*, there you will find fear" (the name *Elohim*, the Lord, being synonymous with fear; as in n.13).

Rebbe Nachman has also quoted the beginning of the verse, "Then you will understand the fear of God...." Understanding is the *sefirah* of *Binah* which, as mentioned, is the source of the *gevurot*. Thus, the full verse can be read: Then you will [bring] the *gevurot* to *Binah*. When? When you find [that you have elevated] this fear up to *daat*.

18. **heart to know.** This is because *Binah* (Understanding) corresponds to the heart. This is a continuation of the previous verse, "Then you will bring the *gevurot* to *Binah*," for the source of the *gevurot*/fear is in *Binah*/heart, and must be felt there. Elsewhere (*Likutey Moharan* I, 154) Rebbe Nachman discusses this same idea and quotes the verse "*Know* it today and bring it back to your heart" (Deuteronomy 4:39).

347   *LIKUTEY MOHARAN #15:2,3*

judgments which *taSiM* (you shall put)...."[12]

As a result, "...to him I will show the salvation of the Lord." This corresponds to fear, as in (Ecclesiastes 12:13), "And the Lord shall you fear."[13] In other words, the aspect of fear ascends from the evil husk and the nations by means of judgment. For, originally, [fear] was clothed in the evil husk. This is why a person is afraid of something—the authorities, thieves, or anything else which causes him to be afraid—because fear has clothed itself in that thing. For if fear had not clothed itself in that thing, the thing itself would not have had the ability to frighten the person.[14]

3. And, the source of fear is *daat* (holy knowledge), as is written in *Etz Chaim* (Shaar Rosh HaShanah 2): *MaNtZPaKh*[15] is located in *Daat* of *Z'er Anpin*.[16] As is written (Proverbs 2:5), "Then you will understand the fear of God, and *daat* of the Lord you will find."[17] And the essence of knowledge is in the heart, as in (Deuteronomy 29:3), "Yet God has not given you a heart to know."[18] The essence of fear is also [in the heart],

---

12. **judgments which taSiM....** Rebbe Nachman adds this verse to show that the "putting" (תשים) of judgments corresponds to the "putting" right (שם) and evaluating of one's ways. Thus, by judging his actions and ways he obviates the other judgments that come from Above.

13. **the Lord shall you fear.** In Hebrew this is *Elohim*, the holy name which indicates strength and judgment, and thus corresponds to fear (see Appendix: Sefirot and Associated Names of God). In this context, the verse reads: **And he that puts right** — judges — **the way, to him I will show the salvation** — revelation or elevation **of the Lord** — fear.

14. **not have had the ability....** See above, note 7.

In review: To experience the *Or HaGanuz* (Hidden Light), the mysteries of the Torah, it is necessary to elevate fear to its source (§1). Fear is elevated through judgment. A person who constantly judges himself obviates judgment from Above. He thus comes to a fear of God which is pure, a fear not clothed in anything external (§2).

15. **MaNtZPaKh....** These are the five end-letters: *mem* (ם), *nun* (ן), *tzadi* (ץ), *peh* (ף), and *khaf* (ך)—מנצפך. As to why these five letters in particular are formed differently when they appear at the end of a word, see *Bereishit Rabbah* (1:11) where it states that they are a testimony to the greatness of Moshe Rabbeinu.

16. **Daat of Z'er Anpin.** The *sefirah* of *Daat* that is part of the Divine persona *Z'er Anpin* consists of the five *chasadim* (benevolences) and five *gevurot* (severities) that emanate from *Chokhmah* and *Binah*, respectively. The *chasadim* are represented by the regular letters. They are called "open" letters because they appear at the beginning or middle of a word and leave an opening for other letters to follow. This alludes to the *chasadim* spreading out and being open to bring lovingkindness into the world. The five *gevurot* are represented by the end-letters, *MaNtZPaKh*. They are called "closed" letters because they appear at the end of the

LIKUTEY MOHARAN #15:3,4

שֶׁאָמְרוּ חֲכָמֵינוּ, זִכְרוֹנָם לִבְרָכָה (קדושין לב:): דָּבָר הַמָּסוּר לַלֵּב,
נֶאֱמַר בּוֹ: "וְיָרֵאתָ מֵאֱלֹקֶיךָ", הַיְנוּ שֶׁיֵּדַע מִמִּי יִתְיָרָא, הַיְנוּ לְיִרְאָה
אֶת הַשֵּׁם הַנִּכְבָּד יִרְאַת הָרוֹמְמוּת:

ד. וּכְשֶׁמַּגִּיעַ לִבְחִינַת דַּעַת, זוֹכֶה לְהַשָּׂגַת הַתּוֹרָה, כְּמוֹ שֶׁכָּתוּב
(משלי ח): "אֲנִי חָכְמָה שָׁכַנְתִּי עָרְמָה", שֶׁשְּׁכוּנַת הַתּוֹרָה אֵצֶל בַּר־
דַּעַת, כְּמוֹ שֶׁכָּתוּב (דְּנִיֵּאל ב): 'קָדְשָׁא־בְּרִיךְ־הוּא יָהֵב חָכְמְתָא
לְחַכִּימִין'.

essence, is the beginning stages of elevating fear to its source. By focusing on the true cause of his fear, rather than its external trappings, he elevates the fear and anxiety that he experiences to *daat*—consciously transforming his "fallen fear" into the fear of Heaven.

The second and higher type of fear of Heaven, known as *yirat haromimut,* is the fear one feels because of God's greatness and exaltedness as the Ruler and Master of the Universe. A person who has advanced to this level does not refrain from sin because he fears Divine retribution. Rather, because he has come to such a sense of awe of the Holy One and, consequently a clear perception of his own insignificance, he is too embarrassed, too petrified, to do anything that would go against the Creator's will. This is the level of fear referred to in the verse quoted in the text, "To fear the glorious name"; it adds completeness, as it were, to God's name and glory. And, while fear of punishment is vitally important, for without it one cannot even enter into the realm of the holy, it is this more exalted fear, the fear of His exaltedness, which is the ultimate goal (*Rabbi Nachman's Wisdom #5; Likutey Moharan I, 185*).

Rebbe Nachman makes it clear that the key for advancing from the *p'chadim* to *yirat haonesh* and ultimately, if one is worthy, to *yirat haromimut,* is the practice of *hitbodedut.* When a person begins his service of God, the fear he experiences is a fear of receiving judgment. As he advances in his devotions and practices *hitbodedut* consistently, thus elevating the fear, he comes to ever deeper insights into the nature of fear, recognizing that all fear is but the manifestation of the *gevurot* in different forms. Ultimately, his *hitbodedut* can bring him to *yirat haromimut,* to the realization—the total and honest realization—that the only one to fear is God Himself.

In review: To experience the *Or HaGanuz* (Hidden Light), the mysteries of the Torah, it is necessary to elevate fear to its source (§1). Fear is elevated through judgment. A person who constantly judges himself obviates judgment from Above. He thus comes to a fear of God which is pure, a fear not clothed in anything external (§2). The source of fear is *daat*; the essence of both is in the heart. This knowledge of whom to fear is the most exalted fear: fear of His exaltedness (§3).

22. **Torah...one who has daat.** "Wisdom" in the verse refers to Torah. Thus, "I, Torah, dwell with [the] cunning"—with the one who has holy knowledge.

23. **wisdom to the wise.** The verse in full reads, "He gives wisdom to the wise, and knowledge to those who have understanding." The obvious question is, If one needs *daat* to acquire

LIKUTEY MOHARAN #15:3,4

as our Sages taught: Of the things which are given over to [i.e., hidden in] the heart, it is said, "And you shall fear your Lord!" (*Kiddushin* 32b).[19] That is, he will know whom to fear[20]—i.e., "To fear the glorious name" (Deuteronomy 28:58), [which is] fear of His exaltedness.[21]

4. When a person achieves the aspect of *daat*, he merits perception of the Torah, as is written (Proverbs 8:12), "I, wisdom, dwell with [the] cunning"—the Torah's dwelling is with the one who has *daat*.[22] As is written, the Holy One "gives wisdom to the wise" (Daniel 2:21).[23]

19. **to the heart...fear your Lord.** There are certain mitzvot, injunctions as well as prohibitions, that are "given over to the heart"—only God knows the true intentions of man's behavior. His fellow man has no way of knowing whether his failure to carry out a positive command or his transgressing a negative one was intentional or not. Thus, for example, a Jew is commanded "not to put a stumbling block [i.e., bad advice] before the [conceptually] blind...," and "to stand up and give honor to a sage..." (Leviticus 19:14,32). Because these involve matters which are hidden in the heart, one can claim to be innocent of any wrongdoing. After giving bad advice and causing his friend, who did not know any better, to stumble in some matter, he can claim he was not aware that there was anything wrong with his suggestion. He can say, "I didn't realize!" and no one—other than God—will ever know. Likewise, he can fail to rise when he sees a sage approaching and then claim, "I didn't see him coming." Who—other than God—will ever know? Therefore, immediately following these commandments the Torah warns, "And you shall fear your Lord!" Thus, the Talmud emphasizes that anything "given over to the heart" requires that we *fear God!* We must remember that God knows even our hidden thoughts and though we may be capable of deceiving our fellow man, the thoughts of man's heart are open before God (*Kiddushin* 32a).

20. **know whom to fear.** One has to elevate this fear to *daat* (holy knowledge), and when he *knows* this, he will know whom to fear.

21. **fear of His exaltedness.** There are three general categories of fear: two within the realm of holiness and which assist in the service of God, and one from which a person must rid himself so he can develop in holiness and come closer to God. This latter type of fear is what Rebbe Nachman referred to in the previous section as *p'chadim* (fright; cf. n.7) and which he elsewhere calls *yirah chitzonit* (extraneous fear; *Likutey Moharan* I, 5:4) and *yirah nefulah* (fallen fear; *ibid.*, 154). In the Rebbe's *Aleph-Bet Book* (*Pachad* A, 33), he writes, "When a person is terrified, it is a sign that the Holy One has hidden His face from him and that he has been beset by stern judgments."

In contrast to the fear and anxiety which one experiences when distant from holiness are the two types of fear of Heaven. The lower form, the fear of punishment for one's sins, is a fundamental prerequisite for anyone seeking to serve God. *Yirat haonesh*, as it is known, indicates that one has an awareness of God's hand manifesting itself in that which he is presently afraid of. He understands that authorities, thieves and the like are nothing more than God's messengers, sent to exact judgment for his having transgressed His will. Indeed, it is precisely through the *p'chadim* and *yirah nefulah* that he is reminded of this. This, in

LIKUTEY MOHARAN #15:4

אֲבָל יֵשׁ שְׁנֵי בְחִינוֹת תּוֹרָה: יֵשׁ בְּחִינַת נִגְלֶה וּבְחִינַת נִסְתָּר; אֲבָל לִבְחִינַת נִסְתָּר אֵינוֹ זוֹכֶה אֶלָּא לֶעָתִיד לָבוֹא, אֲבָל בְּזֶה הָעוֹלָם זוֹכֶה לִבְחִינַת נִסְתָּר עַל־יְדֵי תְּפִלָּה בִּמְסִירַת־נֶפֶשׁ, וְלִתְפִלָּה זוֹכֶה – עַל־יְדֵי תּוֹרָה שֶׁבְּנִגְלֶה, כִּי הַתּוֹרָה שֶׁהִיא בְּנִגְלֶה הִיא בְּחִינַת סִינַי, כְּמוֹ שֶׁאָמְרוּ חֲכָמֵינוּ, זִכְרוֹנָם לִבְרָכָה (בְּרָכוֹת סד.): 'סִינַי וְעוֹקֵר הָרִים, הֵי מִנַּיְהוּ עָדִיף? וְהֵשִׁיבוּ: סִינַי עָדִיף, כִּי הַכֹּל צְרִיכִין לְמָרֵי חִטַּיָּא'; וְהַתּוֹרָה שֶׁבְּנִגְלֶה הַכֹּל צְרִיכִין לָהּ, אֲבָל הַתּוֹרָה שֶׁבְּנִסְתָּר – זְעִירִין אִנּוּן דִּצְרִיכִין לָהּ.

וּבְחִינַת סִינַי הוּא בְּחִינַת שִׁפְלוּת, כְּמוֹ שֶׁאָמְרוּ חֲכָמֵינוּ, זִכְרוֹנָם לִבְרָכָה (סוֹטָה ה.), שֶׁהִנִּיחַ הַקָּדוֹשׁ־בָּרוּךְ־הוּא כָּל הֶהָרִים, וְלֹא נָתַן הַתּוֹרָה אֶלָּא עַל הַר־סִינַי. וַחֲכָמֵינוּ, זִכְרוֹנָם לִבְרָכָה, אָמְרוּ (שָׁם ה:), שֶׁתְּפִלַּת הַשָּׁפֵל אֵין נִמְאֶסֶת, כְּמוֹ שֶׁכָּתוּב (תְּהִלִּים נ"א): "לֵב

(*Berakhot* 32b). These periods of preparation and prayer are explained in the *Shulchan Arukh* (*Orach Chaim* 98:1) as their having reached a level of *hitpashtut hagashmiyut* (literally, shedding the physical). This is why their Torah was preserved in their hearts. It is the concept of fear being elevated to its source, by which one merits the hidden Torah.

25. **revealed Torah...everyone needs.** The Talmud (*loc. cit.*) asks: Whom does the world need more, one with a very broad knowledge of Torah law—"Sinai," or one whose sharp mind enables him to deduce the law—"an uprooter-of-mountains"? Our Sages answer that the person with the broad knowledge is like the one who sells already harvested grain—all people have a need for such an individual. Torah, in general, is called Sinai, for all the laws (broad knowledge) were given there.

Similarly, Rebbe Nachman strongly emphasized the need for studying Jewish law. He said that study of the Codes every single day is an absolute must for every individual (*Rabbi Nachman's Wisdom #29*). The *Shulchan Arukh* states this quite clearly in *Yoreh Deah* 246:4; *Shakh, ibid. 5; Mishneh Berurah* 155:3. It is based on the Talmudic teaching: Whoever studies Torah law every day will merit the Future World (*Niddah* 73a). All this will tie in at the end of the lesson where the Rebbe explains that the Future World *is* the hidden Torah.

26. **few are those who need it.** Or, within the context of the lesson, our perception of the Torah is not on the level to need it—i.e., we have not yet elevated fear to its source so as to merit the hidden Torah.

27. **humble...not rejected....** Thus, when a person studies Torah and comes into the category of Sinai/humility, he can pray properly. Because his heart is broken and contrite, God desires his prayers. When this happens, there are no obstacles and diversions interrupting his prayer, and the humble person is able to pray with great intensity and self-sacrifice (*Parparaot LeChokhmah*).

351   *LIKUTEY MOHARAN #15:4*

However, there are two aspects to the Torah: the aspect of revealed and the aspect of hidden. Although the aspect of hidden will only be [fully] merited in the Future (*Zohar* III, p.152a), still, by means of prayer with self-sacrifice one can merit the aspect of hidden [even] in this world.[24] And the way to merit prayer is through the revealed Torah. This is because the Torah which is revealed corresponds to Sinai, as our Sages taught: "Sinai" or "an uprooter-of-mountains," which is preferable? And they answered, "Sinai" is preferable, for everyone requires the grain merchant (*Berakhot* 4a). The revealed Torah is something which everyone needs.[25] The hidden Torah, however, few are those who need it (*Zohar* III, p.73a).[26]

Now the aspect of Sinai corresponds to humility, as our Sages taught: The Holy One ignored all the mountains and gave the Torah only on Mount Sinai (*Sotah* 5a). And our Sages taught: The prayers of a humble person are not rejected, as in (Psalms 51:19), "A broken and contrite heart You do not despise" (*Sotah* 5b).[27] By praying with self-

---

Torah and he is only given this holy knowledge when he has Torah—for the Holy One gives wisdom/Torah to the wise/those with *daat*—then where does he begin? The answer is: START! Begin by studying Torah, even without *daat*. This Torah study will guide him to the proper paths in life so that, during *hitbodedut*, he can judge himself accordingly (§2 above). Such judgment will elevate him and his fear to the level where he can attain *daat*.

The verse which follows "[He] gives wisdom..." states: "He reveals deep and secret things." This ties in with Rebbe Nachman's next remark that there are two aspects to the Torah: the revealed and the hidden. Thus, after one attains the "wise," the revealed Torah, he is then ready to receive the "secret," the hidden Torah.

24. hidden...prayer with self-sacrifice.... Just as an angel cannot come into this world unless it is clothed in the physical (as was the case with the angels who visited Avraham; Genesis 18:2ff), the Torah, which is far more exalted than even the highest angel, cannot be revealed in this world except by means of concealment. The Torah which we presently have in this world has its origin in *Z'er Anpin*, and its essence is known as the *neshamah* of the Torah. However, there will come a time, the Future, when the layers of concealment will be removed and we will be given an entirely new revelation and deeper understanding of the Word of God (*Zohar* III, 152a). Nevertheless, in this lesson Rebbe Nachman reveals that by "shedding one's garment," it is possible to attain this spiritual revelation even in this world. How? When a person prays with such total self-sacrifice and intensity that he transcends his corporeality and is no longer bound by the constraints of his physical existence, then he can taste the *neshamah* of the *neshamah*, the hidden Torah of *Atik*, the *Or HaGanuz*.

This is in line with the Talmudic teaching that for each of the three daily prayers, the early *chassidim* (men of great piety) would wait an hour before their prayers, pray for an hour, then wait another hour after their prayers. The Talmud asks: If nine hours of the day were spent in prayer, when did they study Torah and earn a living? The answer is that because they were *chassidim*, their knowledge was preserved in their hearts and their work was blessed

LIKUTEY MOHARAN #15:4,5

352

נִשְׁבָּר" וְכוּ'. וְעַל־יְדֵי תְּפִלָּה שֶׁהִיא בִּמְסִירַת־נֶפֶשׁ, שֶׁמְּבַטֵּל כָּל
גַּשְׁמִיּוּתוֹ וְאֵין גְּבוּל, וּכְשֶׁאֵין גְּבוּל, אֲזַי יָכוֹל לְהַשִּׂיג הַתּוֹרָה
שֶׁלֶּעָתִיד, שֶׁהִיא אֵינָהּ גְּבוּל וְאֵין נִתְפֶּסֶת בִּגְבוּל:

ה. וְזֶה שֶׁאָמַר רַבָּה בַּר בַּר־
חָנָה: לְדִידִי חֲזִי לִי הַהִיא
אַקְרוּקְתָּא, דַּהֲוֵי כִּי אַקְרָא
דְהַגְרוֹנְיָא. וְאַקְרָא דְהַגְרוֹנְיָא
כַּמָּה הֲוֵי? שִׁתִּין בָּתֵּי. אֲתָא
תַּנִּינָא בְּלַעַהּ. אֲתָא פּוּשְׁקַנְצָא
וּבְלָעֵהּ לְתַנִּינָא, וּסְלֵיק יָתֵב
בְּאִילָנָא. תָּא חֲזִי כַּמָּה נְפִישׁ חֵילָא דְּאִילָנָא. אָמַר רַב פַּפָּא בַּר
שְׁמוּאֵל: אִי לָאו דַּהֲוֵי הָתָם לָא הֵימְנֵהּ.

רַשְׁבַּ"ם:

אַקְרוּקְתָּא – צְפַרְדֵּעַ. כְּאַקְרָא
דְהַגְרוֹנְיָא – גָּדוֹל הָיָה כְּאוֹתָהּ כְּרַךְ.
וְאַקְרָא דְהַגְרוֹנְיָא כַּמָּה הֲוֵי, שִׁתִּין בָּתֵּי
– תַּלְמוּדָא קָאָמַר לָהּ. אֲתָא תַּנִּינָא –
רַבָּה קָאָמַר לָהּ. פּוּשְׁקַנְצָא – עוֹרֵב
נְקֵבָה. בְּאִילָנָא – עַל עָנָף אֶחָד כְּדֶרֶךְ
הָעוֹפוֹת. לָא הֵימְנִי – לֹא הֶאֱמַנְתִּי.

אַקְרוּקְתָּא – פֵּרֵשׁ רַבֵּנוּ שְׁמוּאֵל: צְפַרְדֵּעַ. וְזֶה בְּחִינַת עֲלִיַּת הַיִּרְאָה
לְשָׁרְשָׁהּ, הַיְנוּ דַּעַת; כִּי צְפַרְדֵּעַ הִיא מִלָּה מֻרְכֶּבֶת: צִפּוֹר דֵּעָה (תָּנָא
דְּבֵי אֵלִיָּהוּ ז' וּבְכַוָּנוֹת הַהַגָּדָה), וְצִפּוֹר הוּא בְּחִינַת יִרְאָה, בְּחִינַת אֶרֶץ,
כְּמוֹ שֶׁכָּתוּב (יְשַׁעְיָהוּ כ"ד): "מִכְּנַף הָאָרֶץ זְמִירוֹת" וְכוּ', וּכְמוֹ

accomplishing self-judgment (nn.6, 23), this is only one, initial, aspect of secluded prayer.
After consistent and dedicated practice of *hitbodedut*, one discovers yet another, higher level.
This is the level at which his *hitbodedut* becomes the intense and devoted prayer through
which the mysteries of the hidden Torah are unlocked (*Mabuey HaNachal*).

In review: To experience the *Or HaGanuz* (Hidden Light), the mysteries of the Torah, it is
necessary to elevate fear to its source (§1). Fear is elevated through judgment. A person who
constantly judges himself obviates judgment from Above. He thus comes to a fear of God
which is pure, a fear not clothed in anything external (§2). The source of fear is *daat*; the
essence of both is in the heart. This knowledge of whom to fear is the most exalted fear: fear
of His exaltedness (§3). Having elevated fear to *daat*, one merits the revealed Torah—
knowledge of its laws—and humility. He is then able to pray with intensity and self-sacrifice.
Through this transcending of corporeality he merits the hidden Torah/the *Or HaGanuz* (§4).

30. **bird...fear/earth....** The word *k'naf*, which means corner, as in the literal translation of
the verse, also means the wing of a bird. Hence, this verse which Rebbe Nachman quotes
from Isaiah can likewise be read: "From the wing of the earth...." Thus, wing/bird is
associated with earth, which is synonymous with fear (§2, n.4).

353 LIKUTEY MOHARAN #15:4,5

sacrifice, a person transcends all his corporeality and has no limitations.[28] And with no limitations, he is then able to perceive the Torah of the Future, which has no limitations and cannot be circumscribed.[29]

5. This is what Rabbah bar bar Chanah recounted: I myself saw this *akrukta* which was as *akra deHagrunia* (the city of Hagrunia). And how large was the city of Hagrunia? sixty houses. A *tanina* (serpent) came by and swallowed it. A *pushkantza* (raven) came by and swallowed the serpent, and then ascended a tree and sat there. Come and see how great was the strength of that tree! Rabbi Papa the son of Shmuel said: Had I not been there, I would never have believed him! (*Bava Batra* 73b).

Rashbam:

akrukta - [Aramaic for frog;] in Hebrew, *tzephardeah*: **as the city of Hagrunia** - it was as large as this city: **And how large was the city of Hagrunia? sixty houses** - the Talmud said this: **A serpent came by** - Rabbah said this: **pushkantza** - [Aramaic for] a female raven; [*orev* in Hebrew]: **a tree** - on one branch, the way birds do: **never have believed** - I would not have believed it:

akrukta — Rashbam explains that this is a *tzephardeah*. This alludes to the elevation of fear to its source, i.e., *daat*. This is because the word *tZePhaRDeAh* is a composite of *tZiPoR* (bird) and *DeAh* (knowledge) (*Tanna d'Bei Eliyahu* 1:7). A bird corresponds to fear/earth, as in (Isaiah 24:16), "From the *knaf* (corner) of the earth we heard songs."[30]

28. **no limitations.** As a result of his humility, which he acquired by studying the revealed Torah, a person is brought to the level of shedding his physical garment. This is the advanced spiritual level known as *bitul* (negation); as far as he is concerned, he does not exist (*Parparaot LeChokhmah*).

29. **...cannot be circumscribed.** As mentioned previously (see n.24), the *Zohar* teaches that the hidden Torah of the Future has its origin in the highest Divine persona, *Atik*. This higher aspect of Torah cannot be encompassed and clothed in any physical form which would allow it to be brought into this world. Because it cannot be contained or circumscribed by anything corporeal, man's mind is incapable of perceiving its great mysteries. However, the humble person who transcends his own corporeality, is, in a sense, no longer attached to or limited by the physical forms of this world. His mind is therefore able to absorb and encompass that which is normally beyond human perception and understanding. Having been freed from these constraints, the hidden Torah is no longer concealed from him.

Elsewhere, Rebbe Nachman taught that by practicing *hitbodedut* one can merit completely eliminating all one's negative character traits (*Likutey Moharan* I, 52). This brings one to the quality of humility which is vital for transcending his corporeality, as mentioned in this lesson. And, whereas earlier *hitbodedut* was explained as the means for

LIKUTEY MOHARAN #15:5

שֶׁכָּתוּב (שָׁם ס): "מִי אֵלֶה" – אוֹתִיּוֹת 'אֱלֹקִים' – כָּעָב תְּעוּפֶינָה" וְכוּ', וְדֵעָה הִיא שֹׁרֶשׁ הַיִּרְאָה.

וְדַמְיָא לְאַקְרָא דְּהַגְרוֹנְיָא – לְשׁוֹן (שָׁם נ"ח): "קְרָא בְגָרוֹן", שֶׁזֶּה בְּחִינַת תּוֹרָה שֶׁבִּנְגְלֶה, כְּמוֹ שֶׁאָמְרוּ חֲכָמֵינוּ, זִכְרוֹנָם לִבְרָכָה (עֵרוּבִין נד.): 'לְמוֹצִיאֵיהֶם בַּפֶּה', כִּי עַל-יְדֵי עֲלִיַּת הַיִּרְאָה לִבְחִינַת דַּעַת, זוֹכִין לַתּוֹרָה שֶׁבִּנְגְלֶה.

וְאַקְרָא דְּהַגְרוֹנְיָא כַּמָּה הֲוָה, שִׁתִּין בָּתֵּי – זֶה בְּחִינַת תְּפִלָּה, כִּי כְּשֶׁאָנוּ קוֹרְאִין לְהַקָּדוֹשׁ-בָּרוּךְ-הוּא בְּתָאֳרִים שֶׁל בָּשָׂר וָדָם, וְהוּא נִמְצָא לָנוּ בְּכָל קָרְאֵנוּ אֵלָיו – זֶה חֶסֶד הַשֵּׁם יִתְבָּרַךְ, כִּי אִם לֹא הָיָה בְּחַסְדֵּי הַשֵּׁם יִתְבָּרַךְ, לֹא הָיָה כְּדַאי לִקְרֹא וּלְכַנּוֹת אֶת הַשֵּׁם יִתְבָּרַךְ בְּתָאֳרִים וּשְׁבָחִים וְתֵבוֹת וְאוֹתִיּוֹת, אֲבָל זֶה הַכֹּל חֶסֶד שֶׁל הַשֵּׁם יִתְבָּרַךְ. וְזֶה: 'שִׁתִּין בָּתֵּי' – זֶה בְּחִינַת חֶסֶד, בְּחִינַת אַבְרָהָם, כְּמוֹ שֶׁכָּתוּב (שִׁיר הַשִּׁירִים ו): "שִׁשִּׁים הֵמָּה מְלָכוֹת", פֵּרֵשׁ רַשִׁ"י:

majestic, can never suffice; neither as thanksgiving nor as praise. Even such descriptive superlatives as great, awesome and exalted, are mere physical conceptions and fall infinitely short of the praise which is His due. Indeed, any attempt which mortal man makes in this area would almost seem to be an act of arrogance, God forbid. What gives man the right to think that he can say anything about God, when anything he does say will be no more than an inadequate anthropomorphic description of the indescribable Holy One? What is it, therefore, that makes us think that we have the means of praising and praying to Him? Thus, Rebbe Nachman concludes that the right which man has to call out to God and refer to Him in the imagery and utterances of human design is nothing less than a gift from the Holy One Himself. It is a supreme act of lovingkindness that the Creator has bestowed upon His creation; providing all created beings with the benefits which stem from *presuming* to relate, thank and praise Him.

It is therefore essential that a person rouse himself to intense prayer, with total self-sacrifice, particularly when mentioning the words of praise which ascribe attributes to the Holy One. By doing so, he will be worthy of attaching himself to holiness and coming closer to God. For in truth, God's greatness is far beyond our conception and the words we utter in His praise can never be adequate; it is only because of His *chesed* (lovingkindness) that we can even mention them at all (*Mai HaNachal*).

35. **lovingkindness, the aspect of Avraham.** Avraham is known as an *ish chesed* (man of lovingkindness). He is the attribute and *sefirah* of *Chesed* incarnate (see Appendix: The Seven Supernal Shepherds).

LIKUTEY MOHARAN #15:5

And, as is written (Isaiah 60:8), "*MI EiLeH* (Who are these)"—the same letters as *ELoHIM*—"that fly as a cloud."[31] And *deah* is the source of fear.[32]

which was as aKRA (the city) of haGRUNia — This is phonetically similar to "*KRA b'GaRUN* (cry out from the throat)" (Isaiah 58:1). This is a reference to the revealed Torah, as our Sages taught: *l'motzI'eihem* (to those who express them) verbally (*Eruvin* 54a). For by elevating the fear to the aspect of *daat,* one merits the revealed Torah.[33]

And how large was the city of Hagrunia? sixty houses — This corresponds to prayer. For when we call out to the Holy One in the imagery of man and He makes Himself available to us "whenever we call upon Him" (Deuteronomy 4:7), this is God's lovingkindness. This is because, were it not for God's kindnesses, it would not be appropriate to call out and make reference to God with imagery, praises, words and letters. But all this is God's lovingkindness.[34] And this is **sixty houses**—corresponding to lovingkindness, the aspect of Avraham.[35] As it is written (Song of Songs 6:8), "There are sixty kingdoms," which

---

31. **who are these...fly....** The *Tikkuney Zohar* (#20, p.42b) teaches: "In the beginning, *Elohim* created" (Genesis 1:1)—*ELoHIM* (אלהים) is *MI EiLeH* (מי אלה), as in (Isaiah 40:26), "Lift your eyes heavenward and see *mi* (who) created *eileh* (these)." And, as explained earlier (§2, n.13), *Elohim* (the Lord) is the holy name which indicates strength and judgment, and thus corresponds to fear. Thus, "Who are these that fly" denotes the connection which *Elohim*/fear has with the *tzipor* (bird).

32. **source of fear.** Hence, the composite word *tZePhaRDeAh* (צפרדע)—*tZiPoR DeAh* (צפור דעה)—alludes to fear and *daat*, with *daat* being the source of fear (§3 above). Cf. *Likutey Moharan* I, 3.

33. **verbally....** The Talmud teaches (*loc. cit.*): "For they are life *l'motzA'eihem* (למצאיהם, to those who find them)" (Proverbs 4:22)—read this *l'motzI'eihem* (למציאיהם, to those who express them) verbally. Thus, our Sages teach that Torah is the source of life for those who speak it openly—*kra begarun*. This corresponds to the revealed Torah, which one may, and should, always speak about and teach, as opposed to the hidden Torah, which must be carefully guarded from those not suited to learn it (cf. *Chagigah* 11b).

Thus, Rabbah bar bar Chanah's recounting that he saw this *tzephardeah* alludes to his having elevated fear to its source, *daat*. This *tzipor deah* was as the *kra begarun*—i.e., through it he merited the revealed Torah.

34. **God's lovingkindness....** The praise which man utters in his attempt to relate to God, to thank Him, and to depict His greatness is just that—an attempt. Our words, no matter how

LIKUTEY MOHARAN #15:5

'זֶה בְּחִינַת אַבְרָהָם'; 'וּבָתֵּי' – 'לְשׁוֹן בָּתֵּי מַלְכוּת'.

וְזֶה (שָׁם ב): "סַמְּכוּנִי בָּאֲשִׁישׁוֹת" – כְּמוֹ שֶׁמְּשִׂימִין אֲשִׁישׁוֹת כְּנֶגֶד אוֹר גָּדוֹל, כְּדֵי לְהִסְתַּכֵּל בָּאוֹר הַגָּדוֹל עַל־יְדֵי אֲשִׁישׁוֹת, כֵּן גָּזַר חַסְדּוֹ לְסָמְךְ אוֹתָנוּ בַּתְּאָרִים וּשְׁבָחִים הָאֵלּוּ. וְזֶה לְשׁוֹן: "סַמְּכוּנִי", שֶׁהוּא בְּחִינַת סָמֶ"ךְ, וּבְחִינַת שִׁשִּׁים הֵמָּה מְלָכוֹת, בְּחִינַת אַבְרָהָם, שֶׁהוּא בְּחִינַת סָמֶ"ךְ בָּתֵּי.

וְאָתָא תִּנְיָנָא וּבָלַע – תִּנְיָנָא זֶה בְּחִינַת נָחָשׁ, שֶׁמֵּסִית אֶת הָאָדָם שֶׁיִּתְפַּלֵּל לְתוֹעֶלֶת עַצְמוֹ, כְּמוֹ: הַב לָנָא חַיֵּי וּמְזוֹנָא, אוֹ שְׁאָר תּוֹעֶלֶת.

וְאָתֵי פּוּשְׁקַנְצָא וּבָלְעֵהּ – פֵּרֵשׁ רַבֵּנוּ שְׁמוּאֵל, עוֹרֵב; וְאָמְרוּ חֲכָמֵינוּ, זִכְרוֹנָם לִבְרָכָה (עֵרוּבִין כב.): 'מִי שֶׁמַּשְׁחִיר פָּנָיו כְּעוֹרֵב וּמִי שֶׁנַּעֲשֶׂה אַכְזָרִי עַל בָּנָיו כְּעוֹרֵב', הַיְנוּ שֶׁמִּתְפַּלֵּל בְּלִי שׁוּם כַּוָּנַת תּוֹעֶלֶת עַצְמוֹ, וְאֵינוּ חוֹשֵׁב לִכְלוּם אֶת עַצְמוֹ, וְנִתְבַּטֵּל כָּל עַצְמוּתוֹ וְגַשְׁמִיּוּתוֹ, וְנִתְבַּטֵּל כְּאִלּוּ אֵינוֹ בָּעוֹלָם, כְּמוֹ שֶׁכָּתוּב (תְּהִלִּים מ"ד):

---

fear to holy knowledge eventually led to the Torah being revealed, the revealed Torah, through Moshe. Having achieved this level, Yocheved and Miriam were able to offer prayers with such intensity that they actually brought stillborn infants back to life (*Shemot Rabbah* 1:19). Miriam was then rewarded with prophecy. She was able to see the future, corresponding to the *Or HaGanuz*, the hidden Torah.

38. ...rely upon this imagery and praise. Though our words of prayer and praise are no better than *ashashot*—creating a reflected image of the True Light and not depicting the True Light Himself—because of God's lovingkindness we are given permission to rely upon our mirrorlike descriptions and representations.

39. SaMKhuni...SaMeKh...houses. "*Samkhuni b'ashishot...*for I am sick with love" can thus be translated: "I can rely upon the mirrorlike imagery and praises to pray to God because of the quality of the sixty houses of Avraham, who is lovingkindness."

Thus, Rabbah bar bar Chanah said that *akra deHagrunia* was as sixty houses. The revealed Torah to which he merited led him to prayer, and because of the quality of *chesed*, he was able to call out to God in praise and thanks.

40. other similar benefits. This is alluded to above (§4) where Rebbe Nachman teaches that, with his humility, a person should nullify his physical desires so that he can attain the level of prayer where he sheds his garment. For when one acquires Torah he merits prayer, but during this prayer he has to detach himself entirely from corporeality (*Biur HaLikutim*).

LIKUTEY MOHARAN #15:5

Rashi explains as referring to Avraham.[36] And **houses** connotes houses of kingship.[37]

This is the meaning of "*samkhuni b'AShiShoT* (support me with the wine jugs)" (Song of Songs 2:5). This is like holding up *AShaShoT* (crystal reflectors) against a powerful light in order to look at the powerful light through the reflectors. Similarly, His lovingkindness decreed that we be supported by [i.e., rely upon] this imagery and praise.[38] And this is the connotation of *SaMKhuni*, it corresponds to *SaMeKh* (sixty), and to "There are sixty kingdoms." This is the aspect of Avraham, for he corresponds to the *samekh* houses.[39]

A tanina came by and swallowed it — *Tanina* indicates the aspect of a serpent. It lures a person into praying for personal benefit, such as, "Give us life and livelihood" (*Tikkuney Zohar*, p.22a), or other [similar] benefits.[40]

A pushkantza came by and swallowed it — Rashbam explains that this is an *orev*. And our Sages taught: [With whom is the Torah to be found?] With the one who makes his face as black as a raven, and one who makes himself cruel to his children as the raven (*Eruvin* 22a). That is, he prays without any concern for personal benefit. He does not consider himself as having any worth, so that all his selfhood and corporeality are eliminated. He is thus negated, as if he were not in

---

36. **sixty kingdoms...Avraham.** Rashi (*loc. cit.*) explains that the "sixty kingdoms" refers to Avraham and his descendants (Yitzchak, his sons and their sons, Yishmael and his sons, and the sons of Keturah). See also *Likutey Moharan* I, 4:9 that the sixty kingdoms are synonymous with the sixty cities (from another of Rabbah bar bar Chanah's stories), and that these sixty correspond to the sixty letters of the Priestly Blessing (Numbers 6:22-26). This too is a reference to Avraham who, aside from being the paragon of lovingkindness, has God's assurance that he "will be a priest forever" (Psalms 110:4). Yet another allusion of the sixty kingdoms is to the sixty tractates of the Oral Law, the revealed Torah.

37. **...houses of kingship.** The Torah tells us that because the Jewish midwives feared God and refused to follow Pharaoh's orders, "He made houses for them" (Exodus 1:21). Our Sages explain that "houses" refers to the House of Priesthood (Aharon), the Levitical House (Moshe) and the House of Kings (King David) (*Sotah* 11b). The "sixty houses" here alludes to houses of kingship, corresponding to the sixty dynasties established from Avraham's descendants.

Further study of the episode of the Jewish midwives in Egypt provides additional connections to our lesson. Pharaoh commanded the midwives (Yocheved and Miriam) to kill all Jewish males at birth—a period of judgment had descended upon the Jews. But the midwives feared God and they refused to comply with Pharaoh's decree. For this, Yocheved merited giving birth to Moshe, who is the concept of *daat* (above, n.16). Yocheved's elevating

LIKUTEY MOHARAN #15:5

358

"כִּי־עָלֶיךָ הֹרַגְנוּ כָל־הַיּוֹם". וְזֶה בְּחִינַת (שִׁיר־הַשִּׁירִים ה): "שְׁחוֹרוֹת כָּעוֹרֵב". וְעַל־יְדֵי זֶה:

סָלֵק וִיתֵב בְּאִילָנָא – שֶׁזּוֹכֶה לִבְחִינוֹת תּוֹרָה שֶׁבְּנִסְתָּר, כְּמוֹ שֶׁכָּתוּב (תְּהִלִּים י"ח): "יָשֶׁת חֹשֶׁךְ סִתְרוֹ", שֶׁסִּתְרֵי־תּוֹרָה – אָדָם זוֹכֶה לָהֶם עַל־יְדֵי חֹשֶׁךְ, הַיְנוּ מְסִירַת־נֶפֶשׁ, שֶׁמַּשְׁחִיר פָּנָיו כָּעוֹרֵב, כִּי הֵם בְּחִינַת חֹשֶׁךְ עַל שֵׁם עֹמֶק הַמַּשָּׂג. וְזֶה בְּחִינַת: 'סָלֵק וִיתֵב בְּאִילָנָא', שֶׁשָּׁם מָדוֹר הַנְּשָׁמוֹת, כְּמוֹ שֶׁכָּתוּב (זֹהַר מִשְׁפָּטִים צט.): 'כָּל נִשְׁמָתִין מֵאִילָנָא רַבְרְבָא נָפְקִין'.

וְהוּא בְּחִינַת עוֹלָם הַבָּא, שֶׁשָּׁם אֲרִיכוּת יָמִים, כְּמוֹ שֶׁכָּתוּב (יְשַׁעְיָהוּ ס"ה): "כִּימֵי עֵץ יְמֵי עַמִּי". וְזֶה זוֹכֶה עַל־יְדֵי תְּפִלָּה, כִּי 'הַקָּדוֹשׁ־

order to develop spiritually, will find a blessing in his studies. He will merit tasting the hidden Torah, the Hidden Light, in all the laws. In addition, "*shchorot k'orev*" alludes to self-sacrifice in prayer, as rising in the morning represents the morning prayers and staying in the evening refers to the evening prayers (*Mai HaNachal*).

44. black...darkness...deep concepts. The mysteries of the Torah are likened to darkness in that they are hidden from general knowledge and are not easily understood due to their great depth. This relates to the person who has "made his face black" by denying himself the physical so as to be worthy of experiencing the *Or HaGanuz* in this world.

Because of God's *chesed*, Rabbah bar bar Chanah was able to pray with intensity and self-sacrifice. Thus, he relates that the raven swallowed the aspect of the serpent—Rabbah bar bar Chanah made his face as black as an *orev* and paid no attention to his physical needs (cf. Lesson #14:9). This made him worthy of having a taste of the hidden Torah.

45. from the Great Tree. This refers to *Binah*, from where the *neshamah* (soul) emanates (*Zohar HaRakia, loc. cit.*). The Great Tree is also an allusion to the Tree of Life, of which the *Zohar* teaches: It corresponds to *Binah* and to the hidden Torah (*Zohar* III, 124b).

46. the World to Come. The Future World is known as *Olam Haba* (the World to Come). In the teachings of the Ari, this name is explained as a reference to the revelation of *mochin* (mentalities) which are in a constant state of "coming." In the Future World there will be an continuous revelation of these *mochin*, whereas presently, in this world, only those who are allowed to taste of the hidden Torah acquire these *mochin*. In addition, of the ten *sefirot*, the lower seven are associated with the seven days of the week, whereas *Binah*, the eighth *sefirah* (starting from the bottom), is associated with *Olam HaBa* (*Etz Chaim* 15:5). *Binah*, as mentioned above (n.17), is the *sefirah* to which fear must be elevated, because it is *Binah* that provides the *MaNtZPaKh*, the *gevurot* in the *Daat* of *Z'er Anpin* (above, n.16). In other words, when one has acquired revealed Torah and prays intensely and with *mesirat nefesh*, he merits having the Torah's mysteries revealed to him. This hidden Torah is synonymous with the World to Come, when the binds of corporeality will be shed entirely.

359   *LIKUTEY MOHARAN #15:5*

this world,[41] as it is written (Psalms 44:23), "For Your sake, we are killed each day."[42] This corresponds to "black as a raven" (Song of Songs 5:11).[43] And through this:

ascended a tree and sat there — This is meriting the aspect of hidden Torah, as is written (Psalms 18:11), "He made darkness *SiTRo* (His hidden place)." A person merits the *SiTRey* (hidden mysteries of) Torah through darkness—i.e., self-sacrifice—for he "makes his face as black as a raven." For [the hidden Torah] corresponds to darkness due to its deep concepts.[44] And this is: **It ascended a tree and sat there.** [The tree] is the dwelling place of the souls, as is written (*Zohar* II, 99a): All the souls emanate from the Great Tree.[45]

And [the hidden Torah] is an aspect of the World to Come,[46] in which there is length of days, as in (Isaiah 65:22), "As the days of a tree, so shall the days of My people be." This is merited through prayer,

---

41. **...negated...in this world.** The raven is known to be a very cruel bird, even to its own offspring (*Ketuvot* 49b). Like the raven, one who would dedicate himself to coming closer to God so that he might experience the *Or HaGanuz* needs to be totally unmerciful towards his own selfhood and corporeality. When praying, he must negate all his physical interests and focus only on the spiritual needs of his soul. Only through this "cruelty" can one merit insight into the hidden Torah.

42. **killed each day.** Rebbe Nachman explains that a day does not go by without each and every person displaying some form of *mesirat nefesh* (self-sacrifice). People give of themselves for someone or something in many different ways, though ultimately, perfected self-sacrifice is only for God. This *mesirat nefesh* is referred to in, "For Your sake, we are killed each day" (*Likutey Moharan* II, 46). This can be better understood in light of this lesson, because it is during prayer—intense prayer—that one must "kill" all selfhood and sacrifice material benefit for God (*Mai HaNachal*).

Elsewhere, Rebbe Nachman says: When people want to become truly religious and serve God, they seem to be overwhelmed with confusion and frustrations.... The more they want to serve God, the more difficulty they encounter. All the enthusiasm that such people have when trying to do good is very precious, even if their goal is not achieved. All their effort is counted like a sacrifice, in the category of, "For Your sake, we are killed each day." This verse also applies to the person who wants to pray but encounters numerous distractions. If he gives himself over entirely to the task, exerting every effort to pray properly, then even if his prayer is not perfect, his very effort is like bringing a sacrifice (*Rabbi Nachman's Wisdom* #12).

43. **black as a raven.** Concerning this expression "*shchorot k'orev*" (black as a raven), the Talmud teaches that Torah resides only with one who rises early and stays late to study and/ or with one who shows no mercy for his physical well-being so that he "blackens" himself with self-abnegation in order to dedicate himself to Torah study (*Eruvin* 22a). This is deduced from the expression itself: *ShChoRoT* (שחורות) denotes *ShaChaRiT* (שחרית, morning), while *ŒReV* (עורב) denotes *EReV* (ערב, evening) (*Rashi, s.v. shemashkim*). The person who arrives at the house of study early morning and stays late into the night, enduring physical hardships in

LIKUTEY MOHARAN #15:5,6 360

בָּרוּךְ־הוּא מִתְאַוֶּה לִתְפִלָּתָן שֶׁל יִשְׂרָאֵל'.

וּכְשֶׁיִּשְׂרָאֵל מִתְפַּלְּלִין לְפָנָיו וּמְמַלְּאִין תַּאֲוָתוֹ, אֲזַי נַעֲשָׂה כִּבְיָכוֹל בִּבְחִינַת אִשָּׁה, שֶׁהוּא מְקַבֵּל תַּעֲנוּג מֵעִמָּנוּ, כְּמוֹ שֶׁכָּתוּב (בְּמִדְבַּר כ"ח): "אִשֵּׁה רֵיחַ נִיחֹחַ לַה'" – עַל־יְדֵי הָרֵיחַ נִיחוֹחַ שֶׁמְּקַבֵּל נַעֲשָׂה בִּבְחִינַת אִשָּׁה, "וּנְקֵבָה תְּסוֹבֵב גָּבֶר" (יִרְמְיָה ל"א), שֶׁהַקָּדוֹשׁ־בָּרוּךְ־הוּא נַעֲשָׂה בִּבְחִינַת מַלְבּוּשׁ נִגְלֶה, הַיְנוּ מִבְּחִינַת שֶׁהָיָה מִתְּחִלָּה בְּנִסְתָּר, עַכְשָׁו נִתְגַּלֶּה עַל־יְדֵי הַתְּפִלָּה, וְקֻדְשָׁא־ בְּרִיךְ־הוּא וְאוֹרַיְתָא כֹּלָּא חַד, וְאָז עַל־יְדֵי הַתְּפִלָּה נִתְגַּלֶּה אוֹרַיְתָא, הַיְנוּ סִתְרֵי אוֹרַיְתָא.

תָּא חֲזֵי כַּמָּה נָפִישׁ חֵילָא דְּאִילָנָא – הַיְנוּ, כַּמָּה נָפִישׁ חֵילָא דְּהַאי סִתְרֵי־תּוֹרָה, שֶׁאֵין יְכוֹלִים לְהִתְלַבֵּשׁ בְּשׁוּם דָּבָר מֻגְבָּל, בְּשׁוּם גּוּף, אֶלָּא בְּמִי שֶׁמַּשְׁחִיר פָּנָיו כְּעוֹרֵב וְנַעֲשָׂה כְּעוֹרֵב עַל בָּנָיו:

ו. וְזֶה בְּחִינַת: 'חֲמִשָּׁה קִנְיָנִים שֶׁקָּנָה בְּעוֹלָמוֹ'.

to the "garment" which the Holy One adorns in order to reveal Himself to the one He is courting.

50. **God and the Torah are one.** So that when God is revealed, so is the hidden Torah.

51. **only in the one ....** Elsewhere, Rebbe Nachman taught that when one transcends earthly interests and attachments, he can grasp the entire Torah. He will not forget what he has learned because his incorporeality enables him to encompass the limitless spirituality of the Torah. But when one brings corporeality to the words of Torah and causes them to take on crass physicality, he will only be able to grasp certain aspects of the Torah, never its entirety. If he attempts to absorb new understanding in his limited mind, he will find that it responds the way anything physical would when full: the old is removed, forgotten in favor of the new (*Likutey Moharan* I, 110).

Thus, Rabbah bar bar Chanah saw the *orev* ascending the tree—he was able to divest himself of his attachment to this world. He ascended to the level of *Binah,* to the World to Come, to the mysteries of the Torah. By transcending his own corporeality, his mind was able to absorb and encompass that which is normally too deep for human perception and understanding. Having been freed from these constraints, the hidden Torah was no longer concealed from him (above, nn.28,29).

In the lesson, we find no explanation of the conclusion of Rabbah bar bar Chanah's story, in which Rabbi Papa the son of Shmuel said: "Had I not been there, I would never have believed him!" Although there is no evidence that Rebbe Nachman ever said anything about this, the Tcheriner Rav (author of the *Parparaot LeChokhmah*) did offer an

LIKUTEY MOHARAN #15:5,6

for the Holy One desires the prayer of the Jewish people (cf. *Chullin* 60b).[47]

And, when the Jews pray before Him and satisfy His desire, then [God], as it were, takes on the aspect of *IShaH* (the feminine). This is because He receives pleasure from us, as is written (Numbers 28:8), "It is an *ISheH* (fire offering), an appeasing fragrance to God." Through the appeasing fragrance that He receives, He takes on the feminine aspect.[48] And, [because] "The female shall court the male" (Jeremiah 31:21),[49] the Holy One takes on the aspect of a "revealed garment." In other words, that aspect which was originally hidden is now revealed through prayer. And, God and the Torah are one (*Zohar* III, 73a).[50] Thus, through prayer, Torah is revealed—i.e., the hidden mysteries of the Torah.

Come and see how great was the strength of that tree! — That is, [come see] how great is the strength of those mysteries of Torah. It cannot be clothed in anything finite or physical, but only in the one who "makes his face as black as a raven" and behaves as a raven to his children.[51]

6. {There are five possessions which the Holy One acquired in His world: Torah is one possession; heaven and earth are one possession; Avraham is one possession; Israel [the Jewish people] is one possession; the Holy Temple is one possession (*Avot* 6:10).}

---

47. **prayer of the Jewish people.** The Talmud (*loc. cit.*) explains this as God's desiring the prayers of specific tzaddikim. In our context, Rebbe Nachman applies this to the prayers of one who has attained such a great degree of humility that he has successfully nullified his own being. His prayers, like those of one with a broken and contrite heart (§4), *are* the prayers of the tzaddikim.

48. **IShaH...ISheH...the feminine aspect.** Every creation falls into one of two categories: either *mashpiah* (giver), the masculine principle; or *nishpah* (receiver), the feminine principle. Vis-a-vis the Holy One, however, all aspects of creation are beneficiaries, while God, who is always providing the world with *shefa*, is the benefactor. Nevertheless, when the Jewish people perform the mitzvot, we provide God with pleasure. Then we become the *mashpiah* and He the *nishpah*, as it were. This is alluded to in, "It is an *isheh* (אשה, a fire offering)... to God." Through our giving and His receiving, God, so to speak, takes on the quality of *ishah* (אשה), the feminine aspect.

49. **female shall court the male.** Although the present custom is for the male to take the active role in seeking a marriage partner (*Kiddushin* 2b), there will come a time, said Yirmiyahu, when this will be reversed, when the woman will court the man. In our context, this relates to when God becomes the beneficiary. Then He, as it were, courts the man who—through self-sacrificing and intense prayer—has provided God with pleasure. How does God court man? He reveals Himself to him. Rebbe Nachman deduces this from the verse itself. The word here translated as "court" is *t'soveiv*, which literally means to surround or envelop. It thus alludes

LIKUTEY MOHARAN #15:6

362

'תּוֹרָה קִנְיָן אֶחָד' – זֶה בְּחִינַת תּוֹרָה שֶׁבְּנִגְלֶה;

'שָׁמַיִם וָאָרֶץ קִנְיָן אֶחָד' – זֶה בְּחִינַת הַעֲלָאַת הַיִּרְאָה לַדַּעַת;

'אָרֶץ' זֶה בְּחִינַת יִרְאָה כַּנַּ"ל, 'וְשָׁמַיִם' זֶה בְּחִינַת דַּעַת, כִּי דַּעַת

הוּא חִבּוּר, כְּמוֹ שֶׁכָּתוּב (בְּרֵאשִׁית ד): "וְהָאָדָם יָדַע". וְזֶה בְּחִינַת

'שָׁמַיִם' – אֵשׁ וּמַיִם מְחֻבָּרִין יַחַד.

'אַבְרָהָם קִנְיָן אֶחָד' – זֶה בְּחִינַת תְּפִלָּה, בְּחִינַת שִׁתִּין בָּתֵּי, שִׁשִּׁים

הֵמָּה מְלָכוֹת כַּנַּ"ל.

'יִשְׂרָאֵל קִנְיָן אֶחָד' – זֶה בְּחִינַת מִשְׁפָּט הַמַּעֲלֶה אֶת הַיִּרְאָה כַּנַּ"ל,

כְּמוֹ שֶׁכָּתוּב (תְּהִלִּים קמ"ז): "חֻקָּיו וּמִשְׁפָּטָיו לְיִשְׂרָאֵל".

'בֵּית-הַמִּקְדָּשׁ קִנְיָן אֶחָד' – זֶה בְּחִינַת סִתְרֵי אוֹרַיְתָא, שֶׁזּוֹכִין לָהֶם

עַל-יְדֵי הַתְּפִלָּה, שֶׁהִיא בְּחִינַת אַבְרָהָם. וְזֶה (שָׁם ע"ח): "הַר זֶה

קָנְתָה יְמִינוֹ", שֶׁזֶּה יָמִין, בְּחִינַת תְּפִלָּה, בְּחִינַת אַבְרָהָם. וְנִקְרָא הַר

עַל שֵׁם עֹמֶק הַמַּשָּׂג; וְנִקְרָא בֵּית-הַמִּקְדָּשׁ, בְּחִינוֹת קֹדֶשׁ, בְּחִינוֹת

רֵאשִׁית; "וְכָל זָר לֹא יֹאכַל קֹדֶשׁ" (וַיִּקְרָא כ"ב) – וְלֹא יֹאכַל בּוֹ

(אש) and *mayim* (מים), alluding to the heaven being a combination of fire and water. Conceptually, this denotes a union between *chasadim* (benevolences) from *Chokhmah* (water) and *gevurot* (severities) from *Binah* (fire), which together form *Daat/daat* (see Lesson #13, n.6). Thus, in the context of the lesson, *shamayim* symbolizes *daat*.

56. **sixty...as above.** See section 5, notes 34-39.

57. **judgments to Israel.** Israel is thus symbolic of judgment, the means by which fear is elevated to its source (§2).

58. **Avraham....** Rebbe Nachman will now show the connection which the Holy Temple has with the hidden Torah. Avraham, as mentioned, represents prayer. As the *ish chesed,* he corresponds to the right side (cf. Lesson #12, n.41).

59. **deep concepts.** As above, the hidden Torah corresponds to darkness, its mysteries have great depth and cannot be easily understood. The verse thus reads: **This mountain** — the deep and hidden Torah, **which his right hand** — prayer — **has acquired.**

60. **holiness/first.** "Israel is holy to God, the first-fruits of his produce..." (Jeremiah 2:3). Holiness is synonymous with first; first-fruits, first-born, "first in Divine thought" (*Bereishit Rabbah* 1:5; cf. Lesson #14:3).

61. **No non-priest may eat....** It is forbidden for someone who is not a *kohein* (priest) to eat from the sacrifices of the Temple. In the context of the lesson, Rebbe Nachman teaches that only the holy, the priest/the man of *chesed*/Avraham, may partake of the Torah's mysteries. However, a person who has not attained the level of intense prayer will not be able to partake of the holy, the *Or HaGanuz.*

363   *LIKUTEY MOHARAN #15:6*

This corresponds to, "There are five possessions which He acquired in His world...."[52]

Torah is one possession — This corresponds to the revealed Torah.

heaven and earth are one possession — This is the aspect of elevating fear to *daat*. "Earth" corresponds to fear, as mentioned above.[53] "Heaven" corresponds to *daat,* because *daat* (knowledge) is union, as in (Genesis 4:1), "The man knew [Chavah, his wife]."[54] And this corresponds to *ShaMaYiM* (heaven): *aiSh* (fire) and *MaYiM* (water) bound together.[55]

Avraham is one possession — This corresponds to prayer, the aspect of sixty houses, "there are sixty kingdoms," as above.[56]

Israel is one possession — This is the aspect of judgment, which elevates fear, as explained. As is written (Psalms 147:19), "His statutes and His judgments to Israel."[57]

The Holy Temple is one possession — This corresponds to the mysteries of the Torah, which are merited through prayer, the aspect of Avraham.[58]

And this is: "This mountain, which His right hand has acquired" (Psalms 78:54). "Right" corresponds to prayer, the aspect of Avraham. And [the hidden Torah] is called "mountain" due to its deep concepts.[59] It is also called Holy Temple, the aspect of holiness/first,[60] [as in] (Leviticus 22:10), "No non-priest may eat that which is holy"[61]—

---

explanation based upon the Rebbe's lesson. The Talmud tells us that Rabbi Papa was the *dayan* (judge) in Pumbedita (*Sanhedrin* 17b). In our context, this alludes to his practicing *hitbodedut*—he was constantly elevating fear to its source by instituting justice. He said, "Had I not been there"—practicing justice, "I would never have believed him"—that there exists such an *akrukta*. He never would have believed Rabbah bar bar Chanah that it is possible to elevate fear to its source, *daat,* and thereby attain the revealed Torah...the ability to pray intensely...and revelations into the hidden Torah. All this was accomplished through *hitbodedut,* the concept of judgment (*Mai HaNachal*).

52. **five possessions....** Rebbe Nachman will now connect the themes of this lesson to the five acquisitions mentioned in *Avot.*

53. **mentioned above.** See section 2 and note 4.

54. **man knew...his wife.** Adam cohabited with Chavah, the concept of union (see below, n.73). So, too, the *sefirah* of *Daat* is not one of the Ten *Sefirot,* but a combination, a union, of *Chokhmah* and *Binah* (see Appendix: The Structure of the Sefirot).

55. **aiSh and MaYiM bound together.** The word *ShaMaYiM* (שמים) is a combination of *aish*

LIKUTEY MOHARAN #15:6,7

364

אֶלָּא מִקְדָּשָׁיו וּמִקְרָאָיו, וּבֵית־הַמִּקְדָּשׁ הוּא בְּחִינַת סִתְרֵי אוֹרַיְתָא:

ז. וְזֶהוּ פֵּרוּשׁ: וְאַתֶּם תִּהְיוּ לִי מַמְלֶכֶת כֹּהֲנִים.
מַמְלֶכֶת – זֶה בְּחִינַת תּוֹרָה שֶׁבְּנִגְלֶה, כִּי "בָּהּ מְלָכִים יִמְלֹכוּ"
(מִשְׁלֵי ח), וּמַלְכוּת הוּא בְּחִינָה נִגְלָה, כִּי 'אֵין מֶלֶךְ בְּלֹא עָם', וְהַכֹּל
צְרִיכִין לְמֶלֶךְ, כִּי הַכֹּל צְרִיכִין לְמָרֵי חִטַּיָּא.

וְכֹהֲנִים – זוֹ בְּחִינַת תְּפִלָּה, בְּחִינוֹת אַבְרָהָם כַּנַּ"ל, כְּמוֹ שֶׁאָמְרוּ
חֲכָמֵינוּ, זִכְרוֹנָם לִבְרָכָה (נְדָרִים לב.), שֶׁאָמַר הַקָּדוֹשׁ־בָּרוּךְ־הוּא
לְאַבְרָהָם: אַתָּה כֹהֵן לְעוֹלָם וְכוּ'.

וְגוֹי קָדוֹשׁ – זֶה בְּחִינַת בֵּית־הַמִּקְדָּשׁ, בְּחִינוֹת תּוֹרָה שֶׁבְּנִסְתָּר,
הַנִּקְרָא קֹדֶשׁ. וְעַל־יְדֵי מַה זוֹכֶה לְאֵלּוּ הַבְּחִינוֹת? עַל־יְדֵי שֶׁיַּעֲלֶה
וִיקַשֵּׁר בְּחִינַת יִרְאָה לִבְחִינַת דַּעַת עַל־יְדֵי בְּחִינַת מִשְׁפָּט כַּנַּ"ל.

this when he offered his son Yitzchak as a sacrifice to God. This corresponds to the cruelty which one must show to one's children, mentioned above (§5:end) (*Biur HaLikutim*).

64. **kings rule.** The verse reads, "With me, kings rule." Our Sages taught: "With me" refers to the Torah (*Gittin* 62a). The verse asserts that the rule of Jewish kings stands on Torah law (*Rashi, loc. cit.*).

65. **revealed...everyone has need of a king....** A king is one who rules openly, a sovereign over subjects. Thus, "kingdom" alludes to the revealed Torah.

Rebbe Nachman points out that everyone has need of a king. Taken in a literal sense, this can be connected to the teaching of our Sages: Pray for the well-being of the kingdom/government. Were it not for the fear which men have for authority, they would swallow each other alive (*Avot* 3:2). Just as people who provide ready grain are vital to society's functioning, so are kings and figures of authority. In the context of the lesson, this can be understood on deeper level. Here, "kings" alludes to the Torah scholars, masters of the revealed Torah, as in the Talmudic teaching from which Rebbe Nachman quoted immediately prior to this: How do you know that the rabbis are called kings? For it is written, "With me, kings rule"—with the Torah, rabbis rule.

66. **priest forever.** See above note 36. The "*kohein*" corresponds to the *sefirah* of *Chesed* and thus to Avraham, the paradigm of *chesed* and the symbol of prayer.

67. **holy nation....** The "holy nation" alludes to the Holy Temple, the concept of the hidden Torah, as above (§6:end).

68. **as above.** See section 2. As explained (n.6), this judgment is the practice of *hitbodedut*.

365   *LIKUTEY MOHARAN #15:6,7*

the only ones that may eat of it are His holy ones and those whom He called [to partake].[62] And the Holy Temple corresponds to the mysteries of the Torah.[63]

7. And this is the explanation of [the opening verse]:

"You will be to Me a kingdom of priests and a holy nation. {These are the *devarim* (words) that you should *daber* (speak) to the Children of Israel.}"

kingdom — This corresponds to the revealed Torah, because with it "kings rule" (Proverbs 8:15).[64] Kingship is the aspect of revealed, for a king without a nation is no king. And everyone has need of a king, because "everyone requires the grain merchant."[65]

priests — This is synonymous with prayer, the aspect of Avraham. As our Sages taught: The Holy One said to Avraham (Psalms 110:4), "You are a priest forever" (*Nedarim* 32b).[66]

and a holy nation — This is the aspect of the Holy Temple—the hidden Torah which is called holy.[67] And how can we merit achieving these aspects? by elevating and binding the aspect of fear to knowledge through the aspect of judgment, as above.[68] And this is:

---

62. **called to partake.** This is a paraphrasing of the verse in Zefaniah (1:7), "For God has prepared a festive meal (offering), He has bid (made holy) His invited guests [to partake]" (see *Metzudat Tzion, loc. cit.*). That is, God calls to those whose prayers He desires, the humble person who prays intensely, with self-sacrifice. This person will taste the Hidden Light.

63. **Holy Temple...mysteries of the Torah.** This refers to the Holy of Holies in the Temple. It was concealed, situated in the innermost section of God's House, and excepting the High Priest on Yom Kippur, no one was permitted to enter. This corresponds to the hidden Torah (*Zohar* III, 33a).

    The five possessions which the Holy One acquired are as follows: 1) *Israel* is the judgment that elevates fear to its source; 2) *heaven and earth* are the source, *daat*; 3) *Torah* is the revealed Torah one attains when he elevates fear to *daat*; 4) *Avraham* is prayer which one merits through the revealed Torah; 5) *the Holy Temple* is the hidden Torah which one merits by praying intensely.

    It is worth noting that it was Avraham who called the site of the Holy Temple "*har HaShem yeiraeh* (the mountain that God will appear upon)" (Genesis 22:14). This ties in with our context in that Avraham symbolizes prayer, through which one can merit insight into the mysteries of Torah. This comes about through *YeiRAeH/YiRAH* (fear), the elevation of which brings one to a taste of the *Or HaGanuz* (*Mai HaNachal*). In addition, Avraham said

LIKUTEY MOHARAN #15:7,8

וְזֶהוּ: **אֵלֶּה הַדְּבָרִים אֲשֶׁר תְּדַבֵּר** – זֶה בְּחִינַת יִרְאָה, הַנִּקְרָא דָּבָר, כִּי עִקַּר הַדִּבּוּר שָׁם הוּא, כְּמוֹ שֶׁאָמְרוּ חֲכָמֵינוּ, זִכְרוֹנָם לִבְרָכָה (בְּרָכוֹת וּ): 'מִי שֶׁיֵּשׁ בּוֹ יִרְאַת־שָׁמַיִם, דְּבָרָיו נִשְׁמָעִים'. מֹשֶׁה – הוּא בְּחִינַת דַּעַת, וְזֶה: 'אֲשֶׁר תְּדַבֵּר' דַּיְקָא; וְזֶה (שְׁמוֹת י"ח): "כִּי יִהְיֶה לָהֶם דָּבָר בָּא אֵלַי", שֶׁיִּשְׂרָאֵל שֶׁהֵם בְּחִינַת מִשְׁפָּט כַּנַּ"ל, הֵם מַעֲלִין וּמְקַשְּׁרִין (הַיִּרְאָה) לִבְחִינַת משֶׁה, לִבְחִינַת דַּעַת. וְזֶה: **אֶל בְּנֵי יִשְׂרָאֵל** – דַּיְקָא, כִּי הֵם בְּחִינַת מִשְׁפָּט, כְּמוֹ שֶׁכָּתוּב: "חֻקָּיו וּמִשְׁפָּטָיו לְיִשְׂרָאֵל".

נִמְצָא, שֶׁעַל־יְדֵי שֶׁמְּקַשְּׁרִין הַיִּרְאָה עַל־יְדֵי מִשְׁפָּט לִבְחִינַת דַּעַת, זוֹכִין לַתּוֹרָה שֶׁל נִגְלֶה, וְעַל־יְדֵי תּוֹרָה שֶׁבְּנִגְלֶה זוֹכִין לִתְפִלָּה, וְעַל־יְדֵי תְּפִלָּה זוֹכִין לְסִתְרֵי אוֹרַיְתָא.

דָּבָר – זֶה בְּחִינַת יִרְאָה, כְּמוֹ שֶׁכָּתוּב (מַלְאָכִי ג): "אָז נִדְבְּרוּ יִרְאֵי ה'":

ח. זֹאת הַתּוֹרָה שַׁיָּךְ עַל פָּסוּק: "עֵינַי בְּנֶאֶמְנֵי אֶרֶץ" וְכוּ'. **עֵינַי** – זֶה בְּחִינוֹת דַּעַת, כְּמוֹ שֶׁכָּתוּב (בְּרֵאשִׁית ג): "וַתִּפָּקַחְנָה עֵינֵי שְׁנֵיהֶם". גַּם דַּעַת הֵם עֶשֶׂר שְׁמוֹת [הֲוַיָ"ה], גִּימַטְרִיָּא שְׁנֵי פְּעָמִים עַיִן כַּיָּדוּעַ.

---

words — through the fear of Heaven — **that you [Moshe]** — when elevated to *daat*, **should speak to the children of Israel** — by means of *hitbodedut*, self-judgment, which elevates fear.

73. **eyes...were opened.** "My eyes" alludes to *daat* (holy knowledge). See Rashi on Genesis 3:7.

74. **ten times the holy name...** As explained, *Daat* of *Z'er Anpin* contains five *chasadim* and five *gevurot* (above, n.16). These ten correspond to 10 variations of the Tetragrammaton, each punctuated by a different vowel point. The Tetragrammaton (יהוה) itself has a numerical value of 26. Thus, the 10 holy names equal 260. The numerical value of the word *ayin* (eye, עין) is half that, 130 (see Appendix: Gematria Chart). Therefore, "And the eyes...were opened" alludes to "twice *ayin*" (plural, 260), the eyes corresponding to *daat*.

75. **faithful...Aharon....** The Midrash (*loc. cit.*) teaches: "My eyes are upon the faithful" (Psalms 101:6)—this alludes to Aharon. God told Moshe to appoint a *kohein*, but Moshe did not know from which tribe to choose this priest. "Choose from your own tribe," God said, for "My eyes are upon the faithful." As the High Priest, Aharon connotes the aspect of judgment. He bore the judgment of Israel upon his heart—through judgment, he elevated fear to its source, to *daat* which is in *Binah* (n.18 above).

LIKUTEY MOHARAN #15:7,8

These are the devarim (words) which you should daber (speak) — This corresponds to fear which is called "word." This is because the essence of speech is there [in fear], as our Sages taught: When a person has fear of Heaven, his words are listened to (*Berakhot* 6b).[69] Moshe is the aspect of *daat*.[70] This is, **which you should daber**—specifically ["*daber*"]! And this is: "If they should have *davar* (a word) between them, they come to me" (Exodus 18:16)—because Israel, who is the aspect of judgment,[71] elevates and binds fear to Moshe, to the aspect of *daat*. And this is:

to the Children of Israel — Specifically! for they are the aspect of judgment, as in, "His statutes and His judgments to Israel."

Thus, by binding fear to the aspect of *daat* through judgment, we merit revealed Torah. Through the revealed Torah we merit prayer. And through prayer, we merit the mysteries of the Torah.

DaVaR — This corresponds to fear, as is written (Malakhi 3:16), "Then those who fear God *niDBRu* (spoke)."[72]

8. This lesson applies to the verse:
"My eyes are upon the faithful of the earth, that they should dwell with Me. He that goes in the way of perfection, he will serve me" (Psalms 101:6).

My eyes — This is the aspect of *daat*, as in (Genesis 3:7), "And the eyes of both of them were opened."[73] Also, *daat* is ten [times] the holy name {*YHVH*}, which is numerically equivalent to twice *ayin* (eye), as is known (see *Etz Chaim, Shaar* 25:2).[74]

the faithful — This is the aspect of Aharon, as is brought in Midrash *Shocher Tov* (#101). And Aharon corresponds to judgment, as in (Exodus 28:30), "Aharon bore the judgment of the Children of Israel."[75]

Aaron wore the Chashen mishpar

---

69. **his words are listened to.** "Words which you should speak" alludes to fear, because when one has fear of Heaven, his words are respected and heeded. In contrast to this, without fear, one's words are not accepted. And, as Rebbe Nachman teaches elsewhere, "Words that are not listened to and heeded are not words at all" (*Likutey Moharan* I, 29:1). It is as if they were never spoken. Thus, a vital ingredient of speech is fear.

70. **Moshe is the aspect of daat.** See above, note 16.

71. **Israel...judgment.** Above, section 6 and note 57.

72. **those who fear God spoke.** In the lesson's context, this verse reads: "Then there is speech, when the words (דברים) are spoken (נדברו) by those who fear God."

We now have a deeper understanding of the lesson's opening verse: **You will be to me a kingdom** — revealed Torah — **of priests** — which brings to prayer, **and a holy nation** — and to the partaking of the Hidden Light, the hidden Torah. How are these achieved? **These are the**

LIKUTEY MOHARAN #15:8

בְּנֶאֱמְנֵי – זֶה בְּחִינַת אַהֲרֹן, כַּמּוּבָא בְּמִדְרַשׁ שׁוֹחֵר טוֹב; וְאַהֲרֹן הוּא בְּחִינַת מִשְׁפָּט, כְּמוֹ שֶׁכָּתוּב (שְׁמוֹת כ"ח): "וְנָשָׂא אַהֲרֹן אֶת מִשְׁפַּט בְּנֵי יִשְׂרָאֵל".

אֶרֶץ – זֶה בְּחִינוֹת יִרְאָה כַּנַּ"ל.

לָשֶׁבֶת עִמָּדִי – זֶה בְּחִינוֹת סִינַי, שִׁפְלוּת, "אֶשְׁכֹּן אֶת דַּכָּא" (יְשַׁעְיָהוּ נ"ז) כַּנַּ"ל.

הֹלֵךְ בְּדֶרֶךְ תָּמִים – זֶה בְּחִינוֹת תְּפִלָּה, בְּחִינַת אַבְרָהָם כַּנַּ"ל, כְּמוֹ שֶׁכָּתוּב (בְּרֵאשִׁית י"ז): "הִתְהַלֵּךְ לְפָנַי וֶהְיֵה תָמִים".

הוּא יְשָׁרְתֵנִי – זֶה בְּחִינַת סִתְרֵי אוֹרַיְתָא, זֶה בְּחִינַת הוּא, בְּחִינוֹת עוֹלָם הַבָּא (זֹהַר וַיֵּצֵא קנד: קנח:):

בָּרוּךְ הַבּוֹחֵר בַּעֲדַת מִי מָנָה, אֲשֶׁר עַד כֹּה עֲזָרָנוּ לִשְׁמֹעַ פְּלָאוֹת כָּאֵלֶּה עַל מַאֲמְרֵי רַבָּה בַּר בַּר־חָנָה. תָּא חֲזִי כַּמָּה נָפִישׁ חֵילֵהּ דְּהַאי אִילָנָא. כְּעַן בִּרְשׁוּתָא דְּמַלְכָּא עִלָּאָה, קֳדָמֵיכוֹן יַסִּיק לְתַמִּידָא אִמְרֵי יָאֵי, רַב טוּב הַצָּפוּן וְגָנוּז בְּמַאֲמָרִין קַדִּישִׁין דְּאַרְיָוָתָא דְּבֵי עִלָּאָה, אִנּוּן מְחַצְּדֵי חַקְלָא דַּהֲווֹ מִשְׁתָּעֵי, דִּי בְּהוֹן גְּנִיזִין עֲטִין קַדִּישִׁין דְּנַפְקִין מֵאוֹרַיְתָא דְּעַתִּיקָא סְתִימָאָה. לְכוּ חֲזוּ מִפְעֲלוֹת ה', דַּרְכּוֹ נִפְלָאָה, רָבָה אִילָנָא וּתְקֵף, וְרוּמֵהּ מָטָא לְצֵית שְׁמַיָּא, וַחֲזוֹתֵהּ לְסוֹף כָּל אַרְעָא, אִנְבֵּהּ סַגִּיא וְחֶזְוֵהּ יָאֵי. שִׁמְעוּ וּתְחִי נַפְשְׁכֶם, וּשְׁאַבְתֶּם מַיִם בְּשָׂשׂוֹן מִמַּעְיְנֵי הַיְשׁוּעָה.

We can now understand this verse as follows: **My eyes** — *daat* — **are upon the faithful of the earth** — to which fear is elevated through judgment/*hitbodedut;* **that they should dwell with Me** — enables one to acquire the revealed Torah which corresponds to Sinai and humility. **He that goes in the way of perfection** — Through humility one comes to intense prayer; **he will serve Me** — and with intense prayer one merits insight into the mysteries of the Torah. He will thus experience a taste of the *Or HaGanuz* that will be revealed in the World to Come.

LIKUTEY MOHARAN #15:8

the earth — This corresponds to fear, as above.[76]

should dwell with Me — This alludes to Sinai, humility; "I dwell with the humble" (Isaiah 57:15), as above.[77]

He that goes in the way of perfection — This is the aspect of prayer, the aspect of Avraham, as is written (Genesis 17:1), "Go before Me and be perfect."[78]

he will serve me — This alludes to the mysteries of the Torah, corresponding to "he," an aspect of the World to Come (Zohar I, 154b).[79]

---

76. **above.** See section 2 and note 4.

77. **dwell with the humble, as above.** See the end of section 4. God resides only with the humble. Of the haughty God says, "I and he cannot abide in the same world" (Sotah 5a). Of the humble He says, "They shall dwell with Me."

78. **be perfect.** This was said to Avraham when he circumcised himself. Hence, perfection/completeness is said in reference to Avraham, who represents intense prayer/complete service (cf. Lesson #14:8).

79. **mysteries of the Torah...he...World to Come.** "You," as a second person pronoun, indicates familiarity and thus connotes the known and revealed Torah. "He," as a third person pronoun, indicates remoteness and thus connotes the mysteries of the hidden Torah (Zohar I, 154b).

LIKUTEY MOHARAN #16:1 — 370

לִיקוּטֵי מוהר"ן סִימָן ט"ז

רַבִּי יוֹחָנָן מִשְׁתָּעֵי: זִמְנָא חֲדָא הֲוָה   רַשְׁבָּ"ם:

קָאָזְלִינַן בִּסְפִינְתָּא, וַחֲזֵינָא הַאי   וְנָפִיק – וְשָׁפַךְ. אוּסְיָא – נְחִירָיו.

כַּוְרָא דְּאַפִּיק רֵישֵׁהּ מִמַּיָּא, וְדַמְיָא   מַבְּרֵי דְסוּרָא – נְהָרוֹת שֶׁבְּסוּרָא.

עֵינֵהּ כִּתְרֵי סַהֲרֵי, וְנָפִיק מַיָּא מִתַּרְתֵּי אוּסְיָא כִּתְרֵי מַבְּרֵי דְסוּרָא

(בָּבָא בַּתְרָא עד.).

וַחֲזֵינָא הַאי כַּוְרָא – שֶׁהוּא הַצַּדִּיק, הַמְכֻנֶּה בְּשֵׁם דָּג, כַּיָּדוּעַ:

דְּאַפִּיק רֵישֵׁהּ מִמַּיָּא, וְדַמְיָא עֵינֵהּ כִּתְרֵי סַהֲרֵי, וְנָפִיק מַיָּא מִתַּרְתֵּי

אוּסְיָא כִּתְרֵי מַבְּרֵי דְסוּרָא – כִּי אִי אֶפְשָׁר לַצַּדִּיק לִהְיוֹת מַחֲשַׁבְתּוֹ

מְשׁוֹטֵט תָּמִיד בְּחָכְמוֹת עֶלְיוֹנוֹת, כִּי לִפְעָמִים צָרִיךְ לָצֵאת לַחוּץ

understandable that he does not want to return to the physical. Yet, he must. As long as God sees fit to keep his soul housed in a body, man—the tzaddik—must never do anything that would lead to his divesting himself of corporeality altogether. God therefore created certain "obstructions," physical hindrances which pull the tzaddik back into the lower levels and away from his being totally immersed in the Divine. Even so, this is only a temporary stage, a means for him to rise to still higher and more unfathomable levels of spirituality. However, when Mashiach comes, all physical obstacles will cease to exist. The tzaddik will then be able to remain permanently attached to the upper levels, the upper wisdom. And, as Rebbe Nachman explains, this tzaddik who encompasses the two Messiahs will then draw all the nations unto him and teach them the word of God.

2. **tzaddik...fish....** The *Mai HaNachal* explains that the sea which Rabbi Yochanan alludes to is the sea of wisdom. Indeed, water is often said to symbolize Torah and wisdom, as in (Isaiah 11:9), "The earth shall be filled with the knowledge of God as the waters cover the sea." Thus, the tzaddik is likened to a fish. Just as a fish spends its life immersed in water, the tzaddik spends his life immersed in the wisdom of the Torah and in cleaving to God.

3. **pondering upper wisdoms.** A tzaddik is not content with a surface or simple understanding of Torah. He is always in search of greater comprehension of God's word, for he knows that this will bring him closer to God Himself. Yet, this level of attachment to and pondering of upper wisdom, a level far greater than the average person can hope for, is not something which even the greatest tzaddik can hope to achieve on a permanent basis. Not now, in any case. As Rebbe Nachman will explain, with the world in its present imperfected state, the tzaddik must remove himself from this *devekut* (cleaving to and longing for God) and engage in mundane matters as well.

LIKUTEY MOHARAN #16[1]

Rabbi Yochanan related: One time, we were travelling by ship and we saw this fish which had raised its head out of the water. His eyes resembled two moons and he *nafitz* (spouted out) water from his two nostrils like the two rivers of Sura *(Bava Batra 74a).*

Rashbam:

spouted out - poured out: **nostrils** - the holes in its nose: **rivers of Sura** - rivers in Syria:

We saw this fish — This is the tzaddik who is called a fish, as is known (cf. *MeOrey Or, dag*).[2]

[handwritten marginalia: Tzadik can't live without Torah. Torah likened to water. tzadik = fish]

[left margin handwritten: w Sifrei Kabbala]

which had raised its head out of the water. His eyes resembled two moons and he spouted out water from his two nostrils like the two rivers of Sura — For it is impossible for the tzaddik to always ponder upper wisdoms.[3] There are times when he has to move outside [of these

---

1. **Likutey Moharan #16.** This lesson was taught on a Shabbat morning some time during the summer of 5563 (1803). A large number of Rebbe Nachman's followers had come to Breslov to be with him. Their gathering was unexpected, as this particular Shabbat was not one of the fixed times when the Rebbe's followers would come together (cf. *Tzaddik* #23). Initially, Rebbe Nachman expressed a certain displeasure and remarked that his followers were making Shabbat gatherings on their own. At the morning gathering he gave this lesson, mentioning that there are seventy nations divided between the domains of Esav and Yishmael. He also spoke of the tzaddik who encompasses the two Messiahs. With so many people pressing around him to hear what he was saying, the table at which the Rebbe was sitting suddenly broke. Rebbe Nachman remarked, "Can it be that there are gentiles sitting around my table? Are these then messianic times that the gentiles should draw close to the tzaddikim in fulfillment of the words, 'And all the nations shall flow unto him' " (Isaiah 2:2)? This was Rebbe Nachman's way, he would even relate his casual conversations to the lesson in which he was involved (*Parparaot LeChokhmah*; *Tzaddik* #132).

Lesson #16 is *leshon Rabbeinu* (see *Likutey Moharan* I, 7, n.1). Unlike the previous lessons, where Rebbe Nachman introduces the theme of his teaching and then shows how it is alluded to in a particular Talmudic tale, here he presents the tale at the outset and only afterwards develops the theme. In light of this brevity, the following passage is offered as an introduction to the lesson:

Man is put into this physical world so that, in his rising above the material, he comes ever closer to God. The paragon of spirituality, the tzaddik, is the one who ascends to the highest levels possible. He is the personification of the complete human being. And, when the tzaddik attains these upper levels, when he sheds corporeality and cleaves to spirituality, it is

LIKUTEY MOHARAN #16:1

לַעֲסֹק בְּדִבְרֵי הָעוֹלָם, כְּמוֹ שֶׁאָמְרוּ חֲכָמֵינוּ, זִכְרוֹנָם לִבְרָכָה (מְנָחוֹת צט.): 'פְּעָמִים בְּטוּלָה שֶׁל תּוֹרָה זוֹ הִיא קִיּוּמָהּ'.

וְכַד אַפִּיק רֵישָׁא רֵמַיָּא מִמַּיָּא – הַיְנוּ כַּד מַפִּיק אֶת עַצְמוֹ מֵחָכְמוֹת עֶלְיוֹנוֹת, אֲזַי:

וְדַמְיָא עֵינֵהּ כִּתְרֵי סִהֲרֵי – כִּי פְּקִיחַת עֵינַיִם מְכֻנִּים עַל שֵׁם הַחָכְמָה, כְּמוֹ שֶׁכָּתוּב (בְּרֵאשִׁית ג): "וַתִּפָּקַחְנָה עֵינֵי שְׁנֵיהֶם". וּכְשֶׁעוֹסֵק בְּחָכְמָתוֹ, אֲזַי עֵינָיו בִּבְחִינַת שֶׁמֶשׁ, וּכְשֶׁמְּסַלֵּק אֶת עַצְמוֹ מֵחָכְמָה עֶלְיוֹנָה, הֲוָה זֶה כְּמוֹ בִּיאַת שֶׁמֶשׁ, וּכְשֶׁבָּא הַשֶּׁמֶשׁ אֲזַי נִשְׁתָּאֲרִים עֵינָיו בִּבְחִינַת סִהֲרֵי, כִּי סִהֲרָא אֵין מְאִירָה אֶלָּא כַּד נִסְתַּלֵּק הַשֶּׁמֶשׁ.

serving God. Reb Yechiel complained that in order to do this, much time would have to be wasted on speaking about mundane matters before one could come to the point. Speaking directly about the need for improving oneself and serving God might otherwise be taken as sermonizing, serving only to alienate the person one is trying to help. Was this waste of time really worth it? The Rebbe responded: Our Sages thought to suppress the Book of Ecclesiastes because it contains seemingly contradictory statements. But, they said, "It starts with words of Torah and ends with words of Torah," and so they let it be (*Shabbat* 30b). Thus, Rebbe Nachman advised his brother to cleverly introduce words of Torah into his casual conversation with people. In this way, not only would he be binding them to God, he would also be 'setting aside Torah in order to preserve it' (cf. *Tzaddik* #377).

See *Likutey Moharan* II, 78 where the Rebbe discusses at length this concept of setting aside or neglecting Torah as sometimes being the way to fulfill it more completely.

6. **from the upper wisdoms.** Water symbolizes upper wisdom (as above, n.2). Thus, just as the fish which Rabbi Yochanan saw raised its head out of the water, the tzaddik must sometimes remove himself—his mind—from pondering the upper wisdom and cleaving to God.

7. **eyes...were opened.** This connotes knowledge (*Rashi*, Genesis 3:7).

8. **wisdom...the sun.** In an earlier lesson (*Likutey Moharan* I, 1:2), Rebbe Nachman taught, "Wisdom is a very great light which shines to an individual in all his ways...just as the sun." Rebbe Nachman then quotes the verse, "The path of the righteous is like the gleam of sunlight" (Proverbs 4:18). When performing his devotions, the tzaddik is likened to the sun, shining very brightly with this heavenly light of the upper wisdom (see Exodus 34:30 that after descending from Mt. Sinai, Moshe's face shone with a brilliant light).

9. **sun having set.** This phrase is also used as a euphemism to indicate passing away (cf. *Likutey Moharan* I, 5:2). The holy Ari explains that descending from one's level of spirituality is comparable to death (*Shaar HaHakdamot* p. 374). Thus, when the tzaddik has to lower himself from his attachment to upper wisdom, it is likened to the sun having set—an aspect of death.

10. **moon only shines when the sun goes down.** The moon complained about being made smaller during Creation and said, "Of what value is a candle by day?" (*Chullin* 60b). The

373   *LIKUTEY MOHARAN #16:1*

wisdoms] and occupy himself with mundane matters.[4] As our Sages taught: There are times when setting aside Torah preserves it (*Menachot* 99b).[5]

when it raised its head out of the water — That is, when he removed himself from the upper wisdoms.[6] Then:

His eyes resembled two moons — Opening the eyes is an expression which indicates wisdom, as in (Genesis 3:7), "And the eyes of the both of them were opened."[7] When he is occupied with wisdom, then his eyes correspond to the sun,[8] but when he removes himself from upper wisdom, it is comparable to the sun having set.[9] And when the sun sets, his eyes take on an appearance corresponding to the moon. This is because the moon only shines when the sun goes down.[10]

conce for og chochmah

4. **mundane matters.** The category of acts considered "mundane matters" can be quite encompassing. Determining what is called mundane depends upon the particular spiritual level which a person has reached. Thus, one who spends his day occupied with seeing to his family's daily needs could justifiably say that any religious act or thoughts of God which he has are a form of *devekut* to the spiritual. Not so the tzaddik. His preoccupation with the upper wisdom of God's word is such that, when he engages in "mundane matters," the tzaddik is actually involved in something which for most of us would be considered a true act of spiritual achievement. Thus, when discussing the tzaddik's simple devotions, Rebbe Nachman teaches elsewhere: The casual conversations of the tzaddikim are very precious...because the true tzaddik lifts up the lower wisdom and binds it to the upper wisdom. This is why the tzaddik will spend time talking to irreligious Jews and gentiles. While engaging such a person in conversation, the tzaddik elevates his own intellect and binds it to God. In doing this, he also elevates the other person's intellect from wherever it is...binding all the words to God, and thereby bringing him to repent (cf. *Likutey Moharan* II, 91). Yet, even this is considered mundane and a setting aside of upper wisdom for the true tzaddik.

5. **...preserves it.** This Rabbinical teaching has numerous applications. Although one may be aware that Torah is the lifeline of the Jew, he realizes that there are times when he must absent himself from Torah study and devotion for a while. He does this so that he will later be able return to his study and devotion with renewed commitment and vigor. Consider, for example, the person who is unwell. Forcing himself to diligently maintain his prescribed schedule of study or rigorous devotional practices might seem praiseworthy to say the least. But, if by doing so he becomes even more ill so that even greater measures are needed to bring about his recovery—measures which ultimately entail a more prolonged absence from study and devotion than might have otherwise been necessary—then his act is not as commendable as it first appeared. Had he set aside his Torah study or demanding practice for a while, he could have "preserved it" in the long run.

    Likewise, there is the person who sees a family member or neighbor behaving improperly or about to commit a sin. If, by taking the time to speak to him or her, he helps his friend or family member become more knowledgeable and remain firm in the face of desire, then he has actually had a hand in preserving the Torah. This is in line with the advice which Rebbe Nachman gave his brother, Reb Yechiel, when encouraging him to speak to others about

LIKUTEY MOHARAN #16:1 374

וְזֶה בְּחִינַת: 'וְעֵינֵינוּ מְאִירוֹת כַּשֶּׁמֶשׁ וְכַיָּרַחַ' – לִפְעָמִים מְאִירוֹת
כַּשֶּׁמֶשׁ, כַּד אֲנַחְנוּ דְּבֵקִים בְּחָכְמָה, וְלִפְעָמִים מְאִירוֹת כַּיָּרַחַ, כַּד
מְסַלְּקִין אֶת עַצְמֵנוּ מִלְשׁוֹטֵט בְּחָכְמָה.

וְנָפִיק מַיָּא מִתְּרֵי אוּסְיָא – הֵם בְּחִינַת תְּרֵין מְשִׁיחִין, שֶׁאֲלֵיהֶם
הָעַכּוּ״ם יִדְרְשׁוּ וְיִמְשְׁכוּ אֶת עַצְמָם אֲלֵיהֶם, כְּמוֹ שֶׁכָּתוּב (יְשַׁעְיָהוּ
ב): "וְנָהֲרוּ אֵלָיו כָּל הַגּוֹיִים". וְזֶה:

'תְּרֵי נְהָרוֹת דְּסוּרָא'. 'סוּרָא' – זֶה בְּחִינַת עַכּוּ״ם, עַל שֵׁם עֲבוֹדָה
זָרָה, כְּמוֹ שֶׁכָּתוּב (שְׁמוֹת ל״ב): "סָרוּ מַהֵר מִן הַדֶּרֶךְ", וְהֵם נִכְלָלִים
בִּשְׁתֵּי אֻמּוֹת: עֵשָׂו וְיִשְׁמָעֵאל. וְעַל-יְדֵי אֵלּוּ תְּרֵין מְשִׁיחִין, שֶׁהֵם
תְּרֵי אוּסְיָא, בְּחִינַת (אֵיכָה ד): "רוּחַ אַפֵּינוּ מְשִׁיחַ ה'", עַל-יָדָם
יִגָּאֲלוּ וְיִמָּשְׁכוּ כִּנְהָרוֹת אֶצְלָם לִלְמֹד דְּבַר ה'.

Israel, lives eternal." He alone will bring God's final redemption, something which will only happen when the lower wisdom has also been rectified.

13. **flow unto him.** River in Hebrew is *nahar*, which in Aramaic means light. That is, the gentile nations will flow unto and draw close to the Mashiach, so that he can enlighten them in the service of God.

14. **strayed from the path.** Sura (סורא) is similar to *saru* (סרו, they strayed). The Jews went astray in embracing idolatry. In this, they resembled the nations. The Messiahs will have to come to rectify their wisdom.

15. **Esav and Yishmael.** During this final exile, there are 70 nations (Genesis 10; cf. *The Living Torah*, pp.21-30): 35 under the domain of Esav (Christianity) and 35 under the domain of Yishmael (Islam). Though the exile is known as the exile of Edom, referring to Esav, the Ishmaelites have and continue to also play a role in subduing the Jewish people (*Eikhah Rabbah* 1:44; *Zohar* III, 246b). In the Kabbalah, these two nations are known as the harshest and hardest *kelipot*. It will take the combined attributes of these two Messiahs to subdue them (*Tikkuney Zohar*, 10 of the 11 last chapters; *Parparaot LeChokhmah*).

16. **the breath of our noses....** Rebbe Nachman taught that the Mashiach's weapon is prayer. With it he will conquer the nations of the world. Rebbe Nachman relates this to the teaching of our Sages that the Mashiach will judge through the power of smell. Mashiach is thus associated with the nostrils, the means by which the *ruach*/prayer is drawn. See also *Likutey Moharan* I, 9:4 and 2:1 where these connections are developed in greater detail.

17. **to learn the word of God.** This appears to mean that Mashiach ben Yosef and Mashiach ben David will subdue the nations with God's word, not with war. Those who have for centuries persecuted His chosen people will be drawn to the true word of God, which, as Rebbe Nachman tells us, is prayer (cf. *Likutey Moharan* II, 1:9).

LIKUTEY MOHARAN #16:1

This corresponds to (Shabbat *Nishmat Prayer*), "And our eyes shine like the sun and the moon." Sometimes they shine like the sun—when we are bound to < the upper > wisdom; and sometimes they shine like the moon—when we remove ourselves from pondering wisdom.[11]

he naFitZ (spouted out) water from his two nostrils — This alludes to the two Messiahs,[12] whom the gentiles will seek out and be drawn to. As is written (Isaiah 2:2), "All the nations shall flow unto him."[13] And this is: *All goyim will be drawn to 2 moshichs / ben Josof + ben Dovod*

the two rivers of Sura — SuRa alludes to the gentiles, on account of [their] idolatry, as in (Exodus 32:8), "*SaRu* (They strayed) quickly from the path."[14] [The gentiles] are embodied in two nations: Esav and Yishmael.[15] And through these two Messiahs—who are the two nostrils, corresponding to "The breath of our noses, the Mashiach of God" (Lamentations 4:20)[16]—[the gentiles] will be redeemed, and they will be drawn to them to learn the word of God.[17]

---

moon objected that as long as the sun's light filled the sky, it—the moon—had been rendered useless. This is what is meant by the blemishing of the moon, synonymous with the lower wisdom, the smaller light (*Likutey Moharan* I, 1:2; *ibid.* II, 91). The Jews, whose calendar follows the lunar cycle, are themselves likened to the moon. This affinity is further manifested in the affect which the actions of the Jewish people have upon the moon. Through their sins, the moon/lower wisdom is blemished and, in the terminology of the Kabbalah, the nations of the world are able to draw nourishment from this lower wisdom (cf. *Likutey Moharan* II, 3, where the moon/lower wisdom is associated with the *Malkhut* of holiness, the lowest of the *sefirot*; see Appendix: The Divine Persona, Alternate Names). In doing this, the nations are able to turn lower wisdom into the wisdom of heresy, giving credence to false beliefs and further subduing the Jews. The tzaddik, who is normally on the level of upper wisdom, must then set aside his personal cleaving to God. To save the Jews, the kingdom of holiness, he must enter the lower wisdom and by doing so, elevate wisdom to its rightful place in holiness (*Mabuey HaNachal*).

11. **like the sun and the moon...** Thus the tzaddik must alternate between upper wisdom and lower wisdom. However, he must be very careful to never become trapped in the mundane matters. Rather, he must keep a careful watch over his "eyes," his wisdom, even in the lower levels, so that he never succumbs to the kingdom of unholiness—i.e., the so called wisdom of heresy, idolatry and philosophical debate.

12. **two Messiahs.** The first Mashiach, the one who will ready the future redemption, will descend from Yosef. He however will not live to see the redemption's completion, which will be brought about by the second Mashiach, a direct descendant of King David. The *Mai HaNachal* adds: Mashiach ben Yosef represents the sun, upper wisdom. This is because Yosef received all his father's wisdom, as in, "Yaakov and Yosef are considered as one" (*Zohar* I, 176b), and Yaakov himself corresponds to the sun (cf. *Bereishit Rabbah* 68:12; cf. *Likutey Moharan* I, 1:2). Mashiach ben David, on the other hand, represents the moon, lower wisdom. This is why when we recite the Blessing of the Moon, we say, "David, the king of

LIKUTEY MOHARAN #16:1

376

וּתְרֵין אֲמִין, עֵשָׂו וְיִשְׁמָעֵאל, אִנּוּן תְּרֵין עֲנָנִין דִּמְכַסִּין עַל הָעֵינִין,
שֶׁאֵין יְכוֹלִין לְהָאִיר תָּמִיד בִּבְחִינַת שֶׁמֶשׁ. וּבִשְׁבִיל זֶה צָרִיךְ
הַצַּדִּיק לְבַטֵּל אֶת דְּבֵקוּתוֹ, כְּדֵי שֶׁלֹּא יִתְגַּבְּרוּ הָאֻמִּין עֵשָׂו
וְיִשְׁמָעֵאל עַל עֵינָיו, וְיִתְבַּטֵּל, חַס וְשָׁלוֹם, חָכְמָתוֹ לְגַמְרֵי.
אֲבָל עַל־יְדֵי תְּרֵין מְשִׁיחִין, שֶׁיְּפוּצוּ מַעְיְנוֹתֵיהֶם חוּצָה, וְיֵהָפֵךְ
לְכֻלָּם שָׂפָה בְרוּרָה, אָז יִתְקַיֵּם (יְשַׁעְיָהוּ ל): "וְהָיָה אוֹר הַלְּבָנָה כְּאוֹר
הַחַמָּה", וְאָז לֹא יִצְטָרֵךְ לְבַטֵּל מִדְּבֵקוּתוֹ.

(מִסִּימָן טוּ עַד כָּאן – לְשׁוֹן רַבֵּנוּ, זִכְרוֹנָם לִבְרָכָה)

21. **pure tongue.** The entire verse reads, "For then I will transform the nations to a pure tongue, that they may all call upon the name of God, to serve Him in unison." See *Metzudat David* that this refers to a common tongue—the holy tongue—through which the peoples of the earth will come to a singular belief in the one God and thus pray to Him with common thought and intent.

22. **moon...as the sun....** Originally, the light of the moon was like the light of the sun. Now, however, the moon has been diminished. Yet there will come a time when the moon will regain its former status and splendor. At such time, the tzaddik will be able to remain permanently absorbed in upper wisdom; his eyes will always shine like the sun. He will no longer be obliged to descend to lower wisdom in order to rectify it, for once the word of God has been accepted by all, it too will shine brightly of its own accord.

The Talmudic passage thus reads:

One time, we were travelling by ship — in the sea of upper wisdom.

We saw this fish — the tzaddik,

which had raised its head out of the water — from upper wisdom.

His eyes resembled two moons — when attached to upper wisdom, his eyes shone like the sun. Even when attached to lower wisdom, they can also shine and bring people back to God, but on a smaller scale. His eyes are then likened to two moons.

he spouted out water — The wellsprings of his teachings are disseminated,

from his two nostrils — from the two Messiahs. The tzaddik who encompasses the qualities of Mashiach ben Yosef and Mashiach ben David (above, n.1) will have the power to subdue the wisdom of the nations.

like the two rivers of Sura — That is, he will subdue idolatry and heresy from the world. Then this tzaddik will be able to remain absorbed in the profound levels of upper wisdom and constantly cleave to God.

The *Mai HaNachal* adds that this singular tzaddik who encompasses the two Messiahs is a reference to Moshe-Mashiach, who is known as Shiloh (see *Likutey Moharan* I, 9:4, n.51).

[handwritten top: ben Yosef (Yaakov) sun =) when Moshiach comes, both same / ben David moon]

377 LIKUTEY MOHARAN #16:1

And the two nations, Esav and Yishmael, are the two clouds which cover the eyes so that they cannot always shine like the sun.[18] Because of this, the tzaddik has to set aside his < resolute > cleaving [to wisdom], so that the nations of Esav and Yishmael do not overpower his eyes and nullify his wisdom entirely, God forbid.[19]

But, through the two Messiahs "whose wellsprings *yaFutZ* (will spread forth)" (cf. Proverbs 5:16),[20] they will all be transformed to a "pure tongue" (cf. Tzefaniah 3:9).[21] Then, "The light of the moon will be as the light of the sun" (Isaiah 30:26), and [the tzaddik] will no longer have to set aside his cleaving [to upper wisdom.][22]

[handwritten left margin: If too much Kedusha revealed forces the Klipot to respond with greater force i.e. s/ts have to keep back some kedusha]

[handwritten across page: why didn't sefirim of avots remain? bec the force of tumah would be so strong (corresponding with to good) & could wipe our Jewish people. bechira / By reducing the power of Kedusha sometimes can make greater Kedushe in long term]

18. cover over the eyes...sun. The "eyes"—wisdom—are meant to shine like the sun. But Esav and Yishmael becloud the truth with false beliefs and heretical doctrine. This is what prevents the tzaddik from permanently remaining Above—keeping his mind attached to the upper wisdom, his entire being cleaving to God.

[handwritten left margin: ↓ why we]

19. nullify wisdom entirely, God forbid. As explained (see n.10), through their sins the Jews cause parts of the lower wisdom to descend, as it were, into the realm of unholiness. This is known as the blemishing of the moon and it allows the nations of the world—symbolized in Esav and Yishmael—to flourish. The credence which this gives to their false beliefs must be countered by the tzaddik. But in order for him to rectify the lower wisdom and the mundaneity of the world, he is obliged to set aside Torah in order to preserve it. For if he allows their influence to go unchecked, unholy wisdom would ascend and even draw from the upper wisdom, God forbid. This could, in effect, totally becloud the tzaddik's eyes. His ability to ascend to upper wisdom would be nullified completely. Therefore, the tzaddik must temporarily set aside the profound perceptions which normally engage his mind and descend to the mundane matters so as to rectify them. For "There are times when setting aside Torah preserves it."

[handwritten left margin: Can't teach non Jews Toral Now but only when]

20. wellsprings will spread forth. Harking back to the story of Rabbi Yochanan, Rebbe Nachman quotes this verse from Proverbs (*loc. cit.*) to show that just as the two nostrils of the fish *naFitZ* (spouted out) water, the wellsprings of the two Messiah's teachings will *yaFutZ* (spread out) to the nations of the world.

Thus, the tzaddik's efforts to ascend and descend to the different levels of wisdom is only necessary now, in this world. However, when Mashiach ben Yosef and Mashiach ben David arrive, the "wellsprings will spread forth...." and their teachings will spread the word of God to even the gentile nations, nullifying all heresy and idolatry. All the nations will be drawn to them and there will be no need to fear the clouds/Esav and Yishmael, for the wisdom of God will prevail (*Mai HaNachal*).

[handwritten left margin: Mashiach comes bac now if we teach non Jew]

[handwritten bottom: Jew, the power of human may be turned against]

APPENDIX

THE ORDER OF THE TEN SEFIROT

THE STRUCTURE OF THE SEFIROT

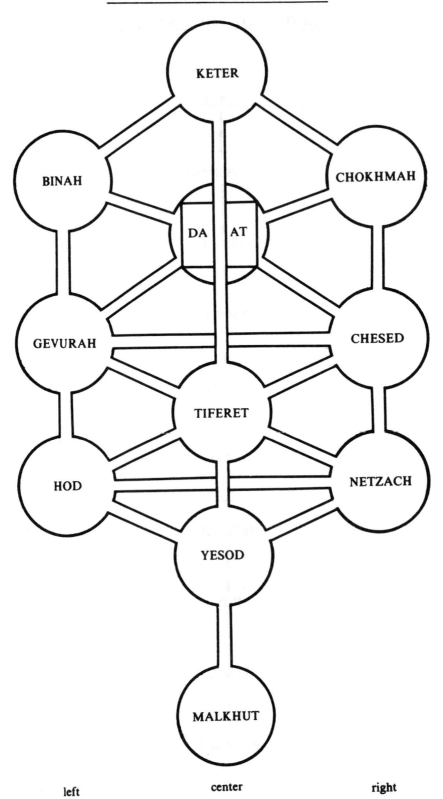

left   center   right

THE PARTZUFIM - THE DIVINE PERSONA

Sefirah	*Persona*
KETER	ATIK YOMIN / ARIKH ANPIN
CHOKHMAH	ABBA
BINAH	IMMA
(Chokhmah + Binah → Daat)	
TIFERET (Chesed, Gevurah, Tiferet, Netzach, Hod, Yesod)	Z'ER ANPIN
MALKHUT	NUKVA of Z'ER ANPIN

Alternate names used in the Kabbalah and our text for Z'er Anpin and Malkhut:

Z'er Anpin: Yaakov, Yisrael Sava, Torah, Written Law, Holy King, Sun.

Malkhut: Leah, Rachel, Prayer, Oral Law, Divine Presence/Shekhinah, Moon.

THE SEFIROT AND MAN

Keter-Crown	Skull
Chokhmah-Wisdom	Right brain
Binah-Understanding	Left brain
(Daat-Knowledge)	(Middle brain)
Chesed-Lovingkindness	Right arm
Gevurah-Strength	Left arm
Tiferet-Beauty	Torso
Netzach-Victory	Right leg
Hod-Splendor	Left leg
Yesod-Foundation	Sexual organ (brit)
Malkhut-Kingship	Mate/feet

Alternatively, Chokhmah corresponds to brain/mind; Binah to heart.

LEVELS OF EXISTENCE

World	Manifestation	Sefirah	Soul	Letter
Adam Kadmon		Keter	*Yechidah*	Apex of *Yod*
Atzilut	Nothingness	Chokhmah	*Chayah*	*Yod*
Beriyah	Thought	Binah	*Neshamah*	*Heh*
Yetzirah	Speech	Tiferet [six sefirot]	*Ruach*	*Vav*
Asiyah	Action	Malkhut	*Nefesh*	*Heh*

World	Inhabitants	T-N-T-A
Adam Kadmon	Tetragrammatons	
Atzilut-Nearness	Sefirot, Partzufim	*Taamim*-Cantillations
Beriyah-Creation	The Throne, Souls	*Nekudot*-Vowels
Yetzirah-Formation	Angels	*Tagin*-Crowns
Asiyah-Action	Forms	*Aotiyot*-Letters

EXPANSIONS OF THE HOLY NAMES OF GOD

YHVH — Expansions of the Tetragrammaton — יהוה

Expansion	Partzuf	Value		Expansion
YOD HY VYV HY	AB	Chokhmah	72	עב	יוד הי ויו הי
YOD HY VAV HY	SaG	Binah	63	סג	יוד הי ואו הי
YOD HA VAV HY	MaH	Z'er Anpin	45	מה	יוד הא ואו הא
YOD HH VV HH	BaN	Malkhut	52	בן	יוד הה וו הה

EHYH — Expansions of the Holy Name EHYeH — אהיה

Expansion	Partzuf	Value		Expansion
ALePH HY YOD HY	KSA	161	קסא	אלף הי יוד הי
ALePH HH YOD HH	KNA	151	קנא	אלף הה יוד הה
ALePH HA YOD HA	KMG	143	קמג	אלף הא יוד הא

THE SEFIROT AND ASSOCIATED NAMES OF GOD

Sefirah	Holy Name
Keter-Crown	*Ehyeh Asher Ehyeh*
Chokhmah-Wisdom	*YaH*
Binah-Understanding	*YHVH* (pronounced *Elohim*)
Chesed-Lovingkindness	*El*
Gevurah-Strength	*Elohim*
Tiferet-Beauty	*YHVH* (pronounced *Adonoy*)
Netzach-Victory	*Adonoy Tzevaot*
Hod-Splendor	*Elohim Tzevaot*
Yesod-Foundation	*Shaddai, El Chai*
Malkhut-Kingship	*Adonoy*

THE SUPERNAL COLORS

Sefirah	Color
Keter-Crown	blinding invisible white
Chokhmah-Wisdom	a color that includes all color
Binah-Understanding	yellow and green
Chesed-Lovingkindness	white and silver
Gevurah-Strength	red and gold
Tiferet-Beauty	yellow and purple
Netzach-Victory	light pink
Hod-Splendor	dark pink
Yesod-Foundation	orange
Malkhut-Kingship	blue

THE SEVEN SUPERNAL SHEPHERDS

Sefirah	Shepherd
Chesed-Lovingkindness	Avraham
Gevurah-Strength	Yitzchak
Tiferet-Beauty	Yaakov
Netzach-Victory	Moshe
Hod-Splendor	Aharon
Yesod-Foundation	Yosef
Malkhut-Kingship	David

HEBREW LETTER NUMEROLOGY — GEMATRIA

100=ק	10=י	1=א
200=ר	20=כ	2=ב
300=ש	30=ל	3=ג
400=ת	40=מ	4=ד
	50=נ	5=ה
	60=ס	6=ו
	70=ע	7=ז
	80=פ	8=ח
	90=צ	9=ט

זכרון נצח

לעילוי נשמת

אבי מורי
ר׳ גרשון ב״ר מרדכי קופל ז״ל
נלב״ע ערב סוכות, י״ד תשרי תשמ״ה

ת.נ.צ.ב.ה.

בעבור שבנו
ר׳ שלמה מרדכי קופל הי״ו
נדב סכום הגון להדפסת הספר הקדוש הזה לעילוי נשמתו

זכרון נצח

לעילוי נשמת

אמי אשה יראת ה׳
מרת חיה בת ר׳ ברוך
אינדיג ע״ה
נלב״ע פסח שני, י״ד אייר תש״ל

ת.נ.צ.ב.ה.

בעבור שבתה
שרה דבורה קופל תחי׳
נדבה סכום הגון להדפסת הספר הקדוש לעילוי נשמתה

זכרון נצח

לעילוי נשמת

הר"ר אליהו חיים
ב"ר קלונימוס קלמן רוזן ז"ל
נלב"ע כ' כסליו תשד"מ

ת.נ.צ.ב.ה.

בעבור שתלמידיו
ר' שלמה מרדכי ב"ר גרשון קופל נ"י
וזוגתו שרה דבורה בת ר' אלתר צבי תחי'
נדבו כל הוצאות הדפסת הספר הקדוש הזה לעילוי נשמתו

זכרון נצח

לעילוי נשמת

הר"ר אברהם ב"ר נפתלי הערץ
שטערינהארץ (כוכב לב) ז"ל
נכד מוהרנ"ת זצ"ל
נלב"ע כ' אלול תשט"ו

ת.נ.צ.ב.ה.

בעבור שתלמידיו
ר' שלמה מרדכי ב"ר גרשון קופל נ"י
וזוגתו שרה דבורה בת ר' אלתר צבי תחי'
נדבו כל הוצאות הדפסת הספר הקדוש הזה לעילוי נשמתו

זכרון נצח

לעילוי נשמת

מורי ורבי

הר"ר צבי אריה בן־ציון

ב"ר ישראל אבא רוזנפלד ז"ל

נלב"ע י"א כסליו תשל"ט

ת.נ.צ.ב.ה.

בעבור שתלמידיו

ר' שלמה מרדכי ב"ר גרשון קופל נ"י

וזוגתו שרה דבורה בת ר' אלתר צבי תחי'

נדבו כל הוצאות הדפסת הספר הקדוש הזה לעילוי נשמתו

ESCAPING PERPETUAL
INSANITY

DIARY OF AN ESSEX BOY

BERNARD O'MAHONEY

Copyright © Bernard O'Mahoney 2021

All rights reserved

The moral right of the author has been asserted

First published in Great Britain in 2021

ISBN 9798731488198

Front Cover: Martin Moore

True Crime Publishing

Dublin

No part of this book may be reproduced or transmitted in any form or by any means without permission in writing from the publisher, except by a reviewer who wishes to quote brief passages in connection with a review written for insertion in a magazine, newspaper or broadcast.

In Memory of

My Friend Natalie

11 April 1973 – 17 May 2018

This world was never meant for one as beautiful as you.

ACKNOWLEDGEMENTS

A huge thank you to all the usual suspects who endure my highs and many lows when I immerse myself in the writing of a book. Roshea, daughter Karis, partner Tommy, daughter Lydia, son Adrian, son Vinney and partner Michaela, son Daine and son Paddy the Laddy. My grandchildren, Charlie-Joe, Alannah Bananas, Micky, Poppy, Good Golly Miss Molly and Tommy. My late mother Anna, wife Emma and brother-in-law El, never forgotten. Last but by no means least, Gavin Spicer, Martin 'Magic' Moore and Mad Andy Byrne.

Bernard O'Mahoney is the bestselling author of Essex Boys, Salford Lads, Essex Boys the New Generation, Bonded by Blood, Fog on the Tyne, Flowers in Gods Garden, Hateland and numerous other acclaimed true crime titles.

O'Mahoney has also written and presented several true crime documentaries for television, including British Gangsters Faces of the Underworld; Series one and two, Essex Boys; The Truth, The Krays; Kill Order and Gangster No 1 - The Freddie Foreman Story. Hollywood star Vinnie Jones plays Bernard O'Mahoney in the movie Rise of the Footsoldier Origins. (2021)

CONTENTS

INTRODUCTION: I, Bernard O'Mahoney   Pg 1

CHAPTER ONE: When the Gunsmoke Cleared   Pg 9

CHAPTER TWO: Won't Get Fooled Again   Pg 31

CHAPTER THREE: Darkness on the Edge of Town   Pg 57

CHAPTER FOUR: Life in a Northern Town   Pg 87

CHAPTER FIVE: Stay Away from the Light.   Pg 113

CHAPTER SIX: Coming Down Again   Pg 141

CHAPTER SEVEN: Porridge   Pg 167

CHAPTER EIGHT: Everybody Hurts   Pg 195

CHAPTER NINE: Hello Darkness My Old Friend   Pg 223

CHAPTER TEN: A Better Day   Pg 253

CHAPTER ELEVEN: No Regrets   Pg 283

CHAPTER TWELVE: The Circle of Life   Pg 305

TEN ESSEX BOYS

Ten ruthless Essex Boys believed anything they wanted to do was fine, Mark Rothermel decapitated a man and then there were nine.

Nine ruthless Essex Boys cast out a mate, Chris Wheatley sought solace in drugs and died and then there were eight.

Eight ruthless Essex Boys will never get to heaven, Larry Johnson stabbed a man to death and then there were seven.

Seven heartless Essex Boys supplied clubbers with their fix, Leah Betts collapsed, Mark Murray fled and then there were six.

Six worried Essex Boys clinging on to survive, Chris Lombard was shot dead and then there were five.

Five desperate Essex Boys know they can never win the war, David King was executed and then there were four.

Four Essex Boys believed that they were Dons, three went to a meeting and then there was one.

One Essex Boy renounced a life of violence, hurt and pain, he now lives happily ever after, fulfilled and sane.

And then...there were none.

*Adapted from the poem; Ten Little Indians, written by Septimus Winner 1868.

INTRODUCTION
I, Bernard O'Mahoney

January 1996: Brookside Café, London Road, Rayleigh, Essex. I am watching eggs chase bacon around a spitting frying pan. A guy sitting at an adjacent table is talking to his wife. I assume it's his wife because she isn't listening. His monotone voice drones on and on about the damp that has appeared on their bathroom ceiling and the health risks they both may now face. She is staring vacantly out of a window, lost in blissful, absolute nothingness. Behind me, I can hear an elderly lady telling a young waitress how Basildon used to be before the war. I too knew Basildon before the war, but I suspect we are thinking of two very different conflicts. The lady is recalling the second world war when brave young men and women gave their all for King and country. The conflict I have in mind, was a bloody drugs war that had ended abruptly when three of my former friends, Craig Rolfe, Pat Tate and Tony Tucker, had been executed. I emphasise the fact that they were former friends, because the friends I once knew, were no more, long before their deaths. Once lucid, rational and trustworthy, class A drugs had transformed them into unreasonable, paranoid, schizophrenic bullies. I first met Tucker at a club in London during the summer of 1992. As we were both doormen, the conversation naturally revolved around door work. Tucker said that he had a contract to provide security for a company called First Continental which owned a chain of nightclubs, Hollywood Romford, Hollywood Ipswich, Club Art Southend and Club UK Wandsworth. He later secured a contract with The Velvet Underground, a popular club in London's West End. They were all undoubtedly great venues to have, but unfortunately for Tucker, most became great rave clubs and all rave clubs became a magnet for drugs. Prior to meeting Tucker, I was given the security contract at a club called Raquel's in Basildon. I had initially worked there as a doorman but my former employer had left and I took over. The door staff that I inherited were not ruthless enough to control what was a very violent venue. Local hardmen had grown up with the doormen, they had attended the same schools, shared the same friends, drank in the same pubs and lived in the same streets. These hardmen, would commit diabolical acts of violence and be ejected from the club. The following weekend, they would be welcomed back as if nothing had happened. It was a gruesome merry go round that ensured Raquel's retained its violent reputation, which in turn ensured that decent people wouldn't dare to set foot in the place. I used to meet Tucker socially at Epping Forest Country Club where I worked on Wednesday and Sunday nights. We had become friends and after learning of my manpower problem, he offered to supply door staff from outside the Basildon area. These men, he explained, would not acknowledge, fear or even be aware of the locals' reputations. 'If the locals want trouble they can have it, my guys won't give a fuck about them,' he explained. Probably not the slickest sales pitch I have ever heard but I accepted his offer and we became partners in running security at Raquel's. Initially things went well, the troublemakers were thrown out, usually headfirst down a concrete stairwell and remained excluded. The reduction in violence attracted genuine party people and that change in clientele attracted interest from rave promoters who were seeking large, trouble-free venues to fill. The rave scene had no place for violence. Clubbers high on what was known as the love drug, (Ecstasy) would dance in unison and embrace one other. Venues like Raquel's that subsequently hosted raves, were engulfed by a tsunami of drugs overnight. Tucker, who had been raised on entrepreneurial Thatcherism, quickly realised that there were vast amounts of money to be made from the drugs which were the backbone of the rave phenomenon. He began ejecting drug dealers from clubs and replacing them with his own. Within a very short period of time Tucker had become, what detectives would later describe as, 'middle management,' in the Essex drug world. His ego swelled in tandem with his bank balance. High on the drugs he had confiscated from rogue dealers in his clubs, Tucker thought he was fucking Superman and mere mortals posed no threat. He believed that he could rob, bully or hurt whoever he wished at will. All superheroes and villains have a side kick, Batman had Robin, The Joker had Harley Quinn and Tony Tucker had Craig Rolfe. He was twelve years younger than Tucker, but had inhabited the drug world for much longer than his 'boss.' Described by many as Tuckers Gofer, Rolfe would chauffer his hero around day – and night – damage people when required and distribute drugs. I personally didn't like the man but in fairness to Rolfe, he didn't like me either.

In the drugs world at that time, there was an abundance of dynamic duos like Tony Tucker and Craig Rolfe. They were small fish in a vast ocean but in their drug addled minds, they were Kings of all they surveyed. Man mountain Pat Tate had become acquainted with Tucker after meeting in a Southend café during the summer of 1994. Tate had just completed a ten-year prison sentence for drug offences and robbing a Happy Eater restaurant following a dispute about the price of his burger and chips. Tate had a serious crack cocaine and heroin habit that he struggled to control. His mood swings were terrifying, one moment he would be laughing and joking, the next he would be frothing at the mouth and threatening to shoot somebody. In one outburst, he had even threatened to kill his own mother. Knowing her son better than most, she took to carrying a note in her pocket which read, 'if anything happens to me, look for my son Pat.' Within a week of meeting Tate, Tucker had started smoking crack cocaine and injecting class A drugs. The incline he and Tate stood on was steep and their inevitable fall therefore, was always going to be more of a headfirst plunge into a dark abyss rather than a mere stumble.

As time passed by, clubbers whose bodies had become accustomed to the effects of ecstasy, were increasing the number of pills they popped in the hope of achieving what was fast becoming an elusive high. Cocaine became the drug of choice for many. Rather than make people feel love, it harvested deep seated paranoia and mindless thuggery. Cocaine gave many people a false sense of invincibility and power. Tucker, Tate and Rolfe were no different, they began talking about controlling the drug trade throughout south-east England and beyond. Tate had met people he deemed useful in prison. Three of these 'useful people' were Darren Nicholls, Mick Steele and Jack Whomes. Steele had a history of importing drugs from the continent and so Tate employed him, Nicholls and Whomes to import cannabis on his and Tucker's behalf. Neither man had the finances required to fund such an operation and so Tate convinced a shady car dealer to invest. On 8 November 1995, Tucker and Tate's first cannabis importation arrived in Essex. It turned out to be substandard and so a refund was demanded. Steele agreed to collect the money from his Dutch supplier. Tate, under the influence of drugs and suffering from acute paranoia, decided Steele had tried to rip him off and so began making threats to kill him. Three days after the dud drug shipment had landed, a policeman's daughter named Leah Betts had collapsed after taking ecstasy at her 18th birthday party. It was reported that the pill had been purchased in Raquel's. The fact that Leah was so young and a policeman's daughter, ensured the story made national headline news. The last thing international drug smugglers need is hordes of investigative journalists, television crews and policemen milling around outside a nightclub which was essentially the center of their operations. But that is precisely what happened and the added pressure made Tucker and Tate even more desperate and volatile. That pressure was increased tenfold when Leah lost her fight for life five days after collapsing. When Tucker heard that one of Leah's friends had been arrested for supplying the pill that ultimately killed her, he urged me to expose him to the press. 'Once he appears in the papers the journalists will fuck off from the club and stop investigating us. I can't have them around at this time,' he had said. I did as Tucker asked and it backfired on us all spectacularly. The man who had been arrested claimed that I threatened to break his legs and burn his house down. Unsurprisingly, the police got to hear about it. Rather than deflect attention away from the club and ourselves, the police and media scrutiny intensified. The more pressure Tucker and Tate were put under, the more irrational they became. Tate told his girlfriend that he was going to take Mick Steele 'up north' and he wouldn't be returning. Fearing Tate would commit murder, Tate's girlfriend warned

Steele about the threat. On 06 December 1995, Tucker, Tate and Rolfe met Mick Steele and drove him to an isolated farm track in the village of Rettendon. In an effort to appease Tate, Steele had told him that a light aircraft carrying one ton of cocaine was scheduled to land in a field. Steele added, that they could rob the cocaine which would compensate Tate, Tucker and their consortium for the importation of the poor-quality cannabis. Driven by greed, Tate didn't question Steeles integrity for one moment. As a Range Rover containing the men made its way slowly down a pothole strewn track, the driver, Craig Rolfe, called out, 'There's a locked gate ahead.' Steele, who was sitting in the back with Tate replied, 'I will get it.' As Steele opened the rear door, Jack Whomes emerged from a nearby hedgerow carrying two shotguns. Whomes handed one to Steele before leaning into the vehicle and shooting Rolfe, Tucker and then Tate in quick succession. In order to fulfill a grisly pact, Steele too shot the men, despite the fact that they were already dead. Whomes then telephoned Darren Nicholls who had been waiting nearby. He picked his blood-spattered colleagues up moments later and they made good their escape. That event I wanted, no, needed to believe, had ended years of misery and violence for a lot of people. As the gun smoke cleared, I could finally embrace what I had craved for so long, routine, everyday life. That is why I was enjoying myself, people watching in a café.

The aroma of the eggs and bacon I was now enjoying was preferable to the smell of fear and violence that had clung to me like a bad smell for the past decade. The man droning on about the damp on his bathroom ceiling was sweet music to my ears and the elderly lady reminiscing about her past was somehow heartening. Surrounded by normality I felt content, happy even. But I should have been acutely aware that normality is in fact an illusion, what is normal for the spider, is chaos for the fly.

8

CHAPTER ONE

When the Gunsmoke Cleared...

07 12 1995: For all the shit I had endured during the reign of the Essex Boys, there was always one factor that ensured I remained involved, I was rarely short of money. Now that door had firmly closed, I had no idea how I was going to support my family from here on in. The only qualification I achieved at school was a red basic swimming badge and so my employment options were at best limited. After leaving the Army aged 21, I had worked in the haulage industry driving tipper lorries around London. I was now living in rural Essex, fifty miles from the capital and so large construction sites simply didn't exist. I therefore needed to either travel great distances to work, or seek out some form of unskilled labour locally. The plan had always been to turn my back on crime and live happily ever after with my partner Debra and our two children, but cracks had begun to appear in our relationship long before the murders at Rettendon. The gang politics, the violence and regular police raids had caused constant rows. My endless apologies and broken promises that followed, became meaningless. It is fair to say that our lack of finances and a mounting pile of unpaid bills didn't help the situation. I felt like a Pelican, whichever way I turned all I

could see was a fucking big bill.

31 12 1995: Chris Wheatley, who had been Tony Tuckers right hand man until Pat Tate crashed onto the scene, rang me and asked if I would work a door with him on New Year's Eve. Debra wasn't with me when I received the call but I could feel her disapproving glare as I momentarily hesitated before answering, 'Yes, no problem.' The event had been organised by Perfect Virtue, the promotions team that had been so successful at Raquel's. They had a large following of good, decent, party people and so the event was trouble free. Chris and I spent the evening talking about the rise and demise of Tucker, Tate and Rolfe, our former friends. Before Tate had been released from prison, Chris had been trusted, respected and relied upon by Tucker. However, Tucker turned out to be one of life's users, you could be his best friend one minute and the next, he would discard you for someone he deemed more useful. Chris Wheatley had certainly been discarded after Tucker was introduced to Tate.

One evening, Chris had been working at Hollywood's nightclub in Romford. Just before closing time, he ejected a man from Basildon named Danny Wright. He claimed that Chris had assaulted him and was naturally upset about it. I knew Danny really well; he was a regular at Raquel's. I can best describe him as a loveable rogue who was always in the thick of the fighting. We fell out several times but there was never any animosity. Danny's uncle, Sid Wright, was a notorious face in the Southend area. When he heard what had happened to Danny, Sid made it known that he was unhappy. Tucker, who didn't relish the prospect of conflict with Sid, turned on Chris and removed him from the door at

Hollywood's. From that moment on, the friendship they had once shared, was no more.

Begrudgingly, Tucker did eventually appoint Chris as head doorman at a venue in Southend called Club Art. When Tucker was murdered, all of the venues he had contracts with 'reviewed' their security arrangements and new companies were employed. At the event on New Year's Eve, Chris and I had discussed the dilemma we faced now that the cash cow had been slaughtered. Chris couldn't see himself doing an 'ordinary' 9-5 job. I, on the other hand, said I wasn't particularly bothered what I did so long as it paid the bills. 'Needs must Chris,' I reasoned, 'do what you have to do for now and something better will always come along in the end.' Sadly, Chris found reinventing himself difficult and used drugs as a crutch. To fund the drugs he took socially, Chris began selling ecstasy, speed and cocaine to friends, but matters inevitably escalated. His social drug use had quickly developed into full blown drug addiction. Chris needed more money to satisfy his habit and so he expanded his drug operation throughout Southend and beyond. The steady stream of additional punters knocking on Chris's front door did not go unnoticed. Fifteen months after Tucker's murder, police raided Chris's flat and seized 30 grammes of cocaine, 3 grammes of amphetamine, 357 ecstasy pills and £950 in cash. A further 170 grammes of cocaine were discovered hidden under the seat of his car. The drugs had an estimated street value of between £10.000 and £17.000. In mitigation, Chris's Barrister told Basildon Crown Court that his client had become addicted to cocaine after losing his job as a doorman. 'Mr. Wheatley had been unable to secure alternative employment because of the reputation of the

'Essex Boys' whom he had been associated with; he had then become dependent on drugs and that caused his marriage to fail.' Chris was sentenced to seven years imprisonment. After serving half of that sentence he was released, but shortly afterwards he collapsed outside a gym in Southend and died. A post-mortem revealed that Chris had been abusing steroids. (Danny Wright was killed in a tragic motorcycle accident in 1999, he was 23 years old. Sid Wright was jailed for twenty-one years in October 2008 for importing two kilos of cocaine and seven semi-automatic firearms. Sid had flown a Cessna light aircraft from Belgium and dropped two packages into a field in Essex. A member of the public had seen 'objects falling from the plane' and alerted the police. They had raced to the scene and stopped a car which was being driven by Douglas Garrod, who had picked up the packages. Sid was arrested shortly afterwards.)02 01 1996: Essex police rang me today to enquire about my well-being. They had been informed, by an anonymous source of course, that I had been shot and my body dumped in a ditch. These stories were becoming so common they barely registered with me. I assured the police that I was neither in a ditch nor dead but I appreciated their concern.

Basildon Council also rang me with news. I was informed that 'following a meeting,' they had decided to ban me from working as a doorman for the next seven years, 'at least.' Again, I was neither surprised nor bothered, events in Essex had left me unemployable in the nightclub security industry. It was time to move on, start afresh but few it seemed, were prepared to let me go quietly.

A man named Rob Chilton, who I had never met, was telling

people that £10.000 had been offered to doormen (employed at Bagley's nightclub in Kings Cross, London) to shoot me. As far as I knew, they had no issue with me, nor I with them. I had been involved in an altercation with the door staff at Bagley's six months prior to the Rettendon murders. A gun had been brandished. It had occurred after a friend of mine had hired out Bagley's for a private event. Dave Tomkins, a drug dealer from Bristol had attended with me. He had been searched in the venue by the door staff. They found drugs, confiscated them and ejected him. I politely explained that the drugs didn't belong to Tomkins, he was just a dealer and they should be returned as the owner was a very unreasonable man. They refused and adopted a threatening manner. Words were exchanged and a gun was pointed at them. It's surprising how intently people are prepared to listen when a firearm is pointing at their head. It was decided that further unpleasantness wasn't necessary. Tomkins could indeed have his drugs returned but we would have to leave. We agreed, and as far as I was concerned that was the end of the matter. After several people had told me what Chilton had been saying, I went to see him at his workplace. As is the norm with such people, when confronted he denied knowing any doormen in London and claimed that he had been falsely accused. I gave him the benefit of the doubt but the very next day I was told he was still making mischief by repeating the same story. I drove to his yard, walked into the Portacabin where he was sat behind a desk and punched him as hard as I could before walking out. As I ambled towards my car, I glanced in the window and saw that Chilton was lying on the floor surrounding by his colleagues who were trying to rouse him. Everyone it seemed, had an opinion or a story to tell about the Essex Boys. The vast majority of such people had never met them and were usually talking shite. Similarly, the death of Leah Betts had spawned a whole host of fucking self-taught chemists who had become 'experts' on illegal drugs overnight. What wasn't open to debate, was the fact that the Essex Boys/Leah Betts saga, had signaled the beginning of the end for the rave culture. It limped on for a while, incapacitated by stringent new licensing laws and harsher restrictions. The authorities watched on like Vultures, eagerly waiting for the phenonium to fall and draw its last breath. The clubbers did not help themselves or disappoint the authorities. Club UK in south London had been one of Tony Tuckers doors. He had not only controlled the security, he charged drug dealers 'rent' and took a percentage of their earnings. Following his death there was a free for all. Dealers descended on the venue in great numbers knowing that they could operate rent free.

12 01 1996: Nineteen-year-old Andreas Bouzis left home to go dancing and never returned. Andreas collapsed in Club UK at 1.40.a.m, just ninety minutes after taking one ecstasy tablet. Medically-trained staff at the club tried in vain to revive him. The following day, in scenes reminiscent of the Leah Betts tragedy, stern faced police officers and his tearful parents held a press conference. Detective Chief Superintendent Roger Couzens announced that a post-mortem examination had revealed Andreas suffered from a congenital heart defect which appeared to have been exacerbated by the drug. Another officer added, 'It seems he could have gone on for years unaware and lived a normal life, but the drug exposed the condition.' Fighting back tears, Andreas's mother Josephine said, 'Andreas was our life, our

family, our love, our reason to live. On Friday night he went to a club, just as your children may have done. Now he is dead, gone forever. I cannot describe our feelings. Yesterday, our son had a future, he had a life ... today he is dead. Families and their love are very precious. Ecstasy tablets destroy families.' Shortly after Andreas Bouzis tragic death, Club UK was forced to close. It felt as if everyone and everything associated with Tony Tucker's empire was slowly being erased from history.

February 1996: Whilst working at Raquel's I had regularly collected debts for a variety of people and businesses. Smithfield Market in Farringdon, London, is the largest wholesale meat market in the UK and one of the largest of its kind in Europe. I collected debts for several years on behalf of many of the traders there. The amounts outstanding were relatively small but most traders were owed money by at least five or more shops. Therefore, I could easily collect in excess of forty debts every week. Most of the other 'work' I did came via a middleman named Carter. Jobs varied from straight debt collection to burning out cars or punishment beatings. In need of finances, I had to accept that my obligation to provide for my family was far more important than my desire to stay out of trouble. I rang Carter to find out if my services could be employed. He explained that things had been relatively quiet since Christmas. However, a guy named Martin Davies from Market Harborough had been ringing him constantly concerning debts that had brought about the closure of his video rental shop. Carter had declined the offer because those type of debts were notoriously tedious and generally not worthwhile. They usually involved a handful of customers or suppliers who owed small amounts of cash. However, I needed to earn something soon and so I asked Carter to ring Davies back as something is always better than nothing.07 03 1996: I drove to Market Harborough with Carter and one of his friends and we met Davies. From the outset I didn't like the guy and decided any money I may collect on his behalf would be confiscated. The majority of the debts he was owed were pitiful amounts ranging from £10 up to £800. I enquired who owed the latter and Davies said that it was a local man named Danny Marlow. Davies gave me Marlow's address and so I went to see him. A lady, who I assumed was his wife, answered the door. I knew instinctively that I was not the first who had called wanting to speak to her spouse. 'He's not here, I don't know where he is or when he will be back,' she said in a well-rehearsed nonchalant manner. Undeterred, I spoke to her neighbours who told me that Marlow was a taxi driver, they also told me where he worked. When I entered the cab office, I asked the controller to contact Marlow, 'give him my number and ask him to call.' Shortly afterwards, Marlow rang me. 'There's no problem, but I need to meet up with you to discuss the money Davies says you owe him,' I said. 'I'm not meeting anyone, I am at work, I don't owe him anything,' Marlow replied. I tried to respond but Marlow had hung up. I did ring him back but my call went straight to voicemail. Rather foolishly, I left a terse message warning Marlow that this problem wasn't going to go away, he needed to meet me and deal with it.' Marlow didn't comply and so I returned to his house. I informed his wife that I would be returning to see her husband later that night. I had no intention of hanging about for a paltry percentage of an £800 debt that Marlow probably couldn't pay in any event. My hope was, either he or his wife would ring the police claiming that they had been threatened. The police would then ring Davies and inform him that if he sent anybody else to Marlow's door, he would be arrested. Davies would then ring Carter and ask him to leave Marlow alone and chase someone else who owed him money. Unfortunately for Davies, whenever I accepted a debt, the conditions always were, I stayed on it until the cash had been collected. If for any reason the person who had hired me changed their mind, they would have to pay me fifty per cent of the debt. Davies would undoubtedly comply with instructions from the police and in doing so, he would have to pay me £400. I had lost the will to run around Market Harborough chasing fools for a pittance and so I headed home with Carter and his friend in tow.

01 05 1996: At 9.a.m I received a telephone call from DC Sandford who was a member of the Major Incident Team with Essex police. He told me that he was working on the Rettendon murder enquiry and he needed to speak to me. I had nothing to hide and so I said, 'tell me where and when.' At mid-day I attended South Woodham Ferrers police station where the bodies of Tucker, Tate and Rolfe had been taken the morning after the murders. DC Chapple and his colleague DC Sandford asked me general questions about my relationship with Tucker, our recent falling out and threats Tucker and Tate had made concerning me. I was honest and told them it was nothing, Tucker and Tate had been telling people that they were looking for me but both knew where I lived, both had my home and mobile numbers. Neither man had been to my address and neither man had telephoned me. 'They used to shout and scream to impress their minions but the reality of the situation is, they had no legitimate reason to

have an issue with me and so nothing was ever going to happen.' At the end of the interview DC Chapple informed me that detectives from Leicestershire were in the next room and they wished to speak to me. I realised that I had been duped into walking into that police station. The questions I had been asked were questions that I had answered previously. I laughed to myself and said to the officers, 'Well show me the way, I don't want to keep them waiting.' As soon as I walked into the adjacent room two plain clothed policemen stood up. They introduced themselves and said that I was not under arrest but they wanted to question me about the murder of Danny Marlow. I was shocked to say the least. The officers explained that when Marlow had finished work on the day that I had spoken to him, he had returned home and got changed. He then walked to a local pub called the Bell where he played pool. At approximately 10.30.p.m the landlord had called Marlow to the bar where he was told there was a phone call for him. Marlow spoke to the caller, who has never been identified. He left the pub approximately ten minutes later. Around 11.p.m a witness near Marlow's home heard two men talking in raised voices. It was apparent that they were arguing. The witness then heard an engine revving and something that sounded wooden clattering to the floor. Danny Marlow was found lying in the road shortly afterwards, he had suffered horrific injuries. The emergency services were called but sadly, the 35-year-old father of two was pronounced dead before he reached hospital. Forty minutes later, a stolen Ford Granada was found burnt out just nine miles away. The officers explained that they had already interviewed Martin Davies and he had said he employed Carter and me to collect his debts. 'We know Danny owed

Davies money and we know Danny was threatened. We have spoken to his wife and retrieved the message from his phone,' they added. I told the officers that whether or not Marlow had been threatened, I had not played any part in his death. Three hours after entering the police station I was taken to my home. I was asked to hand over the small amount of paperwork Davies had given to me relating to Marlow's debt. As the officers were leaving, they warned me, that they would be back in touch soon.

In February 1998, the truth about Marlow's death did eventually come out when two men were charged with his murder. Marlow, a keen snooker player, had bet Peter Marsh, the owner of Market Harborough's Big Break snooker club, that he could beat him in a game. The prize for the winner was the princely sum of forty pounds. Marsh triumphed, but Marlow refused to pay. Marsh told friends that he was going to, 'rip Marlow's head off.' Two years after the game, Marsh hired nightclub doorman Tim Harris to, 'sort Marlow out.' His attempt to do so had gone horribly wrong. Marlow had suffered multiple injuries after being struck by a stolen car Harris was driving. At Nottingham Crown Court Tim Harris was found guilty of manslaughter and sentenced to five years imprisonment. Peter Marsh was jailed for four years for conspiring to commit actual bodily harm.

15 05 1996: Thirty-five-year-old John Marshall went missing from home today. John had been a one-time friend and business partner of Pat Tate. The Essex rumour mill lurched into top gear as soon as word got out that he had disappeared. Like Tate, John was a big man standing at approximately 6ft tall and weighing approximately sixteen

stone. Like Tate, John was a car dealer. Unlike Tate, John's life revolved around his family. He was married to Toni and they had three children. He worked hard, buying and selling high performance vehicles and was on his way to becoming a millionaire. John had terminated his relationship with Tate because he couldn't tolerate his behaviour. Being a decent guy with morals, he had refused Tate's numerous offers to get involved with drugs. On the day he went missing, John had left home between 10.20.a.m and 11.20.a.m for a meeting regarding the purchase of a house in Kent. He had £5000 in cash on him, which he was going to use to pay for a car. John had told his wife that he would be back in a few hours. He had then driven directly to Century Salvage, a scrap yard in Pitsea, Basildon where he purchased parts for a Fiesta. He departed between 12 noon and 1p.m. His car was seen crossing the Queen Elizabeth II bridge into Kent shortly afterwards. John had a dentist appointment in Burns Avenue, Basildon at 3.p.m where he had also arranged to meet a business associate. The £5,000 John had with him was due to be handed over at this meeting but he never arrived. The business associate later told police, 'I tried to call John's mobile number several times but I was unable to get through.' Seven days after leaving home, John Marshall was found dead in the back of his black Range Rover in Thorpewood Avenue, Round Hill, south London. The police said that they thought the car had been dumped there either on Wednesday night or in the early hours of Thursday morning when it was found. John had been shot twice, once in the head and once in the chest. His body had then been bundled into the Range Rover and covered with straw. It was noted that John was a big man, and so it would have taken more than one person to have lifted him into the back of his vehicle. It was thought that he was not shot where he was found. The police said that they were keen to discover where he had been murdered and also who had driven his car from the murder scene to where it was found. John still had the £5,000 in cash on him but the killer was thought to have taken the Range Rover keys, a grey Head sports bag containing all of Johns business documents, two mobile phones and a Patek Philippe 18ct gold watch with a blue face. However, it was never established where the grey Head sports bag had gone missing. John Marshall's car had been dumped with its doors unlocked and a window open, raising the possibility that the Head sports bag could have been taken after the car was abandoned. John's murder remains unsolved.

23 05 1996: The day after John Marshalls body had been discovered, 23-year-old, ex-Raquel's doorman Larry Johnson made his way to Big Hand Mo's pub in Rush Green Romford. I liked Larry a lot, he was a funny, fearless and dangerous guy. I can recall one Christmas Eve lunch time, Larry and Steve Longshanks, another first-class no-nonsense doorman were working at the Buzz Bar, an annex of Raquel's. Basildon town center was awash with drunks and as the day wore on, the jovial Christmas mood turned increasingly dark. Late in the afternoon a group of approximately fifteen men arrived at the Buzz Bar and a fight had broken out after they were refused entry. Greatly outnumbered and without a prayer of winning, Larry and Steve stood their ground and fought to the bitter end. Thankfully, neither suffered serious injury. In another incident Larry had battered fellow Raquel's doorman Dave Done. When Larry had pulled out a knife to stab Done, I had been forced to intervene. Not because I liked Done, it was

more because I liked Larry and didn't want him to end up in prison. Larry was a live wire to say the least and his long-suffering girlfriend had eventually grown tired of his antics. To Larry's dismay she had informed him that their relationship was over but he had refused to accept it. Larry had heard that his now ex-girlfriend had started a relationship with a bouncer named Stephen Poutney who worked at Big Hand Mo's near Romford. So, Larry and a friend had decided to go and visit him. When they arrived at the pub around 8.15.p.m, Larry had pulled out a large knife and placed it on a fence before walking to the door. Shortly afterwards, Larry approached his ex-girlfriend and began talking to her. The conversation became heated and Larry said that he was going to kill Poutney. Alerted by raised voices, two doormen had spoken to Larry after which, he walked outside. Larry retrieved the knife from the fence, returned to the pub and stabbed Stephen Poutney in the left-hand side. Thirty-one-year-old Poutney was rushed to nearby Old Church hospital but he was pronounced dead on arrival. Larry was arrested the following day and charged with murder. On 7 May 1997 Larry was convicted of murder at the Old Bailey and sentenced to life imprisonment with a recommendation that he serve sixteen years.

13 11 1996: One of my few genuine friends in Basildon was arrested for attempting to import two million pounds worth of drugs. His case is a good example of how exaggerated Tucker, Tate and Rolfe's standing was in the Essex underworld. They are portrayed in films as Mafia type Dons who controlled Essex and parts of London. The truth is they were small predatory fish in a relatively small puddle. In the deal that led to their murders, they had invested a paltry

£60.000. Rolfe had invested £7.000, Tucker £20.000 and Tate and a car dealer contributed the rest. That amount of money in the drug trade is equivalent to the loose change you might find down the back of your sofa.

My friend, Mark Chinnock, had a brother-in-law named Roger. He had been arrested at a Basildon hotel in 1994. Police had stormed Rogers room where they found him counting out ecstasy pills and putting them into bags for the dealers at Raquel's. When Roger was sentenced to five years imprisonment, the villains at the top of that particular supply chain demanded their money for the drugs that had been seized. Roger didn't have any money, nor did his family. The villains, who it is said ran north London at the time, were not prepared to listen to excuses, they wanted paying. Mark told me that he had come out of work one day and a junior member of this notorious crime family was waiting for him. 'It was all very friendly. The man was at pains to point out that he understood my position and that it was a shame Roger had been arrested, but he explained that they still wanted their money.' Mark was under no illusions regarding his family's position and so he 'agreed' to import drugs using his own van to pay off the debt. Customs officers followed Mark's vehicle to Amsterdam and when it returned to Basildon it had been stopped, searched and five kilos of cocaine, twenty-four kilos of amphetamine and ten kilos of ecstasy pills had been found. The drugs had been hidden under a false floor. A spokesperson for Customs and Excise later told reporters more than forty officers from the National Investigation Service, police in Belgium and a Dutch specialist police team had been involved in a 'long term investigation which led to the seizure.' That statement proved Mark wasn't stopped by chance. He was probably recruited to drive the drugs into the UK after others involved in the importation realised that they may be being watched. When Mark appeared in court, he was sentenced to twelve years imprisonment.

30 11 1996: One evening, Raquel's doorman Chris Lombard had told me that he was leaving to work elsewhere. 'This place is too much mate, there's grief every night. I have been offered a job in a venue where there isn't much hassle and it's not far from my home,' he had said. I liked Chris, he was a huge guy, his size made him appear intimidating, but in reality, he was quiet, respectful and always remained calm when all around him madness reigned. His family and close friends quite rightly described him as a gentle giant. 'No problem, I understand, you have to do what is best for you, 'I replied. That night we shook hands and I watched him walking away from the club to his car, I never saw him again. I didn't hear of Chris again until Thursday, 5 December 1996. It was almost one year to the day since Tucker, Tate and Rolfe had been blown away. I had stopped at a shop outside Liverpool Street station in London to pick up a newspaper as I had to wait half an hour for a train. I glanced at the front page and then stared in horror. I could not believe what I was looking at nor what I was reading. 'Murdered doing his job' and alongside the headline was a photograph of Chris Lombard. It was reported that Chris had been shot dead and another man had been seriously injured after a hail of gunfire ripped through the Island nightclub reception area where they worked. Chris, 30, was fatally wounded when seven bullets smashed through the glass of a locked door at 3.35.a.m. Five young men had arrived at the venue moments before the doormen had stopped admitting people. They demanded to

be let in but Chris had explained that he was not allowed to do so because the clubs licence prohibited customers entering after a designated time. The men became abusive, threatening and vowed to return. Shortly afterwards, as the door staff chatted, shots rang out and Chris fell. He had been hit once in the head and twice in the chest. He was dead before he hit the floor. The club was just yards from the local police station, but its location had not deterred the gang. The head doorman, Albert St Hiliare, 40, had been shot once in the back, the bullet lodging itself near his spinal cord. A third doorman escaped serious injury when a bullet grazed his neck. Having regained the 'respect' the gang thought they had lost by not being allowed into a nightclub, they scattered like rats into the night. An unmarked police car with a video camera on board, filmed the five men running in all directions – two of them appeared to be carrying weapons. My former friends in the Essex underworld were dropping like flies. I was pleased, really fucking pleased, that I had walked away from all of that shit.10 12 1996: The trial of Steven Packman started today. He had allegedly supplied Leah Betts with the ecstasy pill that claimed her life. I tried hard to take my mind off the publicity I knew the trial would generate. A year had passed since the Rettendon murders, my children were settling in at school, the last thing we needed was more press attention. Need, want or otherwise, it mattered not, the people in the village where we lived were soon provided with plenty of material to fuel gossip. On the opening day of the trial our local newspaper, The Maldon and Burnham Standard reported, 'David Sims, (Manager of Raquel's) told jurors, 'A man called Anthony Tucker was in charge of security at the club and Bernard O'Mahoney, the then head doorman, was

Tuckers right hand man. He (O'Mahoney) wasn't happy Raquel's nightclub had been drawn into the Leah Betts investigation and he was under pressure from his business partner Tony Tucker to sort it out.' It was true that Tucker had urged me to identify Packman (who had already been arrested) to the press. Tucker wanted journalists to stop scrutinising Raquel's and the chain of supply that eventually led to Leah. If the press were made aware that Packman had been arrested, Tucker believed they would focus on him and forget about us. With the benefit of hindsight, Tucker couldn't have been more wrong. I had met Packman with a journalist and the conversation, in which he appeared to confess to supplying Leah was recorded. Rather than simply publishing that story with a photograph of Packman, the journalist gave the recording to the police and named me as the man who had met Packman. That's how I came to be the centre of attention at the trial. Packman claimed that I had threatened to burn down his house and break his legs. His best friend Stephen Smith, who had earlier pleaded guilty to his role in the supply of the drug to Leah, stuck the boot in by claiming that he was more frightened of me than he was of Mike Tyson. (He hadn't met me never mind Mike Tyson) The trial and the publicity, was to say the least, an unpleasant experience. After a week of listening to the evidence, the jury retired to consider its verdict. Despite the fact Packman's best friend Smith, had pleaded guilty and had told the jury that Packman had purchased the drugs in Raquel's before giving them to Leah's friend, the jury were unable to reach a verdict. Much to my dismay, a retrial was ordered. The publicity that followed the trial was ruthless. I was the only person still alive who had been identified as being involved with the so-called Essex Boys 'criminal organisation.' So, I got hit repeatedly by the press with both barrels. I was falsely accused of being a drug dealer. I was called a bastard by Leah Bett's father Paul, who stated on national television that he held me responsible for her death. I was even accused of, 'somehow' being involved in the murders of my former friends. Paul Betts based his allegation on the fact that I was head of security at a club, where everyone concerned, including the police and his daughter Leah, knew drugs were available. It was ridiculous, you don't blame a barman when you choose to get drunk. Raquel's was a rave after all and a rave without drugs is simply not a rave. Of course, I knew drugs were on sale, but I have never sold drugs to anyone. Detective Sergeant Nicholl, one of the investigating officers on Leah's case, told a press conference after the trial, 'in the early stages of the enquiry there was information which led police to suspect O'Mahoney might also be involved in drug dealing at Raquel's. Further enquiries failed to reveal any evidence of that and no charges were ever brought.' Despite Detective Sergeant Nicholls statement, former policeman Paul Betts chose to ignore his ex-colleagues' findings. The publicity his unfounded allegations created resulted in older children telling my children that their father was a murderer. How do you tell your tearful son or daughter to ignore such vile allegations? What could I possibly say when they asked if I had indeed taken a young girl's life? In an effort to stop what was a very damaging smear campaign, I wrote an open letter to Paul Betts which was published in the press. I urged him to confront me on live television so we could debate who really was responsible for his daughter's death but he, unsurprisingly, declined. I say unsurprisingly because six weeks before her death, I had barred Leah from Raquel's as she was underage. Her 18th birthday party had been held at her father's house; which is twenty-five miles from Raquel's. Her father had banned alcohol at the party. Imagine being a student, you invite all of your friends to your 18th birthday party but your father has banned alcohol. Leah and her friends foolishly chose to use ecstasy as a substitute. As Leah was banned from Raquel's, she asked friends to buy the drugs from the club on her behalf. The following week she took a pill at her party in her father's house and collapsed. It was revealed at trial that Leah and some of her guests were smoking cannabis at her party. Her father, a former policeman who was present, claimed that he didn't smell the cannabis that was being smoked in his house. Those are the undisputable facts and he blamed me for her death. The media of course, went along with him for the ride. I did not realise it at the time, but the seeds were being sown for a scenario that would cause my family and I misery for decades to come. Everyone, it seemed, wanted somebody to blame. Tucker, Tate and Rolfe were dead, who else was there to point an accusing finger at?

Other people claiming to be gang members did surface later. Eight years after the murders a guy named Carlton Leach published a book titled 'Muscle.' Leach was a gym buddy/friend of Tuckers who I had met no more than five or six times at various nightclubs. According to his book, he was close to 'Tone.' To add credence to his claim, Leach recalled how two weeks before the murders they had celebrated Tuckers fortieth birthday at Hollywood nightclub in Romford. It must have been quite a party because Tucker died aged thirty-eight. Another individual who claimed to be a 'close friend' of the Essex Boys was Steve Nipper Ellis. He had met Pat Tate in prison and allowed him to live at his flat upon release. During the first six weeks of meeting 'the boys,' Carlton Leach, according to Ellis, had stolen his car, money he gave him to tax the car and several leather jackets. Tucker had stolen a kettle, toaster and other household items from Ellis's flat. These were given to a prostitute who needed the items for her home. Rolfe had then attempted to steal Ellis's motorbike. Tate repaid Ellis's kindness by hiding quantities of drugs in and around his property. Fortunately for Ellis, the police didn't raid his home. Showering their new 'friend' with more love, Tucker and Tate dragged Ellis into his bedroom where Tucker put a gun to his head and threatened to cut his arm or leg off with a butcher's cleaver. After six short weeks Ellis had gone on the run after he learned that Tucker and Tate were planning to murder him. (Clearly not a close 'friend' of anyone in that circle.) In any event, I am not sure you can claim to be 'in the know' with anyone after six weeks, but Ellis clearly holds a different view.

CHAPTER TWO
Won't Get Fooled Again

22 02 1997: I took my son Vinney to watch Chelsea take on Manchester United in the Premier League at Stamford Bridge in south-west London. The game wasn't exactly thrilling, Gianfranco Zola put Chelsea ahead after just two minutes and David Beckham equalised for United in the 68th minute. When the game was over Vinney, who was aged nine at the time, said that he would like to get the United players autographs. I had been telling him how, as a boy, I had waited outside Manchester United games to get the autographs of legendary players like George Best, Denis Law and Bobby Charlton. We walked to the players entrance where steel barriers had been erected and a group of six burly stewards were stood stony faced glaring at approximately thirty young fans and their parents. Eric Cantona, David Beckham and a few other United players came out of the ground and walked towards the team coach. The young children were leaning over the barrier trying to get signatures but the stewards began shouting, 'get back' and shoved the steel barriers into them. Having worked in security for years, I considered their behaviour to be totally unnecessary and dangerous as the children were not posing a threat to anyone. I grabbed one of the stewards by the arm and told him to take it easy but he responded by slapping me across the nose with his glove. A

colleague of his then grabbed me by the shirt. I considered myself to be in danger and so I head butted him full into the face and he fell back, blood pouring from his nose. Vinney was naturally upset by all of this and so I led him away towards my car. The stewards got together and advanced across the car park towards me. There were eight of them at this time. I turned in a threatening manner and they backed off. Rather foolishly, I thought that was the end of the matter and proceeded to my car. Nobody approached me and so I left the car park and drove home.

24 02 1997: The second trial concerning Steven Packman got under way at Norwich Crown Court today. The media had milked the story dry by this stage and so thankfully, my feelings of impending doom proved futile. Press coverage of the proceedings was minimal. After five days the jury retired to consider its verdict, but once more, they failed to agree. The case was dismissed, Steven Packman walked free, his friend Stephen Smith was given a conditional discharge and I was told, that was the end of the matter, I would no longer be required.

03 04 1997: Ever since Leah Betts had collapsed at her father's home I had been pursued and maligned by the media. I didn't respond to some pretty wild and malicious allegations because I understood that grieving people needed to vent their anger. Unfortunately, the less I said the more I gave people free reign to make even more false and damaging allegations. The conclusion of the Betts trial gave the media one last chance to blame me for Leah's death. Banner headlines in national newspapers posing the question, 'Who really killed Leah Betts? ' were accompanied by a full-page

photograph of me. People pointed me out in the village where I lived and my children were constantly being told that their father was a murderer. I had written to several television companies asking them to arrange a live debate between myself and Paul Betts but he refused my offer. I tried to address matters by giving interviews to journalists but they edited or misrepresented the facts to make me appear guilty. I was advised that the only way I could truly have my say was if I wrote a book. 'Only you can edit it and you can cover every issue you choose,' I was told. So, that is what I did. On 3 April 1997 'So This is Ecstasy? was published.

10 04 1997: I have always been a huge fan of The Who. Their 1973 album Quadrophenia was the soundtrack of my chaotic youth. It was later made into a film which told the story of a young man in the 1960's who got caught up in gangs, violence and drugs. Predictably, he ended up dead. The story reminded me of the Essex Boys, working class lads with ideas of grandeur. They too got involved in gangs, violence and drugs and predictably ended up dead. I thought a modern-day version of Quadrophenia based on the Essex Boys story, with a soundtrack of classic rave tunes, would make a great movie. I had a meeting in London with Bill Curbishley, the manager of The Who. He had been instrumental in making Quadrophenia into a film. Bill admired my enthusiasm but he didn't think my idea would work. I touted the idea around several film and television companies but none showed any interest. I say none, but one clearly did, they just kept it from me. I met Jeff Pope at Granada films who seemed keen to hear what I had to say but concluded, like Bill Curbishley that my idea wouldn't work. I left disappointed but I remained confident that the story had the potential to be adapted into a

film. I had encountered similar negativity with my book. Ten or more publishers must have turned it down before it was finally accepted by Mainstream Publishing. One well known true crime publisher I submitted the manuscript to had written back to me saying, 'Essex Boys will never be a book, the story will struggle to fill a page in a newspaper.' I often wonder if he remembers sending me that letter. We've all got a black book full of missed opportunities.

14 04 1997: My former friend Dave Tomkins from Bristol had his appeal heard today at the Royal Courts of Justice in London. I had introduced Tomkins and his friends, Steve and Nathan to Tony Tucker. He had agreed to let the trio deal drugs exclusively in Club UK south London, for a fee of course. Things had gone well, so well in fact that their success attracted the attention of other criminals. Steve and Nathan had their BMW 'confiscated' by a villain in Bristol and Tomkins had his home burgled. I had recovered the BMW but before I could assist Tomkins, he had blasted Stephen Wood, (the man responsible for the burglary) with a shotgun. When questioned by police, Wood and his partner had named Tomkins as the gunman. Tomkins had contacted me and I had sorted out a pub in Basildon where he could live whilst he was on the run. Two weeks later I had travelled to Bristol with another doorman and met Woods. He had a gun put to his head and was advised to retract his statement. Woods complied. Tomkins returned to Bristol where he was charged with shooting Woods and possessing a firearm with intent to cause grievous bodily harm. I had fallen out with Tomkins at this stage over comments he had made behind my back. I went to Bristol prison and attacked him in the visiting room. We haven't spoken since. Tomkins believed that the case

against him would collapse because Woods had retracted his evidence. However, he had overlooked the fact Woods partner had also made a statement. Tomkins was convicted and sentenced to fourteen years imprisonment. At today's appeal, Tomkins's legal team told the judge that at the time of the burglary he had been in Cornwall on holiday with his family. He had received a telephone call informing him that his home had been burgled and ransacked. The caller added, that the burglar was Stephen Wood, a man who was well known to Tomkins. It was suggested that, in view of the state of his home, he should return before the rest of his family in order to clean up what was a diabolical mess. Tomkins travelled home immediately and discovered a scene of utter devastation. The contents of drawers and cupboards had been taken out and smashed. A tin of stain varnish had been poured over the living room carpet. The intruder or intruders had both urinated and defecated in the property. To his horror, Tomkins also discovered that they had defecated in his children's beds and then replaced the covers. Enraged, Tomkins borrowed a shotgun and went with another man to Wood's house, where they banged on the door. Wood opened it. He was struck in the face by the other man, and Tomkins aimed the gun at Woods groin and fired. The judges at the Court of Appeal said that they had seen, 'certain highly relevant material which was not available to the judge who had sentenced Tomkins. That material included a number of reports from the prison where Tomkins was currently serving his sentence. Those reports spoke, 'quite unambiguously of the very great efforts' which Tomkins had made and 'is continuing to make to rehabilitate himself.' In the light of that material, the Appeal Court granted Tomkins a substantial reduction in his sentence. It was reduced to just four years imprisonment. Tomkins 'very great efforts to rehabilitate himself, ' did however, fail to follow him out of the prison gate. Soon after his release, he was imprisoned for five years after pleading guilty to supplying heroin.

18 06 1997: Nearly four months after the incident at Chelsea football club, two police officers called at my home to arrest me. Debra and our children were walking out of the front door to go on the school run when they arrived. I wasn't home and the officers refused to tell Debra why they wanted me. They were very intimidating, saying I had to get in touch, it was urgent and it was in my best interests to comply. When Debra drove the children to school the police followed her. Feeling concerned, she had telephoned me to tell me what was happening. The officers had given her a number to pass on to me and so I called and asked what the fuck they thought they were doing. I was told that I was wanted for assaulting a steward at Chelsea football club, 'We need to see you urgently,' the officer added. I laughed, 'urgently? Well, if it's that urgent why wait four fucking months to contact me?' I lied and told the officer that I was in Liverpool. 'I'm home next week, I can pop in Wednesday if that's ok,' I added. They had little choice and so agreed. When I arrived at Chelsea police station I was formerly charged with assault and bailed to appear at West London Magistrates Court at a later date.

12 07 1997: Despite my retirement from criminality, the police continued to keep one eye on me and my family. I don't know if it was to ensure that Debra and the children didn't come to any harm or if they thought I was up to something, but they were always there, lurking in the background. They would

drive slowly past my house or ring to ask if everything was okay. During one such telephone call, a detective expressed his concern about a firearms incident he claimed had occurred outside my home. Debra told him that she didn't have a clue what he was talking about. The detective was adamant that a colleague from the armed response unit had mentioned that a man in possession of a shotgun had been arrested outside my home. Debra, who was naturally shocked, said that if it was true, we hadn't been informed. When I returned home later that evening, Debra told me what had been said and so I rang the detective concerned. He told me that he didn't have any information to hand but he would look into the matter and get back to me as soon as possible. His parting words were far from reassuring, 'In the meantime Bernie, if I were you, I would be vigilant.' I wasn't going to leave Debra and our children hanging around to find out if some psycho had been near the house with a shotgun. Protecting my family came first, second and third. I could deal with any threat once they were out of harm's way. I didn't have anything in the house that would 'deter' an armed intruder and so I decided to move out until the necessary hardware could be acquired. I assumed that I would be the intended target and so I sent Debra and the children to stay with her parents. I went to my mother's house in Codsall, a small village on the outskirts of Wolverhampton. You cannot live your life running away from people. You have to face threats and violence, but it's no good doing so if you are not mentally and physically prepared. I had to find out who was posing the threat and I had to have the means to defend myself regardless of what they may be armed with. When I arrived in Codsall, I dropped my overnight bag off at my mothers, telephoned Debra to check everything was ok and then I walked to a local shop. On my way back, I saw my friend Hughie having a drink outside a pub called The Crown. Because it was a warm summers day there were plenty of other people enjoying a drink at adjacent tables. I sat down with Hughie and a couple of other lads and started talking about things in general. I had only been there two or three minutes when I noticed a police sergeant walking by. The expression on his face changed when he saw me. He quickened his pace and headed straight for the table where I was sitting. Naturally, everybody stopped what they were doing to look at the officer who was now standing before me with his hands on his hips. 'You've made a name for yourself haven't you O'Mahoney,' he said. 'Are you staying at your mothers? When are you going back to London?'

I sat in silence; grateful I hadn't actually done anything to attract this particular policeman's attention. I stared straight at him with utter contempt. I was thinking, my family are living in fear, people are threatening to kill me and all Sergeant dick head can do is give me grief. After looking him up and down I told him to fuck off and when he arrived, he should fuck off some more. The Sergeant sensed my mood was hostile and wisely walked away. I was extremely embarrassed by the attention he had drawn to me, everybody was looking and talking about what had been said. I told Hughie that I was going home for a while but I would see him later.

At approximately 10.p.m I returned to the pub and remained with Hughie until closing time. After saying our goodbyes, I walked to a nearby Indian restaurant where I purchased a takeaway. The streets were deserted as I made my way back to my mother's home. A police riot van drove slowly down the street but when the driver spotted me, he stopped and called out of his window. 'Alright mate, you been anywhere nice? I had enough on my mind without having to deal with a comedian in uniform. I had been minding my own business and wasn't doing anything to warrant police attention. I told him to grow up or fuck off. The policeman had no intention of doing either, he replied, 'there's no need for that son.' I told him to fuck off again. He unclipped his seat belt and attempted to get out of his vehicle. I held his door shut and told him to stay where he was as I didn't want any trouble. He kept trying to open the door and was threatening to arrest me. Perhaps it was the state of mind I was in after being pestered by so called villains and now this fool? Whatever triggered me, I just flipped. I couldn't take any more of his or anyone else's shit. When I let go of the door, I knew that the officer would leap out and so I was ready for him. As he moved towards me, he held out his hands as if to grab me. I hit him hard across the side of the head with the flat of my hand and as he staggered back, I punched him in the face. He stumbled momentarily and so I slapped him again around the ear. He clutched his head with both hands and fell sideways onto the pavement. I noticed that he wasn't laughing anymore. There was a struggle as his colleague who had been in the passenger seat, jumped on my back. Within minutes I had been overwhelmed by officers who had been summoned to the scene to give assistance. I wasn't surprised that the Sergeant who had confronted me earlier was one of them. I was handcuffed and thrown headfirst into the van. The handcuffs had been fitted so tightly they were cutting into my wrists. My forehead was bleeding and I had three other baton wounds in the back of my head. I later learned that my finger had been broken and I had a large boot shaped bruise on my stomach. At the police station my hands remained cuffed behind my back, I could feel the blood from my wrists running through my hands and fingers. Requests to loosen or remove the cuffs were refused. I was hauled in front of the desk Sergeant and the arresting officer said that I had been detained for using abusive words and threatening behaviour. No mention was made of the assault, perhaps I thought, because I had come off much worse than any of them. I was put in a cell, still handcuffed, and left alone to contemplate my rapidly decreasing good fortune. Throughout the years I had worked at Raquel's, I had never endured bullshit like this, but now I was trying to give up my criminal past, I was being crucified. I lay face down on the wooden bench in my cell. I couldn't lay on my back because my hands were still cuffed behind me. I could feel the blood running down my face from the wounds on my head. A pool of blood began to form on the bench. My wrists were beginning to swell, intensifying my discomfort and pain. Not only were the handcuffs preventing me from laying on my back, they were preventing me from undoing my trousers and I was desperate to use the toilet. Unable to wait any longer, I had to suffer the indignity of urinating myself. As a 14-year-old boy I had been locked in the very same police cell I now found myself in. Over twenty years had passed but nothing had changed. The same anger, the same sense of injustice and the same sense of hopelessness tore through me. My lifelong struggle with authority had certainly buckled and warped me, but the pressure I had been under for the past two years had almost broken me. I couldn't care less what they charged me with, nor did I care that I was in a cell, I just felt so bloody hopeless. Whichever path I chose, they were never going to allow me to succeed. I realised that I was wallowing in self-pity and got angry with myself, embarrassed even. I then heard the rattle of keys which indicated the police were coming for me. I remained face down on the bench and pretended to be asleep. I had done that ever since I was a boy, in my mind I was showing the police that I wasn't worrying about their latest intrusion into my life. The inspection hatch in the cell door dropped down and I could feel the officer's eyes surveying my cell. He slammed the hatch back into position and I listened as his footsteps echoed down the corridor and out of the cell block.

13 07 1997: The cell door opened and the day shift officers were kind enough to take my handcuffs off. The expression on their faces told me that I looked a mess. I was soaked in my own urine, I had blood all over my face, head and chest and my clothing had been torn. I was given the opportunity to wash, offered a cup of tea and then taken out to the custody officer. He formerly charged me with using abusive words, threatening behaviour and, after a theatrical pause, assaulting a police officer.

24 07 1997: Eleven days after being charged with assaulting the officer and using abusive words/threatening behaviour, I had to appear at West London Magistrates Court in London for allegedly assaulting the steward at Chelsea Football Club. In the world of Bernard O'Mahoney I was innocent. I had only retaliated after being slapped across the nose and being grabbed by a couple of over-zealous hard men who thought they could flex their beer guts in front of children.

Unfortunately, the law according to Bernard O'Mahoney was nil and void in the real world. I wasn't sure how I was going to present my defence. The police had mustered six 'upstanding' stewards of impeccable character as witnesses. The 'victim' had been photographed bearing some pretty nasty looking injuries including a fractured eye socket and cheekbone. It certainly didn't look good for me. In the waiting room I noticed that the stewards were sitting with the detective who had arrested me and so I sat immediately behind them. None of the stewards appeared to recognise me and the detective was sitting with his back to me. I could clearly hear every word that they were saying. The steward that I had allegedly headbutted, was telling the detective that he wanted the magistrate to ban me from ever visiting Chelsea's ground again. 'Just in case I bump into him,' he added. The steward then asked the detective what he should do if, 'somebody doesn't get their story straight?' The detective replied, 'Don't worry, it's a Stipendiary magistrate today, she's a good old bird, she will guide you through it.' I stood up and turned around to face the detective and the stewards. 'Trying to get your story straight, are you? The magistrate will guide you, will she? As a police officer I would have thought you would know better than to coach witnesses.' I could see that they were shocked to discover that I had been listening to their conversation. I added to their anguish by informing them that I was going to complain to the Stipendiary magistrate. 'You know the one officer, the good old bird,' I added for spite. I went to the court office and asked the receptionist to call the police as an attempt was being made to pervert the course of justice. At first the receptionist seemed keen to get some toe rag locked up but when I explained that the ringleader was a detective the mood changed. The receptionist said that she would have to seek advice. A few minutes later she told me that it wouldn't be necessary to call the police as the magistrate was going to deal with my complaint. When my case was eventually called, the clerk advised me that I should not make any complaint in open court. I could however question those I was claiming had been involved in matters in the waiting room. When the stewards were called to give evidence, I asked them about their conversation with the detective, some were totally honest, some denied any conversation had taken place and others claimed that they couldn't remember. The incident at the Chelsea ground became secondary as I exposed the witnesses as being unreliable conspirators at best. In less than thirty minutes the trial had ended after the, 'good old bird' dismissed the case against me. The detective and the stewards looked physically sick. On the stairs outside the court, the steward that I had allegedly headbutted got rather upset and lunged at me, but his colleagues held him back. I smiled at him and said, 'You shouldn't take matters so personally, your detective friend should have warned you that there isn't any justice anymore.' I then walked away as he continued to struggle and shout abuse.

11 11 1997: I left home at 4.30.a.m to undertake the three-and-a-half-hour drive to Wombourne Magistrates Court near Wolverhampton. I faced two charges, abusive words/threatening behaviour and assaulting a police officer. My intention was to plead not guilty to both. At 5.20.a.m my vehicle broke down just north of Chelmsford. I had to be in court by 10.a.m or the unforgiving police would undoubtedly charge me with failing to answer my bail. Two charges were

plenty for me to be getting on with, so I rang Debra. Understandably, once she was awake, Debra was far from pleased. I explained that I was stranded and if I didn't get to court on time I would end up in more trouble. Reluctantly, Debra agreed that she would get the children out of bed, pick me up and drive the 173 miles from our home to court. I felt awful about having to ask but, I had no choice. At 8.a.m I rang the police and asked them to inform the officer in charge of the case that I had broken down. 'I may be late if I hit the rush hour traffic in Birmingham, but rest assured, I will be there.' 'No problem, we will pass on your number and if there is a problem, he will contact you, 'they replied. I walked into the court building at 9.55.a.m leaving my two small children and Debra asleep in the car. I found the Usher and explained that I was due in court at 10.a.m. 'Hasn't anybody contacted you Mr. O'Mahoney? The matter has been adjourned until 12 January next year because of a non-disclosure issue,' she said. I may have used expletives relating to sex and travel before walking out. It may have been a genuine administrative error, but my heart told me I was the victim of a juvenile prank. Regardless of the truth, I am in no doubt that the officers involved in the case were made aware that it wouldn't be proceeding prior to 10.a.m that morning. I guess they just 'forgot' to tell me. I can only describe the atmosphere in the car on the three-and-a-half-hour drive home, as 'frosty.'

17 11 1997: Solicitors representing Michael Steele and Jack Whomes, the two men accused of murdering Tucker, Tate and Rolfe contacted me. They wanted to know if I would be willing to make a statement. I failed to see how I could help their clients but agreed I would if I could. They wanted to

know why I had fallen out with the three deceased men and how I knew about the position of the bodies which I had described to the media. I knew, like most people with an interest in the case, because the details had been published in most newspapers at the time of the murders. Two farmers who discovered the bodies had also appeared on television describing the position and posture of the victims in the Range Rover. The murder trial had started three months earlier, it was clearly not going well for the defendants if their legal team were searching for fresh witnesses at this late stage.

12 01 1998: I attended Wombourne Magistrates Court near Wolverhampton today. I stood trial for abusive words/threatening behaviour and assaulting the police officer who had stopped me whilst I was visiting my mother. To his credit, the Sergeant who had initially approached me outside the pub admitted he had walked over 'for no particular reason' to 'chat with me.' He said that he had seen me on television and in the newspapers following the murders of my former associates. The officer I had slapped with my open hand was equally honest. He admitted that he had pulled up next to me for, 'no particular reason.' It was late and I asked him if he had been anywhere nice.' I was representing myself and found it wasn't too difficult to make the magistrates wonder why I had been stopped for no apparent reason on two separate occasions by two different officers within a seven-hour period. I told the court that I had arrived in the village after leaving my home in Essex because the police had informed me that a man had been arrested in possession of a shotgun outside my home. The incident had arisen, police believed, because I had assisted them in the Leah Betts case.

As soon as I arrived in Codsall I had been confronted by a sarcastic police officer in front of members of the public and later that night I had been confronted by another equally sarcastic officer. I was, I said, a man who had snapped under enormous pressure. I was found not guilty of using abusive words and threatening behaviour but guilty of assaulting a police officer. The magistrate said when sentencing me, that although assaulting a police officer was a serious matter, given the circumstances, I would be given a two-year conditional discharge. This meant I would not be punished if I stayed out of trouble for two years. If I was convicted of any offence during that period, I could be brought back to court and sentenced again for the assault. The Prosecution, who had been hoping for a custodial sentence, were seething. The Prosecutor told the magistrate that they wanted £500 in costs from me but this was refused and I was ordered to pay just £100. I had stood in that court room endless times during my formative years and usually departed for home feeling aggrieved or extremely aggrieved in the back of a prison van. On this occasion I felt as if justice had been served. I should not have assaulted the officer but I do believe that on both occasions that evening I had been provoked.

Driving back to Essex, I heard on the radio that Raquel's had closed its doors for good. The management had tried to relaunch the club by replacing Tucker's door staff and renaming it Europa, but they could never erase the stigma the club had or wash the blood out of the carpets.

It was now going to be a Snooker Hall where the locals could enjoy smashing each other's balls around with a wooden stick, no change there then. For all its faults, and it did have many, I do have some very fond memories of that place. I just thank God that walls really can't talk.

20 01 1998: I was in Colchester when I heard on the radio that Michael Steele and Jack Whomes had been found guilty of conspiracy to import cannabis and the murders of Craig Rolfe, Pat Tate and Tony Tucker. Their former friend Darren Nicholls had turned supergrass in lieu of a life sentence. His evidence, supported by a paper trail of Ferry bookings, hire cars, hotels and phone cell site evidence, was crucial. It wasn't however the only evidence. Both Steele and Whomes humiliated themselves as they were cross examined because the web of lies, they had used to manufacture their alibis fell apart under scrutiny. Whomes had told officers during interviews that he had no idea where Rettendon was, but phone cell site evidence had not only placed him in Rettendon on the relevant night, it had placed him in the lane where and at the time, the murders had taken place. Steele had recruited a relative to give him an alibi but she crumbled in the witness box and admitted that she was only repeating times and a date that Steeles solicitor had suggested to her. Craig Rolfe's wife had told police that on the night he died he had said that he was going to meet Steele, or Micky the pilot as he was known and they were planning to rob a shipment of drugs. The very same story Nicholls had told police when he was arrested six months later. Nicholls and Rolfe's wife, had never met. Instead of parading me in front of the jury as a man with a motive for murder, Steele and Whomes legal team had opted for Billy Jasper. Like me, Billy Jasper had been approached at the eleventh hour to give evidence, but unlike me he had little choice. Jasper was in prison at the time and was served with a court order demanding he attend. Initially

he refused to leave the cells below the court, but after several hours he was coaxed into the witness box. Jasper was a drug addict who has been described as a 'serial confessor.' When confined in police cells and withdrawing from drugs, he had a habit of offering evidence to officers in the hope he would be released early so that he could satisfy his habit. Shortly after the Rettendon murders (15 January 1996) Jasper had been arrested by Essex police on an unrelated matter. Without any encouragement, Jasper told the police that he had driven Tucker, Tate and Rolfe's killer to the murder scene. He went on to claim that the assassin was armed with a sawn-off shotgun and a handgun. The police knew instantly that Jasper was lying because the wounds all three men had suffered had not been caused by a handgun or sawn-off shotgun. Ballistic experts had firmly established that all three men had been shot by a full-length pump action shotgun. For clarity, the officers took Jasper to the general area of Rettendon and asked him to point out the lane where he said he had dropped the killer off. Despite driving past the actual lane where the murders took place on two occasions, Jasper failed to point it out. Eventually, he directed officers to a lane nearly two miles away from the crime scene. He was in short, absolutely clueless about the location, the time the crimes were committed and the weapons used. Jasper's confession was laughed out of court and the right men were convicted and sentenced to life imprisonment.

24 03 1998: Essex police arrived at my home and demanded that I dismantle part of a garden wall that I had restored. Approximately one week earlier, I was on my way home from Colchester when I saw several tonnes of builder's waste fly tipped in a lay by. I needed a few house bricks to repair an

old wall at home and so I had loaded about ten in the boot of my car. The police told me that although the bricks didn't appear to have an owner, it was still theft. 'You can either go to court or accept a caution, 'the officer said. What can you say to anyone who could pretend that this was a serious matter, I looked at him with a sense of pity. I wasn't going to argue about a few old bricks that someone had thrown away and so I accepted his caution. He then stood waiting whilst I dismantled part of my wall and put the bricks into the boot of his car. I learned two things from that incident, one, I must be being watched if they did indeed see me take the bricks and two, some people really are fucking sad.

I had been to Colchester that day to see an Irish guy about a job. In the 1980's I had worked for a few Irish firms driving HGV tipper lorries around London. It sounds like a relatively normal job but that industry, at that particular time, was awash with criminals. The East End docklands had been a wasteland for decades and so in the 1980's the Government decided to bulldoze and then rebuild vast swathes of the area. From Liverpool Street Station in the city to Barking in Essex, money was poured in and the work began. Much of the muck/soil that was excavated was destined for what was later to become the Lakeside shopping centre. As the name suggests, a lot of the area they intended to build on was under water and so they needed the muck/soil to fill the lakes. Due to the dense London traffic, if you drove all day, you could only manage three trips from the city to Lakeside. After paying the running costs of the lorry and a driver's wage there was very little profit left. So, ever resourceful, some of the Irish lads began renting huge hangar like warehouses close to the city. A digger would be put inside the empty warehouse and the doors would be closed. Loaded HGV tipper lorries would arrive from the city, the doors would be opened, they would reverse in, tip their twenty tonne loads of muck and drive away. The doors would then be closed again and the digger would heap the muck/soil up to the roof until the warehouse was completely full. Instead of three loads to Lakeside, drivers were doing fifteen to twenty loads per day. I was earning more in a day than most people were earning in a week. The Irish guy I knew had just bought a yard in Colchester and when I went to see him, he offered me a job. The good old days were long gone but there was still some money to be made with tippers and so I accepted his offer.

17 04 1998: A month after starting work for the Irish guy, he told me that a huge development was being built in Peterborough and he had been given the contract to do all of the excavating and muck shifts. Hampton, as the development was known, included the construction of 8,500 new homes with additional schools, local centres and leisure facilities, as well as commercial and retail areas providing more than 12,000 jobs. The Irishman said that he wanted me to go to Peterborough and run the job for him. I shook his hand whilst thinking, the good old days may soon be returning.

11 05 1998: I started work at 7.a.m at Hampton, Peterborough after a two-hour, 95-mile drive from my home in Essex. Finishing work at 6.p.m, it was 8.p.m by the time I got home. Despite the very long days, I enjoyed working in Peterborough. The lads were a good laugh, always playing pranks on one another and so the time flew by. We travelled in two vehicles from Essex, one was a conventional transit

van, the other a two-seater pick-up truck which we used to transport lorry tyres. One of the lads lived at Marks Tay, a small village on the outskirts of Colchester. He chose to sit in the back of the pick-up truck for the journey each morning. At 5.a.m it was still dark and extremely cold and so he used to wear a diver's wet suit which he claimed kept him warm and dry. (I could never understand why he didn't just sit in the back of the transit but being an action man was clearly his thing.) As I reached the outskirts of Colchester one morning, I rang the police and said I had noticed a weird man opposite my home dressed in a rubber suit acting suspiciously. After taking my false name the telephonist told me that they would send a car immediately. I then picked one of the other drivers up. When we arrived at the lay by where we normally picked action man up, I could see two police vehicles parked with their blue lights flashing. I slowed down as if I was curious to see what the police were up to. An officer waved me down and approached my car with action man, who was wearing his rubber wet suit and handcuffs. 'Do you know this gentleman sir? He says that he is waiting for you? ' the officer enquired. 'Definitely not, as you can see this is a two-seater vehicle, we aren't picking anybody up, ' I replied. Action man began shouting and so the policeman told me to go as he turned to lead his prisoner to his car. I still laugh when I think about it today. Action man was released when his wife verified that he lived in the house opposite the lay by where he was arrested and he was en-route to work.

21 06 1998: Tired of commuting, I began staying in Peterborough during the week and returning home on Fridays. Debra, quite rightly was not happy with the situation and told me that our relationship had run its course and

staying together was pointless. I agreed and began looking for alternative accommodation.

In the summer of 1998, I met Emma Turner. We had known one another for some time but we were nothing more than casual friends. Emma and I began meeting socially but even then, it was on a purely friendship basis. It was obvious to us both that we liked one another but every aspect of my life was awash with uncertainty. I wasn't living in Peterborough or Essex but spent my time in both, my belongings were in Debra's house and I couldn't say if things were going to change next week, next month or next year. Romance was most definitely not a priority in my life at that time, but we don't get to choose the day we wake up and realise that someone is the one. Like shit, it just happens.

October 1998: Granada television, who I had approached with an idea about a film, announced it was going to make a movie which was 'inspired by the Rettendon murders' called 'Essex Boys.' A spokesperson for Granada said: 'We have not cast the film yet, but it will be stars of film rather than television. We will start on this in the next few weeks. 'The budget is not finalised. but the film will probably cost several million pounds and locations have not been found. 'We hope we will be shooting some scenes at Rettendon and the rest will be done in other parts of the county. We are looking towards the end of the year for these locations. 'The film, which will take about two months to make, will be about all organised crime, will be purely fiction and will be shown in cinemas throughout the country. 'Shocked? No. Surprised? No. Words simply failed me. This was the company who had told me that a film about events in Essex would never work.

06 01 1999: A journalist from the Observer newspaper contacted me. He wanted to know what I thought about ex-Raquel's doorman Mark Rothermel escaping from a police station in Brazzaville, the capital of the Congo Republic in Africa. I was surprised Mark had been locked up in the Congo, but not surprised he had escaped.

Nicknamed the Colonel by the media, I had always liked Mark, reserved, polite and matter of fact, he didn't suffer fool's, period. He worked for me at Raquel's and we worked together at the Ministry of Sound and Epping Country Club. The Congo is not a location many Essex based bouncers can claim to have had a battle in, but Mark Rothermel is no run of the mill Essex bouncer. The best way I can describe him, is by briefly telling his remarkable story.

Towards the end of 1985 Rothermel had been interviewed by the Essex Chronicle regarding his plans to lead an expedition in the Congo to find a descendent of the dinosaurs called Mokele Mbembe, an African version of the Loch Ness monster, which supposedly inhabited uncharted swamps. Rothermel and Bill Gibbons, a member of Rothermels Operation Congo expedition, flew out to Africa in the spring of 1986. The expedition failed to find the monster, but Gibbons was greatly influenced by an American missionary couple they had met and according to a relative of another member of the expedition he found God in the jungle.

In November 1989, Rothermel had been sentenced to six years imprisonment for assisting in the disposal of a body. Rothermel had been working at Hollywood's in Romford - one of Tony Tucker's doors - with another man, Pierre St Ange.

Pierre and Rothermel had got into a dispute with a D.J there named Bernie Burns. They had lured him to a flat in Ilford where Burns had been strangled. His body was wrapped in a blanket, put in the boot of a car and taken to a quiet wood near Chelmsford. It was there that Rothermel took an axe to the man's body; he hacked off the head and both of his hands so it would be difficult to identify. Rothermel was reported to have told a friend: 'the hands came off easily but the head was more of a problem because of the veins in his neck.' Burns was buried in a shallow woodland grave; his head and his hands have never been recovered.

Police found the mutilated corpse after a tip-off and arrested Rothermel at the same time; he was hiding in a pond up to his neck in water near the grave. Rothermel was found not guilty of murder, not guilty of manslaughter but he received six years imprisonment for the disposal of the body. Pierre St Ange was found not guilty of murder but was sentenced to ten years for manslaughter.

On 6 November 1998 Rothermel was arrested in Brazzaville on suspicion of being a spy. Two months later Rothermel escaped from a police station with forty other people during a fierce gun battle. The Foreign office said he was an 'aid worker' and he had contacted them after the breakout. Following that initial contact, Rothermel had just 'vanished.' Prior to his departure from the UK, Rothermel had told friends that he was travelling to the Congo to go trekking and do 'a bit of charity work.'

However, Mission Aid, the Christian charity Rothermel told friends he had volunteered for, ceased to exist two years earlier. It also emerged that Rothermel had recently spent time in Russia and California – again, apparently, in connection with charity work. Several broadsheet newspapers speculated that Rothermel had actually been working as a spy.

On 3 May 2001 Mark Rothermel made headline news again. On this occasion, one hundred HM Customs and firearms officers had stormed Bawdsey Beach in Suffolk. Overhead, a police helicopter directed the operation. One eye witness told reporters that the scene was, 'like something out of a movie.' The focus of all this attention was Mark Rothermel and his seven-man gang. Rothermel and his second in command, Sean Clarke, had been observed by Customs officers over a period of months carrying out checks of remote beaches in East Anglia. Maps and notes giving marks out of ten for 'good spots' were later recovered. Notes in Rothaermel's handwriting gave Bawdsey ten out of ten for being the ideal site for landing drugs. Two days before his arrest on the Suffolk beach, Rothermel and an accomplice named Brian Richardson, had travelled from Dover to Zeebrugge and then on to Holland where they acquired 3.3kgs of amphetamine and 40kgs of herbal 'skunk' cannabis. Police estimated that the drugs had a street value of almost £60.000. Richardson had met Rothermel whilst working on the door at The Venue, a club in Ilford with which many of the gang had a connection. Rothermel and Richardson had loaded the drugs into a specially designed motorboat in Belgium. It then departed for Bawdsey beach via Point Clear near Clacton. (Ironically, Mick Steele and Jack Whomes had chosen Point Clear to land the drugs they had imported for Tucker, Tate and Rolfe) Rothermel and Richardson then returned to the UK via the

Channel tunnel to await the return of the boat. When the boat landed at around 8.a.m the army of HM Customs and police officers had swooped. Sean Clarke was sentenced to four years imprisonment and Mark Rothermel was given five years.

18 12 1998: Debra and I put our house up for sale, which reinforced the uncomfortable truth that our relationship was terminal. I was still seeing Emma socially but eventually we did become an item. I didn't want to make Debra feel any worse than either of us did, nor did I want to upset our children and so I kept the relationship to myself. Debra isn't stupid, far from it, she knew, we just didn't discuss it. In many ways I think Debra was relieved, our floundering relationship could finally sink.

Aside from my many personal faults, the reputation of the Essex Boys still clung to me like a bad smell. The majority of Basildon residents, including Emma's mother Terry, had heard about me and the events that I was associated with. It was pointless blaming others or trying to disassociate myself because each and every story had been told in newspapers during the various trials. It's fair to say that Terry strongly disapproved of me initially, but after meeting a few times we did get on reasonably well. Maybe, just maybe I thought, I am beginning to put the past behind me.

CHAPTER THREE

Darkness on the Edge of Town

15 01 1999: Emma was due to celebrate her 21st birthday on 18 January and so I took her to Paris for the weekend. We had without doubt an amazing time. Before we knew it, the weekend was over and we were heading home. It was late when we arrived back in Basildon and so I stayed at Emma's flat. I didn't want her to wake up alone on her birthday in any event.

18 01 1999: At 6.a.m I left Emma's flat in Waldringfield, Basildon and headed for home. Two minutes into my journey I had reached a local shopping centre on Whitmore Way. Nothing much happens at that time of morning and so a cluster of police cars and several officers roaming around in the street caught my attention. I instinctively slowed down and saw that officers dressed in forensic suits were on their hands and knees searching an area outside a shop. I assumed someone had been murdered or seriously hurt, this was Basildon after all. I rang Emma and said, 'It looks as if somebody has been topped by the shops.' Emma said that she would no doubt hear the full story when she went around to her mother's house later. When I arrived home, I went

upstairs to shower and get changed. An hour or so later I went into the kitchen and Debra looked far from happy. 'You better ring your girlfriend, ' she said. 'What's brought this on? ' I replied. 'Nothing, she has been texting and ringing your phone ever since you went upstairs, I'd say its urgent.' I will never forget picking up my phone and reading Emma's message, 'Bernie, ring me please, as soon as you can, my mother has been murdered.' Shocks don't come much bigger than that message. I apologised to Debra and explained I had to go back out, 'this is serious, ' I said. I rang Emma and she said that the police had arrested her mother's boyfriend after he had telephoned an ambulance. Emma's mother had been found at the bottom of the stairs in her home with terrible head injuries and quite heavy bruising. Attempts had been made to save her, but she had passed away shortly after reaching the hospital. 'Are you sure, I saw the police and forensic team searching outside the shop near your flat when I left this morning, ' I said. 'I am not sure of anything, I am hearing all sorts, please just get here as quick as you can, ' Emma pleaded. When I did arrive, Emma was understandably distraught. Six years earlier, her father had died after falling down the stairs in the same house where her mother had now died. I spoke to a detective who asked if I would accompany Emma to Basildon hospital as they needed her to identify her mother's body. When we arrived, Emma's friend Karen was waiting for us. Emma embraced Karen and they both broke down. I was finding it hard to take in, I couldn't begin to imagine what Emma was going through. A 21st birthday card in her lounge with the inscription, 'Have a wonderful day, ' from her mother kept coming into my thoughts. It was like a cruel, cruel joke. Three detectives approached us and one asked Emma to accompany them but she refused. 'I can't, I just can't, ' she sobbed. I offered to accompany Emma and this seemed to calm her down. We were taken into a large room and a detective and doctor stood waiting by an open casket. A white shroud covered the body within. 'Are you okay Miss Turner? ' the detective enquired. 'Yes, ' Emma replied. 'Shall we? ' he asked as he held either end of the shroud. 'Ok', Emma said. As the shroud was lifted to reveal her mother, Emma began to sob uncontrollably. I did my best to comfort her but she was inconsolable. There was a deep wound down the left side of Terry's head and face, her nose and eye had been pushed in towards the skull, it was horrific. 'I'm sorry, I have to ask you Miss Turner, is this your mother? 'the detective asked. Choking back tears, Emma confirmed the terrible truth. Emma asked if we could be left alone for a few minutes with her mother and so the detective and the doctor departed. I couldn't imagine what was going through Emma's mind as we stood looking at her mother's badly disfigured face. After a few minutes I said, 'Come on Emma, let's get you home.' Emma didn't answer, she just turned and walked away with me. Having now lost both parents in tragic circumstances at the age of 21, I couldn't leave Emma alone. She needed someone, anyone to be there for her. The nature of her mother's death made grieving all the more difficult, Emma, had so many unanswered questions. The front page of the evening newspaper confirmed Emma's worst fears, 'A south Essex town was today rocked by two murders after the bodies of a mother and a man in his 20's were found in separate incidents.' Although Terry's boyfriend hadn't been charged with murder, detectives were insisting it was indeed murder and charges would follow. The newspaper did resolve the confusion I had about the forensic officers near the shops, that turned out to be a separate murder. The incidents were half a mile apart, or a ten-minute walk and the police had been called to both incidents within twenty minutes of one another. I later learned that a 26-year-old Yardie gangster calling himself Omar Locke had arrived in Basildon from north London and tried to muscle in on the crack cocaine trade. Drug dealer Darren Robinson recruited fellow crack cocaine addict Dennis Twilley to rob Locke and teach him a lesson. When Locke had arrived in Basildon, Robinson bought a rock of crack cocaine from him and invited him into his flat for payment. As soon as Omar walked through the door, Robinson and Twilley threatened him with a hammer. Robinson then slashed Omar across the wrists. Omar backed off, but he backed himself up to a window. In a desperate attempt to get out, Omar smashed the glass and went through the window. Robinson pulled him back and stabbed him in the thigh, the buttock and ankle. The force of one of the knife blows, propelled Omar through the window and onto the street below. Omar managed to crawl and hide in nearby bushes. He was later found by a friend put into a car and driven back to London. Sadly, he bled to death on the way. Detectives investigating Omar's death travelled to Jamaica to discover his true identity after learning he had been using a friend's passport. Detective Inspector Sharpe, who made the trip to Jamaica, told reporters that he had interviewed the real Omar Locke who had worked with his friend Venroy Pinnock on a roadside food bar. Venroy, a promising chef, had decided to visit England to study catering and for some reason obtained a passport in the name of his friend Locke. Detectives revealed that Venroy Pinnock had previously been deported from the US for 'drug-related matters.' Robinson was sentenced to nine years imprisonment for manslaughter and Twilley was jailed for five years after he confessed to robbing Pinnock of Class A drugs. It's hard to understand how two men who had armed themselves and then attacked a man for the purpose of robbing him, were not convicted of murder. Everything about the crime was premeditated. Emma and I were also left bewildered after the police released her mother's boyfriend after three days without charge. We had a meeting with the senior detective in the case who insisted Emma's mother's death was not murder but the result of a terrible accident.

According to the detective, Emma's mother had got up in the night to use the bathroom and tripped on a radio lead that had been left in the hall. 'She fell forward down the stairs and her head struck a radiator which caused the fatal injury,' he said. Neither Emma or I believed that explanation to be true. A neighbour had made a statement claiming she had heard shouting, an argument. 'There was a male and female voice. I then heard a scream, a loud dull thud and silence before the sound of the emergency services arriving approximately half an hour later.' We never got to learn the truth because despite our protestations, the police closed the case. Unsurprisingly, Terry's boyfriend disappeared, he didn't even attend her funeral.

10 05 1999: Debra and our children moved out of the family home as she had acquired her own property in a nearby village. We had found a buyer for our house but the estate agent had warned that it could take up to three months for the sale to go through. Debra, quite rightly, had taken most of

the contents from the house as the children's needs came first. That left me living alone in a large empty property and so I moved back to Basildon to live with Emma.

18 05 1999: Emma and I went for a drink at the Festival Leisure Park in Basildon. This is a large entertainment complex comprising of bars, nightclubs, a bowling alley, cinema and fast-food restaurants. Some of the wittier locals refer to it as 'Bas Vegas.' We had a drink in a couple of the bars and ended up in a nightclub called Jumping Jacks. When we entered the venue, a small, thin, drug-ravished man started shouting 'fucking cunt.' at me. He threw his baseball cap on the floor and repeatedly spat, each time repeating, 'cunt, fucking cunt.' I looked around to see if the man had a responsible adult with him or perhaps a carer because he appeared to be mentally challenged or suffering from some sort of embarrassing disorder. I couldn't see anyone and so I thought it best to ignore the poor wretch. Emma, not used to witnessing such alarming behaviour, clutched my arm and asked me who he was. It was only when the man started shouting about 'grassing Mark Murray up' did I take a closer look and realise it was a wannabe gang'star' named John Rollinson. He liked to be known as Gaffer. I hadn't seen him since I had worked at Raquel's and he had lost a lot of weight. He looked gaunt and thin, no doubt the result of a low life existence, popping pills and feeding a cocaine habit. When you are out with your partner for a drink, you don't really relish the thought of rolling round the floor with a drunk or loud-mouthed druggie. I apologised to Emma and told her we would have a drink at the other end of the bar, but if Gaffer continued to be abusive or offered violence, then I would have to discipline him. Gaffer was in the company of another

man who was also glaring at me and so their actions were twice as despicable. What sort of people start trouble with a man when he is out with his partner having a drink? No doubt Gaffer and his side kick thought that they were 'pwoppa gangsters' who follow the criminal code? So much for showing women respect. Throughout the evening, Gaffer kept glaring down the bar at me and tipping his hat like a comical clown. 'Come on,' I said to Emma, 'I've had enough of this, let's go.' As I walked past Gaffer, the gutless coward squirted me in the face with ammonia. I was temporarily blinded so Emma opened the door for me and I stepped outside. Gaffer had been telling everybody in Essex that he was after me, now that I was temporarily blinded and standing in front of him, he had the best chance he was ever going to get to do me. Gaffer and his friend followed me outside which frightened Emma, so I turned and confronted them. I knew Gaffer was not capable of fighting, so I was expecting him to pull out a weapon. To his friends' credit, he stepped back, making it obvious that he wanted no part in any trouble. As Gaffer advanced, I grabbed his head and shoved him backwards. I was not the slightest bit concerned about what he may try to do, or what he may try to do it with, because I had a double-bladed twelve-inch combat knife down the back of my trousers. If he got within striking distance of me with a weapon, I was more than prepared to bury the knife deep in his chest or head. When I had shoved him backwards, his cap had fallen off. As he approached me again, I could see in his eyes that he was unsure of himself. He pulled out a Jif lemon container, and after lunging forward, he squirted me once more in the face with ammonia. As my eyes began to burn and the red mist rose, I wanted nothing more than to end his miserable and pointless life. I pulled out the knife and raised it. He saw the blade, screamed like a bitch and ran back into the club. 'What the fuck am I doing?' I thought. 'How did I end up getting involved with this fool? I could end up serving a life sentence because some little nobody has decided to attack me.' A bouncer named Michael Kelly who used to work for Tucker in the 1980's came out and told me the police had been called. 'You're on CCTV as well Bernie,' he said. 'You had better make yourself scarce.' I found out later that it was Kelly's door team who had called them. Emma and I tried to get into a taxi but the driver refused to take us and the other taxis in the rank drove away empty. I could see Gaffer hiding in the club foyer behind the bouncers so I knew he wouldn't be troubling me again that night. Emma and I didn't live too far from the Leisure Park, so we decided to walk home. We made our way across the car park to the main road where two police cars pulled up. My mind was racing, I had a certain prison sentence tucked down the back of my trousers and I didn't fancy being locked up for a loser like Gaffer. 'The knife, the knife, how the fuck can I explain away the knife?' I knew everybody had seen it and I knew the CCTV would have recorded me brandishing it, so I knew it was pointless denying its existence. There was only one thing for it, I was going to have to come up with a false but credible story. I pulled out the knife and approached the police officers. 'It's ok officers,' I said, 'I've got the knife.' 'Drop the weapon, drop the weapon,' they began to shout. I laughed and told them it was okay. 'It's not my weapon,' I said. 'I took it off a lunatic.' I threw the knife on the floor. One of the police officers forced my hands behind my back and slapped a pair of handcuffs on. 'You're under arrest for possessing an offensive weapon, ' he said. I asked the police to make sure Emma got home alright. They said they would. They then put me in the back of their car and took me to Basildon police station. By this time my eyes were becoming increasingly painful. They were blood shot and swollen from the effects of the ammonia. Now I had the handcuffs on I was unable to wipe or try to clean them. I asked the officers to remove the cuffs but they refused. I explained to the desk sergeant that I had been squirted with a noxious substance and I needed to wash my eyes out but he said I couldn't do anything until I had seen a doctor. Rightly or wrong, I thought I was only in the police station because I had been attacked for assisting the police in the Betts case. A distinct pattern was forming, I agreed to help them and I am getting shafted by all sides for doing so. My reasonable request for immediate attention to prevent damage to my eyes soon descended into the inevitable argument laced with abuse. Eventually they agreed to remove my handcuffs so that I could wipe my eyes. I was then bundled into a cell and the door was slammed shut. In the early hours of the morning a doctor did come to see me and after examining my eyes he told the police that I needed to go to hospital immediately. The officers who had arrested me were assigned to be my escort. On the way to Basildon hospital, they were making sarcastic comments about myself, Tucker and 'our firm.' I told them that they ought to be careful as I was sick of hearing about Tucker and our so-called fucking firm. 'What do you mean be careful? ' they asked. 'Just be fucking careful because that uniform won't save you, ' I replied. From there on in, relations between myself and the two officers deteriorated rapidly. The accident and emergency department was very busy when we arrived. The officers said that they were not going to let me enter until they had handcuffed me as they had to consider the safety of the public. I told them that I thought it was an unnecessary precaution and I wasn't going to be humiliated by walking around in public with handcuffs on. They insisted that their decision was non-negotiable and so in a fit of temper I lunged at one of them. There was a brief struggle during which I was pushed to the floor. One of the officers sat on me whilst the other twisted my arm and wrist before applying the handcuffs. They then frog marched me into the public waiting room where I was told to sit down. One of the officers then went in search of a nurse. I was extremely embarrassed as everybody in the room was looking at me and whispering to one another. Eventually the officer returned minus a nurse and said that we were going back to Basildon police station. I reminded him that a doctor had said my eyes required urgent medical attention and as yet nobody had looked at them. The officer repeated that we were going back to Basildon police station, placed me in the car and drove off. Half an hour after departing for the hospital I was sitting back in my cell. My eyes were extremely swollen and sore. 'Fuck them, ' I thought. I decided I would lay down, close my burning eyes and hopefully fall asleep.

19 05 1999: I used the tea they kindly gave me for breakfast to wash my eyes out. It helped but they remained painful and my vision was blurred. At approximately 3.p.m a detective came to my cell to take me to the interview room. I had a rough idea of what I was going to say, but I was unaware of how much evidence the police had gathered. I decided I would wait to hear what they had to say before telling my story. The officer interviewing me said that a bouncer at the

club had called the police after a man had ran inside screaming that I had attempted to stab him. The officer added, that they had seized the CCTV footage and it clearly showed me lunging at this man with a large combat knife. I asked the officer if they had the video footage from inside the club, and he said he hadn't as the interior video camera had not been working. As soon as he said that, I knew I was home and dry. I said to him that he only had half of the story. 'What do you mean?' he asked. 'That man attacked me inside the club, sprayed me with ammonia, and pulled out a knife when we started to struggle', I replied. 'When he tried to stab me. I took the knife off him, and fearing for my safety, went outside. The man followed me and was asking me to give him back the knife. I didn't want to, as I thought he would stab me, so I refused. When he came towards me, I pushed him away, but then he attacked me with a Jif lemon container full of ammonia. Having been temporarily blinded, I feared for my safety, I pulled out his knife which I had secreted down the back of my trousers and he ran away screaming. I had pulled out his knife purely to defend myself. When he ran back into the club, I did not run inside after him as the danger had passed. I then stood outside the club for five or ten minutes, no taxis would take Emma and I home, so we walked across the car park. I saw a police car and immediately handed the knife to an officer who arrested me. If you ask the arresting officers, they will tell you I said, 'Its ok, I've got the knife, I took it off a lunatic'. 'But that's not what other people are saying,' the interviewing officer said, 'they're saying it's your knife.' 'Well, you had better get these people to make statements, because it's not my knife, it belongs to the man who attacked me, he owns the knife.' I insisted. The detective said he had spoken to Gaffer and he did not want to make a statement. I reiterated the fact that Gaffer didn't want to make a statement because he had the knife in the first place and he's the one who attacked me. The officer insisted he had other witnesses and therefore I would be charged. 'Fair enough,' I said, 'Fucking charge me'. Clearly frustrated, the officer said, 'okay' and read the following charge to me: 'That without lawful authority or reasonable excuse, I had with me in a public place an offensive weapon, namely a knife.' He also alleged that I had, used or threatened unlawful violence towards another, and my conduct was such as would cause a person of reasonable firmness present at the scene to fear for his personal safety. When he alleged that I had caused a person of reasonable firmness present at the scene to fear for his personal safety, I started laughing. 'How can you call a person reasonable when they are trying to blind you with ammonia?' The officer just looked at me and said, 'those are the charges, have you anything to say?' I did not say a word, but the officer wrote on the charge sheet that I had replied, 'Guilty'. Fortunately for me, the interview was also being recorded on tape. I decided to say nothing about his 'error' because I knew I would be able to use it against the police when the case reached court. I was bailed to appear at Basildon Magistrates and then released. It's hard to explain how depressing an incident like this can be. You go out for a drink with your partner, and you end up being locked up for the best part of twenty-four hours. After your release you spend the next few months agonising over whether or not you will receive a prison sentence. And for what? For some drug-pedalling mendicant who took it upon himself to try and blind me with ammonia in the presence of my girlfriend for no reason. His motive? I had assisted the police who then locked me up and charged me for resisting the attack. My attacker meanwhile, walked free. It is absolutely sickening, and I can fully understand why some people end up serving life-sentences for murdering this type of churl. The law tells you to turn your cheek and walk away, but what is the point of walking away when these low-life's just stab you in the back, cut you, maim you or try to blind you? It is pointless walking away. I should have left him lying in the gutter where he belonged. Once more, the never-ending trauma of going back and forth to court became part of my life. The uncertainty of my future, the pressure of preparing for yet another trial left me marking time in utter misery. That night I sat down with Emma and I suggested leaving Essex for good. The contract in Peterborough had at least ten years to run. We could start afresh, buy our own home, forget about the past. I would miss my children and Emma would miss her sister but Peterborough was less than two hours' drive away, we could visit every weekend if need be. To my surprise Emma took less convincing than I thought, in fact she was really excited about the thought of moving away together. It was agreed that I would look for accommodation and once the matter involving Gaffer had been resolved, we would leave Essex.

21 05 1999: The 1998 – 1999 season was the most successful in the history of Manchester United Football Club. After finishing the previous campaign without winning any titles, in May 1999 they were one game away from winning a treble of trophies, the Premier League, the FA cup and the UEFA Champions League. Victory against Bayern Munich in the Champions League final at the Nou Camp stadium in Barcelona would make them the first side in English football

to achieve such a feat. I had followed United since I was thirteen. The first game I attended was on 13 January 1973, Wolves v United in the FA cup third round. Wolves won 1-0. I loved everything about watching United, the excitement generated by players like Best, Law and Charlton, the roar of the crowd and the camaraderie of the fans. I would hitch hike all over the country to see them. I can remember a night match away at Stoke City. It was pouring with rain and nobody would stop to give me a lift. I arrived back home the following morning just in time for school. I would regularly sleep in Piccadilly Gardens near Manchester Piccadilly train station after night matches at Old Trafford. No hardship or inconvenience deterred me from watching United.

In May 1999 my youngest brother Michael was living in Spain with his family. He was managing a huge farm for a Spanish company near El Puerto de Santa Maria which isn't too far from Cadiz. I rang Michael and arranged for me, Emma and my son Vinney to spend a week with him. Towards the end of that week, we planned to travel up to Barcelona to watch the Bayern v United final. Three days after the incident with Gaffer, we flew to Spain and spent a much-needed stress free week with my brother. I say stress free, there was an 'incident' in Madrid on the overnight train to Barcelona. I purchased sleeper tickets as the journey was over 500 miles and was due to take in excess of twelve hours. When we boarded the train, we found our beds in a small compartment and went to sleep. After a few hours we were awoken by a group of Spanish men who had entered the compartment and started getting undressed. I jumped out of bed and began pushing them out of the door. A scuffle broke out and somebody pulled the emergency cord. A few minutes later the train pulled into Madrid and police boarded the train. The Spanish men were shouting and pointing at me. The police officers drew their guns and I was bundled on to the platform. I tried to protest but they responded with threats. The train then departed leaving me, Emma and Vinney on the platform with our luggage. Apparently in Spain, half a dozen men can sleep in the same compartment as a female they don't know. Peasants.

A European Cup Final in the Nou camp stadium has to be any football fans Valhalla. Despite both clubs receiving only 30,000 tickets, it was estimated that up to 100,000 Manchester United fans travelled to Spain for the final. Many, including me, were able to buy tickets from touts. I paid £1.500 for three tickets which had cost a Barcelona fan just £84 through his club. 90,245 fans were crammed in to the stadium to watch Bayern take on arguably Manchester United's best ever team. After just six minutes United were 1-0 down and a cloud of gloom descended upon the crowd. Our train back to Cadiz was due forty minutes after the game was due to end. Losing was one thing, sitting on a platform until the next train at 10.a.m the following day was another. With minutes to go I said to Emma and Vinney, 'I'm off.' It was one of the worst decisions of my life. As we reached the street, the stadium erupted and people began shouting, 'Sheringham has scored, United are level. 'I tried to get a non-hysterical fan clutching a radio to confirm the news but less than two minutes later the stadium erupted again. Ole Gunnar Solskjær had scored the winner for United. Referee Pierluigi Collina later cited this match as one of the most memorable of his career, and described the noise from the crowd at the end of the game as being like a 'lion's roar.' I had certainly not heard anything like it before or since. It was a remarkable week that I shall never forget.

After returning from Spain, I began preparing myself for a trial concerning the knife incident with Gaffer. I had written to the Crown Prosecution Service after the first two court hearings and asked them to drop the charges. I pointed out that there was little or no evidence to disprove my version of events and only a little to support theirs, but they refused. Changing tact, I made a lot of the fact that the detective who interviewed me had falsely recorded my reply to the charge, a point which may be extremely embarrassing for Essex police should it be aired in open court. Eventually, after a lot of haggling and mind-numbing games, both of the charges. were dropped. The Crown Prosecution Service said that it was not in the public interest to pursue the matter. I also received a formal letter from the manager of the Festival Leisure complex where the incident had taken place. He informed me that I had been banned from entering the complex for life. This meant that I couldn't take my children to the cinema, bowling alley, Pizza Hut or McDonalds. I rang the police and the complex manager and pointed out that I had not been convicted of any offence. I was told that I was not the problem, it was other people. 'You are being banned for your own safety O'Mahoney because it appears people have issues with you or your former friends.' I hadn't felt welcome in Essex for some time, I now had an official letter confirming the fact in fancy bold type.

05 06 1999: Emma and I caught the train to Barking from Basildon to watch England take on Sweden in a European championship qualifying game. Because of the trouble my

presence in Basildon appeared to cause, I thought it would be nice to watch the game in a pub where nobody knew me and have a look around the shops afterwards. If I wasn't being pestered by fools like Gaffer in Basildon I was being bombarded with questions by strangers about the death of Leah Betts or the murders of Tucker, Tate and Rolfe. Whilst we were roaming around Barking, we bumped into a doorman named Mark who used to work for me at Raquel's. We hadn't enjoyed the best working relationship in fact I had beaten him up one night after I felt he had bullied a customer. We were all trying to move on and forget about the past so I shook hands with Mark and apologised about any 'earlier misunderstandings.' Mark told me that he and his partner were running a pub near the market and invited Emma and I there for a drink. We remained in his pub for most of the afternoon catching up on who was doing what and watching the football. At approximately 5.p.m. Emma and I said our goodbyes and headed for the station. We were walking through the market when a very agitated looking man dressed in pyjamas came striding towards us. Before we had a chance to move out of his way, he had collided with Emma who called out, 'be bloody careful.' The next thing I saw, was Emma disappearing backwards and hitting the floor. The man in the pyjamas had wrapped her long hair around his hand, pulled her backwards and was now trying to punch her. I stood behind the man, who was kneeling over Emma, put my left hand under his chin, pulled his head back and began punching him. I was telling him to let go of Emma but he clung on to her hair. The market was packed and so I thought somebody would help but this was Barking, the onlookers just formed a circle to watch. The man was beginning to tire after being punched so many times and so he let Emma's hair go. I tried to put my fingers in his eyes as he turned his head but he just sunk his teeth into me. The pain seared through my fingers and the harder I punched him the harder he bit me. I pushed my hand towards the pavement and his head was forced to follow it. Standing up and stepping back with my back bent double, I began kicking his head repeatedly. Eventually he fell forward and released my hand but I still kept kicking him until eventually, he was motionless. I comforted Emma and walked her over to a nearby telephone box so that she could compose herself. Emma was still brushing handfuls of hair out of her head when the man appeared again. British Telecom had dug a trench to lay cable to the telephone box. The trench was sealed off with red and white tape and various signage. The soil from the trench was piled up nearby. I picked up a piece of 4 x 2 wood which was approximately 3ft long and hit the man around the side of the head with it as hard as I could. There was a sickening thud and an arc of blood flew through the air before he fell backwards and into the trench. 'Oh my God Bernie, you have killed him, ' Emma said. We looked into the very narrow but deep trench. The lunatic in the pyjamas was face up and his arms and legs were pointing straight up at the sky. The trench was so narrow he was unable to move. 'He doesn't look too good, does he? Let's do one.' I said to Emma. We walked briskly out of the market. Emma was terrified that we would both end up in prison and begged me to take her home. I was laughing, but still in total shock about what had happened. Who wouldn't be? We had been attacked by a guy in pyjamas on a busy London street during daylight. We heard police sirens, which is not unusual in Barking, but Emma was convinced that they were in hot pursuit of us. I tried to reason with her but she insisted we wait on a nearby enclosed car park until they had gone. I kept telling Emma that we had acted in self-defence but she was convinced that we would both end up in jail if we didn't remain in the car park. I have no idea how long we were there, I didn't lose track of time, more lost my will to live. At least two hours later, a Mondeo pulled up and a uniformed policeman got out. Emma's face drained of all colour. 'Are you alright? ' the officer enquired. 'Yes sure, we are not from Barking, we parked our car near the train station but can't recall which car park it's on, ' I replied. 'It won't be this one, ' he said, 'this is the police station staff car park, its private.' Emma and I thanked the policeman and walked swiftly away. I laughed at Emma every time I looked at her for the next few days. I could imagine the police hunting for us for hours then returning to the station only to find us hanging about on their private car park. I have no idea what happened to the lunatic or how he managed to dislodge himself from the trench. I was focused on leaving Essex and starting a trouble-free life with Emma.

16 09 1999: Stop the Ride, I Want to Get Off : The Autobiography of Dave Courtney was published today. I didn't know it at the time, but the contents of this book were going to be the root cause of ill feeling between Courtney and I that would last for decades. Courtney (falsely) claimed that he had tried to 'put me out of my misery.' He said that he and his 'gang' had tried to lure me to a party in north London where I was going to be murdered. An attempt was made but it turned out to be little more than a bit of bad street theatre. I had fallen out with a doorman at the Ministry of Sound. Courtney, who had absolutely nothing to do with matters,

elected himself to intervene. I was invited to a party and Courtney asked if I would give his friend a lift. En-route, I sensed something wasn't right. Courtney's friend was on edge and fumbling for something in his jacket. When I noticed Courtney and others were following me in their cars, I knew something wasn't right. I pulled up at a garage, grabbed Courtney's mate and dumped him on the forecourt before driving off. When I looked at where my would-be assailant had been sitting, I saw that he had left behind a large knife. I rang Courtney but he denied being involved in anything underhand. I have met him several times since, visited his home and nothing has been said. I don't know why people feel the need to pad their books out with self-serving bullshit.

03 10 1999: Whilst working at the Epping Country Club and the Ministry of Sound, I had become friends with a man named Darren Pearman. I liked Darren a lot and we began socialising at places like Charlie Chans nightclub in Walthamstow and the Hippodrome in Leicester Square. Despite his butter wouldn't melt looks, Darren would fight anyone he deemed rude or disrespectful. It's fair to say his list of rude and disrespectful people was quite extensive. Since walking away from clubland I had heard that Darren was socialising with a guy named Dave King. Tucker used to have a body building shop in Ilford that sold protein powders, supplements and under the counter steroids. It was there that King had first met Tucker. King was an imposing figure, he was 6ft 2' tall and his muscle-bound frame had been bloated by Tucker's steroids. I had met King briefly through Tucker. I thought the pair were well suited, both were flash and extremely arrogant. King had been imprisoned in the early 90's after he had badly beaten a man before putting him into

the boot of his car. Like Tucker, King was involved with running nightclub doors and the pair occasionally worked as bodyguards for boxer Nigel Benn. Eventually, King launched his own nightclub in Stevenage, Hertfordshire. The Renaissance was a notorious centre for drug dealing and was eventually closed by the local council for non-payment of rent. One former bar manager told a reporter: 'Renaissance was a drugs haven. It was full of them.' As well as violence and drugs, King was linked to the lucrative London trade in stolen watches - earning him the soubriquet 'Rolex Dave.'

In September 1999, Darren and King had gone to Charlie Chans nightclub which was at Walthamstow stadium in north-east London. Like Epping Country Club, the venue was a magnet for celebrities, pop stars and Premier League footballers. It's unclear exactly what happened that night, but there was some sort of dispute involving Darren, King and others. A man was cut by a bottle or glass. The glassing kicked off a big fight and the doormen got involved. Darren and King were ejected from the venue. One of the door staff that night was Ronnie Fuller who lived in Gray's, Essex. His partner was a friend of mine named Larissa Tuit. I was working at the Ministry of sound when Ronnie started work there. Because Larissa was a friend, I got to know Ronnie quite well. He had been a professional wrestler but said he gave it up because every match was fixed. 'The sport is full of villains, I had enough of it, ' he said. After quickly glancing at the guys in our door team I looked at Ronnie and began to laugh. 'You have come to work here to get away from villains? ' It was a strange thing to say, the Ministry door team included Mark Rothermel who had cut a man's head, hands and feet off, Chris Raal, who was wanted in south Africa for allegedly shooting dead a nightclub manager and Peter and Tony Sims, who had been charged with murder after a man was stabbed to death during a fight at a pub in north London. The brothers were acquitted at trial. I can remember saying to Larissa that Ronnie was making a huge mistake getting involved in 'our game' because he was too nice. People rarely listen to advice and so it was with Ronnie. Within a very short period of time, he was mixing with some extremely violent people and giving the impression that he was like them. In that violent, egocentric, testosterone filled world, perceived respect is everything. People get punched, beaten or stabbed for looking at someone, bumping into someone or saying the wrong thing, it's pathetic but that's the way it is. When Darren and King had been ejected from Charlie Chans, they felt humiliated, disrespected and vengeful. It was common knowledge that Ronnie worked at Epping Country Club on Sunday evenings and so a plan was hatched to attack him. When the club opened its doors the following week, three men entered and ordered a drink at the bar. It was too early for them to be searched or scrutinised by the door staff; they were not even on the premises at that time. When the men were sure that nobody was paying them any attention, they walked over to a sofa and secreted a large machete under a seat cushion. Other deadly weapons were hidden in strategic places. Later that night a fight broke out and Ronnie wrestled a weapon from Darren. In the melee, both Darren and his brother were stabbed. Under no circumstances would Darren or his sibling ring the police and so they got into a taxi and ordered the driver to take them to hospital. Sadly, Darren didn't make it, he passed away en-route. He was just 27 years old. Ronnie Fuller and two other men were arrested for

Darren's murder but when the police appealed for witnesses nobody had seen anything. Darren's friends had told the investigating officers, that they would sort matters out themselves. Due to the lack of evidence, Ronnie and the other two men were released without charge. Ronnie knew what was coming, he and Larissa moved house to try and escape the inevitable revenge attack but leaving the planet may have been the only thing that could have saved him.

01 November 1999: Emma and I left Essex and moved to a rented flat in Stanground, Peterborough. It's hard to describe how I felt, it was as if the troubles of the world had been lifted from my shoulders. For the first time in years, I felt free. My feelings of redemption were however, short lived. The local newspaper published a double page story about different aspects of my life for five consecutive days. The information for each 'exclusive' had been gleaned from my books. Approximately fifty yards away from my flat there was a pub called the Carpenters Arms. The clientele were in the main, what I would describe as ' intellectually disabled.' Their grasp of the English language appeared to be limited to, 'What are you fucking looking at? Have you got a fucking problem? And 'Fuck off.' Despite the hostile environment, on the few occasions Emma and I had visited the pub our presence had been largely ignored. Unfortunately, that changed when the newspaper began publishing the stories about me. After entering the pub, I had jokingly renamed the Out-patients Arms, I made my way to the bar and Emma sat down. The barmaid, who was as wide as she was tall, saw me and walked briskly to where I was standing. 'I'm not fucking scared of you, ' she said. 'Sorry, did I miss something? ' I replied. My response was met with a tirade of abuse

interspersed with rambling statements about her not being scared of anyone. 'So what if you knew the Krays, fucking Essex Boy? ' I looked at Emma, shook my head and said its best we leave. That response to the publicity was extreme but not untypical. I cannot and would not want to guess what goes through people's minds, but I assume they somehow felt threatened and wanted me, and more importantly their friends, to know that they were not frightened. I didn't want or need to relive another situation like the one I had endured with Gaffer and so ignoring people and walking away became preferable.

Directly opposite my flat was a pub called The Golden Lion. It too had an ambiance that could only be described as hostile, but I wasn't prepared to barricade myself in at home to appease a few lunatics. One Sunday evening, Emma and I went for a drink and as we entered the pub two men, 'Big Fletch' and Johnny McClair were blocking our path. The landlord, a short overweight Irish man named John was demanding in a raised voice, 'I want you both to leave, will you just go?' McClair and Fletch were clearly intoxicated and telling John in no uncertain terms that they were not going anywhere. John repeatedly asked them to leave and they continued to refuse. The drunken duo were preventing me from getting into the pub and so I looked at Emma, raised my eyes as if to say here we go and said to McClair, 'Look, he isn't going to serve you so why bother arguing? You're stopping us getting in the pub, do everyone a favour and just go.' McClair stepped out of the way and Emma and I walked into the bar. As I passed Fletch he said, 'Who the fuck are you? ' I looked at him and replied, ' This is who I am.' Bang! I punched him in the face and he fell into the doorway. McClair jumped on my back and we began to fight. Fletch, a man mountain, soon got to his feet and began punching me. Fearing I may be overwhelmed by the two men, I picked up a pint glass. At that moment, the pub door burst open and six police officers ran in to separate McClair, Fletch and myself. 'What's going on here? ' they asked. McClair pointed at me and said, 'that wanker started it.' Before he could say another word, I replied, 'What did you say boy, don't get fucking brave just because these have turned up, they won't save you.' 'Fuck off, ' McClair replied. I stepped forward and punched him but before I could hit him again, I was underneath two officers on the floor being handcuffed. I was informed that I was being arrested for assault and after being hauled to my feet I was frog marched out of the pub. I had to laugh, I had popped out for a quiet drink with my girlfriend and had managed to get arrested before reaching the bar. You couldn't fucking make it up. I was taken to Thorpe Wood police station and put in a cell. I was advised that I would be there until at least the following morning. Later that night John the landlord arrived and told the officers what had happened. McClair didn't wish to press charges and so I was released. Sadly, it didn't end there. I wouldn't say that McClair and I were friends but we had always exchanged pleasantries when we would meet. He had been in HMP Stafford for stabbing somebody around the same time I had been there. We therefore had something in common and so it was inevitable that we would have some form of rapport. The problem was we were too alike. McClair was never going to accept his local hard man reputation being belittled by a newcomer. I was never going to accept bad manners or bullying. Initially McClair began telling people that he was going to kill me, but then somebody began ringing my employer and warning the receptionist that I was going to die. That, in my opinion, was a step too far.

One evening I was in the Golden Lion when a local man took me to one side and warned me that McClair was going to 'finish me.' I had heard enough shit, if somebody says that they are looking for me I will save them the trouble and go find them. At closing time, I escorted Emma out of the pub. As we walked across the road to our flat Emma didn't say a word. I am in no doubt that she could sense what was coming because I was physically shaking with temper. After Emma had gone to bed, I sat in the lounge watching the clock. By 11.30.p.m I knew the pub would have been cleared, perhaps drunken McClair would be filling his drunken big mouth with a kebab on the way home? That would add 15-20 minutes to his journey. By 1.a.m I was pretty confident that McClair would be tucked up in bed. After turning out all of the lights I left home with a bread knife tucked into the waistband of my trousers and headed for his house. I don't know why the locals feared him, he had served five years imprisonment for stabbing someone but apart from that all he did was get drunk and shout abuse at people. Scumbag. Psyching myself up for the job in hand I checked the knife was secure in my waistband, opened the garden gate and prepared to launch myself at McClair's front door. 1-2-3 Go! I raced through the open gate and down the path before leaping into the air and kicking open the door. Landing in the hallway, I grabbed my knife and ran upstairs. I entered the first bedroom I reached, turned on the light and prepared to attack McClair in his bed. The room was empty. As I turned and hurried out of the room, I encountered a man dressed in his pyjamas on the landing.

'What the fuck do you think you're doing?' he shouted. 'Where's McClair, where's fucking McClair?' I replied. Looking puzzled the man pulled hard on his pyjama bottoms cord to stop them from falling down and said, 'McClair? McClair doesn't live here, he lives next door.' Without saying another word, I rushed downstairs and kicked open a second front door. McClair had obviously been awakened by the fracas at his neighbour's home because I met him as he walked bleary eyed down the stairs. He screamed as soon as he saw me and tried to run back to his room. I caught him before he reached the landing. After pummelling his face with my fists, I held the bread knife to his throat. 'Apologise you maggot, apologise or fucking die,' I said. 'I'm sorry, I'm sorry I was drunk,' McClair whimpered. A female came out of the bedroom and began shouting at me to leave him alone. The knife had caused a minor cut on McClair's neck and when she saw the blood she began to scream. It was time for me to leave. When I ran out of the house, McClair's neighbour attempted to take a photograph of me. I put my head down and continued to run. When I got home, I washed the knife, hid it in the loft and slipped into bed beside Emma who was fast asleep. The following morning, I went to work, but as it was a Saturday, Emma had remained in bed. At approximately 10.a.m she rang me to say the police had been to our flat and wanted to speak to me. 'They have left a number Bernie, you better ring them,' Emma said. I never did comply with their request and I never heard from them again about the matter. A week later I was approached by a friend of McClair's who said that he wanted to meet me. I said that I would be in the Golden Lion on Friday night and would be happy to meet him. When McClair walked in the pub, he extended his hand and offered to buy me a drink. As far as I was concerned that was the end of the mater and we have been friends ever since.

The Out Patients Arms closed around this time due to a lack of custom and so their clientele (and carers) began to drink in the Golden Lion. This cocktail of mentally challenged drunks and unhinged street fighters was certainly more entertaining to watch than some of the bands the manager booked. Well, that is not entirely true, there was the night an Elvis Presley impersonator came to town. The Golden Lion was packed and Elvis and his entourage of about fifteen fans arrived around 8.p.m. Elvis went into the Ladies toilet to get ready and his assistant prepared some sort of explosive device at the door in preparation for his grand entrance. The DJ then asked the crowd to give the one and only Elvis Presley a warm Golden Lion welcome and then BOOM! There was a loud explosion and Elvis emerged from the Ladies toilet engulfed in a large cloud of white smoke. Dressed all in white with a large cape Elvis launched into 'I'm all shook up.' (He should have saved that particular song for his impending trip to the hospital) Slipping on wraparound sunglasses Elvis began to sing 'Are you lonesome tonight? As he sang, he moved along the bar from girl to girl, some were hugged, the lucky ones got a kiss on the cheek. Unfortunately for Elvis, some of the lads in the Golden Lion had a caveman mentality. Their partners were their property and if approached by another male, fire, clubs or other deadly weapons would be used to fend of the threat. As Elvis leaned towards a pretty young blonde girl her boyfriend bellowed, 'Oi mate, get your hands off my fucking bird.' He then punched Elvis full in the face. As his knees buckled and he crumpled to the floor, Elvis's horrified entourage rushed to his aid. A huge fight broke out and I could see Elvis being dragged around the floor by his cape. Several people were kicking him repeatedly. The Elvis fans were being badly beaten and so they began leaping to safety across the bar. When the police arrived on the car park with sirens blaring, the locals ran out of a side door. Elvis remained motionless, laying by the bar. A false side burn and a blood-stained cape were discarded alongside him. An ambulance was summoned, 'The King' was given first aid and then taken from the pub on a stretcher. Elvis had left the building.

CHAPTER FOUR
Life in a Northern Town

Emma urged me to give the Golden Lion a wide berth for a while and so we began drinking in a pub that was relatively close to home called The White Horse. At first, we were made welcome but soon I heard people talking about 'the Essex Boys' and saw fingers being pointed in my direction. One night an extremely drunk twenty something year old punched me and ran out of the pub. I was sitting on a stool with my back to him and so could do little about it. He had run away by the time I stood up. Another night, a man attacked me with a pool cue for no reason. Unbeknown to him I had learnt a lesson from the previous attack and gone to the pub prepared. An old-fashioned cutthroat razor had been secreted in my jacket pocket. I opened it and moved towards him as he lashed out with the pool cue. The doorman, a friend of mine named Lee, attempted to restrain me in an effort to save my attacker. In the struggle that followed, Lee's arm was slashed. My attacker fled outside, smashed the pub windows with the pool cue and then ran away. (Strange boy) I left the pub with Emma just as the police arrived. They were soon telling Lee that they knew I had an open razor and they knew I had slashed his arm. 'Make a complaint Lee, just say O'Mahoney did it to you, ' they begged. Thankfully Lee refused and the police never bothered me over the incident.

Emma and I reverted to drinking in the Golden Lion where we eventually made lifelong friends with some great characters, Jimmy Dean senior, his son Jimmy Hendrix Dean, a great young fighter and his brother Mad Jack, the clue is in his name! Others included Johnny a down syndrome boy who adored Emma and his father an old school tough guy called Ellie. Great, great people.

Whilst working on the Hampton site I was approached by a guy named Joe who wanted to purchase brick hardcore. Joe explained that he had purchased a large plot of land in a village called Eye. He wanted to cover it with hard core so he could put a mobile home on the plot and eventually build stables and out buildings. Hampton was a disused brickworks and so I had access to endless stocks of hard core. A price was agreed and the following day the lorries began delivering to Joe. The agreement had been that each load would be paid for in cash when the lorry arrived. The first day went according to plan, but on the second day Joe could not be found. I rang him and he told me that he was in Spain. 'Just keep tipping the brick and I will pay you when I get back, ' he said. By the end of the week the job had been completed and Joe owed several thousand pounds. I went down to the site and spoke to his wife who told me that he had left her. I had known Joe was a traveller from the outset and so I knew this was a scam to get out of paying me. It may have worked for him in the past but it wasn't going to work with me. I went to the traveller's site in Peterborough and began knocking caravan doors in search of Joe. I found his father who assured me that Joe would be in touch. Later that day Joe rang and began shouting about me looking for him at his father's home. 'It won't work Joe, I have heard all this shit before, you pay or I will put a machine in your yard on Monday and reload all the brick.' He asked me to meet him at a pub frequented by the travelling community and when I arrived, he paid me. From that day, he became my friend. Joe, I soon learned, did not understand the concept of honesty. Avoiding payment for anything, was the norm for him. Joe saw a 360 excavator for sale in a newspaper and rang the owner. Joe agreed to pay £15.000 in cash if the machine was delivered to his yard. He said that he would be working during the day so any time after 5.p.m would be fine. It was wintertime and so was dark by 4.30.p.m. The man was concerned that it may be dangerous unloading in darkness but Joe assured him that his yard was flood-lit. The following Friday, a low loader drove into Joe's yard and the driver began to unload the machine. When he had done so, Joe counted out the cash and the driver gave him a receipt. Joe then made a point of standing in his caravan doorway and waving at the departing driver. Joe's yard was at the bottom of a lane, at the top there was a gate. When the driver had entered the yard, the gate had been open, but he now saw that it was closed. Climbing out of his cab into the darkness the man thought it may have just swung shut. Just before he reached the gate the man was pushed to the floor and ordered to remain there. As he looked up, he saw a balaclava clad man brandishing a baseball bat. Another man had got into the cab of his lorry and was searching for the cash. When he found it, both men climbed over the gate and ran away into the darkness. The lorry driver got to his feet and ran back down the lane to Joe's caravan. 'I've been robbed, call the police, ' he shouted. Joe feigned shock and rang the police who arrived approximately fifteen minutes later. They knew what had happened as this wasn't the first time that Joe had been a 'witness' to such a crime. They had no proof of any wrongdoing on Joe's behalf and so went through the motions of taking statements before departing. The former owner of the machine rang Joe demanding his machine be returned but Joe explained that the sale had taken place, 'I have a receipt, its mine, what happened after the sale is your drivers' fault, not mine, ' Joe said. It's fair to say that Joe did not give a fuck about other people.

Joe rang me in a panic one day and asked me to drive to a village called Oundle as soon as possible. Oundle is approximately twelve miles from Peterborough and so it didn't take me long to get there. When I arrived, I was met with a scene of utter devastation. Joe had recently stolen a JCB digger and had decided to start up a block paving company. His workforce could best be described as a gang of alcohol dependant, unskilled thugs. After digging the old drive out at a magnificent five-bedroom bungalow, they had gone to the pub for lunch. Joe, who had never driven a JCB, decided to give himself a lesson. Going forward seemed pretty easy but when Joe engaged reverse the machine lurched towards the bungalow. The back digging arm of the JCB struck a large bay window knocking out the main support for the ceiling and roof. Panicking, Joe drove the 8-tonne digger forward dragging much of the structure with him. When I got out of my car, I saw Joe, up to his knees in rubble standing in what was once the owners bedroom. The roof above him sagged and the ceiling had fallen as the supporting structures were gone. 'Perfume, all I can smell is fucking perfume, what am I going to do? ' he said. 'Abandon ship Joe, leave the fucking machine, get in my car and don't come back, ' I replied. Wild eyed, Joe jumped In my car and we sped away leaving the bungalow almost derelict. On another occasion, Joe rang and asked me to meet him at a petrol station near to the traveller's site in Peterborough. When I arrived, he was sitting in a car with three other lads. 'You're coming to Thailand, ' he shouted as I approached their vehicle 'I'm not, ' I replied. 'Oh yes you are, I have bought you a ticket.' Later that evening, I was sitting alongside four travellers on board a plane bound for Bangkok. The plan, according to Joe, was to visit various farms in Thailand which produce premier league birds that are used in cock fighting. We would buy eggs, smuggle them back into the country, incubate them and sell the chicks for a handsome profit. (In May 2017, a 16-month-old fighting cock with a record of three straight victories has been sold in Thailand for one million baht. Approximately £23.500.00p) I leant forward, buried my head in my hands and prayed that I was having a bad dream. When we arrived in Thailand, we booked into a hotel in a city called Pattaya. It is approximately one hundred miles from Bangkok on the east coast.

This was going to be our base for the next week. From there, we set off early each morning to visit farms in jungle like areas near the Khao Chamao-Khao Wong National Park and beyond. The breeders greeted us with enthusiasm and plied us with drink. At one farm we were taken into a wooded area where a round Colosseum type structure had been made entirely from Bamboo. This 'theatre' seated approximately two hundred people.

Throughout the afternoon, the organisers put on cock fights, men fighting men and large Beetle type insects that fought each other, all of which the spectators bet on. It wasn't really my thing, but Joe and the others enjoyed themselves.

At the end of the week Joe had purchased approximately one hundred eggs. He was mindful that they needed to be incubated and so he announced that he was going home. The other lads wanted to stay longer and so I said I would go with Joe to help him carry the eggs through Customs. Our first hurdle was getting back to Bangkok so that we could catch a plane.

On the beach at Pattaya, I remembered that there was a guy who hired out open top second world war jeeps so tourists could drive up and down the sands. The vehicles were badly maintained and certainly not roadworthy.

Nevertheless, the engine turned over and they moved forward when the accelerator was depressed. Joe and I had found our transport to Bangkok. I hired the jeep and confirmed to the owner that I understood I must not leave the beach.

Moments later, I was pulling up outside our hotel and Joe was loading our bags into the rear of the vehicle. Laughing hysterically, Joe and I then headed for the motorway (Route 7) which would take us to the airport and home. Things went well at first but at the halfway point the engine blew and we juddered to an abrupt halt. Joe unloaded our bags whilst I stood at the side of the motorway waving bank notes at drivers.

Within minutes a coach driver had stopped and for a small fee agreed to drop us at the airport. The following day I was walking through Customs at Heathrow carrying a sports bag laden with chicken eggs. I do know some of them later hatched and Joe did make a handsome profit from the chicks he sold.

03 04 2000: My book Essex Boys was published today.

14 05 2000: My book Soldier of the Queen was published today.

10 07 2000: I don't know if Granada Films were offering me an olive branch after making Essex Boys, a film I had coincidently suggested to them. It may not have been the actual story line I had envisaged, but it was certainly based on the same events. I could of course be wrong; they no doubt have an abundance of inspirational thinkers in their company. Whatever, I was invited to the film Premier at Southend where I was introduced to Sean Bean, Alex Kingston, Charlie Creed Mills, Jude Law and his then girlfriend Sienna Miller. It was an enjoyable evening. When the film had ended, we were ushered into a large room where there was a free bar and buffet.

People posed for photographs and exchanged pleasantries; it was all very 'nice.' That was until a female came charging towards me and began shouting about a man called Jesse Gail. 'You bastard O'Mahoney, you implicated him in the murders and he isn't here to defend himself.' It was to say the least embarrassing but fortunately security bundled her out of the door. I sympathised with the lady who was clearly upset about what I had written in my book, but I had not made the allegation. Billy Jasper, the man Whomes and Steele had unsuccessfully tried to use to dupe their jury, had claimed Jesse Gail had paid him £5000 to drive a gunman to Rettendon.

The jury, who watched Jasper squirming in the witness box as he was scrutinised and his story fell apart, saw right through his charade. Jasper was lying and therefore Gale was totally innocent of any involvement and so the lady at the film Premier had every right to be annoyed. But I hadn't implicated Gale, I merely reported what Jasper had alleged in court.

In October 1997 a Range Rover, being driven by Jesse Gale, had 'flew across a crash barrier' on the M20 in Kent. The vehicle landed on the opposite carriageway where it smashed into a Vauxhall Carlton being driven by a 63-year-old man who was accompanied by his 59-year-old wife. The Vauxhall contained two rear seat passengers, a 64-year-old man and his 59-year-old wife. They were on their way home from a day trip to France. 43-year-old Gale and the four occupants of the Vauxhall all died. According to the police, there was nothing wrong with the Range Rover - which was also hit by three oncoming cars. However, at the time of the accident, Jesse Gale was speeding and over the drink-drive limit.

29 08 2000: The atmosphere at Epping Forest Club was still rather tense following the death of Darren Pearman approximately ten months earlier. It was Bank Holiday Monday and 3.000 revellers were crammed into the venue. At 3.a.m, around thirty men began fighting in the car park. The door staff ran out to try and break up the melee, but as they did so, a man took out a gun and shot two of the doormen. One was taken to King George Hospital in Ilford, with a bullet wound to the thigh. The other suffered a stomach wound and

underwent emergency surgery at Whipps Cross Hospital, Leytonstone. Both made a full recovery. Rumour and speculation were rife and everybody was saying that the shootings were connected to Darren's murder. Some thought this was the comeback everyone had been expecting, but they were wrong. This was just a gun toting wannabe from south London who had been shown 'disrespect' when the doormen had refused him entry.

At 7.45am, less than five hours after the shootings in Epping, Ronnie Fuller left home at Parkside in Grays, Essex. Ronnie had taken a job as a Painter and Decorator and was on his way to work. As he reached his white van, which was parked just ten yards from his front door, a man got off a motor scooter with L-plates and approached him. Ronnie had opened the van door and was climbing in when the man pulled out a 9mm pistol. Ronnie saw the gun but at the same time his assassin began squeezing the trigger. Two bullets were fired into Ronnie's body and one into his head. He staggered to the back of his van but the gunman followed and shot him again in the head. Ronnie's partner Larissa later said, ' I went to the door and just saw the guy walking away. He was not in a hurry and walked so casually, it made me think: 'Did you just do that?' 'He wasn't in a hurry to leave and was just pulling his gloves on. He was medium build and was wearing a postman-type jacket, but it was not leather.' Neighbours, alerted by Larissa's screams, fought to save Ronnie as he lay on the driveway bleeding heavily from the head. A neighbour who went to Ronnie's aid told police, 'At 7.35am I heard three loud bangs and ran outside to look. The man's wife was screaming and I went to see if I could help. Then I saw him lying on his side by the car. Several people came to help but no one knew what to do and you couldn't have helped him anyway. There was a lot of blood around his head and he was unconscious but breathing. We had to just sit and wait for the ambulance.' Armed police sealed off the area and an ambulance took Ronnie to Basildon Hospital where he later died. Many believed that Ronnie had been murdered in vain because Darren Pearman's death was later deemed to be lawful. In March 2016, the Metropolitan police issued the following statement, 'After referral to the Crown Prosecution Service it was deemed that the actions of the suspects were lawful in the terms of self-defence and as such the matter was recorded as no crime under Home Office Rule 12.' Ronnie Fullers murder remains unsolved but a secret police document titled Operation Tiberius states, ' In spite of taking extensive precautions to avoid the inevitable retaliation, Fuller was subsequently shot dead by Darren's father, Christopher Pearman. 'There isn't any evidence to suggest that this is true and Christopher Pearman has never been arrested for the crime. He was however arrested, charged and convicted of another murder which took place on 02 May 2006. At approximately 9.p.m 24-year-old Rocky Dawson was shot in the back as he helped his two children into his car outside his parents' home in Hornchurch. Rocky managed to crawl into his mother's house, where he died in her arms. The fatal shots had been fired from a dark-coloured 4x4 and later that evening, a blue Land Rover Freelander was discovered burnt-out nearby. Contract killers Chris Pearman, 63, and James Tomkins, 66, were later jailed for life, but the police believed others were involved in the murder. As a result, Rocky's mother Candy wrote to her son's killers. In 2012 Pearman agreed to see Candy at HMP Frankland, Co

Durham. Pearman claimed he and Tomkins had been paid £5,000 each to kill her other son Ross, by a businessman who suspected he was one of two masked armed robbers who had raided his home. 'The attack was meant for your other boy, but when Rocky came out of the house Tomkins said, 'His brother will do.' Pearman said. Candy later claimed, 'He named a man who he said paid them and why, and I told him that I was going to tell the police. I asked if he would tell them what he told me and he said he would do what he could.' In a later prison letter, Pearman told Candy he had spoken to detectives. 'I told them that I was now doing what I could to make things right by telling them what I knew, and that although I didn't want to do so, if I had to give evidence I would. They said something to the effect that even with my evidence it would be difficult to reopen the case because I couldn't give them evidence that was sufficiently strong enough. I got the impression that the police position was that they had got the man who pulled the trigger on your son, Tomkins, and they had got the mug who had driven the car, me, and so that was the case closed. 'Dave King, the man who had been with Darren Pearman when the initial trouble had started also suffered a violent death. Like his friend Tony Tucker, King thought his size and reputation would make people reluctant to take him on. Again, like Tucker, King became involved in the importation of drugs, but in Kings case it was heroin rather than cannabis. In June 2002 HM Customs intercepted a £100.000 consignment of heroin. King and four other men were subsequently arrested in connection with the seizure. All five men were later charged with various drug offences. One of Kings co-accused was a one-time friend named David Sharma. When proceedings against King were dropped at an early stage, Sharma had shouted out in court that King was a grass. King knew that this allegation would cause him problems and so he offered cash to anyone who was willing to kill Sharma. When Sharma became aware of the contract King had put on his head, he fled to Cannes in the south of France where he went into hiding under a false identity. Sharma told two of his friends about the threat to his life and they offered to have King shot. Those two friends, Roger Vincent and Dave Smith said that they would have King 'wiped out' purely as a favour, no payment would be required. They contracted armed robber Dean Spencer, from Manchester, to carry out the assassination. Spencer armed himself with a Webley .38 pistol and five bullets and went with another man to King's home in Stevenage. But King had been warned about a possible attack and was lying in wait with 'minder' Ian Crocker. The four men were locked in a stand-off outside King's home before Spencer lost his nerve and fled. He was later arrested for an armed robbery and told detectives about the murder plot. 'When I saw how big he was and the fact he was wearing a bulletproof vest, I knew my little gun would be useless against him.' When Vincent and Smith heard that Spencer had 'bottled out' they decided to do the job themselves. Aware that King now knew of the murder plot against him and was routinely wearing a bulletproof vest, they purchased a Hungarian made Kalashnikov AKS-47 machine gun and loaded it with 'full metal jacket' armour piercing bullets. Using a stolen white Transit van and a stolen Mercedes as getaway vehicles, they stalked King until they saw him leaving the Physical Limit gym in Hoddesdon Hertfordshire. In a classic 'drive by' assassination, Roger Vincent sprayed twenty-six shots at King from close range.

Five rounds from the three second burst hit him in the arm, chest and leg. King was dead before he hit the ground. Other bullets were scattered into King's car, his friend Ian Crocker, and into the walls of the gym. Vincent and Smith then sped away and torched their getaway vehicles. But close to the burned-out van, police found a discarded plastic glove. The inside of the glove contained a palm print from Smith. The following day a couple walking on the Norfolk Broads spotted a man hurling a red bag into the water and running away. The walkers waded in and dragged the bag out. To their amazement it contained an AKS-47 assault rifle. The Police were able to prove that the gun, which had previously belonged to the Hungarian Prison Authorities, was the same one used to kill King. On the lip of the curved ammunition clip they found a trace of Smith's DNA. On a towel in the same bag, they found DNA from Vincent. And on another towel, the police found fibres from a unique jute rug which was at a flat used by Vincent. Police also analysed mobile phone transmissions from Hoddesdon to Cannes minutes after the shooting. They believe these were Vincent and Smith calling Sharma to tell him they had murdered King. Sharma, who is wanted for murder in relation to King's execution, has since disappeared and is being hunted across Europe by Interpol. Roger Vincent and David Smith were convicted of murder and sentenced to life imprisonment. The judge recommended that Smith should serve no less than twenty-five years and Roger Vincent thirty years.

27 09 2001: My book The Dream Solution: The Murder of Alison Shaughnessy - and the Fight to Name Her Killer was published today.

27 04 2002: After renting the flat in Stanground for more than two years, Emma and I purchased a house in a Market Deeping, Lincolnshire. It was only five miles from Peterborough city centre and so it was perfect for commuting to work and enjoying trouble free leisure time. Market Deeping is described on a tourist board website as one of the prettiest villages in the county. The Deepings is the collective name given to the towns of Market Deeping, Deeping St James and the two outlying villages of West Deeping and Deeping Gate which all border the banks of the River Welland. The neat, quiet streets are lined with stone-built homes, some pre-dating the 17th century. The Deepings has a long history of habitation going back to prehistoric times. The land is low lying and in the distant past it was frequently covered by the sea as waters rose and receded with each ice age. It is a land upon which roamed such animals as the Mammoth and Woolly Rhinoceros. Little had changed from those prehistoric times when Emma and I arrived there in the spring of 2002. A small number of the locals with obvious tribal instincts, wanted to protect their forgotten world and so viewed us as a threat to their existence. 'Go back to where you came from,' one bitter old lady remarked to Emma, 'we don't want people from outside buying up our homes.' Emma and I worked during the day and at weekends we would travel to Essex so that I could spend time with my children and Emma could visit her sister. This meant that we were rarely home and so we seldom encountered those who vehemently opposed our presence. Six weeks after arriving in the village, I received a phone call from Spalding police station. I was informed that the local Inspector had heard that I had moved into Market Deeping and he wished to meet me. I asked why a Police

Inspector would want to meet me and I was told that there wasn't a problem, however he wanted me to understand 'a few ground rules' so that it remained that way. I thanked the officer for the invitation and explained that I was extremely busy trying to make a living and therefore I wouldn't have time for any informal chats. The call actually concerned me because the police, for whatever reason, considered me a threat despite the fact I hadn't actually done anything. In such an unforgiving climate, people don't usually get much justice if they are ever accused of something. Prejudging a person, deprives them of a fair hearing.

29 06 2002: My son Vinney had never been academic but he was a good worker with a will to succeed. He was having problems at school in Essex and so two days after his 15th birthday, he moved to Market Deeping. Having Vinney at home meant I spent more time in the village. I would drop him off at school, pick him up and take him to various events. One afternoon I went to pick Vinney up and I noticed a police car parked near the school gates. I didn't think anything of it at the time. When Vinney got into my car, I started to drive away but a police officer ran into the road and stood in front of my car. I always keep a Dictaphone in my car and so I switched it to record and held it up so the officer could see it. 'Is this vehicle yours? 'Is this vehicle taxed and insured? Could I have your name and address please? ' I looked at the officer and said, 'You could be killed jumping in front of moving vehicles, do you really think that was necessary? ' The conversation descended into a full-blown argument and so eventually, I just drove off. A few months later, snow had begun to fall and the children were making snowmen and throwing snowballs. Vinney came home and about an hour later a police officer

knocked my door. I recognised him immediately, it was the same officer who had jumped in front of my car outside the school. 'Can I come in, ' he asked. 'Sorry, I am busy at the moment, how can I help? ' I replied. The officer said that it was a serious matter and I really should let him in. Eventually, I relented and showed him into the kitchen. 'It's your son Vinney, I am going to caution him, but if he doesn't accept the caution he will have to go to court.' 'Go to court for what? ' I enquired. Stern faced; the officer told me that Vinney had been throwing snowballs at the side of a house. 'Were there any windows on the side of the house? ' I asked. 'No, it's just a plain wall, but it's still somebody's property.' I honestly could not believe what this grown man was saying to me about a child. 'Let me get this straight, you want to caution a 15-year-old boy for throwing snowballs at a brick wall? Cautions are given for minor crimes when was throwing a snowball at a wall a crime of any description? ' 'Vinney can be arrested and charged if you don't agree, ' the officer replied. I told him to get out of my house before I did something, we would both regret. 'Go on fuck off.' I shouted. He never did arrest Vinney; I knew he wouldn't, because he had no grounds to do so. Unfortunately for me, Lincolnshire police were not finished with me just yet.

18 08 2002: I was at home watching Aston Villa play Liverpool on the television when the phone rang. The caller informed me that he was a policeman and asked if everything was okay as they had received a report of a disturbance. I laughed and said, 'It's a wind up, isn't it? ' but the policeman was adamant. He asked if anybody else was in the house and I told him that my girlfriend was asleep upstairs. The policeman insisted on talking to her, so I called up to Emma and she picked up the

phone in the bedroom. When the policeman asked her about an alleged disturbance, she confirmed what I had said, we were not aware of any disturbance in or around our home. The policeman said okay and put the phone down. The match was approaching half time and so I rang a local takeaway and asked for a Pizza to be delivered. Approximately fifteen minutes later there was a loud knock on the door. I assumed it was the Pizza guy, so I sorted out some cash and went to the front door. When I opened it, approximately eight police officers stood before me looking very agitated. Three of them flicked their extendable batons open. A WPC said that she wanted to come into my home and when I asked why she said, 'There has been a disturbance.' I laughed and said, 'We've just had your people on the phone saying the same thing. My girlfriend is in bed, I am watching a game of football on the television and waiting for a pizza. What is disturbing about that? ' The WPC tried to push her way past me and so I pushed her back outside and told her that she was not welcome. 'You don't have a warrant or a reasonable excuse and so you are not getting in, ' I said before closing the door. Somewhat bewildered, I walked back down the hall towards the lounge. Moments later there was an almighty crash. I knew instinctively it wasn't the Pizza guy. I turned to see that the police had kicked my front door off its hinges. They ran up the hallway and without saying a word began spraying me full in the face with CS gas. I was pushed to the floor, handcuffed and four officers then sat on me. Another struck me repeatedly across the ribs with an extendable baton despite the fact I hadn't said a word or offered any form of resistance. Emma came running downstairs and demanded to know what was going on. The police said that they had received information that I had assaulted somebody and I was under arrest. At no stage had any officer asked my name, but they all certainly knew it. Emma was clearly in shock. She repeatedly told the officers that they were talking total nonsense, that she had been in bed since the early hours of the morning and I hadn't fallen out with anybody, never mind assaulted them. Fearful of their true intentions, Emma plugged in my Dictaphone and recorded herself telling the officers that they were talking rubbish and why. The police responded by contacting headquarters and informing control that they were being recorded. After fifteen minutes of being sat on by four burly officers, who were not quite sure what to do next, I was frogmarched out into the street. Five police vehicles and an ambulance were blocking the road. Their blue flashing lights ensured that everyone in the street was peeping out from behind twitching curtains. I was bundled into a van, taken to Spalding police station, which is twelve miles away, put in a cell until 3.a.m and then released without being questioned or charged. Perhaps I should have gone for that chat when the Inspector invited me?

10 12 2002: Walking through a city centre late at night with a pretty girl can often attract unwelcome comments from drunks. Most people try to ignore them but I don't see why people should be subjected to such behaviour or ignore it. I had been out with Emma and was walking to the taxi rank in Peterborough when a group of drunken lads walked by. One of them made a disgusting remark and so I asked him to apologise. We went through the usual street theatre, 'What are you going to do? Who the fuck are you? Come on then let's have it. Don't hold me back, etc etc...I punched him in his drunken mouth once and he hit the floor. His friends then

began shouting and threatening just as the police arrived. I was asked what had happened and once I had explained, I was told I could leave. As Emma and I walked up the street a police vehicle roared up behind us. An officer got out and said, 'Bernard O'Mahoney, I am arresting you on suspicion of threatening behaviour.' I explained that I had given an account to an officer at the scene and they had let me go. 'I know, but since then we have been told to arrest you, ' the officer replied. I made sure Emma got safely into a taxi and then the police put me in the back of their car. I was taken to Thorpe wood police station and kept in the cells overnight. The following morning, I was taken to Peterborough Magistrates Court where I was fined £150 and ordered to pay £55 costs.

December 2002: Vinney understandably wanted to enjoy Christmas with his mother and sister. Rather than spend the festive period in Market Deeping, I decided to take Emma to Paris. We had been through some challenging times together and each one had brought us closer together. Emma had spent her childhood in care after her mother sought solace in drink following the tragic death of her father. We loved one another and I knew she craved 'real' family life and so I had decided to ask for her hand in marriage. On Christmas eve we went to Notre-Dame Cathedral in Paris.

It is a beautiful building steeped in history, but that night it was more, it really was magical. Because it was Christmas the Cathedral was packed with worshippers and an amazing choir was singing Carols by candlelight. It was there, on the site of one of the greatest love stories ever told, (Quasimodo, the bell-ringer of Notre-Dame Cathedral and Esmeralda a beautiful Gypsy street dancer.) that I asked Emma to marry me and she accepted.

As soon as we returned to Market Deeping Emma began to plan our wedding. We booked Peterborough Cathedral for the service and Barnsdale Hall hotel on Rutland Water for the reception. I genuinely felt like I had turned a corner. Seven years after Leah Betts death and the Rettendon murders I felt happy, life at last began to feel good and problem free.

14 02 2003: John Rollinson's book titled Gaffer was published today. On the front cover readers are warned, 'If you dis me, I swear I will never forget, never forget and have my revenge.' On the inner sleeve it states, 'John 'Gaffer' Rollinson is the most dangerous man in the country. If they issued certificates for brutality, he'd have a masters degree.' I personally would replace the word dangerous with deluded but these sort of true crime books were the new norm. It cannot be denied, the King of spin, Dave Courtney invented the celebrity gang-star. His book had opened the flood gates for every wannabe and never has been to tell their story and some. Publishers had snapped up petty criminals for true crime biographies that were little more than platforms for nobodies to try and convince the public they were in fact somebodies. In his fantasy filled novel Gaffer claimed (falsely) that I had been a prosecution witness at the Rettendon murder trial. He (falsely) claimed that every time someone clicked on a website I once owned, I was paid a fee. He (falsely) claimed that I sold the crime scene photos of the Rettendon murders to the Sunday Sport. On and on Gaffer droned, calling me a bastard and a 'a fucker,' whatever one of them may be. Finally, he said that if he ever found me, he would kill me. This

amusing little man had clearly forgotten the night in Basildon when he ran away from me screaming like a bitch.

14 03 2003: Carlton Leach's book titled Muscle was published today. The ghost writer for Leach's book was Sun journalist Mike Fielder. Ironically, Fielder had also written Gaffer's drivel which had been published just a month earlier. Perhaps that's why the claim on the front cover of Leach's book was equally ridiculous. 'I'm the deadliest bastard you'll ever meet. If you cross me, I'll track you to the ends of the earth and destroy you.' The inevitable attack on me began on page 43. Leach claimed that after Tucker, Tate and Rolfe had been murdered he was trying to work out which people and what events may be significant in relation to their deaths. He claimed one event in particular kept coming to mind. It was the night I was stabbed in the Ministry of Sound. Leach went on to (falsely) claim that I was lying on the toilet floor writhing in agony. Super hero Leach allegedly came to my aid and battered my attacker with an iron bar. The man required 56 stitches. The true story is slightly less gung ho. I had gone to the Ministry of Sound when Raquel's had closed. I was wearing a white shirt and black trousers. When I left the Ministry to drive home, a group of black lads who had been refused entry assumed I worked there and followed me up the street. I sensed something was about to happen and so I stopped and asked if there was a problem. They ran at me and we ended up fighting in a shop doorway. I was stabbed just above my waistband on the right-hand side. I pushed the knifeman into the shop window which broke and set an alarm off. The lads ran off and I walked to my car. I drove home but was admitted to Basildon hospital later the same day. I know there was a lot of drugs around in the 90's so maybe that explains

why Leach's memory is so creative. Joking aside, I genuinely think he is confusing me being stabbed with an incident involving a guy named Marvin Herbert who did stab a Ministry doorman and was then attacked by Leach. I have spoken to Marvin and he is in no doubt whatsoever that the two incidents are unconnected.

25 08 2003: It was Bank Holiday Monday and so Emma and I went for a walk down the village to see what, if anything was happening. The Old Coach House is a large picturesque stone detached pub that sits on the bank of the river Welland. There weren't any seats available outside and so Emma and I entered the bar which was also packed. After buying a drink we made our way through the crowd to a space at the far end of the bar. A group of middle-aged people who had clearly been drinking all day stood next to us. Emma and I were having a private conversation when one of the females from the group butted in. I politely asked her to go away but she became abusive. I eventually told her to fuck off. Initially she did walk away but returned to spit abuse on three further occasions. Emma asked this woman's boyfriend to take her away and in fairness to him, he did. The woman continued to glare at us but we ignored her. I went to the toilet and when I walked back out, I was once more confronted by the abusive woman. She was swearing and shouting and so I told her to fuck off again. One of the males with her said, 'Don't talk to her like that.' I replied, 'I will talk to who I want, how I want.' The man punched me and a fight broke out, involving not only my assailant, but his friends. The bouncers, who I knew, intervened and separated us. One of the men, Ken Burton, was 6ft 4'and proved to be difficult for the door staff to restrain. He was struggling and shouting obscenities at me.

As I was both quiet and calm, the door staff had no reason to be concerned about me. Suddenly, Burton stopped shouting and began screaming. Blood poured from wounds in his neck, face and chest. His friend also started screaming as blood poured from a wound on the bridge of the nose. That wound had been caused by flying glass. Burton's injuries were sustained after he was glassed in the face, neck and chest. It was over in seconds, even he did not see who was responsible as he was struggling with the bouncers. The police were quickly on the scene and I was arrested, questioned and later charged with two counts of wounding with intent. Under legislation that had only recently been introduced, anyone who was 18 or over on or after 01 October 1997 and who was convicted of a second serious violent offence would have a mandatory life sentence imposed upon them. I had previously served two prison sentences for wounding and if convicted of these latest offences I would have a total of four wounding convictions, double the amount required for a life sentence. That didn't mean that I would spend the rest of my life in prison if convicted, but it did mean that after completing a lengthy prison sentence I would be on licence and monitored by the Probation service for the remainder of my days. If those keeping an eye on me decided that I was not living a lifestyle that they approved of, I could be returned to prison at any time. Whichever way I looked at it, a conviction had to be avoided at all costs. To make matters worse, if indeed they could be made worse, Emma and I had set a date to be married. My trial date for the two wounding offences happened to fall one week to the day before what was supposed to be the happiest day of our lives. Emma was distraught, 'how can we invite guests, book a venue and plan a honeymoon if there is no guarantee you're even going to be there,' she reasoned? I did my best to reassure her that everything would turn out fine but after considering the evidence against me, even I began to doubt I could secure a not guilty verdict. Lincolnshire police had appealed for witnesses to the incident in the local newspaper and one man came forward who said that he had seen everything. After giving an almost photographic description of me, the witness went on to say how he had seen the victim stagger backwards after having a glass smashed in his neck. I put on a brave face for Emma but deep down I was convinced that I was doomed.

The trial took place at Lincoln Crown Court, the victim's girlfriend and another man both told the jury they were in no doubt whatsoever that I was the man who had wielded the glass that night. The alleged victim claimed that although he didn't see me hit him with a glass, he 'knew' it was me. Two bouncers were not so sure, they agreed that I had been involved in the fracas but neither could remember me picking up a glass. Other witnesses were so hostile in their attempts to secure a conviction they messed their stories up several times and had to correct themselves. I have unfortunately endured numerous trials and I am of the opinion that the more witnesses against you the better. If one person gives an account of an incident their story cannot be contradicted by others. If ten people give an account of the same story, there will always be discrepancies for your legal team to exploit. The court fell silent as the man who had contacted the police after they had appealed for witnesses took the stand. The prosecution took him through his statement line by line, he was positive that the guilty party was wearing a white shirt and black trousers, he was confident that the man was in his mid-forties, had receding hair and was heavily built. As the fighting factions were pulled apart by the door staff, the witness said he clearly saw this man pick up a glass and stab the victim in the neck, chest and face. Members of the jury glared at me with utter contempt, I was doomed. That was until my barrister began to cross examine the man. He too took the witness through his statement line by line, but at the end of it, he pointed at me and asked if I was the man, he had seen wield a glass that night. 'Definitely not,' replied the witness, 'I remember seeing him on the opposite side of the room.' The court erupted as my friends and family began to cheer. The prosecution and the police looked devastated. They couldn't call their own witness a liar and should have taken steps to check his evidence before summoning him to court. Simply because my description matched that of the assailant did not mean that it was me. An identification parade should have taken place if they were relying so heavily on identification evidence. Dawn Pritchard Prosecuting, offered no further evidence. The judge directed the jury to find me not guilty and ordered my immediate release. As I looked towards my friends and family, I saw Emma sitting at the back of the court weeping tears of joy. A Detective Constable named Garner, who for reasons unknown to me at that time, had taken a personal interest in me, looked as if he too was going to weep. I suspect it was for very different reasons. I later learned, to my cost, that DC Garner had watched the Essex Boy movie, linked it to me and developed an unhealthy interest in bringing me to justice for crimes he believed were not only real, but I was responsible for. I formed the impression that he thought he had just witnessed something untoward at my trial. Whether or not he knew the truth, he certainly made his own mind up about matters, and in my opinion, he developed a deep-seated grudge against me because of it.

30 11 2003: Danny Woollards book titled We Dared was published today. In the early 90's I had driven an articulated lorry full of stolen coffee beans to a bonded warehouse in Liverpool for Danny. The lorry belonged to great train robber Buster Edwards brother. The lorry, a heap of shit, kept breaking down and I arrived in Liverpool when the warehouse had closed. I unhitched the trailer and headed for home. Members of Danny's gang stayed with the trailer. The lorry broke down again near Leicester and so I abandoned it and hitch hiked back to Essex. The following morning Danny's gang were arrested in Liverpool by Customs officers. Buster Edwards, unbeknown to me, had invested in the stolen coffee beans and was left penniless. Facing financial ruin, Buster went to a lock up garage near Waterloo station in London and hung himself. In Danny's book, he blamed me and (falsely) claimed he 'summoned' me to his office but I wouldn't go. I say falsely claimed, because it was his house, he asked me to visit not his office. I went alone and Danny accepted the lorry breaking down wasn't my fault. We went out socially several times after that and the subject never arose again. On 18 November 2013, Danny suffered a heart attack and sadly died whilst visiting Richie Reynolds, a mutual friend in prison.

CHAPTER FIVE

Stay Away from the Light

A distinct pattern in my life was becoming painfully obvious. I had been raised in a small village and ended up being sent to prison twice, once for glassing a man in the neck who was threatening his girlfriend and once for glassing a man who butted into a dispute I was having with another person. I had been arrested for similar incidents when I lived in South Africa, London, Essex, Peterborough and now Market Deeping. My environment and other people were not the problem, it was me and my Fenian temper. I lectured myself about being older, wiser and on being on the threshold of married life, I needed to calm down, but as usual, I wasn't really listening.

04 03 2004: My book Wannabe in my Gang? was published today.

After such a stressful time I decided to book a much-needed holiday for Emma and I. As our departure date drew near, we still hadn't received our tickets and so I rang the travel agents. A female answered, asked my name, our departure date and destination. I gave the required information and was asked to wait a moment. The moment turned into a ten-minute wait. I thought the travel agent had put the phone down and so I hung up and rang again. Exactly the same thing happened again and so I put the phone down and rang yet again. The female dealing with my enquiry eventually broke the news that there was a problem. When I asked what the problem may be, she said that she couldn't find any trace of my booking on their system. I didn't say anything else, I put the phone down, told Emma that we were going out and headed for the door. The red mist was descending rapidly. By the time I had reached the city centre I had worked myself up into a frenzy. I was ranting and raving to myself whilst Emma sat in silence next to me shaking her head. We parked the car and I marched off to the travel agents. Emma followed in my wake.

As soon as I walked in, I asked a female sitting behind a desk to search for my details on her computer. She told me that she was serving somebody else but I said I didn't care. Looking nervously at the customer she was serving, she got up, excused herself and went out to the back of the shop. Moments later she returned with her manager. 'Can I help you Sir? ' she asked. 'Yes, you can, either give me my tickets or my money back,' I replied. The manager asked me for my details and began punching them into the computer. As she was doing so, Emma entered the shop and stood behind me. 'We don't appear to have you on the system Sir,' the manager finally said. I was really wound up by this point. I said, 'I don't care if I am not on your system, I have paid you so either give me the tickets or the cash back now.' Emma started laughing and so I turned and asked her what was so amusing. Ignoring me, Emma looked at the manager and said, 'Sorry, you will have to excuse him, he's actually in the wrong travel agents, we booked it in Thomas Cook opposite.' I mumbled an apology and headed for the door followed by Emma who was crying with laughter.

A few days later, we flew to San Francisco where we spent four days, we then drove to L.A. where we spent three days and then we flew to Hawaii for a week. On one of the last nights in Hawaii, Emma said that she would love to go for a romantic meal on a cruise ship. I will never forget how Emma looked that night, she was beautiful. As the sun set over the ocean, we sat at the captain's table with a breath-taking view of Waikiki beach in front of us. Most of the other diners were loud Americans who were boasting about their wealth and lavish lifestyles. After a few drinks, a waiter brought out a huge silver tray. On it, was some sort of pink, white, red and purple salad. After the waiter placed the tray in the centre of our table all of the Americans began to clap. Emma and I didn't have a clue why they were clapping, but we joined in enthusiastically so as not to appear out of place. When the applause had ended, I put some of the salad on my plate, sprinkled it with salt and began eating it. I had no idea what it was but it tasted okay. Emma looked at me and said, 'Are you sure Bernie, it doesn't look like starters to me.' 'It tastes fine, have some,' I replied. Just as I took another mouthful the waiter rushed over, 'No Sir, no, you must not eat this, it is the table decoration.' I stopped chewing and looked around the dinner table. For a moment everyone was silent and staring at me. They then averted their gaze, clearly disgusted to be dining with such a heathen. Emma was laughing so much she had to excuse herself and go to the ladies. The 'salad' I later learned, was in fact a table display of Hawaiian orchids.

After our holiday Emma and I began to focus on our wedding,

which could now go ahead as planned. I decided to have my stag night in Dublin. Around twenty of us flew there to celebrate the passing of my bachelor status. We visited the Temple Bar district where we drank in several pubs. The atmosphere was good but bordering on a little boisterous. One of our group had got very drunk and began pinching women's bottoms. I've never liked that sort of disrespectful behaviour. I asked him to refrain from doing it in my company. He refused to comply with my polite request and called me an arsehole. Shortly afterwards the bottom-pincher was lying in the street, unconscious with life threatening head injuries. I knew that I had inflicted serious damage as I felt his head 'give' after I foolishly stamped on him. It was a very sobering moment. The Irish police arrived almost immediately and so I stood in a shop doorway with a traveller named Shane. Two officers approached us and demanded to know who we were and what we were doing. I pulled out my Irish passport and said I was waiting for my mother who was shopping. Realising I wasn't 'entirely' English, the mood changed. 'No problem boys, there's been some trouble and we are trying to find the people involved.' Shane and I thanked him, then walked off before disappearing amongst the Dublin shoppers. The injured man had not regained consciousness and so he was rushed to hospital. He was immediately placed in intensive care where doctors diagnosed a fractured skull and two bleeds on the brain. Shane and I made our way to the airport where I rang Emma who was out in Peterborough on her hen night. 'Hi Em, where are you? ' I asked. Emma explained that she had been out for a meal but was now at her friend's house. 'I need you to go home, unplug the landline and wait until either me or Shane rings you on your mobile,' I said.

'What's happened? Emma asked. 'Don't panic just yet, but I think I have killed one of the lads on my stag night,' I replied. Emma, no stranger to drama since meeting me, said that she would leave straight away. There was nothing else I could do until the flight home, so Shane and I went to sleep on benches in the departure lounge. When I awoke a few of the lads from the stag party were sitting nearby and laughing hysterically. Whilst I had been sleeping Shane and others had put deep red lipstick around my mouth and drew countless circles around my eyes and chin. My finger nails had also been painted. When the laughter died down, they told me that the police had arrested sixteen of my stag party and they had all been told that the injured man may die. 'So why are you all laughing? ' I asked. 'We have been imagining you in a police interview room being questioned about an attempted murder with drawings on your face, wearing lipstick and nail varnish, ' came the answer. As funny as the thought may have been, I didn't want to risk ending up in Broadmoor hospital for the criminally insane and so I went to the bathroom to wash it all off. As my stag night guests were released one by one, the news about the injured man grew increasingly grim. We were told that he had undergone emergency surgery to remove blood clots from his brain and he was now fighting for his life. His family were being flown out from England to be at his bedside. It was feared, that even if he pulled through, he may be brain-damaged. Around lunch time the gate opened for passengers to board our flight. Shane and I went into a clothes store, purchased the loudest outfits we could find and made our way to the gate. Two detectives were standing at the entrance looking at each and every male passenger. We were not stopped and so we made our way to our seats. Just before the doors were closed for to take off, the detectives walked up and down the aisle looking at every passenger. Finally, they stepped off the plane and the cabin doors were closed. We were going home. The injured man spent the next six days fighting for his life with his family at his bedside. Emma and I considered cancelling our wedding. We certainly couldn't have gone ahead with it if he had died. We telephoned the man's brother in Dublin every day to check on his condition. Then, on the eve of our wedding, he informed us that his brother had regained consciousness. He said the likelihood was, he would now make a full recovery and be discharged from hospital shortly. He wasn't going to be home in time for my wedding, which in any case he might well have opted to avoid. I am really pleased to say, that he didn't suffer any permanent brain damage, which was a relief to me, him, his family and friends.

15 07 2004: I booked myself and Vinney into the Bull hotel in Peterborough city centre. Custom dictates that the groom should not see his bride before their big day. (The reason being, back when marriages were arranged, the bride and groom weren't allowed to see or meet each other until they were at the altar.) My friends Rachie, Goldie and Ferris all popped down to see me for a 'quiet drink' or so they said. The quiet drink soon descended into drunkenness and when the bar closed, we ordered bottles of champagne on room service.

16 07 2004: At 6.a.m, despite nobody being hungry we all ordered a cooked breakfast which was used as ammunition in a food fight. When we ran out of missiles more food was ordered until the waiter, concerned about the mess, alerted

the manager. The food fight was still in full swing when the manager burst into our room. Goldie, who was drunk out of his mind, was sat in a chair swigging champagne out of a steel tea pot. Rachie, a devout Muslim, lay asleep on the floor, bacon was draped across his forehead and a pork sausage had been stuffed into each ear. 'Out, Out! Get out of my hotel or I will call the police, ' screamed the manager. I stood up to talk to him then realised I was wearing a steel cullender on my head. We all fell about laughing before bombarding the manager with egg, beans and mushrooms. Vinney went after him and returned to say that we had been given one hour to clean the room and get out. I had booked the room for the entire day as Vinney and I had to get dressed for my wedding, but the manager was having none of it. He told us that if we didn't leave, he would call the police. I conceded defeat and Vinney and I had to get dressed on the car park.

The wedding went ahead as planned at Peterborough Cathedral. Approximately two hundred and fifty people attended. I had experienced great difficulty choosing just one best man and so I chose four. One to represent each of the four main places that I had spent my life to date. My school friend Hughie represented my youth in Codsall, Staffordshire. Mad Andy represented the ten years I had lived in south London, Gavin, who had been my closest friend at Raquel's, represented my time in Essex and Rachie, my time in Peterborough. Prior to the service starting, Sinead O'Connor's acapella version of Danny Boy was played in memory of Emma's parents and other family members and friends that had passed.

As Sinead's haunting vocals filled the Cathedral, I scanned

the faces of the two hundred and fifty guests. Violence and hatred had dominated my life and the lives of many of my friends. Yet now at the age of forty-four, I stood at peace with my beautiful wife to be. A new start, a new beginning. We were happy, financially secure and we had overcome every imaginable hurdle to be together, how could Emma and I possibly fail?

17 07 2004: At 9.30.a.m, Emma and I got up to have breakfast with our families and guests. As we began to descend a long winding staircase, we could hear a hotel guest complaining bitterly to the manager. We stopped in our tracks and leant over the banister to listen. Apparently four men had knocked the man's door in the early hours of the morning. The man said he had opened it dressed in his pyjamas and asked what they wanted. One of the men had pulled out a wallet, and shouted, 'Drug squad move away from the door.' When the man had complied, the four men had run into his room, jumped up and down on the bed whilst howling with laughter then ran back out. Emma and I couldn't stop laughing, but worse was yet to come. After breakfast the manager cornered me and Emma and said the police had been called to the hotel during the night. 'Some of your guests were on the roof and others were seen climbing from one room to another via the balconies,' the manager said. 'Somebody could have been seriously injured, killed even,' he added. 'Still could be,' I replied. 'How do you know these people were our guests? ' After a moment of silence he conceded that he didn't. 'If they were not, I apologise, ' he said. Pointing to a window he added, 'but I do know the people on the Golf course in their car are your guests, because they have told me so.' 'Can you please remove them immediately? ' Emma

and I looked out of the window and saw my friend Taffys 4 x 4 parked on one of the greens. Three travellers, too smashed to walk the course, were hacking and slashing golf balls and falling about laughing hysterically. Emma and I went back to our room, I didn't have the heart to spoil my friend's enjoyment. I later learned that one of the travellers had offered a man a line of cocaine that morning as a 'livener.' The man, never one to refuse a freebee, thanked the traveller and hoovered it up with his nose. The traveller immediately fell about laughing but wouldn't reveal just what the joke was. Shortly afterwards, they had all gone to play Golf and whilst on the course the man had started behaving erratically. The traveller had crushed four ecstasy pills into a powder and mixed them with Special K (A trance-inducing anaesthetic). The man had snorted the mixture in one go and was now hallucinating. Golf balls had been smashed into the lake, the car park and the hotel, Taffys 4x4 had torn up the greens as they raced around the course. Emma and I looked at one another and agreed it was time to leave.

We spent our honeymoon in Cancun, Mexico which is one of those beachside paradises most people can only dream about. Miles and miles of pure white sand overlooking the Gulf of Mexico. I am eternally grateful that we were able to go to such a beautiful place and spend time together. When we returned from Mexico, we both did our best to settle into some sort of normal existence. My daughter Karis came to live with us and so our house soon began to feel like a real home.

Nineteen weeks after Emma and I had married, we both fell ill with flu like symptoms. Neither of us were bed ridden, it felt like one of those viruses many people catch each winter. We were confident it would clear up within a few days. I naturally felt for my wife and suggested she take a few days off work, but Emma insisted that she wasn't that ill. She added that she wanted to work as much overtime as possible as she wanted extra money for Christmas. Emma worked hard and late all of that week. Her symptoms didn't appear to get any worse but they didn't disappear either. At the weekend we went out together and had a really good time. On Sunday, we stayed in bed for much of the day recovering. On Monday, we both got up and went into work. At home later that evening, Emma told me she felt really ill. We agreed she wouldn't go to work the next day.

30 11 2004: Emma didn't seem that bad this morning, we even made love. Afterwards, we laughed about possible excuses I could give when I rang in sick for her. In the past, I hadn't always conveyed accurately the details we'd agreed. On one occasion – after she'd instructed me to say she had a bad cold – I'd telephoned her work with the excuse that she sat stranded sixty miles away. I'd said that after visiting her sister in Basildon, she'd gone to drive home only to discover that someone had stolen her car's wheels. I neglected to tell Emma I'd altered the story slightly. Sitting at her work desk next day, with fake cough and theatrical sniffles, she'd been stumped by her boss asking sympathetically if the police had found her wheels. I jokingly called her a skiver as I made up the bed before leaving home. I left fruit-juice, books, magazines and the television's remote-control at her fingertips. At 9.a.m I rang in sick for her. At 10.a.m, I phoned home. She said she felt awful, so I rang the doctor's surgery which stood almost on our doorstep. Thanks to a

cancellation, the doctor could see her in just over an hour. I phoned Emma back to tell her to walk the thirty paces to the doctors. In a weak voice, she replied she couldn't make the appointment because she couldn't get out of bed. I felt so alarmed I left work immediately and headed home. The doctor agreed to come to Emma. I sat on the edge of the bed holding her hand and talking to her until he arrived. Then I left the room and waited downstairs till he'd finished. He diagnosed 'inflamed lungs', and prescribed anti-inflammatories and antibiotics. I went straight across the road to the chemist, who told me to bin the prescription because I could buy the same medication more cheaply off the shelf. I brought the tablets back to Emma, who started taking them. She seemed to pep up a bit, so I returned to work for a few hours. When I got home later that day, Emma told me she felt worse. She looked pale and poorly. I wanted to take her to hospital, but she thought I was overreacting. She insisted she didn't feel bad enough to merit a trip to casualty. I'll never forget her words, 'Stop worrying, Bernie. It's only a cold.'

01 12 2004: I said I wanted to stay at home with Emma, but she ordered me to go to work, insisting she'd survive without me. I spoke to her on the phone during the day. When I got back late afternoon, she asked me, as she often did, to lie in bed with her and Brumble, her beloved teddy bear and almost inseparable companion. She loved watching TV in bed, snuggled up with me and Brumble rather than sitting in front of the screen downstairs. That Wednesday night, we hardly slept at all. She kept saying how awful she felt. I sat up in bed most of the night, holding her hand and stroking her hair.

02 12 2004: At 5.a.m, I kissed Emma goodbye and told her I'd

finish work early to be with her. She said, 'Don't be long, Bernie.' During the day, I rang home to check on her condition. She said she felt a bit better, and we talked about poxy curtains. At 4.p.m, I finished work and went home to find her sitting on the sofa in the front room downstairs. She looked strange. She seemed scared, like she'd seen a ghost. I asked if she was all right. She said, 'I love you, Bernie.' I knew then that something was desperately wrong. She seemed to know that, too. She said again, 'I love you, Bernie,' and added, 'Help me.' I said, 'Don't fuck about, woman. You're scaring me.' She laughed, which came as a relief, but then she repeated the words, 'I love you, Bernie.' I sat next to her with my arm around her, holding one of her hands. Vinney popped his head round the door to ask if everything was all right. Over the next few hours, Emma's condition deteriorated rapidly. I kept wanting to make her a cup of tea, but every time I tried leaving the room, she'd beg me to stay. I made another attempt to get to the kitchen. She said then what I later realised had been her last words, 'Please don't leave me, Bernie. Stay here with me. Don't go now. I love you, Bernie.' Her pleading tone filled me with fear. I guessed something dreadful might be about to happen – and I felt powerless to stop it. I picked her up in my arms, like you'd pick up a child, and held her, trying to reassure her. Suddenly, her eyes rolled in her head. Gripped by a desperate panic, I laid her down gently, then rang the doctor's surgery and implored them to send someone immediately. By now, Vinney had joined us in the front room. I put the phone down, and again held Emma in my arms. All of a sudden, she leant forward. Her upper body stiffened, as if she were having a convulsion or even a heart attack. She seemed to stop breathing. Sick with shock and fear, I rang 999 and told the operator my wife had stopped breathing, though I could still feel a pulse in her neck. I begged for help. The operator instructed me on how to give the kiss of life – and promised an ambulance would soon be there. Vinney helped me lay Emma on the floor. He held her head as I tried desperately to breathe life into her. The 999 operator had stayed on the line. Vinney picked up the phone and began describing what was happening. Then he started passing on further instructions from the operator to me. I felt Emma's heart stop. I shouted at Vinney, 'Tell them her hearts stopped! Tell them her hearts stopped!' The operator told me via Vinney to try to restart her heart by pushing her chest down with the palm of my hand. I did as instructed, crying the whole time, pleading with her to wake up, but I knew my Emma had just died. Sobbing and shouting, I continued doing everything to get her breathing again. But she'd gone. The paramedics arrived swiftly. They set to work urgently, but Emma failed to respond. I slammed the door shut. I said no one could leave until they'd saved my Emmie. They fought for more than an hour to revive her. Eventually, the ambulance crew asked Vinney and I to leave the room so they could place Emma on a stretcher and take her to hospital. When we stepped outside the house the street was illuminated by the blue flashing lights of the ambulance and the paramedics vehicles. Our elderly neighbour came out and asked me what had happened. 'Its Emmie, she's dead, ' I replied. The neighbour began crying when Emma was brought out. She cuddled me and told me to be strong. Vinney and I walked towards my car but before we had reached it, the ambulance had left with sirens blaring. We drove at speed to Peterborough hospital but Emma had already been admitted when we arrived. At the Accident and Emergency department we asked about Emma's whereabouts but we were told to take a seat and wait. A few minutes later a doctor came out, introduced himself and asked me and Vinney to follow him. We walked into a hallway and he paused outside an office with a sign that read, Relatives Room. 'Would you rather I spoke to you alone Mr. O'Mahoney, ' the doctor asked. 'I think I know what you are going to tell me and I would rather my boy be with me, ' I replied. We all went into the room and the doctor said, 'I am sorry, we were unable to save your wife Mr. O'Mahoney, she was pronounced dead at 8.24.p.m. I said I wanted to see her and so he told us to wait outside whilst Emma's body was prepared. When I went back into the waiting room two police officers approached me. 'We need you to make a statement about your wife's death Mr. O'Mahoney,' one said. 'Please don't, not tonight, don't do this to my tonight, ' I replied. 'You can make one here or we will arrest you and you can make one down the station. Your wife was young, she wasn't being treated for any illness and she has died suddenly. It's not us, its procedure,' he said. 'Okay, okay, I will do it,' I replied. When I had finished making a brief statement about Emma's death, I was allowed to see her. I held her hand which was ice cold, I kissed her, told her that I loved her and left.

03 12 2004 – 07 12 2004: These days have been erased from my memory. I know lots of family and friends came to see me, but I don't remember anything about it/them being there.

08 12 2004: I started to think about funeral arrangements because I couldn't bear the thought of Emma lying in a fridge at the hospital over Christmas. Unfortunately, the Coroner

would not release Emma's body until the cause of her death had been determined. I went to the pathologist's office in the afternoon and begged him to carry out his work as soon as possible. I became so distressed and angry at his refusal to do as I demanded, I was escorted from the building by security guards. A few days later, the pathologist performed the post-mortem. I can't bear to think of what he had to do to my beautiful Emma's body, but his work meant he could tell me why she'd died. The first post-mortem was inconclusive and I was told my wife would have to undergo a second procedure. Following the second post-mortem the pathologist told me that a common flu virus had attacked Emma's heart. Normally, this virus just travels round the bloodstream until it's zapped either by antibiotics or the body's own defences. But sometimes, rarely and unpredictably, it attacks the heart. The pathologist told me he'd only ever come across one other case. The victim then had also been a woman in her twenties. He told me that, once the virus had started attacking Emma's heart, nothing could have saved her. She could have been on antibiotics in the best hospital in the world, but she'd still have died.

Later the same day, the police telephoned me and asked if I wanted Emma's clothing which they had seized at the hospital. I replied, 'of course I do.' The policeman added, 'I must tell you, they had to cut her clothing off her body.' 'Keep them,' I replied and put the phone down. I rang a funeral director and booked an appointment so that the necessary arrangements could be made. My brother's partner Carol thankfully accompanied me and helped me to make some extremely difficult decisions. I will forever be in her debt after she volunteered to put Emma in her wedding dress prior to being placed in her coffin. Emma's body had been subjected to huge surgical intrusions during two post-mortems and I know Carol found her task extremely distressing. However, it was important to us all that Emma was cared for by those that loved her rather than some stranger.

13 12 2004: I had to appear at Boston Magistrates Court for a speeding offence. This also happened to be the day when Emma's body was to leave Peterborough and be taken to Staffordshire in preparation for her funeral. I arrived at the court half an hour before proceedings were due to commence. I found the Usher and explained that my wife had died and I needed to get back to Peterborough to oversee her removal. I produced a copy of Emma's death certificate and asked if my case could be heard first. In a rather terse tone, I was informed that I would be called when I was required. I sat at the back of the court feeling extremely distressed and frustrated. Five hours later, at 2.20.p.m, I was called to stand in the dock. I was in a terrible state, I could barely say my name, address and date of birth. I then pleaded guilty to driving at 46mph in a 40mph limit. The Clerk of the court stood up and whispered something to the magistrate who then addressed me. 'Mr. O'Mahoney, it is clear to me that you are not in a mentally fit state to plead, therefore we are going to adjourn this case until January. You may leave now, thank you.' I don't remember driving home, Vinney later told me that he came in and found me sitting on the kitchen floor. I had not been able to see Emma off and I had spent an entire day waiting elsewhere for absolutely nothing. Their lack of humanity hurt me, really hurt me, bastards.

15 12 2004: One day short of five months since our marriage,

and only ten days before Christmas, I buried my wife in her wedding dress. There were still pieces of confetti trapped in her veil. More than 100 people followed the horse-drawn carriage containing her coffin. At the cemetery in Codsall, my four best men – Rachie, Gavin, Andy and Hughie – together with my sons Adrian and Vinney and my brother Michael, helped me carry Emma to her grave. We made our way through the cemetery at a solemn snail's pace. Each step brought me closer to the moment when Emma's body would disappear forever. My sense of dread filled my feet with lead. The coffin too, grew heavier with every second. I felt a stab of pain as I saw ahead of me the mounds of freshly dug earth that would soon cover my beloved Emmie. Slowly, we reached our grim destination. The moment for our final farewell had arrived. As we began to lower Emma to her final resting place, I prayed silently for her. Less than halfway down, the coffin suddenly stopped descending. We raised it slightly, then lowered it again, but the coffin would not go any lower. It was then we realised that the grave was too small. The funeral director was blushing with embarrassment as he tried to apologise. Mad Andy ordered him out of the way and took charge. 'Lift the coffin back up boys, 'Andy said. The funeral director insisted on summoning his own 'grave attendant' but Andy advised him that it wasn't a good idea to identify the fool responsible for this fiasco. Andy then picked up one of the long-handled shovels and said, 'one of you grab the other shovel.' Emma's Uncle Jerry picked up a shovel and he and Andy took turns in digging away the excess earth. Huffing, puffing and ranting loudly, Andy looked up at me at one point and said, 'typical O'Mahoney refusing to do what's expected.' Everyone laughed, which pleased me, because it broke the dreadful atmosphere that had prevailed up until that moment. Ten minutes later, the grave was wide enough to receive Emma's coffin.

After the burial, everyone went to a working man's club near to my mother's house. Ex Wolverhampton Wanderers and Manchester City player Steve Daley was the licensee and he had kindly given me the use of the club free of charge. My Uncle Paul, who had travelled over from Ireland sang a moving version of Danny Boy, the song Emma and I had chosen to remember loved ones before our wedding just a few months earlier. All day, I had to tell myself to stay strong, not just for myself, but for my mother, my children and Emma's sister, Siobhan. I knew Emma wouldn't have wanted me to go to pieces in public. All day, I stifled my tears. Only when everyone had gone home that night did I allow myself to break down. I walked crying through Codsall's empty streets and made my way back to the cemetery. In the darkness, I found Emma's grave and lay down on the thick carpet of flowers that covered her final resting place. Alone again with my Emma, I let my tears fall until I cried myself to sleep. My brother Michael and our uncle Paul found me there at 4.a.m. They lifted me to my feet, put their arms round my shoulders and helped me walk back to my mother's house. I have never felt so alone in my life.

The days following Emma's funeral are an alcohol induced blur. In between bouts of suicidal binge drinking, I would become so distraught I could not physically function. I was unable to think straight or focus on anything properly. I was dreading Christmas day, Emma's presents lay untouched under the tree in the front room, every glimpse of them was a reminder of the fact that she was never coming home. Then again, every object and every scent in my home was a reminder of the terrible event that had taken place in the lounge. It was impossible to control my emotions, I kept breaking down and so I asked the children to go and stay with their mother. Vinney was reluctant to leave me alone at first but when I explained that I wasn't in the mood for any jolliness, good will or endless renditions of Good King fucking Wenceslas he agreed. That same week a man named Adrian Foster and his young assistant came to my house to fit some doors and complete a few odd jobs that Emma and I had wanted doing. To be honest I can't remember Adrian or his mate even being there. I do know that as a gesture of goodwill they refused any form of payment.

24 12 2004: Today, I received a letter from Peterborough District Hospital. In recent years there had been a scandal at Alder Hey Children's hospital in Liverpool which centred on the retention of hearts and organs from hundreds of children. The organs had been removed from babies who died at the hospital without their parents' permission. Dutch pathologist, Dick van Velzen, who was employed at Alder Hey, kept an 11-year-old's head in a jar and left thousands of jars containing children's organs to decay in a musty storeroom. During his time at the hospital, he systematically ordered the 'unethical and illegal stripping' of every organ from every child who had had a post-mortem. The subsequent enquiry resulted in the Human Tissue Act 2004 being made law. This dictates that the next of kin of anybody who undergoes a post-mortem should be informed of the procedures their loved one has had. I can't remember if I was able to finish reading the letter about Emma, it was grotesque and extremely upsetting. They

had opened her chest and removed the top of her head in an effort to find out why she had died. The next clear recollection I have, is waking up in a cell in Spalding police station.

26 12 2004: I don't remember anything about Christmas day, but on Boxing day evening I felt I couldn't remain in the house for a moment longer. There was far too much Yo Ho fucking Ho on the television and so I went outside to sit in my car. I hadn't eaten for days and so I drove into the village and bought a takeaway. I looked at it, put it on the passenger seat and drove home. I didn't want to go into the house or eat and so I sat listening to the radio in my car. I can't say how long I was there because I was weeping uncontrollably. I do know that at some stage, somebody tapped on the driver's door window and shone a torch in my eyes. 'Have you been drinking Sir,' a police officer asked. 'Do yourself a favour and fuck off mate,' I replied, 'My wife has just died and I am not in the mood for your games.' In a statement made later that evening, the officer said, 'O'Mahoney had glazed eyes and slurred speech, he was crying telling us to leave him alone and that his wife had recently died. He kept repeating this. He was drunk. As O'Mahoney had clearly been driving whilst under the influence I decided it would be necessary to breathalyse him. Due to his demeanour, I decided it would be better to wait until other officers arrived. 'My vehicle was in a private parking bay, I did have glazed eyes because I had been crying. I have never been unable to understand why it was 'clear' to this officer that I had been driving whilst under the influence of alcohol. I knew what was coming, reinforcements were on their way and so the police were clearly expecting trouble. I wasn't in the mood to disappoint. I

was asked to get out of my car and when I complied, I recognised the officer as being the one who had arrested me for the wounding offences that I had been acquitted of. 'I want you to get into the back of the police car until other officers arrive,' the officer said. I complied. According to the officer's statement, 'After a few minutes of O'Mahoney being sat in the car, Sgt Gadd and PC Baines arrived from Stamford. Sgt Gadd asked O'Mahoney if he was going to cooperate. O'Mahoney stated that he would not and again talked of his dead wife and how we were in the wrong. He then rolled onto his back on the back seat and drove his legs up and against the nearside rear passenger window, which was closed. He kicked out with great force smashing through the window before sitting up again. I ran around to the window and Sgt Gadd, PC Capp, PC Baines and myself reached in trying to grab O'Mahoney's arms to prevent him assaulting us. Due to O'Mahoney's manner, I sprayed him with a short burst of CS spray which went on his clothing. I saw that PC Capp and Sgt Gadd had also sprayed him. As we restrained his arms, he became more compliant and I said to O'Mahoney, I'm arresting you on suspicion of causing criminal damage to this police vehicle and driving a motor vehicle whilst unfit through drink. There was no reply as we struggled to restrain him. Eventually we handcuffed him to the front with two sets of handcuffs linked and double locked. 'What I failed to understand is this, what exactly was I was supposed to be complying with? I had been asked to get out of my car and sit in a police vehicle which I had done. Then at least four officers were demanding that I comply with what? I was equally puzzled as to why they had to use CS spray to prevent me from assaulting them. I was in the rear of a police car, all of which are fitted with child locks. They were outside the vehicle and so how could I possibly assault them? My version of events naturally differed greatly from the officers. In my statement, I had explained about the death of my wife, burying her just days before Christmas and the state of mind I was in over the Christmas period. I described being outside my home in my car and the police asking me to sit in their vehicle. When other officers arrived at the scene I was, as the officer quite rightly stated, talking about my wife dying and explaining that the officers were wrong to think that I had been drinking. I alleged that one of the officers then said to me, 'fuck you and fuck your nigger loving wife.' My wife's sister is married to a Basildon born and bred black guy and so I took this to be a reference to that fact. The officer I alleged made this remark has always denied it. The police had searched my home during the wounding investigation a few months earlier and so they would have seen photographs of Emma's sister and her black husband. After hearing that unnecessary racist remark, I say, I lost my temper. I couldn't reach any of the officers as I was locked in a car and so I kicked the window out. Understandably, my version of events was disbelieved and I was charged with driving under the influence of alcohol, having no driving licence, no insurance and criminal damage. I laughed when they charged me with no licence and no insurance. Both items were in my vehicle which they had searched. Another trial loomed, but in all honesty, I was beyond caring, I honestly didn't give a fuck anymore, what more could I possibly lose? That didn't mean I wasn't going to fight it.

29 01 2005: A few of my old friends from Wolverhampton had contacted me and asked if I fancied going to London to watch

Wolves take on Arsenal in the FA Cup. The honest answer was I didn't, but they urged me to go saying it would do me good to have a day out. Reluctantly, I agreed. My friends had been working in London and so I met them at Kings Cross station. My eldest son Adrian was with them. We had a few drinks in various pubs before making our way to Highbury. The game was pretty abysmal, Patrick Vieira put Arsenal ahead after 53 minutes when he scored from the spot after Thierry Henry was fouled. In the 82nd minute a Freddie Ljungberg shot from close range made it 2-0. Adrian was meant to catch the train home after the game, he had promised to drive his partner Natalie to work the following morning. However, we went for a drink and one for the road turned into ten. In the early hours of the morning, we checked into a hotel in Euston. I was awoken a few hours later by the sound of my mobile phone ringing. I looked at a clock, saw it was 8.30.a.m and launched my phone across the room. It continued to ring and after going to answering machine, it began to ring again. Reluctantly, I crawled out of bed and picked up the phone. 'You do know its half past eight on a Sunday morning? ' I asked the as yet unknown caller. 'Bernie, its Natalie's brother, is Adrian with you? ' I knew something terrible had happened to Natalie by the tone of his voice. 'Yes, why? What's up? ' I replied. 'A lorry has crashed into Natalie's car; she has been taken to hospital by air ambulance, it's not looking good. Adrian needs to come home.' 'Keep calm,' I said, 'don't worry, I will make sure he gets there.' I woke Adrian up, told him to get dressed and added, 'You need to hurry, there's a problem.' When Adrian was ready, he came out of his room into the corridor and asked what was going on. 'There's been an accident Ade, don't panic because I don't know if it's serious or not.' Before I could finish Adrian broke down, 'Its Nat isn't it? Its Nat,' he said. I rang Natalie's brother and gave the phone to Adrian. Whilst they were talking, I spoke to my friend Leo and he agreed to drive Adrian to the Queen Elizabeth hospital in Birmingham. Natalie had been at my home a few weeks earlier helping me to sort out Emma's possessions. I prayed that she would be okay, she had to be. I was later told that Natalie had been driving along a main road when a lorry had reversed out of a yard straight in front of her. She suffered horrific head injuries and for a while her chances of survival were at best slim. Natalie spent eight long weeks on life support and after that, another four months on a general ward. To his credit, Adrian didn't leave her side. He sat at her bedside during the day and slept in lodgings within the hospital at night. Thankfully Natalie did recover but to this day she still suffers from some of the complications caused by her injuries.

04 02 2005: Just after Emma's funeral Adrian Foster and his twenty-year-old assistant had come to my house to fit doors and carry out other carpentry work. A few days later, Adrian's assistant had left a note for his girlfriend, got into his transit van and driven at full speed into a tree. He died instantly. I didn't know the lad but as he had been working at my home, I felt obliged to attend his funeral. I had booked a flight to Pisa in Italy on the same day as an old school friend had invited me over for the weekend. After the funeral, I drove to Stanstead airport, arriving with only moments to spare. I ran to my departure gate and managed to board the plane just as they were about to secure the aircraft door. The plane looked full so I sat down in the first empty seat I saw. Beside me was

an attractive, young, extremely tall, black girl. 'Sorry about this, I have been to a funeral and had to run to catch the plane, ' I said. The girl introduced herself as Toene, she said that she was a model and was on her way to meet her boyfriend in Italy. Toene and I got on really well, we spent most of the two-hour flight laughing and drinking. When we arrived in Italy, we exchanged numbers and said we would stay in touch. We spoke regularly after that; we would meet up for a drink and became good friends.

A month or so before Emma's death, I had paid a local man named Jim Botham approximately £1.700 in cash to fit skirting boards and wooden floors in an extension at our home. Botham, a former friend, had completed most of the work but after Emma's death he had stayed away and nothing further had been done. I didn't trouble Botham simply because all thoughts of such a trivial matter had left my head when Emma had died. Approximately four months later, I decided that it was time to begin picking up the pieces, I needed to get back to work and get my life in order. I telephoned Botham and he agreed that approximately £500 worth of work was still outstanding. On several occasions he arranged to come to my house but each time he let me down. What I didn't know at that time was Botham was avoiding me because he had run off with Adrian Foster's wife and he believed Foster was a close friend of mine. Foster had done work at my home and we had been out for a drink but I would never have described him as a friend. I personally, couldn't care less about what they got up to in their sordid lives as it wasn't my business.

24 04 2005: I was playing football with a few of the lads in

the beer garden of the Bull pub in Market Deeping. Whilst there, an acquaintance, 'Geordie Sean,' received a call from Jim Botham on his mobile phone. Sean told me that Botham was drunk and ranting about wanting to come over to Market Deeping to sort matters concerning the unfinished work out with me. I asked Sean to call Botham back and tell him not to come as I didn't want to have to debate resolving anything with anybody who was drunk. I knew instinctively that I would end up falling out with Botham. Not only had he broken countless promises to me regarding the work, he had run off with Adrian Fosters live in girlfriend Helen Myers. The latter wasn't my concern but it did reflect upon his character. After setting up home with Myers, Botham had returned to the house she had shared with Foster and removed a washing machine and other electrical goods. Because Botham believed Foster was my friend, he thought I wanted to retrieve these items also. That was never the case, in fact at that stage I wasn't aware that any items had been taken. All I wanted Botham to do, was to either complete the work at my home or return the money I had paid him in advance. Botham told Sean to tell me that he would sort it out. I didn't hear anything from Botham the following day so I rang him several times but he failed to answer. I texted him and eventually he rang me back. I told him that I was going to Paris that weekend with my friend Toene and her nephew, he could either go to my house and complete the work or put the money he owed me through the letterbox. Either course of action would resolve the matter.

29 04 2005: I had to pick Toene and her niece Darnell up from Letchworth in Hertfordshire and so my mind was not focusing on Botham. Our flight was at mid-day and I was

already running late. As I drove down the M11 at speed my phone rang and when I answered Helen Myers said, 'What is going on Bernie, Jim doesn't owe you any money, he did a good job at your house.' If there's one thing I hate, it's a 'man' who hides behind a woman. I admit I was rather rude to Myers, I told her that if her boyfriend wanted to know anything or if he had a problem with me, he should ring me as it wasn't her business. When Myers hung up, I telephoned Botham but true to form he wouldn't answer. As far as I was concerned, he had agreed to repay me and so I switched my phone off and concentrated on getting to Toene on time. I shouldn't have worried, Toene, true to form was running even later than I was. We arrived at Heathrow with moments to spare. It was good to get away from everything back home. I had been drinking far too much since Emma's death but I had felt so bloody lost. I couldn't think of anything else to do which would numb my morbid thoughts and terrible grief. Away from home and all things familiar I was able to temporarily set aside my grief. I am not sure who enjoyed Disneyland Paris the most, myself, Toene or Darnell, regardless we all had a memorable time.

140

CHAPTER SIX

Coming Down Again

01 05 2005: I had wanted to go to Notre Dam Cathedral ever since Emma had died because it was there, where I had proposed to her. Paris was also the first place we had ever travelled abroad together. Emma's mother had been killed on her 21st birthday, the morning after we had returned. It would be an emotional journey for me for many reasons. Disneyland is approximately twenty miles from the centre of Paris. I didn't really want to spoil Toene and Darnell's weekend by asking them to make the journey to Notre Dam for my sake, but fortunately Toene suggested that I go. It was agreed that I would visit the cathedral on our way to the airport. When we arrived in Paris city centre, Toene said she would take Darnell to a park for an hour and I could meet them when I had finished. I was pleased they had chosen not to accompany me because as soon as I saw Notre Dam I became quite emotional. Only two years previous, on Christmas eve, I had held Emma where I now stood and asked her to marry me. In the background a choir had been singing Christmas carols and the cathedral entrance was glowing from the light of hundreds of candles. The memories of that evening came flooding back. Emma had cried tears of joy then; it was my eyes that welled up now. I lit a candle in Emma's memory,

prayed for her and then bought a rosary which I wanted to place on her grave. Leaving that beautiful cathedral literally broke my heart, it felt as if I was leaving something magical behind that Emma and I had shared.

I met Toene and Darnell back at the park as planned and together we headed to the airport. Toene time, as Toene calls it, runs approximately two hours behind whichever time zone she happens to be in. Because she made various de-tours to look at must see things, we arrived at the airport with moments to spare. Our names were still being called over the public address system as we barged through the flight gate which was closing. I had forgotten all about Botham until I switched my phone on after landing at Heathrow. There was a message from Foster who said that Botham had failed to return the possessions that had been taken from his home or pay my money as agreed. Unbeknown to me at this time, Foster had been busy texting and ringing Botham and Myers throughout the weekend. In the texts he falsely claimed that I was going to harm Botham because I didn't like the fact he had started a relationship with Fosters now ex-partner and removed his property.

Foster: 'That Bernie thing is about Botham, not you. He hates him more than you could ever imagine. It's between them, I can't stop that sorry.'

Myers: 'Why? '

Foster: 'Lots of people hate him, he's just one of those sorts of people. He did the dirty on a mate, you don't do that. Forget the stuff. Then I'll tell Bernie to sort it out some other way. '

As time wore on, love sick Foster had become increasingly desperate and the threats to his ex-girlfriend, who he clearly still had feelings for, became more menacing.

Foster: 'Botham is a fucking low life and a snake, he's not getting away with this I am sorry.'

Myers: 'What do you think will happen to him? Honestly? Honestly? Did you ever love me?'

Foster: 'Yes, I love you. I think he will disappear.'

Myers: 'Disappear? How? Is that what you want? Have you asked for this?'

Deeper and deeper Foster dragged me into his sordid relationship wrangle. He had not even spoken to me that day, but he gave Myers the impression that he was in constant contact with me. Myers became so alarmed by his threats that she told Botham that in order to guarantee their safety, they would have to go to the police. Before my flight had landed at Heathrow, Botham and Myers were sitting in a police station making a complaint about me. When I telephoned Foster about the message that he had left for me, he repeated that Botham was adamant that he was not going to pay back the money he owed me and he was not going to return Foster's possessions. I asked Foster where Botham was and he told me that he was visiting an elderly relative at Addenbrookes hospital in Cambridge. I telephoned Botham but Myers answered. I asked her where Botham was and when she replied, 'the hospital,' I hung up. It was Botham I wished to speak to, not the woman he was hiding behind so I rang again. Nobody answered on this occasion and so I telephoned a further three times. Still, nobody answered. Approximately one hundred miles away, and without my knowledge, Foster had started to text Myers again: Foster: 'Helen, if you're in the hospital get out. Bernie has gone nuts, I'm sorry. 'A short time later Foster telephoned Myers and pretended that he wanted to be helpful by warning her that I was driving around looking for them.

Foster: 'Helen, I truly feel for you at this time. I can't stop this. It's about rat boy, not you. Please understand that he is a very hated person whose pissed a lot of people off.' Unaware of what Foster was up to, I continued to text and ring Botham. My messages were not threatening, I was merely asking him to answer his phone so we could sort my money out. Eventually Botham did answer and I asked him what was going on. He hung up so I rang him back twice, but he wouldn't answer. I realised that I was wasting my time and so I drove Toene and Darnell home before heading back home myself. I did not hear from Foster again that night.

02 05 2005: I awoke feeling awful, I wasn't ill, coming back to my house had depressed me. I had spent most of the night thinking about Emma. I couldn't face going to work. I had an appointment with Clive, a Forensic counsellor at 3.30.p.m and so I decided to remain indoors and do a bit of housework before going to see him. At approximately 3.15.p.m I put my coat on and opened the front door to leave. Eight policemen, two with snarling Alsatians straining at their leads stood before me. 'What the fuck is going on? I asked. 'Calm down Bernie, calm down,' one of them replied. 'I don't need to calm down because I've not lost my temper,' I said. 'I am on my way to see a counsellor. Please don't cause me any shit fellas.'

The officer in charge said that he was aware that my wife had died and asked if I could prove I had an appointment with a counsellor. I opened my wallet and handed him my appointment card. 'We need to speak to you at the police station,' the officer said. 'Fair enough, I replied, 'but why turn up mob handed with dogs? ' 'You know the score Bernie,' the officer said, 'we don't want problems like we had on Boxing day.' If we let you keep this appointment, will you come down the nick afterwards? ' 'Of course, no problem, I've got nothing to hide, I will be there,' I assured him. I felt sick when the police had left. Already depressed over Emma and my arrest on Boxing day, I really did not need any more grief from the police. Where the fuck was this all going to end? I had to get my head together, I just had to begin the process of moving on. I told myself that I would go and see the counsellor, go and see the police and then go home, do something normal, maybe take Vinney out for dinner? Tomorrow I would return to work, I would stop sitting at home drinking in the evenings and I would start going to the Gym again. Physical exercise undoubtedly makes you feel better. God knows, I needed to feel better. This was to be my second counselling session. To be honest I could not see how counselling was ever going to help me come to terms with my loss. All I had done on the first session was weep. I felt a complete phony sitting in a room pouring my heart out to a complete stranger. How could he ever understand what Emma and I had? During this second session, the counsellor really surprised me. Out of the blue he told me that that the extreme anger I felt over losing Emma so suddenly and through such a common illness would destroy me if I did not control it. I left the surgery thinking his diagnosis may have already proved to be true. I drove to

Market Deeping police station to meet up with the officers as agreed. I had guessed that they had wanted to talk to me about Botham but that wasn't going to take long. When I went in P.C Capp and P.C. Donaldson walked into the public foyer and said they would have to talk to me at Spalding police station as the paperwork concerning their enquiries was there. I felt like saying something to Capp and Donaldson about the treatment I had received since my arrival in Market Deeping. Capp had been one of the officers who had arrested me for wounding Burton. Capp was also present when my front door had been kicked open and I had been gassed in my own home. Despite Capps enthusiasm, not one of his efforts had resulted in me being convicted of any offence. Capp said it would be better if I drove my own vehicle to Spalding as that would save the time and trouble of waiting for the police to give me a lift home when their enquiries were complete. Spalding police station is about ten miles from Market Deeping and I didn't relish the thought of sharing the journey with Capp and his side kick so I agreed. On the journey to Spalding, Capp stayed right behind me, I felt uncomfortable driving with a police car tailgating me and so I tried slowing down in the hope he would overtake, but he remained in my rear-view mirror. When we arrived at Spalding, I was invited to enter the custody area. As soon as I complied Capp said, 'O'Mahoney, I am arresting you on suspicion of making threats to kill,' he then informed me of my rights and asked me if I understood them. I sensed he was enjoying his moment and so I made no reply. Capp said that because it was such a serious allegation, a detective rather than a police constable, was going to have to deal with me. These detectives, I was assured, were already in the police station and so wouldn't be long. I would therefore be put in a cell for 'ten minutes or so.' As I was escorted to the cell block, I noticed that the time was 5.10.p.m.

At 11.40.p.m my cell door was opened and I was taken to an interview room. PC Capps ten minutes had somehow stretched to six hours and thirty minutes. Pathetic and sad are words that spring to mind. I wasn't going to react angrily if that was their hope, instead I chose not to mention the matter. Two detectives entered the room and introduced themselves as DC Garner and DS Gibbon. I remembered well how disappointed DC Garner had been at Lincoln Crown Court when I had been acquitted of wounding Burton and his friend. Garner had glared at me intently as I celebrated avoiding a mandatory life sentence. I could tell from his demeanour that this was going to be anything but a normal interview. I was questioned about every text message that I had sent to Botham and I gave an explanation about the content of each. None contained a threat to kill anybody. DC Garner made a Freudian slip when he said, 'If you give a reasonable explanation for sending these text messages, it might make them not legal.' DS Gibbon burst out laughing and Garner quickly corrected himself. 'Sorry, sorry, it might make them legal.' 'You were right the first time. You tripped up,' I replied. The interview was concluded and I insisted that my solicitor be present for any further interviews or I would not leave my cell.

03 05 2005: At approximately 1.15.a.m I had been returned to my cell. It was freezing cold, there wasn't any bedding and the light had been left on. I was expected to sleep on a lumpy four-inch-thick plastic mattress but when I lay down, my face

stuck to it. I gave up any thoughts of sleep and sat instead, waiting for the sun to rise. It was daylight when an Inspector came to the cell door and informed me that he was authorising my detention whilst a search of my home was being conducted. 'Is that your Range Rover on the car park outside? ' he asked. 'It is yes,' I replied. 'Well, we are going to have to search that also at some stage,' he said. I'd had niggling concerns about the length of time I'd been kept over what was essentially a civil matter, but the fact that the police were now going to search my home and car really concerned me. Why would the police need to search my home and car in connection with a telephone call? I asked the Inspector if I could ring my teenage son as he would be concerned about my whereabouts. Despite me having the right to make a call, the Inspector said that he was going to refuse me as he thought it 'may interfere with or hamper an ongoing police operation'. The Inspectors answer confirmed to me that this was far more sinister than I had imagined. I asked if I could see the duty solicitor who I knew was in the police station because I had heard her talking to whoever was in the cell next door to me. About an hour after I had made the request, an officer came to my cell. He said I could not see that solicitor as she did not cover the Spalding area and therefore would not be paid if she advised me. I was getting extremely anxious now as the police had no right to deny me access to a solicitor. I asked the officer to ring my solicitor Mr. Cauthery and inform him that I was being held in custody, the officer agreed that he would. I was not worried about the police searching my home. The Range Rover however, was a different matter. I remembered that I had left a combat knife with a 12" blade between the passenger and driver's seat. I knew the police would not believe that I had been using it in the yard to cut ropes for the lorries. It smacks of desperation now, but I actually prayed to Emma to help me, I pleaded with her to stop them from finding it. I knew in my heart that professional competent police officers searching the interior of a car in broad daylight would not fail to find a 12" long knife. What started out as a trivial dispute was quickly escalating into something far more serious. Twenty-four hours after I had been put in the cells my solicitor Mr. Cauthery arrived at the police station. I was taken to an interview room where we discussed the allegation being made against me. Shortly afterwards, DC Garner and another officer named DC Skeath arrived and said they wanted to interview me again. I was convinced they had found the combat knife and were going to ask me if it was anyway connected to my alleged threat to kill Botham. The interview went over the same ground as the first, but I knew from experience the police always save their best until last. I asked DC Garner where the evidence was which proved or even implied that I had threatened to kill anyone. With a straight face, DC Garner claimed that I had telephoned Botham and said, 'Give Adrian his stuff back and put my money through my letterbox. I am going to cut you anyway, do as your told or I will slit your throat.' I would have laughed if it wasn't so serious. I pointed out that the alleged conversation bore no resemblance whatsoever to the tone of the text messages I had sent around the same time. These were non-threatening and simply asked Botham if he would complete the work or return my money. In response DC Garner stated (on tape) that I had then sent a text message which read, 'I am going to kill you, I am going to fucking kill you, why make an agreement and not keep it.' I was in no doubt whatsoever that what DC Garner was claiming, was completely and utterly false. I challenged him to show me the text message and he was unable to do so. When pressed, he claimed that he couldn't read the handwriting on Botham's statement. I told him that I was not going to answer another question until he produced that particular text message. Eventually, he conceded that there wasn't any such text message but, he then claimed that I had made the threat during a phone call. I insisted that too was a lie and such a threat was totally out of context with the messages I had sent. DC Garner must have known that his threats to kill case would be laughed out of court. Desperate, deluded, I know not which, but he then made the most ridiculous claim that he had made throughout the entire process. 'Botham hasn't put this in his statement yet, but he has said that during the phone call when I had threatened to kill him, he had passed the phone to a police officer.' That officer, P.C Kitchen, claimed he looked at the phone and the screen read, 'Call from Bernie,' he then looked at his watch and noted that it was 5.13.p.m. P.C. Kitchen said he heard a male voice that was loud and sounded angry. He added that he heard, 'some of the words, 'Deliver money or I will cut you to pieces you fucking wanker.' I told DC Garner that he was talking absolute rubbish and quite rightly denied that such a conversation had ever taken place. 'This is clearly a crucial part of your case, yet your star witness 'forgot' to mention it in his statement, you're talking nonsense,' I said. DC Garner, now in full irrational mode, shocked everybody in the room when he broke into his next tirade. 'Are you aware of any reputation you have got? ' DC Garner asked. Mr. Cauthrey interjected and reminded DC Garner that reputation is opinion and not evidence. DC Garner claimed that a website mentioning me and the Essex Boys was relevant to this case because it talked about people being in fear of the gang. 'Grow up man, that's referring to a fictional film, it's nothing to do with me, Sean Bean stars in it.' I said. 'Yes, I know, I have seen it, ' DC Garner replied. Mr. Cauthrey interrupted DC Garner again, 'How can this possibly be relevant to this particular enquiry? ' DC Garner, insisted that it was, but he didn't explain how a fictional film I had nothing to do with making, had something to do with me collecting money I was owed. When the interview was over, Mr. Cauthery and I remained in the interview room to discuss what had been alleged. Mr. Cauthery said that he thought I would be charged with making threats to kill but I should be bailed and out of the police station within the hour. I was taken from the interview room and asked to stand in front of Sergeant Brotherton whose job it was to either charge, bail, remand or free me. Brotherton, Garner and Skeath asked Mr. Cauthery if they could be excused for a moment. They then disappeared into a back room leaving Mr. Cauthery and I exchanging puzzled looks. When the beaming trio re-appeared, Sergeant Brotherton addressed me. 'Patrick Bernard O'Mahoney, between the 29th of April 2005 and the 1st of May 2005, at Bourne Lincolnshire, with a view to gain for yourself or another or with intent to cause loss to another, you made an un-warranted demand of payment of money and property from Jim Botham with menaces. This is contrary to section 21 (1) of the theft act 1968. In other words, O'Mahoney, you have been charged with Blackmail, have you anything you wish to say? ' I looked at Mr Cauthery who appeared to be as shocked as I was. I laughed and Mr.

Cauthery shook his head. Unfortunately, the joke was far from over. Sergeant Brotherton told me that he had followed the investigation from the outset, he said he 'knew all about me' and given the nature of the case, he was not going to grant me bail because he believed I would interfere with witnesses. I was going to be kept in police custody and be taken to Grantham Magistrates Court in the morning. I was allowed to make a phone call to my son Vinney who told me that Adrian Foster was also in custody at Spalding police station. I asked Vinney what, if anything, the police had taken from our home? He laughed and said they had taken Emma's phone as evidence. Vinney had told the officers that it wasn't my phone but they did not believe him and seized it. My phone had been next to Emma's, but the cover and battery had been removed so they had assumed it was broken. I had in fact, taken it apart to clean it. Searching and gathering evidence was obviously not the greatest forte of Lincolnshire police.

04 05 2005: When I awoke, I was allowed to have a shower. It was my third day in custody and I'd not been offered the opportunity to wash, shave or change my clothing. I stank. As I was drying myself, an officer unlocked a cell adjacent to the shower cubicle and Foster walked out. He barely looked at me and so I guessed that he must have said things during his interviews that he was now regretting. Today, I assumed, was going to be no better than the previous two days. An appearance in court, dishevelled, facing a trumped-up charge and if the Polls were right, Tony Blair and his Labour government would be voted back in power for a third term. I needed to hear some good news.

Around 9.a.m a Group 4 prison security van came to collect Foster and I. Two female guards lead us out of the police station in handcuffs and then locked us in adjacent cubicles in the van. It was the first opportunity I had to speak to Foster but he wasn't in the mood for talking, his eyes were streaming with tears. He certainly wasn't filling me with confidence. The driver of the prison van got lost before we had even left Spalding town centre and we ended up in a dead-end street on an industrial estate. The drivers mate asked us if we knew the way to Grantham. I was going to send him the opposite way for a laugh but Foster gave him the correct directions. When we finally arrived at Grantham, we were taken into the cell block and put in separate cells. Foster was still reluctant to talk to me so I knew he had blamed me for everything to save himself. Mr. Cauthery was unable to attend court to represent me as he had previously arranged to visit an inmate in prison. In his place, he had sent a Mr. Milligan. Before the hearing convened, I had a meeting with Mr. Milligan who told me that Foster 'had done me no favours.' Because he had cooperated with the police, they were not going to oppose his bail but they were adamant that I should not be released as they were convinced, I would interfere with witnesses. 'I don't know what you have done to them,' he said, 'but they certainly don't like you.' Mr. Milligan advised that my best course of action would be to offer the court a bail address outside Lincolnshire. The court could then make an order as part of my bail conditions that I do not contact any witnesses directly or via a third party and I do not enter Lincolnshire unless attending court. Vinney had already sorted out two alternative bail addresses, my brother Michael in Wolverhampton and my friend Dawn in Cambridgeshire.

Dawn at that time, was a prison officer in top security HMP Whitemoor, so I thought the court may grant me bail at her home address. Mr. Milligan pointed out that I had never been convicted of any offence relating to interfering with witnesses, I owned my own home, I had always been employed and therefore there seemed no reason why my legal right to bail should be denied. Foster and I were taken from the cells to the dock at 11.30. We sat down behind a glass screen flanked by four prison officers. The prosecution said they had no objections to Foster being granted bail. However, there were conditions, he should not contact any of the witnesses and he must reside at his parents' home which was some distance from Market Deeping. Before the court heard my application for bail, Foster was told that he was free to leave the dock. I looked around the court, DC Garner and Helen Myer's parents sat together. Immediately behind them sat Vinney, Geordie Sean and Fosters latest girlfriend Melanie. I looked at Vinney who raised his thumb indicating that he thought I would get bail; I shook my head knowing it was not to be. The prosecutions objections to me being bailed took everyone in the court, including me, by surprise. I was described as a 'gangster with underworld connections.' Police intelligence, the prosecutor said, 'knew that I had paid a Prosecution witness £500 during my trial last year to say that I had not wounded two people with a glass in a pub in Market Deeping.' A contract had been put out to have me attacked by travellers but I was told about it and had it stopped. Police intelligence, (obviously not relevant to the officers who had searched my car and home) indicated that I had serious criminal connections and I had for a number of years been involved in serious crime. I was looking around the courtroom at one stage to see if I could spot this Mafioso type man they were describing. If it was not such a serious matter, I may have laughed. DC Garner was visibly excited, this obviously, was what police work was all about, catching real criminals like those he saw on TV and in films. Rounding up poachers and intoxicated tractor drivers which is the norm in rural Lincolnshire, was clearly not for him. To top his case off, DC Garner had produced a GQ magazine article titled 'Hard Graft.' It had been written about a man named Harry who was an unscrupulous violent debt collector. (DC Garner claimed Harry was me) The magazine was eleven years old and was now being used in a heavily edited form to deprive me of my liberty and my children of their father. My communications with Botham and Myers, the crux of the case, became secondary. Mr. Milligan, on my behalf, asked the Prosecutor if an actor from the film, 'Lock, Stock and Two Smoking Barrels' was arrested by Lincolnshire police, would he be questioned about the 'crimes' he had committed on screen? Mr. Milligan was quite rightly trying to make the point that the scenes portrayed in the film Essex Boys couldn't possibly be attributed to anything I may have done. Unsurprisingly, his noble efforts fell on deaf ears. I honestly found it hard to believe that I was in a British court of law. The District Judge said he would need time to consider whether or not I should be granted bail and so the court adjourned. Ten minutes later I was brought back up from the cells. The judge said he accepted that I was not the Krays, but pictures from a website clearly showed that I had attended the Kray brother's funeral and the Court of Appeal in support of the Rettendon murderers. 'Mr O'Mahoney, despite his denials, is clearly connected with serious criminals. It is my view that if he were to be granted bail he may interfere with witnesses and therefore bail is denied.' As I walked down the steps to the cell block, the guards said they had never heard anything like it before. 'That was more like a 17th century witch trial,' one of them remarked. Another said, 'Fucking hell mate, you aren't going to have us topped for locking you up, are you?' We all laughed, but I had no doubt DC Garner was laughing louder. Mr. Milligan came to see me; he too had been surprised by the 'off the wall' allegations the prosecution had produced as evidence. My next court appearance was going to be the following Thursday at Lincoln Crown Court. Mr. Milligan explained that the prosecution would probably present 'a slightly more temperate case' and I would be allowed to make a fresh application for bail. If that application failed, I would have to remain in prison until the trial which may not take place until November. The only exception would be if there was a dramatic change in circumstances such as new evidence indicating my innocence. If that happened, I could apply for bail to a judge in chambers. That is a hearing that does not take place in open court.

I thanked Mr. Milligan and was returned to my cell to await the prison van that would take me to HMP Lincoln. When we eventually drove away from Grantham Magistrates Court, the driver put on a Bon Jovi CD which was so loud the vehicle vibrated. I'm no fan of Bon Jovi, far from it in fact, but the music and the countryside flashing by the small darkened window of the cubicle I was in, helped me escape from the reality of my ludicrous situation. 'Living on a fucking Prayer indeed. The allegation that I had paid a witness £500 in the Burton wounding trial had troubled me.

According to DC Garner, I had asked a man to ring the police after they had put an appeal in the local newspaper asking for witnesses to come forward. I had then told the man to describe me and the attack on Burton but under no circumstances was he to name me. Finally, I had allegedly told the man to repeat all of this in court but deny I was the guilty party when I was pointed out to him. It was laughable, I wouldn't pay anyone £500.

I guessed that Fosters texts about me making Botham disappear etc... had stoked Botham's fear and he had told the police not only about the texts and phone calls, but every rumour and story he had ever heard about me. The more dirt he served up, the more the police could blacken my character in court and the less chance I would have of getting bail. It all made sense to me now. That is why they had searched my home and car, no doubt they were looking for gold bullion, bodies, drugs and guns!

The prison van slowed as we entered Lincoln city centre. I could see people going about their everyday business. My right to go about my everyday business had been taken away from me by the police and the courts. I began to feel sorry for myself, but just as we pulled up outside the prison gates, I looked across the road and saw the County Hospital. I immediately thought of Natalie who was still in hospital at that time. My situation wasn't so bad after all. I would much rather be going into prison than into a hospital to endure what she was suffering. The main gate of Lincoln prison swung open and the prison van disappeared inside. The driver got out and returned moments later with what I assumed was a security pass. A second inner gate swung open and we entered a courtyard. When the final gate had closed behind me, it felt like the lid of my coffin was being screwed down before I'd even died. I knew the free world I had inhabited was now gone for the foreseeable future. A guard opened the door to my cubicle and lead me still handcuffed, up a short flight of steps into the reception area. As I stood in front of a desk awaiting instructions, the guards and prison officers talked as if I wasn't there. 'O'Mahoney, Patrick Bernard, from Grantham Magistrates Court, remanded,' one of them said. A prison officer sitting at the desk asked my escort to sign a body receipt and I was then told that I am now the responsibility of Her Majesties Prison Lincoln. I was asked my name, address, date of birth, place of birth, what court sent me to prison and did I know why they had sent me? I tried to make light of the situation by saying there appeared to have been some sort of terrible mix up but the officer had heard every joke and clever answer to his questions before. I told the officer what he already had written down on the paperwork in front of him. I was then told to empty my pockets and remove any jewellery I may be wearing. Everything I put on the desk was carefully checked and listed. I then had to sign to say that all of my property had been listed before it was taken away and stored. Without even looking at me, the officer pointed behind me to a room and said, 'wait in there until you are called.' When I entered, five other prisoners were sitting on a bench that ran along the length of the wall. They all acknowledged me with nods and grunts. We were each called out of the room at approximately thirty-minute intervals, I was called last. I was told to stand in front of an officer sitting at a desk and remove all of my upper clothing which was then replaced with prison garb; a light blue T-shirt, blue and white stripped cotton shirt and a grey sweatshirt. I then had to take off my trousers, pants, shoes and socks. These were replaced with boxer shorts, grey track suit bottoms, socks and plastic shoes. As I was a remand rather than a convicted prisoner, I was told that I could keep my own shoes and apply to have my own clothing to wear at a later date. My clothing was logged, signed for and then I had to be photographed before being sent to another room for a medical. A middle-aged woman reeled off a list of questions she had undoubtedly learned off by heart over the years; have you ever self-harmed, have you had a mental illness, have you any form of disability, sexually transmitted disease, are you an alcoholic or drug user? I was asked to provide a urine sample and then, having satisfied herself I was not a risk to myself or others, I was told to sit in another waiting room. Shortly afterwards, a man with a clipboard entered and asked me if I had expected to be sent to prison. When I explained that I hadn't and why, he asked me if I had any young or elderly family members or pets left at home. I told him I hadn't. He asked me to sign a form on his clipboard and then he gave me a white plastic prison identity card which had my name, prison number JB9772 and photograph on. I was then given a spare set of prison clothing, two bed sheets, one pillowcase and one thin blanket. 'Follow me,' a prison officer said, 'I will show you to your room.' Myself and the other prisoners were taken through numerous security doors to 'J' wing where we were told we would have to spend a few days whilst we were being processed. We were offered a meal on a steel tray which I declined upon viewing it. Once the others had finished eating the slop, incorrectly described as a meal, the four inmates with me were put in pairs and allocated a cell. I was put in a cell alone.

05 05 2005: Twenty years ago I had been incarcerated in this very same jail. The regime and conditions had changed dramatically, sadly I had not. Perhaps in my heart I had mellowed. I was certainly not as reckless or as violent as I had been then. But unlike others of my age, I had failed to mature during the last two decades. My inability to settle down, accept responsibility and adapt my social life accordingly had collectively ensured that my youthful, careless attitude had been prolonged. Born in a different age I may have lived a happy fruitful life, securing a trade after school, marriage to Mrs. Ordinary, 2.5 children, Grandfather hood and then off to my eternal rest in some churchyard. Trouble is, the intense fire burning in my delinquent heart didn't even flicker, let alone extinguish. My heart has always ruled my head, that's the way it is, that's the way it's always been and that's why I think I will forever end up getting in trouble.

My cell contained a bunk bed, a toilet, wash basin and colour television. It had been a stressful day so, at 8.p.m I got into bed and fell asleep immediately. The next thing I knew, the cell door crashed open and several prison officers entered. 'Out of bed O'Mahoney, we need to search you and this cell.' Still half asleep, I put on my prison clothes and asked one of the officers the time. 'Half past ten O'Mahoney, stand outside your cell.' As I stepped outside an officer and a dog entered. I had nothing to fear but for some reason I felt anxious. I had been in police custody for three days so it was more than unlikely that I had any drugs or contraband on me. Regardless, an officer searched me as I stood waiting for the search of my cell to be completed. I began to think that those officers conducting the search, who were now behind a closed door, might be planting something. My fears were soon proven to be unfounded; I was told that I could go back to bed.

06 05 2005: This morning has been spent being interviewed and checked by people from various agencies or departments within the prison. Do I have a drug problem? Do I have a drink problem? Do I think I would benefit from an anger management course? Am I religious? Am I suicidal? Do I self-harm? Can I read and write? Am I on medication? Have I ever had any form of mental illness? Do I want to work? What type of work do I want to do? Will I need help with accommodation when I am released? Do I have any form of disease? From seat to seat, department to department I was shuffled, hardly any of the questions were relevant to me. Anything that was relevant, they chose to ignore. I applied to work in the library and being an author, I thought I may have a fair chance of success but they sent me to work on a sewing machine in the tailor's shop. Logical. In the afternoon I was moved to cell number 8 on the ground floor of 'C' Wing. Once more I was housed on my own. This cell did not have a television and as I had no writing or reading material every hour dragged on like an entire day.

Around 8.p.m, just as the daylight was fading, I got into bed to sleep. As soon as I had closed my eyes, the entire wing began to reverberate to the sound of pounding House music. It was a bit like lying on the dance floor of a nightclub in full swing and trying to get some sleep. As well as the music, people were calling out to one another through the cell windows or screaming at the top of their voices as if in pain. I had no idea what was going on, the only thing I knew for sure was I wouldn't be getting much, if any sleep that night.

07 05 2005: I asked one of the inmates what had been going on during the night. 'Landing two mate,' he replied, 'everyone is on de-tox. We call it the cluckers and rattlers landing as they are all trying to come off smack. (Heroin) They either get out of their heads on gear and make a row or they are going through cold turkey (withdrawal symptoms) and they shout, cluck, rattle, smash their cells up or scream the place down.' Great, trust me to get a cell underneath the highway to fucking hell. At 10.30.a.m we were all unlocked for exercise. It isn't exercise as such, but it gets you into the fresh air, something I had not enjoyed for five days. The exercise yard reminded me of a school playground surrounded by a high wire fence. I counted sixty other prisoners out on the yard. Twenty-five of us walked in a clockwise circle whilst the other inmates, under the constant gaze of four security cameras, sat on the floor with their backs against a fence. All of us were dressed in either grey or maroon elasticised prison manufactured tracksuits. Nearly every conversation I overheard seemed to revolve around crimes committed or crimes that may be committed in the future. I'm no better than any man in or out of prison but I chose to keep my own company. I knew that if I did get involved with some of the inmates it would end in tears and undoubtedly, more trouble. To occupy my mind and avoid eye contact, I counted my footsteps as I walked around the exercise yard. One hundred and twenty-six steps long, twenty-five steps wide. 'Bernie, Bernie, ' a voice called out. Oh, shit I thought. When I turned around, I saw a traveller named John Sweeney who knew a few of the travellers that I was friends with around

162

Peterborough. We only had time for a brief conversation before the exercise yard gate opened and we were escorted back to our wings. Because I had not slept much the night before, I went to bed at 7.p.m. My mind was awash with thoughts about different things. Every time that I nodded off, I began to dream. Emma kept appearing, lying next to me, putting her finger to her lips so I did not speak and then smiling. I smiled back at her and she put her arms out to embrace me. The dream was so real, I could feel her in my arms, the tighter I pulled her to me, the warmer and happier I felt. I'm not sure if the detox inmates were 'rattling' that night or if they were playing their music because I never awoke until the following morning.

08 05 2005: My cell door was unlocked and an officer informed me that I had a visit. I knew Vinney would come up to see me. To get to the visiting room I had to walk through 'A' wing and 'B' wing where I had been housed twenty years earlier. 'A' wing was now empty following a riot in October 2002. Trouble had broken out on the first floor at 7.50.p.m, just as association was about to finish. Two hundred and fifty of the prisons five hundred and seventy prisoners were out of the cells under the supervision of only twenty-five officers. A group of prisoners pounced on one of them and forced him into an empty cell. They took his keys before beating him on the head with his own baton. Other officers had gone to their colleague's aid. Two were injured, one suffered a puncture wound from a weapon. The officers withdrew from A wing as the attackers began freeing other prisoners. Within a few minutes they had opened one hundred and fifty cells. The prison officers retreated to the gatehouse whilst reinforcements were called. Inmates smashed toilets,

televisions, lights, and windows. Some moved on to B wing, and then on to C wing. They set fire to bedding and toilet paper. There were two explosions after emergency-breathing apparatus was thrown into the flames. Police from five counties surrounded the prison to prevent a break-out and a no-fly zone above was declared. Some of the inmates who had managed to reach C wing had smashed a large arched window, hurled abuse at onlookers, and taunted police officers. Other prisoners broke into the prison's pharmacy and began taking drugs. Many were later treated after suffering from overdoses. Some prisoners not involved in the riot were so frightened that they dialled 999 pleading for help. Teams of officers from other prisons were bussed in. Wearing riot gear, carrying shields and batons, they entered the prison shortly before midnight and by 4.20.a.m HMP Lincoln was back in the guards' control. A and C wings were completely destroyed, B wing was badly damaged. Reminders of that night were everywhere. Doors hung from their frames and fixtures and fittings were strewn all over the floor. It was as if nobody had bothered to clear up.

As I entered the visiting room Vinney stood up and waved at me. Alistair McDonald and Geordie Sean were with him. We all shook hands and sat down. McDonald was friends with Botham and had been party to numerous conversations that I had with him regarding the work at my home. If the matter went to trial McDonald could be an important witness. Geordie Sean was a mutual acquaintance of me and Botham. He had received the call when Botham said he was coming to Market Deeping to see me to resolve matters, he too could be an important witness. McDonald and Geordie Sean both said, 'You will be out of here in a few days, Botham and Myers want to drop the charges. They have been constantly ringing us, its Foster they are upset with, not you.' I told them that I was not interested in what Botham or Myers had to say. 'They exaggerated their statements so that I would not get bail, as far as I am concerned, they have made their bed, let them lie in it until trial.' 'Where is Foster? ' I asked. 'He was sitting in the pub crying last night,' Vinney replied, 'nobody is talking to him because they know his childish behaviour has had you imprisoned.' This news cheered me up. 'But where is he, I thought he would come and visit me? ' Geordie Sean and McDonald said that Foster would not come because his bail conditions prevented him from doing so. 'That's total bollocks, ' I said, 'tell Foster I need to see him.' I asked Vinney, McDonald and Geordie Sean not to discuss me or the case with Botham, 'in fact avoid him at all costs, this time in here will help me clear my head, my Barrister can deal with Botham at trial.' When the visit was over, I returned to the wing feeling happier about my situation. I knew Botham would chop and change his story; he was just one of those people who didn't think before he opened his mouth. I had told Mr. Cauthery and the police who were interviewing me that he would dither before I was even charged.

CHAPTER SEVEN
Porridge

09 05 2005: The next morning I awoke feeling extremely anxious. However hard I tried to dismiss what I had been told about Botham, the very thought of freedom would not leave my mind. If Botham did go to the police and withdraw his statement, I could be out of prison within a couple of days. I told myself to think the worst, then whatever happens can only be a bonus. I needed to put Botham to the back of my mind. Whilst walking around the exercise yard, I exchanged pleasantries with to two brothers, Martin and Jim Doran who I learned, were Irish travellers. We got on well and knew a lot of the same people.

In the afternoon, I was told that I had a visit. I had no idea who it could be. I was taken over to the waiting area and found the Doran Brothers were also there. Martin had their case papers with him as they were expecting a visit from their solicitor. 'Can you read Bernie, ' Martin asked, 'We have had these statements for weeks but neither of us can read or write and so we haven't got a clue what people have told the police about us.' I told Martin that I would gladly help. The Doran brothers lived in Basildon, where they had purchased a large yard. They had applied to the local council for permission to put six chalets on the land and permission had been granted. They had a block paving business and employed several men as labourers. A man named Chris from Lincolnshire had worked for them for six and a half years. He was paid £30 per day cash in hand and was given food and accommodation in the Doran's yard. Chris had complained to the police that the Doran brothers had treated him like a dog and a slave. He alleged Martin Doran would regularly beat him with a broom handle or punch him in the head or face if he stopped work for a moment's break. On one occasion, Jim Doran was operating a mini digger, Chris alleged that he leant on his shovel to light a cigarette and when Jim saw him, he swung the machine around and smashed the digger bucket into his head causing a gaping wound. Chris alleged the Doran's would not let him go to hospital, as they wanted to finish the drive they were working on. Instead, Martin allegedly went to a local chemist and purchased bandages and sterile strips, the cost of which, he deducted from Chris's wages. Eventually, Chris and his brother Michael, who also worked for the Doran's, ran away from the yard and returned to their native Gainsborough in Lincolnshire. One afternoon, Chris alleged that the Doran brothers turned up at his mother's home and carried him to their Range Rover which was parked outside. Chris said that he was screaming, 'help me, help me' and that the Doran brothers were just laughing. Two mechanics who were working on a car in the street later made statements claiming they tried to free Chris. A few weeks later these statements were withdrawn. The mechanics told police, 'people had asked them to lie about the Doran's.' Whatever was the truth of the matter, Chris ended up back in Essex working for the brothers. A few days later, the Doran's received a phone call from a member of

Chris's family saying the police were looking for him. The brothers immediately took Chris to Colchester police station to allay any fears the police, friends and relatives may have had about him. They told Chris to ring them when he had finished at the police station but he never did call. A week later, Essex police raided their yard and arrested Jim and Martin for kidnap and firearms offences. (A handgun was found in a sealed plastic bag under a hedge during the raid) Their solicitor had told them that they would probably get five years imprisonment if convicted. Despite the allegations of cruelty Chris had made, I really liked the Doran's. I knew that they were not angels but they showed me nothing but respect. My visit never did materialise. Toene had booked it, travelled from London with good intent but had been refused entry because she didn't have photo identification with her. Meeting Toene wherever you may be, is never ever straightforward

10 05 2005: I awoke to find a slip of paper had been pushed under my cell door. 'There will be a lock down search for operational reasons. For the duration of the search there will be no workshops operating nor will the Gymnasium. Visits will take place as usual and a normal regime will be resumed as soon as possible. Thank you for your patience. Lyn Saunders. Governor.'

The rattle of keys, heavy steel doors being unlocked and raised voices indicated that the search had begun. As my door flung open with unnecessary drama, between six and eight officers stood in a semi-circle immediately outside. A black Labrador no doubt trained to sniff out drugs yapped and strained at its lead. The officers, all wearing surgical gloves took a step back as I approached the door. 'Stand outside your cell O'Mahoney' one of the officers barked. As I stepped outside the Labrador and its handler entered my cell. Another officer pushed the door closed so that I could no longer see what was going on inside. I was told to raise my arms and open my legs before being given a thorough search. Moments later, their task complete, I was told to go back in the cell and the heavy steel door slammed shut with a crash. The search team moved from cell to cell. I could not see what they were doing and I could not hear what was being said, but the rattling of the keys, the slamming of the doors and the muffled voices made me think this was a routine search rather than a search targeted at any particular individual or group. Suddenly above the muffled din, I heard the Labrador begin to bark excitedly. A loud roar went up from the inmates on the wing and many began kicking their doors. Inmates were shouting abuse at the officers and encouragement to those whose cell the dog was searching. I later learned a small amount of cannabis had been found on the cluckers landing. Being locked up all day is particularly frustrating for me; I have never been the type of person who does nothing all day. I am actually looking forward to starting work in the prison as it will occupy my mind and get me out of the cell. I enquired when my employment would begin and I was told that it would be in the morning. Everything in prison is always fucking tomorrow. I decided to go to bed early, because the sooner tomorrow came, the better.

11 05 2005: I slept well but once more awoke feeling anxious. I had been in custody for nine days for making a phone call to somebody who had ripped me off. My anxiety soon turned to anger when officers informed me that the tailor's workshop

was being closed so that another operational search could take place. I sat in my cell fuming. One of the officers had noticed that I wasn't in the best of moods. After a few minutes, he opened my cell door and gave me a television. The current prison officers were certainly more humane than some of the dogs that had walked the very same landings twenty years ago.

Only Geordie Sean turned up to visit me this afternoon. My friend Jacquelyn, a barmaid from Market Deeping, had attempted to get into the prison to see me, but Sean had not pre-booked her and so she was refused entry. I asked Sean why Foster had not been to see me. He said that Foster had called at his home earlier and asked if he could use the phone. After making a brief call to his solicitor, Foster told Sean that he had been advised not to visit me. Advising somebody is totally different from forbidding somebody. Foster had got me into this mess and he had walked away on bail. At that moment in time in that visiting room, I loathed him. I had recently lost my wife, my teenage son was at home alone and Foster didn't have the spine to come, look me in the eye and apologise. Sean said Foster had written me an apology and he intended to give it to my solicitor. As far as I was concerned, like Botham, it was an apology too late and one I was not interested in. When I got back to the wing, I rang Debra to check that both Karis and herself were ok.

 Debra said that she was on her way to my house to check that Vinney was coping. She was going to stay the night and attend my court hearing in the morning. My brother Michael and son Adrian were also going to attend. If I was granted bail to live at Michaels address in Wolverhampton, he wanted to be present to tell them he agreed to letting me stay so there couldn't be any 'misunderstandings. '

12 05 2005: Today had significance long before I found myself in this mess. My book Hateland was to be published today. I had been booked to appear on Simon Mayo's BBC 5 live radio programme. The only questions I would be answering today were from the judge and the Clerk of the Court. I awoke at 6.a.m but I couldn't feel excited, something told me that I wasn't going to get bail and go home. I folded up my bedding, folded up my spare set of prison clothing, completed my exercises, washed and waited for my cell door to be opened. It was a beautiful morning as I walked out of the reception area to the prison van. In a desperate moment I imagined Vinney, Adrian, Michael, Debra and I sitting outside a pub in the sunshine having a celebration drink. The jangling of keys, slamming of doors and officers shouting orders soon returned me to reality. I was searched for the fourth time since leaving the wing and then locked in a cubicle in the van. Soon we were driving through the prison gates and making our way along narrow streets to the Crown Court, which is in the grounds of Lincoln castle. When we arrived, I was searched again, handcuffed with two sets off handcuffs and walked less than ten paces to the cell block where the handcuffs were removed. I was then locked in a large holding cell. About an hour later, Mr. Cauthery came to see me with a Barrister. Both seemed confident that I would be granted bail. I desperately wanted to share their enthusiasm but I had witnessed the venom with which the prosecution and police had attacked me at my initial court appearance. I knew they would fight any attempt to release me with equal vigour. At approximately 11.30.a.m I was called into court. Foster was

standing with his back to me at the bottom of a short flight of stairs that led into the dock. I poked him hard in the back and whispered, 'How are you doing Adey boy? ' Sheepishly, he replied, 'Ok, you? ' Before I could answer, he scuttled up the wooden stairs and sat in the dock. I followed him and once seated, I looked towards the public gallery. Vinney, Adrian, Debra and Michael were sitting together. I waved at them and they all smiled or gestured back at me. Less than a year ago I had sat in this dock and turned to wave at Emma. That day she had cried with happiness because I had been acquitted of wounding Burton and his friend. What I would give for Emma to be sitting there again.

Judge Heath entered the court and brought me back rapidly to the here and now. I was told to stand and asked to confirm my name, address and date of birth. With the formalities over, the prosecution indicated that they were not going to contest Foster's bail and so he was told that he was free to go. He left the dock without even looking at me. The prosecutor was less melodramatic than his colleague in Grantham when he described my alleged crime. He also used less inflammatory language when he described me, but he too made it clear that he opposed me being granted bail.

DC Garner sat behind the prosecutor like an over excited child ensuring the illusory knife remained firmly lodged in my back. DC Garner passed notes to the prosecutor and whispered like Judas Iscariot when things didn't appear to be going the prosecutions way. I honestly felt sorry for him; it was pathetic to watch. My barrister said all that he could say on my behalf, but before he had even sat down, Judge Heath said that he believed that I would interfere with witnesses.

Therefore, I would be remanded in custody until the next hearing on 7 July. I thanked Judge Heath for his kind consideration and turned to leave. The officers held me and handcuffed me whilst I was still in the dock. I looked up at my family, 'What a fucking stitch up, ' I called to them, 'Thanks for coming, see you all soon.' Before they could answer, I was led down the stairs and locked in a large holding cell. Approximately thirty minutes later, Mr. Cauthery and my barrister came down to see me. I told them I appreciated their efforts but I wasn't prepared to play Garners pathetic game any longer. I asked Mr. Cauthery to talk to the prosecution to see if any sort of compromise could be reached. 'If they drop the blackmail charge to a lesser, more realistic charge then I will plead guilty. I'm locked up for making a phone call; they can't lock me up for years for that can they? Mr. Cauthery suggested I could face three to five years if convicted of Blackmail, 'it does after all Bernie, carry a maximum sentence of fourteen years imprisonment, ' he said. 'Three years? I replied, 'I wouldn't get that if I had beaten him.' It was agreed an unofficial off the record approach would be made and I would be informed of the response in due course.

By 12.30 I was back in Lincoln prison but it was nearer 4.30.p.m by the time I had been processed and returned to the wing. When I had left that morning, I was told that I would be put back in my old cell if I didn't get bail. However, I was now informed that my cell had been taken by somebody else and I would have to share with another inmate. I said I didn't mind, but when I walked in, I was hit by the stench of an unwashed body and thick cigarette smoke. Having not enjoyed the best day of my life, I wasn't in the mood for being polite. 'I have never smoked,' I told the officer, 'and so I cannot sit in a smoke-filled concrete box with an unwashed dosser.' 'Put me in the punishment block if you wish, but I am not sharing a cell with him.' Moments later, the man was moved out of the cell and after I had cleaned it thoroughly, I moved in.

At 6.p.m I attended Catholic Mass in the prison chapel, only four other inmates and the Priest were present. Halfway through the service the Priest began to talk about a unique opportunity being given to somebody in the Bible. The Priest raised his hands and said, 'Who would not welcome such an opportunity? ' A fool from Yorkshire standing next to me shouted out, 'I would welcome it Father, I would welcome it with open arms and grasp it with both hands.' Quite how this idiot was going to grasp something with both hands whilst his arms were open, I will never know. When the service had ended, another prisoner asked the Priest if he could address the congregation. When he agreed, the man stood in front of us all and proudly announced that he had once had a drink problem. However, since coming to prison he boasted that he hadn't touched a drop. Everybody except me began clapping and shaking his hand. I walked away shaking my head, confused as to how a man serving a prison sentence could do anything but not drink. I decided to save any future prayers for the confines of my cell. After such a stressful day, it was no surprise that I fell asleep as soon as my head touched my pillow.

13 05 2005: I awoke feeling at ease, almost comfortable with my uncomfortable situation. I believed that the case against me would never make it to trial with the current Blackmail charge still in place. By the time I was next due in court, I

would have served over two months in custody. Prisoners only serve half of their sentence and I thought it unlikely I'd be given more than six months for making malicious communications despite what Mr. Cauthery had advised. A few weeks or months in prison would help me clear my head and help me catch up with my writing, which I had ignored since Emma's death.

Today I started work in the tailor's shop operating a sewing machine. My job was to stitch the arms and neck lines onto prison issue T-shirts. I was told that if I produced ten boxes a day, which amounted to approximately two hundred garments, I could earn £6 a week. Visions of an extravagant lifestyle failed to swirl through my mind. After considering the effort required to meet this target, I assured the instructor I wasn't interested in earning £6 per week. 'I'll neither slack nor sweat, I assured him, but your £6 is safe.' To be honest I quite enjoyed being in the tailor shop. The atmosphere was pretty relaxed on the whole and a couple of the lads seemed okay. Whilst having a tea break, I flicked through a discarded copy of the Daily Express. I never read my stars as a rule but I had more time on my hands than usual.

'Because of a superb link between the sun and Saturn, you may meet someone and fall in love. Either way, you should enjoy getting up close and personal. Yes, it's great, but it doesn't solve your immediate problems, even if others offer to whisk you away today. '

The only person who had got up close and personal and wanted me whisked away was DC Garner. Whatever he said or did, I was confident I would never grow to love him.

As I sat at my machine, I noticed a young stocky man who appeared to be agitated. He looked towards me and then strode purposely down the workshop, his eyes remained fixed in my direction. At first, I thought he had a problem with me but as he got closer, I saw that he was glaring at somebody standing beyond me. When he reached the man, he whispered something to him and they both headed off towards the toilets. As they reached the toilet entrance, the young stocky man smashed his fist into the elder man's face and continued to pound him until he fell. Prison officers pulled the pair apart and the younger man walked off. With blood pouring from a wound under his eye, the older man was taken into the office and asked what had happened. He refused to answer any questions and was soon led away to the treatment room to be patched up. The younger man continued working as if nothing had happened. I never saw his injured opponent again.

After work I returned to the wing and an Irish traveller named Rooney approached me. 'Can I have your cornflakes? ' he asked. 'Sorry mate, I have just come in from work, I haven't got any.' I replied. 'Can you get me some later then? ' Rooney asked. 'If we are given cornflakes in the morning, you can certainly have mine.' I said. 'No, you don't understand me,' Rooney pleaded, 'Cornflakes, real fucking cornflakes.' I was beginning to think the man had suffered some sort of mental breakdown but then from behind me I heard people laughing.

When I turned, I saw the Doran brothers doubled up with laughter. Rooney had been trying to purchase cannabis and they had told him I was the man to speak to. The codeword to use when approaching me, was cornflakes. I did laugh because I had genuinely believed Rooney had wanted my breakfast cereal.

As we were queuing for our evening meal, prisoners started shouting, pointing and looking up towards the roof. I instinctively followed their gaze and saw a middle-aged man had climbed up onto the handrail on the fourth-floor landing. He had made a rope out of bed sheets, put a noose around his neck and tied the other end to the handrail. The man spread his arms as if he was going to dive into a swimming pool, then shouted, 'Fuck you, fuck you all,' at the top of his voice. He then went to launch himself to a certain death approximately forty feet below. Fortunately for him, and those of us about to eat our evening meal, a prison officer managed to grab his leg and hang on to him. The would-be suicide victim hit the steel frame that supports the landings with a sickening thud. As other officers struggled to pull the man to safety he began to scream, 'Let me die you fucking cunts, let me fucking die.' Kicking and struggling, the prison officers managed to pull the distraught man to safety before taking him away. A few of the younger prisoners laughed but it was a sight no right-thinking human could fail to have been shocked and saddened by. The man, I later learned, had been imprisoned the day before. Nobody seemed to know any more than that. None of the inmates I asked knew who he was, what he was in for or how long he was serving. It's like that in jail, nobody gives a fuck about anybody but themselves, unless of course, you've got cornflakes.

14 05 2005: When I awoke a slip of paper had been pushed under my cell door informing me that I had a visit that afternoon. I assumed that it would be Vinney. Now that I had

been remanded until July, I had to sort out the money he would need to maintain the general running of our home. I had compiled a list of things for him to do and a list of witnesses I needed to contact for my trial. When I walked into the visiting room, I saw that Vinney had brought Geordie Sean. As soon as I sat down Sean said that Botham had been in touch with him again. I reminded him that I was not interested in Botham, 'I'd much rather you make a statement to my Solicitor about Botham's approaches to you.' I have been imprisoned because the police and a judge think I can't be trusted not to contact prosecution witnesses and the very same witnesses are doing everything they can to contact me via third parties. It makes a complete mockery of the prosecutions objections to me being granted bail. I explained to Sean that if Botham had anything to say he should talk to a solicitor or DC Garner, not me or anybody associated with me.

Sean said that on the day that I had been in court, he had seen Botham in a pub and he was saying that he was going to retract his allegation. He was then going to disappear on holiday to Cyprus so that the police could not pressure him into changing his mind. I don't know why, but I formed the impression that Sean was trying to set me up or somehow compromise me, so I asked him to leave the visiting room. Sean and I had been associates for about four months and he had been friends with Botham for more than a year. His desire to 'help me' didn't feel right. Vinney insisted that Sean wouldn't set me up. However, I couldn't help but think it was odd that he insisted that we talk about Botham when I had made it crystal clear that I did not want to. When the visit was over, I returned to my cell a worried man. Something seemed to be going on, but I couldn't think what it may be. Whatever it was, I was confident that it wasn't going to be of benefit to me.

Shortly after returning from the visit, I was informed that I was being moved again. This time I was going to cell 5 on the first landing of B wing. To my delight, the officer said that I was going to be locked up in a single cell. As I lay in the darkness on my bed that night, I started to think about the police. It actually saddened me that so-called professionals who didn't even know me could form such a one-sided acidic opinion and cause myself and my children so much upset. Shame on them, I think they are tragic.

15 05 2005: The writing paper, envelopes and pens that I had ordered from the prison canteen finally arrived. I spent the day transferring my notes from scraps of paper onto A4 sheets. I started at 7.30.a.m and finally put my pen down at 9.p.m. Writing is the ideal past time to mentally escape from this shit hole. Since losing Emma I have been unable to concentrate enough to write anything of substance and three proposed books remain unfinished. Free from alcohol and other diversions, I have been able to think clearly in prison. Maybe DC Garner has unwittingly done me a favour?

16 05 2005: I awoke at 6.15.a.m. I broke my hand in two places a couple of months ago. I had trapped it in the tailboard of a lorry, gone to hospital, took one look at the queue in the Accident and Emergency department and gone home. I told myself I would get the bones re-set tomorrow but tomorrow never materialised. I decided I would go to the doctor here and get it sorted rather than go to work, but for

some reason, my cell door remained closed until mid-day. When I asked why they had not unlocked me, I was told they had simply forgotten. You can only report sick in the morning unless you're at deaths door and so I went to work in the afternoon. That evening I was allowed out of my cell for my first association period. Two landings are allowed out at a time. We are allowed to play pool on a child size pool table, play table tennis, use the telephone if we have purchased phone credit, have our hair cut, change our bedding and clothing or have a shower. Approximately eighty men are allowed out to share one pool table, one table tennis table, four telephones and six shower cubicles. I queued for twenty minutes to have a shower; nothing was going to deter me from being clean. After washing in a small steel bowl three or four times a day, standing in a hot shower felt like heaven. I also needed a haircut and so I sought out the inmate who had decided to wield the clippers that particular evening. I had been warned that there was usually a scramble for the clippers because whoever was successful in getting them from the office was able to charge other inmates for haircuts. The fee was usually two cigarettes. I told the 'barber' I did not smoke and so we agreed on a pot noodle. He didn't do styles, he said it was a number two shave all over, or nothing. Like all barbers he made small talk whilst cutting swathes across my head. He asked me where I lived, what was I in for and when did I think I would be released. When I asked him the same questions, he told me he was from Boston in Lincolnshire, he had murdered his wife and was serving a life sentence. 'You didn't kill her with a pair of clippers did you mate? ' I asked. He flicked the clippers cable round my neck, laughed and said, 'No, I strangled her with an electrical flex.' We both laughed, me rather nervously.

17 05 2005: I awoke at 6.15.a.m. I have a blister at the top of my backside approximately an inch wide and four inches long. This has been caused by me doing sit ups. The material prison jeans are made of, is so coarse, it has shredded my skin like sandpaper. I have been doing fifty sit ups in the morning and fifty before I go to bed. I only managed five this morning because the blister is bleeding and extremely sore. I will have to knock the exercise on the head until it heals. I definitely feel healthier since coming in here. I have lost two stone in weight since Emma died but that is due to not eating rather than exercising. Having abstained from alcohol for two weeks has definitely helped. I was opened up for work this morning and decided to go rather than get my hand sorted out. I have made friends with a man from Nottingham named Peter. He is about 35 years old, married with four children and the director of a demolition company. A man had an affair with his wife so Peter went to his house and punched him twice. Seven years prior to this incident, Peter had been convicted of handling stolen goods but he hadn't been in trouble since. He told me that he doesn't have to appear in court again until the end of July by which time he will have served three months imprisonment. That is the equivalent of serving a six-month sentence because fifty per cent of your sentence is automatically deducted for good behaviour. I told Peter that I thought he would be freed at his trial as he will have served an appropriate sentence for his crime.

The short stocky man who assaulted another inmate in the tailor's shop was moved into my cell this evening, his name is Darren Barrington. (Name changed) Darren seems okay, he is from Leicester. He tells me in exaggerated terms that he 'beat a guy badly' in the tailor's shop because he owed his friend some tobacco. When I tell Darren, I was aware of the incident because I saw it, he changed tact slightly. The guy is doing life, Darren tells me, 'He kept saying that he had murdered someone but I didn't care.' I am not sure that murdering another human being automatically qualifies you for hard man status but Darren obviously thought so. Now that he had defeated an elderly murderer in a fist fight, Darren thought he had become equally hard, if not harder. Just in case I was in any doubt of Darren's ability to fight, he spent the next hour rambling on about the numerous violent offences he was being held on remand for. None, in my humble opinion, amounted to much more than lager fuelled fisticuffs. (I looked 'Darren' up whilst writing this book, by February 2021 he had accumulated twenty-six criminal convictions for fifty-three offences. In his most recent, Darren and his partner had been shopping and when they arrived home, they had a drink together. Darren became aggressive and started shouting. His partner went into the bedroom and he followed her. Darren pushed her from behind and she fell against a wardrobe, injuring her head. He then started punching her on the left side of the face and kicking her in the ribs. She later told police, 'He was shouting in my ear, you won't be leaving here. 'This will be your last couple of breaths'. He said that Satan had sent me to murder him'.

Darren was imprisoned for 10 months.

18 05 2005: I awoke feeling uncomfortable, my back was really sore, old age advancing no doubt. I went to the doctor and he confirmed that my hand was broken and that I have

very poor circulation which is causing the discolouration of my hand. (It is blue) I am told I will be put on the hospital waiting list. When I return to my cell, Darren has been moved.

A deluded smack head with a hook nose that wouldn't be out of place on the face of some bird like prehistoric creature was lying on my bed. 'Do yourself a favour and get off my bed,' I said as I walked in the cell. 'Chill bro, I always sleep on da top innit? ' I prayed to Jesus, Mary and fucking Joseph to give me strength. 'I cannot emphasise enough the danger you are in at this moment in time, for the last time, get off my fucking bed,' I said. Ali G mumbled something about respect and slithered off my bed onto his. I climbed on to my bed and read a letter from my solicitor. It did very little to alleviate my rising temper, 'he didn't relish our prospects at this stage, of getting the charge dropped to a lesser charge'. It was his experience that cases of this sort do not move very quickly for a number of weeks or even months. He also said that as far as bail is concerned, I have exhausted every avenue for now. 'It will be necessary for us to demonstrate a change of circumstances before we can make another application.' It looked as if I was going to be in here for the long haul. I am worried about my mother; she has not been well lately. God forbid anything happens to her whilst I am in here. I have been told that Botham and Myers went on holiday to Cyprus on Tuesday. I have been watching the news hoping for reports of a plane crash but no such luck yet. I have been in custody for three weeks now, the joke is beginning to wear a little thin. I will of course, overcome whatever they throw at me, but that does not mean I will ever accept it as being justified.

19 05 2005: I am finding it increasingly difficult to sleep. Ali G

is a heroin smoking fucking dick head. He thinks he is a white Jamaican yardie gangster. He talks Patois (Jamaican slang) and struts about like a big man. In reality he is a nobody fucking midget going nowhere fast. I am going to do my best to remain calm, but it's not going to be easy. Ali G spent the night standing on a chair at the window shouting to his divvy mates. In the end I had to tell him to shut up. Thankfully, he complied.

20 05 2005: When I eventually got some peace and quiet last night, I did manage to sleep well. It was more to do with being over tired rather than the 'comfort' of my surroundings. I got up around 6.a.m and completed The Mirror newspaper crossword whilst waiting to be unlocked. Hardly challenging but it killed a few minutes. When they did open the cell door for work, I went to leave the wing but was stopped from doing so. 'Go back to your cell O'Mahoney, the officer said, your being taken to hospital this morning.' About fifteen minutes later, my cell door opened and two officers said they were going to escort me to Lincoln County hospital to have my hand X-rayed. The hospital is literally over the road from HMP Lincoln but regulations stipulate that prisoners have to be transported there and as the prison has no transport of its own, this has to be done using taxis. As I walked to the prison reception area, the two officers escorting me were complaining bitterly about the amount of paperwork they have to complete, how easy prison life had become for inmates and the amount of 'bullshit procedures' they have to adhere to. I had washed and put-on clean clothing thirty minutes before I had left the cell but I had to strip in front of the officers and put on a fresh set of clean clothing before I could be processed. My 'fresh' set of clean clothing was miss

matched and ill fitting. I had a maroon sweatshirt on that was two sizes two small and a grey pair of elasticated track suit bottoms that were so tight nothing was left to the imagination. I prayed I would not encounter too many good-looking Nurses as it could prove to be extremely embarrassing. My Armani trainers were taken from me and I was given a pair of felt slippers with plastic soles. My attire ensured that any opportunity to escape which may arise would definitely be ignored. I would rather serve an extra month in prison than be seen walking the streets in my dodgy outfit. Two pairs of handcuffs were put on me and a third set attached my left wrist to the right wrist of one of the officer's. It all seemed a bit over cautious to me but as the officers kept saying, it was procedure. Once I had been securely shackled to an officer, we walked out of reception to a waiting taxi. I was told to get in the back and then the prison officers got in either side of me. The inner prison gate opened and we drove forward before stopping at the gatehouse. The inner gate closed immediately behind us. My handcuffs were checked to see if they were secure, my identity was checked and then the big wooden gates opened. The taxi drove out of the prison and fifteen seconds later (yes fifteen seconds) we pulled up outside the Accident and Emergency department. It was humiliating walking through the busy hospital manacled to a prison officer. I must have looked like a lunatic in my mis-matched ill-fitting clothes and felt carpet slippers. Everybody was looking, I wanted the ground to open up and swallow me. We followed the signs for the X-ray department and after checking in we sat in the waiting area with half a dozen other patients. The prison officers began talking about the prospect of Lincoln City football club being promoted via the play offs.

Apparently, they were taking a 1-0 lead to Mansfield Town that night from the first leg. (They drew 1-1, Lincoln City were later knocked out in the semi-finals 2-0 by Southend) As they droned on, an attractive blonde girl who I guessed was in her mid-twenties looked over at me and rolled her eyes as if to say, 'b-o-r-i-n-g' and smiled. Holding my shackled hands up, I said to her, 'this is not what it seems, Rupert and I got carried away last night and he has lost the key.' She laughed and said that pink, fluffy handcuffs are safer. I was keen to find out how such a pretty, innocent looking girl could possibly know such a thing but a bed was wheeled out of the X-ray room and she was on her feet and heading towards the guy lying on it before I had a chance to ask her. My brush with normality was over. My name was called out and so the prison officers and I got up and walked into the X-ray room. They removed the handcuff from my right hand but I remained shackled to an officer by my left. The officer pulled up a chair next to mine and his colleague put a heavy green X-ray vest on him. An Australian nurse eyed me with unease and suspicion which made me start laughing. 'Trust me,' I said, 'these two in the funny suits are far more dangerous than me.' Once the X-rays had been taken, I was handcuffed again and we walked out of the hospital into the sunshine to wait for our taxi. An elderly man walked over to where we were standing, looked at me, then at the prison officers. He then shook his head and walked off mumbling to himself. I had noticed that the officer who had not been handcuffed to me had been writing notes every few minutes since we had left the prison. 'What is that you keep writing down,' I asked. 'More bullshit,' he replied, 'I have to make a note of everything we do. I have to decide at the end of it if you have behaved, whether or not you were polite to us and members of the public, everything and anything essentially.' The taxi arrived after about twenty minutes and we got in. Fifteen seconds later we re-entered the prison.

In the afternoon I went into work and spent most of the time talking to Peter. He really made me laugh, he said that on his visits he has to pretend that he believes his wife when she says she wasn't unfaithful. Peter says he knows for sure that she was. 'I have to sit there saying sorry, I must be going divvy, I know you would never do that to me.' His wife replies, 'Yes, Peter, you are a total divvy.' I couldn't stop laughing as Peter ranted, 'I could fucking swing for her. I am sitting there fuming saying I am divvy but I cannot have a go at her or she will divorce me for unreasonable behaviour, take all my money and share it with him.' The more Peter ranted the more I laughed. Peter has four children and although I can understand his feelings of betrayal and pain, I advise him to swallow it, 'Do it for your kids Peter. We all fuck up,' I said, 'If you walk away, you are not going to be happy, take it on the chin and see if she has learned from this episode. Whatever you do, don't let her keep telling you that your divvy, tell her you know the truth and leave it at that.' Eventually, Peter walked away cursing to himself.

I don't know why but this evening I felt really annoyed. I guess it's just this fucking dustbin I am being forced to live in. I rang Vinney who told me that Botham had telephoned the police and dropped the charges before flying off to Cyprus. 'Ringing the police is no fucking good,' I said, 'they won't have logged his call. If he wants to withdraw the allegation he has to do so in writing. Now I have to sit here until the lousy bastard comes back from his holiday.' I slammed the phone down and stormed back to my cell. The wing shook once more as my cell door threatened to leave its hinges. Ali G looked up at me then put his head in a magazine. I climbed up onto the top bunk and sat on my bed ranting to myself. I am absolutely fucking fuming, how I will sleep tonight I will never know. This has certainly not been my best day in this human fucking zoo.

21 05 2005: I have been saddened by the news in a letter from my brother's partner Carol, Emma's headstone has been erected. I really wanted to be there, I don't know why, it was just important to me. At 11.a.m we are all unlocked for exercise. I walk in ever decreasing circles with Peter discussing what we see as the injustices of our cases. I'm pleased Toene is coming to see me this afternoon and that Vinney is driving her to the prison from Peterborough. It's been approximately a week since Botham allegedly rang the police and dropped the charges but nobody appears to have informed my solicitor and I'm pretty certain nobody will be rushing to do so. Because the information came to me third hand, I have decided that in order to prevent any allegations of interfering with witnesses, I am going to ignore the news for now and see if the police or the Crown Prosecution Service mention it to my solicitor.

After lunch myself and thirty-one other prisoners are taken to the visits waiting room. The travellers Martin and Jim are there and they have had good news. The mechanic and his mate/son who initially told police they had witnessed Martin and Jim carrying the alleged kidnap victim to their Range Rover have retracted their statements. They are now saying that the alleged kidnap victim asked them to lie so he could claim compensation. I am really pleased for them although I have warned them that the police do not enjoy having their illusions shattered. It will probably be alleged that the mechanic and his son/mate have been threatened or paid off and therefore the charge will not necessarily be dropped. The waiting room is filled with cigarette smoke and the stench of stale piss from a single urinal. One by one the prisoner's names are called out, one by one they are searched and allowed to pass through into the main visiting area. An hour and twenty minutes pass and only eight of us remain in the room. Toene I know, would be late for her own funeral and so I am not too concerned. At 3.p.m, I am the only one left sitting in the waiting room. Outside prison people call it being stood up, in here they call it being benched. I'm trying not to get annoyed but it's difficult, extremely difficult. Surely, I have made myself clear over the last couple of weeks? If you book a visit and cannot make it, just ring up and cancel it. I keep telling myself Toene will show up or somebody will ring but by 3.30.p.m when the visiting entrance closes nobody has shown or rang. At 4.p.m the humiliation begins as Martin, Jim and other prisoners I know re-enter the waiting room and ask me if I have been benched. To save face I lie and say my visitors telephoned the prison to say they were stuck in traffic. When I get back on the wing I head straight for the telephones and call Vinney. I tell him I want him, the bills from home, the completed list of things I asked him to do, Geordie Sean and Foster on a visit on Wednesday. After that, I don't want anybody to visit me or anybody to mention visiting me again. Before Vinney can answer I slam the phone down and head for my cell. I slam the door so hard the re-enforced glass in the viewing slit cracks. I hate getting annoyed and frustrated in here, you cannot shrug issues off or escape them. Your anger festers, your frustration becomes more intense. I lay on the top bunk trying to read but that is an equally useless distraction. Eventually I lie staring at the blank cell ceiling until I fall asleep.

22 05 2005: I awoke at 5.30.a.m, the shadow of the cell bars on the wall reminds me where I am. Some mornings, for a very, very brief moment I forget. I have always got out of bed immediately after waking up but as Ali G is not awake yet, I consider it unfair to do so. I lie on my back staring at the badly painted ceiling and think. Losing Emma so suddenly was a terrible thing, trying to grieve in here makes it all the more difficult. There are so many regrets, so many things I wish I would have said and done, so many things I wish I had not said and did not do. My father used to say, 'Wish in one hand and shit in the other, see which one gets filled first.' Hardly Aristotle but I accept he had a point.

Around 06.30.a.m the bunk bed rattled which indicates Ali G is awake. I jump down to the floor, fill the stainless-steel sink with cold water, wash and brush my teeth. At 08.30.a.m the cell door is unlocked and by 9.a.m I am heading for work. Same old, same old, or another day up the Queens arse as they say in here. The prison officers in the tailor shop inform us that the jail will be on lockdown tomorrow. That means no work, no visits and we will be left in our cells for twenty-three hours. After work, landings one and two were given one hour association. Because of the queues I only manage to have a shower, exchange my prison clothing and make a few phone calls. Vinney tells me that Toene missed the train on Sunday and sends her apologies, she wants me to call her. The problem with the prison phones is once you have dialled one number you have to wait five minutes after the call has ended before you can ring another. I am guessing it is to prevent inmates from hogging the phone and creating grief with other prisoners in the very long queue. I asked Vinney to call Toene and tell her I will ring her tomorrow.

23 05 2005: Its 5.30.a.m and a flock of scavenging birds are screeching at each other as they fight over food scraps prisoners have thrown from their cells into the yard. My comatose cell mate is still in a narcotic induced stupor. Nothing could awaken him from his slumber. I feel guilty about my rants over missed visits. I should be grateful people make the right noises, offer to come, offer to help and occasionally do so. Life, whether I like it or not, goes on beyond these walls and people have things of their own to do. I am not wiping the slate clean; they could still ring up and cancel the visit when they know they aren't coming. About ten of us were called into work despite the prison being locked down. We were asked to move all of the tables in the workshop so the floors could be washed by a machine. I suppose its preferable to lying in the cell all day. After work, the officer in charge arranged for us all to have an additional shower, a rare treat in this dump. I feel really tired tonight. I have received yet another visiting slip. I am convinced something will go wrong this week, it's just a feeling I have. Not so much to do with visitors, it's something else, something sinister. God, I hope that I am wrong.

24 05 2005: I awoke around 05.30.a.m, a flock of fucking Starlings are driving me insane shrieking at one another. This prison is driving me insane. I have spent the last hour lying on

my back laughing at myself because I cannot stop thinking a ridiculous thought. Why is the storage compartment in front of the passenger seat in a car called a glove box? I have never known anybody who uses it exclusively to store gloves. They usually put CD's, tapes or maps in it. Its fucking mad. The staff at work have been flexing their muscles today. They have banned prisoners from lying on the cloth cutting tables or sitting on the recess floor. Six inmates were given a red card for playing cards. If you get three red cards you lose all of your privileges, association, your television and the like. It's more like fucking school than an adult institution. Whatever happened to good old-fashioned brutality? After dinner I was taken to the visiting room holding cell. When it got to 2.30.p.m, I was beginning to get mildly irate. I had started pacing up and down and muttering to myself when my name was finally called. I was searched and allowed out into the visiting area. I walked past Peter who looked as if he was confessing to being a divvy again to his wife. I laughed and said, 'Hello Pete.' I think he guessed what I was laughing about because he began laughing to. 'You know me Bernie, I am never alright or right,' he replied. Vinney stood up from a table near the back of the room and waved. I could see Geordie Sean and Toene were with him. Foster, was as I expected, absent. Vinney had convinced me to allow Sean to visit as he thought it best to keep him 'on board.' A hostile Geordie Sean may well cause me additional problems. He claimed Botham had told him that he was going to write a letter to the Crown Prosecution Service upon his return from Cyprus repeating his wish to withdraw his allegation. I told Sean that I have no interest in what Botham has to say or what he does. I spent the remainder of the visit talking to my son and Toene. When I returned to the wing I went for a shower. I had to laugh at the conversation the prisoners were having. The general view appeared to be that heroin had destroyed the moral fibre of the criminal fraternity. One said, 'there's no honour or loyalty within the prison community anymore, you used to be able to walk out of your cell and your possessions would be safe. If you don't close your cell door now, they nick everything.' His friend chipped in, 'You can't even have drugs in your cell these days, the smack heads grass you up to win favour with the screws.' They sounded like pensioners reminiscing about the good old days. Heroin has not only destroyed the so-called criminal underworld; it has destroyed a large part of society. The numerous twenty-somethings in this place, who all consider themselves to be 'proper villains' no longer frown upon the scum that snatch handbags or burgle family homes to feed their filthy drug habit. They don't frown upon such 'people' because the very same 'people' are buying the drugs they sell. I conclude that we are all fucking doomed.

CHAPTER EIGHT
Everybody Hurts

25 05 2005: I awoke feeling really annoyed again, God knows why. At work the sewing machine I use kept breaking down which did nothing to improve my mood. By lunch time I had decided I wasn't going to work anymore.

In this prison dustbin you see the same sign everywhere. 'Her Majesty's Prison service serves the public by keeping in custody those committed by the courts. Our duty is to look after them with humanity and to help them lead law abiding and useful lives in custody and after release.' If true, the prison service is failing fucking miserably. If you have manners, work as requested and keep yourself to yourself you are given the worst jobs and are fucked about from breakfast to bedtime. If you behave like a spoilt brat and bowl about like a yob with attitude, the screws suck up to you and give you your own way. Smoking crack and shooting up heroin also helps. In the recess, a group of such scum have been bragging that they are going to stab a young prisoner called Dixon on the yard. According to them, two of their associates who were unexpectedly moved to HMP Leicester for 'security reasons' were grassed by Dixon. They have no evidence of this, they simply dislike Dixon and so they are using this as an excuse to harm him. When we went out for exercise at lunch time three of the recess conspirators attacked Dixon. There isn't any knife and Dixon remains on his feet giving the trio as good as they are giving him. Eventually, the bored looking screws press the panic alarm and half a dozen officers enter the yard to separate the combatants. Dixon refused to leave the yard as he says he has done no wrong. Nobody is taken away, instead the officers decide to end exercise early. When I got back to the cell Ali G had just woken up. I said, 'I am not being funny but if you think you are going to sleep all day and then stay awake all night fine. But it will be done in silence and in the dark. Do we understand each other? '

'Yo, Yo chill brethren,' he replied. I remained silent. I lay down and watched television until I fall asleep.

26 05 2005: I slept well last night probably because I was mentally exhausted. I have been told to remain in my cell today as I have to go to the medical centre on E Wing concerning my broken hand. I hate going anywhere near the place because that is where all of the beasts are housed. Beasts are rapists, child molesters and prisoners who need protection because they have informed on people or owe money. If you make eye contact with a prisoner on that wing they always look down or away. I am taken over there with a prisoner called Bennett, his face and hands are badly burned. He tells me that he and others were stripping an empty factory of lead, copper and other precious metals. Bennett had cut through an electric cable carrying 13.000 volts. He was set on fire; thrown fifteen feet across the floor and the angle grinder he had been holding had melted. Bennett managed to make his own way to hospital where he was

arrested by the police three days later. I asked him if he got a buzz out of committing crime but his brain must have been fried because my bad joke didn't register with him. Bennett just replied, 'No, I hate it actually, I only did it because I was skint.'

'Did some bright spark put you up to it then,' I asked. 'No, it was my idea, I used to work there,' he replied. I gave up trying to be witty and sat in silence waiting to be called. After an hour, a Nurse put her head around the door and called my name. I stood up ready to follow her but she said, 'It's okay, we just wanted to tell you that your X-Rays are not back from the hospital. That is all, wait here and an officer will return you to your wing.' Why they bothered to drag me from one end of the prison to the other to tell me such meaningless news only they will ever know. I thanked the Nurse and awaited my escort.

When I got back to my cell Ali G was sleeping. As the evening wore on, I began to feel tired just as Ali G was waking up. When I laid down to go to sleep, he stood on a chair and began shouting out to his homies through the window. I jumped out of bed, gripped Ali G by the throat and shoved him hard against the wall. 'Listen and listen well you fucking fool, from now on, when I am in this cell, you don't talk to me or anybody else. If you want to sleep all day and stay awake all night, fine. But you do so quietly, lying on your bunk and in the dark. Do you understand?' Ali G nodded. 'Wise boy,' I said, 'If I hear your voice again, it will be shouting fucking help.'

27 05 2005: I awoke at 8.a.m. Ali G had been silent but his homies had been shouting threats at their rivals into the early

hours. The 'ghosting out' (removal) as they call it in here, of the two lads who had attacked Dixon has split opinion on the wing. When my cell door was opened, I fully expected a pitched battle to break out. The sworn enemies from throughout the night, only offered bleary eyed glares at one another. When we went out on to the yard for exercise the glaring continued but battle failed to commence.

Pete tells me that he has had a little good fortune. The man he allegedly assaulted for having an affair with his wife has been boasting at work that he headbutted Pete first. He has also claimed that he beat Pete up. The man works as a hospital porter. His wife, who he happens to be locked in a bitter divorce battle with, also works at the hospital. Two nurses and a doctor who heard him boasting, have told his wife that they are willing to make statements and attend court if necessary. Pete would then be able to plead self-defence. I was really pleased for him; Pete is a decent guy whose only crime is a poor taste in women. When exercise was over, I went to the library. They don't stock too many good books or many books at all for that matter. I ended up choosing comedian Peter Cooks biography. At 1.p.m our landing was unlocked for association. I headed for the showers, the only decent thing in this jail. You try to keep clean, but being forced to live in a shit hole with only a sink at your disposal, it isn't easy. After my shower, I rang Vinney. He tells me that Botham has handed over a signed statement to a mutual friend which he is on his way to collect. Association was ending as we were talking and so I won't be able to find out if it is true until I see Vinney on a visit tomorrow. I am now locked up for the night. It's going to be a long one waiting to hear what, if anything, Botham and possibly Myers have said.

28 05 2005: I awoke around 7.a.m when a prison officer opened the flap in the cell door to do the morning head count. He then slammed it shut as hard as he could. Fucking juvenile. I still felt tired but the wretched Starlings (rats with wings) were screeching and the prison bars do nothing to keep the daylight out. Any hope of sleep is pointless. I suppose the real reason I cannot sleep soundly is because I am anxious to learn what, if anything, Botham and Myers may have said in a fresh statement. The police, or should I say P.C.Capp and D.C Garner will not be happy if it is something that will undermine the case against me. D.C Garner will no doubt be dispatched to try and learn why they have changed their minds and to try and persuade them not to. Ironically, if he does, he will be doing the very same thing he alleged I may do when he opposed my bail. I suppose it's okay for the police to encourage someone to press charges but heinous for a member of the public to encourage someone not to? I am not quite sure how the scales of justice are supposed to be balanced.

Queuing for breakfast I learn that a man two cells down from mine slashed himself during the night. He was serving just six months, or a shit and a shave as they call it in here. The landing cleaners were mopping the blood up as I was returning to my cell. I was told that the man had put a razor blade between his two biggest toes, pushed it in as deep as he could and then slashed upwards along the length of his foot, up his leg to the knee. He is in his twenties, apparently, he has done it several times before. God help him. Who knows what goes on in some of these people's lives and minds? The prison service and the judicial system employs thousands of people in various agencies and services. I think the millions it costs to fund all of that would be better spent in putting trained people into schools. They could identify the children with problems or attitude and get them help or teach discipline. The child would be spared a life of misery, would be victims would be spared physical or some other form of injury or loss and the Government would save millions by not having to lock them up. I mentioned my theory to a prison officer who told me it costs £37.000 per year to house a prisoner in HMP Lincoln. After giving it some thought, I told him that I was willing to stay at a local Travel Lodge which I had worked out would cost £12.500 per year, a saving of £24.500 for the Government. I was politely told to fuck off.

At 2.p.m I was taken to the visiting room. Only Vinney and Rachie had turned up. Botham had changed his mind about giving the statement to his friend. Another mood swing no doubt, the after effect of yet another cocaine binge. I am learning hard lessons about people. When I returned to the wing a fight broke out between two men outside cell 7. (I am in 5) One of the men had a gaping wound across his nose and cheek. I don't know if he has been slashed or just whacked. We were all quickly locked in our cells as the two men were restrained then led away. Moments later, people were shouting out to each other through the cell windows. It seems the fight was part of the ongoing dispute between men loyal to the prisoners who had been ghosted out and Dixon who was attacked in the yard for allegedly grassing them up. No doubt there will be more violence this week unless of course more prisoners get ghosted out.

29 05 2005: I found sleeping difficult again last night, Botham appears to be taunting me. I don't understand why he would

keep contacting people I know to tell them he is withdrawing his complaint. Then, in the next breath, he makes a point of telling them that he hasn't. Perhaps he is trying to cause more trouble for me? I cannot fathom him out. On exercise this morning a huge Asian man collapsed and lay motionless in the yard. An officer ran to his aid, another radioed for the medics. A lot of the prisoners began pointing, jeering and laughing. Word soon got around that the man had received bad news when he had telephoned home. Why anyone would find that funny I will never know. No doubt it was the usual scum bags trying to make themselves look big and clever? Know what I mean? Innit? Pricks. Eventually the medics arrived and took the man away. When I returned to the wing after exercise, two prison officers were standing outside my cell. They told me to enter and then walked in behind me. The surgical gloves that they were wearing indicated to me that I was going to be searched. I was told to take my top clothing off, put it back on, then remove my tracksuit bottoms. After I had complied, I was told to remove my trainers and socks. 'What are you in for O'Mahoney? ' they asked. 'You know, you have my prison file in your hand,' I replied. 'What are you in for? ' he repeated. 'Blackmail and threats to kill,' I replied. I was asked to point out my property in the cell and then I was told to wait outside. After ten minutes Ali G returned from a medical appointment and he was subjected to the same treatment. I later learned that twenty cells had been targeted on the wing because the occupants were suspected of being drug dealers. I prayed the officers hadn't been watching D.C Garners copy of the Essex Boy movie.

30 05 2005: I was awoken by the rain pounding a metal roof near my cell window. 'Everybody Hurts' by REM was being

played loudly in a cell across the yard. Certain songs always take us on a journey, reminding us of people and places. 'Everybody Hurts' reminded me of 1994 and my son Vinney for some unknown reason. Anything that took my mind away from this fool infested shit hole was music to my ears.

31 05 2005: Today has been one of those days. It started off bad and progressively got worse. I decided to read through the evidence that had been disclosed to me. It is far from complete, Fosters evidence remains suspiciously absent. Always a good sign, the police generally stall the disclosure of evidence that undermines their case. I was confident Fosters would. Rather than read what is essentially window dressing, I simply wrote out the times and details of every call and text message they had allowed me to see. The facts told a very different story to the one the police were hoping to tell. At no stage had I threatened to kill Botham, nor had I blackmailed him. I am feeling a little more confident about the case. I am not blind to the fact that the unexpected should always be expected when dealing with the police and the judicial system. I still think my solicitors estimate of a three-year sentence is a little excessive. I have decided that I have had enough of working in the tailor's shop and so I am going to ask to be moved.

01 06 2005: Six months ago tomorrow I lost Emma. What I would do to turn back time. If we had gone to the hospital earlier, could I have saved her? Our G.P Doctor Wilson had told me that the hospital wouldn't have admitted her because she only had flu like symptoms. He may be right but that nagging doubt still haunts me. I guess it always will. Tomorrow is going to be hard, very hard.

They came to take me for a Gym induction course today. It consists of general health questions, safety talks, demonstrations on how to use the equipment and first aid. The latter included giving the kiss of life to a dummy. I felt terrible watching the demonstration. All I could think of was Emma lying stricken on the living room floor and me trying to breathe life into her. The instructor said that we all had to try it but I told him I couldn't and why. Thankfully he said he understood and there wasn't any need for me to take part. I couldn't have done it, stupid I know, but I just couldn't. I managed to weigh myself when I was over at the Gym. I am 16 stone now, that's two and a half stone lighter than when Emma died. The last time I can remember being 16 stone I was at school.

In the afternoon we went back to the Gym. I did a bit of weightlifting and half an hour on the running machine. I surprised myself how far and fast I was able to run. The loss of two and a half stone has obviously been beneficial.

02 06 2005: I awoke thinking of Emma. Today is going to be difficult, especially this evening when like it or not I will be clock watching thinking, six months ago today at this time, that happened, six months ago today at this time, this happened. I know I cannot change what's gone, but that won't stop me wishing I could. Work dragged today; I just couldn't concentrate. At 1.p.m six months ago, I had telephoned Emma and she had said, 'I was just about to call you Bernie.' We had talked about buying a set of made to measure curtains from a local shop. Mundane, but I sat longing to have that conversation again. I didn't bother eating after work, I can't face the slop they serve. I went to my cell to try and sleep. If

anybody thinks that what they have done to me is justice, for what I am alleged to have done, then they must be smoking the same shit as Ali G.

03 06 2005: Despite my best-efforts last night, it was 10.p.m before I finally drifted off to sleep. Ali G has started brewing Hooch to fuel his nocturnal lifestyle. Prisoners get an empty plastic bottle and fill one third of it with water. They then crush an Oxo cube and put that in the bottle. Shake vigorously, then allow to settle overnight. The Oxo cube will separate. White sediment will settle at the bottom of the bottle and brown coloured water at the top. (This is the colouring etc...) Pour the coloured water away and top up the bottle to the halfway mark with clean water. Add chopped up fruit and two or three spoonsful of sugar. Secure the lid tightly and hide the bottle to avoid detection. At night, fill the sink with hot water and submerge the bottle in it to speed up the fermentation process. Each day add another two or three spoonsful of sugar. After four or five days you can add undiluted squash to flavour it. The potion can be consumed at this stage but the prison connoisseurs leave it a little longer adding sugar daily to increase its strength. Some of the lads on the wing are drunk every night of the week. Two in particular are intoxicated more than anybody else. That's not because of prison Hooch, their favourite tipple is Vodka followed by a 'blazing session.' (Smoking heroin) A prison officer they know from outside, smuggles in a plastic bottle full of Vodka twice a week. In return, the officer is given £50 a time. The lads deny they get the drugs from the same source, but both 'blaze' most nights.

Debra and my daughter Karis came to visit me today. It was

good to see them. Karis was laughing and joking which pleased me as she had been upset about my incarceration. The Doran brothers were also receiving a visit and they were sitting at an adjacent table. One of them asked if I wanted a drink of his Ribena. I thought it odd, but the way he was looking at me I guessed it wasn't Ribena. 'Ok, I will have some,' I replied. He drank half the bottle before passing it to me. I took a mouthful and nearly choked. Debra and Karis began to laugh as my head turned blood red. 'What's up? What's up?' they asked. 'Its neat fucking Vodka,' I croaked. I looked over at the Doran's and they were laughing too. I wasn't planning on going to the pub for a few weeks so I thought, why not? I drank the rest of the bottle in one go. For the rest of the visit Debra and Karis continued to laugh because I was all over the place. It had been some time since I had consumed any alcohol and it clearly was having an effect on me. By the time I got back to my cell I was barely able to stand. I clambered on to my bed and immediately fell asleep.

04 06 2005: Slamming steel doors, jangling keys and an officer shouting, 'Kitchen staff, kitchen staff,' woke me from my slumber. I knew it was approximately 7.a.m because that is the time the kitchen staff are unlocked for work. Another visiting slip has been pushed under the cell door. I think Rachie is coming to see me on Sunday but I'm not sure. Today shouldn't be so bad, its Saturday and so there isn't any work. I've got library, Gym, association and Gym again in the afternoon. At Gym this morning we played 5 a side football which was pretty fucking brutal. It struck me after about the tenth kick in the back of my legs that Bernard O'Mahoney was no longer a twenty something wide boy! By the end of the

game, I could taste blood in my mouth and my heart was threatening to explode. It took me a good thirty minutes before I began to feel anywhere near normal again. I missed going to the library because I had been at the gym. I need to get fit more than I need to read so it was an acceptable sacrifice. I hobbled around the exercise yard later that morning with Peter. He told me that he had hired a private detective to work on his case. The detective has told him that his wife is still meeting the man Peter is accused of assaulting. The courts wont grant Peter bail because they say he may interfere with witnesses, but in the meantime, the alleged victim is interfering with Pete's wife. The 'victim' has denied knowing Pete's wife in his statement and so the detective has been instructed to get photographic evidence of them together. I was both saddened and pleased for Peter. He isn't a villain; he has worked hard all of his life to build up a business for his wife and their four children. It has now been proven to him beyond doubt that his wife has betrayed him. At least this awful news will confirm he isn't a divvy, help him to get out of here and he can begin to rebuild his life. When I returned to my cell, Ali G was arguing with a prison officer about him not been taken to the library. He called the officer a prick and when he was asked what he had said he repeated, 'You are a prick.' He then said, 'Don't think I am bothered about you or any other officer in this jail. I have been in and out of prison for years and I don't give a fuck about none of you. The officer replied, 'We will see.' He then asked me if I was going into the cell and when I stepped inside, he slammed the door. The 'we will see' turned out to be an idle threat because nothing happened. That was the problem with people like Ali G, they could mouth off knowing their 'rights' would protect them from violent retribution. He should have had his teeth smashed with a baton the moment he called the officer a prick. Neanderthal justice maybe, but violent people only understand one thing, violence.

I felt a sharp pain in my back when I got up to go to the Gym in the afternoon. I'm not sure if I had pulled or twisted something leaping off the top bunk or if I had damaged it playing football earlier. The sensible thing to do would have been to rest. I have never been accused of being sensible, so I thought I would be able to run it off in the Gym. When I returned from my afternoon exertions I felt okay. I laid down for an hour or so. When I eventually sat up, the pain shot through my spine and I was forced to lie back down. I spent the rest of the evening attempting to get myself into a comfortable position, but the pain was intense.

05 06 2005: I have spent most of the night awake. The dip in the centre of my prison mattress ensures that I cannot ease the pain in my back, which is now glowing because it is so inflamed. Ali G, suffering as all smack heads do, from chronic diarrhoea, added to my misery by stinking the cell out at regular intervals with noxious anal gases.

I will be surprised if I can get out of my bed and onto the floor today, so the gym is definitely out. The old guy overdid it, I think. My imprisonment is not causing me too much anxiety or stress, (My family disagree) which is strange, as it has done in the past. I feel content, almost resigned to my dreadful situation. With no wife or girlfriend to concern myself with and confident Vinney will have paid all of the outstanding household bills, I don't have much to be anxious about. The bastards can't hang me, although I get the impression that if it was an option, they might. The discharge list will have my name on it one day. I am not ashamed about what I am alleged to have done or about the fact that I am in prison. There are others who should be, but I doubt if they are decent enough to be able to acknowledge the depth of their treachery and deceit. We were only on the exercise yard for five minutes today as it poured with rain. When we were told to return to our cells, sixteen prisoners refused to move. One of them was Ali G. 'Ya know what I mean? Innit? Safe. Twat.' The prison officers radioed for reinforcements and soon the yard had been cleared.

Vinney, Rachie and his girlfriend Amanda came to see me today. Amanda was a good friend of Emma's; she wants to visit her grave with me when I am realised. It was good to see her. Vinney has sorted out the majority of the tasks I had asked him to do. Knowing everything is in order with the house and bills is a weight off my mind. I like everything in my life to be up to date, debt is a no, no. If you can't afford something, save, simple. Its Vinney's 18th birthday on the 27th of this month. I have told him to book himself and three friends a weekend abroad. The Doran brothers were on the same visit and ended up steaming drunk again. One of them was so hammered I was sure the prison officers would notice. When it was time to return to the wing, their cousin John Rooney, me and the other Doran brother walked in front, behind and to the side of our drunken friend in an effort to disguise his condition. Once safely back in his cell, he collapsed onto a bed and immediately fell asleep. When I returned to my cell, Ali G said that he and the other fifteen inmates who had refused to leave the yard had been served with a notice. They have all been charged with refusing a lawful order. Form F1145 explained his rights. At section 9, it states that he can write out an explanation of his behaviour and this can then be read out to the prison Governor or the Governor can read it aloud to him. Ali G claimed the Governor was virtually powerless to punish him and his co-accused and so they intended to fuck him about as much as possible. After conversing with one another by shouting, shrieking and laughing out of the windows, the Lincoln sixteen as they are calling themselves, agreed on a strategy. It is their right to receive an information pack about their rights prior to the hearing, which is scheduled for the morning. We are locked up for the night and there are only four-night security officers on the wing. All of the Lincoln sixteen are pressing their emergency bells demanding their information pack. Knowing the night security officers don't have access to the packs the Lincoln sixteen all lodge complaints about their rights being infringed All sixteen then begin writing up the reasons why they refused the alleged lawful order. They have all said that they will demand that the Governor will read their statements to them as is their right. They have also agreed that they will start their statements with their childhood experiences and write as many pages as possible incorporating their parents, upbringing, school etc... To fuck the Governors head up further, they have all agreed to litter their statements with expletives, incorrect spellings and sentences that don't quite make sense. The final 'right' they have agreed to exercise, is their individual right to call all relevant witnesses. All sixteen have agreed to call all of the officers who were present (approximately eight) and their fifteen co-accused. Each prisoner is dealt with separately, so the Governor would, if the rules are adhered to, have to hear approximately 284 people give evidence. It is unlikely proceedings will end tomorrow or even next week if their amusing plan is allowed to be played out. Unfortunately, most of the inmates are full of shit and so it's unlikely they will adhere to the strategy. Ali G and his co-accused think, from what I can hear being shouted out of the windows, that the worst punishment they can get is one week's loss of earnings or one week's loss of canteen. (The weekly right to purchase additional; toiletries, tobacco, confectionary etc...from their private cash) Ali G refuses to work and so has no earnings to lose and the 'goodies' he could be prevented from purchasing for one week can be borrowed from other inmates until he can pay them back the following week. Prison Governors are no longer allowed to add time to your sentence for bad behaviour, although fifty per cent of your sentence is automatically taken off for good behaviour before you have even reached the prison. I am no psychologist but I am guessing that is why inmates abuse and threaten prison officers without fear of retribution.

It's been an eventful and interesting day. The more I read the few case papers I have at my disposal, the 'airtight' case D.C Garner thought he had constructed appears to be springing countless leaks. Like those who built the Titanic, he foolishly believes that his creation will never sink.

06 06 2005: My back is still extremely painful; I think I have trapped a nerve because I get a sharp pain when I move to my right but not my left. Ali G has been awake most of the night writing his statement which he says explains his behaviour. He has completed fourteen sides of A4 paper. I

struggled to read the first page which describes the dire environment he was born into. The grammar was atrocious, the spelling atrocious and the handwriting equally so. The expression, 'Ya know what I mean?' featured heavily throughout as did 'Fed's' (The police) Dissed, (Disrespected) Me drum, (Home/House) and Brethren, (Brother/friends) I would pay good money for a front seat at the hearing today and beyond if all goes according to plan. British justice, eh? The 'best' in the world, not! Human Rights are an admirable thing to ensure justice and equality for the masses, but we should give equal prominence to Human Wrongs and then maybe, just maybe, our streets and prisons wouldn't be infested with the likes of Ali G. He has never done a day's work in his life and doesn't intend to. His net contribution to society...zero.

I have just been informed that I have got a visit from my solicitor. I am taken across to the visiting hall and ushered into a room where my solicitor is already sitting reading my case papers. I like Hugh, he is an old school gentleman, a man of principle and a legal eagle. Little if anything goes unnoticed by his sharp mind and intense scrutiny. He isn't smiling and so I prepare myself for more bad news. Hugh explained that Myers had been in touch with him and alleged my son Vinney had contacted her about the case. Myers had told Botham and he had advised her to go to the police. Myers told Hugh that she wanted to talk to him about her evidence but he quite rightly refused. Fortunately, Vinney had recorded Myers when she rang him and so her false claim was easy to disprove. Myers went on to tell Mr. Cauthery that she wanted to withdraw her evidence.

Despite the fact myself or my friends had not done anything wrong, I was livid. I had known this constant phone calling would end up a mess. I had advised people to ignore Botham and Myers, demanded they tell them to fuck off, but nobody it seemed had listened. Mr. Cauthery did his best to make me realise that I was in an ever-increasing serious situation. He advised that the case against me was far from weak and the 'Essex Boys' evidence I believed was irrelevant, would be difficult to exclude. 'If your convicted Bernie, you will go away for a minimum of three years in my opinion,' he warned. I was frustrated and angry and told him I didn't agree. 'I feel like I am trying to fight this case with both hands tied behind my back, the police have had it all their own way, I need to hit back,' I said. Mr. Cauthery explained that I had to be patient, 'the prosecution has to disclose all of their evidence by 23 June.' 'We can then take stock of the situation,' he advised.

Resigned to my fate, I had no choice but to wait. It will certainly be interesting to read what shit the police have produced for my trial. I have a feeling my co-accused Adrian Foster will make or break this case for me. Before Mr. Cauthery left, he told me that my barrister had withdrawn from the case. Apparently, I had praised him on the internet for the sterling job he had done during the 'glassing trial' involving Burton. The Barrister felt this could appear to any juror that he and I had some sort of unscrupulous relationship. I accepted his professional concerns but in reality, if any inference had been drawn because I had praised his professionalism it would at best be ridiculous. I had been in a fairly upbeat mood prior to the meeting with my solicitor. I don't blame him for being the bearer of bad news. Reality checks are often hard, but I would prefer to be aware of all the facts and potential pitfalls rather than go Into a trial with a false sense of security. I'm confident that more evidence will come out that will assist me, it's safe to assume some will be disclosed that won't. In the meantime, I am stuck on this fucking prison rollercoaster.

06 06 2005: The Lincoln sixteens plan to disrupt their disciplinary hearing appears to have worked. Frustrated by the amount of time the first case had taken, the prison Governor suspended the inmate's sentence of no canteen for a week. This meant that if the inmate behaved for seven days, he wouldn't receive any punishment. However, if he got in trouble, he would be denied canteen for one week. Hardly a punishment, more of an inconvenience. Tired of his mundane task, the Governor ensured that his lenient punishment filtered back to the other inmates who were waiting to be called. When they heard a non-punishment sentence was on the table, most pleaded guilty. As I write this, Ali G and four others are yet to be called. Their cases have been deferred until after lunch.

As time goes on, the pain in my back is increasing. I am barely able to bend down and even walking is difficult. In the afternoon I hobbled around the exercise yard before returning to my cell. To my surprise and utter joy, Ali G had been moved. In his place they have installed Ricky, a 22-year-old lad from Grantham. Much to my dismay, he also smokes. Ricky seems a nice enough kid. I told him that I hated people smoking around me and so if I moved cell, it wasn't anything personal. He tells me that he is serving 18 months for threatening to shoot his wife with an air rifle. They had been married for just seven months when she invited her lover into their home to tell Ricky that she was leaving. Ricky picked up his air rifle and aimed it at his wife's head. Rather wisely, she fled upstairs and called the police. Ricky had never been in trouble before. He committed the offence in December, pleaded guilty and was sentenced three days ago. I feel quite sorry for him. His wife has betrayed him after just seven months of marriage and after a moment of madness he has ended up in here. Whilst Ricky was in full flow about his matrimonial problems Ali G appeared at the cell door and asked him to put his ear next to the serving hatch. Ali G told Ricky that I was his mate which was news to me. He added that I am a good bloke who Ricky should respect. If Ricky didn't, then he would have to answer to Ali G. I feel I ought to shout 'safe' or somefink to Ali G but I pretended I hadn't heard his drivel. I concluded that Ali G was just going through yet another stage in life, the terrible twos clearly being his last. I asked Ali G how he had faired at the disciplinary hearing and he said that everyone was given the loss of canteen sentence which was suspended for one week. 'In other words, fuck all,' he said. He then dropped his bombshell. 'Ya listening B?' 'Yes,' I replied thinking, if only I had a choice. 'Nuffink personal you understand Bro, but I asked the screws to move me to another crib on landing three because me soldier (mate) was on his own innit?' 'No problem,' I replied. 'Safe, respect,' he yelled as he bowled down the landing with the arse of his trousers hanging down near his knees. May God help society when some of these reprobates are released into the general population.

07 06 2005: One month today I will be back in court for pleas and directions. If I plead guilty, they don't have to arrange a trial, if I plead not guilty, they have to estimate how long a

trial could last, book the court for that period, notify potential witnesses and of course decide what evidence they will need and what evidence they won't. It's an administrative hearing. My back feels better this morning. I slept throughout the night so that has to be an improvement. I am locked up with a man who is serving 18 months for pointing a rifle at his wife's head and threatening to shoot her. I am facing three years for allegedly threatening a man on the telephone over money he owed me. He was 150 miles away at the time. Something isn't quite right with our judicial system. A group of lads in the breakfast queue are talking about attacking a man on landing four. He has been featured on the local radio news bulletins. The inmates claim that he broke into a house in Bourne, which is a village near my home in Market Deeping. A sleeping 16-year-old girl was sexually assaulted and when she awoke, she screamed. Her father is said to have run to her aid and he was then stabbed in the neck and chest. The man responsible for such heinous crimes was sentenced to just six years imprisonment. The inmates are quite rightly outraged and are desperate to mete out their own justice. I personally cannot see the culprit being put on normal location in the prison. My guess is, he is on E wing. The lads are insistent that he is on landing four because a prison officer is said to have tipped them off that he is in cell number nineteen. Landings two and four have association tonight, if anything is going to happen to the man, it will happen when he goes for a shower or when his cell door is left open. No doubt I will hear what, if anything, occurred in the morning.

I am lying on my bed writing this diary and there has just been an almighty roar. Everyone is cheering and kicking their steel cell doors. The sound of crashing, banging and raised voices is thunderous. People are shouting, 'Boo Yah, Boo Yah,' whatever the fuck that means. Prison officers have just opened our flap and ordered us to stand back from the door. I can see that they are carrying people out of the wing, I have no idea if they have been restrained or are injured. The inmates are now chanting, 'Kill the screws, take the jail, take the jail.' I am watching a 'mature' prison officer through the narrow door flap, he is looking decidedly unsure. As the sounds of hatred intensify, the prison officers begin to retreat from the wing. The inmates no longer have anyone to direct their anger at, the tactic has the desired effect and the shouting eventually stops. It looks as if I was wrong about the guy being on landing four. They have either attacked him during association or they have beaten up somebody they didn't like the look of as a way of venting their pent-up aggression. Shit happens in prison. The story will no doubt get told a thousand times over in the morning.

08 06 2005: I was awoken at 2.a.m by officers shouting and someone kicking a cell door, screaming and pressing an emergency bell. This device emits a piercing long beep at two second intervals. Either two inmates have fallen out, someone has overdosed or some poor soul has attempted suicide. My cell mate Ricky is extremely worried about the environment the authorities have put him in to be rehabilitated. He looks nervously at me and says that he isn't leaving the cell tomorrow. 'Will I get in trouble? ' he enquires sheepishly. 'Your already in trouble Ricky, you are in jail,' I replied. He has only served five days and has nine months to go. If he is scared whilst standing behind a locked steel door, he is going to find the next nine months terrifying.

The breakfast queue is buzzing with stories from the night before. A young inmate from Birmingham with only twenty days left to serve was charged with refusing to work yesterday. When his door was opened for association last night, he told a prison officer that if he was going to be charged with anything, it may as well be something worthy of punishment. He then walked up the stairs to landing four, stood on the balcony rail and climbed up into the rafters. In the roof there is a steel pulley and chain mounted on a steel girder. The pulley can be slid along the length of the wing. The man disengaged the pulley, hung onto the chain and made his way along the steel girder until he was above the centre of the wing. All of the inmates were cheering him and jeering at the officers who were busy attaching four corners of a safety net to hand rails. During the unrest, an inmate who was out of favour with the 'in crowd' was attacked for reasons unknown.

Officers managed to rescue the battered man and lock everybody else in their cells. I then heard somebody smashing up their wooden furniture. Fragments were then used to smash the glass in the cell inspection flap. When the crashing and banging had stopped, I heard the sound of wood clattering to the floor in the exercise yard. Whoever had smashed their cell up was now throwing the debris out of their window. I later found out that the culprit was none other than my former cell-mate Ali G. Caught up in the 'excitement' of the man climbing into the rafters and another being attacked, Ali G knew that his moment to be acknowledged had arrived. He was later charged with criminal damage and moved to C Wing. No doubt the suspended sentence he received last week will now be activated. Was Ali G remorseful? Not likely, he was in his element strutting around the exercise yard with his pigeon chest stuck out thinking he was Al Capone.

The raised voices that had awoken me at 2.a.m belonged to officers who were urging the man in the rafters to come down. Another inmate who had been awoken by the commotion looked up to find his cell mate hanging from a bedsheet that had been tied to the cell bars. He was taken down, and fortunately survived. I say fortunately, but however callous this may sound, some of the tortured souls in here would probably be better off dead. All in all, last night was undoubtedly an eventful evening.

It's a beautiful day today. After work I walked around the exercise yard thinking about everything that had happened since my wedding just eleven months ago. I wouldn't be buying a Lottery ticket any day soon that's for sure. I received a letter off my mother today, she isn't well, which is a worry. Mom tells me that Emma's headstone is beautiful. I hoped it would be. I had it made in India, the stone has all sorts of crystal embedded in it. Mom always talks to those who have passed when she attends a grave. I laughed when I read, 'I told Emma that you loved her, you missed her and you're in the shit again.'

It's our landings turn for association this evening. When an officer unlocks my cell door, he tells Ricky to pack his belongings as he is being moved to landing three. Fresh air at last is my first thought. I am painfully aware that Ricky may well be replaced by another gang-star like Ali G in the morning. However, tonight I can immerse myself in the beautiful sound of silence and breath reasonably fresh air. I actually feel happy at this moment!

As I wrote the last word of the previous sentence, my cell door opened and Enderby walked in. 'Ello mate, my name is Enderby,' he said. 'Great, but what are you doing in my cell,' I asked. 'I have been told to move in here, the bloke I was with tried to hang himself today and they won't allow two self-harmers to share a cell.' My fucking head fell off, literally.'

Are you telling me that you try to top yourself and they have put you in my cell?' I asked. 'No, I haven't tried for weeks, I am under a psychiatrist now but he insists that I am a risk.' I look at Enderby in disbelief. 'No mate, you are the fucking nutter, I am the person at risk,' I explain. Enderby tells me that he rarely leaves prison. 'I am from Lewisham in south London, my brothers are all serving very long sentences. I moved from London to Grantham because I don't like the jails in London. I am looking at two to three years for threatening to kill a policeman on platform one, Grantham train station. I was carrying an axe, a knife and a hammer. I was on my way to 'do someone' but my girlfriend rang the police to tell them as she didn't want me to get into trouble.' I am laughing to myself writing this, as Enderby struggles to string his sentences together on the bunk below. I do point out that ringing the police to tell them that your boyfriend is armed to the teeth and on his way to 'do someone,' may not be the best way of keeping him out of trouble.

After a minute's silence, Enderby agrees that I may well be right. I shouldn't laugh at the guy really; I should be praying I see the sunrise and hear those fucking Starlings screeching.

Enderby has just announced that he needs to take his medication, Zopiclone to help him sleep and Olanzapine to treat his schizophrenia.

I am coming off Largactil he tells me whilst his mad eyes dart all around the cell. They gave it me to calm me down. I have been prescribed the Zopiclone in its place. (I have stopped laughing at this point, in fact I have become increasingly concerned for my safety)

I am reminded that it was Enderby's cell mate who tried to hang himself in the early hours of this morning. I am beginning to understand how he must have felt and I have only sat through ninety minutes of an audience with Ed Gein. (Ed Gein was a notorious American serial killer who skinned his victim's corpses. He cut their faces off and wore them like masks.) God help Enderby and his victims. I understand that he cannot help having psychiatric problems, but do I really have to have the best seat in the jail to witness them progress?

Enderby has just shouted out that he knows a lifeguard who is scared of water! What the fuck does that actually mean? I am not going to reply, he may think I am asleep. I am tempted to learn more about his mate the lifeguard, I imagine he met him on one of the numerous secure wards he has been held on. Let sleeping dogs lie they say, tonight, 'they' are probably right.

09 06 2005: Well, I am awake and so I obviously survived. Enderby is tossing and turning, no doubt murdering someone in his disturbed sleep. Perhaps that's a tad harsh, he could be swimming a few lengths with his lifeguard mate. There is total silence outside the cell window, it's the first time I have

experienced it in here. Perhaps those flying rats have left town? Birds obviously have a sixth sense concerning impending danger.

I arrived at work in a foul mood, sleep deprivation cannot be helping my mood. Peter tells me that he is fucked off too. His solicitor has advised him that he should expect a custodial sentence and not to bother with the private detective anymore. The standard of advice many prisoners receive from solicitors is pretty dire. Peters' wife and her lover have denied knowing one another. If the Private Investigator can photograph them socialising, it will prove that they have lied in their statements and the case will collapse. How a solicitor can say that line of enquiry is not worth pursuing is beyond me.

222

CHAPTER NINE

Hello Darkness My Old Friend

A new inmate with 'Bommer of Boston' tattooed on the back of his neck has been allocated the machine directly behind me at work. He couldn't wait to tell me that he had been arrested at his grandmother's funeral for murder. 'We were standing watching them lower her coffin into the grave when they jumped on me, 'Bommer boasted. He is in his late twenties, slightly built and has been deprived of basic intelligence. He wears two plastic Rosary's around his neck, I am guessing he isn't considering joining the Priesthood. I find out later these cheap trinkets are the latest must have prison fashion accessories. When I ask Bommer who he had murdered he replied, 'Nobody, they have dropped the charge to manslaughter now.'

'This kid was raping his mother; we beat him up and threw him into the river where he drowned. I didn't ask him if he could swim and when I realised that he was drowning I couldn't jump in to save him because I can't swim either.'

I don't know if the dead boy had attacked his mother or not, but surely the smirking numbskull making the allegation didn't have the right to sentence him to death? I excused myself, not wanting to permit the moron to bask in his own glory. When I got back to the wing my cell door was open and a male nurse was sitting with Enderby. I was asked to wait outside. Each wing in prison has Samaritan trained 'listeners.' These are inmates who are made available day or night to other prisoners who are feeling suicidal or just down and want to talk. The listener on my landing was a Geordie. He told me that Enderby had been talking about hanging himself. An officer joined us and asked me how Enderby had been. I said that in my opinion he wasn't a well man and should be in a hospital, but I'm no doctor. 'He hasn't told me that he wants to top himself, but he did say that his cell mate had tried,' I said. 'Enderby is hard core O'Mahoney, it's not a case of if he will kill himself, it's a case of when,' the officer replied. I felt guilty for laughing at Enderby last night. I also felt guilty for wanting him out of my cell. After twenty minutes the nurse left. Enderby and I went downstairs together to queue for dinner. 'Are you okay mate? ' I asked. 'I will tell you when we get back to the cell,' he replied. 'I am 29, ' Enderby said as he sat down in the cell to eat his egg, burger and chips. 'They are going to move me to the hospital wing after dinner because I want to commit suicide. When I was 19, me and my best friend were walking home one night through Catford, south London. A group of black guys followed us and when we turned off the main road, they pulled out a knife and demanded our money. I managed to run away so they all turned on my friend and he was stabbed to death. It's my fault, I should never have left him.' Enderby said that he had started to drink heavily and suffered, 'some sort of breakdown.' 'I've been sectioned under the Mental Health Act and been in and out of prison ever since, 'he said. 'At

Grantham I was trying to throw myself under a train, a policeman tried to stop me. I struggled and threatened to take him with me if he didn't let go. That's why I have been charged with threats to kill. I was on my way to kill a man who I thought was one of the gang who killed my best friend. My girlfriend knew that I was confused and rang the police.' Enderby slumped forward and began to cry. I really felt for him, what human being wouldn't? I tried to reassure him by saying that he would be better off in hospital. 'Don't beat yourself up mate, ' I said. 'You didn't choose to be ill, did you? It's wrong to punish you for having an illness. ' I could see that Enderby was deep in thought. After a few seconds he turned to me and said, 'No, I didn't choose to be ill, who in their right mind would choose to be fucking mad? ' I laughed until the officers opened the door to take the poor tortured soul away. 'Good luck Enderby, ' I said shaking his hand. Enderby wished me luck with my case and left sandwiched between two nurses. I don't believe Enderby did ever got his own joke, but after the way he had been treated, he had no use for a sense of humour.

I am alone in my cell at last but I don't feel elated, I actually feel quite down. We don't really 'get life' until it hits us head on. I have my health, my family and outside I want for nothing. Okay, I am going through a shit patch at the moment but I have no doubt that it will pass. Enderby and many more like him have no hope out there or in here. They are lost, forgotten. Maybe Enderby is right, maybe he would be better off standing on a chair, tying a bedsheet to the bars, putting the other end around his neck and jumping into the eternal abyss?

10 06 2005: I am standing on a chair looking out of the cell window watching the day dawn. I have no idea what time it is, around 5am I guess. Across the exercise yard I can see the Health Care Unit where Enderby is. I haven't stopped thinking about him. This place is full of troubled and tormented people, their screams of hate and anguish fill the air every night. God help them.

Debra and my daughter Karis are coming to visit me today. I am looking forward to enjoying a normal conversation with them. Work dragged on and on this morning. I have been in the tailor's shop for a month now. It is mind numbing; I need a change of scenery. I feel happier now that I am locked up alone. I have never been comfortable in the company of strangers. After lunch I am taken to the visiting room and thankfully Debra and Karis were on time. I really appreciate them coming as it is a three-hundred-mile round trip to spend ninety minutes with me. Karis leaves school next year and wants to attend an Equestrian College in York where she would live for two years. The basic cost is £15.000 but at the end of it she would have enough qualifications to forge a career with horses. As I don't owe anybody anything, I can afford to pay it for her. Forget houses or cars, the best thing you can give your children is some sort of education. The Doran brothers are on the visit, they are applying for bail on Monday. They asked me to pray for them, I am not sure God has listened to me for years, if ever. I do however, hope they are released.

11 06 2005: It's a miserable grey morning. I believe the guy with the stereo across the yard is employed by the Government to reduce the prison population. Several

mornings a week I am awoken by him as he blasts out yet another depressing tune. I can imagine the likes of Enderby gazing longingly at the bars, should I? Shouldn't I? Michael Stipe then wails on cue, 'When you think you've had too much of this life, ' I then imagine the prison population dropping by one. This morning the D. J's weapon of choice is 'Without You' by Harry Nilsson. 'I can't live, if living is without you, ' it's bound to get at least one inmate swinging.

I asked 'fake tan', my name for a fairly attractive female prison officer with an orange face how Enderby is doing. She tells me that he has been sedated as he became extremely distressed. During our conversation I learn that the prison Health Care Unit is in fact just another cell block. Some of the cells don't even have the now standard television installed. Surely this is not another means of reducing the prison population? Lock a suicidal man alone in a cell with absolutely nothing for him to do or watch. If he is 'lucky' he will be able to hear the moron who plays depressing songs all day. I wouldn't be surprised to find Mr. fucking Happy swinging from a bedsheet in this place.

I have started to read 'Inside Times' a prison newspaper, circulation 35.000. I have no idea why only half of the prison population receive it. It states that two inmates every week take their own lives. Twenty-three people have killed themselves this year in prison, this time last year it was forty-two. At its best, the suicide rate amongst the prison population is twice as high as the general population outside. At its worst, the prison suicide rate has been ten times higher. One of Ali G's associates slapped a Palestinian man across the face on the landing at lunch time. A group of 'gang-stars' had been calling the man a glorified gypsy. 'Your people nicked a bit of land, stuck a few shacks on it and call it home,' one added. He had obviously opted out of learning history at school. The Palestinian man had walked up to a prison officer and pointed out his assailant. The man was led away by officers and the Palestinian continued to walk around as if nothing has happened. I don't know if he is stupid or very brave. It is highly likely that he will be attacked soon for informing on someone so openly and brazenly. Vinney and Toene came to visit me this afternoon. Initially I thought that I had been benched (stood up) but I was the victim of Toene time. An hour late is not bad for her. I was really pleased to see them both regardless. They tell me that my traveller friend Shane has returned from a holiday in Las Vegas and my so-called victims have been bombarding him with calls. Shane is no fool and refused to discuss anything with them. I am once more beginning to feel a little more confident of a just outcome in this case. If the 'victims 'are desperate to talk, they are clearly not relishing the scrutiny that a trial will bring. Me? I have nothing to hide and I certainly don't fear being cross examined in the witness box. Its 4.30.p.m now and I have been locked in my cell for the night. It will be another sixteen hours before my door is opened again.

12 06 2005: I awoke at 06.15.a.m. The screeching Starlings have returned. I put my table next to the arched cell window and climb up on to it so I can see the ground outside. The birds are fighting over the food and rubbish inmates have thrown out of their windows. Scruffy bastards. They have been absent because inmates were tasked to clean up the mess a day or two ago. The rare clean sweep had deprived the scavenging Starlings of their food source. Men in cages

sustaining wild birds is undoubtedly food for thought. I like mornings. The prison is rarely silent but there is something peaceful about day break. I lie on my bed and begin reading a book about the murder of Rap artist Biggie Smalls. It's pretty awful but the library here is at best crap. However, it does stock two books I have written, 'Essex Boys' and 'The Dream Solution. 'At 8.45.a.m the prison D.J began broadcasting to his potential victims. 'The Drugs Don't Work, ' by the Verve is a poignant reminder to many of the inmates of their wasted lifestyles. 'Insomnia' by Faithless awakens the jail judging by the cheers that greet the intro. 'We can't get no fucking sleep, we need to sleep, we can't get no fucking sleep,' the inmates scream out of their cell windows. Maybe the drugs do work after all. I am off to Mass to wish the Doran brothers good luck at court tomorrow. Peter from Mansfield is going to accompany me. It's a weird feeling hoping two of only half a dozen people I like in this place will leave. John Rooney greets me at Mass and lets me know that the prison officers are not allowing the Doran brothers to attend, no reason was given. I was pleased to see Enderby who arrived looking vacant. When I approached him, he shook my hand and smiled. Dry white medication was all around his mouth and he looked as if he had been sleeping in his clothes. I asked him how he was and if he needed anything, he said that he was fine. He didn't appear fine to me, but he was still alive which was a pleasant surprise.

After lunch I went to the Gym. I had reached the stage where if I continued to put it off until tomorrow, I would never go. We are only given one hour and inmates queue to use apparatus so I try to do everything at speed for maximum benefit. I managed thirty minutes on the running machine, chest exercises with weights and 2000 metres on the rowing machine. I am exhausted but I feel so much better for it. How I will feel in the morning is a different matter.

13 06 2005: Another grey day in paradise. Whatever happened to the great British summer? Inmates generally hate hot summer days. They complain bitterly, saying they are locked up and unable to enjoy the sun. I suspect thoughts of their partners roaming the streets unaccompanied and wearing skimpy clothing is too much for some to bear. I spoke to the lady who runs education classes this morning. I am fed up working in the tailor shop. A change will definitely do me good. I am better off learning something, anything rather than sitting robot like at a sewing machine all day. Unfortunately, the lady said that education classes are basic, very basic. 'If you can write your name you are overqualified, ' she warned. I decide to endure my boredom and leave any vacancy for someone who genuinely needs it. I have been told that the Doran brothers were granted bail today. I am really pleased for them and their families. Peter from Mansfield will be out next, I hope. Good luck to them all.

14 06 2005: The D.J over on C Wing has been silent for two days now. His last blast was on Sunday morning. Has he been released, relieved of his stereo, moved or simply grown tired of his music? I shall miss my early morning musical alarm. It's a pity the fucking Starlings haven't gone missing. The bastards are shrieking really loud. It's as if they are mocking me as I lay in my bed writing this. Fake tan and another officer opened my cell door early this morning and asked if I wanted the landing two cleaner's job. Wing cleaner is a much sought-after position in prison. You have access to the

phones and showers all day, extra association and Gym and you are hardly ever locked in your cell during the day. I accepted the job and was told that security would have to assess me. If I am approved, I could start work in two days. Any privileges offered in these places must be taken. If all goes wrong at trial and I get a lengthy sentence, a trustee's job will ensure a low security risk assessment. I will then get sent to a cushy jail. Only fools do their time the hard way. Manipulate the system to make life easier for yourself has to be the way. A fight broke out in the dinner queue this evening. It was the usual suspects who jumped a man in his twenties. He was smashed in the side of the head with a steel tray which sent a cocktail of blood, custard and sponge pudding flying up a nearby wall. It sent the man to the ground. Stunned and oblivious to who had struck him, he was then surrounded, kicked and stamped on. Moments later, it was over and the attackers stood quietly in line as if nothing had happened. Two officers eventually strolled up, saw the man, got him to his feet and led him away. At the Gym this evening, the man's assailants were boasting about attacking him because his brother had allegedly grassed one of their friends. This turned out to be the incident in May when a guy named Dixon was attacked for allegedly grassing up two men who were moved to HMP Leicester. The man who wielded the steel tray in today's attack has now been nicked. This place is getting more like Coronation Street or EastEnders every day. If somebody upsets you, deal with it yourself. If your physically unable to do so invest in a heavy blunt instrument. Simple.

I managed to get thirty minutes on the running machine tonight. I then stood in a freezing cold shower for fifteen minutes. It was pure heaven; showers are definitely the best thing in this dustbin. You certainly take the simple things in life for granted when you are at home. I am down to 15.9 stone now. I need to lose a few more pounds before I am about right for my height and build. Sorting my head out, may take a little longer.

15 06 2005: Another grey morning. They must have cleared up the mess outside the wing yesterday because the screeching shit hawks display team (Starlings) are absent. The D.J remains silent also. This prison never sleeps though. The constant jangling of keys, steel doors crashing shut and muffled voices echoing around the wing is our never-ending soundtrack. Work this morning dragged on and on. I can however suffer it as I will be out of the tailor's shop once my security clearance for the wing cleaning job comes through.

It is lunchtime and I am bored out of my mind. I have tried reading, exercising and watching television, but I simply cannot concentrate on anything. It is freezing cold in this cell, pouring with rain outside and I haven't eaten. An officer watching over the dinner queue told an inmate that the prison buys the food it needs directly from supermarket chains. 'If a batch of food is about to reach its sell by date the prison is offered it cheap,' he explained. 'The trouble is a lot of it has gone off by the time it reaches here.' I immediately lost my appetite and gave my food to Baldrick, a disabled alcoholic from Birmingham who is housed in the cell next to mine. Baldrick was given an ASBO (Anti-Social Behaviour Order) for being drunk and begging. He continued his anti-social behaviour regardless and was imprisoned for three months. Baldrick tells me that he is not going to return to his native

Birmingham as he is too well known by the police. He intends instead, to relocate to Bristol. I always give Baldrick my potato's, bread and pudding. I have a soft spot for him because my Uncle Bernie (Whom I was named after) was an alcoholic. He was kicked to death in February 1985 by persons unknown on the streets of Birmingham. After dinner, my cell door opened and an Asian man was told to enter by a prison officer. 'Your new pad mate O'Mahoney, I hope you are happy together,' he said before closing the door. The man, who was aged about 25-30 years old introduced himself as Max which I thought was an unusual name for an Asian. He told me that he lived in Bolton and had married a British born Asian girl four years ago. The immigration department had since discovered his 'wife ' had married previously and she was engaged to be married to another man in Leicester. 'Max' Patel said that he had been sentenced to twelve months imprisonment. When he completes that sentence, he will be deported back to Bombay. Max had been in an open prison for five months but now he only had a month left to serve, deportation loomed and so the authorities wanted to ensure that he didn't flee. Max looked around the cell and asked me which direction was south-east. 'Look, I get you don't want to be deported mate, but nobody is escaping from any cell that I am in. I want to leave here by the front door so I can get on with my life,' I said. 'No, no, I have to face south-east when I am praying,' Max replied.

During association I rang Toene. She tells me that she is working in Italy on Friday and then she is off to New York on Tuesday. I am gutted about New York as we had planned to go there together. There will be other times, I guess. After association, Bombay Max as I now call him, announces that he has an apology to make. 'I may have to disturb your sleep,' he said. 'You see, I pray five times per day, Fajr (Dawn), Dhuhr (After midday), Asr (Afternoon), Maghrib (Sunset), Isha (Night-time). ' I laughed, 'So long as you don't start smoking crack or smack in here, attempt suicide or chant, 'death to the infidel's,' I couldn't care less what you do.' After Ali G and Enderby I could quite easily endure a man praying. At least Bombay Max had the decency to warn me and apologise in advance, manners go a long way with me. Max tells me that he may be moving onto landing three in the morning. There's an Egyptian Muslim up there with a cell space. Max said that they will be able to pray together. Suits me, I prefer my own company, particularly in here, I hope that they are very happy together.

16 06 2005: Bombay Max woke me at 3.30.a.m sorting his prayer mat out in preparation for sunset an hour later. If it wasn't so early, I may be writing it's good that some people in this world still have beliefs. I felt as if I was intruding on his privacy and so I pretended to be asleep. Before too long, I had dropped back off. I had to see the prison doctor this morning as my hand is turning a deeper shade of blue. Inmates have to see a nurse before being granted an appointment with the doctor. This is to weed out malingerers as the doctor's time is limited, we are told. There's something ironic about telling prisoner's time is limited, but a clever or humorous come back failed me. The nurse informs me that my X-Rays show that I have two breaks in my hand. 'What do you want us to do? ' she enquired. Raising my discoloured, deformed hand, I suggested that it could be reset. The nurse made notes and told me to go and sit in the waiting room. A few minutes later a prison officer informed me that he was

escorting mc back to the wing. 'But I haven't seen the doctor,' I replied. Ignoring me, the officer told me to stand then escorted me back to my cell. Before closing the door, I showed my hand to the officer. Agreeing it 'looked bad,' he said the nurse had said there wasn't any need for me to see the doctor but he was now going to check. An hour has passed, he didn't return, I am assuming that my trip to see the doctor, that never actually occurred, is over. Bombay Max has told me, and so I have no evidence that it is true, that his uncle is a magistrate in Blackburn. He claims this uncle is an acquaintance of Labour M.P Jack Straw, a former Home Secretary who went on to become Secretary of State for Justice. According to Max, prior to his illegal marriage he went to visit his uncle. When he arrived, Jack Straw was present and happened to be talking to the then Prime Minister Tony Blair on the phone. According to Max, he invited his uncle, Jack Straw and Tony Blair to his wedding. A few days later he received a letter from Downing Street thanking him for his invitation but expressing regret that the Prime Minister would be unable to attend. If true, and I haven't seen any proof that it is, Max certainly had some front inviting such people to an illegal ceremony.

When exercise ended this morning, the panic alarm was activated and officers ran towards E wing. Large scale disturbances on that wing are very rare. No doubt the details of events will be revealed on the prison grapevine soon. At lunch time I was informed that I was being moved to landing two tomorrow morning. I have been cleared to work as the wing cleaner and so my time in the tailor's shop has ended. I would have to spend today in my cell. Not only is it good news regarding my employment, landing two means the

Starlings will not be fighting for food outside my window. Fucking things have been driving me mad. A change is as good as a rest they say, but in here it is more. A change for the better in employment is recognition the authorities believe you are making progress and that means you are making your way to a more relaxed jail or the gate and ultimately freedom.

17 06 2005: I was moved to cell two on landing two this morning. A guy named Alfie is already in the cell. Alfie is from Bradford, in his mid-twenties and has been imprisoned for driving whilst disqualified. It's too early to make a judgement, but Alfie seems okay. My job consists of approximately three hours work, sweeping and mopping the landing. At 9.30.a.m I was taken to see the doctor who has finally confirmed that my hand is broken in two places. He said that I am now on a list to see an orthopaedic surgeon at Lincoln hospital. I won't hold my breath. (It never was reset and my right hand is buckled as a result) After lunch I had a visit from a friend who lives in Windsor. She had spoken to Vinney prior to entering the prison and he wanted me to know that Myers and Botham had sent copies of a statement withdrawing their allegations to the Crown Prosecution Service, the police and my solicitor. If true, this means, I can now apply for bail as it would be deemed a change in circumstances in the case. (Having been refused bail I cannot re-apply unless there is a significant change.) I'm still not excited or even hopeful. How can the police and the prosecution stand in court and say straight faced, that I should be locked up because they fear I may contact or harass the alleged victims? It's ludicrous when the alleged victims are constantly ringing my friends and family and writing to police, the prosecution and my solicitor stating

that they don't wish to proceed. What do they believe I am going to do, bully them into wanting to prosecute me? Madness, total madness. I was locked in the waiting area after the visit with Tim Readhead. We have spoken on a few occasions in the past. Tim is a Rastafarian from Sheffield and has a 'chequered history.' His best friend was a Greek Cypriot named Anthony Antoniou. In 1992 Antoniou had started a relationship with Louise Bobb, better known as the award-winning singer Gabrielle. (Dreams, (Can Come True) Rise, Out of Reach) Antoniou had first become acquainted with Gabrielle just as her career was taking off. They met through the music business, but the friendship developed and by July 1994, the singer was pregnant with Antoniou's child. The day after their son was born, Antoniou left Gabrielle rebuking her for being 'fat'. The couple had begun to grow apart when Gabrielle fell pregnant and Antoniou began to change character radically. Almost a year later, Gabrielle was to discover just how extreme that transformation had been. In December 1995 Antoniou and Tim were in Sheffield to meet Walter McCarthy, Antoniou's stepfather. They were to later claim that he had boasted of adulterous affairs and abusing children. There is no evidence to support this claim. McCarthy was invited to travel to Manchester for the day and he accepted. As they drove along the A57, Antoniou started arguing with his stepfather. He pulled up in a lay-by and stabbed his stepfather with a 2ft long Japanese ceremonial sword. Antoniou then dragged the body out of the car and after thirty to fifty blows with the sword, beheaded his victim. Antoniou believed that the brain would still be alive for twenty minutes after death and would be able to understand him. 'I wanted to have a little chat with him,' Antoniou later told police. 'I picked the head up by the hair and placed it on the passenger seat. I talked to him until the twenty minutes was up. I put my two fingers on his nose and mouth to see if he was still breathing. I was convinced he was still alive. Afterwards, I put the head in a bag in the boot. I was in a world of my own. I did not plan it.'

McCarthy was stabbed fifty-two times, an attempt had been made to cut off his left hand, his body was hidden behind rocks in Derbyshire and his head was found 150 miles away in woodland in Bedfordshire. After the killing, Antoniou turned up at Gabrielle's London flat 'out of the blue.' While staying there, he set the car he had used in the killing on fire in a nearby street. Antoniou was later convicted of murdering his stepfather and sentenced to life imprisonment. Tim received twelve years imprisonment for disposing of the body. When I met Tim, he was on remand for allegedly cutting a man's throat in Skegness. Tim didn't deny he had inflicted the injury, but he did say that he had done so in self-defence. If he is convicted, he says that he will get a life sentence because he has two previous wounding convictions. I had faced a similar dilemma, but fortunately a witness who the police thought was describing me, told the jury at Lincoln Crown Court that I was present but hadn't wounded anyone. D.C Garner believed I had planned the collapse of my trial with the witness, I believed and still do, that is why I am being treated so harshly regarding Botham and Myers allegations. The judicial process in this country is no longer about truth, it is a game, you win some and you lose some, there's no place for grudges. DC Garner should just accept that the wisest man often wins. When Tim and I returned to the wing, we saw an inmate known as Cokey bleeding profusely from a deep wound above his eye. Two officers were escorting him to the medical wing. The injury was caused in the tailor shop and so the officers are assuming he was cut with a pair of scissors or a knife. The wing is therefore locked down and searched to ensure weapons haven't been smuggled into inmate's cells. It's annoying, it's frustrating but they insist its necessary. It later transpires that Cokey's friend Adam had hit him during a heated argument. Cokey had fallen backwards and hit his head against a radiator. When questioned, he said that he had simply slipped and so the matter was closed.

Now that I am on the cleaners, I get an additional association period on Friday nights. I met a guy called Bob tonight from Bethnal Green. He is serving 10 years for stealing and selling thirty shotguns and a pallet loaded with ammunition from a warehouse. Just before his current sentence was imposed, Bob served six years for shooting a man in the leg. He had served time with Chris Pearman, father of my late my friend Darren who was murdered at Epping Country Club. Too many of my friends are dead or serving time.

18 06 2005: Alfie jumped out of bed and announced, 'Its 08.10.a.m we are late, we are late. 'I had got up and put the BBC news on at 06.10.a.m so didn't have a clue what he was on about. I have learned that Alfie has started to smoke heroin and so he doesn't know what day it is lately, in fact I would be very surprised if he had any concept of time. So many young lads' experiment with heroin in here, once it gets you, it doesn't let go.

When I am released, whether that be soon or much later, I have to make some harsh decisions about my future whilst considering my children's wellbeing. I would like to return to live near my mother in Codsall, Staffordshire. My wife Emma is also buried there. On the other hand, moving could disrupt Vinney's life. I shall just have to sit down with him and decide what is best when I get out. It's a beautiful day today, certainly too nice to be locked up in prison. In the afternoon I was taken to the visitor's centre with approximately thirty other inmates. One by one they were called in until eventually only three of us remained. I started feeling irate as Vinney had assured me that he would arrive early. When I was finally left alone in a sweltering hot room, full of second-hand smoke and without ventilation the red mist rose. As I began to pace up and down in a futile attempt to subdue my anger an officer opened the visiting room door. 'O'Mahoney? ' he enquired. 'That is correct,' I replied. 'Your son has been refused entry, he is only seventeen and cannot come in without an adult.' It was pointless arguing only to be told rules are rules and so I thanked him and sat down. I am totally fucking frustrated now; I want Monday to come so I can speak to my solicitor about a bail application. I lie on my bed and find it hard to relax or 'lose myself' in a book. Eventually, as darkness engulfs the prison, I drift off to sleep.

19 06 2005: It is yet another beautiful morning. Unfortunately, I cannot see much of it through the bars of my cell. The view is blocked almost entirely by rolls of razor wire that sit on top of the exercise yard fence, which is only a few feet away. The heat in my concrete tomb is unbearable and its only 9.a.m. I have tried telephoning Vinney numerous times but he isn't answering. I am starting to worry as it's a good forty or fifty miles to the prison from our home. The roads are notoriously dangerous and he hasn't held a licence very long. I am hoping

he is okay. I was called to attend church this morning. I didn't realise that it was Father's Day until I arrived. Half a dozen women from a Methodist church have come into the prison to celebrate the occasion. The women were equipped with Tambourines and Bongo drums and wanted to know if any of the inmates wished to play. Tim Redhead picked up the Bongos and another inmate began rattling a Tambourine. The Chapel organ began playing, a woman strummed an acoustic guitar and the others, dressed in identical floral dresses began marching on the spot as they sang. My friend Peter and I couldn't stop laughing. It was like being on the film set of 'One Flew Over the Cuckoo's Nest.' After Church, we went out to the exercise yard. It's a wonderful feeling being able to walk around in the sunshine with your shirt off, albeit in circles with an entourage of psychos and other assorted miscreants. Bombay Max joined Peter and I on the road to nowhere.

Max is finding being locked up alone difficult. He says that the lack of contact with other people is driving him mad. For me, being locked up alone is bliss. I have no idea why; I just prefer my own company and always have done. After exercise and lunch, I managed to get through to my daughter Karis. She tells me that Vinney is fine, he lost his phone on Friday evening. It still rings out so it is probably plugged into the wall of some pub or nightclub. I am anxious waiting for tomorrow when I can ring my solicitor and ask him to apply for bail. I have a feeling he will advise me to wait until next month after we have received the case papers. But I think we have sat back and endured their shit for too long, we need to start fighting this case, go on the fucking offensive. Give it the bastards!

20 06 2005: My first thought when I awake is the call I need to make to my solicitor. As usual in this place, simple tasks are made ridiculously difficult. A prison officer informs me that for security reasons, all of the phones are currently switched off. Undeterred, I decide to get on with my job and try the phone at hourly intervals. Then came my second kick in the ribs, we are told to return to our cells as the wing is being locked down, again for security reasons. At 11.a.m we were opened up and told that we could go on exercise. I spend the next hour walking in circles with Peter and an inmate named Billy. As soon as we are allowed back on the wing, I head for the nearest phone. To my great relief they had been switched back on and eventually, I was put through to my solicitor. I had a bad feeling as I dialled the number, I knew that our opinions regarding the case were going to differ. I asked if he had received the latest statement from the witness. 'I have,' he said, 'and my advice is we ignore it.' I don't recall everything I said, but it's fair to say I lost my temper.' I am in prison because the police and C.P.S say that I am going to interfere with witnesses. Those witnesses say they want to withdraw their statements and you are saying ignore them?' My solicitor, always level headed and astute, warned me that the police would say that the witnesses had been intimidated by my son and friends and they would be arrested. Me, always hot headed, argued that nobody had done anything wrong in relation to the witnesses. 'I am instructing you to apply for bail as soon as possible,' I said. The solicitor said that he would do as I asked and I hung up. Its 6.p.m and I am still raging. Applying for bail if there has been a change in circumstances is a right, not something that is dependent on what the police may think. God, I hate this

fucking game! Its 8.p.m the prison has just erupted following a scene in the television soap EastEnders. I don't watch the programme but apparently, a character called Dennis (Rickman) has had a showdown in the Queen Victoria pub with the Slater family. As the end credits began to roll inmates began cheering, kicking their doors and chanting, 'Dennis, Dennis, Dennis! A funny moment in this unfunny place. We have all been locked up for the night. I have swapped a sleeping pill for two tea bags. I am too stressed out to sleep, so will need it after today's conversation with my solicitor. I need to sleep and wake up in a more positive frame of mind.

21 06 2005: I fell asleep at 10.30.p.m and awoke at 4.a.m. I fell back asleep around 5.a.m and awoke again at 7.a.m. The sleeping pills that inmates swear by are, in my opinion, absolute shite. I have felt lethargic all morning, I can't even be bothered to work. The panic alarm has just sounded and a group of officers are running towards E Wing. We are all locked in our cells for half an hour. When the incident has been dealt with, we learn an inmate had cracked and began smashing his cell up. He was restrained and dragged off to the punishment block on B wing. I started watching Wimbledon today. The last time I tuned in was 1981. John McEnroe defeated Björn Borg in the final. I was a soldier serving in County Fermanagh, Northern Ireland at the time. It doesn't seem like twenty-four years ago. The IRA were a threat to me then, it's just the police I have to contend with these days. Tennis isn't something I would find the time to watch outside but a good three-hour game is ideal in here. The story I was told about the night officer smuggling in Vodka appears to be true. The lads on the wing claim she

also writes sexually explicit letters to two inmates. Alfie began talking to her tonight on association. I mentioned to her that I prefer Jack Daniels but promised I wouldn't make a fuss if she can only get Vodka. An eyebrow was raised in reply but at least she didn't say no. I saw Enderby today going for his medication. He looked vacant but recognised me. Thankfully he is out of hospital and is housed on C Wing. 'I still don't feel well enough to be left alone,' he tells me. No doubt somebody will believe him when he is found swinging from the bars on the end of a bedsheet. The Vodka officer just opened the flap in our cell and said, 'Goodnight lads.' Alfie shouted back, 'Come and tuck me in Miss.' We could hear her laughing as she walked away down the landing. If she is prepared to move drugs from wing to wing, smuggle in Vodka and write sexually explicit letters to inmates, a bottle of Jack Daniels shouldn't be too much of an ask.

22 06 2005: Today marks my fiftieth day in custody for making a telephone call to someone who owes me money. It's yet another beautiful day outside. I have calmed down somewhat following yesterday's difference of opinion with my solicitor. It's inevitable that I will experience highs and lows in here. I just have to take them as they come and deal with them accordingly. When I rang my brothers partner Carol, she tells me that my solicitor had called. He had asked my brother to confirm that I could live at his house if I was granted bail. This enquiry confirms to me that my solicitor is applying for bail as I requested. I haven't done any work this afternoon. They had their £6 (my weekly wage) worth this morning. I am laying on my bed watching yet another Cowboy film. It's all they seem to show on television of late. I have had enough of fucking Cowboys. An officer on the landing has told the

inmates that there is a 'real kiddie fiddler' on the wing. He said he couldn't give his name until he is just about to finish his shift as he doesn't want any comeback on him. By 5.p.m the man's name was circulating around the wing. Shortly afterwards one of the younger hot-headed inmates walked into the man's cell and asked him what he was in for. 'Conspiracy to supply Class A drugs,' the man replied. 'Show me your paperwork because one of the screws says you're a nonce,' the inmate said. The man laughed and said, 'I know who has been talking to you. He has got it in for me. I threatened him on C Wing and was put in the block. When I came out of isolation, he told me that he was going to fuck me up and get me moved to HMP Hull. Here's all the police statements concerning my offence, you won't find anything sexual in there.' The inmates have chosen to believe the man as the police statements support his version of events plus, he had a quantity of heroin that he was prepared to share. It has been agreed that the officer who made the allegation is out of order. Interestingly, they don't consider his conduct wrong because an innocent man could have been badly beaten. They unanimously agree it was wrong because one of their number may have been charged for assaulting the innocent man.

I offered the Vodka officer a bullseye (£50) for a bottle of Jack Daniels tonight. I said it half in jest just in case she took offence and charged me. 'I would do anything for a JD and Coke now, well not anything, but I would pay a bullseye for a bottle.' She laughed and replied, 'What wouldn't you do O'Mahoney, I have read your file.' A few minutes later one of the recipients of her sexually explicit mail came to see me. 'Just to let you know, that's bullshit about her bringing in drink,' he said. 'She moves the odd parcel around the jail and puts on an occasional show (exposes herself) but that's about it.' 'Fair enough, no harm in trying,' I replied. As soon as he had walked away his cell mate told me that he was lying, 'He wants to keep his perks to himself,' he said. I wasn't really bothered about a bottle of Jack Daniels, to be honest it was more about corrupting a screw.

23 06 2005: I couldn't sleep last night, not because I was anxious or excited, it was because Alfie sat up all night watching television. He was one of the inmates who had shared the alleged kiddie fiddler's heroin. It was yet another beautiful morning, I got up at 8.a.m and watched the news before going to work. Today is the day my bail application is due to be heard. I would be lying to myself if I said my mind wasn't occupied with the hearing going on in Lincoln Crown Court in my absence. As they day drags on, every time an officer calls my name my heart leaps. It's a real head fuck not knowing if you will be home in bed this evening or still rotting in here for a few years. I have got Gym at 3.p.m so I can vent my frustration on the machines and weights. I am reminded of Oscar Wilde and the wise words he uttered during an interview in 1894.' What a perfect fiasco is our system of penal administration! ...To punish a man for wrong-doing, with a view to his reformation, is the most lamentable mistake it is possible to commit. If he has any soul at all, such procedure is calculated to make him ten times worse than he was before... It is a sign of a noble nature to refuse to be broken by force.'

That's what 'the system' doesn't get, they think fucking you about and playing mind games will break you. In reality it makes you more determined, more rebellious and more resentful. As I am leaving the Gym, I weigh myself. I'm currently 15 stone 3lbs. I have somehow managed to lose more than a stone a month. I showered, but was still pouring with sweat an hour and a half later. The Gym is definitely the best place to get rid of frustration and anger. I just wish they had a punchbag in there. I will definitely hit 14 stone before I go home.

23 06 2005: Prisoners on the wing are talking about Andy, an inmate who attacked a guy called Corky in the tailor shop. They are saying that he has been nicked along with his cell mate, a junkie named Danny. According to the prison grapevine, one of the cleaners had asked an officer if he could give his friend a bottle of orange squash. Andy and Danny, the intended recipients of the squash were not on association and so their cell door was locked. When the officer opened it to enable the squash to be handed over, he saw that they were both smoking heroin off tin foil. The cell has supposedly been searched and other drug paraphernalia has been found. Both are said to have been taken to the punishment block. I feel much better about my supposedly failed bail application now. (I haven't been told the outcome but if it was successful, I would have been released.) I keep telling myself to stay calm, this is a fucking game, I am in prison for making a phone call not murder.

24 06 2005: I awoke at 6.15.a.m, yet another beautiful morning although rain is forecast for this afternoon. Not for the first time, the prison grapevine has been proven to be the carrier of inaccurate information. Andy and his cell mate Danny were not kept in the block. According to Andy, when the officer had opened their cell door Danny had tried to

prevent the officer from grabbing their drugs by blocking his way. Danny had put the officer in a headlock and began shouting, 'What are you doing, what are you doing, leave my cell mate alone.'

The officer and Danny had fallen to the floor. Danny got to his feet but the officer stayed down having sustained an injury to his shoulder. Andy had thrown the drugs out of the window and then helped the officer to his feet.

A thorough search of the cell unearthed drug paraphernalia but no drugs. Andy and Danny both said that they thought the officer was attacking Andy which is why Danny restrained him. They claimed that a crack pipe and tin foil which had been found, had fallen out of a fresh towel that they had picked up from the stores. Because of the lack of witnesses, neither has been charged with any offence at this stage.

Why their 'friends' shout about their business out of the cell windows every night is beyond me. Surely the prison officers sit and listen to everything that is being said? The injured officer isn't happy, he has been showing everyone a huge black bruise on his shoulder and chest.

I met Pete on the landing, his cell mate has been put in the punishment block. He had been told he was being transferred to an open prison but he refused to go, preferring instead to ' be a soldier and do hard time.' Fucking idiot, he will learn. Andy and Danny have been taken to a police station to be interviewed about assaulting the prison officer. Both were charged and moved to another prison. They will be appearing at a local magistrate's court within the next few days.

I rang my mother tonight, she is okay, she always tells me that she loves me, bless her. God knows I love her too. When I return to my cell for the night, I find Alfie out of his mind on heroin. He tells me that it makes the bars disappear. Half of the prison is on the shit. If I walked out of my cell in the morning, I could buy heroin within two minutes, it's a joke.

25 06 2005: I woke up at 08.a.m, it's a miserable, grey, wet morning. After breakfast, (Two fried eggs and two large tablespoons of beans) I went to the Gym. It was quite busy but I still managed to do 15 minutes on the running machine, 10 minutes on the cross trainer and weights. I am down slightly, to 15 stone 2lb. I didn't leave my cell too much today. I spent most of the time reading. We were all locked in our cells for the night just after 4.p.m. Alfie has slept all day after his heroin binge last night. The cell absolutely stinks because the drugs have given him a bad stomach. He smells like a decaying corpse, why wouldn't he? He fucking is! The inmates began shouting out of their windows about 7.p.m. They say that Andy had been moved to HMP Wandsworth in south London. Danny has been charged with an additional offence, preventing an officer from carrying out his lawful duty. Nobody seems to know what prison he has been moved to.

An unidentified 'gang-star' is shouting out to another prisoner whose girlfriend is acquainted with his outside. They have both been convicted of shoplifting and the 'gang-stars' girlfriend, a repeat offender, has been imprisoned. Initially he was threatening to 'smash' the other prisoner's girlfriend when he was released but he changed tact and began threatening to, 'smash the other prisoner until he was unconscious.' The prisoner being threatened pleaded with the 'gang-star' not to hurt him, at one point he sounded like he was crying. All of the chavs on the wing were shouting, 'Boi, Boi' (Whatever that means) and laughing. It was quite sickening to listen to.

26 06 2005: I awoke at 04.30.a.m feeling dreadful. This emotion happens unexpectedly, but occurs regularly. Without warning I am overwhelmed by the feelings of loss I have experienced since Emma's death. I have been told by numerous people that grieving gets easier but I have my doubts. I don't think people would believe me if I said for a fleeting moment, I forget she is dead, but it's true. I wake up and still half-asleep reach out for her and then boom, I am hit with reality and my heart sinks. I miss her so much and being separated from friends and family in here makes it harder to grieve.

Its 08.30.a.m, we will be unlocked for breakfast soon. I struggle to eat the shit on offer in here and so I try to choose food they can't fuck up. This morning I have two fried eggs and two tinned tomatoes. Later, when I am returning to the wing from the Gym, the young inmate from Birmingham who had climbed into the roof was shouting out of his cell window. He wants everyone to know he was sentenced to an additional thirty-five days imprisonment for his antics. The idiot only had five days left to serve when he did it, some of these lads love it in here. On exercise some inmates are complaining bitterly about the Vodka officer. Apparently, she refused to move their parcels around the wing last night. She has told them that there won't be any more favours until Andy and Danny have been dealt with at court because it was her friend that was assaulted. One or two prisoners had been talking about giving evidence to help them evade justice and I am assuming this is her counter threat. Vinney, Karis and Debra came to see me today. Jimmy Rooney was escorted out of the visiting room by two officers after they claimed he had been passed something by his visitor. I hope he is okay. Vinney gave me copies of Myers and Botham's latest statements. One sentence struck me straight away, 'After deliberating I have decided not to carry on!' Who the fuck do these people think they are? Judges deliberate, alleged victims tell it as it happened. No more, no less. I screwed both statements up and put them in the bin. I relished a trial now.

Two alleged victims who had spent the last few months trying to change their stories, a cop who thinks he heard parts of a conversation and a detective, well my thoughts on him are probably best left unsaid. I don't think a decent barrister would need much effort to dismantle this absurd case. I was allowed to give Vinney his birthday card on the visit rather than post it out. He is 18 tomorrow. Vinney has endured a lot this year, he fought to save Emma with me as she was dying in our home and then aged 17, he was left alone at home after I was imprisoned. It cannot have been easy for him but he is a strong character thankfully, I suppose he has to be.

252

CHAPTER TEN

A Better Day

27 06 2005: I was out on the landing this morning when Alfie called out, 'Bernie, you have got a letter, it looks like it's from your solicitor.' My heart sank, my mind was swarmed with thoughts about what fresh allegations the prosecution may now be making. Botham and Myers statements potentially opened the door for the police to allege that they had been intimidated or otherwise persuaded to discontinue their allegations. When I finally read the letter, I was pleasantly surprised. Judge Heath, who presided over my bail application hadn't refused me, he had adjourned the case for a week so that the police could make 'necessary investigations into the correspondence Botham and Myers had sent to all parties.' Once more my liberty is in the hands of those two. If they tell the truth and say nobody has contacted them and they wish to withdraw their allegations of their own free will, I get bail. If they claim the opposite, I will undoubtedly face additional charges. The letter also informed me that the Prosecution have failed to serve their evidence on my solicitor on time. (26/06/2005) They asked Judge Heath for an additional two weeks to prepare their case but he refused saying that they had been given ample time already. However, not wanting to appear unreasonable he did grant them an additional week. They now have to serve their

papers (All of their evidence) on my solicitor the same day as my bail application is to be considered. I feel now as if we are at least fighting back. For the first time in ages, I slept in the afternoon so I never got to the Gym. I am now wishing I hadn't slept as I will probably be awake all night.

I rang Vinney to wish him happy birthday, he seems in good spirits. I wish I was out there to celebrate with him. It's funny the things you take for granted outside, a drink or a meal with friends, time with your children, these are the things I long to do again. Just before we were locked up for the night an inmate named Green leapt over the handrail of landing four. He ended up on the wire safety mesh which prevents 'jumpers' falling to a certain death. Green was on the net spread eagle fashion and refused to move unless he was allowed to make a phone call. Apparently, he had applied for phone credit, the money had been taken from his account but no credit had been issued. He had asked an officer to look into it, but as is the norm, nothing was done, hence the protest. An officer had activated the panic alarm and his colleagues were soon swarming onto the wing from all over the prison. A senior officer spoke to Green who stood up moments later, leapt over the handrail and ambled down the landing.

The senior officer followed him with about a dozen colleagues in tow. I thought that Green was heading for the punishment block but he walked into the wing office followed closely by the senior officer. The entire wing watched as Green sat down and picked up a phone on the officer's desk. I had to laugh, it was yet another example of this ridiculous regime and system on how to not instil discipline and manners in rebellious young men. If you don't get your own way, cause trouble. Rehabilitation techniques at their worst.

28 06 2005: I awoke around 6.30.a.m. My frustration and anxiety appear once more to have abated. This morning the jail is on lockdown. Alfie made me laugh, he has a dot tattooed on two knuckles. Amongst the criminal fraternity a dot tattooed on each knuckle indicates that you have been to Borstal. (Borstals don't exist anymore. They were institutions for young prisoners) Each of the four dots represent a word, 'All Coppers Are Bastards.' Because Alfie only had two dots I asked if he was unsure about the parentage of police officers. 'No, no, I used to live in Dudley on a huge estate called Wren's nest,' he replied. 'All the lads had two dots on their knuckles and a third between their thumb and index finger.' 'Everyone then knew that you were part of the Wrens nest mob,' beamed Alfie. So how come you only have two Alfie? ' I enquired. 'Because the one between my thumb and index finger hurt too much,' he replied sheepishly.

Exercise was early today. They have erected a sign on the yard which warns, 'Shirts must be worn on exercise. Anybody failing to comply will be issued with a red warning. Any inmate found to be suffering from sunburn as a result of not wearing a shirt will be charged with causing a self-inflicted injury.' I walked around with Bombay Max, Peter and Billy at first. Billy is a fucking twat. If I had to spend any length of time with him, I just know it wouldn't end well. He asked Bombay Max if he was in for selling counterfeit jeans. Max replied, 'no, why? ' Billy sneered at Max and said, 'because that's all you lot are ever in for.' I made some excuse and went to sit with Max's cell mate Mohamed the Egyptian. Bombay Max joined us shortly afterwards. I advised Max to steer clear of Billy in future. 'He's a gutless bastard who will cause trouble for you,' I said. Mohamed has recently been sentenced to twelve months imprisonment for entering the country and working illegally. Approximately seventeen years ago he was living and working in Iraq. During the Iran, Iraq war, the area he was living in came under heavy bombardment and so he and many others fled. Fearing for his life, Mohamed travelled through Jordan and Israel to the Egyptian border. He didn't have a passport or money; in fact, his only possessions were the clothes he was wearing. Mohamed was arrested and later handed over to the military police who accused him of being a terrorist. He was not given access to a solicitor or permitted to contact his family. Mohamed was eventually sent to a notorious military prison where he spent the next fifteen years. Built on the Nile River in 1993 at the southern edge of Cairo and officially named Tora Maximum Security Prison, its reputation has since earned it a different moniker: The Scorpion. Authorities there banned inmates from contacting their families or lawyers for months at a time, held them in degrading conditions, humiliated, beaten, and confined them for weeks in cramped 'discipline' cells. Mohamed managed to escape and made his way to France. He eventually entered the UK via Dover in the back of a lorry. He said he didn't know where he got out but he walked for eight days before arriving in Boston, Lincolnshire. Mohamed worked on a farm for three or four months before being arrested for entering the country illegally. He began to cry as he told us that he hadn't seen or heard from his parents and three sisters in over seventeen years. At the end of his sentence, he is due to be deported back to Egypt where he is still wanted for escaping from prison. I have no idea if the guy is telling the truth or not, if he is, may his God help him. I have a feeling he will never see his family again; I hope that I am wrong.

A 35-year-old from Nottingham nicknamed Shredder came in today. If he had a brain, he would be dangerous. Shredder has a nervous twitch which makes him shudder and hiss like a cat. He told me that he had visited his sister who complained that a man had made sexual advances towards her sixteen-year-old daughter. For eight months the daughter had remained silent, but eventually she confided in her mother. When the mother told Shredder, he had flown into a blind rage, rang his friends and arranged to meet them at the alleged offender's home. They kicked the door down, smashed up furniture and fittings, beat the man and then bundled him into a van. They continued to assault him until they arrived at Shredders sister's home. They dragged the man inside and ordered him to apologise to his alleged victim. The trembling and bleeding man was on his knees in the lounge when the teenager walked in, she looked at the man, looked at Shredder and said, 'that isn't him, I have never seen this man before in my life.' Shredder cleaned the man up whilst apologising profusely. Instead of taking the man back to his home, which he said he had just moved into, Shredder took his victim to hospital. The man thanked Shredder and asked if he would wait until he had been treated as he had no way of getting home. Feeling charitable, Shredder agreed. When the man went to the counter in the A&E department to book in, Shredder took a seat. A few minutes later police officers rushed in and arrested him. Shredder is now facing a lengthy prison sentence for aggravated burglary, criminal damage, wounding with intent and kidnap. He told me that he thinks the judge will be lenient with him because he was kind enough to take the man to hospital. I did point out to Shredder that he only took his blood-soaked victim to hospital after he realised that the man was in fact totally innocent. I don't think the penny dropped, as I looked at Shredders vacant expression, I formed the impression that it never will.

As I am writing this Alfie's heroin is arriving via a cell window on one of the landings above. It is attached to a line (String) that is being slowly lowered. Alfie holds a mirror out through the bars until he can see the line and its deadly cargo. 'Left, left Coxy,' he shouts. Alfie then uses a toilet brush to hook the line and pull it towards him. 'I've got it, I've got it,' he shouts triumphantly. It's going to be a very long night for us both.

29 06 2005: I was awoken by lightening illuminating the cell at 5.40.a.m. Rumbling thunder and torrential rain made it difficult to fall back asleep. I feel absolutely exhausted. Alfie was buzzing off his tits walking up and down the cell and talking to himself until 1.30.a.m which didn't help. I had toast for the first time in months this morning. One of the lads nicked a loaf of bread and a toaster from the officer's rest room. One officer in particular is threatening all manner of distasteful retribution. All of the lads are laughing, advising him that he should call the police. We are all told that if the toaster hasn't been found or returned in working order, 'action' will be taken. At lunchtime the toaster was 'found' in landing four's recess by an officer. It wasn't hidden, it was left out in the middle of the floor. Even some of the officers are laughing about it. Exercise is cancelled because of the rain and so I had a shower and sat talking to Jim Rooney. He told

me he had been drinking Vodka on the last visit but he wasn't removed for that. His visitor had passed him a lump of cannabis which the security camera operator had seen. On his way to the block to be strip searched Rooney had somehow managed to secrete the dope into his backside. He was kept there for two days but they never found the dope. Once left alone, Rooney said that he had removed it from his backside and put it in his mouth before swallowing it. I don't mind admitting, I did feel sick when he was telling me.

My bail application is due to be considered tomorrow at Lincoln Crown Court. I keep telling myself to expect the worst, what will be, will be and countless other useless cliches. However hard I try not to build up my hopes, my disobedient mind reminds me of what tomorrow could bring. Will this be my last night in this bunk, will tomorrow be my last meal in this place, the sooner I fall to sleep tonight the better.

30 06 2005: I awoke at 6.30.a.m. and my first thoughts were, today could be the day I go home. Regardless of whether I am to be released on bail or not, I still have to endure the frustration of waiting in here not knowing what is going on in court. I go to work and try but fail to forget the proceedings. Its 1.p.m. and I haven't heard anything. 3.p.m. still no news. I go to the Gym shortly so at least I can burn off some of my stress and anxiety. On the plus side, the Prosecution have to hand over all of the evidence that they have gathered against me. I cannot wait to read what my co-accused Adrian Foster had to say when interviewed. It's been nagging me for a long time, why would the police believe that I had been hired by him to get his possessions back from Myers and Botham? Its absolute bollocks, but the police obviously believe it's true. It

was 4.30.p.m. by the time I got back to the wing. Naturally, I was extremely disappointed that there hadn't been any news about my bail application. No news indicates the application has failed. Its 6.30.p.m and we have been locked in our cells for the night. Today has been disappointing to say the least but fuck them, I have taken a lot of knocks over the past year and I am still ready to fight on.

01 07 2005: I awoke at 6.40.a.m. Emma was my first thought, my last before falling asleep last night. I feel ashamed complaining about my situation when I think of my 26-year-old wife lying dead in her grave. I have to be more positive, be stronger and look to the future, a future Emma can never have. God love her xxx

02 07 2005: Seven months ago today I lost Emma. I have really missed her recently. At 10.a.m. I received a recorded delivery parcel. It was the Prosecutions papers and a letter from my solicitor. I have not bothered doing my work or going to the Gym as I have been reading every word people have been saying about me. If this wasn't such a serious matter I would laugh. I cannot believe what DC Garner has done to me knowing the facts of the case. I accept that Adrian Foster had told Myers and Botham in numerous text messages and telephone calls that I intended to harm them. D.C Garner had used that part of the evidence during my police interviews to paint a very grim picture indeed. DC Garner pointed out repeatedly that Myers, Botham and Foster were all saying I had blackmailed Botham and Myers and that I had threatened to kill Botham. Surely, nobody could be in any doubt about my guilt? A policeman was produced who allegedly heard me threatening to cut Botham's throat during a telephone call.

After being charged and the 'facts' read out to magistrates, I was never going to be granted bail, hence my current address. However, I could now see that the case was little more than a sinister charade because the most important facts had not been disclosed until this late stage. Foster was no doubt hurt and upset when his partner left him for Botham. I get that. He probably enjoyed causing them distress by threatening them with me. I don't agree with what he did but it explains why he acted in that way. But, when he was interviewed, Foster told the absolute truth. Remarkably, this was never disclosed during my police interviews or during my court appearances. The truth had deliberately been hidden from me and my legal team. Had it not been, I would not have spent one day in this shit hole. I was grieving for my dead wife and my teenage son was left to fend for himself, shame, shame, shame on the bastards. During his police interviews Adrian Foster was repeatedly asked if he had asked me to threaten Botham and Myers. He answered on every occasion that he had neither hired me, encouraged me or even had a conversation with me about threatening anybody. However hard D.C Garner tried to construct his spurious case; Foster totally demolished it by being honest.

D.C Garner: 'So what has Bernie said to give you the impression that he hates him (Botham) more than she (Myers) could ever imagine? '

Foster: 'Well he hasn't...he hasn't said that to me to be honest.'

D.C Garner: 'No? Why did you say that then? '

Foster: 'Well just like I say, I'm probably using my...a bloke I know on my side to sort of, you know, my mates are bigger than your mates sort of thing, you know, so maybe using his name in that way...'

D.C Garner: 'She's saying that at 15:46 she got a text from you stating that Bernie just rang from the airport, wants to know if you have my stuff, what do you want me to tell him, he's back at 7.p.m. '

Foster: 'Yeh, well, I didn't speak to him, I just said that to her, I didn't see him.'

D.C Garner: 'She's saying that she got a text from you saying, 'Helen, if you're in the hospital, get out, Bernie's gone nuts. I'm sorry. '

Foster: 'Possibly, I sent that, but again its...'

D.C Garner: 'Can you explain to me what it means?'

Foster: 'I think it's probably me exaggerating, and you know like, saying...telling her that Bernie's back and were going to come and get the stuff because she hasn't given me it...'

DC Garner: 'Were you with Bernie at the time? '

Foster: 'No.'

If D.C. Garner was in any doubt whatsoever about my alleged involvement in threats being made, Foster reiterated the truth at the end of his interview.

Foster: 'I deny asking Bernie to send any texts and also deny asking Bernie for his help in recovering my property.

'I knew that I would be going home soon but I was also acutely aware that there may well be further attempts to keep me imprisoned. I had to be vigilante, I had to watch everything I did and said...and to whom.

03 07 2005: I don't intend doing any work today or going to the Gym, I will read and re-read the 'evidence' until I identify every untruth in what I now call a conspiracy rather than a prosecution. The police have submitted as evidence photographs of child killers Ian Brady and Myra Hindley and the Taylor sisters. (Michelle Taylor murdered her lovers' wife, her sister Lisa assisted her) The photographs were on my website because I had written books about them. In D.C Garners statement he claims that they are, 'evidence of O'Mahoney's connection with the underworld.' If D.C Garner provides me with the postcode or a map reference for this 'underworld' place I will gladly look it up. I am fairly certain however, that it only exists in the minds of fools, fantasists and dopey detectives who watch too much fucking television.

04 07 2005: It's a miserable day outside, so much for British summertime. Both exercise and Gym have been cancelled. The day, unsurprisingly, is going to seem endless. I have read the conspiracy papers several times now. I try reading them again until the words on the paper blur into one and I fall asleep.

05 07 2005: I awoke at 7.15.a.m. Yet another grey morning in Lincolnshire. I have received a letter from my solicitor who informs me that he isn't going to attend court at my next hearing. (07 July) He doesn't say why, but tells me his assistant will be representing me. I deduce from that the

hearing will be a paper shuffling exercise. The court will just be checking both sides are ready to go to trial. I had a much-needed visit from my friend Debbie today. She lives in Feltham Middlesex and so her journey takes four hours in total by train. It means a lot to me to know that someone is prepared to go to so much trouble to see me. A middle-aged builder named Richard Philp is sitting at an adjacent table. His mother, who is in her 70's, is visiting him. I notice that they are both crying. Philp, according to press reports, is a 'controlling and possessive man who is self-centred and self-absorbed.' He is awaiting trial for the murder of 34-year-old Debbie Newton who was found dead in a dyke close to a lay-by on the A16 near Spilsby, Lincolnshire.

She had been in a relationship with Philp following the death of her husband from cancer in 2000. Philp had moved in with Newton and her two children at their cottage near Skegness in 2002. He was said to be 'distraught' when Newton tired of his possessive, controlling behaviour and ended their relationship. A few weeks later in June 2005, Philp had lured his unsuspecting ex-partner to the lay-by and strangled her. After the killing, Philp returned to his flat where he wrote what was later described as a 'self-indulgent' suicide note, making no mention of his crime, before taking an overdose of pills which did not kill him.

He should have saved his tears for his victim and her now orphan children. None of us know what each day has in store for us. Prisoners, victims, their loved ones, there aren't any winners in the end. I did feel sorry for his mother, she must know that due to her age she is unlikely to ever see her son as a free man again. (Philp was later convicted of murder and sentenced to life imprisonment with a recommendation that he serve at least 12 and half years before he can be considered for parole.)

06 07 2005 My sons Adrian and Vinney came to see me today. We spent the entire visit discussing my prospects at court tomorrow. They are confident, in light of the recently disclosed evidence, that I will be home tomorrow evening. It is a great help when you have your family behind you, they give you strength, the will to fight on when you are down. I know that people experience lows after highs, but tonight I am feeling confident. God willing, I will feel the same way tomorrow night.

07 07 2005: I awoke at 6.40.a.m. its pouring with rain. I lie on my back, close my eyes and pray for Emma. I tell her that I love her, I miss her and I am sorry that I couldn't save her. They came for me at 7.45.a.m. it was soul destroying queuing up with the inmates who were going home. My journey as a convicted prisoner is yet to begin, the finishing line is as yet unknown. We were all told to sit on a bench in the waiting room. Two heroin addicts were discussing which dealer they were going to head to first. One told the other because it was so early, they would have to seek out a 'Big Issue' seller. He explained that many were homeless and so they knew who the street dealers were. They would know someone or somewhere where they could 'score.' Both men were in high spirits talking about antique windows in Lincoln that they intended to steal.

I was called out of the room, told to stand in a cubicle and remove my shirt. I then had to hold up my arms so they could check I had not secreted anything under my armpits. I was told to open my mouth and raise my tongue whilst an officer peered in for foreign objects. After replacing my shirt, I had to take off and hand over my training shoes to be searched. I removed my socks which were turned inside out. Finally, I had to remove my trousers and boxer shorts before bending down. After my humiliation had been completed, I was ushered into an office. A senior prison officer asked who I was, where I was going and did I have any questions? I was then put into 'room 3' with three other inmates. One was due to attend court in Skegness for burglary, one, on crutches, was being released and the third was the young inmate from Birmingham who had climbed into the rafters on the wing. He was appearing at Grantham Magistrates Court for a string of offences ranging from burglary to possessing illegal drugs. Cocky as ever, he was back chatting the prison officers and behaving like a fool. 'What you at court for geezer? ' he enquired. 'An idiot upset me,' I replied. He didn't trouble me again. I was called out of the room and put into the secure prison van. A few minutes later, I was being handcuffed and taken into the cells beneath Lincoln Crown Court. Ten minutes later, I was informed that my solicitor wished to see me. My 'solicitor' turned out to be Mr. Cauthery's secretary. My new Barrister, who I had never spoken to previously, admitted that he hadn't had time to read my case papers. I was told not to worry as I wouldn't be asked to plea today. (Admit or deny the charges against me) Had I been defending myself I would have asked the judge to look at Fosters interview and applied to have the case thrown out. There seemed little point raising points of evidence with a man who hadn't read the case papers, so I returned to my cell. Shortly afterwards, I was called into court number two. Adrian, Vinney and Rachie were the only people in the public gallery. Foster sat in the dock staring straight ahead. I sensed that he was making a determined effort not to make eye contact with me. A security guard was next to Foster which prevented me from sitting alongside him. Recorder Donaldson had been appointed to oversee the proceedings. He told me to listen carefully as the Prosecution wanted to amend the indictment. I honestly thought, that after reading the transcripts of Fosters interviews, they were going to reduce the charges or maybe even drop them altogether. My fucking head fell off when I was told that I was now going to face seven separate charges; four of blackmailing Jim Botham, one of blackmailing Helen Myers, one of attempting to blackmail Jim Botham and one of threatening to kill him. Foster had his indictment amended to one charge of procuring me to make an unwarranted demand for money or goods from Jim Botham with menaces, one charge of procuring me to make an unwarranted demand for money or goods from Helen Myers with menaces and three charges of blackmailing Helen Myers. I could see the police glaring at me, their faces beaming with joy. I looked back at them, smirked, shook my head and mouthed tossers. We were then informed that the case was being adjourned until 29 July. I turned to Foster and said, 'we need to talk.' He replied, 'I cannot come to see you.' He then stared straight ahead as if I wasn't there. I turned to my sons and Rachie as I wasn't sure they had understood what had just happened. All three were shaking their heads and said they would come up to see me soon. I now had to face the uncomfortable truth; I may not be going home for years. I was taken back to the cells where an officer offered me a cup of tea. I thanked him but declined. The same officer told me that there had been a series of explosions in London and a number of people had been killed and injured. The news naturally shocked me, dirty bastards blowing up innocent people. I heard my name being called and moments later I was told that my solicitor wished to see me. I was taken to an interview room where she said that I needed to go through every sentence of every statement. I stopped her and said I had already done so. I then gave her all of my notes. The Barrister arrived and said I needed to 'understand exactly what blackmail meant.' He explained that even if somebody owed me money it would be an unwarranted demand for that money if the person felt threatened. 'You need to consider your position Mr. O'Mahoney. The maximum sentence for blackmail is fourteen years and you now face six blackmail charges and a threat to kill charge which carries a maximum sentence of ten years. Those alone add up to a maximum sentence of ninety-four years. If the judge was super lenient and gave you a tenth of that, you would be sentenced to nine and a half years. You are in trouble Mr. O'Mahoney, big trouble and you need to consider your position.' 'I wouldn't have got that if I had shot him,' I replied. 'But shooting somebody is one charge, you face seven separate serious charges,' he said. I knew exactly what 'consider my position' meant. I was being asked to consider a plea-bargain deal i.e, If I agree to plead guilty, they will ensure I get a reduced sentence. I had heard enough, I picked up my case papers thanked the Barrister for his time and asked the officer to return me to my cell. Moments later, I was handcuffed and led out to the prison van which had been waiting for me. My cuffs were removed and I was locked in a small cubicle. The van pulled up outside HMP Lincoln minutes later. Because of the bomb attacks in London all Government buildings had been locked down. I don't know how long I sat in that sweat box waiting for the threat level to be reduced, but it was several hours. I was eventually led into reception where I was subjected to the same humiliating procedures that I had undergone that morning. When I walked onto the wing I was greeted by Alfie and Pete. Neither could believe the charges I now faced. They told me that there had been a lot of trouble in the prison throughout the day. Asian prisoners were being attacked in retaliation for the bomb attacks in London. I went to check on Bombay Max, thankfully he was okay. I advised him to remain in his cell because idiots were using the attacks as an excuse to cause trouble. Anybody with a grain of sense would know bombs are indiscriminate, Blacks, Whites, Jews, Muslims and Christians could all have been victims of today's atrocity. Tonight, I sat on my bed thinking about the day's events. I had no right to feel bad about my situation. The death toll in London currently stands at thirty-three but it is expected to rise as lots of other people have been injured. There isn't one of those thirty-three who wouldn't swap places with me right now. God help them and their loved ones.

08 07 2005: Nineteen years ago today I walked out of HMP Stafford and caught the train to Basildon, Essex. If I hadn't had made that journey, I would never have taken over security at Raquel's nightclub. If I hadn't taken over security at Raquel's, I wouldn't have been able to offer Tucker a partnership. Tucker wouldn't have had any business in Basildon and therefore was unlikely to have ever met Tate. If, is a huge word we all use too often. So much has happened in

those nineteen years, yet here I am back in prison, back at square one. I have lived every day of my life, done okay for myself but have I moved on, have I matured? Probably not. The clock never stops ticking, I am 45 years old, I need to settle down. I cannot live like a twenty something year old forever. The death toll in London has risen to sixty-five, seven hundred people are reported injured. The Government don't want to admit it, but this country is at war. Trouble is, we don't know who we are fighting.

09 07 2005: Vinney and Rachie came to see me today. Vinney gave me my wedding ring which choked me up at first, but now I have it, I feel content. Maybe it will change my luck? It did me good to sit in the company of people I care about and talk about better times. It's my first wedding anniversary next weekend and I have written something I want read at Emma's grave around the time we exchanged our vows. Vinney said that he would ensure it is done. The Catholic priest in the jail has also agreed to hold a special Mass for Emma. When I return to my cell Alfie is crashed out on his bed. He gets out the day that I am in court. (29th) He has gate fever and is using heroin to keep his mind off things. That's what he says anyway. I can see he is simply addicted to that shit and is descending headfirst into an abyss of misery.

10 07 2005: I slept well last night. I had managed to blag a new mattress out of the stores so now I have two. My old one had a big dip in the middle which caused havoc with my back. The new one, coupled with the old one, is perfect. It's a beautiful day, the sun is a demon. Nobody bothered walking around the exercise yard, it was too hot. Its 4.30.p.m. and we are now banged up until 8.a.m. tomorrow. I am bored out of

my mind. The window warriors are screaming insults and threatening each other. Alfie is talking gibberish to himself. He was watching athletics on television; the volume is turned up high and he is trying to shout over the noise about the race. In the midst of the madness, I try to read one of my own books, 'The Dream Solution.' It's simply too difficult to concentrate. The book does give me food for thought though, so many of my years have undoubtedly been wasted.

11 07 2005: Tim Redhead has been put in the punishment block for three days to 'calm down.' Another black inmate named Green has been shipped out to another prison for unproven allegations regarding drugs. Tim had been going for a shower when 'Fake tan' had told him it was time for bang up. Tim insisted he was having a shower and a stand-off ensued. The panic alarm was activated and when reinforcements arrived Tim walked into his cell. Later in the Gym, Tim was complaining bitterly about 'Fake tan' and his friend Green said that he would get her sorted out. Word had obviously got back to the prison officers via one of the twenty to thirty inmates who were present. Tim was put in the block and Green had been shipped out using the drug allegations as an excuse. I was getting on with my work this morning when another cleaner named Pettit approached me with a prison officer. 'Why don't you use the cleaning machine to clean the floors, it gives a better finish,' Pettit said. 'Because its broken,' I replied. It wasn't, but the lads had told me that if you used the machine a ninety-minute job turned into an all-day affair because it strips the floor. The officers then expect you to polish it by hand.

Pettit insisted the machine wasn't broken and through

clenched teeth I insisted it was. Pettit, a proper fucking nuisance, ignored me and dragged the machine out of the store cupboard. Moments later he started it up and grinned triumphantly at me. I spent the remainder of the morning verbally abusing him. 'It's a fucking job designed to help you pass the time in this dustbin, it's not a career.'

I usually finish work around 9.30.a.m but today I was still going at 2.45.p.m. I missed going to the Gym and so I was less than happy to say the least. Alfie is in a bad way with drugs now, he is smoking the shit in the cell every night. What can I do? If I complained I would be grassing on him. If I have a go at him, we will end up falling out. He has two weeks left in here, let sleeping dogs lie appears to be the best solution.

12 07 2005: My fourth 'new' Barrister is coming to visit me today. Hopefully he will have read my case papers before he starts advising me. Legal visits take place first thing in the morning and so I won't have to use that God forsaken cleaning machine today. At 9.30.a.m. I was taken to the visiting room. My solicitor's assistant and my new Barrister Stephen Spence introduced themselves and quickly got down to business.

I liked Mr. Spence from the outset, he had obviously read the case papers and said that in his opinion the allegations of blackmail and threats to kill were 'a farce.' He was aware that I had made a formal complaint against Lincolnshire police following my arrest on Boxing Day. 'Nothing officially has been said, but it's unlikely you will be given an inch whilst that is ongoing,' he advised. When I asked if it would be helpful if I withdrew my complaint I was told, 'it may open negotiations.'

Mr. Spence said that he did not think a judge would allow evidence about my past to be used. However, if it was, we could use it to our advantage by explaining to the jury the misery my family and I have endured since agreeing to assist police in the Leah Betts case.

Our main objective now is to obtain telephone records that prove I was in touch with Botham long before these alleged offences were committed. We also needed phone records to prove that Myers and Botham had been in contact with my family and friends after my arrest. Mr. Spence said that it was 'incredible' that I had not been granted bail. 'Now that the two alleged victims have withdrawn their statements there is absolutely no reason to keep you in custody,' he said. After a two-hour conference I left feeling incredibly confident about my prospects. I have to accept a trial may not take place until October but that is only three months away.

When I return to my cell Alfie tells me that he has to appear in court in Barnsley tomorrow. He is being called as a witness to a fight involving his friends. Alfie told the prison officers that he doesn't want to go but they have said there is a court order and so he has no choice. There's a 50/50 chance he won't come back to this prison as HMP Doncaster is local to Barnsley. I won't be sorry to see him go.

13 07 2005 Alfie left to attend court in Barnsley today. His head is totally fucked with heroin. It's sad seeing a young man being ravaged by drugs. The cleaning machine blew up this morning. I think whoever may have used it last put the cleaning fluid in the wrong place. When I switched it on smoke began pouring out and then there was a bang. All the

lights on the wing went out because it activated the trip switch in the main fuse box. I complained bitterly to the officers about people interfering with my job. They apologised and said unfortunately, I would have to revert back to cleaning the floors with a mop. I was finished by 10.a.m. today.

I spent the remainder of the morning watching television in my cell. Alfie turned up just after lunch, he only got as far as Mansfield. The officers taking him to Barnsley were contacted and told the trial had been abandoned after all charges against the defendants had been dropped. Alfie was smoking heroin within an hour of his return. My son Vinney is coming to see me tomorrow, I am told my co-defendant Foster is coming with him. It will be interesting to hear what he has to say for himself.

14 07 2005: The officer in charge of the cleaners was ranting and raving about the cleaning machine being broken. He called a cleaners meeting and told us that the machine had cost several thousand pounds of taxpayer's money. 'I want to know which one of you deliberately filled the machine with cleaning fluid,' he asked repeatedly. I had to stifle my laughter when he said, 'O'Mahoney's job is twice as hard now because he has to physically sweep and mop the landing.' I didn't have the heart to tell him that would only be true if O'Mahoney could be bothered to do the job properly. What do these people expect in return for £6 wages per week? The meeting proved fruitless for the investigating officer. He assured me as I was leaving the room that the maintenance guy would try to repair the machine. I sincerely hope that doesn't happen, if it does, I am in no doubt something will happen to the

machine again.

Foster turned up on the visit today with Vinney. He seemed extremely nervous, but I didn't bear him any grudge, it's the police who are fucking me, he is just naïve. I couldn't be annoyed with him. He said that he hasn't read or even seen the statements that have been made against me. It is quite worrying just how little he does know about the case. I was shocked when he revealed that Helen Myers had recently sent him a birthday card signed with love and kisses. He has also been speaking regularly to both Myers and Botham on the phone. They have allegedly said that they would do anything to get me released from prison. They have telephoned the police who say that they cannot talk to them. Regardless, here I remain. Foster said that when we appeared at Lincoln Crown Court, he had used the toilet. (Foster was on bail) D.C Garner and other officers were in the toilet. One had said, 'Who nicked O'Mahoney then? ' D.C. Garner replied, 'I did.' The other officer had laughed and said, 'nice one.' How fucking childish can you get? It's a disgrace that public money is being used to fund this farce and pay for my imprisonment.

When I got back to the wing, Alfie was smashed on smack. He was crouching on the floor beside his bed. I didn't bother asking what planet he thinks he is on. The Priest is dedicating a service to Emma tonight, but the officers have 'forgotten' to unlock me so I cannot go. I ring the cell bell to alert them but I am ignored. There is a thunder and lightning storm tonight, someone in heaven isn't happy.

15 07 2005: Alfie is talking excitedly about being freed from prison. I asked him where he will go to celebrate. 'Me and my

mates just sit in a bus shelter smoking gear and drinking cider,' he replied. Although I am not totally surprised, I am a little. Because 95% of inmates wear identical prison clothing it's impossible to work out the haves and have nots. Homeless inmates are given a compulsory shower when they arrive and are dressed in prison garb. Therefore, they appear no different to the chavs who claim they drive a Ferrari and live with a model. Alfie is 25 years old; he just didn't strike me as the type of guy who sat in a bus shelter smoking and drinking all day. Then again, his real junkie self has come to the fore over the last few weeks. Tim Redhead has been shipped out to HMP Leicester today. I wish him well; he is an okay fella. This time last year, me, Vinney, Fez, Goldie, Shane and Rachie went out for the night. It is tradition that a bride and groom should not see one another the day before their wedding. It was a wild night that continued well into the morning. Thanks for the memory's lads!

16 07 2005: My first wedding anniversary. I awoke at 4.a.m., my mind was awash with thoughts of Emma and our wedding day. I know I keep saying it, but how could so much shit happen in such a short period of time? I went to the Gym this morning and ran harder than I have ran for years. I finished the session on the rowing machine.

I am just below 14 stone 7lb now. A dramatic weight loss (4 stone) over a relatively short period of time. Vinney, my mother and my childhood friend Hughie came to see me today. My mother isn't very well, she looks tired. I sensed that everyone was avoiding talking about the fact it was my wedding anniversary, although Hughie did ask if I had been coping okay 'with today.' I felt really sad when it was time for them to leave, I so much wanted to be walking out of the door with them.

Despite being awake so early I cannot sleep tonight. I am lying on my bunk watching the daylight slowly dim into darkness. I wrap both arms around a pillow and imagine it is Emma. I would do or give anything to hold her just one more time. Tears stream down my face. Finally, all of today's raw emotions overwhelm me.

17 07 2005: Today didn't happen. I didn't want to see or speak to anyone and so I remained in my cell.

18 07 2005 The gang 'stars' on the yard have found a new punchbag. They surrounded a lad in his twenties and accused him of being a grass. They have told him that he is going to get some 'recess therapy,' which means he is going to get beaten up when he visits the toilet/showers. His alleged 'crimes' were not put to him and he neither denied or admitted any wrongdoing and so I assume they all know each other. No doubt he will be considering his future, a move to the protection section on E wing or stay and take the beating. Nothing but mouth-watering choices amongst the criminal fraternity. At 2.30.p.m. as I was waiting to go to the Gym, an officer came to the cell and told me to step outside. As I did so, Alfie walked into the cell and the officer closed the door. 'What's going on? ' I asked. The officer didn't answer, he just walked away. I looked through the hatch and Alfie came to the door. He was clearly drugged out of his mind. 'They caught me blazing in my mates' cell, see if you can find out what's happening,' he said. I didn't think there was anything to find out, he had been caught and would no doubt be charged

and lose his privilege's. As we were talking, an officer walked up the landing and told me to get my possessions together. When I enquired why, he told me that I was being moved to a single cell. As I packed the little I had, the officer was telling Alfie that the substance he had been caught with would be tested. 'You will undergo a drug test and this cell and your possessions will be searched,' he added. I couldn't help but feel elated. Being locked up is bad enough but being locked up with someone who smokes heroin night and day makes life unbearable. If Alfie had any self-respect, he wouldn't fuck about with heroin, if he had any respect for others, he wouldn't pollute the air that they are forced to breath with his vile habit.

Its 8.p.m. I have been locked up for the night. Its absolute bliss to be able to breath clean air and watch what I want on television.

19 07 2005: I awoke this morning at 6.15, it's good to just lie on my bunk undisturbed. I have been approached by the Residential Governor this morning to sit on a new Prison Committee as B-Wing representative. I told him that I am happy to do anything that helps pass the time. I was taken over to E wing where a meeting was being held between all of the wing representatives and members of a civilian independent board. The powers that be want to get some feedback from the inmates and see if positive changes can be made for the better of all. I thought changing the vast majority of the books in the library would be helpful. Very few are of interest to the average prisoner. If inmates could be encouraged to read it would help with their education and relax them. Others complained about the food, the fact

requests are ignored and visiting mothers are not being allowed to bring spare nappies into the prison. We now have to wait until the Governor calls another meeting before he responds to our points. It was the first meeting and I had not had an opportunity to consult with any of the lads on the wing. When the next meeting takes place, I will be able to air some of their grievances and hopefully change a few things for the better. The alleged 'grass' on the wing took two separate hidings today. Six inmates jumped on him when he was walking along landing four. They were all kicking and punching him. After he got up and walked away his attackers stood 'bigging' each other up. Half an hour later, he was attacked again by the same people. Prison officers were suspiciously absent on both occasions. Fair play to the lad, he went out on to the yard at exercise time and he didn't report the attacks. No doubt they will turn on him again when they are bored. I saw Enderby today; he has to appear in court this week. He told me that they had dropped his charge to Affray and so he should walk out of court because of the time he has served on remand. I really hope so. I advised him to move back to London so he will have his family to support him. He kind of acknowledged me, but I didn't think he was really listening.

20 07 2005: I have spent most of today alone. I couldn't be bothered to finish my work; I couldn't be bothered to talk to other people and so I stayed in my cell. Time, unsurprisingly dragged. For reasons unknown, we were all locked in for the 'night' at 4.30.p.m. It will either be staff shortages or some sort of security concern. Who cares? I prefer my own company.

21 07 2005: I awoke at 7.20.a.m. washed and did my press ups which I have started again now I am locked up alone. I applied to see the doctor this morning. I keep losing my balance, feeling dizzy and nauseous. The nurse came for me at 11.a.m. and took me to the medical centre on E wing. My blood pressure was taken and I was told that it was low. The nurse also remarked that I 'looked grey and clammy.' I have now been deemed to have a genuine complaint and can therefore see a doctor. He asked me if I smoked or otherwise took heroin and I said no. He then asked me if my cell mate smoked heroin. Not wanting to inform on Alfie I explained that I was recently moved to a single cell but more than one of my previous cell mates had regularly smoked it. 'I thought so,' he replied, 'you have been passive smoking heroin and it has caused these side effects.' Fucking good eh? I get imprisoned to prevent me pestering people who robbed me and I get poisoned with heroin. (I always thought the doctor's diagnosis was a bit dubious. However, whilst writing this, I did a little research and discovered prisoners and prison staff falling ill after passive smoking heroin is extremely common. In 2018 the Royal College of Nursing reported staff in prisons feeling nauseous, light-headed and some had even fallen unconscious. In at least one case, a nurse had been taken to A&E in an ambulance after passively inhaling spice.)

22 07 2005: Only God knows what Alfie has poisoned me with. I feel really ill today. I must look pretty rough as the nurse who saw me summoned the doctor to my cell. After examining me, he said that I have a 'nasty ear infection' which is why I feel dizzy and nauseous. Apparently, smoking, passive or otherwise, weakens the immune system and damages tissues in the nose and throat, making them more

susceptible to infections that affect the ears too I was given a course of antibiotics (Amoxicillin), some sort of anti-depressant (Paroxetine) and told to rest.

23 07 2005: I attempted to train in the Gym this morning but I was unsteady on my feet and seeing three of everything. Rather than ignore the good doctor's advice, I accept he may be right and return to my bed.

24 07 2005: I have no idea what time I fell asleep last night, it was late, very late. I heard someone laughing this morning whilst saying what sort of fucking name is O'Mahoney? The person kept repeating it and so I walked out of the cell and saw that it was one of a group of 'people' who were on remand for murdering an innocent man.

Paul Bradshaw Kevin Hind and others had attacked a man at a beach barbecue after 'they heard' that he had raped somebody. The victim, Sean Rogers, was beaten with a broomstick, kicked, punched, then dumped in waterway where he drowned. 'What's so funny about O'Mahoney you fucking nobody? ' I enquired. 'Ease up mate, ease up, I am only having a laugh,' he replied. 'Laugh all you want, but don't do so at my expense, now fuck off,' I said. Fucking bullies, I hate them.

25 07 2005: A wet, cold and miserable morning. I still feel spaced out and pretty shit. I am back in court in four days, hopefully there will not be any surprises. A note has been pushed under my door. The prison is being locked down tomorrow, more bullshit no doubt. The last few days have been 'difficult, ' I need to give my head a wobble and start being more positive but it's hard in here.

26 07 2005: We still haven't been told why the jail is on lockdown, it's probably staff shortages. I didn't do a lot today, but what can you actually do in an 8 x 12ft tomb? I'm definitely not myself, I think it's the medication I was prescribed so I have decided to cease taking the tablets. Tomorrows another day I guess, another day nearer to Friday and my day in court. Nearly every hearing to date has gone against me, here's hoping the prosecution get put on their arse at this one.

CHAPTER ELEVEN

No Regrets

27 07 2005: I went on a visit today expecting to see my friend Rachie. I was really surprised therefore to find my friend Jacquelyn from Market Deeping had come to see me instead. To be honest it was nice to sit and chat about everyday stuff rather than trouble and strife. Jacquelyn said that Foster thinks I am going to attack him and therefore he is moving to France. The man is deluded, I don't agree with what he has done to me but I get why he did it. His partner ran away with his friend, he was naturally upset and said things he now regrets. Simple. He's an idiot not a bad person.

28 07 2005: I fell asleep at 9.30.p.m. last night, I was exhausted. The sound of torrential rain woke me at 7.40.a.m. I feel so much better today, not taking the medication has definitely helped. The Toaster has been stolen from the officer's rest room again, so we are all enjoying the luxury of toast this morning. The officers have said that they don't intend searching for it. If it's returned by 5.p.m. nothing will be said. If we are caught with it, the punishment will be severe. I have packed the few possessions I have in preparation for court in the morning. Lincolnshire police have written to me acknowledging the fact I have withdrawn my complaint. It pained me to do so, but the system would never have allowed

me to prevail in any event. This is a game; they dictate the rules.

29 07 2005: I was up at 5.15.a.m and unlocked for court two hours later. Alfie was standing outside my cell; he was still smashed from the night before...and the night before that. I looked at him and laughed. 'Is it that obvious? ' he asked. I have never understood why people on drugs believe they appear normal. 'It's very obvious Alfie, you are ruined,' I said. Alfie didn't give a fuck because he was going home today, back to living with his Grandparents, smoking drugs and drinking strong cider in the bus shelter. I didn't envy him. Pete was also waiting to go to court. We wished each other well and said we would probably see each other on the wing this evening. I went through the now familiar procedure of being strip searched, seeing the Governor and being sent to wait in room three for the prison van. Paul Bradshaw, Kevin Hind and one of their co-defendants were also in the waiting room. One of them was reading extracts from a statement out and laughing. He claimed their victim, Sean Rogers, had slept with his own mother which is why they attacked him. In a sickening outburst he said he was proud to have killed Rogers because he was a nonce. Why are most people who pontificate about morality the lowest form of scum? (Paul Bradshaw was eventually imprisoned for seven years and Kevin Hind eight and a half years for manslaughter, another man was sentenced to twelve months and two women received non-custodial sentences)

When we arrived at Lincoln Crown Court I was locked in cell number two. My Barrister came to see me and explained that it would be a straightforward, 'in, plead and out' matter today.

He then went upstairs to speak to my solicitor. Half an hour later my Barrister re-appeared and said that he had spoken to the prosecution and they were prepared to drop all of the current charges if I agreed to plead guilty to harassing Botham and Myers. The maximum sentence for harassing somebody is five years. The Prosecution also agreed that there wouldn't be any evidence offered that related to my alleged involvement in the Essex Boys/underworld and debt collection business. Finally, there appeared to be light at the end of my very long, dark tunnel. The Barrister said I would be called upstairs into the dock; I should plead not guilty to all of the Blackmail and threats to kill charges but guilty to harassing Botham and Myers. I would then be remanded in custody for 4-6 weeks whilst a pre-sentencing report was prepared. It would be unlikely that I would be sentenced to more than twelve to eighteen months which meant I may be home for Christmas. Fifteen minutes later the prison officers came for me and I was led up a flight of wooden steps and into the dock. I looked over to the public gallery, Vinney, Karis and Debra waved. Foster sat nervously at my side. I called him a few choice names and so a prison officer came and sat between us. When the charges were read out to me, I did as I had been advised, not guilty to all charges relating to Blackmail and threats to kill but guilty to harassing Myers and Botham.

The judge, a wise man, told the Prosecution that now I had plead guilty to the only charge against me, there wasn't any reason he could think of why I would try to interfere with witnesses. Therefore, he was going to grant me bail until sentencing took place in six weeks' time. 'Mr. O'Mahoney, you are free to go for now,' he said. I turned to my children and

Debra in the public gallery and smiled. It was finally over; I was free to go home. If the judge thought I had not served long enough for such a petty crime he wouldn't have bailed me. That fact alone told me I had nothing to fear when I returned for sentencing.

19 08 2005: It only took three weeks for the Probation Service to prepare my pre-sentence report. I had worked all of my life, had two children living at home who were dependant on me and I had served a six-month sentence (Three months served in custody and three months that would have automatically been taken off for good behaviour) for a relatively minor offence. It would not be in the public interest to return me to prison.

The judge agreed, and I was sentenced to twelve months' Probation and ordered to complete 150 hours Community Service. I didn't mind the Probation, all that entailed was seeing someone once a month who asked how you were and if you had any problems. The Community Service order was a different matter. I drove tipper lorries for a living and so argued from the outset that the courts had given me a ridiculous choice: Comply with their order and break the law or ignore their order and break the law.

My probation officer asked me to explain. Under the laws that govern heavy goods vehicle drivers' hours, 'you must take a regular weekly rest of 45 continuous hours in every week.' The Community Service order stated that I had to attend and complete voluntary work in the community every Sunday. 'If I work five days a week driving, then work on a Sunday, it will be illegal for me to drive on Monday as I wouldn't have taken a continuous 45-hour rest,' I said. 'If I refuse to work on Sundays, I will be in breach of the court's order, whatever I do will be illegal. I knew that they wouldn't force me to break the law and I knew they wouldn't force me to give up my job. They did suggest all sorts of unworkable alternatives but eventually, they agreed to have the order quashed.

26 08 2005: A week after I had been sentenced at Lincoln Crown Court, I was driving through Peterborough city centre en-route to my home. I will always remember glancing at the dashboard clock as my phone began to ring. It was 4.26.p.m. 'Is that you Bernie? ' a voice enquired. 'Vinney's had a bad car crash, you had better get to Peterborough hospital.' I was sitting in heavy traffic and so I mounted the pavement and drove as quickly as possible whilst sounding my horn. People were moving out of the way but some were trying to stop me by waving me down. I drove on regardless. When I arrived at the A&E department I ran inside and found myself in the same room where Emma had been declared deceased. Doctors were rushing around and I could see my son on a stretcher with his head and neck in some sort of brace. I went over to him and saw that his face was covered in blood. 'Vinney its Dad? Are you alright? What happened? ' A nurse asked me to sit outside in the waiting room and assured me that he would be fine. When I was eventually let in to see Vinney, he told me that he had not been concentrating as his friends were in the car. His vehicle had strayed on to the opposite side of the carriageway and hit the front offside of a 44-tonne articulated lorry which was travelling in the opposite direction.

I have no idea how he wasn't killed. The off side of his vehicle was torn open like a tin can. Thankfully Vinney only suffered a broken collar bone, a broken toe, severe whiplash and various lacerations to his face. His friends were equally fortunate and apart from a few bumps and bruises, they escaped unscathed.

01 09 2005: Grantham Magistrates Court; I am hoping that this is the final legal issue that has to be resolved before I can get on with my life. I am standing trial for the incident on Boxing Day when I kicked the windows out of a police car and was falsely accused of drink driving. I was guilty of kicking the windows out. I had done so after my late wife had been insulted. I was however innocent of driving whilst under the influence of alcohol and having no licence or insurance. The police alleged that I had refused to take a breath test. My defence was, I was so upset about my wife's death I had little or no memory of events that week never mind that evening. If I had been asked to take a breath test, I certainly wasn't coherent or in any fit state to comply. Dr Wilson, my G.P had been called to give evidence, he had visited my home several times in the days following Emma's death.

He was acutely aware of how hard losing Emma had been for me. Gary Jones, the current editor of the Daily Express and a long-term friend, was also going to give evidence on my behalf. Like Dr. Wilson, Gary knew the effect Emma's death had on me. This was an important trial for my family, if I was found guilty, I would lose my licence. If I lost my licence, I would lose my job and subsequently my income. My children would then be affected, I wasn't going to let that happen without a fight. When I was called into court, I pleaded guilty to damaging the police car but not guilty to all of the other charges. Five police officers gave evidence against me but their testimony was inconsistent and some were shown to be 'mistaken.' It was accepted that one of the officers had made an insulting comment about my wife, but none of the officers appeared to be able to recall what exactly had been said or who had said it.

I genuinely had little memory of Christmas 2004. Unless you have had the misfortune of losing a loved one, you won't thankfully understand. I was therefore quite shocked when a recording of my police interview was played. I was distraught throughout the few minutes of its duration but the officer continued questioning me regardless.

It was apparent to everyone who heard it that I wasn't listening to him, never mind refusing to comply with any request to take a breathalyser test. Dr. Wilson told the court that I had been suffering from a condition known as complicated grief. I had never heard of it, but I now understand that it occurs in about 7% of bereaved people.

People suffering from the condition remember the past and imagine the future through a distressed longing for the person they have lost. They feel hopelessness about the future, waves of painful emotion, and preoccupation with memories of the deceased.

This intense preoccupation makes it difficult for them to recall past and future events that do not include their loved one. It is like all other memories that do not include the deceased are erased from their minds.

Gary Jones gave the court examples of my behaviour/state of

mind that he had witnessed following Emma's death. Nobody in that court room was left in any doubt whatsoever about who was telling the truth and I was quite rightly found not guilty of refusing to take a breath test and driving without a valid licence and insurance. I was fined £200 for damaging the police car. My wife had been dead for ten months, I had endured two separate prosecutions and spent three months in jail, it was time for a new start – a new beginning.

04 09 2005: Three days after my trial, I went for a drink in a pub near my home. I wasn't with anybody and I didn't speak to anybody whilst I was there. Debra had come to visit Vinney and Karis. I had gone out so they could spend some time together. At approximately 11.p.m I left the pub and walked home alone. Vinney's car had been written off in the accident involving the lorry. It had been recovered to a communal parking area near my house because the insurance company wanted to inspect it. As I reached home, I noticed that a group of Vinney's teenage friends were standing around what was left of his car. 'Hello Bernie, I can't believe Vinney walked away from this,' one of them had said. I stood talking to the lads for a few minutes and then said I had to go as Vinney's mother was visiting. As we were saying our goodbyes, I noticed two middle aged men jumping over the car park wall. 'Fucking hell it's those blokes,' one of the lads had said. 'We are going to fucking do you,' the men shouted as they began advancing across the car park. I couldn't quite believe what I was seeing. The men were both in their late 30's and brandishing 14-inch-long kebab knives. 'You don't need fucking knives to take on kids, put them down,' I shouted. Both men turned on me simultaneously. 'Do you want some, do you want some,' they screamed. 'Threaten me with a knife

and you'll fucking die,' I replied before punching one of them. The man I struck raised his kebab knife and lunged at me. I instinctively ducked and the blade went into the back of my shoulder and exited through my chest. Blood pumped out of the wound. I could feel it running down my chest and legs. I knew it was only a matter of time before I passed out and so I knew that I would have to kill my attackers before they killed me. Fortunately, when the other man brandishing a knife saw what his friend had done, he dropped his weapon and ran. I grabbed the man who had stabbed me and began punching him with one hand whilst head butting him in the face. He fought frantically to pull the knife out of my body. Each time he yanked or pulled at the blade, it ripped and tore the wound. I was producing so much adrenaline I could not feel any pain. I bent forward enabling the man to pull the knife out that had skewered my body. Fearing he would stab me again, I hit him as hard as I could and he fell to the ground. I genuinely believed that he was trying to get to his feet to stab me again. I was losing a lot of blood and so knew I had to stop him before I lost consciousness. I began to kick him as hard as I could in the head in order to incapacitate him. I only stopped when he appeared to be dead. I picked up the knife, gave it to one of Vinney's friends for safe keeping and then walked back to my home. When I walked into the kitchen, I asked Debra to get me a drink of Jack Daniels before collapsing. I have no idea what happened after that. I awoke in hospital the following day having undergone emergency surgery. I was told that I had been given five pints of blood. Initially, people were telling me that the man who stabbed me had died. I later learned that he was in Addenbrookes, a specialist hospital in Cambridge that treats brain and head injuries. I wasn't proud of what I had done, but I felt no remorse either, there are many forms of justice. A surgeon told me that the entry wound in my shoulder was six inches in diameter. This was because my attacker had been pulling the knife side to side in an effort to pull it out of my body. The 14-inch blade had passed straight through me. He said it was a miracle that I had survived and the person responsible should be charged with attempted murder as my wounds were undoubtedly life threatening. Lincolnshire police, unsurprisingly thought otherwise.

05 09 2005: I discharged myself from hospital and went to visit my friend Martin in Devon. Whilst there I received a telephone call. A police officer asked where I was because he said they wanted to interview me. 'I am sorry, that's not going to happen, I have had enough trouble over the last few months, I am not going to make a complaint against the guy who stabbed me and I definitely won't give evidence against him so forget it,' I said. 'I don't think you understand, Mr. O'Mahoney, it's you we are going to arrest,' the officer replied. I am tempted to say that I couldn't believe what I had heard but the fact is, I did and I had been half expecting it. Knowing that I could now face a charge of attempted murder or at least wounding, I began ringing people to find out the background to the incident.

I learned that a few hours before I had encountered the men, one of them, 40-year-old Dawson, had been drinking in one of the village pubs. He had started on a 20-year-old man who had retaliated and got the better of him. Dawson, a man who believes that he has a deserved reputation as a hard man, was ejected from the pub. Outside, he picked up a bottle in frustration and hurled it at a passing car which was being driven by a 'mature' lady. Quite rightly upset, the lady had informed her teenage sons what had happened when she arrived home. Her sons had left the house, found Dawson and assaulted him. After being humiliated twice in a short period of time by 'kids,' hardman Dawson went to his brothers flat and kicked the door. His brother's girlfriend answered, Dawson burst in, grabbed two 14-inch kebab type knives and made to leave. When his brother tried to prevent him from doing so, Dawson grabbed him and threatened to kill him. Dawson had then telephoned his friend, another 40 odd year-old hard man and told him what had happened. The pair met and Dawson gave his friend one of the knives. They then set off to find the 'kids' who had humiliated Dawson. Unfortunately for the two men, the 'kids' were Vinney's friends and they happened to be talking to me when Dawson and his friend found them. The rest as they say, is bloody history.

13 09 2005: After learning that the police were looking for me, I contacted Mr. Cauthery my solicitor and he arranged for me to hand myself in at Spalding police station. I was immediately arrested on suspicion of section 18 wounding with intent and interviewed. Seven hours later, I was bailed to reappear at the police station on 30 September pending further enquiries. That night the local newspaper published a story regarding the incident:

'Police have assured Market Deeping residents they are not at risk after a man was stabbed in the early hours of Sunday morning. Armed police were called to Black Prince Avenue on Sunday after reports that an altercation had taken place. Insp

Andy McManus, of Lincolnshire Police said: 'This was not a random attack and the public are not at risk.' The incident occurred due to an escalation of a prior disorder. 'There will be an increased police presence in the town to reassure people. Patrol officers will regularly be visiting the local pubs to ensure that there is no violence or other problems.' Chief Insp Kieran English added: 'Officers responded and dealt with the incident appropriately and at no time were other members of the public at risk.' We will not tolerate acts of violence or those who increase fear within local communities. Our inquiries continue into this incident and we would welcome any information from members of the public.'

I laughed when I read what the police had said, was I expected to tolerate an act of extreme violence? If you stick a 14" blade through a man's body surely there has to be a response?

18 09 2005: I went for a drink in my local pub but the landlord politely informed me that Lincolnshire police had advised all licensees that I should not be served in any licensed premises in the county. This was no temporary ban, the landlord said, it was for life.

At that moment I knew my time in Market Deeping was over. If you are arrested when you are the victim of an attempted murder and you are barred from entering all pubs, some shops and restaurants (Many are licensed) in the county where you live, there really is no point in staying, because further issues will undoubtedly arise in the future. I had only remained there because I couldn't bring myself to sell the home that Emma and I had shared together.

30 09 2005: I arrived at Spalding police station to answer my bail but I was informed that enquiries were ongoing. I was bailed once more until 26 October 2005.

26 10 2005: I arrived at Spalding police station to answer my bail but I was informed that enquiries were still ongoing. I was bailed once more until 29 November 2005.

29 11 2005: I arrived at Spalding police station to answer my bail but I was informed that enquiries were still ongoing. I was bailed once more until 14 December 2005.

14 12 2005: Three months after being stabbed, the police finally cancelled my bail. They told me as I hadn't made a complaint against my attackers they wouldn't be charged. Only twelve months had passed since my wife's death, during that period my life had been turned upside down. Emma would not have wanted me to go through anymore of the shit I had endured and so I rented out my home and left. Prior to me making this decision, Karis had returned to her mother's home in Essex and Vinney had moved in with a friend in Wakefield, Yorkshire. I was alone and so it didn't really matter where I chose to settle. I needed to go someplace where nobody would know me and I could live out the rest of my days in peace.

21 01 2006: It was heart-breaking turning out the lights and closing the front door of the house I had shared with Emma and my children. So many happy memories had been made within those walls, but I knew that it was time to move on. My mother had recently been diagnosed with Alzheimer's disease. Although her illness was in its early stages, I knew it would only be a matter of time before she needed me. I

decided therefore to purchase a house in Harborne, Birmingham which is only fourteen miles from Codsall where my mother lived and my wife was buried. Nobody knew me in Birmingham, yet I was only a thirty-minute drive from the village where I had grown up. I felt that I could enjoy the best of both worlds, solitude in Birmingham and friends just a short distance away if I needed company. I had little contact with anybody other than my mother and children and I felt genuinely content. 2006 began as I had hoped. I visited my mother and my wife's grave every day and threw myself into my work.

11 08 2006: Seven months after moving to Birmingham, I received a late-night call on my mobile phone from a withheld number. 'You murdered Tucker, Tate, Rolfe and Danny Marlow, the taxi driver,' a man with a strong Geordie accent ranted. 'Really?' I replied. 'You'd better go to the police and tell them that the wrong men are in jail then, hadn't you?' 'No,' the Geordie sneered. 'I want £10,000 in cash from you, or I'm going to go to the newspapers with tapes that prove you killed them all.' I told the man, who was clearly intoxicated, that I would pay him the £10,000 he was demanding. However, he would have to pop around to my house to pick up the cash. 'Do you think I'm fucking stupid?' he replied. 'I will give you a time and a place to drop it off.' 'Perhaps I can put it in a bag and leave it in my front garden for you?' I joked. 'Do yourself a favour, you maggot, and fuck off!' I replaced the receiver and thought that would be the end of the matter.

It had been eleven years since my former associates Pat Tate, Tony Tucker and Craig Rolfe had been executed. Our gang's rapid rise, and kamikaze fall, had become the subject of numerous books, television documentaries and feature films. Blatant lies and exaggerated stories have been manufactured by hangers-on, wannabes and never-will-be's since our demise; most are told by people we never even met. As with the Kray gang before us, every chancer and loser in the UK seemed to want to be associated with the Essex Boys firm and its imaginary exploits. I had met the late Danny Marlow. I was interviewed by the police about his death, but I honestly played no part in it. Two men were later convicted and sentenced to life imprisonment for the killing. Two men were also convicted of the triple murders in the Essex Boys case, and they too were sentenced to life imprisonment. Taking into consideration those facts, I failed to see how a drunken Geordie was going to convince the police that they had locked up the wrong men. I knew, of course, that my late-night caller had no intention of contacting the police. I had been receiving regular phone calls for more than a decade from strangers or strange people who were either in awe of my deceased associates or who were abusive and issued death threats because I quite rightly described their heroes as arseholes. It can be a tad annoying and frustrating, and occasionally depressing, but never have I felt threatened. If somebody did intend to cause me serious harm, I am in no doubt that they would not give me the courtesy of a warning. Let me make my position clear here, 26 years have passed since the murders and not one of you have had the bollocks to confront me. Arseholes. The drunken Geordie was not the first person to accuse me of being a murderer, but it was most certainly the first time that somebody had demanded money from me. I put the call down to the evils of drink, drugs or gang-star rap and thought that I would hear no more once the sad wretch had sobered up.

The following morning, I was awoken by the insistent ringing of my mobile phone. Still half asleep, I picked up the handset, but before I had a chance to speak the, caller said, 'Because of your fucking cheek, O'Mahoney, we now want twenty grand or we go to the police and the newspapers.' 'Who the fuck is 'we?' I replied. The man, whom I recognised as the Geordie who had called the night before, screamed, 'I am one of the Conroy's! C-O-N-R-O-Y-S! Have you got that?' I had no idea who the Conroy's were or what business they thought they had with me, and so I asked the man to explain just what his problem was. 'We have proof that you murdered Tucker, Tate, Rolfe and Marlow. We want 20 . . . no, fuck it, 50 thousand off you, or you are going to jail. The people in prison didn't kill them, O'Mahoney. You did.' Rather than debate my innocence or guilt with a mentally challenged monkey, I switched my phone off and tried to get back to sleep. These nuisance calls continued for three weeks, and on each occasion the Geordie became more and more abusive. During the first week, he threatened to cut my eyes out, and the following week he promised an unsavoury death unless I met his increasing demands for more and more cash. Employing the expertise of a friend I was able to trace and identify the man who was harassing me. Rather than deal with him myself and risk a return to prison I went to the police but they refused to do anything.

08 09 2006: After a particularly abusive and threatening early morning call, I rang the police and told them that I was en-route to Pelton in County Durham. 'When I get there, I intend to make a citizen's arrest and bring the man to Birmingham.

His name is Michael Strawbridge and he is 26 years old.' I said. Moments later an Inspector rang me back. He warned me that if I forced anybody into my vehicle I would be arrested for kidnap. I told him that I was sick of being threatened and abused in endless calls. 'I have asked you to intervene but you won't, so fuck you, I will sort it out myself.' I put the phone down but a few minutes later the Inspector called me back. 'Mr. O'Mahoney, there isn't any point in you driving anywhere. I have instructed my colleagues in Durham to arrest Mr. Strawbridge and he will be brought to Birmingham tonight.' A bit unorthodox maybe, but it was one way of getting the police to do the job they are paid to do. When Strawbridge was interviewed at Harborne police station he confessed to making the threatening phone calls and making the demands for money, 'for a laugh.' Unlike me, who was imprisoned for simply telephoning Botham, who did owe me money, Strawbridge, who had demanded thousands of pounds, threatened to cut my eyes out and kill me, was given an £80 instant fine.

In a statement to the press, West Midlands police said, 'A man arrested in connection with a blackmail allegation made by a local man has been released without charge. However, following advice from the Crown Prosecution Service, the man was issued with an £80 fixed penalty for sending false messages by the public electronic communications network causing annoyance, inconvenience and anxiety.' British justice, words fail me, they really do.

03 10 2006: For several days I had felt unwell with flu like symptoms. I also had blurred vision and was passing blood. This morning I suffered what was later diagnosed as a

transient ischemic attack. (Mild stroke) Thereafter, my general health nose-dived. Aged 19, I'd had testicular cancer which resulted in me undergoing surgery. (Orchidectomy) Because of my medical history and the fact I was passing blood, my G.P advised that I should have a colonoscopy to check for bowel cancer.

05 10 2006: My book Bonded by Blood: Murder and Intrigue in the Essex Ganglands was published today.

04 12 2006: Two years ago today I lost Emma, God love her.

06 12 2006: I attended Selly Oak hospital in Birmingham for what is normally a thirty-minute procedure. A colonoscopy involves a doctor inserting a long flexible tube called a colonoscope, or scope, into the rectum which is then slowly guided into the colon. The scope inflates the large intestine with carbon dioxide gas to give the doctor a better view. A small camera mounted on the scope transmits a video image from inside the large intestine to a computer screen, allowing the doctor to carefully examine the intestinal lining. In my case the doctor had difficulty moving the scope as he said it had looped. Eventually, he gave up and I was told the procedure had failed. Shortly afterwards, I was discharged from the hospital. Ten minutes later, I was doubled over in pain as a huge air bubble forced its way from my stomach into my chest, a second air bubble followed immediately afterwards. (This was a build-up of the carbon dioxide gas that had been pumped into me) I did not know it at the time but my stomach had been pushed into my chest and I had suffered a tension pneumothorax. This is when a defect in the diaphragm allows air to flow into the chest cavity. Each

breath allows air in, but none is allowed out. As the pressure builds in the chest, vital organs such as the heart are displaced or unable to function. The force of the air entering my chest had burst my left lung and moved my heart to the right. I somehow managed to make my way home and rang Vinney. Because of the mounting pressure in my chest, I was finding it increasingly difficult to breath and so he suggested that I telephone an ambulance immediately. When I was rushed back into the hospital, Vinney was waiting. A priest was summoned and he gave me the last rites as I lied on a trolley waiting to enter an operating theatre. My son stood watching events in total disbelief; he was told that I was dying. The doctors advised Vinney that all of my family should be notified of my condition as quickly as possible as it was unlikely that I would survive. I underwent emergency surgery and for the next three days I fought for my life in intensive care.

I don't recall much about my time in that ward but I knew that I was seriously ill. I have very brief 'flash-point' memories of me thinking that I was back in the Army. This was because Army personnel were working on the intensive care ward. The Army were flying their casualties from the battlefields in Afghanistan directly to Selly Oak hospital at the time.

I have vague memories of a soldier who had been shot in the face being resuscitated. I could hear some sort of beeping alarm and voices calling out as people crowded around his bed. In the darkness other young men cried or called out to nurses or their loved ones. Death in that intensive care ward was no stranger.

10 12 2006: As I began to recover, I was transferred to the Queen Elizabeth hospital in Birmingham. I was told that once I was stronger, I would have to undergo major surgery to repair the damage that the pneumothorax had caused.

19 12 2006: The operation lasted six hours and I was once more put into intensive care as I struggled to breathe without assistance. I cannot begin to describe the pain I endured during this time; I have not been physically fit since.

22 12 2006: Today I was taken off the ventilator and I can breathe unaided. I say breathe, I feel and sound like a ninety-year-old man who has smoked every day of his life. I don't actually breathe; I gasp for air like a fish out of water.

24 12 2006: Yo Ho Fucking Ho! Its Christmas and I have been moved out of intensive care. It's the front door of this hospital I need to get out of.

25 12 2006:My brother Michael and his partner Carol came to see me. I didn't want them to see me lying in bed like some geriatric basket case and so I clung to a handrail and hobbled to a day room clutching two large containers. These containers collect bodily fluids which pass down drains that have been surgically inserted into the left side of my chest. I tell my brother that I need to get out of the hospital and so he goes in search of a wheelchair. When he returns, he sits me down, throws a blanket over my legs and wheels me down numerous corridors and out the front door to his car. Freedom, this is a huge step for us! We celebrated Christmas day in McDonalds on Bristol Road, Edgbaston. I began to feel ill after a few minutes and so Michael returned me to the hospital.

27 12 2006: After repeatedly telling doctors that I needed to go home, I was finally discharged. I took a taxi to my house in Harborne. Because my torso had been opened from under my left arm to my right hip, the stitches made it impossible for me to stand upright without suffering searing pain. I tried hard to crawl up the stairs to bed but it proved impossible, I was in agony. My friend Jacquelyn from Market Deeping came to visit me and insisted she stay until I could care for myself. A true friend to whom I will be eternally grateful. Jacquelyn made a makeshift bed for me downstairs which I used for several weeks. Things improved, but I would never make a full recovery. Scarring from the operation caused adhesions. These are bands of tissue that have formed around my lungs preventing them from fully inflating. Today my left lung has only one third of its normal capacity, my right lung has 78%. Because my lungs do not function properly, there is a shortage of oxygen in my blood. In an attempt to compensate for this shortage, my heart beats faster. When I am sitting down resting, my heart rate is 137 beats per minute. The average heart rate for my age is 60-100 beats per minute. A specialist has told me it is too dangerous to operate, it is a condition that I will just have to live with.

I am certainly not complaining about my lot because few people in the world have survived what I went through. My case was in fact so rare that it was published in the unusual cases section of the Medical Journal. I will forever be indebted to all of the people who brought me back from the brink of death and to those who helped me along the long road to recovery. For nearly two years I was unable to carry out any form of physical employment and so I concentrated on writing books.

10 02 2008: I travelled to Newcastle to meet Paddy Conroy a notorious villain. We had discussed writing his biography together and I had agreed to visit him. I first became aware of the Conroy family after Michael Strawbridge my would-be blackmailer had claimed to be 'one of their gang.' I liked Paddy and initially we got on well.

01 05 2008 My book Essex Boys, The New Generation was published today.

CHAPTER TWELVE
The Circle of Life

20 10 2008: Whilst working on Paddy Conroy's book, I had travelled regularly to Newcastle Upon Tyne. Usually, I would interview him during the day and then sit in a hotel room all night writing my notes up. One Saturday evening I ended up at a pub in Gateshead where a Buskers night was being held. These are events where members of the public get on stage and sing, play musical instruments or both. I met and began talking to a beautiful girl twenty years my junior named Roshea Tierney. At the time she was at college studying music but, in her teens she had earned a living as a singer having secured a recording contract. Romance was the last thing on my mind when we initially met. However, we got on well and arranged to meet regularly on my trips to the north-east. In time, we both realised that we were meant to be and so inevitably, a relationship blossomed. As is the norm, there were teething problems, but not of our own making. Roshea had two young children, a boy aged eight and a girl aged five. Her ex-partner John, can best be described as a Class A, drug addicted social nuisance. His elder brother George thought he was a gang-star who controlled a huge estate called Leam Lane in Gateshead. The truth is, he was a crack head who couldn't control his bladder never mind Leam Lane. Roshea, like too many women, had encountered problems

with her ex when it came to contact with their children. Her view was, he wasn't the type of person who should see them under any circumstances. This caused serious problems between Roshea, John and his family. When they became aware that I was in a relationship with Roshea, they applied to the family court to have me banned from seeing the children. To ensure the court granted the injunction, they claimed that I was, 'a former Essex Boys gang member and a drug dealer.' For three months I wasn't allowed in Roshea's home whilst the children were there. Once I had been assessed and checked out by the police the ban was lifted immediately. Sadly, that was the beginning of a campaign against me that inevitably affected innocent children.

24 11 2008: After leaving a solicitor's office, Roshea and I caught a taxi home because we did not relish the thought of lugging the large suitcase I had with me on the Metro. (Underground) It was rush hour and the traffic was heavy. We arrived at Roshea's home at approximately 5.50.p.m. Her dog had been home alone all afternoon and so I dropped my suitcase in the hall and put the dog on its lead. Roshea, the dog and I then stepped out to go to the shops via the park. As we entered the street two police officers came running towards us. We were told to give our names and asked where we lived. After identifying ourselves, we were ordered to return to the house and the police followed us inside. Roshea was then accused of assaulting a lady named Shirley Elliott earlier that day (Her father's ex-partner who lived three doors away) and of threatening to 'put her windows through.' The complainant had said, 'Roshea is acting like this because, she is going out with a gangster.' Fortunately, we were able to tell the officers that we had been sitting in a solicitor's office at

the relevant time. We did query the fact that the allegation against Roshea would raise an incident log number which her ex's family could mention in court, (I assume that's why they did it) and the officers said they would - if we were telling the truth - write the alleged incident up accordingly. (The police did contact the solicitor who confirmed that we were in her office at the relevant time and therefore the allegation was entirely false.)

Unfortunately, matters didn't end there, Roshea was physically attacked whilst walking in the park with her children and bricks and other objects were regularly hurled through her windows. I was still living in Birmingham and so Roshea naturally feared for her safety when I wasn't there. There were several 'heated arguments' when I confronted her ex and his brother in the street. I had been warned that if I assaulted anyone it would have a huge impact on the proceedings regarding the children and so for Roshea's and their sake, I refrained from doing so. The less I did, the more the campaign of harassment and intimidation intensified. On a visit to his Grandparents house Roshea's son had his head completely shaved. The Grandparents then contacted social services and claimed that I had held the boy down on his bed and used electric clippers to cut off all of his hair. An investigation was launched but fortunately I was able to prove beyond doubt that I had been in Birmingham on the night they claimed it had happened. When questioned, the boy said that his Grandmother and her neighbour were responsible. On another occasion, Roshea's son had gone missing whilst he was at his Grandparents house. They rang the police and claimed that I had been seen 'abducting him off the street and putting him in the boot of my car.' The police were quite rightly alarmed and rang me wanting to know where I was and with whom. I didn't have a clue what was going on and so I told them that I would drive directly to Gateshead police station. (I had been visiting Roshea so was in the area) When I arrived, I was taken into an office and my car was searched. A female police officer entered the room I was in and informed her colleagues that the missing boy had been found. He had left his Grandparents house without them knowing and walked to a nearby shop. At no stage had he seen or spoken to me. These ridiculous allegations were never ending and they created a lot of stress and worry for Roshea.

03 12 2008: This evening we were sitting in Roshea's home watching television when a large plant pot was hurled through the lounge window. I jumped up and ran outside where I saw Johns older brother George standing in the street. He is a huge man, (6ft 3") but I grabbed hold of him regardless and told him in no uncertain terms what the future held for him if he persisted with his behaviour. He was out of his head on crack cocaine and so I knew I wouldn't get any sense out of him. I went back into the house to check on Roshea and the children and to clear up the mess.

04 12 2008: The evening after I had confronted George, I saw Roshea's fathers ex-partner Shirley in the street. I had a lot of time for Shirley, life had not been kind to her and I thought of her as being vulnerable. George and others like him preyed on vulnerable people and Shirley was an ideal victim. Because she lived opposite Georges parents, he was often in her house exploiting or intimidating her. I told Shirley about the altercation I had with George and warned her to be careful

around him. 'If he carries on the way he is, he is going to get hurt,' I said. Shirley asked me to lend her £10 for a bottle of wine and I obliged. Five minutes later, Roshea and I walked to a nearby shop. As we were returning home, we saw numerous police vehicles with their blue lights flashing parked outside Shirley's house. Snow covered the ground but I could see several people on their knees which I thought was odd considering the sub-zero temperature. As we got nearer, we could see that ambulance staff were working on what appeared to be a body. A few people had come out of their homes and were saying that Shirley Elliott had been stabbed. I then saw that the snow around Shirley's head and waist was soaked in blood. The ambulance crew loaded Shirley onto a stretcher and moments later, the vehicle disappeared into the darkness with its sirens wailing. Two hours later, George and his brother were arrested at Johns flat. John had washed George in bleach to destroy any forensic evidence, but for reasons unknown he was never charged with assisting an offender. George, who had been asleep under a duvet on the sofa, was arrested on suspicion of murder. He was so drugged up he replied to the arresting officers, 'What murder? What are you on about? ' He later told police that he had been trying to stop Shirley taking a carving knife to Roshea's house, where she was going to break the windows following a row. There had been a struggle and he had 'accidently' stabbed her. That may sound like a reasonable explanation to some, but not so when you consider the fact that Shirley suffered sixty-seven separate stab wounds. Bastard, Shirley's death was no accident.

The first trial was halted when Georges ridiculous explanation was exposed as being implausible by expert evidence

(Number of wounds). At a second trial George had hoped to plead guilty with diminished responsibility but this was not accepted and so eventually, albeit reluctantly, George had to plead guilty to murdering a 43-year-old defenceless mother of three, Grandmother and harmless well-liked lady. The judge sentenced him to life imprisonment with a recommendation that he serve a meagre fourteen years before he can be considered for parole. The real reason George attacked Shirley has never been established. However, it is more than likely that it was Shirley who was trying to stop him from going to Roshea's house with a knife and so he had stabbed her in the struggle that ensued. I genuinely rue the day they abolished hanging.

06 12 2008: I told Roshea that neither her or her children would ever be safe living anywhere near such 'people.' You cannot be rational with irrational people, particularly irrational people who are addicted to heroin and crack cocaine. The violence was escalating and all social services would say is, 'Bernard needs to try and be more understanding about vulnerable people with problems.' Hanging about and hoping your family survives some social experiment is not a strategy I was happy to comply with. I urged Roshea to move as soon as possible but added that I would live with her in Gateshead until her and the children were safe.

08 01 2009 My book Wild Thing: The True Story of Britain's Rightful Guv'nor was published today.

09 01 2009: Roshea, her children and I moved into a house in Ryton, Gateshead. It is a relatively affluent area near the banks of the River Tyne. We had been prevented from

moving out of the north-east as the children's father had obtained a Prohibited Steps Order which meant the children had to remain in the area until the final court hearing resolved all issues in dispute. From that moment forth, every delaying tactic possible was employed to drag out the proceedings.

28 05 2009: Good news at last, during these dark times. Roshea has fallen pregnant. We are both overjoyed. We had already been discussing marriage but this news accelerates our plans. Roshea and I have decided to get married before our child is born.

06 08 2009: My book Essex Boy: Last Man Standing was published today.

20 09 2009: Roshea's 31st birthday. We married in the Great Hall at the amazing Alnwick Castle in Northumberland where the Harry Potter movies were made. A beautiful bride, a beautiful setting and an unforgettable day.

15 12 2009: I am now having to live between Birmingham and Ryton because of my mother's deteriorating health. There are fleeting moments when she is lucid, we laugh and we cry together, I am always in awe of her strength. It's heart-breaking sitting talking to her when dementia has robbed her of her memory. I find caring for her a daily struggle for lots of reasons, but I owe my mother my life, literally.

Today I visited my mother and found her in bed unable to move. Mom was complaining bitterly about a pain in her back and so I had summoned an ambulance. When we arrived at New Cross hospital in Wolverhampton, the doctors told me that it was nothing to worry about and I should go home. My mother was admitted to a ward and given a course of antibiotics. Over Christmas her condition appeared to improve.

14 01 2010: I grew up in a house where birthdays were considered to be of little importance. Throughout her life, my mother believed that she had been born on the 14th of January, but as it wasn't of any relevance, she never checked. Today her birthday feels very significant. My mother is in hospital and Roshea is due to give birth to our son Paddy at the Women's hospital in Birmingham. I am really pleased that the doctor has said that they are going to perform a caesarean section today. The staff have taken Roshea down to theatre. I am sitting in the waiting room both excited and nervous. I am surprised when Roshea walks back into the waiting room accompanied by a doctor. I fear something dreadful has happened but he informs me that they had to cancel the procedure as there had been an emergency admission and they needed the theatre. I am naturally disappointed as there is a long line of 'same day births' in my family. (My Granddaughter shares my birthday, my daughter shares my brother's birthday, two of my sons - born more than a decade apart share the same birthday, my eldest son was born the day my Grandmother died, my son Vinney shares his Grandfather's birthday, etc etc...) The main thing is Roshea and our baby are fine, so we return home and prepare to return the following day.

15 01 2010: Roshea gave birth to our son Paddy today. Without doubt, one of the happiest days of our lives.

18 01 2010: I visited my mother regularly at the Royal hospital

in Wolverhampton but this evening I was told that I could not do so as visiting had been banned following the outbreak of a vomiting virus. Over twenty members of staff had already been taken ill with the highly infectious norovirus bug which causes sickness and diarrhoea. I don't know what it was, but I instinctively knew that I had to get into the hospital somehow to see my mother. I walked around the perimeter of the building until I found an open door.

Once inside, I made my way to my mother's ward and slipped un-noticed into her private room. My mother was awake and alert; she smiled when she saw me. It was as if her dementia had been temporarily erased. I sat on her bed, held her hand and we talked. Within an hour my mother had fallen asleep and so I kissed her goodbye before leaving.

19 01 2010: I received a telephone call from the hospital telling me that I should make my way there immediately. When I arrived. my brother Michael and his partner Carol were already at my mother's bedside.

A doctor took me into an office and explained that my mother had kidney failure and it was unlikely that she would survive another day. Michael, Carol and I sat with my mother until the early evening. They had to return home to care for their children and so I was left alone with my mother.

A nurse came in to see me and asked if there was anything that she could do. I told her that if my mother's condition deteriorated, I did not want the doctors to help her. 'Please give her pain killers but do not prolong her misery,' I said. The nurse nodded and left the room.

I held my mother in my arms and despite her being barely conscious I spoke to her throughout the night. I wept as I apologised for all the wrong I had done in my life and all of the upset that I had undoubtedly caused her. I thank God that I was able to have that time alone with her.

20 01 2010: Dark blood began to appear around my mother's mouth which I wiped away. I placed a crucifix in her hand and held her. My mother began to cough as if drowning in her own blood and so I asked a nurse to help her. The nurse looked at me and without saying a word adjusted the bed so my mother was lying flat on her back. Moments later, at 08.31.a.m my heroine lost her brave fight for life. I wiped the blood from her mouth, brushed her hair and then went to inform the staff that she had passed away. Her life had ended as mine had begun, her alone with me and me alone with her. (She had given birth to me alone after collapsing in the street.)

25 01 2010: Whilst arranging my mother's funeral, I had to apply for her birth certificate. I was pleasantly surprised to learn that her belief, that she had been born on the 14th of January was in fact incorrect. Her birth certificate stated that she had in fact been born on the 15th of January, the same day Paddy had been born. (I like to think some sort of divine intervention prevented Paddy from being born on the 14th)

16 07 2010: Six years ago, I married Emma. So much has happened since then. There wasn't any reason for me to remain in Birmingham now that my mother had passed. I am moving to Newcastle today to be with Roshea and her children. Roshea has travelled down to Birmingham with

Paddy to assist me with moving.

As I was loading my worldly goods into the removal truck, I heard Roshea scream and shout, 'No, no!' I ran upstairs and found her sitting on our bed crying. Her brother Elric had just been found dead by her mother; he was 32 years old. Elric had been unwell with flu like symptoms and so he had laid down on the sofa watching television. His mother popped to the shops and when she returned, he was unresponsive. Elric had died from complications with pneumonia.

19 07 2010: I was featured in an episode of the television series, Danny Dyers Deadliest Men.

27 12 2010: A film based on my book Bonded by Blood was released today.

05 05 2011: My book Fog on the Tyne: The Story of Britain's Bloodiest Gang War was published today. This book was originally Paddy Conroy's biography (In the Name of My Father) but relations between Paddy and I had sadly broken down. Paddy regularly smoked Skunk, a powerful form of cannabis with high levels of THC. (Tetrahydrocannabinol, the compound in cannabis that is psychoactive and generates the feeling of being high). Skunk is linked to psychosis-like symptoms such as paranoia and delusions. Paddy undoubtedly suffered from paranoia.

He accused me of planting files on his computer that monitored him. He also believed that I was working for MI5 and interviews for his book were really intelligence gathering exercises. It was pointless continuing to work with Paddy and so we parted company. I rewrote the book and changed the title rather than waste two- or three-years' hard work.

30 04 2011: My book Faces: A Photographic Journey Through the Underworld was published today.

07 07 2011: My book Trouble in Mind was published today.

07 09 2012: Billy 'Boy' Martindale was murdered today. I met Billy whilst writing his father (Lew Yates) book (Wild Thing: The True Story of Britain's Rightful Guv'nor). Lew was an extremely tough guy in his prime. I formed the opinion Billy was jealous of his father's notoriety and resented me for refusing to work on a book about him.

In the weeks leading up to the release of Lew's book, Billy started what became a lengthy internet campaign of harassment against me. He mocked my dead wife, claimed I killed her, contacted my publisher and said his father's book was all lies and regularly telephoned me (when drunk) to threaten to stab, shoot or kill me.

On 15 December 2008 Billy self-published his autobiography, Wanted: My Life on the Run as Billy Boy Yates. Believing he was about to become a household name, Billy's ego slipped into overdrive. He boasted that he had murdered two hit men. He pleaded with well-known villains such as Roy Shaw, Danny Woolard, Billy Frost and Loyalist terrorist Johnny 'Mad Dog' Adair to pose for photographs with him so he could 'prove' that they were his friends. He even had his face tattooed so that he looked 'harder.' Few were fooled by his charade. His partner Tina Joseph later told a court, 'I don't think he was a gangster. He just thought he was one.'

Paul Groves, a rather unremarkable man, had been growing cannabis with Billy at a small holding in High Ongar, Essex. Inevitably there was a dispute about money and Billy began threatening Groves and his family. Groves had gone to Billy's small holding in a rather agitated state to 'sort things out.' He found Billy and his friend Paul Meeking sitting at a table drinking. Billy's children, a boy of fourteen and a girl of six, were playing in and around a caravan nearby. Groves knocked Billy unconscious by punching him four or five times in the head. Billy fell face down onto the table. Meeking tried to protect Billy by hitting Groves with a pick-axe handle. Groves then fought with Meeking, gaining the upper hand by biting him hard in the chest. Groves wrestled the pick-axe handle from Meeking, which he then used to hit him five times: once above the right eye, causing a bad wound, and then to the chest, hip and each knee. Having dealt with Meeking, Groves then returned to the table where Billy remained slumped and motionless. Groves struck Billy twice to the rear of his head with the pick-axe handle causing fatal injuries. Billy's son, who knew Groves well, had heard the first attack on his father and he witnessed the second. Just after his father was hit with the pick-axe handle, he had dialled 999 telling the operator what had happened and who was responsible. Both children witnessed their dead or dying father lying across the table with severe head injuries and brain matter oozing from his badly fractured skull. Groves was later sentenced to life imprisonment with a recommendation that he serve a minimum of 23 years.

03 12 2012: A six-part television series I wrote and presented, British Gangsters: Faces of The Underworld - Series One was released on DVD today.

04 07 2013: My book Wayne Barker: Born to Fight: The Extraordinary Story of a Bare-Knuckle Boxer was published today.

26 07 2013: The case in the family court regarding Roshea's children dragged on for three very long years. We eventually secured a judgement in Roshea's favour. I sympathise with anybody who has to go through the family courts to protect their children. I represented Roshea throughout the often tedious, always draining proceedings which took us on a journey to courts in Gateshead, Sunderland, Newcastle and the Appeal Court in London. It is not something I would like to experience again. Liberal minded social workers and over sympathetic judges were the bane of my every waking hour. Today we finally left the north-east and moved into a house in rural Lincolnshire.

08 07 2015: The first episode of an eight-part television series I wrote and presented, British Gangsters Faces of the Underworld series 2 was broadcast on Quest today. I had interviewed Paddy Conroy for series one and initially he was happy with the way he was portrayed. One of the episodes in series 2 looked at victims of crime and the effect their experiences have had on their lives. One man I interviewed was Phil Berriman. In 1994 he had been charged with importing 3.5 tonnes of cannabis into the UK. Berriman gave a defence of duress claiming that Paddy Conroy had threatened to harm his family if he did not skipper a boat laden with the drugs. Berriman was acquitted at Exeter crown court of all charges but shortly afterwards he was lured to a meeting by alleged associates of Conroy and badly beaten. Berriman sustained 130 separate injuries, required 27 staples

in the back of his head, had broken ribs and his teeth knocked out. As soon as Conroy became aware that Berriman was going to be featured in the programme he began publishing derogatory remarks about me on social media. Initially I defended myself but the more I responded the more intense the abuse became. Conroy then began posting outlandish claims such as I had underage sex with my dead wife. In another outburst Conroy suggested that I might rape his children and I should be charged with raping two sisters I had successfully fought in the High Court over a confession to murder that one of them had made. (The Taylor Sisters) There wasn't in fact any sexual element to the case whatsoever. Conroy's most bizarre claim was that MI5 had planted child pornography on his computer in an effort to get him arrested and discredited.

As soon as the Berriman episode was broadcast Conroy made a complaint to OFCOM that was considered to be so serious that the television channel immediately cancelled the broadcast of the rest of the series. Conroy falsely claimed that all of Berriman's story was untrue and he had not been acquitted following a defence of duress. When Conroy and his followers became aware that the series had been cancelled, they promoted the view that this proved Conroy was telling the truth and I had concocted and manipulated the facts. I cannot begin to describe the abuse, threats and vile allegations I endured because of this. Rapist, paedophile, police informant, MI5 agent and child abuser - you name it, I was falsely and publicly accused of it. I was warned that I would be shot, stabbed, beaten and or be dumped face down in the River Tyne. My wife Roshea was given a threat to life warning after police received intelligence that acid was going to be thrown in her face. During one particularly stressful period I lost control and in desperation offered to fight Conroy to end the dispute. His nephew Michael Conroy rang offering to fight me on Paddy Conroy's behalf. When I enquired what it had to do with him, Michael replied, 'Paddy is an old man, it's not fair you fighting him.' I pointed out that I am actually older than Paddy and so Michael put the phone down. I haven't heard from Paddy since. OFCOM later dismissed Conroy's allegations when they were furnished with the facts and the series was eventually aired.

14 09 2015: A film I wrote and presented, The Krays: Kill Order was released today.

06 12 2015: Twenty years ago today, Tucker, Tate and Rolfe were murdered. My book Essex Boys: The Final Word: No More Myths, No More Lies...the Definitive Story was published today. A film I wrote and presented, Essex Boys: The Truth was also released today.

22 05 2017: A film Bonded by Blood 2: The New Generation, which is based on my book, Essex Boys the New Generation was released today.

03 06 2019: A film I wrote and presented, Gangster Number One, Freddie Foreman was released today.

05 08 2019: A film I wrote and presented, The Feared, Irish Gangsters was released today.

06 10 2020: Pat Tate's former girlfriend Paula 'wild child' Jackson appeared at Basildon Crown Court today charged with possession of an imitation firearm in a public place and

attempting to pervert the course of justice. The court was told that at 2.30am Jackson was seen buying drugs in Southend from the driver of a car. When the car drove off, she produced what appeared to be a handgun in her right hand and aimed it at the vehicle. Jackson who was homeless, had been staying at a hostel and at 7.20am that morning she went into the office and gave the manager four £20 notes. He said, 'she was in a state and she said 'cut the CCTV' and 'if someone asks, say I was here all night.' The manager refused, but Jackson persisted. The police were called and armed officers arrested Jackson. Judge Andrew Hurst told Jackson: 'The streets of Essex are no place for firearms to be brandished around and if anyone is foolish enough to do it, they will get a big shock with a long custodial sentence.' Jackson received four months in prison for the imitation firearm, and eight months for perverting the cause of justice.

04 11 2020: I appeared on the film set of Rise of the Foot Soldier Origins in a cameo role alongside Hollywood star Vinnie Jones who is playing me in the film.

30 12 2020: My book Salford Lads: The Rise and Fall of Paul Massey was published today.

06 03 2021: It has been reported that Jack Whomes one of two men convicted of murdering Tucker, Tate and Rolfe has been released from prison after serving 23 years. He was man enough to shoot the trio but not man enough to admit his crimes. Whomes continues to maintain his innocence. His supporters blame a new suspect every other week without having any evidence whatsoever to support their ridiculous claims. It was Leah Betts's father, me, the police, the military,

Billy Jasper, a north London crime family, a Canning Town Cartel, a family called Blundell, Danny Woolard, Dave Courtney, Kenny Noye, a mysterious Mr. D, Sarah Saunders, the IRA, Steven Ellis, his father Sid Ellis, Damon Alvin, Darren Nicholls and no doubt Colonel Mustard in the study with a candle stick. The case has become a game of modern day Cluedo played by the clueless.

25 03 2021: Tony Tuckers gym buddy Carlton Leach regularly insults me on the internet. The news that Vinnie Jones was playing my character in a film about the Essex Boys appeared to have incensed Leach as his abuse intensified. Since 1990 I have employed various pseudonyms to befriend child killers and paedophiles in the hope of getting them to confess to their vile crimes. To date, the evidence I have gathered has been used to secure murder convictions against Richard Blenkey who murdered 7-year-old Paul Pearson, Shaun Armstrong who murdered 3-year-old Rosie Palmer and David Copeland who murdered Nick Moore, 31, John Light, 32, Andrea Dykes 27 and her unborn baby. (See my book Flowers in Gods Garden) Leach thinks it is hilarious to call me Bernadette, Belinda or Patsy, a reference to the fact that I have often used female pseudonyms to befriend the monsters I am targeting. Today I did wonder if he was laughing with as much gusto at a person using the pseudonym Violet. Violet had been exchanging internet messages with Leach's friend. He had boasted to Violet that the Rise of the Footsoldier movies, which are based loosely on the Essex Boys story, were about him and Leach. He also claimed that he was involved in supplying drugs and guns. Leach's friend was trying to impress 'Violet' who he believed was a 14-year-old child. His intention was that she would

meet and have sex with him. Today, he was arrested when he went to meet Violet who turned out to be a decoy working for an amazing organisation called Broken Dreams Awareness. Based in Essex they track down and bring to justice paedophiles in exactly the same way I have done for the past twenty plus years. Leach's friend was thankfully arrested and Leach, I assume, no longer finds this type of sterling work humorous.

10 04 2021: It has been twelve long years since I have been in any sort of trouble with the police. The last time was in 2009 and that was a trivial matter brought about by a person's ignorance, lack of understanding and civility. I had met my wife off a train in Birmingham and was loading her luggage into my car when a British Rail car park attendant arrived. He began shouting and demanding that I move my car immediately as it was in a no parking zone. I explained that I was there to save my wife walking a considerable distance with heavy luggage. No other cars were in the area and so I wasn't causing anyone to be inconvenienced. He could have allowed me the ten or twenty seconds needed, but as I was carrying the final suitcase to the boot, he blocked my way. Foolishly, I pushed him out of my way. I then put the suitcase in the car and drove off. If he had spoken to me with civility and applied some common sense, it wouldn't have happened. Manner's cost nothing, pushing a car park attendant cost me £200 in fines.

I have managed to avoid trouble for the longest period in my life simply because I avoid interaction with any other people other than my one friend Gavin Spicer and my family. Gavin was the doorman I relied upon most at Raquel's, he plays the same role in my life today. One true friend that cannot be replaced. We speak maybe once a month, meet maybe twice a year for a meal and that's it. Like me, he has tired of the masses and their social media influenced pseudo world. I still get shit from some people, mainly strangers and wannabe 'gang'-stars' who pollute the internet. These morons who are either jealous or seeking notoriety and attention, abuse me in Facebook messages, ring me from withheld numbers and threaten to shoot me, dig my dead wife up or make juvenile videos on you tube which attempt to put me down. They do make me laugh. They remind me of children, name calling in a school playground.

There's not a man amongst them. I try to ignore these fools and dedicate my time to my family. Family is not an important thing to me; it is everything. My family have helped me through hard times, picked me up when I was down and been there for me when it mattered. Despite the many setbacks in my life, I consider myself to be lucky, extremely lucky. I say that because so many of my former friends and associates have been less so.

In the main, this has been because they refused to accept the life we lived was toxic, not glamourous. Instead of walking away and acknowledging their folly, they hung on to the Essex Boys myth hoping the good old days would return. Many of these former friends and associates now litter prisons and graveyards, each and every one of them a grim milestone on a road that took us all to hell.

Printed in Great Britain
by Amazon